Francisco J. Garijo   José C. R[i]que[lme]
Miguel Toro (Eds.)

Advances in Artificial Intelligence – IBERAMIA 2002

8th Ibero-American Conference on AI
Seville, Spain, November 12-15, 2002
Proceedings

Springer

Series Editors

Jaime G. Carbonell, Carnegie Mellon University, Pittsburgh, PA, USA
Jörg Siekmann, University of Saarland, Saarbrücken, Germany

Volume Editors

Francisco J. Garijo
Telefónica Investigación y Desarrollo
Emilio Vargas 6, 28043 Madrid, Spain
E-mail: fgarijo@tid.es

José C. Riquelme
Miguel Toro
Universidad de Sevilla, ETS Ingeniería Informática
Dpto. Lenguajes y Sistemas Informáticos
41012 Seville, Spain
E-mail: {riquelme,mtoro}@lsi.us.es

Cataloging-in-Publication Data applied for

Bibliographic information published by Die Deutsche Bibliothek

Die Deutsche Bibliothek lists this publication in the Deutsche Nationalbibliografie;
detailed bibliographic data is available in the Internet at <http://dnb.ddb.de>.

CR Subject Classification (1998): I.2, F.1.1

ISSN 0302-9743
ISBN 3-540-00131-X Springer-Verlag Berlin Heidelberg New York

Springer-Verlag Berlin Heidelberg New York
a member of BertelsmannSpringer Science+Business Media GmbH

http://www.springer.de

© Springer-Verlag Berlin Heidelberg 2002
Printed in Germany

Typesetting: Camera-ready by author, data conversion by PTP-Berlin, Stefan Sossna e.K.
Printed on acid-free paper   SPIN: 10873146   06/3142   5 4 3 2 1 0

Preface

The 8th Ibero-American Conference on Artificial Intelligence, IBERAMIA 2002, took place in Spain for the second time in 14 years; the first conference was organized in Barcelona in January 1988.

The city of Seville hosted this 8th conference, giving the participants the opportunity of enjoying the richness of its historical and cultural atmosphere.

Looking back over these 14 years, key aspects of the conference, such as its structure, organization, the quantity and quality of submissions, the publication policy, and the number of attendants, have significantly changed. Some data taken from IBERAMIA'88 and IBERAMIA 2002 may help to illustrate these changes.

IBERAMIA'88 was planned as an initiative of three Ibero-American AI associations: the Spanish Association for AI (AEPIA), the Mexican Association for AI (SMIA), and the Portuguese Association for AI (APIA). The conference was organized by the AEPIA staff, including the AEPIA president, José Cuena, the secretary, Felisa Verdejo, and other members of the AEPIA board.

The proceedings of IBERAMIA'88 contain 22 full papers grouped into six areas: knowledge representation and reasoning, learning, AI tools, expert systems, language, and vision. Papers were written in the native languages of the participants: Spanish, Portuguese, and Catalan. Twenty extended abstracts describing ongoing projects were also included in the proceedings.

IBERAMIA 2002 was organized as an initiative of the Executive Committee of IBERAMIA. This committee is in charge of the planning and supervision of IBERAMIA conferences. Its members are elected by the IBERAMIA board which itself is made up of representatives from the following Ibero-American associations: AEPIA (Spain), APPIA (Portugal), AVINTA (Venezuela), SBC (Brazil), SMIA (Mexico), and SMCC (Cuba).

The organizational structure of IBERAMIA 2002 is similar to other international scientific conferences. The backbone of the conference is the scientific program, which is complemented by tutorials, workshops, and open debates on the principal topics of AI.

An innovative characteristic, which differentiates IBERAMIA from other international conferences, is the division of the scientific program into two sections, each with different publication requirements. The paper section is composed of invited talks and presentations of the contributions selected by the PC. Since the 6th conference held in Lisbon in 1998, Springer-Verlag has published the proceedings of the papers section in English as part of the LNAI series.

The open discussion section is composed of working sessions devoted to the presentation of ongoing research being undertaken in Ibero-American countries, and to the discussion of current research issues in AI. Selected papers here are written either in Spanish, Portuguese, or English. The proceedings are published in a local edition.

A total of 345 papers were submitted to IBERAMIA 2002 from 28 different countries, 316 papers submitted to the paper section and the remaining 29 papers to the open discussion section. The number of papers per country and section are shown in the following table:

Country	Paper Section	Open Section	Country	Paper Section	Open Section
Algeria	3		Mexico	21	6
Argentina	2		Peru	1	
Australia	1		Poland	3	
Austria	1		Portugal	20	
Brazil	25	5	Ireland	1	
Canada	3		Romania	2	
Cuba	1		Russia	1	
Chile	3		Slovakia	1	
China	1		Spain	187	17
France	14		The Netherlands	1	
Germany	3		Tunisia	1	
India	2		UK	4	
Italy	3		USA	1	
Japan	1		Venezuela	8	1

Of the 316 papers submitted to the paper section, only 97 papers were selected for publication in the proceedings. The AI topics covered by the submitted papers and the papers accepted can be seen in the following table:

Topic	Submitted	Accepted
Knowledge Representation and Reasoning	66	19
Machine Learning	18	6
Uncertainty and Fuzzy Systems	23	7
Genetic Algorithms	31	9
Neural Nets	38	15
Knowledge Engineering and Applications	3	0
Distributed Artificial Intelligence and Multi-Agent Systems	42	9
Natural Language Processing	33	9
Intelligent Tutoring Systems	13	5
Control and Real time	23	8
Robotics	19	6
Computer Vision	8	4
Total	317	97

The quantity and the quality of the submissions to IBERAMIA have improved since 1988. Furthermore, the number of submissions for the paper section in IBERAMIA 2002 was significantly higher than those of previous conferences. We received 316 submissions, 97 of them (30.5%) were accepted; IBERAMIA 2000 received 156, 49 (32%) were accepted; IBERAMIA'98 received 120, 32 (26%) were accepted.

The evaluation of this unexpectedly large number of papers was a challenge, both in terms of evaluating the papers and maintaining the high quality of preceding IBERAMIA conferences. All these goals were successfully achieved by the PC and the auxiliary reviewers. The acceptance rate was very selective 30.5%. It was in line with that of IBERAMIA 2000, 33%, and with IBERAMIA'98, 26%, the most selective.

A large Spanish participation and a low number of application-oriented papers were also significant characteristics of IBERAMIA 2002. The Spanish AI groups submitted 187 papers (50% of the total), to the paper section. This is a reflection of the growth of AI research in Spain, and the maturity attained over the last 16 years.

The correlation between theoretical research and applications seems unbalanced. In IBERAMIA'88 the large majority of papers, 15 out of a total of 22, detailed applications. A full section with 7 papers was devoted to Expert Systems applications. In IBERAMIA 2002 the large majority of papers selected for presentation were devoted to theoretical aspects of AI.

There is no doubt about the need for theoretical research on the modeling and understanding of the mechanisms of intelligence; however, the power and the validity of theoretical models should be demonstrated outside academic labs. It is necessary to go beyond simulated solutions to real engineering solutions which incorporate the scientific and technological knowledge into useful systems, which are able to one day successfully pass the Turing test.

Bridging the gap between theory and practice and incorporating theoretical results into useful products is still one of the key issues for industrialized countries. In the context of Ibero-America it seems essential that AI researchers accept the challenge of solving real-world problems, making the science and technology based on AI contribute to the progress of our developing communities.

This book contains revised versions of the 97 papers selected by the program committee for presentation and discussion during the conference. The volume is structured into 13 thematic groups according to the topics addressed by the papers.

November 2002

Francisco J. Garijo,   Miguel Toro Bonilla   José C. Riquelme Santos

Acknowledgments

We would like to express our sincere gratitude to all the people who helped to bring about IBERAMIA 2002. First of all thanks to the contributing authors, for ensuring the richness of the conference and for their cooperation in the preparation of this volume.

Special thanks are due to the members of the program committee and reviewers for their professionalism and their dedication in selecting the best papers for the conference. Thanks also to the IBERAMIA Executive Committee for its guidance and continuous support.

We owe particular gratitude to the invited speakers for sharing with us their experiences and their most recent research results.

Nothing would have been possible without the initiative and dedication of the Organizing Committee from the LSI Department at the University of Seville. We are very grateful to all the people who helped in the large variety of organizing tasks, namely Mariano González our web manager, Carmelo del Valle our publicity manager, Roberto Ruiz for his support during August, Paco Ferrer for his help in the preparation of this book, Jesús Aguilar and Rafael M. Gasca for their contribution to the management of the tutorials and workshops, Juan A. Ortega and Raúl Giráldez for their help in the management of local arrangements and financial issues. The Organizing Committee chair Miguel Toro Bonilla and his team did a great job.

We would like to thank Telefónica, and especially Arturo Moreno Garciarán, General Director of Institutional Relationships, for his continuous support of the conference and for sponsoring the production of this book. Thanks very much to Telefónica I+D and its CEO, Isidoro Padilla, for providing the environment and the technical facilities to prepare the book.

Finally, we would like to acknowledge the role of the IBERAMIA 2002 sponsors: Universidad de Sevilla, Vicerrectorado de Extensión Universitaria y Vicerrectorado de Investigación, the Spanish council for research and technology, CICYT, and the Fundación FIDETIA. All of them provided constant support for both the conference organization and the proceedings' publication.

IBERAMIA 2002 Organizing Committee

Program and Scientific Chairman
Francisco J. Garijo
Telefónica I+D
28048 Madrid, Spain

Organization Chairman
Miguel Toro Bonilla
Dpto. Leng. y Sistemas Informáticos
Universidad de Sevilla
Av. Reina Mercedes s/n
41012 Sevilla, Spain

Organization Vice-Chairman
José C. Riquelme Santos
Dpto. Leng. y Sistemas Informáticos
Universidad de Sevilla
Av. Reina Mercedes s/n
41012 Sevilla, Spain

IBERAMIA 2002 Program Committee

Agostino Poggi (Italy)
Alejandro Ceccatto (Argentina)
Alexandro Provetti (Italy)
Alfredo Waitzanfield (Mexico)
Amal El Fallah (France)
Ana García Serrano (Spain)
Ana Paiva (Portugal)
Analia Amandi (Argentina)
Angel P. del Pobil (Spain)
Anna Helena Reali (Brazil)
Antonio Bahamonde (Spain)
Antonio Ferrandez (Spain)
Antonio Moreno (Spain)
Ariadne Carvalho (Brazil)
Carolina Chang (Venezuela)
Claire Nédellec (France)
Ed Durfee (USA)
Elisabeth Andre (Germany)
Enrique Sucar (Mexico)
Federico Barber (Spain)
Fernando Moura Pires (Portugal)
Gabriel Pereira Lopes (Portugal)
Gabriela Henning (Argentina)
Gerardo Ayala (Mexico)

Guillermo Morales Luna (Mexico)
Gustavo Arroyo Figueroa (Mexico)
Hector Geffner (Venezuela)
Jesús Favela Vara (Mexico)
José Maia Neves (Portugal)
José C. Riquelme (Spain)
Juan Flores (Mexico)
Juan M Corchado (Spain)
Kevin Knight (USA)
Marcelo Finger (Brazil)
Maria Cristina Riff (Chile)
Maria Fox (UK)
Michael Huns (USA)
Osvaldo Cairo (Mexico)
Pablo Noriega (Mexico)
Pavel Bradzil (Portugal)
Riichiro Mizoguchi (Japan)
Roque Marin (Spain)
Rosa Vicari (Brazil)
Scott Moss (UK)
Solange Rezende (Brazil)
Stefano Cerri (France)
William B Langdon (UK)
Yves Demazeau (France)

Reviewers

Agostino Poggi
Alejandro Ceccatto
Alexandre S. Simões
Alexandro Provetti
Alfredo Weitzenfeld
Alípio Jorge
Alneu de Andrade Lopes
Amal El Fallah
Amedeo Napoli
Ana García Serrano
Ana Isabel Martinez
Ana Paiva
Analia Amandi
Andre Ponce de Leon
André Riyuiti Hirakawa
Angel P. del Pobil
Anna Helena Reali
Antonio Bahamonde
Antonio Ferrandez
Antonio Morales Escrig
Antonio Moreno
Ariadne Carvalho
Aurora Vizcaino
Beatriz Barros
Begoña Martinez Salvador
Carlos Brizuela
Carlos Carrascosa
Carlos Eduardo Ferreira
Carlos García-Vallejo
Carlos H.C. Ribeiro
Carlos Soares
Carmelo del Valle
Carolina Chang
Claire Nédellec
Ed Durfee
Edson Augusto Melanda
Elisabeth Andre

Enric Cervera i Mateu
Enrique Sucar
Eva Millán
Eva Onaindica
Fabio Paraguaçu
Federico Barber
Fernando Moura Pires
Francisco Ferrer-Troyano
Francisco J. Garijo
Francisco Herrera
Gabriel Pereira Lopes
Gabriel Recatalá Ballester
Gabriela Henning
Gerardo Ayala
Gilles Bisson
Guillermo Morales Luna
Gustavo Arroyo Figueroa
Gustavo Olague
Hector Geffner
Hugo Hidalgo
Jacqueline Brigladori
Jesús Favela Vara
Jesús Aguilar-Ruiz
João Gama
Joaquim Pinto da Costa
Jorge Gomez Sanz
José Maia Neves
José C. Riquelme
José Santos Reyes
Juan Flores
Juan M. Corchado
Juan Pavón Mestras
Kevin Knight
Leliane Nunes de Barros
Luis Hernandez
Luís Torgo
Marcelo Finger

Maria Carolina Monard
Maria Cristina Riff
Maria Fox
Maria Jose Castro
Mariano González Romano
Michael Huns
Michele Sebag
Nathalie Pernelle
Osvaldo Cairo
Pablo Granito
Pablo Noriega
Paulo Azevedo
Pavel Bradzil
Rafael M. Gasca
Raúl Giraldez Rojo
Raul Marin Prades
Reinaldo A.C. Bianchi
Renata Wasserman
Riichiro Mizoguchi
Roberto Marcondes Cesar
Roberto Ruiz-Sánchez
Roque Marin
Rosa Vicari
Roseli A. Francelin
Sandra Maria Aluisio
Scott Moss
Solange Rezende
Stefano Cerri
Thorsten Joachims
Valguima O. Martinez
Vicente Julián
William B. Langdon
Yves Demazeau
Yves Kodratoff
Zhao Liang

Table of Contents

Knowledge Representation and Reasoning

Uncertainty and Fuzzy Systems

Genetic Algorithms

Neural Nets

Distributed Artificial Intelligence and Multi-agent Systems

Natural Language Processing

Intelligent Tutoring Systems

Control and Real Time

Robotics

Computer Vision

Improving Naive Bayes Using Class-Conditional ICA

Marco Bressan and Jordi Vitrià

Centre de Visió per Computador, Dept. Informàtica
Universitat Autònoma de Barcelona, 08193 Bellaterra, Barcelona, Spain
Tel. +34 93 581 30 73 Fax. +34 93 581 16 70
{marco, jordi}@cvc.uab.es

Abstract. In the past years, Naive Bayes has experienced a renaissance in machine learning, particularly in the area of information retrieval. This classifier is based on the not always realistic assumption that class-conditional distributions can be factorized in the product of their marginal densities. On the other side, one of the most common ways of estimating the Independent Component Analysis (ICA) representation for a given random vector consists in minimizing the Kullback-Leibler distance between the joint density and the product of the marginal densities (mutual information). From this that ICA provides a representation where the independence assumption can be held on stronger grounds. In this paper we propose class-conditional ICA as a method that provides an adequate representation where Naive Bayes is the classifier of choice. Experiments on two public databases are performed in order to confirm this hypothesis.

1   Introduction

For years, the most common use of the Naive Bayes Classifier has been to appear in classification benchmarks outperformed by other, more recent, methods. Despite this fate, in the past few years this simple technique has emerged once again, basically due to its results both in performance and speed in the area of information retrieval and document categorization [1,2]. Recent experiments on benchmark databases have also shown that Naive Bayes outperforms several standard classifiers even when the independence assumption is not met [3]. Additionally, the statistical nature of Naive Bayes implies interesting theoretic and predictive properties and, if the independence assumption is held and the univariate densities properly estimated, it is well known that no other classifier can outperform Naive Bayes in the sense of misclassification probability. Attempts to overcome the restriction imposed by the independence assumption have motivated attempts to relax this assumption via a modification of the classifier [4], feature extraction in order to hold the assumption on stronger grounds, and approaches to underestimate the independence assumption by showing it doesn't make a big difference [3,5]. This paper is clearly on the second line of research: we propose a class-conditional Independent Component Analysis Representation

F.J. Garijo, J.C. Riquelme, and M. Toro (Eds.): IBERAMIA 2002, LNAI 2527, pp. 1–10, 2002.

(CC-ICA) together with an appropriate feature selection procedure in order to obtain a representation where statistical independence is maximized. This representation has already proved successful in the area of object recognition and classification of high dimensional data [6].

For multivariate random data, Independent Component Analysis (ICA) provides a linear representation where the projected components (usually called independent components) have maximized statistical independence. Additionally, in many problems the unidimensional densities of the independent components belong to restricted density families, such as supergaussian or subgaussian, exponential densities, etc. This prior knowledge allows a simple parametric approach to the estimations. The success of performing Naive Bayes over an ICA representation has an additional explanation. It has been shown that Naive Bayes performance improves under the presence of low-entropy distributions [5]. In many problems, this is precisely the type of distribution achieved by an ICA representation [7,8,9,10].

In Section 2 we introduce the concept of independence and conditional independence, making some observations that justify the need for class-conditional representations. Here, we also introduce the Bayes Decision scheme and the particular case corresponding to the Naive Bayes classifier. Section 3 introduces Independent Component Analysis (ICA) and explains how it can be employed, through class-conditional representations, to force independence on the random vector representing a certain class. Naive Bayes is adapted to our representation. The problem of estimating the resulting marginal densities is also covered in this section. In Section 4, using the concept of divergence, briefly provides a scheme to select those features that preserve class separability from each representation in order to classify using a restricted set of features. Finally, experiments are performed on the Letter Image Recognition Data, from the UCI Repository [11] and the MNIST handwritten digits database [12]. These experiments illustrate the importance of the independence assumptions by applying the Naive Bayes classifiers to different representations and comparing the results. The representations used are the original representation, a class-conditional PCA representation (since PCA uncorrelates the data, under our line of reasoning, it can be understood as a second-order step towards independence) and finally our CC-ICA representation.

2   Independence and the Bayes Rule

Let X and Y be random variables and $p(x, y)$, $p(x)$, $p(y)$ and $p(x|y)$ be, respectively, the joint density of (X, Y), the marginal densities of X and Y, and the conditional density of X given $Y = y$. We say that X and Y are independent if $p(x, y) = p(x)p(y)$ or equivalently, $p(x|y) = p(x)$. It proves useful to understand independence from the following statement derived from the latter: Two variables are independent when the value one variable takes gives us no knowledge on the value of the other variable. For the multivariate case $(X_1, ..., X_N)$, independence can be defined by extending the first expression as $p(x) = p(x_1)...p(x_N)$.

In the context of statistical classification, given K classes in a D-dimensional space $\Omega = \{C_1, ...C_K\}$ and a set of new features $\mathbf{x_T} = (x_1, ..., x_D)$ we wish to assign $\mathbf{x_T}$ to a particular class minimizing the probability of misclassification. It can be proved that the solution to this problem is to assign $\mathbf{x_T}$ to the class that maximizes the *posterior probability* $P(C_k|\mathbf{x_T}$. The Bayes rule formulates this probability in terms of the likelihood and the prior probabilities, which are simpler to estimate. This transformation, together with the assumption of independence and equiprobable priors results on the Naive Bayes rule,

$$C_{Naive} = \arg \max_{k=1...K} \prod_{d=1}^{D} P(x_d|C_k) \qquad (1)$$

The simplification introduced in (1), transforming one D-dimensional problem into D 1-dimensional problems, is particularly useful in the presence of high dimensional data, where straightforward density estimation proves ineffective [13,14]. Notice that class-conditional independence is required: a representation that achieves global independence of the data (sometimes referred to as "linked independence") is useless in this sense. A frequent mistake is to think that the independence of the features implies class-conditional independence, being Simpson's paradox [15] probably the most well known counterexample. We conclude that in order to assume class-conditional independence, it is not enough to work in an independent feature space. For this particular case, in which class-conditional independence is not true, we now introduce a local representation where this assumption can be held on stronger grounds.

3   Independent Component Analysis

The ICA of an N dimensional random vector is the linear transform which minimizes the statistical dependence between its components. This representation in terms of independence proves useful in an important number of applications such as data analysis and compression, blind source separation, blind deconvolution, denoising, etc. [16,17,10,18]. Assuming the random vector we wish to represent through ICA has no noise, the ICA Model can be expressed as

$$\mathbf{W}(\mathbf{x} - \bar{\mathbf{x}}) = \mathbf{s} \qquad (2)$$

where $\mathbf{x}$ corresponds to the random vector representing our data, $\bar{\mathbf{x}}$ its mean, $\mathbf{s}$ is the random vector of *independent components* with dimension $M \leq N$, and $\mathbf{W}$ is called the *filter* or *projection matrix*. This model is frequently presented in terms of $\mathbf{A}$, the pseudoinverse of $\mathbf{W}$, called the *mixture matrix*. Names are derived from the original blind source separation application of ICA. If the components of vector $\mathbf{s}$ are independent, at most one is Gaussian and its densities are not reduced to a point-like mass, it can be proved that $\mathbf{W}$ is completely determined [19].

In practice, the estimation of the filter matrix $\mathbf{W}$ and thus the independent components can be performed through the optimization of several objective functions such as likelihood, network entropy or mutual information. Though several algorithms have been tested, the method employed in this article is the one known as FastICA. This method attempts to minimize the mutual information by finding maximum negentropy directions, proving to be fast and efficient [18]. Since mutual information is the Kullback-Leibler difference between a distribution and its marginal densities, we would be obtaining a representation where the Naive Bayes rule best approximates the Bayes Rule in the sense of Kullback-Leibler.

As mentioned, global feature independence is not sufficient for conditional independence. In [6] we introduced a class-conditional ICA (CC-ICA) model that, through class-conditional representations, ensures conditional independence. This scheme was successfully applied in the framework of classification for object recognition. The CC-ICA model is estimated from the training set for each class. If $\mathbf{W}_k$ and $\mathbf{s}_k$ are the projection matrix and the independent components for class C_k with dimensions $M_k \times N$ and M_k respectively, then from (2)

$$\mathbf{s}^k = \mathbf{W}^k(\mathbf{x} - \overline{\mathbf{x}^k}) \tag{3}$$

where $\mathbf{x} \in C_k$ and $\overline{\mathbf{x}^k}$ is the class mean, estimated from the training set. Assuming the class-conditional representation actually provides independent components, we have that the class-conditional probability noted as $p^k(\mathbf{s}) \stackrel{def}{=} p(\mathbf{s}^k)$ can now be expressed in terms of unidimensional densities,

$$p(\mathbf{x}|C_k) = \nu_k p^k(\mathbf{s}) = \nu_k \prod_{m=1}^{M_k} p^k(s_m) \tag{4}$$

with $\nu_k = (\int p^k(\mathbf{s})ds)^{-1}$, a normalizing constant. Plugging in (4) in (1) and applying logarithms, we obtain the Naive Bayes rule under a CC-ICA representation,

$$C_{Naive} = \arg \max_{k=1...K} \left(\sum_{m=1}^{M_k} \log P^k(s_{lm}) \right) + \nu_k \tag{5}$$

In practice, classification is performed as follows. Representative features are extracted from the objects belonging to class C_k, conforming training set T_k. T_k is then used to estimate the ICA model and projected into this model. From the projected features, the M_k one dimensional densities are estimated, together with the normalization constants. If we have no prior information on these marginal distributions, nonparametric or semiparametric methods can be used in the one dimensional estimation. Given a test object, its representative features are projected on each class, and the class-conditional likelihoods calculated. The test object is assigned to the class with the highest probability.

As a matter of fact, the nonparametric density estimation is not even necessary, due to the fact that the ICA Model gives us a priori information that can be used in the estimation of the marginal densities of the independent components. In ICA, since progressive maximization of mutual information is achieved in the directions of maximum nongaussianity [20], the resulting marginal distributions are strongly nongaussian. Actually, a close relationship between sparsity and ICA has been pointed out [8,9,7]. Classification can be interpreted in terms of sparsity in the following way. If an independent feature corresponds to an object belonging to a certain class, then a sparse representation for this feature will be provided. This means that the independent components of the projected object will be nearly zero for most values and consequently should have a large probability. Instead, if the object does not belong to the class, it should activate several independent components at the same time when projected and consequently have a low probability. This property is illustrated in Figure (1) for two class-conditional representations obtained in the experiments.

Though several parametric, semi-parametric and nonparametric approaches are possible, the experiments were performed using Laplacian or Gaussian mixtures for estimating the marginal distributions.

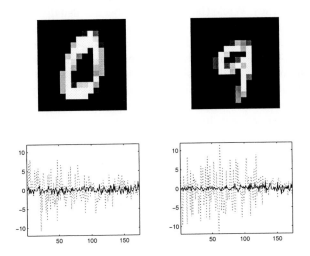

Fig. 1. In top row: representative for MNIST classes "0" and "9". The bottom row plots the features of each representative on its own and on the other's classconditional representations. Sparsity of the first representation (continuous) is observed as well as random feature activation when class belonging is not met (dotted).

4   Feature Selection

The fact the features we are dealing with are statistically independent can also be an advantage in the context of feature selection. Divergence, a frequently used measure for feature selection is additive for statistically independent variables.

Class separability is a standard criterion in feature selection for classification. Measures for class separability are generally obtained from the distance among the previously estimated class-conditional distributions. A commonly used distance measure for (class-conditional) densities, for its connection with information theory, is the Kullback-Leibler distance,

$$KL(C_i, C_j) = \int_\Omega p(\mathbf{x}|C_i) \log \frac{p(\mathbf{x}|C_i)}{p(\mathbf{x}|C_j)} d\mathbf{x} \qquad (6)$$

where $1 \leq i, j \leq K$. The asymmetry of Kullback-Leibler motivates the symmetric measure of divergence, since long ago used for feature selection [21], defined as

$$\hat{D}_{ij} = \hat{D}(C_i, C_j) = KL(C_i, C_j) + KL(C_j, C_i) \qquad (7)$$

Besides being symmetric, divergence is zero between a distribution and itself, always positive, monotonic on the number of features and provides an upper bound for the classification error [22]. The two main drawbacks of divergence are that it requires density estimation and has a nonlinear relationship with classification accuracy. While the second drawback is usually overcomed by using a transformed version of divergence, introduced by Swain and Davis [23,24], the first inconvenient is not present when class-conditional features are independent. For this case, it can be proved that divergence is additive on the features. So, for this particular case, unidimensional density estimation can be performed and the calculation of divergence for a feature subset $S \subseteq \{1, ..., N\}$ (noted by $\hat{D}_{ij}^S$) is straightforward. A very important property besides monotonicity shared by transformed divergence and divergence, is that

$$(n_1 \notin S, n_2 \notin S) \wedge (D_{ij}^{n_1} \leq D_{ij}^{n_2}) \Rightarrow (D_{ij}^{S \bigcup n_1} \leq D_{ij}^{S \bigcup n_1}) \qquad (8)$$

This property of order suggests that, at least for the two class case, the best feature subset is the one that contains the features with maximum marginal (transformed) divergence, and thus provides a very simple rule for feature selection without involving any search procedure.

Although, (transformed) divergence only provides a measure for the distance between two classes there are several ways of extending it to the multiclass case, providing an effective feature selection criterion. The most common method is to use the average divergence, defined as the average divergence over all class pairs. This approach is simple and preserves the exposed property of order for feature subsets, but it is not reliable as the variance of the pairwise divergences increases. A more robust approach is to sort features by their maximum minimum (two-class) divergence. This works fine for small subsets but decays as the size of the subset increases: sorting features by maximum minimum divergence is a very conservative election.

In the CC-ICA context we have K local linear representations, each one making $\mathbf{x}|C_k$ independent. This involves the selection of possibly distinct single features belonging to different representations. We now provide an alternative definition of divergence, adapted to local representations.

The log-likelihood ratio (L) is defined as,

$$L_{ij}(\mathbf{x}) = \log p(\mathbf{x}|C_i) - \log p(\mathbf{x}|C_j) \qquad (9)$$

$L_{ij}(\mathbf{x})$ measures the overlap of the class-conditional densities in $\mathbf{x}$. It can be seen from (7) that $D_{ij} = E_{C_i}(L_{ij}) + E_{C_j}(L_{ji})$ where E_{C_i} is the class-conditional expectation operator. Approximating $E_{C_i}(g(x)) \approx (1/\#C_i)\sum_{x \in C_i} g(x) \overset{def}{=} \overline{g(x)}_{C_i}$, and reordering the terms, we have

$$D_{ij} \approx \left(\overline{\log p(x|C_i)}_{C_i} - \overline{\log p(x|C_i)}_{C_j} \right) + \left(\overline{\log p(x|C_j)}_{C_j} - \overline{\log p(x|C_j)}_{C_i} \right)$$

$$\overset{def}{=} D'_{ij} + D'_{ji}$$

$$(10)$$

D'_{ij} measures the difference in the expected likelihood of classes i and j, assuming all samples are taken from class i. It is no longer symmetric but still additive for conditionally independent variables. Introducing (4) D'_{ij} can be expressed as,

$$D'_{ij} = \nu_i \sum_{m=1}^{M_i} \left(\overline{\log p^i(s_m)}_{C_i} - \overline{\log p^i(s_m)}_{C_j} \right) \overset{def}{=} \nu_i \sum_{m=1}^{M_i} D'^m_{ij} \qquad (11)$$

Divergence is maximized by maximizing both D'_{ij} and D'_{ji}. The asymmetry and locality of the latter will cause different feature subsets on each class representation, meaning that while certain features might be appropriate for separating class C_i from class C_j in the ith representation, possibly distinct features will separate class C_j from class C_i in the jth representation.

Extension to the multiclass case can be performed as with divergence. For instance, having fixed the representation, the average has to be taken over only one index,

$$D'^m_{A_i} = \frac{1}{K-1} \sum_{j=1, j \neq i}^{K} D'^m_{ij} \qquad (12)$$

5   Experiments

A first experiment is performed on the Letter Image Recognition Data [11]. Each instance of the 20000 images within this database represents a capital typewritten letter in one of twenty fonts. Each letter is represented using 16 integer valued features corresponding to statistical moments and edge counts. Training is done on the first 16000 instances and test on the final 4000. There are approximately 615 samples per class in the training set. Fig. (2) illustrates the results of the Naive Bayes Classifier for different representations and feature subsets. The divergence feature selection criterion was used for ICA (a global ICA representation), CC-ICA and ORIG (the original representation), while for PCA, features were selected as ordered by the representation. For all the Naive Bayes Classifiers, the mixture of two gaussians was used to estimate the resulting unidimensional densities. The results of Maximum Likelihood classification on PCA were also included as a reference.

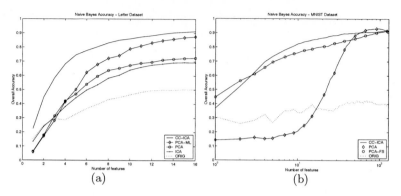

Fig. 2. Naive Bayes performance on the original, PCA (class-conditional), PCA-ML (global), ICA (global) and CC-ICA representations of the Letter (a) and MNIST (b) databases. The importance of the independence assumption on Naive Bayes performance is observed. Notice log-scale on (b)

We can observe in Fig. 2(a) the importance of the independence assumption when using, both Naive Bayes and the divergence criterium. The CC-ICA representation, by seeking this independence, achieves much better results than all the other implementations. To test the feature selection criterion, on this database we also tried Naive Bayes on 10000 random 8-feature combinations for each class, resulting that no combination achieved our classification results (83.17%).

The second experiment was performed on the MNIST handwritten digit database [12], which contains 60000 training and 10000 test samples. The images were resized from 28×28 to 16×16 resulting in 256 dimensional samples. 5000 and 750 samples per digit were randomly chosen for training and test sets, respectively. Overall accuracy using 1 through 128 features is plotted in Fig. 2(b). In all cases, a Naive Bayes classifier was used and the unidimensional densities estimated using the same approach (mixture of three gaussians) for adequate comparison. Also in all cases using simpler estimation methods such as gaussian or nonparametric (frequential) estimation performs worst than the exposed results. In the graph, PCA stands for a class-conditional PCA representation using the features as given by PCA. This approach performs poorly for a low number of features (< 50) but, after 60 features outperforms all the other methods, starting to decrease in performance after 100 features. Using the divergence feature selection criterion on PCA (PCA-FS) improves the performance of Naive Bayes on a PCA representation for a low number of features. CC-ICA obtains the best accuracy when the number of features is less than 60, obtaining an accuracy of .9 with as few of 50 features and .8 with only 9 features. The accuracy of CC-ICA is monotonic on the number of features. Several hypothesis can be thought of when analyzing lower accuracy of CC-ICA with respect to PCA for a large number of features. From the ICA perspective, it is well known that in large dimensions degenerate independent sources can arise. This seems to be our case since, in order to allow a dimensionality of 128, we have included sources with estimated kurtosis as high as 100. This affects both the classifier and the feature selection criterion.

In all cases unidimensional feature densities are estimated using the same approach (gaussian mixtures) for adequate comparison. Also in all cases using simpler estimation methods such as gaussian or nonparametric (frequential) estimation performs considerably worst than the exposed results.

6   Conclusions

The Naive Bayes classifier, though its generally unmet assumptions and notorious simplicity, still performs well over a large variety of problems. In this article, by making use of Independent Component Analysis, we present a class-conditional representation that allows to hold the Naive Bayes independence assumption on stronger grounds and thus improve the performance. Reinforcing the hypothesis is not the only reason for this improvement. It has been shown that Naive Bayes performance has a direct relationship with feature low entropy, and it is also well known that in several cases the independent components have low entropy (supergaussian/sparse distributions). For this representation we also introduce a scheme for selecting those (class-conditional) features most adequate for the task of classification. This scheme takes advantage of the property that states that feature divergence is additive on statistically independent features. Precisely the assumption we will make when using Naive Bayes.

A first experiment is performed in order to show that our proposed representation and feature selection criterion performs well even in low dimensional problems. The second experiment, on the MNIST database, evaluates Naive Bayes improvement in a high dimensional database. In both experiments results are compared against applying Naive Bayes on the original representation and on a PCA representation.

Acknowledgements. This work was supported by MCyT grant TIC2000-0399-C02-01 and the Secretaria de Estado de Educacion, Universidades, Investigacion y Desarrollo from the Ministerio de Educacion y Cultura of Spain.

References

1. Yang, Y., Slattery, S., Ghani, R.: A study of approaches to hypertext categorization. Journal of Intelligent Information Systems. Kluwer Academic Press (2002)
2. Lewis, D.: Naive bayes at forty: The independence assumption in information retrieval. In N'edellec, C., Rouveirol, C., eds.: Proceedings of ECML-98, 10th European Conference on Machine Learning. Volume 1398.25., Springer Verlag, Heidelberg, DE (1998) 4–15
3. Domingos, P., Pazzani, M.J.: On the optimality of the simple bayesian classifier under zero-one loss. Machine Learning **29** (1997) 103–130
4. Turtle, H., Croft, W.: Evaluation of an inference network-based retrieval model. ACM Transactions on Information Systems **9** (1991) 187–222

5. Rish, I., Hellerstein, J., Thathachar, J.: An analysis of data characteristics that affect naive bayes performance. In N'edellec, C., Rouveirol, C., eds.: Proceedings of the Eighteenth Conference on Machine Learning -ICML2001, Morgan Kaufmann (2001) –

6. M.Bressan, D.Guillamet, J.Vitria: Using an ica representation of high dimensional data for object recognition and classification. In: IEEE CSC in Computer Vision and Pattern Recognition (CVPR 2001). Volume 1. (2001) 1004–1009

7. Bell, A., Sejnowski, T.: An information-maximization approach for blind signal separation. Neural Computation 7 (1995) 1129–1159

8. Field, D.: What is the goal of sensory coding? Neural Computation 6 (1994) 559–601

9. Hyvärinen, A.: Sparse code shrinkage: Denoising of nongaussian data by maximum likelihood estimation. Neural Computation 11 (1999) 1739–1768

10. Vigario, R., Jousmäki, V., Hämäläinen, M., Hari, R., Oja, E.: Independent component analysis for identification of artifacts in magnetoencephalographic recordings. Advances in Neural Information Processing Systems 10 (1998) 229–235

11. Blake, C., Merz, C.: Uci repository of machine learning databases (1998)

12. LeCun, Y., Labs-Research, A.: The MNIST DataBase of Handwritten digits. http://www.research.att.com/ yann/ocr/mnist/index.html (1998)

13. Scott, D.W.: Multivariate Density Estimation. John Wiley and sons, New York, NY (1992)

14. Duda, R., Hart, P., Stork, D.: Pattern Classication. John Wiley and Sons, Inc., New York, 2nd edition (2001)

15. Simpson, E.: The interpretation of interaction in contingency tables. Journal of the Royal Statistical Society, Ser. B 13 (1951) 238–241

16. Bell, A., Sejnowski, T.: The 'independent components' of natural scenes are edge filters. Neural Computation 11 (1999) 1739–1768

17. Lee, T., Lewicki, M., Seynowski, T.: A mixture models for unsupervised classification of non-gaussian sources and automatic context switching in blind signal separation. IEEE Transactions on PAMI 22 (2000) 1–12

18. Hyvärinen, A., Karhunen, J., Oja, E.: Independent Component Analysis. John Wiley and Sons (2001)

19. Comon, P.: Independent component analysis - a new concept? Signal Processing 36 (1994) 287–314

20. Hyvärinen, A.: New approximatins of differential entropy for independent component analysis and projection pursuit. Advances in Neural Processing Systems 10 (1998) 273–279

21. Marill, T., Green, D.: On the effectiveness of receptors in recognition systems. IEEE Trans. on Information Theory 9 (1963) 1–17

22. Kailath, T.: The divergence and bhattacharyya distance measures in signal selection. IEEE Trans. on Communication Technology COM-15 1 (1967) 52–60

23. Swain, P., King, R.: Two effective feature selection criteria for multispectral remote sensing. In: Proceedings of the 1st International Joint Conference on Pattern Recognition, IEEE 73 CHO821-9. (1973) 536–540

24. Swain, P., Davis, S.: Remote sensing: the quantitative approach. McGraw-Hill (1978)

Detecting Events and Topics by Using Temporal References

Aurora Pons-Porrata[1], Rafael Berlanga-Llavori[2], and José Ruíz-Shulcloper[3]

[1]Universidad de Oriente, Santiago de Cuba (Cuba)
[2]Universitat Jaume I, Castellón (Spain)
[3]Institute of Cybernetics, Mathematics and Physics, La Habana (Cuba)

Abstract. In this paper we propose an incremental clustering algorithm for event detection, which makes use of the temporal references in the text of newspaper articles. This algorithm is hierarchically applied to a set of articles in order to discover the structure of topics and events that they describe. In the first level, documents with a high temporal-semantic similarity are clustered together into events. In the next levels of the hierarchy, these events are successively clustered so that more complex events and topics can be discovered. The evaluation results demonstrate that regarding the temporal references of documents improves the quality of the system-generated clusters, and that the overall performance of the proposed system compares favorably to other on-line detection systems of the literature.

1 Introduction

Starting from a continuous stream of newspaper articles, the *Event Detection* problem consists in determining for each incoming document, whether it reports on a new event, or it belongs to some previously identified event. One of the most important issues in this problem is to define what an *event* is. Initially, an event can be defined as something that happens at a particular place and time. However, many events occur along several places and several time periods (e.g. the whole event related to a complex trial). For this reason, researchers in this field prefer the broader term of *Topic*, which is defined as an important event or activity along with all its directly related events [5].

A *Topic Detection System* (TDS) is intended to discover the topics reported in the newspaper articles to organize them in terms of these topic classes. In this work we will consider *on-line* systems, which incrementally build the topic classes as each article arrives. Current on-line TD systems have in common that use both the chronological order of articles, and a fast document-clustering algorithm. For example, the system presented in [8] uses the Single-Pass algorithm and a moving time window to group the incoming articles into topics. Moreover, this system defines a similarity function that takes into account the position of the articles in the time window. In [6] the Single-Pass algorithm is applied to a set of document classifiers whose thresholds take into account the temporal adjacency of articles. The UMass system [1] uses an $1NN$ algorithm over the sequence of incoming articles, which has a quadratic time complexity.

F.J. Garijo, J.C. Riquelme, and M. Toro (Eds.): IBERAMIA 2002, LNAI 2527, pp. 11-20, 2002.
© Springer-Verlag Berlin Heidelberg 2002

One drawback of current TD systems is that they make irrevocable clustering assignments. As a consequence, the set of events detected by the system could be different depending on the arrival order of the documents. Another limitation is that they only use the document publication date to locate the occurrences of events.

Our main research interest is to discover the temporal structure of topics and events, that is, to identify not only the topics but also the possible smaller events they comprise. In our opinion, all temporal properties of articles must be further exploited to achieve this purpose. In this sense, we think that the time references extracted from the article texts can be efficiently used to cluster those articles that report about the same event.

In this paper we propose an incremental clustering algorithm for event detection, which makes use of the temporal references in the text of newspaper articles. This algorithm is hierarchically applied to a set of articles in order to discover the structure of topics and events that they describe.

The remainder of the paper is organized as follows: Section 2 presents the representation of documents taking into account their temporal components, Section 3 proposes a new document similarity function for these documents, Section 4 describes the clustering algorithm, and Section 5 describes our experiments. Conclusions and further work are presented in Section 6.

2 Document Representation

The incoming stream of documents that feed our system comes from some on-line newspapers available in Internet, which are automatically translated into XML (eXtended Markup Language). This representation preserves the original logical structure of the newspapers, so that different thematic sections can be distinguished as well as the different parts of the articles (e.g. the title, authors, place, publication date, etc.). Nevertheless, in this work we will use only the publication date and the textual contents of the articles. From them, we define two feature vectors to represent each document, namely:

- *A vector of weighted terms,* where the terms represent the lemmas of the words appearing in the text. Stop words, such as articles, prepositions and adverbs, are disregarded from this vector. Terms are statistically weighted using the normalized term frequency (TF).

  In our work, we do not use the Inverse Document Frequency (IDF) because of the on-line nature of the final detection system. In this context we assume that it does not exist a training corpus to obtain the initial values for the IDF weights.

- *A vector of weighted time entities*, where time entities represent either dates or date intervals expressed in the Gregorian calendar. These entities are automatically extracted from the texts by using the algorithm presented in [3]. Briefly, this algorithm firstly applies shallow parsing to detect the temporal sentences in the text. Afterwards, these temporal sentences are translated into time entities of a formal time model. Finally, those time entities that represent specific dates or date intervals are selected. It is worth mentioning that this tool deals with both absolute (e.g. "10th of April of 1999") and relative time references (e.g. "today", "this week", etc.).

Time entities are statistically weighted using the frequency of their references in the text. From this vector, all the time references that are no relevant to the article are removed, namely: those that are separated more than ten days from the publication date, and those whose frequency is smaller than a tenth part of the maximum in the vector.

Summarizing, each article is represented as follows:

- A vector of terms $T^i = (TF_1^i, \dots, TF_n^i)$, where TF_k^i is the relative frequency of term t_k in the document d^i.

- A vector of time entities $F^i = (TF_{f_1^i}, \dots, TF_{f_{m_i}^i})$, where $TF_{f_k^i}$ is the absolute frequency of the time entity f_k in the document d^i and $k = 1, \dots, m_i$.

3   Document Similarity Measure

Automatic clustering of documents, as in event detection, relies on a similarity measure. Most of the clustering algorithms presented in the literature use the cosine measure to compare two documents. In our case, the aim of the similarity measure is to indicate whether two articles refer to a same event or not. For this purpose we have also taken into account the proximity of the temporal properties of the documents. Thus, we consider that two articles refer to the same event if their contents and time references approximately coincide.

To compare the term vectors of two documents d^i and d^j we use the cosine measure:

$$S_T(d^i, d^j) = \frac{\sum_{k=1}^{n} TF_k^i \cdot TF_k^j}{\sqrt{\sum_{k=1}^{n} TF_k^{i^2}} \cdot \sqrt{\sum_{k=1}^{n} TF_k^{j^2}}}$$

To compare the time vectors of two documents we propose the traditional distance between sets, which is defined as follows:

$$D_F(d^i, d^j) = \min_{f^i \in FR^i, f^j \in FR^j} \left\{ d(f^i, f^j) \right\}$$

where $d(f^i, f^j)$ is the distance between the dates f^i and f^j, and FR^i is the set of all dates f^i of the document d^i that satisfy the following conditions:

- each f^i has the maximum frequency in d^i, that is, $TF_{f^i} = \max_{k=1,\dots,m_i} \left\{ TF_{f_k^i} \right\}$

- each f^i has the minimum distance to the publication date of d^i.

The last condition is not considered when comparing cluster representatives instead of documents.

It is not difficult to see that the set FR^i is not necessarily unitary. The distance d is defined as follows:

- If f^i and f^j are dates, then $d(f^i, f^j)$ is the number of days between f^i and f^j.
- If $f^i = [a, b]$ and $f^j = [c, d]$ are date intervals, then

$$d(f^i, f^j) = \min_{f_1 \in [a,b], f_2 \in [c,d]} \left\{ d(f_1, f_2) \right\}$$

- If f^i is a date and f^j is an interval, then $d(f^i, f^j) = d([f^i, f^i], f^j)$.
- If f^j is a date and f^i is an interval, this function is defined in a similar way.

Finally, the temporal-semantic similarity measure can be defined as follows:

$$S_{time}(d^i, d^j) = \begin{cases} S_T(d^i, d^j) & \text{if } D_F(d^i, d^j) \le \beta_{time} \\ 0 & \text{otherwise} \end{cases}$$

where β_{time} is the maximum number of days that are required to determine whether two articles refer to the same or to different events.

4   Temporal-Semantic Clustering of Documents

Given a document collection ζ we must find or generate a natural structure for these documents in the adopted representation space. This structure must be carried out by using some document similarity measure. In general, the clustering criterion has three parameters, namely: a similarity measure S, a property Π that establishes the use of S, and a threshold β_0. Thus, clusters are determined by imposing the fulfillment of certain properties over the similarities between documents.

According to this, we will consider the following definitions:

Definition 1: Two documents d^i and d^j are β_0-temporal-semantic similar if $S_{time}(d^i, d^j) \ge \beta_0$. Similarly, d^i is a β_0-isolated element if $\forall d^j \in \zeta$, $S_{time}(d^i, d^j) < \beta_0$, where β_0 is an user-defined parameter.

Definition 2 [4]: The set $NU \subseteq \zeta$, $NU \ne \phi$, is a β_0-compact set if:

a) $\forall d^j \in \zeta [d^i \in NU \wedge \underset{\substack{d^t \in \zeta \\ d^t \ne d^i}}{max} \{S_{time}(d^i, d^t)\} = S_{time}(d^i, d^j) \ge \beta_0] \Rightarrow d^j \in NU$.

b) $[\underset{\substack{d^i \in \zeta \\ d^i \ne d^p}}{max} \{S_{time}(d^p, d^i)\} = S_{time}(d^p, d^t) \ge \beta_0 \wedge d^t \in NU] \Rightarrow d^p \in NU$.

c) Any β_0-isolated element is a β_0-compact set (degenerated).

The first condition says that all documents of *NU* has the most β_0-temporal-semantic similar document in *NU*. The second condition says that it does not exist outside of *NU* a document whose the most β_0-temporal-semantic similar document is in *NU*.

Notice that this criterion is equivalent to find the connected components of the undirected graph based on the maximum similarity. In this graph, the nodes are the documents and there is an edge from the node d^i to the node d^j if d^j is the most β_0-temporal-semantic similar document to d^i. This criterion produces disjoint clusters.

4.1 Incremental β_0-Compact Algorithm

In this paper we propose a new incremental clustering algorithm for event detection, called *incremental β_0-compact algorithm*, which is based on Definition 2. Figure 1 presents this algorithm, which works as follows.

Each document d^i has associated the cluster to which it belongs and three fields: $To(d^i)$, which contains its most β_0-temporal-semantic similar document (or documents), the value of this maximum similarity $MaxSimil(d^i)$, and $From(d^i)$, which contains those documents for which d^i is the most β_0-temporal-semantic similar document.

Every time a new document arrives, its similarity with each document of the existing clusters is calculated and its fields are updated (Step 2). Then, a new cluster with the new document is built together with the documents connected to it in the graph of maximum similarity (Step 3 and 4). Every time a document is added to the new cluster, it is removed from the cluster in which it was located before (Step 4).

Finally, in Step 5 the clusters that can potentially become unconnected after Step 4 are reconstructed to form their β_0-compact set.

The worst case time complexity of this algorithm is $O(n^2)$, since for each document, all the documents of the existing clusters must be checked to find the most similar document. The construction of the connected components of the graph based on the maximum similarity in the Steps 4 and 5 is $O(n+e)$, since the graph is represented by its adjacency lists. Here e is the number of edges and, in our case, $e=cn$, where c is the maximum number of documents more similar to a given one.

It is worth mentioning that this clustering algorithm allows the finding of clusters with arbitrary shapes, as opposed to algorithms such as K-means and Single-Pass, which require central measurements in order to generate the clusters, restricting the shapes of these clusters to be spherical. Another advantage of this algorithm is that the generated set of clusters at each stage is unique independently on the arrival order of the documents. As we know the set of all compact sets of a given set is unique [4].

The parameter settings are chosen in practice by mathematical modeling of the problem together with the user-specialist.

4.2 Representation of Clusters

The first time we apply the previous clustering algorithm to the document stream we obtain several clusters with a high temporal-semantic similarity. In this level, the individual events reported by the documents are identified. In the next levels, applying the same clustering algorithm these events are successively clustered. As a consequence, more complex events and topics can be identified. The resulting hierarchy will describe the structure of topics and events taking into account their temporal occurrence. In this work we only deal with the two first levels of this hierarchy, called the *Event Level* and *Topic Level* respectively.

Input: Similarity threshold β_0.

          Similarity measure S_{time} and its parameters.

Output: Document clusters (β_0-compact set) representing the identified events.

Step 1. Arrival of a document d.

          $From(d) = \emptyset$, $To(d) = \emptyset$, $MaxSimil(d) = 0$, $UC = \emptyset$, $DC = \emptyset$.

Step 2. For each existing cluster C' do

          For each document d' in C' do

               (a) Calculate the similarity S_{time} between d and d'.

               (b) If $S_{time} \geq \beta_0$ then

                   If $S_{time} > MaxSimil(d')$ then

                       If $|To(d')| > 1$ then add C' to UC.

                       Update the fields of d': $To(d') = \{ d \}$, $MaxSimil(d') = S_{time}$.

                       Remove d' in $From(d'')$ for all $d'' \in To(d')$.

                       Add d' to $From(d)$.

                       If $C' \notin DC$ add C' to DC else add C' to UC.

                   If $S_{time} = MaxSimil(d')$ then

                       Add d to $To(d')$.

                       Add d' to $From(d)$.

                   If $S_{time} \geq MaxSimil(d)$ then update $MaxSimil(d)$ with S_{time} and $To(d)$ with d'.

Step 3. Create a new cluster C with the document d.

Step 4. If $MaxSimil(d) \neq 0$ then

               Add to C all the documents of the remaining clusters that have in the field To or in the field $From$ some document of C, and remove them from the clusters where they are placed.

Step 5. For each cluster C' of UC do

               (a) Remove C' of the existing cluster list.

               (b) $NewC = \{ d' \}$, d' is a document of C'.

               (c) Add to $NewC$ all the documents of the C' that have in the field To or in the field $From$ some document of $NewC$, and remove them from the C'.

               (d) Add $NewC$ to the existing cluster list

               (e) If $C' \neq \emptyset$ then go to 5(b)

Fig. 1. β_0-compact clustering algorithm

Once the clusters of the *event level* have been calculated and the representatives of each cluster are determined, they are grouped to form the clusters of the next level in the hierarchy.

The representative of a cluster c, denoted as $\bar{c}$, is a pair $(T^{\bar{c}}, F^{\bar{c}})$, in which $T^{\bar{c}}$ is the component of the terms, and $F^{\bar{c}}$ the temporal component. In this work, it is calculated as the average of the cluster's documents:

$$T^{\bar{c}} = \left(T_1^{\bar{c}}, \ldots, T_n^{\bar{c}}\right), \text{ where } T_j^{\bar{c}} = \frac{1}{|c|} \sum_{d^k \in c} TF_j^k \ , \ j \in \{1, \ldots, n\}$$

$$F^{\bar{c}} = \left(F_{f_1}^{\bar{c}}, \ldots, F_{f_s}^{\bar{c}}\right), \text{ where } F_{f_j}^{\bar{c}} = \frac{1}{|c|} \sum_{d^k \in c} TF_{f_j}^k \ , \ j \in \{1, \ldots, s\} \text{ and } s \text{ is the total}$$

number of time entities that describe the documents of this cluster.

In order to reduce the dimension of the cluster representatives, we also truncate their vectors by eliminating the terms (res. dates) whose frequency are lesser than the tenth part of the vector maximum frequency.

5   Evaluation

The effectiveness of the proposed clustering algorithm has been evaluated using a collection of 452 articles published in the Spanish newspaper "El País" during June 1999. We have manually identified 71 non-unitary events, being their maximum size of 16 documents. From these events we have identified 43 topics, whose maximum size is 57 documents. The original collection covers 21 events associated to the end of the war of Kosovo along with their immediate consequences. These events have a high temporal-semantic overlapping, which makes difficult their identification. Table 1 shows some of these events.

Table 1. Sample of Events of the Kosovo war episode.

Event Description	Date Range	#Docs
Peace agreement negotiations	June 07-08	16
Sign of the peace agreement	June 09-11	13
Political reactions in Yugoslavia	June 14-19	16
Serbian troops leave Kosovo	June 10-19	6
Deployment of NATO Troops	June 11-19	13
Return of Albanian refugees to Kosovo	June 16-24	8
Serbian refugees escape from Kosovo	June 14-24	11

To evaluate the clustering results we use two measures of the literature that compare the system-generated clusters with the manually labeled events, namely: the F1-measure and the *Detection Cost* [5].

The F1-measure is widely applied in Information Retrieval Systems, and it combines the precision and recall factors. In our case, the F1-measure of the cluster number j with respect to the event number i can be evaluated as follows:

$$F1(i, j) = 2 \cdot \frac{n_{ij}}{n_i + n_j}$$

where n_{ij} is the number of common members in the event i and the cluster j, n_i is the cardinality of the event i, and n_j is the cardinality of the cluster j.

To define a global measure, first each event must be mapped to the cluster that produces the maximum F1-measure:

$$\sigma(i) = \arg\max_{j} \{F1(i, j)\}$$

Hence, the overall F1-measure [2] is calculated as follows:

$$F1 = \frac{1}{N_{docs}} \sum_{i=1}^{N_{events}} n_i F1(i, \sigma(i))$$

The detection cost is a measure that combines both the miss and false alarm errors between an event i and a system-generated cluster j:

$$C_{DET}(i, j) = P_{miss}(i, j) \cdot P_{topic} + P_{false\_alarm}(i, j) \cdot (1 - P_{topic})$$

where $P_{miss} = (n_i - n_{ij}) / n_i$ and $P_{false\_alarm} = (n_j - n_{ij}) / (N - n_i)$, P_{topic} is the a priori probability of a document belonging to a given event, and N is the collection size.

It is worth mentioning that the P_{topic} probability must be different for each clustering level. This is because of the cluster sizes, which are higher as we add levels to the cluster hierarchy. The higher the average cluster size, the greater the probability of a document belonging to a given cluster is. In our experiments, the P_{topic} for the event level has been estimated in 0.014, and for the topic level it is about 0.025.

Again, to define the final measure, each event must be mapped to the cluster that produces the minimum detection cost:

$$\sigma(i) = \arg\min_{j} \{C_{DET}(i, j)\}$$

The macro-average of this measure (also called *Topic Weighted*) is then defined as follows:

$$C_{DET} = \frac{1}{N_{events}} \sum_{i=1}^{N_{events}} C_{DET}(i, \sigma(i))$$

Figure 2 shows the results for the F1-*measure* and *Detection Cost* at the Event Level with respect to the time threshold β_{time}. These graphics show a dramatic decrement in the system effectiveness when disregarding the temporal component ($\beta_{time} = \infty$). As a consequence, we can conclude that the time component improves notably the quality of the system-generated events. Notice also that the optimal time threshold is different for the two measures.

With regard to the Topic Level, Figure 3 shows the results for the F1-measure and Detection Cost. Although still important, the temporal component has a minor impact over the F1-measure at the topic level, and it does not affect to the Detection Cost.

Finally, we have implemented the three systems mentioned in the introduction and we have evaluated their effectiveness (optimizing their parameters) using the same collection of 452 articles of "El País". In Table 2 we compare the performance of our system with respect to these approaches. As it can be noticed, our system overcomes clearly the other systems in all the performance measures.

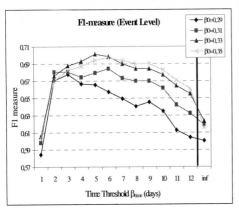
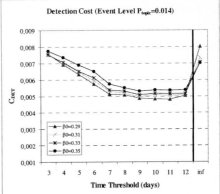

Fig. 2. F1-measure and Detection Cost for the Event Level.

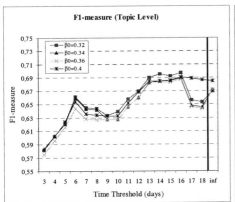
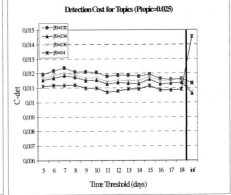

Fig. 3. F1-measure and Detection Cost for the Topic Level.

Table 2. Results for other systems (Event Level)

Approach (best result)	F1-measure	Cdet	
		Topic-weighted	Story-weighted
Umass [1] (β=0.33)	0,6364	0,0121	0,0135
Yang [8] (β=0.1, *window*=150)	0,5885	0,0158	0,0160
Papka [6] (0.1, 0.0005, 80)	0,5003	0,0243	0,0243
Our System (β_0= 0.33, β_{time}=5)	0,7037	0,0074	0,0087

6 Conclusions

In this paper a new similarity measure between documents considering both the temporality and contents of the news has been introduced. Unlike other proposals, the temporal proximity is not just based on the publication date, but it is calculated using a group of dates automatically extracted from the texts of the news [3]. This temporal component characterizes the time span of events and topics, which can be used in a similar way to the Timelines [7] to browse the whole document collection.

A new algorithm for determining a hierarchy of clustered articles is also introduced. In the first level the individual events are identified. In the next levels, these events are successively clustered so that more complex events and topics can be identified. This algorithm is based on the incremental construction of existing β_0-compact sets in the document collection. Its main advantage is that the generated set of clusters is unique, independently of the document arrival order. Our experiments have demonstrated the positive impact of the temporal component in the quality of the system-generated clusters. Moreover, the obtained results for the F1-measure and the detection cost also demonstrate the validity of our algorithm for event detection tasks.

As future work, we will study other methods for calculating the cluster representatives and the inclusion of other article attributes such as the event places. Additionally, we will analyze new incremental algorithms that take into account overlapping topics and events, and we will analyze the conceptual description of the obtained groups at any level of the hierarchy.

Acknowledgements. We acknowledge Dolores Llidó by her helpful collaboration in the presented experiments. This work has been partially funded by the research projects Bancaixa (PI.1B2000-14) and CICYT (TIC2000-1568-C03-02).

References

[1] Allan, J.; Lavrenko, V.; Frey, D.; Khandelwal, V.: Umass at TDT 2000. In Proc. *TDT 2000 Workshop*, 2000.

[2] Larsen, B.; Aone, C.: Fast and Effective Text Mining Using Linear-time Document Clustering. *In KDD'99*, San Diego, California, pp. 16-22, 1999.

[3] Llidó, D.; Berlanga R.; Aramburu M.J.: Extracting temporal references to automatically assign document event-time periods. In Proc. *Database and Expert System Applications 2001*, 62-71, Springer-Verlag, Munich, 2001.

[4] Martínez Trinidad, J. F., Shulcloper J.R., Lazo Cortés, M.: Structuralization of Universes. *Fuzzy Sets and Systems*, Vol. 112 (3), pp. 485-500, 2000.

[5] National Institute of Standards and Technology. The Topic Detection and Tracking Phase 2 (TDT2) evaluation plan. version 3.7, 1998.

[6] Papka, R.: On-line New Event Detection, Clustering and Tracking. Ph.D. Thesis Report, University of Massachusetts, Department of Computer Science, 1999.

[7] Swan R. C.; Allan, J.: Automatic generation of overview timelines. In Proc. *ACM/SIGIR 2000*, pp. 49-56, 2000.

[8] Yang, Y.; Pierce, T.; Carbonell, J.: A Study of Retrospective and On-Line Event Detection. In Proc. *ACM/SIGIR 1998*, pp. 28-36, 1998.

Asymmetric Neighbourhood Selection and Support Aggregation for Effective Classification

Gongde Guo, Hui Wang, and David Bell

School of Information and Software Engineering, University of Ulster
Newtownabbey, BT37 0QB, N.Ireland, UK
{G.Guo, H.Wang, DA.Bell}@ ulst.ac.uk

Abstract. The k-Nearest-Neighbours (kNN) is a simple but effective method for classification. The success of kNN in classification depends on the selection of a "good value" for k. To reduce the bias of k and take account of the different roles or influences that features play with respect to the decision attribute, we propose a novel asymmetric neighbourhood selection and support aggregation method in this paper. Our aim is to create a classifier less biased by k and to obtain better classification performance.
Experimental results show that the performance of our proposed method is better than kNN and is indeed less biased by k after saturation is reached. The classification accuracy of the proposed method is better than that based on symmetric neighbourhood selection method as it takes into account the different role each feature plays in the classification process.

1   Introduction

k-Nearest-Neighbours (kNN) is a non-parametric classification method which is simple but effective in many cases [Hand *et al.*, 2001]. For a data record t to be classified, its k nearest neighbours are retrieved, and this forms a *neighbourhood of t*. Majority voting among the data records in the neighbourhood is used to decide the classification for t. However, to apply kNN we need to choose an appropriate value for k, and the success of classification is very much dependent on this value. In a sense the kNN method is biased by k. There are many ways of choosing the k value, but a simple one is to run the algorithm many times with different k values and choose the one with the best performance. This is a pragmatic approach, but it lacks theoretical justification.

In order for kNN to be less dependent on the choice of k, Wang [wang, 2002] proposed to look at multiple sets of nearest neighbours rather than just one set of k nearest neighbours as we know for a data record t each neighbourhood bears certain support for different possible classes. The proposed formalism is based on probability, and the idea is to aggregate the support for various classes to give a more reliable support value, which better reveals the true class of t. However, in practice the given dataset is usually a sample of the underlying data space, and with limited computing time it is impossible to gather all the neighbourhoods to calculate the support for classifying a new data record. In a sense, the classification accuracy of the CPT method in [Wang, 2002] depends on a number of chosen neighbourhoods and this number is limited. Moreover, for most datasets in practice, features always play different roles with respect to decision attribute. Distinguishing different

F.J. Garijo, J.C. Riquelme, and M. Toro (Eds.): IBERAMIA 2002, LNAI 2527, pp. 21–31, 2002.
© Springer-Verlag Berlin Heidelberg 2002

influences of features on the decision attribute is a critical issue and many solutions have been developed to choose and weigh the features [Wang *et al.*, 1998, Liu *et al.*, 1998, Kononenko, 1994]. In this paper, we propose an asymmetric neighbourhood selection method based on information entropy, which takes into account the different role each feature plays to the decision attribute. Based on these specific neighbourhoods, we propose a simple aggregation method. It aggregates all the support of a set of chosen neighbourhoods to various classes for classifying a new data record in the spirit of kNN.

2   Aggregation Problem

Let Ω be a finite set called a frame of discernment. A *mass* function is m: $2^{\Omega} \to [0,1]$ such that

$$\sum_{X \subseteq \Omega} m(X) = 1 \qquad (2.1)$$

The mass function is interpreted as a *representation* (or *measure*) of *knowledge* or *belief* about Ω, and $m(A)$ is interpreted as a degree of support for A for $A \subseteq \Omega$ [Bell *et al.*, 1996].

To extend our knowledge to an event, A, that we cannot evaluate explicitly for m, Wang [Wang, 2002] defines a new function G: $2^{\Omega} \to [0,1]$ such that for any $A \subseteq \Omega$

$$G(A) = \sum_{X \subseteq \Omega} m(X) \frac{|A \cap X|}{|X|} \qquad (2.2)$$

This means that the knowledge of event A may not be known explicitly in the representation of our knowledge, but we know explicitly some events X that are related to it (i.e., A overlaps with X or $A \cap X \neq \varnothing$). Part of the knowledge about X, $m(X)$, should then be shared by A, and a measure of this part is $|A \cap X| / |X|$.

The mass function can be interpreted in different ways. In order to solve the *aggregation problem*, one interpretation is made by Wang as follows.

Let S be a finite set of class labels, and Ω be a finite dataset each element of which has a class label in S. The labelling is denoted by a function f: $\Omega \to S$ so that for $x \in \Omega$, $f(x)$ is the class label of x.

Consider a class $c \in S$. Let $N = |\Omega|$, $N_c = |\{x \in \Omega | : f(x) = c\}|$, and $M_c = \sum_{X \subseteq \Omega} P(c | X)$.

The mass function for c is defined as m_c: $2^{\Omega} \to [0,1]$ such that, for $A \subseteq \Omega$,

$$m_c(A) = \frac{P(c | A)}{\sum_{X \subseteq \Omega} P(c | X)} = \frac{P(c | A)}{M_c} \qquad (2.3)$$

clearly $\sum_{X \subseteq \Omega} m_c(X) = 1$, and if the distribution over Ω is uniform, then

$M_c = \frac{N_c}{N}(2^N - 1)$. Based on the mass function, the aggregation function for c is

defined as $G_c : 2^{\Omega} \to [0,1]$ such that, for $A \subseteq \Omega$

$$G_c(A) = \sum_{x \subseteq \Omega} m_c(X) \frac{|A \cap X|}{|X|} \tag{2.4}$$

When A is singleton, denoted as a, equation 2.4 can be changed to equation 2.5.

$$G_c(a) = \sum_{x \subseteq \Omega} m_c(X) \frac{|a \cap X|}{|X|} \tag{2.5}$$

If the distribution over Ω is uniform then, for $a \in \Omega$ and $c \in S$, $G_c(a)$ can be represented as equation 2.6.

$$G_c(a) = P(c \mid a)\alpha_c + \beta \tag{2.6}$$

Let C_N^n be the combinatorial number representing the number of ways of picking n unordered outcomes from N possiblities, then, $\alpha_c = \dfrac{1}{M_c} \displaystyle\sum_{i=1}^{N} \dfrac{1}{i^2}(C_{N-1}^{i-1} - C_{N-2}^{i-2})$ and

$\beta = \dfrac{N_c}{M_c} \displaystyle\sum_{i=1}^{N} \dfrac{1}{i^2}(C_{N-2}^{i-2})$.

Let t be a data record to be classified. If we know $P(c|t)$ for all $c \in S$ then we can assign t to the class c that has the largest $P(c|t)$. Since the given dataset is usually a sample of the underlying data space we may never know the true $P(c|t)$. All we can do is to approximate $P(c|t)$.

Equation 2.6 shows the relationship between $P(c|t)$ and $G_c(t)$, and the latter can be calculated from some given events. If the set of events is complete, i.e., 2^Ω, we can accurately calculate $G_c(t)$ and hence $P(c|t)$; otherwise if it is partial, i.e., a subset of 2^Ω, $G_c(t)$ is a approximate and so is $P(c|t)$.

From equation 2.5 we know that the more we know about a the more accurate $G_c(a)$ (and hence $P(c|a)$) will be. As a result, we can try to gather as many relevant events about a as possible. In the spirit of the kNN method we can deem the neighbourhood of a as relevant. Therefore we can take neighbourhoods of t as events. But in practice, the more neighbourhoods chosen for classification, the more computing time it will take. With limited computing time, the choice of the more relevant neighbourhoods is not trivial. This is one reason that motivated us to seek a series of more relevant neighbourhoods to aggregate the support for classification. Also in the spirit of kNN, for a data record t to be classified, the closer a tuple is to t, the more contribution the tuple donates for classifying t. Based on this understanding, to limit the number of neighbourhoods (for example, k) chosen for aggregation, we choose a series of specific neighbourhoods, which we think are relevant to a data item to be classified, for classification. Moreover, for computational simplicity, we modify equation 2.4 to equation 2.7 only keeping the core of aggregation and the spirit of kNN.

$$G_c'(t) = \frac{1}{k} \sum_{i=0}^{k-1} P(c \mid A_i), t \in A_i \tag{2.7}$$

Given a data record t to be classified, we choose k neighbourhoods, $A_0, A_1, \ldots, A_{k-1}$ which satifies $t \in A_0$ and $A_0 \subset A_1 \subset, \ldots, \subset A_{k-1}$. According to equation 2.7 we calculate $G_c^{'}(t)$ for all classes $c \in S$, and classify t as c_i with maximal $G_{c_i}^{'}(t)$, where $c_i \in S$.

Example 1. Given some examples with known classification $S=\{+, -\}$ shown in Fig. 1, three neighbourhoods around t are denoted as A_0 (*blank*), A_1 (*striped*), A_2 (*wavy*), where $A_0 \subset A_1 \subset A_2$. Classify a new point t by counting the '+s', and '-s' respectively, in the neighbourhoods as follows:

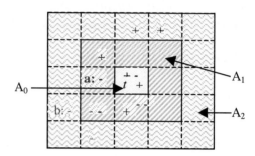

Fig. 1. Three symmetric neighbourhoods

$mass_+(A_0)=2/3$, $mass_-(A_0)=1/3$, $mass_+(A_1)=4/10$, $mass_-(A_1)=6/10$, $mass_+(A_2)=6/14$, $mass_-(A_2)=8/14$

$$G_+(t) = \frac{1}{3}\sum_{i=0}^{2} m_+(A_i) = \frac{1}{3}(2/3 + 4/10 + 6/14) = \frac{1}{3} \times \frac{157}{105} = 0.498$$

$$G_-(t) = \frac{1}{3}\sum_{i=0}^{2} m_-(A_i) = \frac{1}{3}(1/3 + 6/10 + 8/14) = \frac{1}{3} \times \frac{158}{105} = 0.502$$

As $G_-(t) > G_+(t)$, so t is classified with label '-'.

It is clear that a data point close to t plays more contribution to t than a distant one. In Fig. 1 for example, if we only select 3 neighbourhoods to aggregate the support for classification, the contribution of data close to t labelled "-" in A_0 is $\frac{1}{3} \times (\frac{1}{3} + \frac{1}{10} + \frac{1}{14}) = 0.168$ and the data marked 'a' is slight away from t plays $\frac{1}{3} \times (\frac{1}{10} + \frac{1}{14}) = 0.057$ contribution to t as well as another data marked 'b' which is far away from t plays $\frac{1}{3} \times \frac{1}{14} = 0.024$ contribution to t.

In Fig. 1, these neighbourhoods are nested, hence aggregation may count some data points 2 or 3 times in aggragation. This is desirable because points close to the data item to be classified are more influential.

3   Asymmetric Neighbourhood Selecting Algorithm

In [Wang2002], there is no discussion on how to choose the best neighbourhoods for classification. In practice, the given dataset is usually a sample of the underlying data space. It is impossible to gather all the neighbourhoods to calculate the support for classifying a new data record. In a sense, the classification accuracy of the CPT depends on a set of chosen neighbourhoods and the number of neighbourhoods is limited. Moreover, for most datasets in practice, features always play different roles to decision attribute. Distinguishing influences features play to the decision attribute is a critical issue and many solutions have been developed to choose and weigh features. In practice we cannot collect all neighbourhoods to gather the support for classification, so methods to consider the contributions different features make to the decision attribute and select the more relevant neighbourhoods in the process of picking up neighbourhoods are important.

Our motivation in proposing the asymmetric neighbourhood selection method is an attempt to improve classification accuracy by selecting a given number of neighbourhoods with information for classification as possible. In this paper, we use the entropy measure of information theory in the process of neighbourhood selection. We propose a neighbourhood-expansion method by which the next neighbourhood is generated by expanding the previous one. Obviously, the previous one is covered by the later one. In each neighbourhood expansion process, we calculate the entropy of each candidate and select one with minimal entropy as our next neighbourhood. The smaller the entropy of a neighbourhood, the more unbalanced there is in the class distribution of the neighbours, and the more relevant the neighbours are to the data to be classified. More details of our algorithm are presented below.

Let C be a finite set of class labels denoted as $S=(c_1,c_2,\dots,c_m)$, and Ω be a finite dataset denoted as $\Omega=\{d_1, d_2, \dots, d_N\}$. Each element d_i in Ω denoted as $d_i=(d_{i1}, d_{i2}, \dots, d_{in})$ has a class label in S. t is a data record to be classified denoted as $t=(t_1,t_2,\dots,t_n)$. Let $N=|\Omega|$, $N_{c_i}=|\{x\in\Omega: f(x)=c_i\}|$ to all of $c_i\in S$.

Firstly, we project dataset Ω into n-dimensional space. Each data is a point in the n-dimensional space. Then we partition the n-dimensional space into a multi-grid. The partitioning algorithm of our multi-grid is described as follows:

For each dimension of n-dimensional space, if attribute a_i is ordinal, we partition $\mathbf{dom}(a_i)=|a_{imax}-a_{imin}|$ into h equal intervals. h is an option, its value depends on concrete application domains. We use symbol Δ_i to represent the length of each grid of ith attribute, in which $\Delta_i=|a_{imax}-a_{imin}|/h$. If attribute a_i is nominal, its discrete values provide a natural partitioning. At the end of the partitioning process all the data in dataset Ω are distributed into this multi-grid.

Assume A_i is the ith neighbourhood and $G^i=(g_1^i,g_2^i,\dots,g_n^i)$ is the corresponding grid in n-dimensional space, for any ordinal attribute a_j, g_j^i is a interval denoted as $g_j^i=[g_{j1}^i,g_{j2}^i]$. The set of all the data covered by grid $(g_1^i,\dots,[g_{j1}^i-\Delta_j,g_{j2}^i],\dots,g_n^i)$ as well as the set of all the data covered by grid $(g_1^i,\dots,[g_{j1}^i,g_{j2}^i+\Delta_j],\dots,g_n^i)$ will be the candidates for the next neighbourhood selection. If attribute a_j is nominal, g^i_j is a set denoted as $g^i_j = \{ g^i_{j1}, g^i_{j2}, \ldots, g^i_{jq} \}$. For every element $x \in$ **dom**(a_j), where $x \notin g^i_j$, the set of all the data covered by grid $(g^i_1, \ldots, g^i_j \cup \{x\}, \ldots, g^i_n)$ will be the candidates for the next neighbourhood selection.

Given a set of label-known samples, the algorithm to classify a new data record t is described as follows:

Suppose that a data record $t = (t_1, t_2, \ldots, t_n)$ to be classified initially falls into grid $G^0 = (g^0_1, g^0_2, \ldots, g^0_n)$ of n-dimensional space, i.e., $t \in G^0$. To grid G^0, if feature t_j is ordinal, g^0_j represents a interval, denoted as $g^0_j = [g^0_{j1}, g^0_{j2}]$, where $g^0_{j1} = t_j - |\Delta_j|/2$, $g^0_{j2} = t_j + |\Delta_j|/2$. Obviously, t_j satisfies $g^0_{j1} \le t_j \le g^0_{j2}$; if feature t_j is nominal, g^0_j is a set, denoted as $g^0_j = \{ g^0_{jq} \}$, where $t_j = g^0_{jq}$. All the data covered by grid G^0 make up of a set denoted by A_0, which is the first neighbourhood of our algorithm. The detailed neighbourhood selection and support aggregation algorithm for classification is described as follows:

1. Set $A_0 = \{ d_i | d_i \in G^0 \}$
2. For $i = 1$ to $k-1$

    {Find i^{th} neighbourhood A_i with minimal entropy E^i among all the candidates expanding from A_{i-1}}

3. Calculate $G_c(t) = \dfrac{1}{k} \sum\limits_{i=0}^{k-1} (|A^c_i| / |A_i|)$ for all $c \in S$

4. Classify t for c that has the largest $G_c(t)$

In above algorithm, the entropy E^i is defined as follows:

$$E^i = I_{A_i}(c^i_1, c^i_2, \ldots, c^i_m) \frac{|A_i|}{|\Omega|} \qquad (3.1)$$

$$I_{A_i}(c^i_1, c^i_2, \ldots, c^i_m) = -\sum_{j=1}^{m} p_j \log_2(p_j), \text{ where } p_j = \frac{|\{d^i_j | d^i_j \in A_i, f(d^i_j) = c^i_j\}|}{|A_i|} \qquad (3.2)$$

Suppose that A_i and A_j are two neighbourhoods of t having the same amount of entropy, i.e., $I_{A_i}(c^i_1, c^i_2, \ldots, c^i_m) = I_{A_j}(c^j_1, c^j_2, \ldots, c^j_m)$, if $|A_i| < |A_j|$, we believe that A_i is more relevant to t than A_j, so in this case, we prefer to choose A_i to be our next neighbourhood. Also, if two neighbourhoods A_i and A_j of t have the same number of data tuples, we prefer to choose the one with minimal entropy as our next neighbourhood. According to equation 3.2, the smaller a neighbourhood's entropy is, the more unbalanced its class distribution is, and consequently the more information it has for classification. So, in our algorithm, we adopt equation 3.1 to be the criterion for neighbourhood selection. In each expanding process, we select a candidate with minimal E^i as our next neighbourhood.

To grasp the idea here, the best way is by means of an example, so we graphically illustrate the asymmetric neighbourhood selection method here. For simplicity, we decribe our asymmetric neighbourhood selection method in 2-dimensional space.

Example 2. Suppose that a data record x to be classified locates at grid [3,3] in Fig. 2. We collect all the data, which are covered by grid [3.3] (G^0), into a set called A_0 as our first neighbourhood. Then we try to expand our neighbourhood one step in each of 4 different directions respectively (up, down, left, right) and choose a candidate having minimal E^i as our new expanded area, e.g. G^1. Then we look up, down, left, right again and select a new area (e.g. G^2 in Fig. 4). All the data covered by the expanded area make up of the next neighbourhood called A_1 and so on. At the end of the procedure, we obtain a series of asymmetric neighbourhoods e.g. A_2, A_3, ..., as in Fig. 2 to Fig. 4.

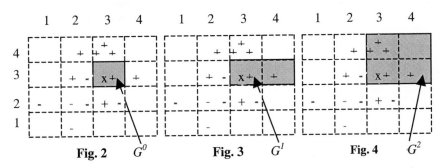

Fig. 2 G^0 Fig. 3 G^1 Fig. 4 G^2

If the data record y to be classified locates at grid [2,3] in Fig. 5, the selection process of 3 asymmetric neighbourhoods is demonstrated by Fig. 5 to Fig. 7. The support aggregation method is demonstrated by **Example 1** in the previous section.

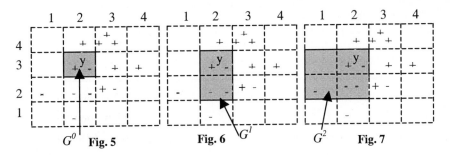

G^0 Fig. 5   Fig. 6 G^1 G^2 Fig. 7

4 Evaluation and Experiment

For experimentation we used 7 public datasets available from the UC Irvine Machine Learning Repository. General information about these datasets is shown in Table 1. The datasets are relatively small but scalability is not an issue when datasets are indexed.

We used the asymmetric neighbourhood selection algorithm introduced in the previous section to select a series of neighbourhoods on 7 public datasets. The experimental results are graphically illustrated in Fig. 8. For each value of *k*, *nok*NN (we use the notation *nok*NN in this paper to label our method) represents the average classification accuracy of aggregating *k* neighbourhoods' support, and *k*NN represents the average classification accuracy of the kth neighbourhood. A comparison of asymmetric *nok*NN and *k*NN is shown in Table 2.

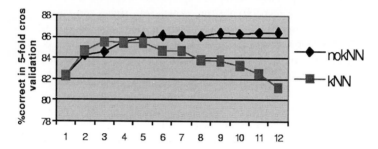

Fig. 8. A Comparison of Asymmetric nokNN and Asymmetric kNN

Table 1. General information about the datasets

Dataset	NA	NN	NO	NB	NE	CD
Iris	4	0	4	0	150	50:50:50
Wine	13	0	13	0	178	59:71:48
Hear	13	3	7	3	270	120:150
Aust	14	4	6	4	690	383:307
Diab	8	0	8	0	768	268:500
Vote	18	0	0	18	232	108:124
TTT	9	9	0	0	958	332:626

In Table 1, the meaning of the title in each column is follows: NA-Number of attributes, NN-Number of Nominal attributes, NO-Number of Ordinal attributes, NB-Number of Binary attributes, NE-Number of Examples, and CD-Class Distribution.

Table 2. A comparison of asymmetric *k*NN and asymmetric *nok*NN in 5-fold cross validation

Dataset	Asymmetric *k*NN				*Nok*NN
	Worst case		Best case		All of 12
	k	%correct	*k*	%correct	%correct
Iris	12	90.67	2	97.33	96.67
Wine	1	83.71	4	96.07	95.51
Hear	12	59.63	3	81.85	83.70
Aust	1	83.04	9	85.51	85.22
Diab	1	68.75	11	76.43	74.48
Vote	8	85.78	3	92.67	91.38
TTT	10	75.78	8	79.65	78.08
Average		78.19		87.07	86.43

From the experimental results it is clear that *k*NN performance varies when different neighbourhoods are used while *nok*NN performance improves with increasing number of neighbourhoods but stabilises after a certain stage. Furthermore the performance of *nok*NN is obviously better than that of *k*NN after stabilisation for each *k*. The experiment further shows that the stabilised performance of *nok*NN is comparable to the best performance of *k*NN within 12 neighbourhoods.

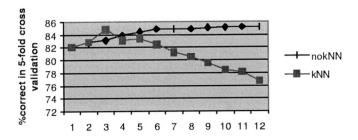

Fig. 9. A Comparison of Symmetric *nok*NN and Symmetric *k*NN

To further verify our aggregation method, we also developed a symmetric neighbourhood selection algorithm, which in each neighbourhood selection process all features are expanded in the same ratio as its domain interval, seeing Fig. 1.

Fig. 9 and Table 3 show that similar results are obtained while using the symmetric neighbourhoods selection method.

Table 3. A comparison of symmetric *k*NN and symmetric *nok*NN in 5-fold cross validation

Dataset	Symmetric *k*NN				*NokNN*
	Worst case		Best case		All of 12
	k	%correct	*K*	%correct	%correct
Iris	12	74.00	1	96.67	96.67
Wine	4	91.01	3	93.82	95.51
Hear	12	55.56	3	75.93	75.93
Aust	12	78.55	3	85.07	83.91
Diab	1	68.62	3	75.52	75.00
Vote	1	85.34	5	92.67	91.38
TTT	12	75.99	9	79.12	77.97
Average		75.58		85.54	85.19

A comparison of asymmetric *nok*NN with symmetric *nok*NN in classification performance is shown in Fig. 10 and a comparison of asymmetric *k*NN with symmetric *k*NN in classification performance is shown in Fig. 11.

It is obvious that the asymmetric neighbourhood selection method is better than the symmetric neighbourhood selection method for both *nok*NN and *k*NN. From the experimental results it is clear that our hypothesis is correct – the bias of *k* can be removed by this method.

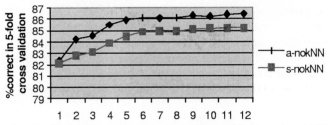

Fig. 10. Comparison of Asymmetric nokNN and Symmetric nokNN

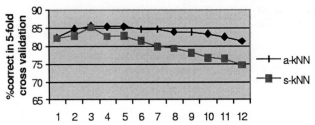

Fig. 11. Comparison of Asymmetric kNN and Symmetric kNN

5   Summary and Conclusion

In this paper we have discussed the existed issues related to the kNN method for classification. In order for kNN to be less dependent on the choice of k, we looked at multiple sets of nearest neighbours rather than just one set of k nearest neighbours. A set of neighbours is called a neighbourhood. For a data record t each neighbourhood bears certain support for different possible classes. Wang addressed a novel formalism based on probability to aggregate the support for various classes to give a more reliable support value, which better reveals the true class of t. Based on [Wang, 2002] method, for specific neighbourhoods using in kNN, which always surround around the data record t to be classified, we proposed a simple aggregation method to aggregate the support for classification. We also proposed an asymmetric neighbourhood selection method based on information entropy which partitions a multidimensional data space into multi-grid and expands neighbourhoods with minimal information entropy in this multi-grid. This method is independent of 'distance metric' or 'similarity metric' and also locally takes into account the different influence of each feature on the decision attribute.

Experiments on some public datasets shows that using *nok*NN the classification performance (accuracy) increases as the number of neighbourhoods increases but stabilises soon after a small number of neighbourhoods; using kNN, however, the classification performance varies when different neighbourhoods are used. Experiments also show that the stabilised performance of *nok*NN is comparable to the best performance of kNN. The comparison of asymmetric and symmetric methods shows that our proposed asymmetric method has better classification performance as it takes into account the different influence of each feature on the decision attribute.

References

[Bell *et al.*, 1996] Bell, D. Guan, J. and Lee, S. (1996) Generalized Union and Project Operations for Pooling Uncertain and Imprecise Information. Data & Knowledge Engineering. 18(1996), pp89-117.

[Hand *et al.*, 2000] Hand, D., Mannila, H., and Smyth, P. (2001). *Principles of Data Mining.* The MIT Press.

[Kononenko, 1994] Kononenko, I., (1994) *Estimating attributes: analysis and extensions of RELIEF.* In *Proceedings of the 1994 European Conference on Machine Learning.*

[Liu, *et al.*,1998] Liu, H., Motoda, H., (1998) *Feature Extraction Construction and Selection: a data mining perspective*, Kluwer Academic Publishers.

[Wang *et al.*, 1998] Wang, H., Bell, D., and Murtagh, F. (1998). *Feature Extraction Construction and Selection a Data Mining Perspective p85-99.* Kluwer Academic Publishers.

[Wang, 2002] Wang, H. (2002) *Nearest Neighbours without k: A Classification Formalism based on Probability*, technical report, Faculty of Informatics, University of Ulster, N.Ireland, UK.

Incremental Learning of Tree Augmented Naive Bayes Classifiers

Josep Roure Alcobé

Departament d'Informàtica i Gestió
Escola Universitària Politècnica de Mataró
Avda. Puig i Cadafalch 101-111
08303 Mataró, Catalonia, Spain
roure@eupmt.es

Abstract. Machine learning has focused a lot of attention at Bayesian classifiers in recent years. It has seen that even Naive Bayes classifier performs well in many cases, it may be improved by introducing some dependency relationships among variables (Augmented Naive Bayes). Naive Bayes is incremental in nature but, up to now, there are no incremental algorithms for learning Augmented classifiers. When data is presented in short chunks of instances, there is an obvious need for incrementally improving the performance of the classifiers as new data is available. It would be too costly, in computing time and memory space, to use the batch algorithms processing again the old data together with the new one. We present in this paper an incremental algorithm for learning Tree Augmented Naive classifiers. The algorithm rebuilds the network structure from the branch which is found to be invalidated, in some sense, by data. We will experimentally demonstrate that the heuristic is able to obtain almost optimal trees while saving computing time.

1 Introduction

Classification plays an important role in the field of machine learning, pattern recognition and data mining. Classification is the task to identify the class labels for instances based on a set of features or attributes. The induction of Bayesian classifiers from data have received a lot of attention within the Bayesian Network learning field [7,3,8].

The simplest Bayesian Classifier is the Naive Bayes [5,11]. It assumes that attributes are independent when the class label is known. Even it is a very strong assumption and it does not hold in many real world data sets, the Naive Bayes classifier is seen to outperform more sophisticated classifiers specially over data sets where the features are not strongly correlated [11].

More recently, a lot of effort has focused on improving the Naive Bayes classifier by relaxing independence assumptions [7,3]. Mainly, these methods infer restricted networks among features from data. In this way, these methods combine some of the Bayesian Networks ability to represent dependencies with the simplicity of Naive Bayes. This sort of classifiers are usually called Augmented Naive Bayes.

Naive Bayes is an incremental classifier. That is, it is able to revise the classifier when new data instances are available, with neither beginning from scratch nor processing

F.J. Garijo, J.C. Riquelme, and M. Toro (Eds.): IBERAMIA 2002, LNAI 2527, pp. 32–41, 2002.

again old data instances. This sort of learning is useful when data instances are presented in streams while the classifier still must work.

When Naive Bayes classifier is augmented, it looses the incremental property as most of the algorithms for inferring Bayesian Networks are batch [2]. In this paper, we use an incremental algorithm for learning tree-shaped Bayesian Networks to obtain an incremental Tree Augmented Naive Bayes classifier. We will show, in this paper, that the incremental version obtains most of times the same accuracy than the batch classifier while saving computational time.

Incremental learning attempts to update current Bayesian Networks in response to newly observed data instances. Langley [10] stated that an algorithm is incremental if (1) it inputs one training experience at a time, (2) does not reprocess any previous data instances, and (3) retains only one knowledge structure in memory.

Each of these three constraints aims at clear objectives. The first wants incremental algorithms to be able to output a Bayesian Network at any moment of the learning process. The second keeps low and constant the time required to process each data instance over all the data set. And finally, the third constraint wants learning algorithms not to do unreasonable memory demands.

2 Bayesian Network Classifiers

Bayesian classifiers have proven to be competitive with other approaches like nearest neighbor, decision trees or neural networks [7]. Bayesian classifiers learn from pre-classified data instances the probability of each attribute X_i given the class label C, $P(X_i|C)$. Then the Bayes rule is used to compute the probability that an example $e = < x_1, \ldots, x_n >$ belongs to a class C_i, $P(C_i|x_1, \ldots, x_n)$. In this way, the class with highest posterior probability is calculated. The independence assumptions among attributes or variables distinguish the different Bayesian classifiers.

2.1 Naive Bayes

The Naive Bayes as discussed by Duda and Hart [5] assume that all attributes are independent given the class label. This classifier can be represented by a simple Bayesian Network where the class variable is the parent of all attributes.

Given the independence assumptions, the posterior probability is formulated as

$$P(C_i|x_1, \ldots, x_n) \propto P(C_i) \prod_k P(x_k|C_i)$$

This simple expression can very efficiently be calculated and it is only needed to estimate $P(C_i)$ and $P(x_k|C_i)$ from data. To do so, we only need to keep a counter for the number of training instances, a counter for each class label, and a counter for each attribute value and class label pair.

Note that to incrementally learn the Naive Bayes classifier we only need to increase the counters as new instances are precessed. See also that the network structure is not learnt from data but fixed before hand. So, we could use the incremental approach proposed by Spiegelhalter et. al [13] in order to incrementally update the conditional probabilities of the classifier.

2.2 Tree Augmented Naive Bayes

The Tree Augmented Naive Bayes (TAN) classifier was introduced [7] in order to improve the performance of the Naive Bayes. The TAN classifier relaxes the independence assumptions having a dependence tree $\mathcal{T}$ among the attributes $x_1, \ldots, x_n$ and maintaining the class variable as a parent of each attribute.

In order to learn the TAN classifier, first it is learned the tree among the attributes and afterwards an arch is added from the class variable to each attribute. To learn the tree structure, it is used the algorithm proposed by Chow and Liu [4].

Given the independence assumptions in the tree $\mathcal{T}$, the posterior probability is

$$P(C_i|x_1,\ldots,x_n) \propto P(C_i) \prod_k P(x_k|x_{j(k)}, C_i)$$

where $x_{j(k)}$ stands for the parent of variable x_k in the tree $\mathcal{T}$, and x_0 for the null variable.

Friedman et al. [7] showed that TAN outperforms Naive Bayes while maintaining the computational simplicity on learning and classifying. We now need to keep a counter for the number of training instances, a counter for each class label, and a counter for each attribute value, parent value and class label triplet.

Note that Chow and Liu's proposal is a batch learning algorithm. In the next section we will explain the Chow and Liu batch algorithm and our incremental approach.

3 Tree-Shaped Bayesian Network Learning

The Chow and Liu's algorithm , CL algorithm from now on, estimates the underlying n-dimensional discrete probability distribution from a set of samples. The algorithm yields as an estimation a distribution of $n-1$ first order dependence relationships among the n variables, forming a tree dependence structure. It builds a maximal cost tree introducing branches into the tree in decreasing cost order.

Our incremental approach revises an already learnt tree-shaped Bayesian Network without processing the old data instances. Roughly speaking, we state that new data invalidates the old tree-shaped structure when the branches are not anymore in decreasing cost order. Then, the tree is rebuilt from the first branch found in a bad position into the order. In this way, our algorithm, can both detect the need of updating and update the current network. We will call our proposal ACO heuristic (Arches in Correct Order).

3.1 Chow and Liu's Batch Algorithm

The Chow and Liu's algorithm uses the mutual information as closeness measure between $P(\mathbf{X})$ and $P_\tau(\mathbf{X})$, where $P(\mathbf{X})$ is the probability distribution from a set of samples, and $P_\tau(\mathbf{X})$ is the tree dependence distribution. It is an optimization algorithm that gives the tree distribution closest to the distribution from the samples. Let us give some notation in order to explain the Chow and Liu's measure and algorithm.

Let $(m_1, \cdots, m_n)$ be a permutation of integers $1, 2, \cdots, n$, let $j(i)$ be a mapping with $0 \le j(i) \le i$, let $\mathcal{T} = (\mathbf{X}, E)$ be a tree where $\mathbf{X}(\mathcal{T}) = \{X_{m_i}|1, 2, \cdots, n\}$ is the set of nodes, $E(\mathcal{T}) = \{(X_{m_i}, X_{m_{j(i)}})|1, 2, \cdots, n\}$ is the set of branches, and where

X_0 is the *null* node. If we now assign the mutual information between two variables, $I(X_{m_i}; X_{m_{j(i)}})$, as a cost to every dependence tree branch, the maximum-cost dependence tree is defined as the tree $\mathcal{T}$ such that for all $\mathcal{T}'$ in $\mathcal{T}_n$, $\sum_{i=1}^{n} I(X_{m_i}; X_{m_{j(i)}}) \geq \sum_{i=1}^{n} I(X_{m_i}; X_{m_{j'(i)}})$. Where $\mathcal{T}_n$ stands for the set of trees with n variables.

Chow and Liu used the Kruskal algorithm for the construction of trees of maximum total cost where $I(X_{m_i}; X_{m_{j(i)}})$ may represent the distance cost from node X_{m_i} to node $X_{m_{j(i)}}$. An undirected graph is formed by starting with a graph without branches and adding a branch between two nodes with the highest mutual information. Next, a branch is added which has maximal mutual information associated and does not introduce a cycle in the graph. This process is repeated until the $(n-1)$ branches with maximum mutual information associated are added as seen in Algorithm 1.

In this paper, we give a direction to all the branches of the tree. We take as the root of the tree one of the nodes of the first branch and the direction of the branches introduced afterwards goes from the node already into the structure to the one recently introduced.

Algorithm 1 CL

Require: a database D on $\mathbf{X} = \{X_{m_1}, \cdots, X_{m_n}\}$ variables
Ensure: $\mathcal{T}$ be a dependence tree structure
    Calculate $SUFF_D(\mathcal{T})$
    $\mathcal{T} = (\mathbf{V}, E)$ the empty tree where $\mathbf{V}(\mathcal{T}) = \{\emptyset\}$ and
    $E(\mathcal{T}) = \{\emptyset\}$
    Calculate costs for every pair $I(X_{m_i}; X_{m_j})$
    Select the maximum cost pair (X_{m_i}, X_{m_j})
    $\mathbf{V}(\mathcal{T}) = \{X_{m_i}, X_{m_j}\}; E(\mathcal{T}) = \{(X_{m_i}, X_{m_j})\}$
    repeat
        $B(\mathcal{T}) = \{(X_{m_i}, X_{m_j}) \mid ((X_{m_i}, X_{m_k}) \in E(\mathcal{T}) \vee (X_{m_k}, X_{m_i}) \in E(\mathcal{T})) \wedge X_{m_j} \notin$
        $\mathbf{V}(\mathcal{T})\}$
        Select the max cost pair (X_{m_i}, X_{m_j}) from $B(\mathcal{T})$
        $\mathbf{V}(\mathcal{T}) = \mathbf{V}(\mathcal{T}) \cup \{X_{m_j}\}$
        $E(\mathcal{T}) = E(\mathcal{T}) \cup \{(X_{m_i}, X_{m_j})\}$
    until $(\mathbf{V} = \mathbf{X})$

3.2 Incremental Algorithm

We introduce some notation before the explanation of our algorithm. Let $N_X^D(x)$ be the number of instances in D where $X = x$. Let $\widehat{N}_X^D$ be the vector of numbers $N_X^D(x)$ for all values of X. We call the vector $\widehat{N}_X^D$ the *sufficient statistics* of the variable X, $suff_D(X)$. In the same way, the *sufficient statistics* of the tree $\mathcal{T}$, $suff_D(\mathcal{T})$, are defined as the set of vectors $\widehat{N}_{X_{m_i}, X_{m_{j(i)}}}$ $\forall i : 0 \leq i \leq n$.

To find the maximal cost tree we need the vector numbers $\widehat{N}_{X_{m_i}, X_{m_{j(i)}}}^D$ for all the pairs of variables in $\mathbf{X}(\mathcal{T})$, we will call this set of numbers $SUFF_D(\mathcal{T})$. Note that $SUFF_{D \cup D'}(\mathcal{T})$ can be calculated as $\widehat{N}_{\mathbf{X}}^D \oplus \widehat{N}_{\mathbf{X}}^{D'}$, where $\oplus$ stands for the addition of vector components.

We divide our algorithm into two steps. In the first step, the algorithm calculates the *sufficient statistics* for both old D and new D' data instances, and in the second, it revises the tree structure according to the new *sufficient statistics*.

In the first step of the algorithm, we assume that *sufficient statistics* of the old data set D are stored. Thus, in order to recover the *sufficient statistics*, $SUFF_{D \cup D'}(\mathcal{T})$, of the whole set of data instances the algorithm does not need to go through the old ones.

The second step uses a heuristic which decides to update the structure only when the arches are not in correct order. When the tree is built for the very first time using the CL algorithm, arches are introduced into the tree structure in decreasing cost order. This order $\mathcal{O}$ is stored. When new data instances D' are presented, the cost $I(X_{m_i}; X_{m_{j(i)}})$ for each branch is calculated again using the new *sufficient statistics* $SUFF_{D \cup D'}(\mathcal{T})$, and only when the order $\mathcal{O}$ does not hold anymore the structure is updated.

Algorithm 2 ACO heuristic

Require: a database D' on $\mathbf{X} = \{X_{m_1}, \cdots, X_{m_n}\}$ variables a tree structure $\mathcal{T}$, an order $\mathcal{O}$ of branches and $SUFF_D(\mathcal{T})$

Ensure: $\mathcal{T}'$ be a dependence tree structure

    Calculate $SUFF_{D \cup D'}(\mathcal{T})$

    $\mathcal{T}' = (\mathbf{V}, E)$ the empty tree where $\mathbf{V}(\mathcal{T}') = E(\mathcal{T}') = \{\emptyset\}$

    Let X_{m_h} be the root of $\mathcal{T}$

    $B(\mathcal{T}) = \{(X_{m_h}, X_{m_j}) \mid (X_{m_h}, X_{m_j}) \in E(\mathcal{T})\}$

    continue=false; k=0

    if $((X_{m_i}, X_{m_j})_{\mathcal{O}(1)} = arg\, max_{(X_{m_r}, X_{m_s}) \in B(\mathcal{T}) \cap E(\mathcal{T})} I(X_{m_r}, X_{m_s}))$ **then**

        $\mathbf{V}(\mathcal{T}') = \{X_{m_h}, X_{m_j}\}; E(\mathcal{T}') = \{(X_{m_h}, X_{m_j})\}$

        continue=true; k=2 be the number of branches added (+ 1)

    end if

    while (*continue*) and ($k \leq |E(\mathcal{T})|$) **do**

        $B(\mathcal{T}_{\mathcal{O}(k)}) = \{(X_{m_i}, X_{m_j}) \mid ((X_{m_i}, X_{m_k}) \in E(\mathcal{T}_{\mathcal{O}(k)}) \vee (X_{m_k}, X_{m_i}) \in E(\mathcal{T}_{\mathcal{O}(k)})) \wedge$
        $X_{m_j} \notin \mathbf{V}(\mathcal{T}_{\mathcal{O}(k)})\}$

        if $((X_{m_i}, X_{m_j})_{\mathcal{O}(k)} = arg\, max_{(X_{m_r}, X_{m_s}) \in B(\mathcal{T}_{\mathcal{O}(k)}) \cap E(\mathcal{T})} I(X_{m_r}, X_{m_s}))$ **then**

            $\mathbf{V}(\mathcal{T}') = \mathbf{V}(\mathcal{T}') \cup \{X_{m_j}\}$

            $E(\mathcal{T}') = E(\mathcal{T}') \cup \{(X_{m_i}, X_{m_j})\}; k$++

        else

            continue=false

        end if

    end while

    if ($k \leq |V(\mathbf{X})|$) **then**

        Continue building $\mathcal{T}'$ using the original CL algorithm

    end if

More precisely our algorithm, see Algorithm 2, inspects the arches in the order $\mathcal{O}$ they were added into the tree. When an arch $(X_{m_i}, X_{m_{j(i)}})_{\mathcal{O}(k)}$ at the k-th position in $\mathcal{O}$ has not the highest cost among all candidate arches present into the former structure, the tree is rebuilt from that arch using the original CL algorithm. Formally, when the arch at the k-th position $(X_{m_i}, X_{m_{j(i)}})_{\mathcal{O}(k)} \neq arg\, max_{(X_{m_k}, X_{m_l}) \in B(\mathcal{T}_{\mathcal{O}(k)}) \cap E(\mathcal{T})} I(X_{m_k}, X_{m_l})$.

Where $\mathcal{T}_{\mathcal{O}(k)}$ stands for the tree built only with the first $k-1$ arches of the order $\mathcal{O}$ and $B(\mathcal{T}_{\mathcal{O}(k)})$ stands for the set of arches that do not introduce any cycle in $\mathcal{T}_{\mathcal{O}(k)}$, $B(\mathcal{T}_{\mathcal{O}(k)}) = \{(X_{m_i}, X_{m_j}) \mid ((X_{m_i}, X_{m_k}) \in E(\mathcal{T}_{\mathcal{O}(k)}) \vee (X_{m_k}, X_{m_i}) \in E(\mathcal{T}_{\mathcal{O}(k)})) \wedge X_j \notin \mathbf{V}(\mathcal{T}_{\mathcal{O}(k)})\}$.

Note, it may happen that (X_{m_i}, X_{m_k}) has the maximum cost among the arches in $B(\mathcal{T}_{\mathcal{O}(k)}) \cap E(\mathcal{T})$ and not among the ones in $B(\mathcal{T}_{\mathcal{O}(k)})$. In such situation, the ACO heuristic and the CL algorithm would not recover the same tree structure.

4   Experiments

We conducted several experiments in order to compare the repeated use of the batch CL algorithm against our incremental ACO heuristic. We presented data instances to both algorithms in chunks of 100. Then we compared the Bayesian Network structures and the classifiers accuracy during all the learning process. We used five well-known datasets from the UCI machine learning repository [12]: Adult (13 attributes, 48.842 instances and 2 classes), Nursery (8 attributes, 12.960 instances and 5 classes), Mushroom (22 attributes, 8.124 instances and 2 classes), DNA (60 attributes, 3.190 instances and 3 classes) and finally Car (6 attributes, 1.738 instances and 4 classes).

We presented the instances to the algorithms in three different kind of orders. Namely, an order where similar instances are consecutive, another where dissimilar instances are consecutive, and finally a random order. We used five different orders of each kind to run both algorithms, and all numbers presented in the tables of this section are the mean and the standard deviation of the quantity being analyzed.

We used these three different kind of orders because it is widely reported in the literature that incremental algorithms may yield different results when the same instances are presented in different orders [10].

4.1   Computational Time Gain

The main objective of the incremental algorithm proposed was to reduce the time spent in learning a new tree structure when the system already learned one from past data. In Table 1, we compare the operations done by the batch and the incremental algorithms.

At the first two columns, we show the number of $I(X; Y)$ calculations, which is the most time consuming function of the learning algorithm. In our implementation, both batch and incremental algorithms calculate the $I(X; Y)$ amounts once, when it is firstly needed, and store them in an array. At the third and fourth columns, we show the number of times the $I(X; Y)$ is recalled. This gives an idea of the number of comparisons the algorithms perform in order to find the arch with highest $I(X; Y)$.

We can see that the number of $I(X; Y)$ calculations and recalls are much higher for the batch algorithm. Note that the number of $I(X; Y)$ calculations and recalls are the same for all runs of the batch algorithm as it always builds the tree structure from scratch, while they are different for the incremental algorithm as it builds the tree structure from the arch found in an incorrect order.

We also note from Table 1 that the more attributes data sets have the greater the gain is. Compare Adult against Nursery and Car results. And also, we can see that the gain grows with the number of data instances (see Adult results). This last point is due to the fact than when many data instances have already been processed, the new data instances slightly modify the probability distribution of the database and therefore the network structure does not need to be updated.

Another cause which may influence the time spent is the order in which the instances are presented. Usually, when similar instances are presented consecutively, the network structures learned from data are not good models of the probability distribution of the entire database. Thereof, the incremental algorithm spends more time as it must update the network structure. We see, at Table 1, that the number of $I(X;Y)$ calculations and recalls are usually higher when similar instances are ordered together.

Table 1. CPU clock ticks and operations spent in learning

		$I(X;Y)$ Calculations		$I(X;Y)$ Recalls	
		Batch	Incremental	Batch	Incremental
Adult	Rand		4801.00 (445.57)		28830.20 (1234.17)
	Sim	25350	4468.40 (564.36)	114400	24727.20 (2826.10)
	Diss		4243.00 (153.88)		19744.60 (5114.83)
Nursery	Rand		1155.40 (271.08)		3305.60 (903.06)
	Sim	2408	1216.80 (359.76)	6622	3411.20 (798.36)
	Diss		1092.80 (246.21)		3304.60 (411.21)
Mush-room	Rand		5702.20 (3085.10)		43269.40 (18451.79)
	Sim	12474	10947.80 (1383.95)	94500	73106.80 (9536.44)
	Diss		8490.40 (1839.75)		56983.20 (12287.89)
DNA	Rand		35827.60 (3042.28)		692008.60 (70438.44)
	Sim	37170	34847.60 (970.70)	754551	652884.80 (51460.44)
	Diss		33489.80 (6154.39)		647897.00 (144846.32)
Car	Rand		87.60 (49.51)		171.60 (100.51)
	Sim	165	106.40 (16.53)	330	218.80 (53.65)
	Diss		77.80 (24.10)		154.00 (74.14)

4.2 Quality of the Recovered Structures

In Figure 1, we show the behavior of our heuristic along the learning process where the algorithm is fed with chunks of 100 data instances, and using a random data order. We compare the structures obtained with our incremental proposal against the ones obtained with the CL batch algorithm.

Graphics present three curves. The first, shows the first arch which is not in decreasing cost order. When the number shown coincides with the number of attributes, it means that all arches are in decreasing cost order and consequently the structure is not updated. This curve gives an idea of when ACO detects that the structure must be updated. The second, shows the number of different arches between the structures learnt by the batch algorithm and the ones learnt by our incremental proposal. This curve gives us an idea of how well ACO approximates the best solution. Finally, the third curve, shows the number of arches that are different between the former and the current tree structure learnt with the batch algorithm. This curve gives an idea of the degree in which the new 100 data instances make the current structure to change.

Looking at the figure, we discover that our incremental algorithm approximates very well the best solution. It is able to detect when the structure should be updated and is updated correctly. The third curve shows that, at the early stages of the learning process, when few data instances have already been processed, the structure changes quite a lot and that the number of changed arches tend to decrease as more data is processed. This is very well seen at the graphic of the DNA dataset. Even in this case the incremental algorithm learns structures very close to the best one. If we look back to Table 1, we can see that the incremental algorithm saves, in this case, little time as it must trigger the CL algorithm very often at firsts arches, building almost the entire tree.

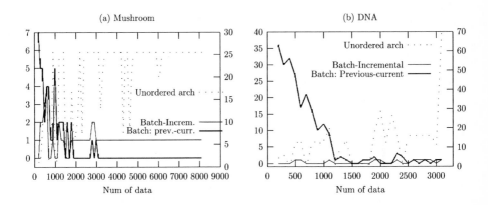

Fig. 1. Quality of recovered structures. Each graphic presents three curves; the first (*Unordered arch*), shows the first arch which is not in decreasing cost order. When the number shown coincides with the number of attributes, it means that all arches are in decreasing cost order. The second (*Batch-Incremental*) shows the number of different arches between the trees learnt by the batch algorithm and the ones learnt with the ACO heuristic. The third curve (*Batch: Previous-current*), shows the number of different arches between the former and the current trees learnt by the batch algorithm. Note that the y axis of the first curve is on the right while the y axis of the second and third curves is on the left.

4.3   Accuracy Curves

In this section, we compare the accuracy curves of the batch and the incremental algorithms when data is presented in the three different orders we explained above. In our experiments, we used two thirds of the data instances to train the classifier and the remainder for testing. In all data orders the test instances were randomly sampled.

In Figure 2, we can see the evolution of the accuracy for the DNA data set. The graphic on the left corresponds to the repeated use of the batch algorithm and the one on the right corresponds to the incremental algorithm.

Note that the shape of both graphics is almost the same. That is, our incremental classifier behaves as well as the batch one. We expected this result as the tree structures yielded by both algorithms are, most of the times, the same as shown in Figure 1.

If we compare the accuracy curves of the three different orders, we can see that the accuracy is best when data is randomly presented, while it is worse when similar instances are presented consecutively. That is due to the fact that when similar instances come together, the classifier is, at the beginning, trained with instances from one single class, and though it is not able to correctly classify instances from other classes. Lately, when new instances from other classes are used to train the classifier its accuracy is improved. Note also that the accuracy of the last learnt classifier is almost the same for the three orders.

We can see at Figure 2 that the classifier accuracy dramatically drops around the 600th instance when similar instances are presented together. That is due to overfitting, that is, the classifier is too specialized to recognize the training instances and it is not able to correctly classify the test ones.

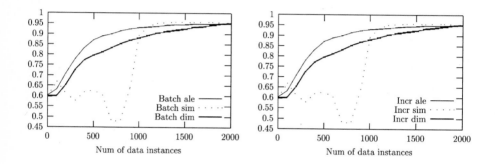

Fig. 2. Accuracy curves. DNA data set.

5   Discussion and Final Conclusions

Previous work on incremental learning of Bayesian Networks have focused on learning general network structures, namely, directed acyclic graphs (DAGs) [1,6,9]. The authors assume that the size of the *sufficient statistics* necessary to recover any possible DAG is very large and thereof it is not feasible to store them in main memory.

We presented in this paper an extension of the CL algorithm in order to incrementally learn tree-shaped Bayesian Networks. We used our algorithm to incrementally learn Tree Augmented Naive Bayes classifiers. We obtained in this way a TAN classifier which is incremental like Naive Bayes.

We claim that our algorithm is very reactive, that is, it is able to quickly detect changes in new data and to correctly update the structure. In Figure 1, we could see that the heuristic is sound in the sense that it triggers the updating process only when changes are actually needed. We could also see in Figure 2 that the accuracy of the incremental classifier is as good as the accuracy of the batch one.

The major benefit of our incremental proposition is that it saves computing time. Even when the tree must be updated the number of calculations and the number of comparisons required is very much reduced each time a branch is checked as correctly ordered. The number of comparisons the CL algorithm must perform to order the arches is $\binom{n}{2} + \sum_{i=2}^{n} i(n-i)$, while in our proposition when the first branch is checked as correct the number of comparisons is reduced by $\binom{n}{2}$ and the number of calculations of mutual information is reduced from $\binom{2}{n}$ to a maximum of $\binom{n-1}{2}$. And when the k-th branch is checked as correct, being $1 < k < n$, the number of comparisons is reduced by $k(n-k)$ and the number of tests is reduced from $\binom{n-k}{2}$ to a maximum of $\binom{n-k-1}{2}$.

References

[1] W. Buntine. Theory refinement on Bayesian networks. In B.D. D'Ambrosio, P. Smets, and P.P. Bonisone, editors, *Proceedings of the Seventh Conference on Uncertainty in Artificial Intelligence*, pages 52–60, 1991.

[2] W. Buntine. A guide to the literature on learning probabilistic networks from data. *IEEE Trans. On Knowledge And Data Engineering*, 8:195–210, 1996.

[3] Jie Cheng and Russell Greiner. Learning bayesian belief network classifiers: Algorithms and system. In *Proceedings of the Canadian Conference on AI*, pages 141–151, 2001.

[4] C.K. Chow and C.N. Liu. Approximating discrete probability distributions with dependence trees. *IEEE Transactions on Information Teory*, 14:462–467, 1968.

[5] R. O. Duda and P. E. Hart. *Pattern Classification and Scene Analysis*. John Wiley & Sons, New York, 1973.

[6] N. Friedman and M. Goldszmidt. Sequential update of Bayesian network structure. In *Proceedings of the Thirteenth Conference on Uncertainty in Artificial Intelligence*, 1997.

[7] Nir Friedman, Dan Geiger, and Moises Goldszmidt. Bayesian network classifiers. *Machine Learning*, 29(2-3):131–163, 1997.

[8] E. Keogh and M. Pazzani. Learning augmented bayesian classifiers: A comparison of distribution-based and classification-based approaches. In FL Ft. Lauderdale, editor, *Proceedings of the seventh International Workshop on Artificial Intelligence and Statistics*, pages 225–230, 1999.

[9] W. Lam and F. Bacchus. Using new data to refine Bayesian networks. In R. López de Mantaras and D. Poole, editors, *Proceedings of the Tenth Conference on Uncertainty in Artificial Intelligence*, pages 383–390, 1994.

[10] P. Langley. Order effects in incremental learning. In P. Reimann and H. Spada, editors, *Learning in humans and machines: Towards an Interdisciplinary Learning Science*. Pergamon, 1995.

[11] Pat Langley and Stephanie Sage. Induction of selective bayesian classifiers. In R. López de Mantaras and D. Poole, editors, *Proceedings of the tenth Conference on Uncertainty in Artificial Intelligence (UAI'94)*, pages 399–406. San Francisco, CA: Morgan Kaufmann.

[12] P.M. Murphy and D.W. Aha. UCI repository of machine learning databases. http://www.ics.uci.edu/ mlearn/MLRepository.html., 1994. Irvine, CA: University of California, Department of Information and Computer Science.

[13] D. J. Spiegelhalter and S. L. Lauritzen. Sequential updating of conditional probabilities on directed graphical structures. *Networks*, 20:579–605, 1990.

A Comparison of PCA and GA Selected Features for Cloud Field Classification

Miguel Macías-Macías[1], Carlos J. García-Orellana[1],
Horacio M. González-Velasco[1], Ramón Gallardo-Caballero[1], Antonio Serrano-Pérez[2]

[1] Departamento de Electrónica e Ingeniería Electromecánica - Universidad de Extremadura,
Avda. de Elvas s/n, 06071. Badajoz, Spain.
(miguel, carlos, horacio, ramon)@nernet.unex.es
[2] Departamento de Física - Universidad de Extremadura,
Avda. de Elvas s/n, 06071. Badajoz, Spain.
(asp)@unex.es

Abstract. In this work a back propagation neural network (BPNN) is used for the segmentation of Meteosat images covering the Iberian Peninsula. The images are segmented in the classes land (L), sea (S), fog (F), low clouds (C_L), middle clouds (C_M), high clouds (C_H) and clouds with vertical growth (C_V). The classification is performed from an initial set of several statistical textural features based on the gray level co-occurrence matrix (GLCM) proposed by Welch [1]. This initial set of features is made up of 144 parameters and to reduce its dimensionality two methods for feature selection have been studied and compared. The first one includes genetic algorithms (GA) and the second is based on principal component analysis (PCA). These methods are conceptually very different. While GA interacts with the neural network in the selection process, PCA only depends on the values of the initial set of features.

1 Introduction

In order to understand and model the radiation balance in the climatic system a very accurate information of the cloud cover is needed. Clouds play an important role reflecting the solar radiation and absorbing thermal radiation emitted by the land and the atmosphere, therefore reinforcing the greenhouse effect. The contribution of the clouds to the Earth albedo is very high, controlling the energy ente-r-ing the climatic system. An increase in the average albedo of the Earth-atmosphere system in only 10 percent could decrease the surface temperature to levels of the last ice age. Therefore, global change in surface temperature is highly sensitive to cloud amount and type.

These reasons make that numerous works about this topic have been published in the last years. Many of them deal with the search of a suitable classifier. Welch [1] used linear discrimination techniques, Lee et al. [2] tested a back-propagation neural network (BPNN), Macías et al. at [3] showed that the classification results obtained with a BPNN were better than those obtained with a SOM+LVQ neural network, and

F.J. Garijo, J.C. Riquelme, and M. Toro (Eds.): IBERAMIA 2002, LNAI 2527, pp. 42-49, 2002.
© Springer-Verlag Berlin Heidelberg 2002

at [4] they used a BPNN to studying the evolution of the cloud cover over Cáceres (Spain) along 1997. Bankert et al. [5] and Tiam et al. [6][7] used a probabilistic neural network (PNN). In [8] linear discrimination techniques, and PNN and BPNN neural networks were benchmarked and the results showed that BPNN achieves the highest classification accuracy.

Other works are related with the search of an initial feature set that allow to obtain reliable classification results. First works used simple spectral features like albedo and temperature. Later works include textural features too since they are less sensitive to the effects of atmospheric attenuation and detector noise that the first ones [9]. In [1] Welch et al. used statistical measures based on gray level co-occurrence matrix (GLCM) proposed by Haralick et al. in [10]. In [6] several image transformation schemes as singular value decomposition (SVD) and wavelet packets (WP's) were exploited. In [11] Gabor filters and Fourier features are recommended for cloud classification and in [6] authors showed that SVD, WP´s and GLCM textural features achieved almost similar results.

In spite of it, the initial set of features and the classifier proposed in each work is very dependent on the origin of the images (season, satellite type, location on the Earth, etc.) that have been used.

In this work we propose a BPNN neural network and GLCM textural features for the segmentation of Meteosat images covering the Iberian Peninsula. The initial GLCM feature set consists of 144 features. Because of the finite size of the prototypes set and in order to remove the redundancy in these features, a selection process has to be used.

In that sense, in [12] Doak identifies three different categories of search algorithms: exponential, sequential and randomised. In [13] Aha et al. use the most common sequential search algorithms for feature selection applied to the clouds classification: the forward sequential selection (FSS) and the backward sequential selection (BSS). In [14], [15] and [16] a genetic algorithm (GA) representative of the randomised category is used for feature selection. They use GA because it is less sensitive than other algorithms to the order of the features that have been selected.

All these algorithms interact with the network in the selection process. Thus, it seems that this process is going to be very dependent of the prototypes selection and classification by the Meteorology experts. This process is particularly problematic in this application, since clouds of different types could overlap on the same pixel of the image. Taking into account this drawback, feature selection algorithms not dependent on the labelled of the prototypes, as principal component analysis (PCA), acquire a notable interest for comparison studies.

Therefore, in this work we want to compare the classification results obtained from the two previously mentioned feature selection methods. In section 2 we show the methodology followed in all the process, namely, the pre-processing stage, a brief of the PCA feature selection algorithm and the characteristics of our GA feature selection algorithm. In section 3 the classification results with both of the feature selection methods are given and finally the conclusion and comments are presented in section 4.

2 Methodology

In this paper images from the geostationary satellite Meteosat are used. This satellite gives multi-spectral data in three wavelength channels. In this work two of them, the visible and infrared channels, are used. The subjective interpretation of these images by Meteorology experts suggested us to consider the following classes: sea (S), land (L), fog (F), low clouds (C_L), middle clouds (C_M), high clouds (C_H) and clouds with vertical growth (C_V).

For the learning step of the neural models, several Meteorology experts selected a large set of prototypes. These are grouped into rectangular zones, of such form that, each of these rectangular zones contains prototypes belonging to the same class. For this selection task a specific plug-in for the image-processing program GIMP was implemented.

In order to compare the classification results obtained by the two feature selection algorithms and to carry out the GA feature selection process, the set of prototypes was divided into a training set, a validation set and a test set. For obtaining an optimal neural network with good generalization, we started from a BPNN with very few neurons in its hidden layer. This network was trained with the training set. The learning process stops when the number of misclassifications obtained on the validation set reaches a minimum. After that, the process was repeated by increasing the network size. The new network is considered optimal if the number of misclassifications over the validation set is lower than the previous one. Finally, we select the optimal feature selection algorithm according to the classification results on the test set.

For the training of the BPNN, the Resilient Backpropagation RProp algorithm descri-bed in [17] is used. Basically this algorithm is a local adaptive learning scheme which performs supervised batch learning in multi-layer perceptrons. It differs from other algorithms since it considers only the sign of the summed gradient information over all patterns of the training set to indicate the direction of the weight update. The different simulations were performed by means of the freeware neural networks simulation program SNNS (Stuttgart Neural Network Simulator).

2.1 Preprocessing Stage

Our final aim is the definition of a segmentation system of images corresponding to different times of the day and different days of the year. Therefore, satellite data must be corrected in the preprocessing stage to obtain physical magnitudes which are cha-r-acteristic of clouds and independent of the measurement process.

From the infrared channel, we obtained brightness temperature information corrected from the aging effects and transfer function of the radiometer. From the visi-ble channel we obtained albedo after correcting it from the radiometer aging effects and considering the viewing and illumination geometry. This correction deals with the Sun-Earth distance and the solar zenith angle at the image acquisition date and time, and the longitude and latitude of the pixel considered. In [7] no data correction is made and an adaptive PNN network is proposed to resolve this issue.

Next, from the albedo and brightness temperature data, which are already characteristic of the cloud, 144 statistical measures based on grey level co-occurrence matrix (GLCM) were computed. These measures constitute the characteristic vector for each pixel in the image. The large dimensionality of this vector and the limited quantity of prototypes available lead us to the case where the sparse data provide a very poor representation of the mapping. This phenomenon has been termed *the curse of dimensionality* [18]. Thus, in many problems, reducing the number of input variables can lead to improved performances for a given data set, even though some information is being discarded. Therefore, this process constitutes one of the fundamentals steps of the preprocessing stage and also one of the most significant factors in determining the performance of the final system.

In the next sections we are going to describe briefly the algorithms used for reducing the dimensionality of the input vector. Two different methods will be applied, GA as representative of the algorithms that select a subset of the inputs and discard the remainder and PCA as representative of the techniques based on the combination of inputs together to make a, generally smaller, set of features.

2.2   PCA Feature Selection

Principal Components Analysis is one of the most known techniques of multivariate analysis [19]. Due to its versatility, this method has been used for many different purposes related to synthesizing information. This method starts with a large set of variables which are highly intercorrelated and defines new uncorrelated variables, which are linear combination of the initial ones, ordered by the information they account for. In this study, the 144 mentioned statistical measures were calculated for 4420 pixel extracted from a set of 20 images chosen to be representative of all types of clouds, land and sea. The distance between selected pixels is, at least, five pixels, which means about 35 km for the region of study. This avoids considering too much redundant information.

Next, a PCA was performed with the correlation matrix of the 144 variables and 4420 cases. The correlation matrix was chosen as the dispersion matrix since the variables have different units. Thus, all variables have the same weight irrespective of their original variance. The most representative principal components (PCs) were selected according to the Kaiser's rule [20]. Then, the variable most correlated to each PC was chosen as representative of the information accounted for by the PC.

Since rotating PCs results in a less ambiguous classification of variables, the PCs were also rotated according to Varimax method [21]. This rotation was chosen since it is widely accepted as being the most accurate orthogonal rotation method.

Thus, finally, two sets of variables were selected, one for the case of unrotated PCs (PCANR) and other for the case of rotated PCs (PCAR).

2.3 GA Feature Selection

The GA algorithm [22] tries to select a subset of features that offer the neural network with the best generalisation by using the prototypes selected and labelled by the experts in Meteorology. That is, the network that, trained with the prototypes of the learning set, achieves the minimum number of misclassifications over the validation set.

For each subset of features the algorithm uses one hidden layer perceptrons where the number of the neurons of the hidden layer changed from 20 till 40. For each topology the training process is repeated 20 times randomizing the weights each time. As fitness we have used the sum of squared error (SSE) over the validation set.

The GA was configured using a cross-over probability of 0.6, a mutation probability of 0.1, a population of 350 individuals, a tournament selection and a steady-state population replacement with a 30% of replacement.

The simulations were done in a Beowulf style cluster with Clustermatic as OS (a patched RedHat 7.2 Linux OS, with *bproc* for cluster management). The cluster is built using on master node, a double Pentium III @ 800 MHz with 1 Gbyte of RAM memory, and 25 nodes, with AMD Athlon @ 900 MHz with 512 Mbytes of memory each. For GA simulations we used the PGAPack [23] simulator with MPI enabled.

3 Results

In order to implement the processes described above, the experts in Meteorology selected 4599 prototypes, 2781 for the training set, 918 for the validation set and 900 for the test set. The prototype selection was made from the Iberian Peninsula Meteosat images corresponding to the years 1995-1998.

In the feature selection process the PCANR algorithm selected 8 variables, the PCAR 17 and the GA gave 13. In table 1 we can observe the set of parameters selected for each algorithm.

Table 1. Parameters selected for each algorithm

Algorithm	Number	Parameters
GA	13	113, 143, 83, 85, 72, 125, 110, 119, 88, 72, 17, 58, 40
PCAR	17	136, 25, 67, 94, 15, 22, 96, 126, 60, 121, 102, 84, 30, 50, 56, 86, 132
PCANR	8	140, 25, 22, 78, 12, 121, 56, 86

Once feature selection is made, we use a BPNN to make the comparison of the algorithms and to make the final classification. In order to select the network with the best generalization for each algorithm we take one hidden layer BPNN with variable number of neurons. We train the neural network with the training set and we calculate the SSE over the validation set each training iteration. The network that reaches a minimum of misclassification over the validation set is chosen as representative for this algorithm.

In the GA case the minimum value for the sum of squared error (SSE) over the validation set was $SSE_v=35$ and this value was reached with 23 neurons in the hidden layer. With the PCAR algorithm $SSE_v=136$ with 24 neurons in the hidden layer and, finally, with the PCANR algorithm we used 48 neurons in the hidden layer to obtain a $SSE_v=196$.

In tables 2,3 and 4 the percentage of success over the seven classes defined in the learning process and the SSE calculated over the three subsets of prototypes by the network representative of each feature selection algorithm can be observed.

Table 2. Classification results over the learning set reached by the networks with the best generalization over the three sets of features.

Algorithm	F	C_L	C_M	C_H	C_V	L	S	SSE_L
				Learning set				
GA	96.4	95.1	94.6	100	96.5	100	100	146
PCAR	87.4	86.1	89.6	98.4	89.2	100	100	347
PCANR	84.2	92.3	93.3	97.8	86.7	94.5	95.0	376

Table 3. Classification results over the validation set reached by the networks with the best generalization over the three sets of features.

Algorithm	F	C_L	C_M	C_H	C_V	L	S	SSE_V
				Validation set				
GA	96.4	96	99.4	98.4	98.9	100	100	35
PCAR	83.2	87.9	88.7	98.4	87.8	90.3	100	136
PCANR	74.3	87.9	79.9	98.4	90	88.2	95.2	196

Table 4. Classification results over the test set reached by the networks with the best generalization over the three sets of features.

Algorithm	F	C_L	C_M	C_H	C_V	L	S	SSE_T
				Test set				
GA	92.7	86.5	77.6	100	75.9	100	100	167
PCAR	84.6	69.7	78.8	97.3	76.8	97.6	100	194
PCANR	62.6	94.2	94.1	91.8	60.7	69.6	99.3	262

4   Conclusions

Since the feature selection algorithm interacts with the network in the selection process for the GA case, the minimum value for the SSE_v is lower than the minimum obtained with the other algorithms. But it also happens that the value of the SSE_T for the GA algorithm is the lowest obtained. Thus we propose the features selected by the GA algorithm to perform the future automatic segmentation of the Iberian Peninsula Meteosat images.

In Figure 1 an example of an Iberian Peninsula Meteosat image segmentation can be observed. For the final classification a new class, the indecision class (I), has been added. We consider that one pixel belongs to a class when the output of the neuron representative of this class is bigger than 0.6 and the others outputs are least than 0.4. In other case the pixel is considered to belong to the indecision class.

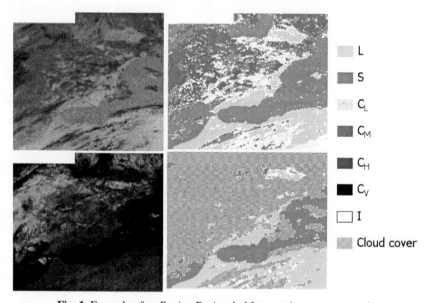

L

S

C_L

C_M

C_H

C_V

I

Cloud cover

Fig. 1. Example of an Iberian Peninsula Meteosat image segmentation.

Acknowledgements. Thanks are due to EUMETSAT for kindly providing the Meteosat data and to project 1FD970723 (financed by the FEDER and Ministerio de Educación).

References

1. Welch, R.M., Kuo K. S., Sengupta S. K., and Chen D. W.: Cloud field classification based upon high spatial resolution textural feature (I): Gray-level cooccurrence matrix approach. J. Geophys. Res., vol. 93, (oct. 1988) 12633-81.
2. Lee J., Weger R. C., Sengupta S. K. And Welch R.M.: A Neural Network Approach to Cloud Classification. IEEE Transactions on Geoscience and Remote Sensing, vol. 28, no. 5, pp. 846-855, Sept. 1990.
3. M. Macías, F.J. López, A. Serrano and A. Astillero: "A Comparative Study of two Neural Models for Cloud Screening of Iberian Peninsula Meteosat Images", Lecture Notes in Computer Science 2085, Bio-inspired applications of connectionism, pp. 184-191, 2001.

4. A. Astillero, A Serrano, M. Núñez, J.A. García, M. Macías and H.M. Gónzalez: "A Study of the evolution of the cloud cover over Cáceres (Spain) along 1997, estimated from Meteosat images", Proceedings of the 2001 EUMETSAT Meteorological Satellite Data Users' Conference, pp. 353-359, 2001

5. Bankert, R. L et al.,: Cloud Classification of AVHRR Imagery in Maritime Regions Using a Probabilistic Neural Network. Journal of Applied. Meteorology, 33, (1994) 909-918.

6. B. Tian, M. A. Shaikh, M R. Azimi, T. H. Vonder Haar, and D. Reinke, "An study of neural network-based cloud classification using textural and spectral features," IEE trans. Neural Networks, vol. 10, pp. 138-151, 1999.

7. B. Tian, M. R. Azimi, T. H. Vonder Haar, and D. Reinke, "Temporal Updating Scheme for Probabilistic Neural Network with Application to Satellite Cloud Classification," IEEE trans. Neural Networks, Vol. 11, no. 4, pp. 903-918, Jul. 2000.

8. R. M. Welch et al., "Polar cloud and surface classification using AVHRR imagery: An intercomparison of methods," J. Appl. Meteorol., vol. 31, pp. 405-420, May 1992.

9. N. Lamei et al., "Cloud-type discrimitation via multispectral textural analysis," Opt. Eng., vol. 33, pp. 1303-1313, Apr. 1994.

10. R. M. Haralick et al., "Textural features for image classification", IEEE trans. Syst., Man, Cybern., vol. SMC-3, pp. 610-621, Mar. 1973.

11. M. F. Aug.eijin, "Performance evaluation of texture measures for ground cover identification in satellite images by means of a neural.network classifier," IEEE trans. Geosc. Remote Sensing, vol. 33, pp. 616-625, May 1995.

12. Doak J. An evaluatin of feature selection methods and their application to computer security (Technical Repor CSE-92-18). Davis, CA: University of California, Department of Computer Science.

13. Aha, D. W., and Bankert, R. L.: A Comparative Evaluation of Sequential Feature Selection Algorithms. Artificial Intelligence and Statistics V., D. Fisher and J. H. Lenz, editors. Springer-Verlag, New York, 1996.

14. Eng Hock Tay F. and Li Juan Cao, A comparative study of saliency analysis and genetic algorithm for feature selection in support vector machines", Intelligent Data Analysis, vol. 5, no. 3, pp. 191-209, 2001.

15. A. Tettamanzi, M. Tomassini. Soft Computing. Integrating Evolutionary, Neural and Fuzzy Systems. Springer, 2001.

16. F.Z. Brill, D.E. Brown and W.N. Martin. Fast genetic selection of features for neural network classifiers. IEEE Transactions on Neural Networks, 3(2): 324-328, 1992.

17. M. Riedmiller, M., Braun, L.: A Direct Adaptive Method for Faster Backpropagation Learning: The RPROP Algorithm. In Proceedings of the IEEE International Conference on Neural Networks 1993 (ICNN 93), 1993.

18. R. Bellman: "Adaptive Control Processes: A Guided Tour". New Jersey, Princeton University Press.

19. I. T. Jolliffe: Principal Component Analysis, Springer-Verlag, 271 pp., 1986.

20. H. F. Kaiser: "The application of electronic computer to factor analysis", Educ. Psycol. Meas., vol. 20, pp.141-151, 1960.

21. H. F. Kaiser, "The Varimax criterion for analytic rotation in factor analysis", Psychometrika, vol. 23, pp. 187-200, 1958.

22. D.E. Goldberg. Genetic Algorithms in Search, Optimization & Machine Learning. Addison Wesley, 1989.

23. D. Levine. Users Guide to the PGAPack Parallel Genetic Algorithm Library. Research Report ANL-95/18. Argonne National Laboratory, 1996.

Filtering Noisy Continuous Labeled Examples*

José Ramón Quevedo Pérez, María Dolores García, and Elena Montañés

Centro de Inteligencia Artificial. Oviedo University. Viesques, E-33271 Gijón, Spain
{quevedo, marilo, elena}@aic.uniovi.es

Abstract. It is common in Machine Learning where rules are learned from examples that some of them could not be informative, otherwise they could be irrelevant or noisy. This type of examples makes the Machine Learning Systems produce not adequate rules. In this paper we present an algorithm that filters noisy continuous labeled examples, whose computational cost is $O(N \cdot logN + NA^2)$ for N examples and A attributes. Besides, it is shown experimentally to be better than the embedded algorithms of the state-of-the art of the Machine Learning Systems.

1 Introduction

In Machine Learning environment the process of learning rules from available labeled examples (training data) is called *training* and the process of applying these learned rules to unlabeled examples (test data) is called *testing*.

An example is represented by a sequence of pairs attribute-value and a label that represents its category. The category can be symbolic or continuous. The examples have the same attributes although some values could be *missing*.

A good performance could be reached supposing that the sets of training and test data have the same distribution of the category over theirs attributes [3].

One of the most difficult tasks when dealing with real problems is to find the attributes more related to the category in the way to define a fixed distribution that a Machine Learning System (*MLS*) could learn. An additional difficulty is the possible presence of noisy examples mainly caused by the collection of them.

In this paper an algorithm that filters noisy continuous labeled examples is presented. It is shown that some *MLS* perform better using the filtered data set than using the original one.

2 Task Definition

This paper describes an algorithm that removes noisy examples from a set of continuous labeled examples producing a subset containing informative ones.

This Noisy Continuos Labeled Examples Filter (*NCLEF*) takes an example e and classifies it as noisy or as informative. This classification is made according to two

---

* The research reported in this paper has been supported in part under MCyT and Feder grant TIC2001-3579

F.J. Garijo, J.C. Riquelme, and M. Toro (Eds.): IBERAMIA 2002, LNAI 2527, pp. 50–59, 2002.
© Springer-Verlag Berlin Heidelberg 2002

errors: the error committed when the current example is taking into account on the data set and the error committed when the current example is removed from the data set. The method employed to evaluate these errors is the continuous version of *knn* [1], it is used with Leaving-One-Out (*LOO*)[12] (See Fig. 1).

It is well known that *knn* is noise sensitive [1], that is, adding a noisy example to the data set the performance of *knn* would be worse. The algorithm described in this paper is based on this idea on a reverse way: "if the removal of an example produces lower error then this example is supposed to be noisy".

The algorithm has two main disadvantages. The first one is that its computacional cost is $O(N \cdot O(knn))=O(N \cdot kAN^2)=O(kAN^3)$ for N examples and A attributes. The second one is the insignificant influence of an example over the *knn*'s error for large data sets. A Divide and Conquer method (*D&C*) is incorporated to overcome these difficulties. The resulting filter adding *D&C*, called *NCLEFDC*, makes its cost be $O(N \cdot logN + NA^2)$.

3   Related Work

This work is related with Example Selection. There are several techniques about Example Selection proposed by Wilson & Martinez [14]; Aha [2]; Aha, Kibler & Albert [1] and Cameron-Jones [5].

Blum and Langley [4] propose at least three reasons for selecting examples: purposes of computational efficiency, high cost of labeling and focusing attention on informative examples. Our algorithm pays attention to the third one in the way that it trends to remove noisy examples and keep informative ones.

Most of the algorithms for Example Selection work only on symbolic labeled examples. There are algorithms to deal with data set containing noisy continuous labeled examples which are embedded in the *MLS* (*M5'* [11], *RT* [9], *Cubist* [8]), but there is no documentation for commercial systems like *Cubist*.

In this paper is compared the performance of using *NCLEFDC* before the *MLS* with the performance of using only those *MLS*.

4   The NCLEFDC Algorithm

The algorithm involves three steps which are detailed in the next subsections: the principle, the iterative algorithm and the incorporation of a *D&C*.

4.1   The Principle

The principle involves the election of the measures employed to decide if an example is noisy or not. A trivial measure could be the *knn*'s error for this example, being the noisiest example that with the highest error. That is true in most cases, but it is not useful since there could be no noisy examples with high error and since it is difficult to find out the meaning of "high error". Fortunately, noisy examples in *knn* entails another very useful feature, namely, adding a noisy example to the data set causes an increasing of the errors of its neighbors (See Figure 1).

Taking into account this last feature, the algorithm sees the effect that an example causes to the error of its neighbors in order to decide if it is noisy or not. The error is approached by means of *LOO* with *knn* over the data set. The error for N examples is denoted by E_N, the error when removing example e from the data set is denoted by $E_{N-1}(e)$ and the error E_N but without considering the error of the example e is denoted by $E'_N(e)$. This latter error is given by equation (1).

$$E'_N(e) = \frac{E_N \cdot N - ErrorKnn(data = DataSet - \{e\}, test = \{e\})}{N-1} \qquad (1)$$

$$SupposedNoisy(e) \Leftarrow E'_N(e) > E_{N-1}(e) \qquad (2)$$

It could be supposed that an example is noisy in the way of equation (2). This means that the presence of this example makes that the *knn*'s error of the examples that take it as its neighbor be bigger than if the example is removed from the data set.

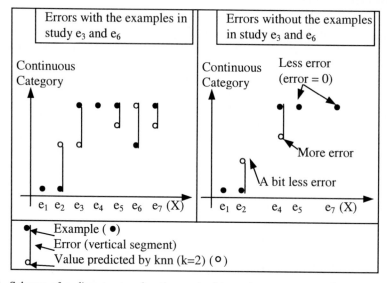

Fig. 1. Schema of a discrete step function and of how the errors vary when examples are removed. Examples e_3 and e_6 have the same error, but e_3 is informative (it is the first example of the next step) and e_6 is noisy. If e_6 is removed the errors of its neighbors (e_5 and e_7) becomes 0, but if e_3 is removed the sum of the error of its neighbors (e_2 and e_4) is higher.

The algorithm requires choosing the value of k for the *knn*. It should not be so small because it is necessary that an example has enough neighbors in order to measure its influence. It should also not be so big because the predictions of *knn* should significantly vary if an example is removed. A good value for k is generally determined via cross-validation [13] but a *bad* value is preferred in order to make *knn* be very noise sensitive. Although the experiments show that the influence of k over *NCLEF* is not so much significant, it is chosen the best one obtained in our experiments, that is: $k=A/2+1$, where A is the number of attributes of the problem.

4.2   The NCLEF Algorithm

The *NCLEF* algorithm based on the principle previously shown tries to remove the example with more error in each iteration. Over this structure it is possible to develop several versions. We prefer to make a prudent version, one that the main objective is to keep informative examples. In this way three aspects of the algorithm are changed. Firstly a new test for noisy examples is proposed. This test, described in equation (3), takes into account the number of examples previously removed in order to avoid removing informative ones. Secondly, the application of the test is limited to examples whose error is above a fixed threshold (*MinError* in equation (4)). Finally, the algorithm ends when it considers the example as not noisy.

$$prudentNoisy(e) \Leftarrow E'_N(e)\frac{N - Examplesremoved}{N} > E_{N-1}(e) \tag{3}$$

$$MinError = \overline{LOO(knn(DataSet))} + \sigma\big(LOO(knn(DataSet))\big) \tag{4}$$

In equation (4) *LOO(knn(DataSet))* is the set of errors of a *LOO* execution on the data set using *knn*. *MinError* is chosen to be the sum of the average and the typical deviation of all LOO executions. The addition of the typical deviation to the average assures that the algorithm only tries to remove examples with high *knn*'s error.

The *NCLEF* algorithm is described as follows.

```
DataSet NCLEF(DataSet DS){
    // Obtain the initial Average Error using knn
    {ExampleMaxErr,AverageErr,DeviationErr}=LOOKNN(DS);
    MinError=AverageErr+DeviationErr;

    for(ite=1;ExampleMaxErr.Error>MinError;ite++){
        // Obtain the Average Error and Example with
        // more error using knn
        {ExampleMaxErrN1,AverageErrN1}=
              LOOKNN(DS-{ExampleMaxErr});
        //If the example is noisy, it is eliminated
        if(prudentNoisy(ExampleMaxErr)){
           DS=DS-{ExampleMaxErr};
           ExampleMaxErr=ExampleMaxErrN1;
           AverageErr=AverageErrN1;
        }
        else break; // the example is not noisy
    } // end of for
    return DS;
} // end of NCLEF
```

Function *LOOKNN* applies *LOO* with *knn* to the data set given as a parameter. It returns the average error, the deviation error and the example with highest error. This information is necessary in function *prudentNoisy* to test if an example is noisy or not.

4.3   Using Divide and Conquer on NCLEF

As *NCLEF* iterates for each example and uses *knn* its order is $O(NCLEF)=$ $O(N \cdot O(knn))=O(N \cdot kAN^2)=O(kAN^3)$. Besides, given that we choose k to be $A/2-1$, then $O(NCLEF)=O(kAN^3)=O(A^2N^3)$ for N examples and A attributes. This order makes *NCLEF* computationally unacceptable. That is the reason why *D&C* is applied.

The new algorithm, called *NCLEFDC*, divides recursively the data set in subsets, then applies *NCLEF* to each subset and finally joins all partial filtered subsets.

The goal is to divide the original data set into subsets where all the neighbors of an example in the original set were in the same subset. As this could be impossible or, at least, very computationally expensive, the *Divide* method based on the following heuristic is used: (1) To take an example e and to calculate its $\| \; \|_1$, (2) to obtain two subsets, one with the examples with more $\| \; \|_1$ than e and the other one with the examples with less $\| \; \|_1$ than e. The algorithm looks for an example that produces two subsets with similar number of elements. The attributes values are normalized between 0 and 1 to avoid the generation of concentric subsets obtained by the application of a norm. Given that all norms are equivalent in finite dimension spaces, $\| \; \|_1$ is chosen due to its faster calculus than euclidean one employed by *knn*.

The order of *NCLEFDC* is $O(NCLEFDC)=O(N/M(O(Divide)+O(knn)))$, where M is the maximum number of the size of the subsets and N/M is the number of subsets.

The order of *Divide* is $O(Divide)=O(N_{DIV}M)$, where N_{DIV} is the number of examples of the data subset. In each execution N_{DIV} could be different, so the average is estimated in the following way: Supposing that *Divide* splits the data set into two subsets with equal number of examples, the algorithm is executed 2^i times, each one with a data set of $N/2^i$ examples in depth i of the recursive algorithm. This is made until $M/2<N/2^L<M$, been L the maximum depth of the recursive algorithm. If M and N are integers such that $0<M<N$ then equation (8) represents an estimation of N_{DIV}. Then $O(Divide)$ and $O(NCLEFDC)$ are given by the equations (9) and (10) respectively.

$$2^L > \frac{N}{M} \Rightarrow 2^{L+1}-1 > \frac{2N}{M}-1 \Rightarrow \frac{N(L+1)}{2^{L+1}-1} < \frac{N(L+1)}{2N/M-1} \tag{5}$$

$$N_{DIV} = \frac{\sum_{i=0}^{L} 2^i \frac{N}{2^i}}{\sum_{i=0}^{L} 2^i} = \frac{N(L+1)}{2^{L+1}-1} \, by(5) < \frac{N(L+1)}{2N/M-1} < \frac{N(L+1)}{N/M} = M(L+1) \tag{6}$$

$$\frac{N}{2^L} > \frac{M}{2} \Rightarrow \frac{2N}{M} > 2^L \Rightarrow \log_2\left(2\frac{N}{M}\right) > L \Rightarrow 1+\log_2\left(\frac{N}{M}\right) > L \tag{7}$$

$$N_{DIV} \, by(6) < M(L+1) \, by(7) < M\left(2+\log_2\frac{N}{M}\right) \tag{8}$$

$$O(Divide) = O(N_{DIV} M) = O\left(M\left(2 + \log_2\left(\frac{N}{M}\right)\right) M \right) = O\left(M^2\left(\log_2\left(\frac{N}{M}\right)\right)\right) \quad (9)$$

$$O(NCLEFDC) = O\left(\frac{N}{M}\big(O(Divide) + O(Knn)\big)\right) = O\left(MN\left(\log_2\left(\frac{N}{M}\right)\right) + NA^2 M \right) \quad (10)$$

Fixing M to be constant in all experimentation, then $O(NCLEFDC)$ is:

$$O(NCLEFDC) = O\big(N \cdot \log_2(N) + NA^2\big) \quad (11)$$

The algorithm does not always split the data set into two subsets with exactly the same number of examples, otherwise it could split into subsets with a proportion between 40%-60%. Then, the base of the logarithm in equation (11) could be lower than 2, but even though the first addend would be always lower that N^2.

The algorithm *NCLEFDC* is described below:

```
DataSet NCLEFDC(DataSet DS,int M){
  // If there are more examples in the data set than M
  // we divide the data set into two subsets
  if(#DS>M) {
  {DS1,DS2}=Divide(DS,M);
    //  The global result is the Union of the partial
    // result of the two recursive calls to NCLEFDC
    return Union(NCLEFDC(DS1),NCLEFDC(DS2));
  } else return NCLEF(DS); // base case
} // End of program


{DataSet DS1,DataSet DS2} Divide(DataSet DS,int M){
  Min=0;
  Max=MaxNormalizedNorm1;
  Example ERand;
  for(iterations=1;iterations<M;iterations++) {
    ERand=RandomExampleBetween(DS,Min,Max);
    above=PercentExamplesWithMoreNorm1(DS,ERand);
    if(above>=40 and above=<60) break; // good solution
    // Redefine search interval
    if(above<40) Max=Norm1(ERand);
    if(above>60) Min=Norm1(ERand);
  } // End of for
  DS1=ExamplesWithLessNorm1(DS,ERand);
  DS2=ExamplesWithMoreNorm1(DS,ERand);
}// End of Divide
```

The function *Divide* searches for an example e whose $\| \|_1$ is a percentile between 40% and 60% in the distribution of all $\| \|_1$. This interval is fixed as an approximation of 'equal number of examples'.

5   Experimental Evaluation

A set of experiments were conducted to compare the performance of *M5'*, *Cubist* and *RT* with and without *NCLEFDC*.

The well known heterogeneous data sets of the Torgo's repository at *LIACC* [10] are used. Each experiment consists of a *Cross Validation (CV)* with 10 folds. Besides, it is employed MLC++[6] with 2032 seed to make the experiments to be repeatable.

The result of a *CV* experiment is the Medium Average Deviation (*MAD*), but in the forward tables it is shown the Relative Medium Average Deviation (*RMAD*) which is the *MAD* divided by the *MAD* of the system that always predicts the average function.

Table 1. List of the data sets of the Torgo's repository. The name, the number of examples (#Ex), the number of attributes (#Att) and the *MAD* of the system that always predict the average function (Av. MAD) are shown for each data set. Each data set is also numbered (N°) to be referred forward using this number.

N° Name	#Ex	#Att	Av.MAD	N° Name	#Ex	#Att	Av.MAD
1 Abalone	4177	8	2,363	16 Diabetes	43	2	2,363
2 Ailerons	13750	40	0,0003	17 Elevators	16599	18	0,0046
3 Airpla.Com.	950	9	5,4852	18 Friedman Ex.	40768	10	4,0648
4 Auto-Mpg	398	4	6,5459	19 Housing	506	13	6,6621
5 Auto-Price	159	14	4600,65	20 Kinematics	8192	8	0,2156
6 Bank 32NH	8192	32	0,0903	21 Machine-Cpu	209	6	96,9004
7 Bank 8FM	8192	8	0,1236	22 MvExample	40768	10	8,8932
8 Cal. Hou.	20640	9	91174,5	23 PoleTele.	15000	48	37,2124
9 Cart Delve	40768	10	3,6069	24 Pumadyn(32)	8192	32	0,0235
10 Census(16)	22784	16	32428,2	25 Pumadyn(8)	8192	8	4,8659
11 Census(8)	22784	8	32428,2	26 Pyrimidines	74	27	0,0957
12 Com.Act	8192	21	10,6326	27 Servo	167	2	1,1662
13 Com.Act(s)	8192	12	10,6326	28 Triazines	186	60	0,1187
14 Delta Ailer.	7129	5	0,0003	29 Wisconsin	198	32	29,6833
15 Delta Eleva	9517	6	0,002				

Table 2 shows that the use of *NCLEFDC* does not improve the performance significantly because the data sets do not have enough noisy examples. Table 3 shows the results when the 10% of training data are changed by noisy examples in each execution of the *CV* (the test data are not modified). Under these circumstances the performance of *Cubist*, *M5'* and *RT* gets better. So *NCLEFDC* removes examples better than the embedded filters that use these systems.

Table 2. *RMAD* of the *MLS* with and without the *NCLEFDC* filter. It is shown the *RMAD* for each data set of Torgo's repository and the average of all *RMADs* (Av.) of a *MLS*.

	Only the systems			NCLEFDC before the systems		
	Cubist 1.10	M5'	RT 4.1	Cubist 1.10	M5'	RT 4.1
1	105,16%	101,12%	100,46%	104,63%	99,89%	100,46%
2	73,88%	66,67%	84,74%	73,88%	66,67%	84,74%
3	39,54%	33,82%	42,62%	39,54%	33,82%	39,14%
4	27,83%	28,01%	48,81%	27,83%	28,01%	48,76%
5	33,07%	31,75%	36,73%	33,65%	30,54%	36,70%
6	34,04%	34,41%	43,17%	34,79%	34,83%	34,45%
7	12,67%	11,69%	16,94%	12,60%	11,76%	17,20%
8	63,48%	64,24%	67,85%	63,06%	64,43%	71,23%
9	100,00%	50,00%	50,00%	100,00%	50,00%	50,00%
10	19,37%	20,64%	24,33%	19,37%	20,43%	24,41%
11	17,88%	18,53%	22,90%	17,88%	18,45%	22,90%
12	50,67%	51,42%	52,40%	50,65%	51,57%	52,39%
13	58,47%	64,45%	70,21%	58,14%	63,23%	70,32%
14	26,38%	28,51%	30,64%	26,81%	28,51%	30,64%
15	15,89%	17,80%	22,65%	15,80%	17,89%	22,65%
16	55,61%	56,17%	66,70%	55,52%	56,17%	66,88%
17	22,07%	22,08%	22,43%	22,07%	22,08%	22,44%
18	6,37%	8,28%	8,78%	6,56%	8,25%	8,76%
19	52,41%	58,01%	57,93%	51,60%	57,47%	57,49%
20	49,67%	54,57%	54,56%	49,28%	54,28%	54,02%
21	38,89%	35,98%	41,68%	35,45%	35,94%	42,08%
22	50,00%	36,96%	52,17%	50,00%	36,96%	52,17%
23	23,83%	26,63%	33,88%	23,83%	26,70%	33,79%
24	100,00%	33,33%	33,33%	100,00%	33,33%	33,33%
25	0,22%	0,97%	12,42%	0,22%	0,97%	12,36%
26	85,17%	81,80%	88,96%	89,89%	81,55%	89,72%
27	101,27%	97,49%	100,56%	101,07%	97,16%	96,76%
28	30,88%	28,16%	40,53%	32,18%	27,57%	42,62%
29	55,00%	55,00%	55,00%	55,00%	55,00%	55,00%
Av.	46,54%	42,02%	47,70%	46,60%	41,84%	47,36%

Table 2 shows that there are no significant differences in the precision when *NCLEFDC* is applied to no noisy data sets. However, the application of *NCLEFDC* to noisy data sets (see Table 3) causes an improvement in the performance.

Table 3. *RMAD* of the *MLS* with and without the *NCLEFDC*. It is shown the *RMAD* for each data set of Torgo's repository and the average of all *RMADs* (Av) of a *MLS*. The data in each execution of a *CV* are modified with a 10% of noisy examples.

	Only the systems			NCLEFDC before the systems		
	Cubist 1.10	M5'	RT 4.1	Cubist 1.10	M5'	RT 4.1
1	98,19%	101,52%	96,18%	98,88%	98,50%	95,58%
2	76,05%	71,01%	90,44%	75,84%	69,85%	90,86%
3	41,22%	50,84%	53,20%	38,84%	40,98%	43,10%
4	54,59%	60,01%	79,86%	39,61%	43,19%	54,45%
5	38,85%	37,01%	43,45%	35,57%	34,32%	40,66%
6	46,13%	42,09%	53,64%	41,18%	40,42%	52,08%
7	19,66%	20,60%	25,72%	15,28%	14,98%	28,02%
8	64,60%	68,83%	73,61%	62,53%	64,25%	75,30%
9	100,00%	50,00%	50,00%	100,00%	50,00%	50,00%
10	35,88%	41,70%	41,97%	27,85%	33,15%	34,19%
11	26,26%	30,44%	34,39%	20,53%	23,55%	28,20%
12	53,01%	54,31%	55,26%	53,04%	53,32%	55,07%
13	64,75%	76,53%	82,57%	57,28%	69,35%	76,34%
14	31,20%	36,32%	37,61%	30,77%	36,32%	37,18%
15	33,94%	40,85%	41,38%	24,13%	32,91%	33,81%
16	58,02%	60,58%	72,82%	57,79%	59,65%	72,77%
17	23,02%	24,10%	26,27%	22,25%	22,50%	24,03%
18	14,27%	18,35%	18,98%	10,52%	12,23%	12,35%
19	57,33%	79,30%	76,55%	48,19%	62,31%	60,37%
20	50,08%	74,08%	73,12%	43,14%	56,42%	56,37%
21	42,11%	41,53%	49,54%	42,59%	39,72%	47,09%
22	52,63%	56,14%	68,42%	45,61%	42,11%	57,89%
23	25,43%	34,82%	44,17%	24,92%	32,48%	41,29%
24	100,00%	33,33%	66,67%	100,00%	33,33%	66,67%
25	7,38%	15,24%	17,32%	3,65%	7,19%	9,65%
26	97,13%	93,53%	95,25%	93,28%	95,74%	98,20%
27	157,47%	156,00%	152,13%	156,73%	152,29%	151,54%
28	45,21%	44,78%	51,63%	42,80%	40,01%	46,15%
29	55,00%	55,00%	60,00%	55,00%	55,00%	60,00%
Av.	54,12%	54,10%	59,73%	50,61%	48,83%	55,15%

6   Conclusions

This paper describes an algorithm that filters noisy continuous labeled examples from a data set. This algorithm uses *knn* to determine if an example is noisy or not. *knn* is helped by *D&C* in order to reduce its computational cost.

The quality of this algorithm has been evaluated by two criteria: the cost associated to the filtering and the accuracy of *M5'*, *Cubist* and *RT* when they use the filtered data set instead of the original one. The cost of the algorithm is $O(Nlog_2N+A^2N)$ where N is the number of examples and A is the number of attributes.

It is shown experimentally that the accuracy of the latter systems is better when they use this filter under the presence of noisy examples. However, the accuracy is the same when there are no noisy examples.

A conclusion is that the performance of *M5'*, *Cubist* and *RT* is worse under the presence of noisy examples. Another conclusion is that in our experiments *NCLEFDC* deals with noisy examples better than the embedded algorithms of the latter systems.

In this paper only basic principles are presented, but a lot remains could be done in this area. We are interested in the following issues: (1) to calculate automatically the stop condition of the *D&C* phase; (2) to extend this idea to a discrete labeled examples; (3) to transfer the use of *knn* as noise detector to the area of feature selection.

References

1. Aha, D.W., Kibler, D., Albert, M.K.: Instance based learning algorithms. Machine Learning, Vol. 6. (1991) 37-66
2. Aha,D.W.: Lazy learning. Kluwer Academic Publishers, Dordrecht. (1997)
3. Blum A.L.: Relevant examples and relevant features: Thoughts from computational learning theory. In AAAI Fall Symposium on 'Relevance'. (1994) 31
4. Blum A.L., Langley. P.:Selection of relevant features and examples in machine learning. Artificial Intelligence. (1997) 245-271
5. Cameron-Jones, R.M.: Instance Selection by encoding length heuristic with random mutation hill climbing. IEEE Proc. of the 8th Australian Joint Conference on AI. World Scientific. (1995) 99-106.
6. Kohavi, R., John, G., Long, R., Manley, D., & Pfleger, K. (1994). MLC++: A machine learning library in C++. In Proc. of the 6th International Conference on Tools with Artificial Intelligence, 740-743. IEEE Computer Society Press.
7. Quinlan, J.R.: Learning with continuous classes. In Proc. 5th Australian Joint Conference on Artificial Intelligence. World Scientific, Singapore, (1992) 343-348.
8. Quinlan, J.R.: Cubist. http://www.rulequest.com/cubist-info.html
9. Torgo. L.: Functional models for regression tree leaves. In Proc. of the 14th International Conference on Machine Learning, Nashville, TN. Morgan Kaufmann. (1997) 385-393
10. Torgo. L: Regression Data Sets Repository at LIACC (University of Porto). http://www.ncc.up.pt/~ltorgo/Regression/DataSets.html
11. Wang, Y., and Witten, I.H.. Inducing model trees for continuous classes. In Poster Papers 9th European Conf. on Machine Learning. Prague, Czech Republic. (1997) 128-137.
12. Weiss, S. M., Kulikowski, C. A.: Computer systems that learn: Classification and prediction methods from statistics, neural nets, machine learning, and expert systems. MorganKaufmann, San Mateo, CA, (1991.)
13. Wettschereck, D., Dietterich, T. G.: Locally adaptive nearest neighbor algorithms in Advances of Neural Information Processing Systems 6. Morgan Kaufmann Publishers. (1994) 184-191
14. Wilson, D.R., Martinez, T.R.: Instance pruning techniques. Proc. of the 14th International Conference on Machine Learning. Morgan Kaufmann, Nashville, TN., (1997) 403-411

Designing Adaptive Hypermedia for Internet Portals: A Personalization Strategy Featuring Case Base Reasoning with Compositional Adaptation

Syed Sibte Raza Abidi

Faculty of Computer Science, Dalhousie University, Halifax B3H 1W5, Canada
sraza@cs.dal.ca

Abstract. In this paper, we propose that the *Case Based Reasoning (CBR)* paradigm offers an interesting alternative to developing adaptive hypermedia systems, such that the inherent analogy-based reasoning strategy can inductively yield a 'representative' user model and the case adaptation techniques can be used for dynamic adaptive personalization of generic hypermedia-based information content. User modeling is achieved by applying an *ontology-guided CBR retrieval technique* to collect a set of similar past cases which are used to form a global user-model. Adaptive personalization is accomplished by a *compositional adaptation technique* that dynamically authors a personalized hypermedia document—a composite of multiple fine-grained *information 'snippets'*—by selectively collecting the most relevant information items from matched past cases (i.e. not the entire past solution) and systematically amalgamating them to realize a component-based personalized hypermedia document.

1 Introduction

Web-mediated information portals routinely suffer from their inability to satisfy the heterogeneous needs of a broad base of information seekers. For instance, web-based education systems present the same static learning content to learners regardless of their individual knowledge of the subject; health information portals deliver the same generic medical information to consumers with different health profiles; and web e-stores offer the same selection of items to customers with different preferences.

A solution to this overly-simplified approach for 'generic' information delivery is the development of *adaptive hypermedia systems*—web-based systems that belong to the class of user-adaptive software systems—that have the ability to adapt their behavior to the goals, tasks, interests and needs of individual users and group of users [1]. An adaptive hypermedia system involves two distinct activities: (a) development of a user model and (b) adaptation of static generic information content to user-specific personalized content [2].

In this paper, we argue that the *Case Based Reasoning (CBR)* paradigm [3] offers an interesting alternative to developing adaptive hypermedia systems [4], such that the inherent analogy-based reasoning strategy can inductively yield a 'representative' user model and the case adaptation techniques can be used for dynamic adaptive personalization of generic hypermedia-based information content [5]. In our work,

F.J. Garijo, J.C. Riquelme, and M. Toro (Eds.): IBERAMIA 2002, LNAI 2527, pp. 60-69, 2002.
© Springer-Verlag Berlin Heidelberg 2002

user modeling is achieved by applying an *ontology-guided CBR retrieval technique* to collect a set of similar past cases which are used to form a global user-model. Adaptive personalization is accomplished via a novel *compositional adaptation technique* that dynamically authors a personalized hypermedia document—a composite of multiple fine-grained *information 'snippets'*—by selectively collecting the most relevant information items from matched past cases (i.e. not the entire past solution) and systematically amalgamating them to realize a component-based personalized hypermedia document. For concept explication purposes, we have chosen the healthcare sector and present an adaptive hypermedia system designed to dynamically author personalized healthcare information hypermedia content based on an individual's current health status/profile. The choice of the application domain is driven by the need for information personalization in the healthcare sector [5, 6, 7], as personalized health maintenance information is deemed to have a significant impact in ensuring wellness maintenance both at the individual and community level.

2   CBR-Mediated Adaptive Personalization

Our CBR-mediated adaptive hypermedia system development approach builds on a corpus of past *cases* specified by medical practitioners. Each case depicts a situation-action construct, such that (a) the situation component defines the local user-model—i.e. an individual's *Health Profile (HP)*—in terms of attribute-value pairs (ideally originating from the individual's electronic medical record); and (b) the action component comprises a corresponding *Personalized Healthcare Information Prescription (PHIP)* that is composed of a number of fine-grain, *Problem-focused (hypermedia) Documents (PD)*. Each PD is designed to contain health maintenance information pertaining to a specific medical problem/issue. Note that the PHIP is a composite of multiple PDs, whereby each constituent PD is prescribed by a medical practitioner in response to some facet (i.e. an attribute-value) of an individual's HP.

2.1 Problem Specification

We argue that one limitation of traditional CBR approaches is that the recommended solution/action to a new problem-situation—i.e. a new case—is taken as the entire solution of the matched past case. In a healthcare information delivery context where information accuracy is paramount it would be rather naive to assume that heterogeneous individuals may have a similar HP or user model! Hence, it is argued that the entire PHIP associated with matched past cases (i.e. existing user-profiles) cannot be regarded as an accurate inferred solution to a new user-model.

In this scenario, adaptive personalization is characterized as the problem of selective collection of only the relevant information 'snippets' from the multiple matched past PHIPs, as opposed to selecting the entire PHIP (which may potentially contain irrelevant or damaging information for a particular individual). We believe that a *component-based* information representation and compilation strategy will ensure that the healthcare content disseminated to an individual is specifically focused towards the individual's prevailing healthcare needs, akin to the kind of personalized service one enjoys from a visit to a medical practitioner [5].

2.2 Our Compositional Adaptation Strategy

We have devised a case adaptation strategy—based on notions of compositional adaptation [8, 9]—that is applicable to the adaptation of a specialized class of cases in which the case solution is a composite of individual *sub-solutions*; where each sub-solution addresses a particular problem-defining attribute of a case. Our compositional adaptation strategy is applicable to dynamic adaptive personalization of hypermedia documents, as it allows the tailoring of a personalized documents via user-profile driven selection of 'generic' information snippets (analogous to sub-solutions) from an ensemble of past-compiled hypermedia documents. The systematic amalgamation of 'relevant' information snippets yields a unified personalized document corresponding to a particular user-model. Figure 1 shows our CBR-mediated compositional adaptation strategy for adaptive hypermedia personalization.

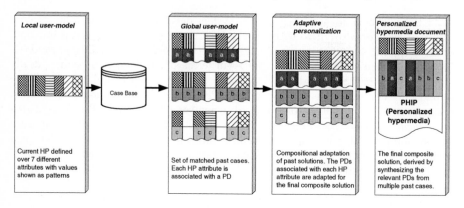

Fig. 1. A pictorial illustration of our CBR-Mediated compositional adaptation based strategy for generating adaptive personalized hypermedia documents.

The rationale for our approach is grounded in the principle that since inter-case similarity is determined at an attribute-level, therefore fine-grained solution adaptation should also be conducted at the attribute-level. By adapting the attribute-specific sub-solutions based on the attribute's similarity measure we ensure that the best matching attribute values impact the most on a selected segment of the solution—i.e. the sub-solution component associated with the attribute—as opposed to impacting the entire solution component [9]. In this way we are able to generate a solution that contains components that reflect the best features—i.e. most relevant information—of similar past solutions.

3   An Algorithm for CBR-Mediated Adaptive Personalization

In this section we will discuss our compositional adaptation algorithm for performing adaptive personalization of hypermedia documents. We will continue with the exemplar application of generating a personalized health information package (PHIP) based on a specific user-model (i.e. an individual's HP).

3.1 Case Representation Scheme

The HP depicts a 'local' user-model defined in terms of a list of health specific attributes as shown in Table 1. The HP, deemed as the problem description in a CBR content, contains multi-valued attributes, where the domain of attribute-values is determined from standard medical resources. In a CBR-context, the PHIP is deemed as the solution component of a case. Structurally, the PHIP is a composite of multiple PDs. Conceptually, each HP attribute is related to at least one PD in the solution component.

Table 1. An exemplar HP illustrating the 7 information groups and their corresponding values.

Acute Disease (AD)	Short-Term Illness (SI)	Current Symptoms (S)	Current Drugs (D)	Allerg-ies (A)	Demograp-hic Data (DD)	Lifestyle Data (LD)
Diabetes-Mellitus Hypertension	Fever	High Temp. Cough Rashes	Panadol Bendryl	Allergic Rhinitis	Age : 56 y Sex : Male Edu.: High	Fitness: N Diet : H Smoke: Y

3.2 User-Modeling: Case Retrieval Procedure

In CBR terms, user modeling involves the generation of a *global user-model* derived based on the similarity between the local user-model (i.e. the HP) and a set of past user-models. Given a local user-model, we retrieve a set of similar past user-models based on similarity measures—referred as **Total Weighted Distance** (**TWD**). The value of the TWD is derived as the sum of the individual **Total Distance** (TD) between the corresponding attributes in the current and past user-models. This process is akin to the case retrieval process in the CBR formalism. To illustrate our case retrieval strategy, Table 2 shows an exemplar current HP; for illustration purposes we will focus on a single HP attribute, namely Acute Disease (AD). In Table 2, the HP section shows that the AD attribute has 3 values (given in uppercase typeface)—each HP attribute-value code is derived as a combination of the *class-code, sub-class-code* and the *element-code* originating from a medical taxonomy. Table 2 also illustrates four matched Past Cases (PC) that are retrieved (note that we show the values for the attribute AD in the past cases in a lowercase typeface).

Table 2. Current HP and 4 matching past cases. Note that only the AD attribute is shown.

	HP			
Current Case	$AD_1 = 1\text{-}1\text{-}002_1$ $AD_2 = 1\text{-}3\text{-}035_2$ $AD_3 = 2\text{-}1\text{-}004_3$			
	PC_1	PC_2	PC_3	$PC_{total} = 4$
Past Cases (PC)	$ad_1 = 1\text{-}1\text{-}002_1$ $ad_2 = 1\text{-}3\text{-}035_2$ $ad_3 = 2\text{-}1\text{-}004_3$	$ad_1 = 1\text{-}2\text{-}021_1$ $ad_2 = 2\text{-}1\text{-}003_2$ $ad_3 = 1\text{-}1\text{-}002_3$	$ad_1 = 1\text{-}1\text{-}020_1$ $ad_2 = 1\text{-}3\text{-}035_2$ $ad_3 = 2\text{-}1\text{-}004_3$	$ad_1 = 3\text{-}1\text{-}002_1$ $ad_2 = 3\text{-}1\text{-}004_2$

A domain-specific *similarity matrix* (as shown in Table 3) is used to determine the attribute-level *Degree of Similarity* (DS)—the DS spans from *perfect match* to *close match* to *weak match* and *no match*—between the current and past HP attribute-values belonging to the same attribute. For instance, the attribute values 1-2-2001 and 1-2-2002 will result in a DS of 'close match' as the class and sub-class codes match, whereas the DS between the attribute values 1-2-2001 and 1-3-3004 is a 'weak match' because only the class code is similar.

Table 3. Similarity Matrix used to determine DS between the current HP and past HP attributes

Degree of Similarity (DS)	Class Code	Sub-Class Code	Element Code	Numeric Value for DS
Perfect Match	√	√	√	1
Close Match	√	√	×	75
Weak Match	√	×	×	25
No Match	×	×	×	100

We trace below the steps involved in the calculation of TWD between a current HP and a set of past HPs, leading to the retrieval of similar past cases.

Step 1 : Determine attribute-level *Distance*.
The idea is to establish equivalence between the current HP and a past case's HP at the attribute level. We calculate the DS between each current HP attribute-value with respect to corresponding attribute-value(s) in each past case's HP. Since each HP attribute can have multiple values, we need to individually determine the DS for each current HP attribute-value. The pseudo code for performing the same is given below; for illustration purposes we consider matching the values for the current HP attribute of 'AD' with the corresponding retrieved past case attribute of 'ad_x'.

```
For P = 1 to PC_total {total is the no. of past cases}

    For J = 1 to AD_N {N = no. of AD values in current HP}

        For K = 1 to ad_m {m = no. of ad values in a past HP}

            compare each AD_J with all ad_K in PC_P using the
            similarity matrix given in table 4 such that

                DS[AD_J, ad_K^P] = similarity_matrix(AD_J, ad_K^P )
```

Step 2 : Find the best matching attribute-value in the past HP.

For each current HP attribute-value, we find the best matching attribute-value(s) in the past cases based on the value of $DS(AD_x, ad_y)$. This is achieved by determining the *Distance* (D) as shown in the pseudo code below:

```
For P = 1 to PC_total

    For J = 1 to AD_N

        For K = 1 to ad_m
```

$$D_{AD_J}^{ad_K^P} = min(DS[AD_J, ad_K^P])$$

where $D_{AD_J}^{ad_K^P}$ implies that AD_J best matches with the attribute-value ad_K in the past case P, and the variable D holds the distance measure between AD_J and ad_K which would be the minimum for all ad values in the past case P. Note that we individually calculate $D_{AD_J}^{ad_K^P}$ for all the past cases. Using the current HP and the set of past cases given in Table 2, we present a trace of the calculation of DS in Table 4.

Step 3 : Calculate the *Total Distance* for each current HP attribute.

For each current HP attribute, we calculate its distance with the corresponding attribute in a specific past case. Since each attribute can have multiple values, the TD is derived via averaging the individual matching D's associated with the multiple attribute-values. Note that a D_{AD} value of 100 refers to a non-match and hence it will not included in the calculation of the TD. We calculate a separate TD for each current HP attribute for all past cases as follows:

```
For P = 1 to PC_total
```

$$TD_{AD}^P = \sum_{K=1}^{N} D_{AD_K}^{ad^P} / N$$

where TD_{AD}^P refers to the total distance of the current HP attribute of AD with the same attribute in the past case P, and N is the number of non-zero D_{AD}. Note that the same procedure is applied to calculate the TD for the other four attributes in the current HP, given as TD_{SI}, TD_S, TD_D and TD_A. In Table 5, we illustrate the calculation of TD for the current HP attribute of AD as per the procedure mentioned above.

Step 4 : Calculate the *Total Weighted Distance* for each past case.

We use the individual TD values for all the current HP attributes with respect to a specific past case to calculate the TWD between the entire current HP and the HP component of a specific past case. The case-level distance is weighted—i.e. the user can modulate the influence of each attribute in the determining the similarity between the current and past HPs.

Step 5: Retrieve similar past cases to form global user model.

Finally, we retrieve all past cases that have a TWD less than a pre-defined threshold.

Table 4. Calculation of DS and TD for the current HP and the set of past cases. The legend $(AD_1 \rightarrow ad_1)$ implies that the attribute value AD_1 matches with value ad_1.

P	J	K	$DS[AD_j, ad^p_k]$	TD_{AD}
1	1	1	1 ($AD_1 \rightarrow ad_1$)	
		2	75	
		3	100	
	2	1	75	1.00
		2	1 ($AD_2 \rightarrow ad_2$)	
		3	100	
	3	1	100	
		2	100	
		3	1 ($AD_3 \rightarrow ad_3$)	
2	1	1	75	
		2	100	
		3	1 ($AD_1 \rightarrow ad_3$)	
	2	1	75 ($AD_2 \rightarrow ad_1$)	33.67
		2	100	
		3	100	
	3	1	100	
		2	25 ($AD_3 \rightarrow ad_2$)	
		3	100	

P	J	K	$DS[AD_j, ad^p_k]$	TD_{AD}
3	1	1	25 ($AD_1 \rightarrow ad_1$)	
		2	75	
		3	100	
	2	1	75	9.00
		2	1 ($AD_2 \rightarrow ad_2$)	
		3	100	
	3	1	100	
		2	100	
		3	1 ($AD_3 \rightarrow ad_3$)	
4	1	1	100	
		2	100	
	2	1	100	100.00
		2	100	
	3	2	100	

Table 5. Calculation of the TWD of the current HP with the HP component of the past cases. The TDs for attribute other than AD are set to 50 for illustration purposes only.

Past Case	TD_{AD}	TD_{SI}	TD_S	TD_D	TD_I	TWD	Case Retrieved (TWD < 55)
PC_1	1.00	50	50	50	50	40.20	√
PC_2	33.67	50	50	50	50	46.73	√
PC_3	9.00	50	50	50	50	41.80	√
PC_4	100.00	50	50	50	50	60.00	×

3.3 Adaptive Personalization via Compositional Adaptation

In the adaptive personalization stage, we personalize the solution component of the retrieved past cases to generate an individual-specific solution—i.e. a PHIP. As per our compositional adaptation approach, for each HP's attribute-value we select the most relevant past sub-solution (which manifests as a specific PD) from the entire solution of the retrieved past cases. The processing sequence is as follows: (i) Each attribute-value of the current HP is mapped to a set of matching attribute-values in the retrieved past cases; (ii) the PD associated with the matching past case's attribute value is selected; and (iii) the set of selected PDs are systematically amalgamated to yield the most representative PHIP. We explain below our compositional adaptation technique, building upon the case retrieval mechanism described earlier.

Step 1: Calculate the *Relative Distance* of each matched current HP value.
We determine the *Relative Distance* (RD) of each current HP attribute-value with respect the attribute-level distance (calculated earlier as D) and case-level distance (calculated earlier as TWD) for each retrieved past case as follows:

```
For P = 1 to PCretrieved
     For K = 1 to N {N = total no. of matched AD value}
```

$$RD_{AD_K}^{ad_x^P} = (D_{AD_K}^{ad_x^P} * W_{Field} + TWD^P * W_{TWD})/(W_{Field} + W_{TWD})$$

where $RD_{AD_K}^{ad_x^P}$ is the relative distance between the current HP attribute-value AD_K and the corresponding attribute-value ad_x in the retrieved past case P (shown in Table 7). Here, we introduce two user-specified weights $W_{Attribute}$ and W_{TWD} to impact the influence of attribute-level and case-level similarity, respectively.

Table 7. Calculation of RD of each AD attribute-value with the corresponding attribute-values in the three retrieved cases.

K	P	TWD^P	ad_x^P	$D_{AD_K}^{ad_x^P}$	$RD_{AD_K}^{ad_x^P}$	AD_K	Temp	$NRD^P{}_{ADK}$
1	1	40.20	1-1-002	1	28.44	1	0.092	0.38
	2		1-1-002	1	33.01			0.33
	3		1-1-020	25	36.76			0.29
2	1	46.73	1-3-035	1	28.44	2	0.086	0.40
	2		1-2-021	75	55.21			0.21
	3		1-3-035	1	29.56			0.39
3	1	41.80	2-1-004	1	28.44	3	0.092	0.38
	2		2-1-003	25	40.21			0.26
	3		2-1-004	1	29.56			0.36

Step 2 : Calculate the Normalized Relative Distance of current HP values.

To acquire a uniform range of RD's over the entire set of current-HP attribute values we calculate the *Normalized Relative Distance* (NRD) of a specific current HP attribute-value (say AD) over the entire set of retrieved past cases (i.e. $PC_{retrieved}$):

```
For K = 1 to ADN
```

$$Temp_{AD_K} = \sum_{P=1}^{PC_{retrieved}} 1/RD_{AD_K}^{ad_x^P}$$

Next, the NRD for the attribute-value AD for a retrieved past case P is calculated:

$$NRD_{AD_K}^{ad_x^P} = 1/(Temp_{AD_K} * RD_{AD_K}^{ad_x^P})$$

where $NRD_{AD_K}^{ad_x^P}$ is the normalized relative distance between the current HP attribute-value AD_K and the attribute-value ad_x in the past case P, shown in Table 7.

Step 3 : Determine the appropriateness of available solution components.

Since each current HP attribute-value can match with one or more past case attribute-value, there exist the possibility that a current HP attribute-value can be associated with multiple PDs. We select the most appropriate PDs (from the set of collected PDs) for each current HP attribute-value. This is achieved by determining the

Appropriateness Factor (AF) of all the available PDs via the aggregation of their NRD over the entire set of retrieved cases in the following manner:

For I = 1 to AD_N

$$AF_{AD_I}^{ad_x^P} = \sum_{P=1}^{PC_{retrieved}} NRD_{AD_I}^{ad_x^P}$$

where $AF_{AD_I}^{ad_x^P}$ is the appropriateness factor for the PD associated with the attribute-value ad_x in the past case P with respect to the current HP attribute-value of AD_I. Next, we compare the AF for each PD against a pre-defined threshold; if the AF of a PD exceeds the threshold then it is included in the final solution.

The Output: A Personalized Document Comprising Multiple Sub-Documents.
Table 8 shows the final calculations of AF for the 9 candidate PDs (note that there are only 6 distinct PDs). For attribute AD_1, we have two distinct candidate PDs: PD 1-1-002 from two past cases—i.e. PC_1 and PC_2; and PD 1-1-020 from PC_3. Since, PD 1-1-002 is recommended by two past cases it has a stronger bias for being included in the final solution, as is reflected by its AF value. In this way, our compositional adaptation strategy favors those PDs that are recommended by multiple past solutions.

Table 8. Selection of the most appropriate PDs based on their AF values. The selection criteria is $AF_{PD} > 0.35$. The selected PDs represent the final solution component (i.e. PHIP).

AD_x	$ad^P \rightarrow PD^P$	NRD	AF_{PD}	Selected PDs as the FINAL SOLUTION
AD_1 (1-1-002)	$ad^1 = 1\text{-}1\text{-}002$	0.38	0.71	√ (1-1-002)
	$ad^2 = 1\text{-}1\text{-}002$	0.33		
	$ad^3 = 1\text{-}1\text{-}020$	0.29	0.28	×
AD_2 (1-3-035)	$ad^1 = 1\text{-}3\text{-}035$	0.40	0.79	√ (1-3-035)
	$ad^3 = 1\text{-}3\text{-}035$	0.39		
	$ad^2 = 1\text{-}2\text{-}021$	0.21	0.21	×
AD_3 (2-1-004)	$ad^1 = 2\text{-}1\text{-}004$	0.38	0.74	√ (2-1-004)
	$ad^3 = 2\text{-}1\text{-}004$	0.36		
	$ad^2 = 2\text{-}1\text{-}003$	0.26	0.26	×

The composition of the final solution (shown in the last column of Table 8) clearly illustrates an adaptive personalization affect whereby the final PHIP comprises three PDs, one each for AD_1, AD_2 and AD_3. The solution for AD_1 is collected from past cases 1 and 2, whereas the solution for AD_2 is collected from past cases 1 and 3. This is in accordance with our compositional adaptation approach that posits the collection of the most appropriate sub-solutions from all the retrieved past cases as opposed to the selection of the entire solution of the most similar past case.

5 Concluding Remarks

In this paper, we have presented an interesting compositional adaptation technique that is applied to problem of adaptive hypermedia design. We conclude that our compositional adaptation approach is well-suited for personalized hypermedia document generation, if the hypermedia document is a composite of multiple fine-grained *information 'snippets'*. In this scenario, we design a personalized hypermedia document by selecting the most appropriate sub-solutions (or information snippets) from all the retrieved past cases. From our experiments, we have determined that (a) the higher the frequency of occurrence of a particular sub-solution across the various retrieved past cases, the higher its appropriateness towards the current solution; and (b) the appropriateness of a particular sub-solution is more accurately determined by taking into account both its individual appropriateness factor and the similarity measure of the entire past case with the current problem description.

Finally, we believe that the said compositional adaptation mediated personalization approach can be used for a variety of applications such as education material personalization based on academic performance, stock market reporting and advice based on user-specific portfolio, tourist information based on user-specific criterion and so on; the only constraint being the availability of a large volume of past cases.

References

1. Brusilovsky, P., Kobsa, A. and Vassileva, J. (Eds): Adaptive Hypertext and Hypertext, Kluwer Academic Publishers, Dordrecht, 1998.
2. Fink, J., Koenemann, J., Noller, S., and Schwab, I.: Putting Personalization into Practice, Communications of the ACM 45:5, 2002.
3. Aamodt A., Plaza E.: Relating Case-Based Reasoning: Foundational Issues, Methodological Variations and System Approaches, AI Communications, 7:1, 1994
4. Bradley, K., Rafter, R. and Smyth, B.: Case-Based User Profiling for Content Personalization. In Brusilovsky, P. et al (Eds): Adaptive Hypertext and Adaptive Web-based Systems. Lecture Notes in Computer Science, 1892, Springer Verlag, Berlin, 2000.
5. Wilke W, Bergmann R.: Techniques and Knowledge Used for Adaptation During Case Based Problem Solving. Lecture Notes in Artificial Intelligence, Vol. 1416. Springer-Verlag, Berlin Heidelberg New York, 1998, pp. 497-505
6. Bental, D., Cawsey, A., Pearson, J., and Jones, R.: Adapting Web-based Information to the Needs of Patients with Cancer. In Proc. Intl. Conf. On Adaptive Hypertext and Adaptive Web-based Systems, Trento, Italy, 2000
7. Abidi S.S.R., Han, C.Y. and Abidi, S.R.: Patient Empowerment via 'Pushed' Delivery of Personalised Healthcare Educational Content Over the Internet. In 10th World Congress on Medical Informatics (MedInfo'2001), London, 2001.
8. Abidi S.S.R., Goh A.: A Personalized Healthcare Information Delivery System: Pushing Customized Healthcare Information Over the WWW. In: Hasman A., Blobel B., Dudeck J., Engelbrecht R., Gell G., Prokosch H. (eds.): Medical Infobahn for Europe. IOS Press, Amsterdam, 2000, pp. 663 – 667
9. Arshadi N., Badie K.: A Compositional Approach to Solution Adaptation in Case-based Reasoning and its Application to Tutoring Library, Proceedings of 8th German Workshop on Case-Based Reasoning. Lammerbuckel, 2000.

Improving Classification Accuracy of Large Test Sets Using the Ordered Classification Algorithm

Thamar Solorio and Olac Fuentes

Instituto Nacional de Astrofísica, Óptica y Electrónica,
Luis Enrique Erro # 1,
72840 Puebla, México
thamy@cseg.inaoep.mx, fuentes@inaoep.mx

Abstract. We present a new algorithm called Ordered Classification, that is useful for classification problems where only few labeled examples are available but a large test set needs to be classified. In many real-world classification problems, it is expensive and some times unfeasible to acquire a large training set, thus, traditional supervised learning algorithms often perform poorly. In our algorithm, classification is performed by a discriminant approach similar to that of Query By Committee within the active learning setting. The method was applied to the real-world astronomical task of automated prediction of stellar atmospheric parameters, as well as to some benchmark learning problems showing a considerable improvement in classification accuracy over conventional algorithms.

1 Introduction

Standard supervised learning algorithms such as decision trees (e.g. [1,2]), instance based learning (e.g. [3]), Bayesian learning and neural networks require a large training set in order to obtain a good approximation of the concept to be learned. This training set consists of instances or examples that have been manually, or semi-manually, analyzed and classified by human experts. The cost and time of having human experts performing this task is what makes unfeasible the job of building automated classifiers with traditional approaches in some domains. In many real-world classification problems we do not have a large enough collection of labeled samples to build an accurate classifier. The purpose of our work is to develop new methods for reducing the number of examples needed for training by taking advantage of large test sets.

Given that the problem setting described above is very common, an increasing interest from the machine learning community has arisen with the aim of designing new methods that take advantage of unlabeled data. By allowing the learners to effectively use the large amounts of unlabeled data available, the size of the manual labeled training sets can be reduced. Hence, the cost and time needed for building good classifiers will be reduced, too. Among the most popular methods proposed for incorporating unlabeled data are the ones based on a generative model, such as Naive Bayes algorithm in combination with the Expectation Maximization (EM) algorithm [4,5,6,7,8]. While this approach has proven

F.J. Garijo, J.C. Riquelme, and M. Toro (Eds.): IBERAMIA 2002, LNAI 2527, pp. 70–79, 2002.

to increase classifier accuracy in some problem domains, it is not always applicable since violations to the assumptions made by the Naive Bayes classifier will deteriorate the final classifier performance [9,10]. A different approach is that of co-training [11,10], where the attributes describing the instances can naturally be divided into two disjoint sets, each being sufficient for perfect classification. One drawback of this co-training method is that not all classification problems have instances with two redundant views. This difficulty may be overcome with the co-training method proposed by Goldman and Zhou [12], where two different learning algorithms are used for bootstrapping from unlabeled data. Other proposals for the use of unlabeled data include the use of neural networks [13], graph mincuts [14], Semi-Supervised Support Vector Machines [15] and Kernel Expansions [16], among others.

In this paper we address the problem of building accurate classifiers when the labeled data are insufficient but a large test set is available. We propose a method called Ordered Classification (OC), where all the unlabeled data available are considered as part of the test set. Classification with the OC is performed by a discriminant approach similar to that of Query By Committee within the active learning setting [17,18,19]. In the OC setting, the test set is presented to an ensemble of classifiers built using the labeled examples. The ensemble assigns labels to the entire test set and measures the degree of confidence in its predictions for each example in the test set. According to a selection criterion examples with a high confidence level are chosen from the test set and used for building a new ensemble of classifiers. This process is repeated until all the examples from the test set are classified.

We present some experimental results of applying the OC to some benchmark problems taken from the UCI Machine Learning Repository [20]. Also, as we are interested in the performance of this algorithm in real-world problems, we evaluate it on a data set obtained from a star catalog due to Jones [21] where the learning problem consists in predicting the atmospheric parameters of stars from spectral indices. Both types of experiments show that using the OC results in a considerable decrease of the prediction error.

2   The Ordered Classification Algorithm

The goal of the OC algorithm is to select those examples whose class can be predicted by the ensemble with a high confidence level in order to use them to improve its learning process by gradually augmenting an originally small training set. How can we measure this confidence level? Inspired by the selection criterion used in previous works within the active learning setting (e.g. [17,18, 19]) we measure the degree of agreement among the members of the ensemble. For real-valued target functions, the confidence level is given by the inverse of the standard deviation on the predictions of the ensemble. Examples with low standard deviation in their predicted target function are considered more likely to be correctly classified by the ensemble, thus these examples are selected and added to the training set. For discrete target functions we measure the confidence level by computing the entropy on the classifications made by the ensemble on the test set. Again, examples with low entropy values are selected for rebuilding the ensemble. The test set is considered as the unlabeled data since they do not have a label indicating their class, so from now on we will use the words unlabeled data and test set to refer to the same set.

Our algorithm proceeds as follows: First, we build several classifiers (the ensemble) using the base learning algorithm and the training set available. Then, each classifier predicts the classes for the unlabeled data and we use these predictions to estimate the reliability of the predictions for each example. We now proceed to select the n previously unlabeled examples with the highest confidence level and add them to the training set. Also, the ensemble re-classifies all the examples added until then, if the confidence level is higher than the previous value then the labels of the examples are changed. This process is repeated until there are no unlabeled examples left. See Table 1 for an outline of our algorithm.

The OC can be used in combination with any supervised learning algorithm. In the experimental results presented here, when the learning task involves real-valued target functions we used Locally Weighted Linear Regression (LWLR) [3]; for discrete-valued target functions we used C4.5 [2]. The next subsections briefly describe these learning algorithms.

2.1   Ensembles

An ensemble of classifiers is a set of classifiers whose individual decisions are combined in some way, normally by voting. In order for an ensemble to work properly, individual members of the ensemble need to have uncorrelated errors and an accuracy higher than random guessing. There are several methods for building ensembles. One of them, which is called *bagging* [22], consists of manipulating the training set. In this technique, each member of the ensemble has a training set consisting of m examples selected randomly with replacement from the original training set of m examples (Dietterich [23]). Another technique similar to bagging manipulates the attribute set. Here, each member of the ensemble uses a different subset randomly chosen from the attribute set. More information concerning ensemble methods, such as boosting and error-correcting output coding, can be found in [23]. The technique used for building an ensemble is chosen according to the learning algorithm used, which in turn is determined by the learning task. In the work presented here, we use bagging when C4.5 [2] is the base learning algorithm; and the one that randomly selects attributes when using Locally Weighted Regression [3].

2.2   The Base Learning Algorithm C4.5

C4.5 is an extension to the decision-tree learning algorithm ID3 [1]. Only a brief description of the method is given here, more information can be found in [2]. The algorithm consists of the following steps:

1. Build the decision tree form the training set (conventional ID3).
2. Convert the resulting tree into an equivalent set of rules. The number of rules is equivalent to the number of possible paths from the root to a leaf node.

Table 1. The ordered classification algorithm

I_s is a matrix whose rows are vectors of attribute values
L_s is the class label
S is the training set, given by the tuple $[I_s, L_s]$
U is the unlabeled test set
A is initially empty and will contain the unlabeled examples added to the training set

1. While $U \neq \oslash$ do:
   - Construct E, the ensemble containing k classifiers
   - Classify U and estimate reliability of predictions
   - V are the n elements of U for which the classification assigned by the ensemble is most reliable
   - $S = S \cup V$
   - $U = U - V$
   - $A = A \cup V$
   - Classify A using E and change the labels of the examples with higher confidence level
2. End

---

3. Prune each rule by removing any preconditions that result in improving its accuracy, according to a validation set.
4. Sort the pruned rules in descending order according to their accuracy, and consider them in this sequence when classifying subsequent instances.

Since the learning tasks used to evaluate this work involve nominal and numeric values, we implemented the version of C4.5 that incorporates continuous values.

2.3   Locally Weighted Linear Regression

LWLR belongs to the family of instance-based learning algorithms. These algorithms build query specific local models, which attempt to fit the training examples only in a region around the query point. They simply store some or all of the training examples and postpone any generalization until a new instance must be classified. In this work we used a linear model around the query point to approximate the target function.

Given a query point $\mathbf{x}_q$, to predict its output parameters $\mathbf{y}_q$, we assign to each example in the training set a weight given by the inverse of the distance from the training point to the query point: $w_i = \frac{1}{|\mathbf{x}_q - \mathbf{x}_i|}$

Let W, the weight matrix, be a diagonal matrix with entries $w_1, \ldots, w_n$. Let X be a matrix whose rows are the vectors $\mathbf{x}_1, \ldots, \mathbf{x}_n$, the input parameters of the examples in the training set, with the addition of a "1" in the last column. Let Y be a matrix whose rows are the vectors $\mathbf{y}_1, \ldots, \mathbf{y}_n$, the output parameters of the examples in the training set. Then the weighted training data are given by $Z = WX$ and the weighted target function is $V = WY$. Then we use the estimator for the target function $\mathbf{y}_q = \mathbf{x}_q^T (Z^T Z)^{-1} Z^T V$.

Table 2. Description of Data sets

name	cases	features	% Cont.	%Discr.
chess	3196	37	0	100
lymphography	148	19	0	100
credit	653	16	60	40
soybean	266	36	0	100
spectral indices	651	24	100	0

3   Experimental Results

In order to assess the effectiveness of the OC algorithm we experimented on some learning tasks taken from the UCI Machine Learning Repository [20] as well as on an astronomical data set of spectral indices due to Jones [21]. In Table 2 we present a description of each data set used.

In all the experiments reported here we used the evaluation technique 10-fold cross-validation, which consists of randomly dividing the data into 10 equally-sized subgroups and performing ten different experiments. We separated one group along with their original labels as the validation set; another group was considered as the starting training set; the remainder of the data were considered the test set. Each experiment consists of ten runs of the procedure described above, and the overall average are the results reported here.

3.1   Benchmark Experiments

We described in this subsection the experiments with the data sets of the UCI Machine Learning Repository. To analyze the effectiveness of the Ordered Classification algorithm we performed three different experiments and compared the resulting accuracy. In the first type of experiment we built an ensemble of classifiers, with seven members, using C4.5 and the training set available. The test set was then classified by this ensemble and the resulting classification error rates are presented in Table 3 under the column named *standard*. In the next type of experiment we built again an ensemble with seven members, C4.5 and the training set available. This time a random selection of n examples from the test set was made and added to the training set until the complete test set was classified. We set $n = \frac{|T|}{10}$, where T is the training set. The error rates for this experiment are also in Table 3 under the feature *random selection*. The column named *OC* presents the results of experimenting using our algorithm. Parameters k and n where set to the same values as the previous experiment.

The main difference between random selection and the OC algorithm is that the former does not measures the confidence level on the predictions of the ensemble, it simply selects randomly which unlabeled examples are going to be added in the training process. We performed the random selection experiment with the purpose of finding if the selection criterion used in the OC algorithm gives better results than simply using labeled examples selected randomly.

Table 3. Comparison of the error rates

	standard	random selection	OC
lymphography	0.2912	0.2668	0.2567
chess	0.0551	0.0523	0.0419
soybean	0.2714	0.2255	0.1947
credita	0.0952	0.0915	0.0848

Unsurprisingly, the error rates of random selection are lower than the traditional C4.5, but in all the learning tasks, the lowest error rates were obtained with our algorithm. We can notice that by incrementally augmenting a small training set we can boost accuracy of standard algorithms. The advantage of using our algorithm over random selection is that we are maximizing the information gained by carefully selecting unlabeled data, and that is the reason why we can improve further classifier accuracy. For these benchmark problems error reductions of up to 29% were attained. Results from Table 3 suggest that the OC algorithm is the best alternative.

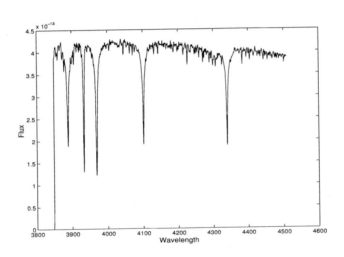

Fig. 1. Stellar spectrum

3.2   Prediction of Stellar Atmospheric Parameters

We introduce here the problem of automated prediction of stellar atmospheric parameters. As mentioned earlier, we are interested in the applicability of our algorithm to real-world problems. Besides, we know that important contributions might emerge from the collaboration of computer science researchers with researchers from different scientific disciplines.

Table 4. Comparison of mean absolute errors in the prediction of stellar atmospheric parameters

	traditional	random selection	OC
Teff[K]	147.33	133.79	126.88
Log g[dex]	0.3221	0.3030	0.2833
Fe/H	0.223	0.177	0.172

In order to predict some physical properties of a star, astronomers analyze its spectrum, which is a plot of energy flux against wavelength. The spectra of stars consists of a continuum, with discontinuities superimposed, called spectral lines. These spectral lines are mostly dark absorbtion lines, although some objects can present bright emission lines. By studying the strength of various absorption lines, temperature, composition and surface gravity can be deduced. Figure 1 shows the spectrum of a star from the data set we are using.

Instead of using the spectra as input data, a very large degree of compression can be attained if we use a measurement of the strength of several selected absorption lines that are known to be important for predicting the stellar atmospheric parameters. In this work we use a library of such measurements, which are called *spectral indices* in the astronomical literature, due to Jones [21]. This dataset consists of 24 spectral indices for 651 stars, together with their estimated effective temperatures, surface gravities and metallicities. It was observed at Kitt Peak National Observatory and has been made available by the author at an anonymous ftp site at the National Optical Astronomy Observatories(NOAO).

For the learning task of predicting stellar atmospheric parameters we used LWLR as the base learning algorithm. Results from the experiments are presented in Table 4, which presents the mean absolute errors for the three types of experiments performed. Each experiment was carried out as explained in the previous subsection. We can observe that the lowest error rates were attained when using our algorithm. An error decrease of up to 14% was reached taking advantage of the large test set available. However, both learners that used unlabeled data outperformed the traditional Locally Weighted Linear Regression Algorithm.

A different experiment was performed to analyze the effect of using the OC algorithm with training sets of different sizes. Figure 2 shows a graphical comparison of predicting the stellar atmospheric parameter metallicity using an ensemble of LWLR and the OC algorithm. From these results we can conclude that even when standard LWLR performs satisfactory well with a large enough training set, OC can take advantage of the test set and outperform accuracy of LWLR.

4   Conclusions

The Ordered Classification algorithm presented here was successfully applied to the problem of automated prediction of stellar atmospheric parameters, as well

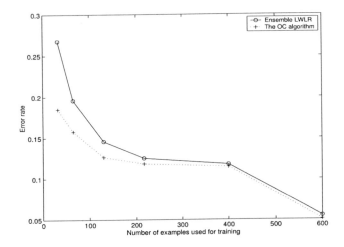

Fig. 2. Error Comparison between an ensemble of C4.5 and the OC algorithm as the number of training examples increases

as evaluated with some benchmark problems proving in both cases to be an excellent alternative when the labeled data are scarce and expensive to obtain.

Results presented here prove that poor performance of classifiers due to a small training sets can be improved upon when a large test set is available or can be gathered easily. One important feature of our method is the criterion by which we select the unlabeled examples from the test set -the confidence level estimation. This selection criterion allows the ensemble to add new instances that will help obtain a better approximation of the target function; but at the same time, this discriminative criterion decreases the likelihood of hurting the final classifier performance, a common situation when using unlabeled data. From experimental results we can conclude that unlabeled data selected randomly improve the accuracy of standard algorithms, moreover, a significant further improvement can be attained when we use the selection criterion proposed in this work.

Another advantage of the algorithm presented here is that it is easy to implement and given that it can be applied in combination with almost any supervised learning algorithm, the possible application fields are unlimited.

One disadvantage of this algorithm is the computational cost involved. As expected, the running time of our algorithm increases with the size of the test set. It evaluates the reliability of every single examples in the test set, thus the computational cost is higher than traditional machine learning approaches. However, if we consider the time and cost needed for gathering a large enough training set, for traditional algorithms, our approach is still more practical and feasible.

Some directions of future work include:

- Extending this methodology to other astronomical applications.
- Performing experiments with a different measure of the confidence level.

– Experimenting with a heterogeneous ensemble of classifiers.
– Performing experiments with other base algorithms such as neural networks.

References

1. J.R. Quinlan. Induction of decision trees. *Machine Learning*, 1:81–106, 1986.
2. J.R. Quinlan. C4.5: Programs for machine learning. 1993. San Mateo, CA: Morgan Kaufmann.
3. Christopher G. Atkeson, Andrew W. Moore, and Stefan Schaal. Locally weighted learning. *Artificial Intelligence Review*, 11:11–73, 1997.
4. A. McCallum and K. Nigam. Employing EM in pool-based active learning for text classification. In *Proceedings of the 15th International Conference on Machine Learning*, 1998.
5. K. Nigam, A. Mc Callum, S. Thrun, and T. Mitchell. Learning to classify text from labeled and unlabeled documents. *Machine Learning*, pages 1–22, 1999.
6. K. Nigam. *Using Unlabeled Data to Improve Text Classification*. PhD thesis, Carnegie Mellon University, 2001.
7. S. Baluja. Probabilistic modeling for face orientation discrimination: Learning from labeled and unlabeled data. *Neural Information Processing Sys.*, pages 854–860, 1998.
8. B. Shahshahani and D. Landgrebe. The effect of unlabeled samples in reducing the small sample size Problem and mitigating the Hughes phenomenon. *IEEE Transactions on Geoscience und Remote Sensing*, 32(5):1087–1095, 1994.
9. F. Cozman and I. Cohen. Unlabeled data can degrade classification performance of generative classifiers. Technical Report HPL-2001-234, Hewlett-Packard Laboratories, 1501 Page Mill Road, September 2001.
10. K. Nigam and R. Ghani. Analyzing the effectiveness and applicabitily of co-training. *Ninth International Conference on Information und Knowledgement Management*, pages 86–93, 2000.
11. A. Blum and T. Mitchell. Combining labeled and unlabeled data with co-training. In *Proceedings of the 1998 Conference on Computational Learning Theory*, July 1998.
12. S. Goldman and Y . Zhou. Enhancing supervised learning with unlabeled data. In *Proceedings O n the Seventeenth International Conference on Machine Learning: ICML-2000*, 2000.
13. M.T. Fardanesh and K.E. Okan. Classification accuracy improvement of neural network by using unlabeled data. *IEEE Transactions on Geoscience und Remote Sensing*, 36(3):1020–1025, 1998.
14. A. Blum and Shuchi Chawla. Learning from labeled and unlabeled data using graph mincuts. *ICML'01*, pages 19–26, 2001.
15. G. Fung and O.L. Mangasarian. Semi-supervised support vector machines for unlabeled data classification. *Optimixation Methods and Software*, (15):29–44, 2001.
16. M. Szummer and T. Jaakkola. Kernel expansions with unlabeled examples. *NIPS 13*, 2000.
17. Y. Freund, H. Seung, E. Shamir, and N. Tishby. Selective sampling using the query by comitee algorithm. *Machine Learning*, 28(2/3):133–168, 1997.
18. S. Argamon-Engelson and I. Dagan. Committee-based sample selection for probabilistic classifiers. *Journal of Artificial Inteligence Research*, (11):335–360, Nov. 1999.

19. R. Liere and Prasad Tadepalli. Active learning with committees for text categorization. In *Proceedings of the Fourteenth National Conference On Artificial Intelligence*, pages 591–596, 1997.
20. C. Merz and P. Murphy. UCI Machine Learning Repository. http://www.ics.uci.edu./~mlearn/MLRepository.html, 1996.
21. L.A. Jones. *Star Populations in Galaxies*. PhD thesis, University of North Carolina, Chapel Hill, North Carolina, 1996.
22. L. Breiman. Bagging predictors. *Machine Learning*, 24(2):123–140, 1996.
23. T. Dietterich. Ensemble methods in machine learning. In *First International Workshop on Multiple Classifier Systems, Lecture Notes in Computer Science*, pages 1–15, New York: Springer Verlag, 2000. In J. Kittler and F. Roli (Ed.).

A Comparative Study of Some Issues Concerning Algorithm Recommendation Using Ranking Methods

Carlos Soares and Pavel Brazdil

LIACC/Faculty of Economics, University of Porto
R. Campo Alegre 823, 4150-180 Porto, Portugal
{csoares,pbrazdil}@liacc.up.pt

Abstract. Cross-validation (CV) is the most accurate method available for algorithm recommendation but it is rather slow. We show that information about the past performance of algorithms can be used for the same purpose with small loss in accuracy and significant savings in experimentation time. We use a meta-learning framework that combines a simple IBL algorithm with a ranking method. We show that results improve significantly by using a set of selected measures that represent data characteristics that permit to predict algorithm performance. Our results also indicate that the choice of ranking method as a smaller effect on the quality of recommendations. Finally, we present situations that illustrate the advantage of providing recommendation as a ranking of the candidate algorithms, rather than as the single algorithm which is expected to perform best.

1 Introduction

The problem selecting an appropriate algorithm for a given data set is commonly recognized as a difficult one [1,2]. One approach to this problem is meta-learning, which aims to capture certain relationships between the measured data set characteristics and the performance of the algorithms. We adopt a framework which uses the IBL algorithm as a meta-learner. The performance and the usefulness of meta-learning for algorithm recommendation depends on several issues. Here we investigate the following hypotheses:

- **data characterization**: can we improve performance by selecting and transforming features that we expect to be relevant?
- **ranking method**: given that there are several alternatives, can we single out one which is better than the others?
- **meta-learning**: are there advantages in using meta-learning, when compared to other alternatives?
- **type of recommendation**: is there advantage in providing recommendation in the form of ranking, rather than recommending a single algorithm?

F.J. Garijo, J.C. Riquelme, and M. Toro (Eds.): IBERAMIA 2002, LNAI 2527, pp. 80–89, 2002.
© Springer-Verlag Berlin Heidelberg 2002

We start by describing the data characteristics used (Section 2). In Section 3, we motivate the choice of recommending a ranking of the algorithms, rather than a single algorithm. We also describe the IBL ranking framework used and the ranking methods compared. Ranking evaluation is described in Section 4. Next, we describe the experimental setting and present results. In Section 6, we present some conclusions.

2   Data Characterization

The most important issue in meta-learning is probably data characterization. We need to extract measures from the data that characterize relative performance of the candidate algorithms, and can be computed significantly faster than running those algorithms. It is known that the performance of different algorithms is affected by different data characteristics. For instance, k-Nearest Neighbor will suffer if there are many irrelevant attributes [3].

Most work on meta-learning uses general, statistical and information theoretic (GSI) measures or *meta-attributes* [2,4]. Examples of these three types of measures are number of attributes, mean skewness and class entropy, respectively [5]. Recently, other approaches to data characterization have been proposed (e.g. *landmarkers* [6]) which will not considered here.

As will be described in the next section, we use the k-Nearest Neighbor algorithm for meta-learning, which, as mentioned above, is very sensitive to irrelevant and noisy attributes. Therefore, we have defined a small set of measures to be used as meta-features, using a knowledge engineering approach. Based on our expertise on the learning algorithms used and on the properties of data that affect their performance, we select and combine existing GSI measures to define *a priori* a small set of meta-features that are expected to provide information about those properties. The measures and the properties which they are expected to represent are:

- The *number of examples* discriminates algorithms according to how scalable they are with respect to this measure.
- The *proportion of symbolic algorithms* is indicative of the preference of the algorithm for symbolic or numeric attributes.
- The *proportion of missing values* discriminates algorithms according to how robust they are with respect to incomplete data.
- The *proportion of numeric attributes with outliers* discriminates algorithms according to how robust they are to outlying values, which are possibly due to noise[1]. An attribute is considered to have outliers if the ratio of the variances of mean value and the α-trimmed mean is smaller than 0.7. We have used $\alpha = 0.05$.
- The *entropy of classes* combines information about the number of classes and their frequency, measuring one aspect of problem difficulty.

---

[1] Note that we have no corresponding meta-attribute for symbolic attributes because none was available.

- The *average mutual information of class and attributes* indicates the amount of useful information contained in the symbolic attributes.
- The *canonical correlation of the most discriminating single linear combination of numeric attributes and the class distribution* indicates the amount of useful information contained in groups of numeric attributes.

More details about the basic features used here can be found in [5]. We note all three proportional features shown above represent new combinations of previously defined data characteristics.

3   Meta-learning Ranking Methods

Here we have used the meta-learning framework proposed in [7]. It consists of coupling an IBL (k-NN) algorithm with a ranking method. The adaptation of k-NN for ranking is simple. Like in the classification version, the distance function is used to select a subset of cases (i.e. data sets) which are most similar to the one at hand. The rankings of alternatives (i.e. algorithms) in those cases are aggregated to generate a ranking which is expected to be a good approximation of the ranking in the case at hand (i.e. is expected to reflect the performance of the algorithms on the data set at hand).

Several methods can be used to aggregate the rankings of the selected neighbors. A ranking method specific for multicriteria ranking of learning algorithms is proposed in [7]. Here we will focus on three ranking methods that take only accuracy into account [8]. These methods represent three common approaches to the comparison of algorithms in Machine Learning, as described next.

Average Ranks Ranking Method. This is a simple ranking method, inspired by Friedman's M statistic [9]. For each data set we order the algorithms according to the measured error rates[2] and assign ranks accordingly. The best algorithm will be assigned rank 1, the runner-up, 2, and so on. Let r_j^i be the rank of algorithm j on data set i. We calculate the *average rank* for each algorithm $\bar{r}_j = \left(\sum_i r_j^i \right) / n$, where n is the number of data sets. The final ranking is obtained by ordering the average ranks and assigning ranks to the algorithms accordingly.

Success Rate Ratios Ranking Method. As the name suggests this method employs ratios of success rates (or accuracies) between pairs of algorithms. For each algorithm j, we calculate $SRR_j = \sum_k \sqrt[n]{\prod_i SR_j^i / SR_k^i} / m$ where SR_j^i is the accuracy of algorithm j on data set i, n is the number of data sets and m is the number of algorithms. The ranking is derived directly from this measure, which is an estimate of the average advantage/disadvantage of algorithm j over the other algorithms. A parallel can be established between the ratios underlying this method and performance scatterplots that have been used in some empirical studies to compare pairs of algorithms [10]

---

[2] The measured error rate refers to the average of the error rates on all the folds of the cross-validation procedure.

Significant Wins Ranking Method. This method builds a ranking on the basis of results of pairwise hypothesis tests concerning the performance of pairs of algorithms. We start by testing the significance of the differences in performance between each pair of algorithms. This is done for all data sets. In this study we have used paired t tests with a significance level of 5%. This is the highest of the most commonly used values for the significance level not only in AI, but in Statistics in general [9]. We have opted for this significance level because we wanted the test to be relatively sensitive to differences but, at the same time, as reliable as possible. We denote the fact that algorithm j is significantly better than algorithm k on data set i as $SR_j^i \gg SR_k^i$. Then, we construct a *win table* for each of the data sets as follows. The value of each cell, $W_{j,k}^i$, indicates whether algorithm j wins over algorithm k on data set i at a given significance level and is determined in the following way:

$$W_{j,k}^i = \begin{cases} 1 & \text{iff } SR_j^i \gg SR_k^i \\ -1 & \text{iff } SR_k^i \gg SR_j^i \\ 0 & \text{otherwise} \end{cases} \qquad (1)$$

Note that $W_{j,k}^i = -W_{k,j}^i$ by definition. Next, we calculate $pw_{j,k}$ for each pair of algorithms j and k, by dividing the number of data sets where algorithm j is significantly better than algorithm k by the number of data sets, n. This value estimates the probability that algorithm j is significantly better than algorithm k. The ranking is obtained by ordering the $pw_j = \left(\sum_k pw_{j,k} \right) / (m-1)$ obtained for each algorithm j, where m is the number of algorithms. The kind of tests underlying this method is often used in comparative studies of classification algorithms.

In Section 5 we present the results of an empirical study addressing the following hypotheses:

- Given the sensitivity of the Nearest-Neighbor algorithm to the quality of the attributes, the subset of meta-features selected is expected to provide better results than the complete set which is commonly used.
- The SRR ranking method is expected to perform better than the other two methods because it exploits quantitative information about the differences in performance of the algorithms.
- Our meta-learning approach is expected to provide useful recommendation to the users, in the sense that it enables them to save time without much loss in accuracy.

The results are obtained with the evaluation methods described in the next section.

4   Evaluation of Rankings and Ranking Methods

Ranking can be seen as an alternative ML task, similar to classification or regression, which must therefore have appropriate evaluation methods. Here we will use two of them. The first one is the methodology for evaluating and comparing ranking methods that has been proposed earlier for meta-learning [8]. The rankings recommended by the ranking methods are compared against the true observed rankings using Spearman's rank correlation coefficient [9]. An interesting property of this coefficient is that it is basically the sum of squared errors, which can be related to the commonly used error measure in regression. Furthermore, the sum is normalized to yield more meaningful values: the value of 1 represents perfect agreement and -1, perfect disagreement. A correlation of 0 means that the rankings are not related, which would be the expected score of the random ranking method. We note that the performance of two or more algorithms may be different but not with statistical significance. To address this issue, we exploit the fact that in such situations the tied algorithms often swap positions in different folds of the N-fold cross-validation procedure which is used to estimate their performance. Therefore, we use N orderings to represent the true ideal ordering, instead of just one. The correlation between the recommended ranking and each of those orderings is calculated and its score is the corresponding average. To compare different ranking methods we use a combination of Friedman's test and Dunn's Multiple Comparison Procedure [9] that is applied to the correlation coefficients.

The second evaluation method is based on an idea which is quite common in Information Retrieval. It assumes that the user will select the top N alternatives recommended. In the case of ranking algorithms, the performance of the top N algorithms of a ranking will be the accuracy of the best algorithm in that set.

5   Results

Before empirically investigating the hypotheses in the beginning of this paper, we describe the experimental setting.

Our meta-data consists of 53 data sets mostly from the UCI repository [11] but including a few others from the METAL project[3] (SwissLife's Sisyphus data and a few applications provided by DaimlerChrysler). Ten algorithms were executed on those data sets[4]: two decision tree classifiers, C5.0 and Ltree, which is a decision tree that can introduce oblique decision surfaces; the IB1 instance-based and the naive Bayes classifiers from the MLC++ library; a local implementation of the multivariate linear discriminant; two neural networks from the SPSS Clementine package (Multilayer Perceptron and Radial Basis Function Network); two rule-based systems, C5.0 rules and RIPPER; and an ensemble method, boosted C5.0. Results were obtained with 10-fold cross-validation using default parameters on all algorithms.

At the meta-level we empirically evaluated the k-NN approach to ranking using a leave-one-out method.

---

[3] Esprit Long-Term Research Project (#26357) *A Meta-Learning Assistant for Providing User Support in Data Mining and Machine Learning* (www.metal-kdd.org).
[4] References for these algorithms can be found in [6].

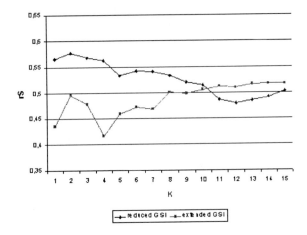

Fig. 1. Mean correlation obtained by SW ranking method for increasing number of neighbors using two sets of GSI data characteristics: reduced and extended.

5.1   Comparison of Data Characterizations

Figure 1 shows the mean average correlation for increasing number of neighbors obtained by SW ranking method using two different sets of meta-features: the reduced set (Section 2) and an extended set with 25 measures used in previous work [7]. We observe that the results are significantly better with the reduced set than with the extended set. We also observe that the quality of the rankings obtained with the reduced set decreases as the number of neighbors increases. This is not true when the extended set is used. These results indicate that the measures selected do represent properties that affect relative algorithm performance. The shape of the curves also indicates that the extended set probably contains many irrelevant features, which, as is well known, affects the performance of the k-NN algorithm used at the meta-level. Similar results were obtained with the other two ranking methods, AR and SRR.

5.2   Comparison of Ranking Methods

In this section we compare the three ranking methods described earlier for two settings of k-NN on the meta-level, k=1 and 5, using the reduced set of meta-features. The 1-NN is known to perform often well [12]. The 5 neighbors represent approximately 10% of the 45 training data sets, which has lead to good results in a preliminary study [7]. Finally we also evaluated a simple baseline setting consisting of applying the ranking methods to all the training data sets (i.e., 52-NN).

In the next section, we analyze the results of concerning the final goal of providing useful recommendation to the users. But first, we will compare the three

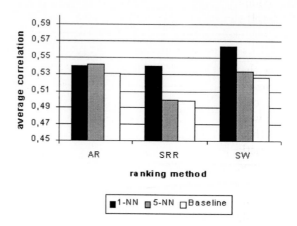

Fig. 2. Comparison of mean average correlation scores ($\bar{r}_S$) obtained with the 1-NN, 5-NN and the baseline (52-NN) combined with the three ranking methods, AR, SRR and SW.

ranking methods to each other. We observe in Figure 2 that for k=1, SW obtains the best result[5]. For k=5, AR is the best method and significantly better than the other two, according to Friedman's test (95% confidence level) and Dunn's Multiple Comparisons Procedure (75% confidence level). Comparing the results of the three baselines, we observe that AR is the best at finding a consensus from a set of very diverse rankings. This is consistent with previous results that showed good performance of AR [8]. The results of SRR are somewhat surprising because earlier results in the baseline setting indicated that it was a competitive method [8]. However, the results presented in that paper were based on less meta-data (only 16 data sets).

Comparing these results to the ones presented in the previous section, we observe that the choice of an adequate data characterization yields larger gains in correlation than the choice of ranking method.

5.3   How Useful Is the Recommendation Provided?

In this section, we start by comparing the gains obtained with the k-NN approach to ranking when compared to the baseline ranking methods. Next, we take a more user-oriented view of the results, by analyzing the trade-off between accuracy and time obtained by the algorithm recommendation method described when compared to cross-validation.

We observe in Figure 2 that meta-learning with k-NN always improves the results of the baseline (52-NN), for all ranking methods. Friedman's test (95%

---

[5] As expected, it not significantly different from the other two ranking methods for k=1, because no aggregation is performed with only one data set.

confidence level) complemented with Dunn's Multiple Comparison Procedure (75% confidence level) shows that most of the differences are statistically significant. The exceptions are the pairs (1-NN, baseline) and (1-NN, 5-NN) in the AR method and (5-NN, baseline) in the SRR method.

We also observe that there is a clear positive correlation between the recommended rankings generated and the ideal rankings. The critical value for Spearman's correlation coefficient (one-sided test, 95% confidence level) is 0.5636. Given that we are working with mean correlation values, we can not conclude anything based on this critical value. However, the fact that the values obtained are close to the statistically significant value is a clear indication that the rankings generated are good approximations to the true rankings.

The evaluation performed so far provides information about the ranking as a whole. But it is also important to assess the quality of the recommendation provided by the meta-learning method in terms of accuracy. Since recommendation is provided in the form of a ranking, we don't know how many algorithms the user will run. We use an evaluation strategy which is common in the field of Information Retrieval, basically consisting in the assumption that the user will run the top N algorithms, for several values of N. This strategy assumes that the user will not skip any intermediate algorithm. This is a reasonable assumption, although, as mentioned earlier, one of the advantages of recommending rankings is that the user may actually skip some suggestions, due to personal preferences or other reasons. In this kind of evaluation, we must take not only accuracy into account but the time required to run the selected algorithm(s). If accuracy is the only criterion that matters, i.e. there are no time constraints, the user should run all algorithms and choose the most accurate.

The cross-validation strategy will be used as a reference to compare our results to. It is the most accurate algorithm selection method (an average of 89.94% in our setting) but it is very time consuming (more than four hours in our setting). As a baseline we will use boosted C5.0, which is the best algorithm on average (87.94%) and also very fast (less than two min.). We also include the Linear Discriminant (LD), which is the fastest algorithm, with an average time of less than five seconds.

The results of the SW method using 1 neighbor and the reduced set of meta-features are presented in Figure 3, assuming the selection of the first 1, 2 or 3 algorithms in the ranking. For each selection strategy (including the baselines), we plot the average loss in accuracy (vertical axis), when compared to CV, against the average execution time (horizontal axis). In the ranking setting, when the algorithm recommended in position N was tied with the one at N+1, we selected, from all the tied algorithms, the ones with the highest average accuracy (in the training data sets) such that exactly N algorithms are executed. The results demonstrate the advantage of using a ranking strategy. Although the Top-1, with an average loss of accuracy of 5.16%, does not seem to be very competitive in terms of accuracy, if the user is willing to wait a bit longer, he/she could use the Top-2 algorithms. The time required is quite good (less than five min., while CV takes more than three hours, on average) and the loss in accuracy

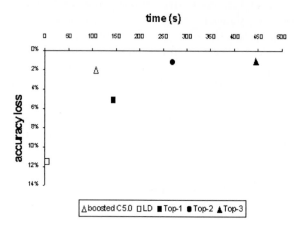

Fig. 3. Evaluation of several algorithm selection strategies (Linear Discriminant, boosted C5.0, Top-1, 2 and 3) according to two criteria (accuracy loss when compared to CV and time). Note that cross-validation takes on average more than three hours.

is only of 1.23%. Running another algorithm, i.e. running the Top-3 algorithms would provide further improvement in accuracy (1.06% loss) while taking only a little longer.

Comparing to the baselines, we observe that even the Top-1 strategy will be much more accurate than LD but the latter is faster. The comparison of Top-1 with boosted C5.0 is, at first sight, not very favorable: it is both less accurate and slower. However, the Top-2 and Top-3 strategies compete well with boosted C5.0: they are both more accurate but take more time (although, as mentioned above, they still run in acceptable time for many applications).

6   Conclusions

We have investigated different hypotheses concerning the design of a meta-learning method for algorithm recommendation. First, we compared a large set of general, statistical and information-theoretic meta-features, commonly used in meta-learning, with one of its subsets, containing measures that represent properties of the data that affect algorithm performance. This selection has significantly improved the results, as would be expected, especially considering that the k-NN algorithm was used at the meta-level. We plan to compare this approach to data characterization with new approaches, like landmarking.

Next, we analyzed a few variants of the recommendation method. We compared two different settings of the k-NN algorithm (k=1 and 5) and three different ranking methods to generate a ranking based on information about the performance of the algorithms on the neighbors. We observed that meta-learning is beneficial in general, i.e. results improve by generating a ranking based on the most similar data sets. The differences in performance between the three ranking methods, although statistically significant in some cases, are not so large as the ones obtained with the selection of meta-features.

Finally, we have compared the results obtained with our ranking approach with the most accurate method for algorithm recommendation, cross-validation (CV) and with boosted C5.0, the best algorithm on average in our set, in terms of accuracy and time. The results obtained show that the strategy of running the Top-2 or 3 algorithms achieves a significant improvement in time when compared to CV (minutes compared to hours) with a small loss in accuracy (approximately 1%). Furthermore, it competes quite well with boosted C5.0, which is faster but less accurate.

References

1. Aha, D.: Generalizing from case studies: A case study. In Sleeman, D., Edwards, P., eds.: Proceedings of the Ninth International Workshop on Machine Learning (ML92), Morgan Kaufmann (1992) 1–10
2. Brazdil, P., Gama, J., Henery, B.: Characterizing the applicability of classification algorithms using meta-level learning. In Bergadano, F., de Raedt, L., eds.: Proceedings of the European Conference on Machine Learning (ECML-94), Springer-Verlag (1994) 83–102
3. Atkeson, C.G., Moore, A.W., Schaal, S. In: Locally Weighted Learning. Volume 11. Kluwer (1997) 11–74
4. Lindner, G., Studer, R.: AST: Support for algorithm selection with a CBR approach. In Giraud-Carrier, C., Pfahringer, B., eds.: Recent Advances in Meta-Learning and Future Work, J. Stefan Institute (1999) 38–47
5. Henery, R.: Methods for comparison. In Michie, D., Spiegelhalter, D., Taylor, C., eds.: Machine Learning, Neural and Statistical Classification. Ellis Horwood (1994) 107–124
6. Pfahringer, B., Bensusan, H., Giraud-Carrier, C.: Tell me who can learn you and i can tell you who you are: Landmarking various learning algorithms. In Langley, P., ed.: Proceedings of the Seventeenth International Conference on Machine Learning (ICML2000), Morgan Kaufmann (2000) 743–750
7. Soares, C., Brazdil, P.: Zoomed ranking: Selection of classification algorithms based on relevant performance information. In Zighed, D., Komorowski, J., Zytkow, J., eds.: Proceedings of the Fourth European Conference on Principles and Practice of Knowledge Discovery in Databases (PKDD2000), Springer (2000) 126–135
8. Brazdil, P., Soares, C.: A comparison of ranking methods for classification algorithm selection. In de Mántaras, R., Plaza, E., eds.: Machine Learning: Proceedings of the 11th European Conference on Machine Learning ECML2000, Springer (2000) 63–74
9. Neave, H., Worthington, P.: Distribution-Free Tests. Routledge (1992)
10. Provost, F., Jensen, D.: Evaluating knowledge discovery and data mining. Tutorial Notes, Fourth International Conference on Knowledge Discovery and Data Mining (1998)
11. Blake, C., Keogh, E., Merz, C.: Repository of machine learning databases (1998) http:/www.ics.uci.edu/~mlearn/MLRepository.html.
12. Ripley, B.: Pattern Recognition and Neural Networks. Cambridge (1996)

Properties and Complexity in Feasible Logic-Based Argumentation for Electronic Commerce

Luís Brito and José Neves*

Departamento de Informática
Universidade do Minho
Braga, Portugal
{lbrito, jneves}@di.uminho.pt
http://alfa.di.uminho.pt/~lbrito
http://www.di.uminho.pt/~jneves

Abstract. Logic-Based Argumentation (LBA) exhibits unique properties and advantages over other kinds of argumentation proceedings, namely: the adequacy to logic-based pre-argument reasoning, similarity to the human reasoning process, reasoning with incomplete information and argument composition and extension. Logic enables a formal specification to be built and a quick prototype to be developed. In order for LBA to achieve feasibility in Electronic Commerce scenarios, a set of properties must be present: self-support, correctness, conjugation, temporal containment and acyclicity. At the same time, LBA is shown to achieve stability in argument exchange (*guaranteed success problem*) and, depending on the definition of *success*, computational efficiency at each round (*success problem*).

Keywords: logic-based argumentation, electronic commerce, success problem, guaranteed success problem.

1   Introduction

The use of logic (be it propositional, extended logic programming, modal or any other sort) enables systems to be modeled with the added benefit of mathematical correctness and avoidance of ambiguity. Logic programming tools even provide a working prototype for the modeled system, amazingly reducing the time between formal specification and prototype development/testing. Argumentation systems benefit from the use of logic for two reasons: the intrinsic logic behind argumentation [1,7] and the already stated benefits in the software development cycle.

---

* José Neves would like to acknowledge the financial support from FCT, given under the project POSI/EEI/13096/2000 – *Um Sistema de Informação com base na Web para acesso a Jurisprudência.*

F.J. Garijo, J.C. Riquelme, and M. Toro (Eds.): IBERAMIA 2002, LNAI 2527, pp. 90–100, 2002.

Electronic Commerce (EC) environments provide an unparalleled arena for the combination of logic and argumentation [5]. Logic provides the formal tools for the sound development of agents and agent reasoning mechanisms. Argumentation provides a way to exchange justified information among business counterparts (be it in Business-to-Consumer – B2C – or Business-to-Business – B2B – scenarios) or even to develop negotiation techniques that aim at shorter times for each deal (with more information present at each stage) [11,16]. However, the feasibility of Logic-Based Argumentation (LBA) for EC can only be determined if two problems are approached:

- **EC-directed properties**: in order for LBA to be feasible for EC, arguments must exhibit properties that may lead to reducing algorithmic complexity, guarantee acyclicity and deliver correction, just to name a few;
- **complexity of success and guaranteed success problems**: once the desired kind of arguments and an algorithm are chosen, feasibility can only be achieved by argumentation procedures which enable success determination and guarantee success with a relatively low cost.

On section 2 a formalization for LBA is presented, together with advantages, mathematical foundations and the proof of each necessary property for EC feasibility. On section 3 the success and guaranteed success problems are stated and the complexity for LBA is presented. Finally, sections 4 and 5 show related work and some conclusions.

The main contributions of this work are: (i) deliver the power of mathematical logic to argumentative procedures in EC; (ii) state the main advantages of LBA; (iii) state and prove some of the most important properties for feasible argumentation; (iv) determine if LBA provides success determination and if success is guaranteed.

2   Logic-Based Argumentation for Electronic Commerce

Although the use of logic has been questioned in the field of argumentation [12], logic-based argumentation still presents a set of characteristics which can not be measured by a simplistic computational efficiency metric, such as [5,6]:

- **adequacy to logic-based approaches to pre-argument reasoning**: some agent development strategies [8,15] define a stage that precedes the instant an agent starts to articulate an argument. This stage is called pre-argument reasoning and enables the agent to reason about such things as the *right to deal* some product or the *right to deal* with some counterpart. Due to the fundamental use of logic as a formalization tool and the manipulation of a logic Knowledge Base (KB) [8] a set of rules is available in order for an argument to be formulated;
- **similarity to the human reasoning processes**: the use of logical mechanisms in reasoning and, in special, such inference mechanisms as *modus ponens*, enable easy construction of rules even by non-experts. On the other hand, the set of available rules (in an agent's KB) is largely human-readable;

- **reasoning with incomplete information**: the use of null values [2,7], in combination with negation as failure, enables the use of incomplete information and a reasoning mechanism that deals with uncertainty (i.e., the *unknown* valuation in clauses). An agent is able to construct arguments where some of the steps are not taken as simple *true* or *false* elements;
- **argument composition and extension**: the set of logical elements (rules) which compose an argument may be extended in order to strengthen the argument conclusion, therefore inumerous compositions might be available, which permits easy adaption to the specific kind of argument intention (e.g., information exchange). On the other hand, taking an argument for A and the insertion of a rule such as $B \leftarrow A$, an argument for B is easily reached;

2.1   Mathematical Foundations

Extended Logic Programming (ELP) is a useful, simple and powerful tool for problem solving. If argumentation in EC-oriented agents is to be addressed through ELP the structure of each agent's KB needs to be defined. This KB is considered to be a collection of organized clauses (logic theory OT') that enable inferencing and, therefore, action justification and argument construction.

Definition 1. (knowledge clause) *The knowledge available in each agent is composed of logic clauses of the form* $r_k : P_{i+j+1} \leftarrow P_1 \wedge P_2 \wedge ... \wedge P_{i-1} \wedge not\, P_i \wedge ... \wedge not\, P_{i+j}.$, *where* $i, j, k \in N_0$, $P_1, ..., P_{i+j+1}$ *are literals; i.e, formulas of the form* p *or* $\neg p$, *where* p *is an atom. In these clauses* r_k, *not*, P_{i+j+1}, *and* $P_1 \wedge P_2 \wedge ... \wedge P_{i-1} \wedge not\, P_i ... \wedge not\, P_{i+j}$ *stand, respectively, for the clause's identifier, the* **negation-as-failure** *operator, the rule's consequent, and the rule's antecedent. If* $i = j = 0$ *the clause (rule) is called* **fact** *and represented as* $r_k : P_1$.

An ELP program (Π_{ELP}) is seen as a set of knowledge clauses as the ones presented above. Arguments are to be constructed from inference sequences over an agent's KB (in fact, a Π_{ELP}). The use of ELP in the KB enables a three-valued approach to logical reasoning [4,2,8] which leads to the possibility of using *null values* to represent incomplete information. These *null values* combined with a meta-theorem solver enable the construction of arguments that rely not only on rules that are *positively triggered* (i.e., their logical valuation after variable instantiation is *true*) but on all the three logical valuations: *true*, *false* and *unknown*. This reasoning over incomplete and unknown information is extremely important in EC scenarios due to the pervasive nature of fuzzy negotiation situations (e.g., agent A is able to deal product P with agent B using the set of conditions C_1, however it is not known if it can do the same thing with a set C_2 – leading to further dialog).

Definition 2. (negotiation argument) *Taking ordered theory* OT', *a negotiation argument is a finite, non-empty sequence of rules* $\langle r_1, ..., demo(r_i, V_i), ..., r_n \rangle$ *such that, for each sequence rule* r_j *with* P *as a part of the antecedent, there is* *a sequence rule r_i ($i < j$) on which the consequent is P (demo(r_i, V_i) represents the meta-theorem solver application over rule r_i and valuation V_i).*

The conclusion of an argument relates to the consequent of the last rule used in that same argument. Therefore, having in mind the use of such premise in further definitions, a formal statement of argument conclusion is to be reached.

Definition 3. (conclusion) *The conclusion of an argument $A_1 = \langle r_1, ..., r_n \rangle$, conc($A_1$), is the consequent of the last rule (r_n) an none other than that one.*

Notice that, through the current definition of *negotiation argument*, it is possible to build *incoherent arguments*; i.e., it is possible to build arguments where there are rules that attack (deny) previous rules stated in the sequence. The formal characterization of coherency is provided in terms of a constraint statement in the form:

Definition 4. (coherency) *An argument $A_1 = \langle r_1, ..., r_n \rangle$ is said to be "coherent" iff $\neg \exists_{a_i, a_j} a_i, a_j \in subarguments(A) \wedge i \neq j : a_i$ attacks a_j.*

Taking into account the two forms of argument attack (*conclusion denial* and *premise denial*), a *conflict* among two opposing agents (e.g., buyer/seller) can be formally stated.

Definition 5. (conflict/attack over negotiation arguments)
Let $A_1 = \langle r_{1,1}, ..., r_{1,n} \rangle$ be the argument of agent 1 and $A_2 = \langle r_{2,1}, ..., r_{2,m} \rangle$ be the argument of agent 2. Then,

(1) A_1 attacks A_2 iff A_1 executes a conclusion denial attack or a premise denial attack over A_2; and
(2) A_1 executes a conclusion denial attack over A_2 iff and conc(A_1) = $\neg$conc(A_2); and
(3) A_1 executes a premise denial attack over A_2 iff $\exists r_{2,j} \in A_2 - conc(A_2)$: conc(A_1) = $\neg r_{2,j}$.

Once coherent arguments are exchanged, a negotiation history (set of exchanged arguments) of the sender agent to the receiver agent can be defined.

Definition 6. (history) *The argumentation history of agent A to agent B is $h_{A \rightarrow B} = \langle A_{1, A \rightarrow B}, A_{2, A \rightarrow B}, ..., A_{n, A \rightarrow B} \rangle$.*

It is also important to state that *argumentation procedures* (i.e., the exchange of arguments amongst agents on a particular issue) should exhibit acyclicity. Once some conclusion has been put forward by one of agents and attacked by a counterpart, that same conclusion can not be put forward and attacked once again due to the danger of an *argumentative cycle*.

Definition 7. (termination) *Given the argumentation histories $h_{A \rightarrow B}, h_{B \rightarrow A}$ and arguments $A_i \in h_{A \rightarrow B}$ and $A_j \in h_{B \rightarrow A}$, $\exists^1_{(i,j)}$ conc(A_i) = $P \wedge$ conc(A_j) = $\neg P$ in order to deliver argumentative acyclicity and termination.*

2.2   Properties

After stating the mathematical foundations of LBA, it is now possible to present and prove a set of theorems that establish its most important features. By proving the validity of such properties, it is possible to ensure that EC-directed arguments based on the present LBA system ensure correction and feasibility. EC needs: arguments which are supported and inferred from the specific knowledge of each agent (self-support property), truthful agents (non-contradiction property), easy to combine arguments (conjugation property), non-monotonous knowledge bases to capture the commercial reality (temporal containment property) and an acyclic line of argument generation (acyclicity property).

In order to prove many of these properties it must be ensured that *stable time intervals* are considered, once if long range reasoning is assumed and given the non-monotonous characteristics of each agent's KB (necessary to faithfully express real-world commerce) contradictory arguments might be generated. The arguments in an LBA system for EC exhibit, therefore, a set of properties presented in terms of the statements:

Theorem 1. (self-support) *Given a stable time interval, argument $A_1 \in h_{A \to B}$ and having $A_1 \vdash P$, then $KB_A \vdash P$.*

Proof. By $A_1 \in h_{A \to B}$ and the definition of *argument*, $A_1 = \langle r_1, ..., r_n \rangle$ being $r_i \in KB_A$. Therefore, $KB_A \supseteq A_1 \vdash P$ and by consequence $KB_A \vdash P$.

It is then proved that agent A can only support its arguments by the knowledge present at its own KB.   □

Corollary 1. *Given a stable time interval, $A_1 \in h_{A \to B}$ and having $conc(A_1) = P$, then $KB_A \vdash P$.*

Theorem 2. (correctness or non-contradiction) *Given a stable time interval, arguments $A_1 \in h_{B \to A}$, $A_2 \in h_{A \to B}$, $A_3 \in h_{A \to C}$, $A_4 \in h_{C \to A}$, argument conclusions $conc(A_1) = \neg P$, $conc(A_2) = P$, $conc(A_3) = P$ and an attack of A_4 over A_3, then $conc(A_4) \neq \neg P$.*

Proof. If an attack of A_4 over A_3 takes place, either the conclusion or the premises of A_3 are denied by A_4. Assuming each situation separately:

- *conclusion attack:* $conc(A_4) = \neg conc(A_3) = \neg P$. Taking into account that $A_4 \subseteq KB_A$, then $KB_A \vdash \neg P$. However, the KB of each agent is coherent and by $conc(A_2) = P$ it is know that $KB_A \vdash P$, therefore it must be stated that $conc(A_4) \neq \neg P$; and
- *premise attack:* $conc(A_4) = \neg Q$ ($Q \in A_3 - [conc(A_3)]$). By the definition of *argument conclusion* and by $conc(A_3) = P$ it is known that $conc(A_4) \neq \neg P$.

It is then proved that agent A is unable to "lie" (i.e., state $\neg P$ after having stated P in the same time frame).   □

Theorem 3. (conjugation) *Given a stable time interval, argument $A_1 \in h_{A \to B}$, argument $A_2 \in h_{A \to B}$, $conc(A_1) = P_1$, $conc(A_2) = P_2$ and a general rule $Q \leftarrow P_1, P_2.$, then argument $A = A_1 \odot A_2 \odot Q \leftarrow P_1, P_2.$ (where $\odot$ stands as the concatenation operator) delivers $conc(A) = Q$.*

Proof. Taking $conc(A_1) = P_1$ and $conc(A_2) = P_2$, then by the definition of *argument* and *argument conclusion*, argument A is valid only if $A' = \langle P_1, P_2, Q \leftarrow P_1, P_2. \rangle$ is valid (due to the fact that the justifications for A_1 and A_2 are independent). Once again, by the definition of *argument*, A' is valid and, by the definition of *argument conclusion*, $conc(A) = Q$.

It is then proved that agent A is able to compose valid arguments into new arguments with combined conclusions. □

Theorem 4. (temporal containment) *Given time instants $t_1 \neq t_2$, KB_{t_1} (the agent's KB at time instant t_1), KB_{t_2} (the agent's KB at time instant t_2), argument $A = \langle r_1, ..., r_n \rangle$, $r_i \in KB_{t_1}$ and $conc(A) = P$, then it can not be concluded that $KB_{t_2} \vdash P$.*

Proof. Proceeding by an absurd reduction proof, assume that with time instants $t_1 \neq t_2$, KB_{t_1}, KB_{t_2}, argument $A = \langle r_1, ..., r_n \rangle$, $r_i \in KB_{t_1}$ and $conc(A) = P$, then *it can* be concluded that $KB_{t_2} \vdash P$. By having, for example, $KB_{t_1} = \{a.; b \leftarrow a, c.\}$, $KB_{t_2} = \{\neg a.\}$, $t_1 \neq t_2$ and $A = \langle a \rangle$, it can be concluded that $conc(A) = a$ and, by the taken assumption, $KB_{t_2} \vdash a$, however by looking at KB_{t_2} is easily seen that $KB_{t_2} \nvdash a$. The initial assumption is, therefore, false.

It is then proved that the fact that an argument is generated at a given time instant, does not mean that the KB of that same agent is able to generate that same argument at a different time instant. □

Theorem 5. (acyclicity) *Given an acyclic KB, then $\forall A, A \in h_{A \to B}$ generated from KB is acyclic.*

Proof. Take the Atom Dependency Graphs [4] ADG_A and ADG_{KB} (i.e., a graph which has ground atoms at each vertex and directed edges labeled with $\langle P_i, P_j, s \rangle$, representing the existence of a rule with P_i at the head, P_j in the body and $s \in \{+, -\}$ if the atom is positive or negative, respectively) derived from the ELP programs present at A and KB, respectively). Having $A \subseteq KB$, if $\forall_i (u_i, u_{i+1}) \in edges(ADG_A)$ (with $u_i \in vertices(ADG_A)$) then $(u_i, u_{i+1}) \in edges(ADG_{KB})$ (with $u_i \in vertices(ADG_{KB})$). If a cycle exists within ADG_A, $\exists_i (u_i, u_i) \in edges(ADG_A)$ and due to $A \subseteq KB$, $\exists_i (u_i, u_i) \in edges(ADG_{KB})$, once ADG_{KB} is acyclic a cycle in ADG_A can not exist.

It is then proved that an acyclic ELP KB (which implies a *terminating program* [4,3]) delivers acyclic (therefore, *terminating*) arguments. □

3   The Success and Guaranteed Success Problems

Although the presented properties show that LBA has the necessary semantic and syntactic soundness to be used in EC environments, it must be proved that computational feasibility is also present. It must be shown that LBA protocols exhibit computational feasibility at each round and, at the same time, stability or termination is reached. These problems are also known as the *success* and *guaranteed success* problems, respectively.

In a negotiation process, through which the acceptability region of each agent is constrained [11], there is an active adversarial process that proceeds by an argument/counter-argument mechanism, where an agent successively attacks another agent's premises or conclusions. On the other hand, there is a different situation where argumentation is used as a way of exchanging justified information and support the decision-making process. Therefore, the *success* and *guaranteed success* problems have to be considered for these two situations.

3.1   The Success Problem

In the case of EC-directed negotiation, success can be measured in many ways (e.g., the number of "victories" over a set of rounds, or the lowest argument length average), however in pragmatic terms victory rarely depends on a successful history of arguments (which serve in adversarial argumentation, as a way to constrain the acceptability space of each agent) but rather on the conclusions of the present round (which may be the last or just a step on the overall argumentation history).

Definition 8. (success)   *A   set   of   exchanged   LBA   arguments* $\bigcup_{i,j \in Agents, i \neq j} h_{i \to j}$ *exhibits* **success** *if* $\bigwedge_{i,j \in Agents, i \neq j} conc_{ext} \left(A_{|h_{i \to j}|} \right) \nvdash \bot$, *where* $conc_{ext}()$, *Agents and* $A_{|h_{i \to j}|}$ *stand, respectively, for the* **extended conclusion**, *the set of involved agents and the last argument sent from agent* i *to agent* j. *The* **extended conclusion** *results from extending the conclusion function by assigning logic values to two specific situations: concession (an agent quits by agreeing with the counterparts' conclusions) and drop-out (an agent quits by refusing to agree with the counterparts' conclusions), formally:*

$$conc_{ext}(A) = \begin{cases} \top, & if\, concession \\ \bot, & if\, drop-out \\ conc(A), & otherwise \end{cases}.$$

Considering that each conclusion is a ground literal, the previous definition of *success* leads to an algorithm that searches for the presence of $\bot$ or the presence of both P and $\neg P$, which can easily be done in $O\left(|Agents|^2\right)$. However, if *success* is defined in terms of the total argument and not only its conclusion, by assuming propositional rules an equivalent to the *logic satisfiability problem* is achieved, which is proven to be NP-complete [20,10]. By assuming DATALOG restrictions, complexity is proven to be EXPTIME-complete [10].

In the case of a non-adversarial argument exchange, the existence of premise and conclusion-denial situations lead to a much easier way to solve the *success* problem. In an EC-directed environment where non-adversarial argumentation occurs (typically B2B situations), each agent presents (in an informative way) what it can deduce from its knowledge about the world, therefore $conc_{ext}()$ on *Definition 8* is to be changed to allow a permanent *success* situation:

$$conc_{ext}(A) = \top.$$

3.2   The Guaranteed Success Problem

Although it is important to determine the eventual *success* at each argumentation round, LBA for EC can only be considered feasible if the *guaranteed success problem* is not computationally intractable; i.e., it is possible to achieve stability on the set of exchanged arguments. The pragmatic characteristics of EC do not support large (or even infinite) argument exchange sets.

In the case of non-adversarial argumentation (e.g., many B2B situations), the necessity to reach a stable situation does not directly arise. Though each agent uses the premise and conclusion denial tools to generate counter-arguments, the aim of such action is not to arrive at an agreement on some knowledge but rather a cooperative information exchange [7]. Therefore, *success is guaranteed* at each round.

Adversarial argumentation is more complex than the non-adversarial one. By considering that each argument was built through the use of a language based on propositional Horn clauses $\mathcal{L}_0^{HC}$, it has been proven that the *guaranteed success problem* for such a language is co-NP-complete [20]. Nonetheless such an approach, the expressiveness from the desired ELP is reduced to propositional logic while maintaining an high algorithmic complexity. However, the set of properties present in LBA (and previously proven) yield an interesting conclusion, that is now stated in the form:

Theorem 6. *Assuming that each round is a stable time interval, then adversarial LBA exhibits* **guaranteed success.**

Proof. Given the stable time interval of a round, *Properties 2 (non-contradiction)* and *5 (acyclicity)*, and *Definition 7 (termination)*, it is easy to conclude that each agent can not generate argumentative cycles through "lies" or arguments with cyclic clauses and, at the same time, it can not incur in the use of arguments which have been denied by a counterpart.

Being n_0 the finite size of the Atom Dependency Graph (i.e., the total number of edges and vertexes) associated with the knowledge of a given agent (ADG_{KB}), the argumentative process proceeds, round by round, on an acyclic argumentative path, progressively constraining the possible set of usable inferences to perform premise and conclusion-denial attacks. Therefore, ADG_{KB} has the number of traversable edges and vertexes, in order to reach some conclusion P, progressively reduced:

$$n_0, n_1, n_2, ..., n_m, \ \ n_0 > n_1 > n_2 > ... > n_m$$

where n_i is the size of the traversable ADG_{KB} at each round. It is then easy to see that, in a number of steps lower than n_0 (therefore finite), no path will be available on ADG_{KB} and a *concession* or *drop-out* occurs. □

4   Related Work

The study of argumentation through mathematical logic (especially ELP) goes back to work done by Loui [14], Simari et al. [18], and by Kowalski and Toni [13]. Formalization through reasoning models happened even earlier by Toulmin [19] and, in philosophical terms, during Classic Antiquity.

The use of LBA in the Law arena, is present in the work of Prakken and Sartor [17]. However, the use in EC scenarios was proposed by Jennings et al. [11]. The formalization and viability study for B2C, B2B and cooperative argumentation was approached by Brito and Neves [5,6] combined with a presentation of a 4-step approach to agent development by Brito et al. [7,9].

A complexity study on the use of logic in negotiation has been presented by Wooldridge and Parsons [20].

5   Conclusions

The use of ELP is important either to formally specify the reasoning mechanisms and the knowledge exchange in EC scenarios, or to quickly develop a working prototype. LBA exhibits a set of characteristics which are unique to this kind of argumentation: it deals with incomplete information and is similar to the human reasoning processes.

A formal way that will endorse adversarial or even cooperative argument exchanges in EC implies that an important set of characteristics need to be present on LBA, namely: self-support, correctness, conjugation, temporal containment and acyclicity. It has been proven that, through the present LBA formalization, the necessary properties are available.

However it is necessary to evaluate, at each round, the *success* of an argumentative procedure and it must be proven that stability is reached at some stage (*guaranteed success*). These questions are extremely important in EC scenarios and condition the feasibility and viability of LBA for EC. It has been proven that for non-adversarial situations the *success* and *guaranteed success* problems are trivially solved. As for adversarial situations, the *success* problem can be reduced to polynomial complexity (depending on the definition of *success*) and there is *guaranteed success*.

References

1. L. Amgoud, N. Maudet, and S. Parsons. Modelling Dialogues using Argumentation. In *Proceedings of the 4th International Conference on Multi-Agent Systems*, Boston, USA, 2000.
2. C. Analide and J. Neves. Representation of Incomplete Information. In *Conferencia da Associacao Portuguesa de Sistemas de Infomnçao (CAPSI)*, Universidade do Minho, Guimaraes, Portugal, 2000.
3. K. Apt and M. Bezem. Acyclic Programs. *Neu Generation Computing*, 9(3,4):335–365, 1991.
4. C. Baral and M. Gelfond. Logic Programming and Knowledge Representation. Technical report, Computer Science Department, University of Texas at El Paso, El Paso, Texas, USA, 1994.
5. L. Brito and J. Neves. Discussing Logic-Based Argumentation in Extended Electronic Commerce Environments. In *Workshop "Adventures in Argumentation" at the 6th European Conference on Symbolic and Quantitative Approaches to Reasoning with Uncertainty (ECSQARU'01)*, Toulouse, France, September 2001.
6. L. Brito and J. Neves. Argument Exchange in Heterogeneous Electronic Commerce Environments. In *Proceedings of the First International Joint Conference on Autonomous Agents and Multiagent Systems AAMAS 2002*, Bologna, Italy, June 2002. ACM Press.
7. L. Brito, P. Novais, and J. Neves. On the Logical Aspects of Argument-based Negotiation among Agents. In Matthias Klush and Franco Zambonelli, editors, *Cooperative Information Agents V, Proceedings of the 5th International Workshop CIA 2001*, number 2182 in Lecture Notes in Artificial Intelligence, pages 178–189, Modena, Italy, September 2001. Springer-Verlag: Heidelberg, Germany.
8. L. Brito, P. Novais, and J. Neves. Temporality, Priorities and Delegation in an E-Commerce Environment. In *Proceedings of the 24th Bled Electronic Commerce Conference (BEedOI)*, Bled, Slovenia, July 2001.
9. L. Brito, P. Novais, and J. Neves. *Intelligent Agent Software Engineering*, chapter The Logic Behing Negotiation: From Pre-Argument Reasoning to Argument-Based Negotiation. IDEA Group, 2002.
10. E. Dantsin, T. Eiter, G. Gottlob, and A. Voronkov. Complaity and Expressive Power of Logic Programming. *ACM Computing Surveys*, 3(33):374–425, 2001.
11. N. Jennings, S. Parsons, P. Noriega, and C. Sierra. On Argumentation-based Negotiation. In *Proceedings of the International Workshop on Multi-Agent Systems*, Boston, USA, 1998.
12. H. Jung, H. Tambe, and S. Kulkarni. Argumentation as Distributed Constraint Satisfaction: Applications and Results. In *Proceedings of the International Conference on Autonomous Agents (Agents01)*, Montreal, Canada, 2001.
13. R. Kowalski and F. Toni. Argument and Reconciliation. In *Proceedings of the International Symposium on the Fifth Generation Computer Systems: Workshop on Legal Reasoning*, pages 9–16, Tokyo, Japan, 1994.
14. R. Loui. Defeat Among Arguments: A System of Defeasible Inference. *Computational Intelligence*, (3):100–106, 1987.
15. P. Novais, L. Brito, and J. Neves. Developing Agents for Electronic Commerce: A Constructive Approach. In *Proceedings of the World Conference on Systemics, Cybernetics and Informatics (SCI2OOl)*, Orlando, Florida, 2001.
16. S. Parsons and N. Jennings. Argumentation and Multi-Agent Decision Making. In *Proceedings of the AAAI Spring Symposium on Intemctive and Mixed-Initiative Decision Making*, pages 89–91, Stanford, USA, 1998.

17. H. Prakken and G. Sartor. Argument-based Logic Programming with Defeasible Priorities. *Journal of Applied Non-Classical Logics*, (7):25–75, 1997.
18. G. Simari, C. Chesñevar, and A. Garcia. Modelling Argumentation in a Logic Programming Setting: Formalization and Logic Properties. In *Workshop "Adventures in Argumentation" at the 6th European Conference on Symbolic and Quantitative Approaches to Reasoning with Uncertainty (ECSQARU'01)*, Toulouse, France, September 2001.
19. S. Toulmin. *The Uses of Arguments*. Cambridge University Press, 1958.
20. M. Wooldridge and S. Parsons. Languages for Negotiation. In *Proceedings of 14th European Conference on Artificial Intelligence (ECAI2000)*, 2000.

A Hybrid CBR Model for Forecasting in Complex Domains

Florentino Fdez-Riverola[1] and Juan M. Corchado[2]

[1] Dpto. de Informática, E.S.E.I., University of Vigo
Campus Universitario As Lagoas s/n., 32004, Ourense, Spain
riverola@uvigo.es
[2] Dpto. de Informática y Automática, University of Salamanca
Facultad de Ciencias, Plaza de la Merced, s/n., 37008, Salamanca, Spain
corchado@usal.es

Abstract. A hybrid neuro-symbolic problem solving model is presented in which the aim is to forecast parameters of a complex and dynamic environment in an unsupervised way. In situations in which the rules that determine a system are unknown, the prediction of the parameter values that determine the characteristic behaviour of the system can be a problematic task. The proposed model employs a case-based reasoning system to wrap a growing cell structures network, a radial basis function network and a set of Sugeno fuzzy models to provide an accurate prediction. Each of these techniques is used in a different stage of the reasoning cycle of the case-based reasoning system to retrieve, to adapt and to review the proposed solution to the problem. This system has been used to predict the red tides that appear in the coastal waters of the north west of the Iberian Peninsula. The results obtained from those experiments are presented.

1 Introduction

Forecasting the behaviour of a dynamic system is, in general, a difficult task, especially when dealing with complex, stochastic domains for which there is a lack of knowledge. In such a situation one strategy is to create an adaptive system which possesses the flexibility to behave in different ways depending on the state of the environment. An artificial intelligence approach to the problem of forecasting in such domains offers potential advantages over alternative approaches, because it is able to deal with uncertain, incomplete and even inconsistent data numerically represented. This paper presents a hybrid artificial intelligence (AI) model for forecasting the evolution of complex and dynamic environments that can be numerically represented. The effectiveness of this model is demonstrated in an oceanographic problem in which neither artificial neural network nor statistical models have been sufficiently successful.

However, successful results have been already obtained with hybrid case-based reasoning systems [1,2,3] used to predict the evolution of the temperature of the water ahead of an ongoing vessel, in real time. The hybrid system proposed in this paper presents a new synthesis that brings several AI subfields

F.J. Garijo, J.C. Riquelme, and M. Toro (Eds.): IBERAMIA 2002, LNAI 2527, pp. 101–110, 2002.

together (CBR, ANN and Fuzzy inferencing). The retrieval, reuse, revision and learning stages of the CBR system use the previously mentioned technologies to facilitate the CBR adaptation to a wide range of complex problem domains and to completely automate the reasoning process of the proposed forecasting mechanism.

The structure of the paper is as follows: first the hybrid neuro-symbolic model is explained in detail, then a case of study is briefly outlined and finally the results are analyzed together with the conclusions and future work.

2   Overview of the Hybrid CBR Based Forecasting Model

In this paper, a method for automating the CBR reasoning process is presented for the solution of complex problems in which the cases are characterised predominantly by numerical information. Figure 1 illustrates the relationships between the processes and components of the proposed hybrid CBR system. The diagram shows the technology used at each stage, where the four basic phases of the CBR cycle are shown as rectangles.

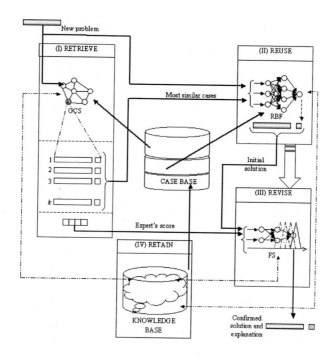

Fig. 1. Hybrid neuro-symbolic model.

The retrieval stage is carried out using a Growing Cell Structures (GCS) ANN [4]. The GCS facilitates the indexation of cases and the selection of those that are most similar to the problem descriptor. The reuse and adaptation of cases is carried out with a Radial Basis Function (RBF) ANN [5], which generates an initial solution creating a forecasting model with the retrieved cases. The revision is carried out using a group of pondered fuzzy systems that identify potential incorrect solutions. Finally, the learning stage is carried out when the real value of the variable to predict is measured and the error value is calculated, updating the knowledge structure of the whole system.

When a new problem is presented to the system, a new problem descriptor (case) is created and the GCS neural network is used to recover from the case-base the k most similar cases to the given problem (identifying the class to which the problem belongs, see Figure 2).

In the reuse phase, the values of the weights and centers of the RBF neural network used in the previous forecast are retrieved from the knowledge-base. These network parameters together with the k retrieved cases are then used to retrain the RBF network and to obtain an initial forecast (see Figure 2). During this process the values of the parameters that characterise the network are updated.

CBR-STAGE	Technology	Input	Output	Process
Retrieval	GCS network.	Problem descriptor.	k similar cases.	All the cases that belong to the same class to which the GCS associates the problem case are retrieved.
Reuse	RBF network.	Problem descriptor. k similar cases.	Initial solution.	The RBF network is retrained with the k retrieved cases.
Revision	Fuzzy systems.	Problem descriptor. Initial solution.	Confirmed solution.	Different Fuzzy sistems are created using the RBF network configuration with different degrees of generalization.
Retain	GCS network. RBF network. Fuzzy systems.	Problem descriptor. Forecasting error.	Configuration parameters of the GCS network, RBF network and Fuzzy systems.	The configurations of the GCS network, the RBF network and the Fuzzy subsystems are updated according to the accuracy of the forecast.

Fig. 2. Summary of technologies employed by the hybrid model.

In the revision phase, the initial solution proposed by the RBF neural network is modified according to the response of the fuzzy revision subsystem (a set of fuzzy models). Each fuzzy system has been created from the RBF network using neurofuzzy techniques [6] as it will be seen later.

The revised forecast is then retained temporarily in the forecast database. When the real value of the variable to predict is measured, the forecast value for the variable can then be evaluated, through comparison of the actual and forecast value and the error obtained (see Figure 2). A new case, corresponding to this forecasting operation, is then stored in the case-base. The forecasting error value is also used to update several parameters associated with the GCS network, the RBF network and the fuzzy systems.

2.1   Growing Cell Structures Operation

To illustrate the working model of the GCS network inside the whole system, a two-dimensional space will be used, where the cells (neurons) are connected and organized into triangles [4]. Each cell in the network (representing a generic case), can be seen as a "prototype" that identifies a set of similar problem descriptors. The basic learning process in a GCS network is carried out in three steps.

In the first step, the cell c, with the smallest distance between its weight vector, w_c, and the actual case, x, is chosen as the *winner cell*. The second step consists in the adaptation of the weight vector of the winning cells and their neighbours. In the third step, a *signal counter* is assigned to each cell, which reflects how often a cell has been chosen as winner. Repeating this process several times, for all the cases of the case-base, a network of cells will be created.

For each class identified by the GCS neural network, a vector of values is maintained (see Figure 1). This vector (to which we will refer as "importance" vector) is initialised with a same value for all its components whose sum is one, and represents the accuracy of each fuzzy system (used during the revision stage) with respect to that class. During revision, the importance vector associated to the class to which the problem case belongs, is used to ponder the outputs of each fuzzy system. For each forecasting cycle, the value of the importance vector associated with the most accurate fuzzy system is increased and the other values are proportionally decreased. This is done in order to give more relevance to the most accurate fuzzy system of the revision subsystem.

Figure 3 provides a more concise description of the GCS-based case retrieval regime described above, where v_x is the value feature vector describing a new problem, confGCS represents the set of cells describing the GCS topology after the training, K is the retrieved set of most relevant cases given a problem and P represents the "importance" vector for the identified prototype.

The neural network topology of a GCS network is incrementally constructed on the basis of the cases presented to the network. Effectively, such a topology represents the result of the basic clustering procedure and it has the added advantage that inter-cluster distances can be precisely quantified. Since such networks contain explicit distance information, they can be used effectively in CBR to represent: (i) an *indexing structure* which indexes sets of cases in the case-base and, (ii) a *similarity measure* between case sets [7].

2.2   Radial Basis Function Operation

Case adaptation is one of the most problematic aspects of the CBR cycle, mainly if we have to deal with problems with a high degree of dynamism and for which there is a lack of knowledge. In such a situation, RBF networks have demonstrated their utility as universal approximators for closely modelling these continuous processes [8].

```
procedure RETRIEVE (input: vₓ, confGCS; output: K, P)
        {
00    begin.
01         CD ← ∅ /* vector of pairs (cell, distance) */
02         for each cell c ∈ confGCS do
03                   compute_distance: dc ← DIS(vₓ, w_c)
04                   assign_cell-distance-pair: CD ← (c, d_c)
05              order_by_distance(CD) /* ascending */
06         for each pair p ← CD do
07                   K ← get_cases_from_cell(p)
08                   if |K| > 0 then
09                            go_to_line 10 /* non-empty cell */
10    end.
        }
```

Fig. 3. GCS-based case retrieval.

Again to illustrate how the RBF networks work, a simple architecture will be presented. Initially, three vectors are randomly chosen from the training data set and used as centers in the middle layer of the RBF network. All the centers are associated with a Gaussian function, the width of which, for all the functions, is set to the value of the distance to the nearest center multiplied by 0.5 (see [5] for more information about RBF network).

Training of the network is carried out by presenting pairs of corresponding input and desired output vectors. After an input vector has activated each Gaussian unit, the activations are propagated forward through the weighted connections to the output units, which sum all incoming signals. The comparison of actual and desired output values enables the mean square error (the quantity to be minimized) to be calculated. A new center is inserted into the network when the average error in the training data set does not fall during a given period.

The closest center to each particular input vector is moved toward the input vector by a percentage a of the present distance between them. By using this technique the centers are positioned close to the highest densities of the input vector data set. The aim of this adaptation is to force the centers to be as close as possible to as many vectors from the input space as possible. The value of a is linearly decreased by the number of iterations until its value becomes zero; then the network is trained for a number of iterations (1/4 of the total of established iterations for the period of training) in order to obtain the best possible weights for the final value of the centers.

Figure 4 provides a more concise description of the RBF-based case adaptation regime, where v_x is the value feature vector describing a new problem, K is the retrieved set of most relevant cases, confRBF represents the previously configuration of the RBF network and f_i represents the initial forecast generated by the RBF.

```
procedure REUSE (input: v*, K, confRBF; output: fi)
    {
00    begin.
01        while TRUE do /* infinite loop */
02            for each case c ∈ K do /* network adaptation using K cases */
03                retrain_network: error ← annRBF(c)
04                move_centers: annRBF.moveCenters(c)
05                modify_weights: annRBF.learn(c) /* delta rule */
06            if (error / |K|) < error_threshold then
07                go_to_line 8 /* end of infinite loop and adaptation */
08        generate_initial_forecast: fi ← annRBF(v*)
09    end.
    }
```

Fig. 4. RBF-based case adaptation.

The working model commented above together with their good capability of generalization, fast convergence, smaller extrapolation errors and higher reliability over difficult data, make this type of neural networks a good choice that fulfils the necessities of dealing with this type of problems. It is very important to train this network with a consistent number of cases. Such consistence in the training data set is guaranteed by the GCS network, that provides consistent classifications that can be used by the RBF network to auto-tuning its forecasting model.

2.3 Fuzzy System Operation

The two main objectives of the proposed revision stage are: to validate the initial prediction generated by the RBF and, to provide a set of simplified rules that explain the system working mode. The construction of the revision subsystem is carried out in two main steps:

(i) First, a Sugeno-Takagi fuzzy model [9] is generated using the trained RBF network configuration (centers and weights) in order to transform a RBF neural network to a well interpretable fuzzy rule system [6].

(ii) A measure of similarity is applied to the fuzzy system with the purpose of reducing the number of fuzzy sets describing each variable in the model. Similar fuzzy sets for one parameter are merged to create a common fuzzy set to replace them in the rule base. If the redundancy in the model is high, merging similar fuzzy sets for each variable might result in equal rules that also can be merged, thereby reducing the number of rules as well. When similar fuzzy sets are replaced by a common fuzzy set representative of the originals, the system's capacity for generalization increases.

In our model, the fuzzy systems are associated with each class identified by the GCS network, mapping each one with its corresponding value of the importance vector. There is one "importance" vector for each class or prototype. These fuzzy systems are used to validate and refine the proposed forecast.

The value generated by the revision subsystem is compared with the prediction carried out by the RBF and its difference (in percentage) is calculated. If the initial forecast does not differ by more than 10% of the solution generated by the revision subsystem, this prediction is supported and its value is considered as the final forecast. If, on the contrary, the difference is greater than 10% but lower than 30%, the average value between the value obtained by the RBF and that obtained by the revision subsystem is calculated, and this revised value adopted as the final output of the system. Finally, if the difference is greater or equal to 30% the system is not able to generate an appropriate forecast. This two thresholds have been identified after carrying out several experiments and following the advice of human experts.

The exposed revision subsystem improves the generalization ability of the RBF network. The simplified rule bases allow us to obtain a more general knowledge of the system and gain a deeper insight into the logical structure of the system to be approximated. The proposed revision method then help us to ensure a more accurate result, to gain confidence in the system prediction and to learn about the problem and its solution. The fuzzy inference systems also provides useful information that is used during the retain stage.

2.4   Retain

As mentioned before, when the real value of the variable to predict is known, a new case containing the problem descriptor and the solution is stored in the case-base. The importance vector associated with the retrieved class is updated in the following way: the error percentage with respect to the real value is calculated, then the fuzzy system that has produced the most accurate prediction is identified and the error percentage value previously calculated is added to the degree of importance associated with this fuzzy subsystem. As the sum of the importance values associated to a class (or prototype) has to be one, the values are normalized. When the new case is added to the case-base, its class is identified. The class is updated and the new case is incorporated into the network for future use.

3   A Case of Study: The Red Tides Problem

The oceans of the world form a highly dynamic system for which it is difficult to create mathematical models [10]. The rapid increase in dinoflagellate numbers, sometimes to millions of cells per liter of water, is what is known as a *bloom* of phytoplankton (if the concentration ascends above the 100.000 cells per liter). The type of dinoflagellate in which this study is centered is the pseudo-nitzschia spp diatom, causing of amnesic shellfish poisoning (known as ASP).

In the current work, the aim is to develop a system for forecasting one week in advance the concentrations (in cells per liter) of the pseudo-nitzschia spp at different geographical points.

The problem of forecasting, which is currently being addressed, may be simply stated as follows:

- **Given**: a sequence of data values (representative of the current and immediately previous state) relating to some physical and biological parameters,
- **Predict**: the value of a parameter at some future point(s) or time(s).

The raw data (sea temperature, salinity, PH, oxygen and other physical characteristics of the water mass) which is measured weekly by the monitoring network for toxic proliferations in the CCCMM (Centro de Control da Calidade
do Medio Marino, *Oceanographic environment Quality Control Centre*, Vigo,
Spain), consists of a vector of discrete sampled values (at 5 meters' depth) of
each oceanographic parameter used in the experiment, in the form of a time series. These data values are complemented by data derived from satellite images
stored on a database. The satellite image data values are used to generate cloud
and superficial temperature indexes which are then stored with the problem descriptor and subsequently updated during the CBR operation. Table 1 shows the
variables that characterise the problem. Data from the previous 2 weeks (W_{n-1},
W_n) is used to forecast the concentration of pseudo-nitzschia spp one week ahead
(W_{n+1}).

Table 1. Variables that define a case.

Variable	Unit	Week
Date	dd-mm-yyyy	W_{n-1}, W_n
Temperature	Cent. degrees	W_{n-1}, W_n
Oxygen	milliliters/liter	W_{n-1}, W_n
PH	acid/based	W_{n-1}, W_n
Transmitance	%	W_{n-1}, W_n
Fluorescence	%	W_{n-1}, W_n
Cloud index	%	W_{n-1}, W_n
Recount of diatoms	cel/liter	W_{n-1}, W_n
Pseudo-nitzschia spp	cel/liter	W_{n-1}, W_n
Pseudo-nitzschia spp (future)	*cel/liter*	W_{n+1}

Our proposed model has been used to build an hybrid forecasting system
that has been tested along the north west coast of the Iberian Peninsula with
data collected by the CCCMM from the year 1992 until the present. The prototype used in this experiment was set up to forecast the concentration of the
pseudo-nitzschia spp diatom of a water mass situated near the coast of Vigo
(geographical area A0 ((42°28.90' N, 8°57.80' W) 61 m)), a week in advance.
Red tides appear when the concentration of pseudo-nitzschia spp is higher than
100.000 cell/liter. Although the aim of this experiment is to forecast the value
of the concentration, the most important aspect is to identify in advance if the
concentration is going to exceed this threshold.

A case-base was built with the above mentioned data normalized between
[-1, 1]. For this experiment, four fuzzy inference systems have been created from
the RBF network, which uses 18 input neurons representing data coming from

the previous 2 weeks (see Table 1), between three and fifty neurons in the hidden layer and a single neuron in the output layer that represents the concentration for the pseudo-nitzschia spp diatom.

The following section discusses the results obtained with the prototype developed for this experiment as well as the conclusions and future work.

4   Results, Conclusions, and Future Work

The hybrid forecasting system has been proven in the coast of north west of the Iberian Peninsula with data collected by the CCCMM from the year 1992 until the present time. The average error in the forecast was found to be 26.043,66 cel/liter and only 5.5% of the forecasts had an error higher than 100.000 cel/liter. Although the experiment was carried out using a limited data set, it is believed that these error value results are significant enough to be extrapolated over the whole coast of the Iberian Peninsula.

Two situations of special interest are those corresponding to the *false alarms* and the *not detected blooms*. The first one happens when the system predicts bloom (concentration of pseudo-nitzschia $\geq$ 100.000 cel/liter) and this doesn't take place (real concentration $\leq$ 100.000 cel/liter). The second, more important, arise when bloom really exists and the system doesn't detect it.

Table 2 shows the predictions carried out with success (in absolute value and %) and the erroneous predictions differentiating the not detected blooms and the false alarms. This table also shows the average error obtained with several techniques. As it can be shown, the combination of different techniques in the form of the hybrid CBR system previously presented, produces better results that a RBF neural network working alone or anyone of the tested statistical techniques. This is due to the effectiveness of the revision subsystem and the retrained of the RBF neural network with the cases recovered by GCS network. The hybrid system is more accurate than any of the other techniques studied during this investigation.

Table 2. Summary of results forecasting pseudo-nitzschia spp.

Method	OK	OK (%)	N. detect.	Fal. alarms	Aver. error (cel/liter)
CBR-ANN-FS	**191/200**	**95,5%**	**8**	**1**	**26.043,66**
RBF	185/200	92,5%	8	7	45.654,20
ARIMA	174/200	87%	10	16	71.918,15
Quadratic Trend	184/200	92%	16	0	70.354,35
Moving Average	181/200	90,5%	10	9	51.969,43
Simp. Exp. Smooth.	183/200	91,5%	8	9	41.943,26
Lin. Exp. Smooth.	177/200	88,5%	8	15	49.038,19

In summary, this paper has presented an automated hybrid CBR model that employs case-based reasoning to wrap a growing cell structures network (for the index tasks to organize and retrieve relevant data), a radial basis function network (that contributes generalization, learning and adaptation capabilities) and a set of Sugeno fuzzy models (acting as experts that revise the initial solution) to provide a more effective prediction. The resulting hybrid model thus combines complementary properties of both connectionist and symbolic AI methods in order to create a real time autonomous forecasting system.

In conclusion, the hybrid reasoning problem solving approach may be used to forecast in complex situations where the problem is characterized by a lack of knowledge and where there is a high degree of dynamism. The prototype presented here will be tested in different water masses and a distributed forecasting system will be developed based on the model in order to monitor 500 km. of the North West coast of the Iberian Peninsula.

This work is financed by the project: *Development of techniques for the automatic prediction of the proliferation of red tides in the Galician coasts, PGIDT-00MAR30104PR*, inside the Marine Program of investigation of Xunta de Galicia. The authors want to thank the support lent by this institution, as well as the data facilitated by the CCCMM.

References

1. Corchado, J. M., Lees, B.: A Hybrid Case-based Model for Forecasting. Applied Artificial Intelligence, 15, num. 2, (2001) 105–127
2. Corchado, J. M., Lees, B., Aiken, J.: Hybrid Instance-based System for Predicting Ocean Temperatures. International Journal of Computational Intelligence and Applications, 1, num. 1, (2001) 35–52
3. Corchado, J. M., Aiken, J., Rees, N.: Artificial Intelligence Models for Oceanographic Forecasting. Plymouth Marine Laboratory, U.K., (2001)
4. Fritzke, B.: Growing Self-Organizing Networks-Why?. In Verleysen, M. (Ed.). European Symposium on Artificial Neural Networks, ESANN-96. Brussels, (1996) 61–72
5. Fritzke, B.: Fast learning with incremental RBF Networks. Neural Processing Letters, 1, num. 1, (1994) 2–5
6. Jin, Y., Seelen, W. von., and Sendhoff, B.: Extracting Interpretable Fuzzy Rules from RBF Neural Networks. Internal Report IRINI 00-02, Institut für Neuroinformatik, Ruhr-Universität Bochum, Germany, (2000)
7. Azuaje, F., Dubitzky, W., Black, N., and Adamson, K.: Discovering Relevance Knowledge in Data: A Growing Cell Structures Approach. IEEE Transactions on Systems, Man and Cybernetics, 30, (2000) 448–460
8. Corchado, J. M., and Lees, B.: Adaptation of Cases for Case-based Forecasting with Neural Network Support. In Pal, S. K., Dilon, T. S., and Yeung, D. S. (Eds.). Soft Computing in Case Based Reasoning. London: Springer Verlag, (2000) 293–319
9. Takagi, T., Sugeno, M.: Fuzzy identification of systems and its applications to modeling and control. IEEE Transactions on Systems, Man, and Cybernetics, 15, (1985) 116–132
10. Tomczak, M., Godfrey, J. S.: Regional Oceanographic: An Introduction. Pergamon, New York, (1994)

Generalized Modifiers as an Interval Scale: Towards Adaptive Colorimetric Alterations

Isis Truck[1], Amel Borgi[1,2], and Herman Akdag[1,2]

[1] LERI, Université de Reims, rue des Crayères – BP 1035
51687 Reims Cedex 2, France
truck@leri.univ-reims.fr
http://www.univ-reims.fr/leri
[2] LIP6, Université P. & M. Curie, 8, rue du Capitaine Scott
75015 Paris, France
{Amel.Borgi,Herman.Akdag}@lip6.fr

Abstract. In this article, new tools to represent the different states of a same knowledge are described. These states are usually expressed through linguistic modifiers that have been studied in a fuzzy framework, but also in a symbolic context. The tools we introduce are called *generalized symbolic modifiers*: they allow linguistic modifications. A first beginning of this work on modifiers has been done by Akdag & al and this paper is the continuation. Our tools are convenient and simple to use; they assume interesting mathematical properties as order relations or infinite modifications and, moreover, they can be seen as an interval scale. Besides, they are used in practice through a colorimetric application and give very good results. They act as a link between modifications expressed with words and colorimetric alterations.

1 Introduction

When imperfect knowledge has to be expressed, modifiers are often used to translate the many states of a same knowledge. For example, we can associate the modifiers "very", "more or less", "a little", etc. with the knowledge "young". These intermediate descriptions have been called by Zadeh [1] *linguistic hedges* or *linguistic modifiers* and have been taken up by Eshragh & al [2] and Bouchon–Meunier [3] notably. It seems to be interesting to define modifiers that would allow to modify values at will for a given application. In this paper, new tools, the generalized symbolic modifiers, are introduced for this kind of modification. These tools have very interesting mathematical properties and are also fully appropriate in practice.

The paper is organized as follows: section 2 is devoted to the different existing approaches about modifiers. In particular, we briefly present modifiers defined in a fuzzy framework [1], [3], [4] but also in a symbolic framework [5]. Our propositions about generalized symbolic modifiers are described in section 3. In particular, we assure that very few conditions are necessary to use and apply them and we explain how they can be considered as an interval scale. In section

F.J. Garijo, J.C. Riquelme, and M. Toro (Eds.): IBERAMIA 2002, LNAI 2527, pp. 111–120, 2002.

4 the application developed is detailed. Indeed, generalized modifiers are very useful in colorimetry and allow to propose adaptive colorimetric alterations. Finally, section 5 concludes this study.

2   Modifiers and Measure Scales

There are especially two kinds of approaches about linguistic modifiers: fuzzy and symbolic approaches. The first ones deal with fuzzy logic and represent the modifiers as modifications of membership functions while the others represent them as modifications of values on a scale basis.

2.1   Context in Fuzzy Logic

Zadeh has been one of the pioneers in this domain [6]. He has proposed to model concepts like "tall" or "more or less high",... with fuzzy subsets and, more precisely, with membership functions. Afterwards, some authors like Desprès have proposed an approach aiming at a classification of the fuzzy modifiers [4]. Desprès has defined classes or families of modifiers: the intensive ones that reinforce the initial value and the extensive ones that weaken it. The figure 1 sums these different cases up.

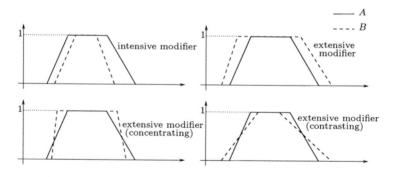

Fig. 1. Examples of modifiers enabling us to go from A to B.

Besides, the modifiers can be studied in a symbolic framework. Let us now have a look at what has been done concerning more symbolic approaches.

2.2   Symbolic Context

Akdag & al suggest to model modifiers in a symbolic context [5], [7]. Indeed, adverbs evaluating the truth of a proposition are often represented on a scale of linguistic degrees. They propose tools, i.e. symbolic linguistic modifiers, to combine and aggregate such symbolic degrees. The authors also introduce the notion of intensity rate associated to a linguistic degree on a scale basis.

Formally, Akdag & al define a symbolic linguistic modifier m as a semantic triplet of parameters. Let a be a symbolic degree and b a scale basis[1]; to a pair (a, b) corresponds a new pair (a', b') obtained by linear transformation depending on m. a' is the modified degree and b' the modified scale basis:

$$(a', b') = f_{m(\text{quantifier,nature,mode})}(a, b)$$

The quantifier (called λ) expresses the strength of the modifier, the nature is the way to modify the scale basis (i.e. dilation, erosion or conservation) and the mode is the sense of modification (weakening or reinforcing). Besides, they associate to each linguistic degree D of range a on a scale b its intensity rate, the proportion $\text{Prop}(D) = a/(b-1)$.

As Desprès, the authors classify their modifiers into two main families:

– weakening modifiers: they give a new characterisation which is less strong than the original one. They are divided into two subfamilies: the ones that erode the basis ($EG(\lambda)$ and $EG(\lambda^{\frac{1}{2}})$) and the ones that dilate the basis ($IG(\lambda)$ and $IG(\lambda^{\frac{1}{2}})$),
– reinforcing modifiers: they give a new characterisation which is stronger than the original one. They are divided into two subfamilies: the eroding ones ($ED(\lambda)$ and $ED(\lambda^{\frac{1}{2}})$) and the dilating ones ($ID(\lambda)$ and $ID(\lambda^{\frac{1}{2}})$).

This is gathered and briefly defined in figure 2 for a best understanding.

2.3   Measure Scales

As we have seen, the symbolic modifiers just introduced above act on scales. That is why it seems now appropriate to look into the existing works about this subject.

Measure scales are often used by statisticians [8] but also by researchers in fuzzy logic, like Grabisch [9]. [8] defines four measure scales that are described below:

The nominal scale. The codes that identify the variable are independent from each other. There is no order relation. Example: sex (F/M), etc.
The ordinal scale. The codes allow us to establish an order relation between them. Example: groups of age (under 18, between 18 to 30, 30 to 50, etc.).
The interval scale. The conditions are the same as in the previous case, but, moreover, the codes must be uniformly distributed on the scale. Example: ambient temperature in °C.
The ratio scale. The conditions are the same as in the previous case, but, moreover, the position of zero is important (absolute zero). Examples: company turnover; programme execution time, etc.

Let us see now our propositions about symbolic modifiers and how they can be considered as measure scales.

---

[1] The authors consider that a degree's scale denoted b represent a finite number of ordered degrees $0, 1, 2, \ldots b-1$. $b-1$ is thus the biggest degree of the scale.

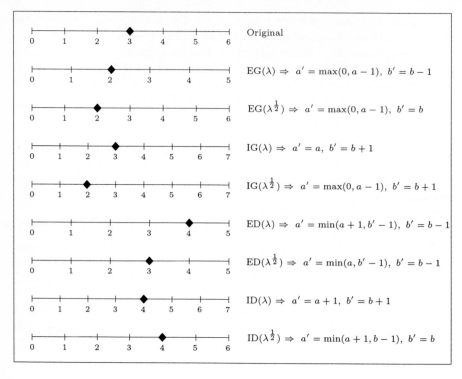

Fig. 2. Summary and comparison of the symbolic linguistic modifiers.

3   Generalized Symbolic Modifiers

Here we propose a generalization of symbolic linguistic modifiers presented in section 2.2. We clarify the role of the quantifier λ and we propose more general families of modifiers, for any given quantifier. Moreover, we establish a link between our modifiers and one of the measure scales studied above.

3.1   Definition

We associate to the notion of modifier a semantic triplet {radius, nature, mode}. The radius ρ ($\rho \in \mathbb{N}^*$) represents the strength of the modifier. As defined in section 2.2, the nature is the way to modify the scale basis (i.e. dilation, erosion or conservation) and the mode is the sense of modification (weakening or reinforcing). The more ρ increases, the more powerful the modifier.

In a more general way, we define a generalized symbolic modifier as a function allowing us to go from a pair (a, b) to a new pair (a', b').

Definition 1 *Let (a, b) be a pair belonging to $\mathbb{N} \times \mathbb{N}^*$. A generalized symbolic modifier with a radius ρ, denoted m or m_ρ is defined as:*

$$\mathbb{N} \times \mathbb{N}^* \to \mathbb{N} \times \mathbb{N}^*$$
$$(a, b) \mapsto (a', b') \quad \text{with} \quad a < b \quad \text{and} \quad a' < b'$$

a is a degree on a uniformely distributed scale b.

The definitions of our modifiers are summarized in the Table 1.

Table 1. Summary of reinforcing and weakening generalized modifiers.

MODE NATURE	Weakening		Reinforcing	
Erosion	$a' = \max(0, a - \rho)$ $b' = \max(1, b - \rho)$	$\mathbf{EW}(\rho)$	$a' = a$ $b' = \max(a + 1, b - \rho)$	$\mathbf{ER}(\rho)$
			$a' = \min(a + \rho, b - \rho - 1)$ $b' = \max(1, b - \rho)$	$\mathbf{ER'}(\rho)$
Dilation	$a' = a$ $b' = b + \rho$	$\mathbf{DW}(\rho)$	$a' = a + \rho$ $b' = b + \rho$	$\mathbf{DR}(\rho)$
	$a' = \max(0, a - \rho)$ $b' = b + \rho$	$\mathbf{DW'}(\rho)$		
Conservation	$a' = \max(0, a - \rho)$ $b' = b$	$\mathbf{CW}(\rho)$	$a' = \min(a + \rho, b - 1)$ $b' = b$	$\mathbf{CR}(\rho)$

3.2 Order Relation

The generalized modifiers assume a partial order relation $\trianglelefteq$. First we define what exactly this relation is.

Preliminary notation: If we consider a modifier m_ρ, a the original degree on a scale b and a' the modified degree on the modified scale b' then we denote:

$$a' = m_\rho(a) \text{ and } b' = m_\rho(b)$$

Definition 2 *Let $m_{\rho,1}$ and $m_{\rho,2}$ be two modifiers. $Prop(m_{\rho,1}) = \dfrac{m_{\rho,1}(a)}{m_{\rho,1}(b) - 1}$ is comparable with $Prop(m_{\rho,2}) = \dfrac{m_{\rho,2}(a)}{m_{\rho,2}(b) - 1}$ if and only if*

$$\begin{cases} Prop(m_{\rho,1}) \leq Prop(m_{\rho,2}) \text{ for any given } a \text{ and } b \\ or \\ Prop(m_{\rho,2}) \leq Prop(m_{\rho,1}) \text{ for any given } a \text{ and } b \end{cases}$$

Definition 3 *Two modifiers $m_{\rho,1}$ and $m_{\rho,2}$ entail an order relation if and only if $Prop(m_{\rho,1})$ is comparable with $Prop(m_{\rho,2})$, for any given a and b. Formally, the relation $\trianglelefteq$ is defined as follows:*

$$m_{\rho,1} \trianglelefteq m_{\rho,2} \Leftrightarrow Prop(m_{\rho,1}) \leq Prop(m_{\rho,2}) \quad \text{for any given } a \text{ and } b$$

Let us note that if a pair of modifiers $(m_{\rho,1}, m_{\rho,2})$ are in relation to each other, the comparison between their intensity rates is possible obviously because these intensity rates are rational numbers but particularly because the unit is the same, for all a and b. Indeed, the degrees are uniformly distributed on the scales. Furthermore, it is easy to see that the binary relation $\lhd$ over the generalized modifiers is a partial order relation as the relation $\leq$.

If we compare the generalized modifiers in pairs, we establish a partial order relation between them that we express through a lattice (cf. figure 3). The relation is only partial because some modifiers can not be compared with some others.

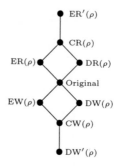

Fig. 3. Lattice for the relation $\lhd$.

3.3 Finite and Infinite Modifiers

Moreover, we can notice that some modifiers can modify the initial value towards infinity. That is the case of two modifiers: $DW(\rho)$ and $DR(\rho)$.

Definition 4 *We define an infinite modifier m_ρ as follows:*

$$m_\rho \text{ is an infinite modifier} \Leftrightarrow \begin{cases} (\forall \rho \in \mathbb{N}^*, \; Prop(m_{\rho+1}) > Prop(m_\rho)) \\ or \\ (\forall \rho \in \mathbb{N}^*, \; Prop(m_{\rho+1}) < Prop(m_\rho)) \end{cases}$$

This means that the modifier will always have an effect on the initial value.

Definition 5 *We define a finite modifier m_ρ as follows:*

$$m_\rho \text{ is a finite modifier} \Leftrightarrow \begin{cases} \exists \rho \in \mathbb{N}^* \text{ such as } \forall \rho' \in \mathbb{N}^* \text{ with } \rho' > \rho \\ Prop(m_{\rho'}) = Prop(m_\rho) \end{cases}$$

This means that, starting from a certain rank, the modifier has no effect on the initial value.

3.4   The Modifiers as an Interval Scale

Our modifiers correspond to one measure scale: the interval one. Indeed, we work on scales with an order relation (the degrees are ordered) and, as it is said in the definition, there is a condition about the degrees' distribution: they are uniformly distributed on the scale.

4   Application

An interesting implementation of our generalized modifiers lies in colorimetrics. We propose a piece of software that is dedicated to colour modification according to colorimetric qualifiers (like "dark", "bright", "bluish"...) and linguistic terms for the modification (as "much more", "a little bit less"...). For example, the user can ask for a red "a little bit more bluish".

4.1   Context

To modify a colour, we modify its colorimetric components expressed in a certain space (either RGB-space for Red-Green-Blue, or HLS-space for Hue-Lightness-Saturation...). The space we have chosen is HLS for many reasons explained in [10]. We increase or decrease the components thanks to our generalized modifiers. We establish a link between the linguistic terms and the symbolic generalized modifiers.

A colour is associated to three symbolic scales, one scale for each colorimetric component. For example, to display on the user's screen a "brighter" green, we can use the modifier $CR(\rho)$ with ρ equal a certain value (depending on the total number of linguistic terms) that increases the value of L (Lightness). The three components H, L and S can be modified at the same time or not, depending on the selected qualifier. Indeed, some qualifiers (like "gloomy", for example) require a modification of only one component, while some others (like "bluish", for example) require modifications of more than one component.

To simplify the modification, we split the range of a component (i.e. [0,255]) into three equal parts, and we split the parts into a certain number of sub-parts — this number depending on the quantity of linguistic terms we have, since each sub-part is associated to a linguistic term. The figure 4 shows a very simple example of qualifiers associated to the component L.

A deeper study of this process is explained in [11] and a comparison between this symbolic approach with a fuzzy one is done in [12].

4.2   Which Modifiers for What Modification?

We can use all kinds of our generalized modifiers in this application. But, it is preferable not to use the infinite ones because the very principle of these modifiers — for example $DR(\rho)$ that reinforces — is never to reach the top of the scale, i.e $b - 1$. It means that, knowing that a component takes its values

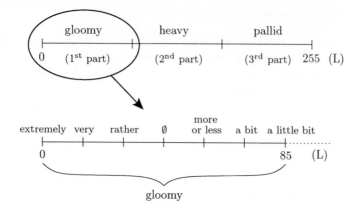

Fig. 4. Qualifiers associated to parts of L space.

between 0 and 255, 255 will never be reached. In fact, with the approximation of the calculus, it will probably be reached, but, theoretically, we don't want to use these modifiers since we do want to reach the maximum.

So, the modifiers we use are the finite ones and, depending on where the initial value of the component is, we use the most powerful modifiers or the less powerful ones.

- In the cases where the initial value of the colorimetric component has to be set to the first or the third part (for example if the user has asked for a *gloomier* or a *more pallid* colour), we use the most powerful modifiers, i.e. ER'(ρ) and/or CR(ρ) and DW'(ρ) and/or CW(ρ),
- In the cases where the initial value of the colorimetric component has to be set to the second part (for example if the user has asked for a *heavier* colour), we use the less powerful modifiers, i.e. ER(ρ) and EW(ρ). The figure 5 shows both cases.

The reason of these choices is simple: the biggest distance between an initial value and the "2nd part" is twice as short as the biggest distance between an initial value and the "1st part" (or the "3rd part"). So, a slow approach when the initial value is close to the value to be reached has been favored. It is a way to compensate the differences between distances.

4.3   Learning for an Adaptive Alteration

As the perception of colours is very subjective, we have added to our software a learning process. Indeed, a "very much more pallid red" for one person can be interpreted as a "little bit more pallid red" or even as a "much heavier red" for another person. That is why it is possible to change the association between the colours modifications (through the generalized symbolic modifiers) and the

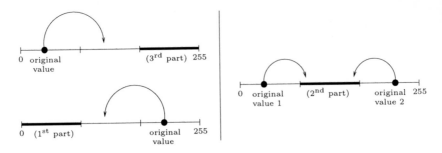

Fig. 5. Left, case of "big jumps" performed by the most powerful generalized modifiers and right, case of "small jumps" performed by the less powerful ones.

linguistic terms. In our application, a linguistic term corresponds to both a qualifier ("pallid", ...) and a linguistic quantifier ("much more", ...). A particular association will reflect the perception of a particular user. This process is carried out thanks to an internal representation of the modifications through a graph. More explanations about that will be given in a further work.

Besides this learning process, one interesting thing is that this process of modification can be done in both directions. Indeed, the user can ask for a certain colour through a linguistic expression and he obtains it, but, on the contrary, from a colour, the software can give a linguistic expression composed of a qualifier and a modifier.

Furthermore, this application could be inserted in another one that would classify pictures by predominant colour, for example.

5   Conclusion

We have presented new symbolic modifiers: the *generalized symbolic modifiers*, coming from the linguistic symbolic modifiers introduced by Akdag & al [5]. We have seen that they embody some good mathematical properties and we notably use them in a colorimetric application.

Moreover, we believe that the modification process can be seen as an aggregation process. Indeed, for us, to modify is equivalent to aggregating an initial value with an expression of the modification. In the colours application, this can be summed up as shown on the figure 6.

The symbol "+" on the figure symbolizes the aggregation process.

The modifiers which have been introduced in this paper can help a lot in an aggregation process. An interesting perspective would be to pursue our research in this domain and imagine an aggregator defined as a composition (in the mathematical sense) of our modifiers.

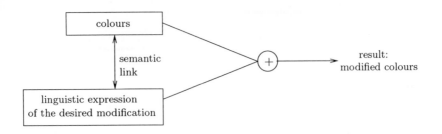

Fig. 6. Link between aggregation and modification.

References

1. L. A. Zadeh, A Fuzzy-Set-Theoretic Interpretation of Linguistic Hedges, Journal of Cybernetics, **2(3)** (1972) 4–34.
2. F. Eshragh and E. H. Mamdami, A general approach to linguistic approximation, International Journal of Man-Machine Studies **11(4)** (1979) 501–519.
3. B. Bouchon–Meunier, Fuzzy logic and knowledge representation using linguistic modifiers, LAFORIA 92/09, Université de Paris VI, Paris (1992).
4. S. Desprès, Un apport à la conception de systèmes à base de connaissances: Les opérations de déduction floues, Université de Paris VI (1988).
5. H. Akdag, N. Mellouli and A. Borgi, A symbolic approach of linguistic modifiers, Information Processing and Management of Uncertainty in Knowledge-Based Systems, Madrid (2000) 1713–1719.
6. L. A. Zadeh, The concept of a linguistic variable and its application to approximate reasoning, Information Science, **8 & 9** (1975).
7. H. Akdag, I. Truck, A. Borgi and N. Mellouli, Linguistic modifiers in a symbolic framework, International Journal of Uncertainty, Fuzziness and Knowledge-Based Systems, Special Issue: Computing with words: foundations and applications **9** (2001) 49–62.
8. G. Baillargeon, Statistique avec applications en informatique, gestion et production, SMG (2000).
9. M. Grabisch, Evaluation subjective, Méthodes, Applications et Enjeux, chap. IV, ECRIN (1997) 137–156.
10. I. Truck, H. Akdag and A. Borgi, Using Fuzzy Modifiers in Colorimetry, SCI 2001, 5th World Multiconference on Systemics, Cybernetics and Informatics, Orlando, Florida, **16** (2001) 472–477.
11. I. Truck, H. Akdag and A. Borgi, A symbolic approach for colorimetric alterations, EUSFLAT 2001, 2nd International Conference in Fuzzy Logic and Technology, Leicester, England (2001) 105–108.
12. I. Truck, H. Akdag and A. Borgi, Colorimetric Alterations by way of Linguistic Modifiers: A Fuzzy Approach vs. A Symbolic Approach, FLA/ICSC-NAISO, Bangor, England (2001) 702–708.

A Conceptual Graph and RDF(S) Approach for Representing and Querying Document Content

R. Carolina Medina Ramírez, Olivier Corby, and Rose Dieng-Kuntz

Acacia project, INRIA Sophia Antipolis, 2004, route des lucioles
06902 Sophia Antipolis CEDEX, France
{cmedina, corby, dieng}@sophia.inria.fr

Abstract. This article describes a first synthesis of a Conceptual Graph and RDF(S) approach for representing and querying document contents. The framework of this work is the ESCRIRE project [1], the main goal of which is to compare three knowledge representation formalisms (KR): conceptual graphs (CG), descriptions logics (DL), and object-oriented representation languages (OOR) for querying about document contents by relying on ontology-based annotations on document content. This comparison relies on an expressive XML-based pivot language to define the ontology and to represent annotations and queries; it consists of evaluating the capacity of the three KR formalisms for expressing the features of the pivot language. Each feature of the pivot language is translated into each KR formalism, which is than used to draw inferences and to answer queries. Our team was responsible on the CG part. The motivation of this paper is to give a first synthesis of the translation process from the pivot language to RDF(S) and CG, to underline the main problems encountered during this translation.

Keywords: Knowledge representation, Conceptual Graphs, Ontologies, RDFS, XML, and Semantic information retrieval.

1   Introduction

Documents available from the Web or from any digital representation constitute a significant source of knowledge to be represented, handled and queried. The main goal of the ESCRIRE project is to compare three knowledge representation (KR) formalisms in the task of annotating and querying document (by using a specific domain ontology). The test base consist of abstracts of biological articles from the Medline database [2]. This annotated base is queried by each KR formalisms (CG, DL, OOR). A pivot language based on XML syntax was specially defined for the comparison. This pivot language is represented by a DTD containing the syntactic rules to describe an ontology and annotations and to query these annotations using an OQL-based format. Besides, the XML and RDF languages are recommended respectively by the World Wide Web consortium to

F.J. Garijo, J.C. Riquelme, and M. Toro (Eds.): IBERAMIA 2002, LNAI 2527, pp. 121–130, 2002.

structure information and to describe any resource on the Web. In [3,4] the impact of using conceptual graphs for indexing and searching information has been studied and analyzed. CG seems to be a good candidate to represent the content of documents. In the following, we would like to stress on the use of conceptual graphs (as an inference mechanism) and on RDF(S) [5,6] language (as an intermediate syntax to represent ontologies and annotations) in the ESCRIRE project. In our experiments we used CORESE, a semantic search engine [7].

The remaining of this paper is structured as follows.In Section 2, we describe briefly the ESCRIRE language. Section 3 presents the translation process from the pivot language to RDF(S) and CGs. In Section 4 we discuss some difficulties encountered during this translation. Section 5 concludes our work.

2   Escrire Language

As explained in the introduction, a *pivot* language was defined (1) to represent a domain ontology, to annotate document contents and to query this base of annotations and (2) to be used as a bridge between the documents constituting the test base and each KR formalism involved in the ESCRIRE project. We recall the main features of this language detailed in [1].

2.1   Description of Domain Ontology

Basically, an ontology is a hierarchy of concepts and relations between these concepts representing a particular application domain. For the ESCRIRE project, a genetic ontology (genes and interactions between these genes) was built and represented by a DTD by one of our colleagues [8]. This DTD defines classes, relation classes, and a subsumption relation organizes these classes into a hierarchy. A class is described by a set of attributes (roles and attributes for the relation classes) the type of which is a class belonging to the ontology (a concrete type, such as integer, string, or Boolean for relation classes attributes). Inside an ontology, a class can be *defined* (i.e. the attribute of the classes are necessary and sufficient conditions for the membership of an individual to this class) or *primitive* (i.e. the attributes of classes are considered as only necessary conditions). For example, the following code represents a relation called *substage*, composed by two roles: SUPERSTAGE and SUBSTAGE the type of which is DEVELOPMENT-STAGE (another class in the ontology). This relation does not have any attribute and it is qualified by properties of transitivity, reflexivity, and antisymmetry.

```
<esc:descbinrel name="substage" transitive="yes" reflexive="yes"
                          antisymmetric="yes">
  <esc:defrole name="superstage">
    <esc:classref name="development-stage"/>
  </esc:defrole>
  <esc:defrole name="substage">
    <esc:classref name="development-stage"/>
  </esc:defrole>
</esc:descbinrel>
```

2.2   Description of Annotations

To each document D_i that belongs to a base of documents corresponds a semantic annotation $Annota_i$ representing the content of D_i. The set of annotations
$Annota_1$, ..., $Annota_n$ is represented in the pivot language and uses the conceptual vocabulary specified into the domain ontology, which is also defined in
the pivot language. In the ESCRIRE project, an annotation describes *genes* (objects) and *interactions* between genes (relations). The objects are described by
attributes (name, class to which they belong to) and the relations are described
by *roles* (domain and range) and attributes (to represent the relation characteristics). For example, the annotation given below describes an interaction between
a *promoter gene* called *dpp* (with dorso-ventral-system type) and a *target gene*,
called *Ubx* (with BX-C type). The effect of the interaction is that the *dpp* gene
inhibits the *Ubx* gene.

```
<esc:relation type="interaction">
   <esc:role name="promoter">
      <esc:objref type="dorso-ventral-system" id="dpp"/>
   </esc:role>
   <esc:role name="target">
      <esc:objref type="BX-C" id="Ubx"/>
   </esc:role>
   <esc:attribute name="effect">
      <esc:value>inhibition</esc:value>
   </esc:attribute>
</esc:relation>
```

2.3   Queries

An ESCRIRE query is similar to an OQL [9] query, and is based on the block
SELECT (values to be shown in the result), FROM (variables typed by a class),
WHERE (constraints to be considered), and ORDERBY (the result order specified
by a list of paths). Logical operators (conjunction, disjunction, and negation) as
well as quantifiers (universal and existential) can be used. For example, the
query given below represents a query to find documents mentioning interactions
between the *Ubx* (ultrabithorax) gene acting as target and, as promoter, the
en (engrailed) gene or the *dpp* (decapentaplegic) gene. The criterion to order
answers is the promoter name.

```
SELECT  I.promoter.name, I.effect
FROM    I:interaction
WHERE   (I.target=OBJREF(gene,'Ubx') AND
        ( I.promoter=OBJREF(gene,'en') OR
          I.promoter=OBJREF(gene,'dpp')) )
ORDERBY   I.promoter.name
```

3   Translation Process: Pivot Language-RDF(S)-CG

In this section, we detail the process of translating ontologies and annotations from pivot language to RDF(S) and conceptual graphs. This double translation has two motivations: (1) RDF(S) and pivot language are languages based on XML, and (2) we used CORESE, a semantic search engine based on CG as its inference mechanism and ontology-based annotations represented in RDF(S). Our translation methodology is based on two mappings: (1) *pivot language* → *RDF(S)* - to map from the ESCRIRE ontology and annotations to RDF Schema and RDF statements - and (2) *RDF(S)* → *CG* - to map from an RDF Schema and RDF statements to the CG support and assertional conceptual graphs. A depth comparison and correspondance between CG and RDF(S) models are studied in [10].

To improve clarity, we give a brief overview of the CG model. A conceptual graph [11,12] is an oriented graph that consists of concept nodes and relations nodes describing relations between this concepts. A concept has a *type* (which corresponds to a semantic class) and a *marker* (which corresponds to an instantiation to an individual class). A marker is either the generic marker $*$ corresponding to the existential quantification or an individual marker corresponding to an identifier; M is the individual markers set.

A relation has only a *type*. Concept types and relation types (of same arity) are organized into hierarchies T_C and T_R respectively. This hierarchies are partially ordered by generalization/specialization relation $\geq$ (resp. $\leq$).

A CG support upon which conceptual graphs are constructed is defined as (T_C, T_R, M). The projection operator permits to compare two conceptual graphs, it enables to determine the generalization relation ($\leq$) between two graphs: $G_1 \leq G_2$ iff there exists a projection π from G_2 to G_1. π is a graph morphism such that the label of a node n_1 of G_1 is a specialization of the label of the node n_2 of G_2 with $n_1 = \pi(n_2)$.

In particular, an RDF Schema (the class hierarchy and property hierarchy) corresponds to a CG support (T_C and T_R respectively) and the RDF statements correspond to assertional conceptual graphs in CG.

3.1   Classes and Relations

Since the pivot language and RDF(S) share an XML syntax, we have implemented the mapping *pivot language* → *RDF(S)* as an XSLT style sheet. ESCRIRE ontology is translated into RDF Schema.

To finish the cycle, the mapping *RDF(S)* → *CG* is carried out by CORESE: RDF statements and RDF Schema are translated respectively into assertional conceptual graphs and into CG support.

The definition and description of *classes* and *relation classes* are represented by RDFS classes (rdfs:Class) and in conceptual graphs like concept types belonging to the T_C hierarchy of the CG support. We reified ESCRIRE *relations* classes because, in CG and RDF(S) models the qualified relations (relations with roles and attributes) are not considered i.e., they are translated into RDFS classes

(Concept types in T_C). *Roles* and *attributes* of ESCRIRE relations are translated into RDF properties (rdf:Property); these properties correspond to relation types in T_R. CORESE can handle relation properties like transitivity, reflexivity, symmetry and inverse property. Currently, the antisymmetric property is not handled in CORESE, we are planning to implement it in a future version of CORESE. The binary relations supported by CORESE do not have roles or attributes. We adapted these algorithms for processing ESCRIRE relations (which contain *roles* and *attributes*). The following example shows the CORESE representation of the *substage* relation declare in Section 2.1.

```
<rdfs:Class rdf:ID="substage">
        <cos:reflexive>true</cos:reflexive>
        <cos:transitive>true</cos:transitive>
</rdfs:Class>

<rdf:Property ID="superstage">
        <rdfs:domain rdf:resource="#substage"/>
        <rdfs:range rdf:resource="#development-stage"/>
</rdf:Property>

<rdf:Property ID="substage">
        <rdfs:domain rdf:resource="#substage"/>
        <rdfs:range rdf:resource="#development-stage"/>
</rdf:Property>

<rdfs:Class rdf:ID="development-stage"/>
```

3.2   Objects and Relations

Objects and relations exist inside annotations and in the ontology. The global object features inside the ontology are always true for all the annotations. We consider as global objects: *objects* and *relations* both of them existing in the ontology and referred in the annotations. These global objects represent common and reusable knowledge for annotations, avoiding redundant information. Figure 1, shows two annotations sharing *antenapedia* gene information, located into the global object base.

Objects and relations existing in annotations (ESCRIRE annotations) are represented as RDF statements corresponding to assertional conceptual graphs. The same translation process is applied to global objects.

A document is represented by an *individual concept*, for example the concept [Document : URL-94008526], is an individual concept with *type field* Document belonging to T_C and *marker field* URL-94008526 belonging to M and representing the URL and document name. The *interaction* relation shown in section 2.2 is represented in RDF and CG in the following way:

Written with RDF syntax:

```
<ns:Interaction>
  <ns:promoter>
     <ns:dorso-ventral-system rdf:about="#dpp"/>
  </ns:promoter>
  <ns:target>
     <ns:BX-C rdf:about="#Ubx"/>
  </ns:target>
  <ns:effect>inhibition</ns:effect>
</ns:interaction>
```

This can be interpreted in CG as:

```
[Interaction : *]->(promoter)->[dorso-ventral-system : dpp]
                ->(target)->[BX-C : Ubx]
                ->(effect)->[literal : inhibition]
```

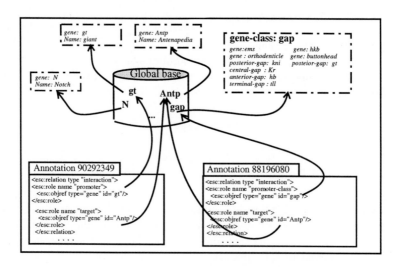

Fig. 1. Annotations sharing global object informations.

3.3   Evaluating Queries

Given a document collection, we have an ESCRIRE annnotation that indexes each document (representing its content). These annotations are translated in RDF statements and into assertional conceptual graphs (annotation graphs), constituting an annotation graph base (AG_{Base}). An ESCRIRE query is translated as a query conceptual graph Q and processed by a CG projection of the query Q on the

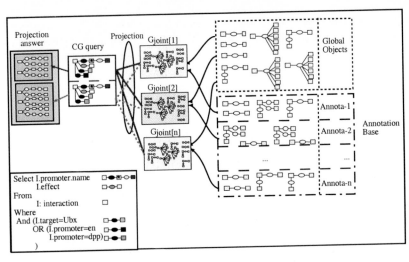

Fig. 2. Query Evaluation using joint graphs.

annotation graph base. The projection operator recovers relevant graphs. Figure 2 shows the process carried out to satisfy a query Q considering the global objects. Equation (1) represents the result set retrieved by projection of the query Q on the conceptual joint graph (G_{joint}). This joint graph is composed of the global graph (representing the global objects) and each annotation graph staying into AG_{Base}. The annotation graph base size is denoted by N.

$$Result = \{\pi\,(Q,\,G_{joint[i]})\mid$$
$$G_{joint[i]} = G_{global\ objects} \cup AG_{Base[i]}\},i \in [1,N] \qquad (1)$$

To compose the joint graph, we select only the relevant arcs of the global graph and the annotation graph. The ϕ operator [11] assigns a first-order formula $\phi(G)$ to each graph G. $\phi(G)$ is a positive, conjunctive and existentially closed formula; therefore, the fact of having the logical disjunction or, implies a special processing because disjunction is not considered in the conceptual graphs formalism (traditional projection). We have implemented the or operator as follows. A query Q is a unique graph if there is not an or operator, otherwise Q is split into several graphs such that, each of those do not contain or operators to be projected on the AG_{Base}. The result corresponding to the query Q is composed of the values selected in the query Q (select part) and by URL of documents [8]. This result is presented to the user by an XSLT style sheet.

4   Discussion: Translation Problems

In this section we would like to stress on problems faced during the translation from the pivot language to RDF(S) and CG.

Defined classes. The distinction between *defined classes* and *primitive classes* exists in CG but it does not exist in RDF(S). An extension of RDF(S) in order to handle *defined classes* and the *primitive classes* remaining of interest in this case. In CORESE, the translation in CG of the pivot language rests on RDF(S), however none of the mappings *pivot language* → *RDF(S)* or *RDF(S)* → *CG* considers it.

Evaluating relation properties. Binary relations are represented as classes and the properties of transitivity, symmetry, reflexivity and inverse property are processed by a specific code in CORESE. Once again, the RDF(S) model could be extended to support the representation of such kind of properties [13]. In CORESE, several extensions of RDF(S) model have been added for enabling to process this kind of meta-properties and enrich the annotation base. A in-depth description and manipulation of meta-properties are studied in [7].

Handling negation queries. Conceptual graphs correspond to an existential, conjunctive and positive logic, thus the negation is not considered in the formalism of simple conceptual graphs. In some models of conceptual graphs one can put a negation ($\neg$) in some contexts [14]. RDF(S) statements are positive and conjunctive, so handling the negation implies yet another type of extension. In the Notio CG platform [15] on which CORESE was developed, the NOT did not exist. We have implemented particular algorithms to process the negation of each ESCRIRE element. Our main algorithm is the following:
Let be Q= $\neg(G_1 \wedge (G_2 \vee G_3))$, where G_1, G_2, G_3 are conceptual graphs. We have to build :

1. A CG query Q' as the normalization of the query Q by the application of Morgan's rules.
2. A positive CG query Q" (without negation graphs) by replacing negative operators (NOT (A=B)) in each G_i by positive ones (A != B). In this way, only positive graphs are ready to be sent to projection. If there is an or operator in Q' we split Q" such as shown in table 1.
3. The result set (R), as the the projection of each graph in Q" on the annotation graph base (AG_{Base}).
4. Validation of R.

The validation process consists of applying the algorithms which process the operator negations (for exemple NOT (A=B)) into the result set R by recalling the original negation criterions.

Evaluating quantifiers. The variables in a query FROM clause are existentially quantified. However, the variables in a WHERE clause can be quantified. In CG, since the logical interpretation of a graph **G** is a first order logical formula $\phi(G)$, positive and existentially quantified, the existential quantifier can be taken into account. Nevertheless, it is not obvious to handle a universal quantification. A

Table 1. Evaluating negative disjunctive queries.

$Q = \neg(G_1 \wedge (G_2 \vee G_3))$	Original Query
$Q' = \neg G_1 \vee (\neg G_2 \wedge \neg G_3)$	Normalization
$Q'' = G'_1 \vee (G'_2 \wedge G'_3)$ where G'_1, G'_2, G'_3 are positive conceptual graphs $G_4 = (G'_2 \wedge G'_3)$	Positive Query
$R_1 = \pi\ (G'_1, AG_{Base})$ $R_2 = \pi\ (G_4, AG_{Base})$	Projection
$R = R_1 \cup R_2$	Validation

way to support it could be to transform a universally quantified formula into the negation of an existentially quantified formula, but this would require a complex extension of the projection operator.

5   Conclusion

In this paper, we have described a pivot language to represent a domain ontology, annotate document contents and to query this base of annotations. Some expressiveness problems encountered during the mappings: (1)*pivot language → RDF(S)* and (2) *RDF(S) → CG* have been discussed. These problems underline the need of expressiveness extensions for RDF(S), in order to support defined classes, relation properties, negation and quantifiers. We also described a technique to treat negative disjunctive queries. For this first experiment, a hundred of 4500 abstracts of biological articles extracted from NIH Medline public database have been considered. We have applied a representative query set to validate all aspects of pivot language. Our future efforts are focused on the analysis of semantic expressiveness extension works for RDF(S) [13] and XML [16], to complete our solution. Finally, in order to extend the ontology we are using the inference mechanism provided by CORESE to build a rule base for retrieving hidden knowledge from annotations in order to be exploited afterwards by query evaluations.

References

1. Rim Al-Hulou, Olivier Corby, Rose Dieng-Kuntz, Jérôme Euzenat, Carolina Medina Ramírez, Amedeo Napoli, and Raphaël Troncy. Three knowledge representation formalisms for content-based manipulation of documents. In *Proc. KR 2002 workshop on Formal Ontology, Knowledge Representation and Intelligent Systems for the World Wide Web (SemWeb), Toulouse, France,* 2002.
2. Medline database. http://www.ncbi.nlm.nih.gov/PubMed.
3. Philippe Martin and Peter Eklund. Knowledge Retrieval and the World Wide Web. *IEEE Intelligent Systems,* 15(3):18–25, 2000.

4. Iadh Ounis and Marius Pasca. RELIEF: Combining Expressiveness and Rapidity into a Single System. In *In Proc. of the 21st annual international ACM SIGIR conference on Research and development in information retrieval (SIGIR'98), Melbourne, Australia*, 1998.

5. Resource Description Framework Model and Syntax Specification. W3C Recommendation, 1999.

6. Resource Description Framework Schema Specification. W3C Candidate Recommendation, 2000.

7. Olivier Corby and Catherine Faron. Corese : A corporate semantic web engine. In *Proc. WWW2002 workshop on Real world RDF and semantic web applications, Hawaii*, 2002.

8. Embedded Structured Content Representation In REpositories: Escrire DTD. http://escrire.inrialpes.fr/dtd/.

9. Roderic G. G. Cattell. The Object Database Standard: ODMG-93. Morgan Kauffman, San Francisco, California, 1994.

10. Olivier Corby, Rose Dieng, and Cédric Hebert. A conceptual graph model for W3C Resource Description Framework. In Bernhard. Ganter and Guy W. Mineau(eds.), editors, *In Proc. of the 8th International Conference on Conceptual Structures (ICCS'00), Darmstadt, Germany*, volume 1867 of *LNAI*. Springer-Verlag, 2000.

11. John F. Sowa. *Conceptual structures: Information Processing in Mind and Machine*. Addison-Wesley, 1984.

12. John F. Sowa. Conceptual Graphs: DpANS. http://concept.cs.uah.edu/CG/Standard.html, 1999.

13. Alexandre Delteil, Catherine Faron-Zuker, and Rose Dieng-Kuntz. Extension of RDF(S) based on the Conceptual Graph Model. In G.Stumme H.S. Delugach, editor, *Proc. of 9th International Conference on Conceptual Structures (ICCS'01)*, volume 2120 of *LNAI*. Springer-Verlag Berlin Heidelberg, 2001.

14. John F. Sowa. Conceptual Graphs summary. In Timothy E. Nagle, Janice A. Nagle, Laurie L. Gerholz, and Peter W. Eklund, editors, *Conceptual Structures: current research and practice*, pages 3–51. Ellis Horwood, 1992.

15. F. Southey and J. G. Linders. Notio - A Java API for developing CG tools. In William M Tepfenhart and Walling Cyre (eds.), editors, *Proc. of 7th International Conference on Conceptual Structures (ICCS'99)*, volume 1640 of *LNAI*. Springer-Verlag, 1999.

16. W3C Publishes Web Ontology Language Requirements Document. http://xml.coverpages.org/ni2002-03-08-d.html.

Automatic Optimization of Multi-paradigm Declarative Programs*

Ginés Moreno

Dep. Informática, UCLM, 02071 Albacete, Spain.
gmoreno@info-ab.uclm.es

Abstract. This paper investigates the optimization by fold/unfold of functional-logic programs with operational semantics based on needed narrowing. Transformation sequences are automatically guided by tupling, a powerful strategy that avoids multiple accesses to data structures and redundant sub-computations. We systematically decompose in detail the internal structure of tupling in three low-level transformation phases (definition introduction, unfolding and abstraction with folding) that constitute the core of our automatic tupling algorithm. The resulting strategy is (strongly) correct and complete, efficient, elegant and realistic. In addition (and most important), our technique preserves the natural structure of multi-paradigm declarative programs, which contrasts with prior pure functional approaches that produce corrupt integrated programs with (forbidden) overlapping rules.

1 Introduction

Functional logic programming languages combine the operational methods and advantages of the most important declarative programming paradigms, namely functional and logic programming. The operational principle of such languages is usually based on *narrowing*. A *narrowing step* instantiates variables in an expression and applies a reduction step to a redex of the instantiated expression. Needed narrowing is the currently best narrowing strategy for first-order (inductively sequential) functional logic programs due to its optimality properties w.r.t. the length of derivations and the number of computed solutions [6], and it can be efficiently implemented by pattern matching and unification.

The fold/unfold transformation approach was first introduced in [10] to optimize functional programs and then used for logic programs [21]. This approach is commonly based on the construction, by means of a *strategy*, of a sequence of equivalent programs each obtained from the preceding ones by using an *elementary* transformation rule. The essential rules are *folding* and *unfolding*, i.e., contraction and expansion of subexpressions of a program using the definitions of this program (or of a preceding one). See [19,15] for more applications of these

---

* This work has been partially supported by CICYT under grant TIC 2001-2705-C03-03 and by Acción Integrada Hispano-Italiana HI2000-0161, and the Valencian Research Council under grant GV01-424.

F.J. Garijo, J.C. Riquelme, and M. Toro (Eds.): IBERAMIA 2002, LNAI 2527, pp. 131–140, 2002.

rules. Other rules which have been considered are, for example: instantiation, definition introduction/elimination, and abstraction. The first attempt to introduce these ideas in an integrated language is presented in [3], where we investigated fold/unfold rules in the context of a strict (*call-by-value*) functional logic language. A transformation methodology for lazy (*call-by-name*) functional logic programs was introduced in [4]; this work extends the transformation rules of [21] for logic programs in order to cope with lazy functional logic programs (based on needed narrowing). The use of narrowing empowers the fold/unfold system by implicitly embedding the instantiation rule (the operation of the Burstall and Darlington framework [10] which introduces an instance of an existing equation) into unfolding by means of unification. [4] also proves that the original structure of programs is preserved through the transformation sequence, which is a key point for proving the correctness and the effective applicability of the transformation system. These ideas have been implemented in the prototype SYNTH ([2]) which has been successfully tested with several applications in the field of Artificial Intelligence ([1,17]).

There exists a large class of program optimizations which can be achieved by fold/unfold transformations and are not possible by using a fully automatic method (such as, e.g., partial evaluation). Typical instances of this class are the strategies that perform *tupling* (also known as *pairing*) [10,13], which merges separate (nonnested) function calls with some common arguments (i.e., they share the same variables) into a single call to a (possibly new) recursive function which returns a tuple of the results of the separate calls, thus avoiding either multiple accesses to the same data structures or common subcomputations, similarly to the idea of *sharing* which is used in graph rewriting to improve the efficiency of computations in time and space [7]. In this paper, we propose a fully automatic tupling algorithm where eureka generation is done simultaneously at transformation time at a very low cost. In contrast with prior non-automatic approaches (tupling has only been semi-automated to some extent [11,12]) where eurekas are generated by a complicate pre-process that uses complex data structures and/or produces redundant computations, our approach is fully automatic and covers most practical cases. Our method deals with particular (non trivial) features of integrated (functional-logic) languages and includes refined tests for termination of each transformation phase. More exactly, we have identified three syntactic conditions to stop the search for regularities during the unfolding phase[1].

The structure of the paper is as follows. After recalling some basic definitions, we introduce the basic transformation rules and illustrate its use by means of interesting tupling examples in Section 2. The next three sections describe the different transformation phases that constitute the core of our tupling algorithm. Finally, Section 6 concludes. More details can be found in [16].

Preliminaries. We assume familiarity with basic notions from term rewriting [7] and functional logic programming [14]. In this work we consider a (*many-sorted*) *signature* Σ partitioned into a set $\mathcal{C}$ of *constructors* and a set $\mathcal{F}$ of

---

[1] The method is not universal but, as said in [19], "one cannot hope to construct a universal technique for finding a suitable regularity whenever there is one".

defined functions. The set of *constructor terms* with *variables* is obtained by using symbols from $\mathcal{C}$ and $\mathcal{X}$. The set of variables occurring in a term t is denoted by $Var(t)$. We write $\overline{o_n}$ for the *list* of objects $o_1, \ldots, o_n$. A *pattern* is a term of the form $f(\overline{d_n})$ where $f/n \in \mathcal{F}$ and $d_1, \ldots, d_n$ are constructor terms. A term is *linear* if it does not contain multiple occurrences of one variable. A term is *operation-rooted* (*constructor-rooted*) if it has an operation (constructor) symbol at the root. A *position* p in a term t is represented by a sequence of natural numbers. Positions are ordered by the *prefix* ordering: $p \leq q$, if $\exists w$ such that $p.w = q$. Positions p, q are *disjoint* if neither $p \leq q$ nor $q \leq p$. Given a term t, we let $\mathcal{FP}os(t)$ denote the set of non-variable positions of t. $t|_p$ denotes the *subterm* of t at position p, and $t[s]_p$ denotes the result of *replacing the subterm* $t|_p$ by the term s. For a sequence of (pairwise disjoint) positions $P = \overline{p_n}$, we let $t[\overline{s_n}]_P = (((t[s_1]_{p_1})[s_2]_{p_2}) \ldots [s_n]_{p_n})$. By abuse, we denote $t[\overline{s_n}]_P$ by $t[s]_P$ when $s_1 = \ldots = s_n = s$, as well as $((t[s_1]_{P_1}) \ldots [s_n]_{P_n})$ by $t[\overline{s_n}]_{\overline{P_n}}$. We denote by $\{x_1 \mapsto t_1, \ldots, x_n \mapsto t_n\}$ the *substitution* σ with $\sigma(x_i) = t_i$ for $i = 1, \ldots, n$ (with $x_i \neq x_j$ if $i \neq j$), and $\sigma(x) = x$ for all other variables x. id denotes the identity substitution.

A set of rewrite rules $l \to r$ such that $l \notin \mathcal{X}$, and $Var(r) \subseteq Var(l)$ is called a *term rewriting system* (TRS). The terms l and r are called the *left-hand side* (lhs) and the *right-hand side* (rhs) of the rule, respectively. A TRS $\mathcal{R}$ is left-linear if l is linear for all $l \to r \in \mathcal{R}$. A TRS is constructor–based (CB) if each left-hand side is a pattern. In the remainder of this paper, a functional logic *program* is a left-linear CB-TRS. A *rewrite step* is an application of a rewrite rule to a term, i.e., $t \to_{p,R} s$ if there exists a position p in t, a rewrite rule $R = (l \to r)$ and a substitution σ with $t|_p = \sigma(l)$ and $s = t[\sigma(r)]_p$.

The operational semantics of integrated languages is usually based on *narrowing*, a combination of variable instantiation and reduction. Formally, $s \rightsquigarrow_{p,R,\sigma} t$ is a *narrowing step* if p is a non-variable position in s and $\sigma(s) \to_{p,R} t$. We denote by $t_0 \rightsquigarrow^*_\sigma t_n$ a sequence of narrowing steps $t_0 \rightsquigarrow_{\sigma_1} \ldots \rightsquigarrow_{\sigma_n} t_n$ with $\sigma = \sigma_n \circ \cdots \circ \sigma_1$ (if $n = 0$ then $\sigma = id$). Modern functional logic languages are based on *needed narrowing* and *inductively sequential* programs.

2   Tupling by Fold/Unfold

Originally introduced in [10,13] for optimizing functional programs, the tupling strategy is very effective when several functions require the computation of the same subexpression. In this case, it is possible to tuple together those functions and to avoid either multiple accesses to data structures or common subcomputations [20]. Firstly, we recall from [4] the basic definitions of the transformation rules. Programs constructed by using the following set of rules are inductively sequential. Moreover, the transformations are strongly correct w.r.t. goals containing (*old*) function symbols from the initial program.

Definition 1. *Let $\mathcal{R}_0$ be an inductively sequential program (the original program). A transformation sequence $(\mathcal{R}_0, \ldots, \mathcal{R}_k)$, $k > 0$ is constructed by applying the following transformation rules:*

Definition Introduction: *We may get program $\mathcal{R}_{k+1}$ by adding to $\mathcal{R}_k$ a new rule ("definition rule" or "eureka") of the form $f(\overline{x}) \to r$, where f is a new function symbol not occurring in the sequence $\mathcal{R}_0, \ldots, \mathcal{R}_k$ and $Var(r) = \overline{x}$.*

Unfolding: *Let $R = (l \to r) \in \mathcal{R}_k$ be a rule where r is an operation-rooted term or $\mathcal{R}_k$ is completely defined. Then, $\mathcal{R}_{k+1} = (\mathcal{R}_k - \{R\}) \cup \{\theta(l) \to r' \mid r \rightsquigarrow_\theta r'$ in $\mathcal{R}_k\}$. An unfolding step where $\theta = id$ is called a normalizing step.*

Folding: *Let $R = (l \to r) \in \mathcal{R}_k$ be a non definition rule, $R' = (l' \to r') \in \mathcal{R}_j$, $0 \le j \le k$, a definition rule[2] and p a position in r such that $r|_p = \theta(r')$ and $r|_p$ is not a constructor term. Then, $\mathcal{R}_{k+1} = (\mathcal{R}_k - \{R\}) \cup \{l \to r[\theta(l')]_p\}$.*

Abstraction: *Let $R = (l \to r) \in \mathcal{R}_k$ be a rule and let $\overline{P_j}$ be sequences of disjoint positions in $\mathcal{FP}os(r)$ such that $r|_p = e_i$ for all p in P_i, $i = 1, \ldots, j$, i.e., $r = r[\overline{e_j}]_{\overline{P_j}}$. We may get program $\mathcal{R}_{k+1}$ from $\mathcal{R}_k$ by replacing R with $l \to r[\overline{z_j}]_{\overline{P_j}}$ where $\langle z_1, \ldots, z_j \rangle = \langle e_1, \ldots, e_j \rangle$ (where $\overline{z_j}$ are fresh variables).*

The following well-known example uses the previous set of transformation rules for optimizing a program following a tupling strategy. The process is similar to [10,11,20] for pure functional programs, with the advantage in our case that we avoid the use of an explicit *instantiation rule* before applying unfolding steps. This is possible thanks to the systematic instantiation of calls performed implicitly by our unfolding rule by virtue of the logic component of narrowing [4].

Example 1. The fibonacci numbers can be computed by the original program $\mathcal{R}_0 = \{R_1 : \texttt{fib(0)} \to \texttt{s(0)}, \ R_2 : \texttt{fib(s(0))} \to \texttt{s(0)}, \ R_3 : \texttt{fib(s(s(X)))} \to \texttt{fib(s(X))} + \texttt{fib(X)}\}$ (together with the rules for addition $+$). Note that this program has an exponential complexity, which can be reduced to linear by applying the tupling strategy as follows:

1. Definition introduction: (R_4) $\texttt{new(X)} \to \langle \texttt{fib(s(X))}, \texttt{fib(X)} \rangle$
2. Unfold rule R_4 (narrowing the needed redex $\texttt{fib(s(X))}$):
   (R_5) $\texttt{new(0)} \to \langle \texttt{s(0)}, \texttt{fib(0)} \rangle$, (R_6) $\texttt{new(s(X))} \to \langle \texttt{fib(s(X))} + \texttt{fib(X)}, \texttt{fib(s(X))} \rangle$
3. Unfold (normalize) rule R_5: (R_7) $\texttt{new(0)} \to \langle \texttt{s(0)}, \texttt{s(0)} \rangle$
4. Abstract R_6: (R_8) $\texttt{new(s(X))} \to \langle Z_1 + Z_2, Z_1 \rangle$ where $\langle Z_1, Z_2 \rangle = \langle \texttt{fib(s(X))}, \texttt{fib(X)} \rangle$
5. Fold R_8 using R_4: (R_9) $\texttt{new(s(X))} \to \langle Z_1 + Z_2, Z_1 \rangle$ where $\langle Z_1, Z_2 \rangle = \texttt{new(X)}$
6. Abstract R_3: (R_{10}) $\texttt{fib(s(s(X)))} \to Z_1 + Z_2$ where $\langle Z_1, Z_2 \rangle = \langle \texttt{fib(s(X))}, \texttt{fib(X)} \rangle$
7. Fold R_{10} with R_4: (R_{11}) $\texttt{fib(s(s(X)))} \to Z_1 + Z_2$ where $\langle Z_1, Z_2 \rangle = \texttt{new(X)}$

Now, the (enhanced) transformed program $\mathcal{R}_7$ (with linear complexity thanks to the use of the recursive function $\texttt{new}$), is composed by rules R_1, R_2, R_7, R_9 and R_{11}.

The classical instantiation rule used in pure functional transformation systems is problematic since it uses most general unifiers of expressions (it is commonly called "minimal instantiation" [11]) and, for that reason, it is rarely considered explicitly in the literature. Moreover, in a functional-logic setting the use of an unfolding rule that (implicitly) performs minimal instantiation may generate corrupt programs that could not be executed by needed narrowing. The reader must note the importance of this fact, since it directly implies that tupling algorithms (that performs minimal instantiation) developed for pure functional programs are not applicable in our framework, as illustrates the following example.

---

[2] A *definition rule* (*eureka*) maintains its status only as long as it remains unchanged, i.e., once it is transformed it is not considered a *definition rule* anymore.

Example 2. Consider a functional-logic program containing the following well-known set of non overlapping rules: $\{\ldots, \texttt{double(0)} \to \texttt{0}, \quad \texttt{double(s(X))} \to \texttt{s(s(double(X)))}, \texttt{leq(0,X)} \to \texttt{true}, \quad \texttt{leq(s(X),0)} \to \texttt{false}, \quad \texttt{leq(s(X),s(Y))} \to \texttt{leq(X,Y)}, \ldots\}$. Assume now that a tupling strategy is started and after some definition introduction and unfolding steps we obtain the following rule: $\texttt{new}(\ldots, \texttt{X}, \texttt{Y}, \ldots) \to \langle \ldots, \underline{\texttt{leq(X,double(Y))}}, \ldots \rangle$. Then, if we apply an unfolding step (over the underlined term) with implicitly performs minimal instantiation before (lazily) reducing it, we obtain:

$$\texttt{new}(\ldots, \texttt{0}, \texttt{Y}, \ldots) \to \langle \ldots, \texttt{true}, \ldots \rangle$$
$$\texttt{new}(\ldots, \texttt{X}, \texttt{0}, \ldots) \to \langle \ldots, \texttt{leq(X,0)}, \ldots \rangle$$
$$\texttt{new}(\ldots, \texttt{X}, \texttt{s(Y)}, \ldots) \to \langle \ldots, \texttt{leq(X,s(s(double(Y))))}, \ldots \rangle$$

And now observe that there exist overlapping rules that loose the program structure. This loss prevents for further computations with needed narrowing. Fortunately (as proved in [4]), our unfolding rule always generates a valid set of program rules by using appropriate (non most general) unifiers before reducing a term. In the example, it suffices with replacing the occurrences of variable X by term s(X) in each rule (as our needed narrowing based unfolding rule does), which is the key point to restore the required structure of the transformed program.

Since tupling has not been automated in general in the specialized literature, our proposal consists of decomposing it in three stages and try to automate each one of them in order to generate a fully automatic tupling algorithm. Each stage may consists of several steps done with the transformation rules presented in section 2. We focus our attention separately in the following transformation phases: definition introduction, unfolding and abstraction+folding.

3   Definition Introduction Phase

This phase[3] corresponds to the so-called eureka generation phase, which is the key point for a transformation strategy to proceed. The problem of achieving an appropriate set of eureka definitions is well-known in the literature related to fold/unfold transformations [10,19,21,5]. For the case of the composition strategy, eureka definitions can be easily identified since they correspond to nested calls. On the other hand, the problem of finding good eureka definitions for the tupling strategy is much more difficult, mainly due to the fact that the calls to be tupled are not nested and they may be arbitrarily distributed in the right hand side of a rule. Sophisticated static analysis have been developed in the literature using dependencies graphs ([11,18]), m-dags ([8]), symbolic trace trees [9] and other intrincated structures. The main problems appearing in such approaches are that the analysis are not as general as wanted (they can fail even although the program admits tupling optimizations), they are time and space consuming and/or they may duplicate some work too[4]. In order to avoid these risks, our approach generates eureka definition following a very simple strategy (Table 1)

---

[3] Sometimes called "tupling" [19], but we reserve this word for the whole algorithm.
[4] This fact is observed during the so-called "program extraction phase" in [19]. This kind of post-processing can be made directly (which requires to store in memory

that obtains similar levels of generality than previous approaches and covers most practical cases. The main advantages are that the analysis is terminating, easy and quickly, and does not perform redundant calculus (like unfolding, instantiations, etc.) that properly corresponds to subsequent phases.

Table 1. Definition Introduction Phase

INPUT: OUTPUT:	Original Program $\mathcal{R}$ and Program Rule $R = (l \rightarrow r) \in \mathcal{R}$ Definition Rule (Eureka) R_{def}
BODY:	1. Let $T = \langle t_1, \ldots, t_n \rangle$ $(n > 1)$ be a tuple where $\{t_1, \ldots, t_n\}$ is the set of operation-rooted subterms of r that are *innermost* (i.e., t_i does not contain operation-rooted subterms) such that each one of them shares at least a common variable with at least one more subterm in T 2. Apply the DEFINITION INTRODUCTION RULE to generate : $$R_{def} = (f_{new}(\overline{x}) \rightarrow T)$$ where f_{new} is a new function symbol not appearing $\mathcal{R}$, and $\overline{x}$ is the set of variables of T

As illustrated by step 1 in Example 1, our eureka generator proceeds as the algorithm in Table 1 shows. Observe that the input of the algorithm is the original program $\mathcal{R}$ and a selected rule $R \in \mathcal{R}$ which definition is intended to be optimized by tupling. In the worst case, every rule in the program could be used as input, but only those that generate appropriate eureka definitions should be considered afterwards in the global tupling algorithm.

One final remark: it is not clear in general neither the number nor the occurrences of calls to be tupled, but some intuitions exist. Similarly to most classical approaches in the literature, we require that only terms sharing common variables be tupled in the rhs of the eureka definition [11,19]. On the other hand, since it is not usual that terms to be tupled contain operation rooted terms as parameters, we cope with this fact in our definition by requiring that only operation-rooted subterms at innermost positions of r be collected. On the contrary, the considered subterms would contain nested calls which should be more appropriately transformed by composition instead of tupling (see [5] for details).

4   Unfolding Phase

During this phase, that corresponds to the so-called *symbolic computation* in many approaches (see a representative list in [19]), the eureka definition $R_{def} =$

---

elaborated data structures, as is the case of symbolic computation trees) or via transformation rules similarly to our method, but with the disadvantage in that case that many folding/unfolding steps done at "eureka generation time" must be redundantly redone afterwards at "transformation time" or during the program extraction phase.

$(f_{new}(\overline{x}) \to T)$ generated in the previous phase, is unfolded possibly several times (at least once) using the original program $\mathcal{R}$, and returning a new program $\mathcal{R}_{unf}$ which represents the unfolded definitions of f_{new} . Since the rhs of the rule to be transformed is a tuple of terms (T), the subterm to be unfolded can be decided in a "don't care" non-deterministic way. In our case, we follow a criterium that is rather usual in the literature ([10,11]), and we give priority to such subterms where recursion parameters are less general than others, as occurs in step 2 of Example 1 (where we unfold the term `fib(s(X))` instead of `fib(X)`). Moreover, we impose a new condition: each unfolding step must be followed by normalizing steps as much as possible, as illustrates step 3 in Example 1.

Table 2. Unfolding Phase

INPUT:	Original Program $\mathcal{R}$ and Definition Rule (Eureka) R_{def}
OUTPUT:	Unfolded Program $\mathcal{R}_{unf}$

| BODY: | 1. Let $\mathcal{R}_{unf} = \{R_{def}\}$ be a program
2. Repeat $\quad$ $\mathcal{R}_{unf}$=UNFOLD$(\mathcal{R}_{unf}, \mathcal{R})$
$\quad$ until every rule $R' \in \mathcal{R}_{unf}$ verifies TEST(R', R_{def})>0 |

As shown in Table 2, the unfolding phase basically consists of a repeated application of the unfolding rule defined in Section 2. This is done by calling function UNFOLD with the set of rules that must be eventually unfolded. In each iteration, once a rule in $\mathcal{R}_{unf}$ is unfolded, it is removed and replaced with the rules obtained after unfolding it in the resulting program $\mathcal{R}_{unf}$, which is dynamically actualized in our algorithm. Initially, $\mathcal{R}_{unf}$ only contains $R_{def} = (f_{new}(\overline{x}) \to T)$. Once the process has been started, any rule obtained by application of the unfolding rule has the form $R' = (\theta(f_{new}(\overline{x})) \to T')$. In order to stop the process, we must check if each rule $R' \in \mathcal{R}_{unf}$ verifies one of the following conditions:

Stopping condition 1: If there are no subterms in T' sharing common variables[5] or they can not be narrowed anymore, then rule R' represents a case base definition for the new symbol f_{new}. This fact is illustrated by step 3 and rule R_7 in Example 1.

Stopping condition 2: There exists a substitution θ and a tuple T'' that packs the set of different innermost operation-rooted subterms that share common variables in T' (without counting repetitions), such that $\theta(T) = T''$[6]. Observe that rule R_6 verifies this condition in Example 1 since, for $\theta = id$ there exists (in its rhs) two an one instances respectively of the terms ocurring in the original tuple, that is, $\theta(T) = T = T'' = \langle \texttt{f(s(X))}, \texttt{f(X)} \rangle$.

---

[5] This novel stopping condition produces good terminating results during the search for regularities since it is more relaxed than other ones considered in the literature.

[6] This condition is related to the so-called *similarity*, *regularity* or *foldability* conditions in other approaches ([19]) since it suffices to enable subsequent abstraction+folding steps which may lead to efficient recursive definitions of f_{new}.

In algorithm of Table 2 these terminating conditions are checked by function TEST, which obviously requires the rules whose rhs's are the intended tuples T and T'. Codes 0, 1 and 2 are returned by TEST when none, the first or the second stopping condition hold, respectively. We assume that, when TEST returns code 0 forever, the repeat loop is eventually aborted and then, the unfolding process returns an empty program (that will abort the whole tupling process too).

5   Abstraction+Folding Phase

This phase follows the algorithm shown in Table 3 and is used not only for obtaining efficient recursive definitions of the new symbol f_{new} (initially defined by the eureka $\mathcal{R}_{def}$), but also for redefine old function symbols in terms of the optimized definition of f_{new}. This fact depends on the rule R to be abstracted and folded, which may belong to the unfolded program obtained in the previous phase ($\mathcal{R}_{unf}$), or to the original program ($\mathcal{R}$), respectively. In both cases, the algorithm acts in the same way returning the abstracted and folded program $\mathcal{R}'$.

Table 3. Abstraction+Folding Phase

INPUT:	Program $\mathcal{R}_{aux} = \mathcal{R}_{unf} \cup \mathcal{R}$ and Definition Rule (Eureka) R_{def}
OUTPUT:	Abstracted+Folded Program $\mathcal{R}'$

| BODY: | 1. Let $\mathcal{R}' = \mathcal{R}_{aux}$ be a program and let R' be an empty rule
2. For every rule $R \in \mathcal{R}_{aux}$ verifying TEST(R, R_{def})=2
$\qquad R'$=ABSTRACT(R, R_{def})
$\qquad R'$=FOLD(R', R_{def})
$\qquad \mathcal{R}'$=$\mathcal{R}' - \{R\} \cup \{R'\}$ |

Firstly we consider the case $R \in \mathcal{R}_{unf}$. Remember that $R_{def} = (f_{new}(\overline{x}) \to T)$ where $T = \langle t_1, \ldots, t_n \rangle$. If $R = (\sigma(f_{new}(\overline{x})) \to r')$ satisfies TEST(R, R_{def})=2, then there exists sequences of disjoint positions[7] $\overline{P_j}$ in $\mathcal{FPos}(r')$ where $r'|_p = \theta(t_j)$ for all p in P_j, $j = 1, \ldots, n$, i.e., $r' = r'[\theta(\overline{t_j})]_{\overline{P_j}}$. Hence, it is possible to apply the abstraction rule described in Section 2 to R. This step is done by function ABSTRACT(R, R_{def}), that abstracts R accordingly to tuple T in rule R_{def} and generates the new rule R': $\sigma(f_{new}(\overline{x})) \to r'[\overline{z_j}]_{\overline{P_j}}$ where $\langle z_1, \ldots, z_n \rangle = \theta(\langle t_1, \ldots, t_n \rangle)$, being $\overline{z_j}$ are fresh variables. This fact is illustrated by step 4 and rule R_8 in Example 1.

Observe now that this last rule can be folded by using the eureka definition R_{def}, since all the applicability conditions required by our folding rule (see Definition 1) are fulfilled. This fact is done by the call to FOLD(R', R_{def}) which returns the new rule: $\sigma(f_{new}(\overline{x})) \to r'[\overline{z_j}]_{\overline{P_j}}$ where $\langle z_1, \ldots, z_n \rangle = \theta(f_{new}(\overline{x}))$.

---

[7] This positions obviously correspond to the set of innermost operation-rooted subterms that share common variables in r'.

Note that this rule (illustrated by rule R_9 and step 5 in Example 1), as any other rule generated (and accumulated in the resulting program $\mathcal{R}'$) in this phase, corresponds to a recursive definition of f_{new}, as desired.

The case when $R \in \mathcal{R}$ is perfectly analogous. The goal now is to reuse as much as possible the optimized definition of f_{new} into the original program $\mathcal{R}$, as illustrate steps 6 and 7, and rules R_{10} and R_{11} in Example 1.

6   Conclusions and Further Research

Tupling is a powerful optimization strategy which can be achieved by fold/unfold transformations and produces better gains in efficiency than other simpler-automatic transformations. As it is well-known in the literature, tupling is very complicated and automatic tupling algorithms either result in high runtime cost (which prevents them from being employed in a real system), or they succeed only for a restricted class of programs [11,12]. Our approach drops out some of these limitations by automating a realistic and practicable tupling algorithm that optimizes functional-logic programs. Compared with prior approaches in the field of pure functional programming, our method is less involved (we do not require complicate structures for generating eureka definitions), more efficient (i.e., redundant computations are avoided), and deals with special particularities of the integrated paradigm (i.e., transformed rules are non overlapping).

For the future, we are interested in to estimate the gains in efficiency produced at transformation time. In this sense, we want to associate a cost/gain label to each local transformation step when building a transformation sequence. We think that this action will allow to drive more accurately the transformation process, since it will help to define deterministic heuristics and automatic strategies.

Acknowledgements. My thanks to María Alpuente and Moreno Falaschi for helpful discussions on transformation strategies. I am specially grateful to German Vidal for critical comments that helped to improve this paper.

References

1. M. Alpuente, M. Falaschi, C. Ferri, G. Moreno, and G. Vidal. Un sistema de transformación para programas multiparadigma. *Revista Iberoamericana de Inteligencia Artificial*, X/99(8):27–35, 1999.
2. M. Alpuente, M. Falaschi, C. Ferri, G. Moreno, G. Vidal, and I. Ziliotto. The Transformation System SYNTH. Technical Report DSIC-II/16/99, UPV, 1999. Available in URL: http://www.dsic.upv.es/users/elp/papers.html.
3. M. Alpuente, M. Falaschi, G. Moreno, and G. Vidal. Safe folding/unfolding with conditional narrowing. In H. Heering M. Hanus and K. Meinke, editors, *Proc. of the International Conference on Algebraic and Logic Programming, ALP'97, Southampton (England)*, pages 1–15. Springer LNCS 1298, 1997.

4. M. Alpuente, M. Falaschi, G. Moreno, and G. Vidal. A Transformation System for Lazy Functional Logic Programs. In A. Middeldorp and T. Sato, editors, *Proc. of the 4th Fuji International Symposyum on Functional and Logic Programming, FLOPS'99, Tsukuba (Japan)*, pages 147–162. Springer LNCS 1722, 1999.

5. M. Alpuente, M. Falaschi, G. Moreno, and G. Vidal. An Automatic Composition Algorithm for Functional Logic Programs. In V. Hlaváč, K. G. Jeffery, and J. Wiedermann, editors, *Proc. of the 27th Annual Conference on Current Trends in Theory and Practice of Informatics, SOFSEM'2000*, pages 289–297. Springer LNCS 1963, 2000.

6. S. Antoy, R. Echahed, and M. Hanus. A Needed Narrowing Strategy. In *Proc. 21st ACM Symp. on Principles of Programming Languages, Portland*, pages 268–279, New York, 1994. ACM Press.

7. F. Baader and T. Nipkow. *Term Rewriting and All That.* Cambridge University Press, 1998.

8. R.S. Bird. Tabulation techniques for recursive programs. *ACM Computing Surveys*, 12(4):403–418, 1980.

9. M. Bruynooghe, D. De Schreye, and B. Martens. A General Criterion for Avoiding Infinite Unfolding. *New Generation Computing*, 11(1):47–79, 1992.

10. R.M. Burstall and J. Darlington. A Transformation System for Developing Recursive Programs. *Journal of the ACM*, 24(1):44–67, 1977.

11. W. Chin. Towards an Automated Tupling Strategy. In *Proc. of Partial Evaluation and Semantics-Based Program Manipulation, 1993*, pages 119–132. ACM, New York, 1993.

12. W. Chin, A. Goh, and S. Khoo. Effective Optimisation of Multiple Traversals in Lazy Languages. In *Proc. of Partial Evaluation and Semantics-Based Program Manipulation, San Antonio, Texas, USA (Technical Report BRICS-NS-99-1)*, pages 119–130. University of Aarhus, DK, 1999.

13. J. Darlington. Program transformation. In J. Darlington, P. Henderson, and D. A. Turner, editors, *Functional Programming and its Applications*, pages 193–215. Cambridge University Press, 1982.

14. M. Hanus. The Integration of Functions into Logic Programming: From Theory to Practice. *Journal of Logic Programming*, 19&20:583–628, 1994.

15. G. Hutton. Fold and Unfold for Program Semantics. In *Proc. of 3rd ACM SIGPLAN Int'l Conf. on Functional Programming, Baltimore, Maryland*, 1998.

16. G. Moreno. Automatic Tupling for Functional–Logic Programs. Technical Report DIAB-02-07-24, UCLM, 2002. Available in URL: http://www.info-ab.uclm.es/personal/gmoreno/gmoreno.htm.

17. G. Moreno. Transformation Rules and Strategies for Functional-Logic Programs. *AI Communications, IO Press (Amsterdam)*, 15(2):3, 2002.

18. A. Pettorossi and M. Proietti. Transformation of Logic Programs: Foundations and Techniques. *Journal of Logic Programming*, 19,20:261–320, 1994.

19. A. Pettorossi and M. Proietti. A Comparative Revisitation of Some Program Transformation Techniques. In O. Danvy, R. Glück, and P. Thiemann, editors, *Partial Evaluation, Int'l Seminar, Dagstuhl Castle, Germany*, pages 355–385. Springer LNCS 1110, 1996.

20. A. Pettorossi and M. Proietti. Rules and Strategies for Transforming Functional and Logic Programs. *ACM Computing Surveys*, 28(2):360–414, 1996.

21. H. Tamaki and T. Sato. Unfold/Fold Transformations of Logic Programs. In S. Tärnlund, editor, *Proc. of Second Int'l Conf. on Logic Programming, Uppsala, Sweden*, pages 127–139, 1984.

SL_{FD} Logic: Elimination of Data Redundancy in Knowledge Representation

Pablo Cordero, Manolo Enciso, Angel Mora, and Inmaculada P. de Guzmán

E.T.S.I. Informática. Universidad de Málaga
29071 Málaga. Spain.
{pcordero,enciso}@uma.es,
{amora,guzman}@ctima.uma.es

Abstract. In this paper, we propose the use of formal techniques on *Software Engineering* in two directions: 1) We present, within the general framework of lattice theory, the analysis of relational databases. To do that, we characterize the concept of f-family (Armstrong relations) by means of a new concept which we call non-deterministic ideal operator. This characterization allows us to formalize database redundancy in a more significant way than it was thought of in the literature. 2) We introduce the *Substitution Logic SL_{FD}* for functional dependencies that will allows us the design of automatic transformations of data models to remove redundancy.

1 Introduction

Recently, there exists a wide range of problems in Software Engineering which are being treated successfully with Artificial Intelligence (AI) techniques. Thus, [5, 6] pursue the integration between database and AI techniques, in [14,16,20] non classical logics are applied to *specification* and *verification* of programs, [19] shows the useful characteristics of logic for Information Systems, [10] introduces an automatic tool that translates IBM370 assembly language programs to C.

Rough set theory [18] can be used to discover knowledge which is latent in database relations (e.g. data mining or knowledge discovery in database [4,12]). The most useful result of these techniques is the possibility of *"checking dependencies and finding keys for a conventional relation with a view to using the solution in general knowledge discovery"* [3]. Moreover, in [13] the authors emphasize that the solution to this classical problem in database theory can provide important support in underpinning the reasoning and learning applications encountered in artificial intelligence. The discovery of keys can also provide insights into the structure of data which are not easy to get by alternative means.

In this point, it becomes a crucial task to have a special kind of formal language to represent data knowledge syntactically which also allows to automate the management of functional dependencies. There exists a collection of equivalent functional dependencies (FD) logics [2,9,15,17,21]. Nevertheless, none of them is appropriate to handle the most relevant problems of functional dependencies in an efficient way. The reason is that their axiomatic systems are not close to automation.

F.J. Garijo, J.C. Riquelme, and M. Toro (Eds.): IBERAMIA 2002, LNAI 2527, pp. 141–150, 2002.
© Springer-Verlag Berlin Heidelberg 2002

In [11,13,15], the authors indicate the difficulties of classical FD problems and they point out the importance of seeking efficient computational methods. In our opinion, an increasing in the efficiency of these methods might come from the elimination of redundancy in preliminary FD specification. Up to now, redundancy in FD sets was defined solely in terms of redundant FD (a FD α is redundant in a given set of FD Γ if α can be deduced from Γ). Nevertheless, a more powerful concept of FD redundancy can be defined if we consider redundancy of attributes within FDs.

In this work we present an FD logic which provides:

- New substitution operators which allows the natural design of automated deduction methods.
- New substitution rules which can be used bottom-up and top-down to get equivalents set of FD, but without redundancy.
- The FD set transformation induced by these new rules cover the definition of *second normal form*. It allows us to use substitution operators as the core of a further database normalization process.

Besides that, we introduce an algebraic framework to formalize the data redundancy problem. This formal framework allows us to uniform relational database definitions and develop the meta-theory in a very formal manner.

2   Closure Operators and Non-deterministic Operators

We will work with posets, that is, with pairs $(A, \leq)$ where $\leq$ is an order relation.

Definition 1. *Let $(A, \leq)$ be a poset and $c : A \to A$. We say that c is a **closure operator** if c satisfies the following conditions:*

- $a \leq c(a)$ and $c(c(a)) \leq c(a)$, for all $a \in A$.
- *If $a \leq b$ then $c(a) \leq c(b)$ (c is monotone)*

*We say that $a \in A$ is c-**closed** if $c(a) = a$.*

As examples of closure operators we have the lower closure operator[1]. Hereinafter, we will say lower closed instead of $\downarrow$-closed. Likewise, we will use the well-known concepts of $\vee$-semilattice, lattice and the concept of ideal of an $\vee$-semilattice as a sub-$\vee$-semilattice that is lower closed. Now, we introduce the notion of non-deterministic operator.

Definition 2. *Let A be a non-empty set and $n \in \mathbb{N}$ with $n \geq 1$. If $F : A^n \to 2^A$ is a total application, we say that F is a **non-deterministic operator with arity** n in A (henceforth, ndo) We denote the set ndos with arity n in A by $\mathcal{N}do_n(A)$ and, if F is a ndo, we denote its arity by $\mathrm{ar}(F)$.*

As usual, $F(a_1, \ldots, a_{i-1}, X, a_{i+1}, \ldots, a_n) = \bigcup_{x \in X} F(a_1, \ldots, a_{i-1}, x, a_{i+1}, \ldots, a_n).$

---

[1] If $(U, \leq)$ is a poset, $\downarrow : 2^U \to 2^U$ is given by $X \downarrow = \bigcup_{x \in X} (x] = \bigcup_{x \in X} \{y \in U \mid y \leq x\}.$

As an immediate example we have that, if R is a binary relation in a non-empty set A, we can see R as an unary ndo in A where $R(a) = \{b \in A \mid (a, b) \in R\}$. We will use the following notation: $R^0(a) = \{a\}$ and $R^n(a) = R(R^{n-1}(a))$ for all $n \geq 1$. Therefore, we say that R is **reflexive** if $a \in R(a)$, for all $a \in A$, and we say that R is **transitive** if $R^2(a) \subseteq R(a)$, for all $a \in A$.[2]

Most objects used in logic or computer science are *defined inductively*. By this we mean that we frequently define a set S of objets as: "the smallest set of objects containing a given set X of atoms, and closed under a given set $\mathcal{F}$ of constructors". In this definition, the constructors are deterministic operators, that is, functions of A^n to A where A is the universal set. However, in several fields of Computer Science the ndos have shown their usefulness. So, the interaction of these concepts is necessary.

Definition 3. *Let A be a poset, $X \subseteq A$ and $\mathcal{F}$ a family of ndos in A. Let us consider the sets $X_0 = X$ and $X_{i+1} = X_i \cup \bigcup_{F \in \mathcal{F}} F(X_i^{\mathrm{ar}(F)})$ We define the **nd-inductive closure** of X under $\mathcal{F}$ as $C\ell_{\mathcal{F}}(X) = \bigcup_{i \in \mathbb{N}} X_i$. We say that X is **closed for** $\mathcal{F}$ if $C\ell_{\mathcal{F}}(X) = X$.*

Theorem 1. *Let $\mathcal{F}$ be a family of ndos in A. $C\ell_{\mathcal{F}}$ is a closure operator in $(2^A, \subseteq)$.*

Example 1. Let $(A, \vee, \wedge)$ be a lattice. The ideal generated by X is $C\ell_{\{\vee, \downarrow\}}(X)$ for all $X \subseteq A$.

3   Non-deterministic Ideal Operators

The study of functional dependencies in databases requires a special type of ndo which we introduce in this section.

Definition 4. *Let F be an unary ndo in a poset $(A, \leq)$. We say that F is a **non-deterministic ideal operator** (briefly **nd.ideal-o**) if it is reflexive, transitive and $F(a)$ is an ideal of $(A, \leq)$, for all $a \in A$. Moreover, if $F(a)$ is a principal ideal, for all $a \in A$, then we say that F is **principal**.*

The following example shows the independence of these properties.

Example 2. Let us consider the followings unary ndos in $(A, \leq)$:

$$F(x) = \{0, x\} \qquad G(x) = \{0\} \qquad H(x) = \begin{cases} (x] & \text{if } x \neq 0 \\ A & \text{if } x = 0 \end{cases}$$

1. F is reflexive and transitive. However, F is not an nd.ideal-o because $F(1)$ is not an ideal of $(A, \leq)$.
2. G is transitive and $G(x)$ is an ideal for all $x \in A$. But, G is not reflexive.
3. H is reflexive and $H(x)$ is an ideal for all $x \in A$. However, H is not transitive because $H(H(a)) = A \nsubseteq H(a) = (a]$.

The following proposition is an immediate consequence of the definition.

---

[2] Or, equivalently, if $R^n(a) \subseteq R(a)$, for all $a \in A$ and all $n \in \mathbb{N} \smallsetminus \{0\}$.

Proposition 1. *Let F be an nd.ideal-o in a poset $(A, \leq)$ and $a, b \in A$. F is a monotone operator of $(A, \leq)$ to $(2^A, \subseteq)$.*

Proposition 2. *Let $(A, \leq)$ be a lattice. The following properties hold:*

1. *Any intersection of nd.ideal-o in A is a nd.ideal-o in A.*
2. *For all unary ndo in A, F, there exists an unique nd.ideal-o in A that is minimal and contains $\mathcal{F}$. This nd.ideal-o is named **nd.ideal-o generated by** $\mathcal{F}$ and defined as $\widehat{F} = \bigcap \{F' \mid F' \text{ is a nd.ideal-o in } A \text{ and } F \subseteq F'\}$.[3]*

Theorem 2. *Let $(A, \leq)$ be a lattice.* $\widehat{}: \mathcal{N}do_1(A) \to \mathcal{N}do_1(A)$ *is the closure operator given by $\widehat{F}(x) = \mathcal{Cl}_{\{F, \vee, \downarrow\}}(\{x\})$.*

Example 3. Let us consider the lattice $(A, \leq)$ and the ndo given by: $F(x) = \{x\}$ if $x \in \{0, c, d, 1\}$, $F(a) = \{b, c\}$ and $F(b) = \{0\}$. Then, $\widehat{F}$ is the principal nd.ideal-o given by: $\widehat{F}(0) = \{0\}$; $\widehat{F}(b) = \{0, b\}$; $\widehat{F}(x) = A$ if $x \in \{a, c, d, 1\}$

We define the following order relation which can be read as "to have less information that".

Definition 5. *Let $(A, \leq)$ be a poset and $F, G \in \mathcal{N}do_1(A)$. We define:*

1. *$F \preccurlyeq G$ if, for all $a \in A$ and $b \in F(a)$, there exist $a' \in A$ and $b' \in G(a')$ such that $a \leq a'$ and $b \leq b'$.*
2. *$F \prec G$ if $F \preccurlyeq G$ and $F \neq G$.*

Among the generating ndo*s* of a given n.d.ideal-o we look for those that do not contain any superfluous information.

Definition 6. *Let $(A, \leq)$ be a poset and $F, G \in \mathcal{N}do_1(A)$. We say that F and G are* $\widehat{}$*-equivalents if $\widehat{F} = \widehat{G}$. We say that F is **redundant** if there exists $H \in \mathcal{O}nd_1(A)$ $\widehat{}$-equivalent to F such that $H \prec F$.*

Theorem 3. *Let $(A, \leq)$ be a poset and $F \in \mathcal{N}do_1(A)$. F is redundant if and only if any of the following conditions are fullfilled:*

1. *there exists $a \in A$ and $b \in F(a)$ such that $b \in \widehat{F_{ab}}(a)$, where F_{ab} is given by $F_{ab}(a) = F(a) \smallsetminus \{b\}$ and $F_{ab}(x) = F(x)$ otherwise.*
2. *there exists $a, b' \in A$ and $b \in F(a)$ such that $b' < b$ and $b \in \widehat{F_{abb'}}(a)$ where $F_{abb'}$ is given by $F_{abb'}(a) = (F(a) \smallsetminus \{b\}) \cup \{b'\}$ and $F_{abb'}(x) = F(x)$ otherwise.*
3. *there exists $a, a' \in A$ and $b \in F(a)$ such that $a' < a$, $b \in \widehat{F}(a')$ and $b \in \widehat{F_{aba'}}(a)$ where $F_{aba'}$ is given by $F_{aba'}(a) = F(a) \smallsetminus \{b\}$, $F_{aba'}(a') = F(a') \cup \{b\}$ and $F_{aba'}(x) = F(x)$ otherwise.*

We woulkd like to remark the fact that condition 1 is present in the database literature, but conditions 2 and 3 are stronger than it[4].

---

[3] If $F, G \in \mathcal{N}do_n(A)$ then $(F \cap G)(a) = F(a) \cap G(a)$.

[4] In fact, previous axiomatic systems can not remove redundancy from FD sets in such an easy (and automatic) way.

4   Nd.ideal-o*s* and Functional Dependencies

In this section we summarize the concepts that are basic over functional dependencies. The existence of conceptual data model with a formal basis is due, principally, to H. Codd [7]. Codd conceives stored data in **tables** and he calls *attributes* the labels of each one of the columns of the table. For each a attribute, $dom(a)$ is the domain to which the values of the column determined by such attribute belong. Thus, if $\mathcal{A}$ is the finite set of attributes, we are interested in $R \subseteq \Pi_{a \in \mathcal{A}} dom(a)$ relations. Each $t \in R$, that is, each row, is denominated *tuple of the relation*. If t is a tuple of the relation and a is an attribute, then $t(a)$ is the a-component of t.

Definition 7. *Let R be a relation over $\mathcal{A}$, $t \in R$ and $X = \{a_1, \ldots, a_n\} \subseteq \mathcal{A}$. The* **projection** *of t over X, $t_{/X}$, is the restriction of t to X. That is, $t_{/X}(a_i) = t(a_i)$, for all $a_i \in X$.*

Definition 8 (Functional Dependency). *Let R be a relation over $\mathcal{A}$. Any affirmation of the type $X \mapsto Y$, where $X, Y \subseteq \mathcal{A}$, is named* **functional dependency** *(henceforth FD) over R.[5] We say that R* **satisfies** *$X \mapsto Y$ if, for all $t_1, t_2 \in R$ we have that: $t_{1/X} = t_{2/X}$ implies that $t_{1/Y} = t_{2/Y}$.*
We denote by FD_R the following set $FD_R = \{X \mapsto Y \mid X, Y \subseteq A, R$ satisfies $X \mapsto Y\}$

In an awful amount of research on Data Bases, the study of Functional Dependencies is based on a fundamental notion: the notion of f-family (*Amstrong's Relation*) which can be characterized in the framework of the lattice theory (and without the strong restriction of working at 2^U level for a U set with finite cardinality) we present in this section.

Definition 9. *Let U be a non.empty set.[6] A f-**family** over U is a relation F in 2^U that is reflexive, transitive and satisfies the following conditions:*

1. *If $(X, Y) \in F$ and $W \subseteq Y$, then $(X, W) \in F$.*
2. *If $(X, Y), (V, W) \in F$, then $(X \cup V, Y \cup W) \in F$.*

Theorem 4. *Let A be a non-empty set and F a relation in 2^A. F is a f-family over A if and only if F is a nd.ideal-o in $(2^A, \subseteq)$.*

Proof. Let us suppose that F is a nd.ideal-o in $(2^A, \subseteq)$. If $Y \in F(X)$ and $W \subseteq Y$, since $F(X)$ is lower closed, we have that $W \in (Y] \subseteq F(X)$. Therefore, the item 1 in definition 9 is true. On the other hand, if $Y \in F(X)$ and $W \in F(V)$ then, by proposition 1, $Y \in F(X) \subseteq F(X \cup V)$ and $W \in F(V) \subseteq F(X \cup V)$. Therefore, since $F(X \cup V)$ is an $\vee$-semilattice, we have that $Y \cup W \in F(X \cup V)$ and the item 2 in definition 9 is true.

Inversely, let us suppose that F is a f-family over A and we prove that F is a nd.ideal-o in $(2^A, \subseteq)$. Since F is reflexive and transitive, we only need to probe that $F(X)$ is an ideal of $(2^{2^A}, \subseteq)$ for all $X \in 2^A$: the item 1 in definition 9 ensures that $F(X)$ is lower closed and, if we consider $V = X$, item 2 ensures that $F(X)$ is a sub-$\cup$-semilattice.

---

[5] This concept was introduced by Codd in 1970.
[6] In the literature, U is finite.

It is immediate to prove that, if R is a relation over A, then FD_R is a f-family (or equivalently, a nd.ideal-o in $(2^A, \subseteq)$) The proof of the inverse result was given by Armstrong in [1]. That is, given a non-empty finite set, U, for all f-family, F, there exists a relation R (named Armstrong's relation) such that $F = FD_R$. The characterization of f-families as nd.ideal-o.s turns the proof of the well-known properties of FD_R in a trivial matter:

Proposition 3. *Let R be a relation over A. Then* [7]

1. *If $Y \subseteq X \subseteq A$ then $X \mapsto Y \in FD_R$.*
2. *If $X \mapsto Y \in FD_R$ then $X \mapsto XY \in FD_R$.*
3. *If $X \mapsto Y, Y \mapsto Z \in FD_R$ then $X \mapsto Z \in FD_R$.*
4. *If $X \mapsto Y, X \mapsto Z \in FD_R$ then $X \mapsto YZ \in FD_R$.*
5. *If $X \mapsto Y \in FD_R$ then $X \mapsto Y - X \in FD_R$.*
6. *If $X \mapsto Y \in FD_R$, $X \subseteq U \subseteq A$ and $V \subseteq XY$ then $U \mapsto V \in FD_R$.*
7. *If $X \mapsto Y, X' \mapsto Z \in FD_R$, $X' \subseteq XY$, $X \subseteq U$ and $V \subseteq ZU$ then $U \mapsto V \in FD_R$.*

Proof. Since FD_R is reflexive and lower closed, we have that $(X] \subseteq FD_R(X)$. That is, (1). Since FD_R is an $\vee$-semilattice, we have (2) and (4). Since FD_R is transitive, we have (3). Since FD_R is lower closed, we have (5).

(6): Effectively, $V \overset{1}{\in} FD_R(XY) \overset{(2)}{\subseteq} FD_R(X) \overset{(1)}{\subseteq} FD_R(U)$.

(7): Effectively, $Z \in FD_R(X') \overset{(1)}{\subseteq} FD_R(XY) \overset{(2)}{\subseteq} FD_R(X) \overset{(1)}{\subseteq} FD_R(U)$. Finally, by (2), $ZU \in FD_R(U)$) and, by (1) we have that $V \in FD_R(U)$.

5   The FDL and SL_{FD} Logics

The above algebraic study and, specifically, the notion of nd.ideal-o (as an equivalent concept to the f-family concept) has guided the definition of the Functional Dependencies Logic (FDL) that we present in this section.

Definition 10. *Given the alphabet $\Omega \cup \{\mapsto\}$ where Ω is an infinite numerable set, we define the language $\mathbf{L}_{FD} = \{X \mapsto Y \mid X, Y \in 2^\Omega \text{ and } X \neq \varnothing\}$* [8].

5.1   The FDL Logic

Definition 11. *FDL is the logic given by the pair $(\mathbf{L}_{FD}, \mathcal{S}_{FD})$ where $\mathcal{S}_{FD}$ has as axiom scheme $Ax_{FD}: \vdash_{\mathcal{S}_{FD}} X \mapsto Y, \quad if Y \subseteq X$* [9] *and the following inference rules:*

$(R_{trans.})$	$X \mapsto Y, \ Y \mapsto Z \vdash_{\mathcal{S}_{FD}} X \mapsto Z$	**Transitivity Rule**
(R_{union})	$X \mapsto Y, \ X \mapsto Z \vdash_{\mathcal{S}_{FD}} X \mapsto YZ$	**Union Rule**

In $\mathcal{S}_{FD}$ we dispose of the following derived rules (these rules appear in [17]):

$(Rg.augm.) \quad X \mapsto Y \vdash_{\mathcal{S}_{FD}} U \mapsto V$, if $X \subseteq U$ and $V \subseteq XY$

Generalized Augmentation Rule

---

[7] If X and Y are sets of attributes, XY denote to $X \cup Y$.

[8] In the literature, attributes must be non-empty. In FD logic, we consider the empty attribute ($\top$) to ensure that the substitution-operators introduced in section 5.2 (see definition 15) are closed.

[9] Particulary $X \mapsto \top$ is an axiom scheme.

$(R_{g.trans.})$ $X{\mapsto}Y,\ Z{\mapsto}U \vdash_{S_{FD}} V{\mapsto}W$, if $Z \subseteq XY,\ X \subseteq V$ and $W \subseteq UV$
Generalized Transitivity Rule

The *deduction* and *equivalence* concepts are introduced as usual:

Definition 12. *Let* $\Gamma, \Gamma' \subseteq \mathbf{L}_{FD}$ *and* $\varphi \in \mathbf{L}_{FD}$. *We say that* φ *is deduced from* Γ *in* S_{FD}, *denoted* $\Gamma \vdash_{S_{FD}} \varphi$, *if there exists* $\varphi_1 \ldots \varphi_n \in \mathbf{L}_{FD}$ *such that* $\varphi_n = \varphi$ *and, for all* $1 \leq i \leq n$, *we have that* $\varphi_i \in \Gamma$, φ_i *is an axiom* Ax_{FD}, *or it is obtained by applying the inference rules in* S_{FD}.
We say that Γ' *is deduced of* Γ, *denoted* $\Gamma \vdash_{S_{FD}} \Gamma'$, *if* $\Gamma \vdash_{S_{FD}} \alpha$ *for all* $\alpha \in \Gamma'$ *and we say that* Γ *and* Γ' *are* S_{FD}-**equivalents**, *denoted* $\Gamma \equiv_{S_{FD}} \Gamma'$, *if* $\Gamma \vdash_{S_{FD}} \Gamma'$ *and* $\Gamma' \vdash_{S_{FD}} \Gamma$

Definition 13. *Let* $\Gamma \subseteq \mathbf{L}_{FD}$ *we define the* S_{FD}-*closure of* Γ, *denoted* $Cl_{FD}(\Gamma)$, *as* $Cl_{FD}(\Gamma) = \{\varphi \in \mathbf{L}_{FD} \mid \Gamma \vdash_{S_{FD}} \varphi\}$

Now is evident the following result.

Lemma 1. *Let* Γ *and* $\Gamma' \subseteq \mathbf{L}_{FD}$. *Then,* Γ *and* Γ' *are* S_{FD}-**equivalentes** *if and only if* $Cl_{FD}(\Gamma) = Cl_{FD}(\Gamma')$.

5.2   The Logic SL_{FD}

Although the system S_{FD} is optimal for meta-theoretical study, in this section, we introduce a new axiomatic system (SL_{FD}) for $\mathbf{L}_{FD}$ more adequate for the applications. First, we define two substitution operators and we illustrate their behaviour for removing redundancy.
Note that the traditional axiomatic system treats the redundancy type described in the item 1. of the theorem 3. We treat in a way efficient, the redundancy elimination described in item 2 and 3 of theorem 3.

Definition 14. *Let* $\Gamma \subseteq \mathbf{L}_{FD}$, *and* $\varphi = X{\mapsto}Y \in \Gamma$. *We say that* φ *is* **superfluous** *in* Γ *if* $\Gamma \backslash \{\varphi\} \vdash_{FD} \varphi$. *We say that* φ *is* **l-redundant** *in* Γ *if exists* $\varnothing \neq Z \subseteq X$ *such that* $(\Gamma \backslash \varphi) \cup \{(X - Z){\mapsto}Y\} \vdash_{S_{FD}} \varphi$. *We say that* φ *is* **r-redundant** *in* Γ *if exists* $\varnothing \neq U \subseteq Y$ *such that* $(\Gamma \backslash \varphi) \cup \{X{\mapsto}(Y-U)\} \vdash_{S_{FD}} \varphi$. *We say that* Γ **have redundancy** *if it have an element* φ *that it is superfluous or it is l-redundant or it is r-redundant in* Γ.

The operators that we will introduce are transformations of S_{FD}-*equivalence*. This way, the application of this operators does not imply the incorporation of *wff*, but the substitution of *wffs* for simpler ones, with an efficiency improvement [10].

Theorem 5. *Given* $X, Y, Z \in 2^{\Omega}$,

$$\{X{\mapsto}Y\} \equiv_{S_{FD}} \{X{\mapsto}(Y - X)\} \ and \ \{X{\mapsto}Y, X{\mapsto}Z\} \equiv_{S_{FD}} \{X{\mapsto}YZ\}$$

The following theorem allow us to introduce the substitution operators.

Theorem 6. *Let* $X{\mapsto}Y, U{\mapsto}V \in \mathbf{L}_{FD}$ *with* $X \cap Y = \varnothing$.

---

[10] It is easily proven that the reduction rule and union rule are S_{FD}-*equivalence* transformations.

(a) *If $X \subseteq U$ then $\{X \mapsto Y, U \mapsto V\} \equiv_{S_{FD}} \{X \mapsto Y, (U - Y) \mapsto (V - Y)\}$. Therefore, if $U \cap Y \neq \varnothing$ or $V \cap Y \neq \varnothing$ then $U \mapsto V$ is l-redundant or r-redundant in $\{X \mapsto Y, U \mapsto V\}$, respectively.*

(b) *If $X \nsubseteq U$ and $X \subseteq UV$ then $\{X \mapsto Y, U \mapsto V\} \equiv_{S_{FD}} \{X \mapsto Y, U \mapsto (V - Y)\}$. Therefore, if $V \cap Y \neq \varnothing$ then $U \mapsto V$ is r-redundant in $\{X \mapsto Y, U \mapsto V\}$.*

Proof. **(a)**

$\Rightarrow)$: [11]

1. $X \mapsto Y$	Hypothesis		1. $U \mapsto X$	Ax_{FD}
2. $(U\text{-}Y) \mapsto Y$	1, $Rg.augm.$		2. $X \mapsto Y$	Hypothesis
3. $(U\text{-}Y) \mapsto (U\text{-}Y)$	Ax_{FD}		3. $U \mapsto Y$	1, 2, $R_{trans.}$
4. $(U\text{-}Y) \mapsto UY$	2, 3, R_{union}		4. $(U\text{-}Y) \mapsto (V\text{-}Y)$	Hypothesis
5. $(U\text{-}Y) \mapsto U$	4, $Rg.augm.$		5. $U \mapsto VY$	3, 4, R_{union}
6. $U \mapsto V$	Hypothesis		6. $U \mapsto V$	2, 5, $Rg.augm.$
7. $(U\text{-}Y) \mapsto V$	5, 6, $R_{trans.}$			
8. $(U\text{-}Y) \mapsto (V\text{-}Y)$	7, $Rg.augm.$			

(b)

$\Rightarrow)$:

1. $U \mapsto V$	Hypothesis		1. $U \mapsto X$	Ax_{FD}
2. $U \mapsto (V - Y)$	1, $Rg.augm.$		2. $X \mapsto Y$	Hypothesis
			3. $U \mapsto Y$	1, 2, $R_{trans.}$
			4. $U \mapsto (V\text{-}Y)$	Hypothesis
			5. $U \mapsto VY$	3, 4, R_{union}
			6. $U \mapsto V$	2, 5, $Rg.augm.$

The above theorems allow us to define two substitution operators as follows:

Definition 15. *Let $X \mapsto Y \in \mathbf{L}_{FD}$, we define $\Phi_{X \mapsto Y}, \Phi^r_{X \mapsto Y} : \mathbf{L}_{FD} \longrightarrow \mathbf{L}_{FD}$, denominated respectively $(X \mapsto Y)$-**substitution operator**, and $(X \mapsto Y)$-**right-substitution operator** (or simply $(X \mapsto Y)$-r-substitution operator):*

$$\Phi_{X \mapsto Y}(U \mapsto V) = \begin{cases} (U - Y) \mapsto (V - Y) & \text{if } X \subseteq U \text{ and } X \cap Y = \varnothing \text{ [12]} \\ U \mapsto V & \text{otherwise} \end{cases}$$

$$\Phi^r_{X \mapsto Y}(U \mapsto V) = \begin{cases} U \mapsto (V - Y) & \text{if } X \nsubseteq U, X \cap Y = \varnothing \text{ and } X \subseteq UV \\ U \mapsto V & \text{otherwise} \end{cases}$$

Now, we can define a new axiomatic system, $\mathcal{S}_{FDS}$, for $\mathbf{L}_{FD}$ with a substitution rule as primitive rule.

Definition 16. *The system $\mathcal{S}_{FDS}$ on $\mathbf{L}_{FD}$ has one axiom scheme:*

Ax_{FDS} : $\vdash X \mapsto Y$, *where $Y \subseteq X$. Particulary, $X \mapsto \top$ is an axiom scheme. The inferences are the following:*

$(R_{\text{frag.}})$	$X \mapsto Y \vdash_{S_{FDS}} X \mapsto Y'$, if $Y' \subseteq Y$	**Fragmentation rule**
$(R_{\text{comp.}})$	$X \mapsto Y, \; U \mapsto V \vdash_{S_{FDS}} XU \mapsto YV$	**Composition rule**
$(R_{\text{subst.}})$	$X \mapsto Y, \; U \mapsto V \vdash_{S_{FDS}} (U\text{-}Y) \mapsto (V\text{-}Y)$, if $X \subseteq U, \; X \cap Y = \varnothing$	**Substitution rule**

Theorem 7. *The $\mathcal{S}_{FD}$ and $\mathcal{S}_{FDS}$ systems on $\mathbf{L}_{FD}$ are equivalent.*

---

[11] In 2 we use $X \subseteq U - Y$ and in 4 we use $Y(U - Y) = UY$.

[12] Notice that $V - Y$ may be $\top$. In this case we will remove the *wff* using axiom Ax_{FD}.

Proof. Let R_{union} be a particular case of $R_{comp.}$, then all we have to do is to prove that $(R_{trans.})$ is a derived rule of $\mathcal{S}_{FDS}$:

1. $X \mapsto Y$	Hypothesis	6. $XY \mapsto (Z-Y)$		4,5, $R_{subst.}$
2. $Y \mapsto Z$	Hypothesis	7. $(Y-X) \mapsto (Y-X)$		Ax_{FDS}
3. $X \mapsto (Y-X)$	1, $R_{frag.}$	8. $X \mapsto (Z-Y)$		3,6, $R_{subst.}$
4. $Y \mapsto (Z-Y)$	2, $R_{frag.}$	9. $X \mapsto ZY$		1,7, $R_{comp.}$
5. $X \mapsto \top$	Ax_{FDS}	10. $X \mapsto Z$		9, $R_{frag.}$

The example 4 shows the advantages of the Φ and Φ^r operators, and the example 5 show how is possible to automate the redundancy remove process.

Example 4. Let $\Gamma = \{ab \mapsto c, c \mapsto a, bc \mapsto d, acd \mapsto b, d \mapsto eg, be \mapsto c, cg \mapsto bd, ce \mapsto ag\}$. We apply the Φ, and Φ^r for obtaining a non redundant *wffs* set and equivalent to Γ. In the following table, we show by rows how we obtain successively equivalent *wff* sets, but with less redundancy. We emphasize with ⎵ both *wffs* that allow to apply the operator. We cross out with ╱ the removed *wff* after the application of the operator. We remark in each row the operator or the rule applied.

$\Phi_{c \mapsto a}(acd \mapsto b)$	$\{ab \mapsto c, c \mapsto a, bc \mapsto d, \cancel{acd \mapsto b}, d \mapsto eg, be \mapsto c, cg \mapsto bd, ce \mapsto ag\}$
$\Phi_{c \mapsto a}(ce \mapsto ag)$	$\{ab \mapsto c, c \mapsto a, bc \mapsto d, cd \mapsto b, d \mapsto eg, be \mapsto c, cg \mapsto bd, \cancel{ce \mapsto ag}\}$
$\Phi^r_{bc \mapsto d}(cg \mapsto bd)$	$\{ab \mapsto c, c \mapsto a, bc \mapsto d, cd \mapsto b, d \mapsto eg, be \mapsto c, \cancel{cg \mapsto bd}, ce \mapsto g\}$
	$\Gamma' = \{ab \mapsto c, c \mapsto a, bc \mapsto d, cd \mapsto b, d \mapsto eg, be \mapsto c, cg \mapsto b, ce \mapsto g\}$

Example 5. Let Γ the FD set showed in the first row of the table.

$\Phi_{b \mapsto c}(bc \mapsto de)+R_{union}$	$\Gamma = \{a \mapsto b, b \mapsto c, ae \mapsto cfh, \cancel{bc \mapsto de}, bd \mapsto ce, afh \mapsto ce,$ $bcd \mapsto aef\}$
$\Phi_{b \mapsto cde}(bd \mapsto ce)^{13}$	$\Gamma = \{a \mapsto b, b \mapsto cde, ae \mapsto cfh, \cancel{bd \mapsto ce}, afh \mapsto ce, bcd \mapsto aef\}$
$\Phi_{b \mapsto cde}(bcd \mapsto aef)+R_{union}$	$\Gamma = \{a \mapsto b, b \mapsto cde, ae \mapsto cfh, afh \mapsto ce, \cancel{bcd \mapsto aef}\}$
$\Phi^r_{ae \mapsto cfh}(b \mapsto acdef)$	$\Gamma = \{a \mapsto b, \cancel{b \mapsto acdef}, ae \mapsto cfh, afh \mapsto ce\}$
$\Phi^r_{ae \mapsto cfh}(afh \mapsto ce)$	$\Gamma = \{a \mapsto b, b \mapsto ade, ae \mapsto cfh, \cancel{afh \mapsto ce}\}$
$R_{g.trans.}$	$\Gamma = \{a \mapsto b, b \mapsto ade, ae \mapsto cfh, \cancel{afh \mapsto e}\}$
	$\Gamma' = \{a \mapsto b, b \mapsto ade, ae \mapsto cfh\}$

Due to space limitations, we can not go further into comparison with other axiomatic systems, nevertheless we would like to remark that $\mathcal{S}_{FDS}$ allow us to design (in a more direct way) an automated and efficient method which remove redundancy efficiently. In this case, the example 4 taken from [21] requires the application of seven $\mathcal{S}_{FD}$ rules in a non deterministic way.

---

[13] Notice that the Φ operator renders $b \mapsto \top$ and we remove it by using axiom Ax_{FDS}.

References

1. William W. Armstrong. Dependency structures of data base relationships. *Proc. IFIP Congress. North Holland, Amsterdam*, pages 580–583, 1974.
2. Paolo Atzeni and Valeria De Antonellis. Relational Database Theory. *The Benjamin/Cummings Publishing Company Inc.*, 1993.
3. D.A. Bell. From data properties to evidence. *IEEE Transactions on Knowledge and Data Engireering*, 5(6):965–968, 1993.
4. D.A. Bell and J.W. Guan. Computational methods for rought classifications and discovery. *J. American Society for Information Sciences*, To appear. Special issue on Data Mining.
5. Elisa Bertino, Barbara Catania, and Gian Piero Zarri. Intelligent Database Systems. *ACM Press. Addison-Wesley*, ISBN 0-201-87736-8, 2001.
6. L. E. Bertossi and J. C. Ferretti. SCDBR: A reasoner for specification in the situation calculus of database updates. In *1st International Conference on Temporal Logic*, Berlin, 1994.
7. Edgar F. Codd. The relational model for database management: Version 2. reading, mass. *Addison Wesley*, 1990.
8. Manuel Enciso and Angel Mora. FD3: A functional dependencies data dictionary. *Proceedings of the Fourth Conference on Enterprise Information Systems (ICEIS). Ciudad Real, Spain*, 2:807–811, 2002 Apr.
9. Ronald Fagin. Functional dependencies in a relational database and propositional logic. *IBM. Journal of research and development.*, 21 (6):534–544, 1977.
10. Yishai A. Feldman and Doron A. Friedman. Portability by automatic translation: A large-scale case study. *Artificial Intelligence*, 107(1):1–28, 1999.
11. Rusell Greiner. Finding optimal derivation strategies in redundant knowledge bases. *Artificial Intelligence*, 50(1):95–115, 1991.
12. J. W. Guan and D. A. Bell. Rough computational methods for information systems. *Artificial Intelligence*, 105:77–103, 1998.
13. J.W. Guan and D.A. Bell. Rough computational methods for information systems. *Artificial Intelligence*, 105:77–103, 1998.
14. Erika Hajnicz. Time structures. formal description and algorithmic representation. In *Lecture Notes in Artificial Intelligence. Num. 1047.* Springer-Verlag, 1996.
15. Toshihide Ibaraki, Alexander. Kogan, and Kazuhisa Makino. Functional dependencies in horn theories. *Artificial Intelligence*, 108:1–30, 1999.
16. Zohar Manna and A. Pnueli. *Temporal verification of reactive systems: Safety.* Springer-Verlag, 1995.
17. Jan Paredaens, Paul De Bra, Marc Gyssens, and Dirk Van Van Gucht. The structure of the relational database model. *EATCS Monographs on Theoretical Computer Science*, 1989.
18. Z. Pawlak. *Rough Set: teoretical aspects of reasoning about data.* Kluwer, 1991. Dordrecht, Netherlands.
19. David Robertson and Jaum Agustí. Lightweight uses of logic in conceptual modelling. *Software Blueprints. ACM Press. Ed. Addison Wesley*, 1999.
20. Alexander Tuzhilin. Templar: a knowledge-based language for software specifications using temporal logic. *ACM Transactions on Information Systems*, 13:269–304, July 1995.
21. Jeffrey D. Ullman. Database and knowledge-base systems. *Computer Science Press*, 1988.

Indeed: Interactive Deduction on Horn Clause Theories

Oscar Olmedo-Aguirre and Guillermo Morales-Luna

Computer Science Section, CINVESTAV-IPN
Av. I. P. N. 2508, 07300 Mexico City, Mexico
{oolmedo,gmorales}@cs.cinvestav.mx

Abstract. We introduce the declarative programming language **Indeed** that uses both deduction and interaction through multi-agent system applications. The language design is addressed by providing a uniform programming model that combines two refinements of resolution along with some control strategies to introduce state-based descriptions. We show that the logical calculus in which the computational model is based is sound and complete. Finally, we compare our approach to others proposed for coupling interaction with automated deduction.

Keywords: Logic programming, interaction, automated theorem proving, Horn clause theories.

1 Introduction

Artificial intelligence, largely based on formal logic and automated reasoning systems, has become increasingly more interactive. As indicated by Wegner [12], dynamic acquisition of interactive knowledge is fundamental to diminish the complexity of interactive tasks, to better their performance, and to better the expressiveness of their modeling. On the other hand, there is a fundamental distinction between deduction and interaction. In high order logics provers, as HOL [4] and, particularly, Isabelle [7], insteraction is meant as a direct user guidance to construct a proof. The kind of interaction we have in mind is closer to the notion shown in [3]: different agents scan a common work-place to pursue with their common goal, e.g. to prove the current theorem.

Models of algorithmic computation, like automated theorem provers and Turing machines, are characterized by their closed and monolithic approach. Their simple observable behavior comprises a three-stage process of interactive input, closed data processing, and interactive output. Nonetheless, modern applications involving collaboration, communication and coordination, require richer behaviors that cannot solely be obtained from algorithmic computation.

In this work, we propose a logic programming language that extends a resolution-based theorem prover with interaction. The computational model

F.J. Garijo, J.C. Riquelme, and M. Toro (Eds.): IBERAMIA 2002, LNAI 2527, pp. 151–160, 2002.

comprises SLD-resolution and UR-resolution, to describe respectively stateless deduction and state-based transitions. The coordination model consists of a transactional global memory of ground facts along with a strategy for the theorem prover to control program execution by syntactically guided rule selection. In addition, the set of support restriction strategy coordinates the input and output of facts with the shared memory, maintaining the coherence of the current state of the computing agent.

Let us briefly explore other approaches that can be compared with ours: resolution theorem provers, constraint logic programming and coordination logic programming.

The resolution-based theorem prover *OTTER* [13,14] comprises a number of refinements of resolution along with a set of control strategies to prune the explosive generation of intermediate clauses. However, OTTER does not account for interaction. The set of all instantaneous descriptions essentially corresponds to the set of support strategy. In OTTER, a clause is selected and removed from the set of support to produce a new set of clauses deduced from the axioms of the theory. Then, after simplifying a new clause by demodulation and possibly discarding it by either weighting, backward or forward subsumption, the new clause is placed back to the set of support.

Concurrent Constraint Programming (CCP) [8] proposes a programming model centered on the notion of constraint store that is accessed through the basic operations 'blocking *ask*' and 'atomic *tell*'. Blocking $ask(c)$ corresponds to the logical entailment of constraint c from the contents of the constraint store: the operation blocks if there is not an enough strong valuation to decide on c. In this respect, the blocking mechanism is similar to the one used in **Indeed** to obtain the set of ground facts that match with the left-hand side of some rule. Besides, the constraint store shares some similarities with the global memory of ground facts. However, operation $tell(c)$ is more restrictive than placing ground atoms in the global memory because constraint c must be logically consistent with the constraint store.

Extended Shared Prolog (ESP) [3] is a language for modeling rule-based software processes for distributed environments. ESP is based in the PoliS coordination model that extends Linda with multiple tuple spaces. The language design seeks for combining the PoliS mechanisms for coordinating distribution with the logic programming Prolog. Coordination takes place in ESP through a named multiset of passive and active tuples. They correspond to the global memory of facts in **Indeed**, although no further distinction between passive and active ground facts is made. ESP also extends Linda by using unification-based communication and backtracking to control program execution. In relation to the theoretical foundations, ESP has not a clean integration of interaction and deduction as suggested by **Indeed** in which the coordination component is given by providing a particular operational interpretation of the memory of facts.

Finally, *abduction* is a form of reasoning, particularly of synthetic inference, where a hypothesis is obtained from the evidence and the rule. In general, abduction is appropriate for reasoning with incomplete information, where hypothesis generation can be viewed as a method to assimilate knowledge to make information more complete. In [5,9] a proof procedure is based upon combining two forms of deduction: backward reasoning with iff-definitions to generate abductive hypothesis and forward reasoning with integrity constraints both to test input for consistency and to test whether existing information is redundant. This interleaved rationality-reactivity approach for a logic-based multi-agent architecture is similar to the followed in Indeed. However, our proposal suggests a language level syntactic guidance for the resolution theorem prover that can be compared to the programming model of the event-condition-action rules on Active Databases. In Indeed, forward rules solely directs the three-stage procedure of observing, thinking and acting on the knowledge base, whereas the abductive proof procedure of Abductive Logic Programming (ALP) is separated in the abductive phase of hypothesis generation and the consistency phase of incrementally check of the integrity constraints. We believe that the computational model of Indeed may lead to simpler and possibly more efficient implementations for a class of problems dealing with incomplete information. Nonetheless, compared to the rich theoretical framework of ALP for the treatment of negative literals in integrity constraints, the only form of negation used in Indeed is negation as failure.

The paper is organized as follows. First we illustrate the forward and backward search schemes that arise from our model with a programming example. Next, we introduce the declarative language: the syntax and the declarative semantics of the programming language.

2   A Programming Example

Dynamic systems can generally be decomposed into a collection of computing agents with local state. The distributed state of the entire system corresponds to the set of local states of each individual agent, whereas the specification of the system behavior is described by the axioms of logical theories. As agents perceive the surrounding environment through *sensors* and act upon it through *effectors*, their interaction can effectively be decoupled by a coordination medium consisting of a multiset of ground facts. By abstracting away interaction from deduction, the inherently complex operational details of sensors and effectors become irrelevant.

As an example, consider the problem of parsing simple arithmetic expressions. The compiler uses the context free grammar (CFG):

$$E \to 0 \mid 1 \mid (E) \mid E + E \mid E \times E$$

where non-terminal E stands for "expression". Ground atoms are used to represent the tokens forming the input expression and to represent well-formed sub-expressions as well.

Table 1 shows theory *Natural* for the natural numbers written in Indeed. This theory uses *backward rules* that have the general form $p \Leftarrow p_1, \ldots, p_n$ with $n \geq 0$. The logical propositions of the theory are built upon infix predicates =,

$<$, and $\leq$, whose recursive definitions are given by pure Prolog clauses $N1$ to $N5$. *Natural* represents the computational component of the interactive parser.

Table 1. Natural numbers using backward rules.

> **theory** *Natural*
> **axioms**
> $[N1]$ $0 + y = y \Leftarrow .$
> $[N2]$ $(x+1) + y = (x+y) + 1 \Leftarrow .$
> $[N3]$ $0 \leq y \Leftarrow .$
> $[N4]$ $(x+1) \leq (y+1) \Leftarrow x \leq y.$
> $[N5]$ $x < y \Leftarrow (x+1) \leq y.$
> **end**

Table 2 shows the theory *Parser* that extends *Natural* written in Indeed. This theory uses *forward rules* that have the general form $p_1, \ldots, p_n \Rightarrow p$ with $n \geq 0$. The rules of *Parser* define a bottom-up parser for simple arithmetic expressions whose syntactic entities are represented by ground atoms. $T(n, x)$ asserts that token x occurs at position n while $E(n1, n2)$, with $n1 \leq n2$, asserts that the sequence of tokens from $n1$ to $n2$ is a well-formed arithmetic expression. It is defined by self-explanatory rules in accordance with the given CFG.

Table 2. Bottom-up parser for arithmetic expressions.

> **theory** *Parser*
> **extends** *Natural*
> **axioms**
> $[P1]$ $T(n, \text{'}0\text{'}) \Rightarrow E(n, n).$
> $[P2]$ $T(n, \text{'}1\text{'}) \Rightarrow E(n, n).$
> $[P3]$ $T(n1, \text{'}(\text{'}), E(n2, n3), T(n4, \text{'})\text{'})$
> $| \; n1 + 1 = n2, n2 \leq n3, n3 + 1 = n4$
> $\Rightarrow E(n1, n4).$
> $[P4]$ $E(n1, n2), T(n3, \text{'}+\text{'}), E(n4, n5)$
> $| \; n1 \leq n2, n2 + 1 = n3, n3 + 1 = n4, n4 \leq n5$
> $\Rightarrow E(n1, n5).$
> $[P5]$ $E(n1, n2), T(n3, \text{'}\times\text{'}), E(n4, n5)$
> $| \; n1 \leq n2, n2 + 1 = n3, n3 + 1 = n4, n4 \leq n5$
> $\Rightarrow E(n1, n5).$
> **end**

Table 3 sketches the interaction of the parser that takes place in the common memory with sensors and effectors, dealing with the rather trivial, although illustrative, string:'(1+0)×1'. Atoms based on predicate T are placed in the memory by sensors and displayed from left to right as they are produced. As soon as the atoms occurring on the left-hand side of some rule of *Parser* become available, the parser removes them and places the atom occurring on the right-hand side of the rule. An effector may take the last produced atom to inform the editor that the analyzed expression is well-formed.

Table 3. Interactive parsing.

$$\Rightarrow T(1, '(')$$
$$\Rightarrow T(2, '1')$$
$$\overset{P2}{\Rightarrow} E(2,2)$$
$$\Rightarrow T(3, '+')$$
$$\Rightarrow T(4, '0')$$
$$\overset{P1}{\Rightarrow} E(4,4)$$
$$\overset{P4}{\Rightarrow} E(2,4)$$
$$\Rightarrow T(5, ')')$$
$$\overset{P3}{\Rightarrow} E(1,5)$$
$$\Rightarrow T(6, '\times')$$
$$\Rightarrow T(7, '1')$$
$$\overset{P2}{\Rightarrow} E(7,7)$$
$$\overset{P5}{\Rightarrow} E(1,7)$$

A transactional memory ensures the 'all-or-nothing' property in the shared resource concurrent access. Intuitively, the interaction parser proceeds as follows:

1. The initial agent's state is given by ground atoms. As no inputs have been detected from sensors, no rules apply and nothing can be deduced.
2. Eventually, after detecting some activity, sensors place in the shared memory the initial readings as ground atoms.
3. The interactive component determines which responses are necessary by selecting an appropriate forward rule whose left-hand side have a match with the contents of the shared memory.
4. Once a forward rule is selected, the reasoning component attempts to prove that its guarding constraints are satisfied.
5. Whenever the drawn conclusions hold, responses are produced by placing the ground atoms of the consequent part into the shared memory.
6. However, if the drawn conclusions are false, another forward rule, if any, is selected. If there is not a successful forward rule available, the agent waits for the reading of appropriate ground atoms obtained from the sensors.
7. Computation continues until no agent can apply a forward rule.

The current content of the memory is a key factor in selecting a forward rule. However, backward rules participate in the decision to apply the rule and the deduction of additional information.

3 Indeed Formal Description

In this section we provide the formal description of our programming language Indeed. First, we present the programming syntax along with the rules of the logical calculus. Then, we show a programming model derived from the inference rules. Finally, we will just point out the soundness and completeness of this particular logic.

3.1 Inference Rules

The names signature of the language comprises a set C of *constructor names* and a set X of *variable names*. The set $T(X)$ of *terms with variables* is the minimal set contaiining $C \cup X$, closed under composition of a constructor with a term sequence. The set T of *ground terms* consists of the terms with no variables. The set $A(X)$ consists of *atoms*, e.g. compositions of predicate symbols with term sequences. The set A of *ground atoms* consists of all atoms with no variables. A *clause* is a disjunction of *literals*, i.e. atoms or negated atoms, and is represented as a set $P = \{p_1, \ldots, p_n\}$. An *unit clause* contains only one atom. A *positive clause* contains no negated atoms. A *negative clause* contains no positive atoms. A *definite clause* contains at most a positive atom. A *goal* consists only of negative atoms and the set of goals is denoted by $G(X)$. A *guarded goal* has the form $P \mid G$ in which the atoms of P are defined by forward rules whereas the atoms of G are defined by backward rules. The set of all guarded atoms is denoted by $GG(X)$. A *substitution* is a map $\sigma : X \to T(X)$ and it admits a natural extension to terms $\sigma : T(X) \to T(X)$.

The theory Ax consists of all backward and forward rules. The theory Bx consists only of the backward rules in Ax. Both, backward and forward rules, have the same declarative reading: $p \Leftarrow P$ and $P \Rightarrow p$ are read p *holds if* P *holds*. In any case, p and P correspond to the *antecedent* and *consequent* parts of the rule. Nonetheless, the operational interpretations of the rule types are remarkably different. Backward rules have a goal directed control strategy, whereas forward rules are driven by unit clauses representing the currently known set of facts. With respect to unit clauses, their procedural interpretations coincide. Indeed, the proposed notation maintains the declarative meaning of clauses and makes explicit both the resolution method and the control strategy to be used. The forward rules denotation of the usual Horn clause logic is extending the expressiveness of classical logic programming languages. Let $Th(Ax)$ and $Th(Bx)$ be the sets of *deduced clauses* from Ax and Bx respectively. Deduction is determined by the application of the *inference rules* shown in Table 4

Backward rules roughly correspond to the procedural interpretation of SLD-resolution, while forward rules can be related to UR-resolution. Both resolutions

Table 4. Inference rules.

Instantiation rules	
$BI: \dfrac{p \Leftarrow P \in \text{Bx} \qquad \sigma : \text{X} \to \text{T(X)}}{p\sigma \Leftarrow P\sigma \in \text{Th(Bx)}}$	$FI: \dfrac{P \mid G \Rightarrow p \in \text{Ax} \qquad \sigma : \text{X} \to \text{T(X)}}{P\sigma \mid G\sigma \Rightarrow p\sigma \in \text{Th(Ax)}}$
Resolution rules	
$BR: \dfrac{\begin{array}{c} p \Leftarrow P \cup \{q\} \in \text{Th(Bx)} \\ q \Leftarrow Q \in \text{Th(Bx)} \end{array}}{p \Leftarrow P \cup Q \in \text{Th(Bx)}}$	$FR: \dfrac{\begin{array}{c} p_1 \cdots p_n \mid G \Rightarrow p \in \text{Th(Ax)} \\ \Leftarrow G \in \text{Th(Bx)} \\ \Rightarrow p_i \in \text{Th(Ax)} \; \forall i \le n \end{array}}{\Rightarrow p \in \text{Th(Ax)}}$

are known to be sound and refutation complete on definite clauses. Furthermore they can be combined with other strategies such as the set of support.

4   Interpretations, Soundness, and Completeness

Let $\mathbf{H}_{\text{Ax}}$ be Herbrand universe of Ax. The Herbrand base $\mathbf{B}_{\text{Ax}}$ for the definite program Ax is the set of all ground atoms formed using predicate symbols composed with ground terms at the Herbrand universe. The relation $\mathbf{A} \models C\sigma$ among a Herbrand algebra $\mathbf{A}$, a substitution σ and a clause C is canonical: C is true when its variables are substituted according to σ. A clause C is true in the interpretation $\mathbf{A}$, written $\mathbf{A} \models C$, if C is true for every substitution. A clause C is not true in the interpretation, $\mathbf{A} \not\models C$, when C is not true for some substitution. When C is an unsatisfiable goal, we may write $\mathbf{A} \models \Leftarrow C$ instead of $\mathbf{A} \not\models C$. Also:

- If $p(t_1, \ldots, t_n)$ is an atom, then $\mathbf{A} \models p(t_1, \ldots, t_n)\sigma$ iff $(t_1\sigma, \ldots, t_n\sigma) \in p_{\mathbf{A}}$.
- $\mathbf{A} \models \{p_1, \ldots, p_n\}\sigma$ iff $\mathbf{A} \models p_i\sigma$ for all $i = 1, \ldots, n$.
- $\mathbf{A} \models (p \Leftarrow P)\sigma$ iff $\mathbf{A} \models P\sigma$ implies $\mathbf{A} \models p\sigma$.
  In particular, $\mathbf{A} \models (p \Leftarrow)\sigma$ iff $\mathbf{A} \models p\sigma$.
- $\mathbf{A} \not\models \Leftarrow$.

For a set S of clauses, $\mathbf{A}$ models S if $\mathbf{A}$ is an interpretation for each clause in S. Given two set of clauses S and T, S *semantically implies* T, $S \models T$, if every model of S is also a model of T. The following is inmediate:

Lemma 1. *Let C and S be sets of definite clauses and G a definite goal. Then,*

1. $C \models C\sigma$ *for any substitution σ*
2. $S \cup \{C\} \models C$
3. $S \models S'$ *and* $S' \models S''$ *imply* $S \models S''$
4. $S \models C$ *implies* $S \models C'$ *if* $C \models C'$

Let us consider the problem to decide whether $\text{Ax} \models C$. Let $\mathcal{I}$ be a Herbrand interpretation for Ax. The monotonic map $T_{\text{Ax}} : 2^{\mathbf{B}_{\text{Ax}}} \to 2^{\mathbf{B}_{\text{Ax}}}$, $\mathcal{I} \mapsto$

$T_{\text{Ax}}(\mathcal{I}) \hat{=} \{p\sigma \in \mathbf{B}_{\text{Ax}} \mid P \Rightarrow p \in \text{Ax}, P\sigma \subseteq \mathcal{I}, \ \sigma : X \to T\}$ progressively determines the set of ground atoms that are logical consequence from the theory. Namely, $T_{\text{Ax}}(\emptyset) = \{p\sigma \mid (\Rightarrow p) \in \text{Ax}$ and σ a ground substitution$\}$ corresponds to the set of all ground facts of the theory. Let:

$$T_{\text{Ax}}^0 \hat{=} \emptyset \ ; \ T_{\text{Ax}}^n \hat{=} T(T_{\text{Ax}}^{n-1}) \text{ if } n > 0 \ ; \ T_{\text{Ax}}^\omega \hat{=} \bigcup_{n=0} T_{\text{Ax}}^n.$$

We may identify the least Herbrand model with the minimal model $\mathbf{A} = T_{\text{Ax}}^\omega$. The *success set* consists of all ground atoms refutable in the backward theory.

4.1   Soundness and Completeness of Forward Deduction

The following propositions are proved strightforwardly:

Proposition 1. *Forward resolution preserves consistency. I.e:*

$$(Ax \models Q \mid G \Rightarrow p \ \& \ Ax \models \ G\sigma \ \& \ Ax \models q\sigma \ \forall q \in Q) \ \Rightarrow \ Ax \models \Rightarrow p\sigma$$

Proposition 2 (Soundness of forward resolution as a deduction calculus). *Any ground atom q derived from* Ax *is a semantic consequence of* Ax.

Also, the following proposition holds:

Proposition 3 (Completeness of forward resolution as a deduction calculus). *If a positive ground atom p has a Herbrand model, then p can be derived from* Ax *by forward resolution.*

Proof. If the positive ground atom p has a Herbrand model then one of the following relations holds:

1. $Ax \models p$
2. T_{Ax}^ω is a model for $\Rightarrow p$
3. By definition of T_{Ax}, there exists a minimal integer n such that $\Rightarrow q\sigma \in T_{\text{Ax}}^n$. Then, there exists a rule $Q \mid G \Rightarrow q$ and a ground substitution σ such that, either $Q\sigma \mid G\sigma \subseteq \emptyset$ if $n = 0$ or $G\sigma : Q\sigma \subseteq T_{\text{Ax}}^{n-1}$ if $n > 0$, with $p = q\sigma$

In any case, it follows directly that $Ax \vdash \Rightarrow p$.

4.2   Computational Model

In this section we will construct a computational model for the previously defined logic. Let $\text{ID} = GG(X) \times (X \to T(X))$ consist of *instantaneous descriptions*, i.e. pairs *id* consisting of a guarded goal and a substitution instantiating the variables appearing at the goal. ID can be provided of two *transition* relations $\lhd, \rhd \subset \mathcal{P}(\text{ID}) \times \mathcal{P}(\text{ID})$ between sets of instantaneous descriptions, each one defining, respectively, the backward and forward computation relations. Transition relations are determined by the rules shown in Table 5.

Table 5. Rules for relation "transition".

$$\boxed{\begin{array}{c}
\textit{Backward computation}\\[4pt]
\hline
\dfrac{p \Leftarrow P \in \mathrm{Bx}}{(\Leftarrow G \cup \{p\sigma_2\}, \sigma_1) \triangleleft (\Leftarrow G\sigma_2 \cup P\sigma_2, \sigma_1\sigma_2)}\\[10pt]
\hline
\textit{Forward computation}\\[4pt]
\hline
\begin{array}{c}
p_1 \cdots p_n \mid G \Rightarrow p \in \mathrm{Ax}\\
(\Leftarrow G, \sigma) \triangleleft^* (\Leftarrow, \sigma)
\end{array}\\
\dfrac{}{I \cup \{(p_1\sigma, \sigma_1), \ldots, (p_n\sigma, \sigma_n)\} \triangleright I \cup \{(\Rightarrow p\sigma, \sigma_1 \cdots \sigma_m\sigma)\}}
\end{array}}$$

Given an instantaneous description $(\Leftarrow \{p\sigma_2\} \cup G, \sigma_1)$, the first transition applies backward resolution over corresponding instances σ_2 of the goal $\{p\} \cup G$ and the rule $p \Leftarrow P$. If more than one backward rule can be applied, just one candidate rules is non-deterministically selected. The second transition applies forward resolution over a set of ground atoms $\{(\Rightarrow p_1\sigma, \sigma_1), \ldots, (\Rightarrow p_n\sigma, \sigma_n)\}$ for some $n > 0$. The transition requires a suitable instance of rule $p_1, \ldots, p_n \mid G \Rightarrow p$ under some substitution σ such that $p_i\sigma = q_i\sigma$ for each $i \in \{1, \ldots, n\}$. Then, a new instantaneous description $(\Rightarrow p\sigma, \sigma_1 \cdots \sigma_n\sigma)$ is obtained if the guarding condition $G\sigma$ has a refutation with σ as the computed answer. If the guard $G\sigma$ fails, another forward rule is selected non-deterministically. Note that σ must lead to a ground goal $G\sigma$. The substitution $\sigma_1 \cdots \sigma_n\sigma$ enables a form of unification- based communication among the computing agents.

Let $\hookrightarrow$ be the refelxive-transitive closure of the union of $\triangleright$ and $\triangleleft$, $\hookrightarrow = (\triangleright \cup \triangleleft)^*$. Then, the correctness of the computational model can be stated as follows:

Proposition 4. *For any* Q, G, p:

$$Ax \models Q \mid G \Rightarrow p \;\Leftrightarrow\; \forall \sigma : (Ax \cup Q \cup G, \sigma) \hookrightarrow (p, \sigma).$$

We have implemented the programming model in a prototype system written in Prolog consisting of a compiler and a small run-time library. The main difficult in this implementation lies in the inherent complexity posed of selecting appropriate forward rules. A forward rule with n antecedents, each one having a set of k atoms realizes a match in time complexity $O(k^n)$ in the worst case. Fortunately, most applications typically have rules with no more than two antecedents. Our architecture adopts an event-driven approach that reduces the complexity in one order, i.e. $O(k^{n-1})$. Although the results are encouraging, we believe that to take full-advantage of this approach, a further improvement in the expressiveness of the language constructs is still necessary.

5   Conclusions

In this paper, we have addressed the problem of coupling interaction in resolution theorem provers. Our experimental programming language Indeed has been designed by distinguishing between state-based descriptions using forward rules and stateless deduction using backward rules. The distinction is important and convenient as the programming model allow us to combine backward and forward rule chaining in a single model. We have shown that our calculus is sound and complete in the limit case in which no interaction occurs.

References

1. M. Belmesk, Z. Habbas and P. Jorrand A Process Algebra over the Herbrand Universe: Application to Parallelism in Automated Deduction. In B. Fronhofer and G. Wrighston. *Parallelization of inference Systems*. LNAI 590. Springer-Verlag. 1990.
2. N. Carriero and D. Gelernter, Linda in Context, *CACM*, 32(4):444-458, Apr 1989.
3. P. Ciancarini Coordinating Rule-Based Software Processes with ESP, *ACM Trans. on Software Engineering and Methodology*, 2(3):203-227, July, 1993.
4. M. J. C. Gordon and T. F. Melham, *Introduction to HOL: A Theorem Proving Environment for Higher-Order Logic*. Cambridge University Press, 1993.
5. A.C. Kakas, R.A. Kowalski and F. Toni, The role of abduction in logic programming. *Handbook of Logic in AI and Logic Programming*, 5:235-324, Oxford University Press, 1998.
6. J.W. Lloyd, *Foundations of Logic Programming*, Springer-Verlag, 1987.
7. T. Nipkow, *Isabelle HOL: The Tutorial*, http://www.in.tum.de/~nipkow/, 1998
8. V.A. Saraswat Concurrent Constraint Programming. *Records of 17th ACM Symposium on Principles of Programming Languages*, 232-245. San Franciso, CA. 1990.
9. F. Sadri and F. Toni, Abduction with Negation as Failure for Active Databases and Agents. E. Lamma and P. Mello eds., *Springer Verlag LNAI*, 1792:49-60, 2000.
10. S. Tahar and P. Curzon, Comparing HOL and MDG: A Case Study on the Verification of an ATM Switch Fabric. *Nordic Journal of Computing*, 6(4):372-402, Winter 1999.
11. R.D. Tennet, *Semantics of Programming Languages*, Prentice Hall Intl., 1991.
12. P. Wegner, Interactive Software Technology, *CRC Handbook of Computer Science and Engineering*, May 1996.
13. L. Wos, R. Overbeek, E. Lusk and J. Boyle, *Automated Reasoning. Introduction and Applications*, McGraw-Hill, Inc., 1992.
14. L. Wos and G. Pieper, *A Fascinating Country in the World of Computing: Your Guide to Automated Reasoning*, World Scientific Publishing Co., 1999.

Restricted Δ-Trees and Reduction Theorems in Multiple-Valued Logics*

Inma P. de Guzmán, Manuel Ojeda-Aciego, and Agustín Valverde

Dept. Matemática Aplicada
Universidad de Málaga
{aciego, guzman, a_valverde}@ctima.uma.es

Abstract. In this paper we continue the theoretical study of the possible applications of the Δ-tree data structure for multiple-valued logics, specifically, to be applied to signed propositional formulas. The Δ-trees allow a compact representation for signed formulas as well as for a number of reduction strategies in order to consider only those occurrences of literals which are relevant for the satisfiability of the input formula. New and improved versions of reduction theorems for finite-valued propositional logics are introduced, and a satisfiability algorithm is provided which further generalise the TAS method [1,5].

1 Introduction

Automated deduction in multiple-valued logic has been based on the notions of *sign* and *signed formula*, which allow one to apply classical methods in the analysis of multiple-valued logics. The main idea is to apply the following bivalued metalinguistic interpretation of multiple-valued sentences: For example, in a 3-valued logic with truth-values $\{0, 1/2, 1\}$ and with $\{1\}$ as the designated value, the satisfiability of a formula φ can be expressed as: *Is it possible to evaluate φ in $\{1\}$?* In the same way, the unsatisfiability of φ is expressed by: *Is it possible to evaluate φ in $\{0, 1/2\}$?* These questions correspond to the study of validity of the signed formulas $\{1\}{:}\varphi$ and $\{0,1/2\}{:}\varphi$, which are evaluated on the set $\{0, 1\}$. In other words, the formulas in a signed logic are constructions of the form $S{:}\varphi$, where S is a set of truth-values of the multiple-valued logic, called the *sign*, and φ is a formula of that logic.

Although there are interesting works on automated deduction for infinitely-valued logics [2,8], we will only be concerned with n-valued logics. The reason for focussing only on the finitely-valued case is that "fuzzy" truth-values (or human preferences) are usually described in a granulated way, by steps in the degree of perception. This is connected to the well-known fact that people can only distinguish finitely many degrees of quality (closeness, cheapness, ...) or quantity in control.

The first works to provide a systematic treatment of sets of truth-values as signs were due to Hähnle in [7] and Murray and Rosenthal in [9]. There, the notion of *signed formula* is formally introduced. In [7] these tools are used in the framework of truth tables,

---

* Research partially supported by Spanish DGI project BFM2000-1054-C02-02 and Junta de Andalucía project TIC-115.

F.J. Garijo, J.C. Riquelme, and M. Toro (Eds.): IBERAMIA 2002, LNAI 2527, pp. 161–171, 2002.

while in [9] they are used to develop another nonclausal proof method *dissolution*. As a result of these works, the use of signed formulas in the field of automated deduction has been extended, and has led to significant advances in this method; therefore, efficient representations for signed formulas are necessary in order to describe and implement efficient algorithms on this kind of formulas.

An approach to the efficient handling of signed formulas that one finds in the literature is the clause form, which allow the extension of classical techniques such as resolution, or Davis-Putnam procedures. Another approach is that of Multiple-Valued Decision Diagrams (MDDs) and its variants [3], but they are not useful for the study of satisfiability because, although they make straightforward its testing, the construction of a restricted MDD for a given formula requires exponential space in the worst case.

Our approach to automated deduction for signed logics follows the TAS methodology [1,5], that is, the application of as much reduction theorems with low complexity as possible before applying a branching rule. The main aim of the paper is of theoretical nature, to provide a TAS-based satisfiability algorithm for signed formulas.

To work with signed formulas, we will follow the approach introduced in [4,6], interpreting signed formulas by means of Δ-trees, that is, trees of clauses and cubes. In this paper, we will be concerned with the metatheory of multiple-valued Δ-trees, not with implementation issues.

2   Reduced Signed Logics and Multiple-Valued Δ-Trees

The notion of *reduced signed logic* is a generalisation of previous approaches, and it is developed in a general propositional framework without reference either to an initially given multiple-valued logic or to a specific algorithm, ie. the definition is completely independent of the particular application at hand. The generalisation consists in introducing a *possible truth values function*, denoted ω, to restrict the truth values for each variable. These restrictions can be motivated by the specific application and they can be managed dynamically by the algorithms. For example, in [10] are used to characterize non-monotonic reasoning systems.

The formulas in the reduced signed logic $\mathbf{S}_\omega$, the *signed logic valued in* $\mathbf{n}$ *by* ω, are built by using the connectives $\wedge$ and $\vee$ on ω-*signed literals* (or simply, literals): if $\mathbf{n} = \{1, \ldots, n\}$ is a finite set of truth-values, $\mathcal{V}$ is the set of propositional variables and $\omega \colon \mathcal{V} \to (2^{\mathbf{n}} \smallsetminus \varnothing)$ is a mapping, called the *possible truth-values function*, then the set of ω-*signed literals* is $\mathrm{LIT}_\omega = \{S{:}p \mid S \subseteq \omega(p), p \in \mathcal{V}\} \cup \{\bot, \top\}$.

In a literal $\ell = S{:}p$, the set S is called the *sign of* ℓ and p is the *variable of* ℓ. The complement of a signed literal $S{:}p$ is $(\omega(p) \smallsetminus S){:}p$ and will be denoted $\overline{S{:}p}$.

The semantics of $\mathbf{S}_\omega$ is defined using the ω-*assignments*. The ω-assignments are mappings from the language into the set $\{0, 1\}$ that interpret $\vee$ as maximum, $\wedge$ as minimum, $\bot$ as falsity, $\top$ as truth and, in addition, satisfy:

1. For every p there exists a unique $j \in S$ such that $I(\{j\}{:}p) = 1$
2. $I(S{:}p) = 1$ if and only if there exists $j \in S$ such that $I(\{j\}{:}p) = 1$

These conditions arise from the objective for which signed logics were created: the ω-assignment I over $S{:}p$ is 1 if the variable p is assigned a value in S; this value must be unique for every multiple-valued assignment and thus unique for every ω-assignment. This is why we sometimes will write $I(\{j\}{:}p) = 1$ as $I(p) = j$.

An important operation in the sequel will be the *reduction* of a signed logic. This operation decreases the possible truth-values set for one or more propositional variables. The reduction will be forced during the application of an algorithm but it can also help us to specify a problem using signed formulas. Specifically, we will use two basic reductions: to prohibit a specific value for a given variable, $[p \neq j]$, and to force a specific value for a given variable, $[p = j]$: If ω is a possible truth-values function, then the possible truth-values functions $\omega[p \neq j]$ and $\omega[p = j]$ are defined as follows:

$$\omega[p \neq j](v) = \begin{cases} \omega(p) \smallsetminus \{j\} & \text{if } v = p \\ \omega(v) & \text{otherwise} \end{cases} \qquad \omega[p = j](v) = \begin{cases} \{j\} & \text{if } v = p \\ \omega(v) & \text{otherwise} \end{cases}$$

If A is a formula in $\mathbf{S}_\omega$, we define the following substitutions:

- $A[p \neq j]$ is a formula in $\mathbf{S}_{\omega[p \neq j]}$ obtained from A by replacing $\{j\}{:}p$ by $\bot$, $\overline{\{j\}{:}p}$ by $\top$, $S{:}p$ by $(S \smallsetminus \{j\}){:}p$ and, in addition, the constants are deleted using the 0-1-laws.
- $A[p = j]$ is a formula in $\mathbf{S}_{\omega[p = j]}$ obtained from A by replacing every literal $S{:}p$ satisfying $j \in S$ by $\top$ and every literal $S{:}p$ satisfying $j \notin S$ by $\bot$; in addition, the constants are deleted using the 0-1-laws.

An immediate consequence is the following: if I is a model of A in $\mathbf{S}_\omega$ and $I(p) \neq j$, then (the restriction of) I is also a model of $A[p \neq j]$ in $\mathbf{S}_{\omega[p \neq j]}$; if I is a model of A in $\mathbf{S}_\omega$ and $I(p) = j$, then I is a model of $A[p = j]$ in $\mathbf{S}_{\omega[p = j]}$.

Throughout the rest of the paper, we will use the following standard definitions. A signed formula A in $\mathbf{S}_\omega$ is said to be *satisfiable* if there is an ω-assignment I such that $I(A) = 1$; in this case I is said to be a *model* for A. Two signed formulas A and B are said to be *equisatisfiable*, denoted $A \approx B$, if A is satisfiable iff B is satisfiable. Two formulas A and B are said to be *equivalent*, denoted $A \equiv B$, if $I(A) = I(B)$ for all ω-assignment I. We will also use the usual notions of clause (disjunction of literals) and cube (conjunction of literals). Given a set of formulas Ω, the notation $\Omega \models A$ means that all models for Ω are also models for A. A literal ℓ is an *implicant* of a formula A if $\ell \models A$. A literal ℓ is an *implicate* of a formula A if $A \models \ell$.

Multiple-valued Δ-trees. The satisfiability algorithm we will describe is based on the structure of multiple-valued Δ-trees. In the classical case, nodes in the Δ-trees correspond to lists of literals; in the multiple-valued case we will exploit a duality in the representation of signed literals in terms of literals whose sign is a singleton. To better understand this duality, let us consider the literal $\{1,4\}{:}p$ in the signed logic $\mathbf{S}_\omega$ where $\omega(p) = \{1, 2, 4, 5\}$, then: $\{1,4\}{:}p \equiv \{1\}{:}p \vee \{4\}{:}p$ and $\{1,4\}{:}p \equiv \overline{\{2\}{:}p} \wedge \overline{\{5\}{:}p}$. This way, we have both a disjunctive and a conjunctive representation of signed literals using the literals $\{j\}{:}p$ and $\overline{\{j\}{:}p}$, which are called *basic literals*. In the sequel, we will use a simpler representation for these literals: $pj =_{def} \{j\}{:}p$ and $\overline{pj} =_{def} \overline{\{j\}{:}p}$.

The basic literals pj are the *positive literals* and their complements, $\overline{pj}$, are the *negative literals*. In the Δ-tree representation we work with lists of positive literals.

Definition 1.

1. *A list/set of positive literals,* λ, *is* saturated *for the variable p if pj* $\in \lambda$ *for all* $j \in \omega(p)$. *(This kind of lists/sets will be interpreted as logical constants.)*
2. *A* Δ-*list is either the symbol* $\natural$ *or a list of positive literals such that it does not have repeated literals and it is non-saturated for any propositional variable.*
3. *A* Δ-*tree* T *is a tree with labels in the set of* Δ-*lists.*

In order to define the operator sgf which interprets a Δ-tree as a signed formula, we should keep in mind that:

1. The empty list, nil, has different conjunctive and disjunctive interpretations, since it is well-known the identification of the empty clause with $\bot$ and the empty cube with $\top$; but anyway it corresponds to the neutral element for the corresponding interpretation. Similarly, we will use a unique symbol, $\natural$, to represent the absorbent elements, $\bot$ and $\top$, under conjunctive and disjunctive interpretation, respectively.
2. A Δ-tree will always represent a conjunctive signed formula, however, its subtrees are alternatively interpreted as either conjunctive or disjunctive signed formulas, i.e. the immediate subtrees of a conjunctive Δ-tree are disjunctive, and vice versa.

Definition 2. *The operator* sgf *over the set of* Δ-*trees is defined as follows:*

1. $\text{sgf}(\texttt{nil}) = \top,\ \text{sgf}(\natural) = \bot,\ \text{sgf}(\ell_1 \ldots \ell_n) = \overline{\ell_1} \wedge \cdots \wedge \overline{\ell_n}$

2. $\text{sgf}\left(\begin{array}{c} \lambda \\ \overbrace{} \\ T_1 \quad \ldots \quad T_m \end{array} \right) = \text{sgf}(\lambda) \wedge \text{dsgf}(T_1) \wedge \cdots \wedge \text{dsgf}(T_m)$

where the auxiliary operator dsgf *is defined as follow:*

1. $\text{dsgf}(\texttt{nil}) = \bot,\ \text{dsgf}(\natural) = \top,\ \text{dsgf}(\ell_1 \ldots \ell_n) = \ell_1 \vee \cdots \vee \ell_n$

2. $\text{dsgf}\left(\begin{array}{c} \lambda \\ \overbrace{} \\ T_1 \quad \ldots \quad T_m \end{array} \right) = \text{dsgf}(\lambda) \vee \text{sgf}(T_1) \vee \cdots \vee \text{sgf}(T_m)$

In short, we will write $\hat{T} = \text{sgf}(T)$ *and* $\overset{\vee}{T} = \text{dsgf}(T)$; *in particular, if* $T = \lambda = \ell_1 \ldots \ell_n$ *we have:* $\overset{\wedge}{\lambda} = \ell_1 \wedge \cdots \wedge \ell_n$ *and* $\overset{\vee}{\lambda} = \ell_1 \vee \cdots \vee \ell_n$.

An important feature of the structure of Δ-tree is that it gives us a means to calculate implicants and implicates, to be used in the reduction transformations below.

Proposition 1. *If* T *is rooted with* λ *and* $pj \in \lambda$, *then:*

$$\text{sgf}(T) \models \overline{pj} \qquad \text{and} \qquad pj \models \text{dsgf}(T)$$

The notions of validity, satisfiability, equivalence, equisatisfiability or model are defined on Δ-trees by means of the sgf operator; for example, a Δ-tree, T is satisfiable if and only if sgf(T) is satisfiable and the models of T are the models of sgf(T).

In [6] we formally introduced operators to define the converse translation: specifically, operators $c\Delta List$, $d\Delta List$ and $\Delta Tree$ are defined. The first two are auxiliary operators (the inverse of the base cases of sgf and dsgf) and $\Delta Tree$ constructs the Δ-tree associated to a general signed formula.

Example 1. In the logic $\mathbf{S}_\omega$ with $\omega(p) = \{1,2,4,5\}$, $\omega(q) = \{1,2,3\}$, $\omega(r) = \{2,5\}$.

- $d\Delta List(\{1,4\}{:}p \vee \{1,2\}{:}q) = p1\,p4\,q1\,q2$
- $c\Delta List(\{1,4\}{:}p \wedge \{1,2\}{:}q) = p2\,p5\,q3$
- $d\Delta List(\{1,4\}{:}p \vee \{2\}{:}r \vee \{2,4,5\}{:}p) = \natural$, for $\{p1, p2, p4, p5, r2\}$ is saturated for p.
- $c\Delta List(\{1\}{:}q \wedge \{1,2,4\}{:}p \wedge \{2\}{:}q) = \natural$, for $\{p5, q1, q2, q3\}$ is saturated for q.

Recall that, as established in [6], a Δ-tree will always be interpreted as a conjunctive signed formula and arbitrary signed formulas are represented by means of lists of Δ-trees;[1] this way, the study of satisfiability can be performed in parallel.

Example 2. The following examples are from $\mathbf{S}_3$, where 3 denotes the constant mapping defined as $3(p) = \mathbf{3}$ for all p.

$$\Delta Tree((\{1,2\}{:}p \vee \{2\}{:}q) \wedge (\{2,3\}{:}p \vee \{1,3\}{:}r)) = \left[\begin{array}{c} \text{nil} \\ \overbrace{} \\ p1p2q2 \quad p2p3r1r3 \end{array} \right]$$

$$\Delta Tree(\{2,3\}{:}q \vee (\{1,2\}{:}p \wedge (\{1,2\}{:}q \vee \{2,3\}{:}p) \wedge (\{3\}{:}q \vee \{1\}{:}p)))$$
$$= \left[q1, \begin{array}{c} p3 \\ \overbrace{} \\ p2p3q1q2 \quad p1q3 \end{array} \right]$$

It is interesting to recall the intrinsic parallelism between the usual representation of cnfs as lists of clauses and our representation of signed formulas as lists of Δ-trees.

3 Restricted Δ-Trees

In multiple-valued logic there is not a notion which captures the well-known definition of restricted clauses of classical logic, in which complementary literals and logical constants are not allowed. We can say that restricted Δ-trees are Δ-trees without *trivially redundant* information. In this section we give a suitable generalisation built on the notion of restricted multiple-valued Δ-tree which is built from its classical counterpart [4].

Definition 3. *The operators* Uni *and* Int *are defined on the set of Δ-lists as follows. If $\lambda_1, \dots, \lambda_n$ are Δ-lists then:*

1. $\mathtt{Uni}(\lambda_1, \dots, \lambda_n) = \natural$ *if either there exists i such that $\lambda_i = \natural$ or $\bigcup_{i=1}^n \lambda_i$ is saturated for some variable p. Otherwise,* $\mathtt{Uni}(\lambda_1, \dots, \lambda_n) = \bigcup_{i=1}^n \lambda_i$.
2. $\mathtt{Int}(\lambda_1, \dots, \lambda_n) = \natural$ *if $\lambda_i = \natural$ for all i.*

---

[1] To help the reading, we will write these lists with the elements separated by commas and using square brackets as delimiters. This way, for example, $p_1 j_1 \dots p_n j_n$ is a Δ-list, and $[p_1 j_1, \dots, p_n j_n]$ is a list of Δ-trees (in which each Δ-tree is a leaf, which turns out to be a singleton Δ-list).

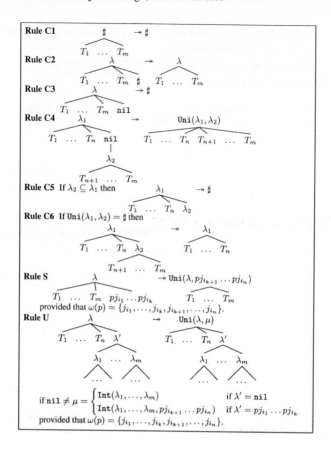

Fig. 1. Rewriting rules to obtain the restricted form

Otherwise, $\text{Int}(\lambda_1, \ldots, \lambda_n) = \bigcap_{\lambda_i \neq \sharp} \lambda_i.$

The following definition gathers the specific situations that will not be allowed in a restricted form: nodes in the Δ-tree which, in some sense, can be substituted by either $\perp$ or $\top$ without affecting the meaning, and also leaves with only one propositional variable; in addition, our restricted trees must have explicitly the implicants and implicates of every subtree in order to perform the reductions based in these objects (see [5]).

Definition 4. *Let T be a Δ-tree.*

1. *A node of T is said to be* conclusive *if it satisfies any of the following conditions:*
   - *It is labelled with $\sharp$, provided that $T \neq \sharp$.*
   - *It is either a leaf or a monary node labelled with* nil, *provided that it is not the root node.*
   - *It is labelled with λ, it has an immediate successor λ' which is a leaf and $\lambda' \subseteq \lambda$.*
   - *It is labelled with λ and* $\text{Uni}(\lambda, \lambda') = \sharp$, *where λ' is the label of its predecessor.*

2. *A leaf in T is said to be* simple *if the literals in its label share a common propositional variable.*

3. *Let λ be the label of a node of T; let λ' be the label of one immediate successor of λ and let $\lambda_1, \ldots, \lambda_n$ be the labels of the immediate successors of λ'. We say that λ can be updated if it satisfies some of the following conditions:*
   - *$\lambda' = \texttt{nil}$ and $\texttt{Int}(\lambda_1, \ldots, \lambda_m) \not\subseteq \lambda$.*
   - *$\lambda' = pj_{i_1} \ldots pj_{i_k}$ and $\texttt{Int}(\lambda_1, \ldots, \lambda_m, pj_{i_{k+1}} \ldots pj_{i_n}) \not\subseteq \lambda$, provided that $\omega(p) = \{j_{i_1}, \ldots, j_{i_k}, j_{i_{k+1}}, \ldots, j_{i_n}\}$.*

   We say that T is updated *if it has no nodes that can be updated.*

4. *If T is updated and it has neither conclusive nodes nor simple leaves, then it is said to be* restricted.

The rewriting rules in Fig. 1 (up to the order of the successors) allow to delete the conclusive nodes and simple leaves of a Δ-tree and in addition, to update the updatable nodes. Note that the rewriting rules have a double meaning; since they need not apply to the root node, the interpretation can be either conjunctive or disjunctive. This is just another efficiency-related feature of Δ-trees: duality of connectives $\wedge$ and $\vee$ gets subsumed in the structure and it is not necessary to determine the conjunctive/disjunctive behaviour to decide the transformation to be applied.

Theorem 1. *If T is a Δ-tree, there exists a list of restricted Δ-trees, $[T_1, \ldots, T_n]$, such that $\texttt{sgf}(T) \equiv \hat{T}_1 \vee \cdots \vee \hat{T}_n$.*

The proof of the theorem allows to specify a procedure to obtain $[T_1, \ldots, T_n]$. Let T' be the Δ-tree obtained from T by exhaustively applying the rules C1, C2, C3, C4, C5, C6, S, and U till none of them can be applied any more, then the list of restricted Δ-trees $[T_1, \ldots, T_n]$, denoted by $\texttt{Restrict}(T)$, is defined as:[2]

1. If $T' = $
$$
\begin{array}{c}
\texttt{nil} \\
| \\
\texttt{nil} \\
\diagup \quad \diagdown \\
T_1 \quad \cdots \quad T_n
\end{array}
$$
then $\texttt{Restrict}(T) = [T_1, \ldots, T_n]$

2. If $T' = $
$$
\begin{array}{c}
\texttt{nil} \\
| \\
\lambda \\
\diagup \quad \diagdown \\
T_1 \quad \cdots \quad T_n
\end{array}
$$
, and $\texttt{dsgf}(\lambda) = S_1{:}p_1 \vee \cdots \vee S_k{:}p_k$ with $p_i \neq p_j$ for every $i \neq j$, then $\texttt{Restrict}(T) = [\texttt{c}\Delta\texttt{List}(S_1{:}p_1), \ldots, \texttt{c}\Delta\texttt{List}(S_k{:}p_k), T_1, \ldots, T_n]$

3. Otherwise, $\texttt{Restrict}(T) = [T']$.

4 Reduction of Δ-Trees

In this section we introduce the reduction theorems used by the TAS algorithm to be given later, which motto is to apply as much reductions with low complexity as possible before applying a branching rule.

---

[2] These patterns correspond to the elimination of a conclusive node at the root, which cannot be deleted by rule C4.

In the statements of the reductions we will use the substitutions $[p = j]$ and $[p \neq j]$, defined on Δ-trees as follows:

Definition 5. *Let T be a Δ-tree.*

1. $[p \neq j]T$ *is the Δ-tree in* $\mathbf{S}_{w[p \neq j]}$ *obtained from T deleting every occurrence of pj in T and, in addition, if a node is saturated for some variable, it is substituted by $\natural$.*
2. $[p = j]T$ *is the Δ-tree in* $\mathbf{S}_{w[p=j]}$ *obtained from T by the applications of the following transformations:*
   a) *If pj is in the root of T, then $[p = j]T = \natural$ (that is, $\mathtt{sgf}([p = j]T) = \bot$).*
   b) *Otherwise, every subtree rooted with a list λ such that $pj \in \lambda$ is deleted and any occurrence of a literal pj' with $j \neq j'$ is also deleted.*
   In addition, if a node is saturated for some variable, it is substituted by $\natural$.

Obviously, these operations on Δ-trees are the same to those on signed formulas:

Lemma 1. *If T is a Δ-tree, then:*
$$\mathtt{sgf}([p = j]T) \equiv \mathtt{sgf}(T)[p = j], \mathtt{sgf}([p \neq j]T) \equiv \mathtt{sgf}(T)[p \neq j].$$

The main result to prove the soundness of the reductions on signed formulas is given below. The theorem allows to drive literals downwards to force either contradictions or tautologies, which can be deleted. In the subsequent corollary we apply the theorem to delete several occurrences of literals; this result is the theoretical support of both the *subreduction* and the *complete reduction*.

Theorem 2. *Let A be a signed formula and η a subformula of A.*

1. *If $A \models \overline{pj}$, then $A \equiv \overline{pj} \wedge A[\eta/\eta \wedge \overline{pj}]$.*
2. *If $pj \models A$, then $A \equiv pj \vee A[\eta/\eta \vee pj]$.*

Corollary 1. *Let A be a signed formula.*

1. *If $A \models \overline{pj}$, then $A \equiv \overline{pj} \wedge A[p \neq j]$, and also $A \approx A[p \neq j]$.*
2. *If $pj \models A$, then $A \equiv pj \vee A[p = j]$.*

The Δ-tree representation is very adequate to apply these properties, because the basic literals in the nodes are either implicants or implicates of the corresponding subformula, as stated in Proposition 1. All the transformations performed by operator $\mathtt{Restrict}$ use just the information of a node and its immediate successors. The next transformation uses "ascending" information, in that nodes are simplified according to information from its ascendants.

Definition 6 (Subreduction). *Let T be a restricted Δ-tree. $\mathtt{SubRed}(T)$ is the Δ-tree obtained form T performing the following transformations in a depth-first traverse:*

1. *If the union of the ascendant nodes of η (including η itself) is saturated for a variable p, then the subtree rooted at η is deleted.*
2. *Otherwise, in a node labelled with λ we delete a literal $pj \in \lambda$ if pj occurs in some proper ascendant of the node.*

Theorem 3. *Let T be a Δ-tree, then* $\mathrm{SubRed}(T) \equiv T$.

The following proposition, which follows easily from the definition of subreduction, states that only the dominant occurrences of literals are present in a subreduced Δ-tree.

Proposition 2. *Let T be a Δ-tree. In every branch of* $\mathrm{SubRed}(T)$ *there is at most one occurrence of each propositional variable. In particular, if ℓ is a literal in* $\mathrm{SubRed}(T)$, *then there is no occurrence of ℓ under ℓ.*

Example 3. We are going to apply the SubRed operator to the following Δ-tree in $\mathbf{S}_\omega$ with $\omega(p) = 5$, $\omega(q) = \{1, 3, 5\}$, $\omega(r) = \{1, 2\}$, $\omega(s) = \{1, 4, 5\}$.

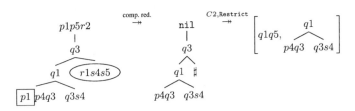

Now we introduce a satisfiability-preserving transformation which, essentially, is a refinement of the subreduction of the Δ-list of the root. Theorem 4 is the Δ-tree formulation of Corollary 1, item 1 (2nd assertion).

Definition 7. *A Δ-tree with non-empty root is said to be* completely reducible.

Theorem 4 (Complete reduction). *If $\lambda \neq \mathrm{nil}$ is the root of T and $pj \in \lambda$, then $T \approx [p \neq j]T$. If I is a model of $[p \neq j]T$ in $\mathbf{S}_{w[p \neq j]}$, then I is a model of T in $\mathbf{S}_\omega$.*

Example 4. Let us consider the initial Δ-tree, T, in Example 3 with the same signed logic. The Δ-tree is completely reducible and thus it is satisfiable iff $[p \neq 1, p \neq 5, r \neq 2]T$ is satisfiable in $\mathbf{S}_{\omega'}$ with $\omega'(p) = \{2, 3, 4\}$, $\omega'(q) = \{1, 3, 5\}$, $\omega'(r) = \{1\}$, $\omega'(s) = \{1, 4, 5\}$. (In fact, it is satisfiable, because the first element in the list is a clause, and $I(q) = 3$ is a model for it).

The TAS Algorithm for Signed Logics: One cannot hope that the reduction strategies are enough to prove the satisfiability of any signed formula. This is only possible after adding a suitable branching strategy, which is based on the Davis-Putnam procedure.

The algorithm handles a list of pairs $[(T_1, \omega_1), \ldots, (T_m, \omega_m)]$, called the *flow*, where the T_i are Δ-trees and ω_i are possible truth values functions. For the satisfiability of a formula A, we set $[T_1, \ldots, T_n] = \Delta\text{Tree}(A)$ and, in the initial list $\omega_i = \mathbf{n}$ for all i.

Given the flow in some instant during the execution of the algorithm, the initial Δ-tree is unsatisfiable iff every T_i is unsatisfiable in $\mathbf{S}_{\omega_i}$, that is $T_i = \natural$ for all i.[3]

1. UPDATING: On the initial list, and after each reduction, the Δ-trees are converted to restricted form.
2. COMPLETE REDUCTION: If some of the elements of the list of tasks is completely reducible, then the transformation is applied and the corresponding logic is reduced.
3. SUBREDUCTION: If no task is completely reducible, then the subreduction transformation is applied.
4. BRANCHING: Finally, if no transformation applies to the list of tasks, then a random task is chosen together with a literal pj to branch on, as follows:

$$[\ldots, (T, \omega), \ldots] \twoheadrightarrow [\ldots, ([p = j]T, \omega[p = j]), ([p \neq j]T, \omega[p \neq j]), \ldots]$$

5   Conclusions and Future Work

A multiple-valued extension of the results obtained for classical logic in [4] has been introduced, which can be seen as the refined version of the results in [5]. As a result it is possible to obtain simpler statements of the theorems and, as a consequence, reduction transformations are more adequately described in terms of rewrite rules.

We have introduced Δ-trees for signed formulas. This allows for a compact representation for well-formed formulas as well as for a number of reduction strategies in order to consider only those occurrences of literals which are relevant for the satisfiability of the input formula. The reduction theorems have been complemented by a Davis-Putnam-like branching strategy in order to provide a decision procedure.

References

1. G. Aguilera, I.P. de Guzmán, M. Ojeda-Aciego, and A. Valverde. Reductions for non-clausal theorem proving. *Theoretical Computer Science*, 266(1/2):81–112, 2001.
2. S. Aguzzoli and A. Ciabattoni. Finiteness in infinite-valued Lukasiewicz logic. *Journal of Logic, Language and Information*, 9(1):5–29, 2000.
3. C. Files, R. Drechsler, and M. Perkowski. Functional decomposition of MVL functions using multi-valued decision diagrams. In *Proc. ISMVL'97*, pages 7–32, 1997.
4. G. Gutiérrez, I.P. de Guzmán, J. Martínez, M. Ojeda-Aciego, and A. Valverde. Satisfiability testing for Boolean formulas using Δ-trees. *Studia Logica*, 72:33–60, 2002.

---

[3] The actual search done by the algorithm is to obtain an element (nil, ω) in the list of tasks. In this case, the input formula is satisfiable by any assignment in $\mathbf{S}_\omega$.

5. I.P. de Guzmán, M. Ojeda-Aciego, and A. Valverde. Reducing signed propositional formulas. *Soft Computing*, 2(4):157–166, 1999.
6. I.P. de Guzmán, M. Ojeda-Aciego, and A. Valverde. Restricted Δ-trees in multiple-valued logics. In *AI - Methodologies, Systems, Applications. AIMSA'02*. Lect. Notes in Computer Science 2443, 2002.
7. R. Hähnle. Uniform notation of tableaux rules for multiple-valued logics. In *Proc. Intl Symp on Multiple-Valued Logic*, pages 238–245. IEEE Press, 1991.
8. D. Mundici and N. Olivetti. Resolution and model building in the infinite-valued calculus of Lukasiewicz. *Theoretical Computer Science*, 200:335–366, 1998.
9. N.V. Murray and E. Rosenthal. Improving tableau deductions in multiple-valued logics. In *Proc. 21st Intl Symp on Multiple-Valued Logic*, pages 230–237. IEEE Press, 1991.
10. D. Pearce, I.P. de Guzmán, and A. Valverde. Computing equilibrium models using signed formulas. In *Proc. 1st Intl Conf on Computational Logic, CL'2000*, Lect. Notes in Artificial Intelligence 1861, pages 688–702, 2000.

Max-CSP Approach for Software Diagnosis

R. Ceballos, Rafael M. Gasca, Carmelo Del Valle, and Miguel Toro

Languages and Computer Systems Department, University of Seville
Computer Engineering Superior Technical School,
Avenida Reina Mercedes s/n 41012 Sevilla(Spain)

Abstract. In software development is essential to have tools for the software diagnosis to help the programmers and development engineers to locate the bugs. In this paper, we propose a new approach that identifies the possible bugs and detect why the program does not satisfy the specified result. A typical diagnosis problem is built starting from the structure and semantics of the original source code and the precondition and postcondition formal specifications. When we apply a determined test case to a program and this program fails, then we can use our methodology in order to obtain automatically the sentence or the set of sentences that contains the bug. The originality of our methodology is due to the use of a constraint-based model for software and Max-CSP techniques to obtain the minimal diagnosis and to avoid explicitly to build the functional dependency graph.

1 Introduction

Software diagnosis allows us to identify the parts of the program that fail. Most of the approaches appeared in the last decade have based the diagnosis method on the use of models (Model Based Diagnosis). The JADE Project investigated the software diagnosis using Model Based Debugging. The papers related to this project use a dependence model based on the source code. The model represents the sentences and expressions as if they were components, and the variables as if they were connections. They transform $Java^{TM}$ constructs into components. The assignments, conditions, loops, etc. have their corresponding method of transformation. For a bigger concretion the reader can consult [10][11].

Previously to these works, it has been suggested the *Slicing* technique in software diagnosis. This technique identifies the constructs of the source code that can influence in the value of a variable in a given point of the program [12][13]. *Dicing*[9] is an extension to this technique. It was proposed as a fault localization method for reducing the number of statements that need to be examined to find faults with respect to *Slicing*. In the last years, new methods [3][5] have arisen to automate software diagnosis process.

In this work, we present an alternative approach to the previous works. The main idea is to transform the source code into constraints what avoids the explicit construction of the functional dependencies graph of the program variables. The following resources must be available to apply this methodology: Source code,

F.J. Garijo, J.C. Riquelme, and M. Toro (Eds.): IBERAMIA 2002, LNAI 2527, pp. 172–181, 2002.
© Springer-Verlag Berlin Heidelberg 2002

precondition and postcondition. If the source code is executed in some of the states defined by the precondition, then it is guaranteed that the source code will finish in some of the states defined by the postcondition. Nothing is guaranteed if the source code is executed in an initial state that broke the precondition.

We use Max-CSP techniques to carry out the minimal diagnosis. A Constraint Satisfaction is a framework for modelling and solving real-problems as a set of constraints among variables. A Constraint Satisfaction is defined by a set of variables $X=\{X_1,X_2...,X_n\}$ associated with a domain, $D=\{D_1,D_2,...,D_n\}$ (where every element of D_i is represented by set of v_i), and a set of constraints $C=\{C_1,C_2,...,C_m\}$. Each constraint C_i is a pair (W_i,R_i), where R_i is a relation $R_i\subseteq D_{i1}x...xD_{ik}$ defined in a subset of variables $W_i\subseteq X$.

If we have a CSP, the Max-CSP aim is to find an assignment that satisfies most constraints, and minimize the number of violated constraints. The diagnosis aim is to find what constraints are not satisfied. The solutions searched with Max-CSP techniques is very complex. Some investigations have tried to improve the efficiency of this problem,[4][8].

To carry out the diagnosis we must use Testing techniques to select which observations are the most significant, and which give us more information. In [1] appears the objectives and the complications that a good Testing implies. It is necessary to be aware of the Testing limits. The combinations of inputs and outputs of the programs (even of the most trivial) are too wide.

The programs that are in the scope of this paper are:

- Those which can be compiled to be debugged but they do not verify the specification Pre/Post.
- Those which are a slight variant of the correct program, although they are wrong.
- Those where all the appeared methods include precondition and postcondition formal specification.

This work is part of a global project that will allow us to perform object oriented software diagnosis. This project is in evolution and there are points which we are still investigating.

The work is structured as follows. First we present the necessary definitions to explain the methodology. Then we indicate the diagnosis methodology: obtaining the PCM and the minimal diagnosis. We will conclude indicating the results obtained in several different examples, conclusions and future work in this investigation line.

2   Notation and Definitions

Definition 1. Test Case(TC): It is a tuple that assigns values to the observable variables. We can use Testing techniques to find those *TCs* that can report us a more precise diagnosis. The Testing will give us the values of the input parameters and some or all the outputs that the source code generates. The inputs that the Testing provides must satisfy the precondition, and the outputs must satisfy the postcondition. The Testing can also provide us an output value which cannot be guaranteed by the postcondition. If this happens, an expert must guarantee that they are the correct values. Therefore, the values obtained by the Testing will be the correct values, and not those that we can obtain by the source code execution. We will use test cases obtained by white box techniques. In example 1a (see figure 3) a test case could be: $TC \equiv \{a=2, b=2, c=3, d=3, e=2, f=12, g=12\}$

Definition 2. Diagnosis Unit Specification: It is a tuple that contemplates the following elements: The Source Code (SC) that satisfies a grammar, the precondition assertion (Pre) and the postcondition assertion (Post). We will apply the proposed methodology to this diagnosis unit using a TC and then, we will obtain the sentence or set of sentences that could be possible bugs.

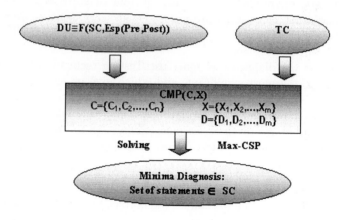

Fig. 1. Diagnosis Process

Definition 3. Observable Variables and Non Observable Variables: The set of observable variables (*Vobs*) will include the input parameters and those output variables whose correct value can be deduced by the TC. The rest of the variables will be non observable variables (*Vnobs*).

Definition 4. Program Constraint-Based Model (PCM): It will be compound of a constraints network C and a set of variables with a domain. The set C will determine the behavior of the program by means of the relationships among the variables. The set of variables set will include (*Vobs*) and (*Vnobs*). Therefore: *PCM(C, Vobs, Vnobs)*

3 Diagnosis Methodology

The diagnosis methodology will be a process to transform a program into a Max-CSP; as it appears in figure 1. The diagnosis process consists of the following steps:

1. Obtaining the PCM:
   - Determining the variables and their domains.
   - Determining the PCM constraints.
2. Obtaining the minimal diagnosis:
   - Determining the function to maximize.
   - Max-CSP resolution.

3.1   Obtaining the PCM

Determining the variables and their domain. The set of variables X={X_1, X_2... ,X_n} (associated to a domain D={D_1,D_2,... ,D_n}) will be compound of *Vobs* and *Vnobs*. The domain or concrete values of each variable will be determined by the variable declaration. The domain of every variable will be the same as the compiler fixes for the different data types defined in the language.

Determining the PCM constraints. The PCM constraints will be compound of constraints obtained from the *Precondition Asserts, Postcondition Asserts* and *Source Code. Precondition Constraints* and *Postcondition Constraints* will directly be obtained from their formal specification. These constraints must necessarily be satisfied, because they express which are the initial and final conditions that a free of bugs source code must satisfy. In order to obtain the *Source Code Constraints*, we will divide the source code into basic blocks like : Sequential blocks (assignments and method calls), conditional blocks and loop blocks. Also, every block is a set of sentences that will be transformed into constraints.

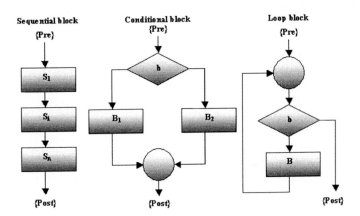

Fig. 2. Basic Blocks

- Sequential blocks: Starting from a sequential block as the one that appears in figure 2, we can deduce that the execution sequence will be: $S_1...S_i...S_n$. The first step will be to *rename the variables*. We have to rewrite the sentences between the precondition and the postcondition in a way that will never allow two sentences to assign a value to the same variable. For example the code *x=a*c; ...x=x+3;... {Post:x =... }* would be transformed into *x1=a*c; ...x2=x1+3;... {Post:x2 =... }*.

Assignments: We will transform the source code assignments into equality constraints.

Method Calls: Our methodology only permits the use of methods calls that specify their precondition and postcondition. At present this specification is viable in object oriented languages as Java 1.4. For every method call, we will add the constraints defined in the precondition and the postcondition of this method to the PCM. When we find a recursive method call, this internal method call is supposed to be correct to avoid cycles in the diagnosis of recursive methods.

Our work is in progress in this point and there are still points that are being investigated. Due to it, we have to suppose that there are only functional methods (those that cannot modify the state of the object which contains the method declaration) and, also, these methods cannot return objects.

- Conditional blocks: We will often find a conditional block as it appears in the figure 2; we can deduce that the sequences will be :

Sequence 1: {Pre }bB$_1${Post} (condition b is true)

Sequence 2: {Pre}¬bB$_2${Post} (condition b is false)

Depending on the test case, one of the two sequences will be executed. Therefore we will treat the conditional blocks as if they were two sequential blocks and we will choose one or the other depending on the test case. Then, we will transform it into constraints that will be part of the PCM. If we compare software diagnosis with the components diagnosis it would be as incorporating one or another component depending on the system evolution; this is something that has not been thoroughly treated in the components diagnosis theory. At this point we introduce improvements to our previous work [2], this methodology allows us to incorporate inequality constraints (in particular those which are part of the condition in the conditional sentences).

- Loop blocks: We will find loop blocks as it appears in figure 2. The sequences will be:

Sequence 1: {Pre}{Post} (none loop is executed)

Sequence 2: {Pre}bB$_1${Post} (1 loop is executed)

Sequence 3: {Pre}b$_1$B$_1$b$_2$B$_2$...b$_n$B$_n${Post} (2 or n loops are executed)

Depending on the test case, one of the three sequences will be executed. To reduce the model to less than n iterations, and to obtain efficiency in the diagnosis process, we propose to add a sentence for each variable that would change value in the loop and would add the necessary quantity (positive or negative) to reach the value of the step *n-1*. The sequence 3 would be like:{Pre}b$_1$βB$_n${Post} where β will substitute B$_1$b$_2$B$_2$...b$_n$.

For every variable X that changes its value in the loop, we will add the constraint $X_{n-1}=X_1+\beta_x$ what would allow us to maintain the value of X_n in the last step, and what would save us the *n-1* previous steps. The value of

β_x will be calculated debugging the source code. The constraints which add the β values cannot be a part of the diagnosis, because they are unaware of the original source code.

3.2   Obtaining the Minimal Diagnosis

Determining the Function to Maximize. The first step will be to define a set of variables R_i that allows us to perform a reified constraint model. A reified constraint will be like $C_i \Leftrightarrow R_i$. It consists of a constraint C_i together with an attached boolean variable R_i, where each variable R_i represents the truth value of constraint C_i (0 means false, 1 means true). The operational semantics are as follows: If C_i is entailed, then $R_i=1$ is inferred; if C_i is inconsistent, then $R_i=0$ is inferred; if $R_i=1$ is entailed, then C_i is imposed; if $R_i=0$ is entailed, then $\neg C_i$ is imposed.

Our objective is that most numbers of these auxiliary variables may take a true value. This objective will imply that we have to maximize the number of satisfied constraints. The solution search will be to maximize the sum of these variables, therefore the function to maximize will be: $\mathrm{Max}(R_1+R_2+...+R_k)$.

Max-CSP resolution. Solving the Max-CSP we will obtain the set of sentences with a smaller cardinality, what caused the postcondition was not satisfied. To satisfy the postcondition we have to modify these sentences. To implement this search we used $ILOG^{TM}$ Solver tools [6]. It would be interesting to keep in mind the works proposed in [8] and [4] to improve their efficiency in some problem cases.

4   Examples of Diagnosis

We have chosen five examples that show the grammar's categories to cover (a subset of the whole $Java^{TM}$ language grammar). To prove the effectiveness of this methodology, we will introduce changes in the examples source code. With these changes the solution won't satisfy the postcondition. The diagnosis methodology should detect these changes, and it should deduce the set of sentences that cause the postcondition non satisfaction.

Example 1 : With this example we cover the grammar's part that includes the declarations and assignments. It will allow us to prove if the methodology is able to detect the dependencies among instructions. If we change the sentence S_5 by *g=y-z*, we will have a new program (named *example 1a*) that won't satisfy the postcondition. The assignments of the source code will be transformed into equality constraints. In example 1a the sentences S_1 to S_5 will be transformed into the result that appears in table 1. As we can observe, the methodology adds 5 equality constraints and the result is assigned in every case to a variable R_i which will be stored if the constraint is satisfied or not. These variables R_i will

```
Example 1:
{Pre: a,b,c,d,e>0}
(--) int x,y,z,f,g;
(S1)  x=a*c;
(S2)  y=b*d;
(S3)  z=c*e;
(S4)  f=x+y;
(S5)  g=y+z;
{Post:f=a*c+b*d
 ∧ g=b*d+c*e}
```

```
Example 2:
{Pre: i>=0;p>0}
(--) public int demo(int n,
int i,int p){
(--)  int s;
(S1)   if (i>n)
(S2)     s=1;
(S3)   else{
(S4)     p=2*p;
(S5)     s=this.demo(n,i+1,p);
(S6)     s=s+p;
(S7)   }
(S8)   return s; }
{Post:s = 1+∑ φ:i≤φ≤n:2^φ}
```

```
Example 3:
{Pre: x>=0;y>=0}
(--) public int mult(int x,int y){
(S1)   int r=x*y;
(S2)   return r; }
{Post:r=x*y}
{Pre: x>=0;y>=0}
(--) public int sum(int x,int y){
(S1)   int r=x+y;
(S2)   return r;
(--) }
{Post:r=x+y}
```

```
Example 4:
{Pre: a>0 ∧ b>0}
(--) int x,y;
(S1)  x=a+b;
(S2)  y=2*b+3;
(S3)  if (x>y)
(S4)      x=2*x;
(S5)  else
(S6)      x=3*x;
{Post:(a+b>2*b+3 ∧ x=2a+2b)
 ∨(a+b<=2*b+3 ∧ x=3a+3*b) }
```

```
{Pre: a>=0;b>=0;c>=0}
(--) public int operate(int a,
int b,int c){
(S1)   int x=object1.mult(a,b);
(S2)   int y=object1.mult(a,c);
(S3)   int f=object2.sum(x,y);
(S4)   return f; }
{Post:f=a*b+a*c}
```

```
Example 5:
{Pre: n>0}
(S1)  int i=0;
(S2)  int p=1;
(S3)  int s=1;
(S4)  while (i<n){
(S5)      i=i+1;
(S6)      p=2*p;
(S7)      s=s+p;}
{Post:s = ∑ φ:0≤φ≤n:2^φ
 ∧ p=2^n }
```

Fig. 3. Examples

be necessary to carry out the search Max-CSP to obtain the minimal diagnosis. These variables R_i will take the value 1 if the constraint is true or the value 0 if it is false.

Using a test case $TC\equiv\{a=2,b=2,c=3,d=3,e=2,f=12,g=12\}$, the obtained minimal diagnosis will include the sentence S_5 that is, in fact, the sentence that we had already changed; and also the sentence S_3. If we change S_3, it won't have any influence in S_4 but it will have influence in S_5, that is the sentence that we had changed. Therefore we will be able to return the correct result changing S_3, and without modifying S_5. It is necessary to emphasize that S_5 also depends on S_2, but a change in S_2 could imply a bug in S_4.

Example 2 : We will use example 2 to validate the diagnosis of recursive methods. We will change the sentence S_4 by $p=2*p+3$, with this change we will obtain the program *example 2a*. The PCM constraints of the examples 2a appear in table 1. The method calls are substituted by the constraints obtained of the postcondition of these method.

The variable R_3 (associated to the method call) should take the value 1 to avoid cycles in the recursive method diagnosis (as we explained in the previous section). In example 2a we will use the test case $TC\equiv\{n=7,i=1,p=1\}$, the diagnosis process reports us the sentences S_6 and S_4; the last one is, in fact, the sentence that we have changed. If we change S_6, we can modify the final result of s variable, and therefore, satisfy the postcondition with only one change.

Example 3 : This example will allow us to validate the diagnosis of non recursive methods. We will change the sentence S_2 by *y=object1.mult(b,c)* in *operate* method, obtaining the program that we will name *example 3a*. The PCM constraints of the example 3a appear in table 1. For example 3a, we show the constraints of *operate* method PCM. The method calls are substituted by the constraints obtained of the postcondition of those methods.

If we apply $TC\equiv\{a=2,b=7,c=3\}$ to the *operate* method (example 3a), we will obtain that the sentences S_1,S_2, and S_3 are the minimal diagnosis. The bug is exactly in S_2 because we called method with wrong parameters b and c instead of a and c. If we change the parameters that are used in the sentences S_1 and S_3, we can neutralize the bug in S_2. An interesting modification of example 3 would be to change the sentence S_3 by *f=sum(x,x)*. If we apply this change, the sentences S_1 and S_3 would constitute the diagnosis result. Now S_2 won't be part of the minimal diagnosis because sentence S_2 does not have any influence on the method result.

Example 4 : This example covers the conditional sentences. We have changed the sentence S_4 by *x=2*x+3*, and we will obtain the *example 4a*. If the inputs are a=6 and b=2, we can deduce that x>y; therefore S_4 will be executed. The result of the transformation of conditional sentence would be the constraint x>y and the transformation of sentence S_4 (in this occasion it is an assignment). We can see the result in table 1.

If we apply $TC\equiv\{a=7,b=2\}$ to example 4a we obtain the sentences S_1 and S_4 as a minimal diagnosis; this last one is in fact the sentence that we have changed. If we change S_1, we can modify the final result of x variable and, consequently, we will satisfy the postcondition. Therefore, it is another solution that would only imply one change in the source code.

Example 5 : We use this example to loop diagnosis. We will change the sentence S_7 by *s=2*s+p* and we will obtain the program *example 5a*. At this example the variables i, p and s change their values inside the loop. If i_0 is the value of i before the loop and i_{n-1} is the value of i in the step n-1, let's name β_i to the difference between i_{n-1} and i_0. Then the instruction $i_{n-1}=i_0+\beta_i$ (which will be before the loop) would allow us to conserve the dependence of the value i_n with previous values, and it would save us the *n-1* previous steps. The constraints which add the values β should not be part of the minimal diagnosis since they are unaware of the original source code. Therefore, the variables R_4,R_5 and R_6 must take the value 1 (as appears in table 1), this will avoid that they would be a part of the minimal diagnosis.

With $TC\equiv\{n=5,\beta_i=4,\beta_p=15,\beta_s=30\}$ we will obtain the sentence S_9 as minimal diagnosis. S_9 is exactly the sentence that we had already changed. The minimal diagnosis does not offer us S_{11} as minimal diagnosis because p takes a correct value (validated by the postcondition), although the value of s variable depends on the value of p variable. The problem is only in the s value, which does not satisfy the postcondition.

Table 1. PCM Examples

Example 1a

Precondition Constraints	Postcondition Constraints	Code Constraints	Observable Variables	Non observable Variables
$a>0$ $b>0$ $c>0$ $d>0$	$f==a*b+b*d$ $g==b*d+c*e$	$R_1==(x==a*c)$ $R_2==(y==b*d)$ $R_3==(z==c*e)$ $R_4==(f==x+y)$ $R_5==(g==y\text{-}z)$	a,b,c,d,e f,g	x,y,z

Example 2a

Precondition Constraints	Postcondition Constraints	Code Constraints	Observable Variables	Non observable Variables
$i>=0$ $p>0$	$s1==1+$ $\sum \phi{:}i0{\leq}\phi{\leq}n{:}2^{\phi}$	$R_1==(i0<=n0)$ $R_2==(p1==2*p0+3)$ $R_3==(s0==1+$ $\sum \phi{:}(i0+1){\leq}\phi{\leq}n{:}2^{\phi})$ $R_3==1$ $R_4==(s1==s0+p1)$	n,i0,p0, p1,s0	s1

Example 3a

Precondition Constraints	Postcondition Constraints	Code Constraints	Observable Variables	Non observable Variables
$a>0$ $b>0$ $c>0$	$f==a*b+a*c$	$R_1==(x==a*b)$ $R_2==(y==b*c)$ $R_3==(f==x+y)$	a,b,c, f	x,y

Example 4a

Precondition Constraints	Postcondition Constraints	Code Constraints	Observable Variables	Non observable Variables
$a>0$ $b>0$	$(a+b>2*b+3 \wedge$ $x2=2a+2b) \vee$ $(a+b<=2*b+3 \wedge$ $x2=3a+3*b)$	$R_1==(x0==a+b)$ $R_2==(y0==2*b+3)$ $R_3==(x0>y0)$ $R_4==(x2==2*x1+3)$	a,b,x2	x0,x1,y0

Example 5a

Precondition Constraints	Postcondition Constraints	Code Constraints	Observable Variables	Non observable Variables
$n>0$	$s2 = \sum \phi{:}0{\leq}\phi{\leq}n{:}2^{\phi}$ $p2=2^{n}$	$R_1==(i0==0)$ $R_2==(p0==1)$ $R_3==(s0==1)$ $R_4==(i0<n)$ $R_5==(i1==i0+ \beta_i)$ $R_6==(p1==p0+ \beta_p)$ $R_7==(s1==s0+ \beta_s)$ $R_5==R_6==R_7==1$ $R_8==(i2==i1+1)$ $R_9==(p2==2*p1)$ $R_{10}==(s2==2*s1+p2)$	n,s2,p2, $\beta_i,\beta_p,\beta_s,$	s0,s1,p0, p1,i0,i1, i2

5   Conclusions and Future Works

In this work we applied Max-CSP techniques to diagnose the software behavior. The explicit construction of the functional dependencies graph (proposed in other methodologies) has been avoided. We used only one TC to carry out the diagnosis, but we think that the use of a greater number of TC will improve our methodology to obtain software diagnosis. The investigation will continue in this line, looking for the way to include the result of several TCs to the diagnosis process of a same program. This will give us a more exact diagnosis. The final objective of our investigation is to extend the methodology to the complete grammar of an object-oriented language.

References

1. Robert V. Binder.: Testing Object-Oriented Systems: Models, Patterms, and Tools. Addison Wesley.
2. R. Ceballos, R. M. Gasca, Carmelo Del Valle y Miguel Toro: Diagnosis basada en modelos para la depuración de software mediante técnicas simbólicas. IV Jornadas de ARCA, Sistemas Cualitativos y Diagnosis, Vilanova i la Geltrú, Spain, June 2002.
3. Khalil, M.: Automated strategies for software diagnosis. The Ninth International Sympsosium on Software Reliability Engineering, Paderborn, Germany, Nov. 1998.
4. K. Kask.: New Search Heuristics for Max-CSP In Proceeding of CP'2000, pg. 262–277, 2000.
5. Khalil, M.: An Experimental Comparison of Software Diagnosis Methods. 25th Euromicro Conference 1999.
6. ILOG: ILOG Solver 4.4 User's Manual. ILOG 1999.
7. J. Larrossa: Algorithms and Heuristics for Total and Partial Constraint Satisfaction. Ph.D dissertation, 1998.
8. J. Larrossa and P. Meseguer.: Partition-based lower bound for max-csp. Proceedings CP, pages 303–315, 1999.
9. Lyle J. R. and Weiser, M.: Automatic bug location by program slicing. Second International Conference on Computers and Applications, Beijing, China, pag. 877–883,June 1987.
10. Cristinel Mateis, Markus Stumptner, Dominik Wieland and Franz Wotawa.: Debugging of Java programs using a model-based approach. DX-99 Work-Shop,Loch Awe, Scotland (1999).
11. Cristinel Mateis, Markus Stumptner, Dominik Wieland and Franz Wotawa.: Extended Abstract – Model-Based Debugging of Java Programs. AADEBUG, August 2000, Munich.
12. Weiser, M.: Programmers Use Slices When Debugging. Communications of the ACM, Vol. 25, No. 7, pp.446-452,1982.
13. Weiser, M.: Program Slicing. IEEE Transactions on Software Engineering SE-10, 4, pp. 352–357, 1984

Local Search Methods for Learning Bayesian Networks Using a Modified Neighborhood in the Space of DAGs

Luis Miguel de Campos[1], Juan Manuel Fernández-Luna[2], and
Jose Miguel Puerta[3]

[1] Dpto. de Ciencias de la Computación e I.A.
Universidad de Granada, 18071 - Granada, Spain
lci@decsai.ugr.es
[2] Dpto. de Informática
Universidad de Jaén, 23071 - Jaén, Spain
jmfluna@ujaen.es
[3] Dpto. de Informática
Universidad de Castilla-La Mancha, 02071 - Albacete, Spain
jpuerta@info-ab.uclm.es

Abstract. The dominant approach for learning Bayesian networks from
data is based on the use of a scoring metric, that evaluates the fitness of
any given candidate network to the data, and a search procedure, that
explores the space of possible solutions. The most efficient methods used
in this context are (Iterated) Local Search algorithms. These methods
use a predefined neighborhood structure that defines the feasible elementary modifications (local changes) that can be applied to a given solution
in order to get another, potentially better solution. If the search space
is the set of directed acyclic graphs (dags), the usual choices for local
changes are arc addition, arc deletion and arc reversal. In this paper we
propose a new definition of neighborhood in the dag space, which uses a
modified operator for arc reversal. The motivation for this new operator
is the observation that local search algorithms experience problems when
some arcs are wrongly oriented. We exemplify the general usefulness of
our proposal by means of a set of experiments with different metrics and
different local search methods, including Hill-Climbing and Greedy Randomized Adaptive Search Procedure (GRASP), as well as using several
domain problems.

1 Introduction

Bayesian Networks (BNs) are graphical models able to represent and manipulate
efficiently n-dimensional probability distributions [18]. A Bayesian network uses
two components to codify qualitative and quantitative knowledge: (a) A directed
acyclic graph (dag), $G = (\boldsymbol{V}, E)$, where the nodes in $\boldsymbol{V} = \{X_1, X_2, \ldots, X_n\}$ represent the random variables from the problem we want to solve, and the topology
of the graph (the arcs in E) encodes conditional (in)dependence relationships

F.J. Garijo, J.C. Riquelme, and M. Toro (Eds.): IBERAMIA 2002, LNAI 2527, pp. 182–192, 2002.

among the variables (by means of the presence or absence of direct connections between pairs of variables); (b) a set of conditional probability distributions drawn from the graph structure: For each variable $X_i \in \mathbf{V}$ we have a family of conditional probability distributions $P(X_i|pa_G(X_i))$, where $pa_G(X_i)$ represents any combination of the values of the variables in $Pa_G(X_i)$, and $Pa_G(X_i)$ is the parent set of X_i in G. From these conditional distributions we can recover the joint distribution over $\mathbf{V}$:

$$P(X_1, X_2, \ldots, X_n) = \prod_{i=1}^{n} P(X_i|pa_G(X_i)) \tag{1}$$

This decomposition of the joint distribution gives rise to important savings in storage requirements. It also allows, in many cases, to efficiently perform probabilistic inference (propagation), i.e., to compute the posterior probability for any variable given some evidence about the values of other variables in the graph [14,18]: The independences represented in the graph reduce changes in the state of knowledge to local computations.

Although in the last years the problem of learning or estimating Bayesian networks from data has received considerable attention, within the community of researchers into uncertainty in artificial intelligence, it is still an active research area. The fact that finding optimal BNs from data is, in general, a NP-Hard problem [7], has motivated the use of heuristic search methods to solve it. The common approach is to introduce a scoring function, f, that evaluates each network with respect to the training data, and then to search for the best network according to this score. Different Bayesian and non-Bayesian scoring metrics can be used [1,6,8,13,17]. The alternative approach, constraint-based, is to search for the network satisfying as much independences present in the data as possible [10,21,19]. Obviously, the decision about which conditional independences are either true or false is made by means of statistical tests. There also exist hybrid algorithms that use a combination of these two methods [1,9,22].

In this paper we focus on Local Search methods, the most efficient methods, and that rely on a neighborhood structure that defines the local rules used to move within the search space. The standard neighborhood in the space of dags uses the operators of arc addition, arc deletion and arc reversal. The main contribution of this paper is the proposal of an alternative definition of neighborhood, which may alleviate some problems of premature convergence to a local optimum due to the difficulty of (locally) improving dags where some arcs are wrongly oriented. We also propose a new algorithm for learning Bayesian network structures, which uses the GRASP (Greedy Randomized Adaptive Search Procedure) metaheuristic [12].

The paper is structured as follows: We begin in Section 2 with some preliminaries. In Section 3 we define the proposed neighborhood structure for searching in the space of dags. Section 4 describes GRASP-BN, a new iterated local search-based learning algorithm that uses Hill-Climbing and a probabilistic version of the algorithm B [5]. In Section 5, we analyze the experimental results obtained by both Hill-Climbing and GRASP-BN (on two different domains, ALARM [3] and INSURANCE [2], and using two different scoring metrics, K2 [8] and BDeu [13]), when these algorithms use the standard neighborhood and the proposed alternative. Finally, Section 6 contains the concluding remarks and some proposals for future research.

2   Local Search Methods for Learning BNs

The problem of learning the structure of a Bayesian network can be stated as follows: Given a training set $D = \{\mathbf{v}^1, \ldots, \mathbf{v}^m\}$ of instances of V, find the dag G^* such that

$$G^* = \arg \max_{G \in \mathcal{G}_n} f(G : D) \tag{2}$$

where $f(G : D)$ is a scoring metric measuring the fitness of any candidate dag G to the dataset D and $\mathcal{G}_n$ is the family of all the dags with n nodes.

Local Search (or Hill-Climbing) methods traverse the search space, starting from an initial solution, by examining only possible local changes at each step, and applying the one that leads to the greatest improvement in the scoring metric. The search process terminates when it is blocked at a local optimum (no local change improves the current solution), although it may be restarted on the basis of either a random modification of the current optimum (by applying a number of local transformations), or a new (random) initial solution. The set of feasible local changes that can be applied to any given solution is determined by the choice of the neighborhood structure. The effectiveness and efficiency of a local search procedure depends on several aspects, such as the neighborhood structure, the fast evaluation of the scoring metric of the neighbors, and the starting solution itself.

As we have already commented, the usual choices for local changes in the space of dags are arc addition, arc deletion and arc reversal, avoiding (in the first and the third case) the inclusion of directed cycles in the graph. Thus, there are $O(n^2)$ possible changes, where n is the number of variables.

An important property of a scoring metric is its decomposability in presence of full data, i.e, the scoring function can be decomposed in the following way:

$$f(G : D) = \sum_{i=1}^{n} f_D(X_i, Pa_G(X_i)) \tag{3}$$

$$f_D(X_i, Pa_G(X_i)) = f_D(X_i, Pa_G(X_i) : N_{x_i, pa_G(X_i)}) \tag{4}$$

where $N_{x_i, pa_G(X_i)}$ are the statistics of the variables X_i and $Pa_G(X_i)$ in D, i.e, the number of instances in D that match each possible instantiation of X_i and $Pa(X_i)$.

The efficiency of the algorithms that search in the space of dags using local methods is mainly due to the property of decomposition that many metrics exhibit: a procedure that changes one arc at each move can efficiently evaluate the improvement obtained by this change. Such a procedure can reuse the computations carried out at previous stages, and only the statistics corresponding to the variables whose parent set has been modified need to be recomputed.

3   A Modified Neighborhood Structure in the Space of Dags

By monitoring a typical local search algorithm for learning BNs as it progresses, we have observed some situations where it gets into troubles. Let us explain these situations by means of the following example:

Example: Consider the network with four variables displayed in Figure 1(a). From this network we have generated a database containing 1000 instances of these variables using logic sampling. The value of the K2 metric for this database and this network is also shown in the figure. A Hill-Climbing algorithm could obtain the network in Figure 1(b). None of the possible transformations of this network, using the classical operators of addition, deletion and reversal of an arc improves the K2 value (the best neighbors are displayed in Figures 1(c)-(e)), so that it is a local maximum. ◇

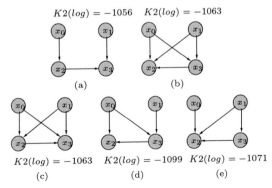

Fig. 1. Problems with the classical neighborhood when an arc is wrongly directed.

This behavior is common for many local search-based learning algorithms: When they mistake the direction of some arc connecting two nodes[1], then the algorithms tend to 'cross' the parents of these nodes to compensate the wrong orientation; the resultant configuration is quite stable, in the sense that no local transformation produces a better network and, therefore, it may be difficult to scape from this local maximum. In the previous example, the wrong orientation of the arc linking the variables X_2 and X_3 is the cause of the problem.

A possible solution for this problem could be to carry out the search process in a different space. For example, we could use the space of equivalence classes

---

[1] This situation may be quite frequent at early stages of the search process.

of dags, to postpone the decisions about the direction of the links until we have more information. Recently, the possibility of searching in the dag space, but including some characteristics relative to equivalence classes of dags, has been considered [15]. This method uses an operator, called RCAR (Repeated Covered Arc Reversal), which iteratively inverts a prefixed (random) number of *covered* arcs[2]. Then, a Hill-Climbing algorithm is fired to obtain a new local maximum, and the whole process is iterated a fixed number of times. We are going to follow a different approach, by modifying the neighborhood structure, i.e., changing the classical operators used to move in the space of dags.

The classical neighborhood of a dag G is $\mathcal{N}(G) = \mathcal{N}_A(G) \cup \mathcal{N}_D(G) \cup \mathcal{N}_R(G)$, being $\mathcal{N}_A(G)$, $\mathcal{N}_D(G)$ and $\mathcal{N}_R(G)$ the links subsets for added, deleted and inverted respectively. Our proposal implies to modify the reversal operator and, therefore, the redefinition of the neighborhood $\mathcal{N}_R(G)$

The new definition of $\mathcal{N}_R(G)$ states that, for any given arc $X_j \rightarrow X_i$ in G, if its extreme nodes share some parent, then we delete the current parents of both nodes, invert the arc and add, as the new parents for each node, any subset of the old parents of either node. The idea is to give the algorithm the opportunity of 'uncrossing' the parents of two nodes which have been connected in the wrong direction, without being limited to move only one arc every time, for example the dags (a) in the figure 1 could be a dag neighbor of the graph (b).

Note that, for any arc $X_j \rightarrow X_i \in G$, the number of possible 'reversals' is now $O(2^{2p})$, with $p = |Pa_G(X_i) \cup Pa_G(X_j)| - 1$, instead of only one. Therefore, the number of neighbors of a dag may increase exponentially. Nevertheless, in practice the number of parents of a node is not usually high, so we expect that the computational cost will not be excessive[3]. In any case we could limit the cardinality of the new parent sets (which is a common practice for other algorithms [8,16]). Note also that, although the new reversal operator may change more than one arc, the number of parent sets that are modified is still two, hence we only have to recompute two statistics to evaluate the corresponding neighbor.

4   A Grasp-Based Learning Algorithm

GRASP [20] is a multi-start or iterative metaheuristic in which each iteration consists basically of two phases: construction and local search. The construction phase builds a feasible solution, whose neighborhood is investigated until a local optimum is found during the local search phase. The best overall solution is kept as the result. In this section we develop an algorithm for learning Bayesian network structures using GRASP, which will be called GRASP-BN.

A general GRASP algorithm works as follows: At each iteration of the construction phase, a solution is built using a greedy randomized process: it incorporates elements to the partial solution under construction from a restricted

---

[2] An arc $X_j \rightarrow X_i$ in a dag G is covered if $Pa_G(X_i) = Pa_G(X_j) \cup \{X_j\}$. A covered arc may be inverted and the resultant dag is equivalent to G.

[3] Our experiments in the next section support this assertion.

candidate list (RCL). The elements in this list are selected from all the feasible candidate elements according to a greedy evaluation function. The element to be incorporated into the partial solution is randomly selected from those in the RCL. Once the selected element is incorporated to the partial solution, the candidate list is updated and their elements are reevaluated. When a solution is finally obtained, the second phase fires a local search algorithm starting from this solution. These two phases are repeated a given number of iterations.

Our GRASP-BN algorithm will use, in its second phase, a Hill-Climbing (HC) search in the space of dags, for some neighborhood structure and some metric f. For the first phase, we are going to create a randomized version of the algorithm B [5].

Algorithm B is a greedy search heuristics. It starts with an empty dag G and at each step it adds the arc with the maximum increase in the (decomposable) scoring metric f, avoiding the inclusion of directed cycles in the graph. The algorithm stops when adding any valid arc does not increase the value of the metric. The gain obtained by inserting a feasible arc $X_j \rightarrow X_i$ in G can be evaluated efficiently by means of the difference $f_D(X_i, Pa_G(X_i) \cup \{X_j\}) - f_D(X_i, Pa_G(X_i))$. At each step, after inserting in G the best valid arc, $X_j \rightarrow X_i$, the algorithm identifies and discards the new unfeasible arcs by searching for the ancestors and descendants of X_i. After that, as the value $f_D(X_i, Pa_G(X_i))$ has been modified, the algorithm recomputes the new values of $f_D(X_i, Pa_G(X_i) \cup \{X_k\}) - f_D(X_i, Pa_G(X_i))$ for any valid arc $X_k \rightarrow X_i$.

The probabilistic version of this algorithm that we propose is the following: instead of always selecting the best arc, we will use a stochastic decision rule that selects the best arc with probability p_0, and with probability $1 - p_0$ each arc $X_j \rightarrow X_i$ in the restricted candidate list RCL (that will contain all the feasible candidate arcs which produce an improvement) will be selected with a probability $p(X_j \rightarrow X_i)$ proportional to its merit:

$$\begin{cases} \arg\max_{X_j \rightarrow X_i \in RCL} \{f_D(X_i, Pa_G(X_i) \cup \{X_j\}) - f_D(X_i, Pa_G(X_i))\} & u \leq p_0 \\ X_l \rightarrow X_r, & u > p_0 \end{cases} \quad (5)$$

where u is a random number uniformly distributed in $[0,1]$, p_0 is the parameter that determines the relative importance of *exploitation* versus *exploration*, and $X_l \rightarrow X_r$ is an arc in RCL randomly selected according to the following probabilities:

$$p(X_l \rightarrow X_r) = \frac{f_D(X_r, Pa_G(X_r) \cup \{X_l\}) - f_D(X_r, Pa_G(X_r))}{\sum_{X_j \rightarrow X_i} f_D(X_i, Pa_G(X_i) \cup \{X_j\}) - f_D(X_i, Pa_G(X_i))} \quad (6)$$

We have to remark that this probabilistic version of the algorithm B could also be used at the initialization stages of other stochastic search algorithms (as Genetic Algorithms, Estimation of Distribution Algorithms and Ant Colonies).

5   Experimental Results

In this section we will evaluate experimentally the usefulness of the proposed neighborhood, as well as the GRASP-BN algorithm. We have selected two test domains: ALARM [3] and INSURANCE [2]. For ALARM we have used the first 3,000 cases of the classical ALARM database (which contains 20,000 cases). For INSURANCE, we have generated three databases with 10,000 cases each by means of probabilistic logic sampling (in this case we show the average of the results obtained for the three databases).

In our experiments we have used two decomposable metrics: K2 [8] and BDeu [13,5] (both in logarithmic version). For BDeu, we use an equivalent sample size equal to 1. We have implemented two versions of a Hill-Climbing algorithm, using the classical definition of neighborhood (HCc) and the proposed modification (HCm). The initial solution of the search process is the empty network in all the cases. Experiments with other two forms of initialization (the networks obtained by the algorithms K2SN [11] and PC [21]) were also carried out, obtaining results similar to the ones displayed for the empty network. The GRASP-BN algorithm has also been implemented using the two neighborhood structures (GRASP-BNc and GRASP-BNm). The parameter determining the number of iterations has been fixed to 15, and the one to trade-off between exploration and exploitation is $p_0 = 0.8$.

The following performance measures have been computed: (1) Measures of quality (effectiveness) of the learned network: (K2) and (BDeu) the value of the corresponding metric for the best network found by the algorithm; the number of arcs added (A), deleted (D) and inverted (I) when we compare the learned network with the true network. (2) Measures of efficiency of the algorithm: (EstEv) the number of different statistics evaluated during the execution of the algorithm; (TEst) the total number of statistics used by the algorithm. Note that this number can be considerably greater than EstEv. By using hashing techniques we can store and efficiently retrieve any statistics previously calculated, so that it is not necessary to recompute them. This avoids many accesses to the database and improves the efficiency; (NVars) the average number of variables that intervene in the computed statistics.

The results obtained by HCc and HCm using the K2 and BDeu metrics are shown in Table 1.

The results of the experiments with the algorithms GRASP-BNc and GRASP-BNm is shown in Table 2 for the ALARM domain, and in Table 3 for the INSURANCE domain. In all the cases, the displayed values represent the averages and the standard deviations of 10 executions of each algorithm. We also give information about the best individuals found in all the executions.

We can see that, in all the cases, the results obtained by an algorithm when it uses the new definition of neighborhood are considerably better than the ones offered by the same algorithm using the classical neighborhood[4], in terms of

---

[4] Except in one case, where we obtain the same results.

Table 1. Results of HCc and HCm using the K2 and BDeu metrics.

	ALARM		INSURANCE	
	HCc	HCm	HCc	HCm
K2	-14425.62	-14414.55	-57998.10	-57934.61
A	6	4	10.33	7.67
D	4	2	11.67	11.00
I	3	2	7.67	7.67
EstEv	3375	3336	2050	2169
TEst	1.54E+05	1.56E+05	7.66E+04	8.32E+04
NVars	2.99	2.93	3.09	3.08
	HCc	HCm	HCc	HCm
BDeu	-33109.47	-33109.47	-133393.03	-133326.27
A	3	3	7.67	7.00
D	2	2	10.00	10.00
I	2	2	10.00	10.67
EstEv	3300	3284	1995	2100
TEst	1.47E+05	1.49E+05	7.15E+04	8.80E+04
NVars	2.88	2.87	2.99	3.04

Table 2. Results of GRASP-BNc and GRASP-BNm for ALARM, using the K2 and BDeu metrics.

	GRASP-BNc			GRASP-BNm		
	μ	σ	Best	μ	σ	Best
K2	-14429.92	18.51	-14414.55	-14404.23	2.52	-14401.91
A	7.20	2.44	4	2.80	1.55	1
D	2.70	0.95	2	1.10	0.32	1
I	4.30	2.54	2	1.20	1.03	0
EstEv	13306	1228		13148	1061	
TEst	5.83E+05	8.85E+03		9.09E+05	9.12E+04	
NVars	4.01	0.05		3.93	0.08	
	μ	σ	Best	μ	σ	Best
BDeu	-33190.14	10.17	-33165.90	-33105.05	4.24	-33101.14
A	5.50	1.18	6	1.40	0.97	1
D	2.00	0.00	2	1.30	0.48	1
I	4.50	0.85	3	1.00	1.41	0
EstEv	12317	759		12769	735	
TEst	5.56E+05	5.23E+04		8.80E+05	6.00E+04	
NVars	3.87	0.07		3.85	0.03	

effectiveness (with respect to both the value of the metric[5] and the number of erroneous arcs). For comparative purposes, the respective K2 and BDeu values of the true networks for the corresponding databases are -14412.69 and -33113.83 for ALARM, and -58120.95 and -133160.47 for INSURANCE. The corresponding values for the empty networks, which may serve as a kind of scale, are -26008.08 and -59889.80 for ALARM, and -93593.76 and -215514.96 for INSURANCE.

With respect to the efficiency of the algorithms, we are going to focus in the number of different statistics evaluated (EstEv) and the number of variables involved (Nvars): Most of the running time of a scoring-based learning algorithm

---

[5] Note that we are using log versions of the metrics, so that the differences are much greater in a non-logarithmic scale.

Table 3. Results of GRASP-BNc and GRASP-BNm for INSURANCE, using the K2 and BDeu metrics.

	GRASP-BNc			GRASP-BNm		
	μ	σ	Best	μ	σ	Best
K2	-57950.53	53.29	-57857.90	-57835.23	30.30	-57779.41
A	10.63	2.11	7	4.57	2.36	4
D	12.27	1.01	10	9.40	1.19	9
I	8.90	3.53	2	3.13	2.34	2
EstEv	7702	626		9135	840	
TEst	2.41E+05	2.74E+04		6.45E+05	9.34E+04	
NVars	3.98	0.06		3.97	0.06	
	μ	σ	Best	μ	σ	Best
BDeu	-133143.92	165.52	-132814.06	-132763.92	100.64	-132592,25
A	6.60	1.92	3	2.23	1.28	0
D	9.97	1.79	7	8.07	0.91	8
I	7.43	2.61	7	2.87	1.96	1
EstEv	7768	923		9011	1095	
TEst	2.54E+05	3.85+04		6.62E+05	1.61E+05	
NVars	3.87	0.09		3.88	0.08	

is spent in the evaluation of statistics from the database, and this time increases exponentially with the number of variables. So, an approximate measure of the time complexity of an algorithm is EstEv $* 2^{\mathrm{NVars}}$. We can observe that the values of NVars are almost identical and the values of EstEv are not sensibly different for the two versions of each algorithm: The values of EstEv in the ALARM domain are even lower when we use the new neighborhood, whereas the opposite is true for INSURANCE. The total number of statistics used is systematically larger with the new neighborhood, even considerably larger in some cases, but as we have already commented, using hashing techniques we can access very quickly to previously computed statistics, so that the time required to compute *new* statistics dominates completely. Therefore, the running times of the algorithms using the two neighborhoods are comparable.

These results increase our confidence in the usefulness and applicability of the proposed neighborhood for any learning algorithm that searches locally in the space of dags, no matter which metric or which type of local search is used.

The comparison between HC and GRASP is favorable to the later (except in the case of using the classical neighborhood with ALARM), at the expense of increasing the running times. Particularly, GRASP-BN equipped with the new neighborhood structure offers excellent results. Moreover, the low standard deviations obtained in this case are noteworthy, indicating that this algorithm seems to be quite stable.

6   Concluding Remarks

In this paper we have proposed a new definition of neighborhood for the space of directed acyclic graphs, which copes with the problems that local search-based learning algorithms encounter when some arcs are wrongly oriented. Our experiments, carried out with different metrics, databases and local search techniques, support the conclusion that the new neighborhood structure improves the performance of the algorithms systematically, without significantly increasing their complexity.

We have also developed another learning algorithm, based on the GRASP metaheuristic, that uses a probabilistic version of the algorithm B in the construction phase, to initialize the local search phase. This algorithm, in conjunction with the new neighborhood structure, obtained excellent results in our experiments.

For future research, in addition to carry out a more systematic experimentation and comparative analysis, we also plan to study several variants of the new operator for arc reversal (e.g., using the intersection of the parent sets in place of their union or applying the operator only to covered arcs).

Acknowledgements. This work has been supported by the Spanish Ministerio de Ciencia y Tecnología (MCYT) under projects TIC2001-2973-CO5-01 and TIC2001-2973-CO5-05.

References

1. S. Acid and L.M. de Campos. A hybrid methodology for learning belief networks: Benedict. *International Journal of Approximate Reasoning*, 27(3):235–262, 2001.
2. J. Binder, D. Koller, S. Russell, and K. Kanazawa. Adaptive probabilistic networks with hidden variables. *Machine Learning*, 29(2):213-244, 1997.
3. I.A. Beinlich, H.J. Suermondt, R.M. Chavez, and G.F. Cooper. The ALARM monitoring system: A case study with two probabilistic inference techniques for belief networks. In *Proceedings of the Second European Conference on Artificial Intelligence in Medicine*, 247–256, 1989.
4. R.R. Bouckaert. Bayesian Belief Networks: From Construction to Inference. PhD. Thesis, University of Utrecht, 1995.
5. W. Buntine. Theory refinement of Bayesian networks. In *Proceedings of the Seventh Conference on Uncertainty in Artificial Intelligence*, 52–60, 1991.
6. W. Buntine. A guide to the literature on learning probabilistic networks from data. *IEEE Transactions on Knowledge and Data Engineering*, 8:195–210, 1996.
7. D.M. Chickering, D. Geiger, and D. Heckerman. Learning Bayesian networks is NP-Complete. In D. Fisher and H. Lenz, Eds., *Learning from Data: Artificial Intelligence and Statistics V*, Springer-Verlag, 121–130, 1996.
8. G.F. Cooper and E. Herskovits. A Bayesian method for the induction of probabilistic networks from data. *Machine Learning*, 9(4):309–348, 1992.
9. D. Dash and M. Druzdel. A hybrid anytime algorithm for the construction of causal models from sparse data. In *Proceedings of the Fifteenth Conference on Uncertainty in Artificial Intelligence*, 142–149, 1999.
10. L.M. de Campos and J.F. Huete. A new approach for learning belief networks using independence criteria. *International Journal of Approximate Reasoning*, 24:11–37, 2000.
11. L.M. de Campos and J.M. Puerta. Stochastic local search algorithms for learning belief networks: Searching in the space of orderings. *Lecture Notes in Artificial Intelligence*, 2143:228–239, 2001.

12. T.A. Feo and M.G.C. Resende. Greedy randomized adaptive search procedures. *Journal of Global Optimization*, 6:109–133, 1995.
13. D. Heckerman, D. Geiger, and D.M. Chickering. Learning Bayesian networks: The combination of knowledge and statistical data. *Machine Learning*, 20:197–244, 1995.
14. F.V. Jensen. *An Introduction to Bayesian Networks*. UCL Press, 1996.
15. T. Kocka and R. Castelo. Improved learning of Bayesian networks. In *Proceedings of the Seventeenth Conference on Uncertainty in Artificial Intelligence*, 269–276, 2001.
16. P. Larrañaga, M. Poza, Y. Yurramendi, R. Murga, and C. Kuijpers. Structure learning of Bayesian networks by genetic algorithms: A performance analysis of control parameters. *IEEE Transactions on Pattern Analysis and Machine Intelligence*, 18(9):912–926, 1996.
17. W. Lam and F. Bacchus. Learning Bayesian belief networks. An approach based on the MDL principle. *Computational Intelligence*, 10(4):269–293, 1994.
18. J. Pearl. *Probabilistic Reasoning in Intelligent Systems: Networks of Plausible Inference*. Morgan Kaufmann, San Mateo, 1988.
19. J. Pearl and T.S. Verma. Equivalence and synthesis of causal models. In *Proceedings of the Sixth Conference on Uncertainty in Artificial Intelligence*, 220–227, 1990.
20. M.G.C. Resende and C.C. Ribeiro. Greedy randomized adaptive search procedures. In F. Glover and G. Kochenberger, Eds., *State of the Art Handbook in Metaheuristics*, Kluwer. To appear.
21. P. Spirtes, C. Glymour, and R. Scheines. *Causation, Prediction, and Search*. Lecture Notes in Statistics 81, Springer Verlag, 1993.
22. M. Singh and M. Valtorta. Construction of Bayesian network structures from data: A brief survey and an efficient algorithm. *International Journal of Approximate Reasoning*, 12:111–131, 1995.

A Quasi-Metric for Machine Learning[*]

Miguel A. Gutiérrez-Naranjo, José A. Alonso-Jiménez, and
Joaquín Borrego-Díaz

Dept. of Computer Science and Artificial Intelligence – University of Sevilla
{magutier, jalonso, jborrego}@us.es

Abstract. The subsumption relation is crucial in the Machine Learning systems based on a clausal representation. In this paper we present a class of operators for Machine Learning based on clauses which is a *characterization* of the subsumption relation in the following sense: The clause C_1 subsumes the clause C_2 iff C_1 can be reached from C_2 by applying these operators. In the second part of the paper we give a formalization of the closeness among clauses based on these operators and an algorithm to compute it as well as a bound for a quick estimation.

1 Introduction

In a Machine Learning system based on clausal logic, the main operation lies on applying an operator to one or more clauses with the hope that the new clauses give a better classification for the training set. This generalization must fit into some relation of order on clauses or sets of clauses. The usual orders considered in Machine Learning based on clauses are the subsumption order, denoted by $\succeq$, and the implication order $\models$. Most of the systems use the subsumption order to carry out the generalization, in spite of the implication order is stronger, i.e., if the clause C_1 subsumes the clause C_2, $C_1 \succeq C_2$, then $C_1 \models C_2$. The reason for choosing the subsumption order is easy: The subsumption between clauses is decidable, whereas the implication order is not [10].

Therefore the subsumption between clauses is the basic relation of order in the generalization processes in Machine Learning with clausal representation, but how is this generalization carried out? The subsumption relation was presented by G. Plotkin [7]. In his study about the lattice structure induced by this relation on the set of clauses, he proved the existence of the *least general generalization* of two clauses under subsumption and defined the *least generalization under relative subsumption*. Both techniques are the basis of successful learning systems on real-life problems.

Later, different classes of operators on clauses, the so-called refinement operators, were studied by Shapiro [9], Laird [4] and Nienhuys-Cheng and de Wolf [11] among others. In their works, the emphasis is put on the specialization operators, which are operators such that the obtained clause is implied or subsumed by the

---

[*] Work partially supported by the MCyT project TIC 2000-1368-C03-0 and the project TIC-137 of the *Plan Andaluz de Investigación*.

F.J. Garijo, J.C. Riquelme, and M. Toro (Eds.): IBERAMIA 2002, LNAI 2527, pp. 193–203, 2002.
© Springer-Verlag Berlin Heidelberg 2002

original clause, and the generalization operators are considered the *dual* of the first ones.

In this paper we present *new* generalization operators for clausal learning, the Learning Operators under Subsumption (LOS) which allow us to generalize clauses in the subsumption order, i.e., if C is a clause, $\{\Delta/x\}$ is a LOS and $C\{\Delta/x\}$ is the output clause, then $C\{\Delta/x\}$ subsumes C.

This property states that the LOS are *operators of generalization* under subsumption in the set of clauses, but the main property of these operators is that the LOS represent a *characterization* by operators of the subsumption relation between clauses in the following sense: If C_1 and C_2 are clauses, C_1 subsumes C_2 if and only if there exists a finite sequence (a *chain*) of LOS $\{\Delta_1/x_1\}, \ldots, \{\Delta_n/x_n\}$ such that

$$C_1 = C_2\{\Delta_1/x_1\} \ldots \{\Delta_n/x_n\}$$

If C_1 subsumes C_2, we know that the set of chains of LOS from C_2 to C_1 is not empty, but in general the set has more than one element.

The existence of a non-empty set of chains gives us the idea for a formalization of *closeness* among clauses as the length of the shortest chain from C_2 to C_1, if C_1 subsumes C_2, and infinity otherwise.

This mapping, which will be denoted by dc, is the algebraic expression of the subsumption order: for every pair of clauses, C_1 and C_2, C_1 subsumes C_2 if and only if $dc(C_2, C_1)$ is finite. Since the subsumption order is not symmetric, the mapping dc is not either. Therefore dc is not a metric, but a *quasi-metric*.

Finally, dc is computable. We give in this paper an algorithm which calculates the quasi-distance between two clauses and present a bound which allows to estimate the closeness between clauses under the hypothesis of subsumption.

2   Preliminaries

From now on, we will consider some fixed first-order language $\mathcal{L}$ with at least one function symbol. Var, $Term$ and Lit are, respectively, the sets of variables, terms and literals of $\mathcal{L}$. A *clause* is a finite set of literals, a *program* is a finite set of clauses and $\mathbb{C}$ is the set of all clauses.

A *substitution* is a mapping $\theta : S \to Term$ where S is a finite set of variables such that $(\forall x \in S)[x \neq \theta(x)]$. We will use the usual notation $\theta = \{x/t : x \in S\}$, where $t = \theta(x)$, $Dom(\theta)$ for the set S and $Ran(\theta) = \cup\{Var(t) : x/t \in \theta\}$. A pair x/t is called a *binding*. If A is a set, then $|A|$ is the cardinal of A and $\mathcal{P}A$ its power set. We will denote by $|\theta|$ the number of bindings of the substitution θ. The clause C *subsumes* the clause D, $C \succeq D$, iff there exists a substitution θ such that $C\theta \subseteq D$.

A *position* is a non-empty finite sequence of positive integers. Let $\mathbb{N}^+$ denote the set of all positions. If $t = f(t_1, \ldots, t_n)$ is an atom or a term, t_i is the term at position i in t and the term at position $i\hat{\ }u$ in t is s if s is at position u in t_i. Two positions u and v are *independent* if u is not a prefix of v and vice versa. A set of positions P is *independent* if $(\forall u, v \in P)[u \neq v \Rightarrow u$ and v are independent$]$ and the set of all positions of the term t in L will be denoted by $Pos(L, t)$. If t is a term (resp. an atom), we will denote by $t[u \leftarrow s]$ the term (resp. the atom) obtained by grafting the term s in t at position u and, if L is a literal, we will write $L[P \leftarrow s]$ for the literal obtained by grafting the term s in L at the independent set of positions P.

3   The Operators

In the generalization process, when a program P is too specific, we replace it by P' with the hope that P' covers the examples better than P. The step from P to P' is usually done by applying an operator to some clause C of P. These operators can be defined as mappings from $\mathbb{C}$ to $\mathbb{C}$ where $\mathbb{C}$ is the set of clauses of the language. Before giving the definition of the operator, we will give some intuition with an example.

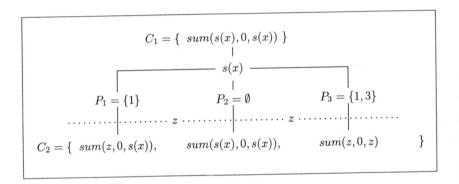

Fig. 1. Example of generalization

Consider the one–literal clause $C_1 = \{L\}$ with $L = sum(s(x), 0, s(x))$. In order to generalize it with respect to the subsumption order, we have to obtain a new clause C_2 such that there exists a substitution θ verifying $C_2\theta \subseteq C_1$. For that, we firstly choose a term t in L, say $t = s(x)$, then we choose several subsets of $Pos(L, t)$, e.g. $P_1 = \{1\}, P_2 = \emptyset, P_3 = \{1, 3\}$ and a variable not occurring in L, say z, and finally we build the clause $C_2 = \{L[P_i \leftarrow z] \mid i = 1, 2, 3\} = \{sum(z, 0, s(x)), sum(s(x), 0, s(x)), sum(z, 0, z)\}$. Obviously $\theta = \{z/s(x)\}$ satisfies $C_2\theta \subseteq C_1$ (see Fig. 1).

If the clause has several literals, for example, $C_1 = \{L_1, L_2, L_3\}$, with $L_1 = num(s(x))$, $L_2 = less\_than(0, s(x))$ and $L_3 = less\_than(s(x), s(s(x)))$, the operation is done with all literals simultaneously. First, the same term is chosen in every literal of C_1, say $t = s(x)$. Then, for each literal $L_i \in C_1$, some subsets of $Pos(L_i, t)$ are chosen, e.g.,

$$P_1^* = \{\emptyset, \{1\}\} \subseteq \mathcal{P}Pos(L_1, t)$$
$$P_2^* = \emptyset \subseteq \mathcal{P}Pos(L_2, t)$$
$$P_3^* = \{\{1, 2 \cdot 1\}, \{1\}\} \subseteq \mathcal{P}Pos(L_3, t)$$

After taking a variable which does not occur in C_1, say z, the following sets are built

$$L_1 \xrightarrow{\quad P_1^* \quad} \{num(s(x)), num(z)\}$$

$$L_2 \xrightarrow{\quad P_2^* \quad} \emptyset$$

$$L_3 \xrightarrow{\quad P_3^* \quad} \{less\_than(z, s(z)), less\_than(z, s(s(x)))\}$$

Finally, the clause C_2 is the union of these sets, i.e.,

$$C_2 = \{num(s(x)), num(z), less\_than(z, s(z)), less\_than(z, s(s(x)))\}$$

and $C_2\{z/s(x)\} \subseteq C_1$. In our general description, we will begin with a study of the relations between substitutions and grafts.

Definition 1. *Let L be a literal and t a term. The set of positions P is called* compatible *with the pair $\langle L, t \rangle$ if $P \subseteq Pos(L, t)$.*

Definition 2. *Let P^* be a set whose elements are sets of positions. Let L be a literal and t a term. P^* is called* compatible *with the pair $\langle L, t \rangle$ if every element of P^* is compatible with $\langle L, t \rangle$*

For example, if $L = sum(s(x), 0, s(x))$ and $t = s(x)$, then $P_1 = \{1\}$, $P_2 = \emptyset$ and $P_3 = \{1, 3\}$ are compatible with $\langle L, t \rangle$ and $P_4 = \{1 \cdot 1, 2\}$ and $P_5 = \{1, 4 \cdot 3\}$ are not. If $P_1^* = \{P_1, P_2, P_3\}$ and $P_2^* = \{P_2, P_4\}$, then P_1^* is compatible with $\langle L, t \rangle$ and P_2^* is not.

The next mappings are basic in the definition of our operators. As we saw in the example, the key is to settle a set of sets of positions for each literal, all them occupied by the same term. This one is done by the following mappings.

Definition 3. *A mapping $\Delta : Lit \to \mathcal{PPN}^+$ is called an* assignment *if there exists a term t such that, for every literal L, $\Delta(L)$ is compatible with the pair $\langle L, t \rangle$.*

Note that the term t does *not* have to be unique, for example, consider the *identity* assignment $(\forall L \in Lit)[\Delta(L) = \{\emptyset\}]$, the *empty* assignment $(\forall L \in Lit)[\Delta(L) = \emptyset]$ or any mixture of both.

The assignments map a literal into a set of sets of positions. Each element of this set of positions will produce a literal, and the positions are the places where the new term is grafted. If $\Delta : Lit \to \mathcal{PPN}^+$ is an assignment of positions and s is a term, we will denote by $L\{\Delta(L)/s\}$ the set of literals, one for each element $P \in \Delta(L)$, obtained by grafting s in L at P. Formally

$$L\{\Delta(L)/s\} = \{L[P \leftarrow s] \mid P \in \Delta(L)\}$$

For example, if $L = sum(s(x), 0, s(x))$, z is a variable, P_1^* is taken from the above example and Δ is an assignment such that $\Delta(L) = P_1^*$ then

$$
\begin{aligned}
L\{\Delta(L)/z\} &= \{L[P \leftarrow z] \mid P \in \Delta(L)\} \\
&= \{L[P \leftarrow z] \mid P \in P_1^*\} \\
&= \{L[P_1 \leftarrow z]\}, L[P_2 \leftarrow z], L[P_3 \leftarrow z]\} \\
&= \{sum(z, 0, s(x)), sum(s(x), 0, s(x)), sum(z, 0, z)\}
\end{aligned}
$$

We can now define our Learning Operators under Subsumption.

Definition 4. *Let Δ be an assignment and x a variable. We say that the mapping*

$$
\{\Delta/x\} : \mathbb{C} \longrightarrow \mathbb{C}
$$
$$
C \mapsto C\{\Delta/x\} = \bigcup_{L \in C} L\{\Delta(L)/x\}
$$

is a Learning Operator under Subsumption (LOS) *if for all literal L, if $\Delta(L) \neq \emptyset$ then $x \notin Var(L)$.*

Turning back to a previous example, if $C = \{L_1, L_2, L_3\}$, with $L_1 = num(s(x))$, $L_2 = less\_than(0, s(x))$, $L_3 = less\_than(s(x), s(s(x)))$, and the assignment

$$
\Delta(L) = \begin{cases}
P_1^* = \{\emptyset, \{1\}\} & \text{if } L = L_1 \\
P_2^* = \emptyset & \text{if } L = L_2 \\
P_3^* = \{\{1, 2 \cdot 1\}, \{1\}\} & \text{if } L = L_3 \\
\emptyset & \text{otherwise}
\end{cases}
$$

and considering the variable z as the variable to be grafted, then

$$
C\{\Delta/z\} = \{num(s(x)), num(z), less\_than(z, s(z)), less\_than(z, s(s(x)))\}
$$

These operators allow us to generalize a given clause and go up in the subsumption order on clauses as we see in the next theorem.

Theorem 1. *Let C be a clause and $\{\Delta/x\}$ a LOS. Then $C\{\Delta/x\} \succeq C$.*

As we pointed above, the LOS define an operational definition of the subsumption relation. The last result states one way of the implication. The next theorem claims that all the learning processes based on subsumption of clauses can be carried out only by applying LOS.

Theorem 2. *Let C_1 and C_2 be two clauses such that $C_1 \succeq C_2$. Then there exists a finite sequence (a chain) $\{\Delta_1/x_1\}, \ldots, \{\Delta_n/x_n\}$ of LOS such that*

$$
C_1 = C_2\{\Delta_1/x_1\} \ldots \{\Delta_n/x_n\}
$$

For example, if we consider $C_1 = \{p(x_1, x_2)\}$ and $C_2 = \{p(x_2, f(x_1)), p(x_1, a)\}$ and the substitution $\theta = \{x_1/x_2, x_2/f(x_1)\}$. Then $C_1\theta \subseteq C_2$ holds and therefore $C_1 \succeq C_2$. Decomposing θ we can get $\sigma_1 = \{x_2/x_3\}$, $\sigma_2 = \{x_1/x_2\}$, $\sigma_3 = \{x_3/f(x_1)\}$ and $C_1\sigma_1\sigma_2\sigma_3 \subseteq C_2$ holds. Hence, considering the assignments

$$
\begin{aligned}
\Delta_1(p(x_2, f(x_1))) &= \{\{2\}\} \quad \text{and} \quad \Delta_1(L) = \emptyset \ \text{ if } L \neq p(x_2, f(x_1)) \\
\Delta_2(p(x_2, x_3)) &= \{\{1\}\} \quad \text{and} \quad \Delta_2(L) = \emptyset \ \text{ if } L \neq p(x_2, x_3) \\
\Delta_3(p(x_1, x_3)) &= \{\{2\}\} \quad \text{and} \quad \Delta_3(L) = \emptyset \ \text{ if } L \neq p(x_1, x_3)
\end{aligned}
$$

we have $C_1 = C_2\{\Delta_1/x_3\}\{\Delta_2/x_1\}\{\Delta_3/x_2\}$. Note that if we consider the assignment $\Delta(p(x_1,a)) = \{\{2\}\}$ and $\Delta(L) = \emptyset$ if $L \neq p(x_1,a)$, then $C_1 = C_2\{\Delta/x_2\}$ also holds.

4   A Quasi-Metric Based on Subsumption

The operational characterization of the subsumption relation given in the previous section gives us a natural way of formalizing the *closeness* among clauses. As we have seen, if $C_1 \succeq C_2$ then there exists *at least* one chain of LOS from C_2 to C_1 and we can consider the length of the shortest chain from C_2 to C_1.

Definition 5. *A chain of LOS of length n from the clause C_2 to the clause C_1 is a finite sequence of n LOS $\{\Delta_1/x_1\}, \{\Delta_2/x_2\}, \ldots, \{\Delta_n/x_n\}$ such that*

$$C_1 = C_2\{\Delta_1/x_1\}\{\Delta_2/x_2\}\ldots\{\Delta_n/x_n\}$$

If $C_1 = C_2$, we will consider that the empty chain, *of length zero, maps C_2 into C_1. The set of all the chains from C_2 to C_1 will be denoted by $\mathbf{L}(C_2, C_1)$ and $|\mathcal{C}|$ will denote the length of the chain $\mathcal{C}$.*

Following the geometric intuition, if we consider these chains as *paths* from C_2 to C_1, we formalize the *closeness* between clauses as the shortest path C_2 to C_1. If C_1 does not subsume C_2, we will think that C_1 cannot be reached from C_2 by applying LOS, so both clauses are separated by an infinite distance.

Definition 6. *We define the mapping $dc : \mathbb{C} \times \mathbb{C} \to [0, +\infty]$ as follows:*

$$dc(C_2, C_1) = \begin{cases} min\{|\mathcal{C}| \ : \ \mathcal{C} \in \mathbf{L}(C_2, C_1)\} & \textit{if } C_1 \succeq C_2 \\ +\infty & \textit{otherwise} \end{cases}$$

The subsumption relation is not symmetric, so the mapping dc is not either. Instead of being a drawback, this property gives an algebraic characterization of the subsumption relation, since for any two clauses, $C_1 \succeq C_2$ iff $dc(C_2, C_1) \neq +\infty$.

Definition 7. *A quasi–metric on a set X is a mapping d from $X \times X$ to the non–negative reals (possibly including $+\infty$) satisfying:*

- $(\forall x \in X)\, d(x,x) = 0$
- $(\forall x, y, z \in X)\, d(x,z) \leq d(x,y) + d(y,z)$
- $(\forall x, y \in X)\, [d(x,y) = d(y,x) = 0 \Rightarrow x = y]$

Notice that a quasi–metric satisfies the conditions to be a metric, except for the condition of symmetry. The next result states the computability of dc and provides an algorithm to compute it.

Theorem 3. *dc is a computable quasi–metric.*

Proof (Outline). Proving that dc is a quasi-metric is straightforward from the definition. The proof of the computability is split in several steps. Firstly, for each substitution θ we define the set of the splittings up:

$$Split(\theta) = \left\{ \sigma_1 \ldots \sigma_n : \begin{array}{l} \sigma_i = \{x_i/t_i\} \quad x_i \notin Var(t_i) \\ (\forall z \in Dom(\theta))[z\theta = z\sigma_1 \ldots \sigma_n] \end{array} \right\}$$

with $length(\sigma_1 \ldots \sigma_n) = n$ and $weight(\theta) = min\{length(\Sigma) \,|\, \Sigma \in Split(\theta)\}$. The next equivalence holds

$$dc(C_2, C_1) = \begin{cases} 0 & \text{if } C_1 = C_2 \\ 1 & \text{if } C_1 \neq C_2 \text{ and } C_1 \subseteq C_2 \\ min\{weight(\theta) \,|\, C_1\theta \subseteq C_2\} & \text{if } C_1 \succeq C_2 \text{ and } C_1 \not\subseteq C_2 \\ +\infty & \text{if } C_1 \not\succeq C_2 \end{cases}$$

Input: A non-empty substitution θ
Output: An element of $Split(\theta)$
Set $\theta_0 = \theta$ and $U_0 = Dom(\theta) \cup Ran(\theta)$
Step 1:
    If θ_i is the empty substitution
        Then stop
        Otherwise: Consider $\theta_i = \{x_1/t_1, \ldots, x_n/t_n\}$ and go to **Step 2**.
Step 2:
    If there exists $x_j \in Dom(\theta_i)$ such that $x_j \notin Ran(\theta_i)$
        Then for all $k \in \{1, \ldots, j-1, j+1, \ldots, n\}$ let t_k^* be a term
    such that $t^k = t_k^*\{x_j/t_j\}$ Set
    $\theta_{i+1} = \{x_1/t_1^*, \ldots, x_{j-1}/t_{j-1}^*, x_{j+1}/t_{j+1}^*, \ldots, x_n/t_n^*\}$
    $\sigma_{i+1} = \{x_j/t_j\}$
    $U_{i+1} = U_i$
        set i to $i+1$ and go to **Step 1**.
        Otherwise: Go to **Step 3**.
Step 3:
    In this case let z_i be a variable which does not belong to U_i and set
    $U_{i+1} = U_i \cup \{z_i\}$
choose $j \in \{1, \ldots, n\}$ y let T be a subterm of t_j such that T is not a variable
belonging to U_{i+1}. Then, for all $k \in \{1, \ldots, n\}$ let t_k^* be a term
    such that $t^k = t_k^*\{z/T\}$. Set
    $\theta_{i+1} = \{x_1/t_1^*, \ldots, x_n/t_n^*\}$
    $\sigma_{i+1} = \{z/T\}$
set i to $i+1$ and go to **Step 1**.

Fig. 2. The algorithm to compute the subset of $Split(\theta)$

We can decide if $C_1 \succeq C_2$ and, if it holds, we can get the finite set of all θ such that $C_1\theta \subseteq C_2$, so to conclude the theorem we have to give an algorithm which computes $weight(\theta)$ for each θ. The Fig. 2 shows a non-deterministic algorithm which generates elements of $Split(\theta)$. We prove that the algorithm finishes and for all $\Sigma \in Split(\theta)$ the algorithm outputs a Σ^* verifying $length(\Sigma^*) \leq length(\Sigma)$.

The previous theorem provides a method for computing dc, but deciding whether two clauses are related by subsumption is an NP-complete problem [1], so, from a practical point of view we need a quick estimation of the quasi-metric before deciding the subsumption. The next result settles an upper and lower bounds for the quasi-metric under the assumption of subsumption.

Theorem 4. *Let C_1 and C_2 be two clauses such that $C_1 \not\sqsubseteq C_2$. If $C_1 \succeq C_2$ then*

$$|Var(C_1) - Var(C_2)| \leq dc(C_2, C_1) \leq min\{2 \cdot |Var(C_1)|, |Var(C_1)| + |Var(C_2)|\}$$

Proof (Outline). For each θ such that $C_1\theta \subseteq C_2$, θ has at least $|Var(C_1) - Var(C_2)|$ bindings and we need at least one LOS for each binding, hence the first inequality holds. For the second one, if $C_1\theta \subseteq C_2$ then we can find n substitutions $\sigma_1, \dots, \sigma_n$ with $\sigma_1 = \{x_i/t_i\}$ and $x_i \notin Var(t_i)$ such that $C_1\sigma_1 \dots \sigma_2 \subseteq C_2$ verifying $n = |\theta| + |Ran(\theta) \cap Dom(\theta)|$. The inequality holds since $Ran(\theta) \subseteq Var(C_2)$, $Dom(\theta) \subseteq Var(C_1)$ and $|\theta| \leq Var(C_1)$.

If $C_1 = \{p(x_1, x_2)\}$, $C_2 = \{p(a, b)\}$ and $C_3 = \{p(f(x_1, x_2), f(x_2, x_1))\}$ then

$$dc(C_2, C_1) = |Var(C_1) - Var(C_2)| = 2$$
$$dc(C_3, C_1) = min\{2 \cdot |Var(C_1)|, |Var(C_1)| + |Var(C_2)|\} = 4$$

The above examples show that these bounds cannot be improved.

5   Related Work

The problem of quantifying the closeness among clauses has already been studied previously by offering distinct alternatives of solution to the problem. In the literature, a metric is firstly defined on the set of literals and then, the Hausdorff metric is used to get, from this metric, a metric on the set of clauses. This approach has two drawbacks. On the one hand, the Hausdorff metric exclusively depends on the extreme points, on the other, these literals are considered isolated: the possible relations among the literals of the same clause are not considered. Next we will see an example.

In [6], Nienhuys-Cheng defines a distance for ground atoms

- $d_{nc,g}(e, e) = 0$
- $p/n \neq q/m \Rightarrow d_{nc,g}(p(s_1, \dots, s_n), q(t_1, \dots, t_m)) = 1$
- $d_{nc,g}(p(s_1, \dots, s_n), p(t_1, \dots, t_n)) = \frac{1}{2n} \sum_{i=1}^n d_{nc,g}(s_i, t_i)$

and then, she uses the Hausdorff metric to define a metric on sets of ground atoms

$$d_h(A, B) = max\left\{ \max_{a \in A}\{\min_{b \in B}\{d_{nc,g}(a, b)\}\}, \max_{b \in B}\{\min_{a \in A}\{d_{nc,g}(a, b)\}\} \right\}$$

The aim of this distance was to define a distance between Herbrand interpretations, so $d_{nc,g}$ was only defined on ground atoms. In [8], Ramon and Bruynooghe extended it to handle non–ground expressions:

- $d_{nc}(e_1, e_2) = d_{nc,g}(e_1, e_2)$ if e_1, e_2 are ground expressions
- $d_{nc}(p(s_1, \ldots, s_n), X) = d_{nc}(X, p(s_1, \ldots, s_n)) = 1$ with X a variable.
- $d_{nc}(X, Y) = 1$ and $d_{nc}(X, X) = 0$ for all $X \neq Y$ with X and Y variables.

This metric can be easily extended to literals: If A and B are atoms, we consider $d_{nc}(\neg A, B) = d_{nc}(A, \neg B) = 0$ and $d_{nc}(\neg A, \neg B) = d_{nc}(A, B)$. By applying the Hausdorff metric to d_{nc} we have a metric d_h on clauses. We have implemented dc and d_h with Prolog programs. The following example allows us to compare this metric with our quasi-metric.

For all $n \geq 0$, consider the clauses

$$C_n \equiv sum(s^{n+1}(x_1), s^n(y_1), s^{n+1}(z_1)) \leftarrow sum(s^n(x_1), s^n(y_1), s^n(z_1))$$
$$D_n \equiv sum(s^{2n+1}(x_2), s^{2n}(y_2), s^{2n+1}(z_2)) \leftarrow sum(s^{2n}(x_2), s^{2n}(y_2), s^{2n}(z_2))$$

and the substitution $\theta_n = \{x_1/s^n(x_2), y_1/s^n(y_2), x_3/s^n(y_3)\}$. Then $C_n\theta_n = D_n$ for all n and hence, $C_n \succeq D_n$. The next table shows the values of the quasi-metric $dc(C_n, D_n)$ and the metric of Hausdorff $d_h(C_n, D_n)$ for several values of N as well as the time of computation on a Pentium III 800 Mhz. in an implementation for SWI-Prolog 4.0.11.

N	$dc(C_n, D_n)$		$d_h(C_n, D_n)$	
	Seg	Q–dist	Seg	Dist
64	0.02	3	0.11	$\sim 2.7\,10^{-20}$
128	0.06	3	0.21	$\sim 1.4\,10^{-39}$
256	0.1	3	0.43	$\sim 4.3\,10^{-78}$
512	0.26	3	0.93	$\sim 3.7\,10^{-155}$
1024	0.67	3	2.03	$\sim 2.7\,10^{-309}$

It can be easily calculated that, for all $n \geq 0$, $dc(C_n, D_n) = 3$. If we use the Hausdorff metric d_h based on d_{nc} we have that, for all $n \geq 0$

$$d_h(C_n, D_n) = \frac{1}{2^{n+1}}$$

which tends to zero in spite of the subsumption relation holds for all n.

In the literature, it can be found other formalizations of the closeness among clauses (e.g. [3] or [8]), but in all them there exists a strong dependence on the distance between individual elements.

6   Conclusions and Future Work

In the nineties, the success reached in real-life problems by learning systems based on clausal representation encouraged the development of techniques of generalization, most of them designed *ad hoc* for a specific problem. The operators presented in this paper[1] might be a significant improvement in the field. The operators are not related to any specific system, they can be easily implemented and used in any system. But the main property is that the LOS are sufficient for all generalization process of clauses based on subsumption. As we have proved, the LOS are a *complete* set of generalization operators: If C_1 subsumes C_2 then C_1 can be reached from C_2 by solely applying LOS.

In the second part of the paper we define a quasi-metric on the set of clauses and give an algorithm to compute it and a method for a quick estimation. The process of quantifying qualitative relations (as subsumption) is a hard and exiting problem which arises in many fields of Computer Science (see [5]) which is far from a complete solution. We present a contribution to its study by defining a quasi-metric on the set of clauses in a natural way, as the minimum number of operators which map a clause into another. As we have seen, this quasi-metric considers the clauses as members of a net of relations via subsumption and overcomes the drawbacks found in others formalizations of closeness.

Finally the definition of quasi-metric is completed with an algorithm to compute it and a bound for a quick estimation. This estimation can be a useful tool for the design of new learning algorithms based on subsumption.

References

1. M.R.Garey and D.S. Johnson: Computers and Intractability: A Guide to the Theory of NP-Completeness. Freeman, New York, 1979.
2. M.A. Gutiérrez-Naranjo, J.A. Alonso-Jiménez and J. Borrego-Díaz: A topological study of the upward refinement operators in ILP. In: Proceedings of the 10th International Conference on Inductive Logic Programming, Work in progress track, 2000.
3. A. Hutchinson: Metrics on Terms and Clauses. Proceedings ECML–97, Prague, April 1997 (Springer).
   ftp://ftp.dcs.kcl.ac.uk/pub/ tech-reports/ tr96-11.ps.gz
4. P.D. Laird: Learning from Good and Bad Data. Kluwer Academic Publishers, 1988
5. R. Lowen: Approach Spaces, the Missing Link in the Topology-Uniformity-Metric Triad. Oxford Mathematical Monographs, Oxford University Press, 1997.
6. S-H. Nienhuys-Cheng: Distance between Herbrand interpretations: a measure for approximations to a target concept. Technical Report EUR–FEW–CS–97–05. Department of Computer Science, Erasmus University, the Netherlands, 1997.
   http://www.few.eur.nl/few/research/pubs/cs/1997/eur-few-cs-97-05.pdf
7. G.D. Plotkin: A Note on Inductive Generalization. In Machine Intelligence 5, pp.: 153–163. Edinburgh University Press, Edinburgh, 1970.
8. J. Ramon and M. Bruynooghe: A framework for defining distances between first–order logic–objects. Report CW 263, Department of Computer Science, Katholieke Universiteit Leuven, May 1998.
   http://www.cs.kuleuven.ac.be/publicaties/rapporten/cw/CW263.ps.gz
9. E.Y. Shapiro: Inductive Inference of Theories from Facts. Technical Report 624, Department of Computer Science, Yale University, New Haven, CT, 1981

---

[1] A preliminary version of these operators appeared in [2].

10. M. Schmidt-Schauss. Implication of clauses is undecidable. Theoretical Computer Science, 59-3, pp. 287–296, 1988.
11. P.R.J. van der Laag, S.-H. Nienhuys-Cheng: Completeness and properness of refinement operators in Inductive Logic Programming. Journal of Logic Programming, Vol 34, n.3, pp.: 201–225, March 1998

Shared Ensemble Learning Using Multi-trees[*]

Victor Estruch, Cesar Ferri, Jose Hernández-Orallo, and
Maria Jose Ramírez-Quintana

DSIC, UPV, Camino de Vera s/n, 46020 Valencia, Spain.
{vestruch, cferri, jorallo, mramirez}@dsic.upv.es

Abstract. Decision tree learning is a machine learning technique that
allows accurate and comprehensible models to be generated. Accuracy
can be improved by ensemble methods which combine the predictions
of a set of different trees. However, a large amount of resources is
necessary to generate the ensemble. In this paper, we introduce a new
ensemble method that minimises the usage of resources by sharing the
common parts of the components of the ensemble. For this purpose,
we learn a decision multi-tree instead of a decision tree. We call this
new approach shared ensembles. The use of a multi-tree produces an
exponential number of hypotheses to be combined, which provides
better results than *boosting/bagging*. We performed several experiments,
showing that the technique allows us to obtain accurate models and
improves the use of resources with respect to classical ensemble methods.

Keywords: Decision-tree learning, Decision support systems, Boosting,
Machine Learning, Hypothesis Combination, Randomisation.

1 Introduction

From the different machine learning approaches which are currently being applied with successful results, decision tree learning [16] is considered to be a
paradigm with an optimal trade-off between the quality and the comprehensibility of the models learned.

A method that has recently been exploited to improve the accuracy of simple
classifiers consists in the combination of a set of hypotheses (or ensemble) [3].
Well-known techniques for generating and combining hypotheses are boosting [8,
18], bagging [1,18], randomisation [4], stacking [19] and windowing [17]. Although
accuracy is significantly increased, "the large amount of memory required to store
the hypotheses can make ensemble methods hard to deploy in applications"[12].
One way to partially overcome this limitation could be to share the common
parts of the components of the ensemble.

In a previous work [5], we presented an algorithm for the induction of decision
trees which is able to obtain more than one solution. To do this, once a node has

---

[*] This work has been partially supported by CICYT under grant TIC2001-2705-C03-
01, Generalitat Valenciana under grant GV00-092-14, and Acción Integrada Hispano-
Austriaca HU2001-19.

been selected for splitting, the other possible splits at this point are suspended and stored until a new solution is required. This way, the search space is a multi-tree rather than a tree which is traversed thus producing an increasing number of solutions as the execution time increases. Since each new solution is built following a suspended node at an arbitrary place in the multi-tree, our method differs from other approaches such as the *boosting* method or the *bagging* method [1,8,18] which induce a new decision tree for each solution. Therefore, a multi-tree is not a forest [10] because a multi-tree shares the common parts of different trees (*shared ensemble*), whereas a forest is just a collection of trees.

Other works have attempted to generate a forest of 'different' trees, either semantically/vertically (by changing the weights of examples, e.g. boosting [8, 18], or the sample, e.g. bagging [1]) or syntactically/horizontally (by selecting attribute samples for each tree). Specifically, this latter approach has been presented independently by [9,10], under the name pseudo-randomly selected feature subspaces, and by [20], under the name stochastic attribute selection committees. In both cases, the idea is to pseudo-randomly select a subset of attributes, to learn a first classifier, and then, to select another subset of attributes and learn a second classifier, and so on. Next, the elements from the set of decision tree classifiers (the forest) are combined. A related technique has been presented by Breiman in [2].

The main aim of both the horizontal and vertical approaches is to obtain better accuracy in the combination. There have also been attempts to combine horizontal and vertical approaches, such as the work from [21]. In [4], a ran-domised method has been introduced in the construction of the tree (random split criterion) and has been shown to be competitive w.r.t. boosting and bagging.

In this paper, we focus on the combination of hypotheses from the multi-tree approach in order to obtain accurate models. The use of this structure allows more hypotheses to be combined than in other combination methods using the same resources. Several hypothesis-fusion strategies are defined and evaluated experimentally. We also include a comparison between our approach and some well-known ensemble methods.

The paper is organised as follows. In Section 2, we introduce the multi-tree structure. Section 3 discusses different ways to combine the components of a shared ensemble. Section 4 presents several experiments showing that the approach effectively generates accurate models. Finally, Section 5 summarises and presents some future work.

2   Multi-tree Structure

In this section, we present the multi-tree structure, and we discuss the different criteria required to construct it.

The construction of decision trees is performed in two different steps [17]:

- **Tree Construction:** The entire decision tree is constructed in this phase. The process is driven by a splitting criterion that selects the best split. The selected split is applied to generate new branches, and the rest of the splits are discarded. The algorithm stops when the examples that fall into a branch belong to the same class.

- **Pruning**. This phase consists in the removal of useless parts of the tree. There are two options: *pre-pruning*, when the process is performed during the construction of the tree, or *post-pruning*, when the pruning is performed by analysing the leaves once the tree has been built.

Thus, decision trees are built in an eager way, which makes it possible for the quick construction of a model. However, it may produce bad models because of bad decisions.

In [5], we have defined a new structure in which the rejected splits are not removed, but stored as *suspended* nodes. The further exploration of these nodes after the first solution is built permits the extraction of new models from this structure. For this reason, we call it a decision multi-tree, rather than a decision tree. Since each new model is obtained by continuing the construction of the multi-tree, these models share their common parts. A decision multi-tree can also be seen as an AND/OR tree [13,15], if one considers the split nodes as being OR-nodes and considers the nodes generated by an exploited OR-node as being AND-nodes.

To populate a multi-tree, we need to specify a criterion that selects one of the suspended nodes. In [6], we presented and evaluated some possible criteria, such as topmost, bottom, or random. Our experimental results showed that random is a trade-off between speed and quality.

Once the multi-tree has been built, we can use it for two different purposes: to select one or *n* comprehensible models (decision trees) according to a selection criterion (Occam, MDL, ...), or to use the multi-tree as an ensemble whose components can be combined. In this paper, we address the latter.

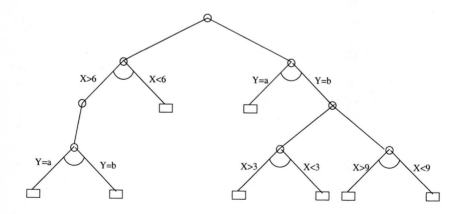

Fig. 1. Selection of a single decision tree from the multi-tree structure.

Figure 1 shows a decision multi-tree. OR-nodes are represented with an arc and leaves are represented by rectangles. Three different models are exhibited in this multi-tree since two suspended nodes have been exploited.

The decision multi-tree approach presents some interesting features. First, the number of solutions grows exponentially wrt. the number of suspended OR-nodes that are exploited. Secondly, the solutions share some of their parts. The percentage of the shared quantity depends on the depth of the suspended OR-node that is exploited. Exploring deep suspended nodes in the bottom areas of the multi-tree causes the generation of models that share many of their conditions; therefore they could be very similar. However, the exploration of OR-nodes in the top positions of the multi-tree produces solutions which are different enough.

3   Shared Ensemble Combination

In this section, we address the question of how to combine different solutions in a multi-tree. Given several classifiers that assign a probability to each prediction (also known as soft classifiers), there are several combination methods or fusion strategies. Let us denote by $p_k(c_j|x)$ an estimate of the posterior probability that classifier k assigns class c_j for example x. In decision tree learning, the $p_k(c_j|x)$ depends on the leaf node where each x falls. More precisely, these probabilities depend on the *proportion* of training examples of each class that have fallen into each leaf node during training. The reliability of each leaf usually depends on the *cardinality* of the leaf.

Let us define a *class vector* $v_{k,j}(x)$ as the vector of training cases that fall in each node k for each class j. For leaf nodes, the values would be the training cases of each class that have fallen into the leaf. To propagate these vectors upwards to internal nodes, we must clarify how to propagate through AND and OR nodes. This is done for each new unlabelled example we want to make a prediction for. For the OR-nodes, the answer is clear: an example can only fall through one of its children. Hence, the vector would be the vector of the child where the example falls. AND-nodes, however, must do a fusion whenever different alternate vectors occur. This is an important difference in shared ensembles: fusion points are distributed all over the multi-tree structure. Following [11], we have considered several fusion strategies that convert m class vectors into one combined vector Ω_j:

- **sum:** $\Omega_j = \sum_{k=1}^{m} v_{k,j}$
- **arithmetic mean:** $\Omega_j = \sum_{k=1}^{m} \frac{v_{k,j}}{m}$
- **product:** $\Omega_j = \prod_{k=1}^{m} v_{k,j}$
- **geometric mean:** $\Omega_j = \sqrt[m]{\prod_{k=1}^{m} v_{k,j}}$
- **maximum:** $\Omega_j = \max_k(v_{k,j})$
- **minimum:** $\Omega_j = \min_k(v_{k,j})$

There have been some studies to determine which strategy is better. In particular, [11] concludes that, for two-class problems, minimum and maximum are the best strategies, followed by average (arithmetic mean).

In addition, we have devised some transformations to be done to the original vectors at the leaves before its propagation:

- **good loser** : $v'_{k,j}(x) = \sum_j v_{k,j}(x)$ if $j = \texttt{argmax}(v_{k,j}(x))$ and 0 otherwise
- **bad loser:** $v'_{k,j}(x) = v_{k,j}(x)$ if $j = \texttt{argmax}(v_{k,j}(x))$ and 0 otherwise.
- **majority:** $v'_{k,j}(x) = 1$ if $j = \texttt{argmax}(v_{k,j}(x))$ and 0 otherwise.
- **difference:** $v'_{k,j}(x) = v_{k,j}(x) - \sum_{i \neq j} v_{k,j}(x)$

For example, the following table shows the results of applying the transformations to two vectors.

Original	Good loser	Bad loser	Majority	Difference
{ 40, 10, 30 }	{ 80, 0, 0 }	{ 40, 0, 0}	{ 1, 0, 0 }	{ 0, -60, -20 }
{ 7, 2, 10 }	{ 0, 0, 19 }	{ 0, 0, 10 }	{ 0, 0, 1 }	{ -5, -15, 1 }

In the next section, we show an experimental evaluation of these fusion and transformation methods for problems with more than two classes.

4   Experiments

In this section, we present an experimental evaluation of our approach, as it is implemented in the SMILES system [7]. SMILES is a multi-purpose machine learning system which (among many other features) includes the implementation of a multiple decision tree learner.

For the experiments, we used GainRatio [17] as splitting criterion and we chose a random method [6] for populating the shared ensemble (after a solution is found, a suspended OR-node is woken at random). Pruning is not enabled.

The experiments were performed in a Pentium III-800Mhz with 180MB of memory running Linux 2.4.2. We have used several datasets from the UCI dataset repository [14]. Table 1 shows the dataset name, the size in number of examples, the number of classes and the number of nominal and numerical attributes.

Since there are many sources of randomness, we performed the experiments by averaging 10 results of a 10-fold cross-validation. This makes a total of 100 runs for each pair composed of a method and a dataset.

4.1   Evaluation of Fusion and Vector Transformation Techniques

Table 2 shows the mean accuracy and the standard deviation using the different fusion techniques introduced in Section 3 for each dataset. We summarise the results with the geometric means for each technique.

The techniques studied are *sum, product, maximum, minimum,* and *arithmetic mean,* all of which use the original vectors. In the table, we do not include the experiments with *geometric mean* because they are equivalent to the results

Table 1. Information about datasets used in the experiments.

#	Dataset	Size	Classes	Nom.Attr.	Num.Attr.
1	Balance-scale	625	3	0	4
2	Cars	1728	4	5	0
3	Dermatology	358	6	33	1
4	Ecoli	336	8	0	7
5	Iris	150	3	0	4
6	House-votes	435	2	16	0
7	Monks1	566	2	6	0
8	Monks2	601	2	6	0
9	Monks3	554	2	6	0
10	New-thyroid	215	3	0	5
11	Post-operative	87	3	7	1
12	Soybean-small	35	4	35	0
13	Tae	151	3	2	3
14	Tic-tac	958	2	8	0
15	Wine	178	3	0	13

Table 2. Comparison between fusion techniques.

#	Arit.		Sum.		Prod.		Max.		Min.	
	Acc.	Dev.	Acc.	Dev.	Acc.	Dev.	Acc.	Dev.	Acc.	Dev.
1	80.69	5.01	81.24	4.66	76.61	5.04	83.02	4.76	76.61	5.04
2	91.22	2.25	91.25	2.26	83.38	3.65	90.90	2.09	83.38	3.65
3	94.17	4.06	94.34	3.87	89.06	5.19	94.00	4.05	89.06	5.19
4	80.09	6.26	79.91	6.13	76.97	7.14	80.09	6.11	76.97	7.14
5	95.63	3.19	95.77	3.18	93.28	3.71	95.93	2.81	93.28	3.71
6	94.53	5.39	94.20	5.66	94.00	5.34	94.47	5.45	94.40	5.34
7	99.67	1.30	99.71	1.18	81.00	8.60	99.89	0.51	81.00	8.60
8	73.35	5.86	73.73	5.82	74.53	5.25	77.15	5.88	74.53	5.25
9	97.87	2.00	97.91	1.80	97.58	2.45	97.62	1.93	97.58	2.45
10	94.52	4.25	93.76	5.10	92.05	5.71	92.57	5.43	92.05	5.71
11	62.50	16.76	63.25	16.93	61.63	17.61	67.13	14.61	61.63	17.61
12	97.50	8.33	97.50	9.06	97.75	8.02	94.75	11.94	97.75	8.02
13	63.60	12.59	64.33	11.74	62.00	12.26	63.93	12.03	62.00	12.26
14	81.73	3.82	82.04	3.78	78.93	3.73	82.68	3.97	78.93	3.73
15	94.06	6.00	93.88	6.42	91.47	7.11	92.53	6.99	91.47	7.11
Geomean	85.83	4.72	85.99	4.71	82.53	5.93	86.40	4.52	82.55	5.93

of *product*. The multi-tree was generated by exploring 100 suspended OR-nodes, thus giving thousands of possible hypotheses (with much less required memory than 100 non-shared hypotheses). According to the experiments, the best fusion technique was *maximum*. Thus, we will use this fusion method to study the effect of applying the transformations on the vector.

Table 3 illustrates the results for accuracy using the *original* vector and the *good loser*, *bad loser*, *majority* and *difference* transformations. According to these

Table 3. Comparison between vector transformation methods.

#	Max + Orig		Max + Good		Max + Bad		Max + Majo.		Max + Diff.	
	Acc.	Dev	Acc.	Dev	Acc.	Dev	Acc.	Dev	Acc.	Dev
1	83.02	4.76	83.02	4.76	83.02	4.76	67.84	6.61	83.02	4.76
2	90.90	2.09	90.90	2.09	90.90	2.09	81.48	3.22	90.90	2.09
3	94.00	4.05	94.00	4.05	94.00	4.05	79.97	7.98	94.00	4.05
4	80.09	6.11	80.09	6.11	80.09	6.11	78.21	6.07	80.09	6.11
5	95.93	2.81	95.93	2.81	95.93	2.81	89.44	4.84	95.93	2.81
6	94.47	5.45	94.47	5.45	94.47	5.45	91.47	6.90	94.47	5.45
7	99.89	0.51	99.89	0.51	99.89	0.51	77.58	6.29	99.89	0.51
8	77.15	5.88	77.15	5.88	77.15	5.88	83.42	5.06	77.15	5.88
9	97.62	1.93	97.62	1.93	97.62	1.93	90.40	4.02	97.62	1.93
10	92.57	5.43	92.57	5.43	92.57	5.43	89.14	6.74	92.57	5.43
11	67.13	14.61	67.13	14.61	67.13	14.61	68.25	15.33	67.00	14.60
12	94.75	11.94	94.75	11.94	94.75	11.94	50.75	28.08	94.75	11.94
13	63.93	12.03	63.87	12.14	63.93	12.03	60.93	11.45	65.13	12.53
14	82.68	3.97	82.68	3.97	82.68	3.97	68.26	4.35	82.68	3.97
15	92.53	6.99	92.53	6.99	92.53	6.99	78.41	11.25	92.53	6.99
Gmean	86.40	4.52	86.39	4.53	86.40	4.52	76.11	7.19	86.49	4.54

experiments, all transformations get very similar results, except from *majority*. We will use the combination *max + difference* in the following experiments.

4.2   Influence of the Size of the Multi-tree

Let us study the influence of the size of the multi-tree, varying from 1 to 1,000 explored OR-nodes. Table 4 shows the accuracy obtained using the shared ensembles depending on the number of OR-nodes opened. The results indicate that the greater the population of the multi-tree the better the results of the combination are.

4.3   Comparison with Other ensemble Methods

Figure 2 presents an accuracy comparison among our method (*multi-tree*), the *boosting* method and the *bagging* method (*multi-tree* and *bagging* without pruning) for the mean of all the 15 datasets, depending on the number of iterations. We have employed the Weka[1] implementation of these two ensemble methods.

Although our method initially obtains lower results with few iterations, with a higher number of iterations it surpasses the other two systems. Probably the slow increase of accuracy in the multi-tree method is due to the random selection of the OR-nodes to be explored.

Nevertheless, the major advantage of the method can be appreciated by looking at the consumption of resources. Figure 3 shows the average training

---

[1] http://www.cs.waikato.ac.nz/~ml/weka/

Table 4. Influence of the size of the multi-tree.

#	1 Acc.	1 Dev.	10 Acc.	10 Dev.	100 Acc.	100 Dev.	1000 Acc.	1000 Dev.
1	76.82	4.99	77.89	5.18	83.02	4.76	87.68	4.14
2	89.01	2.02	89.34	2.20	90.90	2.09	91.53	2.08
3	90.00	4.72	91.43	4.67	94.00	4.05	94.00	4.05
4	77.55	6.96	78.58	6.84	80.09	6.11	80.09	6.11
5	93.63	3.57	94.56	3.41	95.93	2.81	95.56	2.83
6	94.67	5.84	94.27	5.69	94.47	5.45	95.00	5.14
7	92.25	6.27	96.45	4.15	99.89	0.51	100.00	0.01
8	74.83	5.17	75.33	5.11	77.15	5.88	82.40	4.52
9	97.55	1.89	97.84	1.86	97.62	1.93	97.75	1.92
10	92.62	5.22	93.43	5.05	92.57	5.43	90.76	5.89
11	60.88	17.91	63.00	15.88	67.00	14.60	68.13	15.11
12	97.25	9.33	96.00	10.49	94.75	11.94	95.50	10.88
13	62.93	12.51	65.00	12.19	65.13	12.53	65.33	12.92
14	78.22	4.25	79.23	4.03	82.68	3.97	84.65	3.34
15	93.12	6.95	93.29	6.31	92.53	6.99	92.99	5.00
Gmean	83.88	5.52	84.91	5.30	86.49	4.54	87.47	4.47

time depending on the number of iterations (1-300) for the three methods. Note that, as expected, the time increase of *bagging* is linear. *Boosting* behaves better with high values because the algorithm implemented in Weka trickily stops the learning if it does not detect a significant increase in accuracy. Finally, SMILES presents a sub-linear increase of required time due to the sharing of common components of the multi-tree structure.

5 Conclusions

This work has presented a novel ensemble method. The main feature of this technique is the use of a structure called multi-tree that permits sharing common parts of the single components of the ensemble. For this reason, we call it *shared ensemble*.

Several combination methods or fusion strategies have been presented, as well as class vector transformation techniques. The effectiveness of these methods has also been examined by an experimental evaluation. We have also investigated the importance of the size of the multi-tree w.r.t. the quality of the results obtained.

Finally we have compared the new ensemble method with some well-known ensemble methods, namely *boosting* and *bagging*. The accuracy results for the new method are quite encouraging: although our results are initially worse than the other two methods, when the number of iterations is increased, the new approach equals and even excels the other methods. Nevertheless, as we have shown, it is in the use of resources where the shared ensembles offer an important advance. Our system is very appropiate for complex problems where other ensemble methods such as *boosting* or *bagging* require huge amounts of memory and time.

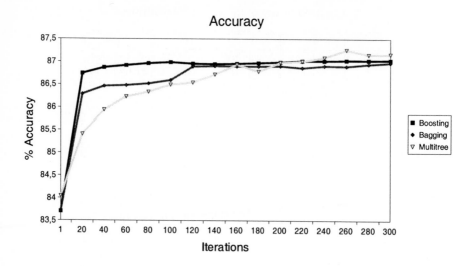

Fig. 2. Accuracy comparison between ensemble methods.

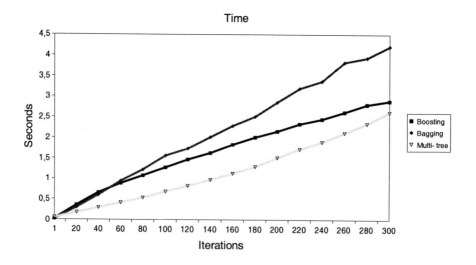

Fig. 3. Time comparison between ensemble methods.

As future work, we propose the study of a new strategy for generating trees. This strategy would be different from the current random technique we have employed to explore OR-nodes, and would probably be based on the semantic discrepancy of classifiers. This technique would provide a way to improve the results of our ensemble method with few iterations.

References

1. Leo Breiman. Bagging predictors. *Machine Learning*, 24(2):123–140, 1996.
2. Leo Breiman. Random forests. *Machine Learning*, 45(1):5–32, 2001.
3. T. G Dietterich. Ensemble methods in machine learning. In *First International Workshop on Multiple Classifier Systems*, pages 1–15, 2000.
4. Thomas G. Dietterich. An experimental comparison of three methods for constructing ensembles of decision trees: Bagging, Boosting, and Randomization. *Machine Learning*, 40(2):139–157, 2000.
5. C. Ferri, J. Hernández, and M.J. Ramírez. Induction of Decision Multi-trees using Levin Search. In *Int. Conf. on Computational Science, ICCS'02*, LNCS, 2002.
6. C. Ferri, J. Hernández, and M.J. Ramírez. Learning multiple and different hypotheses. Technical report, D.S.I.C., Universitat Politécnica de Valéncia, 2002.
7. C. Ferri, J. Hernández, and M.J. Ramírez. SMILES system, a multi-purpose learning system. http://www.dsic.upv.es/~flip/smiles/, 2002.
8. Y. Freund and R.E. Schapire. Experiments with a new boosting algorithm. In *the 13th Int. Conf. on Machine Learning (ICML'1996)*, pages 148–156, 1996.
9. Tim Kam Ho. Random decision forests. In *Proc. of the 3rd International Conference on Document Analysis and Recognition*, pages 278–282, 1995.
10. Tim Kam Ho. C4.5 decision forests. In *Proc. of 14th Intl. Conf. on Pattern Recognition, Brisbane, Australia*, pages 545–549, 1998.
11. Ludmila I. Kuncheva. A Theoretical Study on Six Classifier Fusion Strategies. *IEEE Trans. on Pattern Analysis and Machine Intelligence*, 24(2):281–286, 2002.
12. Dragos D. Margineantu and Thomas G. Dietterich. Pruning adaptive boosting. In *14th Int. Conf. on Machine Learning*, pages 211–218. Morgan Kaufmann, 1997.
13. N.J. Nilsson. *Artificial Intelligence: a new synthesis*. Morgan Kaufmann, 1998.
14. University of California. UCI Machine Learning Repository Content Summary. http://www.ics.uci.edu/~mlearn/MLSummary.html.
15. J. Pearl. *Heuristics: Intelligence search strategies for computer problem solving*. Addison Wesley, 1985.
16. J. R. Quinlan. Induction of Decision Trees. In *Read. in Machine Learning*. M. Kaufmann, 1990.
17. J. R. Quinlan. *C4.5: Programs for Machine Learning*. Morgan Kaufmann, 1993.
18. J. R. Quinlan. Bagging, Boosting, and C4.5. In *Proc. of the 13th Nat. Conf. on A.I. and the 8th Innovative Applications of A.I. Conf.*, pages 725–730. AAAI/MIT Press, 1996.
19. David H. Wolpert. Stacked generalization. *Neural Networks*, 5(2):241–259, 1992.
20. Zijian Zheng and Geoffrey I. Webb. Stochastic attribute selection committees. In *Australian Joint Conference on Artificial Intelligence*, pages 321–332, 1998.
21. Zijian Zheng, Geoffrey I. Webb, and K.M. Ting. Integrating boosting and stochastic attribute selection committees for further improving the performance of decision tree learning. In *Proc. of 10th Int. Conf. on Tools with Artificial Intelligence (ICTAI-98), IEEE Computer Society Press*, pages 216–223, 1998.

A GRASP Algorithm for Clustering

J.R. Cano[1], O. Cordón[2], F. Herrera[2], and L. Sánchez[3]

[1]Dept. of Software Engineering
University of Huelva, 21071 La Rabida (Huelva), Spain
Jose.cano@diesia.uhu.es
[2] Dept. of Computer Science and A.I.
University of Granada, 18071-Granada, Spain
{ocordon,herrera}@decsai.ugr.es
[3] Dept. of Computer Science
University of Oviedo, Oviedo, Spain
luciano@lsi.uniovi.es

Abstract. We present a new approach for Cluster Analysis based on a Greedy Randomized Adaptive Search Procedure (GRASP), with the objective of overcoming the convergence to a local solution. It uses a probabilistic greedy Kaufman initialization for getting initial solutions and K-Means algorithm as a local search algorithm. We compare it with some typical initialization methods: Random, Forgy, Macqueen and Kaufman. The new approach obtains high quality solutions for the benchmark problems.

1 Introduction

Clustering is a basic process to human understanding. The grouping of related objects can be found such diverse fields as statistics, economics, physics, psychology, biology, pattern recognition, engineering, and marketing [3,5].

The Clustering problem involves partitioning a set of entities into a given number of subsets and finding the location of a centre for each subset in such a way that a dissimilarity measure between entities and centres is minimized. K-Means is one of the most known clustering algorithms. Although it is known for its robustness, it can fall in local optimal solutions easily. It is widely reported that the K-Means algorithm suffers from initial starting conditions effects: initial clustering and instance order as shown in [4].

In this contribution, we propose a Greedy Randomized Adaptive Search Procedure (GRASP) [2] applied to the Clustering problem, using K-Means as local search procedure. Our algorithm tries to eliminate the classical problem of the K-Means algorithm, hold up solutions in local optima, by permitting a higher exploration and exploitation of the search space, with a medium computational cost.

In order to do that, the paper is organized as follows. Section 2 introduces a background on clustering, K-means and initialization approaches. Section 3 presents the GRASP approach to clustering. Section 4 shows the experiments and their analysis, and finally, Section 5 points out some concluding remarks.

F.J. Garijo, J.C. Riquelme, and M. Toro (Eds.): IBERAMIA 2002, LNAI 2527, pp. 214–223, 2002.

2 Background

A common problem in cluster analysis is partitioning objects into a fixed number of groups to optimize an objective function-based clustering. These objects are measured along several features that characterize them. Patterns can be viewed as vectors in a high dimensional space, where each dimension corresponds to one feature.

In this section we introduce the formalization of clustering, the K-Means algorithms, and four initialization approaches.

2.1 Clustering Problem

The clustering problem can be formalized as follows [1]: Considering N entities e_i, each with an associated weight w_i (i=1,..,N), we search for k centres c_j (j=1,...,k) minimizing:

$$f(c_1,..., c_k) = \sum_{i=1}^{N} \min_j \left(w_i d\left(e_i, c_j \right) \right)$$

where $d(e_i,c_j)$ measures the dissimilarity between e_i and c_j. In our case, where the entities are described by their co-ordinates in $\Re^m$, $d(e_i,c_j)$ is the Euclidean distance. Basically, clustering is a combinatorial optimization problem.

Let

Q be set containing all objects to be clustered,

C be the set of all feasible clustering of Q,

J: C → $\Re$ be the internal clustering criterion,

then the problem involves

Minimize J(c) subject to c ∈ C.

The complexity of the clustering problem is given by different factors:

1. The clustering is an NP-HARD problem. Therefore, an exhaustive approach is not practicable due to the exponential number of the potential partitions of the input data. The number of possible partitions of N elements into k clusters is given by

$$\prod(k, N) = \frac{1}{k!} \sum_{j=1}^{k} (-1)^{k-j} \binom{k}{j} (j)^N.$$

2. The clustering complexity grows if the number of groups is unknown. In such a case he number of solutions becomes:

$$\prod(k, N) = \sum_{i=1}^{k} \frac{1}{i!} \sum_{j=1}^{i} (-1)^{i-j} \binom{i}{j} (j)^N.$$

3. It is very difficult to translate the concept of 'similarity' into a unique mathematical model, but this depends on the clustering goal.

Due to these reasons, trying to get a global optimal solution by means of an efficient and robust method is difficult. Thus, there is a considerable interest in the design of new heuristics to solve large-sized practical clustering problems.

2.2 K-Means Algorithm

K-means evaluates a set of k selected objects, which are considered representatives for the k clusters to be found within the source set of N objects. Given the set of representative objects, the remaining objects are assigned to the nearest representative one, using a chosen distance measure.

The philosophy is that a better set of clusters is obtained when the k representative objects are more centrally located in the cluster they define. For this reason, a suitable objective function to be minimized is the sum of the distances from the respective centers to all the other objects of the same cluster. The function value depends on the current partition of the database $\{C_1,...,C_k\}$:

$$ J : \prod_k (\Omega) \to \Re $$

with $\pi_k(\Omega)$ being the set of all partitions of the database $\Omega=\{e_1,...,e_N\}$ in k non-empty clusters. Each instance e_i of the N instances in the database Ω is an m-dimensional vector.

The K-Means algorithm finds locally optimal solutions using the Euclidean distance in the clustering criterion. This criterion is sometimes referred to as square-error criterion. Therefore, it follows that:

$$ J(\{C_1,...,C_k\}) = \sum_{i=1}^{k} \sum_{j=1}^{k_i} \left\| e_{ij} - c_i \right\| $$

where k is the number of clusters, k_i the number of objects of the cluster i, e_{ij} is the j-th object of the i-th cluster and c_i is the centroid of the i-th cluster defined as:

$$ c_i = \frac{1}{k_i} \sum_{j=1}^{k_i} e_{ij}, i = 1,...,k $$

The pseudo-code for this algorithm is:

1. Select an initial partition of the database in k clusters $\{C_1,...,C_k\}$
2. Calculate cluster centroids, using the expression of its definition.
3. For every e_i in the database and following the instance order DO
   - Reassign instance e_i to its closest cluster centroid. Hence, $e_i \in C_s$ is moved to C_t if $\|e_i - c_t\| \le \|e_i - c_s\|$ for all t=1,...,k, t≠s.
   - Recalculate centroids for those clusters.
4. If cluster membership is stabilized then stop else go to *step 3*.

The K-Means algorithm has the drawbacks:

- It assumes that the number of clusters k in the database is known, which is not necessarily true.
- It is especially sensitive to initial starting conditions: initial clusters and instance order.
- It converges finitely to a local minimum, defined by a deterministic mapping from the initial conditions to the final solution.

2.3 Initialization Approaches

The second problem, sensitivity to initial conditions, may be mitigated using different values of k, some instance orders and different initialization methods.

In this section we describe four initialization approaches [4]. Each one generates k initial clusters following some kind of heuristic and produces a different K-Means response.

These four classical methods are:

- *Random*: Divides the database into a partition of K randomly selected clusters.
- *Forgy:* k instances of the database (seeds) are chosen at random and the rest of the instances are assigned to the cluster represented by the nearest seed.
- *Macqueen:* k instances of the database (seeds) are chosen at random. Following the instance order, the rest of the instances are assigned to the cluster with the nearest centroid. After each assignment, a recalculation of the centroid has to be carried out.
- *Kaufman:* The initial clustering is obtained by the successive selection of representative instances. The first representative is chosen to be the most centrally located instance in the database. The rest of representative instances are selected according to the heuristic rule of choosing the instances that promise to have around them a higher number of the rest of instances and that are located as far as possible from the previously fixed ones.

Differences between these initialization methods are:

- Random and Forgy generate an initial partition independently of the instance order.
- Macqueen generates an initial partition that depends on the instance order.
- Kaufman is the only deterministic one, based on a greedy approach.

3 GRASP Approach to the Clustering Problem

In this section we introduce the GRASP approach and present its application to clustering.

3. 1   Greedy Randomized Adaptive Search Procedure (GRASP)

A generic GRASP pseudo-code is shown as follows [2]:

```
Procedure grasp( )
  InputInstance();
  For GRASP stopping criterion not satisfied
      ConstructGreedyRandomizedSolution(Solution);
      LocalSearch(Solution);
      UpdateSolution(Solution,BestSolutionFound);
  Rof
  Return(BestSolutionFound);
End grasp;
```

In the construction phase, a feasible solution is iteratively constructed, choosing one element at a time. At each construction algorithm iteration, the choice of the next element to be added is determined by ordering all elements in a candidate list with respect to a greedy selection function. This function measures the benefit of selecting each element. The probabilistic component of a GRASP is characterized by randomly choosing one of the best candidates in the list, but not necessarily the top one. The list of the best candidates is called the restricted candidate list (RCL) and has dimension l. This choice technique allows different solutions to be obtained at each GRASP iteration, but does not necessarily compromise the power of the adaptive greedy component of the method.

The GRASP construction phase pseudo-code is:

```
Procedure ConstructGreedyRandomizedSolution(Solution)
    Solution={ };
    For Solution construction not done
        MakeRCL(RCL);
        s = SelectElementAtRandom(RCL);
        Solution = Solution ∪ {s};
        AdaptGreedyFunction(s);
    Rof
End ConstructGreedyRandomizedSolution;
```

The solutions generated by a GRASP construction algorithm are not guaranteed to be locally optimal with respect to simple neighborhood solutions. Hence, it is almost always useful to apply a local search to attempt to improve each constructed solution. A local search algorithm works in an iterative fashion by successively replacing the current solution by a better solution in the neighborhood of the current one. The key to success for a local search algorithm involves a suitable choice for a neighborhood structure, efficient neighborhood search techniques, and the starting solution.

Finally, the GRASP local search phase pseudo-code is shown:

```
Procedure Local (P,N(P),s)
    For s not locally optimal
            Find a better solution t ∈ N(s);
            Let s=t;
    Rof
    Return (s as local optimal for P)
End local
```

with P being a problem (clustering in our case), $N(P)$ being a mechanism to obtain neighbors for P, and s being a solution for P.

3.2 A Proposal on GRASP for the Clustering Problem

Following the generic GRASP structure, it is easy to adapt the algorithm to the clustering problem using the greedy Kaufman method.

The stopping criterion is defined in terms of the maximum number of iterations, whilst the K-Means is introduced as a local search algorithm.

To construct the greedy randomized solution, the Kaufman initialization [3] is taken as a base, because it is a greedy deterministic initialitation algorithm. Using the Kaufman criterion, the RCL list is generated by the most promising objects for each center of the solution and one of those candidates is randomly selected.

A generic pseudo-code of the GRASP construction phase for clustering is:

Step 1. Select the most centrally located instance as the first seed.
Step 2. FOR every non selected instance e_i DO
      Step 2.1.FOR every non selected instance e_j DO
        Calc $C_{ji} = \max(D_j - d_{ji}, 0)$ where $d_{ji} = \|e_i - e_j\|$
        and $D_j = \min_s d_{sj}$ being s one of the
        selected seeds
      Step 2.2. Calculate the gain of selecting e_i
          by $\Sigma_j C_{ji}$
Step 3. MakeRCL(RCL) by selecting the l instances e_i which maximizes $\Sigma_j C_{ji}$
Step 4. SelectElementAtRandom(RCL)
Step 5. If there are k selected seeds THEN stop ELSE go to Step 2.
Step 6. For having a clustering assign each nonselected instance to the cluster
      represented by the nearest seed.

When the k objects have been taken, the local search (K-Means in this case) is applied taking the clustering obtained as initialization. Then, we compare the local solution cost obtained with the best solution cost found so far, and we take the best. This process continues until all the iterations have been done.

The use of K-Means offers an efficient and low computational cost method to obtain relatively good solutions, but converges to a local minimum. The GRASP construction phase corrects this problem, performing a wide space exploration search. Note that our algorithm constitutes a new initialization method for K-Means, which better explores the search space.

4 Experimental Results

Next, we present the sample process, the results obtained in our experiments, and an analysis.

4.1 Sampling Process

The performance of our algorithm is studied with various instance sets, trying to get conclusions independent of the problem. Four real-world databases are considered:

- Glass, which has 214 instances, 9 attributes and 7 clusters that can be grouped in 2 bigger classes.
- Titanic, which has 2200 instances, 4 attributes and 2 classes.
- Segmentation Image, which has 2310 instances, 19 attributes and 7 classes.
- Pima, which has 768 instances, 8 attributes and 2 classes.

Since the K-Means algorithm strongly depends on initial conditions, this problem of initial starting conditions is mitigated using different values of k and some instance orders.

The following initial number of clusters have been considered:

- Glass: k= 7, 10
- Titanic: k= 4, 10
- Segmentation Image: k= 6, 12
- Pima: k= 6, 10

First, we applied three K-Means variants (each one with its own initialization: Random, Forgy and Macqueen). The sampling process followed is based on the combination of four initial partitions and four instance orders (see [4]) and taking the best result of those sixteen runs.

This process is executed ten times and the following values are taken: arithmetic mean, standard deviation and the best solution.

On the other hand, the evaluation of K-Means with Kaufman initialization has been done using 10 random instance orders of each problem. Although Kaufman initialization seems to be a completely deterministic initialization method, this is not completely true. When one instance has the same Euclidean distance to two cluster centers, this instance will be associated to the first of them. If we have some instances in this situation, their order will modify the evolution of the k centers.

The proposed GRASP algorithm is studied using sixteen iterations in each execution (running sixteen K-means). Ten executions of the GRASP algorithm are made, getting the arithmetic mean, the standard deviation and the best solution from those executions. The RCL size used is fifteen ($l = 15$), which is flexible enough to obtained optimal solutions due the database sizes. Therefore, in order to compare GRASP evaluation with the remaining K-Means initialization methods, we use the same number of K-Means runs than GRASP iterations for every execution of Random, Forgy and Macqueen initialization methods.

4.2. Results

Experimental results are presented in Tables 1-8.

Table 1. Glass results, k=7

	Arithmetic mean	Standard Deviation	Best Solution
Random	206.632	0.704	205.307
Forgy	206.493	0.723	205.889
Macq.	206.635	0.676	205.889
Kaufm.	211.658	0	211.158
GRASP	205.239	0.486	204.992

Table 2. Glass results, k=10

	Arithmetic mean	Standard Deviation	Best Solution
Random	179.042	2.670	175.945
Forgy	176.710	1.205	176.044
Macq.	177.144	1.389	176.044
Kaufm.	188.691	0	188.691
GRASP	176.058	0.089	175.945

Table 3. Titanic results, k=4

	Arithmetic mean	Standard Deviation	Best Solution
Random	1110.034	19.662	1080.426
Forgy	1437.635	297.603	1282.327
Macq.	1442.327	301.718	1282.327
Kaufm.	1170.012	0	1170.012
GRASP	1071.458	1.368	1070.661

Table 4. Titanic results, k=10

	Arithmetic mean	Standard Deviation	Best Solution
Random	880.530	71.877	670.166
Forgy	992.681	82.042	930.914
Macq.	991.914	84.564	930.914
Kaufm.	340.696	0	340.696
GRASP	329.234	4.196	327.234

Table 5. Segmentation Image results, k=6

	Arithmetic mean	Standard Deviation	Best Solution
Random	158581.932	470.346	158141.047
Forgy	158261.497	626.579	157923.297
Macq.	158334.78	321.169	157923.297
Kaufm.	159233.335	0.0178	159233.297
GRASP	158246.504	312.505	157917.547

Table 6. Segmentation Image results, k=12

	Arithmetic mean	Standard Deviation	Best Solution
Random	117819.845	3263.117	114229.797
Forgy	114244.441	7.570	114237.953
Macq.	115645.357	8.724	114237.842
Kaufm.	114248.172	0	114248.172
GRASP	114221.817	1.066	114220.75

Table 7. Pima results, k=6

	Arithmetic mean	Standard Deviation	Best Solution
Random	29415.066	15.681	29403.762
Forgy	29426.369	14.519	29403.762
Macq.	29428.447	15.117	29403.762
Kaufm.	30729.2	0.013	30729.195
GRASP	29403.763	0.001	29403.762

Table 8. Pima results, k=10

	Arithmetic mean	Standard Deviation	Best Solution
Random	24287.956	134.991	24120.801
Forgy	24136.125	26.718	24117.748
Macq.	24137.881	23.687	24117.748
Kaufm.	24340.811	0	24340.811
GRASP	24127.770	7.929	24117.748

4.3 Analysis

Comparing results, we notice that Forgy and Macqueen usually give very similar results. They seem to have the same behaviour, keeping the same or similar local minimum. Their results improve those given by Random initialization, with any number of clusters, except in the Titanic database. Thus, both Forgy and Macqueen initialization respond better than Random, with this difference more significant when k grows.

It is clear that Kaufman initialization by itself does not obtain the best results compared to the classical initialization methods. We conclude that the heuristic used in Kaufman initialization needs a more flexible centroid selection to reach this global optimum.

Finally, we compare the results obtained from GRASP with the remaining K-Means initialization methods. As said, this comparison is feasible because we are comparing ten GRASP runs versus ten sampling processes runs (16 K-Means runs with different initialization approaches). This comparison is based on effectiveness and robustness:

- If we study each table we notice that GRASP gets the best results in every problem for all initial numbers of clusters k. GRASP is the most effective algorithm, because it is doing a better exploration of the search space than K-Means using Kaufman initialization can do by itself.

- On the other hand, GRASP presents similar robustness (small values for the standard deviation) to Kaufman K-Means in most of the cases, and better robustness than the remaining approaches.

Although GRASP is computationally a little more demanding than the remaining K-Means initializations with the same number of runs/iterations (due to the computational time needed by the construction phase), GRASP induces the K-Means algorithm to present a better performance and a more robust behaviour.

5 Concluding Remarks

The K-Means algorithm suffers from its dependence on initial conditions which under certain conditions leads to a local minimum. We present a GRASP algorithm based on Kaufman initialization to avoid this drawback.

The GRASP algorithm has been empirically compared with four classical initialization methods (Random, Forgy, Macqueen and Kaufman) being the most effective algorithm.

References

1. M.R. Anderberg, Cluster Analysis and Applications, Academic Press, 1973.
2. T.A. Feo and M.G.C. Resende, Greedy Randomized Adaptive Search Procedure, Journal of Global Optimization 2 (1995) 1-27.
3. L. Kaufman and P.J. Rousseeuw, Finding Groups in Data. An Introduction to Cluster Analysis. Wiley, 1990.
4. J.M. Peña, J.A. Lozano, and P. Larrañaga, An empirical comparison of four initialization methods for the K-Means algorithm. Pattern Recognition Letters 20 (1999) 1027-1040.
5. S. Theodoridis and K. Koutroumbas, Pattern Recognition. Academic Press, 1999.

An Analysis of the Pheromone Q-Learning Algorithm

Ndedi Monekosso and Paolo Remagnino

Digital Imaging Research Centre
School of Computing and Information Systems
Kingston University, United Kingdom
{n.monekosso, p.remagnino}@kingston.ac.uk

Abstract. The Phe-Q machine learning technique, a modified Q-learning technique, was developed to enable co-operating agents to communicate in learning to solve a problem. The Phe-Q learning technique combines Q-learning with synthetic pheromone to improve on the speed of convergence. The Phe-Q update equation includes a belief factor that reflects the confidence the agent has in the pheromone (the communication) deposited in the environment by other agents. With the Phe-Q update equation, speed of convergence towards an optimal solution depends on a number parameters including the number of agents solving a problem, the amount of pheromone deposited, and the evaporation rate. In this paper, work carried out to optimise speed of learning with the Phe-Q technique is described. The objective was to to optimise Phe-Q learning with respect to pheromone deposition rates, evaporation rates.

1 Introduction

In situations where building a partial or complete model of a complex problem and/or environment is impractical or impossible, learning to solve the problem may be the only solution. In addition, it is often convenient when solving complex or large problems, to break down the problem into its component parts, and each part dealt with separately. This technique is often seen in nature and one such example is the ant foraging behaviour. The ant colony exhibits a collective problem solving ability [4,9]. Complex behaviours emerge from the interaction of the relatively simple behaviour of individual ants. A characteristic that multi-agent systems seek to reproduce. The ant colony exhibits among other features, co-operation and co-ordination, and communicate implicitly by depositing pheromone chemicals. The ant foraging for food will deposit a trail of pheromone. The problem for the ants is to find the shortest path between the nest and the food source whilst minimising energy. The Phe-Q algorithm was inspired by the search strategies of foraging ants, combining reinforcement learning [3,19] with synthetic pheromone. Reinforcement learning has been applied with some success to classical A.I. problems. With this technique, the agent learns by trial and error. Phe-Q algorithm is described in [16]. The performance of the Phe-Q agent is dependent on a few factors namely pheromone deposition and diffusion rates, pheromone evaporation rate. Furthermore, in the context of multiple agents cooperating to solve a problem, there is an optimum number of agents required to maximise speed of learning whilst minimising computational requirements. An investigation into the learning factors of the Phe-Q agent was carried out. The results are presented in this paper.

F.J. Garijo, J.C. Riquelme, and M. Toro (Eds.): IBERAMIA 2002, LNAI 2527, pp. 224–232, 2002.

Section 2 briefly describes ant foraging behaviour and presents some related work inspired by ant foraging mechanisms. Section 3 describes the Phe-Q learning algorithm. In Section 4, optimisation of the Phe-Q parameters is discussed. Experiments and results obtained in optimising the algorithm are presented in Sections 5 and 6 respectively. In Section 7 the results are analysed and finally the paper concludes in Section 8.

2   Ant Behaviour and Related Work

Ants are able to find the shortest path between the nest and a food source by an auto catalytic process [1,2,14]. This process comes about because ants deposit pheromones along the trail as they move along in the search for food or resources to construct a nest. The pheromone evaporates with time nevertheless ants follow a pheromone trail and at a branching point prefer to follow the path with higher concentrations of pheromone. On finding the food source, the ants return laden to the nest depositing more pheromone along the way thus reinforcing the pheromone trail. Ants that have followed the shortest path are quicker to return the nest, reinforcing the pheromone trail at a faster rate than those ants that followed an alternative longer route. Further ants arriving at the branching point choose to follow the path with the higher concentrations of pheromone thus reinforcing even further the pheromone and eventually all ants follow the shortest path. The amount of pheromone secreted is a function of an angle between the path and a line joining the food and nest locations [5]. So far two properties of pheromone secretion were mentioned: aggregation and evaporation [18]. The concentration adds when ants deposit pheromone at the same location, and over time the concentration gradually reduces by evaporation. A third property is diffusion [18]. The pheromone at a location diffuses into neighbouring locations.

Ant behaviour has been researched not only for the understanding of the species but also as an inspiration in developing computational problem-solving systems. A methodology inspired by the ant behaviour was developed in [8,11,13]. Some of the mechanisms adopted by foraging ants have been applied to classical NP-hard combinatorial optimisation problems with success. In [10] Ant Colony Optimisation is used to solve the travelling salesman problem, a quadratic assignment problem in [13], the job-shop scheduling problem in [7], communication network routing [6] and the Missionaries and Cannibals problem in [17].

In [12] Gambardella suggests a connection between the ant optimisation algorithm and reinforcement learning (RL) and proposes a family of algorithms (Ant-Q) related to Q-learning. The ant optimisation algorithm is a special case of the Ant-Q family. The merging of Ant foraging mechanisms and reinforcement learning is also described in [15]. Three mechanisms found in ant trail formation were used as exploration strategy in a robot navigation task. In this work as with the Ant-Q algorithm, the information provided by the pheromone is used directly for the action selection mechanism.

Another work inspired by ant behaviour is reported in [21]. It is applied to a multi-robotic environment where the robots transport objects between different locations. Rather than physically laying a trail of synthetic pheromones, the robots communicate path information via shared memory.

3   Pheromone-Q Learning

The Phe-Q technique combines Q-Learning [22] and synthetic pheromone, by introducing a belief factor into the update equation. The belief factor is a function of the synthetic pheromone concentration on the trail and reflects the extent to which an agent will take into account the information lay down by other agents from the same co-operating group. Reinforcement learning and synthetic pheromone have previously been combined for action selection [15,21]. The usefulness of the belief factor is that it allows an agent to selectively make use of implicit communication from other agents where the information may not be reliable due to changes in the environment. Incomplete and uncertain information are critical issues in the design of real world systems, Phe-Q addresses this issue by introducing the belief factor into the update equation for Q-Learning.

The main difference between the Q-learning update equation and the pheromone-Q update equation is the introduction of a belief factor that must also be maximised. The belief factor is a function of synthetic pheromone. The synthetic pheromone ($\Phi(s)$) is a scalar value (where s is a state/cell in a grid) that comprises three components: aggregation, evaporation and diffusion. The pheromone $\Phi(s)$ has two possible discrete values, a value for the pheromone deposited when searching for food and when returning to the nest with food. The belief factor (B) dictates the extent to which an agent believes in the pheromone that it detects. An agent, during early training episodes, will believe to a lesser degree in the pheromone map because all agents are biased towards exploration. The belief factor is given by (1)

$$B(s_{t+1}, a) = \frac{\Phi(s_{t+1})}{\sum_{\sigma \in N_a} \Phi(\sigma)} \tag{1}$$

where $\Phi(s)$ is the pheromone concentration at a cell, s, in the environment and N_a is the set of neighbouring states for a chosen action a. The Q-Learning update equation modified with synthetic pheromone is given by (2)

$$\hat{Q}_n(s_t, a) \longleftarrow (1 - \alpha_n)\hat{Q}_{n-1}(s_t, a) +$$
$$\alpha_n(r_t + \gamma \prime \cdot max_{a'}(\hat{Q}_{n-1}(s_{t+1}, a') +$$
$$\xi B(s_{t+1}, a')) \tag{2}$$

where the parameter, ξ, is a sigmoid function of time (*epochs* $\geq$ 0). The value of ξ increases as the number of agents successfully accomplish the task at hand. It can be shown that the pheromone-Q update equation converges for a non-deterministic MDP. [1]

4   Optimal Choice of Parameters

The objective is to automate the procedure of fine tuning the many parameters that influence the speed of convergence of Phe-Q learning. In the following discussion, it is assumed that the Q-learning constants α and γ are already optimised. The parameters

---

[1] The proof follows those of Jakkola [20] and Bertsekas [3], assuming that the value function V depends also on the belief factor B: $V_n(s_{t+1}) = max_a(Q_n(s_{t+1}, a) + \xi B(s_{t+1}, a))$.

that influence the speed of learning are the number of agents, pheromone secretion rate, pheromone diffusion rate, pheromone evaporation rate and the pheromone saturation level. Other variable that were found experimentally to influence the convergence were the coefficients of the sigmoid (function of time) that modulates the belief function. The pheromone distribution in the grid environment is a function of the number of agents in the grid. It is also a function the diffusion of across cells and the evaporation. The pheromone distribution in turn affects the belief function. From equation (1), the belief value depends on the pheromone saturation level. The fine tuning of the parameters for optimum speed of convergence requires a function to minimise. Convergence was also proven empirically by plotting the root mean square of the error between Q values obtained during successive epochs. The function chosen to minimise was the area under the convergence curve. The graph in Figure 1 shows a convergence curve for a Phe-Q learning agent.

First brute force exhaustive search with coarse data was investigated followed by finer data. The purpose of the exhaustive search was to sample the state space and determine if the state space was convex. The values of the parameters were constrained to reduce the search space. With a relatively small space using the selection of the parameters mentioned above an exhaustive search was found to be feasible.

5   Experimental Set-Up

Evaluation of the modified updating equation for Phe-Q and comparison with the Q-learning update were presented in [16]. The objective in this paper is to present results of investigations into the fine tuning of the parameters upon which speed of convergence depends.

For the experiments reported the agent environment is a $N \times N$, grid where $N = 20$. Obstacles are placed on the grid within cells, preventing agents from occupying the cell. The obstacles were placed such that the goal state was occluded. The agents are placed at a starting cell (the nest) on the grid. The aim is for the agents to locate the 'food' sources occupying a cell in the grid space and return to the starting cell. The agents move from cell to cell in the four cardinal directions, depositing discrete quantities of pheromone in each cell. The two pheromone values (one associated with search for the food source φ_s and the other associated with the return to the nest φ_n) are parameters to fine tune. The pheromone aggregates in a cell up to to a saturation level, and evaporates at a rate (evaporation rate φ_e) until there is none remaining if the cell pheromone is not replenished by an agent visiting the cell. Equally the pheromone diffuses into neighbouring cells at a rate (diffusion rate φ_d), inversely proportional to the manhattan distance.

Each agent has two goal tasks represented each by a Q-table. One task is to reach the 'food' location, and the second task is to return to the nest. Before release into the 'world' agents have no a-priori knowledge of the environment, nor location of nest or resource, etc. More than one agent can occupy a cell. A cell has associated a pheromone strength, $\Phi \in [0, 255]$. Pheromone is de-coupled from the state at the implementation level so that the size of the state space is an $N \times N$. The grids used (N=10 and 20), result in a state space sufficiently small for a lookup table to be used for the Q values.

The agent receives a reward of 1.0 on completing the tasks. Each experiment consists of a number of agents released into the environment and running in parallel until convergence.

6 Results

Convergence was demonstrated empirically by plotting the Root Means Square (RMS) of the error between successive Q-values against epochs (an epoch is a complete cycle of locating food and returning to the nest). The RMS curves for Phe-Q in Figure 1 show convergence. In a 20x20 grid space, the performance degrades with approximately 30 agents. The graph in Figure 2 shows the RMS curves for increasing number of Phe-Q agents maintaining a constant grid size (for clarity only the RMS curves for 5, 40, and 60 agents are shown on the graph). Between 5 and 20 agents, convergence is comparable for the Phe-Q agents. Above that number, the trend is towards slower convergence. As

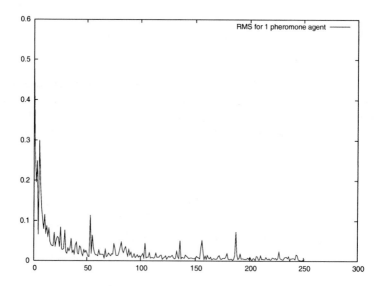

Fig. 1. RMS curve for one Phe-Q agent

mentioned previously, the objective is to maximise speed of convergence. One way to achieve this is to minimise the area under the RMS curves. The area is a function of independent variables : number of agents, pheromone deposition, diffusion and evaporation. Some constraints are imposed on these variables. These are shown in Table 1. For example, pheromone secretion is a positive scalar, so are evaporation and diffusion. A minimum number of agents in a Multi-Agent system is two. These factors determine the lower bound. To impose upper bounds, results previously obtained were analysed. In a 20 by 20 grid, performance degrades beyond 25 to 30 agents [16]. An upper bound of

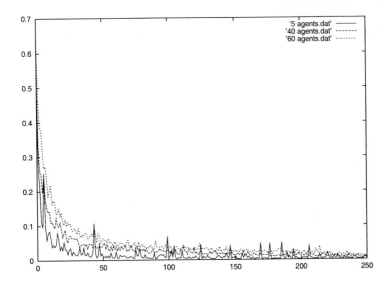

Fig. 2. Performance scaling: 5, 40, 60 agents

20 agents was used. It was also noted that as the number of agents increase, the unit of pheromone secreted (to achieve a performance better than Q-learning) must be reduced. Conversely as the number of agents increase, the unit of evaporation must be increased. Results show that for a given number of agents there is an optimum parameter set. Table 2

Table 1. Constraints on parameters

Parameter	Agent #	φ_s	φ_n	φ_e
Lower bound	2	0	4	0.8
Upper bound	20	1.0	12	2.0

below shows the optimum parameter values for 5, 10, 15 and 20 agents. Of the four cases, the system with 5 agents performs better for the particular scenario (grid size, obstacle layout, goal location). For a given problem, too high or too low a pheromone secretion (maintaining a fixed evaporation) produces somewhat degraded results as shown in Figure 3 (slower convergence and noisy Q values). The role of the evaporation is to balance the pheromone secretion. The results in the table show the best performance for each case, the optimal parameters produces (approximately) only slightly worse performance for 10 and 15 agents. The final choice of which parameter set (i.e. number of agents) to use will therefore depend on the computational load. As might be expected, the higher the number of agents, the greater the computational load. The next step was to select the optimal parameter set using computational time as a constraint. Table 3 below shows the relative computational times using the parameters shown in table 2.

Table 2. Optimum values for parameters

Parameter			
Agent #	φ_s	φ_n	φ_e
5	0.8	5.0	0.8
10	0.4	5.0	0.8
15	0.0	5.0	1.6
20	0.0	1.0	0.8

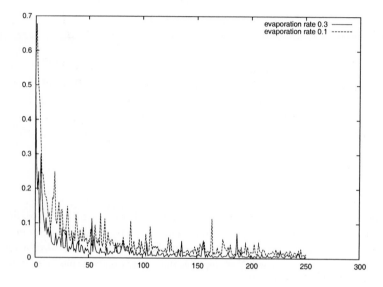

Fig. 3. The role of evaporation

Table 3. Computational load w.r.t. number of agents

Agent #	Time
5	1.0
10	1.76
15	2.53
20	3.23

7   Discussion

The synthetic pheromone guides the agents. It is implicit communication. The information exchange via pheromone enables the agents to learn quicker however there is a price to pay for this information sharing. Too much information i.e. too high a pheromone deposition rate or too low a pheromone evaporation rate causes not unexpectedly poorer results especially in the earlier learning stages where agents are 'mislead' by other exploring agents. Therefore the parameters choice must be such as to minimise the 'misleading' effect whilst maximising learning. Evaporation is key to reducing agents being mislead in the exploratory phases.

Results show that the required number of agents to optimise learning (achieving a 59% decrease in the area under the RMS curve over Q-learning) is relatively low, this means that the computational load can be maintained low.

8   Conclusions

The work described in this paper set out to investigate the tuning of parameters to achieve optimum learning with the Phe-Q technique in the context of a multi-agent system. By bounding the search space, an exhaustive search was carried. Results confirm the relationships between pheromone deposition and evaporation rates and that evaporation is necessary to prevent 'misleading' information to be received by co-operating agents. An important result concerns the number of agents required to achieve optimum learning. This number is lower than previously expected. An important factor since an increase in agents greatly increases computational times.

References

1. R. Beckers, J. L. Deneubourg, S. Goss, and J. M. Pasteels. Collective decision making through food recruitment. *Ins. Soc.*, 37:258–267, 1990.
2. R. Beckers, J.L. Deneubourg, and S. Goss. Trails and u-turns in the selection of the shortest path by the ant lasius niger. *Journal of Theoretical Biology*, 159:397–4151, 1992.
3. D.P. Bertsekas and J.N. Tsitsiklis. *Neuro-Dynamic Programming.* Athena Scientific, 1996.
4. E. Bonabeau, M. Dorigo, and G. Theraulaz. *Swarm intelligence, From Natural to Artificial Systems.* Oxford University Press, 1999.
5. M. C. Cammaerts-Tricot. Piste et pheromone attraction chez la fourmi myrmica ruba. *Journal of Computational Physiology*, 88:373–382, 1974.
6. G. Di Caro and M. Dorigo. Antnet: a mobile agents approach to adaptive routing. Technical Report: IRIDIA/97-12, Universite Libre de Bruxelles, Belgium. citeseer.nj.nec.com/dicaro97antnet.html.
7. A. Colorni, M. Dorigo, and V. Maniezzo. Ant system for job-shop scheduling. *Belgian Journal of OR, statistics and computer science*, 34:39–53, 1993.
8. A. Colorni, M. Dorigo, and G. Theraulaz. Distributed optimzation by ant colonies. In *Proceedings First European Conf. on Artificial Life*, pages 134–142, 1991.
9. J.L. Deneubourg and S. Goss. Collective patterns and decision making. *Ethol. Ecol. and Evol.*, 1:295–311, 1993.
10. M. Dorigo and L. M. Gambardella. Ant colony system: A cooperative learning approach to the travelling salesman problem. *IEEE Trans. on Evol. Comp.*, 1:53–66, 1997.
11. M. Dorigo, V. Maniezzo, and A. Colorni. The ant system: Optimization by a colony of cooperatin agents. *IEEE Trans. on Systems, Man, and Cybernetics*, 26:1–13, 1996.
12. L. M. Gambardella and M. Dorigo. Ant-q: A reinforcement learning approach to the traveling salesman problem. In *Proc. 12Th ICML*, pages 252–260, 1995.
13. L. M. Gambardella, E. D. Taillard, and M. Dorigo. Ant colonies for the qap. *Journal of Operational Research society*, 1998.
14. S. Goss, S. Aron, J.L. Deneubourg, and J. M. Pasteels. Self-organized shorcuts in the argentine ants. *Naturwissenschaften*, pages 579–581, 1989.

15. L. R. Leerink, S. R. Schultz, and M. A. Jabri. A reinforcement learning exploration strategy based on ant foraging mechanisms. In *Proc. 6Th Australian Conference on Neural Nets*, 1995.

16. N. Monekosso and P. Remagnino. Phe-q: A pheromone based q-learning. In *AI2001:Advances in Artificial Intelligence, 14Th Australian Joint Conf. on A.I.*, pages 345–355, 2001.

17. H. Van Dyke Parunak and S. Brueckner. Ant-like missionnaries and cannibals: Synthetic pheromones for distributed motion control. In *Proc. of ICMAS'00*, 2000.

18. H. Van Dyke Parunak, S. Brueckner, J. Sauter, and J. Posdamer. Mechanisms and military applications for synthetic pheromones. In *Proc. 5Th International Conference Autonomous Agents, Montreal, Canada*, 2001.

19. R. S. Sutton and A.G. Barto. *Reinforcement Learning*. MIT Press, 1998.

20. T.Jaakkola, M.I.Jordan, and S.P.Singh. On the convergence of stochastic iterative dynamic programming algorithms. *Neural Computation*, 6:1185–1201, 1994.

21. R. T. Vaughan, K. Stoy, G. S. Sukhatme, and M. J. Mataric. Whistling in the dark: Cooperative trail following in uncertain localization space. In *Proc. 4Th International Conference on Autonomous Agents, Barcelona, Spain*, 2000.

22. C. J. C. H. Watkins. *Learning with delayed rewards*. PhD thesis, University of Cambridge, 1989.

SOAP: Efficient Feature Selection of Numeric Attributes

Roberto Ruiz, Jesús S. Aguilar-Ruiz, and José C. Riquelme

Department of Computer Science. University de Seville.
Avda. Reina Mercedes S/n. 41012 Sevilla, Spain.
{rruiz,aguilar,riquelme}@lsi.us.es

Abstract. The attribute selection techniques for supervised learning, used in the preprocessing phase to emphasize the most relevant attributes, allow making models of classification simpler and easy to understand. Depending on the method to apply: starting point, search organization, evaluation strategy, and the stopping criterion, there is an added cost to the classification algorithm that we are going to use, that normally will be compensated, in greater or smaller extent, by the attribute reduction in the classification model. The algorithm (SOAP: Selection of Attributes by Projection) has some interesting characteristics: lower computational cost (O(mn log n) m attributes and n examples in the data set) with respect to other typical algorithms due to the absence of distance and statistical calculations; with no need for transformation. The performance of SOAP is analysed in two ways: percentage of reduction and classification. SOAP has been compared to CFS [6] and ReliefF [11]. The results are generated by C4.5 and 1NN before and after the application of the algorithms.

1 Introduction

The data mining researchers, especially those dedicated to the study of algorithms that produce knowledge in some of the usual representations (decision lists, decision trees, association rules, etc.), usually make their tests on standard and accessible databases (most of them of small size). The purpose is to independently verify and validate the results of their algorithms. Nevertheless, these algorithms are modified to solve specific problems, for example real databases that contain much more information (number of examples) than standard databases used in training. To accomplish the final tests on these real databases with tens of attributes and thousands of examples is a task that takes a lot of time and memory size.

It is advisable to apply to the database preprocessing techniques to reduce the number of attributes or the number of examples in such a way as to decrease the computational time cost. These preprocessing techniques are fundamentally oriented to either of the next goals: feature selection (eliminating non-relevant attributes) and editing (reduction of the number of examples by eliminating some of them or calculating prototypes [1]). Our algorithm belongs to the first group.

In this paper we present a new method of attribute selection, called SOAP (Selection of Attributes by Projection), which has some important characteristics:
- Considerable reduction of the number of attributes.
- Lower computational time O(mn log n) than other algorithms.

F.J. Garijo, J.C. Riquelme, and M. Toro (Eds.): IBERAMIA 2002, LNAI 2527, pp. 233–242, 2002.

- Absence of distance and statistical calculations: correlation, information gain, etc.
- Conservation of the error rates of the classification systems.

The hypothesis on which the heuristic is based is: "place the best attributes with the smallest number of label changes". The next section discusses related work. Section 3 describes the SOAP algorithm. Section 4 presents the results. Which deal with several databases from the UCI repository [4]. The last section summarises the findings.

2   Related Work

Several authors defined the feature selection by looking at it from various angles depending on the characteristic that we want to accentuate. In general, attribute selection algorithms perform a search through the space of feature subsets, and must address four basic issues affecting the nature of the search: 1) Starting point: forward and backward, according to whether it began with no feautures or with all features. 2) Search organization: exhaustive or heuristic search. 3) Evaluation strategy: wrapper or filter. 4) Stopping criterion: a feature selector must decide when to stop searching through the space of feature subsets. A predefined number of features are selected, a predefined number of iterations reached. Whether or not the addition or deletion of any feature produces a better subset, we also stop the search, if an optimal subset according to some evaluation function is obtained.

Algorithms that perform feature selection as a preprocessing step prior to learning can generally be placed into one of two broad categories: wrappers, Kohavi [9], which employs a statistical re-sampling technique (such as cross validation) using the actual target learning algorithm to estimate the accuracy of feature subsets. This approach has proved to be useful but is very slow to execute because the learning algorithm is called upon repeatedly. Another option called filter, operates independently of any learning algorithm. Undesirable features are filtered out of the data before induction begins. Filters use heuristics based on general the characteristics of the data to evaluate the merit of feature subsets. As a consequence, filter methods are generally much faster than wrapper methods, and, as such, are more practical for use on data of high dimensionality. FOCUS [3], LVF [18] use class consistency as an evaluation meter. One method for discretization called Chi2 [17]. Relief [8] works by randomly sampling an instance from the data, and then locating its nearest neighbour from the same and opposite class. Relief was originally defined for two-class problems and was later expanded as ReliefF [11] to handle noise and multi-class data sets, and RReliefF [16] handles regression problems. Other authors suggest Neuronal Networks for an attribute selector [19]. In addition, learning procedures can be used to select attributes, like ID3 [14], FRINGE [13] and C4.5 [15]. Methods based on the correlation like CFS [6], etc.

3   SOAP: Selection of Attributes by Projection

3.1   Description

To describe the algorithm we will use the well-known data set IRIS, because of the easy interpretation of their two-dimensional projections.

Three projections of IRIS have been made in two-dimensional graphs. In Fig. 1 it is possible to observe that if the projection of the examples is made on the abscissas or ordinate axis we can not obtain intervals where any class is a majority, only can be seen the intervals [4.3,4.8] of Sepallength for the Setosa class or [7.1,8.0] for Virginica. In Fig. 2 for the Sepalwidth parameter in the ordinate axis clear intervals are not appraised either. Nevertheless, for the Petalwidth attribute is possible to appreciate some intervals where the class is unique: [0,0.6] for Setosa, [1.0,1.3] for Versicolor and [1.8,2.5] for Virginica. Finally in Fig. 3, it is possible to appreciate the class divisions, which are almost clear in both attributes. This is because when projecting the examples on each attribute the number of label changes is minimum. For example, it is possible to verify that for Petallength the first label change takes place for value 3 (setosa to Versicolor), the second in 4.5 (Versicolor to Virginica). there are other changes later in 4.8, 4,9, 5,0 and the last one is in 5.1.

SOAP is based on this principle: to count the label changes, produced when crossing the projections of each example in each dimension. If the attributes are in ascending order according to the number of label changes, we will have a list that defines the priority of selection, from greater to smaller importance. SOAP presumes to eliminate the basic redundancy between attributes, that is to say, the attributes with interdependence have been eliminated. Finally, to choose the more advisable number of features, we define a reduction factor, RF, in order to take the subset from attributes formed by the first of the aforementioned list.

Before formally exposing the algorithm, we will explain with more details the main idea. We considered the situation depicted in Fig. 2: the projection of the examples on the abscissas axis produces a ordered sequence of intervals (some of then can be a single point) which have assigned a single label or a set of them: {[0,0.6] Se, [1.0,1.3] Ve, [1.4,1.4] Ve-Vi, [1.5,1.5] Ve-Vi, [1.6,1.6] Ve-Vi, [1.7,1.7] Ve-Vi, [1.8,1.8] Ve-Vi, [1.9,2.5] Vi}. If we apply the same idea with the projection on the ordinate axis, we calculate the partitions of the ordered sequences: {Ve, R, R, Ve, R, R, R, R, R, R, R, R, R, Se, R, Se, R, Se}, where R is a combination of two or three labels. We can observe that we obtain almost one subsequence of the same value with different classes for each value from the ordered projection. That is to say, projections on the ordinate axis provide much less information that on the abscissas axis.

In the intervals with multiple labels we will consider the worst case, that being the maximum number of label changes possible for a same value.

The number of label changes obtained by the algorithm in the projection of each dimension is: Petalwidth 16, Petallength 19, Sepallenth 87 and Sepalwidth 120. In this way, we can achieve a ranking with the best attributes from the point of view of the classification. This result agrees with what is common knowledge in data mining, which states that the width and length of petals are more important than those related to sepals.

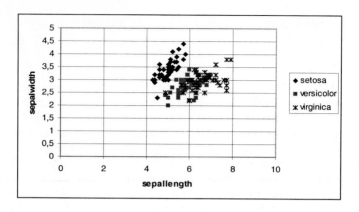

Fig. 1. Two-dimensional representation

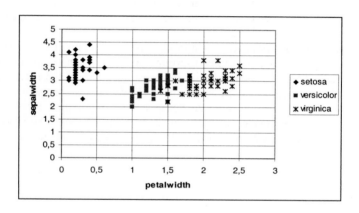

Fig. 2. Two-dimensional representation

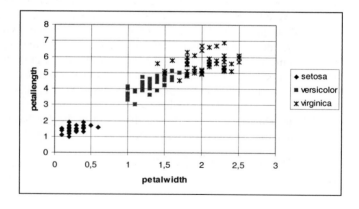

Fig. 3. Two-dimensional representation

3.2   Definitions

Definition 1: Let the attribute A_i be a continuous variable that takes values in $I_i=[min_i,max_i]$. Then, A is the attributes space defined as $A=I_1 \times I_2 \times \cdots \times I_m$, where m is the number of attributes.

   Definition 2: An example $e \in E$ is a tuple formed by the Cartesian product of the value sets of each attribute and the set C of labels. We define the operations att and lab to access the attribute and its label (or class): *att*: E x N $\rightarrow$ A and *lab*: E $\rightarrow$ C, where N is the set of natural numbers.

   Definition 3: Let the universe U be a sequence of example from E. We will say that a database with n examples, each of them with m attributes and one class, forms a particular universe. Then $U=<u[1],...,u[n]>$ and as the database is a séquense, the access to an example is achieved by means of its position. Likewise, the access to j-th attribute of the i-th example is made by $att(u[i],j)$, and for identifying its label $lab(u[i])$.

   Definition 4: An ordered projected sequence is a sequence formed by the projection of the universe onto the i-th attribute. This sequence is sorted out in ascending order.

   Definition 5: A partition in subsequences is the set of subsequences formed from the ordered projected sequence of an attribute in such a way as to maintain the projection order. All the examples belonging to a subsequence have the same class and every two consecutive subsequences are disjointed with respect to the class. Henceforth, a subsequence will be called a partition.

   Definition 6: A subsequence of the same value is the sequence composed of the examples with identical value from the i-th attribute within the ordered projected sequence.

3.3   Algorithm

The algorithm is very simple and fast, see Fig. 4. It operates with continuous variables as well as with databases which have two classes or multiple classes. In the ascending-order-task for each attribute, the QuickSort algorithm is used [7]. This algorithm is O(n log n), on average. Once ordered by an attribute, we can count the label changes throughout the ordered projected sequence. NumberChanges in Fig. 5, considers whether we deal with different values from an attribute, or with a subsequence of the same value. In the first case, it compares the present label with that of the following value. Whereas in the second case, where the subsequence is of the same value, it counts as many label changes as are possible (function ChangesSameValue).

   The k first attribute which NCE (number of label changes) under NCE_{lim} will be selected. NCE_{lim} is calculated applying the follow equation:

$$NCE_{lim}=NCE_{min}+(NCE_{max}-NCE_{min})*RF \qquad (1)$$

RF: reduction factor.

```
Input: E training (n examples, m attributes)
Output: E reduced (n examples, k attributes (k<=m))
        For each attribute a_i with i in {1..m}
            E_i  ← QuickSort(E_i,a_i)
            NCE_i ← NumberChanges(E_i,a_i)
        NCE Attribute Ranking
        Select the k first
```

Fig. 4. SOAP algorithm

```
Input: E training (n examples, m attributes)
Output: number of label changes
        For each example e_j ∈ E with j in {1..n}
            If att(u[j],i) ∈ Subsequence same value
                labelChanges += ChangesSameValue()
            Else
                If lab(u[j]) <> lab(u[j+1])
                    labelChanges++
```

Fig. 5. NumberChanges algorithm

4   Experiments

In order to compare the effectiveness of SOAP as a feature selector for common machine learning algorithms, experiments were performed using twelve standard data sets form the UCI collection [4]. The data sets and their characteristics are summarized in Table 3. The percentage of correct classification with C4.5 and 1NN, averaged over ten ten-fold cross-validation runs, were calculated for each algorithm-data set combination before and after feature selection by SOAP (RF 0.35 and 0.25), CFS and ReliefF (threshold 0.05). For each train-test split, the dimensionality was reduced by each feature selector before being passed to the learning algorithms. The same fold were used for each feature selector-learning scheme combination.

To perform the experiment with CFS and ReliefF we used the Weka[1] (Waikato Environment for Knowledge Analysis) implementation.

Table 1 shows the results for attribute selection with C4.5 and compares the size (number of nodes) of the trees produced by each attribute selection scheme against the size of the trees produced by C4.5 with no attribute selection. Smaller trees are preferred as they are easier to interpret, but accuracy is generally degraded. The table shows how often each method performs significantly better (denoted by ○) or worse (denoted by ●) than when performing no feature selection (column 2 and 3). Throughout we speak of results being significantly different if the difference is statistically at the 5% level according to a paired two-sided t test. Each pair of points

[1] http://www.cs.waikato.ac.nz/~ml

consisting of the estimates obtained in one of the ten, ten-fold cross-validation runs, for before and after feature selection. For SOAP, feature selection degrades performance on four datasets, improves on one and it is equal on seven. The results are similar to ReliefF and a little worse than those provided by CFS. From this table it can be seen that SOAP produces the smallest trees, it improves C4.5´s performances on nine data sets and degrades it on one.

Tables 1 and 2 show the average for two execution of SOAP (RF 0.35 and 0.25, equation 1).

Table 1. Result of attribute selection with C4.5. Accuracy and size of trees. ○,● Statistically significant improvement or degradation (p=0.05).

Data Set	Original Ac.	Size	SOAP Ac.	Size	CFS Ac.	Size	RLF Ac.	Size
balance-scale	78,18	81,08	57,94 ●	6,28 ○	78,18	81,08	78,29	81,54
breast-w	95,01	24,96	94,84	21,62 ○	95,02	24,68	95,02	24,68
diabetes	74,64	42,06	74,34	8,56 ○	74,36	14,68 ○	65,10 ●	1,00 ○
glass	68,18	46,34	66,78	46,10	69,35	40,90 ○	68,97	30,32 ○
glass2	78,71	24,00	78,90	16,32 ●	79,82	14,06 ○	53,50 ●	1,70 ○
heart-stat	78,11	34,58	79,56	28,20 ○	80,63 ○	23,84 ○	82,33 ○	14,78 ○
ionosphere	89,83	26,36	90,06	22,52 ○	90,26	23,38 ○	89,91	22,72 ○
iris	94,27	8,18	94,40	8,12	94,13	7,98	94,40	8,16
segment	96,94	80,98	90,94 ●	110,68 ●	96,35 ●	73,92 ○	96,93	80,66
sonar	74,28	27,98	70,72 ●	13,18 ○	74,38	28,18	70,19 ●	9,74 ○
vehicle	71,83	139,34	52,84 ●	22,26 ○	66,42 ●	106,60 ○	66,22 ●	137,42
waveform	75,36	592,92	77,47 ○	485,26 ○	77,18 ○	513,78 ○	75,51	217,72 ○
Average (35)	81	94	77	66	81	79	78	53
Average (25)			77	59				

Table 2. Result of attribute selection with 1NN. Average number of features selected, the percentage of the original features retained and the accuracy. ○,● Statistically significant improvement or degradation (p=0.05).

Data Set	Original Atts	Ac.	SOAP Atts	%	Ac.	CFS Atts	%	Ac.	RLF Atts	%	Ac.
balance-scale	4	86,56	1,39	35	57,98 ●	4,00	100	86,56	4,00	100	86,56
breast-w	9	95,25	6,00	67	94,16 ●	8,97	100	95,24	8,05	89	95,35
diabetes	8	70,35	2,99	37	70,16	3,11	39	70,07	0,00	0	34,90 ●
glass	9	70,28	3,94	44	73,04 ○	6,30	70	74,25 ○	3,39	38	63,83 ●
glass2	9	77,79	4,72	52	80,37	3,95	44	83,07 ○	0,32	4	54,29 ●
heart-stat	13	75,59	7,11	55	77,74	6,26	48	78,37 ○	6,27	48	78,89 ○
ionosphere	34	86,78	31,55	93	87,07	12,30	36	89,72 ○	30,88	91	87,49
iris	4	95,27	2,00	50	96,33	1,93	48	95,60	4,00	100	95,27
segment	19	97,13	7,00	37	91,29 ●	5,66	30	97,00	15,04	79	97,19
sonar	60	84,47	5,42	9	70,63 ●	17,84	30	83,56	3,89	6	68,61 ●
vehicle	18	69,48	1,09	6	46,50 ●	7,45	41	62,86 ●	5,81	32	61,28 ●
waveform	40	73,59	12,99	32	79,33 ○	14,85	37	79,13 ○	5,77	14	73,09
Average (35)	19	82	7	43	77	8	52	83	7	50	75
Average (25)			6	35	75						

Table 2 shows the average number of features selected, the percentage of the original features retained and the accuracy of 1NN. SOAP is a specially selective algorithm compared with CFS and RLF. If SOAP and CFS are compared, only in one dataset (ionosphere) is the number of characteristics significantly greater than those selected by CFS. In five data sets there are no significant differences, and in six, the number of features is significantly smaller than CFS. Compare to RLF, only in glass2 and diabetes, SOAP obtains more parameters in the reduction process (threshold 0.05 is not sufficient). It can be seen (by looking at the fifth column) that SOAP retained 43% (35%) of the attributes on average. Figure 6 shows the average number of feature selected by SOAP, CFS and ReliefF as well as the number present in the full data set.

Table 3. Discrete class data sets with numeric attributes. Time in milliseconds.

Data Set	Original Instances	Atts	Clases	SOAP t-ms	CFS t-ms	RLF t-ms
1 balance-scale	625	4	3	10	17455	561
2 breast-cancer	699	9	2	10	40	1322
3 diabetes	768	8	2	10	30	1422
4 glass	214	9	7	0	20	160
5 glass2	163	9	2	0	10	80
6 heart-statlog	270	13	2	10	10	281
7 ionosphere	351	34	2	10	120	1202
8 iris	150	4	3	0	10	40
9 segment	2310	19	7	40	521	29362
10 sonar	208	60	2	10	100	771
11 vehicle	846	18	4	10	70	3956
12 waveform	5000	40	3	210	2434	282366
Sum				320	20820	321523

It is interesting to compare the speed of the attribute selection techniques. We measured the time taken in milliseconds[2] to select the final subset of attributes. SOAP is an algorithm with a very short computation time. The results shown in Table 3 confirm the expectations. SOAP takes 320 milliseconds in reducing 12 datasets whereas CFS takes more than 20 seconds and RLF almost 6 minutes. In general, SOAP is faster than the other methods and it is independent of the classes number, a factor that excessively affects CFS, as it is possible to observe in the set "segment" with seven classes. Also it is possible to be observed that ReliefF is affected very negatively by the number of instances in the dataset, it can be seen in "segment" and "waveform". Eventhough these two datasets were eliminated, SOAP is more than 200 times faster than CFS, and more than 100 times than ReliefF.

5 Conclusions

In this paper we present a deterministic attribute selection algorithm. It is a very efficient and simple method used in the preprocessing phase A considerable reduction of the number of attributes is produced in comparison to other techniques. It does not

---

[2] This is a rough measure. Obtaining true cpu time from within a Java program is quite difficult.

need distance nor statistical calculations, which could be very costly in time (correlation, gain of information, etc.). The computational cost is lower than other methods O(m·n·log n).

In later works, we will focus our research on the selection of the subset of attributes once they have been obtained. Finally we will try to adapt SOAP to databases with discrete attributes where redundant features have not been eliminated.

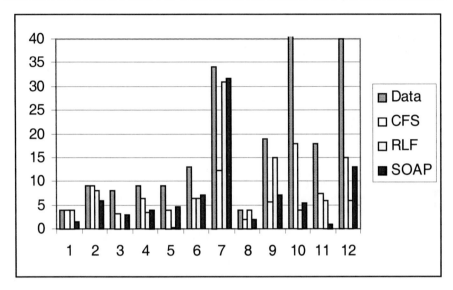

Fig. 6. Average number of feature selected.

Acknowledgments. This work has been supported by the Spanish Research Agency CICYT under grant TIC2001-1143-C03-02.

References

[1] Aguilar-Ruiz, Jesús S., Riquelme, José C. and Toro, Miguel. Data Set Editing by Ordered Projection. Intelligent Data Analysis Journal. Vol. 5, n°5, pp. 1-13, IOS Press (2001).
[2] Almuallim, H. and Dietterich, T.G. Learning with many irrelevant features. In Proceedings of the Ninth National Conference on Artificial Intelligence. pp. 547-552. AAAI Press (1991).
[3] Almuallim, H. and Dietterich, T.G. Learning boolean concepts in the presence of many irrelevant features. Artificial Intelligence, 69(1-2):279-305 (1994).
[4] Blake, C. and Merz, E. K. UCI Repository of machine learning databases (1998).
[5] Brassard, G., and Bratley, P. Fundamentals of algorithms. Prentice Hall, New Jersey (1996).
[6] Hall M.A. Correlation-based feature selection for machine learning. PhD thesis, Department of Computer Science, University of Waikato, Hamilton, New Zealand (1998).
[7] Hoare, C. A. R. QuickSort. Computer Journal, 5(1):10-15 (1962).

[8]   Kira, K. and Rendell, L. A practical approach to feature selection. In Proceedings of the Ninth International Conference on Machine Learning. pp. 249-256, Morgan Kaufmann (1992).

[9]   Kohavi, R. and John, G. H. Wrappers for feature subset selection. Artificial Intelligence, 97, 273-324 (1997).

[10] Koller, D. and Sahami, M. Toward optimal feature selection. In Proceedings of the Thirteenth International Conference on Marching Learning. pp. 284-292, Morgan Kaufmann (1996).

[11] Kononenko, I. Estimating attibutes: Analisys and extensions of relief. In Proceedings of the Seventh European Conference on Machine Learning. pp. 171-182, Springer-Verlag (1994).

[12] Modrzejewski, M. Feature selection using rough sets theory. In Proceedings of the European Conference on Machine Learning. pp. 213-226, Springer (1993).

[13] Pagallo, G. and Haussler, D. Boolean feature discovery in empirical learning. Machine Learning, 5, 71-99 (1990).

[14] Quinlan, J. Induction of decision trees. Machine Learning, 1(1), 81-106 (1986).

[15] Quinlan, J. C4.5: Programs for machine learning. Morgan Kaufmann (1993).

[16] Robnik-Šikonja, M. and Kononenko, I. An adaption of relief for attribute estimation in regression. In Proceedings of the Fourteenth International Conference on Machine Learning. pp. 296-304, Morgan Kaufmann (1997).

[17] Setiono, R., and Liu, H. Chi2: Feature selection and discretization of numeric attributes. In Proceedings of the Seventh IEEE International Conference on Tools with Artificial Intelligence (1995).

[18] Setiono, R., and Liu, H. A probabilistic approach to feature selection-a filter solution. In Proceedings of International Conference on Machine Learning, 319-327 (1996).

[19] Setiono, R., and Liu, H. Neural network feature selectors. IEEE Trans. On Neural Networks, 8(3), 654-662 (1997).

Designing Fuzzy Relations in Orthogonal Persistence Object-Oriented Database Engines

Miguel Ángel Sicilia[1], José Antonio Gutiérrez[2], and Elena García[2]

[1] Computer Science Dept. Carlos III University,
Avd. Universidad 30,
28911, Leganés, Madrid. Spain
msicilia@inf.uc3m.es
[2] Computer Science Dept. University of Alcalá
Ctra. Barcelona km. 33.600.
28871, Alcalá de Henares, Madrid. Spain
{jantonio.gutierrez, elena.garciab}@uah.es

Abstract. Semantic relations between concepts or data are common modelling devices in various knowledge representation approaches. Fuzzy relations can be defined as fuzzy subsets of the cartesian product of a number of domains, extending the notion of crisp relation. Associations in object-oriented modelling – and more specifically in the Unified Modelling Language – can be interpreted as crisp relations on the classifiers they connect, and thus the concept of association can be extended to its fuzzy counterpart by representing a fuzzy relation on the classes involved in the association. In this paper, the resolution form of a fuzzy relation is described as a convenient way to represent fuzzy associations in object-oriented programming languages, thus enabling an efficient practical representation mechanism for them. Specific cases of fuzzy relations can also be dealt with by adding semantic constraints to fuzzy associations. One of the most interesting cases is that of similarity relations, which essentially generalize the notion of object equality to the fuzzy case. Fuzzy relations can be stored in orthogonally persistent object databases by using the described fuzzy association design, as illustrated in this paper with a case study that uses the db4o persistence engine.

1   Introduction

A number of research groups have investigated the problem of modelling fuzziness (in a broad sense, including imprecision and uncertainty, as defined in [14]) in the context of object-oriented databases (OODB) [4], and some of their results include research implementations on top of commercial systems [15]. Nonetheless, currently no commercial system is available that supports fuzziness explicitly in its core physical or logical model, and existing database standards regarding object persistence sources - ODMG [3] and JDO [13] – do not support neither fuzziness nor any other kind of generalized uncertainty information representation [9]) – in their data models.

F.J. Garijo, J.C. Riquelme, and M. Toro (Eds.): IBERAMIA 2002, LNAI 2527, pp. 243–253, 2002.

Nonetheless, imperative OODB application programming interfaces stay very close to the semantic and syntax of the object-oriented programming languages in which they're embedded – see, for example, [2] – facilitating the construction of research prototypes that extend commercial systems by adding a software layer acting as a proxy filter [5] for the underlying non-fuzzy languages.

Relations between concepts are very common constructs in diverse knowledge representation approaches, including modern ontology-description languages [7], and as such, they require specific physical representation mechanisms to be efficiently handled by application software. In this work, we describe our approach for the design of fuzzy relations in orthogonally persistent OODBs, evolved from earlier work [6]. More specifically, we concentrate on the design of associations between database (or model) entities, and on the specific case of similarity relations.

The paper is structured as follows: in section 2, we describe a case study that extends the db4o database engine interfaces to include general-purpose fuzzy associations, a concept that can be considered an extension of the ODMG relationship construct [3]. In section 3, a prototype version for the extensions proposed in this work is described. The prototype is tested on the fully functional db4o community edition, which can be freely redistributed in non-commercial applications. Finally, some conclusions and future work are included in section 4.

2   Fuzzy Relations and Object-Oriented Associations

2.1   Relations and Associations

A crisp relation represents the presence or absence of interconnectedness between the elements of two or more sets. This concept is referred to as association when applied to object oriented modelling. According to the Unified Modelling Language (UML) [10] – the most widely used object-oriented modelling notation –, an association defines a semantic relationship between *classifiers*[1], and the instances of an association can be considered a set of tuples relating instances of these classifiers, where each tuple value may appear at most once. A binary association may involve one or two fuzzy relations (i.e. the unidirectional and bidirectional cases), although due to the semantic interpretation of associations, they're in many cases considered to convey the same information (i.e. the association between authors and books is interpreted in the same way despite the navigation direction).

Since it's common practice to develop object-oriented software from previously defined UML models, we can consider UML semantics as a model from which associations are implemented in specific object-oriented programming languages, by the process of *association design*, which essentially consists in the

---

[1] A classifier is an UML term referring to classes and class-like model elements that describe sets of entities.

selection of the concrete data structure that better fits the requirements of the association (see, for example, [12]).

2.2   Fuzzy Relations

Fuzzy relations are generalizations of the concept of crisp relation in which various degrees of strength of relation are allowed [8]. A binary fuzzy relation R is defined as a fuzzy subset of that cartesian product as denoted in (1).

$$R = \{((x,y), \mu_R(x,y))|(x,y) \in X \times Y\} \tag{1}$$

We'll restrict ourselves to the binary case, since it's the more common case in database applications. Note that even in the recent UML version 1.4, the definition of association relationship is considered to be ill defined [11]. Nonetheless, in this work, we'll consider associations as literal tuples between model elements that hold an additional value representing their membership grade to the association. This assumption implies some constraints in the implementation of bidirectional associations, since both association ends should be aware of updates on the other one.

A common representation for fuzzy relations is an n-dimensional array [8], but this representation does not fit well in the object paradigm, in which a particular object (element of one of the domains in the relation) only is aware of the tuples to which it belongs (the links), and uses them to navigate to other instances. We have extended the association concept to design fuzzy relations attached to classes in a programming language, so that a particular instance has direct links (i.e. 'knows') to instances associated with it. Access to the entire relation (that is, the union of the individual links of all the instances in the association) is provided as a class responsibility, as will be described later.

3   Design Case Study

The db4o[2] object database system is a lightweight OODB engine that provides a seamless Java language binding (it uses reflection run-time capabilities to avoid the need to modify existing classes to make their instances storable) and a novel *Query-By-Example* (QBE) interface based on the results of the SODA[3] – Simple Object Data-base Access – initiative.

Associations are stored in its Java native form in db4o, and therefore, special support for fuzzy associations can be designed by using different standard object oriented design techniques.

---

[2] Available at http://www.db4o.com
[3] Information available at http://www.odbms.org/soda/

3.1 Designing Binary Associations

The membership values of the relation must be kept apart from the instances of the classes that participate in the association. A first approach could be that of building *Proxies* for the instances – which will hold a reference to the instance at the other side of the association and the membership grade – and storing them in a standard collection. The main benefit of this approach is its simplicity, since only a class called for example *FuzzyLink* (FL from now on) solves the representation problem, and it's enough for the case of association with cardinality one. We used this first approach for comparison purposes with our final design.

A drawback of the FL approach for associations with multiple cardinalities is that the responsibility of preserving relation properties is left to the domain-class designer. This is one of the reasons that pushed us to a second approach in which the collection semantics - and not the element semantics - are extended. The base

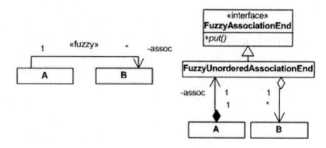

Fig. 1. Unidirectional Binary Association Design

of our fuzzy collection framework is a *FuzzyAssociationEnd* (FAE) interface that defines common behavior for all fuzzy associations. Concrete classes implement that interface to provide different flavors of associations. In this work, we'll restrict our discussion to a *FuzzyUnorderedAssociationEnd* (FUAE) class. The class diagram in Figure 1 shows how a unidirectional fuzzy association[4] from class A to class B can be designed with our framework.

It should be noted that the *put* method can be used both to add and remove objects from the relation - the latter case can be carried out by specifying a zero membership (we have considered in this implementation that zero membership is equivalent to the lack of a link). Since many associations that store different information may exist between the same pair of classes, associations must be named. The class-instance *FUAE* is responsible for maintaining a collection of the associations that are maintained as instances of it (i.e., this behavior is modelled as a class responsibility). These different associations are represented by instances a *FuzzyUnorderedAssociation* (FUA) class. Therefore, *FUA* instances represent entire generic associations and store the union of the links that belong to it. An example of an association *User-Subject* called *'is-interested-in'* may be coded in Java as follows:

---

[4] We have used a *fuzzy* UML stereotype to mark fuzzy associations.

```
public class Subject{
   public String _name;
   public FuzzyUnorderedAssociationEnd _fasoc;
   public Subject(String name){
      _name = name;
      _fasoc = new FuzzyUnorderedAssociationEnd
                    ("isInterestedIn", false);
   }
   public void registerInterest(Object o, double mu){
     _fasoc.putLink(o, mu);
   }
   public Iterator interestedPeople(){
      return _fasoc.values().iterator();
   }
   /...
}
```

Iterations may be performed on the links with an specialization of the *Iterator* interface that returns the elements wrapped in *FuzzyElement* instances, as illustrated in the following code fragment.

```
for (Iterator it=xml.interestedPeople();it.hasNext(); ){
  FuzzyElement e = (FuzzyElement) it.next();
  System.out.println(e.getGrade()+(User)e.getObject());
}
```

3.2 Representation Details

In our design, links are indexed with their membership values as keys, using sets to hold links with the same value (see Fig. 2). In order to turn feasible this approach, real values representing membership values should be stored with a reasonable precision. Note that more than five decimal numbers is seldom needed in common applications (that is, a tuple with $\mu_R = 0.50001$ is hardly distinguishable from another with $\mu_R = 0.5000$).

The union of all *FUAE* that belong to the same association is maintained in a *FUA* instance. These instances are stored as a class member of the *FUAE* class (see Fig.3), so that integrity is preserved in insertion and removal of links. This design also enables an easy maintenance of integrity if the association is implemented in both directions.

The use of dictionaries with fixed precision-membership values as keys provides performance benefits in common operations on fuzzy sets, like $\alpha - cuts$, outperforming common container classes (bags, sets and lists). The rationale behind this organization is that association traversal would be often done by specifying a minimum membership grade, that is, to obtain an element of the partition of the fuzzy relation.

This way, we are representing the relation by its resolution form (2).

$$R = \bigcup_\alpha \alpha R_\alpha, \forall \alpha \in \Lambda_R \qquad (2)$$

248   M.Á. Sicilia, J.A. Gutiérrez, and E. García

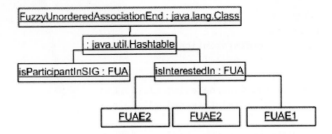

Fig. 2. *FUA* instances as the union of *FUAE* ones

where Λ_R is the level set of R , R_α denotes an $\alpha-cut$ of the fuzzy relation and αR_α is a fuzzy relation as defined in (3).

$$\mu_{\alpha R_\alpha}(x,y) = \alpha \cdot \mu_{R_\alpha}(x,y) \tag{3}$$

The implementation is an extension of Java's `HashMap` collection, which essentially substitutes the add behavior with that of a link operation that is sketched as follows:

```
public Object link(Object key, Object value){
 if (key.getClass() == Double.class){
    double mu = ((Double)key).doubleValue();
    // truncates to current precision:
    mu = truncateTo(mu);
    // Get the set of elements with the given mu:
    HashSet elements=(HashSet)this.get( new Double(mu) );
    if ( elements == null ){
        HashSet aux = new HashSet();
        aux.add(value);
        super.put(new Double(mu), aux);
    }else
        elements.add(value);
    }
    // Inform the association that a new link has been added:
    if (association !=null)
        association.put(key, this, value);
    return null;
}
```

Figure 3 illustrates our described design by showing a *"is-interested-in"* relation between the set U of the users of a Web site and the set S of subjects of the page it serves.

Some common operations found are: obtaining the interest of a user in a specific subject, obtaining the set of subjects a user is interested in and obtaining the set of users which match a specific preference profile (that are interested in a set of subjects). Note that often associations require a specific ordering (i.e. insertion by an specific attribute). Specializations of the classes of our library are expected to add those behaviors.

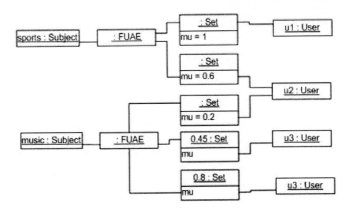

Fig. 3. An example *'is interested in'* fuzzy relation

3.3   Similarity Relations

Similarity relations can be considered as an extension of the concept of equality, and can be implemented as special reflexive fuzzy associations with added support for similarity semantics. A fuzzy similarity relation is a reflexive, symmetric and transitive fuzzy relation, where reflexivity and symmetry are defined as in (4).

$$\mu_R(x, x) = 1 \qquad (4)$$

$$\mu_R(x, y) = \mu_R(y, x)$$

The transitivity property is usually implemented as max-mix transitivity according to the formula in (5).

$$\mu_R(x, y) \leq max_{z \in D}[min(\mu_R(x, z), \mu_R(z, y))] \qquad (5)$$

Our approach is that of storing similarity relations defined on a class with crisp boundaries - other approaches define similarity on attribute values for non-crisp classes [1]. In our framework, a *function object* is required at similarity relation construction to specify the concrete transitivity formula (i.e. substituting the inequality with a specific value). An overloaded *put* method version inserts links in the similarity relation without the explicit specification of a membership value. The actual value is derived from the existing ones in the relation, if possible, through the transitive formula.

An overloaded version of **db4o** the query interface (the *ObjectContainer.get()* method) provides access to similarity-enriched QBE queries and gives explicit access to fuzzy associations as well. QBE queries with similarity comparison operators can be constructed by extending the notion of **SODA** query constraints with fuzzy comparison operators. As the *ObjectContainer* class acts as a factory for its instances, we've extended it through delegation – the class is called *Fuzzy-ObjectContainer* (FOC)–. Basically, when a object whose class holds a similarity relation is passed as a template to method *get* in FOC, not only the instance is retrieved, but also all the similarity related instances. Another version of *get* that takes an additional parameter allows the query to specify a minimum similarity grade for the instances retrieved.

3.4   Performance Considerations

The cardinality of the level set of a fuzzy association with precision m is bounded by $10^m - 1$, and therefore, the number of sets of links with the same membership value in an association is always below or equal to that number. In a degenerate case, the number of links L in the association would be equal to the number of sets, but this is not a common case. In cases in which the number of links is much greater than the number of different membership values, the efficiency of operations that query subsets of the relation increases significantly.

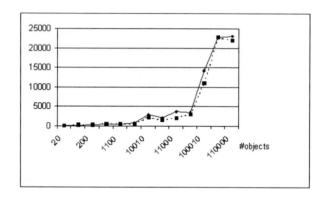

Fig. 4. Iteration retrieval time and total number of objects

Theoretically, the navigational nature of object databases and persistence engines are well suited to operations that only require the physical retrieval of a number of objects, like the retrieval of elements by a membership grade or threshold.

We have carried out several experiments to try to understand the performance behavior of our design. We used a unidirectional fuzzy association from *Subjects* to *Users*, measuring systematically the *retrieval* time[5] (understood as the time required to query the association and traverse all its links) for increasing cardinalities of users, subjects and links between them (the membership values for the links were randomly generated and the number of links was always above the number of users or subjects). The memory requirements of the Java virtual machine constrained the measures to *total object count* (users + subjects) below 10,000 (in the experiment, the number of links was the max(#users, #subjects)).

---

[5] On a Windows XP machine with 256MB RAM and Pentium IV 1500MHz processor.

The first finding was that retrieval times increased significantly with total object count above four thousand objects approximately, as showed in Figure 4. We also observed that retrieval time increased slightly less with increases in the number instances of *User* than with increases on *Subject* (which holds the data structure). The dashed line in Figure 4 summarizes the measures of an alternative implementation using Java `LinkedList` to store the link collection. As showed in that figure, no significant performance overhead is added with our approach from simpler ones. Nonetheless, the retrieval by membership values or by membership threshold ($\alpha - cuts$) is significantly improved (this is theoretically clear from asymptotic analysis, due to the $O(1)$ efficiency of search in `HashSet`). Figure 5 compares the retrieval time increase with the number of links

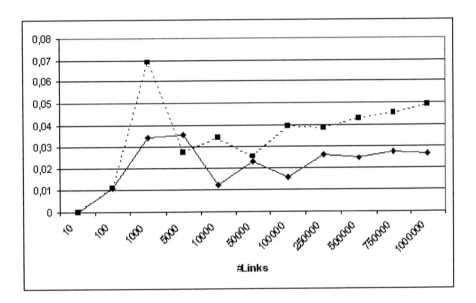

Fig. 5. Random $\alpha - cut$ retrieval time increase and number of links.

stored, when retrieving randomly generated $\alpha - cuts$. The efficiency decrease is significantly lower in the *FUAE* implementation than in the linked list ones for large number of links. Sorting the list by membership reduces retrieval time in the medium case, but it still has worse performance than our approach. The `activationDepth` parameter of db4o is an important factor in these results. It must be reduced from the default 5 value to 2 or 1 to obtain a significant improvement, since with the default, the entire object graph is always retrieved. In addition, and for large cardinalities, we have found performance improvements in retrieval time of links by membership value, in comparison to experiments carried out on relational-like persistence managers (specifically, *Microsoft Access 2000*).

4   Conclusions and Future Work

The resolution form of a fuzzy relation is a convenient way of representing and subsequently storing fuzzy associations in orthogonal persistence engines. Additional constraints on link insertion semantics can be added to obtain specialized relations like similarity relations. This association design approach provides improved performance in operations that involve link retrieval by membership value, and adds no significant time overhead in common collection iteration processes.

Future work should address a more detailed empirical evaluation on a number of different object persistence systems, and a refinement of the current structure to directly represent $\alpha - cuts$ as objects, which could improve the current approach in retrieving elements by specifying a membership threshold.

Acknowledgements. Thanks to Carl Rosenberg from db4o that assisted us in some technical aspects od the storage in the db4o database engine.

References

1. Aksoy, D. Yazici, A. George, R.: Extending similarity-based fuzzy object-oriented data model. Proc. of the 1996 ACM symposium on Applied Computing SAC (1996), 542-546
2. Atkinson, M. P., Daynes, L., Jordan, M.J., Printezis, T., Spence, S.: An Orthogonally Persistent Java. ACM Sigmod Record, 25, 4 (1996).
3. Cattell, R. G. G. (ed.): The Object Data Standard: ODMG 3.0. Morgan Kaufmann Publishers (2000).
4. De Caluwe, R. (ed.): Fuzzy and Uncertain Object-Oriented Databases: Concepts and Models. Advances in Fuzzy Systems, Applications and Theory, V, 13 (1998).
5. Gamma, E., Helm, R., Johnson, R., Vlissides, J.: Design Patterns: Elements of Reusable Object Oriented Design. Addison Wesley (1995).
6. Gutierrez, J. A., Sicilia, M. A., Garcia, E.: Integrating fuzzy associations and similarity relations in object oriented database systems. Proc. Intl. Conf. On Fuzzy Sets Theory and its Applications (2002), 66-67.
7. Horrocks, I.: DAML+OIL: A Reason-able Web Ontology Language. Proc. 8th Intl. Conference on Extending Database Technology (2002), 2-13.
8. Klir, G.J., Folger, T.A.: Fuzzy Sets, Uncertainty and Information. Prentice Hall (1988).
9. Klir, G., Wierman, M.: Uncertainty-Based Information: Elements of Generalized Information Theory. Springer-Verlag (1998).
10. Object Management Group: OMG Unified Modeling Language Specification, Version 1.3 (1999).
11. Stevens, P.: On Associations in the Unified Modelling Language, Proc. of UML2001. Springer-Verlag (2001).
12. Rumbaugh, J., Blaha, M., Premerlani, W., Eddy, F., Lorenson, W.: Object Oriented Modelling and Desing. Prentice Hall (1996).
13. Russell, C. et al: Java Data Objects (JDO) Version 1.0 proposed final draft, Java Specification Request JSR000012 (2001).

14. Smets, P.: Imperfect information: Imprecision-Uncertainty. Uncertainty Management in Information Systems: From Needs to Solutions. Kluwer Academic Publishers (1997), 225-254.
15. Yazici, A., George, R., Demet Aksoy, D.: Design and Implementation Issues in the Fuzzy Object-Oriented Data Model. Information Sciences, 108, 1-4 (1998), 241-260.

An Interactive Framework for Open Queries in Decision Support Systems

Juan A. Fernández del Pozo and Concha Bielza

Decision Analysis Group, Technical University of Madrid,
Campus de Montegancedo, Boadilla del Monte, 28660 Madrid, Spain
{jafernandez,mcbielza}@fi.upm.es

Abstract. We have recently introduced a method for minimising the
storage space of huge decision tables faced after solving real-scale
decision-making problems under uncertainty [4]. In this paper, the
method is combined with a proposal of a query system to answer expert
questions about the preferred action, for a given instantiation of decision table attributes. The main difficulty is to accurately answer queries
associated with incomplete instantiations. Moreover, the decision tables
often only include a subset of the whole problem solution due to computational problems, leading to uncertain responses. Our proposal establishes
an automatic and interactive dialogue between the decision support system and the expert to extract information from the expert to reduce
uncertainty. Typically, the process involves learning a Bayesian network
structure from a relevant part of the decision table and the computation
of some interesting conditional probabilities that are revised accordingly.

1   Introduction

In problems of decision-making under uncertainty, the model evaluation outputs
are decision tables with the optimal alternatives. In our case, the model is an
influence diagram [11], i.e. a directed acyclic graph which has proven to be very
useful in this context. Therefore, the evaluation of an influence diagram yields,
for every decision time, an associated decision table with the information about
which is the best alternative, i.e., the alternative with the maximum expected
utility, for every combination of variables (outcomes of random variables and/or
other past decisions). The evaluation algorithm determines which these variables
are. Let us consider a decision table as a set of attributes (a multidimensional
array) that determine the optimal action, policy or response. Then, an essential
issue is to minimise its storage space, which typically grows enormously in real-
scale problems. Each table may have up to millions of rows and typically, more
than twenty columns, and the results of the decision problem, therefore, rely on
a combinatorial knowledge representation space.

In [4], we introduce $KBM2L$ lists to address this problem. The main idea
stems from how computers manage multidimensional matrices: computer memory stores and manages these matrices as linear arrays, and each position is a

F.J. Garijo, J.C. Riquelme, and M. Toro (Eds.): IBERAMIA 2002, LNAI 2527, pp. 254–264, 2002.

function of the order chosen for the matrix dimensions. KBM2L lists are new list-based structures that optimise this order in the sense of putting equal responses in consecutive positions in order to achieve compact storage.

During usual decision support system (DSS) operation, the expert user will query the system about which is the best recommendation for a given set of attributes. In this paper, we propose a query system based on the KBM2L framework. Section 3 describes different types of queries and elaborates on the difficulties involved. Section 4 addresses the situation of a closed query, with the whole set of attributes instantiated (a record). Section 5 tackles more general and complex queries –open queries–. The procedure combines compact decision tables with learning, information access and information retrieval processes. Section 6 uses a real medical DSS to illustrate all kinds of open queries. The last section is a summary and suggests further research.

2   KBM2L Lists for Knowledge Synthesis

As mentioned above, KBM2L lists store the information of a decision table as a vector, much in the manner computers work. A decision table is a set of attributes. If we assume discrete attribute domains, then an order, natural or conventional, in the values of these domains may also be assumed. The attributes can also be arranged in different orders always maintaining the same information. A *base* is a vector whose elements are the attributes in a specific order. An *index* is a vector whose elements are the values of the attributes of the base, interpreted as the coordinates with respect to the base.

Therefore, the decision table as a multidimensional matrix maps into an array as follows [8]. Given a cell of the table with coordinates $\mathbf{c} = (c_0, c_1, ..., c_n)$, we define $f : \mathcal{R}^{n+1} \rightarrow \mathcal{R}$, such that

$$f(c_0, c_1, ..., c_n) = c_0 \prod_{i=1}^{n} D_i + c_1 \prod_{i=2}^{n} D_i + ... + c_n = q \tag{1}$$

where q is the $\mathbf{c}$-offset with respect to the first element of the table in a given base, D_i denotes the cardinal of the i-th attribute domain $(i = 0, 1, ..., n)$, and $\prod_{j=i+1}^{n} D_j$ is called its *weight* w_i. The vector of weights is $\mathbf{w} = (w_0, w_1, ...w_n)$ with $w_k = w_{k+1}D_{k+1}$, $w_n = 1$ and $k = 0, 1, ..., n - 1$. Their algebraic interpretation is that they are the coefficients that multiply the coordinates in (1), like radix powers in the number value expression. We can use relationship (1) to access all the table values. Without loss of generality, suppose c_i has $0,1,2,...D_i - 1$ as its possible outcomes and, hence, possible values for q are $0,1,2,...,w_0D_0 - 1$.

Rather than looking at the way the cells can be enumerated depending on the base, we now consider their content, namely, the DSS proposals. The list often contains sets of *consecutive* cells leading to the *same* optimal policy, as the optimal decisions present some level of knowledge granularity. The memory savings come from storing only one cell (or equivalently its offset) per set, e.g.

its last cell. This last cell together with the common policy, representing a set of records *(cell,policy)*, is called *item*. The shorter resulting list composed of items is a $KBM2L$ list [4]. It is somewhat related to the way sparse matrices are managed. Each item is denoted as $<offset, policy|$, where the $<$ symbol reflects item offsets increasing monotony and $|$ reflects granularity.

Good KBM2L lists search for bases with few items, grouping identical policies as far as possible into consecutive offsets. We have implemented a genetic and a variable neighbourhood algorithm to guide this search, as well as efficient heuristics for some time-consuming associated processes [5]. A list of minimum length means a table of minimum memory requirements. Moreover, this list also serves as a means of high-level explanation and validation, finding out relationships between groups of attributes and system proposals. [4] illustrates a medical problem. Therefore, this knowledge synthesis is useful from both a physical and a semantic point of view.

3   Queries

The expert decision-maker uses decision tables as a knowledge base (KB). In a typical session, expert and DSS accomplish these tasks: (A) formulate a query in the KB domain; (B) translate it into the KB formalism; (C) implement the response retrieval; (D) build the response efficiently; (E) communicate the response(s) and/or suggest improvements, and wait for user feedback.

As far as tasks (A) and (B) are concerned, there is a wide range of possible query formulations. We propose a simple classification of queries into two groups depending on whether the whole set of attributes is instantiated –*closed* query– or not –*open* query–. A closed query corresponds to a user who issues a specific and defined query, as she knows all the information about the attributes. An open query is more general, since it includes undefined attribute values, because they may be difficult or expensive to obtain or because they are unreliable. This classification is similar to the one given in [9], although [9] deals with GIS (Geographical Information Systems) and focuses more on data efficient updating and access from a physical point of view (merely as a database), than from a logical point of view (as a knowledge base).

Queries are stated as attribute instantiations and, therefore, they are related to the index. A response in terms of the optimal policy is expected. However, an added difficulty is optimal policy ignorance.

Let us explain this point in further detail. The complete evaluation of the decision-making problem may be so costly (in terms of time and memory requirements) that we have to resort to solving a set of subproblems instead, each one as the result of instantiating some random variables [1]. This subproblem set may not be exhaustive, implying unknown optimal policies for some attribute combinations, i.e. those associated with unsolved subproblems. This is common in large decision-making problems. In fact, the optimal KBM2L construction process also operates with unknown policies and subproblems. It firstly (sequentially or in parallel) evaluates all the subproblems, and then the resulting partial decision tables are sequentially added to the KBM2L list by means of a learning mechanism that optimises the list as new knowledge is entered (i.e., before reading the next partial table). Each stage in the addition process supposes a better item organisation and facilitates future additions [5].

In short, we distinguish not only between closed and open queries, but also between known and unknown or uncertain responses. The different scenarios are analysed in the following sections, thus completing tasks (C)-(E).

4 Closed Queries

The whole set of attributes is instantiated for closed queries. Then, the system only needs to look for the corresponding KBM2L list element and retrieve the optimal policy, which is presented to the user as the response. The mechanism is as follows.

Let $A_0, ...A_n$ be the attributes and $\Omega_0, ..., \Omega_n$ their respective domains. Ω_R denotes policy domain. Let $\mathbf{Q}$ denote a closed query, i.e. $\mathbf{Q} = (a_0, ..., a_n), a_i \in \Omega_i, i = 0, ..., n$. Suppose the optimal KBM2L list has been achieved with respect to base $B = (A_0, ...A_n)$ and $\mathbf{w}$ is its respective weight vector. If this list has h items, then the list is $< q_0, r_0| < q_1, r_1| \cdots < q_h, r_h|$, where $0 \leq q_i \leq w_0 D_0 - 1, q_i < q_{i+1} \forall i$ (offsets), $r_i \in \Omega_R, r_i \neq r_{i+1} \forall i$ (policies). The response retrieval procedure (task (C) above) consists of projecting $\mathbf{Q}$ into the offset space $\{0, 1, ..., w_0 D_0 - 1\}$ and deriving its policy from the KBM2L list. Namely, if $\langle \cdot, \cdot \rangle$ denotes scalar product, we compute $\langle \mathbf{Q}, \mathbf{w} \rangle = f(\mathbf{Q}) = q$, and whenever $q \in (q_{i-1}, q_i]$ it implies that the response is r_i.

If r_i is unknown, then an efficient solution is to call the influence diagram evaluation and solve the respective subproblem that makes r_i known.

Finally, response r_i displayed by the system to the expert may be completed by asking for an explanation. The expert is not only interested in knowing which is the best recommendation for a certain case, but also in concise, consistent explanations of why it is optimal, hopefully, translated into her own domain language. Explanations are also useful as a sensitivity analysis tool for validating the DSS. Explanations are constructed via two clearly different parts of the indices an item represents. The first part is the *fixed* (constant) part of the indices. The fact that these components take the same value for the respective attributes somehow *explains* why the policy is also the same. Therefore, the set of attributes of the fixed part can be interpreted as the explanation of the policy. The second part, complementary to the first, is the *variable* part: the records do not share the same values and, therefore, the attributes are unimportant information for the item policy [4].

5 Open Queries

We have seen that the expert is an agent interested in the optimal policy for the decision-making problem and she queries the system. Expert and DSS have a dialogue consisting of queries, responses and explanations. For closed queries, the expert receives definite and accurate responses. For open queries, this task is harder due to expert imprecision. Not all attributes are instantiated. Possible reasons may be the unreliability of some attribute values, missing knowledge, their high extraction cost or simply an interest in making a complex query concerning the whole ranges of (some) attributes. For example, in medical settings, the physician often has access to administrative data like sex, age, etc., but may have no access to (or confidence) attributes like the first treatment received or some test results. Also, she may be interested in asking for all possible patient weight intervals. Thus, an open query is, e.g. $OQ = (*, a_1, *, ..., a_n)$, where $*$ denotes non-instantiated attribute values.

In principle, the DSS looks up the respective KBM2L list elements and retrieves the optimal policy (or policies) to be presented to the user as the response. Suppose, as above, that the optimal KBM2L list has been achieved with respect to base $B = (A_0, ...A_n)$ and the query is open with respect to attributes i and j, i.e., the query is $OQ = (a_0, a_1, ..., *_i, ..., *_j, ..., a_n)$. Actually, OQ is a set of closed queries Q_i, namely,

$$OQ = \{(a_0, a_1, ..., x, ..., y, ..., a_n) : x \in \Omega_i, y \in \Omega_j\} = \bigcup_{i=1}^{D_i \times D_j} Q_i.$$

Then, the response retrieval procedure would consist of applying the technique described in Section 4 to each Q_i, computing $\langle Q_i, w \rangle = f(Q_i) = p_i$, to give an offset set $P = \{p_1, p_2, ..., p_{D_i \times D_j}\}$, with the respective responses $S = \{s_1, s_2, ..., s_{D_i \times D_j}\}$.

There exist four possible situations: (i) all s_i are equal and known; (ii) all s_i are equal but unknown; (iii) there are at least two different values among s_i's and they are known; (iv) there are at least two different values among s_i's but some s_i's are unknown. *Situation (i)* implies an accurate response (s_i) and the DSS does not require additional interaction with the expert. The remaining situations involve various possible responses and/or uncertain responses requiring a refinement to be helpful for the expert. It is here that tasks (D) and (E) pointed out in Section 3 play an important role.

The information for the expert comprises two sets P and S, jointly involving simple KB records. They have been extracted from the optimal base. Note that base is the best base for the *whole KB*, both minimising storage requirements and maximising knowledge explanation performance. Notwithstanding, this base may not be useful with respect to the *part* of the KB concerning the open query.

Attribute weight changes depending on its position within a base, and the further to the right the position, the smaller the weight is. We propose moving query open attributes towards positions to the right. The query is the same, but its attribute order implies working in a new base, with open attributes moved towards the smallest weight positions. From a semantic viewpoint, this movement also agrees with the idea of consigning open attributes to less important positions as the query seems to indicate, that is, the expert has not assigned a value to and does not show a significant interest in these attributes. The new base will be called *operative* base, which gives an operative KBM2L. There are several possible operative bases, all of which are valid. We can choose the base leading to less computational effort when changing the base and transposing the knowledge, after trying a few bases in linear time.

A base change may be interpreted as a change in the query and response points of view. For the DSS, the optimal base represents a good organisation of the whole KB content. For the expert, the operative base provides an organised view of the responses to her open query, as consecutive records. This base will be optimal for explaining the responses. It illustrates how a query may be difficult in one base and easier in another base. It bears a resemblance to human domains, where a query is simple for an expert but hard for non-experts. An expert has a good problem description: a good conceptual model, few relevant facts, and a good information organisation that allows fact analysis and explanation. Indeed, this is why she is an expert.

Now, working on the operative base, new offset set P' will include consecutive p_i''s and we can introduce some rules based on distances in the offset space to make more accurate recommendations to the expert.

Situation (ii) may seem surprising since the DSS is asked for something which is unknown, because the associated subproblems have not been evaluated. Nevertheless, we will try to provide a solution. Specifically, situation (ii) may be solved by predicting that the response is associated with the nearest offset to P' based on the Euclidean distance in the offset space, i.e. in $\{0, 1, ..., w_0 D_0 - 1\}$, as follows. Let p^l, p^u be the minimum and maximum offsets, respectively, included in P'. Suppose q^l is the maximum offset with known policy (say r) that precedes p^l in the operative KBM2L list. Likewise, q^u is the minimum offset with known policy (say s) that follows p^u in the operative KBM2L list. All records that match (p', s), with $p' \in P', s \in S$, belong to the same item in the operative KBM2L list, while, offsets q^l and q^u are located at its adjoining items. Then, we compute $d_1 = |p^l - q^l|$ and $d_2 = |p^u - q^u|$. If $d_1 < d_2$, then the response is r; otherwise the response is s.

Situation (iii) presents different policy values in S. We may give an immediate answer to the expert based on statistics over the policy value distribution (median, mode, etc.). However, more intelligent responses will be preferred. As a first proposal, let us call it Algorithm $\mathcal{A}1$, the DSS asks the expert to instantiate the open attribute further to the left with respect to the optimal base. It will be the most efficient attribute for reducing response uncertainty. That is, it will have the greatest weight among all the open attributes, implying more likelihood of belonging to the fixed part of the item indices, which is what explains a fixed policy. Thus, the further to the left the attribute, the more likely the query is to lead to less responses that are different. If necessary, then, the instantiation of the second further to the left open attribute would be requested, and so on. This approach will fit problems with many attributes but with few open attributes.

For many open attributes, say more than 10, we have enough information to make automatic inferences via a learning process. Thus, we propose focusing once again on the operative KBM2L records of interest and learning the probabilistic relationships among the attributes *and* the policy from these records. The structure to be learnt is a Bayesian network (BN) (see e.g. [10]), as it has a clear semantics for performing many inference tasks necessary for intelligent systems (diagnosis, explanation, learning...). Then, the resulting structure will provide a basis for starting a DSS/expert dialogue to lend insight into the problem and refine the query in the light of new evidence until the response satisfies the expert.

For the sake of simplicity, let $\mathbf{X} \subset \mathcal{R}^{n_1}, \mathbf{Y} \subset \mathcal{R}^{n_2}, n_1 + n_2 = n$ denote, respectively, instantiated and non-instantiated attributes of the query. Our Algorithm $\mathcal{A}2$ follows the steps:

S0. Initialise $\mathbf{X}^0 = \mathbf{X}, \mathbf{Y}^0 = \mathbf{Y}$

S1. DSS extracts data (records) matching $\mathbf{X}^0$ from the operative KBM2L

S2. DSS learns a BN from data (structure and conditional probabilities)

S3. DSS computes $P(R = r | \mathbf{X}^0), \forall r \in \Omega_R$ on the BN. Expert fixes a decision criterion, usually a distribution mode, to choose among r's. Let m^0 be this value. It will be evidence to be propagated through the network.

S4. DSS computes $P(Y_j = y | R = m^0, \mathbf{X}^0), \forall j = 1, ..., n_2, \forall y \in \Omega_{Y_j}$ on the BN. Expert fixes a decision criterion, usually minimum variance, to choose among Y_j's. Let $\widetilde{\mathbf{Y}}^0$ be the resulting vector of Y_j's, with coordinates given by expert instantiations, like e.g., the Y_j mode.

S5. Extend vector $\mathbf{X}^0$ as $\mathbf{X}^1 = \mathbf{X}^0 \cup \widetilde{\mathbf{Y}}^0$. Set $\mathbf{Y}^1 = \mathbf{Y}^0 \setminus \widetilde{\mathbf{Y}}^0$.

Steps *S3* and *S4* are repeated until the expert is satisfied or $\mathbf{Y}^j$ has few components and Algorithm $\mathcal{A}1$ is called to continue. If the algorithm stops at $\mathbf{X}^j$, then m^j is the response returned. The expert can always revise decisions made at *S3* and *S4* of the last iteration whenever she does not agree with the current outputs. Moreover, the DSS will be on the watch for and warn the expert about probabilities conditioned to impossible events (registered in the DSS).

A BN (see a review in [2]) is learned in Step *S2* via a structure learning algorithm, where the K2 algorithm [3] is the standard. K2 is a greedy parent search algorithm using a Bayesian score to rank different structures. Thus, an ordering on the nodes is assumed, and for each node, K2 returns its most probable parents given the data. The algorithm works on quite reasonable data sizes, as in the context we propose. Indeed, we may even have quite large sizes, requiring a sample to be used to be computationally tractable.

Expert decision criteria at Steps *S3* and *S4* might be different. They are expert choices. With the suggested criteria: (a) at Step *S3*, we choose the most likely response given the instantiated attribute set for the query; and (b) at Step *S4*, we choose the attribute(s) in which we have more confidence or the attribute(s) wiggling less than a fixed threshold. Then, they are instantiated in the query as their mode, giving rise to a new, more accurate, query. Posterior steps allow continuous probability updating.

The DSS talks via the BN and its probabilities, giving, firstly, information about the response and, secondly, about the likelihood of each open attribute, given the response chosen by the expert. This support for both responses and queries allows the expert to re-state and improve her query until it is more defined, leading to more accurate answers. This is task (E) mentioned above.

Situation (iv) also presents different policy values in S, some of which, however, may be unknown. Unknown policies are the result of having a system that can legitimately be termed knowledge based, due to its significant size [6], with the impossibility of being completely solved. The expert plays an important role in deciding which part of the problem should be solved, suggesting which is the core she is interested in. As a consequence, her queries are likely to bear on this core, thus having a known response. Thus, situation (iv) can be solved like situation (iii), trying to avoid unknown policies via, e.g. Algorithm $\mathcal{A}1$.

6   Example from a Medical DSS

Open queries and the respective responses and explanations are the basic dialogue elements in the expert/DSS interaction. We now describe how the dialogue is developed in typical sessions. Our decision-making problem concerns a doctor who has to make a decision about a patient admission and two possible therapy actions [4,1], i.e. three alternatives: r_0: no admission, r_1: 12-hours observation, r_2: 12-hours phototherapy. The decision table has 12 attributes, see Table 1, and $82,944$ records. The optimal base is $B = (A_0, A_1, ..., A_{11})$, with respective weights $\mathbf{w} = (27648, 13824, 6912, 3456, 1152, 576, 192, 64, 16, 8, 4, 1)$. Our KB has $1,656$ items distributed over $27,736$ known records and $55,208$ unknown records. Each query will be coded according to the optimal base order.

Table 1. Attributes and domains

Attributes	Domains
Concentration of Bilirubin(A_0)	Normal(0), Pathological(1), VeryPathol.(2)
Child's(A_1) & Mother's(A_9) Rh	Negative(0), Positive(1) Factor
Primiparous?(A_2)	Primiparous(0), Multiparous(1)
Delivery with Instruments?(A_3)	Natural(0), Instrumental(1)
MotherAge(A_4)	15-18(0), 19-35(1), >35(2)
Child(A_5) & Mother(A_{10}) Coombs'	Negative(0), Positive(1) Test
5MinApgarTest(A_6)	0-3(0), 4-7(1), 8-10(2) level
Concentration of Hemoglobin(A_7)	Normal(0), Pathological(1), VeryPathol.(2)
BirthWeight(A_8)	0.5-1.0(0), 1.0-1.5(1), 1.5-2.5(2), >2.5(3) kg
Jaundice(A_{11}) Yellow(Y) skin	Normal(0), Y.(1), Y.-Feet(2), Pumpkin-Y.(3)

Situation (i): doctor queries $(0,0,0,0,0,0,1,0,*,*,*,*)$, with four open attributes on the right-hand side, thus coinciding the optimal and operative bases. The response is that r_1 is the optimal policy. Its explanation is the index fixed part of the corresponding item, that is, A_0 is $0,\ldots,A_7$ is 0, see Table 2.

Situation (ii): doctor queries $(0,0,0,0,0,1,2,0,3,*,*,*)$. In this case, the response and its explanation are not available (NA) as the query covers only unknown responses, see Table 2. Then, the closest offsets with known responses are found. It follows that $q^l = 447, q^u = 1151$, both with policy r_1. Hence, $d_1 = 561, d_2 = 128$, and the response is r_1. q^u is located at an item with 64 records, from offset 1151 to offset 1215. The index fixed part of this item is $(0,1,2,3,4,5,6,7)$, with values $(0,0,0,0,1,0,0,0)$, which is the r_1 explanation.

Table 2. Query details for situations (i), (ii), (iii) and (iv)

	Situation (i)	Situation (ii)
open query	$(0,0,0,0,0,0,1,0,*,*,*,*)$	$(0,0,0,0,0,1,2,0,3,*,*,*)$
min index	$(0,0,0,0,0,0,1,0,0,0,0,0)$	$(0,0,0,0,0,1,2,0,3,0,0,0)$
max index	$(0,0,0,0,0,0,1,0,3,1,1,3)$	$(0,0,0,0,0,1,2,0,3,1,1,3)$
p^l, p^u offsets	192, 255	1008, 1023
fixed part	$(0,\ldots,7)$	NA explanation
response	r_1	unknown

	Situation (iii)	Situation (iv)
open query	$(0,0,1,0,1,1,*,*,*,*,*,*)$	$(0,0,0,0,0,0,0,*,*,*,*,*)$
min index	$(0,0,1,0,1,1,0,0,0,0,0,0)$	$(0,0,0,0,0,0,0,0,0,0,0,0)$
max index	$(0,0,1,0,1,1,2,2,3,1,1,3)$	$(0,0,0,0,0,0,0,2,3,1,1,3)$
p^l, p^u offsets	8640, 9215	0, 191
fixed part	$(0,\ldots,3)$ for r_1	$(0,\ldots,7)$ for r_1
	$(0,\ldots,4)$ for r_2	NA explanation for unknown
response	r_1 or r_2	r_1 or unknown

Situation (iii): doctor queries $(0,0,1,0,1,1,*,*,*,*,*,*)$, with six open attributes, see Table 2. There are two possible responses, each one with its own explanation. Algorithms $\mathcal{A}1$ or $\mathcal{A}2$ could be called.

For $\mathcal{A}1$, the DSS suggests the doctor to instantiate one of the six open attributes, being A_6 an efficient attribute to start with, as it is further to the left. If it is not possible, doctor would be asked for $A_7, \ldots, A_{11}$ values, in this order, trying to minimise the current alternative set size. In this case, doctor says A_6 is 0, and the DSS answers r_2 is the optimal policy. With only one policy, the session ends. The explanation is $(0,0,1,0,1)$, see Table 2.

Situation (iv): doctor queries $(0,0,0,0,0,0,0,*,*,*,*,*)$. The possible responses are r_1 or unknown, see Table 2. To apply $\mathcal{A}1$, the requested attribute order would be $A_7, \ldots, A_{11}$. Doctor says A_7 is 0, DSS answers r_1, and the session ends. The explanation is $(0,0,0,0,0,0,0,0)$, see Table 2.

We only illustrate Algorithm $\mathcal{A}2$ for situation (iii), since the record set involved by the open query in situation (iv) is too small so as to learn a BN. Situation (iii) query involves more than 500 records. The K2 algorithm was embedded in our main program that manages KBM2L lists. Probability calculi were carried out with Hugin Expert Software [7], once our output was exported to Hugin input format. The BN has a naive-Bayes structure, with the five explanation nodes (from A_0 to A_4) directed to the policy node. The BN gives probabilities $0, 0.014, 0.986$ to r_0, r_1 and r_2, respectively, given the data. Doctor chooses the mode, i.e. $m^0 = r_2$, with explanation $(0,0,1,0,1)$ as above. The session ends as doctor is satisfied, not requiring the $\widetilde{\mathbf{Y}}^0$ computation.

7   Conclusions and Further Research

One of the most important DSS facilities is to answer user queries. We have proposed a query system based on the KBM2L framework. Information is efficiently accessed and retrieved to construct the response. The optimal and operative bases allow the records involved in a query to be organised from different perspectives. General queries leading to imprecise responses are addressed via an attributes/policy relationship learning process, where the interaction with the expert is required to arrive at a satisfactory response, with lower uncertainty. Our approach provides the KB definite exploitation for the DSS since queries, responses and explanations are properly performed.

Despite the power of our iterative scheme of progressive knowledge elicitation, future research might focus on allowing queries with constrained rather than non-instantiated attributes, covering initial beliefs about the attributes. Also, more effort could be employed in determining good operative bases if there is more than one. Two criteria could be: minimum computational effort to obtain the new KBM2L and minimum item fragmentation. Finally, rather than directly allowing the expert to choose a decision criterion in Algorithm $\mathcal{A}2$, we could previously implement a search within the tree of possible sessions, i.e. possible r-y-r-$y \cdots$ (response r and instantiated attributes y) sequences. This would filter possibilities that will not satisfy expert expectations, facilitating her choices.

References

1. Bielza, C., Gómez, M., Ríos-Insua, S., Fdez del Pozo, J.A.: Structural, Elicitation and Computational Issues Faced when Solving Complex Decision Making Problems with Influence Diagrams. Comp. & Oper. Res. **27** (2000) 725–740
2. Buntine, W.L.: A Guide to the Literature on Learning Probabilistic Networks from Data. IEEE Trans. on Knowledge and Data Engin. **8** (1996) 195–210
3. Cooper, G.F., Herskovits, E.: A Bayesian Method for the Induction of Probabilistic Networks from Data. Machine Learning **9** (1992) 309–347
4. Fernández Pozo, J.A., Bielza, C., Gómez, M.: Knowledge Organisation in a Neonatal Jaundice DSS. In: Crespo, J., Maojo, V., Martín, F. (eds.): Medical Data Analysis. Lecture Notes in Computer Science, Vol. 2199. Springer, Berlin (2001) 88–94
5. Fernández del Pozo, J.A., Bielza, C., Gómez, M.: Heuristics for Multivariate Knowledge Synthesis. Technical Report #3-UPM. (2002)
6. Henrion, M., Breese, J.S., Horvitz, E.J.: Decision Analysis and Expert Systems. Artif. Intell. Magazine **12** (1991) 64–91
7. Hugin Expert Software: http://www.hugin.com

8. Knuth, D.E.: The Art of Computer Programming, Vol. 1: Fundamental Algorithms. Addison-Wesley, Reading (1968)
9. Martinez, C., Panholzer, A., Prodinger, H.: Partial Match Queries in Relaxed Multidimensional Search Trees. Algorithmica **29** (2001) 181–204
10. Pearl, J.: Probabilistic Reasoning in Intelligent Systems. Morgan Kaufmann, San Mateo CA (1988)
11. Shachter, R.D.: Evaluating Influence Diagrams. Oper. Res. **34** (1986) 871–882

Integration of Fault Detection and Diagnosis in a Probabilistic Logic Framework

Luis E. Garza[1], Francisco Cantú[1], and Salvador Acevedo[2]

Center for Artificial Intelligence[1], Department of Electrical Engineering[2]
Monterrey Institute of Technology
CETEC Tower, 5th floor, 2501 Garza Sada Avenue
Monterrey, NL, 64849, Mexico
Phone: (+52-8) 328-4197, Fax: (+52-8) 328-4189
{legarza,fcantu,sacevedo}@campus.mty.itesm.mx

Abstract. In this paper we formalize an approach to detect and diagnose faults in dynamic industrial processes using a probabilistic and logic multiagent framework. We use and adapt the Dynamic Independent Choice Logic (DICL) for detection and diagnosis tasks. We specialize DICL by introducing two types of agents: the alarm processor agent, that is a logic program that provides reasoning about discrete observations, and the fault detection agent that allows the diagnostic system to reason about continuous data. In our framework we integrate artificial intelligence model-based diagnosis with fault detection and isolation, a technique used by the control systems community. The whole diagnosis task is performed in two phases: in first phase, the alarm processor agent reasons with definite symptoms and produces a subset of suspicious components. In second phase, fault detection agents analyze continuous data of suspicious components, in order to discriminate between faulty and non-faulty components. Our approach is suitable to diagnose large processes with discrete and continuous observations, nonlinear dynamics, noise and missing information.

Keywords: Reasoning models; Uncertainty management; intelligent agents

1 Introduction

In any industrial process or system real faults are masked by dozens of symptoms, which are really a cascaded effect of the major faults. The intrinsic uncertainty in the information requires an intelligent system, to interpret the data and diagnose the abnormal components of the process.

In recent years much research has been devoted to the diagnosis of industrial processes. Most of the industrial implementations of diagnostic systems focus on either qualitative or quantitative techniques. The first, although perform well with definite observations, are weak to analyze continuous observations (e.g. sensors readings). The quantitative techniques focus on the analysis of continuous

F.J. Garijo, J.C. Riquelme, and M. Toro (Eds.): IBERAMIA 2002, LNAI 2527, pp. 265–274, 2002.
© Springer-Verlag Berlin Heidelberg 2002

data and have weak inference engines for discrete data. They normally include mathematical models that are hard to obtain for many processes. This make quantitative approaches very difficult to use in real systems.

Other fault diagnosis methods based on neural networks and fuzzy logic, have both their own limitations. Neural networks represent black box models that do not provide more relevant information than the one contained in the output. In neural networks is also difficult to integrate knowledge from other sources. Fuzzy-based approaches can not deal with missing information in explicit form, and the overall dimension of rules, may blow up strongly even for small components or processes.

The nature of industrial processes, composed of both, discrete and continuous data, suggests the use of hybrid diagnostic engines. Additionally, the diagnostic system has to be able to handle noise, nonlinearities and missing information.

In this paper we show how to make a structured integration of FDI techniques [3], with artificial intelligence model-based diagnosis, within the probabilistic logic framework given by the Dynamic Independent Choice Logic. To analyze discrete signals we are using a model-based diagnosis approach. Model-based diagnosis is based on the fact that a component is faulty if its correct behavior, given by a stored model, is inconsistent with the observations. To deal with continuous signals, we use a fault detection and isolation (FDI) approach, commonly used by the control systems community, that includes dynamic probabilistic models. We have substituted the FDI classical models, such as differential equations or ARMA models, with dynamic probabilistic models, in order to deal with noisy, highly non-linear models, possibly with missing data inputs. These models have simple structure and inference engine, and provide a good approximation to the real signals. A main characteristic of our models, is that we learn the structure (causal model), and the parameters (Lagrange coefficients), from raw data without any preprocessing stage. The raw data may include noise and missing data. The probabilistic models have an accuracy enough to allow the discrimination between the steady state of the process and different mode faults. We apply our method in a simulated industrial-strength power transmission network.

2   Description of the Approach

The main relevant aspects of our approach are:

1. We adopt as a diagnostic strategy, the repair-man perspective [11], where the aim of the diagnostic search is the location of the root-cause of the disturbance. Once the affected area is located by using a set of initial observations, more specific information is analyzed (e.g. sensor signals) to isolate the abnormal components.
2. We modularize the fault detection and diagnosis tasks with the introduction of agents. In our approach, there are three types of agents: *Nature* is regarded as an agent that provides stochastic assumptions about components

behavior. The *Alarm Processor* (AP) agent produces a set of explanations consistent with first observed symptoms. *Fault Detection* (FD) agents associated to every component in the process, are modeled as dynamic agents specifying how streams of sensor data entail fault decisions. The output of the AP agent represents a partial diagnosis to be confirmed by FD agents (see figure 1).

3. The signals produced by sensors located in the candidate components of the system, are analyzed by FD agents. Every component has and FD agent that represents a transduction from inputs (the sensor values) into outputs (the fault/no-fault decision). Transductions represent an abstraction of dynamic systems.

4. The fault detection agent incorporates a predictive causal model, representing the no-fault behavior of the component. The model structure is generated from steady-state data, with a Bayesian learning algorithm. This model includes the temporal relationships between process signals. The model delivers a probability distribution over the forecast variable states, computed with a maximum entropy classifier algorithm.

5. The FD agent compares the one-step ahead prediction of the no-fault model and the stream of data provided by the sensors. The residual analysis gives an indication of the component behavior (normal/abnormal).

6. The logic programs representing the agents, are axiomatized in *phase space* [2] in a similar manner to the event calculus.

7. The specification for a FD agent is not evaluated as a logic program that needs to do arbitrary computation reasoning about the past. We know the data from sensors have been already received, and the reasoning about the fault decision depends on the processing of the received inputs.

8. We use the Dynamic Independent Choice Logic (DICL) [9], with a discrete time structure, as the framework to develop the fault detection and diagnosis approach. We benefit from the compact knowledge representation of logic, the handling of uncertainty with probabilities, the modularization capabilities, and the ability to represent temporal relations of the DICL.

3   Representation

The dynamic independent choice logic is a theory built upon a general model of agents interacting in an environment [9]. We assume a discrete time structure $\mathcal{T}$, that is totally ordered and has a metric over intervals. A *trace* is a function from $\mathcal{T}$ into some domain $\mathcal{A}$. A *transduction* is a function from input traces into output traces, that is causal in the sense that the output at time t can only depend in inputs at times t' where $t' \leq t$. An agent is a specification of a transduction. A *state* is the information that needs to be remembered in order for the output to be a function of the state and the current inputs.

We modify slightly the definition of a dynamic ICL stated in [9], to introduce the diagnostic dynamic independent choice logic (DDICL) [4]:

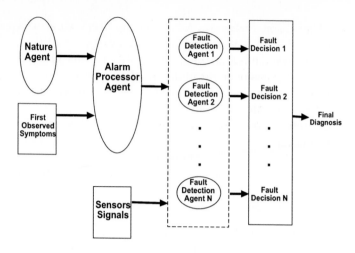

Fig. 1. Agents based Diagnosis

Definition 1. A **diagnostic dynamic independent choice logic theory** (DDICL) is a tuple $\langle \mathcal{A}, \mathcal{C}_0, \mathcal{F}_{AP}, \mathcal{P}_0, \mathcal{ASM}_a \rangle$, where

- $\mathcal{A}$ is a finite set of agents containing three types of agents: *Nature*, *Alarm Processor*, and *Fault Detection* agents,
- $\mathcal{C}_0$, **Nature's choice space**, is a choice space with alternatives controlled by nature,
- $\mathcal{F}_{AP}$, is the logic program specification for the Alarm Processor agent. This agent generates a set of explanations consistent with first observed symptoms.
- $\mathcal{P}_0$ is a function $\bigcup \mathcal{C}_0 \to [0,1]$ such that $\forall \chi \in \mathcal{C}_0 \ \sum_{\alpha \in \chi} \mathcal{P}_0(\alpha) = 1$,
- $\mathcal{ASM}_a$ is a function on $\mathcal{A} - 0 - AP$ such that $\mathcal{ASM}_a$ is an agent specification module for Fault Detection agent a.

We extend the definition for an *Agent Specification Module* (definition 2.1 given in [8]) with the notion of *probabilistic observation function*, to specify a fault detection agent:

Definition 2. An agent specification module for FD agent $a \neq \{0, AP\}$, written $\mathcal{ASM}_a$, is a tuple $\langle \mathcal{I}, \mathcal{O}, \mathcal{R}, \mathcal{L}, \mathcal{F}_a, \phi \rangle$ where

- $\mathcal{I}$ is a set of fluents called the **inputs**. They specify what sensor values are available at various times. The range the input trace is the cross product of the ranges of the fluents in the inputs.
- $\mathcal{O}$, is a set of fluents called the **outputs**. An output is a propositional fluent that specifies a decision about the existence of a fault in a component at various times.
- $\mathcal{R}$, is a set of fluents called the **recallable** fluents. These are fluents whose previous values can be recalled.

- $\mathcal{L}$, is as set of fluents called the **local** fluents. These are fluents that are neither inputs, outputs nor recallable.
- $\mathcal{F}_a$ is an acyclic logic program. $\mathcal{F}_a$ specifies how the outputs are implied by the inputs, and perhaps previous values of the recallable fluents, local fluents, arithmetic constraints and other non-temporal relations as intermediaries.
- ϕ, is the **probabilistic observation function**, $\phi : Q \rightarrow \mathcal{P}_V$, mapping observation states into a distribution over predicted states.

In this paper we emphasize the description of the fault detection agents. The details about the alarm processor agent can be found in [4].

3.1 Dynamics Modeling

The specification for an FD agent, makes use of probabilistic functions as a means of modeling the steady-state dynamics of sensor measurements. The sensor measurements are discretized in fixed bins. The model represents the no-fault behavior of the associated component.

To implement the function ϕ, we developed a forecast modeling approach [4], with the statistical inference engine based on the maximum entropy principle [13] (see figure 2). The steady state causal models (structure and parameters) are learned offline from discretized process data. When a stream of sensor data needs to be analyzed, the inference engine provides a probability distribution over discrete states of the sensor variable. The probabilistic inference amounts to the computation of:

$$P[V = v|Q = q] = \frac{exp\left(\sum_{i=1}^{N} \gamma(Q_i = q_i, V = v)\right)}{\sum_{v'=1}^{K} exp\left(\sum_{i=1}^{N} \gamma(Q_i = q_i, V = v')\right)} \tag{1}$$

where

- Q is a finite nonempty set of observation states,
- V is a finite nonempty set of predicted states.

The subset of Lagrange multipliers $\{\gamma(Q_i = q_i, V = v), i = 1, \ldots, N, q_i = 1, \ldots, |A_i|, v = 1, \ldots, K\}$ are learned in an offline manner with a deterministic annealing algorithm.

Equation 1 is an approximate solution based on the method proposed by Cheeseman to find the maximum entropy joint probability mass function (pmf) consistent with arbitrary lower order probability constraints. The method by Yan and Miller uses a restriction of joint pmf support (during learning) to a subset of the feature space (training set support). The small size of the training set support maintains the learning times quite tractable.

The comparison between the prediction given by the sensor steady state model and the stream of data, delivers a set of residuals that provide information about possible faulty modes.

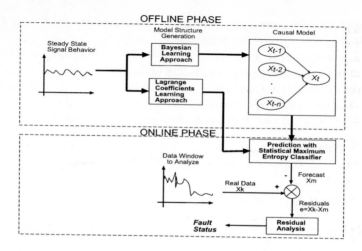

Fig. 2. Structure of a Fault Detection Agent

3.2 Temporal Logic Definitions

We specify FD agents with acyclic logic programs and predicates that explicitly refer to time. The acyclicity corresponds to temporal ordering (if t_1 and t_2 are time points and $t_1 < t_2$, then the acyclic index for t_1 is lower than acyclic index for t_2). Every temporal predicate refers to the value of a fluent in a given time point. A *fluent* is a function that depends on time.

Every fault detection agent has a local time scale, what give us the ability to represent the different dynamics in large processes.

To recall the past values of fluents, we extend the version of temporal predicates defined in [8], to allow the recalling of values beyond previous time point (values of fluent Fl at time point $t - n$, where $n > 1$) :

was(Fl, Val, T_n, T) is a predicate that specifies that recallable fluent Fl was assigned value Val at time T_n.

$$was(Fl, Val, T_n, T) \leftarrow time(T_n) \wedge T_n < T \wedge set(Fl, Val, T_n) \wedge$$
$$\sim reset\_before(Fl, T_n, T).$$

where $reset\_before(Fl, T_n, T)$ is true if fluent Fl was assigned a value in the interval (T_n, T):

$$reset\_before(Fl, T_n, T) \leftarrow time(T_2) \wedge T_n < T_2 \wedge T_2 < T \wedge$$
$$set(Fl, Val2, T_2).$$

now(Fl, Val, T) is a predicate that specifies that recallable fluent Fl has value Val at time T.

$$now(Fl, Val, T) \leftarrow set(Fl, Val, T).$$
$$now(Fl, Val, T) \leftarrow \sim \exists V_1 set(Fl, V_1, T) \wedge was(Fl, Val, T_1, T).$$

$set(Fl, Val, T_n)$ is a predicate that specifies that recallable fluent Fl has value Val at time T. This predicate implements the reading of sensor values received up to the time of failure.

$time(T)$ specify that T corresponds to a point in a discrete, linear time scale.

4   Example

We show the details of our method with a small power network (see figure 3). This network, represents the interconnection of the different components. The *buses* are nodes where industrial or domestic users are connected. The *lines* allows the transference of electrical power between *buses*. The *breakers* help to isolate a fault event from the rest of the network.

The breakers are the main protection for one bus and the backup protection for the bus at the other end of the line. For instance, breaker *Br12*, is the main protection for *bus 1* and the backup protection for *bus 2*. This scheme of backup protection allows the isolation of a fault, even in the case of a malfunction in the main breaker.

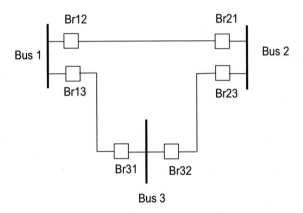

Fig. 3. Single line diagram of a small power network

We assume the buses (nodes) are the only source of faults and there is only one type of fault (e.g., three phase-to-ground fault). The fault persists during the time span of the diagnosis. The first symptoms are the alarms indicating the status of protection breakers (e.g., *open* or *failed to open*). There is also a possibility that the status of some breakers is unknown.

We axiomatise this as follows:

Nature's Alternatives C_0

$$C_0 = \{bus1(faulted) : 0.01,$$
$$bus1(ok) : 0.99, bus2(faulted) : 0.02,$$

$$bus2(ok) : 0.98, bus3(faulted) : 0.025,$$
$$bus3(ok) : 0.975\}$$
$$\{c\_br12\_open(open, faulted, ok) : 0.99, \ldots,$$
$$c\_br32\_open(open, faulted, faulted) : 0.98\}$$

Alarm Processor Facts $\mathcal{F}_{AP}$.

$br12(StBr) \leftarrow bus1(Stbus1) \wedge bus2(Stbus2) \wedge c\_br12\_open(StBr, Stbus1, Stbus2)$
$br21(StBr) \leftarrow bus2(Stbus2) \wedge bus1(Stbus1) \wedge c\_br21\_open(StBr, Stbus2, Stbus1)$
$br13(StBr) \leftarrow bus1(Stbus1) \wedge bus3(Stbus3) \wedge c\_br13\_open(StBr, Stbus1, Stbus3)$
$br31(StBr) \leftarrow bus3(Stbus3) \wedge bus1(Stbus1) \wedge c\_br31\_open(StBr, Stbus3, Stbus1)$
$br23(StBr) \leftarrow bus2(Stbus2) \wedge bus3(Stbus3) \wedge c\_br23\_open(StBr, Stbus2, Stbus3)$
$br32(StBr) \leftarrow bus3(Stbus3) \wedge bus2(Stbus2) \wedge c\_br32\_open(StBr, Stbus3, Stbus2)$

All the axiomatisation above refers to the same time T_a, when the alarms where received (ignoring small delays). For this reason T_a was omitted from the clauses.

FD Agent Module
Agent Facts $\mathcal{F}_{bus1}$.

$$val(Voltage\_bus1\_model, V_{b1}^{m}, T) \leftarrow was(Voltage\_bus1\_real, V_{b1}^{R1}, T-1, T) \wedge$$
$$was(Voltage\_bus1\_real, V_{b1}^{R5}, T-5, T) \wedge$$
$$c\_voltage\_bus1\_model(V_{b1}^{m}, V_{b1}^{R1}, V_{b1}^{R5})$$
$$val(Residual\_Voltage\_bus1, R_{Vb1}, T) \leftarrow now(Voltage\_bus1\_model, V_{b1}^{m}, T) \wedge$$
$$now(Voltage\_bus1\_real, V_{b1}^{R}, T) \wedge$$
$$R_{Vb1} = V_{b1}^{m} - V_{b1}^{R}$$
$$fault\_bus1(yes, T) \leftarrow now(Residual\_voltage\_bus1, R_{Vb1}, T) \wedge$$
$$R_{Vb1} > \lambda_{Vb1}$$
$$fault\_bus1(no, T) \leftarrow now(Residual\_voltage\_bus1, R_{Vb1}, T) \wedge$$
$$R_{Vb1} < \lambda_{Vb1}$$

We omit the specification for the fault detection agents at *bus 2* and *bus 3*, because is similar to the above presented.

The stream of data received from voltage sensors, starts at T_i and ends at T_f. We assume nothing regarding the frequency of data sampling as long as we can distinguish between normal and abnormal behavior, analyzing the data. The only assumption is that $T_i < T_a < T_f$, that is the voltage sensors data are related to the alarms received. This allow us to represent different time scales in each fault detection agent.

The structure of the predictive causal model for the variable voltage of component *bus*1, was generated offline from steady-state data, with a suitable Bayesian learning algorithm (we use the algorithm given in [1]). In this case the output of the algorithm delivers that fluent $Voltage\_bus1\_model$ depends on past observations of fluent $Voltage\_bus1\_real$ at times $T - 1$ and $T - 5$. The stochastic part of the agent is achieved by the function

$$\phi \quad c\_voltage\_bus1\_model(V_{b1}^m, V_{b1}^{R1}, V_{b1}^{R5})$$

that maps the set of past observations $\{V_{b1}^{R1}, V_{b1}^{R5}\}$ to V_{b1}^m.

We have applied our approach in a simulated industrial-scale electrical power network. The estimation of the fault location is difficult due to the presence of multiple faults, the overwhelming number of alarms generated, and the possibility of malfunction of protective devices.

The simulated electrical power network has 24 buses, 34 lines and 68 breakers. We have tested our approach with multiple events, multiple types of faults and missing information on sensors. More details are given in [5]. The accuracy of our method to identify the real faulted components was higher than 70 %.

5   Related Work

The concept of diagnosis agents in technical processes was applied in [7]. In Lauber's work, the agent is based on a dynamic Bayesian network (DBN) for reasoning over time. The structure of the DBN was built with reliability engineering methods (e.g. failure mode and effects analysis). Our agents handle the dynamics of the environment with a more general class of dynamic networks (i.e. We allow non-Markovian forecast models), whose structure was built with algorithms that learn Bayesian networks. HybridDX [10] is a diagnostic system used in aeronautics, that include model-based diagnosis and continuous and discrete simulations of continuous processes. To model the dynamics in HybridDX, they use physical causal models that are frequently not known in analytical form or too complicated for calculations. In [12], Sampath presents a hybrid approach that incorporates the concept of virtual sensors and discrete events diagnosis. The analysis of sensor signals is performed by using different techniques, such as spectral analysis, principal components analysis and statistical discrimination. This approach assumes single fault scenarios and does not address the problem of incomplete sensor data.

6   Conclusions

We have presented a diagnostic system framework that integrates: the dynamic independent choice logic with multiple agents, probabilistic forecast models, and fault detection and isolation techniques. We split the diagnosis task in two

phases: the first phase is performed by the alarm processor (AP) agent that actu-
ates as the disturbed area locator. The output of AP agent is a set of component
candidates to be confirmed as real faulted components by the second phase. The
second phase is performed by fault detection agents, that analyze the behavior
of sensor measurements. The FD agent incorporates a one step-ahead forecast
model describing the no-fault model of the component. The analysis of residuals, computed from the differences between the no-fault model and the sensor
measurements, give the final decision about the fault in a component.

References

1. J. Cheng, D. Bell, and W. Liu (1998). Learning bayesian networks from data:
   An efficient approach based on information theory. Technical Report, Dept. of
   Computing Science, University of Alberta, Alberta CA.
2. T. Dean, and M. Wellman (1991). *Planning and control.* San Mateo, Calif.: Morgan
   Kaufmann, 1991.
3. P. Frank (1990). Fault diagnosis in dynamic systems using analytical and knowledge based redundancy–a survey and new results. *Automatica* 30: 789–804.
4. L. Garza (2001). Hybrid Systems Fault Diagnosis with a Probabilistic Logic Reasoning Framework . PhD Thesis, Instituto Tecnológico y de Estudios Superiores
   de Monterrey, Monterrey, N.L., December 2001.
5. L. Garza, F. Cantú, and S. Acevedo (2002). Fault Diagnosis in Industrial Processes
   with a Hybrid Diagnostic System. In Springer *LNAI Proc. of the MICAI 2002*,
   pages 436–445, Mérida, Yuc., México, April 2002.
6. R. Isermann (1997). Supervision, fault-detection and fault-diagnosis methods – an
   introduction. *Control Engineering Practice*, **5** (5): 639–652.
7. J. Lauber, C. Steger, and R. Weiss (1999). Autonomous agents for online diagnosis
   of a safety-critical system based on probabilistic causal reasoning. In *Proc. Fourth
   Intl. Symposium on Autonomous Decentralized Systems 1999*, pags. 213–219.
8. D. Poole (1995). Logic programming for robot control. In *Proc. 14 th International
   Joint Conference on AI, Montreal, August, 1995*, 150–157.
9. D. Poole (1997). The Independent choice logic for modeling multiple agents under
   uncertainty . *Artificial Intelligence*, **94**:7–56.
10. G. Provan and D. Elsley (2000). Software Toolkit for Aerospace Systems Diagnos-
    tics. In*IEEE Aerospace Conf. Proc. 2000*, Vol. 6, pp. 327–335.
11. J. Rasmussen (1993). Diagnostic reasoning in action. *IEEE Transactions on Sys-
    tems, Man, and Cybernetics*, **23**, 4: 981–991.
12. M. Sampath (2001). A Hybrid Approach to Failure Diagnosis in Industrial Systems.
    In *Proc. of the ACC 2001*, pp. 2077–2082.
13. L. Yan, and D. Miller (2000). General statistical inference for discrete and mixed
    spaces by an approximate application of the maximum entropy principle. *IEEE
    Trans. On Neural Networks*, **11** (3): 558–573.

Series-Parallel and Tree-Decomposition Approaches for Fuzzy Constraint Networks

Alfonso Bosch[1], Francisco Guil[1], Carmen Martinez[1], and Roque Marin[2]

[1] Dpto. de Lenguajes y Computacion
Universidad de Almeria
04120 Almeria (Spain)
{abosch, fguil, cmcruz}@ual.es

[2] Dpto. de Ingenieria de la Informacion y las Comunicaciones
Universidad de Murcia
Campus de Espinardo
30071 Espinardo (Murcia, Spain)
roque@dif.um.es

Abstract. In this work, we present a Disjunctive Fuzzy Constraint Networks model for continuous domains, which generalizes the Disjunctive Fuzzy Temporal Constraint Networks model for temporal reasoning, and we propose the use of the series-parallel and tree-decomposition approaches for simplifying its processing. After a separate empirical evaluation process of both techniques, a combined evaluation process over the same problem repository has been carried out, finding that series-parallel problems practically subsume tree-decomposable problems.

1   Introduction

Fuzzy Constraint Networks (FCN) model, introduced in [14,16], allows expressing simple constraints, representing them by means of a convex and normalized possibility distribution over real numbers. Fuzzy constraints allow combining precise and imprecise information, which can be also qualitative and quantitative. This model is suitable for temporal reasoning and other continuous domains where the combination of such constraint types is required. A fuzzy model allows intermediate consistency degrees, and to quantify the possibility and necessity of a relationship or query.

Fuzzy constraints are used in several contexts, such as medical systems, phytosanitary control, and other domains [1,15,25].

In certain tasks, such as planning, a more general model is needed, where constraints can be convex or not. Then, the FCN model is enhanced, allowing the definition of a constraint with a finite set of possibility distributions, normalized and convex, obtaining the Disjunctive Fuzzy Constraint Networks (DFCN) model. For temporal reasoning, this model extends the TCSP (Temporal Constraint Satisfaction Problems) framework proposed by Dechter [8], and it allows constraints such as "Irrigation *is much before* or *a little after* than Treatment", and subsumes the Vilain & Kautz point algebra (PA) [22]. This framework allows representing all the possible

F.J. Garijo, J.C. Riquelme, and M. Toro (Eds.): IBERAMIA 2002, LNAI 2527, pp. 275-284, 2002.
© Springer-Verlag Berlin Heidelberg 2002

relationships between time points, between intervals and between time points and intervals, and their disjunctions (without managing repetitive patterns).

The aim of this framework is to contribute to constraint-based reasoning under uncertainty for continuous domains, using fuzzy CSPs (Constraint Satisfaction Problems) for search and querying, mixing different filtering techniques and backtrack search.

The main drawback of DFCN is its computational inefficiency, because generally these networks are non-decomposable networks [7,24], needing backtracking to find a solution [11,12,23]. Determining the consistency and computing the minimal network are also exponential. With small problems, this is not a drawback, but in order to generalize the use of the model in a general scope, it would be interesting to simplify its processing, if possible. The idea is to explore different approaches to be used before applying backtracking.

One approach is to try avoiding backtracking, using the topology of the problem graph [8]. Another one is decomposing the network into subproblems that can be solved separately. A third approach is to apply preprocessing, reducing the original network and testing the problem consistency [20,21].

The remainder of this paper is organized as follows. Section 2 presents the DFCN model; Section 3 presents two approaches for managing constraint networks: series-parallel networks and tree decomposition; section 4 presents the empirical evaluation and the analysis of the results; and section 5 summarizes the conclusions and presents the future work.

2   The Disjunctive Fuzzy Constraint Networks Model

A disjunctive fuzzy constraint network (DFCN) L^d consists of a finite set of $n+1$ variables $X_0, \ldots, X_n$ (X_0 as origin for problem variables), whose domain is the set of real numbers R, and a finite set of disjunctive binary constraints L_{ij}^d among these variables. X_0 is a variable added to use only binary constraints, and it can be assigned to an arbitrary value (for simplicity's sake, this value is usually 0).

A disjunctive binary constraint L_{ij}^d among variables X_i, X_j is defined with a finite set of possibility distributions, $\{\pi_{ij}^1, \pi_{ij}^2, \ldots, \pi_{ij}^k\}$ normalized and convex [9], defined over the set of real numbers R; for $x \in R$, $\pi_m(x) \in [0,1]$ represents the possibility that a quantity m can be precisely x.

A value assignation for variables X_i, X_j, $X_i=a$; $X_j=b$, a, $b \in R$, satisfies the constraint L_{ij}^d iff it satisfies one of its individual constraints:

$$\exists \pi_{ij}^p \in L_{ij}^d \ / \ \pi_{ij}^p (b-a) > 0 \tag{1}$$

The maximum possibility degree of satisfaction of a constraint L_{ij}^d for an assignment $X_i = a$, $X_j = b$ is

$$\sigma_{ij}^{\max}(a,b) = \max_{1 \le p \le k} \pi_{ij}^{p}(b-a) \tag{2}$$

A constraint L_{ij}^{d} among variables X_i, X_j defines a symmetric constraint L_{ji}^{d} among X_j, X_i, and the lack of a constraint is equivalent to the universal constraint π_U. A DFCN can be represented with a directed graph, where each node corresponds to a variable and each arc corresponds to a constraint between the connected variables, omitting symmetric and universal constraints. The set of possible solutions of a DFCN L^d is defined as the fuzzy subset from R^n associated to the possibility distribution given as:

$$\pi_S(v_1,...,v_n) = \min_{\substack{0 \le i \le n \\ 0 \le j \le n}}(\sigma_{ij}^{\max}(v_i,v_j) \tag{3}$$

An n-tuple $V = (v_1, ...v_n) \in R^n$ of precise values is an σ-possible solution of a DFCN L^d if $\pi_S(V) = \sigma$. We say that a DFCN L^d is consistent if it is 1-consistent, and it is inconsistent if it does not have any solution.

Given a DFCN L^d, it is possible to find out several networks which are equivalent to L^d. We can obtain this networks using the composition and intersection operations, defined in [3] for temporal reasoning. Among all the equivalent networks, there is always a network M^d DFCN that is minimal. This network contains the minimal constraints. If M^d contains an empty constraint, L^d is inconsistent. If p if the maximum of possibility distributions in each constraint, and the network has q disjunctive constrains and n variables, then the minimal network M^d of a DFCN L^d can be obtained with a complexity O($pqn3$), where $n3$ is the cost of solving each case non disjunctive FCN [16]. Due to this exponential complexity, we need to find a more practical approach.

3   Series-Parallel Networks and Tree Decomposition

It is well known that topological characteristics of constraint networks can help to select more effective methods to solve them, and there are previous studies about this topic [6,8]. These characteristics have been examined for both FCN and DFCN models; in this work, we will focus only in topics involved with disjunctive problems, because they are exponential. The selected approaches are series-parallel networks and tree-decomposition.

3.1   Series-Parallel Networks

A network is series-parallel [18] in respect to a pair of nodes i,j if it can be reduced to arc (i,j) applying iteratively this reduction operation: a) select a node with a degree of two or less; b) remove it from the network; c) connect its neighbours. A network is series-parallel if it is series-parallel in respect to every pair of nodes. The basic algorithm for checking if a network is series-parallel has an O(n^3) complexity, and there is a more efficient algorithm that checks this property with an O(n) complexity [26], applied to fault-tolerant networks (IFI networks).

If a DFCN is series-parallel, the path consistent network is the minimal network, although the intersection and composition operations are non-distributive [26]. As a subproduct of checking if a network is series-parallel, a variable ordering is obtained, when deleting the nodes. Applying directional path-consistency (DPC) algorithm [8] in the reverse order, a backtrack-free network is obtained and the minimal constraint between the first two variables of the ordering too. This can be interesting when we need only to compute a minimal constraint for two variables, and not the minimal network, as in LaTeR [5]. In addition, if the network is series-parallel, we can decide absolutely whether the network is consistent, by applying DPC algorithm in the reverse order.

Figure 1 shows a series-parallel network. It can be reduced to any of its arcs applying the reduction process.

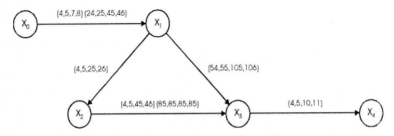

Fig. 1. Example of series-parallel network

However, the network shown in Figure 2 is not series-parallel, because there is not any admissible reduction sequence for any arc. We can see easily that the only node with grade less or equal to two is X_0.

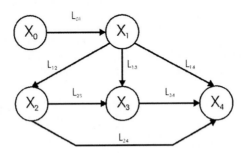

Fig. 2. Example of non series-parallel network

The proposed algorithm for checking if a network is series-parallel (a variant of the algorithm proposed in [26]) is:

SP (Series-Parallel) Algorithm

```
Input:   A Fuzzy Constraint Network.
Output:  A node removal sequence.


begin
   for each i=0..n Calculate-degree (i)
   NodeQueue = {nodes with degree 1 and 2}
   While (NodeQueue <> Ø and |V| > 3)
      begin
       node = Extract(NodeQueue)
       V <- V - {node}
       if Degree(node) = 1
          then Degree(Neighbour(node))  --
       if Degree(Neighbour(node)) = 2
          then Introduce(NodeQueue, Neighbour(node))
          else if Connected(Neighbours(node))
                  then Degree(Neighbours(node))  --
       if Degree(Neighbours(node)) = 2
          then Introduce(NodeQueue, Neighbours(node))
          else E <- E + {NeighboursArc(node)}
      end
   if (NodeQueue = Ø and |V| > 3)
      then exit ("The network is not series-parallel")
end
```

Fig. 3. Series-parallel algorithm

The algorithm ends when the queue is empty or there are three nodes left in the network. If the queue is empty, the reduction process has finished. In such case, if there are more than three nodes, the network is not series-parallel, because there are at least four nodes with a degree greater than two (there is a graph that is homomorphic to K_4 [26]).

3.2 Tree Decomposition

We stated that general DFCN are not tractable when searching the minimal network and finding a solution, but both problems are tractable when a DFCN has a tree structure. Then, it seems adequate to study the possibility of removing redundancies from a DFCN to extract (if it is possible) a tree representing a relative DFCTN equivalent to the original one.

Tree-decomposition is proposed by Meiri *et al.* [17] for discrete CSPs, and it can be extended to DFCN. If a tree T^d can be extracted from a path-consistent network by means of arc removal, the tree T^d represents exactly the original network. Otherwise, if a tree representation cannot be extracted, the algorithm stops and notifies this fact. The tree extraction using arc removal will be possible only when the path-consistent network is also minimal. In addition, if the path-consistent network is minimal, we can state that if the algorithm cannot find the tree decomposition, then there is no tree representation.

The tree decomposition method consists of removing redundant constraints from the original network, until a tree that exactly represents the network without information loss is found [2,17,19]. The algorithm works as follows: Given a path-consistent DFCN, it examines each triplet of variables, identifying the redundancies of each triplet, assigning weights to the arcs depending on the found redundancies. The generated tree, T^d, is a maximum weight spanning tree (MWST) respect to these weights. The last step is to verify that T^d represents truly the original network. If T^d does not represent truly the original network, removed arcs can be added again, until both networks become equivalent. This algorithm has a polynomial cost, and when applied to a minimal disjunctive network, it determines whether the network is decomposable or not.

We proposed an algorithm [2] that generates a tree T^d with these characteristics. If a tree can be extracted from a path-consistent network using arc removal, the tree T^d represents exactly the original network. Otherwise, if tree representation cannot be extracted, the algorithm stops and notifies this fact. The tree extraction using arc removal will be possible only when the path-consistent network is also minimal. In addition, if the path-consistent network is minimal, we can state that if the algorithm cannot find the tree decomposition, then there is no tree representation. The algorithm extends the proposal of Meiri *et al.* [17] for discrete CSPs, and it is depicted in [19].

4   Empirical Evaluation and Results

We have conducted an empirical evaluation process, generating sets of random DFCN with different characteristics, preprocessing them with PC-2 (Path-Consistency) algorithm from Mackworth [13], and applying Tree Decomposition (TD) and Series-Parallel (SP) algorithms.

The parameters used in our problem generator are n (the number of variables), R (the range of the constraints), p (the number of possibility distributions in each constraint), q (the connectivity of the graph), T (the tightness of the constraints) and F (the fuzziness of the constraints). All the constraints generated in each problem have the same number of possibility distributions. The values selected for the first test battery were $n= 4 - 40$; $R= 600$; $p= 1,2,4,8,16,32$; $q= 0.1,0.3,0.5$; $T= 0.1,0.5,0.9$.

The first analysis of the results obtained in the TD evaluation process is presented in [2]. In [4], we analyzed deeper the behaviour of TD, and presented a first analysis of SP, over a new battery of problems generated with the same parameter set. When analyzing the results, we observed that the overall trend of SP was similar to the corresponding of TD: when increasing the problem size, the number of problems where these heuristics succeed diminished. The main found difference was that, in every category, the number of SP problems was always greater than TD problems.

These results lead us to make a combined evaluation of both approaches, testing the SP algorithm over the same battery of path-consistent problems used as input for TD evaluation. Figure 4 shows the overall trend of both algorithms. Note that SP curve is always over TD curve. The bars show the number of path-consistent problems for each number of variables.

The next question is to check the relationship between the two approaches, that is, to know whether a TD problem is also SP, and vice versa. Figure 5 shows the fraction of the four possible cases: 0-0 represents the problems that are neither TD nor SP. 1-1 represents the problems that are both TD and SP. 0-1 represents the problems that are SP but not TD. In addition, 1-0 represents the problems that are TD but not SP. The last case is the most interesting one, because practically there are not problems with this pattern. Looking in depth the result database, there are only five isolated problems TD that are not SP into a population of 25068 problems. In addition, 3551 problems that are SP but not TD, and 5005 problems are SP and TD. Then, the overall fraction of SP problems represents a 34.13 %, versus a 19.98 % for TD.

From this analysis, we propose using SP as standard approach, because it runs with a lower time and memory requirements, and practically subsumes the TD approach.

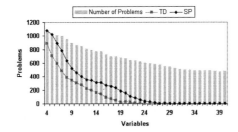

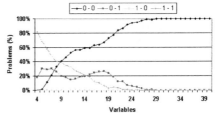

Fig. 4. Number of PC, TD, and SP problems vs. Variable Number.

Fig. 5. Comparative analysis of TD and SP problems v. Variable Number. (TD-SP)

The interest of determining whether a FCN is SP consists on avoiding the need of backtracking. First, the consistency of the problem can be determined with DPC (Directional Path-Consistency) algorithm [8], using the inverse node removal sequence. The output network from DPC can be used to obtain a solution without backtracking, also using the inverse removal sequence. In addition, if the minimal network is needed, it can be computed applying PC-2.

Figure 6 shows the minimal network for the sample FCN shown in Figure 1, obtained with PC-2. Using this information, we can obtain a solution for this network, using the removal sequence {0,2,4,3,1}. We instantiate the variables in this order: X_1, X_3, X_4, X_2, and X_0. A 1-possible solution is:

$X_1 = 5$
$X_3 = 60$
$X_4 = 65$
$X_2 = 15$
$X_0 = 0$

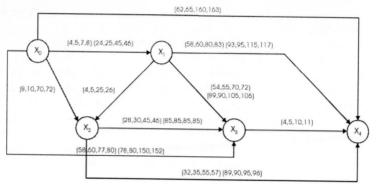

Fig. 6. Minimal network obtained with PC-2

5   Conclusions and Future Work

In this work, we have proposed the DFCN model for constraint networks in continuous domains. Among the candidate techniques for managing these networks, we have selected tree-decomposition and series-parallel networks, carrying out two evaluation processes. First, we made an independent evaluation of both approaches. The analysis of this process leads us to carry out a combined evaluation process. After a detailed study of the results of the last one, we can say that SP has a greater success than TD, and SP practically subsumes TD. In addition, SP presents a lower complexity, and it offers all the features of TD: obtaining solutions without backtracking and computing the minimal network with path-consistency algorithms. Moreover, problem consistency and solutions can be determined and obtained using directional path-consistency, with a complexity lower than general path-consistency.

As future work, we propose to study the application of SP for decomposing the networks onto two types of subnetworks: SP subproblems, which could be solved with the techniques applied for SP, and non-SP subproblems, which could be solved with backtracking. This could be an alternative to other decomposition approaches proposed by our group [3] and other standard techniques, as nonseparable components [10].

Another proposal could be a deeper study of cases of problems that are TD and not SP, trying to find a pattern of this type of problems, where TD can be useful.

All this information could be used to select the better approach for each particular network.

Acknowledgements. The authors would like to thank the anonymous reviewers for their helpful comments on preliminary versions of this paper.

This work is partially supported by an EC FEDER Program grant (1FD97-0255-C03-03) and a Spanish MCYT Program grant ((TIC2000-0873-C02-02).

References

1. S. Barro, R. Marín, and A.R. Patón, "A model and a language for the fuzzy representation and handling of time", *Fuzzy Sets and Systems*, 61, 1994, pp. 153-175.
2. A. Bosch, M. Torres, I. Navarrete, and R. Marín, "Tree Decomposition of Disjunctive Fuzzy Temporal Constraint Networks". *Proc. of Computational* Intelligence*: Methods and Applications CIMA'2001*, ICSC-NAISO, Bangor (UK), 2001, #1714-066, 7 pages.
3. A. Bosch, M. Torres, R. Marín. Reasoning with Disjunctive Fuzzy Temporal Constraint Networks. TIME-2002, Manchester (UK), 8 pages., 2002 (accepted).
4. A. Bosch, C. Martínez, F. Guil, R. Marín. Solving Fuzzy Temporal Problems Without Backtracking.. Eurasian-2002, Teherán (Irán), 10 pages., 2002 (accepted).
5. V. Brusoni, L. Console, B. Pernici, and P. Terenziani, "LaTeR: a general purpose manager of temporal information", *Methodologies for intelligent systems 8*, LNCS 869, Springer, 1994, pp. 255-264.
6. R. Dechter, "Enhancement Schemes for Constraint Processing: Backjumping, Learning and Cutset Decomposition." *Artificial Intelligence* 41, Elsevier, 1990, pp. 273-312.
7. R. Dechter, I. Meiri, and J. Pearl, "Temporal constraint networks", *Artificial Intelligence* 49, Elsevier, 1991, pp. 61-95.
8. R. Dechter, and J. Pearl, "Network-based heuristics for constraint-satisfaction problems", *Artificial Intelligence*, 34, Elsevier, 1987, pp. 1-38
9. D. Dubois, H. Prade, *Possibility Theory: An approach to computerized processing of uncertainty*, Plenum Press, New York, 1988.
10. S. Even, *Graph Algorithms*. Computer Science Press, Rockville, MD, 1979.
11. E. Freuder, "A sufficient condition for backtrack-free search", *Journal of the ACM* 29, 1, ACM Press, 1982, pp. 24-32.
12. G. Kondrak, and P. van Beek, "A Theoretical Evaluation of Selected Backtracking Algorithms", *Artificial Intelligence* 89, Elsevier, 1997, pp. 365-387.
13. A. Mackworth, "Consistency in networks of relations", *Artificial Intelligence* 8, Elsevier, 1977, pp. 99-118.
14. R. Marín, S. Barro, A. Bosch, and J. Mira, "Modelling the representation of time from a fuzzy perspective", *Cybernetics and Systems*, 25, 2, Taylor&Francis, 1994, pp. 207-215.
15. R. Marín, S. Barro, F. Palacios, R. Ruiz, and F. Martin, "An Approach to Fuzzy Temporal Reasoning in Medicine", *Mathware & Soft Computing*, 3, 1994, pp. 265-276.
16. R. Marín, M. Cardenas, M. Balsa, and J. Sanchez, "Obtaining solutions in fuzzy constraint networks", *Int. Journal of Approximate Reasoning*, 16, Elsevier, 1997, pp. 261-288.
17. I. Meiri, R. Dechter, and J. Pearl, "Uncovering trees in constraint networks", *Artificial Intelligence*, 86, Elsevier, 1996, 245-267.
18. U. Montanari, "Networks of constraints: fundamental properties and applications to picture processing", *Information Science*, 7, 1974, pp. 95-132.
19. I. Navarrete, R. Marín, and M. Balsa, "Redes de Restricciones Temporales Disyuntivas Borrosas", *Proceedings of ESTYLF'95*, Murcia, European Society for Fuzzy Logic and Technology, (Spain), 1995, pp. 57-63
20. E. Schwalb, and R. Dechter, "Coping With Disjunctions on Temporal Constraint Networks", *Proc. American Association Artificial Intelligence'93*, AAAI, Washington, 1993, pp. 127-132.
21. E. Schwalb, and R. Dechter, "Processing Disjunctions in Temporal Constraint Networks", *Artificial Intelligence* 93, Elsevier, 1997, pp. 29-61.
22. E. Schwalb, and L. Vila, "Temporal Constraints: A Survey", *Constraints* 3 (2/3), 1998, pp. 129-149.
23. K. Stergiou and M. Koubarakis, "Backtracking Algorithms for Disjunctions of Temporal Constraints", *Artificial Intelligence* 120, Elsevier, 2000, pp. 81-117.
24. E. Tsang, *Foundations of Constraint Satisfaction*, Academic Press, London, 1993.

25. Túnez, S.; Del Aguila, I.; Bienvenido, F.; Bosch, A. y Marín, R.(1996). Integrating decision support and knowledge-based system: application to pest control in greenhouses. Procedings 6th International Congress for Computer Technology in Agriculture (ICCTA'96), pp. 417-422. Wageningen.
26. J.A. Wald, and C.J. Colburn, "Steiner Trees, Partial 2-Trees and Minimum IFI Networks", *Networks,* 13, 1983, pp. 159-167.

Change-Detection Using Contextual Information and Fuzzy Entropy Principle

Maria Luiza F. Velloso[1] and Flávio J. de Souza[2]

[1]Department of Electronics Engineering, [2]Department of Computer Engineering
Uerj –Rio de Janeiro State University
Rua São Francisco Xavier, 524
20550-013, Rio de Janeiro,
BRAZIL
Phone: +55 21 2587 7442
mlfv@centroin.com.br, fjsouza@eng.uerj.br,

Abstract. This paper presents an unsupervised change detection method for computing the amount of changes that have occurred within an area by using remotely sensed technologies and fuzzy modeling. The discussion concentrates on the formulation of a standard procedure that, using the concept of fuzzy sets and fuzzy logic, can define the likelihood of changes detected from remotely sensed data. The fuzzy visualization of areas undergoing changes can be incorporated into a decision support system for prioritization of areas requiring environmental monitoring. One of the main problems related to unsupervised change detection methods lies in the lack of efficient automatic techniques for discriminating between changed and unchanged pixels in the difference image. Such discrimination is usually performed by using empirical strategies or manual trial-and-error procedures, which affect both, the accuracy and the reliability of the change-detection process. To overcome such drawbacks, in this paper, we propose an automatic technique for the analysis of the difference image. Such technique allows the automatic selection of the decision threshold. We used a thresholding approach by performing fuzzy partition on a two-dimensional (2-D) histogram, which included contextual information, based on fuzzy relation and maximum fuzzy entropy principle. Experimental results confirm the effectiveness of proposed technique.

1 Introduction

There has been a growing interest in the development of automatic change-detection techniques for the analysis of multitemporal remote sensing images. In the literature, two main approaches to the change-detection problem have been proposed: the supervised and the unsupervised. The former is based on supervised classification methods, which require the availability of a multitemporal ground truth in order to derive a suitable training set for the learning process of the classifiers. Although this approach exhibits some advantages over the unsupervised one, the generation of an appropriate multitemporal ground truth is usually a difficult and expensive task. Consequently, the use of effective unsupervised change-detection methods is

F.J. Garijo, J.C. Riquelme, and M. Toro (Eds.): IBERAMIA 2002, LNAI 2527, pp. 285-293, 2002.

fundamental in many applications in which a ground truth is not available. The unsupervised system approach is attractive for classifications tasks due to its self-organizing, generalizable, and fault-tolerant characteristics. In contrast to the supervised systems, the unsupervised system does not rely on user-defined training data and it is a advantageous characteristic because, frequently, there are not specialists in remote sensing or geoprocessing in the staff of city councils near sites that require environmental monitoring. Traditional methods of change detection using either air- or satellite-borne remotely sensed data also can be broadly divided in two categories: pre-classification and post-classification. Jensen [1] states that post-classification comparison of changes is the most commonly used method for quantitative analysis. It requires a complete classification of the individual dates of remotely sensed data, whereupon the operator produces a matrix of change that identifies 'from–to' land cover change classes. The main drawback with this method is errors in the individual data classification map will also be present in the final change detection. On the other hand, pre-classification methods detect changes due to variations in the brightness values of the images being compared. In any of the pre-classification approaches, the critical step relies on selecting appropriate threshold values in the lower and upper tails of the histogram representing values of change. This is so that areas of change can be accurately separated from those where no changes have occurred within the period of time considered. In all studies that create a change image, the value at which the threshold is set is somewhat arbitrary. In this paper, we work on one of the unsupervised change-detection techniques so-called "difference image". These techniques process the two multispectral images acquired at two different dates in order to generate a further image - the difference image. The values of the pixels associated with land cover changes present values significantly different from those of the pixels associated with unchanged areas. Changes are then identified by analyzing the difference image. In the widely used change vector analysis (CVA) technique [2], [3], [4], several spectral channels are used and, for each pair of corresponding pixels "spectral change vector" is computed as the difference between the feature vectors at the two times. Then, the pixel values in the difference image are associated with the modules of the spectral change vectors. So, the unchanged pixels present small gray-level values, whereas changed pixels present rather large values. In spite of their simplicity and widespread use, the described above change-detection methods exhibit a major drawback: a lack of automatic and nonheuristic techniques for the analysis of the difference image. An intuitive approach is to apply a grayscale threshold on the difference image – assume that the pixel values of the changed pixels are generally higher than the values of the unchanged pixels. If the histogram of the difference image is bimodal showing a peak for unchanged pixels and a peak for changed pixels, the appropriate value for the threshold can be either manually selected or statistically determined. However, due to the large variability on the change types and noise on the images, segmentation based on a single threshold usually performs poorly. Many methods have been proposed to select the thresholds automatically [5]. Most bilevel thresholding techniques can be extended to the case of multithresholding, therefore, we focus on a bilevel thresholding technique in this paper. The proposed approach will automatically determine the fuzzy region and find the thresholds based on the maximum fuzzy entropy principle. It involves a fuzzy partition on a two-dimensional (2-D) histogram where a 2-D fuzzy entropy is defined .The proposed thresholding technique is adapted from the presented in [6]. In order to minimize computational costs we proposed an simplified adaptation of the fuzzy partition and fuzzy entropy.

This paper is organized as follows. The next section presents the procedure used to generate the 2-D histogram. Section 3 describes the thresholding method used for segmentation in this work. Section 4 describes an evaluation experiment and discusses the results.

2   The 2-D Histogram

Let us consider two multispectral images, X1 e X2 acquired in the same geographical area at two different times, t1 e t2. Let us assume that such images have been coregistered. Let X represents the values of the pixels in the difference image obtained by applying the CVA technique to X1 and X2. For the sake of simplicity, the proposed technique will be presented in the context of the CVA method. However, a generalization to other methods based on the difference image is straightforward. In order to obtain a 2-D histogram of the difference image, we define the local average of a pixel, f(x; y), as the average intensity of its four neighbors denoted by g(x; y):

$$g(x,y) = \frac{1}{4}\left[f(x,y+1)+f(x,y-1)+f(x+1,y)+f(x-1,y)\right]+0.5. \qquad (1)$$

A 2-D histogram can be viewed as a full Cartesian product of two sets X and Y, where X represents the gray levels of the difference image, f(x,y), and Y represents the local average gray levels, g(x,y): X=Y={0,1,2,...,L-1}, where L-1 is the higher level of intensity. This 2-D histogram is an array (L X L) with the entries representing the number of occurrences of the pair (f(x; y); g(x; y)). The pixels having the same intensity but different spatial features can be distinguished in the second dimension (local average gray level) of the 2-D histogram.

3   The Thresholding Method

Four fuzzy sets, ChangedX, NotChangedX, ChangedY, and NotChangedY, were defined based on the S-function and the corresponding Z-function as follows:

$$
\begin{aligned}
ChangedX &= \sum_{x \in X} \frac{\mu ChangedX(x)}{x} = \sum_{x \in X} \frac{S(x,a,b)}{x} \\[4pt]
ChangedY &= \sum_{y \in Y} \frac{\mu ChangedY(y)}{y} = \sum_{y \in Y} \frac{S(y,a,b)}{y} \\[4pt]
NotChangedX &= \sum_{x \in X} \frac{\mu NotChangedX(x)}{x} = \sum_{x \in X} \frac{Z(x,a,b)}{x} \\[4pt]
NotChangedY &= \sum_{y \in Y} \frac{\mu NotChangedY(y)}{y} = \sum_{y \in Y} \frac{Z(y,a,b)}{y}
\end{aligned}
\qquad (2)
$$

In [6] the S-function is defined with three parameters. In order to minimize computational costs we used a S–shaped membership function, defined as

$$S(x,a,b) = \begin{cases} 0 & \text{if } x \le a \\ 2\left(\dfrac{x-a}{b-a}\right)^2 & \text{if } a < x \le (a+b)/2 \\ 1 - 2\left(\dfrac{b-x}{b-a}\right)^2 & \text{if } (a+b)/2 < x \le b \\ 1 & \text{if } x \ge b \end{cases}, \tag{3}$$

and Z(x)=1 – S(x). The parameters a and b locate the extremes of the sloped portion of the curve, and Figure 1 shows a plot of a S-function with a=1 and b=8.

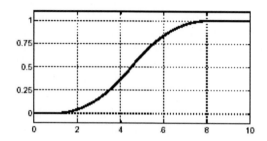

Fig. 1. A plot of a S-function with parameters a=1 and b=8.

The fuzzy relation Changed is a subset of the full Cartesian product space $X \times Y$, i.e., Changed = ChangedX × ChangedY $\subset X \times Y$

$$\mu Changed(x, y) = min(\mu ChangedX(x), \mu ChangedY(y)). \tag{4}$$

Similarly, NotChanged = NotChangedX × NotChangedY $\subset X \times Y$

$$\mu NotChanged(x, y) = min(\mu NotChangedX(x), \mu NotChangedY(y)). \tag{5}$$

Let A be a fuzzy set with membership function $\mu A(x_i)$, where $x_i, i = 1,..., N$, are the possible outputs from source A with the probability $P(x_i)$. The fuzzy entropy of set A is defined as [7]

$$H_{fuzzy}(A) = -\sum_{i=1}^{N} \mu A(x_i) P(x_i) log(P(x_i)) \tag{6}$$

The image is divided in two blocks, NotChangedBlock, with $\mu NotChanged(x, y) > 0$, and ChangedBlock, with $\mu Changed(x, y) > 0$. The total image entropy is defined as

$$H(image) = H(NotChanged) + H(Changed). \tag{7}$$

In [6] the not changed block was divided into a nonfuzzy region R_{NC} and a fuzzy region R_{NCF}. Similarly, the changed block was composed of a nonfuzzy region R_C and a fuzzy region R_{CF}, and four entropies were computed:

$$H(R_C) = -\sum_{(x,y)\in R_{CF}} \frac{\eta_{xy}}{\sum\limits_{(x,y)\in R_C} \eta_{xy}} . log\left(\frac{\eta_{xy}}{\sum\limits_{(x,y)\in R_C} \eta_{xy}}\right) \tag{8}$$

$$H(R_{CF}) = -\sum_{(x,y)\in R_{CF}} \mu Changed(x,y) . \frac{\eta_{xy}}{\sum\limits_{(x,y)\in R_{CF}} \eta_{xy}} . log\left(\frac{\eta_{xy}}{\sum\limits_{(x,y)\in R_{CF}} \eta_{xy}}\right) \tag{9}$$

$$H(R_{NCF}) = -\sum_{(x,y)\in R_{NCF}} \mu NotChanged(x,y) . \frac{\eta_{xy}}{\sum\limits_{(x,y)\in R_{NCF}} \eta_{xy}} . log\left(\frac{\eta_{xy}}{\sum\limits_{(x,y)\in R_{NCF}} \eta_{xy}}\right) \tag{10}$$

$$H(R_{NC}) = -\sum_{(x,y)\in R_{NC}} \frac{\eta_{xy}}{\sum\limits_{(x,y)\in R_{NC}} \eta_{xy}} . log\left(\frac{\eta_{xy}}{\sum\limits_{(x,y)\in R_{NC}} \eta_{xy}}\right) \tag{11}$$

where η_{xy} is the element in the 2-D histogram which represents the number of occurrences of the pair (x; y). The membership functions $\mu Changed(x,y)$ and $\mu NotChanged(x,y)$ are defined in (4) and (5), respectively. The probability computations $\eta_{xy} / \sum \eta_{xy}$ in the four regions are independent of each other and depend on a and b parameters. In order to simplify and minimize the computational costs we defined only one region for each block. The two entropies are computed:

$$H(Changed) = -\sum_{(x,y)} \mu Changed(x,y) . \frac{\eta_{xy}}{\sum\limits_{(x,y)} \eta_{xy}} . log\left(\frac{\eta_{xy}}{\sum\limits_{(x,y)} \eta_{xy}}\right) \tag{12}$$

$$H(NotChanged) = -\sum_{(x,y)} \mu NotChanged(x,y) . \frac{\eta_{xy}}{\sum\limits_{(x,y)} \eta_{xy}} . log\left(\frac{\eta_{xy}}{\sum\limits_{(x,y)} \eta_{xy}}\right) \tag{13}$$

It should be notice that the probability computations $\eta_{xy} / \sum \eta_{xy}$ are the same for both entropies. These computations do not depend on the parameters a and b and can be executed only once. With

$$\mu Changed(x,y) = min(\mu ChangedX(x), \mu ChangedY(y)), \text{ and}$$

$$\mu NotChanged(x) = 1 - \mu Changed(x),$$

we can compute H as

$$H = -\sum_{(x,y)} \left(1 - |\mu NotChanged(x) - \mu Changed(x)|\right) \cdot \frac{\eta_{xy}}{N} \cdot log\left(\frac{\eta_{xy}}{N}\right) \tag{14}$$

where N is the total number of pixels in difference image. Then maximize H is maximize

$$H = \sum_{(x,y)} |\mu NotChanged(x) - \mu Changed(x)| \cdot \frac{\eta_{xy}}{N} \cdot log\left(\frac{\eta_{xy}}{N}\right) \tag{15}$$

To find the best set of a and b is an optimization problem, which can be solved by: heuristic searching, simulated annealing, genetic algorithm, etc. In our approach the optimal solution can be found by direct searching. The proposed method consists of the following four major steps:
1) Make the difference image;
2) Find the 2-D histogram of the difference image;
3) Perform fuzzy partition on the 2-D histogram;
4) Compute the fuzzy entropy.
Steps 1) and 2) needs to be executed only once while steps 3) and 4) are performed iteratively for each set of (a; b). The optimum (a; b) determines the fuzzy region (i.e., interval [a; b]). The threshold is selected as the crossover point of the membership function which has membership 0.5 implying the largest fuzziness. Once the threshold vector (s; t) is obtained, it divides the 2-D histogram into four blocks, i.e., a Not Changed block, a Changed block, and two noise (edge) blocks. In order to minimize commission errors the Changed areas extraction method is expressed as

$$f_{s,t}(x,y,changed) = \begin{cases} 1 & f(x,y) > t \wedge g(x,y) > s \\ 0 & otherwise. \end{cases}$$

4   Experimental Results

In order to evaluate the robustness of the proposed technique for the analysis of the difference image, we considered a synthetic data set artificially generated. An image acquired by the Landsat-7 Thematic Mapper (TM) sensor, composed of bands 3, 4 and 5, in the middle west of Brazil was used as the reference image. In particular a section (700x700 pixels) of a acquired scene was selected. This image was assumed to be X1 image of the data set. The X2 image was artificially generated from the reference one. A first version of the X2 image was obtained by inserting some changes in the X1 image in order to simulate land cover variations. Then the histogram of the resulting image was slightly shifted to simulate different light conditions in the two images. Finally, two versions of the X2 image were generated by adding different realizations of zero-mean Gaussian noise to the X2 image (Signal-to-Noise-Ratio (SNR=20 and 10 dB). For simplicity, we assumed the spatial independence of the noise components in the images. As an example, Fig. 2(a) shows the band 4 of the reference image, X1. The map of the areas with simulated changes is presented in Fig. 2(b). For the two pairs of synthetic images considered, the corresponding difference images were obtained by applying the Change Vector Analysis (CVA) technique [5], [8], [10]. CVA technique is one of spectral change detection techniques that involves the transformation of two original images to a new single-band or multi-band images, in which the areas of spectral change are highlighted. For each pair of images considered, a single-band image was created based on the corresponding difference image. In order to produce spectral change data, only the magnitude value of difference multiband image vector was used. The threshold vectors were (62, 62) and (65,65) for the dataset with SNR=20 dB and 10 dB, respectively.

(a)   (b)

Fig. 2. Synthetic data set utilized in the experiments. (a) Band 4 of the reference image, (b) map of the areas with simulated changes used as the reference map in the experiments.

In order to interpret classification accuracies we used two descriptive measures: the overall accuracy and the Kappa coefficient. The overall accuracy is computed by dividing the total number of correctly classified pixels by the total number of reference pixels. Kappa coefficient of agreement is a measure for overall thematic classification accuracy and ranges from 0 to 1. It is a measure of the difference between the actual agreement between reference data and an automated classifier and the chance agreement between the reference data and a random classifier. A true agreement (observed) approaches 1, and chance agreement approaches 0. A Kappa coefficient of 0 suggests that a given classification is no better than a random assignment of pixels [14].
Tables 1, and 2 show the confusion matrix for the datasets with SNR=20 dB and 10 dB, respectively.

Table 1. Confusion Matrix for the dataset with SNR = 20 dB.

	Not Changed (Reference)	Changed (Reference)
Not Changed (Classified)	479131	1939
Changed (Classified)	0	8930

Table 2. Confusion Matrix for the dataset with SNR = 10 dB.

	Not Changed (Reference)	Changed (Reference)
Not Changed (Classified)	479131	2064
Changed (Classified)	0	8805

Table 3 resumes the results and presents the overall accuracy and the Kappa coefficient for the two datasets. The worst performance was obtained by the dataset with SNR=10 dB, Kappa coefficient 0.89, and the best performance was obtained by the dataset with SNR=10 dB with a Kappa coefficient equal to 0.90.

We can note that resulted errors were only omission errors, as expected, and the noise level did not affect significantly the performance of the algorithm.

Table 3. Results for two datasets.

	Kappa-coefficient	Overall Accuracy
SNR = 20 dB	0.90	99.60 %
SNR = 10 dB	0.89	99.57 %

5   Conclusions

The proposed method presents some improvements in the field of change detection and visualization of the certainty and magnitude of changes. In addition, a system to prioritize areas targeted for map and database revision based on a manager's criteria of a cost-effective threshold of change is presented. A 2-D fuzzy partition characterized by parameters a, and b is proposed which divides a 2-D histogram into two fuzzy subsets "changed" and "not changed." For each fuzzy subset, one fuzzy entropy is defined based on the fuzziness of the regions. The best fuzzy partition was found based on the maximum fuzzy entropy principle, and the corresponding parameters a, and b determines the fuzzy region [a; b]. The threshold is selected as the crossover point of the fuzzy region.

Further research should be conducted to test the potential improvements associated with such approach. Another selection of membership functions could be used, the possibility of using different parameters for the membership functions relative to X and Y sets could be experimented. In spite of the simplicity adopted, even the case characterized by high level of noise, the experimental results confirm the effectiveness of the presented technique.

References

1. Jensen, J. "Principles of change detection using digital. remote sensor data". In: Star, Estes, McGwire Eds., Integration of Geographic Information Systems and Remote Sensing. Cambridge Univ. Press, pp. 37–54, 1997.
2. Johnson, R. D.; Kasischke, E. S. "Change Vector Analysis: a Technique for the Multispectral Monitoring of Land Cover and Condition", International Journal of Remote Sensing, No.19, pp. 411–426, 1998.
3. Malila, W. A., "Change Vector Analysis: An Approach for Detecting Forest Changes with Landsat", Proceedings of the Machine Processing of Remotely Sensed Data Symposium, Ann Arbor, ERIM, pp. 326–335,1980.
4. Zhan, X.; Huang, C.; Townshend, R. de F.; Hansen, M.; Dimiceli, C.; Sholberg, R.; Hewson-Sacardeletti, J.; Tompkins, A. "Land Cover Detection with Change Vector in the Red and Near-Infared Reflectance Space", Geoscience and Remote Sensing Symposium, 2000 IEEE International.
5. P. K. Sahoo, S. Soltani, A. K. C.Wong, and Y. Chen, "A survey of thresholding techniques," Comput. Vis., Graph., Image Process., vol. 41, pp. 233–260, 1988.
6. H. D. Cheng, Y. H. Chen, and X. H. Jiang, " Thresholding Using Two-Dimensional Histogram and Fuzzy Entropy Principle", IEEE Transactions on Image Processing, Vol. 9, No. 4, pp. 732–735, 2000.
7. L. A. Zadeh, "Probability measures of fuzzy events," J. Math. Anal. Applicat , vol. 23, pp. 421–427, 1968.
8. Leondes, C. T., "Image Processing and Pattern Recognition", Academic Press, 1998.
9. Lunetta, R. S.; Elvidge, C. D., "Remote Sensing Change Detection", Ann Arbor Press, 1998.
10. C. A. Murthy and S. K. Pal, "Histogram thresholding by minimizing graylevel fuzziness," Inform. Sci., vol. 60, pp. 107–135, 1992.
11. Jensen, J., 1996. Introductory Digital Image Processing: A Remote Sensing Perspective, 2nd edn. Prentice-Hall, Englewood Cliffs, NJ, 330 pp.
12. Mathers, P. M., Computer Processing of Remotely-Sensed Images, John Wiley & Sons, 1999.
13. Chavez, P.S., Mackinnon, D.J. "Automatic Detection of Vegetation Changes in the Southwestern United States Using Remotely Sensed Images", Photogrammetric Engineering and Remote Sensing, Vol 60, pp. 571–583, 1994.
14. Lillesand and Kieffer "Remote Sensing and Image Interpretation", 4th Edition, John Wiley & Sons, Inc., 2000.

Improving Simple Linguistic Fuzzy Models by Means of the Weighted COR Methodology

Rafael Alcalá[1], Jorge Casillas[2], Oscar Cordón[2], and Francisco Herrera[2]

[1] Department of Computer Science, University of Jaén,
E-23071 Jaén, Spain
alcala@ujaen.es
[2] Department of Computer Science and A.I., University of Granada,
E-18071 Granada, Spain
{casillas, ocordon, herrera}@Springer.de

Abstract. In this work we extend the Cooperative Rules learning methodology to improve simple linguistic fuzzy models, including the learning of rule weights within the rule cooperation paradigm. Considering these kinds of techniques could result in important improvements of the system accuracy, maintaining the interpretability to an acceptable level.

1 Introduction

One of the problems associated with Linguistic Modeling is its lack of accuracy when modeling some complex systems. It is due to the inflexibility of the concept of linguistic variable, which imposes hard restrictions to the fuzzy rule structure. To overcome this problem, many different possibilities to improve the Linguistic Modeling have been considered in the specialized literature. All of these approaches share the common idea of improving the way in which the linguistic fuzzy model performs the interpolative reasoning by inducing a better cooperation among the rules in the learned model. There are different ways to induce rule cooperation in the learning process [2,6,7].

In [2], a new learning methodology was proposed as a first strategy to improve *simple linguistic fuzzy models*, preserving their structure and descriptive power, and inducing a better cooperation among the fuzzy rules: the Cooperative Rules (COR) methodology. The learning philosophy was based on the use of *ad hoc data-driven methods*[1] to determine the fuzzy input subspaces where a rule should exist and a set of candidate consequents assigned to each rule. After that, a combinatorial search was carried out in the set of candidate consequents to obtain a set of rules with good cooperation among them. In [1,3], different combinatorial search techniques were considered with this aim.

On the other hand, other technique to improve the rule cooperation is the use of weighted fuzzy rules [4,8,11], in which modifying the linguistic model

---

[1] A family of efficient and simple methods guided by covering criteria of the data in the example set

F.J. Garijo, J.C. Riquelme, and M. Toro (Eds.): IBERAMIA 2002, LNAI 2527, pp. 294–302, 2002.
© Springer-Verlag Berlin Heidelberg 2002

structure an importance factor (weight) is considered for each rule. By means of this technique, the way in which these rules interact with their neighbor ones could be indicated.

In this work, we propose the hybridization of both techniques to obtain weighted cooperative fuzzy rules. Thus, the system accuracy is increased while the interpretability is maintained to an acceptable level. To do that, we present the Weighted COR (WCOR) methodology, which includes the weight learning within the original COR methodology.

To learn the subset of rules with the best cooperation and the weights associated to them, different search techniques could be considered [9]. In this contribution, we will consider a Genetic Algorithm (GA) for this purpose.

This extended methodology can be intended as a meta-method over any other ad hoc data-driven learning method, developed to improve simple linguistic fuzzy models by considering the way in which the fuzzy rules interact. Depending on the combination of this technique with different ad hoc data-driven methods, different learning approaches arise. In this work, we will consider the Wang and Mendel's method [10] (WM) for this purpose —approach guided by examples—.

The paper is organized as follows. In the next section the said specific ways to improve the rule cooperation are introduced, reviewing the original COR methodology. In Sect. 3, the WCOR methodology to obtain weighted cooperative rules is proposed. Experimental results are shown in Sect. 4, whilst some concluding remarks are pointed out in Sect. 5.

2   Preliminaries

2.1   The COR Methodology

The COR methodology is guided by example covering criteria to obtain antecedents (fuzzy input subspaces) and candidate consequents [2]. Following the WM approach this methodology presents the following learning scheme:

Let $E = \{e_1, \ldots, e_l, \ldots, e_N\}$ be an input-output data set representing the behavior of the problem being solved —with $e_l = (x_1^l, \ldots, x_n^l, y^l)$, $l \in \{1, \ldots, N\}$, N being the data set size, and n being the number of input variables—. And let $\mathcal{A}_j$ be the set of linguistic terms of the i-th input variable —with $j \in \{1, \ldots, n\}$— and $\mathcal{B}$ be the one of the output variable.

1. *Generate a candidate linguistic rule set.* This set will be formed by the rule best covering each example (input-output data pair) contained in the input-output data set. The structure of each rule, RC^l, is obtained by taking a specific example, e_l, and setting each one of the rule variables to the linguistic label associated to the fuzzy set best covering every example component, i.e.,

$$RC_l = \mathsf{IF}\ X_1\ \text{is}\ A_1^l\ \text{and}\ \ldots\ \text{and}\ X_n\ \text{is}\ A_n^l\ \mathsf{THEN}\ Y\ \text{is}\ B^l,$$

with

$$A_j^l = arg\ \max_{A' \in \mathcal{A}_j} \mu_{A'}(x_j^l)\ \text{ and }\ B^l = arg\ \max_{B' \in \mathcal{B}} \mu_{B'}(y^l).$$

2. *Obtain the antecedents R_i^{ant} of the rules composing the final linguistic model and a set of candidate consequents $C_{R_i^{ant}}$ associated to them.* Firstly, the rules are grouped according to their antecedents. Let $R_i^{ant} = $ IF X_1 is A_1^i and ... and X_n is A_n^i be the antecedents of the rules of the i-th group, where $i \in \{1, \ldots, M\}$ (with M being the number of groups, i.e., the number of rules finally obtained). The set of candidate consequents for the R_i^{ant} antecedent combination is defined as:

$$C_{R_i^{ant}} = \{B_k \in \mathcal{B} \mid \exists e_l \text{ where } \forall j \in \{1, \ldots, n\}, \forall A_j' \in \mathcal{A}_j,$$
$$\mu_{A_j^i}(x_j^l) \geq \mu_{A_j'}(x_j^l) \text{ and } \forall B' \in \mathcal{B}, \mu_{B_k}(y^l) \geq \mu_{B'}(y^{l^i})\} \ .$$

3. *Perform a combinatorial search among the sets $C_{R_i^{ant}}$ looking for the combination of consequents with the best cooperation.* An improvement in the learning process consists of adding a new term to the candidate consequent set corresponding to each rule, the *null consequent $\mathcal{N}$*, such that $C_{R_i^{ant}} = C_{R_i^{ant}} \cup \mathcal{N}$, $i = 1, \ldots, M$. If this consequent is selected for a specific rule, such rule does not take part in the model finally learned.

Since the search space tackled in step 3 of the algorithm is usually large, it is necessary to use approximate search techniques. In [3] four different well-known techniques were proposed for this purpose. In this work we will consider a GA as search technique.

2.2   The Use of Weighted Linguistic Rules

Using rule weights [4,8,11] has been usually considered to improve the way in which the rules interacts, improving the accuracy of the learned model. In this way, rule weights suppose an effective extension of the conventional fuzzy reasoning system that allow the tuning of the system to be developed at the rule level [4,8].

When weights are applied to complete rules, the corresponding weight is used to modulate the firing strength of a rule in the process of computing the defuzzified value. From human beings, it is very near to consider this weight as an importance degree associated to the rule, determining how this rule interacts with its neighbor ones. We will follow this approach, since the interpretability of the system is appropriately maintained. In addition, we will only consider weight values in $[0, 1]$ since it preserves the model readability. In this way, the use of rule weights represents an ideal framework for extended LM when we search for a trade-off between accuracy and interpretability. In order to do so, we will follow the weighted rule structure and the inference system proposed in [8]:

IF X_1 is A_1 and ... and X_n is A_n THEN Y is B with $[w]$,

where X_i (Y) are the linguistic input (output) variables, A_i (B) are the linguistic labels used in the input (output) variables, w is the real-valued rule weight, and *with* is the operator modeling the weighting of a rule.

With this structure, the fuzzy reasoning must be extended. The classical approach is to infer with the FITA (First Infer, Then Aggregate) scheme and compute the defuzzified output as the following *weighted sum*:

$$y_0 = \frac{\sum_i m_i \cdot w_i \cdot P_i}{\sum_i m_i \cdot w_i},$$

with m_i being the matching degree of the i-th rule, w_i being the weight associated to the i-th rule, and P_i being the characteristic value of the output fuzzy set corresponding to that rule. In this contribution, the center of gravity will be considered as characteristic value and the *minimum t-norm* will play the role of the implication and conjunctive operators.

A simple approximation for weighted rule learning would consist in considering an optimization technique to derive the associated weights of the previously obtained rules (e.g., by means of ad hoc data-driven methods as WM, or even COR).

3   The WCOR Methodology

It is clear that the said two approaches improve the accuracy of the learned model since they induce a good cooperation among rules. Moreover, they present complementary characteristics. However, due to the strong dependency between the consequent selection and the learning of the associated weights, the said two step-based technique to obtain weighted rules is not the most useful to obtain weighted cooperative rules.

Therefore, we need to include the learning of rule weights in the combinatorial search process of cooperative rules within the COR methodology. In this way, the selection of the set of consequents with the best cooperation and the learning of the weights associated to the obtained rules should be made using global criteria that jointly consider the action of both, consequents and weights.

In this section, we present the WCOR methodology to obtain weighted cooperative rules. With this aim, we include the weight derivation within the cooperative rule learning process.

3.1   Operation Mode

This methodology involves an extension of the original COR methodology. Therefore, WCOR consists of the following steps:

1. *Obtain the antecedents R_i^{ant} of the rules composing the final linguistic model and a set of candidate consequents $C_{R_i^{ant}}$ associated to them.*
2. *Problem representation.* For each rule R_i we have:

$$R_i^{ant}, \ C_{R_i^{ant}}, \text{ and } w_i \in [0, 1].$$

Since R_i^{ant} is kept fixed, the problem will consist of determining the consequent and the weight associated to each rule. Two vectors of size M (number of rules finally obtained) are defined to represent this information, c_1 and c_2, where,

$$c_1[i] = k_i \mid B_{k_i} \in C_{R_i^{ant}}, \; and$$
$$c_2[i] = w_i, \; \forall i \in \{1, \ldots, M\},$$

except in the case of considering rule simplification, in which $B_{k_i} \in C_{R_i^{ant}} \cup \mathcal{N}$.

In this way, the c_1 part is an integer-valued vector in which each cell represents the index of the consequent used to build the corresponding rule. The c_2 part is a real-valued vector in which each cell represents the weight associated to this rule. Finally, a problem solution is represented as follows:

$$c = c_1 \; c_2$$

3. *Perform a search on the c vector, looking for the combination of consequents and weights with the best cooperation.* The main objective will be to minimize the *mean square error:*

$$\text{MSE} = \frac{1}{2 \cdot N} \sum_{l=1}^{N} (F(x_1^l, \ldots, x_n^l) - y^l)^2,$$

with $F(x_1^l, \ldots, x_n^l)$ being the output inferred from the current model when the example e_l is used and y^l being the known desired output.

3.2   Genetic Algorithm Applied to the WCOR Methodology

The proposed GA performs an approximate search among the candidate consequents with the main aim of selecting the set of consequents with the best cooperation and simultaneously learning the weights associated to the obtained rules. The main characteristics of the said algorithm are presented in the following:

- *Genetic Approach* — An elitist generational GA with the Baker's stochastic universal sampling procedure.
- *Initial Pool* — The initial pool is obtained by generating a possible combination at random for the c_1 part of each individual in the population. And for the c_2 part, it is obtained with an individual having all the genes with value '1', and the remaining individuals generated at random in $[0, 1]$.
- *Crossover* — The standard two-point crossover in the c_1 part combined with the max-min-arithmetical crossover in the c_2 part. By using the max-min-arithmetical crossover, if $c_2^v = (c[1], \ldots, c[k], \ldots, c[n])$ and $c_2^w = (c'[1], \ldots, c'[k], \ldots, c'[n])$ are crossed, the next four offspring are obtained:

$$c_2^1 = ac_2^w + (1-a)c_2^v, \qquad\qquad c_2^2 = ac_2^v + (1-a)c_2^w,$$
$$c_2^3 \text{ with } c_3[k] = \min\{c[k], c'[k]\}, \quad c_2^4 \text{ with } c_4[k] = \max\{c[k], c'[k]\},$$

with $a \in [0, 1]$ being a parameter chosen by the GA designer.

In this case, eight offspring are generated by combining the two ones from the c_1 part (two-point crossover) with the four ones from the c_2 part (max-min-arithmetical crossover). The two best offspring so obtained replace the two corresponding parents in the population.

– *Mutation* — The operator considered in the c_1 part randomly selects a specific fuzzy subspace ($i \in \{1, \ldots, M\}$) almost containing two candidate consequents, and changes at random the current consequent k_i by other consequent k_i' such that $B_{k_i'} \in C_{R_i^{ant}}$ and $k_i' \neq k_i$. On the other hand, the selected gene in the C_2 part takes a value at random within the interval $[0, 1]$.

4   Experiments

To analyze the behavior of the proposed method, we have chosen a real-world problem to estimate the length of low voltage lines for an electric company [5].

4.1   Problem Description

Sometimes, there is a need to measure the amount of electricity lines that an electric company owns. This measurement may be useful for several aspects such as the estimation of the maintenance costs of the network, which was the main goal in this application [5]. Since a direct measure is very difficult to obtain, the consideration of models becomes useful. In this way, the problem involves finding a model that relates the *total length of low voltage line* installed in a rural town with the *number of inhabitants* in the town and the *mean of the distances from the center of the town to the three furthest clients* in it. This model will be used to estimate the total length of line being maintained.

To do so, a sample of 495 rural nuclei has been randomly divided into two subsets, the training set with 396 elements and the test set with 99 elements, the 80% and the 20% respectively. Both data sets considered are available at *http://decsai.ugr.es/~casillas/fmlib/*.

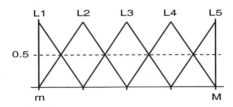

Fig. 1. Linguistic fuzzy partition representation.

Finally, the linguistic partitions considered are comprised by *five linguistic terms* with triangular-shaped fuzzy sets giving meaning to them (see Fig. 1). The corresponding labels, $\{L_1, L_2, L_3, L_4, L_5\}$, stand for very small, small, medium, large and very large, respectively.

4.2   Methods

We will compare the accuracy of different linguistic models generated from our algorithm, named WCORWM [2], to the ones generated from the following methods: the well-known ad hoc data-driven WM method [10], a *method looking for the cooperation among rules* (CORWM) [2,3] and an *algorithm for weighted rule learning* WRL. Table 1 presents a short description of each of them.

Table 1. Methods considered for comparison.

Ref.	Method	Description
[10]	WM	A well-known ad hoc data-driven method
[3]	CORWM	GA Application to the COR methodology (WCOR c_1 part)
—	WRL	Weighted rule learning GA on WM and CORWM (WCOR c_2 part)
—	WCORWM	The proposed algorithm following the WCOR methodology

The values of the parameters used in all of these experiments are presented as follows [3]: 61 individuals, 1,000 generations, 0.6 as crossover probability, 0.2 as mutation probability per chromosome, and 0.35 for the a factor in the max-min-arithmetical crossover.

4.3   Results and Analysis

The results obtained by the analyzed methods are shown in Table 2, where $\#R$ stands for the number of rules, and MSE_{tra} and MSE_{tst} respectively for the error obtained over the training and test data. The best results are in boldface.

Notice that, adding weights (WRL) to the rule sets previously learned with other methods is not sufficient. It is due to the strong dependency among the learned rules and the weights associated to them. Therefore, we need to include the learning of rule weights within the rule learning process to allow an optimal behavior.

The results obtained by WCORWM improve the ones with the remaining techniques. Moreover, an appropriated balance between approximation and generalization (with and without rule simplification) has been maintained.

---

[2] With and without rule simplification

[3] With these values we have tried easy the comparisons selecting standard common parameters that work well in most cases instead of searching very specific values for each method

Table 2. Results obtained in the low voltage line problem.

Method	#R	MSE$_{tra}$	MSE$_{tst}$	2nd stage: W$_{RL}$ MSE$_{tra}$	MSE$_{tst}$
WM	13	298,450	282,029	242,680	252,483
CORWM	13	221,569	196,808	199,128	175,358
WCORWM	13	**160,736**	161,800		
Considering rule simplification					
CORWM	11	218,675	196,399	198,630	176,495
WCORWM	12	161,414	**161,511**		

In the case of the simplified models, it seems that the original COR methodology removes more rules than the desired ones, achieving slight improvements
in the results. The use of rule weights takes advantage of rules that at first should
be removed improving the way in which they interact.

The decision tables of the models obtained by COR and WCOR are presented in Fig. 2. Each cell of the tables represents a fuzzy subspace and contains
its associated output consequent, i.e., the correspondent label together with its
respective rounded rule weight in the case of WCOR. These weights have been
graphically showed by means of the grey colour scale, from black (1.0) to white
(0.0).

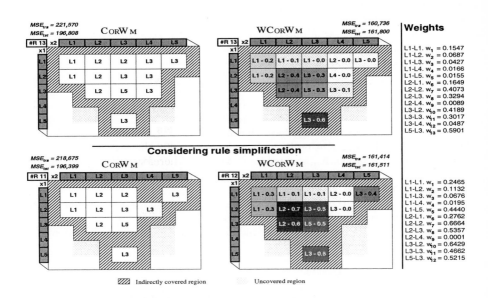

Fig. 2. Decision tables of the obtained models.

In these tables we can observe as the use of weighted rules provokes slight changes in the consequents, improving the cooperation among the rules so obtained. Moreover, we can see as the rule in the subspace L1-L4 is maintained when an appropriate interaction level is considered.

5   Concluding Remarks

In this work, we present a methodology to obtain weighted cooperative rules based on the rule cooperation paradigm presented in [2]. To do that, the learning of rule weights has been included within the combinatorial search of cooperative rules. A GA to learn cooperative rules and their associated weights has been developed for this purpose.

The proposed method has been tested in a real-world problem, improving the behavior of the basic linguistic models and the ones considering cooperative rules. Moreover, an appropriated balance between approximation and generalization has been maintained by the proposed methodology.

References

1. Alcalá, R., Casillas, J., Cordón, O., Herrera, F.: Improvement to the cooperative rules methodology by using the ant colony system algorithm. Mathware & Soft Computing **8:3** (2001) 321–335
2. Casillas, J., Cordón, O., Herrera, F.: COR: A methodology to improve ad hoc data-driven linguistic rule learning methods by inducing cooperation among rules. IEEE Transactions on Systems, Man, and Cybernetics—Part B: Cybernetics (2002). To appear
3. Casillas, J., Cordón, O., Herrera, F.: Different approaches to induce cooperation in fuzzy linguistic models under the COR methodology. In: Bouchon-Meunier, B., Gutiérrez-Ríos, J., Magdalena, L., Yager, R.R. (Eds.): Techniques for Constructing Intelligent Systems. Springer-Verlag, Heidelberg, Germany (2002)
4. Cho, J.S., Park, D.J.: Novel fuzzy logic control based on weighting of partially inconsistent rules using neural network. Journal of Intelligent Fuzzy Systems **8** (2000) 99–110
5. Cordón, O., Herrera, F., Sánchez, L.: Solving electrical distribution problems using hybrid evolutionary data analysis techniques. Applied Intelligence **10** (1999) 5–24
6. Cordón, O., Herrera, F.: A proposal for improving the accuracy of linguistic modeling. IEEE Transactions on Fuzzy Systems **8:4** (2000) 335–344
7. Ishibuchi, H., Nozaki, K., Yamamoto, N., Tanaka, H.: Selecting fuzzy if-then rules for classification problems using genetic algorithms. IEEE Transactions on Fuzzy Systems **9:3** (1995) 260–270
8. Pal, N.R., Pal, K.: Handling of inconsistent rules with an extended model of fuzzy reasoning. Journal of Intelligent Fuzzy Systems **7** (1999) 55–73
9. Pardalos, P.M., Resende, M.G.C.: Handbook of applied optimization. Oxford University Press, NY (2002)
10. Wang, L.X., Mendel, J.M.: Generating fuzzy rules by learning from examples. IEEE Transactions on Systems, Man, and Cybernetics **22** (1992) 1414–1427
11. Yu, W., Bien, Z.: Design of fuzzy logic controller with inconsistent rule base. Journal of Intelligent Fuzzy Systems **2** (1994) 147–159

A Semiquantitative Approach to Study Semiqualitative Systems

Antonio Ortega, Rafael M. Gasca, Miguel Toro, and Jesús Torres

Departamento de Lenguajes y Sistemas Informáticos
University of Seville
Avda. Reina Mercedes s/n – 41012 – Sevilla (Spain)
{ortega,gasca,mtoro,jtorres}@lsi.us.es

Abstract. In this paper is proposed a semiquantitative methodology to study models of dynamic systems with qualitative and quantitative knowledge. This qualitative information may be composed by: operators, envelope functions, qualitative labels and qualitative continuous functions. A formalism is also described to incorporate this qualitative knowledge into these models. The methodology allows us to study all the states (transient and stationary) of a semiquantitative dynamic system. It also helps to obtain its behaviours patterns. The methodology is applied to a logistic growth model with a delay.

1   Introduction

Models of dynamic systems studied in science and engineering are normally composed of quantitative, qualitative, and semiquantitative knowledge. Different approximations have been proposed when the qualitative knowledge is taken into account: transformation of non-linear to piecewise linear relationships, Monte Carlo method, constraint logic programming, probability distributions, causal relations, fuzzy sets, and combination of all levels of qualitative and quantitative abstraction [5], [9].
We are interested in the study of dynamic systems with quantitative and qualitative knowledge. All this knowledge should be taken into account when these models are studied. Different levels of numeric abstraction have been proposed in the literature: purely qualitative [6], semiquantitative [5] [8], numeric interval [14] and quantitative. The proposed methodology transforms a semiquantitative model into a family of quantitative models. A semiquantitative model may be composed of qualitative knowledge, arithmetic and relational operators, predefined functions (log,exp,sin,...), numbers and intervals.

A brief description of the proposed methodology is as follows: a semiquantitative model is transformed into a set of quantitative models. The simulation of every quantitative model generates a trajectory in the phase space. A database is obtained with these quantitative behaviours or trajectories. Techniques of Knowledge Discovery in Databases (KDD) are applied by means of a language to carry out queries about the qualitative properties of this time-series database. This language is also intended to classify the different qualitative behaviours of our model. This

F.J. Garijo, J.C. Riquelme, and M. Toro (Eds.): IBERAMIA 2002, LNAI 2527, pp. 303–312, 2002.
© Springer-Verlag Berlin Heidelberg 2002

classification will help us to describe the semiquantitative behaviour of a system by means of a set of hierarchical rules obtained by means of machine learning algorithms.

The term KDD [1] is used to refer to the overall process of discovering useful knowledge from data. The problem of knowledge extraction from databases involves many steps, ranging from data manipulation and retrieval to fundamental mathematical and statistical inference, search and reasoning. Although the problem of extracting knowledge from data (or observations) is not new, automation in the context of databases opens up many new unsolved problems.

KDD has evolved, and continues to evolve, from the confluence of research in such fields as databases, machine learning, pattern recognition, artificial intelligence and reasoning with uncertainty, knowledge acquisition for expert systems, data visualization, software discovery, information retrieval, and high-performance computing. KDD software systems incorporate theories, algorithms, and methods from all of these fields.

The term data mining is used most by statisticians, database researchers and more recently by the business community. Data mining is a particular step in the KDD process. The additional steps in KDD process are data preparation, data selection, data cleaning, incorporation of appropriate prior knowledge and proper interpretation of the results of mining ensure the useful knowledge is derived from the data [11]. A detailed descriptions of these steps may be found in [10].

The originality of our approach is that it combines in a proper way qualitative reasoning with machine learning techniques. This approach is appropriate to study all the states (transient and stationary) of a semiquantitative dynamic system. It also appropriated to obtain its behaviours patterns. However, some behaviours maybe not found with this approach, mainly, those behaviours obtained with narrowed domains of the parameters.

2   The Methodology

There has been a great deal of previous research studying the stationary state of a system, however, it is also necessary to study transient states. For example, it is very important in production industrial systems to improve their efficiency. Both states of a semiquantitative dynamic system may be studied with the proposed methodology. The methodology is shown in Figure 1.

Starting from a dynamic system with qualitative knowledge, a semiquantitative model S is obtained. A family of quantitative models F is obtained from S by means of the application of some transformation techniques which are bellow described.

Stochastic techniques are applied to choose a model $M \in F$. Every model M is quantitatively simulated obtaining a trajectory, which is composed by the values of all variables from its initial value until its final value, and the values of the parameters. Therefore, it contains the values of these variables in the transient and stationary states of the system.

A database of quantitative trajectories T is obtained with these quantitative behaviours. A language is proposed to carry out queries about the qualitative properties of the set of trajectories included in the database. A labelled database is obtained with the classification of these trajectories in according to a criterion.

Qualitative behaviour patterns of the system may be automatically obtained from this database by applying machine learning based on genetic algorithms. These algorithms are described in [2].

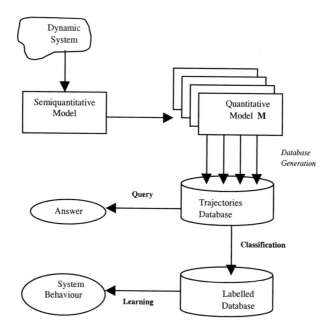

Fig. 1. Proposed methodology

3   Semiquantitative Models

A semiquantitative model S is represented by

$$\Phi(dx/dt, x, q, t), \ \ x(t_0) = x_0, \ \ \Phi_0(q, x_0) \tag{1}$$

being $x \in \mathfrak{R}^n$ the set of state variables of the system, q the parameters, t the time, dx/dt the variation of the state variables with the time, Φ constraints depending on $dx/dt, x, q, t$ and Φ_0 the set of constraints with initial conditions.

If the methodology is applied, the equations of the dynamic system (1) are transformed into a set of constraints among variables, parameters and intervals. In this paper, we are interested in those systems that may be expressed as (2) when the transformation rules are applied

$$dx/dt = f(x, p, t), \ \ x(t_0) = x_0, \ \ p \in I_p, \ \ x_0 \in I_0 \tag{2}$$

where p includes the parameters of the system and new parameters obtained by means of the transformation rules, f is a function obtained by applying the transformation rules, and I_p, I_0 are real intervals. The equation (2) is a family F of dynamic systems depending on p and x_0.

3.1 Qualitative Knowledge

Our attention is focused on those dynamic systems where there may be qualitative knowledge in their parameters, initial conditions and/or vector field. They constitute the semiquantitative differential equations of the system.

The representation of the qualitative knowledge is carried out by means of operators, which have associated real intervals. This representation facilitates the integration of qualitative and quantitative knowledge in a simple way, and the incorporation of knowledge from the experts [4].

Qualitative knowledge may be composed of qualitative operators, qualitative labels, envelope functions and qualitative continuous functions. This qualitative knowledge and its transformation techniques are now detailed.

Qualitative Operators

These operators are used to represent qualitative parameters and initial conditions. They may be unary U and binary B operators. Every qualitative operator op is defined by means of an interval I_{op}, which is supplied by the experts.

Each qualitative magnitude of the system has its own unary operators. Let U_x be the unary operators for a qualitative variable x, i.e. $U_x=\{VN_x, MN_x, LN_x, APO_x, LP_x, MP_x, VP_x \}$. They denote for x the qualitative labels *very negative, moderately negative, slightly negative, approximately zero, slightly positive, moderately positive, very positive* respectively. Let r be a new generated variable and let I_u be an interval defined in accordance with [13], then the transformation rule for a unary operator is as follows

$$op_u(e) \equiv \{r \in I_u , \ e - r = 0\} \tag{3}$$

Let e_1, e_2 be two arithmetic expressions, and let op_b be a binary operator. The expression $op_b(e_1, e_2)$ denotes a qualitative relationship between e_1 and e_2. Binary qualitative operators are classified into:

☐ Operators related to the difference $\geq, =, \leq$ being their transformation rules:

$$e_1 = e_2 \equiv \{ \ e_1 - e_2 = 0 \ \}$$
$$e_1 \leq e_2 \equiv \{ \ e_1 - e_2 - r = 0, \ r \in [-\infty, 0] \ \} \tag{4}$$
$$e_1 \geq e_2 \equiv \{ \ e_1 - e_2 - r = 0, \ r \in [0, +\infty] \ \}$$

☐ Operators related to the quotient $\{«, -<, \sim, \approx, », Vo, Ne,...\}$. The following transformation rule is applied:

$$op_b(e_1, e_2) \equiv \{e_1 - e_2 * r = 0 , \ r \in I_b \tag{5}$$

where I_b is an interval defined according to [7].

In order to maintain the consistency of the model, it is necessary to add constraints to guarantee the relation among the absolute and relative order of magnitude operators. in the general case [12].

Envelope Functions

An envelope function $y=g(x)$ represents the family of functions included between two defined real functions, a upper one $U: \Re \Rightarrow \Re$ and a lower one $L: \Re \Rightarrow \Re$.

$$\langle L(x), U(x), I \rangle, \qquad \forall x \in I: L(x) \leq U(x) \tag{6}$$

where I is the definition domain of g, and x is the independent. The transformation rule applied to (6) is

$$g(x) = \alpha L(x) + (1 - \alpha) U(x) \text{ with } \alpha \in [0,1] \tag{7}$$

where α is a new variable. If $\alpha=0 \Rightarrow g(x)=U(x)$ and if $\alpha=1 \Rightarrow g(x)=L(x)$ and any other value of α in $(0,1)$ stands for any included value between $L(x)$ and $U(x)$.

Qualitative Continuous Functions

A qualitative continuous function $y=h(x)$ represents a set of constraints among the values of y and x according to the properties of h. It is denoted by

$$y=h(x), \quad h \equiv \{P_1, s_1, P_2, \ldots, s_k-_1, P_k\} \tag{8}$$

being P_i the points of the function. Every P_i is defined by means of (d_i, e_i) where d_i is the qualitative landmark associated to the variable x and e_i to y. These points are separated by the sign s_i of the derivative in the interval between two consecutive points. A monotonous qualitative function is a particular case of these functions where the sign is always the same $s_1=\ldots=s_k-_1$.

The transformation rules of a qualitative continuous function are applied in three steps:

1. *Normalization*:

   The definition of the function is completed and homogenised using these continuity properties:

   ☐ a function that changes, its sign between two consecutive landmarks passes through a landmark whose value in the function is zero

   ☐ a function whose derivative changes, its sign between two consecutive landmarks passes through a landmark whose derivative is zero

   The definition of any function (Equation 8) is always completed with: the extreme points $(-\infty, +\infty)$, the points that denote the cut points with the axes, and where the sign of the derivative changes (a maximum or a minimum of h).

2. *Extension*:

   The definition of these functions is enriched by means of an automatic process, which incorporates new landmarks or qualitative labels. This extension is carried out to diminish the uncertainty in the definition of the function.

   The number of new landmarks included between each two consecutive original landmarks may be always the same. With this consideration, we don't loose the statistical representativity of the selected quantitative samples obtained for this function.

3. *Transformation*

A qualitative function h is transformed into a set of quantitative functions H. The algorithm **ChooseH** is applied to obtain H.

```
ChooseH (h)
    for each monotonous region in h
          segment={Pm, ..., Pn}
          choose a value for every Pi in the segment
                verifying the constraints of h
```

This algorithm divides h into its segments. A *segment* is a sequence of consecutive points $\{P_m,...,P_n\}$ separated by means of those points whose landmark $e_i=0$ or where $s_i \neq s_{i+1}$. The segments divide the function into their monotonous regions where their landmarks e_i have the same sign. The algorithm applies stochastic techniques to choose every quantitative function of H. These techniques are similar to the Monte Carlo method, however, the values obtained must satisfy the constraints of h. We use a heuristic that applies a random uniform distribution to obtain the values for every landmark of P_i.

4   Database Generation

A family F of quantitative models has been obtained when the transformation rules described in section 3.1 have been applied to the semiquantitative model S. This family depends on a set of interval parameters p and functions H defined by means of a set of quantitative points. Every particular model M of F is selected by means of stochastic techniques, and it is quantitatively simulated. This simulation generates a trajectory r that is stored into the database T.

The following algorithms are applied to obtain T.

```
ChooseModel (F)
    for each interval parameter or variable of F
            choose a value in its interval for it
    for each function h of F
            H:=ChooseH(h)
```

```
Database generation T
    T:={ }
    for i=1 to N
            M:=ChooseModel(F)
            r:= QuantitativeSimulation(M)
            T:=T ∪ r
```

being N the number of simulations to be carried out, and it is defined in accordance with the section 7. Therefore, N is the number of trajectories of T.

5   Query/Classification Language

In this section, we propose a language to carry out queries to the trajectories database. It is also possible to assign qualitative labels to the trajectories with this language.

5.1   Abstract Syntax

Let T be the set of all trajectories r stored in the database. A query Q is: a quantifier operator $\forall, \exists, \aleph$ applied on T, or a basic query $[r,P]$ that evaluates *true* when the trajectory r verifies the property P.

The property P may be formulated by means of the composition of other properties using the Boolean operators $\land, \lor, \neg$.

Table 1. Abstract Syntax of the Language

$$
\begin{array}{llll}
Q: \forall\ r \in T \bullet [r,P] & P:\ P_b & P_b:\ P_d \\
\quad |\ \exists\ r \in T \bullet [r,P] & \quad |\ P \land P & \quad |\ f(L(F)) \\
\quad |\ \aleph\ r \in T \bullet [r,P] & \quad |\ P \lor\ P & \quad |\ \forall t{:}F \bullet F \\
\quad |\ [r,p] & \quad |\ \neg P & \quad |\ \exists t{:}F \bullet F \\[2ex]
& P_d:\ EQ & F:\ F_b & F_b:\ e_b \\
& \quad |\quad CL & \quad |\ F\ \&\ F & \quad |\ e \in I \\
& & \quad |\ F\,|\,F & \quad |\ u(e) \\
& & \quad |\ !\,F & \quad |\ b(e,e) \\
\end{array}
$$

A basic property P_b may be: a predefined property P_d, a Boolean function f applied to a list L of points or intervals that verifies the formula F, or a quantifier $\forall, \exists$ applied to the values of a particular trajectory for a time t. This time may be: an instant of time, a unary time operator (i.e. a range of time), a predefined time landmark, or the list of times where the formula F is verified.

A defined property P_d is the one whose formulation is automatic. They are queries commonly used in dynamic systems. There are two predefined: EQ is verified when the trajectory ends up in a stable equilibrium; and CL when it ends up in a cycle limit.

A formula F may be composed of other formulas combined by means of Boolean operators $\&, |, !$.

A basic formula F_b may be: a Boolean expression e_b, or if a numeric expression e belongs to an interval, or a unary u or binary b qualitative operator.

5.2   Semantics

The semantics of every instruction of this language is translated into a query on the database. The techniques applied to carry out this transformation come from the development of compilers of language programming. A query $[r,P]$ is *true* when trajectory r verifies the property P. Semantics of a query with a quantifier depends on its related quantifier. If it is $\forall$, a Boolean value *true* is returned when all the trajectories $r \in T$ verify P. If it is $\exists$ then *true* is returned when there is at least one trajectory $r \in T$ that verifies the property P. If the quantifier is $\aleph$ then returns the number of trajectories of T that verifies P.

Let $\forall t: F_1 \bullet F_2$ be a basic property which is *true* if during the time that F_1 is satisfied, all the values of r verify F_2. For $\exists$ quantifier is *true* when at least a value of r that satisfies F_1, also satisfied F_2. In order to evaluate a formula F, it is necessary to substitute its variables for their values. These values are obtained from T.

5.3   Classification

A classification rule is formulated as a set of basic queries with labels, and possibly other expressions

$$[r,P_A] \Rightarrow A,e_{n1},\dots \qquad\qquad [r,P_b] \Rightarrow B,e_{n2},\dots \qquad \dots \qquad (9)$$

A trajectory r is classified with a label η if it verifies the property P_η.

Let $[r,P_A] \Rightarrow A,e_{AI}$ be a classification rule. A trajectory $r \in T$ is classified with the label A if it verifies property P_A. The result of evaluating e_{AI} for this trajectory is also stored into the database.

6   A Logistic Growth Model with a Delay

It is very common to find growth processes where an initial phase of exponential growth is followed by another phase of asymptotic approach to a saturation value. The following generic names are given: logistic, sigmoid, and s-shaped processes. This growth appears in those systems where the exponential expansion is truncated by the limitation of the resources required for this growth. They abound in the evolution of bacteria, in mineral extraction, in world population growth, in epidemics, in rumours, in economic development, the learning curves, etc.

In the bibliography, these models have been profusely studied. There is a bimodal behaviour pattern attractor: A stands for normal growth, and O for decay (Figure 5.b).

Differential equations of the model S are

$$\Phi \equiv \begin{cases} dx/dt=x(n\ r-m),\ y=delay_\tau(x),\ r>0, r=h(y), \\ h \equiv \{(-\infty,-\infty),+,(d_0,0),+,\ (0,1),+,\ (d_1,e_0),\ -,(1,0),\ -\ (+\infty,-\infty)\} \end{cases} \quad (10)$$

being n the increasing factor, m the decreasing factor, and h a qualitative function with a maximum point at (x_1,y_0). The initial conditions are

$$\Phi_0 \equiv \{\ x_0 \in [LP_x,MP_x],\ LP_x(m),LP_x(n),\ \tau \in MP_\tau,VP_\tau\} \quad (11)$$

where LP,MP,VP are qualitative unary operators for x, τ variables.

We would like to know:
1. if an equilibrium is always reached
2. if there is an equilibrium whose value is not zero
3. if all the trajectories with value zero at the equilibrium are reached without oscillations.
4. To classify the database according to the behaviours of the system.

We apply our approach to this model. Firstly, the transformation rules are applied,

$$\Phi \left\{ \begin{array}{l} dx/dt = x(n\ r - m),\ y = delay_\tau(x),\ x > 0,\ r = H(y), \\ H,\ x_0 \in [0,3],\ m,n \in [0,1],\ \tau \in [0.5,10] \end{array} \right. \tag{12}$$

where H has been obtained by applying *Choose H* to h, and the intervals are defined in accordance with the experts' knowledge. The algorithm *Database generation T* returns the trajectories database.

The proposed queries are formulated as follows:

1. $r \in T \bullet [r, EQ]$

2. $r \in T \bullet [r, EQ \wedge \exists\, t: t \approx t_f \bullet !APO_x(x)]$

3. $\forall\, r \in T \bullet [r, EQ \wedge \exists\, t: t \approx t_f \bullet APO_x(x) \wedge \quad length(dx/dt = 0) = 0\ ]$

4. being APO_x a unary operator of x. The list of points where $dx/dt = 0$ is the list with the maximum and minimum points. If length is 0 then there are not oscillations.

   We classify the database by means of the labels:

   $[r, EQ \wedge length(dx/dt = 0) > 0 \wedge\ \exists\, t: t \approx t_f \bullet !APO_x(x)] \Rightarrow recovered,$

   $[r, EQ \wedge length(dx/dt = 0) > 0 \wedge\ \exists\, t: t \approx t_f \bullet APO_x(x)] \Rightarrow retarded,$

   $[r, EQ \wedge \exists\, t: t \approx t_f \bullet APO_x(x)] \qquad\qquad \Rightarrow extinction,$

They correspond to the three possible behaviour patterns of the system (Fig. 6). They are in accordance with the obtained behaviours when a mathematical reasoning is carried out [3].

7   Conclusions and Further Work

In this paper, a methodology is presented in order to automate the analysis of dynamic systems with qualitative and quantitative knowledge. This methodology is based on a transformation process, application of stochastic techniques, quantitative simulation, generation of trajectories database and definition of a query/classification language. There is enough bibliography that studies stationary states of dynamic systems. However, the study of transient states is also necessary. These studies are possible with the proposed language.

The simulation is carried out by means of stochastic techniques. The results are stored in a quantitative database. It may be classified by means of the proposed language. Once the database is classified, genetic algorithms may be applied to obtain conclusions about the dynamic system.

In the future, we are going to enrich the query/classification language with: operators for comparing trajectories among them, temporal logic among several times of a trajectory, more type of equations, etc.

Acknowledgments. This work was partially supported by the Spanish Interministerial Committee of Science and Technology by means of the program DPI2001-4404-E.

References

1. Adriaans P. and Zantinge D. Data Mining. *Addison Wesley Longman.* (1996).
2. Aguilar J., Riquelme J.M. and Toro M. Decision queue classifier for supervised learning using rotated hiperboxes, *Lecture Notes in Artificial Intelligence* 1484: 326–336 (1998).
3. Aracil J., Ponce E., and Pizarro L. Behaviour patterns of logistic models with a delay, Mathematics and computer in simulation No 44, 123–141 (1997).
4. Gasca R.M. Razonamiento y Simulación en Sistemas que integran conocimiento cualitativo y cuantitativo, *Ph.D. diss., Seville University.*(1998).
5. Kay H. Refining imprecise models and their behaviours. *Ph.D. diss., Texas University,* (1996).
6. Kuipers B.J. Qualitative reasoning. Modelling and simulation with incomplete knowledge, *The MIT Press*, (1994)
7. Mavrovouniotis M.L. and Stephanopoulos G. Formal Order-of-Magnitude Reasoning. *Process Engineering Computer Chemical Engineering*, No. 12, 867-880, (1988).
8. Ortega J.A., Gasca R.M., and Toro M. Including qualitative knowledge in semiquantitative dynamic systems. *Lecture Notes in Artificial Intelligence* No.1415, 329–338, (1998).
9. Ortega J.A., Gasca R.M., and Toro M. Behaviour patterns of semiquantitative dynamic systems by means of quantitative simulations *The 16th International Joint Conference on Artificial Intelligence* Qualitative and Model based Reasoning for Complex Systems and their Control, Stockholm (Sweden), 42–48, (1999)
10. Ortega J.A. Patrones de comportamiento temporal en modelos semicualitativos con restricciones. *Ph.D. diss., Dept. of Computer Science, Seville Universit,* (2000).
11. Rastogi R. and Shim K. Data mining on large databases. *Bell laboratories.* (1999).
12. Travé-Massuyès, L., Prats F., Sánchez M., Agell N. Consistent Relative and Absolute Order-of-Magnitude Models, *In Proc. Of 16th International Workshop on Qualitative Reasoning, 185–192,* (2002).
13. Travé,-Massuyès L., Dague Ph., and Guerrin F. Le raisonement qualitativ pour les sciences de l'ingénieur, *Hermes Ed.* (1997)
14. Vescovi M., Farquhar A., and Iwasaki Y., Numerical interval simulation: combined qualitative and quantitative simulation to bound behaviours of non-monotonic systems. *Proceedings of 14th International Joint Conference on Artificial Intelligence*, 1806–1812, (1995).

Multi-objective Optimization Evolutionary Algorithms Applied to Paroxysmal Atrial Fibrillation Diagnosis Based on the k-Nearest Neighbours Classifier

Francisco de Toro[1], Eduardo Ros[2], Sonia Mota[2], and Julio Ortega[2]

[1] Departamento de Ingeniería Electrónica, Sistemas Informáticos y Automática,
Universidad de Huelva, Spain
ftoro@uhu.es
[2] Departamento de Arquitectura y Tecnología de Computadores,
Universidad de Granada, Spain
{eduardo,sonia,julio}@atc.ugr.es

Abstract. In this paper, multi-objective optimization is applied to determine the parameters for a k-nearest neighbours classifier that has been used in the diagnosis of Paroxysmal Atrial Fibrillation (PAF), in order to get optimal combinations of *classification rate*, *sensibility* and *specificity*. We have considered three different evolutionary algorithms for implementing the multi-objective optimization of parameters: the *Single Front Genetic Algorithm* (SFGA), an improved version of SFGA, called *New Single Front Genetic Algorithm* (NSFGA), and the *Strength Pareto Evolutionary Algorithm* (SPEA). The experimental results and the comparison of the different methods, done by using the hypervolume metric, show that multi-objective optimization constitutes an adequate alternative to combinatorial scanning techniques.

1 Introduction

Whilst most real-world optimization problems require the simultaneous optimization of multiple, often competing, criteria (or objectives). These problems are known as MOP (*Multi-objective Optimization Problems*) [1].The notion of *optimum* has to be re-defined in this context and instead of aiming to find a single solution; a procedure for solving MOP should determine a set of good compromises or *trade-off* solutions, generally known as *Pareto optimal solutions* from which the decision maker will select one. These solutions are optimal in the wider sense that no other solution in the search space is superior when all objectives are considered. In addition, evolutionary Algorithms (EAs) have the potential to finding multiple Pareto optimal solutions in a single run and have been widely used in this area [2] Recently the importance of *elitism*, supported experimentally [2,3], *secondary population* and adequate *diversity maintaining techniques* has focused the attention of researches [4]. In that sense, some of the authors have presented elsewhere the SFGA [5] and the NSFGA[6] that continue exploring the benefits of the aforementioned concepts.

The Atrial Fibrillation is the heart arrhythmia that causes most frequently embolic events that may generate cerebrovascular accidents. In this paper is described how the aforementioned techniques are applied to an open real world problem: Paroxysmal

F.J. Garijo, J.C. Riquelme, and M. Toro (Eds.): IBERAMIA 2002, LNAI 2527, pp. 313–318, 2002.

Atrial Fibrillation Diagnosis based on Electrocardiogram (ECG) traces without explicit Atrial Fibrillation episodes [7]. Recently has finished an international initiative that addressed this problem concluding that an automatic PAF diagnosis scheme is possible with a reasonable efficiency. The different proposed diagnosis approaches within the Computers in Cardiology Challenge 2001 [7] were focused on achieving high classification rates. But the use of ECGs (non invasive exploration method) for the diagnosis motivates the possibility of using this diagnosis scheme in routinely cardiac examinations. If the application reaches high accuracy detecting PAF patients (high sensibility), even with a lower capability of accurate diagnosis with healthy subjects (lower specificity), positive diagnosis would motivate more complete explorations. Therefore it can be considered a MOP in which is has interest to optimize the **classification rate** and the **sensibility** (see section 2).

In this paper section 2 describes the PAF diagnosis problem, Section 3 reviews both SFGA and NSFGA. Experimental results for SFGA, NSFGA and SPEA which is one of the State-of the-art evolutionary algorithms for MOPs, are given in section 4. Finally concluding remarks are summarized in Section 5.

2   PAF Diagnosis Based on the K-Nearest Neighbor Classifier

A public database for PAF diagnosis applications is available [8]. It is composed by registers obtained of 25 healthy individuals and 25 patients diagnosed with PAF. An automatic algorithm capable of discriminating registers of these two groups with a certain accuracy is the challenge addressed in the present paper. For this purpose 48 parameters have been extracted of each ECG register [9] obtaining a 48 component vector that characterizes each subject $(p_1, ..., p_{48})$.

A modular classification algorithm based on the K-nearest neighbours has been used for this application and described in detail in [10]. The labelled vectors work as references of the classification system. For each new non-labelled vector, the Euclidean distances to the labelled vectors are calculated. The labels of the K-nearest neighbours are consulted and the final label is calculated through a voting scheme as the label of the majority of the K-nearest neighbours. In this way the classification algorithm is modular, new parameters can be added easily, only the dimension considered in the Euclidean distance calculation step has to be modified. The modularity of the classification algorithm enables automatic parameter scanning techniques. Using the 48 parameters in the classification scheme is highly inefficient, therefore a parameter selection stage is necessary to select a subset of parameters with which the best classification performances are reached.

In order to be able to automatically modify the selection of the different parameters in the classification scheme the input pattern has been multiplied by a filter vector (F), i.e. $I=(p_1 f_1, ..., p_{48} f_{48})$. Where the filter components f_i lie within the interval [0,1]. These filter components represent the chromosome of the different solutions optimized by the evolutionary algorithms.

For biomedical diagnosis applications, the final diagnostic of a specific disease for a patient can be **ill** (suffering of a certain pathology) or **healthy** (free of this concrete pathology). This means that the classification result for PAF diagnosis can be:

True Positive (TP). The algorithm classifies as PAF patient a real PAF patient.

True Negative (TN). The algorithm classifies a healthy subject as healthy.

False Positive (FP). The algorithm classifies as PAF patient a healthy subject
False Negative (FN). The algorithm classifies as healthy subject a PAF patient.
With these cases different functions of interest can be defined (1) : *Classification rate*
(CR), *Sensibility* (SE) and *Specificity* (SP).

$$CR = \frac{TP+TN}{TP+TN+FP+FN} \; ; \; SE = \frac{TP}{TP+FN} \; ; \; SP = \frac{TN}{TN+FP} \tag{1}$$

Note that the *Sensibility* represents the ratio between the detected ill patients and the
total ill patients. While the *Specificity* represents the ration between the detected
healthy subjects and the total healthy subjects.

Due to the small size of the training database (25 patients and 25 healthy subjects),
the evaluation of the classification rate is calculated in 50 cycles with the method
leaving one out. In this way, in each cycle, one vector is selected as test element. This
vector is classified according to the scheme described above with the other 49 labelled
vectors as classification references. In each cycle are actualised the classification
results in four counters: True_Positive (TP), True_Negative (TN), False_Positive (FP)
and False_Negative (FN). The final classification rate (CR), the sensibility (SE) and
the specificity (SP) are finally calculated with these counters that accumulate the
classification results of the 50 cycles

It is worthy to mention that MOEAs generate a population of different solutions.
This must be seen as an added advantage because some of these solutions will be
more appropriate than other for certain patients suffering from other cardiac
pathologies. This other current pathologies may invalidate some solutions based on
certain parameters that are unreliable for these patients. Therefore a population of
solutions instead of a single one is desirable.

3   Single Front Evolutionary Algorithms

The *Single front Genetic Algorithm* (SFGA) [5], previously proposed by some of the
authors, implements a elitist selection procedure in which only the non-dominated
(and well-diversified) individuals in the current population are copied to the mating
pool for recombination purposes (see Figure 1.a) The preservation of diversity in the
population is ensured by means of a filtering function, which prevents the crowding
of individuals by removing individuals according to a given *grid* in the *objective*
space. The filtering function uses the distance evaluated in the objective space. That
approach has been proved very effective when applied to Zitzler test functions in
comparison to other similar algorithms using a more complex selection scheme to
produce the mating pool.

In the *New Single front genetic algorithm* (Figure 1.b) [6], some features has
been added to the original SFGA. Firstly an external archive keeps track of the best-
ever solutions found during the running of the algorithm. A selection procedure
produces a mating pool of size S by randomly choosing individuals from the external
set and the filtered current population. The variation operators produces the offspring
that is copied to the next population. The updating procedure adds the first front of
ND individuals in the current population and deleting from the archive the dominated
individuals.

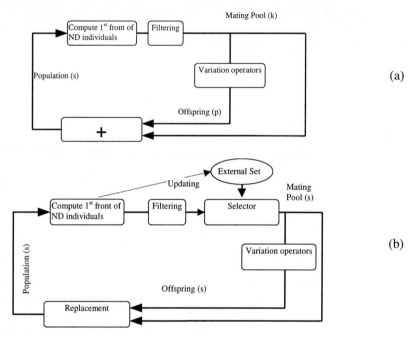

Fig. 1. Description of SFGA (a) and NSFGA (b).

Results of the mentioned algorithms compared to the ones obtained by SPEA [10] are shown in the next section.

4   Experimental Results

For performance comparison, the hypervolume metric [3] for maximization problems has been used. For the sake of simplicity just S metric is shown. S(Ai) is the volume of the space that is *dominated* [1] by the set Ai. All of the algorithms were executed with the same initial population. The filter parameter, ft, is set to 0.01, the mutation probability per gene is 0.01 and the crossover probability is 0.6. Each Algorithm (see Table 1) is executed for 3 objectives (section 4.1) and 2 objectives (section 4.2). After preliminary trials 100 iterations seems to be enough for the algorithms to converge. All algorithms are executed the aforementioned number of iterations except where indicated.

4.1   Three Objectives: Classification Rate, Sensibility, and Specificity

Although these three objectives are linearly dependent, this section can illustrate the performance gain obtained by selecting two of these objectives in section 4.2.

In this case, best Performance was obtained by SPEA with K=1, (the average of the three best Classification rates was 86% with 88% as average Sensibility and

81.3% average Specificity).The results are similar to the ones obtained by combinatorial scanning techniques [11].

Table 1. Performance of the algorithms for 3 and 2 objectives

Popsize	K	$SFGA_3$	$SFGA_2$	$NSFGA_3$	$NSFGA_2$	$SPEA_3$	$SPEA_2$
100^1	1	0.53632	0.68640	0.66259	**0.82720**	**0.68147**	0.77360
	3	0.44256	0.73600	**0.65910**	0.75280	0.58732	**0.78800**
	5	0.47980	0.65120	0.61958	0.77200	**0.68371**	**0.83680**
	7	0.53262	0.65280	0.55104	**0.77200**	0.59222	0.73920
	9	0.46086	0.62400	**0.59136**	0.72080	0.57862	**0.72160**
100	1	0.49795	0.65360	0.66259	0.72160	**0.68147**	**0.73840**
	3	0.44256	**0.71760**	0.50048	**0.71760**	0.57203	**0.71760**
	5	0.47804	0.63520	0.52041	0.67120	**0.64313**	**0.73520**
	7	0.51200	0.62400	**0.55104**	0.68880	**0.55104**	**0.72000**
	9	0.45907	0.60800	**0.55104**	0.67200	0.53504	**0.69840**
50	1	0.49612	0.80960	0.63571	**0.82800**	0.68147	0.70560
	3	**0.50048**	**0.75440**	**0.50048**	0.69920	0.44460	0.65920
	5	0.55936	0.59200	0.42150	0.61920	**0.61203**	**0.65040**
	7	**0.51558**	0.63840	0.46364	0.63840	0.51072	**0.65360**
	9	0.44179	0.59040	**0.53267**	**0.67200**	0.53260	0.63840
30	1	0.68806	0.65600	0.61958	0.68880	**0.73449**	**0.70560**
	3	0.45926	0.69920	**0.48672**	**0.71520**	0.46700	0.64400
	5	0.48838	0.60480	0.53446	**0.67120**	0.53632	0.63840
	7	0.51072	0.59200	0.48153	**0.65520**	0.51200	0.61840
	9	0.43776	**0.66880**	0.46086	0.56080	**0.55212**	**0.66800**

4.2 Two Objectives: Classification Rate and Sensibility

The whole diagnosis scheme is based on ECG traces, therefore on a non invasive exploration process. In this context, a high sensibility is more desired than a high specificity for the same classification rate. This means, that such an automatic PAF diagnosis application could be applied in routinely explorations, in this way, positive PAF diagnosis would motivate more complex diagnosis processes. Because of that we have focused on optimizing the classification rate and sensibility of the algorithm.

In the two objectives optimization scheme the best Performance was obtained by SPEA with K=5, (the average of the three best Classification rates was 82% with 94.7% as average Sensibility, for these solutions the a posteriori calculated Specificity average is 69.3%). In this case, it is observed that the Sensibility increases significantly, although the classification rate decreases, this can be of interest to detect possible PAF patients among the general population in preventive examinations.

---

[1] 1000 iterations

5   Concluding Remarks

Optimization of the three algorithms can be seen as a global optimization, while when only two performance indicators are taken into account (CR and SE) the process is focused on optimizing SE (although this would produce a decrease in SP) and CR. The obtained results are of the same range to the ones reached by combinatorial scanning processes [11] but the techniques applied in this paper have two intrinsic advantages: it represents a multi-path search approach, and the generation of a population of different trade-off solutions instead of a single one can provide some flexibility to the medical specialist. These two characteristics are common to all the evolutionary algorithms applied in this paper.

Acknowledgements. This paper has been supported by the Spanish *Ministerio de Ciencia y Tecnología* under grant TIC2000-1348.

References

[1]   Carlos A. Coello Coello. *An Updated Survey of GA-Based Multiobjective Optimization Techniques*, Technical Report Lania-RD-98-08, Laboratorio Nacional de Informática Avanzada (LANIA), 1998.

[2]   Parks, G.T. and I. Miller. *"Selective breeding in a multiobjective genetic algorithm"*. In A.E. Eiben, T. Bäck, M. Schoenauer, and H.-P. Schwefel (Editos).5th International Conference on Parallel Problem Solving from Nature (PPSN-V), Berlin, Germany, pp. 250–259. Springer.

[3]   Eckart Zitzler, Kalyanmoy Deb, and Lothar Thiele. *Comparison of Multiobjective Evolutionary Algorithms: Empirical Results*, Technical Report 70, Computer Engineering and Networks Laboratory (TIK), Swiss Federal Institute of Technology (ETH) Zurich, Gloriastrasse 35, CH-8092 Zurich, Switzerland, December 1999.

[4]   Laumans M., Zitzler E., Thiele L.: *On the Effects of Archiving Elitism, and Density Based Selection in Evolutionary Multi-objective Optimization.* 1st Conference on Evolutionary Multiobjective Optimization, pp 181–197. Springer-Verlag, 2001.

[5]   F. de Toro; J.Ortega.; J.Fernández; A.F.Díaz. PSFGA: A parallel Genetic Algorithm for Multiobjective Optimization. 10th Euromicro Workshop on Parallel and Distributed Processing. Gran Canaria, January 2002

[6]   F. de Toro, E Ros, S Mota, J Ortega: Non-invasive Atrial disease diagnosis using decision rules: A Mutiobjetive Optimization approach. 8th Iberoamerican Conference on Artificial Intelligence (IBERAMIA2002), November 2002, Sevilla, Spain.

[7]   http://www.cinc.org/LocalHost/CIC2001_1.htm

[8]   http://physionet.cps.unizar.es/physiobank/database/afpdb/

[9]   Mota S., Ros E., Fernández F.J., Díaz A.F., Prieto, A.: ECG Parameter Characterization of Paroxysmal Atrial Fibrillation. 4th International Workshop on Biosignal Interpretation (BSI2002), 24th-26th June , 2002, Como, Italy.

[10] Zitzler, E.; Thiele, L.: An Evolutionary algorithm for multiobjective optimization: The strength Pareto approach, Technical Report No. 43 (May 1998), Zürich: Computer Engineering and Networks Laboratory, Switzerland.

[11] Ros E., Mota S., Toro F.J., Díaz A.F. and Fernández F.J.: Paroxysmal Atrial Fibrillation: Automatic Diagnosis Algorithm based on not fibrillating ECGs. 4th International Workshop on Biosignal Interpretation (BSI2002), 24th–26th June , 2002, Como, Italy.

Population Studies for the Gate Matrix Layout Problem

Alexandre Mendes[1], Paulo França[1], Pablo Moscato[2], and Vinícius Garcia[1]

[1]Faculdade de Engenharia Elétrica e de Computação
Universidade Estadual de Campinas
C.P. 6101, 13083-970, Campinas, Brazil
{smendes, franca, jacques}@densis.fee.unicamp.br

[2]School of Electrical Engineering and Computer Science
University of Newcastle
Callaghan, NSW, 2308, Australia
moscato@densis.fee.unicamp.br

Abstract. This paper addresses a Very Large Scale Integrated (VLSI) design problem that belongs to the NP-hard class. The Gate Matrix Layout problem has strong applications on the chip-manufacturing industry. A Memetic Algorithm is employed to solve a set of benchmark instances, present in previous works in the literature. Beyond the results found for these instances, another goal of this paper is to study how the use of multiple populations and different migration strategies affects the algorithm's performance. This comparison has shown to be fruitful, sometimes producing a strong performance improvement over single population approaches.

1 Introduction

The use of multiple populations in Evolutionary Algorithms (EAs) gained increased momentum when computer networks, multi-processors computers and distributed processing systems (such as workstations clusters) became widespread available. Regarding the software issue, the introduction of PVM, and later MPI, as well as web-enabled, object-oriented languages like Java also had their role. As most EAs are inherently parallel methods, the distribution of the tasks is relatively easy for most applications. The workload can be distributed at an individual or a population level; the final choice depends on how complex are the computations involved. In this work we do not use parallel computers, or workstations networks. The program runs in a sequential way on a single processor, but populations evolve separately, simulating the behavior of a parallel environment. With several populations evolving in parallel, larger portions of the search space can be sampled, mainly because each population will inspect a different part of it. Furthermore, any important information found can be shared between them through migration of individuals. These factors make the parallel search much more powerful than the single population-based one.

F.J. Garijo, J.C. Riquelme, and M. Toro (Eds.): IBERAMIA 2002, LNAI 2527, pp. 319–328, 2002.

2   A VLSI Optimization Problem: Gate Matrix Layout

The Gate Matrix Layout problem is a NP-hard problem [3] that arises in the context of physical layout of Very Large Scale Integration (VLSI). It can be stated as: suppose that there are g gates and n nets on a gate matrix layout circuit. Gates can be described as vertical wires holding transistors at specific positions with nets interconnecting all the distinct gates that share transistors at the same position. An instance can be represented as a 0-1 matrix, with g columns and n rows. A number one in the position (i, j) means a transistor must be implemented at gate i and net j. Moreover, all transistors in the same net must be interconnected. The superposition of interconnections will define the number of tracks needed to build the circuit. The objective is to find a permutation of the g columns so that the superposition of interconnections is minimal, thus minimizing the number of tracks. The figure below shows a possible solution for a given instance, with 7 gates and 5 nets, and how to go from the 0-1 matrix representation to the circuit itself.

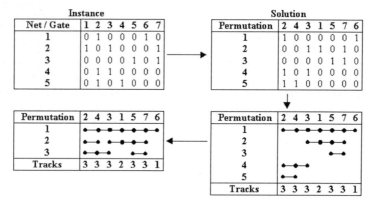

Fig. 1. The translation from a given instance's solution into the real circuit.

In the example, the permutation of the columns was <2-4-3-1-5-7-6>. After the interconnection of all transistors, represented by the horizontal lines, we calculate the number of tracks needed to build each gate. This number is the sum of positions used in each column. The number of tracks needed to build the circuit is its maximum. More detailed information on this problem can be found in [4].

3   Memetic Algorithms

Since the publication of John Holland's book, „*Adaptation in Natural and Artificial Systems*", the field of *Genetic Algorithms,* and the larger field of *Evolutionary Computation,* were definitely established as new research areas. Other pioneer works would also be cited, but since Holland's work they became increasingly conspicuous in many engineering fields and in Artificial Intelligence problems. In the mid 80's, a new class of *knowledge-augmented GAs*, also called *hybrid GAs*, began to appear in the computer science literature. The main idea supporting these methods is that of making use of other forms of „knowledge", *i.e.* other solution methods already available for the problem at hand. As a consequence, the resulting algorithms had little resemblance with biological evolution analogies. Recognizing important differences and similarities with other population-based approaches, some of them were categorized as *Memetic Algorithms* (MAs) in 1989 [7][9].

3.1 Population Structure

It is illustrative to show how some MAs resemble the cooperative problem solving techniques that can be found in some organizations. For instance, in our approach we use a *hierarchically structured population* based on a complete ternary tree. In contrast with a non-structured population, the complete ternary tree can also be understood as *a set of overlapping sub-populations* (that we will refer to as *clusters*).

In Figure 2, we can see that each cluster consists of one *leader* and three *supporter* individuals. Any leader individual in an intermediate layer has both leader and supporter roles. The leader individual always contains the best solution – considering the number of tracks it requires – of all individuals in the cluster. This relation defines the population hierarchy. The number of individuals in the population is equal to the number of nodes in the complete ternary tree, *i.e.* we need 13 individuals to make a ternary tree with 3 levels, 40 individuals to have 4 levels, and so on. The general equation is $(3^n - 1)/2$, where n is the number of levels.

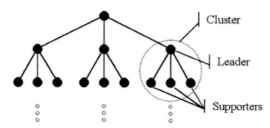

Fig. 2. Diagram of the population structure.

Previous tests comparing the tree-structured population with non-structured approaches are present in [1]. They show that the ternary-tree approach leads to considerably better results, and with the use of much less individuals. In this work, we decided not to address this issue again due to space limitations.

3.2 Representation and Crossover

The representation chosen for the VLSI problem is quite intuitive, with the *chromosome* being composed of alleles assuming different integer values in the $[1, n]$ interval, where n is the number of columns of the associated 0-1 matrix. The crossover tested is a variant of the well-known *Order Crossover* (OX) called *Block Order Crossover* (BOX). After choosing two parents, fragments of the chromosome from one of them are randomly selected and copied into the offspring. In a second phase, the offspring's empty positions are sequentially filled using the chromosome of the other parent. The procedure tends to perpetuate the *relative order* of the columns, although some modifications in this order might occur.

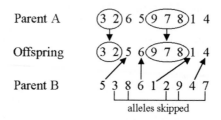

Fig. 3. Block Order Crossover (BOX) example.

In Figure 3, *Parent A* contributes with two pieces of its chromosome to the offspring. These parts are thus copied to the same position they occupy in the parent. The blank spaces are then filled with the information of *Parent B*, going from left to right. Alleles in *Parent B* already present in the offspring are skipped; being copied only the non-repeated ones. The average contribution percentage of each parent is set at 50%. This means that the offspring will be created using information inherited in equal proportion from both parents.

The number of new individuals created every generation is two times the number of individuals present in the population. This crossover rate, apparently high, is due to the offspring acceptance policy. The acceptance rule makes several new individuals be discarded. Thus after several tests, with values from 0.5 to 2.5 we decided to use 2.0. The insertion of new solutions in the population will be later discussed (see section 3.6).

3.3 Mutation

A traditional mutation strategy based on the swapping of columns was implemented. Two positions are selected uniformly at random and their values are swapped. This mutation procedure is applied to 10% of all new individuals every generation.

We also implemented a *heavy mutation* procedure. It executes the job swap move $10.n$ times in each individual – where n is the number of gates – except the best one. This procedure is executed every time the population diversity is considered to be low, *i.e.* it has converged to individuals that are too similar (see section 3.6).

3.4 Local Search

Local search algorithms for combinatorial optimization problems generally rely on a neighborhood definition that establishes a relationship between solutions in the configuration space. In this work, two neighborhood definitions were chosen. The first one was the *all-pairs*. It consists of swapping pairs of columns from a given solution. A *hill-climbing* algorithm can be defined by reference to this neighborhood: starting with an initial permutation of all columns, every time a proposed swap reduces the number of tracks utilized, it is confirmed and another cycle of swaps takes place, until no further improvement is achieved. As the complexity to evaluate each swap is considerably high, we used a reduced neighborhood, where all columns are tested for a swap, but only with the closer ones. Following this, we try swapping all columns only with their 10 nearest neighbors, to the left and to the right. This number is not so critical, but we noticed a strong degradation in performance when values around 5 or lower were utilized.

The second neighborhood implemented was the *insertion* one. It consists of removing a column from one position and inserting it in another place. The hill-climbing iterative procedure is the same regardless the neighborhood definition. In this case, we also utilized a reduced neighborhood. Each column was tested for insertion only in the 10 nearest positions.

Given the large size of the all-pairs and insertion neighborhoods, and the computational complexity required to calculate the objective function for each solution, we found it convenient to apply the local search only on the best individual, located at the top node of the ternary tree, after each generation is completed.

3.5 Selection for Recombination

The recombination of solutions in the hierarchically structured population can only be made between *a leader and one of its supporters within the same cluster*. The recombination procedure selects any leader uniformly at random and then it chooses - also uniformly at random - one of the three supporters.

3.6 Offspring Insertion into the Population

After the recombination and the mutation take place, the acceptance of the new offspring will follow two rules:

- The offspring is inserted into the population *replacing the supporter* that took part in the recombination *that generated it*.
- The replacement occurs *only if* the fitness of the new individual *is better than* the supporter.

If during an entire generation no individual was accepted for insertion, we conclude that the population has converged and *apply the heavy mutation procedure*. Moreover, after the each generation the population is restructured. The hierarchy states that the fitness of the leader of a cluster must be lower than the fitness of the leader of the cluster just above it. The adjustment is done comparing the supporters of each cluster with their leader. If any supporter is found to be better than its respective leader, they swap their places. Considering the problem addressed in this work, the higher is the position that an individual occupies in the tree, the fewer is the number of tracks it requires to build the circuit it represents.

4   Migration Policies

For the study with multiple populations, we had to define how individuals migrate from one population to another. There are three population migration policies:

- **0-Migrate**: No migration is used and all populations evolve in parallel without any kind of communication or solutions exchange.
- **1-Migrate**: Populations are arranged in a ring structure. Migration occurs in all populations and the best individual of each one migrates to the population right next to it, replacing a randomly chosen individual – except the best one. Every population receives only one new individual.
- **2-Migrate**: Populations are also arranged in a ring structure. Migration also occurs in all populations, but the best individual of each one migrates to both populations connected to it, replacing randomly chosen individuals – except the best ones. Every population receives two new individuals.

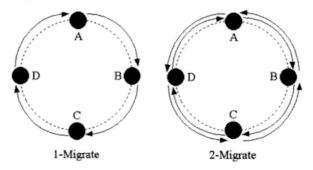

1-Migrate   2-Migrate

Fig. 4. Diagrams of the two migration policies.

5   Computational Tests

The population tests were executed in two different ways. The first one was to verify the influence of the number of populations on the algorithm's performance. For this evaluation, the number of populations varied from one up to five. The second test evaluated the influence of migration, with the three migration policies being applied. The tests are divided into five instances and for each one we executed the whole set of configurations ten times. The stop criterion was a time limit, fixed as follows: 30 seconds for W2, V4470 and X0; 90 seconds for W3 and 10 minutes for W4. The difference between the maximum CPU times is due to the dimension of the instances and takes into account the average time to find high-quality solutions. If larger CPU times were utilized, especially for the smaller instances, most configurations would return excellent results, weakening any performance comparison among them.

In Table 1, we show some information on the instances we utilized in this work. We have one small, three medium and a large instance. In the literature it is difficult to find hard instances. In ref. [4], we found the most extensive computational tests, with a total of 25 instances. However, most of them were too small and easy to solve using the MA. Considering their sizes, only V4470, X0, W2, W3 and W4 had more than 30 gates and for this reason we concentrated our studies on them.

Table 1. Information on the instances.

Instance	Gates	Nets	Best known solution
W2	33	48	14
V4470	47	37	9
X0	48	40	11
W3	70	84	18
W4	141	202	27

Next we show the results of the MA implemented (see Tables 2 to 6). Four numbers are utilized to describe the results for each configuration (see Figure 5). In clockwise order we have: in boldface, the best solution found for the number of tracks for that instance. Next in the sequence, we display the number of times this solution was found in ten tries. Below it, there is the worst value found for the configuration, and finally, in the lower-left part of the cell, is the average value found for the number of tracks.

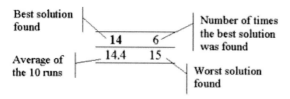

Fig. 5. Data fields for each configuration.

Table 2. Results for the W2 instance.

W2	Number of populations									
	1		**2**		**3**		**4**		**5**	
0-Migrate	**14**	9	**14**	10	**14**	8	**14**	9	**14**	5
	14.1	15	14.0	14	14.2	15	14.1	15	14.5	15
1-Migrate			**14**	10	**14**	9	**14**	8	**14**	5
			14.0	14	14.1	15	14.2	15	14.5	15
2-Migrate			**14**	9	**14**	5	**14**	6	**14**	4
			14.1	15	14.5	15	14.4	15	14.6	15

Table 3. Results for the V4470 instance.

V4470	Number of populations								
	1		2		3		4		5
0-Migrate	**9**	2	**9**	1	**9**	2	**10**	10	**10**	9
	10.1	11	10.0	10	10.0	11	10.0	10	10.1	11
1-Migrate			**9**	2	**9**	1	**9**	2	**10**	8
			10.1	11	10.0	11	9.9	11	10.2	11
2-Migrate			**9**	2	**9**	1	**9**	1	**10**	6
			9.9	11	10.2	11	10.1	11	10.4	11

Table 4. Results for the X0 instance.

X0	Number of populations								
	1		2		3		4		5
0-Migrate	**11**	7	**11**	6	**11**	7	**11**	7	**11**	3
	11.4	13	11.4	12	11.3	12	11.5	13	11.7	12
1-Migrate			**11**	6	**11**	6	**11**	6	**11**	3
			11.5	13	11.6	13	11.4	12	11.9	13
2-Migrate			**11**	7	**11**	4	**11**	3	**11**	5
			11.5	13	12.0	13	11.9	13	11.8	14

Table 5. Results for the W3 instance.

W3	Number of populations								
	1		2		3		4		5
0-Migrate	**18**	1	**18**	2	**18**	1	**19**	1	**19**	2
	21.1	26	20.1	23	20.1	22	20.3	22	20.8	22
1-Migrate			**18**	3	**18**	1	**18**	2	**18**	2
			20.0	23	20.1	23	20.2	22	20.0	22
2-Migrate			**18**	1	**18**	2	**18**	1	**18**	1
			20.2	23	21.1	25	20.3	23	21.3	23

Table 6. Results for the W4 instance.

W4	Number of populations								
	1		2		3		4		5
0-Migrate	**29**	3	**29**	2	**29**	2	**30**	4	**32**	1
	31.5	36	31.1	33	31.4	35	32.1	36	33.7	35
1-Migrate			**28**	2	**28**	1	**28**	2	**29**	3
			31.4	34	31.2	35	30.6	35	31.9	36
2-Migrate			**29**	2	**29**	3	**29**	1	**31**	1
			32.5	36	31.7	35	33.4	35	35.1	38

Firstly, we should explain two aspects of randomized search algorithms: exploitation and exploration. Exploitation is the property of the algorithm to thoroughly explore a specific region of the search space, looking for any small improvement in the current best available solution(s). Exploration is the property to explore wide portions of the search space, looking for promising regions.

With no migration, we observed more instability in the answers, expressed by worst solutions and averages found for the instances W3 and W4. On the other hand, the 1-Migrate appeared to better balance exploitation and exploration, with good average and worst solution values. The 2-Migrate policy did not perform so well, with a clear degradation of these two parameters. A too strong exploitation, in detriment of the exploration shall have caused this. Thus we concluded that migration should be set at medium levels, represented by the 1-Migrate.

The second aspect to be analyzed is the number of populations. Although it is not clear what configuration was the best, the use of only one is surely not the best choice since several multi-population configurations returned better values.

All the best values previously found in the literature, presented in Table 1, were reached by the MA, except the W4. An increase in the CPU time, from 10 to 60 minutes, trying to reach the 27-track value did not work out, too. That time limit was fixed after we verified that the best results for W4, presented in [5], took several hours to be found using an equipment which performance was comparable to ours.

As even with a longer CPU time the algorithm did not succeed, we decided to enlarge the local search neighborhood, increasing the number of positions to be tested from 10 to 20 (see section 3.4). With this change the algorithm finally succeeded to find the best solution in three times out of ten.

Table 7. Results for instance W4 with a 60-minute CPU time limit and the augmented local search neighborhood.

Test #	Best solution found	CPU time required to reach the solution
1	27	2,141.0
2	28	1,791.9
3	29	855.7
4	29	532.4
5	27	1,788.7
6	29	560.8
7	28	1,791.0
8	31	2,908.1
9	27	3,002.5
10	28	600.9

6   Conclusions

This work presented a study on multiple-population approaches to solve the gate matrix layout problem. We used a Memetic Algorithm as the search engine. The results were very encouraging and the best multi-population configuration found was four populations evolving in parallel and exchanging individuals at a medium rate. The five instances utilized were taken from real-world VLSI circuit layout problems and the solutions rivaled with those previously found in the literature. Another strong point is that the method utilized is included in a framework for general optimization called

NP-Opt [6]. That means a general purpose MA was successful in solving a very complex optimization problem, competing head to head with a specific method, especially tailored for this problem. Future works should include the use of parallel techniques to distribute the populations and/or individuals through a computer network and the extension of this study to other NP problems to verify if the results hold as well.

Acknowledgements. This work was supported by „Fundação de Amparo à Pesquisa do Estado de São Paulo" (FAPESP – Brazil) and „Conselho Nacional de Desenvolvimento Científico e Tecnológico" (CNPq – Brazil). The authors also thank Alexandre Linhares, for his relevant remarks and comments, and for providing us with the VLSI instances.

References

1. França, P. M., Mendes, A. S. and Moscato, P.: A memetic algorithm for the total tardiness Single Machine Scheduling problem. European Journal of Operational Research, v. 132, n. 1 (2001) 224–242
2. Hu, Y. H. and Chen, S. J.: GM_Plan: A gate matrix layout algorithm based on artificial intelligence planning techniques. IEEE Transactions on Computer-Aided Design, v. 9 (1990) 836–845
3. Lengauer, T.: Combinatorial algorithms for integrated circuit layout. John Wiley & Sons, New York (1990)
4. Linhares, A.: Synthesizing a Predatory Search Strategy for VLSI Layouts, IEEE Transactions on Evolutionary Computation, v. 3, n. 2 (1999) 147–152
5. Linhares, A., Yanasse, H. and Torreão, J.: Linear Gate Assignment: a Fast Statistical Mechanics Approach. IEEE Transactions on Computer-Aided Design on Integrated Circuits and Systems, v. 18, n. 12 (1999) 1750–1758
6. Mendes, A. S., França, P. M. and Moscato, P.: NP-Opt: An Optimization Framework for NP Problems. Proceedings of POM2001 – International Conference of the Production and Operations Management Society (2001) 82–89
7. Moscato, P.: On Evolution, Search, Optimization, Genetic Algorithms and Martial Arts: Towards Memetic Algorithms. Caltech Concurrent Computation Program, C3P Report 826. (1989)
8. Nakatani, K., Fujii, T., Kikuno, T. and Yoshida, N.: A heuristic algorithm for gate matrix layout. Proceedings of International Conference of Computer-Aided Design (1986) 324–327
9. Moscato, P. and Norman, M. G.: A 'Memetic' Approach for the Traveling Salesman Problem. Implementation of a Computational Ecology for Combinatorial Optimization on Message-Passing Systems, Parallel Computing and Transputer Applications, edited by M. Valero, E. Onate, M. Jane, J.L. Larriba and B. Suarez, Ed. IOS Press, Amsterdam (1992) 187–194

New Generic Hybrids Based upon Genetic Algorithms

Michael Affenzeller

Institute of Systems Science
Systems Theory and Information Technology
Johannes Kepler University
Altenbergerstrasse 69
A-4040 Linz – Austria
ma@cast.uni-linz.ac.at

Abstract. In this paper we propose some generic extensions to the general concept of a Genetic Algorithm. These biologically and sociologically inspired interrelated hybrids aim to make the algorithm more open for scalability on the one hand, and to retard premature convergence on the other hand without necessitating the development of new coding standards and operators for certain problems. Furthermore, the corresponding Genetic Algorithm is unrestrictedly included in all of the newly proposed hybrid variants under special parameter settings. The experimental part of the paper discusses the new algorithms for the Traveling Salesman Problem as a well documented instance of a multimodal combinatorial optimization problem achieving results which significantly outperform the results obtained with a conventional Genetic Algorithm using the same coding and operators.

1 Introduction

Many problems that are treated by Genetic Algorithms belong to the class of NP-complete problems. The advantage of Genetic Algorithms when being applied to such problems lies in the ability to search through the solution space in a broader sense than heuristic methods that are based upon neighborhood search. Nevertheless, also Genetic Algorithms are frequently faced with a problem which, at least in its impact, is quite similar to the problem of stagnating in a local but not global solution. This drawback, called premature convergence in the terminology of Genetic Algorithms, occurs when the population of a Genetic Algorithm reaches such a suboptimal state that the genetic operators can no longer produce offspring that outperform their parents (e.g. [5]).

During the last decades plenty of work has been investigated to introduce new coding standards and operators in order to overcome this essential handicap of Genetic Algorithms. As these coding standards and the belonging operators often are quite problem specific, we try to take a different approach and look upon the concepts of Genetic Algorithms as an artificial self organizing process in a biologically and sociologically inspired generic way in order to improve

F.J. Garijo, J.C. Riquelme, and M. Toro (Eds.): IBERAMIA 2002, LNAI 2527, pp. 329–339, 2002.

the global convergence behaviour of Genetic Algorithms independently of the actually employed implementation.

In doing so we have introduced an advanced selection model for Genetic Algorithms that allows adaptive selective pressure handling in a way quite similar to Evolution Strategies[2]. Based upon this enhanced GA-model two further generic extensions are discussed:

(1) The concept of segregation and reunification of subpopulations aims to assure an independent development of building blocks in very different regions of the search space in order to improve global convergence. The algorithm divides the population into subpopulations. These evolve independently until their fitnesses stagnate. By this approach of width-search, building blocks, which would disappear early in case of standard Genetic Algorithms, are evolved in different regions of the search space at the beginning and during the evolutionary process. In contrast to the Island Models for Genetic Algorithms[16], in our case the single subpopulations grow together again in case of stagnating fitness in order to end up with a final population containing as much essential building blocks as possible.

(2) The second newly introduced concept allows the dynamic usage of multiple crossover operators in parallel in order to somehow imitate the parallel evolution of a variety of species that are struggling for limited resources. This strategy seems very adopted for problems which consider more than one crossover operator - especially if the properties of the considered operators may change as evolution proceeds.

As an important property of all the newly introduced hybrids it has to be pointed out that under special parameter settings the corresponding GA/GAs is/are unrestrictedly included in the new hybrids. The experimental part discusses the new algorithms for the Traveling Salesman Problem as a very well documented instance of a multimodal combinatorial optimization problem. In contrast to all other evolutionary heuristics known to the author that do not use any additional problem specific information, we obtain solutions close to the best known solution for all considered benchmarks (symmetric as well as asymmetric benchmark problems).

2   The Variable Selective Pressure Model

Similar to any other conventional Genetic Algorithm (e.g.[9]) we use a population of fixed size that will evolve to a new population of the same size by selection, crossover, and mutation.

What we additionally have done is to introduce an intermediate step in terms of a so-called virtual population of variable size where the size of the virtual population usually has to be greater than the population size. This virtual population is created by selection, crossover, and mutation in the common sense of Genetic Algorithms. But like in the context of Evolution Strategies, only a certain percentage of this intermediate population will survive.

This handling of selective pressure in our context is mainly motivated by (μ, λ)-Evolution Strategies where μ parents produce λ descendants from which the best μ survive. Within the framework of Evolution Strategies, selective pressure is defined as $s = \frac{\mu}{\lambda}$, where a small value of s indicates high selective pressure and vice versa (for a detailed description of Evolution Strategies see for instance [12]). Even if the interaction between the variable selective pressure within our new model and the notion of temperature within the scope of Simulated Annealing is quite different in detail, we have adopted this notation. Applied to our new Genetic Algorithm, this means that from $|POP|$ (population size) number of parents $|POP| \cdot T$ ((size of virtual population) $> |POP|$, i.e. $T > 1$) descendants are generated by crossover and mutation from which the best $|POP|$ survive as illustrated in Fig. 1.

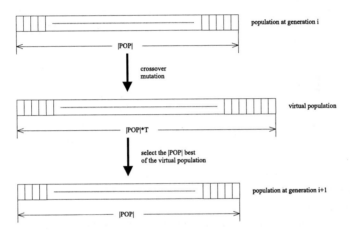

Fig. 1. Evolution of a new population with selective pressure $s = \frac{1}{T}$ for a virtual population built up in the sense of a (μ, λ)-Evolution Strategy.

Obviously we define selective pressure as $s = \frac{|POP|}{|POP| \cdot T} = \frac{1}{T}$, where a small value of s, i.e. a great value of T, stands for high selective pressure and vice versa. Equipped with this enhanced GA-model it is quite easy to adopt further extensions based upon a controllable selective pressure, i.e. it becomes possible either to reset the temperature up/down to a certain level or simply to cool down the temperature in the sense of Simulated Annealing during the evolutionary process in order to steer the convergence of the algorithm.

Biologically interpreting this (μ, λ)-Evolution Strategy like selective pressure handling, for Genetic Algorithms this means, that some kind of 'infant mortality' has been introduced in the sense that a certain ratio of the population ($|POP| \cdot T - |POP| = |POP| \cdot (T - 1)$) will never become procreative, i.e. this weaker part of a population will not get the possibility of reproduction. Decreasing this 'infant mortality', i.e. reducing the selective pressure during the evolutionary process also makes sense in a biological interpretation because also in nature stronger and higher developed populations suffer less from infant mortality.

From the point of view of optimization, decreasing the temperature during the optimization process means that a greater part of the search space is explored at the beginning of evolution - whereas at a later stage of evolution, when the average fitness is already quite high, a higher selective pressure is quite critical in that sense that it can easily cause premature convergence. Operating with a temperature converging to zero, this (μ, λ)-Evolution Strategy like selective pressure model for Genetic Algorithms acts like the corresponding Genetic Algorithm with generational replacement. Moreover, implementing the analogue to the $(\mu + \lambda)$-Evolution Strategy denotes the other extreme of immortal individuals. However, also the implementation of this strategy is quite easy to handle with our model by just copying the old population into the virtual population. Other replacement mechanisms, like elitism or the goldcage-model for example, are also easy to implement by just adding the best individuals respectively the best individual of the last generation to the virtual population.

3   Hybrid GA-Concepts Based upon the Variable Selective Pressure Model

When applying Genetic Algorithms to complex problems, one of the most frequent difficulties is premature convergence. Roughly speaking, premature convergence occurs when the population of a Genetic Algorithm reaches such a suboptimal state that the genetic operators can no longer produce offspring that outperform their parents (e.g. [5]).

Several methods have been proposed to combat premature convergence in the context of Genetic Algorithms (e.g. [4], [6]). These include the restriction of the selection procedure, the operators and the according probabilities as well as the modification of fitness assignment. However, all these methods are heuristic in nature. Their effects vary with different problems and their implementation strategies need ad hoc modifications with respect to different situations.

A critical problem in studying premature convergence is the identification of its occurrence and the characterization of its extent. Srinivas and Patnaik [14], for example, use the difference between the average and maximum fitness as a standard to measure premature convergence and adaptively vary the crossover and mutation probabilities according to this measurement. As in the present paper, the term 'population diversity' has been used in many papers to study premature convergence (e.g. [13]) where the decrease of population diversity is considered as the primary reason for premature convergence. Therefore, a very homogeneous population, i.e. little population diversity, is considered as the major reason for a Genetic Algorithm to prematurely converge.

The following generic extensions that are built up upon the variable selective pressure model primarily aim to avoid or at least to retard premature convergence in a general way.

3.1   Segregative Genetic Algorithms (SEGA)

In principle, our new SEGA introduces two enhancements to the general concept
of Genetic Algorithms. The first is to bring in a variable selective pressure, as
described in section 2, in order to control the diversity of the evolving population.
The second concept introduces a separation of the population to increase the
broadness of the search process and joins the subpopulation after their evolution
in order to end up with a population including all genetic information sufficient
for locating the region of a global optimum.

The aim of dividing the whole population into a certain number of subpopulations (segregation) that grow together in case of stagnating fitness within those
subpopulations (reunification) is to combat premature convergence which is the
source of GA-difficulties. This segregation and reunification approach is a new
technique to overcome premature convergence [1], [3].

Whereas Island Models for Genetic Algorithms (e.g. in [16]) are mainly driven
by the idea of using simultaneous computer systems, SEGA attempts to utilize
migration more precisely in order to achieve superior results in terms of global
convergence. The principle idea is to divide the whole population into a certain
number of subpopulations at the beginning of the evolutionary process. These
subpopulations evolve independently from each other until the fitness increase
stagnates because of too similar individuals within the subpopulations. Then
a reunification from n to $(n-1)$ subpopulations is done. Roughly spoken this
means, that there is a certain number of villages at the beginning of the evolutionary process that are slowly growing together to bigger cities, ending up
with one big town containing the whole population at the end of evolution. By
this approach of width-search, building blocks in different regions of the search
space are evolved at the beginning and during the evolutionary process, which
would disappear early in case of standard genetic algorithms and whose genetic
information could not be provided at a later date of evolution when the search
for global optima is of paramount importance.

Monitoring the behaviour of a Genetic Algorithm when applied to optimization problems shows that the average fitness as well as the fitness of the best
member of the actual population often stagnates at a certain point of the evolution process even if the actual fitness is wide off the mark of a potentially
best or at least a best-known solution (premature convergence). Furthermore it
appears that Genetic Algorithms prematurely converge to very different regions
of the solution space when repeatedly running a Genetic Algorithm. Moreover it
is known from GA-theory[9], that extending the population size does not help to
avoid premature convergence. In fact, depending on the problem-type and the
problem-dimension there is a certain population size, where exceeding this population size doesn't effect any more improvements in the quality of the solution.

Motivated by these observations, we have developed an extended approach to
Genetic Algorithms where the total population is split into a certain number of
subpopulations or villages, all evolving independently from each other (segregation) until a certain stage of stagnation in the fitness of those subpopulations is

reached. Then, in order to bring some new genetic information into each village, the number of villages is reduced by one which causes new overlapping-points of the villages. Fig. 2 shows a schematic diagram of the described process. This process is repeated until all villages are growing together ending up in one town (reunification).

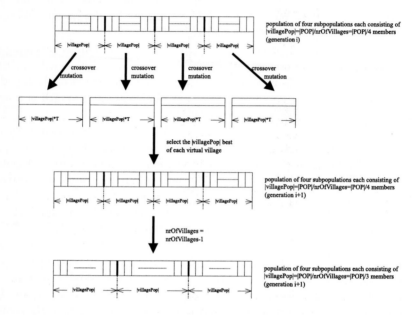

Fig. 2. Evolution of a new population for the instance that four subpopulations are merged to three.

The variable selective pressure is of particular importance if the number of subpopulations is reduced by one because this event brings new diversification into the population. In this case a higher selective pressure is reasonable, i.e. if reunifying members of neighboring villages, the temperature is reset to a higher level in order to cool down to 1 as the new system of subpopulations evolves. While the number of villages decreases during evolution, it is recommended to reset the selective pressure to a higher level because the genetic diversity of the emerging greater subpopulations is growing.

SEGA uses a fixed number of iterations for termination. Depending on this total number of iterations and the initial number of subpopulations (villages), the dates of reunification may statically be calculated at the beginning of the evolutionary process as done in the experimental result section. Further improvements, particularly in the sense of running time, are possible, if, in order to determine the dates of reunification, a dynamic criterion for the detection of stagnating genetic diversity within the subpopulations is used.

Again, like in the context of the variable selective pressure model which is included in SEGA as well, it should be pointed out that a corresponding Genetic Algorithm is unrestrictedly included in the SEGA when the number of subpopulations (villages) and the cooling temperature are both set to 1 at the beginning of the evolutionary process. Moreover, the introduced techniques also do not use any problem specific information.

3.2   Dynamic Habitat Adaptation

Genetic Algorithms as well as its most common variants consider the evolution of a single species, i.e. crossover can be done between all members of the population. This supports the aspect of depth-search but not the aspect of width-search. Considering natural evolution, where a multiplicity of species evolve in parallel, as a role model, we could introduce a number of crossover operators and apply each one to a certain subpopulation. In order to keep that model realistically it is necessary to choose the size of those subpopulations dynamically, i.e. depending on the actual success of a certain species its living space is expanded or restricted. Speaking in the words of Genetic Algorithms, this means that the size of subpopulations (defined by the used crossover and mutation operators) with lower success in the sense of the quality function is restricted in support of those subpopulations that push the process of evolution.

But as no Genetic Algorithm known to the author is able to model jumps in the evolutionary process and no exchange of information between the subpopulations takes place, the proposed strategy would fail in generating results superior to the results obtained when running the Genetic Algorithms with the certain operators one after another. Therefore, it seems reasonable to allow also recombination of individuals that have emerged from different crossover operators, i.e. the total population is taken into account for each crossover operator and the living space (habitat) of each virtual subpopulation is defined by its success during the last iterations as illustrated in Fig. 3.

Exemplarily considering the properties of the OX (order crossover) and the ERX (edge recombination crossover) operators for crossover it is reported (e.g. in [9]) that the OX-operator significantly outperforms the ERX-operator in terms of speed whereas the ERX-operator surpasses OX in terms of global convergence. Dynamically using multiple crossover operators in parallel utilizes the 'fast' OX-operator for a long evolution period until the performance in terms of solution quality of ERX outperforms OX at a later stage of evolution. Even more, experiments have shown that the described strategy significantly surpasses the results obtained when just using one single operator in terms of solution quality.

Anyway, this dynamic (self-organizing) strategy seems particularly suitable for situations where a couple of crossover operators whose properties are not exactly known are taken into account.

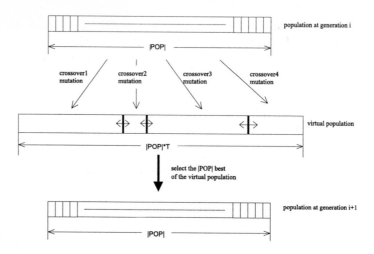

Fig. 3. Evolution of a new population for the instance that four crossover operators are used in parallel.

4   Experimental Results

In our experiment, all computations are performed on a Pentium III PC with 256 megabytes of main memory. The programs are written in the Java programming language.

Even if ongoing experimental research on a variety of problems shows quite similar results it would go beyond the scope of the present paper to present all these tests. So we just give a short summary of the results obtained by SEGA on a selection of symmetric as well as asymmetric TSP benchmark problem instances taken from the TSPLIB [11] using updated results[1] for the best, or at least the best known, solutions. In doing so, we have performed a comparison of SEGA with a conventional GA using exactly the same operators for crossover and mutation and the same parameter settings and with the COSA-algorithm [15] as an established and successful ambassador of a heuristic especially developed for routing problems. For the tests the parameters of COSA are set as suggested by the author in [15]. Both, GA and SEGA use a mutation probability of 0.05 and a combination of OX-crossover and ERX-crossover [9] combined with the golden-cage population model, i.e. the entire population is replaced with the exception that the best member of the old population survives until the new population generates a better one (wild-card strategy). Within SEGA, the described strategies are applied to each subpopulation. The results of a test presented in the present paper start with 32 villages (subpopulations), each consisting of 64 individuals, i.e. the total population size is set to 2048 for SEGA (as well as for COSA and GA). Table 1 shows the experimental results of SEGA

---

[1] Updates for the best (known) solutions can for example be found on
 ftp://ftp.zib.de/pub/Packages/mp-testdata/tsp/tsplib/index.html

(with dynamic habitat adaptation), COSA, and GA concerning various types of problems in the TSPLIB. For each problem the algorithms were run ten times. The efficiency for each algorithm is quantified in terms of the relative difference of the best's individual fitness after a given number or iterations to the best or best-known solution. In this experiment, the relative difference is defined as relativeDifference $= (\frac{Fitness}{Optimal} - 1) * 100\%$. These examples demonstrate the predominance of the new SEGA (together with an adaptive steering of OX and ERX operators) compared to the standard-GA. The preeminence of SEGA, especially when being compared to the rather problem specific COSA heuristic, becomes even more evident, if asymmetric benchmark problems are considered.

Table 1. Experimental results of COSA, GA (using OX or ERX for crossover) and the new SEGA together with a dynamic combination of OX- and ERX crossover.

Problem	Iter.No.	Average difference(%)			
		COSA	GA_{OX}	GA_{ERX}	GA_{new}
eil76(symm.)	5000	6.36	17.56	7.62	0.32
ch130(symm.)	5000	14.76	84.54	32.44	0.35
kroA150(symm.)	5000	20.91	102.40	71.97	0.74
kroA200(symm.)	10000	48.45	95.69	117.11	1.24
br17(asymm.)	200	0.00	0.00	0.00	0.00
ftv55(asymm.)	5000	44.22	41.34	23.52	0.27
kro124p(asymm.)	10000	26.78	30.61	15.49	0.48
ftv170(asymm.)	15000	187.34	87.12	126.22	1.09

5   Conclusion

In this paper an enhanced Genetic Algorithm and two upgrades have been presented and exemplarily tested on some TSP benchmarks. The proposed GA-based techniques couple aspects from Evolution Strategies (selective pressure), Simulated Annealing (temperature, cooling) as well as a special segregation and reunification strategy with crossover, mutation, and selection in a general way, so that established crossover and mutation operators for certain problems may be used analogously to the corresponding Genetic Algorithm. The investigations in this paper have mainly focused on the avoidance of premature convergence and on the introduction of methods which make the algorithm more open for scalability in the sense of convergence versus running time. Concerning the speed of SEGA, it has to be pointed out that the superior performance concerning convergence requires a higher running time, mainly because of the the greater population size $|POP|$ required. This should allow to transfer already developed GA-concepts to increasingly powerful computer systems in order to achieve better results. Using simultaneous computers seems especially suited to increase the performance of SEGA. Anyway, under special parameter settings the corresponding Genetic Algorithm is fully included within the introduced concepts achieving a performance only marginally worse than the performance of the equivalent Genetic Algorithm. In other words, the introduced models can be interpreted as a superstructure to the GA model or as a technique upwards compatible to Genetic Algorithms. Therefore, an implementation of the new algorithm(s) for a certain problem should be quite easy to do, presumed that the corresponding Genetic Algorithm (coding, operators) is known.

However, the efficiency of a variable selective pressure certainly depends on the genetic diversity of the entire population. Ongoing research indicates that it could be a very fruitful approach to define the actual selective pressure depending on the actual genetic diversity of the population.

References

1. Affenzeller, M.: A New Approach to Evolutionary Computation: Segregative Genetic Algorithms (SEGA). Connectionist Models of Neurons, Learning Processes, and Artificial Intelligence, Lecture Notes of Computer Science 2084 (2001) 594–601
2. Affenzeller, M.: Transferring the Concept of Selective Pressure from Evolutionary Strategies to Genetic Algorithms. Proceedings of the 14th International Conference on Systems Science 2 (2001) 346–353
3. Affenzeller, M.: Segregative Genetic Algorithms (SEGA): A Hybrid Superstructure Upwards Compatible to Genetic Algorithms for Retarding Premature Convergence. Internatinal Journal of Computers, Systems and Signals (IJCSS), Vol. 2, Nr. 1 (2001) 18–32
4. Cobb, H.J., Grefenstette J.J.: Genetic Algorithms for Tracking Changing Environment. Proceedings of the Fifth International Conference on Genetic Algorithms (1993) 523–530
5. Fogel, D.B.: An Introduction to Simulated Evolutionary Optimization. IEEE Trans. on Neural Networks 5(1) (1994) 3–14
6. Goldberg, D. E.: Genetic Alogorithms in Search, Optimization and Machine Learning. Addison Wesley Longman (1989)
7. Holland, J. H.: Adaption in Natural and Artificial Systems. 1st MIT Press ed. (1992)
8. Kirkpatrick, S., Gelatt Jr., C.D., Vecchi, M.P.: Optimization by Simulated Annealing. Science 220 (1983) 671–680
9. Michalewicz, Z.: Genetic Algorithms + Data Structures = Evolution Programs. 3rd edn. Springer-Verlag, Berlin Heidelberg New York (1996)
10. Rechenberg, I.: Evolutionsstrategie. Friedrich Frommann Verlag (1973)
11. Reinelt, G.: TSPLIB – A Traveling Salesman Problem Library. ORSA Journal on Computing 3 (1991) 376-384
12. Schöneburg, E., Heinzmann, F., Feddersen, S.: Genetische Algorithmen und Evolutionsstrategien. Addison-Wesley (1994)
13. Smith, R.E., Forrest, S., Perelson, A.S.: Population Diversity in an Immune System Model: Implications for Genetic Search. Foundations of Genetic Algorithms 2 (1993) 153–166
14. Srinivas, M., Patnaik, L.: Adaptive Probabilities of Crossover and Mutation in Genetic Algorithms . IEEE Transactions on Systems, Man, and Cybernetics 24(4) (1994) 656–667

15. Wendt, O.: Tourenplanung durch Einsatz naturanaloger Verfahren. Deutscher Universitätsverlag (1995)
16. Whitley, D.: A Genetic Algorithm Tutorial. Statistics and Computing 4 (1994) 65–85

Genetic Algorithms and Biological Images Restoration: Preliminary Report

Simone J. M. Ribeiro[1] and João C. P. da Silva[2]

[1] Instituto de Biofísica Carlos Chagas Filho, Universidade Federal do Rio de Janeiro, UFRJ,
CEP 21949-900, Rio de Janeiro, RJ, Brasil
simone@biof.ufrj.br
[2] Dept. de Ciência da Computação, Instituto de Matemática, Universidade Federal do Rio de
Janeiro, UFRJ, Caixa Postal 68530, CEP 21945-970, Rio de Janeiro, RJ, Brasil
jcps@ufrj.br

Abstract. The purpose of this work is to investigate the application of genetic algorithms [9] on biological images restoration. The idea is to improve images quality generated by Atomic Force Microscopy (AFM) technique [1] and by Cidade et al. [3] restoration method in a way that they can be used to analyze the structures of a given biological sample.

1   Introduction

Genetic algorithms (GAs) [9] provide computer models based on the principle of natural selection and have been used in a variety of optimization/search problems. In this work, we will investigate the use of GAs as a method to biological image restoration problem.

The biological images we are interested in restoring are generated through AFM (Atomic Force Microscopy) technique [1]. This technique allows one to generate atomic resolution images as well as measuring forces at nanometer range [1], which represent the interactions between a tip and a (biological or not) sample. As we will present in section 2, the resolution of those images will depend on the tip used to scan the sample.

Cidade et al. [3] presented an approach to AFM image restoration using a combination of Tikhonov's regularization approach [11] and the gradient method [18]. Despite of the significative improvement of image quality, this approach has some limitations (see section 2.2). In this paper, we will investigate the use of AGs in two ways : (i) as a restoration method, using the AFM image as the starting point of the process; and (ii) as a refinement method, where the AGs will be used to improve an image quality generated by Cidade et al [3] approach.

This work is organized as follows : in section 2, we will present some basic concepts about AFM technique [1], image restoration and genetic algorithms [9]; in section 3, we will describe how image restoration problem will be represented in genetic terms; and in section 4, we will present some preliminary experimental results.

F.J. Garijo, J.C. Riquelme, and M. Toro (Eds.): IBERAMIA 2002, LNAI 2527, pp. 340–349, 2002.

2   Basic Definitions

In this section, we will present some basic concepts about atomic force microscopy, image restoration and genetic algorithms.

2.1   Atomic Force Microscopy (AFM)

The Atomic Force Microscopy (AFM) technique has been used in a variety of areas such as electronics, chemical and biology, and therefore the materials under investigation can vary from semiconductors to biological membranes. Using the AFM technique allows one to generate atomic resolution images as well as measuring forces at nanometer range [1].

The AFM technique was first used by Binnig et al. [1] and it consists in attaching a tiny shard of diamond onto one end of a tiny strip of gold foil, suspended by a mobile beam, called a cantilever. The diamond tip is pressed against the surface while the sample is scanned beneath the tip. The force between the tip and the sample is measured indirectly by tracking the deflection of the cantilever and analysing it in a detection system (see Fig. 1). The force between the tip and the sample surface is very small, usually less than 10^{-9} N.

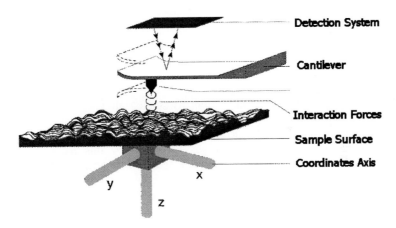

Fig. 1. The AFM System

The most common detection system works emitting an optical beam that is reflected from the mirrored surface on the backside of the cantilever onto a position-sensitive photodetector. In this arrangement, a small deflection of the cantilever will tilt the reflected beam and will change the position of the beam on the photodetector. As the tip scans the sample surface, moving up and down according to its contours, the laser beam is reflected and the photodetector measures the variations in the beam. The idea is to measure quantitatively the sample rugosity and generate tridimensional topological maps of its surface.

The resolution of AFM images (i.e., the blurring added to AFM images) depends on the tip and sample geometry. That means the smaller and thinner the tip is, the more precise is the scanning. (see Fig. 2).

(a)   (b)

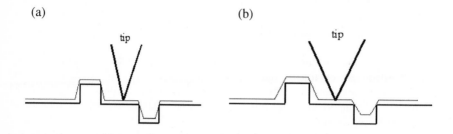

Fig. 2. A thinner tip (a) scans the sample surface more precisely than tip on (b)

Compared to conventional microscopes, the AFM technique is more efficient in many aspects, such as the images obtained are tridimensionals and, in the case of biological samples, we do not need to prepare the sample through expensive processes before scanning. To simplify the presentation, in this work we will consider only bidimensional AFM images, that is, an AFM image will be represented by a 256x256-matrix of pixels, each one vary from 0 to 255 (which correspond to 256 gray values of the AFM pallete).

2.2   Image Restoration

Due to the tip geometry as well as the extremelly small scale involved in the process of scanning biological sample, the images generated by the AFM technique do not correspond precisely to the sample surface. As we saw above, a considerable blurring effects and noise are added to the images generated by this technique. Image restoration intends to improve these blurred images (which means minimizing the blurring and the additive noise) making them closer to the original ones.

Formally, we can express the image restoration problem as follows :

$$y = Bx + n \qquad (1)$$

where y represents, in our case, the image obtained using the AFM technique, x the original image without blurring, B a compact operator, described by a point-spread function matrix of the imaging system and n the additive noise, usually of Gaussian type. As the blurred image y and the compact operator B are known, we are interested in solving the inverse problem :

$$x = B^{-1} y \qquad (2)$$

that can be solved as a finite dimensional optimization problem in which we minimize a functional such as

$$L(x) = \left|\left| y - Bx \right|\right|^2 \qquad (3)$$

known as least squares method [11].

Cidade et al. [3] used Tikhonov's regularization approach [11] to image restoration of biological samples generated by the AFM technique. The Tikhonov's regularization functional is constructed from (3) as follows :

$$Q(\hat{x}) = \frac{1}{2}\|y(i,j) - \sum_{k=-N}^{N}\sum_{l=-N}^{N}b(k,l)\hat{x}(i+k,j+l)\|^2 - \alpha S \quad (a>0, i,j=1,2,...M) \quad (4)$$

where $y(i,j)$ corresponds to one pixel of the AFM image (located at (i,j) in the correspondent matrix), $b(k,l)$ is the point-spread function matrix (with dimension 2N x 2N), $\hat{x}$ is the estimate value of the original image that we want to restore and αS is the regularization term. The parameter α determines the trade-off between the accuracy and stability of the solution. When $\alpha = 0$, we have the least squares equation (3), otherwise, we should calculate S, which is any prior function that imposes no correlation on the image. To simplify the presentation, we will take $\alpha = 0$.

The approach used in [3] was the gradient method which consists in determine the critical point equation $\partial Q/\partial \hat{x} = 0$, obtaining a system of non-linear equations [22] with 65536 equations (since each image is formed by 256x256 pixels). To solve this system of non-linear equations, [3] used the iterative multivariable Newton-Raphson method, including also a gain factor γ to stabilize the iterative process. The system of linear equation obtained from this process is solved using the Gauss-Seidel method[1]. For more details on this approach of image restoration, see [3].

In Fig. 3, we present an original image obtained by AFM technique before restoration process (Fig. 3a), the image after a restoration process based on filters that usually accompany commercial microscope (Fig. 3b), like Wiener filter (which is based on Fourier Transform technique (FFT) - see [21]) and an image (Fig. 3c) restored through the gradient method [3]. In the case of FFT restoration, the brusque variations of colors in the image can be eliminated, which means that relevant informations of the sample can be lost. In this case, the contrast as well as the additive noise should be pained, which can be result in a waste of brightness of the sample.

We can observe the improvement in the contrast of the processed image through Tikhonov's regularization together the multivariable Newton-Raphson method compared to the processed image through FFT.

Despite of the significative improvement of image quality, the gradient method is not capable of good results for point-spread function matrix with dimension greater than 3x3 (indeed, the best results [3] were obtained for matrix of dimension 3x3).

2.3 Genetic Algorithms (GAs)

Genetic algorithms (GAs) provide computer models based on the principle of natural selection and can be applied as optimization/search algorithms. Initially, we have to define a representation of the (candidate) solution for a given problem. In GAs, a

---

[1] For lack of space, we omit the definitions of gradient, iterative multivariable Newton-Raphson and Gauss-Seidel methods. See [18]

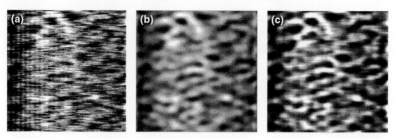

Fig. 3. (a) AFM image before restoration process; (b) AFM image restored through FFT; (c) AFM image restored through gradient method

candidate solution (called an *individual*) is represented as *chromosome*, which is a finite-length string of characters over a finite alphabet Σ. We say that an alphabet Σ is *binary* when $|\Sigma| = 2$. Each character in the chromosome is called a *gene*.

Any finite set of individuals is called a *population*. Once we have defined the representation of the individuals for a given problem, we have to define an *initial population* P_0 that is usually generated at random. From this initial population P_0 and from a set of operators, GAs generate successive populations (called *generations*) intending to improve the quality of the individuals over time, which means to improve the quality of the candidate solutions.

The operators used to pass from one generation to another are : *reproduction, crossover* and *mutation. Reproduction* is a process in which given a population P, each individual $i \in P$ is evaluated according to an *objective or fitness function f*. The fitness value of an individual i (f_i) is then used to define the *total fitness* $F = \Sigma f_i$, the *fitness probability* $p_i = f_i /F$ and the *expected count* $EC = n\, p_i$, where $n = |P|$. Doing this, the individuals of P are ranking according to EC in a way that the best individual (higher EC values) have more probability of being choose to survive into the next generation. Following this ranking, an intermediary population *IP* (*mating pool*) is created and crossover and mutation operators are applied on them.

The *crossover operator* acts in two steps. First, it selects uniformly at random two individuals of the mating pool (with probability P_c) , namely i_1 and i_2. Considering that each individual has a chromosome length k (i.e., $|i_1| = |i_2| = k$), an integer $m \in [1,k-1]$ is selected uniformly at random and it represents the *crossover site*. Two new individuals, namely i'_1 and i'_2, are created as follows: individual i'_1 (resp., i'_2) has between the positions 1 and m and between the positions $m+1$ and k the same genes that, respectively, individual i_1 (resp., i_2) has between 1 and m and individual i_2 (resp., i_1) has between $m+1$ and k. For example, consider i_1 as the 4-bit string 1010 and i_2 as the 4-bit string 0101. Therefore, the crossover site should be selected from the interval [1,3]. For example, if the crossover site is 2, we will have as new individuals in the next generation 1001 (i'_1) and 0110 (i'_2).

The *mutation operator* modifies a single gene in the chromosome of an individual with a small probability P_m. For example, consider a binary alphabet $\Sigma = \{0,1\}$ and an individual i in the mating pool. Applying the mutation operator to i on a gene with value 1 means that such gene turns into 0 and this new individual will be in the next generation.

3   GAs and Image Restoration

To apply GAs to image restoration, the first step is to define the representation of the individuals we will use. In our case, each individual in a population will correspond to an AFM image. As defined above, the AFM images are formed by a 256x256 matrix of pixels, each one varying from 0 to 255 (corresponding to the gray values of the AFM pallete). We will use a binary alphabet $\Sigma = \{0,1\}$ and each pixel will be represent by a 8-bit string. Therefore, an AFM image can be seen as a string over $\{0,1\}$ with length equals to (8x256x256) bits.

To generate the initial population P_0 with k individuals we will proceed as follows : let i be an AFM image (obtained from a scanning sample or from the gradient method proposed in [3]). Each one of the k individuals of P_0 will be generated from i by changing at random its contrast and brightness (one, both or none of them). To change the image brightness, an integer x is randomly selected from a brightness interval $B = [-b, b]$ and such number is added to each pixel q of i. For example, let q be a pixel with value 150 and $B = [-10,10]$. If we select $x = 7$ from B, the new value of pixel q will be 157 and in the case we select x = -3 from B, the new value of pixel q will be 147.

To change image contrast, an integer x is randomly selected from the contrast interval $C = [0, c]$ and each pixel q of i is updated as follows : if $q \in [0,128)$, the new value of pixel q is $(1- 0,01*x)*q$; if $q \in (128,255]$, the new value of pixel q is $(1+ 0,01*x)*q$. For example, given a pixel $q = 150$ and $C = [0,15]$, selecting $x = 10$ from C, the new value of q will be 165. Note that in the case the selected pixel q is 128, its value remains the same.

Once the initial population P_0 is created, each image $i' \in P_0$ is evaluated using as fitness function Tikhonov's regularization functional (equation 4 – section 2.2) with $\alpha = 0$. Note that, in our case, the best individuals will be that with lower values of f_i since we are interested in obtaining the image that is closer to the original one (without blurring).

Finally, we have to define the reproduction and crossover operators (at the moment, we are not dealing with mutation). The reproduction operator is defined as follows : the individuals of P_0 are ranking according to its expected count EC and then an intermediary population IP is constructed in such a way that the best individuals appear in IP with more copies than the others.

We define two kinds of crossover operators : *image* and *pixel crossover*. In the *image crossover*, the crossover site s is chosen from the interval [0,255] and represents a row in the AFM image (that is, a row in the 256x256 matrix of pixels). For example, suppose we have the images i_1 and i_2, and the crossover site $s = 97$. The two new individuals i'_1 and i'_2 will be construct as follows : i'_1 will be formed by the rows 0 to 96 of image i_1 and rows 97 to 255 of image i_2; and i'_2 will be formed by the rows 0 to 96 of image i_2 and rows 97 to 255 of image i_1.

Pixel crossover is applied on each pixel of the selected images. This means that since each pixel is represented by a 8-bit string, the interval that we will use to determine the crossover site will range from 1 to 7. Once we have selected two image, i_1 and i_2, and a crossover site $s \in [1,7]$, the crossover operator is applied as follows : for all $x, y \in [0,255]$, exchange bits between the (x, y)-pixel of i_1 and (x, y)-pixel of i_2.

Note that considering one image as a whole (one string with length 8x256x256), we have 256x256 crossover sites.

Consider the following example to illustrate the crossover operator : let i_1 and i_2 be the selected images to crossover and $s = 3$ be the crossover site. If the pixels (15,176) of i_1 and i_2 are respectively (| marks the crossover site) : (15,176)-pixel of i_1 = 001 | 00111 and (15,176)-pixel of i_2 = 101 | 10101, the resulting pixels after the crossover will be : (15,176)-pixel of i_1 = 001 | 10101 and (15,176)-pixel of i_2 = 101 | 00111.

4   Preliminary Experimental Results

In our preliminary experiments, we used as *original image* (i.e., the image we intend to obtain after the restoration process) the one shown in Fig 4. The original image was intentionally blurred to simulate an *AFM image* obtained from a scanning process of a sample. Using this image and applying Cidade et al [3] approach, we obtained the *gradient image*. We chose that blurred image to restore instead of one obtained through a scanning process of a biological sample because this allows us to measure how near we are of the original image.

For each one of those images (the AFM and the gradient images), we generated the initial population according to the previous section. Some results are shown in table 1 and 2. In both cases, we used $B = [-20,20]$ as brightness interval, $C = [0,20]$ as contrast intervals, crossover probability equals 80%, and 30 individuals in each generation.

Fig. 4. Original image

The values above represent the ratio between the *Mean Square Error* (Weisman et al. [24]) *MSE1* calculated for the original image and the best individual of the last generation, and the *MSE2* calculated for the original image and the initial image (AFM image in table 1 and Gradient image in table 2). As we can see, we obtain (in the best case) a gain of 7% on the brightness and contrast of the considered images.

Table 1. AFM image

# Generations	Image Crossover		Pixel Crossover	
	% Average Restoration	% Best Restoration	% Average Restoration	% Best Restoration
10	97,81	95,40	98,26	95,33
20	97,70	92,90	97,09	92,53
30	99,08	95,50	98,84	95,32
40	97,83	95,20	96,57	94,31
50	96,97	94,44	97,33	95,03

Table 2. Gradient image

# Generations	Image Crossover		Pixel Crossover	
	% Average Restoration	% Best Restoration	% Average Restoration	% Best Restoration
10	97,29	94,70	98,00	95,95
20	97,57	94,97	97,67	94,46
30	96,95	94,51	98,80	96,01
40	97,31	94,76	98,34	94,01
50	96,80	93,23	97,66	93,90

Similar results are obtained when the number of individuals and the crossover probability are increased, and worst results are obtained when the brightness and/or contrast intervals are increased.

As the images obtained using the gradient method is closer to the original image and they can not be improved using this method, the results above suggest that AG could be used as a refinement method of gradient images. At the moment, we are researching alternatives to increase image quality (especially for AFM images) using different fitness functions and reproduction operators. We are also investigating use the term αS (eq. 3 – section 2.2) and restrict crossover operator to parts of the images.

5   Conclusions and Future Works

In this work, we applied genetic algorithms [9] on the biological images restoration problem. We considered two types of images to be restored : those generated by AFM technique (AFM image) [1] and those generated by gradient restoration method [3] applied to AFM images (gradient image). Preliminary results showed an improvement on image quality, a gain (in the best case) of 7% on the brightness and contrast of the considered images. That can be considered a good result for gradient images (since those images can not be improved through the gradient method [3]) and suggests that AG's could work better as a refinement method than as a restoration method.

At the moment, we are studying alternatives to increase image quality (specially for AFM images) such as : (i) using different fitness functions and selection operators,

(ii) include the term αS (eq. 3 – section 2.2) in the used fitness function, and (iii) restrict crossover operator to parts of the images. We will also consider point-spread function matrix with dimension greater than 3x3, since for that kind of matrix the gradient method did not obtain good results.

References

[1]   Binnig, G., Quate, C. F., Gerber, C. H.; *Atomic Force Microscope*; *Phys. Rev. Lett.* 56(9), 930–933 (1986)

[2]   Chacón, P.; Morán, F.; Díaz, J. F.; Pantos, E. and Andreu, J. M.; *Low-Resolution Structures of Proteins in Solution Retrieved from X-Ray Scattering with a Genetic Algorithm*; *Biophysical Journal,* Volume 74 June (1998)

[3]   Cidade, G.A.G., Roberty, N. C., Silva Neto, A. J. e Bisch, P. M.; *The Restoration of AFM Biological Images Using the Tikhonov's Method - the Proposal of a General Regularization Functional for Best Contrast Results*, Acta Micr., v. 10, pp.157–161 (2001)

[4]   Dandekar, T., and P. Argos; *Folding the main chain of small proteins with the genetic algorithm*; *J. Mol. Biol.* 236:844–861 (1994)

[5]   Dandekar, T.; *Improving Protein Structure Prediction by New Strategies: Experimental Insights and the Genetic Algorithm*; (1997)

[6]   Goldberg, David E.; *Genetic Algorithms in Search, Optimization and Machine Learning*; Addison-Wesley (1989)

[7]   Goldberg, David E.; *A Note on Boltzmann Tournament Selection for Genetic Algorithms and Population-Oriented Simulated Annealing*; C. Sys. 4, 445–460 (1990)

[8]   Gultyaev, A. P., F. H. D. van Batenburg, and C. W. A. Pleij; *The computer simulation of RNA folding pathways using a genetic algorithm*; *J. Mol. Biol.* 250:37–51 (1995)

[9]   Holland, John. H.; *Adaptation In Natural and Artificial Systems*; Ann Arbor, Michigan: The University of Michigan Press (1975)

[10]   Jiang, Tianzi and Evans,D. J.; *Image Restoration by Combining Local Genetic Algorithm with Adaptive Pre-Conditioning*; *In. Jap. Comp. Math.*, v. 76, 279–295 (2001)

[11]   Kress, R., *Applied Mathematical Sciences,* 82, Springer Verlag (1989)

[12]   Li, Xiaodong, Jiang, Tianzi and Evans, D. J.; *Medical Image Reconstruction using a Multi-Objective Genetic Local Search Algorithm*; *International Japanese Computer Math.*, Vol 74, 301–314 (2000)

[13]   Mahfoud, Samir W.; *An Analysis of Boltzmann Tournament Selection*; Department of Computer Science, University of Illinois (1994)

[14]   May, Kaaren; Stathaki, Tania; Constantinides, Anthony; *A Simulated Annealing Genetic Algorithm for Blind Deconvolution of Nonlinearly Degraded Images*; *Signal Processing and Digital Systems Section*; Imperial College of Sci., Tech. and Med. (1996)

[15]   Oei, Christopher K.; Goldberg, David E. and Chang, Shau-Jin; *Tournament Selection, Niching, and the Preservation of Diversity*; Illinois Genetic Algorithms Laboratory (1991)

[16]   Pelikan, Martin and Goldberg, David E.; *Genetic Algorithms, Clustering, and the Breaking of Symmetry*; Illinois Genetic Algorithms Laboratory, Department of General Engineering, (2000)

[17]   Rudolph, Günter.; *Convergence Analysis of Canonical Genetic Algorithms*; *IEEE Transactions on Neural Networks*, pp. 96–101, Jan (1994)

[18]   Ruggiero, M. A. G.e Lopes, V. L. da R.; *Cálculo Numérico – Aspectos Teóricos e Computacionais*; Makron Books (1997)

[19] Spears, William M. and Anand, Vic; *A Study of Crossover Operators in Genetic Programming*; Navy Center for App. Res. in AI & The Mass. Ins. of Tech. (1991)

[20] Spears, William M.; *Crossover or Mutation?*; Navy Center for Applied Research in Artificial Intelligence, Naval Research Laboratory, Washington, D.C. (1992)

[21] Tanenbaum, A.S.; *Computer Networks*; Prentice-Hall, Inc. (1996)

[22] Tikhonov,A.N. and Arsenin,V.Y.;*Solutions of Ill-Posed Problems*,Wiley, N. Y. (1977)

[23] Thierens, Dirk; *Scalability Problems of Simple Genetic Algorithms*; Department of Computer Science, Utrecht University, Netherlands (1999)

[24] Weisman *et all*, *Application of morphological pseudoconvolutions to scanning-tunneling and atomic force microscopy*, SPIE Proc., V. 1567, App. of Digital Image Proc. XIV, 1991, pp.88–90

[25] Willet, P; *Genetic algorithms in molecular recognition and design*;Trends Biol. 13: 516 –521 (1995)

Evolution of Multi-adaptive Discretization Intervals for a Rule-Based Genetic Learning System

Jaume Bacardit and Josep Maria Garrell

Intelligent Systems Research Group
Enginyeria i Arquitectura La Salle,
Universitat Ramon Llull,
Psg. Bonanova 8, 08022-Barcelona,
Catalonia, Spain, Europe. {jbacardit,josepmg}@salleURL.edu

Abstract. Genetic Based Machine Learning (GBML) systems traditionally have evolved rules that only deal with discrete attributes. Therefore, some discretization process is needed in order to teal with real-valued attributes. There are several methods to discretize real-valued attributes into a finite number of intervals, however none of them can efficiently solve all the possible problems. The alternative of a high number of simple uniform-width intervals usually expands the size of the search space without a clear performance gain. This paper proposes a rule representation which uses adaptive discrete intervals that split or merge through the evolution process, finding the correct discretization intervals at the same time as the learning process is done.

1 Introduction

The application of Genetic Algorithms (GA) [10,8] to classification problems is usually known as Genetic Based Machine Learning (GBML), and traditionally it has been addressed from two different points of view: the Pittsburgh approach, and the Michigan approach, early exemplified by LS-1 [20] and CS-1 [11], respectively. The classical knowledge representation used in these systems is a set of rules where the antecedent is defined by a prefixed finite number of intervals to handle real-valued attributes. The performance of these systems is tied to the right election of the intervals.

In this paper we use a rule representation with adaptive discrete intervals. These intervals are splitted and merged through the evolution process that drives the training stage. This approach avoids the higher computational cost of the approaches which work directly with real values and finds a good discretization only expanding the search space with small intervals when necessary. This representation was introduced in [1] and the work presented in this paper is its evolution, mainly focused on generalizing the approach and simplifying the tuning needed for each domain.

This rule representation is compared across different domains against the traditional discrete representation with fixed intervals. The number and size of

F.J. Garijo, J.C. Riquelme, and M. Toro (Eds.): IBERAMIA 2002, LNAI 2527, pp. 350–360, 2002.
© Springer-Verlag Berlin Heidelberg 2002

the fixed intervals approach is obtained with two methods: (1) simple uniform-width intervals and (2) intervals obtained with the Fayyad & Irani method [7], a well-known discretization algorithm. The aim of this comparison is two-fold: measure the accuracy performance and the computational cost.

The paper is structured as follows. Section 2 presents some related work. Then, we describe the framework of our classifier system section 3. The adaptive intervals rule representation is explained in section 4. Next, section 5 describes the test suite used in the comparison. The results obtained are summarized in section 6. Finally, section 7 discusses the conclusions and some further work.

2   Related Work

There are several approaches to handle real-valued attributes in the Genetic Based Machine Learning (GBML) field. Early approaches use discrete rules with a large number of prefixed uniform discretization intervals. However, this approach has the problem that the search space grows exponentially, slowing the evolutionary process without a clean accuracy improvement of the solution [2] Lately, several alternatives to the discrete rules have been presented. There are rules composed by real-valued intervals (XCSR [22], [4], COGITO [18]). MOGUL [5], uses a fuzzy reasoning method. This method generates sequentially: (1) fuzzy rules, and then (2) fuzzy membership functions. Recently, GALE [15] proposed a knowledge independent method for learning other knowledge representations like instance sets or decision trees. All those alternatives present better performance, but usually they also have higher computational cost [18].

A third approach is to use a heuristic discretization algorithm. Some of these methods work with information entropy [7], the χ^2 statistic [14] or multi-dimensional non-uniform discretization [13]. These algorithms are usually more accurate and faster than the uniform discretization. However, they suffer a lack of robustness across some domains [1].

3   Framework

In this section we describe the main features of our classifier system. GAssist (*Genetic Algorithms based claSSIfier sySTem*) [9] is a Pittsburgh style classifier system based on GABIL [6]. Directly from GABIL we have borrowed the representation of the discrete rules (rules with conjunctive normal form (CNF) predicates), the semantically correct crossover operator and the fitness computation (squared accuracy).

Matching strategy: The matching process follows a "if ... then ... else if ... then..." structure, usually called *Decision List* [19].

Mutation operators: The system manipulates variable-length individuals, making more difficult the tuning of the classic gene-based mutation probability. In order to simplify this tuning, we define p_{mut} as the probability i of mutating an individual. When an individual is selected for mutation (based on p_{mut}), a random gene is chosen inside its chromosome for mutation.

Control of the individuals length: Dealing with variable-length individuals arises some serious considerations. One of the most important ones is the control of the size of the evolving individuals [21]. This control is achieved ins GAssist using two different operators:

- *Rule deletion.* This operator deletes the rules of the individuals that do not match any training example. This rule deletion is done after the fitness computation and has two constraints: (a) the process is only activated after a predefined number of iterations, to prevent a massive diversity loss and (b) the number of rules of an individual never goes below a lower threshold. This threshold is assigned to the number of classes of the domain.
- *Selection bias using the individual size.* Selection is guided as usual by the fitness (the accuracy). However, it also gives certain degree of relevance to the size of the individuals, having a policy similar to multi-objective systems. We use tournament selection because its local behavior lets us implement this policy. The criterion of the tournament is given by an operator called "size-based comparison" [2]. This operator considers two individuals similar if their fitness difference is below a certain threshold (d_{comp}). Then, it selects the individual with fewer number of rules.

4   Discrete Rules with Adaptive Intervals

This section describes the rule representation based on discrete rules with adaptive intervals. First we describe the problems that traditional discrete rules present. Then, we explain the adaptive intervals rules proposed and the changes introduced in order to enable the GA to use them.

4.1   Discrete Rules and Unnecessary Search Space Growth

The traditional approach to solve problems with real-valued attributes using discrete rules has been done using a discretization process. This discretization can be done using algorithms which determine the discretization intervals analyzing the training information or we can use a simple alternative like using an uniform-width intervals discretization. In the latter method, the way to increase the accuracy of the solution is to increase the number of intervals. This solution brings a big problem because the search space to explore grows in an exponential degree when more intervals are added. The improvement in accuracy expected increasing the number of intervals does not exist sometimes, because the GA spends too much time exploring areas of the search space which do not need to be explored.

   If we find a correct and minimal set of intervals, the solution accuracy will probably increase without a huge increase of the computational cost.

4.2   Finding Good and Minimal Intervals

Our aim is to find good discretization intervals without a great expansion of the search space. In order to achieve this goal we defined a rule representation [1] with discrete adaptive intervals where the discretization intervals are not fixed. These intervals are evolved through the iterations, merging and splitting between them.

To control the computational cost and the growth of the search space, we define the next constraints:

- A number of "low level" uniform and static intervals is defined for each attribute called *micro-intervals*.
- The adaptive intervals are built joining together *micro-intervals*.
- When we split an interval, we select a random point in its *micro-intervals* to break it.
- When we merge two intervals, the value of the resulting interval is taken from the one which has more *micro-intervals*. If both have the same number of *micro-intervals*, the value is chosen randomly.
- The number and size of the initial intervals is selected randomly.

The adaptive intervals as well as the split and merge operators are shown in figure 1.

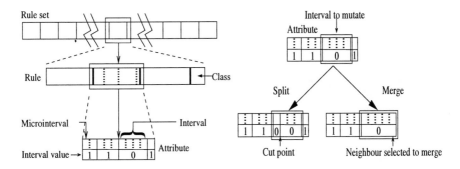

Fig. 1. Adaptive intervals representation and the split and merge operators.

To apply the split and merge operators we have added to the GA cycle two special phases applied to the offspring population after the mutation phase. For each phase (split and merge) we have a probability (p_{split} or p_{merge}) of applying a split or merge operation to an individual. If an individual is selected for splitting or merging, a random point inside its chromosome is chosen to apply the operation.

Finally, this representation requires some changes in some other parts of the GA:

- The crossover operator can only take place in the attribute boundaries.

– The "size-based comparison" operator uses the length (number of genes) of the individual instead of the number of rules, because now the size of a rule can change when the number of intervals that it contains change. This change also makes the GA prefer the individuals with fewer intervals in addition to fewer rules, further simplifying them.

4.3   Changes to the Adaptive Intervals Rule Representation

One of the main drawbacks of the initial approach was the sizing of the number of *micro-intervals* assigned to each attribute term of the rules. This parameter is difficult to tune because it is domain-specific.

In this paper we test another approach (*multi-adaptive*) which consists in evolving attribute terms with different number of *micro-intervals* in the same population. This enables the evolutionary process to select the correct number of micro-intervals for each attribute term of the rules. The number of *micro-intervals* of each attribute term is selected from a predefined set in the initialization stage.

The initialization phase has also changed. In our previous work the number and size of the intervals was uniform. We have changed this policy to a total random initialization in order to gain diversity in the initial population.

The last change introduced involves the split and merge operators. In the previous version these operators were integrated inside the mutation. This made the sizing of the probabilities very difficult because the three operators (split, merge and mutation) were coupled. Using an extra recombination stage in this version we eliminate this tight linkage.

5   Test Suite

This section summarizes the tests done in order to evaluate the accuracy and efficiency of the method presented in this paper. We also compare it with some alternative methods. The tests were conducted using several machine learning problems which we also describe.

5.1   Test Problems

The selected test problems for this paper present different characteristics in order to give us a broad overview of the performance of the methods being compared. The first problem is a synthetic problem (*Tao* [15]) that has non-orthogonal class boundaries. We also use several problems provided by the University of California at Irvine (UCI) repository [3]. The problems selected are: Pima-indians-diabetes (*pima*), *iris*, *glass* and breast-cancer-winsconsin (*breast*). Finally we will use three problems from our own private repository. The first two deal with the diagnosis of breast cancer based of biopsies (*bps* [17]) and mammograms (*mamm* [16]) whereas the last one is related to the prediction of student qualifications (*lrn* [9]). The characteristics of the problems are listed in table 1. The partition of the examples into the train and test sets was done using the *stratified ten-fold cross-validation* method [12].

Table 1. Characteristics of the test problems.

Dataset	Number of examples	real attributes	discrete attributes	classes
tao	1888	2	-	2
pima	768	8	-	2
iris	150	4	-	3
glass	214	9	-	6
breast	699	-	9	2
bps	1027	24	-	2
mamm	216	21	-	2
lrn	648	4	2	5

5.2   Configurations of the GA to Test

The main goal of the tests are to evaluate the performance of the adaptive intervals rules representation. In order to compare this method with the traditional discrete representation, we use two discretization methods, the simple uniform-width intervals method and the Fayyad & Irani method [7].

We analyze the adaptive intervals approach with two types of runs. The first one assigns the same number of *micro-intervals* to all the attribute terms of the individuals. We call this type of run **adaptive**. In the second one, attributes with different number of *micro-intervals* coexist in the same population. We well call this type **multi-adaptive**.

The GA parameters are shown in table 2. The reader can appreciate that the sizing of both p_{split} and p_{merge} is the same for all the problems except the tao problem. Giving the same value to p_{merge} and p_{split} produce solutions with too few rules and intervals, as well as less accurate than the results obtained with the configuration shown in table 2. This is an issue that needs further study.

Another important issue of the p_{split} and p_{merge} probabilities for some of the domains is that they are greater than 1. This means that for these domains at least one split and merge operation will be surely done to each individual of the population. Thus, p_{split} and p_{merge} become expected values instead of probabilities. The tuning done produces a reduction of the number of iterations needed.

6   Results

In this section present the results obtained. The aim of the tests was to compare the method presented in the paper in three aspects: accuracy and size of the

Table 2. Common and problem-specific parameters of the GA.

Parameter	Value
Crossover probability	0.6
Iter. of rule eliminating activation	30
Iter. of size comparison activation	30
Sets of *micro-intervals* in the multi-adaptive test	5,6,7,8,10,15,20,25
Tournament size	3
Population size	300
Probability of mutating an individual	0.6

Code	Parameter
#iter	Number of GA iterations
d_{interv}	Number of intervals in the uniform-width discrete rules
a_{interv}	Number of *micro-intervals* in the adaptive test
d_{comp}	Distance parameter in the "size-based comparison" operator
p_{split}	Probability of splitting an individual (one of its intervals)
p_{merge}	Probability of merging an individual (one of its intervals)

Problem	Parameter					
	#iter	d_{interv}	a_{interv}	d_{comp}	p_{merge}	p_{split}
tao	600	12	48	0.001	1.3	2.6
pima	500	4	8	0.01	0.8	0.8
iris	400	10	10	0.02	0.5	0.5
glass	750	4	8	0.015	1.5	1.5
breast	325	5	10	0.01	3.2	3.2
bps	500	4	10	0.015	1.7	1.7
mamm	500	2	5	0.01	1	1
lrn	700	5	10	0.01	1.2	1.2

solutions as well as the computational cost. Foreach method and test problem we show the average and standard deviation values of: (1) the cross-validation accuracy, (2) the size of the best individual in number of rules and intervals per attribute and (3) the execution time in seconds. The tests were executed in an AMD Athlon 1700+ using Linux operating system and C++ language. The results were also analyzed using the two-sided t-test [23] to determine if the two adaptive methods outperform the other ones with a significance level of 1%. Finally, for each configuration, test and fold, 15 runs using different random seeds were done. Results are shown in table 3. The column titled t-test show a • beside the Uniform or Fayyad & Irani method if it was outperformed by the adaptive methods. The adaptive methods were never outperformed in the tests done, showing a good robustness.

The results are summarized using the ranking in table 4. The ranking for each problem and method is based on the accuracy. The global i rankings are computed averaging the problem rankings.

Table 3 shows that in two of the tests the best performing method was the Fayyad & Irani interval discretization technique. However, in the rest of the tests its performance is lower, showing a lack of robustness across different domains. The two adaptive tests achieved the best results of the ranking. Nevertheless, the goal of improving the rule representation with the *multi-adaptive* configuration has not been achieved. It is only better than the original *adaptive* configuration in three of the eight test problems. The computational cost is clearly the main

Table 3. Mean and deviation of the accuracy (percentage of correctly classifier examples), number of rules, intervals per attribute and execution time for each method tested. Bold entries show the method with best results for each test problem. A • mark a significant out-performance based on a t-test

Problem	Configuration	Accuracy	Number of Rules	Intervals per Rule	Time	t-test
tao	Uniform	93.7±1.2	8.8±1.6	8.3±0.0	36.0±3.5	
	Fayyad	87.8±1.1	**3.1±0.3**	3.4±0.1	**24.2±1.4**	•
	Adaptive	**94.6±1.3**	22.5±5.6	7.7±0.4	96.6±14.7	
	Multi-Adaptive	94.3±1.0	19.5±4.9	6.0±0.6	94.5±13.9	
pima	Uniform	73.8±4.1	6.3±2.2	3.7±0.0	**23.2±2.8**	
	Fayyad	73.6±3.1	6.6±2.6	2.3±0.2	26.4±3.0	
	Adaptive	**74.8±3.5**	6.2±2.6	2.0±0.4	56.2±9.4	
	Multi-Adaptive	74.4±3.1	**5.8±2.2**	**1.9±0.4**	59.7±8.9	
iris	Uniform	92.9±2.7	3.8±1.1	8.2±0.0	**5.2±0.7**	
	Fayyad	94.2±3.0	**3.2±0.6**	2.8±0.1	5.5±0.1	
	Adaptive	94.9±2.3	3.3±0.5	**1.3±0.2**	9.2±0.4	
	Multi-Adaptive	**96.2±2.2**	3.6±0.9	**1.3±0.2**	9.0±0.8	
glass	Uniform	60.5±8.9	8.7±1.8	3.7±0.0	**13.9±1.5**	
	Fayyad	**65.7±6.1**	8.1±1.4	2.4±0.1	14.0±1.1	
	Adaptive	64.6±4.7	**5.9±1.7**	**1.7±0.2**	35.1±5.2	
	Multi-Adaptive	65.2±4.1	6.7±2.0	1.8±0.2	38.4±5.0	
breast	Uniform	94.8±2.6	4.8±2.5	4.6±0.0	6.5±1.0	
	Fayyad	95.2±1.8	4.1±0.8	3.6±0.1	**5.8±0.4**	
	Adaptive	**95.4±2.3**	2.7±1.0	1.8±0.2	15.7±2.1	
	Multi-Adaptive	95.3±2.3	**2.6±0.9**	**1.7±0.2**	17.4±1.5	
bps	Uniform	77.6±3.3	15.0±7.0	3.9±0.0	50.8±9.0	
	Fayyad	80.0±3.1	7.1±3.8	2.4±0.1	**37.7±6.0**	
	Adaptive	**80.3±3.5**	**4.7±3.0**	2.1±0.4	106.6±21.1	
	Multi-Adaptive	80.1±3.3	5.1±2.0	**2.0±0.3**	115.9±20.5	
mamm	Uniform	63.2±9.9	2.6±0.5	2.0±0.0	**7.8±1.0**	
	Fayyad	65.3±11.1	**2.3±0.5**	2.0±0.1	8.5±0.7	
	Adaptive	**65.8±5.3**	4.4±1.7	**1.8±0.2**	27.6±4.9	
	Multi-Adaptive	65.0±6.1	4.4±1.9	1.9±0.2	27.4±5.5	
lrn	Uniform	64.7±4.9	17.8±5.1	4.9±0.0	29.2±4.0	
	Fayyad	**67.5±5.1**	14.3±5.0	4.4±0.1	**26.5±3.4**	
	Adaptive	66.1±4.6	14.0±4.6	3.6±0.3	58.9±7.9	
	Multi-Adaptive	66.7±4.1	**11.6±4.1**	**3.4±0.2**	53.9±7.2	

Table 4. Performance ranking of the tested methods. Lower number means better ranking.

Problem	Fixed	Fayyad	Adaptive	Multi-Adaptive
tao	3	4	1	2
pima	3	4	1	2
iris	4	3	2	1
glass	4	1	3	2
breast	4	3	1	2
bps	4	3	1	2
mam	4	2	1	3
lrn	4	1	3	2
Average	3.25	2.625	1.625	2
Final rank	4	3	1	2

drawback of the adaptive intervals representation. The Fayyad & Irani method is in average 2.62 times faster than it.

7 Conclusions and Further Work

This paper focused on an adaptive rule representation as a a robust method for finding a good discretization. The main contribution done is provided by the used of adaptive discrete intervals, which can split or merge through the evolution process, reducing the search space where it is possible. The use of a heuristic discretization method (like the Fayyad & Irani one) outperform the adaptive intervals representation in some test problem. Nevertheless, the performance increase is not significant. On the other hand, when the adaptive intervals outperform the other methods, the performance increase is higher, showing a better degree of robustness.

The overhead of evolving discretization intervals and rules at the same time is quite significant, being its main drawback. Beside the cost of the representation itself (our implementation uses twice the memory of the discrete representation for the same number of intervals) the main difference is the significant reduction of the search space achieved by a heuristic discretization.

Some further work should use the knowledge provided by the discretization techniques in order to reduce the computational cost of the adaptive intervals representation. This process should be achieved without losing robustness. Another important point of further study is how the value of p_{split} and p_{merge} affect the behavior of the system, in order to simplify the tuning needed for each domain.

Finally, it would also be interesting to compare the adaptive intervals rule representation with some representation dealing directly with real-valued attributes, like the ones described in the related work section. This comparison should follow the same criteria used here: comparing both the accuracy and the computational cost.

Acknowledgments. The authors acknowledge the support provided under grant numbers 2001FI 00514, CICYT/Tel08-0408-02 and FIS00/0033-02. The results of this work were partially obtained using equipment cofunded by the *Direcció General de Recerca de la Generalitat de Catalunya (D.O.G.C. 30/12/1997)*. Finally we would like to thank Enginyeria i Arquitectura La Salle for their support to our research group.

References

1. Jaume Bacardit and Josep M. Garrell. Evolution of adaptive discretization intervals for a rule-based genetic learning system. In *Proceedings of the Genetic and Evolutionary Computation Conference (GECCO-2002) (to appear)*, 2002.
2. Jaume Bacardit and Josep M. Garrell. Métodos de generalización para sistemas clasificadores de Pittsburgh. In *Proceedings of the "Primer Congreso Iberoamericano de Algoritmos Evolutivos y Bioinspirados (AEB'02)"*, pages 486–493, 2002.
3. C. Blake, E. Keogh, and C. Merz. Uci repository of machine learning databases, 1998. Blake, C., Keogh, E., & Merz, C.J. (1998). UCI repository of machine learning databases (www.ics.uci.edu/mlearn/MLRepository.html).

4. A. L. Corcoran and S. Sen. Using real-valued genetic algorithms to evolve rule sets for classification. In *Proceedings of the IEEE Conference on Evolutionary Computation*, pages 120–124, 1994.
5. O. Cordón, M. del Jesus, and F. Herrera. Genetic learning of fuzzy rule-based classification systems co-operating with fuzzy reasoning methods. In *International Journal of Intelligent Systems, Vol. 13 (10/11)*, pages 1025–1053, 1998.
6. Kenneth A. DeJong and William M. Spears. Learning concept classification rules using genetic algorithms. *Proceedings of the International Joint Conference on Artificial Intelligence*, pages 651–656, 1991.
7. Usama M. Fayyad and Keki B. Irani. Multi-interval discretization of continuous-valued attributes for classification learning. In *IJCAI*, pages 1022–1029, 1993.
8. David E. Goldberg. *Genetic Algorithms in Search, Optimization and Machine Learning*. Addison-Wesley Publishing Company, Inc., 1989.
9. Elisabet Golobardes, Xavier Llorà, Josep Maria Garrell, David Vernet, and Jaume Bacardit. Genetic classifier system as a heuristic weighting method for a case-based classifier system. *Butlletí de l'Associació Catalana d'Intel.ligència Artificial*, 22:132–141, 2000.
10. John H. Holland. *Adaptation in Natural and Artificial Systems*. University of Michigan Press, 1975.
11. John H. Holland. Escaping Brittleness: The possibilities of General-Purpose Learning Algorithms Applied to Parallel Rule-Based Systems. In *Machine learning, an artificial intelligence approach. Volume II*, pages 593–623. 1986.
12. Ron Kohavi. A study of cross-validation and bootstrap for accuracy estimation and model selection. In *IJCAI*, pages 1137–1145, 1995.
13. Alexander V. Kozlov and Daphne Koller. Nonuniform dynamic discretization in hybrid networks. In *Proceedings of the 13th Annual Conference on Uncertainty in AI (UAI)*, pages 314–325, 1997.
14. H. Liu and R. Setiono. Chi2: Feature selection and discretization of numeric attributes. In *Proceedings of 7th IEEE International Conference on Tools with Artificial Intelligence*, pages 388–391. IEEE Computer Society, 1995.
15. Xavier Llorà and Josep M. Garrell. Knowledge-independent data mining with fine-grained parallel evolutionary algorithms. In *Proceedings of the Genetic and Evolutionary Computation Conference (GECCO-2001)*, pages 461–468. Morgan Kaufmann, 2001.
16. J. Martí, X. Cufí, J. Regincós, and et al. Shape-based feature selection for microcalcification evaluation. In *Imaging Conference on Image Processing, 3338:1215-1224*, 1998.
17. E. Martínez Marroquín, C. Vos, and et al. Morphological analysis of mammary biopsy images. In *Proceedings of the IEEE International Conference on Image Processing (ICIP'96)*, pages 943–947, 1996.
18. José C. Riquelme and Jesús S. Aguilar. Codificación indexada de atributos continuos para algoritmos evolutivos en aprendizaje supervisado. In *Proceedings of the "Primer Congreso Iberoamericano de Algoritmos Evolutivos y Bioinspirados (AEB'02)"*, pages 161–167, 2002.
19. Ronald L. Rivest. Learning decision lists. *Machine Learning*, 2(3):229–246, 1987.
20. Stephen F. Smith. Flexible learning of problem solving heuristics through adaptive search. In *Proceedings of the 8th International Joint Conference on Artificial Intelligence (IJCAI-83)*, pages 421–425, Los Altos, CA, 1983. Morgan Kaufmann.
21. Terence Soule and James A. Foster. Effects of code growth and parsimony pressure on populations in genetic programming. *Evolutionary Computation*, 6(4):293–309, Winter 1998.

22. Stewart W. Wilson. Get real! XCS with continuous-valued inputs. In L. Booker, Stephanie Forrest, M. Mitchell, and Rick L. Riolo, editors, *Festschrift in Honor of John H. Holland*, pages 111–121. Center for the Study of Complex Systems, 1999.
23. Ian H. Witten and Eibe Frank. *Data Mining: practical machine learning tools and techniques with java implementations*. Morgan Kaufmann, 2000.

An Immunological Approach to Combinatorial Optimization Problems

Vincenzo Cutello and Giuseppe Nicosia

University of Catania,
Department of Mathematics and Computer Science
V.le A. Doria 6, 95126 Catania, Italy
{cutello,nicosia}@dmi.unict.it

Abstract. In this work we use a simplified model of the immune system to explore the problem solving feature. We consider only two immunological entities, antigens and antibodies, two parameters, and simple immune operators. The experimental results shows how a simple randomized search algorithm coupled with a mechanism for adaptive recognition of hardest constraints, is sufficient to obtain optimal solutions for any combinatorial optimization problem.

Keywords: Immune Algorithms, Evolutionary Computation, Combinatorial Optimization, NP-complete problems.

1 Immunological Computation

The Immune System (IS) has to assure recognition of each potentially dangerous molecule or substance, generically called antigen, that can infect the host organism. The IS first recognizes it as *dangerous* or extraneous and then mounts a response to eliminate it. To detect an antigen, the IS activates a recognition process. Moreover, the IS only has finite resources and often very little time to produce antibodies for each possible antigen [1].

Our Immune Algorithm is based on the *theory of the clonal selection* first stated by Burnet and Ledeberg in 1959 [2]. This theory suggests that among all the possible cells with different receptors circulating in the host organism, only those who are actually able to recognize the antigen will start to proliferate by duplication (cloning). The increase of those population and the production of cells with longer expected life-time assures the organism a higher specific responsiveness to that antigenic pattern, establishing a defense over time (immune memory). In particular, on recognition, B and T memory cells are produced. Plasma B cells, deriving from stimulated B lymphocytes, are in charge of the production of antibodies targeting the antigen.

This mechanism is usually observed when looking at the population of lymphocytes in two subsequent antigenic infections. The first exposition to the antigen triggers the *primary response*. In this phase the antigen is recognized and memory is developed. During the *secondary response*, that occurs when the same

F.J. Garijo, J.C. Riquelme, and M. Toro (Eds.): IBERAMIA 2002, LNAI 2527, pp. 361–370, 2002.

antigen is encountered again, a rapid and more abundant production of antibodies is observed, resulting from the stimulation of the cells already specialized and present as memory cells. The *hypermutation* phenomenon observed during the immune responses is a consequence of the fact that the DNA portion coding for the antibodies is subjected to mutation during the proliferation of the B lymphocytes. This provides the system with the ability to generate diversity.

The IS from an information processing point of view [3] can been considered like a problem learning and solving system. The antigen is the problem to solve, the antibody is the generated solution. At beginning of the primary response the antigen-problem is recognized by partial candidate solution (the B cell receptor). At the end of the primary response the antigen-problem is defeated-solved by candidate solutions (antibody or a set of antibodies in the case of multimodal optimization). Consequently the primary response corresponds to a training phase while the secondary response is the testing phase where we will try to solve problems similar to the original presented in the primary response [4].

The new field of *Immunological Computation* (or Artificial Immune System) attempts to use methods and concepts such ideas to design immunity-based system applications in science and engineering [5]. Immune Algorithms (IA) are adaptive systems in which learning takes place by evolutionary mechanisms similar to biological evolution.

The paper is organized as follows: in section 2 we describe the proposed Immunological Algorithms (IA), in 3 we define the test bed where we verify the IA's performance and report simulations' results. In section 4 we reports about other related works and finally in 5 we highlight some future directions.

2   Immune Algorithms

Following the track of the computer experiments performed by Nicosia *et al.* [4] we focus our attention to the problem solving ability of the immune system and present a new immune algorithm. Our approach uses a simplified model of the immune system to explore the problem solving feature. We consider only two entities: antigens and antibodies. The antigen is the combinatorial optimization problem and the antibody is the candidate solution. Antigen is a set of variables that models the problem. Antibodies are modeled as binary strings of length l.

The input is the antigen problem, the population size (d) and the number of clones for each cell (dup). The set $S^{d \times l}$ denotes a population of d individuals of length l, and it represents the space of feasible and unfeasible candidate solutions. After a random initialization and evaluation of cell populations $P^{(0)}$, the loop iterates the cloning of all antibodies, each antibodies produce dup clones, generating the population P^{clo}. T denotes a termination criterion, that is, the algorithm terminates if a solution is found, or a maximum number of evaluations is reached. Next step is to mutate a random bit for each antibody in P^{clo} generating the population P^{hyp}. The mechanism of mutation of the cell receptor is modeled by a random process with parameter l, i.e. the length of the cell receptor. This immunological operator is important because it modifies continuously the receptors in presence like a neural network whose structure (the layers, the number and the nature of neurons) would change in time. After the evaluation of P^{hyp} at time t the algorithm selects the best d antibodies from $(P^{hyp} \sqcup P^{(t)})^1$ (a simple elitist strategy) and creates the new set $P^{(t+1)}$). The output is basically the candidate solutions-clones that have solved-recognized the antigen. A pseudo-code version of the algorithm is given below.

Immune Algorithm
$t := 0$;
Initialize $P^{(0)} = \{x_1, x_2, ..., x_d\} \in S^{d \times l}$
Evaluate $P^{(0)}$;
while (T($P^{(t)}$)= 0) *do*
    $P^{clo} :=$ Cloning $(P^{(t)}, dup)$;
    $P^{hyp} :=$ Hypermutation (P^{clo});
    Evaluate (P^{hyp});
    $P^{(t+1)} :=$ Select the d highest affinity individual $(P^{hyp} \sqcup P^{(t)})$;
    $t := t + 1$;
od

This simplistic view does not represent a strong limitation because in general one can give whatever meaning to the bit string representing the candidate solution and use much more complicated mutation operator than the simple bit-flip, e.g., any map $f : \{0,1\}^l \to \{0,1\}^l$ could determine a different search algorithm. The underlying evolutionary *engine* remains the same.

In evolutionary computation the selection of an appropriate population size is important and could greatly affect the effectiveness and efficiency of the optimization performance. For this reason EA's with dynamic population size achieve better convergence rate and discover as well any gaps or missing tradeoff regions at each generation [6].

All evolutionary algorithms need to set an optimal population size in order to discover and distribute the *nondominated individuals* along the Pareto front [7]. If the population size is too small, EAs may suffer from *premature convergence*, while if the population size is too large, undesired computational overwork may be incurred and the waiting time for a fitness improvement may be too long in practice. We propose here a simple search algorithm with only two parameters d and dup. The correct setting of these parameters allows to discover the non-dominated individuals without using dynamic population. We observe that the evolutionary engine uses a process of *expansion and reduction*. The expansion from population $P^{(t)}$ with $\mid d \mid$ individuals into population P^{hyp} with $\mid d \times dup \mid$ individuals is performed by cloning and hypermutation operators, the reduction from P^{hyp} with $\mid d \times dup \mid$ into $P^{(t+1)}$ with $\mid d \mid$ is performed by means of a selection operator. The expansion phase explores the fitness landscape at a given generation t, the reduction phase decides which individuals to select for the next generation $t + 1$.

---

[1] Note that this is a multi-set union, since we want to allow an individual to appear more than once.

3   NP-Complete Problems

To test our algorithm we chose two NP-complete problems.

3.1   The Minimum Hitting Set Problem

An instance of the Minimum Hitting Set problem consists of a collection S of subsets of a finite set U and a positive integer $k \leq\mid U \mid$. Question: Is there a subset $U' \subseteq U$, with $\mid U' \mid\leq k$, such that U' contains at least one element from each subset in S? This problem is NP-complete. Indeed, membership to NP can be easily observed, since a guessed proposed hitting set U' can be checked in polynomial time. NP-hardness is obtained by polynomial reduction from the Vertex Cover [8].

We work with a fitness function that allows us to allocate feasible and unfeasible candidate solutions.

$$f_{hs}(\boldsymbol{x}) = Cardinality(\boldsymbol{x}) + (\mid S \mid -Hits(\boldsymbol{x}))$$

The candidate solution must optimize both terms. Each population member $\boldsymbol{x}$ must minimize the size of set U' and maximize the number of hit sets. If $(\mid S \mid -Hits(\boldsymbol{x})) = 0$, $\boldsymbol{x}$ is a hitting set, that is a feasible solution.

The used fitness gives equal opportunity to the evolutionary process to minimize both terms. For example, if we have a collection S of 50000 sets and the following two individuals: $\boldsymbol{x}_1$, with $Cardinality(\boldsymbol{x}_1) = 40$, $Hits(\boldsymbol{x}_1) = 49997$, $f_{hs}(\boldsymbol{x}_1) = 43$; $\boldsymbol{x}_2$, with $Cardinality(\boldsymbol{x}_2) = 42$, $Hits(\boldsymbol{x}_2) = 49999$, $f_{hs}(\boldsymbol{x}_2) = 43$, it is difficult to decide which individual is the best, the choice is crucial and strongly influences the subsequent search in the landscape.

We test our IA by considering randomly generated instances of the Minimum Hitting Set problem. Fixed $\mid U \mid= 100$ we construct two types of instances with $\mid S \mid$ equal respectively to 1000 and 10000 (denoted by "hs100-1000" and "hs100-10000"). The third instance, $\mid S \mid= 50000$ ("hs-100-50000") is a very hard instances for the Minimum Hitting Set problem[2]. The best solution found has cardinality 39 [9].

Our experimental results are reported in table 1. One can see the best hitting set found by the IA for each instance, the parameter values and the average number of evaluations to solutions (AES). For each problem instance we performed 100 independent runs. We also provide the number of minimal hitting sets found.

By inspecting the results, one can also see that increasing the values of d and dup, the number of optimal solutions found increases as well, and in turn, the average number of fitness evaluations. Last column shows that for hard instances, even if we increase the population size and decrease the dup, the number of found solutions decreases. In figure 1, we show the 3D graphic of a set of numerical simulation. To understand the algorithm's behavior when changing the

---

[2] All the three instances are available at
http://www.dmi.unict.it/~ cutello/eracop.html

Table 1. Minimum Hitting Set Instances

	hs100-1000		hs100-10000		hs100-50000	
d	25	100	50	200	50	200
dup	15	30	15	15	15	10
$best$	6	6	9	9	39	39
$\#min$	1	3	3	5	3	2
AES	2275	18000	6800	27200	45050	98200

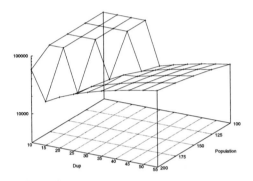

Fig. 1. 3D representation of experimental results, with dimensions: d, dup and AES

parameters, we performed a set of experiments on a simple Hitting Set instance, "hs100-1000", in which d and dup are given several values.

The problem solving ability of the algorithm depends heavily upon the number of individuals we "displace" on the space $S^{d \times l}$ and on the duplication parameter dup. The population size varies from 100 to 200 while dup from 10 to 55. The Z axis shows the average number of evaluations to solutions (we allowed $T_{max} = 100000$ evaluations and performed 100 independent runs). The population d strongly influences the number of solutions found. Indeed, when increasing d the number of nondominated solutions found increases. On the other hand, the average number of fitness function evaluation also increases. The value of dup influences the convergence speed.

In figure 2, we can see the fitness function values for the optimization process in action during the first 70 generations. The minimum hitting set is obtained at generation 60. Subsequently, other antibodies with the same cardinality are discovered, completing the set of (found) nondominated solutions.

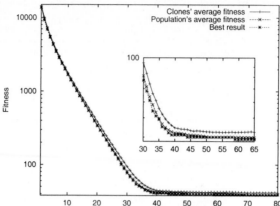

Fig. 2. Fitness function versus generations. Y axis is in log scale and origin is fixed at X-value 39.

3.2   The 3-SAT Problem

3-SAT is a fundamental NP-complete problem in propositional logic [8]. An instance of the 3-SAT problem consists of a set V of variables, a collection C of clauses over V such that each clause $c \in C$ has $\mid c \mid = 3$. The problem is to find a satisfying truth assignment for C. The 3-SAT, and in general K-SAT, for $K \geq 3$, is a classic test bed for theoretical and experimental works.

The fitness function for 3-SAT is very simple, it computes only the number of satisfied clauses

$$f_{sat}(x) = \ \#\text{SatisfiedClauses}(C, x)$$

For our experiments, we used A. van Gelder's 3-SAT problem instance generator, MKCNF.C[3]. The program mkcnf.c generates a "random" constant-clause-length CNF formula and can force formulas to be satisfiable. For accuracy, we perform our tests in the transition phase, where the hardest instances of the problem are located [10]. In this case we have $\mid C \mid = 4.3 \mid V \mid$. The generated instances are the following:

(i1) "sat30-129" number of variables 30, number of clauses 129 and random seed 83791 (mkcnf.c's input parameter useful to reproduce the same formula),
(i2) "sat30-129" (83892),
(i3) "sat30-129" (83792),
(i4) "sat40-172" with $\mid C \mid = 40$, $\mid V \mid = 172$ and random seed 62222, and
(i5) "sat50-215" with random seed 82635.

---

[3] Available by anonymous ftp at
ftp://dimacs.rutgers.edu/pub/challenge/satisfiability/contributed/UCSS/instances

Table 2. 3-SAT Instances

	(i1)	(i2)	(i3)	(i4)	(i5)
d	50	50	50	50	75
dup	20	30	20	30	15
AES	14632	292481	11468	24276	50269

The experimental results for the above 3-SAT instances are shown in table 2. We underline that for each instance we performed 50 independent runs.

To conclude, we note that the first three instances involve different formulae with the same number of variables and clauses. We can observe that among difficult formulae, there are even more difficult ones (at least for our algorithm), as the different number of evaluations proves. Such a phenomenon can be observed also for formulae with a higher number of variables and clauses. In determining a truth assignment AES grows proportionally to the difficulty of satisfying the formula.

Table 3. 3-SAT Instances

Case	$\|V\|$	$\|C\|$	Randseed	SuccessR	AES	SuccessR	AES
1	30	129	83791	1	2708	1	6063
2	30	129	83892	0.94	22804	0.96	78985
3	30	129	83792	1	12142	1	31526
4	40	172	83792	1	9078	1	13328
5	40	172	72581	0.82	37913	1	2899
6	40	172	62222	1	37264	0.94	82031
7	50	215	87112	0.58	17342	1	28026
8	50	215	82635	1	42137	1	60160
9	50	215	81619	0.26	67217	0.32	147718
10	100	430	87654	0.32	99804	0.06	192403
11	100	430	78654	0.04	78816	0.44	136152
12	100	430	77665	0.32	97173	0.58	109091

In table 3 we show the result of the last set of experiments. In this case we use the immune algorithm with a SAW (stepwise adaptation of weights) mechanism [11]. A weight is associated with each clause, the weights of all clauses that remains unsatisfied after T_p generation are incremented ($\delta w = 1$). Solving a constraint with a high weight gives high reward and thus the more pressure is given on satisfying those constraints, *the hardest clauses*. In the table, the parameter $SuccessR$ represents the number of times that the formula is satisfied. The last two columns refer to experimental results in [12] performed with an evolutionary algorithms with SAW mechanism. The table shows that the IA with SAW mechanism, outperforms in many cases the results in [12], both in terms of success rate and computational performance, i.e. a lower number of fitness evaluations.

General remark about the obtained results. Last set of experimental results shows how a simple randomized search algorithm coupled with a mechanism for adaptive recognition of hardest constraints, is sufficient to obtain optimal solutions for any combinatorial optimization problem. Proving the above statement, is the major goal of our research. The above is, obviously, consistent with the latest assumptions in Evolutionary Algorithms, that the most important features are the fitness function and the crossover operator.

4   Related Works

The *clonal selection algorithm* described in [13] represent a straightforward usage of the ideas upon which the theory of the clonal selection is stated in [2]. The clonal selection is itself a Darwinian evolution process so that similarities with Evolution Strategies and Genetic Algorithms are natural candidates. Our immune algorithm, instead, does not use proportional cloning and hypermutation inversely proportional to fitness value. We designed and use very simple cloning and hypermutation operators. Moreover, there is neither a *birth operator* to introduce diversity in the current population nor a mutation rate (p_m) to flip a bit, B cells memory, nor threshold m_c to to clone the best cells in the present population. We had simplified the immunological approach in order to better analyze and predict the algorithm's dynamics.

In this sense, also the approach described in [14] is similar to ours in that the solution is found by letting a population of unbiased potential solutions to evolve in a fitness landscape. Indeed, we are able to find similar results to their numerical experiments. The general philosophy agreement is expressed by using similar coding scheme, evaluation functions and the three immunological operators, i.e. selection, cloning and mutation.

Finally, one can observe similarities between our immune algorithm and the $(\mu + \lambda)$ evolution strategies using ranking selection [15].
Major differences with the above mentioned paradigms are cited below.

1. We consider relevant for the searching ability:
   a) the size of the recognizing clones (the parameter dup), since it determines the size of the fitness landscape explored at each generation,
   b) the number of individuals (d) since it determines the problem solving capacity. This is in contrast with most of the artificial evolution methods where a typical fixed population's size of *a thousand or less* individuals is used [16].
2. We consider only two immunological entities, antigens and antibodies, two parameters, dup and d, and simple immune operators.

5   Conclusions

One relevant disadvantage of our IA is that the search process may stop with a local minimum, when you are working with a small population size and a duplication parameter not sufficiently large. Moreover, the computational work increases proportionally to the size of these parameters. This slows down the search process in the space of feasible solutions although it gives better chances of finding good approximations to optimal solutions. The selection operator makes use of elitism, which on one hand speeds up the search, but on the other hand, may force the population to get trapped around a local minimum, reducing the diversity. In conclusion, our algorithm is simple, efficient and it is certainly suitable for further studies and tests and a deep theoretical analysis.

Acknowledgments. GN gratefully acknowledge the Italian Universities Consortium Computing Center (CINECA) and University of Catania project "Young Researcher" for partial support.

References

1. Perelson, A. S., Weisbuch, G., Coutinho, A. Eds.: Theoretical and Experimental Insights into Immunology. New York, NY: Springer-Verlag (1992).
2. Burnet, F. M.: The Clonal Selection Theory of Acquired Immunity. Cambridge, U.K.: Cambridge Univ. Press (1959).
3. Forrest, S., Hofmeyr, S. A.: Immunology as Information Processing. Design Principles for Immune System & Other Distributed Autonomous Systems. New York: Oxford Univ. Press, SFI Studies in the Sciences of Complexity (2000).
4. Nicosia, G., Castiglione, F., Motta, S.: Pattern Recognition by primary and secondary response of an Artificial Immune System. Theory in Biosciences **120** (2001) 93–106.
5. Dasgupta, D. Ed.: Artificial Immune Systems and their Applications. Berlin, Germany: Springer-Verlag (1998).
6. Tan, K. C., Lee, T. H., Khor, E. F.: Evolutionary Algorithms with Dynamic Population Size and Local Exploration for Multiobjective Optimization. IEEE Transactions on Evolutionary Computation **5** (2001) 565–588.
7. Coello Coello, C. A.: An Updated Survey of GA-Based Multiobjective Optimization Techniques. ACM Computing Survey **32** (2000) 109–143.
8. Garey, M. R., Johnson, D. S.: Computers and Intractability: a Guide to the Theory of NP-completeness. New York: Freeman (1979).
9. Cutello, V., Mastriani, E., Pappalardo, F.: An Evolutionary Algorithm for the T-constrained variation of the Minimum Hitting Set Problem. Proc. of the IEEE World Congress on Computational Intelligence. Honolulu, HI (2002).
10. Mitchell, D., Selman, B., Levesque, H. J.: Hard and easy distributions of SAT problems. Proc. of the AAAI. San Jose, CA (1992) 459–465.
11. Eiben, A. E., van der Hauw J. K., van Hemert J. I.: Graph coloring with adaptive evolutionary algorithms. J. of Heuristics **4** (1998) 25–46.
12. Bäck, T., Eiben, A. E., Vink, M. E.: A superior evolutionary algorithm for 3-SAT. Proc. of the 7th Annual Conference on Evolutionary Programming. Lecture Notes in Computer Science **1477** (1998) 125–136.

13. De Castro, L. N., Von Zuben, F. J.: The Clonal Selection Algorithm with Engineering Applications. Workshop Proc. of the Genetic and Evolutionary Computation Conference (GECCO'00). Las Vegas, NV: Morgan Kaufmann (2000) 36–37.
14. Forrest, S., Perelson, A., Allen, L., Cherukuri, R.: Self-Nonself discrimination in a computer. Proc. of the IEEE Symposium on Research in Security and Privacy. Oakland, CA: IEEE Press (1994) 202–212.
15. Rogers, A., Prügel-Bennett, A.: Genetic Drift in Genetic Algorithm Selection Schemes. IEEE Transactions on Evolutionary Computation **3** (1999) 298–303.
16. Brooks, R.: The relationship between matter and life. Nature **409** (2001) 409–411.

A Genetic Algorithm for Solving a Production and Delivery Scheduling Problem with Time Windows*

Jose Manuel Garcia, Sebastian Lozano, Fernando Guerrero, and Ignacio Eguia

Escuela Superior de Ingenieros, Camino de los Descubrimientos, s/n, 41092 Seville, Spain;
jmgs@esi.us.es

Abstract. This paper deals with the problem of selecting and scheduling a set of orders to be processed by a manufacturing plant and immediately delivered to the customer site. Constraints to be considered are the limited production capacity, the available number of vehicles and the time windows within which orders must be served. We describe the problem relating it to similar problems studied in the literature. A genetic algorithm to solve the problem is developed and tested empirically with randomly generated problems. Comparisons with an exact procedure and a tabu search procedure show that the method finds very good-quality solutions.

1 Introduction

This paper addresses the problem of scheduling a given set of orders by a homogeneous vehicle fleet and under the assumption that orders require be manufactured immediately before be delivered to the customer site. Hence, each order requires manufacturing material in a production plant and delivering it to a predetermined location during a time window.

This problem arises frequently in environments where the distribution stage is connected to the production stage because of the absence of end product inventory. These environments usually involve products with perishable character. For instance, we could mention the ready-mix concrete manufacturing. In this process, materials that compose concrete mix are directly loaded and mixed-up in the drum mounted on the vehicle, and this one is immediately delivers to the customer site since there does not exist an excessive margin of time available before solidification concrete.

We assume that all requests are known in advance. For the manufacturing of orders we have a single plant with limited production capacity. We consider production capacity as the number of orders can be prepared simultaneously, i.e. the production order is considered as a continuous process that requires one unit of capacity during its processing time.

* This research has been financed by the Spanish Ministry of Science and Technology under contract no. DPI2000-0567.

F.J. Garijo, J.C. Riquelme, and M. Toro (Eds.): IBERAMIA 2002, LNAI 2527, pp. 371–380, 2002.

In the distribution stage of an order three consecutive phases are considered: order delivery, order unload and vehicle return trip. Each vehicle may deliver any order, but no more than one order at a time. It is also assumed that the order size is smaller than the vehicle capacity. Hence, the distribution stage of an order can be considered as a single process, which is performed without interruption, and that commences immediately after the end of the production stage. Moreover, as all of the processing times (production and distribution times) are known with certainty, each time window $[a'_i, b'_i]$ can be translated to a starting time window $[a_i, b_i]$(Fig. 1).

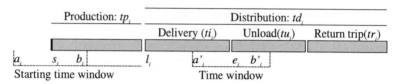

Fig. 1. Order activity

In order to consider the relevance of the perishable character of this kind of product, an ideal due date e_i is assumed within the time window $[a'_i, b'_i]$. We also can translate each ideal due date to a ideal start time s_i within the starting time window $[a_i, b_i]$. In Fig.1 are represented all order data. Thus, tp_i denotes production time and td_i distribution time (as sum of delivery time ti_i, unload time tu_i and return trip time tr_i).

As in the problem we have performed a situation in which the plant have a limited production capacity C and there exist a finite number of vehicles V, it may happen that it is not feasible to satisfy all requests within their time windows. Hence, we will consider as objective function to maximize the value of orders that are selected to be served, assuming that when an order is not served at its ideal due date, a decrease of the order original value, proportional to the deviation, is due. Let W_i be the profit associated with serving order i at instant e_i and let w_i^- and w_i^+ be earliness and tardiness penalties which are used to decrease the profit or value when order i is served prior to or after s_i, respectively. Thus, when an order is served at instant s_i+r, the profit of order i becomes $W_i - (r-s_i)w_i^+$.

Table 1 shows an example problem. Orders are all represented in Fig. 2, shading those that have been selected in the optimal solution, considering production capacity $C=1$ and number of vehicles $V=2$.

Table 1. Example problem.

	tp_i	td_i	s_i	a_i	b_i	W_i	w_i^-	w_i^+
Order 1	2	6	3	2	3	12	1	1
Order 2	2	11	4	3	4	20	1	1
Order 3	2	6	4	3	5	10	1	1
Order 4	3	6	13	12	14	13	2	1
Order 5	1	5	16	15	17	10	1	1

Optimal solution was found by means of processing of order 1, 3, 4 and 5. Order 3 had to be delayed one time period on its ideal start time. The maximal profit obtained was 44.

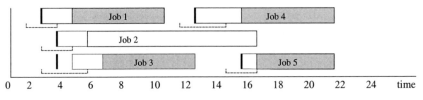

Fig. 2. Order activity

The paper is organized as follows. In section 2 a review of related scheduling problems is presented. Section 3 proposes a genetic algorithm for solving the problem. Computational results are showed in Section 4. Finally, the conclusions of the study are drawn.

2   Literature Review

In terms of job scheduling theory, a production and delivery scheduling problem with time windows (PDSPTW) can be seen as a two-station flow shop with parallel machines, no wait in process and a different due date for each job. The first station would be the production plant, which is composed of a number of identical machines equal to the plant capacity. The second station is composed of a number of identical machines equal to the number of vehicles. Each job would correspond with the production and distribution of each order.

The flow shop with multiple processors (FSMP), also called flexible flow lines scheduling, involves sequencing of a set of jobs in a set of processing stations. All jobs must be processed on each station in the same order. At each station, a job can be processed on any machine. A no-wait scheduling problem occurs in industrial environments in which a product must be processed from start to finish, without any interruption between the stages that compose its performance. FSMP with no-wait in process has been studied by several authors (see [1] and [2]). Both in FSMP and FSMP with no-wait in process, researchers consider objectives of satisfying measures of performance that involve the processing of all jobs. It is assumed that any job can be processed at any time, that is, jobs have an infinite starting time window. In most of the cases, the objective is to minimize the makespan. When due dates and weights for jobs are considered, objectives are to minimize the weighted tardiness or similar measures of performance. As a different case, in [3] is studied a problem with two stages and no-wait in process whose objective is to maximize the set of jobs to be processed. Nevertheless, due dates are not considered for the jobs but a finite scheduling time.

Instead, in this paper we present a scheduling problem where the objective is to find a subset of jobs with maximum total value that can be completed within their time windows. What makes the problem different from other scheduling problems is that the orders served must satisfy time requirements imposed by customers. Scheduling problems that focus on the problem of finding a subset of jobs with maximum total value assuming due dates are the fixed job scheduling problem (FSP) [4] and the variable job scheduling problem (VSP) [5] and [6]. However, these problems consider a single stage for the processing of jobs, so these cases would correspond to a particular case of PDSPTW where the production capacity was unlimited or we had a number unlimited of vehicles.

3   GA for Solving PDSPTW

Genetic algorithms [7] are search and optimisation algorithms based on the Darwinian theory of evolution. Essentially, a GA is an iterative procedure that maintains a population of a few individuals that represent problem solutions. An initial population is generated at random or heuristically. During each iteration, the individuals are evaluated and given a fitness value. From each iteration to the next, a new population, with the same size, is generated by evolutionary operations such as selection, crossover and mutation. In the following, we will describe the representation and operations employed in our GA.

3.1   Individual Representation: Genotype and Phenotype

An important concept is the strict separation of problem constraints and evolutionary method. Such separation results in two completely different views of an individual. On the one hand, there exist the phenotype representation for the problem in order to evaluate the individual by fitness function. On the other hand, the genotypic representation is what the genetic algorithms works upon, that is, the encoded representation over which the evolutionary operators are applied.

A string will be used to represent the genotype of an individual. The length of the string corresponds with the number of jobs. Each string position, also denoted as gene, corresponds to one job, and contains the time period in which the job should start. This time period is defined with respect to ideal start due date of the job. Figure 3 shows the genotype representation of an individual for a problem with 5 jobs. For that individual, job 2 should start at instant s_i-1, job 3 at instant s_i+1 and the rest of jobs on their ideal start times.

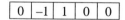

Fig. 3. Genotype representation

Let r_i the start value of order i in a individual. The profit w_i of each order can be calculated as follow: $w_i = \{W_i + r_i w_i^-$ if $r_i < 0$ or $W_i - r_i w_i^+$ if $r_i \geq 0\}$

We have not guarantee that all the orders can be served using those starting instants, therefore a subset of orders that maximize the total profit is to be searched. This situation represents a production and delivered scheduling problem with fixed starting times [8]. In that problem is also hard to find optimal solutions as the number of jobs increases, so we concentrate on a fast heuristic that yields satisfactory solutions. The heuristic exploits the observation that PDP can be modelled as a minimum cost flow problem if the production capacity is enough to process all the orders at he production stage. Hence, here constraints associated with not preparing simultaneously a number of orders greater that the production capacity are not considered.

The construction of the underlying direct graph G used to solve this PDP can be described as follow: Each job i is represented in G by two nodes, l_i and f_i that correspond to start time period and end time period of the distribution stage. There also is an arc associated with each job, from the node corresponding to l_j to the node corresponding to f_j. This arc has an upper capacity of one on the amount of flow that can be transported, and associated costs of $-w_i$. Furthermore, there is an arc from every node f_i to every node l_j as long as $l_j \le f_i$ with zero costs and capacity equals one. Moreover, and start node s is connected to all the nodes s_i and all nodes f_i are connected to an ending node e with zero cost and one unit of capacity.

If we inject V (i.e. the number of vehicles) units of flow in node s, the optimal solution to the minimum cost flow problem in G will obtain a schedule for a subset of orders of maximum total value. A order i is served if and only if in the solution to the minimum cost flow problem one unit of flow passes through the arc (l_i, f_i). Fig. 4 shows the graph G corresponding to genotype showed in Fig. 3 and referred to the problem represented in Table 1 for a number of vehicles $V=2$.

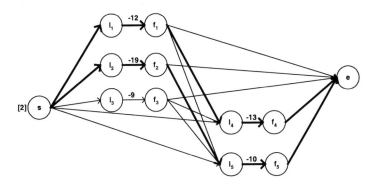

Fig. 4. Graph G corresponding to genotype of Fig 3.

The thick lines in G denote the minimum cost flow path. Orders to be served are 1, 2, 4 and 5.

Once a solution is obtained for G, production process feasibility of the orders selected is checked. For this task, we make use of Kroon's lemma on the Fixed Job Scheduling Problem (FSP) [4], to give a necessary and sufficient condition for the existence of a feasible schedule for all orders selected:

Let O_s be the set of orders selected. A feasible schedule including all orders belong to O_s exist if and only if the maximum order overlap of O_s in plant is less than or equal to the plant capacity C.

Suppose orders are to be processed in the time-interval $[0,T]$, the maximum order overlap is defined as follows: $L = \max \{L_t: 0 \le t \le T\}$ with $L_t = \{i \in O_s: s_i \le t \le l_i-1\}$

Fig. 5. Production stage for orders selected in graph G of Fig. 4

In Fig. 5 the bars indicate the production time (tp_i) of the orders selected previously. For this case L equals 2. It is clear that if and only if $C \ge 2$ can all orders be processed in the plant.

If the maximum order overlap of O_s exceeds C, then the solution provided for the minimum cost flow problem is not feasible. In this case, the heuristic will try to find a subset of orders with maximum total profit that can be processed with capacity C. This problem becomes equivalent to the Maximum Fixed Job Scheduling Problem (Max. FSP). This problem has been considered by a number of authors including Arkin and Silverberg [9], Kroon, Salomon and Van Wassenhove [4] and Gabrel [6], who show that it can be solved by a minimum cost flow algorithm.

The construction of the graph G' that we use in this paper is more direct than the constructions proposed for those authors, and can be described as follows. The set $R = \{r_p: p = 1, ..., P\}$ is used to represent all starting times of the jobs belong to O_k in chronological order. The set of nodes of the graph is in one-to-one correspondence with the set R plus a finish node. There is an arc from each node to the following with zero costs and unlimited capacity. Furthermore, there are arcs from each node to the node corresponding to the first order which could be produced by the plant once it has finished the production of the order origin of the arc. These arcs can carry only one unit of flow and have a cost equal to $-w_i$. At the leftmost node, C units of flow are injected which must reach the finish node. As an example, Fig. 6 shows the graph corresponding to the data of Fig. 5 for a production capacity of one.

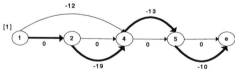

Fig. 6. Graph associated to the example of Fig. 5

Once the optimal solution to this minimum cost flow problem is obtained, let set E denote the set of orders belonging to O_s that have not been selected ($E=\{1\}$ for the example). For each order $j \in E$, we modify the graph G, constructed initially, in order to forbid that order j can be processed. To this end, we just need to assign capacity zero to the arc that joins l_j with f_j. With this new graph G, all the process described above is repeated again until a feasible solution is found.

3.2 Population Reproduction and Selection

Two techniques of population reproduction are currently used in the field of genetic algorithms: generational and steady-state. Briefly, generational reproduction replaces the entire population at each iteration, while steady-state reproduction replaces only a few members at a time.

In our algorithm we have used the steady-state technique, replacing one individual at each iteration. Therefore, at each iteration a new individual is generated using the operators described below. At each iteration an operator will be selected to generate an new individual. For this selection each operator will have a probability of being chosen.

To select the member to be deleted, we use an approach based on the exponential ranking [10] of the individuals within the population. Exponential ranking assigns a chance of being deleted equals to p to the worst individual (worst fitness). If it is not selected, then the next to the last also has a p chance, and so on.

3.3 Crossover and Mutation Operators

Crossover is the most important recombination operator for generating new individuals, i.e., new search points. It takes two individuals called parents and produces a new individual called the offspring or child by swapping parts of the parents. We have used the following procedure to get the child: There are two randomly selected parents p1 and p2. The child is built with next rule: Let p1(i) be gene i in p1. For each i from 1 to n, if p1(i) = p2(i) then child(i) = p1(i), else child(i) is a random value in the interval [p1(i), p2(i)].

In Fig. 7 we can see an example of crossover operator.

p1	2	-1	0	1	0
p2	1	-1	1	-1	0
Child	Rnd[1,2]	-1	Rnd[0,1]	Rnd[-1,1]	0

Fig. 7. Crossover operator

We also employ a standard mutation operator that randomly selects an individual to modify and then randomly choose a new value for one of its positions. This operator helps the GA to maintain diversity in the population to avoid premature convergence.

4 Computational Results

The first stage in our computational experience involved the construction of a set of problems. Afterwards, we will compare GA results with previous results obtained using both an exact method and a tabu search approach.

4.1 Generation of Problems

To construct a set of instance we used as main parameters the average order overlap (number of orders that may be processed simultaneously) in the production stage (PSO) and distribution stage (DSO). Thus, values considered for PSO and DSO were within the intervals (1.50, 1.60) and (5,6) respectively.

Problem sizes used were $n = 20$, 25, 30 and 40 orders. Ten instances were generated for each problem size. Time windows $[a_i, b_i]$ for every problem were generated randomly with sizes between 1 and 5 time periods. The time horizon of the problems has been considered dependent on the number of orders in the problem according to the following intervals: [1,55] (20 orders); [1,65] (25 orders) ; [1,75] (30 orders); [1,95] (40 orders). Order values w_i were randomly generated randomly within the interval [10,100] and penalties both for earliness w_i^- and tardiness w_i^+ were randomly selected within the interval [0,2]. To allow for different levels with regard to capacity C and number of vehicles V, the pairs of values $(C,V) = (1,2)$, $(2,2)$ and $(2,3)$ were considered for each problem.

4.2 Exact Method and Tabu Search Approach

To test the performance of the algorithm, we initially solved the same set of problems using a graph-based exact procedure and a tabu search approach [11]. The exact procedure builds a graph G that collects all feasible solutions to the problem by means of a simple evaluation method of feasible states in the scheduling of orders. The maximal weighted path from start node to end node in G is the optimal solution to the problem.

The tabu search approach is based on exchange moves. A neighbour of a solution is obtained by replacing a order selected by another order/orders that is/are not selected in that solution. Moreover, remove moves are also allowed. Each problem was running five times and the number of iterations was 5000.

4.3 GA Parameters

We used the following GA parameters:
   Initial population obtained randomly.
   Population size: 20
   Probability of mutation: 0.4
   Probability p in the exponential ranking: 0.2
   Number of iterations: 1000

4.4 Summary of Results

Tables 2 and 3 shows the summary of results using the three approaches. The percentage errors have been computed with respect to the optimal solution values (obtained through the graph-based procedure). We have taken averages over the 10 instances in each problem size n. All running times are given in CPU seconds on an Intel Pentium III 850 MHz.

Table 2. Results

n	(C,V)	TS Approach		GA Procedure	
		Avge. Error (%)	N. optimal solutions found	Avge. Error (%)	N. Optimal solutions found
20	(1,2)	0.00	10	0.28	9
20	(2,2)	1.28	6	0.00	10
20	(2,3)	0.06	9	0.03	8
25	(1,2)	0.90	9	0.32	7
25	(2,2)	1.20	8	0.23	8
25	(2,3)	0.24	9	0.02	9
30	(1,2)	0.24	8	0.41	7
30	(2,2)	0.81	7	0.37	7
30	(2,3)	0.30	7	0.13	8
40	(1,2)	0.37	7	0.22	2
40	(2,2)	0.30	6	0.31	3
40	(2,3)	0.50	1	0.24	3

Table 3. Computation times

N	(C,V)	Average Computation Time in CPU seconds		
		TS	GA	Exact Method
20	(1,2)	7	97	73
20	(2,2)	9	99	15
20	(2,3)	11	100	1496
25	(1,2)	9	128	278
25	(2,2)	10	132	47
25	(2,3)	13	137	1957
30	(1,2)	11	196	194
30	(2,2)	14	205	118
30	(2,3)	16	210	6898
40	(1,2)	14	304	97
40	(2,2)	17	310	163
40	(2,3)	27	319	13314

TS found optimal solutions in 87 of the 120 test problems. GA found optimal solutions in 81 instances. However, the total average error was equals 0.05% for TS and 0.02% for GA.

With regard to the average of computation times, the exact method took longer time than TS and GA, showing TS the best times.

5   Conclusions

In this paper, we have studied a type of no-wait production and delivery scheduling problem with time windows. A Genetic Algorithms procedure for solving this problem has been proposed. The quality of this solution has been empirically compared with the optimal solution produced by a graph-based exact solution method and a tabu search approach. Computational results indicate that the GA finds solutions of very good quality.

References

1. Hall N.G. and Sriskandarajah C.: A survey of machine scheduling problems with blocking and no-wait in process. Operations Research, 44, (1996) 510–525.
2. Sriskandarajah C.: Performance of scheduling algorithms for no-wait flowshops with parallel machines. European Journal of Operations Research, 70, (1993) 365–378.
3. Ramudhin A. and Ratliff H.D.: Generating daily production schedules in process industries. IIE Transactions, 27, (1995) 646–656.
4. Kroon L.G., Salomon M. and Van Wassenhove L. N.: Exact and approximation algorithms for the operational fixed interval scheduling problem. European Journal of Operational Research, 82, (1995) 190–205.
5. Gertsbakh I. and Stern H.: Minimal Resources for Fixed and Variable Job Schedules. Operations Research, 26 (1), (1978) 68–85.
6. Gabrel V.: Scheduling jobs within time windows on identical parallel machines: New model and algorithms. European Journal of Operations Research, 83, (1995) 320–329.
7. Goldberg, D. E.: Genetic Algorithms in Search, Optimization, and Machine Learning. (1989). New York, NY: Addison-Wesley.
8. Garcia J. M., Smith K., Lozano S. and Guerrero F.: A Comparison of GRASP and an Exact Method for Solving a Production and Delivery Scheduling Problem. Proceedings of the International workshop on Hybrid Intelligent Systems HIS'2001, Adelaide, Australia. (2001).
9. Arking E.M., Silverberg E.B.: Scheduling jobs with fixed start and end times. Discrete Applied Mathematics 18, (1987) 1–8.
10. Kaufmann, M.: Fundations of Genetic Algorithms. Edited by Gregory J.E. Rawlins, San Mateo California, (1991).
11. Garcia J. M., Smith K., Lozano S., Guerrero F. and Calle M.: Production and Delivery Scheduling Problem with Time Windows. Proceedings of The 30-th International Conference on Computers and Industrial Engineering, Tynos Island, Greece (2002) 263–268.

A Prediction System for Cardiovascularity Diseases Using Genetic Fuzzy Rule-Based Systems*

O. Cordón[1], F. Herrera[1], J. de la Montaña[2], A.M. Sánchez[3], and P. Villar[3]

[1] Dept. of Computer Science and A. I., Univ. of Granada, 18071 – Granada, Spain,
ocordon,herrera@decsai.ugr.es
[2] Lab. of Nutrition and Food Science, University of Vigo, 32004 – Ourense, Spain,
jmontana@uvigo.es
[3] Dept. of Computer Science, University of Vigo, 32004 – Ourense, Spain,
amlopez,pvillar@uvigo.es

Abstract. In this paper we present a fuzzy rule-based system to predict cardiovascularity diseases. The input variables of the system are the most influent factors for that type of diseases and the output is a risk prediction of suffering from them. Our objective is to get an accurate prediction value and a system description with a high degree of interpretability. We use a set of examples and a design process based on genetic algorithms to obtain the components of the fuzzy rule-based system.

1 Introduction

Cardiovascularity diseases are the main cause of mortality in "western countries". Their prediction is a very complex problem because they are influenced by many factors. The most important of these are diet, age, genetic predisposition, smoking, sedentary life, etc. The development of a cardiovascularity disease takes long time before the first symptoms appear and many times it is too late for the patient. So, it is important to take an adequate preventive action to identify and modify the risk factors associated.

In this contribution, we use a fuzzy rule-based system (FRBS) as a means to determine a prediction to suffer from a cardiovascularity disease. As it is difficult for an expert to design the FRBS due to its complexity, we derive it from a learning process using numerical information. In this paper, we have used a genetic algorithm as learning mechanism, so dealing with a genetic fuzzy rule-based system [6]. Moreover, an important objective of this work is to obtain models that can be interpretable. That is the aim for using FRBS.

This paper is organized as follows. Sections 2 and 3 show some preliminaries about cardiovascularity diseases and FRBSs, respectively. Section 4 presents the problem description. The learning method used to obtain the FRBS is briefly described in Section 5. Section 6 presents some experimental results as well as the

---

* This research has been supported by CICYT PB98-1319

F.J. Garijo, J.C. Riquelme, and M. Toro (Eds.): IBERAMIA 2002, LNAI 2527, pp. 381–391, 2002.
© Springer-Verlag Berlin Heidelberg 2002

complete description of a simple FRBS for cardiovascularity disease prediction. Finally, in Section 7, some conclusions are pointed out.

2   Cardiovascularity Diseases

The main factors that influence the appearance of a cardiovascularity disease [8, 9] are shown next:

- **Diet.** From the fifties, epidemiological studies have proven the existence of a direct relationship between the amount and type of fatty consumed and the serum levels of *cholesterol* and *triglycerides*, that are considered as the most important factors in the development of cardiovascularity diseases.

  The cholesterol total amount is the sum of the cholesterol amount associated to the three types of *lipoproteins* more abundant in the blood: very low density lipoproteins (VLDL), low density ones (LDL) and high density ones (HDL). It is useful to distinguish between the cholesterol associated to the LDL (*LDL-cholesterol*) and to the HDL (*HDL-cholesterol*). The LDL-cholesterol is a clear risk factor to suffer from a cardiovascularity disease. On the other hand, the HDL-cholesterol is good to prevent it due its antiatherogenic quality.

  Diet plays a very important role in the serum levels of any type of cholesterol. The main aspect is the amount of fatty in the diet and the type of fatty acids present in the blood. There are three main types of fatty acids:

  - Saturated Fatty Acids (SFA), that increase the cholesterol levels found in the blood, specially the LDL-cholesterol.
  - Monounsaturated Fatty Acids (MUFA), that are conferred a neutral or slightly beneficial effect over the cholesterol levels.
  - Polyunsaturated Fatty Acids (PUFAS), that origin a reduction of the cholesterol concentration, specially of the LDL-cholesterol.

- **Hypertension.** High values of the diastolic blood pressure predispose to a heart attack and other cardiovascularity diseases.
- **Smoking**. The tobacco consum (specially cigarettes) constitutes and important risk factor for the development of cardiovascularity diseases.
- **Obesity.** The obesity is a negative factor for the health. Some studies connect the weight increase with a progressive increment of the serum levels of cholesterol and triglycerides. The degrees of obesity are classified trough the Body Mass Ratio (BMR) that is defined as the division of the weight of an individual (in Kgs.) by its square height (in metres).
- **Sedentary.** A slight physycal activity produces possitive effects over the cardiovascularity system. On the other hand, a sedentary life increases the obesity and the amount of LDL-cholesterol.
- **Age.** Unlike the previous factors, age can not be modified, but it is very important as it can directly affect to them.

3   Fuzzy Rule-Based Systems

FRBSs [13] constitute an extension of classical rule-based systems, as they deal with fuzzy rules instead of classical logic rules. In this approach, fuzzy IF-THEN rules are formulated and a process of fuzzification, inference and defuzzification leads to the final decision of the system (see Fig. 1). The FRBS is then considered as an approach used to model a system making use of a descriptive language based on Fuzzy Logic with fuzzy predicates. The fuzzy rules used –also called linguistic rules– have the following structure [10]:

$$\text{IF } X_1 \text{ is } A_1 \text{ and ... and } X_n \text{ is } A_n \text{ THEN } Y \text{ is } B_i$$

with $X_1, \ldots, X_n$ and Y being the input and output linguistic variables, respectively, and $A_1, \ldots, A_n$ and B being linguistic labels, each one of them having associated a fuzzy set defining its meaning.

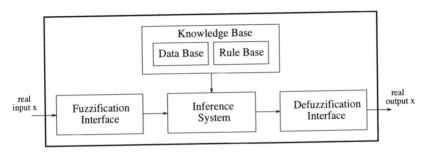

Fig. 1. Generic structure of a descriptive Fuzzy Rule-Based System

The main characteristic of this type of fuzzy systems is the interpretability of the resulting model. The knowledge base of the FRBS is composed of a collection of rules together with a description of the semantics of the linguistic terms contained in these rules. Of course, if the number of rules is excessively high, the global interpretability of the model decreases, although it is possible to perform a local intepretation for the output of a given input data pair analysing only the rules fired for that input data pair.

Although sometimes the fuzzy rules can be directly derived from expert knowledge, different efforts have been made to obtain an improvement on the system performance by incorporating learning mechanisms guided by numerical information to define them, the Rule Base (RB), and/or the membership functions, the Data Base (DB), associated to them. Most of them have focused on the RB learning, using a predefined DB [3,12]. This operation mode makes the DB have a significant influence on the FRBS performance [1,4].

The usual solution to improve the FRBS performance by dealing with the DB components involves a tuning process of the preliminary DB definition once the RB has been derived [1], maintaining the latter unchanged. In opposite to this *a posteriori* DB learning, there are some approaches that learn the different DB components *a priori* [4,5], thus allowing it to both adjust the membership functions and learn the optimal number of linguistic terms for each variable. This will be the approach followed in this paper to design the FRBS.

4   Building Our Prediction System

The first step to design a prediction system for cardiovascularity diseases is to decide which variables will be considered. If all the risk factors were taken into account, a very large set of example data pairs would be needed and it would be difficult to get an FRBS with good performance and a high degree of interpretability, i.e. with a low number of rules and a low number of labels per variable.

For that reason, we only consider the most influent risk factors: the different cholesterol levels, the triglycerides level and the age. The remaining factors are individual habits that the experts only consider for a small increment o decrement of the risk prediction associated to the main risk factors. The most important of these "secondary" factors have been aggregated into a single variable called *habits*. Therefore, our system will have six input variables and one output variable that are described as follows:

- *Cholesterol*: Total cholesterol level present in the blood (in *mg/dl*). Range: $[100 - 350]$
- *LDL-cholesterol*: Serum LDL-cholesterol level (in *mg/dl*). Range: $[100 - 210]$
- *HDL-cholesterol*: Serum HDL-cholesterol level (in *mg/dl*). Range: $[10 - 200]$
- *Triglycerides*: Triglycerides level present in the blood (in *mg./dl*). Range: $[140 - 160]$
- *Age*: Age of the individual (in years). Range: $[20, 80]$
- *Habits*: This variable takes values in $\{1, \ldots, 48\}$. The higher the value, the worse the habits (from the point of view of the disease prevention). A value in the range $\{1 - 12\}$ indicates beneficial factors that reduce the risk of suffering a cardiovascular disease. Values in $\{13 - 24\}$ represent habits that can be considered "neutral" over the risk prediction. The range $\{25 - 37\}$ indicates slightly damaging habits. Finally, values in $\{38 - 48\}$ indicate a dangerous increment of the risk of suffering a cardiovascular disease. The selected habits are shown next:
  - High consum of PUFAS (greater than 33 *gr/day*)
  - High consum of SFA (greater than 33 *gr/day*)
  - Body Mass Ratio (BMR), defined by the relation between the weight of an individual (in kgs.) and the square of its height (in meters). Two ranges are considered: $20 < BMR < 30$ and $BMR > 30$
  - Habitual smoker (more than 10 cigarettes per day)
  - Cholesterol consumed per day (*cholest./day*) in miligrams. Three ranges are considered: *cholest./day* $< 200mgs$, $200mgs <$ *cholest./day* $< 300mgs$ and *cholest./day* $> 300mgs$

- Physical activity. It implies to make daily exercises, even if they are slight.

Table 1 shows the correspondency between each value of this variable and the concrete habits of the individual.
- *Risk prediction*: The output variable is a numeric real value ($[0 - 10]$) that indicates an estimation of the risk to suffer from a cardiovascularity disease. The higher the value, the higher the risk.

Our method uses numerical information for the learning process. Unfortunately, it is very difficult to obtain data from real patients. It would imply frequent studies of the biochemical parameters of many healthy people (from the cardiovascular diseases point of view) with different serum levels, age and habits, and to wait (sometimes many years) for a possible development of a cardiovascular disease. So, the examples have been generated *ad hoc* by an expert trying to produce an uniformly distributed set covering a great range of possible situations. The obtained set is composed of 2594 data pairs and it has been randomly divided into two subsets, a training data set with 2335 elements (90%) and a test data one with 259 elements (10%).

5   Learning Process to Derive the FRBS

We use the genetic fuzzy rule-based system proposed in [5] to learn the KB of the FRBS associated to our prediction system for the risk to suffer a cardiovascularity disease. We will refer that process as **GFS** (Genetic Fuzzy System). **GFS** is composed of two methods with different goals:

- A Genetic Algorithm (GA) [11] to learn the DB that allows us to define:
  - The number of labels for each linguistic variable (granularity).
  - The variable domain (working range), allowing a brief enlargement of the initial domain.
  - The form of each fuzzy membership function (triangular-shaped) in non-uniform fuzzy partitions using a non-linear scaling function.
- A quick *ad hoc data-driven method* [3] that derives the RB considering the DB previously obtained. It is run from each DB definition generated by the GA. In this paper we use the inductive method proposed in [12].

There are three steps that must be done to evaluate each chromosome:

1. Generate the fuzzy partitions (DB) for all the linguistic variables using the information contained in the chromosome.
2. Generate the RB by running the fuzzy rule learning method considering the DB obtained.
3. Calculate the fitness function. First the Mean Square Error (MSE) over the training set is calculated from the KB obtained (genetically derived DB + RB). This value will be used as a base of the chromosome fitness value:

$$MSE = \frac{1}{2|E|} \sum_{e_l \in E} (ey^l - S(ex^l))^2$$

Table 1. Variable *habits*: correspondency of the 48 values with the habits considered

Value	high consum PUFAS	high consum SFA	BMR between 20-30	BMR greater 30	Smoker	< 200 mgs. choles./day	200 − 300 mgs. choles./day	> 300 mgs. choles./day	Phisi- cally activ
1	x		x			x			x
2	x		x		x	x			x
3	x		x			x			
4	x		x		x	x			
5	x		x				x		x
6	x		x		x		x		x
7	x		x				x		
8	x		x		x		x		
9	x		x					x	x
10	x		x		x			x	x
11	x		x					x	
12	x		x		x			x	
13	x			x		x			x
14	x			x	x	x			x
15	x			x		x			
16	x			x			x		
17	x			x			x		x
18	x			x	x		x		x
19	x			x	x		x		
20	x			x	x	x			
21	x			x				x	x
22	x			x				x	x
23	x			x				x	
24	x			x	x			x	
25		x	x			x			x
26		x	x		x	x			x
27		x	x			x			
28		x	x		x	x			
29		x	x				x		x
30		x	x		x		x		x
31		x	x				x		
32		x	x		x		x		
33		x	x					x	x
34		x	x		x			x	x
35		x	x					x	
36		x	x		x			x	
37		x		x		x			x
38		x		x	x	x			x
39		x		x		x			
40		x		x	x	x			
41		x		x			x		x
42		x		x	x		x		x
43		x		x			x		
44		x		x	x		x		
45		x		x				x	x
46		x		x	x			x	x
47		x		x				x	
48		x		x	x			x	

with E being the example set, $S(ex^l)$ being the output value obtained from the FRBS when the input variable values are $ex^l = (ex_1^l, \ldots, ex_n^l)$, and ey^l being the known desired output value.

In order to improve the generalization capability and the interpretability of the final FRBS, we will lightly penalize FRBSs with a high number of rules to obtain more compact linguistic models. Therefore, once the RB has been generated and its MSE over the training set (MSE_{tra}) has been calculated, the fitness function is calculated in the following way [7]:

$$F_C = \omega_1 \cdot MSE_{tra} + \omega_2 \cdot N\_Rules$$

with N_Rules being the number of rules and ω_1, ω_2 two weighting factors.

6   Experimental Results

We have run the **GFS** process with different initial seeds, using various ranges for the granularity values across the interval $\{2, 9\}$. **GFS** allows us to obtain FRBSs with a different trade-off between accuracy and interpretability reducing the maximum value for the granularity and changing the values of the fitness function weigths (parameters ω_1 and ω_2). The genetic parameters considered are the following: number of generations=1000, population size=100, crossover probability=0.6, mutation probability=0.1. We have also considered other types of learning methods in order to compare with the results obtained by **GFS**. We run the following methods:

- Linear Regression.
- Neural Networks (NN): A three layer perceptron, using conjugate gradient plus weight decay as learning rule. Different values for the number of units in the hidden levels were considered. The table of results shows results of two NN, the one with the best MSE_{tra} and the one with the best MSE_{tst}
- A representative process of the usual way to derive an FRBS: The Wang and Mendel's rule generation method plus a DB tuning process (WM + Tuning). As usual, all the variables have the same granularity. We run the WM method for all the possible numbers of labels considered ($\{2, \ldots, 9\}$) and the best results considering the MSE_{tra} was obtained with nine labels while the best result over the MSE_{tst} was obtained with four labels. We have used the genetic tuning process proposed in [2] to refine the preliminary DB of both FRBSs once the RB has been derived.

Linear regression obtains models that can not be considered totally interpretables, while the Neural Networks are not interpretables. Both are shown in order to compare the accuracy of the method proposed for modelling the prediction system (**GFS**). The best results obtained are presented in Table 2, which contains the following columns:

- **Method**: Process used to model the prediction system
- **Granularity**: Number of labels per variable (for FRBS learning methods)
- **N_Rules**: Number of rules of the FRBS RB (for FRBS learning methods)
- **MSE$_{tra}$**: MSE over the training data set
- **MSE$_{tst}$**: MSE over the test data set

Table 2. Best results obtained

Method	Granularity	N_Rules	MSE_{tra}	MSE_{tst}
Linear Regression	- - - - - - -	-	0.0741	0.0683
NN 6-20-1	- - - - - - -	-	0,0445	0,0691
NN 6-5-1	- - - - - - -	-	0.0639	0.0645
WM + Tuning	9 9 9 9 9 9 9	2222	0.0785	2,8523
	4 4 4 4 4 4 4	913	0.1347	0.1589
GFS	9 5 6 4 5 3 9	319	0.0451	0.0474
	9 8 7 5 4 4 9	133	0.0611	0.0606
	7 2 3 2 3 4 6	43	0.0883	0.0892
	5 4 3 3 2 2 5	31	0.1042	0.0996
	5 3 3 3 3 3 5	23	0.1274	0.1171

As can be observed, many learning methods obtain good results as regards the prediction ability of the resulting model. The best result in MSE_{tra} has been obtained using a multilayer perceptron with 20 units in the hidden level, although there is only a small difference respect to the best result obtained with **GFS**. The best result in MSE_{tst} has been obtained using the **GFS** process considering the interval $\{3, \dots, 9\}$ as possible granularity values. So, the prediction ability of the models obtained by **GFS** are enoughly demonstrated. Regarding to the usual process to derive a FRBS (WM + Tuning), the choice of a high number of labels produces good results in MSE_{tra} but clearly leads to an overfitting as can be observed in the great value obtained for MSE_{tst}.

The table collects different FRBSs obtained from the **GFS** process, some of them with good results in the MSE columns and others with low values in the granularity and number of rules. Of course, the latter present greater degrees of interpretabilñity than the former. As said, it is possible to obtain FRBSs with good accuracy or great interpretability by changing the range of the granularity levels and the weigthing factors in the fitness function of the GA. The most accurate FRBSs present more rules and a higher granularity level than the most interpretable FRBSs displayed.

In order to show an example of the composition of an FRBS for the problem, the most simple FRBS of Table 2 (FRBS with 21 rules) are described. A typical consequence when a learning method is forced to obtain FRBS with a few rules is the inplicit elimination of the input variables with lesser relevance, that is, if one variable has the same label in all the rules, it has not influence in the prediction ability. So, we will ignore two variables in the description of this FRBS (*LDL-Cholesterol* and *Tryglicerides*). Figure 2 shows the DB (fuzzy partitions for all the relevant variables in this specific FRBS including the new domain limits learned by **GFS**). In order to improve the readability of the RB, if two rules only differ in one input label (the reamining input variables and the output variable have the same linguistic term), they are depicted as a single rule including the two different labels connected with the operator OR. Therefore, the RB is composed of the following rules:

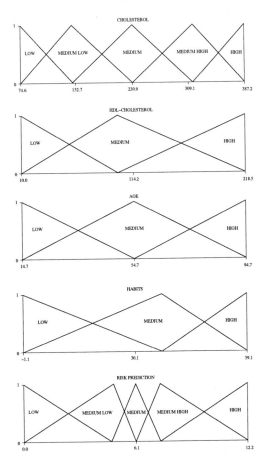

Fig. 2. Fuzzy partitions

R_1_2: IF Cholesterol is *HIGH* and HDL-cholesterol is *HIGH* and Age is *MEDIUM*
and Habits is (*LOW* or *MEDIUM*) THEN Risk is *MEDIUM*

R_3_4: IF Cholesterol is *HIGH* and HDL-cholesterol is *HIGH* and Age is *HIGH*
and Habits is (*LOW* or *MEDIUM*) THEN Risk is *MEDIUM*

R_5_6: IF Cholesterol is *HIGH* and HDL-cholesterol is *MEDIUM* and Age is *MEDIUM*
and Habits is (*LOW* or *MEDIUM*) THEN Risk is *MEDIUM HIGH*

R_7_8: IF Cholesterol is *HIGH* and HDL-cholesterol is *MEDIUM* and Age is *HIGH*
and Habits is (*LOW* or *MEDIUM*) THEN Risk is *MEDIUM HIGH*

R_9: IF Cholesterol is *HIGH* and HDL-cholesterol is *HIGH* and Age is *LOW*
and Habits is *MEDIUM* THEN Risk is *MEDIUM*

R_10_11: IF Cholesterol is *MEDIUM HIGH* and HDL-cholesterol is *HIGH* and Age is *MEDIUM*
and Habits is (*LOW* or *MEDIUM*) THEN Risk is *MEDIUM LOW*

R_12_13: IF Cholesterol is *MEDIUM HIGH* and HDL-cholesterol is *MEDIUM* and Age is *HIGH*
and Habits is (*LOW* or *MEDIUM*) THEN Risk is *MEDIUM*

R_14_15: IF Cholesterol is *MEDIUM HIGH* and HDL-cholesterol is *MEDIUM* and Age is
MEDIUM and Habits is (*LOW* or *MEDIUM*) THEN Risk is *MEDIUM*

R_16: IF Cholesterol is *MEDIUM HIGH* and HDL-cholesterol is *HIGH* and Age is *HIGH* and Habits is *MEDIUM* THEN Risk is *MEDIUM*

R_17: IF Cholesterol is *MEDIUM HIGH* and HDL-cholesterol is *HIGH* and Age is *HIGH* and Habits is *LOW* THEN Risk is *MEDIUM LOW*

R_18_19: IF Cholesterol is *MEDIUM* and HDL-cholesterol is *MEDIUM* and Age is *MEDIUM* and Habits is (*LOW* or *MEDIUM*) THEN Risk is *MEDIUM LOW*

R_20_21: IF Cholesterol is *MEDIUM* and HDL-cholesterol is *MEDIUM* and Age is *HIGH* and Habits is (*LOW* or *MEDIUM*) THEN Risk is *MEDIUM LOW*

R_22_23: IF Cholesterol is *MEDIUM LOW* and HDL-cholesterol is *MEDIUM* and Age is (*MEDIUM* or *HIGH*) and Habits is *LOW* THEN Risk is *MEDIUM LOW*

7   Concluding Remarks

We have proposed an FRBS to predict the risk of suffering from a cardiovascular disease. The learning process uses a GA for deriving the DB and a simple RB generation method to learn the rules. The FRBS learning process allows us to choose the main characteristic desired for the prediction model: good accuracy or good interpretability. As future works, we will try to design an FRBS to predict the risk taking all the human habits as a base. This new approach could be more interesting for the nutrition specialist in order to advise the patients.

References

1. Bonissone, P.P., Khedkar, P.S., Chen, Y.T.: Genetic algorithms for automated tuning of fuzzy controllers, a transportation aplication, Proc. Fifth IEEE International Conference on Fuzzy Systems (FUZZ-IEEE'96) (New Orleans, 1996) 674–680.
2. Cordón, O., Herrera, F.: A three-stage evolutionary process for learning descriptive and approximative fuzzy logic controller knowledge bases from examples, International Journal of Approximate Reasoning 17(4) (1997) 369-407.
3. Casillas, J., Cordón, O., Herrera, F.: COR: A methodology to improve ad hoc data-driven linguistic rule learning methods by inducing cooperation among rules, IEEE Tr. on Systems, Man, and Cybernetics-Part B: Cybernetics (2002). To appear.
4. Cordón, O., Herrera, F., Villar, P.: Analysis and guidelines to obtain a good uniform fuzzy partition granularity for fuzzy rule-based systems using simulated annealing, International Journal of Approximate Reasoning 25(3) (2000) 187–216.
5. Cordón, O., Herrera, F., Magdalena, L., Villar, P.: A genetic learning process for the scaling factors, granularity and contexts of the fuzzy rule-based system data base, Information Science 136 (2001) 85–107.
6. Cordón, O, Herrera, F., Hoffmann, F., Magdalena, L.: Genetic fuzzy systems. Evolutionary Tuning and Learning of Fuzzy Knowledge Bases, (World Scientific, 2001).
7. Ishibuchi, H., Nozaki, K., Yamamoto, N., Tanaka, H.: Selecting fuzzy if-then rules for classification problems using genetic algorithms, IEEE Tr. on Fuzzy Systems 3(3) (1995) 260–270.
8. Mahan, L.K., Scott-Stump, S.: KRAUSE'S Food, Nutrition and Diet Therapy, (W.B. Saunders, 1996).
9. Mann, J.: Diseases of the heart and circulation: the role of dietary factors in aetiology and management, in: J.S. Garrow and W.P.I. James, Eds., Human nutrition and dietetics, (1993) 619–650.

10. Mamdani, E.H.: Applications of fuzzy algorithm for control a simple dynamic plant, Proceedings of the IEEE 121(12) (1974) 1585–1588.
11. Michalewicz, Z.: Genetic Algorithms + Data Structures = Evolution Programs, (Springer-Verlag, 1996).
12. Wang, L.X., Mendel, J.M.: Generating fuzzy rules by learning from examples, IEEE Tr. on Systems, Man, and Cybernetics 22 (1992) 1414–1427.
13. Zadeh, L.A.: Outline of a new approach to the analysis of complex systems and decision processes, IEEE Tr. on Systems, Man, and Cybernetics 3(1) (1973) 28–44.

Multiple Crossover per Couple with Selection of the Two Best Offspring: An Experimental Study with the BLX-α Crossover Operator for Real-Coded Genetic Algorithms

F. Herrera[1], M. Lozano[1], E. Pérez[2], A.M. Sánchez[3], and P. Villar[3]

[1] Dpto. de Ciencias de la Computación e Inteligencia Artificial, Escuela Técnica Superior de Ingeniería Informática, Universidad de Granada
{herrera, lozano}@decsai.ugr.es

[2] Grupo de Ingeniería Industrial, ETS de Ingeniería Industrial, Universidad de Valladolid
elena@eis.uva.es

[3] Dpto. de Informática, Escuela Superior de Ingeniería Informática, Universidad de Vigo
{amlopez, pvillar}@uvigo.es

Abstract. In this paper, we propose a technique for the application of the crossover operator that generates multiple descendants from two parents and selects the two best offspring to replace the parents in the new population. In order to study the proposal, we present different instances based on the BLX-α crossover operator for real-coded genetic algorithms. In particular, we investigate the influence of the number of generated descendants in this operator, the number of evaluations, and the value for the parameter α. Analyzing the experimentation that we have carried out, we can observe that it is possible, with multiple descendants, to achieve a suitable balance between the explorative properties associated with BLX-α and the high selective pressure associated to the selection of the two best descendants.

1 Introduction

An important objective in the development of the genetic operators is to keep a suitable balance between exploration and exploitation, and therefore, to obtain good solutions in the searching process. In this paper, we study real-coded genetic algorithms (RCGAs) ([10]) paying special attention to the way the crossover operator is applied, in order to achieve the balance between exploration and exploitation.

There are different proposals of crossover operators and, particularly, there are crossover operators that generate three ([15]) and four descendants ([8,9]) from two parents and then, they select the two best descendants to replace the parents in the population. In these works, the operators with multiple descendants, more than two descendants

F.J. Garijo, J.C. Riquelme, and M. Toro (Eds.): IBERAMIA 2002, LNAI 2527, pp. 392–401, 2002.

from two parents, present a better behavior than the operators with only two descendants, and achieve a good balance between exploration and exploitation.

According to these ideas, in this paper, we present a proposal for the generation of multiple descendants using the BLX-α crossover operator ([4]) for RCGAs, which operates over two parents, selecting the two best ones to replace the parents in the new population.

The BLX-α operator has associated a high exploration, which induces a high diversity among the descendants. Therefore, this operator allows big differences among the descendants and among them and their parents. On the other hand, the possibility of generating multiple descendants and afterwards selecting the two best ones introduces a high selective pressure.

Due to these reasons, we present the proposal of multiples descendants for the BLX-α crossover operator, introducing a higher selective pressure on this operator with the selection of the two best descendants. With this combination, we can achieve an effective balance between exploitation and exploration and therefore, better solutions may be reached.

We have set up the paper as follows. In Section 2, we describe the BLX-α crossover operator and analyze its behavior when it generates two descendants for different values of α and different population sizes. In Section 3, we present the proposal of multiple descendants and selection of the two best. In Section 4, the experimental study and the analysis of the operator according to the number of generated descendants and to the value of the α parameter is showed. In Sections 5, we study the importance of selecting the two best descendents. In Section 6, we investigate the performance of the model proposed for different numbers of evaluations. Finally, some conclusions are presented in Section 7.

2   The BLX-α Crossover Operator for RCGAs

Let us assume that $C_1 = (c_1^1,..., c_n^1)$ and $C_2 = (c_1^2,..., c_n^2)$ are two real-coded chromosomes to be crossed, then BLX-α generates two offspring, $H_k = (h_1^k,..., h_i^k,..., h_n^k)$, k =1,2, where h_i^k is a randomly (uniformly) chosen number from the interval $[c_{min} - I\alpha, c_{max} + I\alpha]$, where $c_{max} = \max \{c_i^1, c_i^2\}$, $c_{min} = \min \{c_i^1, c_i^2\}$, and $I = c_{max}-c_{min}$. Figure 1 shows the effect of this operator.

It is important to emphasize that this crossover operator is based on the random generation of genes from the associated neighborhood of the genes in the parents. With this technique for the generation of genes, offspring are generated that can defer among them and also among them and their parents. In this sense, this operator presents a high exploration in the generation of the descendants.

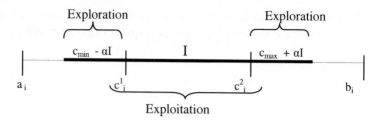

Fig. 1. Interval of random generation for a gene with BLX-α

We study empirically the behavior of BLX-α with different values for α (0.0, 0.1, 0.3, 0.5, and 0.7) and for the population size (N=61 and N=100). In these experiments, BLX-α generates two descendants, which replace the parents in the population.

We have considered thirteen frequently used test functions: Sphere model, Schwefel's problem, Generalized Rastrigin's function, Griewangk's function, Expansion of F10, Generalized Rosenbrock's function, system of linear equations, frequency modulation sounds parameter identification problem, polynomial fitting problem, Ackley's function, Bohachevsky's function, Watson's function, and Colville's function. The formulation of these problems may be found in [11,13]. These functions defer with respect to some characteristics like continuity, modality or dimensions. In this way, the interval of possible situations is wide enough to reach a good level of robustness in experimentation. The dimension of the search space is 25.

A generational GA model is assumed that applies the non-uniform mutation operator ([12]). The selection probability calculation follows linear ranking ([1]) and the sampling algorithm is the stochastic universal sampling ([2]). The elitist strategy is considered as well. We executed all the algorithms 30 times, each one with a maximum of 100000 evaluations. The crossover probability is 0.6 and the probability of updating a chromosome by mutation is 0.1.

Tables 1 and 2 present a summary of the results with 61 and 100 chromosomes, respectively. We have compared, using t-test (at 0.05 level of significance), the best result achieved by the operator, according to the value of α, with the rest of results using the other α values for each function. These tables show the percentages over the total of functions in which the operator has obtained the best results. Each column has the following information:

– **BA / BT**: Best Average / Best Test. Percentage of evaluation functions in which the crossover operator has obtained the best average value and continues being the best one after the application of the t-test.
– **BA / ST**: Best Average / Similar Test. Percentage of evaluation functions in which the crossover operator has obtained the best average value and, at least there is another crossover operator that does not present significant differences after the application of the t-test.

– **TB**: Percentage of evaluation functions in which the crossover operator presents better results without considering the information that we have obtained by the application of the t-test. This percentage is the result of the addition of the two previous columns.

– **ST / NBA**: Percentage of evaluation functions in which the crossover operator shows a similar behavior to the best crossover operator after the application of the t-test, although it does not obtain the best average value.

– **T B / S**: Percentage of evaluation functions in which the crossover operator shows the best behavior or similar to the best. This percentage is the result of the addition of the two previous columns.

According to these results, we can observe that BLX-α achieves the best result when α is 0.3, independently of the population size. This value allows some descendants in the exploration intervals to be generated, introducing diversity in the population. We have compared the results obtained with each parameter, for the different population sizes, and we have observed that the results are better with 61 chromosomes.

Table 1. Results obtained by BLX-α with different values of α and $N=61$

Crossover	BA/BT	BA/ST	TB	ST/NBA	T B/S
BLX-0.0	0%	7.69%	7.69%	38.45%	46.14%
BLX-0.1	0%	0%	0%	53.83%	53.83%
BLX-0.3	38.45%	53.83%	92.28%	0%	92.28%
BLX-0.5	0%	0%	0%	38.45%	38.45%
BLX-0.7	0%	0%	0%	7.69%	7.69%

Table 2. Results obtained by BLX-α with different values of α and $N=100$

Crossover	BA/BT	BA/ST	TB	ST/NBA	T B/S
BLX-0.0	7.69%	0%	7.69%	30.76%	38.45%
BLX-0.1	0%	0%	0%	53.83%	53.83%
BLX-0.3	30.76%	53.83%	84.59%	15.38%	100%
BLX-0.5	0%	7.69%	7.69%	7.69%	15.38%
BLX-0.7	0%	7.69%	7.69%	7.69%	15.38%

3   Generation of Multiple Descendants and Selection of the Two Best

In this section, we propose to increase the number of descendants generated by the BLX-α operator, leading to the mechanism of generation of multiple descendants with the selection of the two best to replace the parents in the new population. It will be denoted as GMD+STB.

The GMD+STB is possible by means of an unique operator or by the hybridization of different crossover operators, using a different operator for each descendant or group of descendants. In this paper, we will use an unique operator, BLX-α, to obtain all the descendants, and we will consider the possible extensions for future works.

The mechanism proposed generates 4, 6, 8 ,16, 32, 64, and 128 descendants for each pair of parents, and selects the two best (operator 2-2-2, 2-4-2, 2-6-2, 2-8-2, 2-16-2, 2-32-2, 2-64-2, and 2-128-2, respectively) to be included in the new population. Figure 2 shows graphically the working scheme of this mechanism.

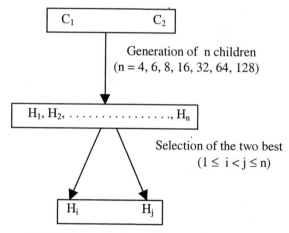

Fig. 2. Scheme for the mechanism of GMD+STB

The generation of multiple descendants from two parents has been considered in different proposals. In [5,6], multiple descendants are generated from two parents using different crossover operators, introducing all the descendants in the new population (MCPC model). In [7], a single offspring from the multiple crossovers (MCPC and MCMP) is selected and inserted in the next population. In [14], the generation of multiple descendants is proposed, selecting the two chromosomes for the next population from the named family, the parents and their children (MGG model). In [3], a generalization of this model is presented. In this case, one of the chromosomes is the best one of the population and another is selected by a classical sampling mechanism (or various ones in the case of multiple parents) and, taking them as point of departure, multiple descendants are generated; finally, the two best chromosomes of the family are selected (G3 model).

The proposal defers from these models because it has a selection of descendants and the parents do not participate in the selection process.

4 The BLX-α Crossover Operator with GMD+STB

In this section, we study empirically the effects of the GMD+STB, when the number of descendant is incremented, for the BLX-α operator with α = 0.5, 0.3, and 0.1. These values allow to use intervals of exploration and produce different levels of diversity. The population size is 61. Tables 3, 4, and 5, and Figure 4, present a summary of the results for the parameters 0.5, 0.3, and 0.1 respectively. These tables show the percentages over the total of functions in which the operator, according to the number of descendants, has obtained the best results.

Table 3. Results obtained by BLX-0.5 with GMD+STB

BLX 0.5	BA/BT	BA/ST	TB	ST/NBA	T B/S
2-2-2	0%	0%	0%	23.07%	23.07%
2-4-2	0%	15.38%	15.38%	30.76%	46.14%
2-6-2	0%	7.69%	7.69%	46.14%	53.83%
2-8-2	23.07%	23.07%	46.14%	30.76%	76.90%
2-16-2	7.69%	23.07%	30.76%	30.76%	61.52%
2-32-2	7.69%	15.38%	23.07%	23.07%	46.14%
2-64-2	0%	0%	0%	30.76%	30.76%
2-128-2	0%	0%	0%	30.76%	30.76%

Table 4. Results obtained by BLX-0.3 with GMD+STB

BLX 0.3	BA/BT	BA/ST	TB	ST/NBA	T B/S
2-2-2	0%	0%	0%	30.76%	30.76%
2-4-2	0%	15.38%	15.38%	23.07%	38.45%
2-6-2	0%	7.69%	7.69%	30.76%	38.45%
2-8-2	0%	30.76%	30.76%	30.76%	61.52%
2-16-2	0%	23.07%	23.07%	61.52%	84.59%
2-32-2	0%	15.38%	15.38%	46.14%	61.52%
2-64-2	0%	7.69%	7.69%	53.83%	61.52%
2-128-2	0%	30.76%	30.76%	15.38%	46.14%

Table 5. Results obtained by BLX-0.1 with GMD+STB

BLX 0.1	BA/BT	BA/ST	TB	ST/NBA	T B/S
2-2-2	0%	0%	0%	23.07%	23.07%
2-4-2	7.69%	0%	7.69%	15.38%	23.07%
2-6-2	0%	30.76%	30.76%	38.45%	69.21%
2-8-2	23.07%	38.45%	61.52%	30.76%	92.28%
2-16-2	0%	7.69%	7.69%	7.69%	15.38%
2-32-2	0%	0%	0%	15.38%	15.38%
2-64-2	0%	0%	0%	7.69%	7.69%
2-128-2	0%	0%	0%	23.07%	23.07%

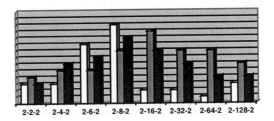

Fig. 4. Results of BLX-α with GMD+STB for α = 0.1, 0.3, and 0.5

According to the Tables 3-5 and the Figure 4, we may see that BLX-α with GMD+STB achieves the best results when the number of descendants is eight, for α=0.1and α=0.5, and sixteen for α=0.3. The results improve gradually as the descendants number increases until 8 or 16 descendants are reached. From this number onwards, the results are progressively worse. It is clear that a high number of descendants produces a worse behavior. A higher number of descendants produces a higher selective pressure, which induces a loss of diversity.

Since each parameter obtains the best results with a different number of descendants, we have compared BLX-0.1and BLX-0.5 with eight descendants, and BLX-0.3 with sixteen descendants, with the aim of deciding which of them is the best. Table 6 shows this comparison.

Table 6. Comparison between different parameters and descendants number

Crossover	BA/BT	BA/ST	TB	ST/NBA	T B/S
BLX-0.1 (2-8-2)	0%	46.14%	**46.14%**	15.38%	**61.52%**
BLX-0.3 (2-16-2)	38.45%	23.07%	**61.52%**	15.38%	**76.9%**
BLX-0.5 (2-8-2)	0%	46.14%	**46.14%**	15.38%	**61.52%**

We observe that the best results are obtained when the α parameter is 0.3 and the operator generates sixteen descendants.

5   Study of the Selection of Descendents: STB versus Selection of All Descendents

The objective of this section is to study the importance of the STB strategy as mechanism for selecting the descendents that are introduced in the population. In order to do this, we attempt to determine whether the generation of multiple descendents may work adequately along with a different strategy. In particular, we investigate an approach where all the descendents generated for every pair of parents are included in the new population. The pairs of parents that do not generate descendents, according to the crossover probability, are incorporated in the population, as well. The process finishes when the population reaches 61 elements. We have carried out the experiments with BLX-α, assuming α=0.5, which is the most standard value ([4]). Table 7 shows the results achieved using different values for the number of descendents.

The alternative strategy does not obtain suitable results when multiple descendents are generated. This does not occur with the STB strategy (Section 3), which has arisen as a powerful technique for working together with the generation of multiple descendents (Section 4).

Table 7. Results obtained by the BLX-0.5 with the new strategy investigated

Num. Desc.	BA/BT	BA/ST	TB	ST/NBA	T B/S
2	92.28%	7.69%	100%	0%	100%
4	0%	0%	0%	0%	0%
6	0%	0%	0%	0%	0%
8	0%	0%	0%	0%	0%
16	0%	0%	0%	0%	0%
32	0%	0%	0%	0%	0%
64	0%	0%	0%	7.69%	7.69%

6 Study with Different Numbers of Evaluations

In this section, we analyze whether the results obtained by GMD+STB may be influenced by the number of evaluations considered. We have carried out additional experiments with different values for the number of evaluations (50000, 150000, and 200000).

Figure 5 shows the percentages in which BLX-0.5 with GMD+STB has obtained the best results with 50000, 100000, 150000, and 200000 evaluations (according to the number of descendants).

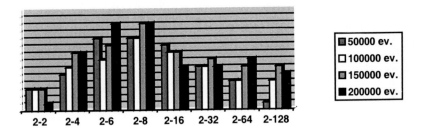

Fig. 5. BLX-0.5 with GMD+STB for 50000, 100000, 150000, and 200000 evaluations.
We may remark that the generation of multiples descendants achieves good results independently of the number of evaluations. This property is limited by a particular offspring number. If too many descendants are generated, the selective pressure is very high after the selection of the two best ones. In this way, a disproportionate balance is produced between the exploration of the mechanism of generation of children and the exploitation associated with the selection of the two best ones.

7 Conclusions

We may conclude that the proposal of multiple descendants achieves good results. With the GMD+STB model, the 2-8-2 and 2-16-2 mechanisms for BLX-α obtains better results than the operators with a higher number of descendants, reaching a suitable balance between diversity and selective pressure.

Furthermore, we have conducted experiments with GMD+STB considering others crossover operators for RCGAs. For crossover operators that show exploitation properties, such as the arithmetical crossover operator, the increment of the number of descendants produce an increment of the selective pressure, and no good results are obtained. In contrast, the crossover operators that have exploration properties achieved good results.

References

1. J.E. Baker: Adaptative Selection Methods for Genetic Algorithms. Proc. Of the First Int. Conf. On Genetic Algorithms and their Applications. J.J. Grefenstette (Ed.) (L. Erlbraum Associates, Hillsdale, MA, 1987), 14–21.
2. J.E. Baker: Reducing bias and inefficiency in the selection algorithm. Proc. Of the Second Int. Conf. On Genetic Algorithms and their Applications, J.J. Grefenstette, Ed., Hillsdale, NJ: Lawrence Erlbaum, 1987, 14–21.
3. K. Deb, D. Joshi, A. Anand: Real Coded Evolutionary Algorithms with Parent-Centric Recombination. KanGAL Report Number 20001003. Indian Institute of Technology, Kanpur, 2001.
4. L.J. Eshelman, J.D. Schaffer: Real-Coded Genetic Algorithms and Interval-Schemata. Foundations of Genetic Algortihms 2, L.D. Whitley (Ed.) (Morgan Kaufmann Publishers, San Mateo, 1993), 187–202.
5. S. Esquivel, R. Gallard, Z. Michalewicz: MCPC: Another Approach to Crossover in Genetic Algorithms. Actas del Primer Congreso Argentino de Ciencias de la Computación, 1995, 141-150.
6. S. Esquivel, A. Leiva, R. Gallard: Multiple Crossover per Couple in Genetic Algorithms. Proc. of the 4th IEEE Int. Conf. on Evolutionary Computation (ICEC'97), Indianapolis, USA, 1997, 103–106.
7. S. Esquivel, S. Ferrero, R. Gallard, C. Salto, H. Alfonso, M. Schütz: Enhanced Evolutionary Algorithms for Single and Multiobjective Optimization in the Job Shop Scheduling Problem. Journal of Knowledge Based Systems 15:1-2 (2002) 12–25.
8. F. Herrera, M. Lozano, J.L. Verdegay: Dynamic and Heuristic Fuzzy Connectives-Based Crossover Operators for Controlling the Diversity and Convergence of Real Coded Genetic Algorithms. International Journal of Intelligent Systems 11 (1996) 1013–1041.
9. F. Herrera, M. Lozano, J.L. Verdegay: Fuzzy Connectives Based Crossover Operators to Model Genetic Algorithms Population Diversity. Fuzzy Sets and Systems 92:1 (1997) 21–30.
10. F. Herrera, M. Lozano, J.L. Verdegay: Tackling Real-Coded Genetic Algorithms: Operators and Tools for the Behaviour Analysis. Artificial Intelligence Review 12 (1998) 265–319.

11. F. Herrera, M. Lozano: Gradual Distributed Real-Coded Genetic Algorithms. IEEE Transactions on Evolutionary Computation 4:1 (2000) 43–63.
12. Z. Michalewicz: Genetic Algorithms + Data Structures = Evolution Programs. Springer-Verlag, New York (1992).
13. R.C. Reynolds, C. Chung: Knowledge-Based Self-Adaptation in Evolutionary Programming Using Cultural Algorithms. Proc. 1997 IEEE International Conference on Evolutionary Computation, IEEE Press, 1997, 71–76.
14. H. Satoh, M. Yamamura, S. Kobayashi: Minimal Generation Gap Model for GAs Considering Both Exploration and Exploitation. Proc. Of IIZUKA: Methodologies for the Conception, Design and Application of Intelligent Systems, 1996, 494–497.
15. A. Wright: Genetic Algorithms for Real Parameter Optimization. Foundations of Genetic Algorithms I, G.J.E. Rawlin (Ed.) (Morgan Kaufmann, San Mateo,1991), 205–218.

Adaptive Random Fuzzy Cognitive Maps

Jose Aguilar

CEMISID, Dpto. de Computación, Facultad de Ingeniería, Av. Tulio Febres.
Universidad de los Andes, Mérida 5101, Venezuela
aguilar@ing.ula.ve

Abstract. A fuzzy cognitive map is a graphical means of representing arbitrarily complex models of interrelations between concepts. The purpose of this paper is to describe an adaptive fuzzy cognitive map based on the random neural network model. Previously, we have developed a random fuzzy cognitive map and illustrated its application in the modeling of processes. The adaptive fuzzy cognitive map changes its fuzzy causal web as causal patterns change and as experts update their causal knowledge. Our model carries out inferences via numerical calculation instead of symbolic deduction. We show how the adaptive random fuzzy cognitive map can reveal implications of models composed of dynamic processes.

1   Introduction

Modeling a dynamic system can be hard in a computational sense. Many quantitative techniques exist. Well-understood systems may be amenable to any of the mathematical programming techniques of operations research. Insight into less well-defined systems may be found from the statistically based methods of data mining. These approaches offer the advantage of quantified results but suffer from two drawbacks. First, developing the model typically requires a great deal of effort and specialized knowledge outside the domain of interest. Secondly, systems involving significant feedback may be nonlinear, in which case a quantitative model may not be possible. What we seek is a simple method that domain experts can use without assistance in a "first guess" approach to a problem. A qualitative approach is sufficient for this. The gross behavior of a system can be observed quickly and without the services of an operations research expert. If the results of this preliminary model are promising, the time and effort to pursue a quantitative model can be justified. Fuzzy cognitive maps are the qualitative approach we shall take.

Fuzzy Cognitive Maps (FCMs) were proposed by Kosko to represent the causal relationship between concepts and analyze inference patterns [7, 9]. FCMs are hybrid methods that lie in some sense between fuzzy systems and neural networks. So FCMs represent knowledge in a symbolic manner and relate states, processes, policies, events, values and inputs in an analogous manner. Compared either experts system and neural networks, it has several desirable properties such as: it is relative easy to use for representing structured knowledge, and the inference can be computed by

F.J. Garijo, J.C. Riquelme, and M. Toro (Eds.): IBERAMIA 2002, LNAI 2527, pp. 402–410, 2002.

numeric matrix operation instead of explicit IF/THEN rules. FCMs are appropriate to explicit the knowledge and experience which has been accumulated for years on the operation of a complex system. FCMs have gained considerable research interest and have been applied to many areas [3, 4, 8, 10]. However, certain problems restrict its applications. A FCM does not provide a robust and dynamic inference mechanism, a FCM lacks the temporal concept that is crucial in many applications and a FCM lacks the traditional statistical parameter estimates.

The Random Neural Network (RNN) has been proposed by Gelenbe in 1989 [5, 6]. This model does not use a dynamic equation, but uses a scheme of interaction among neurons. It calculates the probability of activation of the neurons in the network. The RNN has been used to solve optimization and pattern recognition problems [1, 2, 6]. Recently, we have proposed a FCM based on the random neural model [3]. The problem addressed in this paper concerns the proposition of an adaptive FCM using the RNN. We describe the Adaptive Random Fuzzy Cognitive Map (ARFCM) and illustrate its application in the modeling of dynamic processes. Our ARFCM changes its fuzzy causal web as causal patterns change and as experts update their causal knowledge. We shall use each neuron to model a concept. In our model, each concept is defined by a probability of activation, the dynamic causal relationships between the concepts (arcs) are defined by positive or negative interrelation probabilities, and the procedure of how the cause takes effect is modeled by a dynamic system. This work is organized as follows, in section 2 the theoretical bases of the RNN and of the FCM are presented. Section 3 presents the ARFCM. In section 4, we present applications. Remarks concerning future work and conclusions are provided in section 5.

2   Theoretical Aspects

2.1   The Random Neural Network Model

The RNN model has been introduced by Gelenbe [5, 6] in 1989. The model consists of a network of n neurons in which positive and negative signals circulate. Each neuron accumulates signals as they arrive, and can fire if its total signal count at a given instant of time is positive. Firing then occurs at random according to an exponential distribution of constant rate r(i). Each neuron i of the network is represented at any time t by its input signal potential $k_i(t)$. A negative signal reduces by 1 the potential of the neuron to which it arrives (inhibition) or has no effect on the signal potential if it is already zero; while an arriving positive signal adds 1 to the neuron potential. Signals can either arrive to a neuron from the outside of the network or from other neurons. A signal which leaves neuron i heads for neuron j with probability $p^+(i,j)$ as a positive signal (excitation), or as negative signal with probability $p^-(i,j)$ (inhibition), or it departs from the network with probability d(i). Positive signals arrive to the ith neuron according to a Poisson process of rate $\Lambda(i)$. Negative signals arrive to the ith neuron according to a Poisson process of rate $\lambda(i)$. The main property of this model is the excitation probability of a neuron i, q(i), which satisfy the non-linear equation:

$$q(i) = \lambda^+(i)/(r(i)+\lambda^-(i)) \qquad (1)$$

where, $\lambda^+(i) = \sum_{j=1}^n q(j)r(j)p^+(j,i)+\Lambda(i)$, $\lambda^-(i) = \sum_{j=1}^n q(j)r(j)p^-(j,i)+\lambda(i)$. The synaptic weights for positive $(w^+(i,j))$ and negative $(w^-(i,j))$ signals are: $w^+(i,j) = r(i)p^+(i,j)$ and $w^-(i,j) = r(i)p^-(i,j)$. Finally, $r(i) = \sum_{j=1}^n [w^+(i,j) + w^-(i,j)]$.

To guarantee the stability of the RNN, the following is a sufficient condition for the existence and uniqueness of the solution in the equation (1)

$$\lambda^+(i) < [\, r(i) + \lambda^-(i)]$$

2.2 Fuzzy Cognitive Maps

FCMs combine the robust properties of fuzzy logic and neural networks [7, 9]. A FCM is a fuzzy signed oriented graph with feedback that model the worlds as a collection of concepts and causal relations between concepts. Variable concepts are represented by nodes. The graph's edges are the casual influences between the concepts. In general, a FCM functions like associative neural networks. A FCM describes a system in a one-layer network which is used in unsupervised mode, whose neurons are assigned concept meanings and the interconnection weights represent relationships between these concepts. The fuzzy indicates that FCMs are often comprised of concepts that can be represented as fuzzy sets and the causal relations between the concepts can be fuzzy implications, conditional probabilities, etc. A directed edge E_{ij} from concept C_i to concept C_j measures how much C_i causes C_j. In general, the edges E_{ij} can take values in the fuzzy causal interval $[-1, 1]$ allowing degrees of causality to be represented: i) $E_{jk}>0$ indicates direct (positive) causality between concepts C_j and C_k. ii) $E_{jk}<0$ indicates inverse (negative) causality between concepts C_j and C_k, iii) $E_{jk}=0$ indicates no relationship between C_j and C_k.

In FCM nomenclature, model implications are revealed by clamping variables and using an iterative vector-matrix multiplication procedure to assess the effects of these perturbations on the state of a model. A model implication converges to a global stability, an equilibrium in the state of the system. During the inference process, the sequence of patterns reveals the inference model. The simplicity of the FCM model consists in its mathematical representation and operation. So a FCM which consists of n concepts, is represented mathematically by a n state vector A, which gathers the values of the n concepts, and by a n*n weighted matrix E. Each element E_{ij} of the matrix indicates the value of the weight between concepts C_i and C_j. The activation level A_i for each concept C_i is calculated by the following rule:

$$A_i^{new} = f(\sum_{j=1}^n A_j^{new} E_{ji})+ A_i^{old} \qquad (2)$$

A_i^{new} is the activation level of concept C_i at time t+1, A_j^{old} is the activation level of concept C_j at time t, and f is a threshold function. So the new state vector A, which is computed by multiplying the previous state vector A by the edge matrix E, shows the effect of the change in the activation level of one concept on the other concepts. A

FCM can be used to answer a "what-if" question based on an initial scenario that is represented by a vector $S_0 = \{s_i\}$, for $i=1 \ldots n$, where $s_i=1$ indicates that concept C_i holds completely in the initial state, and $s_i=0$ indicates that C_i does not hold in the initial state. Then, beginning with $k=1$ and $A=S_0$ we repeatedly compute A_i. This process continues until the system convergence (for example, when $A_i^{new}=A_i^{old}$). This is the resulting equilibrium vector, which provides the answer to the "what if" question.

3   The Adaptive Random Fuzzy Cognitive Maps

Our previous RFCM improves the conventional FCM by quantifying the probability of activation of the concepts and introducing a nonlinear dynamic function to the inference process [3]. Similar to a FCM, concepts in RFCM can be causes or effects that collectively represent the system's state. The value of W_{ij} indicates how strongly concept C_i influences concept C_j. $W^+_{ij} > 0$ and $W^-_{ij}=0$ if the relationship between the concepts C_i and C_j is direct, $W^-_{ij} > 0$ and $W^+_{ij}=0$ if the relationship is inverse, or $W^+_{ij}=W^-_{ij}=0$ if doesn't exist a relationship among them. The quantitative concepts enable the inference of RFCM to be carried out via numeric calculations instead of symbol deduction.

The new aspect introduce by the ARFCM is the dynamic causal relationships. That is, the values of the arcs are modified during the runtime of the FCM to adapt them to the new environment conditions. The quantitative concepts allow us develop a feedback mechanism that is included in the causal model to update the arcs. In this way, with the ARFCM we can consider on-line adaptive procedures of the model like real situations. Our ARFCM change their fuzzy causal web during the runtime using neural learning laws. In this way, our model can learn new patterns and reinforce old ones. To calculate the state of a neuron on the ARFCM (the probability of activation of a given concept C_j), the following expression is used [3]:

$$q(j) = \min\left\{\lambda^+(j), \max\left\{r(j), \lambda^-(j)\right\}\right\} \tag{3}$$

where
$$\lambda^+(j) = \max_{i=1,n}\left\{\min\left\{q(i), W^+(i,j)\right\}\right\}$$

$$\lambda^-(j) = \max_{i=1,n}\left\{\min\left\{q(i), W^-(i,j)\right\}\right\}$$

Such as, $\Lambda(j)=\lambda(i)=0$. In addition, the fire rate is:

$$r(j) = \max_{i=1,n}\left\{W^+(i,j), W^-(i,j)\right\} \tag{4}$$

The general procedure of the RFCM is the following:

1. Define the number of neurons (the number of neurons is equal to the number of concepts).
2. Call the Initialization phase
3. Call the Execution phase.

3.1 The Initialization Procedure

In this phase we must define the initial weights. The weights are defined and/or update according to the next procedures:

i)   *Based on expert's opinion:* each expert defines its FCM and we determine a global FCM. We use two formulas to calculate the global causal opinion:

$$E_{ji}^{G} = \max_{e}\left\{E_{ji}^{e}\right\}, \ \forall \ e=1, \ NE \ \text{(number of experts); or} \ E_{ji}^{G} = \sum_{e=1}^{NE} b_{e}E_{ji}^{e}\,/\,NE,$$

where E_{ji}^{e} is the opinion of the expert e about the causal relationship among C_j and C_i, and b_e is the expert's opinion credibility weight. Then, a) If $i \neq j$ and if $E^{G}_{ij}>0$, $W_{ij}^{+} = E_{ij}^{G}$ and $W_{ij}^{-} = 0$, b) If $i \neq j$ and if $E^{G}_{ij}<0$, $W_{ij}^{-} = E_{ij}^{G}$ and $W_{ij}^{+} = 0$, c) If i=j or if $E^{G}_{ij}=0$, $W_{ij}^{+} = W_{ij}^{-} = 0$. The causal relationship (E_{ji}^{e}) is caught from each expert from the interval [0, 1].

ii)   *Based on measured data:* In this case we have a set of measures about the system. This information is the input pattern: $M=\{D_1, ..., D_m\} = \{[d_1^{1}, d_1^{2}, ..., d_1^{n}], ..., [d_m^{1}, d_m^{2}, ..., d_m^{n}]\}$, where d_j^{i} is the value of the concept C_j measured at time t. In this case, our learning algorithm follows the next mechanism:

$$W_{ji}^{t} = W_{ji}^{t-1} + \eta\left(\Delta d_{j}^{t}\Delta d_{i}^{t}\,\Big/\,\Delta^{+}d_{i}^{t}\Delta^{+}d_{j}^{t}\right)$$

where $\Delta d_{j}^{t} = d_{j}^{t} - d_{j}^{t-1}$ $\Delta d_{i}^{t} = d_{i}^{t} - d_{i}^{t-1}$

$\Delta^{+}d_{j}^{t} = d_{j}^{t} + d_{j}^{t-1}$ $\Delta^{+}d_{i}^{t} = d_{i}^{t} + d_{i}^{t-1}$

η is the learning rate.

3.2 The Execution Phase

The ARFCM can be used like an associative memory. In this way, when we present a pattern to the network, it will iterate until generate an output close to the information keeps. This phase consists on the iteration of the system until the system convergence. The input is an initial state $S_0 = \{s_1, ..., s_n\}$, such as $q^{0}(1)=s_1, ..., q^{0}(n)=s_1$ and $s_i \in [0, 1]$ (set of initial values of the concepts). The output $Q^{m}=\{q^{m}(1), ..., q^{m}(n)\}$ is the prediction of the ARFCM such as m is the number of the iteration when the system converge. During this phase, the ARFCM is trained with a reinforced learning law. The weights of edges leaving a concept are modified when the concept has a nonzero state change (the weight of edge among two concepts is increased if they both increase or both decrease, and the weight is decreased if concepts move in opposite directions):

$$W_{ij}^{t} = W_{ij}^{t-1} + \eta\left(\Delta q_{i}^{t}\Delta q_{j}^{t}\right) \tag{5}$$

where Δq_i^t is the change in the ith concept's activation value among iterations t and t-1.

It is an unsupervised method whose computational load is light. In this way, we take into account the dynamic characteristics of the process. The algorithm of this phase is:

1. Read input state Q^0
2. Until system convergence
    2.1 Calculate q(i) according to the equation (3)
    2.2 Update W^t according to the equation (5)

4 Experiment

In this section we illustrate the ARFCM application. A discrete time simulation is performed by iteratively applying the equation (3) to the state vector of the graph. At the beginning, we must define an initial vector of concept states, and the simulation halts if an equilibrium state is reached. To test the quality of our approach, we compare it with the Kozko FCM [4, 9].

4.1 First Experiment: Virtual Worlds

Dickerson and Kosko proposed a novel use for FCMs [4, 8]. They employed a system of three interacting FCMs to create a virtual reality environment populated by dolphins, fish, and sharks. [9] refines the Dickerson and Kosko's approach to be used the FCM to model the "soft" elements of an environment in concert with an expert system capturing the procedural or doctrinal – "hard" elements of the environment. In their paper, they present a FCM modeling a squad of soldiers in combat. This is a good example where we can use a dynamic model to caught ideas like: an army needs several battles to know the strength of its enemy before a decisive battle. We introduce these aspects in this experiment. The concepts in this map are: i) Cluster (C_1): the tendency of individual soldiers to close with their peers for support, ii) Proximity of enemy (C_2), iii) Receive fire (C_3), iv) Presence of authority (C_4): command and control inputs from the squad leader, v) Fire weapons (C_5), vi) Peer visibility (C_6): the ability of any given soldier to observe his peers, vii) Spread out (C_7): dispersion of the squad, viii) Take cover (C_8): the squad seeking shelter from hostile fire, ix) Advance (C_9): the squad proceeding in the planned direction of travel with the intent of engaging any encountered enemy forces, x) Fatigue (C_{10}): physical weakness of the squad members.

In the hybrid system we suggest, the presence of authority concept would be replaced by an input from an expert system programmed with the enemy's small unit infantry doctrine and prevailing conditions. Similarly, the proximity of the enemy would be an input based on the battlefield map and programmed enemy locations.

Table 1. The edge connection initial matrix for the virtual word experiment.

	C_1	C_2	C_3	C_4	C_5	C_6	C_7	C_8	C_9	C_{10}
C_1	0	0	0	0	0	1	-1	0	0	0
C_2	1	0	1	0	1	0	0	1	0	0
C_3	1	0	0	1	-0.1	0	0	1	0	1
C_4	-1	0	0	0	0	0	1	-1	1	0
C_5	0	-0.5	-0.12	0	0	0	0	0	0	0.2
C_6	0	0	0	0	0	0	0	-0.7	1	0
C_7	-1	0	-0.5	0	0	0	0	0	0	0
C_8	1	0	0	1	-0.7	1	0	0	-1	-1
C_9	0	1	0	0	0	0	0	0	0	1
C_{20}	0	0	0	0	-0.5	0	0	0	0	0

Here, however, we give them initial inputs and allow them to vary according to operation of the FCM. In addition, during the runtime we introduce results of previous battles. The table 2 presents the results for the initial states 0 0 0 1 0 1 1 0 1 0.

Table 2. The results for the virtual word experiment.

Input	Kosko FCM	DFRCM	Iteration
0001011010	0001011010	0.2 0.4 0.7 0.6 0.5 0.6 0.6 0.4 0.6 0.4	1
	1111010101	1 0.6 0.6 0.6 0.5 0.1 0.4 0.6 0.6 0.8	2 *
	1011010110	0.6 0.6 0.6 0.6 0.5 0.1 0.4 0.6 0.8 0.8	3
	1111010011	0.8 1 1 0.6 0.8 0.1 0.2 0.8 1 1	4 *
	0110110011	0.8 1 0.8 1 0.8 0 1 0.8 1 0.8	5
	0111000011	1 1 0.8 1 0.8 0 0 0.8 1 0.8	6
	0111100011		7
	1111100111		8

We define the starting state S_0=(0 0 0 1 0 1 1 0 1 0) i.e., presence of authority, peer visibility, spread out and advance are present, but all other concepts are inactive. The system stabilizes to the state S_8 (Kozko model) or state S_6 (ARFCM). The introduction of new information during the runtime doesn't affect the convergence of our system (we obtain the same result of Kozko). The first * consists of clamping the first concept (Cluster) because the soldiers are closed with their peers. The second * clamps proximity of enemy, receive fire, and fatigue because that are new conditions that are observed from the environment. This is reasonable system operation and suggests the feasibility of FCMs as simple mechanisms for modeling inexact and dynamic behavior that is difficult to capture with formal methods.

4.2 Second Experiment: A Simple Model of a Country

In this experiment we present a model to determine the risk of a crisis in a country. The operative concepts are: i) Foreign inversion (C_1): the presence of a strong foreign inversion. ii) Employ rate (C_2): The level of employ on the country. iii) Laws (C_3): the presence or absence of laws. iv) Social problems (C_4): the presence or absence of social conflict on the country. v) Government stability (C_5): a good relationship be-tween the congress, the president, etc. The edge connection matrix (E) for this map is given in table 3.

Table 3. The edge connection matrix for the country model.

	Foreign inversion	Employ Rate	Laws	Social problems	Government stability
Foreign inversion	0	0.8	0	0	0
Employ Rate	0	0	0	-06	0.8
Laws	0.4	0	0	-0.8	0
Social problems	0	0	0	0	-0.8
Government stability	0.6	0	0	0	0

In the system we give initial inputs and during the runtime we introduce results of new events (laws, social problems, etc.). The table 4 presents the results for different initial states

Table 4. The results.

Input	Kosko FCM	ARFCM	Iteration
1 0 0 1 0	1 1 0 1 0	0.6 0.6 0.2 0.2 0.6	1
	1 1 0 0 0	0.8 0.8 0.2 0.2 0.8	2
	1 1 0 1 0	0.8 0.8 0.1 1 0.8	3*
	1 1 0 1 1	0.9 0.8 0.1 0 0.8	4
	1 1 0 1 0		5
	1 1 0 0 1		6
1 0 1 1 0	1 1 1 1 0	0.7 .0.7 0.8 0 0.2	1
	1 1 0 0 0	0.8 1 0.6 0 0.1	2*
	1 0 1 0 0	0.9 .0.8 0.9 0 0	3
	1 1 1 0 0		4
	1 1 1 0 0		5

Clamping two antithetical concepts allows to test the implications of one or more competing concepts. To illustrate, we begin by clamping C_1 and C_4 (S_0=(1 0 0 1 0)) – a strong foreign inversion can generate more employment and maybe solve social problems. The * consists of reclamping the fourth concept because the social prob-lems continue. Despite of the foreign inversion, we have an unstable government due to the social problems (the system reaches an equilibrium state of (1 1 0 0 1)). With S_0=(1 0 1 1 0) foreign inversion and social problems remain clamped, but we also clamp the ability to have a good law system. Now, the second * clamps employ rate because is observed a high employ rate. The system reaches an equilibrium state of 1 1 1 0 0 – A peaceful country at the social level but one unstable government.

We could study the different states of the concepts during the inference process (S_1, S_2). This example suggests the social problem is the main factor to have an unstable government. Obviously, our goal in analyzing this model was not to determine policy choices for a country. Rather, we tried to illustrate the advantages of the ARFCM to this sort of analysis. The nature of the domain is such that a quantitative model is difficult to construct, if not impossible. Resorting to qualitative measures permitted us to rapidly construct a model and analyze a variety of alternative policy options. Our results indicate that ARFCMs quickly come to an equilibrium regardless of the complexity of the model.

5   Conclusions

In this paper, we have proposed an adaptive FCM based on the RNN, the ARFCM. We show fusing the RFCM with a traditional reinforced learning algorithm can yield excellent results. The ARFCM may be rapidly adapted to changes in the modeled behavior. It is a useful method in complex dynamic system modeling. We do not observe any inconsistent behavior of our ARFCM with respect to the previous FCMs. Our ARFCM exhibit a number of desirable properties that make it attractive: i) Provide qualitative information about the inferences in complex dynamic models, ii) Can represent an unlimited number of reciprocal relationships, iii) Is based on a reinforced learning procedure, iv) Facility the modeling of dynamic, time evolving phenomena and process, v) Has a high adaptability to any inference with feedback. Another important characteristic is its simplicity, the result of each ARFCM's cycles is computed from the equation (3). The ease of construction and low computational costs of the ARFCM permits wide dissemination of low-cost training aids. In addition, the ability to easily model uncertain systems at low cost and with adaptive behavior would be of extraordinary value in a variety of domains.

References

1. Aguilar, J. Definition of an Energy Function for the Random Neural to solve Optimization Problems, Neural Networks, Vol. 11, Pergamo, (1998) 731–738.
2. Aguilar, J. Learning Algorithm and Retrieval Process for the Multiple Classes Random Neural Network Model. Neural Processing Letters, Vol. 13, Kluwer Academic Publishers, (2001) 81–91.
3. Aguilar, J. A Fuzzy Cognitive Map Based on the Random Neural Model. Lecture Notes in Artificial Intelligence, Vol. 2070, Springer-Verlag, (2001) 333–338.
4. Dickerson J., Kosko B. Virtual Worlds as Fuzzy Dynamic Systems. in Technology for Multimedia, (B. Sheu, editor), IEEE Press (1996).
5. Gelenbe E. Random neural networks with positive and negative signals and product form solution, Neural Computation, Vol. 1, (1989) 502–511.
6. Gelenbe E. Theory of the random neural network model, Neural networks: Advances and Applications (E. Gelenbe editor), North-Holland, Pays-Bas (1991).
7. Kosko B. Fuzzy Cognitive Maps, Int. Journal of Man-Machine Studies, Vol. 24, (1986) 65–75.
8. Kosko B., Dickerson J. Fuzzy virtual worlds. AI Expert, (1994) 25–31.
9. Kosko B. Fuzzy Engineering, Prentice-Hall, New Jersey (1999).
10. Miao Y., Liu C. On causal inference in Fuzzy Cognitive Map, IEEE Transaction on Fuzzy Systems, Vol. 8, (2000) 107–120.

Convex Hull in Feature Space for Support Vector Machines

Edgar Osuna[1] and Osberth De Castro[2]

[1] Departamento de Computación
Universidad Simón Bolívar
Aptdo 89000, Caracas 1080-A
Venezuela
eosuna@bancomercantil.com

[2] Departamento de Electrónica y Circuitos
Universidad Simón Bolívar
Aptdo 89000, Caracas 1080-A
Venezuela
odcastro@usb.ve

Abstract. Some important geometric properties of Support Vector Machines (SVM) have been studied in the last few years, allowing researchers to develop several algorithmic aproaches to the SVM formulation for binary pattern recognition. One important property is the relationship between support vectors and the Convex Hulls of the subsets containing the classes, in the separable case. We propose an algorithm for finding the extreme points of the Convex Hull of the data points in feature space. The key of the method is the construction of the Convex Hull in feature space using an incremental procedure that works using kernel functions and with large datasets. We show some experimental results.

1 Introduction

In the formulation of a **SVM** [1,2], we find that in feature space the decision surface is always an hyperplane, and the classifier is always written in terms of data instances that belongs to the outside of the *boundaries* of the classes. More specifically, in the separable case, the boundaries of the classes *contain* the instances of solution (support vectors), therefore we only need the points on those boundaries. The boundaries of the data can be obtained from the Convex Hull of each class. In particular, we only need the extreme points (vertices) of the Convex Hull. We show a particular aproach to find these extreme points in feature space, using the so called kernel functions, a key part of **SVM**s formulation. The application area for our method includes incremental training [3, 4], parallel training, and reduction of the run time complexity of **SVM**s [5,6, 7]. Related work on convex geometry for **SVM**s geometry has been developed recently [8,9,10].

F.J. Garijo, J.C. Riquelme, and M. Toro (Eds.): IBERAMIA 2002, LNAI 2527, pp. 411–419, 2002.
© Springer-Verlag Berlin Heidelberg 2002

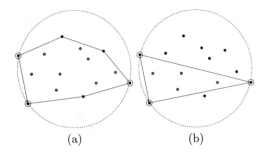

Fig. 1. (a) Relationship between the Convex Hull of a set of points and the smallest hypersphere containing the same points. (b) The first Convex Hull obtained by finding the smallest hypersphere.

1.1   Support Vector Machines for Pattern Recognition

A Support Vector Machine (**SVM**) is a general optimal model for learning from examples that has become practical in the last five years. This model for pattern recognition is based on the Structural Risk Minimization Principle and VC theory, focused on finding the optimal decision surface in terms of the linear function

$$f(\mathbf{x}) = \text{sgn} \sum_{i=1}^{\mathcal{S}} \alpha_i \mathcal{K}(\mathbf{x}, s_i) + b \tag{1}$$

Where $\mathcal{K}$ maps the decision function into a high dimensional *feature space* in which it becomes linear. For example, $\mathcal{K}$ can convert $f(\mathbf{x})$ into a polynomial classifier using $\mathcal{K}(\mathbf{x}, \mathbf{y}) = (\mathbf{x} \cdot \mathbf{y} + 1)^p$, or a Radial Basis Learning Machine using a gaussian form, or a Multilayer Neural Network if we use a sigmoidal $\mathcal{K}(\mathbf{x}, \mathbf{y})$ [1]. These kernel functions can be used under certain conditions. The more intuitive condition is that $\mathcal{K}$ must satisfy $\mathcal{K}(\mathbf{x}, \mathbf{y}) = \varPhi(\mathbf{x}) \cdot \varPhi(\mathbf{y})$ where $\varPhi$ is a non linear map to some inner product space in which the linear function lives. When the hyperplane is on input space, $\mathcal{K}(\mathbf{x}, \mathbf{y}) = \mathbf{x} \cdot \mathbf{y}$.

The usual aproach to train **SVM**s is to solve a quadratic optimization problem with linear constrains, starting from the problem of finding the hyperplane in feature space which maximizes the distance between the class boundary in the separable case. The non separable case is solved by including error penalty variables which transtate in the formulation by creating an upper bound on the QP variables.

2   Finding the Extreme Points of a Convex Hull in Feature Space

The problem of finding the Convex Hull of a set of points in feature space (also called kernel space) is manageable only if the choosen method is able to make all the calculations using the kernel function instead of mapping the points explicitly in feature space. The kernel functions can be used by writing all the formulations in terms of inner products of data points, which can later be replaced by kernel function evaluations to obtain the final feature space formulation.

Let $\mathcal{L} \in \mathbb{R}^N$ be the set of points. The convex hull of a set of points $\mathcal{L}$ is defined by the set $\mathcal{C} = conv(\mathcal{L})$ that satisfy

$$conv(\mathcal{L}) = \{\mathbf{x} \in \mathcal{L} \mid \mathbf{x} = \sum_{i=1}^{\ell} \lambda_i \mathbf{x}_i\} \text{ where } \sum_{i=1}^{v} \lambda_i = 1, \text{ and } \lambda_i \geq 0 \quad (2)$$

Thus, $\mathcal{C}$ are the set of points of $\mathcal{L}$ that can be generated by convex combinations of some subset of elements $\mathcal{V} \in \mathcal{L}$. This subset $\mathcal{V}$ is the set of extreme points of $\mathcal{L}$, and the vertices of the smallest convex polyhedron containing $\mathcal{L}$. The method we show in this paper finds the subset $\mathcal{V}$.

2.1   Finding the Extreme Points $\mathcal{V}$

In order to find $\mathcal{V}$, we use an incremental algorithm that uses the following ideas:

1. Checking the containment of a point in a Convex Hull can be done by: **1.** Solving a convex quadratic optimization program formulated in terms of inner products, so it can be solved in feature space, or **2.** Solving a linear program that tries of find a separating hyperplane between a point and the rest of the data set.
2. Using a measure of the distance to the center of the smallest hypersphere containing $\mathcal{L}$ gives us admissible spatial knowledge in order to use heuristic procedures to find $\mathcal{V}$.

These ideas take us to an incremental algorithm that constructs the set $\mathcal{V}$ based on the iterative inclusion of points in a candidate set of extreme points $\mathcal{V}_0$, based on whether it can be written as a convex combination of the points on $\mathcal{V}_0$. We use a *from outside to inside* inclusion order defined by the distance of the point to the center of the smallest hypersphere containing $\mathcal{L}$. We do this until we have checked all the points. At the end, the algorithm has a candidate $\mathcal{V}_0$ containing the solution $\mathcal{V}$ and some *extra* interior points near the boundaries of the Convex Hull defined by $\mathcal{V}$. De final step is a *one against all* check, to discard the *extra* interior points.

Initial Condition. The most important condition is choosing the first $\mathcal{V}_0$. It can be shown that the points lying on the surface of the smallest hypersphere containing $\mathcal{L}$ are also in $\mathcal{V}$ (see figure 1(b)), then our first $\mathcal{V}_0$ are these points. The calculation of this hypersphere was done using a large scale incremental implementation in feature space previously used with other aplications using **SVMs** [11,6]. In what follows, given a set $\mathcal{L}$, we will call the points on the surface of the smallest hypersphere containing $\mathcal{L}$, *SphereSet*$(\mathcal{L})$.

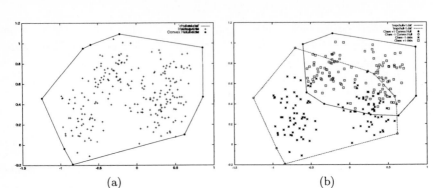

(a)   (b)

Fig. 2. (a) The Convex Hull of the Ripley dataset.(b) The Convex Hulls for classes $+1$ and -1 on Ripley dataset.

The Algorithm. Let $\mathcal{V}$ be the set of extreme points of $\mathcal{L}$, and $\mathbf{x} \in \mathcal{L}$. Suppose that we have the functions $SphereSet(\mathcal{L})$ and $SphereSort(\mathcal{L})$. The first returns the subset of $\mathcal{L}$ lying on the surface of the smallest sphere containing $\mathcal{L}$, and the second returns a descending sort list of $\mathcal{L}$ by the distance to the center of the same sphere. We have also the function $CheckPoint(\mathbf{x}, \mathcal{V})$ returning $TRUE$ if $\mathbf{x}$ belongs the interior of the Convex Hull defined by $\mathcal{V}$. In what follows, $\mathcal{V}_0$ is a set of candidate extreme points.

$ExtremePoints(\mathcal{L})$.

1. Initialize $\mathcal{V}_0 = \{Sphere(\mathcal{L})\}$, and $\mathcal{V} = \emptyset$
2. Create the sorted list $\mathcal{L}^* = \{SphereSort(\mathcal{L})\} - \mathcal{V}_0$
3. Until $\mathcal{L}^*$ is empty

   – Get first $\mathbf{x} \in \mathcal{L}^*$, update $\mathcal{L}^* = \mathcal{L}^* - \{\mathbf{x}\}$
   – If $(CheckPoint(\mathbf{x}, \mathcal{V}_0) = FALSE)$ then $\mathcal{V}_0 = \mathcal{V}_0 \cup \{\mathbf{x}\}$

4. Until $\mathcal{V}_0$ is empty

   – Get next $\mathbf{x} \in \mathcal{V}_0$
   – If $(CheckPoint(\mathbf{x}, \mathcal{V}_0 - \{\mathbf{x}\}) = FALSE)$ then $\mathcal{V} = \mathcal{V} \cup \{\mathbf{x}\}$

At step 4, $\mathcal{V}_0 = \mathcal{V} + \mathcal{A}$, where $\mathcal{A}$ is a set of extra points near the surface of the boundaries of the Convex Hull, and $\mathcal{V}$ the set of extreme points. $\mathcal{A}$ is eliminated in 4. The Algorithm passes once through all $\mathcal{L}$, and twice on $\mathcal{V}_0$. The advantage of this algorithm is that it never uses all the points on a $CheckPoint()$ operation, and the biggest set used is $\mathcal{V}_0$. In most cases, the *from outside to inside* incremental procedure allows us to obtain a small set $\mathcal{A}$. In the following sections we give some remarks on the mathematical formulation in feature space for the functions used by the algorithm.

3   Feature Space Mathematics

In this section we present the mathematical formulation that allows us to use the previous algorithmic aproach in feature space. Thus, we analize the functions used in the section 2.1 on input and feature space.

3.1   Finding the Hypersphere of $\mathcal{L}$

We use the same formulation used in [11,6]. The problem of finding the radius of the smallest sphere containing $\mathcal{L}$ is solved by minimizing the largest distance R between a variable center point $\mathbf{a}$ and every point $\mathbf{x}$.

$$\min_{\mathbf{a}} \max_{i=1,\dots,\ell} R(\mathbf{a}, \mathbf{x}_i) \tag{3}$$

Which can be written in dual form as:

$$\max_{\mathbf{\Lambda}} \sum_{i=1}^{\ell} \lambda_i \mathcal{K}(\mathbf{x}_i, \mathbf{x}_i) - \mathbf{\Lambda}^T Q \mathbf{\Lambda} \text{ where } Q_{ij} = \mathcal{K}(\mathbf{x}_i, \mathbf{x}_j) \tag{4}$$

$$\text{with constrains} \quad \mathbf{\Lambda}^T \mathbf{1} = 1, \; -\mathbf{\Lambda} \leq 0$$

Where $\mathcal{K}(\mathbf{x}, \mathbf{y})$ is the kernel functions making the implicit mapping to feature space for $\mathbf{x}$ and $\mathbf{y}$ and computing their dot product. The solution of this QP yields the sphere radius R, the set of points lying on the surface (points whose coefficient are $\lambda > 0$), and a representation for the center $\mathbf{a}$ (as a linear combination of the points on the surface). The distance from any point $\mathbf{y}$ to the center a can be obtained by:

$$d(\mathbf{a}, \mathbf{y}) = \sqrt{\sum_{i,j}^{s} \alpha_i \alpha_j \mathcal{K}(\mathbf{x}_i, \mathbf{x}_j) + \mathcal{K}(\mathbf{y}, \mathbf{y}) - 2 \sum_i \alpha_i \mathcal{K}(\mathbf{x}_i, \mathbf{y})} \tag{5}$$

Where $\mathcal{S}$ is the set of surface points, $\mathbf{x} \in \mathcal{S}$, and α are the variables in (4).

3.2   Checking a Point y in a Convex Hull $\mathcal{C}$ Defined by $\mathcal{V}$

In this section we show a couple of formulations that allow us to check in feature space the containment of a point in the interior of the Convex Hull $\mathcal{C}$ defined by the vertices $\mathcal{V}$.

Writing a point as a Convex Combination in feature space. We have formulated this problem as a linearly constrained convex quadratic optimization program that minimizes an error measure between $\mathbf{y}$ itself and the aproximation of convex combinations of points in $\mathcal{V}$. If we can minimize this measure to cero, $\mathbf{y}$ can be written as a convex combination of $\mathbf{x} \in \mathcal{V}$. Formally,

$$\min_{\lambda_i} f(\mathbf{y}, \lambda) = \left(\mathbf{y} - \sum_{i=1}^{v} \lambda_i \mathbf{x}_i \right)^2 \text{ with } \sum_{i=1}^{v} \lambda_i = 1, \text{ and } \lambda_i \geq 0, \; \mathbf{x}_i \in \mathcal{V} \tag{6}$$

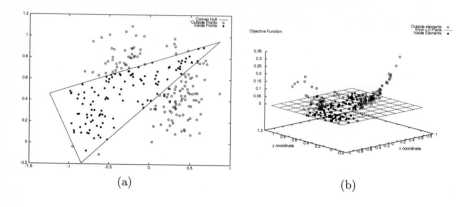

Fig. 3. (a) *Checkpoint* Test on all the Ripley data set for a first Convex hull obtained using the hypersphere calculation from section 3.1. (b) Values of the objective function when $ChecPoint(\mathbf{x}, \mathcal{V}_0)$ is formulated as a QP in section 3.2 the test.

Which can be reduced to an expression in terms of inner products in input space as:

$$\min_{\Lambda} \ f(\mathbf{y}, \Lambda) = \mathbf{y}^T\mathbf{y} + \Lambda^T\mathbf{Q}\Lambda - 2\sum_{i=1}^{v}\lambda_i\mathbf{x}_i^T\mathbf{y} \qquad \text{where } Q_{ij} = \mathbf{x}_i\mathbf{x}_j \qquad (7)$$

$$\text{with constrains } \Lambda^T\mathbf{1} = 1, \ -\Lambda \leq 0, \ \mathbf{x}_i \in \mathcal{V}$$

We can traslate this QP to the feature space form replacing the inner products by kernel functions, obtaining:

$$\min_{\Lambda} \ f(\mathbf{y}, \Lambda) = \mathcal{K}(\mathbf{y}, \mathbf{y}) + \Lambda^T\mathbf{Q}\Lambda - 2\sum_{i=1}^{v}\lambda_i\mathcal{K}(\mathbf{x}_i, \mathbf{y}) \qquad \text{where } Q_{ij} = \mathcal{K}(\mathbf{x}_i, \mathbf{x}_j) \quad (8)$$

$$\text{with constrains } \Lambda^T\mathbf{1} = 1, \ -\Lambda \leq 0, \ \mathbf{x}_i \in \mathcal{V}$$

When we evaluate a point $\mathbf{y}$ outside $\mathcal{C}$, the final objective function is $f^*(\mathbf{y}, \Lambda) > 0$. If $\mathbf{y}$ is inside the polyhedron defined by $\mathcal{C}$ then $f^*(\mathbf{y}, \Lambda) = 0$. Figure 3 shows an experimental demonstration in the 2d dataset Ripley[1]. Figure 2(b) shows the Convex Hull for each class of points (Ripley is a binary classification dataset).

Finding an extreme point using a Separating hyperplane. The hyperplane separating a point $\mathbf{x}_i \in \mathcal{L}$ from the rest $\{\mathcal{L}\} - \mathbf{x}_i$, must satisfy

$$\mathbf{w} \cdot \mathbf{x}_i + b <= 0 \qquad (9)$$

$$\mathbf{w} \cdot \mathbf{x}_j + b >= 0 \ \forall j \neq i$$

In order to formulate the problem of finding this hyperplane for any point in $\mathcal{L}$, not only the extreme points, we introduce penalty variables P for each point in

---

[1] Available on ftp://markov.stats.ox.ac.uk/pub/neural/papers

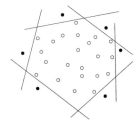

Fig. 4. Separating hyperplanes and the extreme points. We can see that for the interior points the hyperplane can't be found.

$\mathcal{L}$. Therefore, we can formulate a problem wich tries to minimize P_i for every point. Formally,

$$\min_{\lambda,b,P_i} \sum_{i=1}^{\ell} P_i \tag{10}$$

with constrains $\sum_{j=1}^{\ell} \lambda_j \mathbf{x}_j \cdot \mathbf{x}_i + b - P_i <= 0$

$$\sum_{j=1}^{\ell} \lambda_j \mathbf{x}_j \cdot \mathbf{x}_z + b + P_z >= 0 \; \forall z \neq i, \; P_z, P_i >= 0$$

Since the problem has the form of dot products, we can replace all of these operations with kernel functions, obtaining the feature space formulation

$$\min_{\lambda,b,P_i} \sum_{i=1}^{\ell} P_i \tag{11}$$

with constrains $\sum_{j=1}^{\ell} \lambda_j \mathcal{K}(\mathbf{x}_j, \mathbf{x}_i) + b - P_i <= 0$

$$\sum_{j=1}^{\ell} \lambda_j \mathcal{K}(\mathbf{x}_j, \mathbf{x}_z) + b + P_z >= 0 \; \forall z \neq i, \; P_z, P_i >= 0$$

In this formulation the variables b and λ_j are free $\forall j$. It's easy to see that eq. (11) solves the problem for the point $\mathbf{x}_i$ in $\mathcal{L}$. At the end of the minimizing process, if we can minimize all the penalties P_i to cero, the hyperplane separating $\mathbf{x}_i$ from the rest has been found, and we can say that $\mathbf{x}_i$ is an extreme point of $\mathcal{L}$.

4   Conclusions and Final Remarks

In this paper we have shown a procedure to compute the set of extreme points defining the Convex Hull of a data set in feature space. The difference with previous convex hull computation algorithms used in the **SVM** arena [3,12] is that our aproach doesn't need explicit knowledge of dimensionality or explicitly mapping the data points in feature space. A first application area for our method is incremental and parallel training speedup, where work reported in [3,4] could be extended to feature space very easily, although some extensions would need to be worked out to include non-separable data. A second possible application would be reduction **SVM** run time complexity [5,6,7], since, for example, some misclassified support vectors could in principle be rewritten as convex combination of extreme points of the data that are already support vectors. Another interesting property of the method is its dimensionality independence as a general geometric Convex Hull extreme points algorithm, when compared with other algorithms like Quickhull [13], and divide and conquer methods.

One important drawback to be dealt with in this topic is that the complexity of the convex hull and the number of extreme points have an exponential dependence on the dimensionality of the feature space. We have used data in 2 and 3 dimensions to test the algorith, but the adaptation of this aproach to be used in large scale applications and higher dimension feature spaces is subject of further work.

Acknowledgments. Edgar Osuna also works in the Risk Management Department of Banco Mercantil, Caracas, Venezuela. We would like to thank José Ramírez for his useful comments.

References

1. V. Vapnik. *The Nature of Statistical Learning Theory.* Springer, New York, 1.995.
2. C. Cortes and V. Vapnik. Support vector networks. *Machine Learning*, 20:273 – 297, 1995.
3. D. Caragea, A. Silvescu, and V. Honavar. Agents that learn from distributed dynamic data sources. In *Proceedings at The Fourth International Conference on Autonomous Agents*, pages 53–60, Barcelona, Catalonia, Spain, 2000.
4. N. A. Syed, H. Liu, and K. Kay Sung. Incremental learning with support vector machines. In J. Debenham, S. Decker, R. Dieng, A. Macintosh, N. Matta, and U. Reimer, editors, *Proceedings of the Sixteenth International Joint Conference on artificial Intelligence IJCAI-99*, Stockholm, Sweden, 1.999.
5. C. Burges. Simplified support vector decision rules. In Lorenza Saitta, editor, *Proceedings or the Thirteenth International Conference on Machine Learning*, pages 71 – 77, Bari, Italia, 1.996.
6. C. Burges. A tutorial on support vector machines for pattern recognition. *Data Mining and Knowledge Discovery*, 2(2):121–167, 1998.
7. E. Osuna and F. Girosi. Reducing the run-time complexity of support vector machines. *Advances in Kernel Methods, Support Vector Learning*, 1998.
8. K. Bennett and E. Bredensteiner. Duality and geometry in SVM classifiers. In *Proc. 17th International Conf. on Machine Learning*, pages 57–64. Morgan Kaufmann, San Francisco, CA, 2000.
9. K. Bennett and E. Bredensteiner. Geometry in learning. In C. Gorini, E. Hart, W. Meyer, and T. Phillips, editors, *Geometry at Work*, Washington, D.C., 1997. Mathematical Association of America.
10. S. S. Keerthi, S. K. Shevade, C. Bhattacharyya, and K. R. K. Murthy. A fast iterative nearest point algorithm for support vector machine classifier design. *IEEE-NN*, 11(1):124, 2000.
11. E. Osuna. *Support Vector Machines: Trainig and Applications, PhD Thesis.* MIT, Cambridge, 1.998.

12. C.B. Barber, D.P. Dobkin, and H. Huhdanpaa. Quickhull algorithm for convex hulls. *ACM Transactions on Mathematical Software*, 22(4), 1996.
13. C. Bradford Barber, David P. Dobkin, and Hannu Huhdanpaa. The quickhull algorithm for convex hulls. *ACM Transactions on Mathematical Software*, 22(4):469–483, 1996.

Applying Neural Networks and Genetic Algorithms to the Separation of Sources

Fernando Rojas [1], M.R. Alvarez [1], C.G. Puntonet [1], and Ruben Martin-Clemente [2]

[1] Dpto. Arquitectura. y Tecnología de Computadores. University of Granada (Spain)
{frojas, mrodriguez, carlos}@atc.ugr.es
[2] Area de Teoria de la Señal, University of Sevilla (Spain)
ruben@cica.es

Abstract. This paper presents a new adaptive procedure for the linear and non-linear separation of signals with non-uniform, symmetrical probability distributions, based on both simulated annealing (SA) and competitive learning (CL) methods by means of a neural network, considering the properties of the vectorial spaces of sources and mixtures, and using a multiple linearization in the mixture space. Also, the paper proposes the fusion of two important paradigms, Genetic Algorithms and the Blind Separation of Sources in Nonlinear Mixtures (GABSS). From experimental results, this paper demonstrates the possible benefits offered by GAs in combination with BSS, such as robustness against local minima, the parallel search for various solutions, and a high degree of flexibility in the evaluation function. The main characteristics of the method are its simplicity and the rapid convergence experimentally validated by the separation of many kinds of signals, such as speech or biomedical data.

1 Introduction

Blind Source Separation (BSS) consists in recovering unobserved signals from a known set of mixtures. The separation of independent sources from mixed observed data is a fundamental and challenging signal-processing problem [2], [6], [7], [14]. In many practical situations, one or more desired signals need to be recovered from the mixtures only. A typical example is speech recordings made in an acoustic environment in the presence of background noise and/or competing speakers. This general case is known as the *Cocktail Party Effect*, in reference to human's brain faculty of focusing in one single voice and ignoring other voices/sounds, which are produced simultaneously with similar amplitude in a noisy environment. Spatial differences between the sources highly increase this capacity. The source separation problem has been successfully studied for linear instantaneous mixtures [1], [4], [12], [14] and more recently, since 1990, for linear convolutive mixtures. References [10., [17], [19] clearly explain the nature of the problem, previous work, purpose, and contribution of the paper. The nonlinear separation of sources has been addressed in [3], [8], [13].

In the framework of independent component analysis, ICA, many kinds of approaches have been presented concerning the blind separation of sources, with appli-

F.J. Garijo, J.C. Riquelme, and M. Toro (Eds.): IBERAMIA 2002, LNAI 2527, pp. 420–429, 2002.

cations to real problems in areas such as communications, feature extraction, pattern recognition, data visualization, speech processing and biomedical signal analysis (EEG, MEG, fMRI, etc), considering the hypothesis that the medium where the sources have been mixed is linear, convolutive or non-linear. ICA is a linear transformation that seeks to minimise the mutual information of the transformed data, $\mathbf{x}(t)$, the fundamental assumption being that individual components of the source vector, $\mathbf{s}(t)$, are mutually independent and have, at most, one Gaussian distribution. The 'Infomax' algorithm of Bell and Sejnowski [2] is an unsupervised neural network learning algorithm that can perform blind separation of input data into the linear sum of time-varying modulations of maximally independent component maps, providing a powerful method for exploratory analysis of functional magnetic resonance imaging (fMRI) data. Also using the maximization of the negentropy, ICA 'Infomax' algorithm is used for unsupervised exploratory data analysis and for general linear ICA applied to electroencephalograph (EEG) monitor output. Many solutions for blind separation of sources are based on estimating a separation matrix with algorithms, adaptive or not, that use higher-order statistics, including minimization or cancellation of independence criteria by means of cost functions or a set of equations, in order to find a separation matrix [10]. ICA is a promising tool for the exploratory analysis of biomedical data. In this context, a generalized algorithm modified by a kernel-based density estimation procedure has been studied to separate EEG signals from tumour patients into spatially independent source signals, the algorithm allowing artifactual signals to be removed from the EEG by isolating brain-related signals into single ICA components. Using an adaptive geometry-dependent ICA algorithm, Puntonet et al. [14] demonstrated the possibility of separating biomedical sources, such as EEG signals, after analyzing only the observed mixing space, due to the almost symmetric probability distribution of the mixtures. The general case of a nonlinear mixture of sources is shown in the following figure:

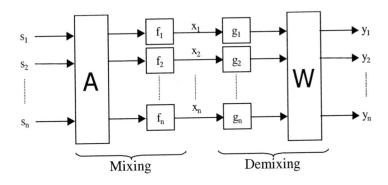

Fig. 1. Nonlinear mixing and demixing model.

2   Hybridization of Competitive Learning and Simulated Annealing

2.1   Algorithm Description

Fig. 1 shows that the mixing system is divided into two different phases: first a linear mixing and then, for each channel i, a nonlinear transfer part. The unmixing system is the inverse, first we need to approximate the inverse of the nonlinear function in each channel g_i, and then unmix the linear mixing by applying W to the output of the g_i nonlinear function.

$$y_i(t) = \sum_{j=1}^{n} w_{ij} g_j(x_j(t))$$

(1)

In different approaches, the inverse function g_j is approximated by a sigmoidal transfer function, but because of certain situations where the human expert does not give the a priori knowledge about the mixing model, a more flexible nonlinear transfer function based on odd polynomial of P-th order is used:

$$g_j(x_j) = \sum_{k=1}^{P} g_{jk} x_j^{2k-1}$$

(2)

where $\overline{g_j} = \lfloor g_{j1}, ..., g_{jP} \rfloor$ is a parameter vector to be determined. In this way, the output sources are calculated as:

$$y_i = \sum_{j=1}^{n} w_{ij} \sum_{k=1}^{P} g_{jk} x_j^{2k-1}$$

(3)

Nevertheless, computation of the parameter vector $\overrightarrow{g_j}$ is not easy, as it presents a problem with numerous local minima. Thus we require an algorithm that is capable of avoiding entrapment in such a minimum. As a solution to this first unmixing stage, we propose the hybridization of genetic algorithms. We have just used new meta-heuristics, as simulated annealing and genetic algorithms for the linear case [5], [15], [16], but in this paper we will focus in a more difficult problem as is the nonlinear BSS. We propose an original method for independent component analysis and blind separation of sources that combines adaptive processing with a simulated annealing technique, and which is applied by normalizing the observed space, $\mathbf{x}(t)$, in a set of concentric p-spheres in order to adaptively compute the slopes corresponding to the independent axes of the mixture distributions by means of an array of symmetrically distributed neurons in each dimension. A preprocessing stage to normalize the observed space is followed by the processing or learning of the neurons, which estimate the high density regions in a way similar, but not identical to that of self organizing maps. A simulated annealing method provides a fast initial movement of the weights towards the independent components by generating random values of the weights and minimizing an energy function, this being a way of improving the performance by speeding up the convergence of the algorithm. The main process for competitive learning when a neuron approaches the density region, in a p-sphere $\rho(k)$ at time t, is given by:

$$w_i(\rho_k, t+1) = w_i(\rho_k, t) + \alpha(t) \cdot f(e(\rho_k, t), w_i(\rho_k, t)) \tag{4}$$

with $\alpha(t)$ being a decreasing learning rate. Note that a variety of suitable functions, $\alpha()$ and $f()$, can be used. In particular, a learning procedure that activates all the neurons at once is enabled by means of a factor, $K(t)$, that modulates competitive learning as in self-organizing systems, i.e.,

$$w_i(\rho_k, t+1) = w_i(\rho_k, t) + \alpha(t) \cdot sign[e(\rho_k, t) - w_i(\rho_k, t)] \cdot K_i(t);$$
$$K_i(t) = \exp(-\eta^{-1}(t) \left\| w_i(\rho_k, t) - w_i^*(\rho_k, t) \right\|^2) \; i^* \subseteq i \in \{1, \dots, 2p\} \tag{5}$$

Simulated annealing is a stochastic algorithm that represents a fast solution to some combinatorial optimization problems. As an alternative to the competitive learning method described above, we first propose the use of stochastic learning, such as simulated annealing, in order to find a fast convergence of the weights around the maximum density points in the observation space $x(t)$. This technique is effective if the chosen energy, or cost function, E_{ij}, for the global system is appropriate. The procedure of simulated annealing is well known [16]. It is first necessary to generate random values of the weights and, secondly, to compute the associated energy of the system. This energy vanishes when the weights achieve a global minimum, the method thus allowing escape from local minima. For the problem of blind separation of sources we define an energy, E, related to the four-order statistics of the original p sources, due to the necessary hypothesis of statistical independence between them, as follows:

$$E = \sum_{i=1}^{p-1} \sum_{j=i+1}^{p} < cum_{22}^2(s_i(t), s_j(t)) > \tag{6}$$

where $cum_{22}(s_i(t), s_j(t))$ is the 2x2 fourth-order cumulant of $s_i(t)$ and $s_j(t)$, and $<x(t)>$ represents the expectation of $x(t)$. In spite of the fact that the technique presented in Section 2.2 is fast, the greater accuracy achieved by means of the competitive learning shown in Section 2.1 led us to consider a new approach. An alternative method for the adaptive computation of the $W\rho_k$ matrix concerns the simultaneous use of the two methods, competitive learning and simulated annealing. Now, a proposed adaptive rule of the weights is the following:

$$w_{ij}(\rho_k, t+1) = w_{ij}^{SA}(\rho_k, t) \cdot \beta(t) + w_{ij}^{CL}(\rho_k, t) \cdot (1 - \beta(t)) \tag{7}$$

2.2 Simulation Results

In Figure 2, we show the first simulation, that corresponds to the synthetic non-linear mixture presented by Lin and Cowan [9], for sharply peaked distributions, the original sources being digital 32-bit signals.

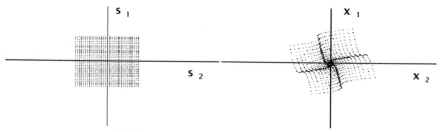

Fig. 2. Non-linear mixture of p=2 sources.

As shown in Figure 3, good estimation of the density distribution is obtained with 20000 samples, and using n=4 p-spheres (p=2).

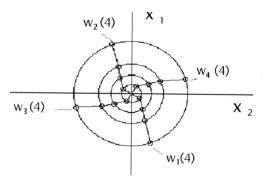

Fig. 3. Network Estimation with SA and CL.

3 Genetic Algorithms

3.1 Algorithm Description

Genetic Algorithms (GAs) are nowadays one of the most popular stochastic optimization techniques. They are inspired by the natural genetics and biological evolutionary process. The GA evaluates a population and generates a new one iteratively, with each successive population referred to as a generation. Given the current generation at iteration t, G(t), the GA generates a new generation, G(t+1), based on the previous generation, applying a set of genetic operations. The GA uses three basic operators to manipulate the genetic composition of a population: reproduction, crossover and mutation [5]. Reproduction consists in copying chromosomes according to their objective function (strings with higher evaluations will have more chances to survive). The crossover operator mixes the genes of two chromosomes selected in the phase of reproduction, in order to combine the features, especially the positive ones of them. Mutation is occasional; it produces with low probability, an alteration of some gene values in a chromosome (for example, in binary representation a 1 is changed into a 0 or vice versa). To perform the GA, first is very important to define the fitness function (or contrast function in BSS context). This fitness function is constructed having in mind that the output sources must be independent from their nonlinear mixtures. For this purpose, we must utilize a measure of independence between random variables. Here, the mutual information is chosen as the measure of independence. Evaluation functions of many forms can be used in a GA, subject to the minimal requirement that the function can map the population into a partially ordered set. As stated, the evaluation function is independent of the GA (i.e., stochastic decision rules). Unfortunately, regarding the separation of a nonlinear mixture, independence only is not sufficient to perform blind recovery of the original signals. Some knowledge of the moments of the sources, in addition to the independence, is required. A similar index as proposed in [16] and [18], is used for the fitness function that approximates mutual information:

$$I(y) \approx -\log|W| - \sum_{i=1}^{n} E\left[\sum_{k=1}^{P} (2k-1)g_{ik} x_i^{2k-2}\right] + \sum_{i=1}^{n} H(y_i) \qquad (8)$$

Values near to zero of mutual information (8) between the y_i imply independence between those variables, being statically independent if $I(y)=0$. In the above expression, the calculation of $H(y_i)$ needs to approximate each marginal probability density function (pdf) of the output source vector y, which are unknown. One useful method is the application of the Gram-Charlier expansion, which only needs some moments of y_i as suggested by Amari et al. [1] to express each marginal pdf of y as:

$$H(y_i) \approx \frac{\log(2\pi e)}{2} - \frac{\left(k_3^i\right)^2}{2 \cdot 3!} - \frac{\left(k_4^i\right)^2}{2 \cdot 4!} + \frac{3}{8}\left(k_3^i\right)^2 k_4^i + \frac{1}{16}\left(k_4^i\right)^3 \qquad (9)$$

where $k_3^i = m_3^i$, and $k_4^i = m_4^i - 3$.

The approximation of entropy (9) is only valid for uncorrelated random variables, being necessary to preprocess the mixed signals (prewhitening) before estimating its mutual information. Whitening or sphering of a mixture of signals consists in filtering the signals so that their covariances are zero (uncorrelatedness), their means are zero, and their variances equal unity. The evaluation function that we compute will be the inverse of mutual information in (8), so that the objective of the GA will be maximizing the following function in order to increase statistical independence between variables:

$$eval\_function(y) = \frac{1}{I(y)} \qquad (10)$$

There is a synergy between Genetic Algorithms and Natural Gradient descent. Given a combination of weights obtained by the genetic algorithms for the nonlinear functions expressed as G= [g1, ..., gn], where the parameter vector that defines each function g_j is expressed by $g_j = [g_{j1}, ..., g_{jp}]$, it is necessary to learn the elements of the linear unmixing matrix W to obtain the output sources y_j. For this task, we use the natural gradient descent method to derive the learning equation for W as proposed in [18]:

$$\Delta W \propto \eta \left| I - \Phi(y)y^T \right| W \tag{11}$$

where

$$\Phi(y) = F_1(k_3, k_4) \circ y^2 + F_2(k_3, k_4) \circ y^3$$

$$F_1(k_3, k_4) = -\frac{1}{2}k_3 + \frac{9}{4}k_3 \cdot k_4 \tag{12}$$

$$F_2(k_3, k_4) = -\frac{1}{6}k_4 + \frac{3}{2}k_3^2 + \frac{3}{4}k_4^2$$

and $\circ$ denotes the Hadamard product of two vectors. The typical genetic operators are crossover and mutation, that will be used for the manipulation of the current population in each iteration of the GA. The crossover operator is „Simple One-point Crossover". The mutation operator is „Non-Uniform Mutation" [11]. This operator presents the advantage when compared to the classical uniform mutation operator, of performing less significant changes to the genes of the chromosome as the number of generations grows. This property makes the exploration-exploitation trade-off be more favorable to exploration in the early stages of the algorithm, while exploitation takes more importance when the solution given by the GA is closer to the optimal solution.

3.2 Simulation Results

To provide an experimental demonstration of the validity of GABSS, we will use a system of three sources. Two of the sources are sinusoidal, while the third is a random signal, uniformly distributed in [-1, 1] (uniform noise). The independent sources and the 3x3 mixture matrix are:

$$s(t) = \begin{bmatrix} \sin(2\pi \cdot 30t + 6 \cdot \cos(2\pi \cdot 6t)), \\ sign[\sin(2\pi \cdot 20t)], \\ rand(t) \end{bmatrix} \quad A = \begin{bmatrix} 0.6420 & 0.5016 & 0.4863 \\ 0.3347 & 0.82243 & -0.6150 \\ 0.3543 & -0.3589 & 0.542 \end{bmatrix} \tag{13}$$

The nonlinear distortion are selected as:
1: $f_1(x) = Tanh(x)$,   2: $f_2(x) = Tanh(0.8x)$,   3: $f_3(x) = Tanh(0.5x)$
The goal of the simulation was to analyse the behaviour of the GA and observe whether the fitness function thus achieved is optimised; with this aim, therefore, we studied the mixing matrix obtained by the algorithm and the inverse function. When

the number of generations reached a maximum value, the best individual from the population was selected and the estimated signals u were extracted, using the mixing matrix W, and the inverse function. Figure 4 represents the 1000 samples from the original signals. Figure 5, on the left, represents the mixed signals, and on the right shows the separated signals obtained with the proposed algorithm. As it can be seen signals are very similar to the original ones, up to possible scaling factors and permutations of the sources. Figure 6, on the left, compares the approximation of the functions g_i to the inverse of f_i and Figure 6, on the right, shows the joint representation of the original, mixed and obtained signals. In this practical application, the population size was $population_{size} = 20$ and the number of generations was $generation_{number} = 40$. Regarding genetic operators parameters, crossover probability per chromosome was $p_c = 0.8$ and mutation probability per gene was $p_m = 0.01$. As an special parameter for the non-uniform mutation operator $b=5$.

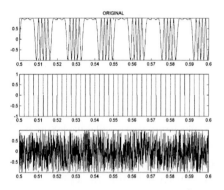

Fig. 4. Original signals

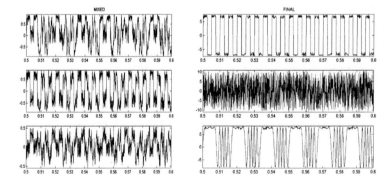

Fig. 5. Mixed signals (left) and separated signals (right).

4 Conclusion

We have shown a new, powerful adaptive-geometric method based on competitive unsupervised learning and simulated annealing, which finds the distribution axes of the observed signals or independent components by means of a piecewise linearization in the mixture space, the use of simulated annealing in the optimization of a four-order statistical criterion being an experimental advance. The algorithm, in its current form, presents some drawbacks concerning the application of simulated annealing to a high number, p, of signals, and the complexity of the procedure $O(2^p p^2 n)$ for the separation of nonlinear mixtures, that also depends on the number, n, of p-spheres. In spite of these questions that remain open, the time convergence of the network is fast, even for more than two subgaussian or supergaussian signals, mainly due to the initial simulated annealing process that provides a good starting point with a low computation cost, and the accuracy of the network is adequate for the separation task, the competitive learning being very precise, as several experiments have corroborated. Besides the study of noise, future work will concern the application of this method to independent component analysis with linear and nonlinear mixtures of biomedical signals, such as in Electroencephalograph and functional Magnetic Resonance Imaging, where the number of signals increases sharply, making simulated annealing suitable in a quantized high-dimensional space. Despite the diversity of the approaches to blind separation of sources, the fundamental idea of the source signals being statistically independent remains the single most important assumption in most of these schemes. The neural network approach has the drawback that it may be trapped into local minima and therefore it does not always guarantee optimal system performance.

This article discusses, also, a satisfactory application of genetic algorithms to the complex problem of the blind separation of sources. It is widely believed that the specific potential of genetic or evolutionary algorithms originates from their parallel search by means of entire populations. In particular, the ability of escaping from local optima is an ability very unlikely to be observed in steepest-descent methods. Although to date, and to the best of the authors' knowledge, there is no mention in the literature of this synergy between GAs and BSS in nonlinear mixtures, the article shows how GAs provide a tool that is perfectly valid as an approach to this problem.

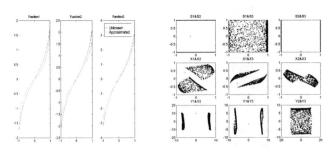

Fig. 6. Comparison of the unknown f_i^{-1} and its approximation by g_i (left), and representation of the original (S), mixed (X), and obtained (Y) signals (right).

Acknowledgement. This work has been partially supported by the CICYT Spanish Project TIC2000-1348 and TIC2001-2845.

References

1. S-I. Amari, A.Cichocki, H.Yang, „A New Learning Algorithm for Blind Signal Separation", In Advances in Neural Information Processing Systems, vol.8, (1996).
2. A. Bell & T.J. Sejnowski: An Information-Maximization Approach to Blind Separation and Blind Deconvolution. Neural Computation 1129–59 (1995).
3. G.Burel, „Blind separation of sources: A nonlinear neural algorithm", Neural Networks, vol.5, pp. 937–947, (1992).
4. J.F.Cardoso, „Source separation using higher order moments", Proc. ICASSP, Glasgow, U.K. May (1989), pp. 2109–2212.
5. D.E. Goldberg, "Genetic Algorithms in Search, Optimization and Machine Learning", AddisonWesley, Reading, MA, (1989).
6. Hyvärinen, J. Karhunen y E.Oja, Independent Component Analysis. J. Wiley-Interscience. (2001).
7. A.Hyvärinen and E.Oja, A fast fixed-point algorithm for independent component analysis. Neural Computation, 9 (7), pp.1483–1492, (1997).
8. T-W.Lee, B.Koehler, R.Orglmeister, „Blind separation of nonlinear mixing models", In IEEE NNSP, pp. 406–415, Florida, USA, (1997).
9. J.K.Lin, D.G.Grier, J.D.Cowan, „Source separation and density estimation by faithful equivariant SOM", in Advances in Neural Information Processing Systems. Cambridge, MA: MIT Press, (1997), vol.9.
10. A.Mansour, C.Jutten, P.Loubaton, „Subspace method for blind separation of sources in convolutive mixtures", in Proc. EUSIPCO, Trieste, Italy, (1996), pp. 2081-2084.
11. Z. Michalewicz, Genetic Algorithms + Data Structures = Evolution Programs, Springer-Verlag, New York USA, Third Edition, (1999).
12. A.V. Oppenheim, E. Weinstein, K.C. Zangi, M. Feder, and D. Gauger. Single-sensor active noise cancellation. IEEE Trans. on speech and audio processing, 2(2):285–290, (1994).
13. P.Pajunen, A.Hyvarinen, J.Karhunen, „Nonlinear blind source separation by self-organizing maps", in Progress in Neural Information Processing: Proc. IONIP'96, vol.2. New York, (1996), pp. 1207–1210.
14. C.G.Puntonet, A.Prieto, "Neural net approach for blind separation of sources based on geometric properties", Neurocomputing, 18 (3), (1998), pp. 141–164.
15. A.Taleb, C.Jutten, „Source Separation in Post-Nonlinear Mixtures", IEEE Transactions on Signal Processing, vol.47 no.10, pp. 2807–2820 (1999).
16. Y.Tan, J.Wang, J.M.Zurada, „Nonlinear Blind Source Separation Using a Radial Basis Function Network", IEEE Trans. On Neural Networks, vol.12, no.1, pp.124-134, (2001).
17. H.L.N.Thi, C.Jutten, „Blind sources separation for convolutive mixtures", Signal Process., vol.45, pp. 209–229, (1995).
18. H.H.Yang, S.Amari, A.Chichocki, „Information-theoretic approach to blind separation of sources in non-linear mixture", Signal Processing, vol.64, (1998), 291–300.
19. D.Yellin, E.Weinstein, „Multichannel signal separation: Methods and analysis", IEEE Trans. Signal Processing, vol.44, pp. 106–118, Jan. (1996).

A Neural Associative Pattern Classifier

Francisco J. López Aligué, Isabel Acevedo Sotoca, Ignacio Alvarez Troncoso,
Carlos J. García Orellana, and Horacio González Velasco

Dept. of Electronics, Faculty of Sciences, University of Extremadura, Avda. de Elvas, s/n. 06071
Badajoz, Spain. aligue@unex.es

Abstract. In this work, we study the behaviour of the Bidirectional Associative
Memory (BAM) in terms of the supporting neural structure, with a view to its
possible improvements as a useful Pattern Classifier by means of class associations
from unknown inputs, once mentioned classes have been previously defined by
one or even more prototypes. The best results have been obtained by suitably
choosing the training pattern pairs, the thresholds, and the activation functions
of the network's neurones, by means of certain proposed methods described in
the paper. In order to put forward the advantages of these proposed methods, the
classifier has been applied on an especially popular hand-written character set
as the well-known NIST#19 character database, and with one of the UCI's data
bases. In all cases, the method led to a marked improvement in the performance
achievable by a BAM, with a 0% error rate.

1 Introduction

We present a design for a two-layer neural network, adapted from the conventional BAM
structure, and specifically aimed at the classification of characters in the strong presence
of noise or distortion. To achieve classification results that are completely error free, we
defined a method of prototype selection in the training set, and a new formulation of the
thresholds and the activity function of the neurons of the network. The classifier was
tested on two widely accepted databases - NIST #19 and UCI. In all cases, even under
unfavourable conditions, the success rate was 100%.

The application of associative memories to Pattern Recognition has been one of the
most popular lines of research for some time now. Some significant theoretical studies
in this field appeared in the sixties (see [1] , [2] and [3]). A network model was first
established in work by Kosko [4] and showed a high degree of immunity to noise and
distortions. After these first studies, there appeared operational neural models known as
Willshaw models, which incorporated Hebbian learning in binary synapses and hetero-
associative one-step retrieval [5]. There followed a number of developments aimed at
improving the efficiency of these associative memories, with an analysis of all potential
modifications of the elements of the process and of the retrieval methods [6].

Different training methods were described in the years following Kosko's original
work to attempt to ensure the recognition of all the pairs presented to a BAM. Two
encoding strategies were proposed in [7]: multiple training and dummy augmentation.
Then the recovery of all the pairs was guaranteed using the multiple training method

F.J. Garijo, J.C. Riquelme, and M. Toro (Eds.): IBERAMIA 2002, LNAI 2527, pp. 430–439, 2002.
© Springer-Verlag Berlin Heidelberg 2002

[8], and the same method was applied to the "back-propagation" algorithm for use in associative memories [9].

At around the same time, a method based on Housenholder transformations was proposed [10] to ensure that the pairs give rise to energy function minima. In doubling the number of connections, this method has the drawback that the evolution of the network may enter a cycle and not converge to a stable state. An improvement was later proposed in [11] which ensured convergence by avoiding such cycles. Two learning algorithms were proposed in [12] which improved Kosko and Wang's results. Amongst other later methods, we might cite that of Arthithan & Dasgupta [13] who approach the problem of the network's recognition of all the pairs and its behaviour with respect to noise. Other forms of altering the characteristics of a BAM may be found in the literature (see [14] , [15] , [16] and [17]). Recently, a three-layer feedforward implementation has been proposed [18] which guarantees secure recall for a determined number of associated pairs, and one finds in [19] one of the last attempts to increase a BAM's recall capacity. An extensive review of the state-of-the art of all the methods used up to now can be found in [20].

For the Associative Memories implemented by means of neural networks, there have been studies of methods of improving their capacity for storage and retrieval as a function of the neuron thresholds for the case of totally interconnected networks [21], for partially connected networks, which are closer to real biological structures [22], and even for such specific structures as cellular neural networks, ([23] , [24]).

2   Architecture of the Classifier System

There are two clearly differentiated units in our system. On the one hand there is an optional geometrical-type preprocessor responsible for eliminating the topological components in cases in which the image aspect of the input character to be classified is important, as is the case with alphanumeric characters, certain kinds of images, etc. On the other hand, after this pre-processor, there is the neural network itself responsible for the definitive classification of the input. Basically then, this is a two-layer, BAM-type associative memory, in which the inputs of each layer's neurons are totally connected to the outputs of the previous layer's neurons, but there exist no sideways connections within any given layer. The neurons of the first layer (the "input" layer in conventional BAM nomenclature) are defined by the expression

$$y_j = F(I_j) = F(\sum_{i=1}^{N} m_{ji} \cdot x_{ki} - \theta_l) \tag{1}$$

where "I_j" represents the excitation coming from the second layer's neurons. With respect to the latter, the main difference is that the threshold term "θ_j" does not appear in their function. The significance of this will be seen below. Neither is the function F(.) the same. Whereas for the second layer, the usual sigmoid or the step functions are used, for the first we chose a multi-step function for the reasons that we will present below in discussing the "dead zone". The network functions under the control of a supervisory unit which, when it detects that the input has been assigned to a class, halts the oscillating cycle that is characteristic of this type of memory. This network is conceived for classification of its inputs, so that, unlike the typical BAM formulation, and even though it is a hetero-associative type of memory, the second character set is fixed beforehand and corresponds to what we shall denominate a set of "class" vectors $\{V_i\} = (V_{i1}, V_{i2}, \dots, V_{i26})$, that belongs to a canonical structured set with equidistance 2 as in [25], so that one and only one of its components - that which indicates the numeral of the class - is "1" and the rest are "0":

$$
\begin{aligned}
V_1 &= (1, 0, 0, \dots, 0) \\
V_2 &= (0, 1, 0, \dots, 0) \\
V_3 &= (0, 0, 1, \dots, 0) \\
&\ \ \vdots \\
V_{26} &= (0, 0, \dots, 0, 1)
\end{aligned}
$$

Thus, for example, we construct the pairs

$$\{A, V_1\}, \{B, V_2\}, \dots \{Z, V_{26}\}. \tag{2}$$

then we obtain a new set of pairs $\{X_1, Y_1\}, \{X_2, Y_2\}, \dots, \{X_{26}, Y_{26}\}$, where $\{X_i\}$ is the set of vectors obtained by bipolarization from the prototype set $\{A, B, C, \dots, Z\}$ and $\{Y_i\}$ the bipolar vectors computed from the class vectors $\{V_1, V_2, V_3, \dots, V_{26}\}$. We thus have the Relation Matrix constructed according to its original definition, but with elements that are much easier to calculate, since, from (2), we have

$$M = \sum_{i=1}^{N} X_i^T \cdot Y_i = \begin{pmatrix} m_{11} & \cdots & m_{1N} \\ \vdots & \ddots & \vdots \\ m_{P1} & \cdots & m_{PN} \end{pmatrix} \tag{3}$$

due to the fact that one is dealing with class vectors, one can verify that the column vectors of the relation matrix have the following structure:

$$m_i^T = X_i^T + \sum_{\substack{j=1 \\ j \neq i}}^{N} X_j^{cT} \tag{4}$$

where X_i^{cT} is the conjugate vector of X_i^T.

At this point, let us suppose that a prototype A_k, $k = 1, \dots, Q$, is presented at the first layer, and A_k belongs to class "j". Since, as was stated above, the first layer has Q neurons with P inputs each, each neuron receives an excitation resulting from equation (5) which is:

$$I_j = \sum_{\substack{i=1 \\ j=1,\dots,Q}}^{P} x_{ki} \cdot m_{ij} = X_k \cdot m_j = X_k(X_j^T + \sum_{\substack{l=1 \\ l \neq j}}^{Q} X_l^{cT}). \tag{5}$$

This constitutes the complete expression that defines the excitation which each neuron of a layer receives from the other layer. We shall see that this expression will be highly useful in the following section.

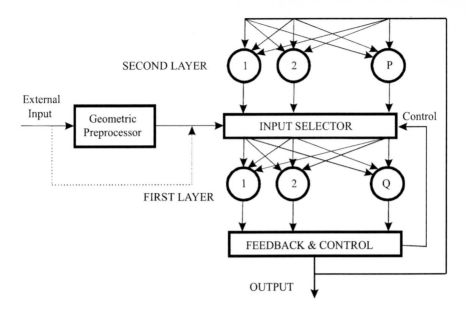

Fig. 1. Block Diagram of the proposed pattern classifier

Figure 1 shows the block diagram of our classifier. The external input can be fed into the memory either directly or by way of the geometrical preprocessor.

For this purpose, we take advantage of the input selection unit which also serves to switch the signals that arrive at the first layer, selecting between the external input – the first activation of the BAM - and the outputs from the second layer – the normal running cycle. In accordance with its definition, the first layer (so called the input layer) has N neurons, the same number as classes, and the second layer (the feedback layer) has P neurons, corresponding to the dimension of input characters to be classified. Each neuron of the first layer has P inputs, one for every output of the second layer, whereas the neurons of the second layer have N inputs, connected to the outputs of the N neurons of the first layer. With this arrangement, imposed by the classical definition of the BAM, the number of neurons and the inputs are perfectly known from the outset. The remaining point is to decide the threshold θ_j of the neural functions, as well as the particular form of the activity function F(.). This will be the main objective of the following section.

3   The Adaptive Mechanism

The reason for this classifier's success resides in its adaptive process, which really begins with the selection of the training set. Indeed, the process of training the network is initiated with the selection of prototypes, with one prototype being chosen for each class. The choice is made by the method of greatest difference, seeking those characters, which provoke the greatest excitation I_j in the neuron of their class, and the least in the others. This process is performed under the control of a specific subprogram, and only takes place at the moment of choosing the classes that one wants to use. In this way, with all the prototypes not belonging to class "j", we have the maximum excitation at the j-neuron with $\mathbf{X_k} \in \mathbf{A_k} \neq$ Prototype $\mathbf{A_j}$,

$$MaxI_k = Max(\sum_{i=1}^{P} w_{ij} \cdot x_{ki}) \qquad (6)$$

which means that the maximum of the excitation coming from the prototypes of the class differs from the excitation for the prototypes of the remaining classes by at least a quantity that can be calculated as

$$\varepsilon_j = I_j - Max\ I_k. \qquad (7)$$

We can now define the specific function of each of the first layer's neurons:

$$y_j = F(\sum_{i=1}^{P} w_{ij} \cdot x_i - (\varepsilon_j - \chi)) \qquad (8)$$

This replaces the initial definition (1). A "fudge" term χ has been introduced into this equation which avoids the possibility that there may at some moment appear an input of another class but of greater similarity to the prototype than those used in the initial calculation.

4   The Dead Zone

One of the other possible ways of increasing the networks' storage capacity is to alter the shape of the activity function. Examples in the literature are the improvements of the models produced by changing the traditional function to one that is non-monotonic [26], or even using networks with a low activity level. We shall now analyze the improvement in classical performance given by changing the activity function to a form similar to that of multi-step activation functions ([27] , [28]) or even more similar to the ternary neurons [29]. Stability is the main problem that arises, together with the elimination of the noise and distortions that have been studied so far. If we present the network with an arbitrary external input, it will begin to oscillate in attempting to stabilize at a point of minimum energy near that input. If the neurons are excessively sensitive, it may occur that this result is not attained, in that any variation in the excitation provoked by a variation in the input alters sharply and unforeseeably the value of the output. We should therefore try to restrict, within certain limits for each class, the states of excitation to which the neurons should respond. It is a matter of endowing the neurons of the system with a variable degree of stability so that they are able to maintain the output constant against distorted inputs without having to completely reprogram the neural network, and so that the said neurons do not fire by mistake in response to inputs that are highly distorted or noisy. In order to modulate the sensitivity of the neurons, we propose defining a safety margin for each class, to thereby ensure that the neurons responsible for the prototype classification do not generate outputs of value "+1" in response to the prototypes of the other classes. To this end, we choose the following model of neuron function:

$$F(x) = \begin{cases} +1 & \text{if } x > \eta^+ \\ 0 & \text{if } \eta^- \le x \le \eta^+ \\ -1 & \text{if } x \le \eta^- \end{cases} \tag{9}$$

Figure 2 shows the plot of this function. With the introduction of the dead zone term into

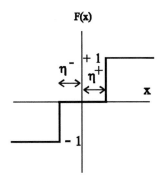

Fig. 2. The neuronal function with the dead zone term η

the neuron function, we get the neurons to fire within the limits learnt as the "allowed excitation limits of the class". In this way, the response to the presence of an unknown input to the network will be closer to the response that we have stored for the prototype of its class. With this premise, one can expect that the network will have a maximum degree of efficiency for pattern classification, since we have two ways to suppress the overlap noise and ensure convergence of the network - the threshold and the dead zone. The general output function for the first-layer neurons will now be put into the following form:

$$y_j = F(I_j, \eta_j) = \begin{cases} +1 & \text{if } I_j > \eta^+ \\ 0 & \text{if } \eta^- \le I_j \le \eta^+ \\ -1 & \text{if } I_j \le \eta^- \end{cases} \tag{10}$$

with the conditions $Max\{I_i\} \le \eta_j^-$; $min\{I_j\} \ge \eta_j^+$; $i \ne j$, where $\{I_i\}$ is the strongest excitation received from the prototypes of the other classes, as was defined in (6), while min $\{I_j\}$ is the minimum excitation provoked by some prototype of the class "j" in question. In this equation, F is the neural function defined in Equation (9) and η_j is each neuron's dead zone term.

5   Results

To evaluate our system's performance, we first chose one of the most widely used and universally accepted character sets, the NIST#19 (see [30]), handwritten character database,

Table 1. Classification success rate (per cent) in a scan of the threshold value $\Delta\theta$ (in hundreds) on characters of the NIST alphabet. Here, θ_j^{ini} is an a priori defined threshold value

		$\Delta\theta$							
Prot.	θ_j^{ini}	0	20	40	80	90	100	115	130
a	17384	4	100	100	100	100	100	25	0
b	17820	0	10	100	100	100	100	45	0
c	17176	0	85	100	100	100	95	25	0
d	18056	0	90	100	100	100	100	50	0
e	18012	0	65	100	100	100	100	80	0
f	16096	0	35	100	100	100	100	100	15
g	16366	0	15	100	100	100	100	55	0
h	17548	0	0	100	100	100	100	909	0
i	16242	0	100	100	100	100	100	75	0
j	14370	0	95	100	100	100	100	0	0
k	18666	0	70	100	100	90	95	0	0
l	18646	20	100	100	100	100	100	65	0
m	18194	70	100	100	100	95	35	0	0
n	17298	20	100	100	100	100	60	0	0
o	16276	0	100	100	100	100	100	85	0
p	14992	0	65	100	100	100	100	100	0
q	16524	0	95	100	100	100	100	85	20
r	16406	0	90	100	100	100	100	100	90
s	16904	0	80	100	100	100	95	30	0
t	16134	0	0	100	100	100	100	95	0
u	15844	5	70	100	100	100	95	30	0
v	14244	0	75	100	100	100	100	70	0
w	15520	25	100	100	100	90	75	15	0
x	15976	0	45	100	100	95	50	0	0
y	16436	0	35	100	100	100	95	20	0
z	15636	25	100	100	100	95	90	55	0

and then, as a completely different case to study, which means that we do not handle inputs with a topologically-characterized structure, we tested our improved BAM as Pattern Classifier on a database of the also well-known UCI (see [31]). As a simple test example, we chose the DISPLAY 1 database, consisting of a set of binary "characters" representing either the excitation state or extinction state of the lighting segments which form a common lighting diode-based display. In all the cases, a 100% level of success was attained, even in the presence of up to 40% noise. The processing speed was high: more than 200 characters per second on a personal computer running a Pentium III at 600 MHz.

The NIST#19 database is a collection prepared by the National Institute of Standards and Technology of the USA from earlier databases. It contains binary images of 3699 forms filled in in long-hand, and 814 255 alphanumeric characters taken from those forms. The isolated characters are 128x128 pixels in size, and are grouped into 62 classes which correspond to the upper and lower case letters of the English alphabet and the digits "0" to "9". This database may be regarded as the most widely accepted selection of characters for the training and testing of optical character recognition systems.

The characters are grouped into divisions according to how they were extracted from the forms. Examples of these divisions are: by writer, by position in the form (the box for dates, etc.), and, of most interest for our purposes, by class, with a selection of the same character (the letter "a", or the number "7", for instance) from different writers. The forms used consisted of 34 fields: name and date, city/state, 28 digit fields, a field of lower case letters, another of upper case, and finally a paragraph taken from the constitution of the USA written freestyle. The writers were personnel from the Census Bureau from all the states of the US and high-school students in Bethesda, Maryland. We formed the Training Set using a pseudo-random selection program, taking a single character for each letter from the character files of the NIST#19 database. The Test Set was constructed using all the remaining elements from each of the files used for the previous selection. Given that the NIST files contain around 400 characters each, the components of the test set clearly constitute an ample and varied spectrum of images on which to test the neural network's capacities in classification tasks.

Finally, Table 1 lists the results obtained on the whole test set as the threshold is varied of the different neurons associated with each class. The table gives the correct classification results in a rail-to-rail threshold scan on each group of characters of the NIST alphabet. The equation governing the threshold scan is $\theta_j = \theta_j^{ini} + \Delta\theta$ where $\Delta\theta$ is expressed in hundreds. Thus the threshold of, for instance, the class "a" neuron varies between 17 384 (the value obtained from the character used as prototype) and 30 384 (= 17 384 + 13 000).

As a completely different case of study, which means that we do not manage inputs with a topological-characterized structure, we have tested our improved BAM as Pattern Classifier on a database of the too well known UCI [31]. Concretely, and as a simple test example, we have chosen the DISPLAY 1 database, constituted by a set of binary "characters" representing either the excitation state or extinction state of the lighting segments which form a common lighting diode-based Display.

The obtained results can be seen at Table 2.

Table 2. Success rates (also in %)for the different noise inputs obtained with the DISPLAY 1 database

Stochastic Noise	Classification Success
0	100
10	100
30	85
40	78

It is important to see, that a noise around 40% means a variation of the statement of the led set that form the digit in the display, over a half of them, leading the system (in most of cases) to a misclassification state of the net for the corrupted input character, due to the fact, that it is formed by 7 attributes, since, coincidences between inputs become unsolvable, being the input involved in such a distortion level. In [31] can be found the obtained results for this database using several techniques of Pattern Classification:

1. With 200 training and 5000 test instances:
   - Optimal Bayes classification rate: 74%
   - CART decision tree: (resubstitution estimate)   71%
   - Nearest Neighbour Algorithm: 71%
2. With 2000 training and 500 test instances:
   - C4 decision tree algorithm: (pessimistic pruning)   72.6%
3. With 400 training and 500 test cases:
   - IWN system: (And-OR algorithm)   73.3%

Acknowledgements. The authors wish to express their gratitude to the Spanish C.I.C.Y.T. and to the Junta de Extremadura for their support of this work through grants TIC2001-0881 and 2PR01-A007, respectively.

References

[1] Steinbuch, K.: Die Lernmatrix. Kybernetik. **1** (1991) 36-45
[2] Anderseon, F. A.: A Simple Neural Network Generating an inter-ctive Memory. Mathematical Biosciences. **14** (1972) 197-220
[3] Kohonen, T.: Associtive Memory: A System-heoretical Approach. Springer Verlag, New York (1977)
[4] Kosko, B.: Bidirectional Associative Memories. IEEE Trans. on Systems, Man and Cybernetics **18(1)** (1988) 49–60
[5] Willshaw, D. J., Buneman, O. P., Longuet, H. C.: Nonholographic Associative Memory. Nature **222** (1969) 960–962. Reprinted in Anderson & Rosenfeld (eds.), Neurocomputing: Foundation of Research, MIT Press, Cam. (1998)
[6] Sommer, F.T., Palm, G.: Improved Bidirectional Retrieval of Sparse Patterns Stored by Hebbian Learning. Neural Networks **12(2)** (1999) 281–297
[7] Wang, Y. F., Cruz, J. B., Mulligan, J. H.: Two Coding Strategies for Bidirectional Associative Memory. IEEE Trans. on Neural Networks **1(1)** (1991) 81–82
[8] Wang, Y. F., Cruz, J. B., Mulligan, J. H.: Guaranteed Recall of all Trainig Patterns for Bidirectional Associative Memory. IEEE Trans. on Neural Networks **2(6)** (1991) 559–567
[9] Wang, Y. F., Cruz, J. B., Mulligan, J. H.: Multiple Trainig Concept for Back-Propagation Neural-Networks for use in Associative Memories. Neural Networks **6** (1993) 1169-1175
[10] Leung, C. S., Cheung, K. F.: Householder Encoding for Discrete Bidirectional Associative Memory.Proc. of the IJCNN'91 **1** (1991) 124–137
[11] Leung. C. S.: Encoding Method for Bidirectional Associative Memory Using Projection on Convex Sets. IEEE Trans. on Neural Networks **4(5)** (1993) 879–881
[12] Zhuang, X., Huang, Y., Chen, S-S.: Better Learning for Bidirectional Associative Memory. Neural networks **6** (1993) 1131–1146
[13] Arthithan, G., Dasgupta, G.: On Problem of Spurious Patterns in Neural Associtive Memory Models. IEEE Trans. on Neural Networks **8(6)** (1997) 1483–1491
[14] WJeng, Y. C., Teh. C. C.: Modified Intraconnected Bidirectional Associtive Memory. IEE Electronic Letters **27(20)** (1998) 1818–1819

[15] Lee, D.L.: Generalized Intraconnected Bidirectional Associtive Memories. IEE Electronic Letters **34(8)** (1998) 736–738

[16] Heekuck, O. H., Kothari, S. C.: Adaptation of the Relaxation Method for Learning in Bidirectional Associative Memory. IEEE Trans. on Neural Networks **5(4)** (1994) 576–583

[17] Simpson, P. K.: Higher-Ordered and Intraconnected Bidirectional Associtive Memories. IEEE Trans. on System, Man and Cybernetics 2 **20(3)** (1990) 637–653

[18] Park, J., Kim, H-Y, Park, Y., Lee, S-W.: A Synthesis procedure for Associtive Memories Based on Space-varying cellular Neural Networks. Neural Networks **14(1)** (2001) 107–113

[19] Muller, P., Rios, D.: Issues in Bayesian Analysis of Neural Network Models. Neural Computation **10** (1995) 571–592

[20] Arica, N., Yarman-Vural, T.: An Overview of Character recognition Focused on Off-line Handwriting.IEEE Trans. on Systems, MAn and Cybernetics - Part C. **31(2)** (2001) 216–233

[21] Wu, Y., Pados, D. A.: A Feedforward Bidirectional Associtive Memory. IEEE Trans. on Neural Networks **11(4)** (2000) 859–866

[22] Nadal, J. P., Toulouse, G.: Information Storage in Sparsely Coded Memory Nets. Network **1** (1990) 61–74

[23] Buckingham, J., Willshaw, D.: On Setting Unit Thresholds in an Incompletely Connected Associtive Net. Networks **4** (1993) 441–459

[24] Chua, L. O., Yang, L.: Cellular Neural Networks: Theory and Applications. IEEE Trans. on Circuits and Systems **35** (1988) 1257–1290

[25] Kumar, S.: Memory Anhilitaion of Structured Maps in Bidirectional Associtive Memories. IEEE Trans. on Neural Networks **11(4)** (2000) 1023–1038

[26] Crespi, B.: Storage Capacity of Non-monotonic Neurons. Neural Networks **12(10)** (1999) 1376–1389

[27] Alippi, C., Piuri, V., Sami, M.: Sensitivity to Errors in Artificial Neural Networks: A Behavioral Approach. Proc. of the IEEE Intl. Symp. on Circuits and Systems. (1994) 1376–1389

[28] Kretzschmar, R., Karayannis, N. B., Richner, H.: NEURO-BRA: A Bird Removal for Wind Profiler Data Based on Quantum Neural Networks. Proc. of the IJCNN'2000,4 (2000) 373–378

[29] Bollé, D., Domínguez, D. R., Amari, S. I.: Mutual Information of Sparsely Coded Associtive Memory with Self-Control and Ternary Neurons. Neural Networks **13 (4-5)** (2000) 455–462

[30] NIST Special Data Base #19: Image Processing Group. Advanced Systems Division. National Institute of Standards and Technology.(1995)

[31] Merz, C. J., Murphy, P. M.: UCI Repository of Machine Learning Databases. (1998). Available at http://www.ics.uci.edu/~mlearn/MLRepository.html

[32] Quinlan, J. R.: Simplifying Decision Trees. International Journal of Man-Machine Studies, (1987)

[33] Tan, M., Eshelman, L.: Using Weighted Networks to Represent Classificatioin Knowledge in Noysi Domains. Morgan Kaufmann (eds.), Proc. of the 5th Intl. Conf. on Machine Learning (1988) 121–134

Rule Extraction from Radial Basis Function Networks by Using Support Vectors

Haydemar Núñez[1,3], Cecilio Angulo[1,2], and Andreu Català[1,2]

[1]Dept. of Systems Engineering, Polytechnical University of Catalonia
Avda. Victor Balaguer s/n E-08800 Vilanova i la Geltrú, Spain
{hnunez,cangulo}@esaii.upc.es
[2]LEA-SICA. European Associated Lab.
Intelligent Systems and Advanced Control
Rambla de l'Exposió s/n E-08028 Vilanova i la Geltrú. Spain
andreu.catala@upc.es
[3]Universidad Central de Venezuela. Facultad de Ciencias. Escuela de
Computación. Caracas, Venezuela
hnunez@kuaimare.ciens.ucv.ve

Abstract. In this paper, a procedure for rule extraction from radial basis function networks (RBFNs) is proposed. The algorithm is based on the use of a support vector machine (SVM) as a frontier pattern selector. By using geometric methods, centers of the RBF units are combined with support vectors in order to construct regions (ellipsoids or hyper-rectangles) in the input space, which are later translated to if-then rules. Additionally, the support vectors are used to determine overlapping between classes and to refine the rule base. The experimental results indicate that a very high fidelity between RBF network and the extracted set of rules can be achieved with low overlapping between classes.

1 Introduction

Neural networks (NNs) have been considered powerful universal predictors. They have shown very good performance in solving complex problems. However, one of their main drawbacks is that they generate black box models: Trained NNs do not have the ability to explain, in an understandable form, the process by of which the exit takes place. In the last years, there has been a widespread activity aimed to redressing this situation by extracting the embedded knowledge in trained neural networks in the form of symbolic rules [1],[5],[20],[21]. In addition to provide NNs with explanatory power, these rule extraction methods have other several purposes: knowledge acquisition for symbolic AI systems, data exploration, development of hybrid architectures [23] and improved adequacy for data mining applications [15],[24].

In this paper, a procedure for rule extraction from radial basis function networks (RBFNs) is proposed. RBF networks [2],[10],[11],[16],[17] have gained considerable attention as an alternative to multilayer perceptrons (MLPs) trained by the backpropagation algorithm. The advantages of RBF networks, such as linearity in the parameters and the availability of fast and efficient training methods have been noted

F.J. Garijo, J.C. Riquelme, and M. Toro (Eds.): IBERAMIA 2002, LNAI 2527, pp. 440–449, 2002.
© Springer-Verlag Berlin Heidelberg 2002

in many publications. The local nature of RBF networks makes them an interesting platform for performing rule extraction (in contrast with the distributed nature of the knowledge representation in MLPs). However, the basis functions overlap to some grade in order to give a relatively smooth representation of the distribution of training data [2],[16]. This overlapping is a shortcoming for rule extraction.

Few rule extraction methods directed to RBF networks have been developed until now [3],[9],[12],[13]. To avoid the overlapping, most of them are using special training regimes [9],[12] or special architectures [3] in order to guarantee that RBF nodes are assigned and used by a single class. Our algorithm does not suppose any training method or special architecture; it extracts rules from an ordinary RBF network. In order to solve the overlapping, a support vector machine (SVM) is used [4],[6],[22]. The decision functions of SVMs are constructed from a subset of the training data called support vectors (SV). These vectors lie in the proximity of the classification border. Therefore, we use the SVM as a frontier pattern selector. Support vectors are used in our algorithm in two forms: (1) to delimit ellipsoids constructed in the input space, which will be translated to rules, (2) to determine overlapping between classes and to refine the rule base.

This paper is organized as follows: the foundations of the RBF networks are exposed in the next section. The rule extraction method is described in section 3. Then, section 4 describes experimental results of our method, applied to several data sets. Finally, we present the conclusions and future work.

2 Radial Basis Function Networks

A RBF network consists on feedforward architecture, with an input layer, a hidden layer of basis functions and an output layer of linear units. The response of the output units is calculated using Eq. 1. Each unit k in the hidden layer has a center o prototype v_k. The corresponding nonlinear activation function ϕ_k expresses the similarity between any input pattern x and the center v_k by means of a distance measure. Weight w_{ik} represents the connection between the hidden unit k and the output unit i and w_{i0} the threshold value of output unit i. The most commonly employed radial basis function is the Gaussian. In this case, the center v_k of the function ϕ_k defines the prototype of input cluster k and the variance σ_k the size of the covered region in the input space.

$$f_i(x) = \sum_{k=1}^{m} w_{ik}\phi_k\left(\frac{\|x - v_k\|}{\alpha_k}\right) + w_{i0} \tag{1}$$

Training on RBF networks is a fast two-stage procedure: (1) Unsupervised learning of basis function parameters; that is, the centers v_k and widths σ_k are either fixed a priori or selected based on the x-values of the training examples. (2) Supervised learning of weights via linear least squares. In order to select the centers, it is possible to use several approaches. One of them consists on taking every training sample as a center. This usually results in overfitting, unless penalty is added to the empirical risk functional. Most methods select centers as representative prototypes via methods as k-means o SOM. Other approaches include modeling the input distribution as a mixture model and estimating the centers via the EM algorithm; and a greedy strategy for sequential addition of new basis functions centered on each training sample. The widths σ_k of the RBF units are determined using various P-nearest-neighbor heuristics, to achieve a certain amount of response overlap between each RBF unit and its neighbors, so that a smooth and continuous interpolation of the input space is obtained.

3 Rule Extraction Algorithm

Our proposal for rule extraction from RBF networks is based on the use a support vector machine as a frontier pattern selector. Support vectors establish the boundaries between classes. Using geometric methods, the centers of the RBF nodes are combined with the support vectors in order to determine the boundaries of regions defined in the input space (ellipsoids or hyper-rectangles). Each region will define a rule with its corresponding syntax (Fig. 1): equation rules, which correspond to mathematical equations of the ellipsoids and interval rules, associated with hyper-rectangles defined from parallel ellipsoids to the coordinate axes.

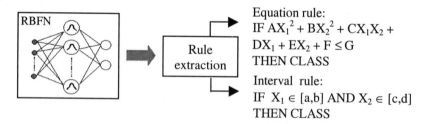

Equation rule:
IF $AX_1^2 + BX_2^2 + CX_1X_2 + DX_1 + EX_2 + F \leq G$
THEN CLASS

Interval rule:
IF $X_1 \in [a,b]$ AND $X_2 \in [c,d]$
THEN CLASS

Fig. 1. Rule extraction from RBF networks

In order to establish the activation range of the rules, we will not use the width parameter of RBF units because this value is determined to produce a certain overlapping degree between these nodes. Some rule extraction methods use it [3], but they add it a correction factor, which they establish empirically. Other methods use genetic algorithms to establish the activation range of the rules [9]. In this study, the ellipsoids (and its activation range) that will be translated to rules are constructed in the following form:

The center of the RBF unit will be the center of the ellipsoid. Then, the algorithm selects one support vector from the associated data to the RBF node (step 3 of below algorithm describes how to establish this partition). The chosen support vector will be the one with the maximum distance to the center. The straight line defined by these two points is the first axis of the ellipsoid. The rest of the axes and the associated vertices are determined by simple geometry. There are three possibilities to define those vertices: (a) with the support vectors themselves, (b) derived from support vectors or (c) with the farthest point to the center. In order to construct hyper-rectangles, a similar procedure is followed. The only difference is that parallel lines to the coordinate axes are used to define the axes of the associated ellipsoid. By using support vector we establish the border of the ellipsoids. Next, the rule extraction algorithm is described in detail:

1. Train SVM on data set.
2. A class label is assigned for each center of RBF units. Output value of the RBF network for each center is used in order to determine this class label.
3. By assign each input pattern to their closest center of RBF node according to the Euclidean distance function, a partition of the input space is made. As it described above, the distance between an input pattern and the center of RBF node determines the activation of the hidden unit. When assigning a pattern to its closest center, this one will be assigned to the RBF node that will give the maximum activation value for that pattern.
4. For each node an ellipsoid with the associated partition data is constructed.
5. Once determined the ellipsoids, they are transferred to rules.

This procedure will generate a rule by each node. Nevertheless, when step 3 is executed, data of different classes could be present in the partition of RBF unit. In this case, the algorithm will generate a rule by *each present class* in the partition with the following procedure:

By each partition
- To construct an ellipsoid with the data of the *same class* of the center of the RBF node.
- For the rest of the data, to determine the mean of the data of each class. Each mean is used as center of its class in order to construct an ellipsoid with the associated data.

In this way, the algorithm will generate one or more rules by RBF node. The number of rules by node will depend on the number of present classes in the activation region of the node. Fig. 2 shows an example of the regions generated by the algorithm.

In order to eliminate or to reduce the overlapping that could exist between ellipsoids of different classes, an overlapping test is applied. Overlapping test verifies if a support vector from another class exits within the ellipsoid. Because the support vectors are the points nearest to decision limit, the presence of these within an ellipsoid of different class is a good indicator of overlapping.

If the overlapping test is positive, the ellipsoid is divided. In order to divide an ellipsoid the following procedure is made:
- To determine two new partitions with the data associated to the ellipsoid. This is made using the k-means algorithm [8], which finds two new prototypes or centers.
- By each prototype an ellipsoid using the associated partition data is constructed.

This procedure will allow to refine the rule base and to reduce the overlapping between classes. When the ellipsoids are divided, more specific rules are generated in order to exclude data from other classes. This procedure can be executed of iterative form; depending of the number of iterations, two or more partitions by ellipsoids can be obtained. The maximum number of iterations can be established by user. Thus, it is possible to control the number of generated rules by RBF node. In some methods, this refinement is made applying a contraction algorithm to eliminate overlapping between regions of different classes [3]. Others, do not solve this overlapping, but they extract special rules that indicate how the nodes between different classes are sharing [13] or they extract fuzzy rules [18].

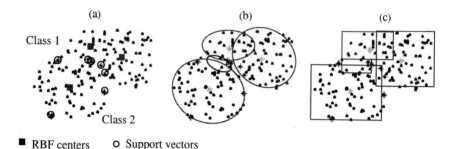

Fig. 2. (a) Data, RBF centers and support vectors. (b) Ellipsoids and (c) Hyper-rectangles generated by the algorithm. Because data of different classes exist in the associated partition, two regions are generated from one RBF node of class 2.

3.1   Data Matching and Classification

Once extracted the rules, the system classifies an example by assigning it the class of the nearest rule in the knowledge base [7], [19]. The distance between a rule and an example is defined as follows. Let $E = (e_1, e_2, ..,e_n)$ be an example with value e_i for the ith attribute, the distance $D(R,E)$ between an equation rule R and E is defined as the result of evaluating the mathematical equation ellipsoid on the example E. In the

$$\delta_i = \begin{cases} 0 & \text{if } r_{i,lower} \leq e_i \leq r_{i,upper} \\ e_i - r_{i,upper} & \text{if } e_i > r_{i,upper} \\ r_{i,lower} - e_i & \text{if } e_i < r_{i,lower} \end{cases}$$

cases of an interval rule the definition of $D(R,E)$ is based on a component distance δ_i for the ith attribute

Here $r_{i,lower}$ and $r_{i,upper}$ are interval limits for the ith attribute in the rule. Then

$$D(R,E) = \sum_{i=1}^{N} \delta_i$$

If an example is covered by several rules, we use the following heuristic to resolve this overlapping: to choose the class of the most specific ellipsoid or hyper-rectangle containing the example; that is, the one with the smallest volume in the input space [19],[24]. For interval rules, this volume $V(R)$ is calculated as follows

$$V(R) = \prod_{i=1}^{N} L_i \qquad \text{where} \quad L_i = r_{i,upper} - r_{i,lower}$$

For comparing the associated volumes with equation rules, a volume index is used instead of the volume. This index is calculated as the product of the all half axes of the ellipsoid

$$V(R) = \prod_{i=1}^{N} radii_i$$

4 Experimental Results

In order to evaluate the performance of the rule extraction algorithm, we carried out two kinds of experiments: with artificial data sets and data sets from the UCI repository [14]. In the first case, 9 artificial samples were generated randomly (each one constituted by 160 training data and 100 test data). Different overlapping degrees between classes were guaranteed for these samples. Afterwards, a RBF network using only training data determined the decision function for each sample (Fig. 3). Finally, the rule extraction algorithm was applied. Tables 1 and 2 show the results obtained for RBF error, rule base error, overlapping percentage on training data (DS) and on test data (TS) and the number of generated rules (NR).

In order to visualize the effect of the overlapping test on the rule performance, results obtained when extracting rules without applying the test and later applying it are showed in the tables. In the last case, only the evaluation parameter values of rules where these values were improved by overlapping test were showed.

In the second experiment, we applied the rule extraction method to three data sets from UCI repository: Iris, Wine and breast cancer Wisconsin. Table 3 shows their characteristics. In this case, the performance of the generated rules was quantified with the following measures:

- *Error (Err)*: This is the classification error provided by the rules on test set.
- *Consistency (Co)*: It is the percentage of the test set for which network and the rule base output agree.
- *Coverage (Cv)*: The percentage of examples from a test set covered by the rule base.
- *Overlapping (Ov)*: It is the percentage of examples from test set covered by several rules.
- *Number of extracted rules (NR)*.

Tables 4, 5 and 6 show the prediction error of the RBF network and the performance values of the extracted rule base. The data were obtained by averaging over stratified ten-fold cross-validation. Our results show a high agreement between the values obtained from the rule base and those obtained from the RBF network. Only few rules are necessary. It should be emphasized that the consistency percentage between the rule base and the RBF networks is very high. Additionally, a low overlapping percentage between classes is obtained when overlapping test is applied. Bellow, we show an example of obtained interval rules for Iris data set.

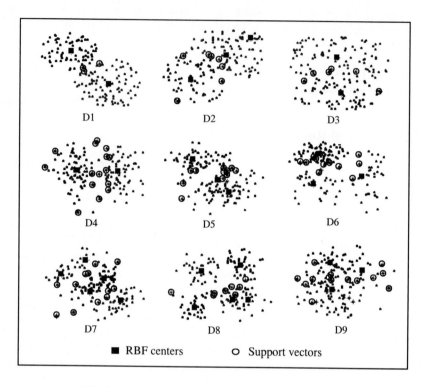

Fig. 3. Artificial data sets, RBF centers and support vectors

Table 1. Results of equation rules for artificial data sets

DATA	RBF error	RBF nodes	Without overlapping test				With overlapping test			
			Error	DS	TS	NR	Error	DS	TS	NR
D1	0.00	2	0.01	0.00	0.00	3	-	-	-	-
D2	0.01	4	0.02	2.50	5.00	5	0.01	0.00	0.00	6
D3	0.03	2	0.02	3.75	3.00	4	0.02	0.63	0.00	6
D4	0.03	2	0.08	22.50	20.00	4	0.04	6.25	6.00	8
D5	0.07	3	0.09	3.75	6.00	5	-	-	-	-
D6	0.02	3	0.02	0.00	0.00	5	-	-	-	-
D7	0.04	5	0.04	1.88	0.00	8	-	-	-	-
D8	0.09	5	0.05	10.63	9.00	7	0.03	2.5	2.00	10
D9	0.01	3	0.03	5.00	5.00	5	0.01	0.63	0.00	6

R1:   IF $X_1 \in$ [4.30,5.84] AND $X_2 \in$ [2.30,4.40] AND $X_3 \in$ [1.00,1.90] AND $X_4 \in$ [0.20,0.60]   THEN Iris setosa   (error: 0.00)

R2:   IF $X_1 \in$ [5.39,7.00] AND $X_2 \in$ [2.20,3.40] AND $X_3 \in$ [2.96,4.70] AND $X_4 \in$ [1.00,1.87]   THEN Iris versicolour   (error: 0.06)

R3:   IF $X_1 \in$ [4.90,6.30] AND $X_2 \in$ [2.20,3.00] AND $X_3 \in$ [4.80,5.10] AND $X_4 \in$ [1.65,2.00]   OR

    IF $X_1 \in$ [6.20,7.96] AND $X_2 \in$ [2.50,3.30] AND $X_3 \in$ [5.10,7.25] AND $X_4 \in$ [1.60,2.50]   THEN Iris virginica   (error: 0.00)

Where: X_1 = sepal length, X_2 = sepal width, X_3 = petal length, X_4 = petal width.

Table 2. Results of interval rules for artificial data sets.

DATA	RBF Error	RBF Nodes	Without overlapping test				With overlapping test			
			Error	DS	TS	NR	Error	DS	TS	NR
D1	0.00	2	0.04	1.25	1.00	3	0.02	0.00	1.00	4
D2	0.01	4	0.04	3.75	4.00	5	0.03	0.00	0.00	7
D3	0.03	2	0.03	3.13	2.00	4	0.02	2.00	0.00	8
D4	0.03	2	0.19	13.75	9.00	4	0.07	1.88	1.00	8
D5	0.07	3	0.14	29.38	43.00	5	0.12	5.63	7.00	9
D6	0.02	3	0.03	0.00	0.00	6	-	-	-	-
D7	0.04	5	0.04	4.38	0.00	8	-	-	-	-
D8	0.09	5	0.09	3.75	3.00	7	0.05	2.5	2.00	9
D9	0.01	3	0.04	1.25	0.00	5	-	-	-	-

Table 3. Data sets and their characteristics.

Data sets	Samples	Attributes	Classes
Iris	150	4	3
Wisconsin	699	9	2
Wine	178	13	3

Table 4. Results for Iris data set.

RBF error: 0.040		RBF nodes: 4.7			
Rules	*Err*	*Co*	*Cv*	*Ov*	*NR*
Equation	0.060	95.33	74.00	0.67	6.3
Interval	0.067	96.00	74.67	1.33	6.9

Table 5. Results for Wisconsin data set.

RBF error: 0.030			RBF nodes: 2.2		
Rules	*Err*	*Co*	*Cv*	*Ov*	*NR*
Equation	0.035	97.79	89.60	4.83	7.2
Interval	0.056	93.67	93.98	6.50	7.7

Table 6. Results for Wine data set.

RBF error: 0.011			RBF nodes: 3.2		
Rules	*Err*	*Co*	*Cv*	*Ov*	*NR*
Equation	0.034	97.77	66.43	2.74	7.6
Interval	0.046	95.38	81.30	5.32	8.4

5   Conclusions and Future Work

The proposed rule extraction algorithm allows transform the RBF network into a rule-based classifier. By using support vectors it is possible to delimit the regions that will be translate to rules and to determine overlapping between regions of different classes.

The extracted rules provided good classification results on the three data sets. They are showing high accuracy on test comparable with the RBF networks. In general, the obtained consistency values show that the rule base captures most of the information embedded in the RBF network with little class overlapping and high coverage of the data.

The number of generated rules will depend on overlapping degree between RBF nodes. In order to exclude data from other class, numerous rules could be generated. Nevertheless, to reduce the rule base, simplification algorithms can be applied. Another possibility, that we are developing, is to realize this simplification at the moment for extracting rules assigning each input data to their closest center of its class.

References

1. Andrews, R., Diederich, J., Tickle, A.: A Survey and Critique of Techniques for Extracting Rules from Trained Artificial Neural Networks. Knowledge-Based Systems. **8** (6) (1995) 373–389
2. Bishop, C.: Neural Networks for Pattern Recognition. Oxford University Press, Inc., New York (1995)
3. Brotherton, T., Chadderdon, G., Grabill, P.: Automated Rule Extraction for Engine Vibration Analysis. Proc. 1999 IEEE Aerospace Conference. Vol. 3 (1999) 29–38
4. Cortes, C., Vapnik, V.: Support-Vector Networks. Machine Learning. **20** (1995) 237-297.
5. Craven, M. Shavlik, J.: Using Neural Networks for Data Mining. Future Generation Computer Systems. **13** (1997) 211–229

6. Cristianini, N., Shawe-Taylor, J.: An Introduction to Support Vector Machines and other kernel-based learning methods. Cambridge University Press, Cambridge (2000)
7. Domingos, P.: Unifying Instance-Based and rule-Based Induction. Machine Learning. **24** (1991) 141–168
8. Duda, R. O., Hart, P. E., Stork, D.G.: Pattern Recognition. John Wiley & Sons, Inc., New York (2001)
9. Fu, X., Wang, L.: Rule Extraction by Genetic Algorithms Based on a Simplified RBF Neural Network. Proc. of the 2001 Congress on Evolutionary Computation. Vol. 2 (2001) 753–758
10. Girosi, F., Poggio, T.: Networks and the best approximation property. Biological Cybernetics. **63** (1990) 169–176
11. Haykin, S.: Neural Networks: A comprehensive foundation. Macmillan, New York (1994)
12. Huber, K., Berthold, M.: Building Precise Classifiers with Automatic Rule Extraction. Proc. IEEE International Conference on Neural Networks. Vol 3 (1995) 1263–1268
13. McGarry, K., Wermter, S., MacIntyre, J.: Knowledge Extraction from Local Function Networks. Proc. IJCAI. (2001) 765–770
14. Merz, C. J., Murphy, P. M.: UCI Repository for Machine Learning Data-Bases. Irvine, CA: University of California, Department of Information and Computer Science, http://www.ics.uci.edu/~mlearn/MLRepository.html] (1998)
15. Mitra, S., Pal, S. K., Mitra, P.: Data Mining in Soft Computing Framework: A survey. IEEE Transactions on Neural Networks. **13** (1) (2002) 3–14.
16. Moody, J., Darken, C.J.: Fast Learning in Networks of Locally-Tuned Processing Units. Neural Computation. **1** (1989) 281–294
17. Park, J., Sandberg, I.W.: Universal approximation using radial basis function networks. Neural Computation. **3** (2) (1991) 246–257
18. Roger, J.-S., Sun, C.-T.: Functional Equivalence Between Radial Basis Function Networks and Fuzzy Inference Systems. IEEE Transactions on Neural Networks. **4** (1) (1993) 156–158
19. Salzberg, S.: A Nearest Hyperrectangle Learning Method. Machine Learning. **6** (1991) 251–276
20. Tickle, A., Maire, F., Bologna, G., Andrews, R.; Diederich, J.: Lessons from Past, Current Issues, and Future Research Directions in Extracting the Knowledge Embedded Artificial Neural Networks,.In: Wermter, S., Sun, R. (eds): Hybrid Neural Systems. Springer-Verlag, Berlin (2000)
21. Tickle. A., Andrews, R., Mostefa, G., Diederich, J.: The Truth will come to light: Directions and Challenges in Extracting the Knowledge Embedded within Trained Artificial Neural Networks. IEEE Transactions on Neural Networks. **9** (6) (1998) 1057–1068
22. Vapnik, V.: Statistical Learning Theory. John Wiley&Sons, Inc., New York (1998)
23. Wermter, S. Sun, R. (eds): Hybrid Neural Systems. Springer-Verlag, Berlin (2000)
24. Witten, I. H., Frank, E.: Data Mining. Practical Machine Learning Tools and Techniques with Java Implementations. Academic Press, San Diego (1999)

Empirical Performance Assessment of Nonlinear Model Selection Techniques

Elisa Guerrero Vázquez, Joaquín Pizarro Junquera, Andrés Yáñez Escolano, and
Pedro L. Riaño Galindo

Grupo Sistemas Inteligentes de Computación
Dpto. Lenguajes y Sistemas Informáticos
Universidad de Cádiz
11510 Puerto Real, Spain
{elisa.guerrero,joaquin.pizarro,pedro.galindo,
andres.yaniez }@uca.es
http://www2.uca.es/grup-invest/sic/

Abstract. Estimating Prediction Risk is important for providing a way of
computing the expected error for predictions made by a model, but it is also an
important tool for model selection. This paper addresses an empirical
comparison of model selection techniques based on the Prediction Risk
estimation, with particular reference to the structure of nonlinear regularized
neural networks. To measure the performance of the different model selection
criteria a large-scale small-samples simulation is conducted for feedforward
neural networks.

1 Introduction

The choice of a suitable model is very important to balance the complexity of the
model with its fit to the data. This is especially critical when the number of data
samples available is not very large and/or is corrupted by noise. Model selection
algorithms attempt to solve this problem by selecting candidate functions from
different function sets with varying complexity, and specifying a fitness criterion,
which measures in some way the lack of fit. Then, the class of functions that will
likely optimize the fitness criterion is selected from that pool of candidates.

In regression models, when the fitness criterion is the sum of the squared
differences between future observations and models forecasts, it is called Prediction
Risk. While estimating Prediction Risk is important for providing a way of estimating
the expected error for predictions made by a model, it is also an important tool for
model selection [11].

Despite the huge amount of network theory and the importance of neural networks
in applied work, there is still little published work about the assessment on which
model selection method works best for nonlinear learning systems. The aim of this
paper is to present a comparative study of different model selection techniques based
on the Minimum Prediction Risk principle in regularized neural networks.

F.J. Garijo, J.C. Riquelme, and M. Toro (Eds.): IBERAMIA 2002, LNAI 2527, pp. 450–459, 2002.
© Springer-Verlag Berlin Heidelberg 2002

Section 2 studies the Generalized Prediction Error for nonlinear systems introduced by Moody [7] which is based upon the notion of the effective number of parameters. Since it cannot be directly calculated, algebraic or resampling estimates are reviewed taking into account regularization terms in order to control the appearance of several local minima when training with nonlinear neural networks.

Results varying the number of hidden units, the training set size and the function complexity are presented in the Simulation results section. Conclusions follow up.

2 Model Selection Techniques

The appearance of several local minima in nonlinear systems suggests the use of regularization techniques, such as weight decay, in order to reduce the variability of the fit, at the cost of bias, since the fitted curve will be smoother than the true curve [9]. Regularization adds a penalty Ω to the error function ε to give:

$$\hat{\varepsilon} = \varepsilon + \lambda \Omega \tag{1}$$

where the decay constant λ controls the extent to which the penalty term Ω influences the form of the solution.

In particular, weight decay consists of the sum of the squares of the adaptive parameters in the network where the sum runs over all weights and biases:

$$\Omega = \frac{1}{2} \sum_i w_i^2 \tag{2}$$

It has been found empirically that a regularizer of this form can lead to significant improvements in network generalization.[1]

Prediction Risk measures how well a model predicts the response value of a future observation. It can be estimated either by using resampling methods or algebraically, by using the asymptotic properties of the model.

Algebraic estimates are based on the idea that the resubstitution error ε_{Res} is a biased estimate of the Prediction Risk ε_{PR}, thus the following equality can be stated:

$$\varepsilon_{PR} = \varepsilon_{Res} + \text{Penalty\_Term} \tag{3}$$

where the penalty-term represents a term which grows with the number of free parameters in the model. Thus, if the model is too simple it will give a large value for the criterion because the residual training error is large, while a model which is too complex will have a large value for the criterion because the complexity term is large. The minimum value for the criterion represents a trade-off between bias and variance.

According to this statement different model selection criteria have appeared in the statistics literature for linear models and unbiased nonlinear models, such as Mallow's CP estimate, the Generalized Cross-Validation (GCV) formula, Akaike's Final Prediction Error (FPE) and Akaike's Information Criteria (AIC) [5], etc. For general nonlinear learning systems which may be biased and may include weight decay or other regularizers Moody [7] was the first to introduce an estimate of Prediction Risk, the Generalized Prediction Error (GPE), which for a data sample of size n can be expressed as:

$$GPE(\lambda) = \mathcal{E}_{Res} + 2\hat{\sigma}^2 \frac{\hat{p}_{eff}(\lambda)}{n} \qquad (4)$$

where $\hat{\sigma}^2$ is an estimate of the noise variance on the data and the regularization parameter λ controls the effective number of parameters peff(λ) of the solution. As suggested in [6] it is not possible to define a single quantity which expresses the effective number of weights in the model. peff(λ) usually differs from the true number of model parameters p and depends upon the amount of model bias, model nonlinearity, and our prior model preferences as determined by λ and the form of the regularizer. See [6] for a detailed determination of peff(λ) and $\hat{\sigma}^2$.

The effective number of parameters can then be used in a generalization of the AIC for the case of additive noise, denoted by Murata as NIC (Network Information Criterion) [8]. The underlying idea of NIC is to estimate the deviance for a data set of size n, compensating for the fact that the weights were chosen to fit the training set:

$$NIC = n * \log(\mathcal{E}_{Res}) + 2 * \hat{p}_{eff}(\lambda) \qquad (5)$$

Alternatively, data resampling methods, such as k-fold Cross-validation (kCV) or bootstrap estimation make maximally efficient use of available data, but they can be very CPU time consuming for neural networks. A nonlinear refinement of CV is called 10NCV [7].

In both, kCV and kNCV, the dataset is randomly split into k mutually exclusive folds or subsets of approximately equal size. The training process is repeated k times, each time leaving out one of the k subsets to test, but kNCV uses as starting point weights of a network trained on all available data rather than random initial weights for retraining on the k subsets.

We consider that models which minimize GPE, NIC, kCV and kNCV are optimal in the average loss sense. We can use these criteria to select a particular model from a set of possible models.

3 Simulation Results

This paper focuses on feedforward neural networks with a single layer of units with hyperbolic tangent activation functions. Architectures considered are limited to single hidden layer networks because of their proven universal approximation capabilities and to avoid further increasing complexity.

The networks were trained by ordinary least-squares using standard numerical optimisation algorithms for H hidden units ranging from 1 to M. The training algorithm was Levenberg-Marquardt. For a network with H hidden units, the weights for the previously trained network were used to initialise H-1 of the hidden units, while the weights for the Hth hidden unit were generated from a pseudorandom normal distribution. The decay constant λ was fixed to 0.002.

All simulations were performed 1000 times, each time generating a new different data set of size N. Model selection results were averaged to reduce the influence of model variability on network size selection by introducing the possibility of escaping local minima.

We used artificially generated data from the following target functions:

$$y = 1.8*tanh(3.2*x + 0.8)- 2.5*tanh(2.1*x + 1.2)- 0.2*tanh(0.1*x - 0.5)+\xi \quad (6)$$

$$y = -5*x^5 - 1.8*x^4 + 23.27*x^3 + 8.79*x^2 -15.33*x - 6 + \xi \quad (7)$$

where $x \in [-2,2]$ and ξ is a Gaussian zero mean, i.i.d. sequence which is independent of the input with variance $\sigma=0.5$.

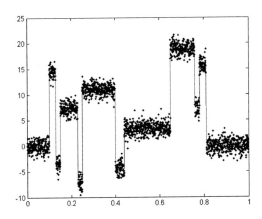

Fig. 1. Low-noise and noise-free block functions from Donojo-Johnstone benchmarks

Alternatively, in order to study a case of higher nonlinearity we considered the low-noise block function from the Donoho-Jonstone benchmarks (fig. 1).These benchmarks have one input, high nonlinearity and random noise can be added to produce an infinite number of data sets. Sarle [10] checked that the MLP easily learned the block function at all noise levels with 11 hidden units and there was overfitting with 12 or more hidden units when training with 2048 samples.

We assume that among the candidate models there exists model M_c that is closest to the true model in terms of the expected Prediction Risk, $E[PR](M_c)$. Suppose a model selection criterion selects model M_k which has an expected Prediction Risk of $E[PR](M_k)$. Observed efficiency is defined as the ratio that compares the Prediction Risk between the closest candidate model, M_c, and the model selected by some criterion M_k.

$$observed \quad efficiency = \frac{PR(M_c)}{PR(M_k)} \qquad (8)$$

Tables from 1 to 9 show observed efficiency for different target functions when the numbers of training examples are 25, 50 and 100.

First column shows the number of hidden units, ranging from 1 to 10 hidden units for hyperbolic tangent target function (6) and for the 5th degree target function (7), and models ranging from 1 to 20 for low-noise block target function. For each of the 1000 realizations the criteria select a model and the observed efficiency of this selection is recorded, where higher observed efficiency denotes better performance.

Next columns show the counts for the different model selection criteria: NIC, 10NCV, 10CV, GPE and the Prediction Risk (PR) computed over a sample size of 2000. These results are one way to measure consistency, and we might therefore expect the consistent model selection criteria to have the highest counts. Last two rows show the mean observed efficiency and the rank for each criterion. The criterion with the highest averaged observed efficiency is given rank 1 (better) while the criterion with the lowest observed efficiency is given rank 4 (lowest of the 4 criteria considered).

Table 1. Simulation results for a data sample size of N=25 and target function (6)

Models	NIC	10NCV	10CV	GPE	PR
1	1	10	7	2	4
2	431	646	653	567	790
3	158	180	155	156	137
4	87	63	85	83	28
5	60	23	24	43	13
6	39	11	8	27	7
7	39	11	10	19	5
8	25	8	12	15	6
9	29	9	11	19	3
10	131	39	35	69	7
Efficiency	0.8080	0.9030	0.9090	0.8480	1.0
Rank	4	2	1	3	

Table 2. Simulation results for N=50 and target function (6)

Models	NIC	10NCV	10CV	GPE	PR
1	0	0	0	0	0
2	529	713	741	631	851
3	164	161	132	149	120
4	86	54	48	65	11
5	55	29	24	45	6
6	47	13	13	31	3
7	22	3	7	13	2
8	15	4	8	10	1
9	22	8	10	17	1
10	60	15	17	39	5
Efficiency	0.8891	0.9521	0.9520	0.9125	1.0
Rank	4	1	2	3	

Table 3. Simulation results for N=100 for target function (6)

Models	NIC	10NCV	10CV	GPE	PR
1	0	0	0	0	0
2	607	702	692	668	873
3	146	165	168	136	106
4	74	66	64	66	12
5	72	33	28	58	4
6	33	14	12	26	2
7	23	2	7	15	0
8	12	5	8	7	0
9	5	1	9	5	0
10	28	12	12	19	3
Efficiency	0.9438	0.9743	0.9716	0.9529	1.0
Rank	4	1	2	3	

Table 4. Simulation results for N=25 and target function (7)

Models	NIC	10NCV	10CV	GPE	PR
1	0	56	60	1	44
2	1	96	77	7	29
3	18	191	149	62	89
4	41	222	185	148	233
5	60	142	151	144	240
6	63	92	125	125	159
7	86	71	85	112	75
8	108	51	67	98	51
9	178	35	55	127	37
10	445	44	46	176	43
Efficiency	0.6820	0.7782	0.7573	0.7370	1.0
Rank	4	1	2	3	

Table 5. Simulation results for N=50 and target function (7)

Mod	NIC	10NCV	10CV	GPE	PR
1	0	0	0	0	1
2	0	4	2	1	3
3	13	75	32	18	16
4	101	264	219	165	239
5	138	248	278	221	351
6	119	161	185	158	199
7	111	103	113	118	103
8	133	53	78	102	46
9	147	53	57	105	20
10	238	39	36	112	22
Efficiency	0.7866	0.8783	0.8558	0.8272	1.0
Rank	4	1	2	3	

Tables 1, 2 and 3 show that for experimental function (6) all methods select models with 2 and 3 hidden units, 10NCV and 10CV perform almost the same, but both are superior to GPE and NIC. In all the experiments NIC averaged observed efficiency has the last position on the ranking.

Table 6. Simulation results for N=100 and target function (7). NCV, CV and GPE favor models from 4 to 8 hidden units while NIC favors more overfitted models

Models	NIC	10NCV	10CV	GPE	PR
1	0	0	0	0	0
2	0	0	0	0	0
3	1	7	1	1	1
4	152	251	113	184	203
5	207	268	329	270	408
6	191	193	223	199	213
7	126	117	132	117	105
8	109	81	96	91	41
9	113	52	56	76	17
10	101	31	50	62	12
Efficiency	0.9114	0.9491	0.9190	0.9250	1.0
Rank	4	1	3	2	

Table 7. Simulation results for N=25 and low-noise block target function, when the sample size is very small model selection tasks are more difficult, in this case NIC shows a very high variance on the observed efficiency

Models	NIC	10NCV	10CV	GPE	PR
1	0	76	69	0	20
2	2	177	146	2	114
3	0	236	235	4	204
4	12	145	158	31	165
5	26	112	96	44	150
6	73	82	83	120	87
7	79	54	45	126	75
8	103	44	43	146	49
9	96	17	38	121	40
10	61	12	12	99	28
11	88	8	10	50	18
12	75	1	9	59	4
13	48	3	6	17	8
14	33	2	5	19	6
15	31	5	4	20	2
16	26	6	6	17	3
17	26	1	7	15	2
18	27	2	6	14	3
19	37	6	5	16	6
20	157	11	17	80	16
Efficiency	0.7251	0.8046	0.8233	0.7319	1.0
Rank	4	2	1	3	

Tables 4, 5 and 6 show that for experimental function (7) observed efficiency increases as the sample size grows. 10NCV is the most underfitting method for a sample size of 25, while NIC and GPE favor overfitted models.

In contrast to the previous results, we next considered a problem that has a much higher nonlinearity, the low-noise block function. Tables 7, 8 and 9 show that NIC outperforms 10NCV and 10CV when the sample size is 100 while with N=50 all methods perform almost the same. The averaged observed efficiency always grows as the simple size increases.

Table 8. Simulation results for N=50 and low-noise block target function. All criteria show a similar averaged observed efficiency, but 10NCV and 10CV tend to more underfitted models than NIC and GPE

Models	NIC	10NCV	10CV	GPE	PR
1	0	3	2	0	0
2	0	28	18	0	9
3	0	71	89	0	22
4	0	173	138	0	65
5	8	188	187	8	120
6	8	111	97	12	112
7	30	81	71	44	96
8	44	66	85	60	102
9	75	83	70	106	91
10	96	41	64	125	72
11	135	36	52	126	98
12	97	33	47	116	56
13	99	30	14	100	30
14	88	19	10	69	34
15	60	3	13	52	18
16	49	5	4	44	20
17	33	6	5	24	11
18	35	6	10	23	11
19	30	9	7	24	10
20	113	8	17	67	23
Efficiency	0.8269	0.8208	0.8358	0.8322	1.0
Rank	2	1	4	3	

From all the experimental results we can conclude that the performance differences are not great between 10NCV and 10CV, but 10NCV seems to perform better in almost all the sample sizes. 10CV is more computationally demanding than 10NCV. This fact leads us to prefer 10NCV rather than 10CV.

In general, there is not best model selection method. Depending on the particular problem one technique can outperforms another. When N is large, all methods give reasonable efficiency results but crossvalidation-based criteria seem to be slightly better. However, when it comes to the case where N=50 and 100 and high nonlinearity is present, NIC and GPE outperform 10NCV and 10CV. The algebraic estimate of Prediction Risk is also more attractive from the computational perspective. However, it is important to note that the theory of NIC relies on a single well-defined minimum to the fitting function, and it can be unreliable when there are several local minima [8]. Among the different cases presented in this paper GPE shows a more reliable behavior with not great differences between the best technique and GPE.

Table 9. Simulation results for N=100 and low-noise block target function. GPE and NIC show a higher averaged observed efficiency, and favor models from 11 to 16 hidden units, while 10CV and 10NCV models ranging between 9 and 14 hidden units

Models	NIC	10NCV	10CV	GPE	PR
1	0	0	0	0	0
2	0	0	0	0	0
3	0	0	0	0	0
4	0	12	17	0	1
5	0	30	42	0	5
6	0	75	55	2	8
7	6	60	42	4	33
8	14	66	36	14	25
9	23	90	68	27	45
1	42	92	91	58	96
11	114	112	120	140	97
12	118	72	87	138	99
13	114	84	78	105	97
14	127	79	87	137	135
15	103	66	75	106	102
16	98	44	49	93	77
17	65	30	27	56	68
18	62	16	47	52	27
19	41	29	20	25	27
20	73	43	59	43	58
Efficiency	0.9326	0.8484	0.8581	0.9319	1.0
Rank	1	3	4	2	

Conclusions

The performance of different model selection techniques based on the Prediction Risk estimation in nonlinear regularized neural networks has been studied. We determined relative performance by comparing GPE, NIC, 10NCV and 10CV against each other under different simulated conditions. Which is the best among these competing techniques for model selection is not clear. They can behave quite differently in small sample sizes and directly depend on the nonlinearity of the task.

The similar performance between 10CV and 10NCV lead us to prefer 10NCV since the computational cost is lower. NIC favors overfitted models when low nonlinearity is present while 10NCV favors underfitted models, even in high nonlinearity cases. Although the observed efficiency of GPE is not always the best, it gives reliable results for all the cases and, as well as 10NCV, it provides good estimates of the prediction risk at a lower computational cost.

Acknowledgements. This work has been supported by the Junta de Andalucía (PAI research group TIC-145).

References

1. Bishop C. M.: Neural networks for pattern recognition. Clarendon Press, Oxford (1995)
2. Brake, G., Kok J.N. Vitányi P.M.B.: Model Selection for Neural Networks: Comparing MDL and NIC. In: Proc. European Symposium on Artificial Neural Networks, Brussels, April 20–22 (1994)
3. Larsen J., Hansen L.K.: Generalization performance of regularized neural network models. Proc. IEEE Workshop: Neural Networks for Signal Processing IV, Piscataway, New Jersey (1994) 42–51
4. Lawrence S., Giles C.L., Tsoi A.C.: What Size of Neural Network Gives Optimal Generalization? Convergence Properties of Backpropagation. Technical Report. UMIACS-TR-96-22 and CS-TR-3617. Institute of Advanced Computer Studies. University of Mariland. (1996)
5. McQuarrie A., Tsai C.: Regression and Time Series Model Selection. World Scientific Publishing Co. Pte. Ltd. (1998)
6. Moody, J.: The effective number of parameters: an analysis of generalization   and regularization in nonlinear learning systems. NIPS (1992) 847–854
7. Moody, J.: Prediction Risk and Architecture Selection for Neural Networks. In Cherkassky, V., Friedman, J. H., and Wechsler, H., editors, From Statistics to Neural Networks: Theory and Pattern Recognition Applications, NATO ASI Series F. Springer-Verlag (1994)
8. Murata N., Yoshizawa S., Amari S.: Network Information Criterion – Determining the Number of Hidden Units for an Artificial Neural Network Model. IEEE Transactions on Neural Networks (1994) 5, 865–872
9. Ripley B.D. Statistical Ideas for Selecting Network Architectures. Neural Networks: Artificial Intelligence & Industrial Applications, eds. B. Kappend and S. Gielen. Springer, Berlin (1995) 183–190
10. Sarle W.: Donojo-Jonhstone benchmarks: neural nets results (1999) ftp: //ftp.sas.com/pub/neural/dojo/dojo.html
11. Zapranis A., Refenes A.: Principles of Neural Model Identification, Selection and Adequacy: with applications to financial economics. (Perspectives in neural computing). Springer-Verlag London (1999)

An Efficient Neural Network Algorithm for the p-Median Problem

Enrique Dominguez Merino and José Muñoz Perez

Department of Computer Science, E.T.S.I. Informatica, University of Malaga
Campus de Teatinos s/n. 29071 Malaga, Spain
{enriqued, munozp}@lcc.uma.es

Abstract. In this paper we present a neural network model and new formulation for the p-median problem. The effectiveness and efficiency of our algorithm under varying problem sizes are analyzed in comparison to conventional heuristic methods. The results for small-scale problems (less than 100 points) indicate that our implementation of algorithm is effective. Furthermore, we also have applied our algorithm to solve large-scale problems, demonstrating that a simple recurrent neural network, with an adapted formulation of the problem, can generate good solutions in a few seconds.

1   Introduction

One of the most popular problems in the facility location literature is the p-median problem. This model locates p facilities in some space (such as Euclidean plane or a network) that will attend n demand points. The objective of the model is to minimize the total (weighted) distance between the demand points and the facilities.

Kariv and Hakimi [20] showed that the p-median problem on a general network is NP-hard. This has resulted in the development of heuristic solution techniques in an effort to solve large-scale problems to near-optimality with a reasonable computational effort. Perhaps the most popular p-median heuristic was developed by Teitz and Bart [27]. This is a node-exchange procedure that attempts to improve the objective function value at each iteration. It is a simple to implement and it produces relatively good solutions to smaller problems when it is applied with multiple starting solutions.

There are more sophisticated heuristics for the p-median problem. A number of solution procedure have been developed for general networks. Most of the proposed procedures have been based on mathematical programming relaxation and branch-and-bound techniques. However, recently have been developed new procedure based on tabu search, neural networks, genetic algorithms and tree search. Thus, some proposed procedures include tree search (Christofides and Beasley [3], Bartezzaghi and Colorni [1]), lagrangian relaxation coupled with branch & bound (Narula, Ogbu and Samuelsson [24], Galvao [13]), tabu search (Ohlemüller [23]), heuristic and decision techniques (Hribar and Daskin [20], Hansen, Mladenovic and Taillard , Drezner and Guyse [18]), as well as Kohonen maps (Lozano, Warrior, Onieva and Larrañeta [23]).

F.J. Garijo, J.C. Riquelme, and M. Toro (Eds.): IBERAMIA 2002, LNAI 2527, pp. 460–469, 2002.
© Springer-Verlag Berlin Heidelberg 2002

Researchers have focused recently on the design of modern heuristics to solve the p-median problem. Modern heuristics can generate better results than the simple node-exchange procedure. But this modern heuristics usually are laborious and difficult to understand and to implement.

We have designed a simple neural network (such as Hopfield neural network) that generates good solutions to the p-median problem, comparable in quality to those of the node-exchange heuristics.

The rest of this paper is organized as follow: Section 2 describes the problem and gives a preliminary analysis. Section 3 shows how to apply a simple recurrent neural network to the problem. Section 4 contains illustrative and comparative simulation results. Finally, section 5 provides a summary and conclusions.

2   Problem Formulation

The p-median problem is well known and it has been studied during years. The p-median problem concerns the location of p facilities (medians) in order to minimize the total weighted distance between the facilities and the demand points. This problem is a multi-facility extension of the Weber problem which is widely accepted as the first formalized facility location problem in the literature. Operational generalizations of the problem have been investigated by Cooper [1] using iterative approximation methods. ReVelle and Swain [26] provided an integer programming formulation for the discrete P-median problem, which is given below

Minimize

$$\sum_{i=1}^{N}\sum_{j=1}^{N}d_{ij}x_{ij} \tag{1}$$

Subject to:

$$\sum_{j=1}^{N}x_{ij}=1 \quad i=1,...N \tag{2}$$

$$\sum_{j=1}^{N}x_{jj}=P \tag{3}$$

$$x_{ij}\le x_{jj} \quad i=1,..N; j=1,..N \tag{4}$$

where
  N is the considered number of points
  P is the number of facilities or medians
  d_{ij} is the distance (cost) between the demand point i and the facility j

$$x_{ij} = \begin{cases} 1 & \text{if the point } i \text{ is associated with the facility } j \\ 0 & \text{otherwise} \end{cases}$$

$$x_{jj} = \begin{cases} 1 & \text{if the point } j \text{ is a facility} \\ 0 & \text{otherwise} \end{cases}$$

The restriction (2) prevents that a demand point i is free, that is to say that does not have any facility associated to him. The restriction (3) establishes the number of facilities or medians. The last condition (4) assures the coherence of the solutions, a demand point i cannot be associated to the facility j ($x_{ij} = 1$) and in the point j not to be established a facility ($x_{jj} = 0$).

To the above formulation they have been applied numerous and different algorithms, but we do not know anyone that has been applied a neural network like the Hopfield network, because the restriction (4) not you ready to their application.

For that reason, in this paper we intends a new more appropriate formulation to the p-median problem:

Minimize

$$\sum_{i=1}^{N}\sum_{j=1}^{N}\sum_{q=1}^{P} d_{ij} S_{iq}^{1} S_{jq}^{2} \tag{5}$$

Subject to:

$$\sum_{q=1}^{P} S_{iq}^{1} = 1 \quad i = 1,..N \tag{6}$$

$$\sum_{j=1}^{N} S_{jq}^{2} = 1 \quad q = 1,..P \tag{7}$$

where

N is the number of points

P is the number of facilities (medians) to locate

d_{ij} is the distance among the points i and j

$$S_{iq}^{1} = \begin{cases} 1 & \text{if the point } i \text{ is associated with the group } q \\ 0 & \text{otherwise} \end{cases}$$

$$S_{jq}^{2} = \begin{cases} 1 & \text{if } j \text{ is a facility of the group } q \\ 0 & \text{otherwise} \end{cases}$$

Notice the existence of two types of neurons: S_{iq}^{1} (allocations neurons) and S_{jq}^{2} (facilities location neurons). Even, it is observed that the restrictions are much simpler that in the previous formulations. With the restriction (6) we only allow that a point associates to an only group, and with the condition (7) we make sure that in each group there is only one facility or median.

3   Competitive Recurrent Neural Network Model

The proposed neural network consists of a single layer of N interconnected binary neurons or processing elements. Each neuron i has an input h_i and an output $S_i \in \{0,1\}$. In order to design a suitable neural network for this problem, the key step is to construct an appropriate energy function E for which the global minimum is simultaneously a solution of the above formulation. The simplest approach to constructing a desired energy function is the penalty function method. The basic idea in this approach is to transform the constrained problem into an unconstrained one by adding penalty function terms to the objective function (5). These terms cause a high cost if any constraint is violated. More precisely, some or all constraints are eliminated by increasing the objective function by a quantity which depends on the amount by which the constraints are violated. That is, the energy function of the neural network is given by the Liapunov energy function defined as

$$E = \sum_{i=1}^{N}\sum_{j=1}^{N}\sum_{q=1}^{P} d_{ij} S_{iq}^1 S_{jq}^2 + \lambda_1 \sum_{i=1}^{N}\left(1 - \sum_{q=1}^{P} S_{iq}^1\right)^2 + \lambda_2 \sum_{q=1}^{P}\left(1 - \sum_{j=1}^{N} S_{jq}^2\right)^2 \tag{8}$$

where $\lambda_i > 0$ are penalty parameters that they determine the relative weight of the constraints. The penalty parameters tuning is an important problem associated with this approach.

In order to guarantee a valid solution and avoid the parameter tuning problem, we will divide our neural network in disjoint groups according to the two restrictions, that is, for the P-median problem with N points, we will have N groups, according to restriction (6), plus P groups, according to restriction (7). Then, we will reorganize our neurons in two matrices (one matrix per neuron type) where a group is represented by a row or column of the matrix according to neuron type.

$$
\begin{array}{ccccll}
S_{11}^1 & S_{12}^1 & \cdots & S_{1P}^1 & \rightarrow & \text{group 1} \\
S_{21}^1 & S_{22}^1 & \cdots & S_{2P}^1 & \rightarrow & \text{group 2} \\
\vdots & \vdots & \ddots & \vdots & & \vdots \\
S_{N1}^1 & S_{N2}^1 & \cdots & S_{NP}^1 & \rightarrow & \text{group N}
\end{array}
$$

$$
\begin{matrix}
S_{11}^2 & S_{12}^2 & \cdots & S_{1N}^2 \\
S_{21}^2 & S_{22}^2 & \cdots & S_{2N}^2 \\
\vdots & \vdots & \ddots & \vdots \\
S_{P1}^2 & S_{P2}^2 & \cdots & S_{PN}^2 \\
\downarrow & \downarrow & & \downarrow
\end{matrix}
$$

group $N+1$ group $N+2$ group $N+P$

Fig. 1. Neurons organization of the neural network for the P-median problem with N points. This shows two matrices, the first matrix contains the allocation neurons and the second contains the location neurons. The allocation neurons inside same group are in the same row of the matrix, and the location neurons inside same group are in the same column

In this model one and only one neuron per group must have one as its outputs, so the penalty terms are eliminated from the objective function. The neurons inside same group are updated in parallel. Then we can introduce the notion of group update. Observe that the groups are updated sequentially. Then, the energy function of the neural network is reduced to

$$
E = \sum_{i=1}^{N} \sum_{j=1}^{N} \sum_{q=1}^{P} d_{ij} S_{iq}^1 S_{jq}^2 \tag{9}
$$

Applying a gradient descent method, we obtain the inputs of the neurons of the network

$$
h_{iq}^1 = -\frac{\partial E}{\partial S_{iq}^1} = -\sum_{j=1}^{N} d_{ij} S_{jq}^2 \tag{10}
$$

$$
h_{jq}^2 = -\frac{\partial E}{\partial S_{jq}^2} = -\sum_{i=1}^{N} d_{ij} S_{iq}^1 \tag{11}
$$

The dynamics of the neural network are given by

$$
S_{iq}^1(k+1) = \begin{cases} 1 & \text{if } h_{iq}^1(k) = \max_{1 \le r \le P} \{h_{ir}^1(k)\} \\ 0 & \text{otherwise} \end{cases} \tag{12}
$$

$$
S_{jq}^2(k+1) = \begin{cases} 1 & \text{if } h_{jq}^2(k) = \max_{1 \le i \le N} \{h_{iq}^2(k)\} \\ 0 & \text{otherwise} \end{cases} \tag{13}
$$

then the energy function is guaranteed to decrease (see [12]). Thus, this energy decrease is maximized at every time. The following procedure describes the proposed algorithm based on the above neural network.

1. Set the initial state by randomly setting the output of one neuron in each group to be one and all the others neurons in the group to be zero.
2. Evaluate the initial value of the energy function (9).
3. Select a group g
4. Compute the inputs of the neurons in the group g, by (10) if $1 \leq g \leq N$ or by (11) otherwise.
5. Interchange the activated neuron in the group with the neuron with maximum input.
6. Repeat from step 3 until the neurons with the maximum input in each group are activated.

On step 3 we select a group randomly or sequencely. On step 5, if there are different neurons with the maximum input value, the algorithm must randomly select one of them.

Fig. 2 illustrates the energy decrease for a small-scale problem. In the first iterations, the curve slope is pronounced due to this energy decrease is maximized at every iteration. In fact, a good solution is obtained from iteration 400 with minimal error. In this case, the optimal solution is reached at 1003rd iteration.

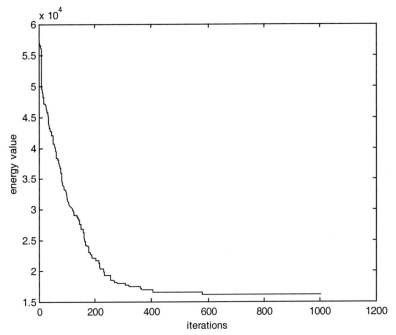

Fig. 2. Graphical representation of the values of the energy function on every iteration step in the 5-medians problem with 100 demand points

4   Simulations Results

A random number generator has been used to generate the two-dimensional points. All points are distributed uniformly within the unit square.

For a comparison, we tested all algorithms on an Origin 2000 computer (Silicon Graphics Inc.). The computation of the optimal solutions has been carried out with an exact algorithm [13], using *branch & bound.*

We choose to compare the performance of proposed algorithm (NN) with the performance of the interchange algorithm proposed by Teizt and Bart [27] (T&B), since T&B is very simple to understand and implement, and it produces good solutions with limited computational effort. We recognize, however, that it is possible to generate better solutions for some instances of the p-median problem using other heuristics, such as langrangian relaxation or tabu search.

We first compare our implementation of NN with T&B and random search (RS) on several small-scale problems. Table 1 lists the comparison of results from different algorithms with optimal solutions. For each instance, which it is represented by a row in the table, 50 randomly problems are generated and tested. T&B and N&N report 100% of optimality for their 50 randomly generated problems with 75 demand points ($N=75$) and 5 medians ($P=5$). The average error figures in the table represent the average percentage deviation from the best solution calculated by an exact algorithm [13].

Table 1. Results for the three algorithms applied to small scale problems

N (demand points)	P (medians)	NN Avg. Error (%)	T&B Avg. Error (%)	RS Avg. Error (%)
75	5	0.00	0.00	0.10
75	10	0.00	0.09	0.12
75	20	0.10	0.17	0.30
100	5	0.00	0.05	0.10
100	10	0.01	0.21	0.25
100	20	0.09	0.39	0.41

RS is the fastest among these algorithms because there is virtually no processing overhead involved. RS performs so well in these cases because the difference between the number of feasible solutions evaluated and the total number of solutions is similar. However, RS is not likely to perform similarly well for larger problems due to size of the solution space. It is included here only to demonstrate that a simple random search method can generate good solutions for small-scale problems in less time.

In Table 2 we compare the iterations and time of NN and T&B for the same problems. In this table we demonstrate that our implementation of NN produce better results in less time due to less number of iterations. Parallelism of the neural networks justified the less number of iterations, since the input of each neuron is calculated in parallel. In addition, our neural network is divided in groups and all neurons in the same group are parallel updated in only one iteration. Although an iteration of NN is slower than an iteration of T&B, our implementation of NN needs less time due to the great difference of iterations between NN and T&B. For example, the first row of Table 2 shows that T&B is faster than our NN, nevertheless our NN needs much less iterations to obtain optimal results. For the rest of problems evaluated, the time of NN is lower than the time of T&B due to the less increase of iterations.

Table 2. Comparison of NN with T&B for small scale problems

N (demand points)	P (medians)	NN		T&B	
		Avg. Iterations	Avg. Time (s)	Avg. Iterations	Avg. Time (s)
75	5	1246	0.74	7051	0.68
75	10	1445	1.00	15253	1.47
75	20	1432	0.93	21422	2.01
100	5	1254	0.81	10965	1.05
100	10	1583	1.20	28199	2.52
100	20	2230	2.15	33241	3.14

The increase of average error or gap is another important characteristic. Fig. 3 shows the increase of average error according to number of medians for instances of randomly problems with 200 demand points. In this case, we test 100 randomly large-scale problems to evaluate the error. This figure illustrates the good results obtained. In fact, our implementation of NN guarantees a solution with 99.4% of optimality for 50-medians problems with 200 demand points. Note that, this large-scale problem has more than $4.5 \cdot 10^{47}$ feasible solutions and the solution is calculated in a few seconds, less than 4 seconds.

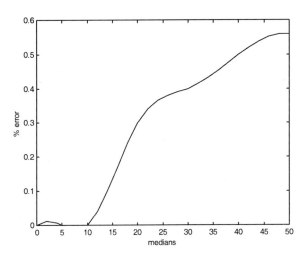

Fig. 3. Graphical representation of the relative error (gap) with 200 demand points

5   Conclusions

In this paper, we applied a neural network to solve the p-median problem. Our objective was to exploit the features of neural networks and demonstrate that a simple recurrent neural network can generate good solutions to location-allocations problems.

With the proposed mathematical model, we have tried to reduce the complexity of the problem that was observed in the resolution of the same one with other formulations. Besides the simplicity of this formulation, a decrease of the number of variables has been gotten, with the rising improvement in the yield of the methods or algorithms to apply. Also, the utility of the neural networks has been shown to treat optimization problems. Although, the proposed model guarantees that every converged state of neural network is equivalent to a feasible solution, and tuning the penalty parameters is not needed. Based on our computational tests, we believe that neural networks have the potential to be useful heuristic for the p-median problem.

In summary, in this paper we have achieved related with success two research areas, Localization and Neural Networks, to solve a classic NP-complete optimization problem, demonstrating this way, the fruitful existent cooperation among these areas.

References

[1]   E. Bartezzaghi, A. Colorni (1981), "A search tree algorithm for plant location problems", *European Journal of Operational Research 7, 371–379*

[2]   M.J. Canós, C. Ivorra, V. Liern (1999), "An exact algorithm for the fuzzy problem p-mediates", *European Journal of Operational Research 116, 80–86*

[3]   N. Christofides, J.E. Beasley (1982), "A tree search algorithm for the problem p-mediates", *European Journal of Operational Research 10, 196–204*

[4]   L. Cooper (1963), "Location-Allocation Problems", *Operations Research 11, 331–343*

[5]   E. Dominguez, J. Muñoz (2001), "Solving the m-median problem with a neural network", *Proc. of IX CAEPIA (Conference of the Spanish Associations for the Artificial Intelligence) Gijon, Spain*

[6]   Zvi Drezner (ed.) (1995), "Facility location: To survey of applications and methods", *Springer*

[7]   Zvi Drezner, Jeffery Guyse (1999), "Application of decision analysis to the Weber facility location problem", *European Journal of Operational Research 116, 69–79*

[8]   G. Galán Marín, J. Muñoz Pérez (1999), "A Net n-parallel Competitive Neuronal for Combinatory Optimization", *Proc. of VIII CAEPIA (Conference of the Spanish Asociations for the Artificial Intelligence) Murcia, Spain, vol. 1, 98–106*

[9]   G. Galán Marín, J. Muñoz Pérez (1999), "A Design of a Neuronal Network for the resolution of the problem of the Four Colors", *Have Ibero-American of Artificial Intelligence 8, 6–17*

[10]   G. Galán Marín, J. Muñoz Pérez (2000), "An improved Neural Network Algorithm for the Bipatite Subgraph Problem", *Proc. of International Conference on Computational Intelligence and Neuroscience, Atlantic City, NJ USES*

[11]   G. Galán Marín, J. Muñoz Pérez (2000), "Finding Near-Maximum Cliques with Competitive Hopfield Networks", *Proc. of International ICSC Symposium on Neural Computation, Berlin, Germany*

[12]   G. Galán Marín, J. Muñoz Pérez (2001), "Design and Analysis of Maximum Hopfield Networks", *IEEE Trans. On Neural Networks 12 (2), 329–339*

[13]   Roberto D. Galvao (1980), "A dual-bounded algorithm for the problem p-mediates", *Operations Research*

[14]   M.R. Garey, D.S. Johnson (1979), "Computers and intractability: To guide to the theory of NP-completeness", *W.H. Freeman and Co., New York*

[15]   S.L. Hakimi (1964), "Optimum locations of switching centers and absolute centers and medians of to graph", *Operations Research 12, 450–459*

[16]   S.L. Hakimi (1965), "Optimum distribution of switching centers in to communication network and some related graph theoretic problems", *Operations Research 13, 462–475*

[17]   P. Hanjoul, D. Peeters (1985), "A comparison of two dual-based procedures for solving the p-median problem", *European Journal of Operational Research 20, 386–396*

[18]   Pierre Hansen, Nenad Mladenovic, Eric Taillard (1998), "Heuristic solution of the multisource Weber problem ace to problem p-mediates", *Operations Research Letters 22, 55–62*

[19]   J.J. Hopfield, D.W. Tank (1985), "Neural computation of decisions in optimization problems", *Biological Cybernetics 52, 141–152*

[20]   Michelle Hribar, Mark S. Daskin (1997), "A dynamic programming heuristic for the problem p-mediates", *European Journal of Operational Research 101, 499–508*

[21]   Kariv O. and Hakimi S.L. (1979) "An Algorithmic Approach to Network Location Problem. Part 2: The p-Median". SIAM J. Appl. Math., Vol. 37, pp. 539–560.

[22]   Love, Robert F., Morris, James G. and Wesolowsky, George O. (1998) "Facilities Location Models & Methods", *North-Holland*

[23]   S. Lozano, F. Guerrero, L. Onieva, J. Larrañeta (1998), "Kohonen maps for solving to class of location-allocation problems", *European Journal of Operational Research 108, 106–117*

[24]   Subhash C. Narula, Ugonnaya I. Ogbu, Haakon M. Samuelsson (1977), "An algorithm for the problem p-mediates", *Operations Research 25, 709–713*

[25]   M. Ohlemüller (1997), "Taboo search for large location-allocation problems", *Journal of the Operational Research Society 48, 745–750*

[26]   C. ReVelle, R. Swain (1970), "Central facilities location", *Geographical Analysis, 2, 30–42*

[27]   M. B. Teitz, P. Bart (1968), "Heuristic methods for estimating the generalized vertex median of a weighted graph", *Operations Research 16, 955–961*

Improving Cellular Nonlinear Network Computational Capabilities

Víctor M. Preciado

Departamento de Electrónica e Ingeniería Electromecánica,
Universidad de Extremadura, E-06071 Badajoz, Spain
vpdiaz@unex.es

Abstract. The Cellular Neural Network (CNN) is a bidimensional array of analog dynamic processors whose cells interact directly within a finite local neighborhood [2]. The CNN provides an useful computation paradigm when the problem can be reformulated as a well-defined task where the signal values are placed on a regular 2-D grid (i.e., image processing) and direct interaction between signal values are limited within a *local neighborhood*. Besides, local CNN connectivity allows its implementation as VLSI chips which can perform image processing based in local operations at a very high speed [5]. In this paper, we present a general methodology to extend actual CNN operations to a large family of useful image processing operators in order to cover a very broad class of problems.

1 Introduction

The Cellular Neural Network Universal Machine (CNN-UM) is a programmable neuroprocessor having real-time power implemented in a single VLSI chip [8]. This neurocomputer is a massive aggregate of regularly spaced nonlinear analog cells which communicate with each other only through their nearest neighbors. Local connectivity allows its implementation as VLSI chips that can operate at a very high speed and complexity [5]. This fact makes the CNN an useful computation paradigm when the problem can be reformulated as a task where the signal values are placed on a regular 2-D grid, and the direct interaction between signal values are limited within a finite local neighborhood [2]. This cellular structure and the local interconnection topology not only resemble the anatomy of the retina, indeed, they are very close to the operation of the eye [10], especially when photosensors are placed over each tiny analog processor. Several of these tiny processors have been placed on a chip, which is also called visual microprocessor or cellular processor. In this paper, a methodology to extend local CNN computation capabilities to a very broad class of global operators is presented. In Section II, the cellular neural network mathematical model and the architecture of the CNN-Universal Machine prototyping system is introduced, as well as some standard CNN operators (also called templates). Sections III and IV describe a general method for implementing any type of piecewise-linear output

F.J. Garijo, J.C. Riquelme, and M. Toro (Eds.): IBERAMIA 2002, LNAI 2527, pp. 470–480, 2002.

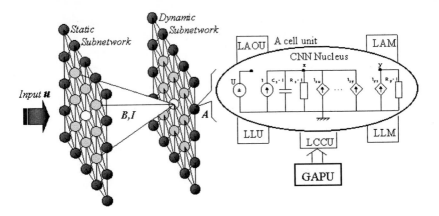

Fig. 1. Structure of the CNN dynamical network (left) and electrical scheme of each cell (right).

function and how we can perform integral and wavelet transforms on the CNN-UM framework. In Section V, several examples demonstrating the operation and run-time of the algorithm are discussed. Finally, Section VI gives a brief conclusion.

2   Description of the CNN-UM

The CNN-Universal Machine (CNN-UM) architecture [8] is an *analogic* spatio-temporal array computer wherein analog spatio-temporal dynamics and logic operations are combined in a programmable framework. A computational infrastructure exists in order to interface this computing analog technology to digital systems.

The elementary instructions and the algorithm techniques are absolutely different from any digital computers because elementary instructions (templates) perform complex spatio-temporal nonlinear dynamics phenomena by varying the local interconnection patterns in the array.

2.1   Nonlinear Dynamics of the Network

CNN dynamics can be electronically emulated by a single capacitor which is coupled to neighbouring cells through nonlinear controlled sources as can be seen in Fig. 1. The dynamics of the array can be described by the following set of nonlinear differential equations

$$\frac{d}{dt}x_{i,j}(t) = -x_{i,j}(t) + \sum_{k,l \in N_r} A_{k,l} y_{i+k,j+k}(t) + \sum_{k,l \in N_r} B_{k,l} u_{i+k,j+k}(t) + I \quad (1)$$

$$y(x) = \frac{1}{2}\left[|x-1| - |x+1|\right] \quad (2)$$

Input, state and output, represented by $u_{i,j}$, $x_{i,j}$ and $y_{i,j}$ are defined on $0 \leq i \leq N_1$ and $0 \leq i \leq N_2$ and N_r represents the neighborhood of the cell with a radius r as $N_r = \{(k,j) : \max\{|k-i|, |l-j|\} \leq r\}$. Due to implementability concerns, the template neighborhood radius is generally restricted to be as small as possible, and templates are applied in a space-invariant manner (A and B are the same for every cell).

2.2   Universal Machine Capabilities

The elementary image processing tasks performed on the input data by a single template can be combined to obtain more sophisticated operation mode on the CNN Universal Machine. The machine uses the simple CNN dynamics (1) in a time multiplexed fashion by controlling the template weights and the source of the data inputs for each operation.

The CNN-UM extends the CNN core of each cell in two main parts: *(a)the array of extended CNN cells* and *(b)the Global Analogic Programming Unit (GAPU)*. Several extra elements extend the CNN nucleus (core cell) computational capabilities to a Universal Machine: *4 Local Analog Memories (LAM)* consisting in a few continuous (analog) values are stored in the LAM in each cell; *4 Local Logic Memories (LLM)* which are several binary (logic) values stored in the LLM at each cell; *a Local Logic Unit (LLU)* which executes a simple programmable multi-input/single-output analog operation; and a *Local Comunication and Control Unit (LCCU)* which receives the messages from the central (global) "commander" (the GAPU) and programs the extended cells accordingly.

2.3   Local Processing Capabilities

In image processing applications, two independent input signal arrays $S_1(ij) = u_{i,j}(t)$ and $S_2(ij) = x_{i,j}(0)$ can be mapped onto the CNN, while the output signal array $S_o(ij)$ is associated with $y_{i,j}$. The generic input can be time varying, but the initial state $x_{i,j}(0)$ is usually fixed.

A lot of computational examples about capabilities of image processing on the cellular neural network can be found in the literature [1], [9], [7]. In the following one, it will be illustrated how CNN output exclusively depend on local properties (e.g., average gray level, intensity or texture). The processing is based on using several templates defined as $TEM_k = \{A^k; B^k; I^k\}$ where $A^k B^k$ are 3×3 convolution matrices and I^k is a biasing scalar.

From an input image Fig. 2(a), we can perform a linear low-pass filtering by convoluting with $TEM_1 = \{A_{ij}^1 = 0; B_{ij}^1 = 0.1(1+\delta_{2j}\delta_{2i}); I^k = 0, \forall i, j\}$. Then we can use the feedback convolution matrix A for thresholding the image by means of $TEM_2 = \{A_{ij}^2 = 2\delta_{2j}\delta_{2i}; B_{ij}^1 = 0; I^k = z^*, \forall i, j\}$ where z^* is the value of the threshold. In the following stage, a border extraction template $TEM_2 = \{A_{ij}^2 = 2\delta_{2j}\delta_{2i}; B_{ij}^1 = -1(1+9\delta_{2j}\delta_{2i}); I^k = -0.5, \forall i, j\}$ is used. It can be noted how the template extract the binary borders: matrix B controls the dynamics of the CNN convoluting the input image by a linear high-pass filter. The design

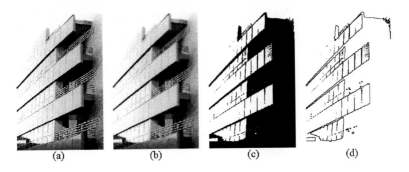

(a)   (b)   (c)   (d)

Fig. 2. An example of image processing capabilities on the Cellular Neural Network. (a)-(b) Input image and output after the low pass filter. (c) Thresholding of (b) with template in the normalized scale $[-1, 1]$. (c) Border detection.

of these templates is based in the geometric aspects of the matrices involved in the nonlinear differential equation (Eq. 1).

In these templates it can be seen how both linear classical filtering and dynamically evolving templates are based on convolution of a image with a 3×3 matrix, this fact makes CNN-UM ill-conditioned for achieving global operations over the whole image (e.g., integral/wavelet transforms or statistical operations).

3   PWL Approximation on the CNN-UM

When considering the VLSI CNN chip model, we deal with the output function (Eq. 1). In this Section, we present a software-based method to implement any non-linear output function on current CNNUM chips by superposition of simple piecewise-linear (PWL) saturation blocks in order to approximate any given continuous functions. This approximation is the basis of a novel method for accomplishing global operations on the implemented chip.

3.1   Notation

The following notation is used. δ_{ij} denotes Kronecker delta, $B_{z_o,r}$ denotes de open ball $B_{z_o,r} := \{z \in Z : \|z - z_o\| < r\}$, $\|\cdot\|$ is the weighted Euclidean norm defined as $\|z\| = \left(\sum_{i=1}^{n} \omega_i z_i^2\right)^{1/2}$, $\omega_i > 0$, $\|\cdot\|_\infty$ the weighted infinity norm, $\Delta h_i := h_{i+1} - h_i$, $\Sigma h_i := h_{i+1} + h_i$ and the simbol ' denotes differentiate on variable x.

3.2   Infinite Norm Criterion

In this paper, a superposition $\overline{f}(x)$ of PWL saturation functions is considered

$$\overline{f}(x) = \sum_{i=1}^{\sigma} \left(\frac{1}{b_i} y(a_i x - c_i) + m_i \right) \tag{3}$$

where $y(x)$ is the function defined in (Eq. 2); $a_i, b_i, c_i, m_i \in \mathbb{R}$ are the parameters of the structure. Basically, (Eq. 3) it is a nonlinear combination of linear affine lines, $\pi_i := \frac{1}{2} \left[|(a_i x - c_i) - 1| - |(a_i x - c_i) + 1| \right], i \in [1, \sigma]$.

Now, the problem under study can be stated as follows: Given a smooth function $f : S \to \mathbb{R}$, where $S \subset \mathbb{R}$ is compact, we want to design a PWL function $\overline{f}$ that minimizes the error between them in some sense. Formally, given a fixed number ε we want to find the optimal parameter vector $\theta^* = [a_i^*, b_i^*, c_i^*, m_i^*]$ that makes the objective functional $\mathfrak{J} := \left\| f(x) - \overline{f}(x) \right\|_\infty = \varepsilon \quad \forall x \in S$. The method used to obtain the PWL function is based on theorem 1

Theorem 1. *Let $f(x)$ be a function defined in the open subset (x_i, x_{i+1}); $x_i, x_{i+1} \in \mathbb{R}$ and $P_n(x)$ a polynomial of degree n. Then $P_n(x)$ minimizes $\left\| f(x) - P_n(x) \right\|_\infty$ if and only if $f(x) - P_n(x)$ takes the value $\varepsilon := \max(|f(x) - P_n(x)|)$ at least in n+2 points in the interval (x_i, x_{i+1}) with alternating sign.*

Remark 1. In manifold cases, the condition required by the previous theorem can be analytically expressed. This is the case when $f(x)$ is a concave or convex function in the approximating interval.

Theorem 2. *Let $f(x)$ be a function with $f'' > 0$ in the interval (x_1, x_2), $x_1, x_2 \in \mathbb{R}$ and $P_1(x) := Mx + B$. Then $P_1(x)^1$ minimizes $\left\| f(x) - P_1(x) \right\|_\infty$ if and only if $M = \Delta f / \Delta x_1$; $B = \frac{1}{2} \left[f(x_2) + f(x_a) - \Delta f_i / \Delta x_i (x_a + x_2) \right]$ where x_a is obtained by solving $f'(x_a) = \Delta f_i / \Delta x_i$*

Proof. It follows from theorem 1 that it must be three points x_1, x_2, x_3 in (x_i, x_{i+1}) which maximize $E(x) := f(x) - P_1(x)$. This condition implies that x_2 is an intermediate point in the interval (x_i, x_{i+1}) with $E'(x)|_{x=x_2} = 0$; this is the same that $f'(x)|_{x=x_2} = M$. Since $f''(x) \geq 0$, $f'(x)$ is a growing function strictly and can equate M only once, this means that x_2 is the only one intermediate point in the interval. Thus $x_1 = x_{i-1}$ and $x_2 = x_i$. Applying the results in theorem 1, we obtain $f(x_i) - P_1(x_i) = - [f(x_2) - P_1(x_2)] = f(x_{i+1}) - P_1(x_{i+1})$. By solving these equations we can conclude

$$ M = \frac{\Delta f_i}{\Delta x_i}; \ B = \frac{1}{2} \left[f(x_{i+1}) + f(x_a) - \frac{\Delta f_i}{\Delta x_i} (x_a + x_{i+1}) \right] $$

Corollary 1. *Under the previous conditions the infinity norm is given by the following expression $\varepsilon = f(x) - \left[\frac{\Delta f_i}{\Delta x_i} x + \frac{1}{2} \left(f(x_{i+1}) + f(x_{ai}) - \frac{\Delta f_i}{\Delta x_i}(x_{ai} - x_{i+1}) \right) \right]$*

Theorem 3. *Let $f(x)$ be a function with $f''(x) \geq 0$ in the interval (x_a, x_b), $x_a, x_b \in \mathbb{R}$, ε an arbitrary small real number and $\overline{f}(x) = \sum_{i=1}^{\sigma} \pi_i$, where $\pi_i := \frac{1}{2} \left[|(a_i x - c_i) - 1| - |(a_i x - c_i) + 1| \right], i \in [1, \sigma]; a_i, b_i, c_i, m_i \in \mathbb{R}, i \in [1, \sigma]$. Then $\overline{f}(x)$ makes $\left\| f(x) - \overline{f}(x) \right\|_\infty = \varepsilon^*$ minimizing σ if the parameters of $\overline{f}(x)$ fulfill the following conditions*

---

[1] This straight line is called *Chebyshev line* in the literature.

$$a_i = 2/ \Delta x_i, \; b_i = 2/ \Delta f_i, \; c_i = \Sigma x_i/ \, 2, \; i \in [1, \sigma];$$
$$m_1 = \Sigma f_i/ \, 2 - \varepsilon^*, \; m_j = \Sigma f_j/ \, 2 - f(x_j) - \varepsilon^*, \; j \in [2, \sigma] \qquad (4)$$

where x_i is defined by the following set of discrete equations

$$\varepsilon^* - \frac{1}{2}\left[x_i + \frac{\Delta f_i}{\Delta x_i}(x_{ai} - x_i) - f(x_{ai}) \right] = 0, \; f'(x_{ai}) = \frac{\Delta f_i}{\Delta x_i}$$

Proof. In order to demonstrates this theorem we can express π_i as

$$\pi_i := \begin{cases} m_i - b_i^{-1}, \; \forall x \in \left[c_i + a_i^{-1}, \infty \right) \\ m_i + \frac{\Delta f_i}{\Delta x_i}(x - c_i), \; \forall x \in B_{c_i, a_i^{-1}} \\ m_i + b_i^{-1}, \; \forall x \in \left(-\infty, c_i - a_i^{-1} \right] \end{cases}$$

Replacing the values of the parameters given in the statement of the theorem

$$\pi_i := \begin{cases} \delta_{1i}\left(f(x_i) - \varepsilon^* \right), \; \forall x \in \left[c_i + a_i^{-1}, \infty \right) \\ \delta_{1i}\left(f(x_i) - \varepsilon^* \right) + \frac{\Delta f_i}{\Delta x_i}(x - x_i), \; \forall x \in B_{c_i, a_i^{-1}} \\ \delta_{1i}\left(f(x_i) - \varepsilon^* \right) + \Delta f_i, \; \forall x \in \left(-\infty, c_i - a_i^{-1} \right] \end{cases}$$

If we consider $x_a \in (x_j, x_{j+1})$ and expand $\overline{f}(x_a)$ taking into account the value of ε^* and the shape of π_i with the parameters given in the theorem it is obtained

$$\begin{aligned} \overline{f}(x_a) &:= \pi_1 + \textstyle\sum_{i=2}^{j-1} \pi_i + \pi_j + \textstyle\sum_{i=j+1}^{\sigma} \pi_i \\ &= (f(x_1) - \varepsilon^*) + \textstyle\sum_{i=2}^{j-1} \Delta f_i + \left[\frac{\Delta f_j}{\Delta x_j}(x - x_j) \right] \\ &= f(x_j) - \varepsilon^* + \frac{\Delta f_j}{\Delta x_j}(x - x_j) \\ &= \frac{\Delta f_i}{\Delta x_i}x + \frac{1}{2}\left[f(x_{i+1}) + f(x_a) - \frac{\Delta f_i}{\Delta x_i}(x_a + x_{i+1}) \right] \end{aligned}$$

this is the equation of the *Chebyshev line* that approximated $f(x)$ in the interval (x_j, x_{j+1}) with $\| f(x) - P_1(x) \|_\infty = \varepsilon^*$ as it was expressed in corollary 4.

Corollary 2. *Since the PWL function is continuous in the intervals (x_i, x_{i+1}) and the term $\sum_{i=j+1}^{\sigma} \pi_i$ is null in the expansion of $\overline{f}(x_a)$ performed in the previous proof, it can be affirmed that $\lim_{\Delta x \to 0} f(x_i + \Delta x) = \lim_{\Delta x \to 0} f(x_i - \Delta x)$, and $\overline{f}(x)$ is a PWL continuous function.*

Remark 2. Theorem 3 gives us the possibility of approximating any contiuous function $f(x)$ with $f''(x) \geq 0$ by means of a PWL function as defined by $\overline{f}(x)$ with an arbitrary infinite norm ε^*. Besides, the intervals of the approximation function can be obtained in a forward way if we know the analytical expression of $f(x)$, by means of solving the uncoupled discrete equations stated at the final of theorem 3.

The functional proposed in this paper is an alternative to the $(f(x) - \overline{f}(x))^2$ functional studied in several papers [3], [4]. This cuadratic criterion yields a nonlinear optimization problem characterized by the existence of several local minima. One practical technique used to solve this problem consist in the use of iterative algorithms which produce new random search direction when a local minimum in reached. This fact emphasize the advantage of the direct method based on theorem 3 to design the intervals of approximation opposite to the annealing iterative method needed in the minimization of the cuadratic norm.

3.3   Approximation of Useful Functions

In this point it will be analytically derived the parameter vector θ^* for several concrete functions that will be used in the process of performing integral transformation on the CNN. In this approximation it will be used a value $\varepsilon^* = 2^{-7}$ because of the physical implementation of the CNN-UM chip allows an analog accuracy of this magnitude.

In the case of $f(x)$ being a logarithmic or exponential function, the discrete equation in theorem 3 yields the following implicit discrete equations

$$\ln\left(\frac{\Delta x_i}{\Delta \ln_i}\right) + \left(\frac{\Delta \ln_i}{\Delta x_i}\right) x_i - \ln(x_i) - 1 = 2\varepsilon^* \tag{5}$$

$$\frac{\Delta \exp_i}{\Delta x_i}\left[\ln\left(\frac{\Delta \exp_i}{\Delta x_i}\right) + x_i + 1\right] - \exp(x_i) \tag{6}$$

where $\Delta \ln_i = \ln(x_{i+1}) - \ln(x_i)$, $\Delta \exp_i = \exp(x_{i+1})\exp(x_i)$ and $\varepsilon^* = 2^{-7}$. Both equation can be easily solved by standard numerical methods in order to obtain in a sequential and forward way the neighboring points of the intervals that construct the PWL approximating function $\overline{f}(x)$. Similar equation can be obtained for the functions x^2 and $\tan^{-1}(x)$. The parameter vector defined as $\theta^* := [a_1^*, b_1^*, c_1^*, m_1^*, a_2^*, b_2^*, ...]$ can be easily obtained as it was shown in theorem 3

- $ln(x)$; $x_i = \{0.368, 0.608, 1.004, 1.657, 2.735\}$ in the interval limited by the conditions[2] $f(x_1) = -1$, $f(x_\sigma) = 1$.
- $exp(x)$; $x_i = \{-2, -1.5, -1, -0.310, 0.202, 0.610, 0.949, 1.239, 1.699, 1.856, 2\}$
- x^2; $x_i = \{0, 0.354, 0.708, 1.062\}$
- $\tan^{-1}(x)$; $x_i = \{0, 0.697, 1.425, 2.672, 5.617, 16.963\}$

3.4   Algorithmic Description of the PWL Approximation

The stages in the approximation process are: (i) modification of the saturation PWL original saturation as defined in (Eq. 2) to adopt it to every interval obtained previously and (ii) superposition of these modified saturation in order to obtain $\overline{f}(x)$.

---

[2] The reason for selecting these intervals will be shown in the following section.

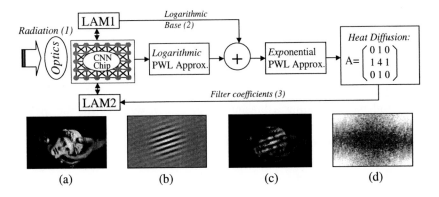

Fig. 3. Algorithmic diagram of the Integral Transformation.

The original saturation function $y(x)$ is modified by the affine transformation given by $\frac{1}{b_i}y(a_ix - c_i) + m_i$. This transformation translates the corners from (-1,-1) and (1,1) to $(c_i - \frac{1}{a_i}, m_i - \frac{1}{b_i})$, $(c_i + \frac{1}{a_i}, m_i + \frac{1}{b_i})$. This transformation is performed on the CNN by means of the following two templates run in a sequential way $TEM_{PWL^k,1} = \left\{A_{ij}^2 = 0; B_{ij}^1 = a_k\delta_{2j}\delta_{2i}); I^k = -a_kc_k ,\forall i,j\right\}$, $TEM_{PWL^k,2} = \left\{A_{ij}^2 = 0; B_{ij}^1 = b_k^{-1}\delta_{2j}\delta_{2i}); I^k = m_k ,\forall i,j\right\}$.

The way to obtain the desired approximating function is by shaping the output saturation by templates given by $TEM_{PWL^k,1}$ and $TEM_{PWL^k,2}$ with the coeficients obtained in the manifold stages needed to approximate the function. Once we have modified the first stage, we apply this shaped output to the input image and save the result into the LAM, then the second stage is modified and the same input image is passed through this saturation and the results is added to the value previously saved in the LAM. Making this process through every stage we finally obtain the image processed by a point operation that approximately performs a desired function $f(x)$.

4   Gabor Transform Computation

This Section describes the design of a CNNUM program which compute the output of integral transforms. The base of the algorithm is described in Fig. 3. In this figure can be seen how the input image is directly irradiated on the Chip surface through the optical devices and sensed by the photosensors implemented on the silicon. Once we have the image in the LAM $I(x,y)$, we perform the approximation of the logarithmic function $\overline{\ln}(I(x,y) + 1.5)$, adding a bias on the whole image to translate the swing of analog values into the interval $(0.5, 2.5)$ where the logarithmic approximation is valid. Then we add in the LAM the logarithmically shaped image with the logarithmic base $B_{\log}(x,y) := \ln(B(x,y) + 1.5)$, where B(x,y) is the transformation base used. Then we pass this results through an exponential approximation stage to obtain

$$\overline{exp}\left[\overline{\ln}(I(x,y)+1.5)+\ln(B(x,y)+1.5)\right]$$
$$= (I(x,y)+1.5)\,(B(x,y)+1.5)$$
$$= I(x,y)B(x,y)+1.5(I(x,y)+B(x,y))+1.5^2$$

It is easy to correct this result to obtain the product by simply substracting the term $1.5(I(x,y)+B(x,y))+1.5^2$ which is computing scaling the addition of input and base including a biasing term. Lastly, we perform the averaging by means of a template that emulated the PDE of temperature diffusion. This template gives us the value of the correlation between the image and the base and the value of the transform at the frequency point of the base is directly calculated.

5 Experimental Results

In this section, it is presented a Gabor transform example providing run-time of the algorithm. Gabor filters has been used as preprocessors for different tasks in computer vision and image processing [6]. Gabor filters exists or signal of arbitrary dimension where an n-dimensional signal is defined to be a mapping from $\mathbb{R}^n$ to $\mathbb{R}$ or $\mathbb{C}$. For n-dimensional signals, the impulse response $g(\overrightarrow{x})$ of a two-dimensional Gabor filter is a complex exponential modulated by an n-dimensional Gaussian

$$g(x,y) = \frac{1}{\sqrt{2\pi}\sigma}e^{-(x^2+y^2)/2\sigma^2}e^{j(\omega_{xo}x+\omega_{yo}y)}$$

which is tuned to spatial frequency $(\omega_{xo},\omega_{yo})$. This filter responds maximally to edges which are oriented at an angle $\theta = \tan^{-1}(\omega_{yo}/\omega_{xo})$ where θ is defined to be an angle between the horizontal axis and the line perpendicular to the edge.

Several illustrative images obtained along the transformation process are showed in Fig. 3. In table 1, we compare this architecture considering the processing time of different elementary steps in CNN and digital technologies. In our comparison we define equivalent operations between the parallel CNN and the serial processors.

6 Conclusions

In this paper, we have introduced the equations that govern the complex CNN spatio-temporal dynamics and the CNNUM computational infrastructure implemented on silicon. After this, we have presented a general technique that allows us to approximate any nonlinear output function on the CNNUM VLSI Chip. For this purpose, we have given a theoretical analysis of an approximation technique based on the infinity norm criterion. Also, the advantages of this technique have been compared with the cuadratic error criterion. Lastly, we have used this technique to implement the algorithm on the fully parallel architecture in order to implement Gabor filters. The main motivation of this work is to

Table 1. Comparision table of execution times of the different imaging processors (grey scale and 64 × 64 image resolution).

Run-time of elementary steps			Sub-tasks of the algorithm	
	CNN 100nsec	PC @4, 1GHz		CNN 100nsec
$I/O\ image$	6 μ sec	10 μ sec	Logarithmic approximation	24,4 μ sec
Conversion LLM/LAM	100 nsec		Exponential approximation	61 μ sec
Binary Save/Load	6 μ sec		Biasing	6,1 μ sec
Arithmetic operation	100 nsec	9 μ sec	PDE (Heat diffusion)	8 μ sec
Logical	50 nsec	8 μ sec	Image LAM transfer	6 μ sec
Convolution 3 × 3	1,4 μ sec	32 μ sec	Coefficient LAM transfer	6 μ sec

release CNNUM emphanalogic (analog+logic) architecture from using emphdigital computers when CNN image processing computing capabilities are unable to perform any required nonlinear filtering step or global transformation.

References

1. K.R. Crounse, and L.O. Chua, "Methods for image processing and pattern formation in cellular neural networks: A tutorial," *IEEE Trans. Circuits Syst.,* Vol. 42, no. 10, 1995.
2. L. O. Chua, and L. Yang. "Cellular neural networks: Theory". *IEEE Trans. Circuits Syst.,*vol. 35, no. 10. pp. 1257–1272, 1988.
3. L.O. Chua, and R.L.P.Ying, "Canonical piecewise-linear analysis," *IEEE Trans. Circuits Syst.,* vol. CAS-30, pp. 125–140, 1983.
4. J.N. Lin, H. Xu, and R. Unbehahuen, "A generalization of canonical piecewise-linear functions," *IEEE Trans. Circuits Syst.,* vol. 41, no. 1, pp. 345–347, 1994.
5. G. Liñán, S. Espejo, R. Domínguez-Castro, and A. Rodríguez-Vázquez, "The CN-NUC3: an Analog I/O 64 x 64 CNN Universal Machine with 7-bit Analog Accuracy", IEEE Int. Workshop on Cellular Neural Networks and their Applications (CNNA'2000), pp. 201–206.
6. S. Marceljia, "Mathematical description of the responses of simple cortical cells," *J. Opt. Soc. Amer.,* vol. 70, pp.1297–1300, 1980.
7. V.M. Preciado, "Real-time wavelet transform for image processing on the cellular neural network universal machine", *Lecture Notes in Computer Science,* Vol. 2085, pp. 636–643. Springer-Verlag, 2001.
8. T. Roska, A. Zarandy, S. Zold, P. Foldesy, and P. Szolgay, "The computational infrastructure of the analogic CNN computing - Part I: The CNN-UM Chip prototyping system", *IEEE Trans. Circuits Syst.,* vol. 46, no. 1, pp. 261–268, 1999.

9. P.L.Venetianer, F.Werblin, T.Roska, and L.O.Chua, "Analogic CNN algorithms for some image compression and restoration tasks", *IEEE Trans. Circuits Syst.*, vol. 42, no. 5, 1995.
10. F. Werblin, T. Roska, and L. O. Chua, "The analogic cellular neural network as a bionic eye," *Int. J. circuit Theory Appl.*, vol. 23, no. 6, pp. 541–549, 1995.

Learning to Assess from Pair-Wise Comparisons[1]

J. Díez[1], J.J. del Coz[2], O. Luaces[2], F. Goyache[1], J. Alonso[2], A.M. Peña[3], and
A. Bahamonde[2]

[1] SERIDA-CENSYRA-Somió, C/ Camino de los Claveles 604,
E-33203 Gijón (Asturias), Spain.
{Jdiez, fgoyache}@serida.org
[2] Centro de Inteligencia Artificial. Universidad de Oviedo at Gijón, Campus de Viesques,
E-33271 Gijón (Asturias), Spain.
{juanjo, oluaces, jalonso, antonio}@aic.uniovi.es,
[3] Facultad de Ingeniería. Universidad Distrital Francisco José de Caldas, Bogotá, Colombia.

Abstract. In this paper we present an algorithm for learning a function able to assess objects. We assume that our teachers can provide a collection of pair-wise comparisons but encounter certain difficulties in assigning a number to the qualities of the objects considered. This is a typical situation when dealing with food products, where it is very interesting to have repeatable, reliable mechanisms that are as objective as possible to evaluate quality in order to provide markets with products of a uniform quality. The same problem arises when we are trying to learn user preferences in an information retrieval system or in configuring a complex device. The algorithm is implemented using a growing variant of Kohonen's Self-Organizing Maps (growing neural gas), and is tested with a variety of data sets to demonstrate the capabilities of our approach.

1 Introduction

Generally speaking, quality assessment is a complex matter: what we usually need to evaluate are the desirable traits of an object by means of a single number. Frequently though, this number does not strictly reflect an absolute value, but rather the relative quality of the object with respect to others. This is especially true for objects of a biological origin; their quality is dependent on a not always well defined group of multisensorial properties resulting from their chemical composition, the natural structure of the food elements, their interaction and the way in which they are perceived by human senses [13]. This situation becomes even more complex when we consider quality grading of food products from the viewpoint of experts or consumers. Since no detailed grading specifications exist, experts may adopt a quality profile that considerably exceeds that expected by the consumer [2]. The requirements of consumers are usually based on single attributes that characterize primary senses.

---

[1] The research reported in this paper has been supported in part under MCyT and Feder grant TIC2001-3579

F.J. Garijo, J.C. Riquelme, and M. Toro (Eds.): IBERAMIA 2002, LNAI 2527, pp. 481–490, 2002.
© Springer-Verlag Berlin Heidelberg 2002

Consequently, the literature reflects disagreement between quality assessments obtained through consumer or expert panels [2, 9].

However, the food industry needs to supply markets with uniform quality products to satisfy consumer demands for normalized quality. Furthermore, if possible, food producers would like to know what the objective (chemical and physical) basis of the assessed quality is from the customer viewpoint so as to improve the acceptability of their products.

The straightforward way to build computable procedures to assess objects is to collect a set of representative assessment events and then to apply a machine learning algorithm that employs regression like CUBIST [6], M5' [16, 20], SAFE (System to Acquire Functions from Examples) [15] or BETS (Best Examples in Training Sets) [7]. However, our experience with biological objects [9, 10] tells us that the complexity of the assessment task means that the repeatability of human evaluations tends to be low. Hence, the reliability of the training material is poor, despite experts having been trained exhaustively and having accumulated a large, valuable body of knowledge used for assessing [12].

Experts or consumers are perfectly able to prefer one object to another, but usually fail when they are asked to label products with a number. There is a kind of *batch effect* that often biases the assessment; human assessors try to number the differences in a relative sense, comparing products with the other partners in the batch. Thus, a product surrounded by worse things will probably obtain a higher assessment than if it were presented with better products. However, although we may find unacceptable individual variability in the absolute number obtained to assess the quality of a given product, the relative position obtained in a batch is quite constant.

In this paper we present a new approach to learning functions capable of assessing objects starting from reliable training material. Our training sets are formed by pairs of object descriptions, given by continuous attributes, where the first one has been considered worse than the second. The goal is then a function able to quantify the quality of objects as coherently as possible with the pair-wise ordering supplied as the training set.

The core idea is to consider each training instance as an indication of a direction where we can find an increase in quality. Thus, the vectorial difference of compared products is interpreted as a kind of coding of the local behavior of the assessment function. In this way, the learning algorithm is a clustering that uses a growing version [8] of Kohonen's Self-Organizing Maps (SOM) [11], where each cell encapsulates a regression rule.

After presenting the geometrical motivations of the algorithm followed by the implementation details, we close the paper with a section devoted to presenting the experimental results obtained with our assessment learner.

2 Geometrical Motivation of the Algorithm

Let **u** and **v** be vectors describing the features of two objects that our experts compare, resulting in **u** being *worse* than **v**; in symbols, **u** < **v**. Then, we seek a function f such that f(**u**) < f(**v**). If we assume that f behaves linearly, at least in the surroundings of our vectors, we have to find a vector **w** such that

$$f_w(\mathbf{u}) = \mathbf{u} \cdot \mathbf{w} < \mathbf{v} \cdot \mathbf{w} = f_w(\mathbf{v}) \tag{1}$$

where, for vectors **z** and **t,** we represent their inner product by **z·t**.

From a geometrical point of view, function f_w represents the distance to the hyperplane $\mathbf{u} \cdot \mathbf{w} = 0$; i.e. the hyperplane of vectors perpendicular to $\mathbf{w}$. If we search for $\mathbf{w}$ considering only normalized vectors (i.e. $\|\mathbf{w}\| = 1$), the largest difference between $f_w(\mathbf{u})$ and $f_w(\mathbf{v})$ values is reached when $\mathbf{w}$ is the normalized vector in the direction of $(\mathbf{v}-\mathbf{u})$. In fact,

$$f_w(\mathbf{v}-\mathbf{u}) = (\mathbf{v}-\mathbf{u}) \cdot \mathbf{w} \leq \|\mathbf{v}\text{-}\mathbf{u}\| \cdot \|\mathbf{w}\| = \|\mathbf{v}\text{-}\mathbf{u}\| = (\mathbf{v}-\mathbf{u}) \cdot (\mathbf{v}-\mathbf{u})/\|\mathbf{v}\text{-}\mathbf{u}\| = f_{(\mathbf{v}-\mathbf{u})/\|\mathbf{v}\text{-}\mathbf{u}\|}(\mathbf{v}-\mathbf{u}) \quad (2)$$

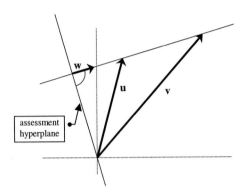

Fig. 1. Given two objects represented by vectors $\mathbf{u}$ and $\mathbf{v}$, if $\mathbf{u}$ is worse than $\mathbf{v}$, the normal vector in the direction of the difference, $\mathbf{w} = (\mathbf{v}\text{-}\mathbf{u})/\|\mathbf{v}\text{-}\mathbf{u}\|$, defines a hyperplane, the distance from which is a suitable local assessment function

In the general case we start from a family of *comparisons*

$$\{\mathbf{u}_i < \mathbf{v}_i : i = 1, \dots, n\} \quad (3)$$

and wish to induce a function f, with local linear behavior, and which hopefully is capable of distinguishing as often as possible that $\mathbf{u}_i$ is worse than $\mathbf{v}_i$, because $f(\mathbf{u}_i) < f(\mathbf{v}_i)$. The algorithm proposed in this paper uses the geometrical intuition introduced in this section as the basic building block of such a function f. Hence, the main task of the algorithm will be to combine the local guidelines suggested by each comparison supplied in the training set.

3 The Algorithm: Clustering Partial Functions

In line with the discussions presented in the previous section, the comparison examples of (3) give rise to a set of 2n *pairs* of vectors as follows:

$$\{((\mathbf{v}_i - \mathbf{u}_i)/\|\mathbf{v}_i - \mathbf{u}_i\|, \mathbf{u}_i): i = 1, \dots, n\} \cup \{((\mathbf{v}_i - \mathbf{u}_i)/\|\mathbf{v}_i - \mathbf{u}_i\|, \mathbf{v}_i): i = 1, \dots, n\} . \quad (4)$$

If $(\mathbf{w}, \mathbf{u})$ is such a pair, we understand it to be a suggestion of a regression rule indicating that the assessment of a vector $\mathbf{z}$ is

$$f_w(\mathbf{z}) \text{ if } \mathbf{z} \text{ is in the neighborhood of } \mathbf{u} \ . \tag{5}$$

Given that $f_w(\mathbf{z}) = \mathbf{z} \cdot \mathbf{w}$, we will usually identify $\mathbf{w}$ with the linear *function* f_w. Likewise, we will refer to $\mathbf{u}$ as the *conditions* of the rule. For short, we write $\mathbf{w} \leftarrow \mathbf{u}$

In general, we are pursuing an assessment function f defined by parts of the whole attribute space. In other words, our assessment function will be given by a list of regression rules

$$(\mathbf{w}_1 \leftarrow \mathbf{u}_1); (\mathbf{w}_2 \leftarrow \mathbf{u}_2); \ldots; (\mathbf{w}_m \leftarrow \mathbf{u}_m) \tag{6}$$

that must be evaluated by means of a minimal distance criterion. In symbols, the function f that is finally induced will work as follows for an arbitrary vector $\mathbf{z}$.

$$f(\mathbf{z}) = \mathbf{w}_k \cdot \mathbf{z} \qquad \text{if } \| \mathbf{z} - \mathbf{u}_k \| \leq \| \mathbf{z} - \mathbf{u}_j \|, \forall j = 1, \ldots, m \tag{7}$$

A first attempt to define the list of regression rules (6) is to consider the whole set of pairs $(\mathbf{w}, \mathbf{u})$ defined in (4), but these rule set must be improved: it is too big and may contain a lot of noise. Therefore, the idea of our learning algorithm (see Algorithm 1) is to cluster similar conditions $\mathbf{u}$, and then to attach a function $\mathbf{w}$ according to the functions of the pairs of the same cluster (see Figure 2). To this end, we use a growing version of Kohonen's Self-Organizing Maps (SOM) [11]: growing neural gas (*GNG*) of Fritzke [8]. This approach has the advantage that we do not need to define a priori configuration parameters like SOM layout dimensions or the radius used throughout the adaptation.

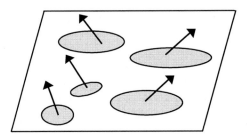

Fig. 2. The clusters of partial functions represents, in each node, an environment in the attribute space of the objects to be assessed, drawn in gray in the picture, and a vector pointing in the direction to measure the assessments. In other words, the map represents a set of regression rules to be applied by means of a nearest-distance criterion

The GNG graph starts with two nodes $\mathbf{u}_1$, $\mathbf{u}_2$ representing two points in the domain of the assessment function, in each iteration step a new node is added trying to fit better this space. The number of steps (N) followed by *GNG* conditions the granularity of the regression rules. By default, N is the number of comparisons divided by 10.

Once we have a number of clusters represented by $\mathbf{u}_1, \mathbf{u}_2, \ldots, \mathbf{u}_m$, we consider the set of comparisons $(\mathbf{t}_2 < \mathbf{t}_1)$ where each $\mathbf{t}_k$ is closer to the same $\mathbf{u}_i$ than to any other $\mathbf{u}_j$. These comparisons will be used to compute a local linear approximation of the assessment function in the surroundings of $\mathbf{u}_i$.

The procedure followed to find a linear function with coefficients $\mathbf{w} = (a_1, \ldots, a_d)$ is taken from OC1 [14] only slightly modified for this purpose. In fact, what we are looking for is a vector $\mathbf{w}$ such that $\mathbf{w} \cdot (\mathbf{t}_1 - \mathbf{t}_2) > 0$ as many times as possible. We can start with $\mathbf{w}$ being the average of the normalized differences

$$\mathbf{w} = (a_1, \ldots, a_d) = \mathsf{Average}\{(\mathbf{t}_1 - \mathbf{t}_2)/\|\mathbf{t}_1 - \mathbf{t}_2\| : \mathbf{t}_1 > \mathbf{t}_2 \ \& \ \mathbf{t}_1, \mathbf{t}_2 \in \mathsf{cluster}(\mathbf{u}_i)\} \ . \tag{8}$$

Now we try to improve the coefficients a_m, one at a time. The key observation is that for each normalized difference $(\mathbf{t}_1 - \mathbf{t}_2)/\|\mathbf{t}_1 - \mathbf{t}_2\| = (x_1, \ldots, x_d)$ we have that

$$\mathbf{w} \cdot (\mathbf{t}_1 - \mathbf{t}_2) = \Sigma(a_i * x_i : i = 1..d) > 0 , \tag{9}$$

when $x_m > 0$, is equivalent to

$$a_m > -(a_1 x_1 + a_2 x_2 + \ldots + a_{m-1} x_{m-1} + a_{m+1} x_{m+1} + \ldots + a_d x_d) / x_m = U \tag{10}$$

or the opposite when $x_m < 0$. When $x_m = 0$, the value of the coefficient a_m does not matter. So, for fixed values of all other coefficients, each equation (10) represents a constraint on the values of a_m. Therefore, we sort all U values and consider as possible setting for a_m the midpoints between each pair of consecutive U's. We select the a_m that satisfies the greater number of constraints. Following the procedure of OC1, we iterate this step in order to adjust all the coefficients until no further optimisation can be achieved.

If the number of clusters is high, for instance whenever we use the default value for N, the number of training examples divided by 10, then the previous approach inspired in OC1 can be skipped (the results are quite similar). We can simply update the function $\mathbf{w}$ attached to a cluster $\mathbf{u}$ as the average of the functions $\mathbf{w}'$ of pairs $(\mathbf{w}', \mathbf{u}')$ whose winner node is $\mathbf{u}$.

In any case, the regression rules so found need a final improvement process. The idea is that $\mathbf{w} \leftarrow \mathbf{u}$ may correctly resolve assessments of objects near $\mathbf{u}$. That is, when $\mathbf{t}_1 > \mathbf{t}_2$, and both $\mathbf{t}_1$ and $\mathbf{t}_2$ are near $\mathbf{u}$, $\mathbf{w}$ was devised for obtaining $\mathbf{w} \cdot (\mathbf{t}_1 - \mathbf{t}_2) > 0$. But $\mathbf{w}$ may fail when one of the objects is going to be assessed by another rule $\mathbf{w}' \leftarrow \mathbf{u}'$. To solve these situations we are going to look for adequate *slope modifiers* a and independent terms b such that the function of the regression rule will now be

$$a \, (\, \mathbf{w} \cdot \square \,) + b \leftarrow \mathbf{u} \ . \tag{11}$$

The procedure followed to find a and b for each regression rule is almost the same that we have just described for adjusting the coefficients a_m of each w. The only difference is that now we consider comparisons where only one of the objects is near the condition of the rule to be improved.

Function LEARN TO ASSESS COMPARISONS FROM EXAMPLES (LACE)
        (comparisons set $\{\mathbf{u}_i < \mathbf{v}_i:\ i=1,\ldots,n\}$, number of steps N) {

$$E = \left\{ \left(\frac{\mathbf{v}_i - \mathbf{u}_i}{\|\mathbf{v}_i - \mathbf{u}_i\|}, \mathbf{u}_i \right):\ i=1,\ldots,n \right\} \cup \left\{ \left(\frac{\mathbf{v}_i - \mathbf{u}_i}{\|\mathbf{v}_i - \mathbf{u}_i\|}, \mathbf{v}_i \right):\ i=1,\ldots,n \right\};$$

    // To have comparable values in [0,1]
    Normalize each component of conditions $\mathbf{u}_i$ and $\mathbf{v}_i$ in E pairs;
    // Now, we cluster the conditions of E examples
    GNG(conditions(E), steps = N); //by default N = $|E|/(2*10)$
    Let $(\mathbf{w}_1,\mathbf{u}_1)$, $(\mathbf{w}_2,\mathbf{u}_2),\ldots,(\mathbf{w}_m,\mathbf{u}_m)$ be the nodes of the graph
        where w_i are the average values of the training
        instances having node i as the nearest one
    //the next loop can be safety skipped when N is high
    for each node $(\mathbf{w}_i,\ \mathbf{u}_i)$ in graph **do** {
        //notice that the function w_i is an arbitrary value
        $\mathbf{w}_i$ = Ocl$\{\mathbf{t}_1 - \mathbf{t}_2:\ (t_2 < t_1)\ \&\&\ \|u_i,t_1\| \le \|u_j,t_1\|\ \&\&\ \|u_i,t_2\| \le \|u_j,t_2\|\ j \ne i\}$
    }
    improve relative slopes and independent terms of regression rules;
    return regression rules;
}

Algorithm 1. The algorithm that learns to assess from pair-wise comparison examples (LACE)

4 Experimental Results

In order to test the validity of our approach we conducted a number of experiments. The idea is to deal with assessment problems where we know *a priori* the kind of results that we would like to obtain.

To illustrate the way that our algorithm works, we start with a simple problem. Let us consider objects describable by only one continuous attribute **x** with values in [0, 1], and having as *true* assessment function the parabola ta(x)= -x(x-1), see Figure (3, a). To build a training set of comparisons E, we generated 3000 pairs (x1,x2) with values in [0,1], and we added to E the pair (x1,x2) if ta(x1) > ta(x2), and we added (x2,x1) otherwise. Our algorithm learned from E the function f drawn in Figure (3, b). Notice that while the actual values of f(x) and ta(x) are quite different, the relative values are almost the same. In fact, building a test set of comparisons using the same procedure followed for E, we only found that the 0.03% of the pairs were erroneously ordered by f.

A second package of experiments (see Table 1) was carried out with objects describable by two continuous attributes: **x** and **y**. Once an assessment function had been fixed, the objects were randomly generated as 2-dimensional points in the stated rectangles; once we have generated two such objects, they are written in the comparison set, the worse one (according to the corresponding goal assessment function) first. We additionally generated another test set of comparisons, changing the random seed. Both sets had 3000 pairs. The errors reported are the percentage of test pairs that were misplaced by the assessment function learned by our algorithm. These data sets should be easy problems for our learner, and in fact were so, as can be seen in the scores reported in Table (1): However, we can appreciate significantly better scores when the regions with different assessment behavior are separated.

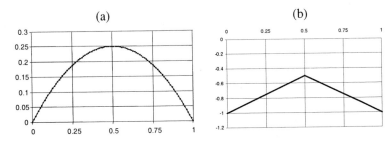

Fig. 3. The objects to be assessed are described by x ∈ [0, 1]. (a) The true assessment is ta(x) = -x(x-1). (b) The function learned by our algorithm f. Only 1 of the 3000 test pairs is erroneously ordered by f

Table 1. Experiments carried out with goal functions defined by two linear subfunctions with separate domains. The original objects to be assessed were vectors in the rectangles [0, 999] × [0,999] in the first two rows, and for the other two [200,299] × [0,999], and [700,799] × [0,999]. Both training and test sets have 3000 elements. We used only 3 steps to adapt the underlying GNG graph

Goal functions	Error
$f(x,y) = \begin{cases} x+10y & x \leq 500 \\ 10x+y & x > 500 \end{cases}$	4.83%
$f(x,y) = \begin{cases} x+y & x \leq 500 \\ x-y & x > 500 \end{cases}$	5.46%
$f(x,y) = \begin{cases} x+10y & x \in [200,299] \\ 10x+y & x \in [700,799] \end{cases}$	0.23%
$f(x,y) = \begin{cases} x+y & x \in [200,299] \\ x-y & x \in [700,799] \end{cases}$	0.20%

Finally, we used some publicly available regression datasets in an attempt to deal with almost *real-world* data. We built training and test sets providing comparisons between the class values of pairs of examples instead of training on their class labels as in the conventional setting; for each example we randomly selected other 10 examples, 8 of them were placed in the training set and the other 2 went to the test set. In order to compare the achievements of LACE, we used two well-known regression learners: M5' [16, 20], and Cubist [6]. We trained M5' and Cubist with the whole dataset, that is considering not only the description of the objects, but the numeric class too. To test what they learned, we compared the values provided for each component of the comparison. The scores so found are reported in Table (2).

Let us remark that the comparative reported in Table (2) is not fair for our LACE. The reason is that regression learners have access to the true numerical classes for *all test examples,* while LACE can only see pairs where there are differences, but without knowing the amount of those differences. As was pointed out in the introduction, in *real-world* cases we will not have the numeric classes and so we will not able to use M5' or Cubist.

Table 2. Error scores of our learner in publicly available regression datasets in addition to the parabola dataset described above. The *CPU*, *Body fat* were dowloaded from Cubist URL [6], while *Boston housing*, and *Liver disorders* can be found at UCI Repositoty [1]. The number of steps followed by GNG was the default value, i.e., the number of training comparisons divided by 10. Notice that LACE reached only 0.03% errors when N was 3 in the parabola dataset

dataset	Cubist	M5'	LACE
CPU	13.16%	11.00%	11.48%
Boston Housing	8.99%	9.19%	7.01%
Body fat	17.26%	15.48%	11.10%
Liver disorders	31.59%	31.30%	14.63%
Parabola	0.86%	9.13%	3.93%
Average	14.37%	15.22%	9.63%

5   Related Work

Tesauro tackled a similar problem in [17] for finding a function able to select the most preferable alternative in his famous backgammon player. His proposal was to enforce a symmetric neural network architecture consisting of two separate subnetworks, one for each object in the comparison. In addition, he enforced that both subnetworks have the same weights (only multiplied by -1 in the output layer). However, this restriction in the training mechanism only worked properly with perceptron networks, at least in his application field. Other perceptron approaches are described in [18,19].

In information retrieval, user preferences were modelled by means of *preference predicates* learned from a set of comparisons [3, 4, 5]. This is a quite different approach since our aim is to obtain a function able to assess grader preferences with a number; for our purposes it is not enough to know which object is preferable. Additionally, once you have a preference predicate, to order a set of objects is a NP-hard problem [5] since the transitivity of the learned predicate is not guaranteed at all.

6   Conclusions

In this paper, we have presented a new approach to obtaining sound assessment functions of objects. Our approach allows us to make use of a kind of knowledge capable of satisfactorily ranking a set of objects from the best to the worst, but that fails in assessing the 'goodness' of a single object with an absolute number. Assessments carried out in an absolute way are strongly affected by a batch effect in the sense that they tend to number the quality of an object with respect to the other objects in a batch, but not in an absolute sense, as we hope for when we assign a number to quality. This situation is characteristic of biological objects, and especially in the food industry, in which the rules for deciding the degree of quality of a product are not usually well defined, but the ranking of products is quite constant and well accepted on the part of consumers and market operators.

From a computational point of view, we have to obtain a float function from training sets without categorical or continuous classes. The problem has been tackled with a growing modification of Kohonen's SOM based on a geometrical intuition of the transformations that should be applied to the training data. The algorithm thus built was tested with both artificial and real-world data in order to show the abilities of the method proposed. The results reflect a very high degree of accuracy.

The limitations of our approach, which should be overcome in a future work, have to do with the granularity of the underlying GNG graph that clusters training data. Additionally, we hope that an improvement in the placement of conditions ($\mathbf{u}$) in regression rules ($\mathbf{w} \leftarrow \mathbf{u}$) would provide a better performance of solutions with a lower number of steps, see Tables 1 and 2.

References

1. Blake, C., Merz, C. J.: *UCI Repository of machine learning databases* [http://www.ics.uci.edu/~mlearn/MLRepository.html].   Irvine,   CA: University   of California, Department of Information and Computer Science (1998)
2. Bollen A.F., Kusabs N.J., Holmes G. and Hall M.A.: Comparison of consumer and producer perceptions of mushroom quality. Proc. Integrated View of Fruit and Vegetable Quality International Multidisciplinary Conference, W.J. Florkowski, S.E. Prussia and R.L. Shewfelt (eds.), Georgia (2002) 303–311
3. Branting, K.L., Broos, P.S.: Automated Acquisition of User Preferences. International Journal of Human-Computer Studies, (1997) 46:55–77.
4. Branting, K.L.: Active Exploration in Instance-Based Preference Modeling, Proceedings of the Third International Conference on Case-Based Reasoning (ICCBR-99), Germany (1999)
5. Cohen, W.W., Shapire, R.E., Singer, Y.: Learning to order things. Journal of Artificial Intelligence Research (1999) 10, 243–270
6. Cubist (2000). Release 1.09, http://www.rulequest.com/cubist-info.html
7. Del Coz, J. J., Luaces, O., Quevedo, J. R., Alonso, J., Ranilla, J., Bahamonde, A.: Self-Organizing Cases to Find Paradigms. Lecture Notes in Computer Sciences, Springer-Verlag, Berlin (1999) Vol. 1606, 527–536
8. Fritzke, B.: A growing neural gas network learns topologies, Advances in Neural Information Processing Systems 7, G. Tesauro, D. S. Touretzky and T. K. Leen (eds.), MIT Press, Cambridge MA (1995) 625–632
9. Goyache, F., Bahamonde, A. Alonso, J., López, S., Alonso, J., del Coz J.J., Quevedo, J.R., Ranilla, J., Luaces, O., Alvarez, I., Royo, L. and Díez J.: The usefulness of Artificial Intelligence techniques to assess subjective quality of products in the food industry. Trends in Food Science and Technology, in press (2002)
10. Goyache, F., del Coz, J.J., Quevedo, J.R., López, S., Alonso, J., Ranilla, J., Luaces, O., Alvarez, I. and Bahamonde, A.: Using artificial intelligence to design and implement a morphological assessment system in beef cattle. Animal Science (2001), 73: 49–60
11. Kohonen, T.: Self-Organizing Maps. Springer Series of Information Science. Springer-Verlag, Berlin (1995)
12. Kusabs N., Bollen F., Trigg L., Holmes G., Inglis S.: Objective measurement of mushroom quality. Proc. New Zealand Institute of Agricultural Science and the New Zealand Society for Horticultural Science Annual Convention, Hawke's Bay, New Zealand (1998)
13. Meilgaard, M., Civille, G.V., Carr, B.T.: Sensory evaluation techniques. CRC Press, Inc., Boca Raton, Florida (1987)

14. Murthy, S. K., Kasif, S., Salzberg, S.: A system for induction of oblique decision trees. Journal of Artificial Intelligence Research, (1994) 2, 1–32
15. Quevedo, J.R., Bahamonde, A.: Aprendizaje de Funciones Usando Inducción sobre Clasificaciones Discretas. Proceedings CAEPIA'99 VIII Conferencia de la Asociación Española para la Inteligencia Artificial, Murcia, Spain (1999) Vol. I, 64–71
16. Quinlan, J. R.: Learning with continuous classes. Proceedings 5th Australian Joint Conference on Artificial Intelligence. World Scientific, Singapore, (1992), 343–348.
17. Tesauro, G.: Connectionist learning of expert preferences by comparison training. In Advances in Neural Information Processing Systems, Proceedings NIPS'88, MIT Press (1989) 99–106
18. Utgoff, J. P., Clouse, J.: Two kinds of training information for evaluation function learning. In Proceedings AAAI'91, MIT Press (1991) 596–600
19. Utgoff, J.P., Saxema, S.: Learning preference predicate. In Proceedings of the Fourth International Workshop on Machine Learning, Morgan Kaufmann, San Francisco (1987) 115–121
20. Wang Y., Witten I.H.: Inducing of Model Trees for Predicting Continuous Classes. Proceedings of European Conference on Machine Learning. Prague, Czech Republic (1997) 128–137.

Forecasting Time Series Combining Machine Learning and Box-Jenkins Time Series

Elena Montañés[1], José R. Quevedo[1], Maria M. Prieto[2], and César O. Menéndez[3]

[1] Artificial Intelligence Center. Viesques E-33271. Gijón
{elena,quevedo}@aic.uniovi.es
[2] Energy Department. Viesques E-22271. Gijón
manuelap@correo.uniovi.es
[3] Mathematics Department. Llamaquique. E-33007. Oviedo
Asturias (Spain)
omar@orion.ciencias.uniovi.es

Abstract. In statistics, Box-Jenkins Time Series is a linear method widely used to forecasting. The linearity makes the method inadequate to forecast real time series, which could present irregular behavior. On the other hand, in artificial intelligence FeedForward Artificial Neural Networks and Continuous Machine Learning Systems are robust handlers of data in the sense that they are able to reproduce nonlinear relationships. Their main disadvantage is the selection of adequate inputs or attributes better related with the output or category. In this paper, we present a methodology that employs Box-Jenkins Time Series as feature selector to Feedforward Artificial Neural Networks inputs and Continuous Machine Learning Systems attributes. We also apply this methodology to forecast some real time series collected in a power plant. It is shown that Feedforward Artificial Neural Networks performs better than Continuous Machine Learning Systems, which in turn performs better than Box-Jenkins Time Series.

Keywords. Forecasting, Box-Jenkins Time Series, Neural Networks, Continuous Machine Learning Systems

1 Introduction

Time series are widely analyzed and forecasted by means of Box-Jenkins Time Series (*BJTS*). This method considers that the time series has been generated by a stochastic process and all techniques which obtain them are conducted to identify this generator. Then, the model is estimated and verified and finally once it has been accepted it is applied to forecast future values of the time series. The model identifies some characteristics of the time series, as the trend and the seasonality and gives an expression that relates the current value of the time series data with its historical ones that are more relevant. The main disadvantage is that these relations are linear which often conducts to inadequate predictions when treating with real world time series. They are also unable to explain sudden changes in the time series.

Alternatively, the use of artificial intelligence techniques, like Feedforward Artificial Neural Networks (*FANN*) and Continuous Machine Learning Systems

F.J. Garijo, J.C. Riquelme, and M. Toro (Eds.): IBERAMIA 2002, LNAI 2527, pp. 491–499, 2002.

(*CMLS*), to forecast time series results promising due to its capacity to handle amounts of data and to reproduce nonlinear relations between inputs and output in *FANN* and between attributes and category in *CMLS*. They are also capable to predict sudden variations. The main and difficult task is to find out which inputs or attributes better define the output or category.

Taking advantage of the best properties of *BJTS* on one hand and of *FANN* and *CMLS* on the other, we propose a methodology that combines them in the way that *BJTS* are used to identify adequate inputs or attributes for *FANN* and for *CMLS* respectively. We apply this methodology to several real physical time series collected in a power plant.

The remainder of this paper is as follows: In section 2 *BJTS*, *FANN* and *CMLS* are briefly detailed, in section 3 the combination of the latter methods are explained, the application of the methodology and the discussion of the results is made in section 4, and finally the conclusions and future work are exposed in section 5.

2   Box-Jenkins Time Series, Neural Networks, and Machine Learning Systems

In this section *BJTS*, *FANN* and some *CMLS* are briefly detailed.

2.1 Box-Jenkins Time Series

The most general *BJTS* are Seasonal Autoregressive Integrated Moving Average (*SARIMA($p^*,d^*,q^*,P^*,D^*,Q^*,s^*$)*), which assume that the mean is zero. The expression of a *SARIMA* time series is given by eq. (1):

$$\phi_{p*}(B)\Phi_{P*}(B^{s^*})(1-B^{s^*})^{D^*}(1-B)^{d^*}y_t = \theta_{q*}(B)\Theta_{Q*}(B^{s^*})a_t \qquad (1)$$

where ϕ_{p*}, Φ_{P*}, θ_{q*} and Θ_{Q*} are the autoregressive p^*-order, the seasonal autoregressive P^*-order, the moving average q^*-order and the seasonal moving average Q^*-order operators, B is the backward shift operator, y_t is the original time series and a_t is white noise time series.

The seasonality s^* is taken by means of the periodogram as the component whose amplitude is significantly greater. The parameters d^* and D^* are simultaneously varied until the trend and the seasonality are removed. Then, a new time series called differenced time series x_t is obtained and given by eq. (2).

$$x_t = (1-B^{s^*})^{D^*}(1-B)^{d^*}y_t \qquad (2)$$

The autocorrelation and the partial autocorrelation functions (*ACF* and *PACF*) are used to choose p^* and q^* (for the differenced time series) and P^* and Q^* (for the differenced time series taking the values corresponding to s^*-multiple indexes) [2].

The autoregressive, seasonal autoregressive, moving average and seasonal moving average operators are given by eqs. (3)-(6):

$$\phi_{p*}(B)x_t = x_t + b_{1,p}x_{t-1} + ... + b_{p,p}x_{t-p} = w_t \tag{3}$$

$$\Phi_{P*}(B^{s*})w_t = w_t + b_{1,P}w_{t-s} + ... + b_{P,P}w_{t-P \cdot s} = z_t \tag{4}$$

$$\Theta_{Q*}(B^{s*})z_t = z_t + b_{1,Q}z_{t-s} + ... + b_{Q,Q}z_{t-Q \cdot s} = r_t \tag{5}$$

$$\theta_{q*}(B)r_t = r_t + b_{1,q}r_{t-1} + ... + b_{q,q}r_{t-q} \tag{6}$$

The coefficients $b_{i,j}$ are estimated based on the methodology shown in [3] and [13]. The *ACF* and *PACF* of the residual time series are used to validate the model to check that the residual time series can be regarded as a white noise time series [19].

2.2 Neural Networks

The most common neural networks are *FANN*, which have the neurons structured in layers. The neurons of a layer can only be connected to neurons of the following layer but not to neurons of the same layer. The incorporation of hidden layers and a transfer function furnishes these neural networks with enough flexibility to solve difficult problems, thus reproducing the nonlinear dependence of the variables.

The logistic function was taken as node function, because it is bounded, monotonous increasing and differentiable and these properties assure the convergence of the weight estimation method [8]. One hidden layer was also chosen since the data partially defines a continuous function and one hidden layer is sufficient to approximate this kind of function [6]. The number of neurons in the hidden layer was obtained by iteratively constructing a sequence of *FANNs* $S_d \subset S_{d+1} \subset ... \subset S_{d+m}$,

where d is the number of inputs and m is the maximum number of neurons in the hidden layer, which was fixed at 10 and S_i is the set of *FANNs* with a hidden layer and i neurons in this layer. The mean squared error adding and without adding an additional term, which improves the forecasting error, was taken as the error function. The addition of this term is called regularization [15]. The mean of the squared weights was chosen as the additional term. The expression of the resulting error function is given by eq. (7).

$$E\left(w_1,..., w_{N_{pe}}\right) = \frac{1}{2}\sum_{j=1}^{N_{de}}\left[d_j - o_j\right] + \frac{1}{N_{pe}}\sum_{j=1}^{N_{pe}}w_j^2 \tag{7}$$

where w_j are the weights to be estimated, N_{de} is the number of data used to obtain the model, d_j is the desired neural network output, o_j is the current neural network output and N_{pe} is the number of weights

The method chosen for the weight estimation was the conjugate gradient method [4], [10], [16] and [11] with the Fletcher-Reeves update [9] combined with Charalambous' search [5] for one-dimensional minimization. In the conjugate gradient algorithms a search is performed along conjugate directions, which produces faster convergence than the basic steepest descent algorithm. These methods require only a little more storage than the simpler algorithms, so they are often a good choice for networks with a large number of weights. An iteration of the method is shown in eq. (8) and eq. (9):

$$w_{k+1} = w_k + \alpha_k p_k \tag{8}$$

$$p_k = -g_k + \beta_k p_{k-1} \tag{9}$$

where w_k is the vector $(w_1,..., w_{N_{pe}})$ in the kth-iteration, p_k is the conjugate gradient direction in the kth-iteration, g_k is the gradient direction in the kth-iteration and α_k is the optimal size step after linear minimization in the kth-iteration.

The various versions of conjugate gradient are distinguished by manner in which the constant β_k is computed. For the Fletcher-Reeves update, the procedure is given by equation (10):

$$\beta_k = \frac{g_k^T g_k}{g_{k-1}^T g_{k-1}} \tag{10}$$

This is the ratio of the squared of the norm of the current gradient to the squared of the norm of the previous gradient. The storage requirements of this update are lower than others.

The validation model is carried out by taking some data that are not used to obtain the model and checking that the error committed in the forecasting is lower than a given value.

2.3   Continuous Machine Learning Systems

CMLS take a set of examples and learn a set of regression rules or regression trees from them. The examples are described as a sequence of pairs attribute-value and a category.

These techniques are widely applied to different areas with excellent results; an example can be found in [12]. The versatility, robustness and accuracy of these systems make them adequate to be applied to forecasting.

One of the most important problems of applying this kind of systems is to select a set of informative attributes [1]. Although it is supposed that they are able to deal with irrelevant attributes if its number is high, it is recommended to carry out an attribute selection.

The *CMLS* employed in this paper are *m5'* [20], *Cubist* [17] and *RT* [18]. *m5'* is "a rational reconstruction of *m5*", which produces regression trees. *Cubist* is a commercial system that produces regression rules. *RT* is a learning system that can handle multiple regression problems based on samples of data and the resulting models have the form of a regression tree.

3   Combination of Box-Jenkins Time Series, Feedforward Artificial Neural Networks, and Continuous Machine Learning Systems

In this section it is explained the methodology that combines *BJTS*, *FANN* and *CMLS*.

As it was previously exposed the most general *BJTS* is *SARIMA*, whose parameters are $p^*, d^*, q^*, P^*, D^*, Q^*, s^*$. These parameters are employed to identify the inputs or attributes of *FANN* and *CMLS*. Firstly, the meaning of these parameters is briefly detailed:

- The parameter p^* is the number of relevant delays of the time series respect to the current instant.
- The parameter d^* is the order of differentiation which allows to remove the trend of the time series.
- The parameter q^* is the number of relevant delays of the white noise time series respect to the current instant (this time series appear in the model of *BJTS*)
- The parameter s^* is the seasonality.
- The parameter P^* is the number of relevant delays with s^*-multiple indexes of the time series respect to current instant.
- The parameter D^* is the order of differentiation which allows to remove the seasonality of the time series.
- The parameter Q^* is the number of relevant delays with s^*-multiple indexes of the white noise time series respect to the current instant (this time series appear in the model of *BJTS*)

In most time series P^* and Q^* are rarely positive [3]. Besides, the parameters associated to the white noise are not taken into account due to the fact that *FANN* and *CMLS* already deal with noise. On the other hand, in Neural Networks and Machine Learning it is accepted the fact that it is desirable that the distribution of the train and the test data be the same. This occurs only when the time series does not have trend, although it has seasonality. This is the reason why D^* is not necessary to be considered. Then, our methodology only takes into account p^*, d^* and s^*.

Firstly, it is necessary to remove the trend, so the time series is differentiated according to eq. (11).

$$x_t = (1 - B)^{d^*} y_t \tag{11}$$

Then, p^* delays respect to the current instant and p^* delays respect to the seasonality s^* are considered as inputs or attributes of the *FANN* and *CMLS* as expressed in eq. (12).

$$(t - c_{p^*}, t - c_{p^*-1}, \dots, c_1, t - c_{s^*+p^*-1}, t - c_{s^*+p^*-2}, \dots, c_{s^*}) \tag{12}$$

Algorithmically, the procedure is as follows:

```
{ForecastedTimeSerieFANN, ForecastedTimeSerieMLS}
FORECAST (TimeSeries TS) {
    //Obtain BJTS parameters
    {p*, d* and s*} = BJTSParameters (TimeSeries TS);
```

```
//Differentiate the time series according d*
DifferentiatedTS=Differenciate(TS, d*);

//Obtain p* delays respect to the current instant and
//respect to the seasonality and the current instant
DataInputsOutputs=Delays(DifferenciatedTS,p*, s*);

//Apply FANN of CMLS to the differentiated time series
//to obtain the forecasted time series
return {FANN(DifferentiatedTS),CMLS(DifferentiatedTS)};

} //end of FORECAST
```

4 Application and Results

Pressures, temperatures and mass flow rates simultaneously registered every 10 minutes from a seawater refrigerated power plant condenser subject to tide effects between 8-6-98 and 14-6-98 (1008 data) are used to compare the performance of *BJTS*, *FANN* and *CMLS*. The last two days (288 data) were removed for the *test*.

The implementation was carried out using the *Matlab 5.3 NAG Foundation Toolbox* [14] and *Neural Network Toolbox* [7] and *Cubist* [17], *M5'* [20] and *RT* [18].

Table 1 shows the *BJTS* and the inputs or attributes of *FANN* and *CMLS*.

In the *BJTS*, the seasonality obtained from the periodogram was a day ($s^* = 144$). The seasonality is removed by differencing the original time series ($D^*=1$). However, it was not necessary to remove the trend ($d^*=0$). The moving averaged components are zero ($q^*=0$ and $Q^*=0$). Only nonseasonal, autoregressive components were identified ($p^*>0$ and $P^*=0$).

The Medium Average Deviation (*MAD*) is a common measure of the performance, but it is adequate to use the Relative Medium Average Deviation (*RMAD*) which is the *MAD* divided by the *MAD* of the system that always predicts the average function (*Av. MAD*). This measure removes the effect of the dimension of the variables. In Table 2 it is shown the *MAD* of the system that always predicts the average function for each time series.

In Table 3 it is shown the *RMAD* forecasting errors for *BJTS*, *FANN* without and with term regularization and some *CMLS* when the real values of the delays are used to forecast the next value of the time series (*TO 1*). It is also shown the best (*BEST*) *RMAD* for each time series.

In Table 4 it is shown the *RMAD* forecasting errors for *BJTS*, *FANN* without and with term regularization and some *CMLS* when the forecasted values of the delays are used to forecast the next value of the time series (*TO N*). It is also shown the best (*BEST*) *RMAD* for each time series.

Table 1. *BJTS* and the inputs or attributes of *FANN* and *CMLS*. The value c_i in $(c_1, c_2,..., c_m)$ is the number of delays with respect to the current instant t

	Time Serie $(p^*,d^*,q^*,P^*,D^*,Q^*,s^*)$	FANN and CMLS $(c_1, c_2,..., c_m)$
$\dot{M}_c$	(1,0,0,0,1,0,144)	(1,144)
T_{dl}	(1,0,0,0,1,0,144)	(1,144)
p_{tes1}	(1,0,0,0,1,0,144)	(1,144)
p_{stlp}	(2,0,0,0,1,0,144)	(1,2,144,145)
T_{stlp}	(1,0,0,0,1,0,144)	(1,144)
p_{cp}	(1,0,0,0,1,0,144)	(1,144)
T_{hot}	(1,0,0,0,1,0,144)	(1,144)
Δp	(1,0,0,0,1,0,144)	(1,144)
L_{ch}	(2,0,0,0,1,0,144)	(1,2,144,145)
$T_{w,i}$	(2,0,0,0,0,0,0)	(1,2)
$T_{w,o}$	(1,0,0,0,1,0,144)	(1,144)

Table 2. *MAD* of the system that always predicts the average function

	Mc	T_{dl}	p_{tes1}	p_{stlp}	T_{stlp}	p_{cp}	T_{hot}	Δp	L_{ch}	$T_{w,i}$	$T_{w,o}$
MAD	47.22	3.20	0.03	0.40	2.30	6.97	2.39	61.82	0.79	0.25	1.91

Table 3. *RMAD* for *BJTS*, *FANN* whitout and with term regularization, some *CMLS* (Cubist, M5' and RT) and the best *RMAD* when *TO 1*

	BJTS	FANN		MLS			BETTER
		-Reg	+Reg	Cubist	M5'	RT	
Mc	13.18%	10.89%	14.72%	10.99%	10.67%	16.79%	10.67%
T_{dl}	10.52%	9.31%	12.03%	9.39%	9.55%	15.31%	9.31%
p_{tes1}	11.39%	8.71%	9.38%	7.68%	7.86%	12.61%	7.68%
p_{stlp}	9.70%	7.03%	14.01%	7.17%	7.11%	15.13%	7.03%
T_{stlp}	51.89%	31.21%	30.65%	29.92%	31.167%	35.60%	29.92%
p_{cp}	13.65%	12.35%	14.26%	12.41%	12.32%	18.59%	12.32%
T_{hot}	12.29%	11.30%	12.06%	11.13%	11.14%	16.97%	11.13%
Δp	22.43%	17.41%	19.04%	17.61%	17.84%	22.96%	17.41%
L_{ch}	20.87%	16.78%	22.05%	15.80%	16.66%	20.46%	15.80%
$T_{w,i}$	12.31%	12.31%	13.49%	16.57%	16.62%	23.99%	12.31%
$T_{w,o}$	14.02%	12.45%	15.08%	12.84%	12.73%	18.28%	12.45%
Av.	17.48%	13.61%	16.07%	13.77%	13.97%	19.70%	13.27%

Table 4. *RMAD* for *BJTS*, *FANN* whitout and with term regularization, some *CMLS* (*Cubist*, *M5'* and *RT*) and the best *RMAD* when *TO N*

	BJTS	FANN		MLS			BETTER
		-Reg	+Reg	Cubist	M5'	RT	
Mc	60.13%	90.58%	53.16%	86.07%	119.74%	117.30%	53.16%
T_{dl}	58.99%	97.97%	53.90%	133.03%	121.88%	150.34%	53.90%
p_{tes1}	62.66%	89.13%	64.67%	129.63%	116.96%	121.63%	62.66%
p_{stlp}	70.19%	57.50%	68.89%	111.89%	66.96%	122.42%	57.50%
T_{stlp}	111.74%	97.84%	96.30%	99.95%	123.15%	235.94%	96.30%
p_{cp}	56.75%	79.77%	54.11%	117.16%	94.21%	126.79%	54.11%
T_{hot}	56.36%	93.05%	53.85%	124.96%	119.29%	129.08%	53.85%
Δp	88.55%	90.14%	87.24%	99.33%	94.77%	114.56%	87.24%
L_{ch}	84.00%	73.58%	79.92%	97.73%	90.86%	152.25%	73.58%
$T_{w,i}$	86.62%	48.63%	47.90%	138.96%	98.75%	106.38%	47.90%
$T_{w,o}$	63.82%	94.77%	57.86%	92.60%	99.04%	137.10%	57.86%
$Av.$	72.71%	83.00%	65.25%	111.94%	104.15%	137.62%	63.46%

Looking at results in Table 3 it is noticed that *FANN* without regularization term outperforms *BJTS* for all time series. However, *FANN* with regularization and *BJTS* are similar. *Cubist* and *M5'* do the same except for $T_{w,i}$, although the difference is insignificant. *Cubist* and *M5'* are also better than *FANN* with regularization. The performance of *FANN* without regularization, *Cubist* and *M5'* are similar. However, the results of *RT* are worse even than *BJTS*.

Looking at results in Table 4 it is noticed that *FANN* with regularization term outperforms *BJTS* and *CMLS* for all time series. However, *CMLS* do not have learned well given that most of the *RMAD* are above the 100%, that is the *MAD* is worse than the *MAD* of the function that predicts the average. *FANN* without regularization are worse than *BJTS* and *FANN* with regularization.

5 Conclusions

This paper describes the employment of the widely used forecasting technique *BJTS* to identify the inputs of *FANN* or the attributes of *CMLS*. This methodology is then applied to some time series collected in a seawater refrigerated power plant condenser subject to tide effects.

The use of *BJTS* as a feature selector to *FANN* and *CMLS* results promising since these latter techniques reaches significantly more accurate than *BJTS*. *Cubist* (a *CMLS*) performs the best although *M5'* (another *CMLS*) and *FANN* also give good results.

FANN without regularization, *Cubist* and *M5'* outperform *BJTS* when the real values of the delays are used to forecast the next value of the time series. However, *FANN* with regularization is the only system that outperforms *BJTS* when the forecasted values of the delays are used to forecast the next value of the time series. In this latter case *CMLS* does not learn correctly.

As future work we are interested in exploiting the power of *FANN* and *CMLS* to deal with different variables at the same time, that is, to incorporate other variables as inputs or attributes, fact that is computational unacceptable for *BJTS*.

Acknowledgements. The research reported in this paper has been supported in part under MCyT and Feder grant TIC2001-3579. FICyT and Hidroeléctrica del Cantábrico also made this research possible under the grants PA-TDI96-01, PC-TDI98-01, and PA-TDI99-05.

References

1. Blum A.L., Langley. P.:Selection of relevant features and examples in machine learning. Artificial Intelligence. (1997) 245–271
2. Brockwell P.J., Davis R.A, Introduction to Time Series and Forecasting. New York: Springer-Verlag, 1996.
3. Box G.E.P., Jenkins G.M., Reinsel C. Time Series Analysis, Forecasting and Control. New Jersey: Holden-Day (Revised Edition), 1976.
4. Ciarlet P.G. Introduction L`analyse Numèrique Matricielle et L`optimisation. París: Masson, 1982.
5. Charalambous C. Conjugate Gradient Algorithm for Efficient Training of Artificial Neural Networks. IEEE Proceedings, 1992;139(3):301–310.
6. Cybenko G. Approximations by Superpositions of a Sigmoidal Function. Mathematics of Control, Signals y Systems, 1992;2(4):303–314.
7. Demuth H., Beale M. Neural Network Toolbox for Use with Matlab. Massachusetts: The MathWorks, 1998.
8. Fine T. L. Feedforward Neural Network Methodology. New York: Springer Verlag, 1999.
9. Fletcher R., Reeves C.M. Function Minimization by Conjugate Gradient. Computer Journal, 1964;7:149–154.
10. Fletcher R. Practical Methods of Optimisation. New York: John Wiley, 1992.
11. Glowinski R. Numerical Solutions of Non-linear Problems and Variational Inequalities. New York: Springer-Verlag, 1987.
12. Goyache, F.; Coz, J. J. del; Quevedo, J. R.; López, S.; Alonso, J.; Ranilla, J.; Luaces, O.; Alvarez, I.; Bahamonde, A.: Using artificial intelligence to design and implement a morphological assessment system in beef cattle. Animal Science, Vol. 73 (2001), pp. 49–60.
13. Marquardt D. W. An Algorithm for Least-squares Estimation of Nonlinear Parameters. J. Soc. Indust. Appl. Math., 1963;11:431.
14. Numerical Algorithms Group. NAG Foundation Toolbox for Use with Matlab. Massachusetts: The MathWorks, 1995.
15. Poggio T., Girosi F. Networks for Approximation and Learning. In Proc. IEEE, 1990;1481–1497.
16. Polak E. Optimisation Algorithms and Consistent Approximations. New York: Springer-Verlag, 1997.
17. Quinlan, J.R.: Cubist. http://www.rulequest.com/cubist-info.html
18. Torgo. L.: Functional models for regression tree leaves. In Proc. of the 14th International Conference on Machine Learning, Nashville, TN. Morgan Kaufmann. (1997) 385–393
19. Uriel E. and Peiró A. Introducción al análisis de series temporales. Madrid: AC, 2000.
20. Wang, Y., and Witten, I.H.. Inducing model trees for continuous classes. In Poster Papers 9th European Conf. on Machine Learning. Prague, Czech Republic. (1997) 128–137.

Gaussian Synapse Networks for Hyperspectral Image Segmentation

J.L. Crespo, R.J. Duro, and F. López-Peña

Grupo de Sistemas Autónomos, Universidade da Coruña, Spain
crespo@cdf.udc.es, {richard, flop }@udc.es

Abstract. In this work we have made use of a new type of network with non linear synapses, Gaussian Synapse Networks, for the segmentation of hyperspectral images. These structures were trained using the GSBP algorithm and present two main advantages with respect to other, more traditional, approaches. On one hand, through the intrinsic filtering ability of the synapses, they permit concentrating on what is relevant in the spectra and automatically discard what is not. On the other, the networks are structurally adapted to the problem as superfluous synapses and/or nodes are implicitly eliminated by the training procedure.

1 Introduction

Remote land observation has been going on for decades. Until recently, most of these observations were carried out through multispectral imagery. Due to limited number of bands of these images, that is, their low spectral resolution, similar land covers could not be differentiated, thus reducing their applicability. To overcome these limitations, imaging spectrometry was developed to acquire images with high spectral resolution. This type of spectrometry is usually called hyperspectral imaging. Hyperspectral images can be defined as those that cover the 400-2500 nm (near infrared to visible) wavelength band with a number of samples between 50 and 250. This corresponds to a sampling of wavelengths in the order of 0.01 micrometers, which is adequate to describe the spectral variability of most surfaces in this wavelength range. This type of technology is relatively new, but we can find a number of commercially available hyperspectral sensors. Staenz [1] lists 14 current instruments with more than 100 spectral bands in this wavelength range. These sensors are mounted on specially prepared airplanes and, depending of the conditions of flight, a hyperspectral pixel can correspond to an area between 15 and 300 square meters, approximately.

The main advantage of hyperspectral imaging with respect to classical remote sensing is the large amount of information it provides. Unfortunately, like in all remote sensing techniques, it still presents the problem of removing the effects induced by whatever is present between the target and the sensor, that is, the atmosphere.

The influence of the atmosphere may be divided into two groups of effects: Those that are spatially and temporally constant and those that are not. In the first

F.J. Garijo, J.C. Riquelme, and M. Toro (Eds.): IBERAMIA 2002, LNAI 2527, pp. 500–508, 2002.

category we can include the absorption and scattering by CO_2, N_2, CH_4 and O_2 (well mixed in the atmosphere), and in the second, those elements that could vary in certain circumstances (like water vapor, ozone and aerosols –dust, water droplets and haze-). To eliminate such influences, it is necessary to make a transformation of the measured radiances into reflectances [2]. There are two possible ways to obtain such a transformation: by radiative transfer models or using ground truth. The use of radiative transfer models is not satisfactory in most cases as the necessary information on atmospheric conditions is seldom available, consequently the reflectance accuracy is limited by the simulation of the atmosphere which turns out to be a hard and resource consuming task due to the combined effects enumerated earlier. As an example of this problem, Goetz [3] assumes that surface reflectance varies linearly with wavelength in the spectral range from approximately 1.0 micrometers to 1.3 micrometers. They develop an estimate of surface reflectance and atmospheric water vapor using reflectance data at high spectral resolution (of the order of 10 nm). If we look into their discussion on the physics underlying this problem and the motivation for addressing it, we can see how complex it becomes. Therefore the procedure used (regression by linear least squares) was very time consuming. Gao and Goetz [3] state that retrievals of water vapor for 20,000 spectra from the Advanced Visible Infrared Imaging Spectrometer (AVIRIS) [4] require 200 minutes of processing on their computers.

The ground truth approach measures the reflectance at selected ground control points at the time of the remotely sensed image. Alternatively it can provide in situ classifications of some targets instead of measuring their reflectances [5]. This last approach has been used in this study.

From the data processing viewpoint and although theoretically the use of hyperspectral images should increase our abilities to identify various materials, the classification methods used for multispectral images are not adequate and the results are not as good as desired. This is because most methods used are statistically based on decision rules determined by training samples. As the number of dimensions in the feature space increases, the number of training samples needed for image classification also increases. If the number of training samples is insufficient as is usually the case in hyperspectral imaging, statistical parameter estimation becomes inaccurate.

Different authors have proposed methods to improve the classification results. One line of research is based on statistical theory to extract important features from the original hyperspectral data prior to the classification. In this case, the objective is to remove the redundant information without sacrificing significant information. A group of these methods are compared using classification performance in [6]. They are principal component analysis [7], discriminant analysis feature extraction [8], and decision boundary feature extraction [9]. The basic idea is not new, if we concentrate only on what is relevant, the classification is a lot easier. This is the approach we have followed in this paper, but instead of designing a statistical method to do it, we propose an Artificial Neural Network architecture and training algorithm that implement a procedure to concentrate on what is relevant and ignore what is not in an automatic manner straight from the training set. In addition, this structure has proven to be very effective in discriminating different categories within hyperspectral images without any atmospheric correction. The only preprocessing the image underwent was to remove the offset through a subtraction of the average pixel value. In the following sections, we will describe the network, provide a brief overview of its training procedure and we will test its classification abilities using one of the benchmark hyperspectral processing images, the Indian Pines image obtained by AVIRIS. This spectrometer is flown on a high altitude aircraft and it acquires image data in 224 spectral bands over the spectral range 0.4 to 2.5 micrometers, at approximately 0.01 micrometers resolution, for each of 614 samples (pixels) per image line.

2 Structure of the Network and GSBP

The architecture employed in this type of networks is very similar to the classical Multiple Layer Perceptron. In fact, the activation functions of the nodes are simple sigmoids. The only difference is that each synaptic connection implements a gaussian function determined by three parameters: its center, its amplitude and its variance:

$$g(x) = A * e^{B(x-C)^2} \tag{1}$$

To train this structure we have developed an extension of the backpropagation algorithm, called Gaussian Synapse Backpropagation (GSBP) [10]. In what follows we will provide a brief overview of it.

First, as in any other backpropagation algorithm, we must determine what the outputs of the different layers are. We must also define the error with respect to the target values we desire and backpropagate it to the parameters determining the synaptic connections, in this case the three parameters that correspond to the gaussian function. In order to do this, we must obtain the gradients of the error with respect to each one of the parameters for each synapse. Consequently, if we define the error as the classical sum of the squares of the differences between what we desire and what we obtain:

$$E_{tot} = \sum_k \frac{1}{2}(T_k - O_k)^2 \tag{2}$$

And as the outputs of the neurons in the output and hidden layers are:

$$O_k = F\left(\sum_j h_j A_{jk} e^{B_{jk}(h_j - C_{jk})^2}\right) = F\left(O_{Net_k}\right) \tag{3}$$

$$h_j = F\left(\sum_i I_i A_{ij} e^{B_{ij}(I_i - C_{ij})^2}\right) = F\left(h_{Net_j}\right) \tag{4}$$

If we now calculate the gradients of the error with respect to each one of the parameters of the gaussians in each layer we obtain the following equations that will be used for the modification of the gaussian corresponding to each synapses every iteration. In the ouput layer the gradient of the error with respect to A_{jk} is:

$$\frac{\partial E_{tot}}{\partial A_{jk}} = h_j(O_k - T_k)F'(O_{Netk})e^{B_{jk}(h_j - C_{jk})^2} \tag{5}$$

In the case of $\mathbf{B_{jk}}$, and $\mathbf{C_{jk}}$ we obtain:

$$\frac{\partial E_{tot}}{\partial B_{jk}} = h_j (O_k - T_k) F'(O_{Netk}) A_{jk} (h_j - C_{jk})^2 \, e^{B_{jk} (h_j - C_{jk})^2} \tag{6}$$

$$\frac{\partial E_{tot}}{\partial C_{jk}} = -2 h_j A_{jk} B_{jk} (O_k - T_k) F'(O_{Netk})(h_j - C_{jk}) \, e^{B_{jk} (h_j - C_{jk})^2} \tag{7}$$

For the hidden layer we have:

$$\Theta_j = \frac{\partial E_{tot}}{\partial h_{Netj}} = \frac{\partial E_{tot}}{\partial h_j} \frac{\partial h_j}{\partial h_{Netj}} = \frac{\partial E_{tot}}{\partial h_j} F'(h_{Netj}) \tag{8}$$

and the variation of the error with respect to $\mathbf{A_{ij}}$, $\mathbf{B_{ij}}$ and $\mathbf{C_{ij}}$ is:

$$\frac{\partial E_{tot}}{\partial A_{ij}} = I_i \Theta_j \, e^{B_{ij} (I_i - C_{ij})^2} \tag{9}$$

$$\frac{\partial E_{tot}}{\partial C_{ij}} = -2 \Theta_j I_i A_{ij} B_{ij} (I_i - C_{ij}) \, e^{B_{ij} (I_i - C_{ij})^2} \tag{10}$$

$$\frac{\partial E_{tot}}{\partial B_{ij}} = \Theta_j I_i A_{ij} (I_i - C_{ij})^2 \, e^{B_{ij} (I_i - C_{ij})^2} \tag{11}$$

3   Segmentation System

The segmentation system we have constructed is presented in figure 1. It consists of a set of Gaussian synapse based networks working in parallel over the spectral dimension of each pixel of the image. These detectors produce a detection probability surface associated with the category they have been trained for. Obviously, a pixel may be assigned a detection probability by two or more detectors. This may be due to several causes: non discriminant training sets, very similar spectra, mixtures of categories within the same pixel (take into account that depending on the altitude of the flight and the spatial resolution of the instrument a pixel may represent very large areas areas), noise, etc. Thus, after going through the detectors, each pixel is characterized by a detection probability vector and the way this detection vector is used will depend on the application. Consequently, to decide on the final label assigned to the pixel, all the detectors send their information to a final decision module. The final decision will be made depending on the desires of the user. For instance, the decision module may be trained to choose the most likely category for the pixel or to assign combinations of detections to new categories so that the final image indicates where there is doubt or even prioritize some types of detections when searching for particular objectives such as minerals.

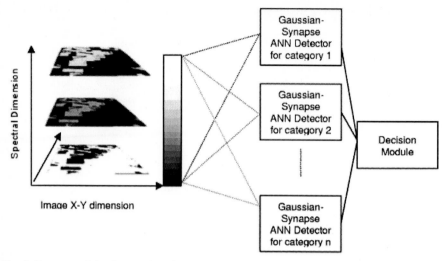

Fig. 1. Structure of the detector based segmentation system. The spectral cube is scanned in the x-y dimension and each spectrum is processed by the different detectors in parallel. The decision module constructs the final detection image.

4 Experimental Results

The spectra used for this work correspond to the Indian Pines 1992 image obtained by the Airborne Visible/Infrared Imaging Spectrometer (AVIRIS) developed by NASA JPL which has 224 contiguous spectral channels covering a spectral region form 0.4 to 2.5 μm in 10 nm steps. It is a 145 by 145 pixel image with 220 spectral bands that contains a distribution of two-thirds of agricultural land and one-third of forest and other elements (two highways, a rail line and some houses and smaller roads). The ground truth available for this image [11] designates 16 not mutually exclusive classes. This scene has been studied by Tadjudin and Landgrebe [8][12], and also by Gualtieri et al. [13].

Instead of the atmospheric correction model used by these authors, we have started with a very simple preprocessing stage consisting in subtracting the average of the pixels in the whole image in order to eliminate offsets. The final spectra for each pixel are quite complex and misleading. As shown in figure 2 spectra corresponding to the same category may be much different than spectra from different categories. Consequently, the use of systems that incorporate the ability to obtain non linear divisions of the input space is needed. This is the context in which the Gaussian synapse networks have been used.

We have built seven networks for detecting categories in the Indian Pines image. The detectors were trained for: Soybean, Corn, Grass-Pasture, Grass-Trees, Hay-windrowed, Wheat and Woods. We group the different types of soybean and corn that were present in original image because the only difference between the types is the

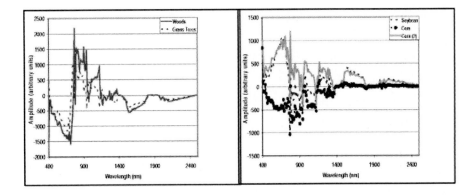

Fig. 2. In the left, two similar spectra corresponding to different categories. Right, two different spectra corresponding to the same category vs. a spectrum from a different category.

amount of weeds. We don't use more categories because there were insufficient number of pixels to train a network.

The training set used for all the detectors contained different numbers of pixels corresponding to the different categories (Soybean, 220; Corn, 350; GP, 220; GT, 292; HW, 320; Wheat , 130; Woods, 450). These training points were extracted from certain regions of the image, but the tests were carried out over the whole image in order to prove the generalization capabilities of the networks. In fact only less than 1% of the points of the image were used as training pixels.

The networks initially consist of 220 inputs, corresponding to the different spectral bands of AVIRIS. Due to the non-physical character of the pre-processing stage, unlike many other authors that manually reduce the number of spectral bands to facilitate the detector's work, we have decided to use the whole spectrum and let the network decide what is relevant. There are two hidden layers, with 18 nodes each, and one output layer corresponding to the presence or absence of the category. The training process consisted of 50 epochs in every case, with the same values for the training coefficients: 0.5 for amplitude training, 2 for variance training, and 0.5 for center training.

In figure 3 and for the purpose of providing an idea of the operation of the individual networks, we present the outputs of three of the detectors after scanning the hyperspectral image. The detectors correspond to the categories of grass pasture, soybean and wheat. There are pixels that are detected to different degrees by more than one of the detectors and in figure 4 we present the results after going through the final decision module. In this case, the figure corresponds to a maximum likelihood decision, which does not take into account any neighbourhood information. We also provide the ground-truth image in the NASA-JPL set for Indian Pines.

Several considerations may be made about these results. First of all, we must indicate that the ground truth provided had enormous areas without any labels. In the original ground truth image this areas were called background. The labelling provided

506   J.L. Crespo, R.J. Duro, and F. López-Peña

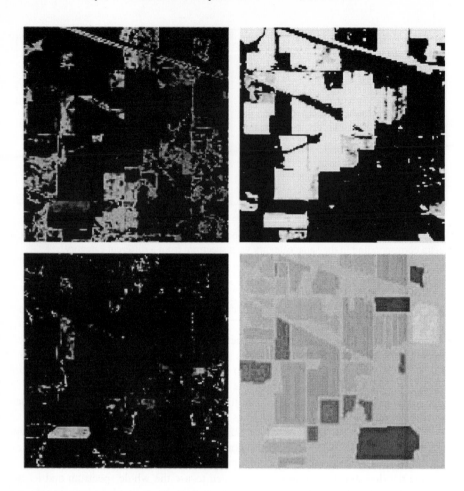

Fig. 3. Information provided by three of the detectors over the whole image. Top left: Grass pasture. Top Right: Soybean. Bottom left: Wheat. Bottom right: Ground truth.

by our system for these areas was very good and consistent with the indications found by other authors [8][13]. In addition, the ground truth is not detailed in the sense that there are elements within the labelled zones that were not indicated, such as roads, pathways, trees within other types of areas, etc. The system consistently detects these features. The network performs a very good classification of the whole image including all of the image regions that were no used in training at all. The only problem in the classification is the double label obtained in corn and soybean regions, where both detectors indicate the presence of their species. This is because the image was taken when the plants were only three or four weeks old and only occupied 5% of the areas labelled as soybean and corn. Corn and Soybean plants at this age are very similar from a spectroscopic point of view. Grass and wheat also present a similar problem and a double label is also obtained in some regions.

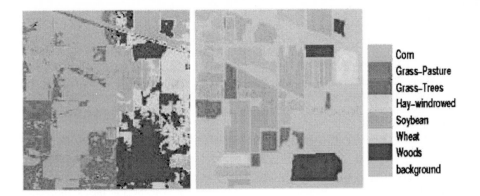

Fig. 4. From right to left. Color code of the categories, ground truth obtained in the literature for this categories and result of our networks with a final maximum likelihood decision module in segmenting the image

5   Conclusions

In this paper we have considered the application of Artificial Neural Networks with High-Order Gaussian Synapses and a new algorithm for training them, Gaussian Synapses Backpropagation (GSBP), to the segmentation of hyperspectral images. The structure of the segmentation system implies the use of Gaussian Synapse based networks as detectors act in parallel over the hyperspectral images providing each providing a probability of the presence of its category in each pixel. The inclusion of gaussian functions in the synapses of the networks allows them to select the appropriate information and filter out all that is irrelevant. The networks that result for each detector are much smaller than if other network paradigms were used and require a very small training set due to their great generalization capabilities. The final segmentation is made by a decision module that is trained depending on the type of segmentation desired. In the case of hyperspectral images and using a maximum likelihood decision module, the segmentation performed is quite good taking into account that no atmospheric modeling has been performed and, consequently, we are basically segmenting the image straight from the sensor. This makes the procedure very adequate for reducing the amount of processing required for this type of sensing strategies.

Acknowledgements. This work was supported by the MCYT of Spain (Pr. N. TIC2000-0739C0404).

References

[1]   Staenz, K., Canadian Activities in Terrestrial Imaging Spectrometry. 994 Annual Report, Canada Centre for Remote Sensing. (1995) 68.

[2]   Wiemker R., Speck A., Kulbach D., Spitzer H., Bienlein J., Unsupervised Robust Change Detection on Multispectral Imagery Using Spectral and Spatial Features. Proceedings of the Third International Airborne Remote Sensing Conference and Exhibition, Copenhagen, vol. I, ERIM, Ann Arbor (1997) 640–647.

[3]   Gao, B-C., and Goetz, A.F.H. Column Atmospheric Water Vapor and Vegetation Liquid Water Retrievals From Airborne Imaging Spectrometer Data, J. Geophys. Res., 95, (1990) 3549–3564.

[4]   Vane, G. T., First Results of the Airborne Visible/Infrared Imaging Spectrometer (AVIRIS), SPIE, Vol 834 Imaging Spectroscopy, (1987) 166–174.

[5]   Rencz A. (Editor). Manual of Remote Sensing. John Wiley and Sons, Inc. New York, 1999.

[6]   Hsu, P.H. and Tseng, Y.H. Feature Extraction for Hyperspectral Image. Proceedings of the 20th Asian Conference on Remote Sensing, Vol. 1, (1999) 405–410.

[7]   Schowengerdt, R.A.. Remote Sensing: Models and Methods for Image Processing, Academic Press. (1997).

[8]   Tadjudin, S. and Landgrebe, D. Classification of High Dimensional Data with Limited Training Samples. PhD Thesis and School of Electrical & Computer Engineering Technical Report TR-ECE 98-8, Purdue University. (1998).

[9]   Lee, C. and Landgrebe, D. Feature Extraction and Classification Algorithms for High Dimensional Data. TR-EE 93-1, Purdue University. (1993).

[10] Duro, R.J., Crespo, J.L., and Santos, J.: Training Higher Order Gaussian Synapses. LNCS, Vol. 1606 Springer-Verlag, Berlín (1999) 537–545.

[11] Landgrebe, D. Indian Pines AVIRIS Hyperspectral Reflectance Data: 92av3c. available at http://makalu.jpl.nasa.gov/locator/index.html. (1992).

[12] Tadjudin, S. and Landgrebe, D. Covariance Estimation for Limited Training Samples. Int. Geoscience and Remote Sensing Symp. Seattle, (1998).

[13] Guatieri, J.A., Bechdol, M., Chettri, S., Robinson, J.W., Garegnani, J., Vermeulen, A. and Antonille, S. From Spectra to Cassification. Extended paper of the presentation at 1st International Symposium on Hyperspectral Analysis, Caceres, Spain. (2000).

An Associative Multivalued Recurrent Network

Enrique Mérida-Casermeiro[1], José Muñoz-Pérez[2], and M.A. García-Bernal[2]

[1] Dept. Matemática Aplicada
[2] Dept. Lenguaje y Ciencias de la Computación.
Universidad de Málaga.
merida@ctima.uma.es, {munozp,magb}@lcc.uma.es

Abstract. This paper shows that the multivalued recurrent neural model (MREM) can be used as an autoassociative memory (multivalued counterpart of Hopfield network). The architecture of the proposed family of networks is inspired from bipolar Hopfield's neural network (BH).

We have modified the function of energy of the bipolar Hopfield model by a new function of the outputs of neurons that we are naming *function of similarity* as it measures the similarity between the outputs of neurons. When binary neurons are considered and the function product is used as a function of similarity, then the proposed model is identical to that of Hopfield.

We have studied a method to load a set of patterns into the network. That method corresponds to the Hopfield's one when bipolar neurons are been considered.

Finally we show that an augmented network avoids the storage of undesirable patterns into the network, as the well-known effect of loading the opposite pattern into the Hopfield's network. For this new storage technics an expression that allows to set bounds to the capacity of the network is obtained.

1 Introduction

Neural networks can be classified into two types according to output signals. One has a continuous value for output signals and other has a binary value. In 1982 J.J. Hopfield introduced a powerful two-state neural network model [2] for content addressable memory. In 1984, he introduced the analog version of his model [3] that has been widely used in order to solve combinatorial optimization problems.

While the continuous Hopfield net model is a powerful generalization of the binary model, the size of the state space increases drastically and the energy function is hence likely to have more local minima than in the discrete model.

However there exists other powerful generalization of the binary model to discrete neurons, that is, the node outputs belong to a discrete set of values. Basically there are four different multivalued type Hopfield neuron models.

- **Q-Ising neuron:** The state of a Q-Ising neuron is represented by a scalar (see [13]). The interaction energy between two neurons is expressed as a

F.J. Garijo, J.C. Riquelme, and M. Toro (Eds.): IBERAMIA 2002, LNAI 2527, pp. 509–518, 2002.
© Springer-Verlag Berlin Heidelberg 2002

function of the product of these scalars. In this model the states are ordered from a minimum to a maximum.

- **Phasor neuron:** The states of a phasor or clock neuron is expressed by a complex vector on the unit circle (see [11] and [4]). The interaction between two neurons is written as a function of the real part of the product of these vectors.
- **Potts neuron:** The different states are expressed by an n-dimensional vector (see [5] and [14]). The interaction energy between two neurons is a function of the scalar product between the vectors that represent their states.
- **Discrete neuron:** The state of that neuron is an integer from $\{1, 2, \ldots, N\}$ (see [1] and [12]). The interaction between neurons is expressed by the sign function.

Multivalued type Hopfield neural networks are been used in [4], [7], [15] and [1] as content addressable memory, but they lead to a very complex representation and the obtained results are similar to standard models that uses more simple neurons. In [1], Erdem and Ozturk introduce the MAREN model that is also used to solve combinatorial optimization problems. In [12] Ozturk and Abut propose the SOAR model as an extension to MAREN and uses it to image classification.

In this paper, we present the MREM neural network model inspired in BH network. The neurons are multivalued and their output can be any element of a finite set $\mathcal{M} = \{m_1, m_2, \ldots, m_N\}$ that can be a numerical or qualitative one, so any order is demanded for the $\mathcal{M}$ set. The interaction between neurons is expressed by the similarity function that produces any numerical value. It leads to a better representation of interaction energy between neurons that SOAR and MAREN models since in those models most of the information enclosed in the multivalued representation is missed by the sign function that produces only values in $\{-1, 0, 1\}$.

It must be pointed out that the MREM model has a big flexibility and allows a good representation for most of combinatorial problems without fine-tuning of parameters, as most others models do [8],[9],[10]. The flexibility of this model can be observed since the four types of neurons before expressed and standard binary $\{0, 1\}$ and bipolar $\{-1, 1\}$ Hopfield models are particular instances of MREM.

In this paper it is shown the MREM model as a content addressable memory and applied to load and retrieve some patterns into/from the network by the Hebb's rule. Other applications can be seen in [8],[9],[10].

In section 2, the discrete version of MREM model is presented and some of its properties are derived. In section 3, the properties of the model as a content addressable memory is shown. Section 4 studies the capacity of the network. Finally we present our conclusions in section 5.

2   The Finite MREM Model of Neural Network

Let $\mathcal{H}$ be a recurrent neural network formed by P nodes (neurons) where the state of each neuron is defined by its output V_i, $i \in \mathcal{I}$, $\mathcal{I} = \{1, 2, \ldots, P\}$

and it takes values in any finite set $\mathcal{M}$. This set can be a numerical set (for example: $\mathcal{M} = \{1, 2, \ldots, N\}$), or a non numerical one (for example: $\mathcal{M} = \{red, green, blue\}$).

The state of the network, at time k, is given by a P-dimensional vector, $V(t) = (V_1(t), V_2(t), \ldots, V_P(t)) \in \mathcal{M}^P$.

The network is fully connected and w_{ij} is the weight of the connection from jth to the ith node. The behavior of the network can be characterized by its energy function that is given by the following expression

$$E = -\frac{1}{2} \sum_{i=1}^{P} \sum_{j=1}^{P} w_{ij} f(V_i, V_j) + \sum_{i=1}^{P} \theta_i(V_i)$$

where $i, j \in \mathcal{I}$ and f, θ_i are functions: $f : \mathcal{M} \times \mathcal{M} \to \mathcal{R}$ and $\theta_i : \mathcal{M} \to \mathcal{R}$.

The function $f(V_i, V_j)$ can be consider as a measure of similarity between the outputs of the ith and jth neurons. The most simple similarity function is

$$f(x, y) = \delta(x, y) = \begin{cases} 1 & x = y \\ 0 & x \neq y \end{cases} \quad \forall x, y \in \mathcal{M}$$

that is, the function only takes the value 1 if the two neurons have the same state. Others similarity functions are $f(x, y) = -Ad(x, y) + B$, where $A, B \in \mathcal{R}$, $A > 0$ and $d(x, y)$ is any function distance.

If we consider $f(V_i, V_j) = V_i V_j$, $\theta_i(V_i) = \theta_i V_i$ and $\mathcal{M} = \{-1, 1\}$ then the BH model is obtained (when $\mathcal{M} = \{0, 1\}$ we obtain the binary one). It can be easily seen due to the energy function in the Hopfield network is $E = -\frac{1}{2} \sum_{i=1}^{P} \sum_{j=1}^{P} w_{ij} V_i V_j + \sum_{i=1}^{P} \theta_i V_i$, where θ_i are real constants (thresholds).

The others models can be easily obtained:

- The MAREN or discrete model is obtained when $\mathcal{M} = \{1, 2, \ldots, N\}$ and $f(V_i, V_j) = sgn(V_i - V_j)$, where $sgn(x)$ is -1, 0, 1 if $x < 0$, $x = 0$ or $x > 0$ respectively.
- In the Phasor model $\mathcal{M}$ is the set of complex roots the equation $z^n - 1 = 0$, and $f(V_i, V_j) = Re(V_i V_j)$, where $Re(z)$ is the real component of z.
- Q-Ising model of neurons uses a finite subset of real numbers as $\mathcal{M}$ and the product function as $f(V_i, V_j)$.
- Potts neuron model has some vertices of $[0, 1]^N$ (or $[-1, 1]^N$) as $\mathcal{M}$ and uses the scalar product of vectors as f, that is, $f(V_i, V_j) = \langle V_i, V_j \rangle$.

Since thresholds will not be used for content addressable memory, henceforth we will consider θ_i be the zero function for all $i \in \mathcal{I}$.

The similarity function has not any restriction, but in most applications it usually verifies three properties that in advance we referred to them as *similarity conditions*. These conditions are

1) $\forall x \in \mathcal{M}$, $f(x, x) = c$, where c is a real number.
2) $f(x, y)$ is symmetric: $\forall x, y \in \mathcal{M}$, $f(x, y) = f(y, x)$
3) $\forall x \neq y \quad f(x, y) \leq c$

If $\mathcal{M}$ is a discrete set, the similarity function is defined by an $N \times N$ matrix, F, where $F_{ij} \in \mathcal{R}$ measures the similarity between the elements m_i and m_j, for $m_i, m_j \in \mathcal{M}$.

In this way, the network $\mathcal{H}$ can be represented by a threesome $\mathcal{H} = (\mathcal{M}, W, F)$ and the energy function:

$$E = -\frac{1}{2} \sum_{i=1}^{P} \sum_{j=1}^{P} w_{ij} F_{V_i, V_j} \qquad (1)$$

When $f(x, y)$ verifies the similarity conditions then F is a symmetric matrix, $F_{ii} = c$ and $F_{ij} \leq c \, (i \neq j)$.

2.1   Dynamic of MREM Network

We have considered discrete time and asynchronous dynamic, where only a neuron is updated at time t. The next state of the interrogated neuron will be the one that makes the lowest value of the energy function.

Let us consider some total order in $\mathcal{M}$, (since it is a finite set we can select any from the $N!$ possible ones), and suppose that a is the index of the interrogated neuron at time t, then at time t+1, the state of neuron i for $i \neq a$, is equal to the previous one ($V_i(t+1) = V_i(t), \forall i \neq a$). In order to determine the next state of neuron a, we define the potential increment.

Definition 1. *We define the potential increment of a-th neuron, at time t, when it takes the state l:*

$$U_{a,l}(t) = \frac{1}{2} \sum_{i=1}^{i=P} \left[w_{ai} F_{l, V_i(t)} + w_{ia} F_{V_i(t), l} \right] - \frac{1}{2} w_{aa} F_{ll} \qquad (2)$$

So, the potencial increment of neuron a is a vector U_a with N components.

Expression (2) is formed by terms in (1) that are affected by changes of a-th neuron, with different sign.

We use the following updating rule:

$$V_a(t+1) = l \Leftrightarrow U_{a,l}(t) \geq U_{a,i}(t), \ \forall i \in \mathcal{M} \qquad (3)$$

when there exist several components with the maximum value, we select the minimum among them by the total order supposed on $\mathcal{M}$. So we shall avoid cycles among states of equal energy.

When similarity conditions are verified by $f(x, y)$ then expression (2) is reduced to: $U_{a,l}(t) = \frac{1}{2} \sum_{i=1}^{i=P} (w_{ai} + w_{ia}) F_{V_i(t), l} - \frac{c}{2} w_{aa}$

Moreover, since the term $-\frac{c}{2} w_{aa}$ is a constant for all possible states of neuron a, it is not necessary to consider this term, when we are looking for the maximum in (3). So, the updating rule is given by:

$$V_a(t+1) = l \Leftrightarrow U^*_{a,l}(t) \geq U^*_{a,i}(t), \ \forall i \in \mathcal{M} \qquad (4)$$

where $U_{a,l}^*(t) = \frac{1}{2} \sum_{i=1}^{i=P} (w_{ai} + w_{ia}) F_{V_i(t),l}$ and it can be called *reduced potential increment* of neuron a when it takes value l.

It has been proved that the MREM model with this dynamics always converges to a minimal state [8].

3   The MREM as a Recurrent Model

Suppose $X = (x_k)_{k \in K}$ be a set of patterns that we want to be loaded into the neural network, that is, they must correspond to minimal energy states. Suppose that, at first, all the states of the network have the same energy $W = 0$, then in order to load a pattern X, we must modify the components of the W matrix to obtain that X be the state of the network with minimal energy.

So we calculate $\frac{\partial E}{\partial w_{ij}} = -\frac{1}{2} f(x_i, x_j)$ and we modify the components of matrix W to reduce the energy of state X by $\Delta w_{ij} = -\alpha \frac{\partial E}{\partial w_{ij}} = \frac{\alpha}{2} f(x_i, x_j), (\alpha > 0)$, so for $\alpha = 2$, it results $\Delta w_{ij} = f(x_i, x_j)$. Summarizing overall the patterns, we obtain:

$$W_{ij} = \sum_{k \in K} f(x_{ki}, x_{kj}) \tag{5}$$

that is a generalization of the *Hebb's postulate of learning* because the weight w_{ij} between neurons is increased in correspondence with their similarity. It must be pointed out that usually the Hebb's learning rule is used with the product function between the neuron outputs.

When bipolar neurons are used and $f(x, y) = xy$, it will be obtained the well-known rule of learning of patterns in the Hopfield's network, but now the outputs of neurons in equation 3 have been extended to any discrete set $\mathcal{M}$.

To recover a loaded pattern, the network is initialized with the known part of that pattern. The network dynamic will converges to a minimal state that is the answer of the network. Usually this stable state is next to the initial one.

Lemma 1. *Given a network $\mathcal{H}$, if we modify the weight matrix W by ΔW then a state V of the network will modify its energy function by*

$$\Delta E = \frac{-1}{2} \sum_{i=1}^{i=P} \sum_{j=1}^{j=P} \Delta w_{ij} f(V_i, V_j)$$

It can be easily proved by subtracting $E' - E$, where E' is the energy with the matrix $W' = W + \Delta W$.

Definition 2. *Given a state V of the network and a similarity function f, we define its **associated matrix** G_V as the $P \times P$ matrix with $G_{ij} = f(V_i, V_j)$. Moreover we define its **associated vector** G_V, as the vector with P^2 components obtained by expanding the matrix G_V as a vector $(G_{ij} = G_{j+P(i-1)})$.*

Lemma 2. *When in a multivalued network* $\mathcal{H}$ *with weight matrix* W*, a pattern* X_k *have been loaded by equation 3, then:*

$$\Delta E_V = -\frac{1}{2}\langle G_{X_k}, G_V \rangle = -\frac{1}{2}||G_{X_k}||\,||G_V||cos(\alpha)$$

where $\langle . \rangle$ *represents the Euclidean scalar product and* α *is the angle between the associated vectors of pattern* X_k *and the state* V*.*

Proposition 2 can be easily proved from Proposition 1.

When the image space of the similarity functions is $\{-1,1\}$, then for all state S and pattern X_k, result $||G_{X_k}|| = ||G_S|| = P$. So it will be obtained by proposition 2 that $\Delta E_S = -\frac{P^2}{2}cos(\alpha)$.

This expression points out that the states with associated vector more similar to G_{X_k} will decrease more its energy. But, can different states have the same associated state?, the answer is affirmative and it produces the well-known effect of loading the opposite state $(-X_k)$ by the BH network.

Proposition 2 justifies that others Hopfield's model (continuous and binary) are not used for content addressable memory since associated patterns to states have different modulus.

Example 1: For the BH network $\mathcal{M} = \{-1,1\}$, $f(x,y) = xy$, so if the vector $x = (-1,1,-1)$ has been loaded, then the associated vector of x is $G_x = (1,-1,1,-1,1,-1,1,-1,1)$, but the associated vector of $-x = (1,-1,1)$ is also G_x. So when the BH network load the pattern x the energy of states with associated vector more similar to G_x is reduced and the opposite state is also loaded. States with local minimum energy and no associated with input patterns are denoted as *spurious states*.

Example 2: Consider $\mathcal{M} = \{R,G,B\}$, (R=red, G=green, B=blue), and the similarity function $f : \mathcal{M} \times \mathcal{M} \to \{-1,1\}$, that verifies: $f(R,R) = f(G,G) = f(B,B) = 1$ and $f(R,G) = f(G,R) = f(R,B) = f(B,R) = f(G,B) = f(B,G) = -1$. To load the pattern $x = (B,G,R,B)$ into the network, the associated matrix is:

$$G_x = \begin{pmatrix} f(B,B) & f(B,G) & f(B,R) & f(B,B) \\ f(G,B) & f(G,G) & f(G,R) & f(G,B) \\ f(R,B) & f(R,G) & f(R,R) & f(R,B) \\ f(B,B) & f(B,G) & f(B,R) & f(B,B) \end{pmatrix} = \begin{pmatrix} 1 & -1 & -1 & 1 \\ -1 & 1 & -1 & -1 \\ -1 & -1 & 1 & -1 \\ 1 & -1 & -1 & 1 \end{pmatrix} \Rightarrow$$

$G_x = (1,-1,-1,1,-1,1,-1,-1,-1,-1,1,-1,1,-1,-1,1)$ is the associated vector, but there exist some others patterns with the same associated vector (those ones V with $V_1 = V_4$, $V_1 \neq V_2 \neq V_3$ and $V_1 \neq V_3$). So all the patterns $(G,R,B,G), (G,B,R,G), B,R,G,B), R,B,G,R$ and $R,G,B,R)$ have the same associated vector than x. The previous effect (spurious states) usually is an undesirable one. Next we will show a trick to avoid it.

Definition 3. *Suppose* $X = (x_1,x_2,\ldots,x_P)$ *is a pattern which must be loaded into the network and* $\mathcal{M} = \{m_1,m_2,\ldots,m_N\}$*, then we say that its* **augmented pattern** $(\hat{X})$ *is a vector in* $\mathcal{M}^{P+N}$ *which components are:*

$$\hat{x}_i = \begin{cases} x_i & i \le P \\ m_{i-P} & i > P \end{cases}$$

Theorem 1. *The function $\Psi : \hat{X} \to G_{\hat{X}}$, which applies its associated vector to an augmented pattern, is injective.*

Let $\hat{X} = (x_1, x_2, \ldots, x_P, m_1, m_2, \ldots, m_N)$ and $\hat{Y} = (y_1, y_2, \ldots, y_P, m_1, m_2, \ldots, m_N)$ be the augmented vectors of $X = (x_1, \ldots, x_P)$ and $Y = (y_1, \ldots, y_P)$ that verify $\Psi(\hat{X}) = \Psi(\hat{Y})$, or equivalently $G_{\hat{X}} = G_{\hat{Y}}$.

The $P + 1$ to $P + N$ components of $G_{\hat{X}}$ are $f(x_1, m_1)$, $f(x_1, m_2)$, $\ldots, f(x_1, m_N)$. If $x_1 = m_j$, since $G_{\hat{X}} = G_{\hat{Y}}$, it results $1 = f(x_1, m_j) = f(y_1, m_j) \Rightarrow y_1 = m_j$.

Repeating the reasoning with kP+(k-1)N+1 to k(P+N) components ($1 \le k \le P$), we obtain $x_k = y_k$ and the function will be injective.

So, to load a pattern X where $x_i \in M = \{m_1, m_2, \ldots, m_N\}$, we can load into the network its augmented pattern $\hat{X}$. The state $\hat{X}$ will be the only one that maximizes the decrement of energy. The new N neurons can be consider false or no implemented since they have always the same value. Only the weight associated with them w_{ij} must be considered.

For example, to load the vector $X = (-1, 1, -1)$ by a BH network, we can augment the given vector with $x_4 = -1$, $x_5 = 1$ and to use a network with five neurons (two false ones), to load $\hat{X} = (-1, 1, -1, -1, 1)$. The minimal states of the new network are related to $\hat{X}$ and $-\hat{X}$. When in the retrieve phase the network is stabilizes in any of them, the original pattern can be obtained by considering that both corresponds to a state V with $V_1 = V_3 = V_4$, $V_2 = V_5$, and we know $V_4 = \hat{X}_4 = -1$ and $V_5 = \hat{X}_5 = 1$.

4   Capacity

Similarly to the analysis of a Hopfield network storage capacity [6], storage capacity of a multivalued associative memory is calculated by the estimation of probability of an error in the network response. So, we suppose that K patterns have been loaded into the network and the state V^* coincides with a loaded pattern, but state V^λ is a state that coincides with V^* except component λ.

From equations 1 and 3, we obtain the energy of any state V from:

$$-2E(V) = \sum_{i=1}^{P+N} \sum_{j=1}^{P+N} \sum_{k=1}^{K} f(X_{k,i}, X_{k,j}) f(V_i, V_j) \tag{6}$$

For simplicity we consider the component that is different between states V^* and V^λ is the first one. Denoting by $D = 2\Delta E = 2(E(V^\lambda) - E(V^*))$, results that if $D > 0$, the corresponding component is obtained without error when the state V^λ is introduced into the network. From equation 6 results:

$$D = \sum_{i=1}^{P+N} \sum_{j=1}^{P+N} \sum_{k=1}^{K} f(X_{k,i}, X_{k,j}) f(V_i^*, V_j^*) - \sum_{i=1}^{P+N} \sum_{j=1}^{P+N} \sum_{k=1}^{K} f(X_{k,i}, X_{k,j}) f(V_i^\lambda, V_j^\lambda)$$

Since $V_j^* = V_j^\lambda$ for all $j > 1$ we obtain that only terms with $i = 1$ or $j = 1$ are different in the expressions of the energy for the states V^* and V^λ. Moreover since the similarity function is symmetric and $f(V_1, V_1) = 1$, for any state V, so we obtain the next expression for D:

$$D = 2 \sum_{i=2}^{N+P} \sum_{k=1}^{K} f(X_{k,1}, X_{k,i})(f(V_1^*, V_i^*) - f(V_1^\lambda, V_i^\lambda))$$

Let X_{k_0} be the loaded pattern that coincides with V^* then:

$$D = 2 \sum_{i=2}^{N+P} f(V_1^*, V_i^*)(f(V_1^*, V_i^*) - f(V_1^\lambda, V_i^\lambda)) +$$

$$+2 \sum_{i=2}^{N+P} \sum_{k \neq k_0}^{K} f(X_{k,1}, X_{k,i})(f(V_1^*, V_i^*) - f(V_1^\lambda, V_i^\lambda))$$

For all i the expression $f(V_1^*, V_i^*)f(V_1^*, V_i^*) = 1$.

The expression $\sum_{i=P+1}^{P+N} f(V_1^*, V_i^*)f(V_1^\lambda, V_i^\lambda) = N - 4$, since last components of the augment patterns are $\{m_1, m_2, \ldots, m_N\}$ there exist $m_p \neq m_q$ with $V_1^* = m_p$ and $V_1^\lambda = m_q$, then for $i \in \{p, q\}$, $f(V_1^*, V_i^*)f(V_1^\lambda, V_i^\lambda) = -1$ and for $i \notin \{p, q\}$ that expression is 1.

To calculate the value for $2 \leq i \leq P$ we consider random patterns whose components are uniformly distributed, so the value of $f(V_1^*, V_i^*)f(V_1^\lambda, V_i^\lambda)$ is a random variable ϕ with distribution: $p(\phi = -1) = \frac{2}{N}$ and $p(\phi = 1) = \frac{N-2}{N}$. It is shown in table 1, so $\mu = E(\phi) = \frac{N-4}{N}$ and its variance is $V(\phi) = \frac{8(N-2)}{N^2}$. The first term of D results $2((N+P-1) - (N-4) - \sum_{i=2}^{P} \phi_i) = 2(P+3 - \sum_{i=2}^{P} \phi_i)$.

Table 1. Distribution of ϕ.

First term	Second term	Probability	Value
$V_1^* = V_i^*$	$V_1^\lambda = V_i^\lambda$	0	1
$V_1^* = V_i^*$	$V_1^\lambda \neq V_i^\lambda$	$\frac{1}{N}$	-1
$V_1^* \neq V_i^*$	$V_1^\lambda = V_i^\lambda$	$\frac{1}{N}$	-1
$V_1^* \neq V_i^*$	$V_1^\lambda \neq V_i^\lambda$	$\frac{N-2}{N}$	1

To evaluate the second term of D, let X_k and V^* be a random pattern and a random state respectively. For a given pattern X_k the expression:
$A = f(X_{k,1}, X_{k,i})(f(V_1^*, V_i^*) - f(V_1^\lambda, V_i^\lambda))$, $(2 \leq i \leq P)$ is a random variable ξ of distribution: $p(\xi = 2) = p(\xi = -2) = \frac{1}{N}$ and $p(\xi = 0) = \frac{N-2}{N}$, as it is shown in table 2(left). The mean and variance of ξ is $E(\xi) = 0$ and $V(\xi) = \frac{8}{N}$.

Hence, $\sum_{i=2}^{P} \sum_{k \neq k_0}^{K} f(X_{k,1}, X_{k,i})(f(V_1^*, V_i^*) - f(V_1^\lambda, V_i^\lambda)) = \sum_{l=1}^{(P-1)(K-1)} \xi_l$.

The expression $B = \sum_{i=P+1}^{i=P+N} f(X_{k,1}, X_{k,i})(f(V_1^*, V_i^*) - f(V_1^\lambda, V_i^\lambda))$ is newly the random variable ξ because $X_{k,i} = V_i^* = V_i^\lambda$ when $i > P$, so denoting

Table 2. Distribution of A and B.

T1	T2	T3	Probability	Value
$X_{k,1} = X_{k,j}$	$V_1^* = V_i^*$	$V_1^\lambda = V_i^\lambda$	0	0
$X_{k,1} = X_{k,j}$	$V_1^* = V_i^*$	$V_1^\lambda \neq V_i^\lambda$	$\frac{1}{N^2}$	2
$X_{k,1} = X_{k,j}$	$V_1^* \neq V_i^*$	$V_1^\lambda = V_i^\lambda$	$\frac{1}{N^2}$	-2
$X_{k,1} = X_{k,j}$	$V_1^* \neq V_i^*$	$V_1^\lambda \neq V_i^\lambda$	$\frac{N-2}{N^2}$	0
$X_{k,1} \neq X_{k,j}$	$V_1^* = V_i^*$	$V_1^\lambda = V_i^\lambda$	0	0
$X_{k,1} \neq X_{k,j}$	$V_1^* = V_i^*$	$V_1^\lambda \neq V_i^\lambda$	$\frac{N-1}{N^2}$	2
$X_{k,1} \neq X_{k,j}$	$V_1^* \neq V_i^*$	$V_1^\lambda = V_i^\lambda$	$\frac{N-1}{N^2}$	-2
$X_{k,1} \neq X_{k,j}$	$V_1^* \neq V_i^*$	$V_1^\lambda \neq V_i^\lambda$	$\frac{(N-1)(N-2)}{N^2}$	0

T1	T2	Probability	Value
p=r	q=r	0	0
p=r	q≠r	$\frac{1}{N}$	2
p≠r	q=r	$\frac{1}{N}$	-2
p≠r	q≠r	$\frac{N-2}{N}$	0

$X_{k,1} = m_r$, $V_1^* = m_p$ and $V_1^\lambda = m_q$, $(m_q \neq m_p)$, we obtain it from table 2(right). Hence we obtain that: $\sum_{i=P+1}^{N+P} \sum_{k \neq k_0}^{K} f(X_{k,1}, X_{k,i})(f(V_1^*, V_i^*) - f(V_1^\lambda, V_i^\lambda))$ is a sum of $K - 1$ independent random variables $B = \sum_{l=(P-1)(K-1)+1}^{P(K-1)} \xi_l$.

Summarizing all terms we obtain: $D = 2(P + 3 - \sum_{i=2}^{P} \phi_i + \sum_{l=1}^{P(K-1)} \xi_l)$. According with the Lindenberg-Levy central limit theorem, for high values of P and K, the distribution of $\sum_{l=1}^{P(K-1)} \xi_l$ becomes a Gaussian with mean zero and variance $P(K-1)\frac{8}{N}$ and $\sum_{i=2}^{P} \phi_l$ becomes another Gaussian with mean $\frac{(P-1)(4-N)}{N}$ and variance $(P-1)\frac{8(N-2)}{N^2}$.

The probability of error when V^λ is introduced into the network is:

$$P_e = prob(D < 0) = prob(P + 3 < \psi) \tag{7}$$

where $\psi \to N(\mu, \sigma)$ with $\mu = \frac{(P-1)(4-N)}{N}$ and $\sigma = \sqrt{\frac{8(P-1)(N-2)}{N^2} + \frac{8P(K-1)}{N}}$.

The parameter of capacity α is usually defined as the quotient between the maximum number of pattern to load into the network and the number of used neurons that obtains an acceptable error probability (usually $P_e^{max} = 0.05$), here $\alpha = \frac{K}{P} \Rightarrow K = \alpha P$. From equation 7, it is possible obtain the value for α for a given P_e. Here we obtain the value $\alpha = 0.1864$ (similar to the well known value 0.15 for BH) when $P_e = 0.05$, $N = 4$ and $P = 1000$ by replacing K for αP and considering that for $Z = \frac{P+3-\mu}{\sigma} = z_{0.05} = 1.645 \Rightarrow P(P_e > Z) = 0.05$

It must be pointed out that for a given parameter α the loaded patterns are multivalued and them contains much more information than binary ones.

5   Conclusions

We have shown the discrete MREM network, it generalizes all existing type Hopfield models with multivalued neurons.

We have studied a method to load patterns into the network, so the model performs as an content addressable memory. The loaded patterns correspond to minimal energy (stable) states. When the network is initialized with similar states, the network converges to a minimal energy state that usually is near from its initial one.

518   E. Mérida-Casermeiro, J. Muñoz-Pérez, and M.A. García-Bernal

The well-known effect of loading into the BH network the opposite pattern $-X$ jointed to X, has been explained in terms of the changes of the energy function on them. Similar effects occurs with the proposed network. But, a method to avoid that usually undesirable result has been shown. This method needs a network with $P + N$ neurons to load an N-dimensional pattern. This could be seen as the price one pays for avoiding to load undesirable patterns.

We have studied the capacity of the network, obtaining an expression where the parameter of capacity of the network can be obtained.

References

1. Mahmut H. Erdem & Y. Ozturk, *A New family of Multivalued Networks*, Neural Networks **9,6**, pp. 979–989,1996.
2. J.J. Hopfield, *Neural networks and physical systems with emergent collective computational abilities*, Proc. of National Academy of Sciences USA,**79**, 2254–2558,1982.
3. J.J. Hopfield, *Neurons with graded response have collective computational properties like those of two-state neurons*, Proceedings of the National Academy of Sciences USA,**81**, 3088–3092, 1984.
4. Stanislaw Jankowski, Andrzej Lozowski and Jacek M. Zurada. *Complex-Valued Multistate Neural Associative Memory*. IEEE Transactions on Neural Networks **7** n° 7 1491–1496, Nov. 1996.
5. L. Gislén, C. Peterson and B. Söderberg. *Complex Schedulling with Potts Neural Networks*. Neural Computation. **9**, 805–831 (1992).
6. John Hertz, Anders Krogh and Richard G. Palmer *Introduction to the theory of neural computation*. Lecture Notes Volume I. Addison Wesley, 1991.
7. Kohring, G.A., *On the Q-state Neuron Problem in Attractor Neural Networks*. Neural Networks, Vol **6**, 573–581, 1993.
8. E. Mérida Casermeiro, *Red Neuronal recurrente multivaluada para el reconocimiento de patrones y la optimización combinatoria*, Ph.D. dissertation. Univ. Málaga, Spain, (in spanish), 2000.
9. E. Mérida Casermeiro, G. Galán Marín, J. Muñoz Pérez. An Efficient Multivalued Hopfield Network for the Traveling Salesman Problem. Neural Processing Letters **14**, 203–216, Dec. 2001.
10. E. Mérida Casermeiro, J. Muñoz Pérez, R. Benítez Rochel. A recurrent multivalued neural network for the N-queens problem. Lecture Notes in Computer Science **2084**, 522–529, 2001.
11. A.J. Noest. *Discrete-state phasor neural nets*. Physical Review **A38** 2196–99, 1988.
12. Yusuf Ozturk and Hüseyin Abut. *System of Associative Relationship (SOAR)*. Proceedings of ASILOMAR'97. Pacific Grove, CA. (1997).
13. H. Rieger. *Storing an extensive number of grey-toned patterns in a neural network using multistate neurons*. Journal of Physics. **A23**, L1273-79 (1990).
14. F.Y. Wu. *The Potts Model* Reviews of Modern Physics. **54(1)**, (1982).
15. Jacek M. Zurada, Ian Cloete and Etienne van der Poel. Generalized Hopfield networks for associative memories with multi-valued stable states. Neurocomputing **13**, 135–149 (1996).

Machine Learning Models for Online Dynamic Security Assessment of Electric Power Systems

Claudio M. Rocco and José A. Moreno

Universidad Central, Facultad de Ingeniería, Apartado 47937, Caracas 1040A, Venezuela
{rocco,jose}@neurona.ciens.ucv.ve

Abstract. In this paper we compare two machine learning algorithms (Support Vector Machine and Multi Layer Perceptrons) to perform on-line dynamic security assessment of an electric power system. Dynamic simulation is properly emulated by training SVM and MLP models, with a small amount of information. The experiments show that although both models produce reasonable predictions, the performance indexes of the SVM models are better than those of the MLP models. However the MLP models are of considerably reduced complexity.

1 Introduction

An important task in the real-time operation of an electric power system is to accurately assess the dynamic response during a system disturbance [1]. In this case, it is important to evaluate the system robustness to establish effective emergency control measures such as under frequency load shedding, in order to prevent system collapse [2,3].

The dynamic behavior of the electric power system, usually analyzed using time-domain simulation methods or Lyapunov´s stability theory is a very time demanding task. Based on simulation results, the state of the system is classified as "secure/insecure". Due to the computationally cost involved and the repetitive use of dynamic simulators, large efforts have been made toward developing fast algorithms to deal with the prediction of the system dynamic behavior.

In the literature several approaches have been presented to address the definition of these algorithms: pattern recognition [4], neural networks [2], decision tree [5], regression trees [6] and associative dichotomous classification [1]. In this work, empirical models, built by training a Support Vector Machine (SVM) and a Multi Layer Perceptron (MLP) are compared. SVM provides a new approach to the two-category classification problem ("secure/insecure")[7] whereas MLP is one of the most common applied method. To our best knowledge, the SVM approach has not been yet used to evaluate on-line dynamic behavior.

The paper is organized as follows: In section 2 the methods used in this paper are introduced, section 3 presents the proposed approach to assess the dynamic response of an electric power system and, finally section 4 presents and compares the results.

F.J. Garijo, J.C. Riquelme, and M. Toro (Eds.): IBERAMIA 2002, LNAI 2527, pp. 519–525, 2002.

2   Global Machine Learning Models

2.1 Support Vector Machine

Support Vector Machines provide a novel approach to the two-category classification problem [7]. The methods have been successfully applied to a number of applications ranging from particle identification, face identification and text categorization to engine detection, bioinformatics and data base marketing. The approach is systematic and properly motivated by statistical learning theory [8].

SVM is an estimation algorithm ("learning machine") in which the training phase involves optimization of a convex cost function, hence there are no local minima to complicate the learning process. Testing is based on the model evaluation using the most informative patterns in the data (the support vectors). Performance is based on error rate determination as test set size tends to infinity [9].

Suppose X_i is a power system state vector whose components represent the variables that are going to characterize a given operating condition, and y_i is the result of applying a dynamic simulation model (DSM): $y_i = DSM(X_i)$. Additionally, if X_i is a secure state then $y_i = 1$, otherwise $y_i = -1$.

Consider a set of N training data points $\{(X_1,y_1), \ldots (X_N,y_N)\}$. The main idea is to obtain a hyperplane that separates secure states from insecure states in this space, that is, to construct the hyperplane H: $y = w \cdot X\text{-}b = 0$ and two hyperplanes parallel to it:

$$H_1: y = w \cdot X\text{-}b = +1 \text{ and } H_2: y = w \cdot X\text{-}b = -1 \tag{1}$$

with the condition, that there are no data points between H_1 and H_2, and the distance between H_1 and H_2 (the margin) is maximized. Figure 1 shows such case [10].

The quantities w and b are the parameters that control the function and are referred as the weight vector and bias [8].

The problem can be formulated as:

$$\begin{aligned} &\text{Min } \tfrac{1}{2}\, w^T w \\ &w,b \end{aligned} \tag{2}$$

$$\text{s.t}\quad y_i(w \cdot X\text{-}b) \geq 1$$

This is a convex, quadratic programming problem in (w, b), in a convex set. Using the Lagrangian formulation, the constraints reduce to those on the Lagrange multipliers themselves. Additionally a consequence of this reformulation, is that the training data will only appear in the form of dot product between data vectors [7]. Introducing Lagrange multipliers $\alpha_1, \ldots, \alpha_N \geq 0$, a Lagrangian function for the optimization problem can be defined:

$$L_p(w,b,\alpha) = \tfrac{1}{2}\, w^T w - \Sigma_i\,(\alpha_i y_i(w \cdot Xi\text{-}b) - \alpha_i) \tag{3}$$

Now L_p must be minimized with respect to w and b with the condition that the derivatives of L_p with respect to all the α_i, vanish and $\alpha_i \geq 0$ [7]. This formulation corresponds to a convex quadratic programming problem, with a convex objective function. Additionally those points that satisfy the constraints also form a convex set.

So the following "dual" problem can be formulated: Maximize L_p, subject to the constraints that the gradient of L_p with respect to w and b vanish and $\alpha_i \geq 0$. The stationarity conditions give the following relations [7]:

$$\mathbf{w} = \Sigma_i \, \alpha_i y_i \, \mathbf{X}_i \qquad\qquad (4)$$

$$\Sigma_i \, \alpha_i y_i = 0 \qquad\qquad (5)$$

From here, substituting in (3) the Wolfe dual formulation [7,8,11] is obtained:

$$L_D = \Sigma_i \, \alpha_i - \tfrac{1}{2} \Sigma_{ij} \, \alpha_i \alpha_j y_i y_j \, \mathbf{X}_i \cdot \mathbf{X}_j \qquad\qquad (6)$$

Solving for α_i and computing b gives $\mathbf{w} = \Sigma_i \, \alpha_i y_i \mathbf{Xi}$.

Once a SVM has been trained it is simple to determine on which side of the decision boundary a given test pattern $\mathbf{X}^*$ lies and assign the corresponding class label, using sgn $(\mathbf{w} \cdot \mathbf{X}^* - b)$.

When the maximal margin hyperplane is found, only those points which lie closest to the hyperplane have $\alpha_i > 0$ and these points are the support vectors, that is, the critical elements of the training set. All other points have $\alpha_i = 0$. This means that if all other training points were removed and training was repeated, the same separating hyperplane would be found [7]. In figure 2, the points a, b, c, d and e are examples of support vectors [10].

Small problems can be solved by any general-purpose optimization package that solves linearly constrained convex quadratic programs. For larger problems, a range of existing techniques can be used [8].

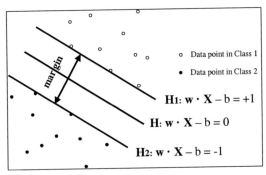

Fig. 1. Decision hyperplanes generated by a linear SVM [10]

If the surface separating the two classes is not linear, the data points can be transformed to another high dimensional feature space where the problem is linearly separable.

The algorithm that finds a separating hyperplane in the feature space can be obtained in terms of points in input space and a transformation function $\Phi(\cdot)$. It is not necessary to be explicit about the transformation $\Phi(\cdot)$ as long as it is known that a *kernel function* $\mathbf{K(X_i, X_j)}$ is equivalent to a dot product in some other high dimensional feature space [7,8-13]. A kernel function must satisfy Mercer's theorem [11], there are many kernel functions that can be used this way, for example [7,8]:

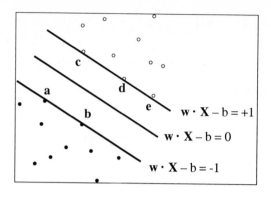

Fig. 2. Example of support vectors [10]

$K(X_i,X_j) = e^{-\|Xi-Xj\|^2/2\sigma^2}$ the Gaussian radial basis function kernel
$K(X_i,X_j) = (X_i \cdot X_j + ml)^p$ the polynomial kernel
$K(X_i,X_j) = \tanh(\beta(X_i \cdot X_j))$ the hyperbolic tangent kernel

With a suitable kernel, SVM can separate in feature space the data that in the original input space was non-separable. This property implies that nonlinear algorithms can be obtained by using proven methods that handle linearly separable data sets [11].

The choice of the kernel is a limitation of the support vector approach. Some work has been done on limiting kernels using prior knowledge [11]. In any case, the SVM with lower complexity should be preferred.

2.2   Multi Layer Perceptrons [14]

A multi layer perceptrons is a kind of artificial neural networks composed of layers of differentiable parametric non-linear functions, in general, sigmoid or hyperbolic tangent.

From a mathematical point of view, an MLP model with only one output unit is defined by a non-linear weighted combinations of m hyperbolic tangents of weighted sums of the input vector:

$$f(x;\theta) = \tanh\left(\sum_i \tanh(x \bullet w_i + b_i) \bullet w_{is} \right) + b_s \qquad (7)$$

where the estimated output is a function of the input vector and the parameters θ: w_i, w_{is}, b_s.

The set of parameters can be estimated by minimizing an error cost function. The most common errors measure used is the mean squared error between the desired output and the estimated outputs, for a given training set:

$$Q = \Sigma(y_i - f(x;\theta))^2 \qquad (8)$$

For this case, a gradient descent algorithm based on the computation of the partial derivative of the error function with respect to all the parameters can be used to estimate the parameters. The gradient descent can be executed for each parameter by an iterative process of the form:

$$\theta(t+1) = \theta(t) + \lambda \partial Q / \partial \theta \qquad (9)$$

where $\lambda < 1$ is the learning rate.

A disadvantage of this model is that the optimization process can get stuck in a local optimum.

2.3 Performance Evaluation

The performance of a binary classifier is measured using sensitivity, specificity and accuracy indexes [15]:

$$sensitivity = \frac{TP}{TP + FN}$$

$$specificity = \frac{TN}{TN + FP}$$

$$accuracy = \frac{TP + TN}{TP + TN + FP + FN}$$

where:

TP=Number of True Positive classified cases (The learning machine correctly classifies)

TN=Number of True Negative classified cases (The learning machine correctly classifies)

FP= Number of False Positive classified cases (The learning machine labels a case as positive while it is a negative)

FN= Number of False Negative classified cases (The learning machine labels a case as negative while it is a positive)

For power system dynamic evaluation, sensitivity gives the percentage of correctly classified secure states and the specificity the percentage of correctly classified insecure states.

3 Proposed Approach

In order to apply the previous models in power system dynamic evaluations, two data sets are built (training and testing) and only different states are selected, that is there are no replicated states in the data sets.

Each power system state is represented by a vector $\mathbf{X}_i$ whose components represent the variables that are going to characterize a given operating condition. As suggested in [3], the following variables were considered: the active and reactive power of all generators, spinning reserve, active and reactive load, among other. As the DSM will be replaced by a machine learning model the data set is built by sampling the configuration space of the electric power system. A random system state is generated by varying the values of the previously mentioned variables and applying the DSM.

A system state $\mathbf{X}_i$ is classified as insecure if the minimum frequency that the system experiments after a disturbance is less that a specific value.

4 Example

The system to be studied is the 60 Hz power system of an oil company in Venezuela, with several types of gas-fired units and a meshed 115 kV transmission network. An equivalent system with a total of 18 variables was considered. A system state is classified as insecure if the frequency is less than 59.3 Hz.

The training data set consists on 770 samples (596 states were secure and only 174 were insecure), whereas the testing data set consists on 3018 states: 2735 states were secure and only 283 were insecure.

In the SVM approach different kernels were tried. The optimization required in the training phase was performed using the Sequential Minimal Optimization approach discussed in [13]. The best SVM found corresponds to a second order polynomial kernel, with ml=4, based on 131 support vectors. This SVM model completely separates the training set, and shows good generalization capacity.

In the MLP, the architecture used consists on an 18 dimension input vector, one hidden layer of variable unit number and one output unit. The best MLP had one hidden layer with 14 processing units. It is interesting to note that the best MLP did not separate completely the training data set, achieving an accuracy of 93.50 %.

In order to compare mathematical similar models, experiments with an hyperbolic tangent kernel were carried out.

Table 1 presents the performance results for both models over the testing data set.

Table 1. Performance Results for different models

Model	Support Vectors	Number of parameters	Sensitivity %	Specificity %	Accuracy %
SVM, p=2	131	2359	94.92	91.88	94.63
SVM tanh	228	4105	96.05	82.33	94.76
MLP m=14	-------	281	92.83	84.45	90.63

It is interesting to note the SVM models are superior to the MLP model, since the performance indexes are higher. In the most similar models from a mathematical point of view (SVM with a hyperbolic tangent kernel and MLP), the SVM model shows a better sensitivity and accuracy than the MLP model, while the specificity is very similar.

5 Conclusions

This paper has evaluated on-line dynamic security assessment of electric power system based on two machine learning models. In the example presented both models, built from a small sample of the state space, produce dynamic evaluation with a satisfactory accuracy. However, SVM models outperform in all cases the best MLP. Nevertheless, from a complexity point of view, MLP models are less complex since they depend on smaller number of parameters.

References

1. Sobajic D.J., Pao Y.: "On-Line Transient Stability Evaluation by Associative Dichotomous Classification", *IEEE Transaction on Power Systems,* Vol 4, Feb. 1989
2. Mitchell M., Peças Lopes J.A., Fidalgo J.N., McCalley J.: "Using a Neural Network to Predict the Dynamic Frequency Response of a Power System to an Under-Frequency Load Shedding Scenario", IEEE Summer Meeting, 2000
3. Hatziargyriou N., Peças Lopes J.A., Karapidakis E., Vasconcelos M.H.: "On-Line Dynamic Security Assessment of Power Systems in Large Islands with High Wind Power Penetration", PSCC'99, 13th Power System Computational Conference, Vol 1, Trondheim, Norway, June 1999
4. Rapid Analysis of Transient Stability, IEEE Publication, 87TH0169-3-PWR, 1987
5. Hatziargyriou N., Papathanassiou S., Papadopulos M.: "Decision Trees for Fast Security Assessment of Autonomous Power Systems with large Penetration from Renewables", IEEE Transaction on Energy Conversion, Vol. 10, No. 2, June 1995
6. Vasconcelos M.H., Peças Lopes J.A.: "Pruning Kernel Regression Trees for Security Assessment of the Crete Network", ACAI'99, Workshop on Application of Machine Learning, July 1999
7. Burges C.: "A tutorial on Support Vector Machines for Patter Recognition", http://www.kernel-machines.org/
8. Cristianini N., Shawe-Taylor J.: "*An introduction to Support Vector Machines*", Cambridge University Press, 2000
9. Campbell C.: "Kernel Methods: A survey of Current Techniques", http://www.kernel-machines.org/
10. http://www.ics.uci.edu/~xge/svm/
11. Campbell C.: "An Introduction to Kernel Methods", In R.J. Howlett and L.C. Jain, editors, *Radial Basis Function Networks: Design and Applications*, page 31. Springer-Verlag, Berlin, 2000
12. Schölkopf B.: Statistical Learning and Kernel Methods, http:/research.Microsoft.com/~bsc
13. Platt J.:"Fast Training of Support Vector Machines using Sequential Minimal Optimization", http://www.research.microsoft.com/~jplatt
14. Hertz J., Krogh A., Palmer R.: "*Introduction to the Theory of Neural Computation*", Addison-Wesley, Redwood City, 1991
15. Veropoulos K., Campbell C., Cristianini N.: "Controlling the Sensitivity of Support Vector Machines", *Proceedings of the International Joint Conference on Artificial Intelligence, Stockholm, Sweden, 1999 (IJCAI99)*, Workshop ML3, p. 55–60.

On Endmember Detection in Hyperspectral Images with Morphological Associative Memories

Manuel Graña[1], Bogdan Raducanu[1], Peter Sussner[2], and Gerhard Ritter[3]

[1] Dept. CCIA, Universidad Pais Vasco, Spain,
ccpgrrom@si.ehu.es,
[2] Institute of Mathematics, Statistics and Scientific Computing, State University of
Campinas, Brazil
[3] Center for Computer Vision and Visualization, University of Florida, USA.

Abstract. Morphological Associative Memories (MAM) are a construct similar to Hopfield Associative Memories defined on the $(R, +, \vee, \wedge)$ algebraic system. The MAM posses excellent recall properties for undistorted patterns. However they suffer from the sensitivity to specific noise models, that can be characterized as erosive and dilative noise. We find that this sensitivity may be made of use in the task of Endmember determination for the Spectral Unmixing of Hyperspectral Images.

1 Introduction

Passive remote sensing evolution has produced measurement instruments with ever growing spectral bread and resolution. Multispectral sensing allows the classification of pixels, however the recognition that pixels of interest are frequently a combination of material has introduced the need to quantitatively decompose the pixel spectrum into their constituent material spectra. Hyperspectral sensor measurements in hundreds of spectral bands allow to perform such "spectral unmixing" [9]. The reasons for the mixture of several spectra in a single pixels are (1) the spatial resolution of the sensor implies that different land covers are included in the area whose radiance measurement results in an image pixel, and (2) distinct materials are intimately mixed (e.g.: a beach). The second situation is independent of the sensor spatial resolution and produces non-linear mixtures, which are difficult to analyze. The first situation produces mixtures which, often, can be adequately modeled by a linear mixing model. In this paper we assume that the linear model is correct, and we present an approach to the detection of endmembers for spectral unmixing in hyperspectral image processing through the application of Morphological Associative Memories.

Research efforts trying to introduce elements of mathematical morphology in the domain of the Artificial Neural Networks involve a small community but are sustained in time. In short definition Morphological Neural Networks are those that involve somehow the maximum and/or minimum (supremum and infimum) operators. Some fuzzy approaches are included in this definition. The kind of

F.J. Garijo, J.C. Riquelme, and M. Toro (Eds.): IBERAMIA 2002, LNAI 2527, pp. 526–535, 2002.
© Springer-Verlag Berlin Heidelberg 2002

Morphological Neural Networks range from patter classifiers [2], [12], [20], [28], target detection [5], [6], [14], [27], to associative memories for image restoration [16], [17], [18].

The basis for the learning algorithms is the computation of the gradient of functions that involve max/min operators [13],[27], [28], [29]. An antecedent for these works is the adaptive construction of morphological filters [1], [21]. Some authors [12], [13] propose the composition of the network with a mixture of morphological and linear operators in the nodes. The Morphological Associative Memories (MAM) [16], [17], [18] are the morphological counterpart of the Correlation Associative Memories (CAM) [10] and the well known Hopfield Associative Memories [7]. Like the CAM, MAM are constructed as correlation matrices but with the substitution of the conventional matrix product by a Min or Max matrix product from Image Algebra [19]. Dual constructions can be made using the dual Min and Max operators. We propose a procedure that involves the application of MAM to detect new patterns, but the training proceeds on line adding the patterns to the already identified patterns,

The structure of the paper is as follows: In section 2 we review the definition of the linear mixing model. Section 3 provides a review of basic results of MAM's. Section 4 gives our algorithm of endmember selection for remote sensing hyperspectral images. Section 5 presents some experimental results of the proposed algorithm. Section 6 gives our conclusions and directions of future work.

2   The Linear Mixing Model

The linear mixing model can be expressed as follows:

$$\mathbf{x} = \sum_{i=1}^{M} a_i \mathbf{s}_i + \mathbf{w} = \mathbf{S}\mathbf{a} + \mathbf{w}, \tag{1}$$

where $\mathbf{x}$ is the d-dimension received pixel spectrum vector, $\mathbf{S}$ is the $d \times M$ matrix whose columns are the d-dimension endmembers $\mathbf{s}_i, i = 1, .., M$, $\mathbf{a}$ is the M-dimension fractional abundance vector, and $\mathbf{w}$ is the d-dimension additive observation noise vector. The linear mixing model is subjected to two constraints on the abundance coefficients. First, to be physically meaningful , all abundance coefficients must be non-negative $a_i \geq 0, i = 1, .., M$. Second, to account for the entire composition the abundance coefficients must be fully additive $\sum_{i=1}^{M} a_i = 1$.

Often the process of spectral unmixing is performed on transformations of the data intended to reduce the computational burden [9] or to enhance some properties of the data [8]. We do not apply any dimension reduction transformation here. The task of endmember determination is the focus of this paper. In an already classical paper [4], Craig starts with the observation that the scatter plots of remotely sensed data are tear shaped or pyramidal, if two or three spectral bands are considered. The apex lies in the so-called dark point. The endmember detection becomes the search for non-orthogonal planes that enclose the data forming a minimum volume simplex, hence the name of the method.

Besides its computational cost the method requires the prespecification of the number of endmenbers. Another step to the automatic endmember detection is the Conical Analysis method proposed in [8] and applied to target detection. The extreme points in the data after a Principal Component transform are the searched for endmember spectra. The method is geometrically similar to the Craig's one but does not require costly linear programming. It also requires the prespecification of the desired number of endmembers. Another approach is the modeling by Markov Random Fields and the detection of spatially consistent regions whose spectra will be assumed as endmembers [15]. A quite standard approach to endmember determination is the use of standard libraries of spectra [9]. This approach requires great expertise and a prori knowledge of the data. Finally, there are interactive exploration algorithms that are supported by specific software packages.

Once the endmembers have been determined the last task is the computation of the inversion that gives the fractional abundance and, therefore, the spectral unmixing. The simplest approach is the unconstrained least squared error estimation given by:

$$\widehat{\mathbf{a}} = \left(\mathbf{S}^T \mathbf{S}\right)^{-1} \mathbf{S}^T \mathbf{x}. \tag{2}$$

The abundance coefficients that result from this computation do not fulfill the non-negative and full aditivity conditions. It is possible to enforce each condition separately, but rather difficult to enforce both simultaneously [9]. As our aim is to test an endmember determination procedure, therefore we will use unconstrained estimation (2) to compute the abundance images. We will show intensity scaled and shifted images of the abundance coefficients to evaluate our results.

3 Morphological Associative Memories

The work on Morphological Associative Memories stems from the consideration of an algebraic lattice structure $(\mathbb{R}, \vee, \wedge, +)$ as the alternative to the algebraic $(\mathbb{R}, +, \cdot)$ framework for the definition of Neural Networks computation [16] [17]. The operators $\vee$ and $\wedge$ denote, respectively, the discrete max and min operators (resp. sup and inf in a continuous setting). The approach is termed morphological neural networks because $\vee$ and $\wedge$ correspond to the morphological dilation and erosion operators, respectively. Given a set of input/output pairs of pattern $(X, Y) = \left\{ \left(\mathbf{x}^\xi, \mathbf{y}^\xi \right) ; \xi = 1, .., k \right\}$, an heteroassociative neural network based on the pattern's crosscorrelation [10], [7] is built up as $W = \sum_\xi \mathbf{y}^\xi \cdot \left(\mathbf{x}^\xi \right)'$. Mimicking this construction procedure [16], [17] propose the following constructions of HMM's:

$$W_{XY} = \bigwedge_{\xi=1}^{k} \left[\mathbf{y}^\xi \times \left(-\mathbf{x}^\xi \right)' \right] \qquad M_{XY} = \bigvee_{\xi=1}^{k} \left[\mathbf{y}^\xi \times \left(-\mathbf{x}^\xi \right)' \right] \tag{3}$$

where $\times$ is any of the $\boxtimes$ or $\boxtimes$ operators. Here $\boxtimes$ and $\boxtimes$ denote the max and min matrix product, respectively defined as follows:

$$C = A \boxtimes B = [c_{ij}] \Leftrightarrow c_{ij} = \bigvee_{k=1..n} \{a_{ik} + b_{kj}\}, \qquad (4)$$

$$C = A \boxtimes B = [c_{ij}] \Leftrightarrow c_{ij} = \bigwedge_{k=1..n} \{a_{ik} + b_{kj}\}. \qquad (5)$$

It follows that the weight matrices W_{XY} and M_{XY} are lower and upper bounds of the max and min matrix products $\forall \xi; W_{XY} \leq \mathbf{y}^{\xi} \times \left(-\mathbf{x}^{\xi}\right)' \leq M_{XY}$ and therefore the following bounds on the output patterns hold $\forall \xi; W_{XY} \boxtimes \mathbf{x}^{\xi} \leq \mathbf{y}^{\xi} \leq M_{XY} \boxtimes \mathbf{x}^{\xi}$, that can be rewritten $W_{XY} \boxtimes X \leq Y \leq M_{XY} \boxtimes X$. A matrix A is a $\boxtimes$-perfect ($\boxtimes$-perfect) memory for (X, Y) if $A \boxtimes X = Y$ ($A \boxtimes X = Y$). It can be proven that if A and B are $\boxtimes$-perfect and $\boxtimes$-perfect memories, resp., for (X, Y), then W_{XY} and M_{XY} are also $\boxtimes$-perfect and $\boxtimes$-perfect, resp.: $A \leq W_{XY} \leq M_{XY} \leq B$. Therefore $W_{XY} \boxtimes X = Y = M_{XY} \boxtimes X$. Conditions of perfect recall of the stored patterns are given by the following theorems proved in [16],[17]:

Theorem 1. *Perfect recall of HMM. The matrix W_{XY} is $\boxtimes$-perfect if and only if $\forall \xi$ the matrix $\left[\mathbf{y}^{\xi} \times \left(-\mathbf{x}^{\xi}\right)'\right] - W_{XY}$ contains a zero at each row. Similarly, the matrix M_{XY} is $\boxtimes$-perfect if and only if $\forall \xi$ the matrix $\left[\mathbf{y}^{\xi} \times \left(-\mathbf{x}^{\xi}\right)'\right] - M_{XY}$ contains a zero at each row.*

Theorem 2. *Perfect recall of AMM. Both erosive and dilative AMM's have the perfect recall property: $W_{XX} \boxtimes X = X = M_{XX} \boxtimes X$, for any X.*

These results hold when we try to recover the output patterns from the noise-free input pattern. To take into account the noise, a special definition of the kinds of noise affecting the input patterns is needed. Let it be $\widetilde{\mathbf{x}}^{\gamma}$ a noisy version of $\mathbf{x}^{\gamma}$. If $\widetilde{\mathbf{x}}^{\gamma} \leq \mathbf{x}^{\gamma}$ then $\widetilde{\mathbf{x}}^{\gamma}$ is an eroded version of $\mathbf{x}^{\gamma}$, alternatively we say that $\widetilde{\mathbf{x}}^{\gamma}$ is subjected to erosive noise. If $\widetilde{\mathbf{x}}^{\gamma} \geq \mathbf{x}^{\gamma}$ then $\widetilde{\mathbf{x}}^{\gamma}$ is a dilated version of $\mathbf{x}^{\gamma}$, alternatively we say that $\widetilde{\mathbf{x}}^{\gamma}$ is subjected to dilative noise. Morphological memories are very sensitive to these kinds of noise. The conditions of *robust* perfect recall for W_{XY}, i.e. the retrieval of $\mathbf{y}^{\gamma}$ given a noisy copy $\widetilde{\mathbf{x}}^{\gamma}$, are given in [16], [17]. The dilative HMM W_{XY} is robust against controlled erosions of the input patterns while the erosive HMM M_{XY} is robust against controlled dilations of the input patterns. At present we are more concerned by the conditions for perfect recall of noisy patterns of AMM:

Corollary 1. *Given patterns X, the equality $W_{XX} \boxtimes \widetilde{\mathbf{x}}^{\gamma} = \mathbf{x}^{\gamma}$ holds when the noise affecting the pattern is erosive $\widetilde{\mathbf{x}}^{\gamma} \leq \mathbf{x}^{\gamma}$ and the following relation holds $\forall i \exists j_i; \widetilde{x}_{j_i}^{\gamma} = x_{j_i}^{\gamma} \vee \left(\bigvee_{\xi \neq \gamma} \left(x_i^{\gamma} - x_i^{\xi} + x_{j_i}^{\xi}\right)\right)$. Similarly, the equality $M_{XY} \boxtimes \widetilde{\mathbf{x}}^{\gamma} = \mathbf{x}^{\gamma}$ holds when the noise affecting the pattern is dilative $\widetilde{\mathbf{x}}^{\gamma} \geq \mathbf{x}^{\gamma}$ and the following relation holds: $\forall i \exists j_i; \widetilde{x}_{j_i}^{\gamma} = x_{j_i}^{\gamma} \wedge \left(\bigwedge_{\xi \neq \gamma} \left(x_i^{\gamma} - x_i^{\xi} + x_{j_i}^{\xi}\right)\right)$.*

The AMM will fail in the case of the noise being a mixture of erosive and dilative noise. To obtain general robustness the kernel method has been proposed [16], [18], [22]. In order to characterize kernels and to obtain a constructive definition, the notion of morphological independence and strong morphological independence is introduced in [18], here we distinguish erosive and dilative versions of this definition:

Definition 1. *Morphological independence. Given a set of pattern vectors* $X = \left(\mathbf{x}^1, ..., \mathbf{x}^k\right)$, *a pattern vector* $\mathbf{y}$ *is said to be morphologically independent of* X *in the erosive sense if* $\mathbf{y} \nleq \mathbf{x}^\gamma; \gamma = \{1, .., k\}$, *and morphologically independent of* X *in the dilative sense if* $\mathbf{y} \ngeq \mathbf{x}^\gamma; \gamma = \{1, .., k\}$. *The set of pattern vectors* X *is said to be morphologically independent in either sense when all the patterns are morphologically independent of the remaining patterns in the set.*

The strong morphological independence is introduced in [18] to give a construction for minimal kernels with maximal noise robustness. For binary valued vectors, morphological independence and strong morphological independence are equivalent. For the current application we want to use AMM as detectors of the set extreme points, to obtain a rough approximation of the minimal simplex that covers the data points. We need to establish first a simple fact in the following remark:

Remark 1. Given a set of pattern vectors $X = \left(\mathbf{x}^1, ..., \mathbf{x}^k\right)$ and the erosive W_{XX} and dilative M_{XX} memories constructed from it. Given a test pattern $\mathbf{y} \notin X$, if $\mathbf{y}$ is morphologically independent of X in the erosive sense, then $W_{XX} \boxtimes \mathbf{y} \notin X$. Also, if $\mathbf{y}$ is morphologically independent of X in the dilative sense, then $M_{XX} \boxtimes \mathbf{y} \notin X$.

The endmembers that we are searching for are the corners of a high dimensional box centered at the origin of the space (we will perform a simple correction of the mean of the data). They are morphologically independent vectors both in the erosive and dilative senses, and they enclose the remaining vectors. The endmember detection process would apply the erosive and dilative AMM's constructed from the already detected endmembers to detect the new ones as suggested by the previous remark. Working with integer valued vectors, a desirable property is that vectors already inside the box defined by the endmembers would be detected as such. However, given a set of pattern vectors $X = \left(\mathbf{x}^1, ..., \mathbf{x}^k\right)$ and the erosive W_{XX} and dilative M_{XX} memories constructed from it. If a test pattern $\mathbf{y} < \mathbf{x}^\gamma$ for some $\gamma \in \{1, .., k\}$ would give $W_{XX} \boxtimes \mathbf{y} \notin X$. Also, if the test pattern $\mathbf{y} > \mathbf{x}^\gamma$ for some $\gamma \in \{1, .., k\}$ then $M_{XX} \boxtimes \mathbf{y} \ngeq \notin X$. Therefore, working with integer valued patterns the detection of the morphologically independent patterns would be impossible. However, if we consider the binary vectors obtained as the sign of the vector components, then morphological independence would be detected as suggested by the above remark. Let us denote by the expression $\mathbf{x} > \mathbf{0}$ the construction of the binary vector $(\{b_i = 1 \text{ if } x_i > 0; b_i = 0 \text{ if } x_i \leq 0\}; i = 1, .., n)$.

4   The Detection of Spectral Endmembers

The endmembers of a given hyperspectral image under the linear mixture assumption correspond to the vertices of the minimal simplex that encloses the data points. The region of the space enclosed by a set of vectors simultaneously morphologically independent in both erosive and dilative senses is a high dimensional box. Therefore, the search for the extremes in the morphological sense gives the high dimensional box that best approaches the minimal simplex that encloses the data points. The approach in this paper is to use AMM's as the mechanism to evaluate the morphological independence condition. Let us denote $\{\mathbf{f}(i,j) \in \mathbb{R}^d; i = 1, .., n; j = 1, .., m\}$ the hyperspectral image, $\boldsymbol{\mu}$ and $\boldsymbol{\sigma}$ the vectors of the mean and standard deviations of each band computed over the image, α the noise correction factor and E the set of endmembers discovered. We perform first a correction of the mean of the data, so that it will be centered about the origin, to ease the detection of the directions where the extreme points lye. The standard deviation of the data at each band is taken as an estimation of the additive noise standard deviation. To test the morphological independence we apply the AMM to the pixel spectra after the addition and subtraction of $\alpha\boldsymbol{\sigma}$. This procedure is intended to avoid the detection of small fluctuations around the mean as endmember directions. The confidence level α controls the amount of flexibility in the discovering of new endmembers.

The steps in the procedure are the following:

1. Compute the zero mean image $\{\mathbf{f}^c(i,j) = \mathbf{f}(i,j) - \boldsymbol{\mu}; i = 1, .., n; j = 1, .., m\}$.
2. Initialize the set of endmembers $E = \{\mathbf{e}_1\}$ with a pixel spectra randomly picked from the image. Initialize the set of morphologically independent binary signatures $X = \{\mathbf{x}_1\} = \{(e_k^1 > 0; k = 1, .., d)\}$
3. Construct the AMM's based on the morphologically independent binary signatures: M_{XX} and W_{XX}. Define orthogonal binary codes Y for the endmembers and construct the identification HMM[1]: M_{XY}.
4. For each pixel $\mathbf{f}^c(i,j)$
   a) compute the vector of the signs of the Gaussian noise corrections $\mathbf{f}^+(i,j) = (\mathbf{f}^c(i,j) + \alpha\boldsymbol{\sigma} > 0)$ and $\mathbf{f}^-(i,j) = (\mathbf{f}^c(i,j) - \alpha\boldsymbol{\sigma} > 0)$
   b) compute $y^+ = M_{XY} \boxtimes (M_{XX} \boxtimes \mathbf{f}^+(i,j))$
   c) compute $y^- = M_{XY} \boxtimes (W_{XX} \boxtimes \mathbf{f}^-(i,j))$
   d) if $y^+ \notin Y$ and $y^- \notin Y$ then $\mathbf{f}^c(i,j)$ is a new endmember to be added to E, go to step 3 and resume the exploration of the image.
   e) if $y^+ \in Y$ and $\mathbf{f}^c(i,j) > \mathbf{e}_{y+}$ the pixel spectral signature is more extreme than the stored endmember, then substitute $\mathbf{e}_{y+}$ with $\mathbf{f}^c(i,j)$.
   f) if $y^- \in Y$ and $\mathbf{f}^c(i,j) < \mathbf{e}_{y-}$ the pixel is more extreme than the stored endmember, then substitute $\mathbf{e}_{y-}$ with $\mathbf{f}^c(i,j)$.
5. The final set of endmembers is the set of original spectral signatures $\mathbf{f}(i,j)$ of the pixels selected as members of E.

---

[1] Although we have no formal proof of the perfect recall of the HMM when the input patterns are morphologically independent, it is very likely and fits nicely to use the HMM as the endmember identifier. In practice, we search the set X directly.

5   Experimental Results

The spectra used for this work correspond to the Indian Pines 1992 image obtained by the Airborne Visible/Infrared Imaging Spectrometer (AVIRIS) developed by NASA JPL which has 224 contiguous spectral channels covering a spectral region form 0.4 to 2.5 mm in 10 nm steps. It is a 145 by 145 pixel image with 220 spectral bands that contains a distribution of two-thirds of agricultural land and one-third of forest and other elements (two highways, a rail line and some houses and smaller roads). The ground truth available for this image [11] designates 16 mutually exclusive classes of land cover. Examples of studies about the application of supervised classification algorithms to this image are [3], [24], [25], [26]. Figure 1 shows the ground truth as identified in [11], [25]. Many specific characteristics are hidden in the background class. The distribution of the cover classes was drawn approximately, so there is a non negligible amount of erroneously labeled pixels in the ground truth. The results of the supervised classification show a great deal of details [3], [25]. As we do not have the permission to reproduce these results we present in figure 2 some false color renderings based on different band selections. These images highlight some spatial distributions of land cover that are consistently identified by diverse works on supervised classification.

We have applied our method to the endmember detection starting with different initializations of the endmember set. In all cases the number of detected endmembers was in the range from 8 up to 15. The control parameter α was set at values between 2 and 1.6, the lower the values the greater the number of endmember detected. The image pixels were processed once. As the endmember detection is an unsupervised process, although we have a ground truth we don't have any proper performance measure, unlike the supervised classification case. The validation of the quality of the results must be by observation of the resulting abundance images. In these images white correspond to high values and black to low values (may be negative). We present in figure 4 abundance images resulting from an execution of the algorithm.

For instance, the endmember #1 seems to be a good detector for oats, whose ground truth spatial situation can be appreciated in figure 1. Abundance image 1 highlights the ground truth patch, but also several straight lines that may correspond to borders between land lots and to the side trees of roads. Endmember #5 appears to be specialized in cultivated lands, it highlights the oats but also the other crops, it gives very dark response on the woods while endmember #7 is a good detector of woods and grass, according to the ground truth and the results of supervised classification [25]. If we take into account that the data was gathered when the crops were very low, a feasible interpretation of the results is that endmember #5 is detecting the soil, while endmember #7 detects the green cover of the woods and the grass. This discussion is aimed to show that the endmembers detected may have some physical meaning and some value in the analysis and interpretation of the image.

Fig. 1. The Indian Pines image ground truth

Fig. 2. Some false color renderings of the image based on different selections of the bands that correspond to the RGB.

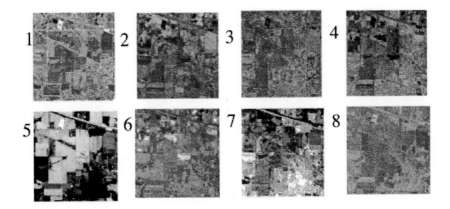

Fig. 3. Abundance images computed using the endmembers obtained with a typical instance of our algorithm. The endmembers are not reproduced for lack of space.

6 Conclusions and Further Work

We have proposed an algorithm for endmember detection in hyperspectral images based on the noise sensitivity of the Autoassociative Morphological Memories (AMM). The procedure does not need the a priori setting of the number of endmembers. Its flexibility in the discovering of endmembers is controlled by the amount of noise correction introduced in the pixel spectral signature. Experimental results on the Indian Pines image have demonstrated that the procedure gives a reasonable number of endmembers with little tuning of the control parameter (α), and that these endmembers have physical meaning and may serve for the analysis of the image.

Further work must be addressed to experimentation with other multi and hyperspectral images to further validate the approach. Also, research into the realization of learning processes on morphological neural networks for this task is a promising research venue. It involves the shift from binary classification as performed by the min/max networks into morphological category representative detection (clustering).

Acknowledgements. The authors received partial support from the Ministerio de Ciencia y Tecnologia projects MAT1999-1049-C03-03, TIC2000-0739-C04-02 and TIC2000-0376-P4-04, B. Raducanu received a predoctoral grant from the University of The Basque Country (UPV/EHU).

References

1. Asano A., K. Matsumura, K. Itoh, Y. Ichioka, S. Yokozeki, (1995) Optimization of morphological filters by learning, Optics Comm. 112 : 265–270
2. Carpenter G.A., S. Grossberg, D.B. Rosen, (1991) Fuzzy ART: Fast stable learning of analog patterns by an adaptive resonance system, Neural Networks 4:759–771,
3. Crespo J.L., R. Duro, Hyperspectral Image Segmentation through Gaussian Synapse Networks , submitted ICANN'2002
4. Craig M., Minimum volume transformations for remotely sensed data, IEEE Trans. Geos. Rem. Sensing, 32(3):542–552
5. Gader P.D., M.A. Khabou, A. Kodobobsky (2000) Morphological regularization neural networks, Pattern Recognition 33 pp. 935–944
6. Graña M., B. Raducanu. (2001) On the application of morphological heteroassociative neural networks. Proc. Int. Conf. on Image Processing (ICIP), I. Pitas (ed.), pp. 501–504, Thessaloniki, Greece, October , IEEE Press.
7. Hopfield J.J., (1982) Neural networks and physical systems with emergent collective computational abilities, Proc. Nat. Acad. Sciences, vol. 79, pp. 2554–2558,
8. Ifarraguerri A., C.-I Chang, (1999) Multispectral and Hyperspectral Image Analysis with Convex Cones, IEEE Trans. Geos. Rem. Sensing, 37(2):756–770
9. Keshava N., J.F. Mustard Spectral unimixing, IEEE Signal Proc. Mag. 19(1) pp. 44–57 (2002)
10. Kohonen T. , (1972) Correlation Matrix Memory, IEEE Trans. Computers, 21:353–359,
11. Landgrebe D. , Indian Pines AVIRIS Hyperspectral Reflectance Data: 92av3c, 1992. The full data set is called Indian Pines 1 920612B available at http://makalu.jpl.nasa.gov/locator/index.html.
12. Pessoa L.F.C , P. Maragos, (1998) MRL-filters: a general class of nonlinear systems and their optimal design for image processing, IEEE Trans. on Image Processing, 7(7): 966–978,

13. Pessoa L.F.C , P. Maragos (2000) Neural Networks with hybrid morphological/rank/linear nodes: a unifying framework with applications to handwritten character recognition, Patt. Rec. 33: 945–960
14. Raducanu B. , M. Graña, P. Sussner.(2001) Morphological neural networks for vision based self-localization. Proc. of ICRA2001, Int. Conf. on Robotics and Automation, pp. 2059–2064, Seoul, Korea, May , IEEE Press.
15. Rand R.S., D.M.Keenan (2001) A Spectral Mixture Process Conditioned by Gibbs-Based Partitioning, IEEE Trans. Geos. Rem. Sensing, 39(7):1421-1434
16. Ritter G. X., J. L. Diaz-de-Leon, P. Sussner. (1999) Morphological bidirectional associative memories. Neural Networks, Volume 12, pages 851–867,
17. Ritter G. X., P. Sussner, J. L. Diaz-de-Leon. (1998) Morphological associative memories. IEEE Trans. on Neural Networks, 9(2):281–292,
18. Ritter G.X., G. Urcid, L. Iancu, (2002) Reconstruction of patterns from moisy inputs using morphological associative memories, J. Math. Imag. Vision submitted
19. Ritter G. X., J.N. Wilson, Handbook of Computer Vision Algorithms in Image Algebra, Boca Raton, Fla: CRC Press
20. Rizzi A., M. ,F.M. Frattale Mascioli, (2002) Adaptive resolution Min-Max classifiers, IEEE trans Neural Networks 13 (2):402–414.
21. Salembier P. (1992) Structuring element adaptation for morphological filters, J. Visual Comm. Image Repres. 3: 115–136
22. Sussner P., (2001) Observations on Morphological Associative Memories and the Kernel Method, Proc. IJCNN'2001, Washington DC, July
23. Sussner P. (2002) , Generalizing operations of binary autoassociative morphological memories using fuzzy set theory, J. Math. Imag. Vision submitted
24. Tadjudin, S. and D. Landgrebe, (1998). Classification of High Dimensional Data with Limited Training Samples. PhD Thesis and School of Electrical & Computer Engineering Technical Report TR-ECE 98–8, Purdue University.
25. Tadjudin, S. and D. Landgrebe,(1999) Covariance Estimation with Limited Training Samples, IEEE Trans. Geos. Rem. Sensing, 37(4):2113–2118,
26. Tadjudin, S. and D. Landgrebe, (2000) Robust Parameter Estimation for Mixture Model, IEEE Trans. Geos. Rem. Sensing, 38(1):439–445,
27. Won Y., P. D. Gader, P.C. Coffield, (1997) Morphological shared-weight neural network with applications to automatic target detection, IEEE Trans. Neural Networks, 8(5): 1195–1203,
28. Yang P.F., P. Maragos, (1995) Min-Max Classifiers: learnability, design and application, Patt. Rec. 28(6):879–899
29. Zhang X.; C. Hang; S. Tan; PZ. Wang, (1996) The min-max function differentiation and training of fuzzy neural networks, IEEE trans. Neural Networks 7(5):1139–1150,

Application of Learning Machine Methods to 3D Object Modeling*

Cristina García and José Alí Moreno

Laboratorio de Computación Emergente,
Facultades de Ciencias e Ingeniería,
Universidad Central de Venezuela.
{cgarcia, jose}@neurona.ciens.ucv.ve
http://neurona.ciens.ucv.ve/Laboratorio

Abstract. Three different machine learning algorithms applied to 3D object modeling are compared. The methods considered, (Support Vector Machine, Growing Grid and Kohonen Feature Map) were compared in their capacity to model the surface of several synthetic and experimental 3D objects. The preliminary experimental results show that with slight modifications these learning algorithms can be very well adapted to the task of object modeling. In particular the Support Vector Machine Kernel method seems to be a very promising tool.

1   Introduction

Object modeling is a very important technique of computer graphics and has been matter of study for more than two decades. The technique has found a broad range of applications, from computer-aided design and computer drawing to image analysis and computer animation. In the literature several approaches to object modeling can be found. One approach is to look for a rigid model that best fits the data set, an alternate one is to deform a model to fit the data. The latter ones are known as dynamically deformable models. They were first introduced by Kass, Witkin and Terzopoulos [1] and have created much interest since then because of their clay like behavior. A complete survey can be found in [2].

To achieve 3D object modeling, it is desirable that the applied method show a great flexibility in terms of shape and topology representation capacity. A deformable model with this characteristic is the simplex mesh developed by Delingette [3], [4]. It is a non-parametric deformable model, that can take virtually any shape of any topology with a very low computational cost as compared to other deformable models with the same flexibility. It is well known that several machine learning algorithms are able to induce efficiently, in a more or less automatic manner, surfaces and topology preserving mappings on arbitrary

---

* This research was supported by the Fondo Nacional de Ciencia, Tecnología e Innovación (FONACIT) under project G-97000651.

F.J. Garijo, J.C. Riquelme, and M. Toro (Eds.): IBERAMIA 2002, LNAI 2527, pp. 536–545, 2002.
© Springer-Verlag Berlin Heidelberg 2002

dimensional noisy data. The proposed approach to 3D object modeling takes advantage of this low cost surface representation capacity inherent to these learning algorithms.

In this paper we describe the application of the Support Vector Kernel Method (SVM) [5], the Kohonen Self-Organizing Feature Maps [6] and the Growing Grid [7] machine learning algorithms to model objects from data sets that contain information from one or more 3D objects. In general the application of the algorithms start with a cloud of 3D data points and no a priori information regarding the shape or topology of the object or objects in the scene. These data points are applied to the learning algorithms, that with simple modifications on the learning rules, generate adaptively a surface adjusted to the surface points. In case of the Kohonen Feature Map and the Growing Grid, a K-means clustering algorithm, with as many prototype vectors as objects in the scene, is initially applied to the data. Next, a spherical network is initialized in the neighborhood of each prototype vector, in the interior of the clouds of points. Finally the learning rule is applied and the networks deform and grow (Growing Grid) until they reach stability at the surface of the clouds of points. In case of the Support Vector Kernel Method the data points are mapped to a high dimensional feature space, induced by a Gaussian kernel, where support vectors are used to define a sphere enclosing them. The boundary of the sphere forms in data space (3D) a set of closed surfaces containing the clouds of points. As the width parameter of the Gaussian kernel is increased, these surfaces fit the data more tightly and splitting of surfaces can occur allowing the modeling of several objects in the scene. At the end of each of these processes we will have a model for each object.

The organization of the paper is as follows: in the second section, an overview of the applied learning machine methods and their modifications for 3D object modeling are discussed. In the third section experimental results are presented and finally in the fourth section the conclusions and further work are described.

2   Learning Machine Methods

3D Object modeling is an ill defined problem for which there exist numerous methods [2], [8], [9], [10]. In the present approach, learning machine methods that produce data clustering are applied to surface modeling. These clustering methods can be based on parametric models or can be non-parametric. Parametric algorithms are usually limited in their expressive power, i.e. a certain cluster structure is assumed. In this work experiments of surface modeling with three non-parametric (Kohonen Feature Map, Growing Grid and SVM Kernel Method) clustering algorithms are presented and compared. In what follows a brief discussion of each learning method is made.

2.1   Support Vector Kernel Method

The idea behind the application of the support vector formalism [5] to object modeling follows the SVM clustering method in [11]. Let $\{\mathbf{x}\}$ be a data-set of N

3D points representing the objects in the scene. Using a nonlinear transformation Φ from the input 3D space to some high dimensional feature space, we look for the smallest enclosing sphere of radius R described by the constraints:

$$\|\Phi(\mathbf{x}_i) - \mathbf{a}\|^2 \leq R^2 \qquad \forall i . \tag{1}$$

Where use is made of the Euclidean norm and $\mathbf{a}$ is the center of the sphere. Soft constraints are incorporated by adding slack variables ξ_i

$$\|\Phi(\mathbf{x}_i) - \mathbf{a}\|^2 \leq R^2 + \xi_i \quad \xi_i \geq 0 \qquad \forall i . \tag{2}$$

This problem is solved in the formalism of Lagrange by introducing and minimizing the Lagrangian

$$L = R^2 - \sum_i (R^2 + \xi_i - \|\Phi(x_i) - \mathbf{a}\|^2)\,\beta_i - \sum_i \xi_i \mu_i + C \sum_i \xi_i . \tag{3}$$

Where μ, β are positive Lagrange multipliers, C is a constant and the last term is a penalty term.

The stationarity of the Lagrangean with respect to R and ξ_i leads to the following relations:

$$\sum_i \beta_i = 1 . \tag{4}$$

$$\mathbf{a} = \sum_i \beta_i \Phi(\mathbf{x}_i) . \tag{5}$$

$$\beta_i = C - \mu_i . \tag{6}$$

The Karush, Kuhn and Tucker complementary conditions result in:

$$\xi_i \mu_i = 0 . \tag{7}$$
$$(R^2 + \xi_i - \|\Phi(\mathbf{x}_i) - \mathbf{a}\|^2)\,\beta_i = 0 . \tag{8}$$

From these relations it is easy to verify that a point $\mathbf{x}_i$ with $\xi_i > 0$ is outside the sphere in feature space, such points have $\mu_i = 0$ and $\beta_i = C$. A point with $\xi_i = 0$ is inside or on the surface of the sphere in feature space. To be on the surface it must have β_i not equal to zero. Points with $0 < \beta i < C$ will be referred to as Support Vectors.

The above relations allow the derivation of the Wolf dual of the Lagrangian:

$$W = \sum_i \beta_i \langle \Phi(\mathbf{x}_i) \cdot \Phi(\mathbf{x}_i) \rangle - \sum_{i,j} \beta_i \beta_j \langle \Phi(\mathbf{x}_i) \cdot \Phi(\mathbf{x}_j) \rangle . \tag{9}$$

and the problem is solved by maximizing the dual. The dot products $\langle \Phi(\mathbf{x}_i) \cdot \Phi(\mathbf{x}_j) \rangle$ can be conveniently replaced by a suitable Mercer kernel $K(\mathbf{x}_i, \mathbf{x}_j)$ in this way the Wolf dual can be rewritten as

$$W = \sum_i \beta_i K(\mathbf{x}_i, \mathbf{x}_i) - \sum_{i,j} \beta_i \beta_j K(\mathbf{x}_i, \mathbf{x}_j) . \tag{10}$$

The Lagrange multipliers β_i are obtained by maximizing this expression. This is computationally done by the application of the Sequential Minimal Optimization (SMO) algorithm [12].

In the approach to object modeling with SVM the Gaussian kernel is employed, with q as the width parameter

$$K(\mathbf{x}_i, \mathbf{x}_j) = \exp(-q\|\mathbf{x}_i - \mathbf{x}_j\|^2) \, . \tag{11}$$

In feature space the square of the distance of each point to the center of the sphere is

$$R^2(\mathbf{x}) = \|\mathbf{\Phi}(\mathbf{x}) - \mathbf{a}\|^2 \, . \tag{12}$$

The radius of the sphere is

$$R = \{R(\mathbf{x}_i) \mid \mathbf{x}_i \text{ is a support vector}\} \, . \tag{13}$$

In practice the average over all support vectors is taken. The surface of the clouds of points in 3D data space is given by the set:

$$\{\mathbf{x} \mid R(\mathbf{x}) = R\} \, . \tag{14}$$

2.2   Kohonen Feature Map

The Kohonen Feature Map [6] is an unsupervised learning machine that typically consists of one layer of processing units in a network of constrained topology. In its learning phase the weight vectors are randomly initialized. During learning, for every input vector the Best Matching Unit (BMU) is determined. The BMU and a number of units in a neighborhood of the BMU, in the constrained topological network, are adjusted in such a way that the weight vectors of the units resemble more closely the input vector. The weight vectors $\mathbf{w}_j(t)$ of the units surrounding the BMU are adjusted less strongly, according to the distance they have to the BMU, applying the Kohonen Learning Rule:

$$\mathbf{w}_j(t+1) = \mathbf{w}_j(t) + \varepsilon(t)\, \Phi_{ij}(t)\, (\mathbf{x}(t) - \mathbf{w}_j(t)) \, . \tag{15}$$

where the learning rate $\varepsilon(t)$ is a linear time decreasing function, $\mathbf{x}(t)$ is the input vector at time t, and $\Phi_{ij}(t)$ is the neighborhood function with the form:

$$\Phi_{ij}(t) = \exp\left(\frac{-|j - i|^2}{\sigma^2(t)}\right) \, . \tag{16}$$

Here j is the position of the BMU in the topological network and i the position of a unit in its neighborhood. The width parameter $\sigma(t)$ is also a linear time decreasing function. It can be noted that since the learning rate and the width parameter both decrease in time the adjustments made on the weight vectors become smaller as the training progresses. On a more abstract level, this means that the map will become more stable in the later stages of the training.

It can be appreciated that the result of learning is that the weight vectors of the units resemble the training vectors. In this way the Kohonen Feature Map produces a clustering of the n-dimensional input vectors onto the topological network.

In order to model the surface of the input data points, two modifications to the Kohonen Feature Map are introduced: (a) The constrained topological network chosen is a spherical grid. (b) the weight vectors of the BMU and its neighbors are actualized only if the input vector is external to the actual spherical grid. The implementation used three different rates to decrease parameters ε and σ: a first rapid stage, a middle slower but longer stage and a final short fine tuning stage.

2.3   Growing Grid Method

This model [7] is an enhancement of the feature map. The main difference is that the initially constrained network topology grows during the learning process. The initial architecture of the units is a constrained spherical network with a small number of units. A series of adaptation steps, similar to the Kohonen learning rule, are executed in order to update the weight vectors of the units and to gather local error information at each unit. This error information is used to decide where to insert new units. A new unit is always inserted by splitting the longest edge connection emanating from the unit with maximum accumulated error. In doing this, additional units and edges are inserted such that the topological structure of the network is conserved.

The implemented process involves three different phases: an initial phase where the number of units is held constant allowing the grid to stretch, a phase where new units are inserted and the grid grows, and finally a fine tuning phase.

3   Experimental Results

The learning algorithms for modeling are applied on several synthetic objects represented in the form of clouds of 3000 points each obtained from the application of a 3D lemniscate with 4, 5 and 6 foci. The initial and final parameters used for the Kohonen Feature Map were: $\varepsilon_0 = 0.5$, $\varepsilon_f = 0.0001$, $\sigma_0 = 4$, $\sigma_f = 0.01$, with a total of 10^5 iterations. For the Growing Grid: $\varepsilon_0 = 0.05$, $\varepsilon_f = 0.001$, and a constant $\sigma = 0.7$, the iteration number is distributed as: 10 x Unit number in the stretching phase; 200 x Unit number in the growing phase, and 200 x Unit number for fine tuning. The parameters in the SVM algorithm are $C = 1.0$ and $q = 2$ (Fig. 1 and Fig. 3), $q = 4$ (Fig. 2), and $q = 0.00083$ (Fig. 4) and $q = 3.33$ (Fig. 5).

In Fig. 1 the original surface (5 foci lemniscate) and the surface models resulting from the application of the three learning methods (a) Kohonen Feature Map (b) Growing Grid and (c) SVM algorithms are shown. The Kohonen Map consisted on a spherical topological network with 182 units initialized in the interior of the cloud of points. The Growing Grid was also a spherical network with 6 initial units initialized in the interior of the cloud, the network was grown up to 162 units. The SVM model was constructed with 49 support vectors. It can be appreciated that the three algorithms achieve a reasonable modeling of the original object. The best results are produced by the Growing Grid and SVM methods.

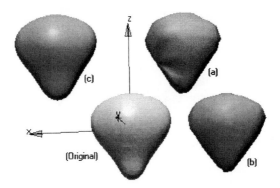

Fig. 1. Results of the three machine learning methods in the modeling of a surface from a solid generated by a 5 foci lemniscate. (*a*) Kohonen Feature Map (*b*) Growing Grid and (*c*) SVM Kernel method

In Fig. 2 the original surface (6 foci lemniscate) and the surface models resulting from de application of the three learning methods (a) Kohonen Feature Map (b) Growing Grid and (c) SVM algorithms are shown. The Kohonen Map consisted on a spherical topological network with 266 units initialized in the interior of the cloud of points. The Growing Grid was also a spherical network with 6 initial units initialized in the interior of the cloud and grown up to 338 units. The SVM model was constructed with 77 support vectors. It can be appreciated that again in this experiment the three algorithms achieve a reasonable modeling of the original object. The best results are produced by the Growing Grid and SVM methods.

In Fig. 3 the original surface (4 foci lemniscate) and the surface models resulting from the application of the two learning methods Growing Grid (a-c) and SVM (b) algorithms are shown. In these experiments the object is of particular interest since it consists of two parts joined by a point, an approximation to a scene of two separate objects. For the experiment leading to Fig. 3(a), a single Growing Grid initialized as a spherical network with 6 initial units in the center of the cloud of points was used. The network was grown up to 134 units. It is clear that the model produced in this case is not a good one. In order to overcome this deficiency the data is initially clustered by a K-means algorithm with two prototype vectors. Then two Growing grids, similar to the latter, are initialized in the neighborhood of the prototype coordinates. A better model, shown in Fig. 3(c), is then obtained. The SVM model was constructed with 38 support vectors. In this experiment both the Kohonen feature Map and the single Growing Grid do not produce good models of the surface. However, it can

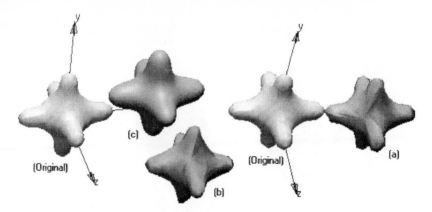

Fig. 2. Results of the three machine learning methods in the modeling of a surface from a solid generated by a 6 foci lemniscate. (*a*) Kohonen Feature Map (*b*) Growing Grid and (*c*) SVM Kernel method

be appreciated that the SVM method and the multiple Growing Grids achieve reasonable models and are superior.

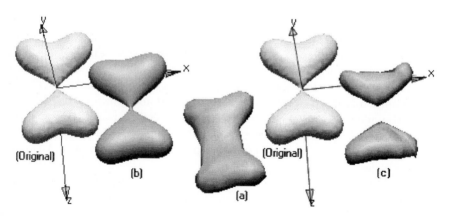

Fig. 3. Results of two machine learning methods in the modeling of a surface from a solid generated by a 4 foci lemniscate. (*a*) Growing Grid and (*b*) SVM Kernel method (*c*) Double Growing Grid

In Fig. 4 the original surface (experimental data from the left ventricle of a human heart echocardiogram) and the surface models resulting from the application of the two learning methods (a) Growing Grid and (b) SVM algorithms are shown. For this case the Growing Grid was a spherical network with 6 initial units initialized in the interior of the cloud of points. The network was grown up 282 units. The SVM model was constructed with 46 support vectors.

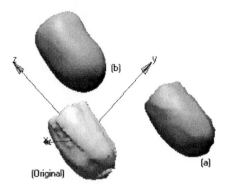

Fig. 4. Results of two machine learning methods in the modeling of a surface from experimental data (left ventricle of a human heart echocardiogram). (*a*) Growing Grid and (*b*) SVM Kernel method

In Fig. 5 the original surface (4 foci disconnected lemniscate) and the surface models resulting from de application of the two learning methods (a) Double Growing Grid and (b) SVM algorithms are shown. In these experiments the methods are applied to two separate objects in the scene. In the application of the Growing Grid algorithm an initial clustering step with a two prototype K-means algorithm is carried out. Then two Growing Grids initialized as spherical networks with 6 units in the neighborhood of the prototype coordinates are evolved. The grids are grown up to 240 units each. The SVM model was constructed with 50 support vectors. It can be appreciated that both the SVM method and the multiple Growing Grids achieve reasonable good models in this multiple object case.

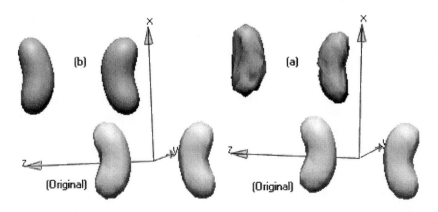

Fig. 5. Results of two machine learning methods in the modeling of a surface from a solid generated by a 4 foci disconnected lemniscate (Two separate objects). (*a*) Double Growing Grid and (*b*) SVM Kernel method

In Table 1 the average execution times for the three machine learning algorithms, measured on a Pentium III 500 MHz. Processor, are shown. It is to be appreciated that the execution time for the Growing Grid method is an order of magnitude greater than those of the other two methods. In any case the computational costs of the algorithms are reasonably low.

Table 1. Average execution times for the three machine learning methods

Figure	Method	Parameters	Time
Fig. 1	Kohonen Feature Map	182 units	22 seg
	Growing Grid	162 units	219 seg
	SVM	49 SVs	32 seg
Fig. 2	Kohonen Feature Map	266 units	33 seg
	Growing Grid	338 units	344 seg
	SVM	77 SVs	37 seg
Fig. 3	Growing Grid	134 units	133 seg
	SVM	38 SVs	26 seg
Fig. 4	Growing Grid	282 units	492 seg
	SVM	46 SVs	5 seg
Fig. 5	Double Growing Grid	484 units	640 seg
	SVM	50 SVs	42 seg

4   Conclusions and Future Work

This work compared the application of three machine learning algorithms in the task of modeling 3D objects from a cloud of points that represents either one or two disconnected objects. The experiments show that the Kohonen Feature Map and the Growing Grid methods generate reasonable models for single objects with smooth spheroidal surfaces. If the object possess pronounced curvature changes on its surface the modeling produced by these methods is not very good. An alternative to this result is to allow the number of units in the network to increase together with a systematic fine tuning mechanism of the units in order to take account of the abrupt changes on the surface. This modifications are theme of further work in case of the Growing Grid algorithm.

On the other hand, the experimental results with the Support Vector Kernel Method are very good. In the case of single smooth objects the algorithm produces a sparse (small number of support vectors) model for the objects. A very convenient result for computer graphics manipulations. This extends to the case with two objects in which the method is able to produce models with split surfaces. A convenient modification of the SVM algorithm would be to include a better control on the number of support vectors needed in the model. This possibility could hinder the rounding tendency observed in the SVM models and allow the modeling of abrupt changes of the surface as seen on the data of the echocardiogram.

To model several objects, with the Kohonen and Growing Grid methods, a good alternative is to evolve multiple networks conveniently initialized in the interior of the clouds of points of each object. To this end, an initial K-means clustering algorithm, with as many prototypes as objects in the scene, is applied to the data. The networks are then initialized in the neighborhood of the coordinates of the prototypes.

The considered data sets for multiple objects are not a representation of a real scene. In a real scene the clusters of data points will be connected by background information (walls and floor). The future work will also include the extension of the actual algorithms to make them applicable to real scenes.

Finally it must be noted that in all cases the computational costs of the algorithms are reasonably low, a fact that can lead to real time implementations.

Acknowledgements. Gratitude is expressed to Guillermo Montilla for allowing us the use of his Virtual Vision Machine software, available at http://www.cpi.uc.edu.ve/Pagina%20VVM/index.htm

References

1. Kass, M., Witkin, A., Terzopoulos, D.: Snakes: Active contour models. Int. J. Of Computer Vision **2** (1998) 321–331
2. Gibson, S.F.F, Mirtich, B.: A Survey of Deformable Modeling in Computer Graphics. Mitsubishi Electric Research Laboratory Technical Report (1997)
3. Delingette, H.: Simplex Meshes: A General Representation for 3D Shape Reconstruction. Technical Report 2214, INRIA, France (1994)
4. Delingette, H.: General Object Reconstruction based on Simplex Meshes. Technical Report 3111, INRIA, France (1997)
5. Cristianini, N., Shawe-Taylor, J.: An Introduction to Support Vector Machines. Cambridge University Press (2000)
6. Kohonen, T.: Self-Organization Associative Memory. 3rd edn. Springer-Verlag, Berlin (1989)
7. Fritzke, B.: Some Competitive Learning Methods. Institute for Neural Computation, Ruhr-Universität Bochum, Draft Report (1997)
8. Bro-Nielsen, B.: Active Nets and Cubes. Technical Report, Institute of Mathematical Modeling Technical University of Denmark (1994)
9. Metaxas, D.: Physics-based Deformable Models: Applications to Computer Vision, Graphics, and Medical Imaging. Kluwer Academic, Boston (1997)
10. Yoshino, K., Kawashima, T., Aoki, Y.: Dynamic Reconfiguration of Active Net Structure. Proc. Asian Conf. Computer Vision (1993) 159–162
11. Ben-Hur, A., Horn, D., Siegelmann, H. T., Vapnik, V.: A Support Vector Method for Clustering. International Conference on Pattern Recognition (2000)
12. Platt, J.: Fast Training of Support Vector Machines Using Sequential Minimal Optimization. http://www.research.microsoft.com/ jplatt

Enriching Information Agents' Knowledge by Ontology Comparison: A Case Study

Gustavo A. Giménez-Lugo[1], Analia Amandi[2], Jaime Simão Sichman[1], and Daniela Godoy[2]

[1] Laboratório de Técnicas Inteligentes
Escola Politécnica da Universidade de São Paulo
Av. Prof. Luciano Gualberto, 158 tv. 3
05508-900 São Paulo, SP, Brazil
{gustavo.lugo,jaime.sichman}@poli.usp.br
[2] Universidad Nacional del Centro de la Prov. de Bs. As.
Facultad de Ciencias Exactas - ISISTAN Research Institute
C.P. 7000 - Tandil, Buenos Aires, Argentina
{amandi,dgodoy}@exa.unicen.edu.ar

Abstract. This work presents an approach in which user profiles, represented by ontologies that were learned by an interface agent, are compared to foster collaboration for information retrieval from the web. It is shown how the interface agent represents the knowledge about the user along with the profiles that were empirically developed. Departing from a specific matching model, briefly presented here, quantitative results were achieved by comparing such particular ontologies in a fully automatic way. The results are presented and their implications are discussed. We argue that an agent's knowledge can be enriched by other agents navigation experiences, possibly helping in connecting and reconciliating distinct knowledge views while preserving a degree of privacy.

1 Introduction

Information agents applied to Information Retrieval(IR) try to detect users preferences to help them in information search tasks. The registered preferences, considered as user profiles, are used as guides in the search processes. An active research field tries to improve the results of this type of agents, working generally isolated, through cooperation. Such an approach, in the form of Multi-Agent Systems (MAS), would foster knowledge sharing, allowing access to the results of other agents experiences that could potentially enrich the results achieved by individual agents. To pave the way for knowledge sharing it is necessary to determine the form by which recorded preferences can be compared.

The PersonalSearcher agent [5], was designed to assist users to filter information during Internet search sessions and to keep profiles that can be treated as ontologies. The agents were initially designed to run as stand-alone systems. An alternative to improve their search performance is to acquire knowledge about themes that are related to the ones that appear in a particular profile, possibly

F.J. Garijo, J.C. Riquelme, and M. Toro (Eds.): IBERAMIA 2002, LNAI 2527, pp. 546–555, 2002.

available with other agents, acting as part of a MAS, although no documents should be automatically exchanged to better preserve the user privacy. The first step in this direction is to compare quantitatively concepts that belong to different user profiles, on their current form. This is the aim of the experiences that are related in this work, describing the experimental results obtained with the implementation of an algorithm for comparing different user profiles, considering the way this knowledge is stored by PersonalSearcher agents. The chosen similarity measure is the MD3 [18] model, that takes into account the words that describe a concept and also its semantic neighborhood. This model is briefly described along with the modifications that were necessary for its adoption.

The work is organized as follows: section 2 presents basic concepts related to information agents; section 3 outlines the model used to quantify the similarity between concepts of different user profiles (ontologies) and shows the implemented algorithm that screens the compared ontologies to map those concepts that may be suitable for an eventual sharing. Next, section 4 details the experimental conditions concerning the selection of the test collections used to generate the profiles and later compare them, as well as the modifications needed to adapt the similarity model to the characteristics of the PersonalSearcher profile representation. Section 5 discusses the results along with implications concerning related work. Finally, section 6 presents the conclusions about this experiment.

2   Information Agents

Agents are usually processes that run continously, know what to do and when to intervene. Agents communicate with other agents, asking solicitations and executing the requested tasks. According to [8], an agent has a long list of properties, among which can be highlighted: *autonomy*, *social hability*, *reactivity* and *proactivity*. Due to the enormous ammount of information accessible through the Internet, and the short time a user generally has to find relevant information, a type of agent that has been widely researched is the so called *intelligent information agent* [9,12,10,16,3]. They are defined in [9] as computational software entities that can access one or multiple information sources that are distributed and heterogeneous and can acquire, mediate and mantain proactively relevant information on behalf of the user or other agents, preferably in a *just-in-time* fashion. They can be, in general, *cooperative* and *non-cooperative*. Additionally, both types can be *rational*, *adaptive* and *mobile*. Recommender agents are a special case of information agents. Two methods that are commonly used in recommender agents, based on Machine Learning(ML) and making part of a MAS applied to IR, are [16,3]:

- *Content based approaches*: agents seek for items that are similar to those preferred by the user, comparing content. Rooted in the IR domain, they are popular for textual data and can be applied succesfully to isolated users;
- *Collaborative approaches*: or *social learning* [13]. They assume that there is a group of users of the system, computing the similarity between users (not items) and recommending items that similar users have found interesting.

The performance of such systems crucially depends on the type of modeling used to represent their users.

2.1 User Profiles

Each agent in a MAS can be considered to have a particular vision of its environment. This vision can be made explicit through an ontology. An ontology is defined in [7] as a logical theory which gives an explicit, partial account of a conceptualization. Furthermore, a conceptualization is an intensional semantic structure which encodes the implicit rules constraining the structure of a piece of reality [7]. Thus, an ontology is a compromise with a specific conceptualization of the world. Guarino's definition refines another definition given by Gruber [6], stating that an ontology is a explicit specification of a conceptualization.

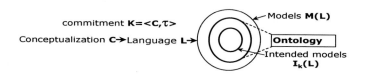

Fig. 1. Relating ontologies, language and conceptualization [7].

The use of ontologies to explain implicit knowledge is a viable approach to overcome the problem of semantic heterogeneity. Interoperability between agents can be achieved reconciliating the different world views through the compromise to a common ontology [19]. Also, information agents can use ontologies to represent explicitly isolated user profiles [17,1], which is the view adopted in this work concerning the profiles generated by the PersonalSearcher agent.

2.2 PersonalSearcher

The PersonalSearcher [5] agent is dedicated to the task of retrieving information from the web. It uses Case Base Reasoning to build a profile of the thematic preferences of the user, using an approach detailed in [5]. This profile is automatically generated and it is incremental, being used to expand the user requests with relevants terms, as well as to filter relevant pages from the set of results obtained from general purpose search engines like Google, Yahoo or Altavista.

The profiles are generated by the agent watching the user's search behaviour. Parameters as the time dedicated to read a document, its source address, content, etc. are taken into account to describe the document as a *case* which is compared to previously recorded cases. When a certain degree of similarity is reached between cases, they are grouped into a cluster. Clusters are monitored, and when the chosen parameters remain invariant, a group of words is taken to generate a *theme*, that will be used from then on to reduce the space of options when verifying if a document retrieved from the web is relevant for the user. A theme has an associated *preference* value, ranging from zero to one. The preference value is given by the time spent by an user reading the cases that are classified under a theme, when compared to the overall reading time of the user. The themes successively generated by the PersonalSearcher agent are hierarchically organized. The thematic hierarchies, or *theme trees*, can be considered as representing particular ontologies. This way, themes can be treated as *concepts* having *features*, actually words that describe them.

3   Ontological Matching as a Quantitative Measure of Profile Similarity

In the literature there are some works that deal with the comparison of ontologies [15,4,14] referencing specific tools for the construction of complex ontologies with the intervention of human experts. On the other hand, in [18] it is presented a relatively simple model, called MD3, to compare ontologies, that allows a completely automated comparison, combining three forms of similarity measurement. Furthermore, it can be applied with some modifications to the hierarchies that appear in the PersonalSearcher user profiles or even to more detailed ontologies. Even though the use of the MD3 model can cause some precision loss in the results, when a society of information agents is considered it is essential that the comparison process could be made effectively with the highest degree of automation, so to avoid a situation in which the user is continously asked to decide upon conflicts that would distract her/him from her/his real goals. The MD3 model evaluates the similarity between classes belonging to different concept hierarchies. It was used as a basis to allow the comparison of profiles of different users of PersonalSearcher. It considers that two independent concept hierarchies (ontologies) are connected through a more general (imaginary) class as it appears in figure 2.a).

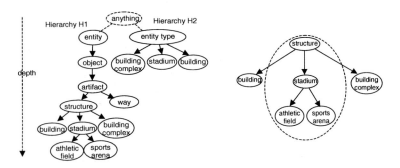

Fig. 2. a)Connecting two ontologies using a common imaginary root (left); b)semantic neighborhood with $r=1$ for $stadium^{H1}$, containing 4 classes (rigth) [18].

The MD3 model combines *feature-matching* and *semantic distance*. The global similarity value $S(a, b)$ between two concepts a and b, belonging to different ontologies, say p and q, is given by the following equation:

$$S(a^p, b^q) = w_l * S_l(a^p, b^q) + w_u * S_u(a^p, b^p) + w_n * S_n(a^p, b^q) \qquad (1)$$

S_l, S_u and S_n denote the lexical, feature and semantic neighborhood similarities between the concepts a and b, and w_l, w_u and w_n are the weights of each component when calculating the global similarity value. As the lexical similarity can be influenced by polysemy, the feature and semantic neighborhood similarities should be used. The values of w_l, w_u and w_n depend on the characteristics of the ontologies to be compared and they must add up to one. However, only common specification aspects can be used to verify the degree of similarity. E.g., if an ontology labels a concept with symbols that carry no information about it (say "ABC0027"), the lexical similarity is useless. In the similarity functions $S_i(a^p, b^q)$, a and b are classes (in the case of PersonalSearcher, *themes*) and i denotes the type of similarity (lexical, feature and semantic neighborhood). Let A and B be the sets of features of a^p and b^q. The *matching* process determines the cardinality of the intersection and the difference between A and B.

$$S_i(a^p, b^q) = \frac{|A \cap B|}{|A \cap B| + \alpha(a^p, b^q) * |A - B| + (1 - \alpha(a^p, b^q)) * |B - A|} \qquad (2)$$

The value of α is calculated using the *depth* of the classes in the connected hierarchies: $\alpha(a^p, b^q) = \begin{cases} \frac{depth(a^p)}{depth(a^p)+depth(b^q)} & \text{If } depth(a^p) \leq depth(b^q) \\ 1 - \frac{depth(a^p)}{depth(a^p)+depth(b^q)} & \text{If } depth(a^p) > depth(b^q) \end{cases}$

An important aspect is that the similarity $S(a^p, b^q)$ between concepts is not a necessarily symmetric relation [18], e.g. "a *hospital* is similar to a *building*" is more generally accepted than the expression "a *building* is similar to a *hospital*".

To calculate the semantic neighborhood similarity is considered the notion of *semantic neighborhood*, that is the set of classes which distance to a given class is within a specified *radius*. The semantic neighborhood of a class contains the given class, as can be seen in fig. 2.b). Formally: $N(a^o, r) = \{c_i^o\}$, where a^o and c_i^o are classes of an ontology o, r is the radius and $N(a^o, r)$ is the semantic neighborhood of a^o. Furthermore, $\forall c_i^o \in N(a^o, r)$, $d(a^o, c_i^o) \leq r$. This notion of similarity is based on shallow matching, associated to the evaluation of the immediate neighborhood of a class, i.e. the *radius* is of value 1.

Given two concepts a^p and b^q from ontologies p and q, where $N(a^p, r)$ has n concepts and $N(b^q, r)$ has m concepts, and the intersection of the two neighborhoods is denoted by $a^p \cap_n b^q$, the value of $S_n(a^p, b^q, r)$ is calculated by:

$$\frac{|a^p \cap_n b^q|}{|a^p \cap_n b^q| + \alpha(a^p, b^q) * \delta(a^p, a^p \cap_n b^q, r) + (1 - \alpha(a^p, b^q)) * \delta(b^q, a^p \cap_n b^q, r)} \qquad (3)$$

where $\delta(a^p, a^p \cap_n b^q, r) = \begin{cases} |N(a^p, r)| - |a^p \cap_n b^q| & \text{If } |N(a^p, r)| > |a^p \cap_n b^q| \\ 0 & \text{In other case} \end{cases}$

The intersection between the neighborhoods is approximated by the similarity of classes within them: $a^p \cap_n b^q = \left[\sum_{i \leq n} \left(max_{j \leq m} S(a_i^p, b_j^q) \right) \right] - \varphi *$ $S(a^p, b^q) with$

$$\varphi = \begin{cases} 1 & \text{If } S(a^p, b^q) = max_{j \leq m} \ S(a^p, b_j^q) \\ 0 & \text{In other case} \end{cases}$$

As $S(a^p, b^q)$ is asymmetric, $a^p \cap_n b^q$ also is. The similarity between two classes a_i^p and b_j^q, from the neighborhoods of a^p and b^q is calculated using lexical and attribute similarity, with equal weights (0.50): $S(a_i^p, b_j^q) = w_l * S_l(a_i^p, b_j^q) + w_u * S_u(a_i^p, b_j^q)$. From here on, $S_n(a^p, b^q)$ should be read as $S_n(a^p, b^q, 1)$.

3.1 Comparison Algorithm

Using the MD3 model, a comparison algorithm was implemented. It has two procedures, $Trav\_1$ and $Trav\_2$, shown in fig 3, being both essentially breadth-first traversals of the PersonalSearcher user profiles theme trees. $Trav\_1$ traverses the first profile $profile\_1$, considered as a *reference*. $Trav\_2$ receives a node of $profile\_1$, with its neighborhood, and compares it with all the concepts in $profile\_2$. The MD3 model was adjusted as follows:

- As a profile concept label carries no information (e.g. "SBJ48"), w_l is set to zero: $S(a^p, b^q) = 0.0 * S_l(a^p, b^q) + 0.5 * S_u(a^p, b^p) + 0.5 * S_n(a^p, b^q)$;
- Theme features have associated weights that affect the values of $|A \cap B|$, $|A - B|$ and $|B - A|$ in eq. 2 when calculating feature similarity. In eq. 2 the cardinality is an integer, now is a real number. A possible interpretation is that the values have attached a confidence degree. A feature is now denoted by an ordered pair indicating the weight of the feature for a concept;
- When two *isolated themes* (i.e. themes that are linked to the root and have no children) are compared, only the feature similarity is calculated.

4 Experimental Results

The described model, implemented as part of the algorithm, was applied to sample user profiles, acquired feeding PersonalSearcher with subsets of test collections of web pages. The profiles correspond to fictitious users. This approach was taken to ensure repeatability, as several parameters can be used to tune the PersonalSearcher theme generation: threshold to add a case to a cluster; number of cases included in a cluster without introducing changes in the set of candidate attribute words (used to transform a cluster into a theme); threshold to classify a case under a theme; threshold to choose a word to be a candidate attribute.

The used collections were made publicly available by the CMU Text Classification Group: the first, more structured, called $WebKB$, has 8282 pages collected in 1997 from Computer Science Departments of four USA Universities, organized into 7 main directories with 5 subdirectories each; the second, rather

```
Procedure 1 Trav_1(profile_1, profile_2)      | Procedure 2 Trav_2(node, queue_neighb,profile_2)
queue_1.add(profile_1.root)                   | queue_2.add(profile_2.root)
while queue_1 not empty do                     | while queue_2 not empty do
   node_1← queue_1.head                        |    node_2← queue_2.head
   for k=1 to num_children(node_1) do          |    for m=1 to num_children(node_2) do
   child_k ← next_child(node_1)                |       child_m ← next_child(node_2)
   queue_1.add(child_k)                        |       queue_2.add(child_m)
   queue_neighb.initialize()                   |       queue_neighb_2.initialize()
   queue_neighb.add(node_1)                    |       queue_neighb_2.add(node_2)
   queue_neighb.add(child_k)                   |       queue_neighb_2.add(child_m)
   for j=1 to num_children(child_k) do         |       for n=1 to num_children(child_m) do
      queue_neighb.add(next_child(child_k))    |          queue_neighb_2.add(next_child(child_m))
   end for                                     |       end for
   Trav_2(child_k, queue_neighb, profile_2)    |       element_queue.sim=S(node,queue_neighb,child_m,queue_neighb_2)
   end for                                     |       node.queue_sim.add(element_queue)
   queue_1.retrieve(node_1)                    |    end for
end while                                       |    queue_2.retrieve(node_2)
                                               | end while
```

Fig. 3. Traversal procedures used in the comparison process.

flat, called *Sector*, has 9548 pages distributed homogeneously into 105 directories corresponding each to an industrial activity sector. The subsets used to fed PersonalSearcher were: 973 pages from one of the 7 main directories of the *WebKB* collection; 521 pages from 5 directories of the *Sector* colection. From here on, citing a collection denotes the used subset. Three profiles, shown in fig. 4, were generated: *UserONE*, using *Sector* as input. Its structure is rather flat, containing just 6 *isolated themes*(i.e., a theme linked to the root, having no children), neither of which is subclassified under another; *UserTWO*, using *WebKB* as input. It is more structured than *UserONE*, with 5 themes, 2 of which are subcategories of more general themes; and *UserTHREE*, obtained feeding initially *Sector* followed by *WebKB*. The order is relevant as it affects the theme generation. A sample concept is shown with its features in table 4.

Table 1. A sample concept from the PersonalSearcher *UserONE* profile

Theme label	Theme preference	Feature (feature weight)
SBJ24	(0.08)	profil(1.0), innov(1.0) corpor(1.0), entertain(1.0) fall(1.0), lodgenet(1.0) sioux(1.0), employ(1.0)

The comparison of the generated profiles was performed in two steps. Initially, each one of the three profiles was compared with itself, in order to have reference cases. Next, they were compared with each other. Each concept of the *reference* ontology keeps a list of the concepts of the other ontology upon with it has a similarity value above a threshold than can be set by the user. Additionally, the preference degree of a theme can be taken into account, causing the similarity to be multiplied by it, decreasing the similarity value. The observations confirmed the predictions stating that the similarity is non-symmetric. Still,

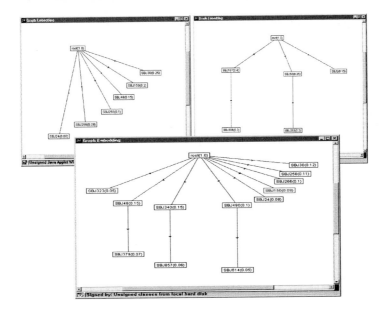

Fig. 4. *UserONE* (upper left), *UserTWO* (upper rigth) and *UserTHREE* (down).

identical themes received relatively high similarity values. The lower similarity value for identical themes was 0.50, resulting from feature similarity, with gradually higher values for correspondingly similar semantic neighborhoods. *Isolated themes* (see section 3.1) reached a similarity of 1.0. Sample comparison results are shown in fig. 5 and in table 4.

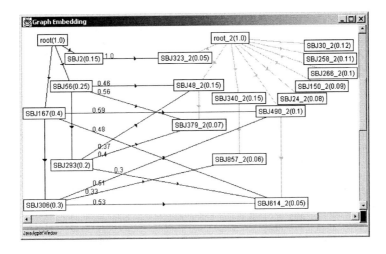

Fig. 5. Similarity links values when comparing *UserTWO* with *UserTHREE*.

Table 2. Relations and similarity link values between sample concepts, from fig. 5

UserTWO theme	UserTHREE theme	Similarity value	Direct relation
SBJ2	*SBJ323 2*	1.00	Identical features
SBJ56	*SBJ379 2*	0.56	Identical features
SBJ167	*SBJ490 2*	0.59	Identical features
SBJ293	*SBJ614 2*	0.30	The 4 *SBJ614 2* features are a subset of the 9 *SBJ293* features

5   Discussion and Related Work

At the present stage, PersonalSearcher user profiles still need improvements in order to have a more accurate representation of the user knowledge, a problem that is common to fully automated knowledge acquisition approaches.

In this sense, a confidence degree can be worked out for the acquired concepts as part of further work on the acquisition of the profiles. Anyway, the comparison process shown in this work doesn't need modifications to manipulate more detailed and accurate ontologies and will only benefit from better acquisition results, as far as the PersonalSearcher representation model remains the same.

There are few related works reporting the representation and comparison of individual user ontologies mantained by agents as user profiles. The CAIMAN [11] system represents ontologies only as vectors of words, on the other hand PersonalSearcher favors the representation of ontologies in a way that is suitable to cope with a frame based knowledge representation model like OKBC [2], enabling a much richer representation that allows to take advantage of the relations that can be made explicit in a hierarchical structure. In DOGGIE [20], agents exchange full documents to learn new concepts, a highly desirable but rather restricting approach, e.g. for privacy reasons; our approach overcomes much of the associated problem because it allows the exchange of (portions of) structured knowledge, i.e. ontologies, without exposing the actual user documents.

6   Conclusions

We have shown an approach in which a quantitative comparison of user profiles, considered as ontologies maintained by information agents, was implemented. We plan to apply the results in a MAS system for IR in which existing interface agents' reasoning capabilities will be extended to support a model in the context of a cooperative MAS in which different degrees of knowledge sharing (say single features, concepts or whole ontologies) will be possible.

Acknowledgements. Part of this work was done while the first author was studying at the ISISTAN Research Institute/UNCPBA, Tandil, Bs.As., Argentina, funded by CAPES, Brazil, CAPES/SCyT cooperation program, grant

BEX 0510/01-7. The third author is partially financed by CNPq, Brazil, grant 301041/95-4; and by CNPq/NSF PROTEM-CC MAPPEL project, grant number 680033/99-8.

References

1. J. Chaffee and S. Gauch. Personal ontologies for web navigation. In *CIKM*, 2000.
2. V. Chaudhri, A. Farquhar, R. Fikes, P. Karp, and J. Rice. OKBC: A programmatic foundation for knowledge base interoperability. In *AAAI-98*, 1998.
3. T. Finin, C. Nicholas, and J. Mayfield. Agent-based information retrieval. In *IEEE ADL'98, Advances in Digital Libraries Conference '98*, 1998.
4. N. Fridman and M. Musen. An algorithm for merging and aligning ontologies: Automation and tool support. In *AAAI Workshop on Ontology Mangmt.*, 1999.
5. D. Godoy and A. Amandi. PersonalSearcher: An intelligent agent for searching web pages. In *7th IBERAMIA and 15th SBAI. LNAI 1952*. M. C. Monard and J. S. Sichman eds., 2000.
6. T. Gruber. Towards principles for the design of ontologies used for knowledge sharing. *Intl. Journal of Human and Computer Studies*, 43(5/6):907–928, 1995.
7. N. Guarino. Formal ontological distinctions for information organization, extraction, and integration. In *Information Extraction: A Multidisciplinary Approach to an Emerging Inf. Technology. LNAI 1299*. M. T. Pazienza(ed). Springer, 1997.
8. N. Jennings and M. Wooldridge. Applications of intelligent agents. In *Agent Technology: Foundations, Applications and Markets*. Jennings, N. and Wooldrigde, M.(eds.). Springer Verlag., 1998.
9. M. Klusch. Intelligent information agents. In *Third European Agent Systems Summer School. Advanced Course on Artificial Intelligence ACAI-01.*, 2001.
10. M. Kobayashi and K. Takeda. Information retrieval on the web. *ACM Computing Surveys*, 32(2):144–173, 2000.
11. M. S. Lacher and G. Groh. Facilitating the exchange of explicit knowledge through ontology mappings. In *14th FLAIRS Conf.* AAAI Press, May 2001.
12. A. Y. Levy and D. S. Weld. Intelligent internet systems. *Artificial Intelligence*, 118(1-2):1–14, 2000.
13. P. Maes. Agents that reduce work and information overload. *ACM Comm.*, 1994.
14. D. McGuinness, R. Fikes, J. Rice, and S. Wilder. An environment for merging and testing large ontologies. In *Proc. of the KR2000 Intl. Conf.*, 2000.
15. P. Mitra, G. Wiederhold, and M. Kersten. A graph oriented model for articulation of ontology interdependendies. In *VII EDBT Conference*, 2000.
16. D. Mladenic. Text-learning and related intelligent agents: a survey, 1999.
17. A. Pretschner. *Ontology Based Personalized Search. MSc. Thesis*. Kansas Univ., USA, 1999.
18. M. A. Rodríguez. *Assessing semantic similarity among spatial entity classes. PhD. Thesis*. University of Maine, USA, May, 2000.
19. H. Wache, T. Vögele, U. Visser, H. Stuckenschmidt, G. Schuster, H. Neumann, and S. Hübner. Ontology-based integration of information – a survey of existing approaches. In *IJCAI Workshop on Ontologies and Information Sharing*, 2001.
20. A. B. Williams and Z. Ren. Agents teaching agents to share meaning. In *Proc. of the 5th Intl. Conf. on Autonomous Agents*. ACM, May 2001.

Negotiation among Autonomous Computational Agents

Fernando Lopes[1], Nuno Mamede[2], A. Q. Novais[1], and Helder Coelho[3]

[1]INETI, DMS, Est. Paço do Lumiar, 1649-038 Lisboa, Portugal
{fernando.lopes, augusto.novais}@ineti.pt
[2]IST, Avenida Rovisco Pais, 1049-001 Lisboa, Portugal
Nuno.Mamede@acm.org
[3]UL, FC, DI, Campo Grande, 1700 Lisboa, Portugal
hcoelho@di.fc.ul.pt

Abstract. Autonomous agents are being increasingly used in a wide range of applications. Most applications involve or require multiple agents operating in complex environments and, over time, conflicts inevitably occur among them. Negotiation is the predominant process for resolving conflicts. Recent interest in electronic commerce has also given increased importance to negotiation. This paper presents a generic negotiation model for autonomous agents that handles multi-party, multi-issue and repeated rounds. The model is based on computationally tractable assumptions.

1 Introduction

Autonomous agents operate in complex environments and, over time, conflicts inevitably occur among them. Conflict resolution is crucial for achieving coordination. The predominant process for resolving conflicts is negotiation. Recent interest in electronic commerce has also given increased importance to negotiation. This paper presents a generic negotiation model for autonomous agents that handles multi-party, multi-issue, and repeated rounds. The components of the model are: (i) a prenegotiation model, (ii) a multilateral negotiation protocol, (iii) an individual model of the negotiation process, (iv) a set of negotiation strategies, and (v) a set of negotiation tactics. The model is based on computationally tractable assumptions.

This paper builds on our previous work [7, 8, 9, 10]. In these papers, we presented the prenegotiation model, introduced the individual model of the negotiation process, and defined a number of negotiation tactics. In this paper, we present a multilateral negotiation protocol, continue the description of the individual model and introduce a set of negotiation strategies.

The remainder of the paper is structured as follows. Section 2 presents a generic model of individual behavior for autonomous agents. The model forms a basis for the development of negotiating agents. Section 3 presents a generic model of negotiation for autonomous agents. Finally, related work and concluding remarks are presented in sections 4 and 5, respectively.

F.J. Garijo, J.C. Riquelme, and M. Toro (Eds.): IBERAMIA 2002, LNAI 2527, pp. 556–565, 2002.

2   Autonomous Agents

Let *Agents* be a set of autonomous agents. This section briefly describes the features of every agent $ag_i \in Agents$ (see [7, 8] for an in-depth discussion).

The agent ag_i has a set $B_i = \{b_{i1},...\}$ of beliefs and a set $G_i = \{g_{i1},...\}$ of goals. Beliefs represent information about the world and the agent himself. Goals represent world states to be achieved.

The agent ag_i has a library $PL_i = \{pt_{i11},...\}$ of plan templates representing simple procedures for achieving goals. A plan template $pt_{ikl} \in PL_i$ is a 6-tuple that includes a header, a type, a list of conditions, a body, a list a constraints, and a list of statements [8]. The header is a 2-tuple: $header_{ikl} = <pname_{ikl}, pvars_{ikl}>$, where $pname_{ikl}$ is the name of pt_{ikl} and $pvars_{ikl}$ is a set of variables. The library PL_i has composite plan templates specifying the decomposition of goals into more detailed subgoals, and primitive plan templates specifying actions directly executable by ag_i.

The agent ag_i is able to generate complex plans from the simpler plan templates stored in the library. A *plan* p_{ik} for achieving a goal $g_{ik} \in G_i$ is a 3-tuple: $p_{ik} = <PT_{ik}, \leq_h, \leq_t>$, where $PT_{ik} \subseteq PL_i$ is a list of plan templates, $\leq_h$ is a binary relation establishing a hierarchy on PT_{ik}, and $\leq_t$ is another binary relation establishing a temporal order on PT_{ik}. The plan p_{ik} is represented as a hierarchical and temporally constrained And-tree. Plan generation is an iterative procedure of: (i) plan retrieval, (ii) plan selection, (iii) plan addition, and (iv) plan interpretation [8].

At any instant, the agent ag_i has a number of plans for execution. These plans are the plans adopted by ag_i and are stored in the *intention structure* $IS_i = [p_{i1},...]$. For each plan template pt_{ikl} in p_{ik}, the header of pt_{ikl} is referred as *intention* int_{ikl}.

The agent ag_i often has information about the agents in *Agents*. This information is stored in the *social description* $SD_i = \{SD_i(ag_1),...\}$. Each entry $Sd_i (ag_j) = <B_i(ag_j), G_i(ag_j), I_i(ag_j)>$, contains the beliefs, goals and intentions that ag_i believes ag_j has.

3   The Negotiation Model

Let $Ag = \{ag_1,...,ag_i,...,ag_n\}$, $Ag \subseteq Agents$, be a set of autonomous agents. Let $P_{Ag} = \{p_{11},...,p_{ik},...,p_{nn}\}$ be a set of plans of the agents in Ag including intentions $I_{Ag} = \{int_{111},...,int_{ikm},...,int_{nnn}\}$, respectively. Let the intentions in I_{Ag} represent commitments to achieve exclusive world states. In this situation, there is a conflict among the agents in Ag. This section presents a domain-independent description of a computational model of negotiation.

3.1   Preparing and Planning for Negotiation

The prenegotiation model defines the main tasks that each agent $ag_i \in Ag$ must attend to in order to prepare and plan for negotiation. A brief description of these tasks follows (see [9] for an in-depth discussion).

Negotiation Problem Structure Generation. A negotiation problem NP_{ik} from the perspective of ag_i is a 6-tuple: $NP_{ik}=<ag_i,B_i,g_{ik},int_{ikm},A,I_A>$, where B_i is a set of beliefs, $g_{ik} \in G_i$ is a goal, $p_{ik} \in P_{Ag}$ is a plan of ag_i for achieving g_{ik}, $int_{ikm} \in I_{Ag}$ is an intention of p_{ik}, $A=Ag-\{ag_i\}$ and $I_A=I_{Ag}-\{int_{ikm}\}$. The problem NP_{ik} has a *structure* $NPstruct_{ik}$ consisting of a hierarchical And-Or tree. Formally, $NPstruct_{ik}$ is a 4-tuple: $NPstruct_{ik}=<NPT_{ik},\leq_h,\leq_t,\leq_a>$, where $NPT_{ik} \subseteq PL_i$ is a list of plan templates, $\leq_h$ and $\leq_t$ have the meaning just specified, and $\leq_a$ is a binary relation establishing alternatives among the plan templates in NPT_{ik}. The nodes of the And-Or tree are plan templates. The header of the root node describes the *negotiation goal* g_{ik}.

The structure $NPstruct_{ik}$ is generated from plan p_{ik} by an iterative procedure involving: (i) problem structure interpretation, (ii) plan decomposition, (iii) goal selection, (iv) plan retrieval, and (v) plan addition [9]. $NPstruct_{ik}$ defines all the solutions of NP_{ik} currently known by ag_i. A *solution* is a plan that can achieve g_{ik}.

Issue Identification and Prioritization. The negotiation issues of ag_i are obtained from the leaves of $NPstruct_{ik}$. Let $L_{ik}=[pt_{ika},...]$ be the collection of plan templates constituting the leaves of $NPstruct_{ik}$. The header ($pname_{ikl}$ and $pvars_{ikl}$) of every plan template $pt_{ikl} \in L_{ik}$ is called a fact and denoted by f_{ikl}. Formally, a *fact* f_{ikl} is a 3-tuple: $f_{ikl}=<is_{ikl},v[is_{ikl}],r_{ikl}>$, where is_{ikl} is a *negotiation issue* (corresponding to $pname_{ikl}$), $v[is_{ikl}]$ is a value of is_{ikl} (corresponding to an element of $pvars_{ikl}$), and r_{ikl} is a list of arguments (corresponding to the remaining elements of $pvars_{ikl}$). Let $F_{ik}=\{f_{ika},...f_{ikz}\}$ be the set of facts of $NPstruct_{ik}$. The *negotiating agenda* of ag_i is the set of issues $I_{ik}=\{is_{ika},...,is_{ikz}\}$ associated with the facts in F_{ik}. The interval of legal values for each issue $is_{ikl} \in I_{ik}$ is represented by $D_{ikl}=[min_{ikl},max_{ikl}]$.

For each issue is_{ikl}, let w_{ikl} be a number called *importance weight* that represents its importance. Let $W_{ik}=\{w_{ika},...,w_{ikz}\}$ be the set of normalized importance weights of the issues in I_{ik}. The *priority* of the issues in I_{ik} is defined as their importance.

Limits and Aspirations Formulation. Limits and aspirations are formulated for each issue. The *limit* for issue is_{ikl} is represented by lim_{ikl} and the initial *aspiration* by asp^0_{ikl}, with $lim_{ikl},asp^o_{ikl} \in D_{ikl}$ and $lim_{ikl} \leq asp^o_{ikl}$.

Negotiation Constraints Definition. Constraints are defined for each issue $is_{ikl} \in I_{ik}$. *Hard constraints* are linear constraints that specify threshold values for issues. They cannot be relaxed. The hard constraint hc_{ikl} for is_{ikl} has the form: $hc_{ikl}=(is_{ikl}\geq lim_{ikl},$ $flex=0)$, where $flex=0$ represents null flexibility (inflexibility). *Soft constraints* are linear constraints that specify minimum acceptable values for issues. They can be relaxed. The soft constraint sc_{ikl} for is_{ikl} has the form: $sc_{ikl}=(is_{ikl}\geq asp^0_{ikl}, flex=n)$, where $flex=n$, $n\in N$, represents the degree of flexibility of sc_{ikl}.

Negotiation Strategy Selection. The agent ag_i has a library $SL_i=\{str_{i1},...\}$ of negotiation strategies and a library $TL_i=\{tact_{i1},...\}$ of negotiation tactics. *Negotiation strategies* are functions that define the tactics to be used at the beginning and during the course of negotiation (see subsection 3.4). *Negotiation tactics* are functions that define the moves to be made at each point of the negotiation process (see subsection 3.5). Strategy selection is an important task and must be carefully planned [3, 12, 13]. In this paper, we assume that ag_i selects a strategy $str_{ik}\in SL_i$ accordingly to his experience.

3.2 A Multilateral Negotiation Protocol

The protocol defines the set of possible tasks that each agent ag_i can perform at each point of the negotiation process. A negotiation strategy specifies a task from the set of possible tasks. A *global* description of the negotiation process follows.

The process starts with ag_i communicating a negotiation proposal $prop_{ikm}$ to all the agents in $A=Ag-\{ag_i\}$. A *negotiation proposal* is a set of facts (see subsection 3.3). Each agent $ag_j\in A$ receives $prop_{ikm}$ and may decide either: (i) to accept $prop_{ikm}$, (ii) to reject $prop_{ikm}$ without making a critique, or (iii) to reject $prop_{ikm}$ and making a critique. A *critique* is a statement about issue priorities.

The process of negotiation proceeds with ag_i receiving the responses of all the agents in A. Next, ag_i checks whether a negotiation agreement was reached. If the proposal $prop_{ikm}$ was accepted by all the agents in A, the negotiation process ends successfully. In this case, ag_i informs the agents in A that an agreement was reached. Otherwise, ag_i can act either: (i) by communicating a new proposal $prop_{ikm+1}$, or (ii) by acknowledging the receipt of all the responses.

The process continues with the agents in A receiving the response of ag_i. If ag_i decides to communicate a new proposal $prop_{ikm+1}$, each agent $ag_j\in A$ may again decide: (i) to accept $prop_{ikm+1}$, or (ii) to reject $prop_{ikm+1}$ without making a critique, or (iii) to reject $prop_{ikm+1}$ and making a critique. If ag_i decides to acknowledge the receipt of the responses, the process continues to a new *round* in which another agent $ag_k\in Ag$ communicates a proposal to all the agents in $A_k=Ag-\{ag_k\}$. This is repeated for other agents in Ag.

3.3 The Negotiation Process (Individual Perspective)

The individual model of the negotiation process specifies the tasks that each agent must perform in order to negotiate in a competent way. These tasks (or processes) are shown in Fig. 1 for the specific case of an agent $ag_i \in Ag$ that communicates a negotiation proposal. Let NP_{ik} represent ag_i's perspective of a negotiation problem and $NPstruct_{ik}$ be the structure of NP_{ik}. A description of the main processes follows.

Negotiation Proposal Generation. This process generates the set of initial negotiation proposals $INPS_{ik}$ satisfying the requirements imposed by $NPstruct_{ik}$. The generation of $INPS_{ik}$ is performed through an iterative procedure involving: (i) problem interpretation, (ii) proposal preparation, and (iii) proposal addition [10]. In brief, problem interpretation consists of searching $NPstruct_{ik}$ for any solution p_{ik} of NP_{ik} and selecting the primitive plan templates $ppt_{ik}=\{pt_{ika},\dots,pt_{ikp}\}$ of p_{ik}. Proposal preparation consists of determining a *negotiation proposal* $prop_{ikm}=\{f_{ika},\dots,f_{ikp}\}$, *i.e.*, a set of facts corresponding to the headers of the plan templates in ppt_{ik}. Proposal addition consists of adding $prop_{ikm}$ to $INPS_{ik}$.

The preparation of a proposal $prop_{ikm}$ partitions the set F_{ik} of facts into: (i) subset $prop_{ikm}$, and (ii) subset $pcompl_{ikm}=\{f_{ikp+1},\dots,f_{ikz}\}$, called *proposal complement* of $prop_{ikm}$. The facts in $prop_{ikm}$ are fundamental for achieving the negotiation goal g_{ik}. They are the *inflexible facts* of negotiation, for proposal $prop_{ikm}$. The negotiation issues $Iprop_{ikm}=\{is_{ika},\dots,is_{ikp}\}$ associated with these facts are the *inflexible issues*. On the other hand, the facts in $pcompl_{ikm}$ are not important for achieving g_{ik}. They are the *flexible facts* of negotiation, for proposal $prop_{ikm}$. The issues $Icompl_{ikm}=\{is_{ikp+1},\dots,is_{ikz}\}$ associated with these facts are the *flexible issues*.

Feasible and Acceptable Proposal Preparation. This process generates the set of feasible proposals $IFPS_{ik}$, $IFPS_{ik} \subseteq INPS_{ik}$, and the set of acceptable proposals $IAPS_{ik}$, $IAPS_{ik} \subseteq IFPS_{ik}$. Let $prop_{ikm}=\{f_{ika},\dots,f_{ikp}\}$ be a negotiation proposal. Let $Iprop_{ikm}=\{is_{ika},\dots,is_{ikp}\}$ be the set of issues associated with the facts in $prop_{ikm}$. Let $HCprop_{ikm}=\{hc_{ika},\dots,hc_{ikp}\}$ and $SCprop_{ikm}=\{sc_{ika},\dots,sc_{ikp}\}$ be the sets of hard and soft constraints for issues in $Iprop_{ikm}$, respectively. A negotiation proposal $prop_{ikm} \in INPS_{ik}$ is *feasible* if the issues in $Iprop_{ikm}$ satisfy the set $HCprop_{ikm}$ of hard constraints. A feasible proposal $prop_{ikm}$ is *acceptable* if the issues in $Iprop_{ikm}$ satisfy the set $SCprop_{ikm}$ of soft constraints.

Feasible Proposal Evaluation. This process computes a score for each proposal in $IFPS_{ik}$ using an *additive scoring function* and orders the proposals in descending order of preference. Let $W_{ik}=\{w_{ika},\dots,w_{ikp}\}$ be the set of importance weights of the issues in $Iprop_{ikm}$. Let $C_{ikm}=(v[is_{ika}],\dots,v[is_{ikp}])$ be the values of the issues in $Iprop_{ikm}$ (C_{ikm} is called a *contract*). For each issue $is_{ikl} \in Iprop_{ikm}$ defined over the interval $D_{ikl}=[min_{ikl},$

max_{ikl}], let V_{ikl} be a *component scoring function* that gives the score that ag_i assigns to a value $v[is_{ikl}] \in D_{ikj}$ of is_{ikl}. The score for contract C_{ikm} is given by [13]:

$V(C_{ikm}) = \sum_{j=a}^{p} w_{ikj} V_{ikj} (v[is_{ikj}])$. The proposal $prop_{ikm}$ is identified with contract C_{ikm}

and both have the same score.

Feasible Proposal Selection. This process selects a feasible proposal $prop_{ikm} \in IFPS_{ik}$. The negotiation strategy str_{ik} of ag_i dictates a tactic $tact_{ik} \in TL_i$ to use. The tactic $tact_{ik}$ specifies a particular proposal $prop_{ikm}$.

Feasible Proposal Modification. This process computes a new proposal $prop_{ikm+1}$ from a rejected proposal $prop_{ikm}$. The strategy str_{ik} defines one or two tactics $tact_{ik}, tact_{ik+1} \in TL_i$. The tactics modify $prop_{ikm}$ to make it more acceptable.

3.4 Negotiation Strategies

This subsection describes two classes of strategies, called concession and problem solving strategies.

Concession strategies are functions that define the opening negotiation and concession tactics. In this paper, we consider three sub-classes of strategies:

1. *starting high and conceding slowly* – model an optimistic opening attitude and successive small concessions;
2. *starting reasonable and conceding moderately* – model a realistic opening attitude and successive moderate concessions;
3. *starting low and conceding rapidly* – model a pessimistic opening attitude and successive large concessions.

The starting high and conceding slowly strategies are formalized by analogous functions. For instance, a strategy *SH01* is formalized by a function:

$sh\_strategy\_01(state, TL_i, F) = tact_{ik} \mid$

         if: *state* ="*initial*" then: $tact_{ik}$="*starting_optimistic*"

         else: $tact_{ik}$="*const_factor_tact*" $\wedge$ F=0.1

where *state* is the state of the negotiation, $F \in [0,1]$ is the *concession factor*, $tact_{ik}$ is the tactic specified by the strategy, *starting_optimistic* is an opening negotiation tactic, and *const_factor_tact* is a constant concession factor tactic (see subsection 3.5). The strategies in the other subclasses are formalized by similar functions.

Problem solving strategies define the opening negotiation, concession and compensation tactics. In this paper, we consider two sub-classes of strategies:

1. *low priority concession making* – model a realistic opening attitude, large concessions on issues of low priority and small concessions on other issues;
2. *low priority concession making with compensation* – these strategies are similar to previous strategies; however, concessions are interleaved with compensations.

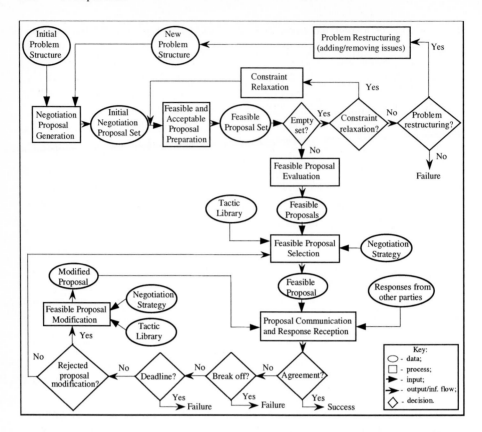

Fig. 1. The negotiation process (perspective of every agent that communicates a proposal)

Low priority concession making strategies partition the set I_{ik} of issues into: (i) subset I_{ik+}, corresponding to higher priority issues, and (ii) subset I_{ik-}, corresponding to the remaining issues. Again, the strategies in this sub-class are formalized by analogous functions. For instance, a strategy *LP01* is formalized by a function:

$lp\_strategy\_01(state, TL_i, I_{ik}, F_1, F_2) = (tact_{ik}, I_{ik+}, tact_{ik+1}, I_{ik-}) |$

> if: *state* ="*initial*" then: $tact_{ik}$="*starting_realistic*" $\wedge$ $tact_{ik+1}$="*nil*"
> else: $I_{ik}= I_{ik+} + I_{ik-} \wedge \forall it_{ikj} \in I_{ik+}$, $tact_{ik}$="*const_factor_tact*" $\wedge F_1$=0.10 $\wedge$
> $\forall it_{ikj} \in I_{ik-}$, $tact_{ik+1}$="*const_factor_tact*" $\wedge F_2$=0.35

where *state* and *const_factor_tact* have the meaning just specified, F_1 and F_2 are constants, $tact_{ik}$ and $tact_{ik+1}$ are the tactics defined by the strategy, and *starting_realistic* is an opening negotiation tactic (see subsection 3.5). The formalization of the strategies in the other sub-class is essentially identical to that.

3.5   Negotiation Tactics

This section describes two classes of tactics, called opening negotiation and concession tactics.

Opening negotiation tactics specify a proposal to submit at the beginning of negotiation. Let $IFPS_{ik}$ and $IAPS_{ik}$ be the sets of feasible and acceptable proposals of ag_i, respectively. Let $INAPS_{ik}=IFPS_{ik}-IAPS_{ik}$. Let $Vprop_{ikh}$ be the score of proposal $prop_{ikh} \in IAPS_{ik}$. Let $Aprop^0_{ikh}$ be the set of initial aspirations of ag_i for issues in $prop_{ikh}$ and $VAprop^0_{ikh}$ be the score of $Aprop^0_{ikh}$. Let $Dif_{ikh}= |Vprop_{ikh}-VAprop^0_{ikh}|$. Similarly, let $Vprop_{ikh+1}$ be the score of proposal $prop_{ikh+1} \in INAPS_{ik}$. Let $Aprop^0_{ikh+1}$ be the set of initial aspirations of ag_i for issues in $prop_{ikh+1}$ and $VAprop^0_{ikh+1}$ be the score of $Aprop^0_{ikh+1}$. Let $Dif_{ikh+1}= |Vprop_{ikh+1}-VAprop^0_{ikh+1}|$. We consider three tactics:

1. *starting optimistic* – specifies the proposal $prop_{ik1}$ with the highest score;
2. *starting realistic* – specifies either: (i) proposal $prop_{ikh}$ with the lowest score, if $Dif_{ikh} \leq Dif_{ikh+1}$, or (ii) proposal $prop_{ikh+1}$ with the highest score, if $Dif_{ikh} > Dif_{ikh+1}$;
3. *starting pessimistic* – specifies the proposal $prop_{ikn}$ with the lowest score.

The three tactics are formalized by similar functions. For instance, the tactic starting optimistic is formalized by the following function:

$$starting\_optimistic(IFPS_{ik})=prop_{ik1} \mid \forall prop_{ikj} \in IFPS_{ik}, Vprop_{ik1} \geq Vprop_{ikj}$$

Concession tactics are functions that compute new values for each issue. In this paper, we consider two sub-classes of tactics: (i) *constant concession factor tactics*, and (ii) *total concession dependent tactics*. In each sub-class, we consider five tactics:

1. *stalemate* – models a *null* concession on is_{ikj};
2. *tough* – models a *small* concession on is_{ikj};
3. *moderate* – models a *moderate* concession on is_{ikj};
4. *soft* – models a *large* concession on is_{ikj};
5. *compromise* – models a *complete* concession on is_{ikj}.

Let $prop_{ikm}$ be a proposal submitted by ag_i and rejected. Let $v[is_{ikj}]_m$ be the value of is_{ikj} offered in $prop_{ikm}$. Let lim_{ikj} be the limit for is_{ikj}. Let $v[is_{ikj}]_{m+1}$ be the new value of is_{ikj} to be offered in a new proposal $prop_{ikm+1}$. Let V_{ikj} be the component scoring function for is_{ikj}. The *constant concession factor tactics* are formalized by a function *const_factor_tact* which takes $v[is_{ikj}]_m$, a constant w, lim_{ikj} and another constant cte as input and returns $v[is_{ikj}]_{m+1}$, *i.e.*,

$$const\_factor\_tact(v[is_{ikj}]_m,w,lim_{ikj},cte)= v[is_{ikj}]_{m+1} \mid$$

$$v[is_{ikj}]_{m+1}=v[is_{ikj}]_m + (-1)^w F \mid lim_{ikj} - v[is_{ikj}]_m \mid \wedge F=cte$$

where $w=0$ if V_{ikj} is monotonically decreasing or $w=1$ if V_{ikj} is monotonically increasing and F is the concession factor. The five tactics are defined as follows: the stalemate tactic by $F=0$, the tough tactic by $F \in \,]0,0.2]$, the moderate tactic by $F \in \,]0.2,0.3]$, the soft tactic by $F \in \,]0.3,0.4]$, and the compromise tactic by $F=1$.

The *total concession dependent tactics* are similar to the previous tactics, but F is a function of the total concession. Let $v[is_{ikj}]_0,...,v[is_{ikj}]_m$, be the values of is_{ikj} successively offered by ag_i, with $V_{ikj}(v[is_{ikj}]_{h-1}) \geq V_{ikj}(v[is_{ikj}]_h)$, $0 \leq h \leq m$. The *total concession Ctotal* made by ag_i on is_{ikj} is: $Ctotal = |v[is_{ikj}]_0 - v[is_{ikj}]_m|$. These tactics are formalized by a function $tcd\_tactics$ which takes $v[is_{ikj}]_m$, w, lim_{ikj}, a constant $\lambda \in R^+$, $Ctotal$ and $v[is_{ikj}]_0$ as input and returns $v[is_{ikj}]_{m+1}$, *i.e.*,

$tcd\_tactics(v[is_{ikj}]_m,w,lim_{ikj},\lambda,Ctotal,v[is_{ikj}]_0)=v[is_{ikj}]_{m+1}|$

$$v[is_{ikj}]_{m+1} = v[is_{ikj}]_m + (-1)^w \, F \, |lim_{ikj} - v[is_{ikj}]_m| \, \wedge$$
$$F = 1 - \lambda \, Ctotal \, / \, |lim_{ikj} - v[is_{ikj}]_0|$$

4 Related Work

The design of negotiating agents has been investigated from both a theoretical and a practical perspective. Researchers following the theoretical perspective attempt mainly to develop formal models. Some researchers define the modalities of the mental state of the agents, develop a *logical* model of individual behavior, and then use the model as a basis for the development of a formal model of negotiation or argumentation (e.g., [6]). However, most researchers are neutral with respect to the modalities of the mental state and just develop formal models of negotiation (e.g., [5]). Generally speaking, most theoretical models are rich but restrictive. They made assumptions that severely limit their applicability to solve real problems.

Researchers following the practical perspective attempt mainly to develop *computational* models, *i.e.*, models specifying the key data structures and the processes operating on these structures. Some researchers start with a model of individual behavior, develop or adopt a negotiation model, and then integrate both models (e.g., [11]). Again, most researchers prefer to be neutral about the model of individual behavior and just develop negotiation models (e.g., [1]). Broadly speaking, most computational models are based on ad hoc principles. They lack a rigorous theoretical grounding. Despite these, some researchers believe that it is necessary to develop computational models in order to use agents in real-world applications [14]. Accordingly, we developed a computational negotiation model.

As noted, most researchers have paid little attention to the problem of how to integrate models of individual behavior with negotiation models. However, it is one of the costliest lessons of computer science that independently developed components resist subsequent integration in a smoothly functioning whole [2]. Accordingly, we developed a model that accounts for a tight integration of the individual capability of planning and the social capability of negotiation.

We are interested in negotiation among both self-motivated and cooperative agents. Our structure for representing negotiation problems is similar to decision trees and goal representation trees [4], but there are important differences. Our approach does not require the quantitative measures typical of decision analysis. Also, our approach is based on plan templates and plan expansion, and not on production rules and forward or backward chaining. In addition, our formulae for modeling concession tactics are similar to the formulae used by Faratin *et al.* [1]. Again, there are important differences. The total concession criterion is not used by other researchers and our formulae: (i) assure that the agents do not negotiate in bad faith, and (ii) model important experimental conclusions about human negotiation.

5   Discussion and Future Work

This article has introduced a computational negotiation model for autonomous agents. There are several features of our work that should be highlighted. First, the model is generic and can be used in a wide range of domains. Second, the structure of a negotiation problem allows the direct integration of planning and negotiation. Also, this structure defines the set of negotiation issues. Third, the model supports problem restructuring ensuring a high degree of flexibility. Problem restructuring allows the dynamic addition of negotiation issues. Finally, the negotiation strategies are motivated by human negotiation procedures [3, 12]. Our aim for the future is: (i) to extend the model, and (ii) to finish the experimental validation of the model.

References

1. Faratin, P., C. Sierra, N. Jennings, "Negotiation Decision Functions for Autonomous Agents", *Robotics and Autonomous Systems*, 24(3-4), 1998, 159-182.
2. Hayes-Roth, B. "On Building Integrated Cognitive Agents: A Review of Allen Newell's Unified Theories of Cognition." *Artif. Intell.*, 59(1-2), 1992, 329-341.
3. Lewicki, R., D. Saunders, J. Minton, *Neg. Readings, Exercises-Cases*, McGraw Hill, 1999.
4. Kersten G., W. Michalowski, S. Szpakowicz Z. Koperczak, 1991, "Restruturable Representations of Negotiation", *Management Science*, 37(10), 1991, 1269-1290.
5. Kraus, S., J. Wilkenfeld, G. Zlotkin, "Multiagent Negotiation Under Time Constraints", *Artif. Intell.*, 75, 1995, 297-345.
6. Kraus, S., K. Sycara, A. Evenchik, "Reaching Agreements Through Argumentation: a Logical Model and Implementation", *Artif. Intell.*, 104, 1998, 1-69.
7. Lopes, F., N. Mamede, H. Coelho, A. Q. Novais, "A Negotiation Model for Intentional Agents", *In Multi-Agent Systems in Production*, Elsevier Science, 1999, 211-216.
8. Lopes, F., N. Mamede, A. Q. Novais, H. Coelho, "Towards a Generic Negotiation Model for Intentional Agents", *In Agent-Based Inf. Systems*, IEEE Comp. Press, 2000, 433-439.
9. Lopes, F., N. Mamede; A. Q. Novais, H. Coelho, "Conflict Management and Negotiation Among Intentional Agents", *In Agent-Based Simulation*, SCS-Europe, 2001, 117-124.
10. Lopes, F., N. Mamede, A. Q. Novais, H. Coelho, "Negotiation Tactics for Autonomous Agents." *In Internet Robots, Systems, Applications.* IEEE Comp. Press, 2001, 708-714.
11. Muller, J., *The Design of Intelligent Agents*, Springer-Verlag, 1996 (LNAI 1177).
12. Pruitt, D., *Negotiation Behavior*, Academic Press, 1981.
13. Raiffa, H., *The Art and Science of Negotiation,* Harvard University Press, 1982.
14. Rao, A. "Integrated Agent Architecture: Execution and Recognition of Mental-States." *In Distrib. Artif. Intell. Archit. Modelling*, Springer-Verlag, 1995, 159-173 (LNAI 1087).

Interface Agents Development in MASA for Human Integration in Multiagent Systems

Ammar Lahlouhi[1], Zaidi Sahnoun[2], Med Lamine Benbrahim[1], and
Abdelouahab Boussaha[1]

[1] MASA Group, Department of computer science, University of Biskra, Biskra, DZ-07000,
Algeria
ammarlahlouhi@yahoo.fr
[2] Lire laboratory, Department of computer science, University of Constantine, Constantine,
DZ-25 000, Algeria

Abstract. The base of research works, on interface agents, is the client-server concept, where they regarded them as humans' assistants in the use of software. This vision does not permit the foundation, in a coherent way, of the human-software cooperation. In this paper, we propose a cooperation-based approach; of interface agents' development for multi-agent systems. Abstractly, we consider the human as an agent H that assumes one or more roles. Conceptually, we associate to the human a software F that holds the H's objective. F is a software agent qualified as interface agent. However, F has neither human's intellectual abilities nor its resources' exploitation. We supplement this lack by F-human interaction. The agent H will then be consisted of F completed by the human's intellectual abilities and his resources' exploitation. H cooperates with other software agents and the development of F will follow a multi-agent development methodology.

1 Introduction

The base of the research works undertaken on interface agents (see [14], for research works survey on interface agents) is the traditional concept of client-server. They see the human as a client and qualify him as a user whereas they see the interface agent as a humans server, for the use of software systems (tools). Consequently, the interface agent must have some characteristics of intelligence, to better serve the human. This is what makes dominate aspects of traditional artificial intelligence (natural language interface, intelligent assistance, comprehension, learning...).

In this paper, we propose a different viewpoint, co-operation based approach. We try to clarify the usual approach and its disadvantages, in section 2. We then introduce the co-operation based approach and its advantages, in section 3. In the remaining sections, we show how we can concretize this approach and how we materialized it in MASA project.

2 Usual Approach

Usually, the human uses software systems through tool invocation. For that, he determines its objective and plans the actions enabling him to reach it. We can subdivide these

F.J. Garijo, J.C. Riquelme, and M. Toro (Eds.): IBERAMIA 2002, LNAI 2527, pp. 566–574, 2002.

actions in two classes: those must do by the human and those must do by the software system. Since the human is intelligent, its plan is fuzzy. It revises it according to its requirements by remaking actions, adding new actions...

2.1 Human Detention of Actions Plan

In this situation, it is the human, which holds its plan, and ensures its execution. The latter consists of: (1) sequencing plan actions, (2) execution of the actions intended for him, and (3) Demand to software system, through an interface, to execute the actions, that he reserved for it.

2.2 Disadvantages

The disadvantages of this approach are numerous. We can cite: (1) Interface development is based on an interminable research of a general valid model for the use of any software system by any human role, (2) Many inconsistencies in the use and/or sequencing tools, (3) Does not make possible to the designer to exploit the humans intellectual abilities to serve the objective of the system to be developed, and (4) The plan detention and its execution by the human is embarrassed, unproductive, causes errors in plan execution and its foundation...

3   Co-operation Based Approach

In the co-operation based approach, we consider, abstractly, the human as an agent H that assumes one or more roles. Conceptually, we associate to the human a software F that holds the H's objective. F is a software agent qualified as interface agent. However, F has neither human's intellectual abilities nor its resources' exploitation. We supplement this lack by F-human interaction. The agent H will then be consisted of F completed by the human's intellectual abilities and his resources' exploitation. H cooperates with other software agents.

3.1   Actions Plan Detention by Interface Agent

In this approach, actions plan, qualified of individual task, must be explicit. Its base is organization's roles that the agent H must assume in the MAS. It is then determined during MAS design so that MAS functioning was coherent.

It is the responsibility of the interface agent to hold the individual task, and to ensure its execution. This execution consists of: (1) sequencing actions plan, (2) Demand to the human to execute actions intended for him, and (3) Demand to software agents to execute actions which are intended for them.

3.2   Sharing Tasks between Software Agents and the Human

In this approach, we can share the tasks, in a coherent way, between software agents and human agent. We can charge the software agents by: (1) Execution of tasks concerning the data processing automation: calculations, storage, research..., and (2) Making certain decisions.

Whereas, we can charge the human agents by: (1) Achieving treatments of intelligent tasks, (2) Making certain decisions, and (3) Achieving actions on the environment, external to software system, decided by the software system.

3.3   Advantages and Disadvantages

The advantages of this approach are numerous. We can cite those, which allow us to: (1) Use multi-agents systems techniques of co-operation, for the derivation of the necessary characteristics of the agent H and, consequently, those of the agent F, (2) Profit the MAS from the intellectual abilities of the humans, (3) Manage human co-operation through a network...

Its disadvantage lie in the need of preliminary planning. However, we can consider this disadvantage also as an advantage, since it ensures a rigorous development of software systems.

4   Interfaces and Agents

We can classified the solutions proposed for combining of agent and interfaces as follows:

1. Interface agent for traditional applications: The human interacts with the software system as it does it usually. The interface agent observes all its actions while advising it and proposing him solutions for possible difficulties, which it will encounter.
2. Traditional interface for multiagent systems: The human interacts directly with the agents of multi-agents system through a traditional interface.
3. Interface agents for multiagent systems: It is an integration of the human in the multiagent system. We consider the human as a system's component (agent) whose it plays one or more roles in a given organization.

4.1   Interface Agents for Traditional Applications

In this case, the interface agent behaves as an assistant who must be intelligent, convivial, understanding, learning, and communicating in natural language.... This approach is that proposed by Maes [4], [5], improved by several interface agents collaboration for learning from several users by Lashkari [6] and by introducing the autonomy by Lieberman [1], [2], [3] and continued by Rich and its colleagues [7], [8], [9], [10], [11].

Several works, of this class, treat the learning of the interface agents from users actions [4], [5], [11], [13].

In this vision, the software system is heterogeneous, i.e., it comprises components based on agent technology and traditional components. The interface agents adaptation, to traditional components, makes that they do not satisfy agents minimal characteristics.

4.2   Traditional Interfaces for Multiagent Systems

It is the approach followed by the MAS developers whose interfaces do not constitute their concern. The role of these interfaces is to assist the human, as in the previous approach, in the use of the various agents. The base of this approach is, generally, the object-based interfaces approach.

In this latter, one presents objects, materialized by icons, representing accessible software system objects, to the human. The later chooses icons and, using a global or contextual menu, he invokes methods of these objects accessible to him.

In this case, the agents are viewed as objects. What is not coherent with the agent concept. Moreover, the software system cannot profit, explicitly and coherently, from humans intellectual abilities and/or humans actions on the environment. It cannot manage, either, the co-operation between the human, since it regard them as users.

4.3   Interface Agents for Humans Integration in Multiagent Systems

We distinguish, in this case, two environments: (1) Virtual or software and (2) Real or physical. The human agent and the interface agent (the particular software F, explained in section 3) are associated to constitute only one agent. The interface agent wraps the human and represents it in the virtual environment, so that it uses humans capacities to serve software agents. In the other hand, the human wraps the interface agent and represents it in the real environment.

5   MASA: Multiagent Modeling of Systems with Autonomous and Heterogeneous Components

5.1   MASA Project

MASA Project consists of three poles: MASA-Meta-model, MASA-Applications and MASA-Method. The autonomy characterization, in MASA-Meta-model, constitutes its strong point where it makes it possible to support heterogeneous agents (physical, software and human). The applications of MASA, MASA-Applications, include several types. They are important applications but they also have the role of the evaluation, validation, correction, improvement and enriching MASA-Meta-model and MASA-Method.

5.2   MASA-Method Methodology

MASA-method is an organizational methodology. Its specificity is the characterization of the organization as being a couple (Structure, Objective) rather than as an only structure, as other multi-agents organizational methodologies consider it. That is what clarifies the development of agents co-operation.

Cooperation's development. We adopted the procedural description of the objective and we qualified it of global task. We then approached the co-operation as follows:

1. Global task description in Colored Petri Nets (CPN) which ensures actions synchronization,
2. Distribution of this global task on the various agents to derive agents individual tasks. This produces a set of synchronized CPN (CPN-S) which each one constitutes a description of an agent's individual task.

MASA-Method's Process. The process of MASA-Method consists of three phases:

Organizational phase. Consists of: (1) Set the organization's objective to produce the objective's informal expression, (2) From this later, determine the organization's structure to produce the organization's structure, and (3) Formalize the objective's expression, using the organization's structure.

Modeling phases. Consists of: (1) Using the organization's structure, distribute the roles on agents, (2) Determine agents' sensors and effectors to constitute communication links between them and to produce MAS's structure, and (3) Distribute the organization's objective on agents, in accordance with roles distribution, to produce MAS's model.

Implementation phase. Consists of: (1) Implement the agents' expertise and their mental states, of the MAS's model, to produce MAS's architecture and (2) Implementation of the MAS's architecture to produce the final MAS.

5.3   Human Agents and Interface Agents in MASA

In MASA, we consider the human, from abstract view, as an agent of the complete multiagent system. To integrate the human agents with software agents, we associate to each of them an interface agent as explained in section 3.

6   Interface Agents in MASA

In MASA, agent characteristics are the following: (1) Sensors and effectors, (2) Resources, (3) State, (4) Expertise, and (5) Individual task. In the following subsections, we describe how we can derive these characteristics for interface agents.

6.1   Interface Agent

We attribute the human agents characteristics to the interface agent as follow:

1. Sensors and effectors are those of agent-human communication,
2. Resources: The interface agent has not the human agents resources but it acts on via the human agent it self, by demanding him to act on them,
3. State is an abstract of the human mental state (see sect. 6.2),
4. Expertise: The expertise procedures are not exactly those, which the human uses (see sect. 6.3),
5. Individual task (see sect. 6.4, for its derivation).

6.2   Interface Agent State Detention

We can consider two solutions: (1) Memorize the state by the interface agent, or (2) Its detention by the human. The difficulty of the first solution is in that the interface agent is not able to memorize all types of information. The difficulty of the second is that the software system will not assist the human in memorizing and presenting certain data and/or results.

In MASA, we propose a combination of the two approaches: Memorizing the information, which the representation is acceptable (cost consideration, feasibility...) and leave the others with the human. The decision, on the adoption of a solution or the other for particular information, is lifted to the MAS designer.

6.3   Expertise Procedures

A procedure of an interface agent expertise must make possible to communicate, to the human, the procedure name and, to present to him the procedure's data and/or to receive from him the results of its execution.

If the communication means, with the human, are the usual ones (keyboard, screen, mouse...) the displaying of the data and/or the entry results can be complex. They can be formatted texts, graphs and/or images. In this case, the associated procedure must use tools enabling it to display these data and/or to assist the human to enter these results.

An expertise's procedure of an interface agent, which is implemented like a method of an active object, can be then described as follows: (1) Display procedure name, (2) Display its data if there is any and (3) Recover results if there is any.

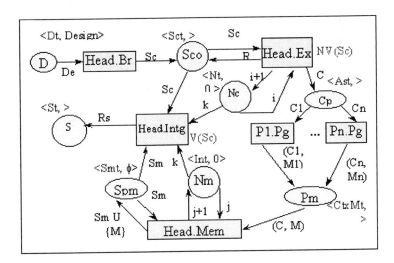

Fig. 1. Programming team's global task

6.4 Individual Task

In MASA, we derive the individual task from the CPN description of the global task, indifferently, as those of all agents. We show that aspect in the application example (See section 7).

7 Example: Project's Head as Interface Agent in the Programming Process

The programming process belongs to the software development process. This last knew a significant turning in the middle of the Eighties with the article of Osterweil [12] entitled "Software processes are software too". Osterweil considered the software process as being a complex software system whose development must follow the software development process it self.

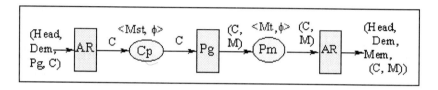

Fig. 2. Individual tasks of a Technician extracted from the programming team's global task

7.1 Multiagent System for Conceptual Models Programming

The organization's global task must answer the question "how to program a design?" We can make this by a team of programmers who program conceptual models. We choose here an organization in team in which a team's head supervise the programmers.

The global task, which its formal description is given in fig. 1, can be described informally as follows: (1) Break up (Br) the design into components, (2) Allot components to programmers, (3) a programmer, holding a component, program (Pg) this component and produces a module, (4) when all components were programmed, the team's head integrates (Intg) modules and produces resulted software.

7.2 Interface Agent: Project's Head

The individual task of a technician, wich represents a programmer role, is given in fig. 2 and that of the project's head, wich represents a team's head role, is given in fig. 3. The expertise of the project's head comprises procedures Br, Extract a component (Ex), Memirize a module (Mem) and Intgr. The base of the derivation of the expertise's procedure is how it displays the procedure name and its entry parameters and how it recovers the results. For example, for the procedure Br, the project's head interface agent must: (1) Displays the message "Breaks up the following design:", (2) Displays the design D, and (3) invokes the tool allowing the human to enter the decomposition result that is a set of components (Scos).

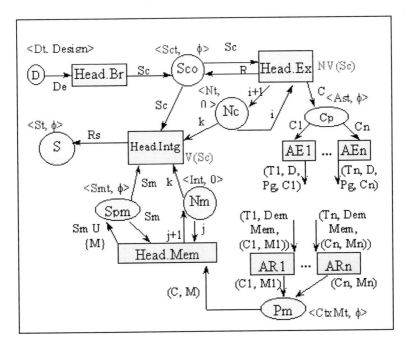

Fig. 3. Individual tasks of the Project's head extracted from the programming team's global task

8   Related Works

We view other interface agents approaches [2], [4], [6], [9], [10] as a particular case of the cooperation based approach. We can show this by introducing agents, in the MAS, in accordance to the cooperation-based approach, that assure particular roles of assistance, supervising... In addition, our approach allows remedying disadvantages of usual approaches and it has many advantages, like those which we explained in the section 3. Among its other advantages, we can cite the simplification of the human-software system interaction. The approach reduces this to the only communication of the operations names, data and results.

It is our opinion; that our approach allows also a harmonious integration of any kind of physical agents such as robots. This is not the case of other approaches. However, we did not study the robot integration with human and/or software agents, for the moment.

9   Conclusion

We validated the cooperation-based approach in a multiagent modeling of software development process as explained earlier, in this paper. The interface agent development systematic and causes no particulars difficulties. The multiagent development process, based on MASA-Method, directs this development. This later is a difficult task that we work to simplify it by systemizing, assisting and/or automating stages of this development. This is the MASA projects objective.

References

1. Henry Lieberman, Integrating User Interface Agents with Conventional Applications, International Conference on Intelligent User Interfaces, San Francisco, January 1998.
2. Henry Lieberman, Autonomous Interface Agents, In Proceedings of the ACM Conference on Human Factors in Computing Systems, CHI '97 (pp. 67-74). ACM Press, 1997
3. Henry Lieberman, Christopher Fry, Louis Weitzman, Exploring the Web with Reconnaissance Agents, Communications of the ACM August 2001/Vol. 44, No. 8.
4. Maes, P., and Robyn Kozierok, Learning Interface Agents, AAAI Conference, 1993.
5. Max Edward Metral, Design of a Generic Learning Interface Agent, Department of Electrical Engineering and Computer Science, Bachelor of Science in Computer Science and Engineering, MIT, Thesis supervised by Patricia E. Maes, May 1993.
6. Yezdi Lashkari, Max Metral, Pattie Maes, Collaborative Interface Agents, Proceedings of AAI '94 Conference, Seattle, Washington, August 1994.
7. Charles Rich, Window Sharing with Collaborative Interface Agents, SIGCHI Bulletin, Vol. 28, No. 1, January 1996, pp. 70-78.
8. Charles Rich, Candace L. Sidner, Segmented Interaction History in a Collaborative Interface Agent, Third Int. Conf. on Intelligent User Interfaces, Orlando, FL, January 1997.
9. Charles Rich, Candace L. Sidner, COLLAGEN: A Collaboration Manager for Software Interface Agents, TR-97-21a March 1998, Merl-A Mitsubishi Electric Research Laboratory, http://www.merl.com
10. Charles Rich, Candace L. Sidner, COLLAGEN: When Agents Collaborate with People, First Int. Conf. on Autonomous Agents, Marina del Rey, CA, February 1997.
11. Neal Lesh Charles Rich Candace L. Sidner, Using Plan Recognition in Human-Computer Collaboration, TR-98-23 December 1998, Merl-A Mitsubishi Electric Research Laboratory, http://www.merl.com
12. L. J. Osterweil, "Software Processes are Software Too", In Proceedings of the Ninth International Conference of Software Engineering, pages 2–13, Monterey CA, March 1987.
13. Anandeep S. Pannu, Katia Sycara, A Learning Personal Agent for Text Filtering and Notification, The Robotics Institute, School of Computer Science, Carnegie Mellon University.
14. Stuart E. Middleton, Interface agents: A review of the field, Technical Report Number: ECSTRñIAM01-001, ISBN: 0854327320, http://www.ecs.soton.ac.uk/˜sem99r, Intelligence, Agents and Multimedia group (IAM group), University of Southampton.

Comparing Distributed Reinforcement Learning Approaches to Learn Agent Coordination

Reinaldo A.C. Bianchi and Anna H.R. Costa

Laboratório de Técnicas Inteligentes – LTI/PCS
Escola Politécnica da Universidade de São Paulo
Av. Prof. Luciano Gualberto, trav. 3, 158. 05508-900 São Paulo – SP, Brazil.
{reinaldo.bianchi, anna.reali}@poli.usp.br
http://www.lti.pcs.usp.br/

Abstract. This work compares the performance of the Ant-ViBRA system to approaches based on Distributed Q-learning and Q-learning, when they are applied to learn coordination among agent actions in a Multi Agent System. Ant-ViBRA is a modified version of a Swarm Intelligence Algorithm called the Ant Colony System algorithm (ACS), which combines a Reinforcement Learning (RL) approach with Heuristic Search. Ant-ViBRA uses *a priori* domain knowledge to decompose the domain task into subtasks and to define the relationship between actions and states based on interactions among subtasks. In this way, Ant-ViBRA is able to cope with planning when several agents are involved in a combinatorial optimization problem where interleaved execution is needed. The domain in which the comparison is made is that of a manipulator performing visually-guided *pick-and-place* tasks in an assembly cell. The experiments carried out are encouraging, showing that Ant-ViBRA presents better results than the Distributed Q-learning and the Q-learning algorithms.

1   Introduction

Based on the social insect metaphor for solving problems, the use of Swarm Intelligence for solving several kinds of problems has attracted an increasing attention of the AI community [2,3]. It is an approach that studies the emergence of collective intelligence in groups of simple agents, and emphasizes the flexibility, robustness, distributedness, autonomy and direct or indirect interactions among agents.

The most common Swarm Methods are based on the observation of ant colonies behavior. In these methods, a set of simple agents, called ants, cooperate to find good solutions to combinatorial optimization problems. As a promising way of designing intelligent systems, researchers are applying this technique to solve problems such as: communication networks, combinatorial optimization, robotics, on-line learning to achieve robot coordination, adaptive task allocation and data clustering.

One possible manner of coordinating agent actions in a Multi Agent System is using the Ant-ViBRA system [1]. It is a Swarm Algorithm that combines the

F.J. Garijo, J.C. Riquelme, and M. Toro (Eds.): IBERAMIA 2002, LNAI 2527, pp. 575–584, 2002.

Reinforcement Learning (RL) approach with Heuristic Search to solve combinatorial optimization problems where interleaved actions need to be performed. The Ant-ViBRA is a modification of a well known Swarm Algorithm – the Ant Colony System (ACS) Algorithm [6] – which was adapted to cope with planning when several agents are involved.

In order to better evaluate the results of the Ant-ViBRA system, this work compares the system performance with the ones obtained using a Distributed Q-learning (DQL) algorithm proposed by [7] and the Q-learning algorithm [8].

The domain in which this comparison is made is that of a manipulator performing visually guided *pick-and-place* tasks in an assembly cell. The system optimization goal is to minimize the execution time by reducing the number of movements made by the robotic manipulator, adapting in a timely fashion to new domain configurations.

The remainder of this paper is organized as follows. Section 2 describes the pick-and-place task domain used in this work. Section 3, 4, and 5 present the Q-Learning, the Distributed Q-Learning, and the Ant-ViBRA algorithm, respectively. Section 6 presents the experimental setup, the experiments performed in the simulated domain, and the results obtained. Finally, Section 7 summarizes some important points learned from this research and outlines future work.

2   The Application Domain

The pick-and-place domain can be characterized as a complex planning task, where agents have to generate and execute plans, to coordinate its activities to achieve a common goal, and to perform online resource allocation. The difficulty in the execution of the pick-and-place task rests on possessing adequate image processing and understanding capabilities and appropriately dealing with interruptions and human interactions with the configuration of the work table. This domain has been the subject of previous work [4,5] in a flexible assembly cell.

In the pick-and-place task, given a number of parts arriving on the table (from a conveyor belt, for example), the goal is to select pieces from the table, clean and pack them. The pieces can have sharp edges as molded metal or plastic objects usually presents during their manufacturing process. To clean a piece means to remove these unwanted edges or other objects that obstruct packing. In this way, there is no need to clean all pieces before packing them, but only the ones that will be packed and are not clean. In this work, pieces to be packed (and eventually cleaned) are named tenons and the desired place to pack (and eventually clean) are called mortises.

While the main task is being executed, unexpected human interactions can happen. A human can change the table configuration by adding (or removing) new parts to it. In order to avoid collisions, both the cleaning and packing tasks can have their execution interrupted until the work area is free of collision contingencies.

The pick-and-place domain is a typical case of a task that can be decomposed into a set of independent tasks: packing (if a tenon on the table is clean, pick it up with the manipulator and put it on a free mortise); cleaning (if a tenon or mortise have sharp edges, clean it before packing) and collision avoidance.

One of the problems to be solved when a task is decomposed into several tasks is how to coordinate the task execution. Since collision avoidance is an extremely reactive task, its precedence over cleaning and assembly tasks is preserved. This way, only interactions among packing and cleaning are considered. The packing subtask is performed by a sequence of two actions – *Pick-Up* followed by *Put-Down* – and the cleaning subtask applies the action *Clean*. Actions and relations among them are:

- *Pick-Up*: to pick up a tenon. After this operation only the *Put-Down* operation can be used.
- *Put-Down*: to put down a tenon over a free mortise. In the domain, the manipulator never puts down a piece in a place that is not a free mortise. After this operation both *Pick-Up* and *Clean* can be used.
- *Clean*: to clean a tenon or a mortise, removing unwanted material to the trash can and maintaining the manipulator stopped over it. After this operation both *Pick-Up* and *Clean* can be used.

The coordination problem of the task execution, given a certain table configuration in the pick-and-place domain, becomes a routing problem that can be modeled as a combinatorial TSP Problem, since the goal here consists in minimize the total amount of displacement performed by the manipulator during the task execution. We have used three different reinforcement learning algorithms to learn the agent coordination policy that minimizes the routing problem for a given table configuration: Q-Learning, DQL and Ant-ViBRA. These algorithms are discussed in the next sections.

3   Q-Learning

Reinforcement Learning (RL) algorithms have been applied successfully to the on-line learning of optimal control policies in Markov Decision Processes (MDPs). In RL, learning is carried out on-line, through trial-and-error interactions of the agent with the environment. On each interaction step the agent senses the current state s of the environment, and chooses an action a to perform. The action a alters the state s of the environment, and a scalar reinforcement signal r (a reward or penalty) is provided to the agent to indicate the desirability of the resulting state.

The task of an RL agent is to learn a policy $\pi : S \rightarrow A$ that maps the current state s into the desirable action a to be performed in s. One strategy to learn the optimal policy π^* is to allow the agent to learn the evaluation function $Q : S \times A \rightarrow \mathcal{R}$. Each $Q(s, a)$ value represents the expected cost incurred by the agent when taking action a at state s and following an optimal policy thereafter.

The Q-learning algorithm [8] iteratively approximates Q, provided the system can be modeled as an MDP, the reinforcement function is bounded, and actions are chosen so that every state-action pair is visited an infinite number of times. The Q learning rule is:

$$Q(s,a) \leftarrow Q(s,a) + \alpha[r(s,a) + \gamma \max_{a'} Q(s',a') - Q(s,a)] \tag{1}$$

where: s is the current state, a is the action performed in s, $r(s,a)$ is the reinforcement received after performing a in s, s' is the new state, γ is a discount factor $(0 \leq \gamma < 1)$, and α is the learning rate $(\alpha > 0)$.

4   Distributed Q-Learning

A recent Distributed Reinforcement Learning algorithm is the Distributed Q-learning algorithm (DQL), proposed by Mariano and Morales [7]. It is a generalization of the traditional Q-learning algorithm described in the previous section where, instead of a single agent, several independent agents are used to learn a single policy.

In DQL, all the agents have a temporary copy of the state-action pair evaluation functions of the environment, which is used to decide which action to perform and that are updated according to the Q-Learning update rule.

These agents explore different options in a common environment and when all agents have completed a solution, their solutions are evaluated and the best one receives a reward. The DQL algorithm is presented in table 1.

Table 1. The general DQL algorithm [7].

Initialize $Q(s,a)$ arbitrarily
Repeat (for n episodes)
    Repeat (for m agents)
        Initialize s, copy $Q(s,a)$ to $Qc^m(s,a)$
        Repeat (for each step of the episode)
            Take action a, observe r, s'
            $Qc^m(s,a) \leftarrow Qc^m(s,a) + \alpha[\gamma \max_{a'} Qc^m(s',a') - Qc^m(s,a)]$
            $s \leftarrow s'$
        Until s is terminal
    Evaluate the m solutions
    Assign reward to the best solution found
    $Q(s,a) \leftarrow Q(s,a) + \alpha[r + \gamma \max_{a'} Q(s',a') - Q(s,a)]$

---

5   Ant-ViBRA

Ant-ViBRA is a modification of the ACS algorithm in order to cope with different sub-tasks, and to plan the route that minimizes the total amount of displacement performed by the manipulator during its movements to execute the pick-and-place task.

5.1   The ACS Algorithm

The ACS Algorithm is a Swarm Intelligence algorithm proposed by Dorigo and Gambardella [6] for combinatorial optimization based on the observation of ant colonies behavior. It has been applied to various combinatorial optimization problems like the symmetric and asymmetric traveling salesman problems (TSP and ATSP respectively), and the quadratic assignment problem. The ACS can be interpreted as a particular kind of distributed RL technique, in particular a distributed approach applied to Q-learning [8]. In the remaining of this section TSP is used to describe the algorithm.

The ACS represents the usefullness of moving to the city s when in city r in the $\tau(r, s)$, called *pheromone*, which is a positive real value associated to the edge (r, s) in a graph. It is the ACS counterpart of Q-learning Q-values. There is also a *heuristic* $\eta(r, s)$ associated to edge (r, s). It represents an heuristic evaluation of which moves are better. In the TSP $\eta(r, s)$ is the inverse of the distance δ from r to s, $\delta(r, s)$.

An agent k positioned in the city r moves to city s using the following rule, called state transition rule [6]:

$$s = \begin{cases} \arg\max_{u \in J_k(r)} \tau(r, u) \cdot \eta(r, u)^\beta & \text{if } q \leq q_0 \\ S & \text{otherwise} \end{cases} \tag{2}$$

where:

- β is a parameter which weighs the relative importance of the learned pheromone and the heuristic distance values ($\beta > 0$).
- $J_k(r)$ is the list of cities still to be visited by the ant k, where r is the current city. This list is used to constrain agents to visit cities only once.
- q is a value chosen randomly with uniform probability in [0,1] and q_0 ($0 \leq q_0 \leq 1$) is a parameter that defines the exploitation/exploration rate: the higher q_0 the smaller the probability to make a random choice.
- S is a random variable selected according to a probability distribution given by:

$$p_k(r, s) = \begin{cases} \dfrac{[\tau(r, u)] \cdot [\eta(r, u)]^\beta}{\sum_{u \in J_k(r)} [\tau(r, u)] \cdot [\eta(r, u)]^\beta} & \text{if } s \in J_k(r) \\ 0 & \text{otherwise} \end{cases} \tag{3}$$

This transition rule is meant to favor transition using edges with a large amount of pheromone and which are short.

Ants in ACS update the values of $\tau(r, s)$ in two situations: the local update step (applied when ants visit edges) and the global update step (applied when ants complete the tour).

The ACS local updating rule is:

$$\tau(r, s) \leftarrow (1 - \rho) \cdot \tau(r, s) + \rho \cdot \Delta\tau(r, s) \tag{4}$$

where: $0 < \rho < 1$ is a parameter (the learning step), and $\Delta\tau(r, s) = \gamma \cdot \max_{z \in J_k(s)} \tau(s, z)$.

The ACS global update rule is:

$$\tau(r, s) \leftarrow (1 - \alpha) \cdot \tau(r, s) + \alpha \cdot \Delta\tau(r, s) \tag{5}$$

where: α is the pheromone decay parameter (similar to the discount factor in Q-Learning), and $\Delta\tau(r, s)$ is a delayed reinforcement, usually the inverse of the length of the best tour. The delayed reinforcement is given only to the tour done by the best agent – only the edges belonging to the best tour will receive more pheromones (reinforcement).

The pheromone updating formulas intends to place a greater amount of pheromone on the shortest tours, achieving this by simulating the addition of new pheromone deposited by ants and evaporation. The ACS algorithm is presented in table 2.

Table 2. The ACS algorithm (in the TSP Problem).

Initialize the pheromone table, the ants and the list of cities.
Repeat (for n episodes) /* an Ant Colony iteration */
    Repeat (for m ants) /* an ant iteration */
        Put each ant at a starting city.
        Repeat (for each step of the episode)
            Chose next city using equation (2).
            Update list J_k of yet to be visited cities for ant k.
            Apply local update to pheromones using equation (4).
        Until (ants have a complete tour).
    Apply global pheromone update using equation (5).

5.2 The Ant-ViBRA Algorithm

To be able to cope with a combinatorial optimization problem where interleaved execution is needed, the ACS algorithm was modified by introducing: (i) several pheromone tables, one for each operation that the system can perform, and; (ii) an extended $J_k(s, a)$ list, corresponding to the pair state/action that can be applied in the next transition.

A priori domain knowledge is intensively used in order to decompose the pick-and-place problem into subtasks, and to define possible interactions among subtasks. Subtasks are related to pick-and-place actions (*Pick-Up*, *Put-Down* and *Clean* – see section 2), which can only be applied to different (disjunct) sets of states of the domain.

The use of knowledge about the conditions under which every action can be applied reduces the learning time, since it makes explicit which part of the state space must be analyzed before performing a state transition.

In Ant-ViBRA the pheromone value space is decomposed into three subspaces, each one related to an action, reducing the search space. The pheromone space is discretized in "actual position" (of the manipulator) and "next position" for each action. The assembly workspace configuration perceived by the vision system defines the position of all objects and also the dimensions of the pheromone tables.

The pheromone table corresponding to the *Pick-Up* action has entries "actual position" corresponding to the position of the trash can and of all the mortises, and entries "next position" corresponding to the position of all tenons. This means that to perform a pick-up, the manipulator is initially over a mortise (or the trash can) and will pick up a tenon in another place of the workspace.

In a similar way, the pheromone table corresponding to the *Put-Down* action has entries "actual position" corresponding to the position of the tenons and entries "next position" corresponding to the position of all the mortises. The pheromone table corresponding to the *Clean* action has entries "actual position" corresponding to the position of the trash can and of all the mortises, and entries "next position" corresponding to the position of all tenons and all mortises.

The $J_k(s, a)$ list is an extension of the $J_k(r)$ list described in the ACS. The difference is that the ACS $J_k(r)$ list was used to record the cities to be visited, assuming that the only action possible was to move from city r to one of the cities in the list.

To be able to deal with several actions, the $J_k(s, a)$ list records pairs (*state/actions*), which represent possible actions to be performed at each state. The Ant-ViBRA algorithm introduces the following modifications to the ACS algorithm:

- Initialization takes care of several pheromone tables, the ants and the $J_k(s, a)$ list of possible actions to be performed at every state.
- Instead of directly choosing the next state by using the state transition rule (equation 2), the next state is chosen among the possible operations, using the $J_k(s, a)$ list and equation (2).
- The local update is applied to pheromone table of the executed operation.
- When cleaning operations are performed the computation of the distance δ takes into account the distance from the actual position of the manipulator to the tenon or mortise to be cleaned, added by the distance to the trash can.
- At each iteration the list $J_K(s, a)$ is updated, pairs of (*state/actions*) already performed are removed, and new possible pairs (*state/actions*) are added.

The next section presents experiments of the implemented system, and results where the performance of Ant-ViBRA, DQL and Q-learning are compared.

6   Experimental Description and Results

Ant-ViBRA was tested in a simulated domain, which is represented by a discrete 10x10 workspace where each cell in this grid presents one of the following six configurations: one tenon, one mortise, only trash, one tenon with trash on it, one mortise with trash on it, one tenon packed on one mortise, or a free cell.

Experiments were performed considering different configurations of the workspace, learning successfully action policies in each experiment under the assembly task domain. In order to illustrate the results we present three examples. In all of them, the goal is to find a sequence in which assembly actions should be performed in order to minimize the distance traveled by the manipulator grip during the execution of the assembly task. One iteration finishes when there is no more piece left to be packed, and the learning process stops when the result becomes stable or a maximum number of iterations is reached. All three algorithms implemented *a priori* domain knowledge about the position of the pieces in order to reduce the state space representation, reducing the search space.

In the first example (figure 1) there are initially 4 pieces and 4 tenons on the border of a 10x10 grid. Since there is no trash, the operations that can be performed are to pick up a tenon or put it down over a mortise. The initial (and final) position of the manipulator is over the tenon located at (1,1).

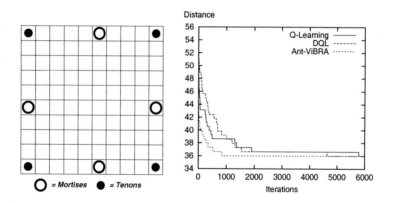

Fig. 1. Configuration of example 1 (left) and its results (right).

In this example, the average of 25 episodes of the Ant-ViBRA algorithm took 844 iterations to converge to the optimal solution, which is 36 (the total distance between pieces and tenons). The same problem took 4641 steps in average to achieve the same result using the Distributed Q-learning and 5787 steps using the Q-learning algorithm. This shows that the combination of both reinforcement learning and heuristics yields good results.

The second example (figure 2) is similar to the first one, but now there are 8 tenons and 8 mortises spread in a random disposition on the grid. The initial position of the manipulator is over the tenon located at (10,1). The result (see figure 2-right) is also better than that performed by both the DQL and the Q-learning algorithm.

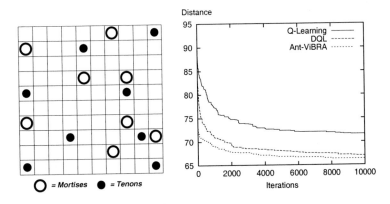

Fig. 2. Configuration of example 2 (left) and its results (right).

Finally, example 3 (figure 3) presents a configuration where the system must clean some pieces before performing the packing task. The tenons and mortises are on the same position as example 1, but there are trashes that must be removed over the tenon in the position (1, 10) and over the mortise (6, 1). The initial position of the manipulator is over the tenon located at (1,1). The operations are pick up, put down and clean. The clean action moves the manipulator over the position to be cleaned, picks the undesired object and puts it on the trash can, located at position (1, 11). Again, we can see in the result shown in figure 4-right that the Ant-ViBRA presents better results.

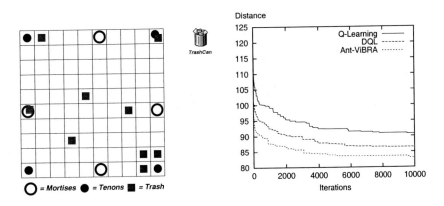

Fig. 3. Configuration of example 3 (left) and its results (right).

In the 3 examples above the parameters used were the same: exploitation/exploration rate is 0.9, the discount factor γ is set at 0.3, the maximum number of iterations allowed was set to 10000 and the results are the average of

25 episodes. For both the Q-learning and the DQL, the learning rate α is set at 0.1. In a similar way, the learning step ρ is set at 0.1 for the Ant-ViBRA. The experiments were implemented on a AMD K6-II-500MHz, with 256 MB RAM memory, using Linux and GNU gcc.

7   Conclusion

The experiments carried out show that the Ant-ViBRA algorithm was able to minimize the task execution time (or the total distance traveled by the manipulator) in several configurations of the pick-and-place workspace. Besides that, the learning time of the Ant-ViBRA was also small when compared to the Distributed Q-Learning and Q-Learning techniques.

Future works include the implementation of an extension of the Ant-ViBRA algorithm in a system to control teams of mobile robots performing foraging tasks, and the exploration of new forms of composing the experience of each agent to update the pheromone table after each iteration.

Acknowledgements. This research was conducted under the NSF/CNPq-ProTeM CC Project MAPPEL (grant no. 68003399-8) and FAPESP Project AACROM (grant no. 2001/14588-2).

References

[1] R. A. C. Bianchi and A. H. R. Costa. Ant-vibra: a swarm intelligence approach to learn task coordination. *Lecture Notes in Artificial Intelligence - XVI Brazilian Symposium on Artificial Intelligence – SBIA'02*, 2002.

[2] E. Bonabeau, M. Dorigo, and G. Theraulaz. *Swarm Intelligence: From Natural to Artificial Systems*. Oxford University Press, New York, 1999.

[3] E. Bonabeau, M. Dorigo, and G. Theraulaz. Inspiration for optimization from social insect behaviour. *Nature 406 [6791]*, 2000.

[4] A. H. R. Costa, L. N. Barros, and R. A. C. Bianchi. Integrating purposive vision with deliberative and reactive planning: An engineering support on robotics applications. *Journal of the Brazilian Computer Society*, 4(3):52–60, April 1998.

[5] A. H. R. Costa and R. A. C. Bianchi. L-vibra: Learning in the vibra architecture. *Lecture Notes in Artificial Intelligence*, 1952:280–289, 2000.

[6] M. Dorigo and L. M. Gambardella. Ant colony system: A cooperative learning approach to the traveling salesman problem. *IEEE Transactions on Evolutionary Computation*, 1(1), 1997.

[7] C. Mariano and E. Morales. A new distributed reinforcement learning algorithm for multiple objective optimization problems. *Lecture Notes in Artificial Intelligence*, 1952:290–299, 2000.

[8] C. J. C. H. Watkins. *Learning from Delayed Rewards*. PhD Thesis, University of Cambridge, 1989.

Empowered Situations of Autonomous Agents

Fabiola López y López and Michael Luck

Department of Electronics and Computer Science
University of Southampton. Southampton, SO17 1BJ, UK
{flyl00r,mml}@ecs.soton.ac.uk

Abstract. Identifying situations in which power exists is an ability that agents can exploit when they must interact with one another. In particular, agents can take advantage of empowered situations to make other agents satisfy their goals. The aim of this paper is to identify situations in which power might exist through the roles agents play in a society as well as the powers that emerge from their own capabilities. However, unlike other models in which power is eternal and absolute, in our model power is always considered as being *dynamic*.

1 Introduction

Identifying situations in which power exists is an ability that agents can exploit when they need to interact with one another. In particular, agents can take advantage of empowered situations to make other agents satisfy their goals. That is, one of the advantages for agents in a society is that they can overcome their limited capabilities by using the capabilities of others and, in this way, satisfy goals that might otherwise not be achieved. However, given that agents are autonomous, the benevolent adoption of goals cannot be taken for granted since agents can choose not to adopt them [15], and therefore a mechanism to influence them must be used. One effective means of doing this is by using the power that some agents have not only due to their own capabilities [4], but also by being in particular situations in the society where they exist.

According to Ott [18], *power* can be defined as the latent ability to *influence* the actions, thoughts or emotions of others and, consequently, it is the potential to get people to do things the way you want them done. Translating these concepts to the context of agents, we can say that powers are expressed through an agent's capabilities to change the beliefs, the motivations, and the goals of others. However, power exists only if the other agents allow being influenced. That is, power involves a bilateral relationship between two agents, the one who exerts the power and the one on whom the power is exerted [9]. What is important to understand now is both where the power of agents comes from and why some agents become influenced.

Towards this end, the main objective of this paper is to analyse the situations in which power can be identified, whereas situations in which agents are influenced are left for future work. Unlike other models in which power is eternal and absolute, in our model power is always considered as being *dynamic*. That is, powers appearing in a particular situation might not exist in another, and they cannot be exerted over all agents, but a particular subset of agents. In addition, our model always considers powers of agents as being related to the goals of target agents (i.e. those to be influenced). We start our

F.J. Garijo, J.C. Riquelme, and M. Toro (Eds.): IBERAMIA 2002, LNAI 2527, pp. 585–595, 2002.

discussion by defining autonomous agents and norms in Section 2. After that, powers existing in a society are described in Section 3, whereas powers that are result of agents' capabilities are discussed in Section 4. Finally, both conclusions and future work are presented.

2   Agents and Norms

In this section, we describe the basic blocks from which to build up our theory of power relationships, and which underpin several aspects not included in this paper, but described elsewhere [14,16]. In particular, we adopt the SMART *agent framework* described in [8] and, in what follows, we use the Z specification language to construct a formal model. Z is based on set-theory and first order logic, with details available in [21]. For brevity, however, we will not elaborate the use of Z further.

In the SMART *agent framework*, an *attribute* represents a perceivable feature of the agent's environment, which can be represented as a predicate or its negation. Then, a particular *state* in the environment is described by a set of attributes, *actions* are discrete events that change the state of the environment when performed, a *goal* represents situations that an agent wishes to bring about, and *motivations* are desires or preferences that affect the outcome of the reasoning intended to satisfy an agent's goals. For the purposes of this paper, we formally describe environmental states, actions and goals. Details of the remaining elements are not needed, so we consider them as given sets.

$$[Attribute, Motivation]$$

$$EnvState == \mathbb{P}_1 \, Attribute; \qquad Action == EnvState \rightarrow EnvState$$
$$Goal == \mathbb{P}_1 \, Attribute$$

In addition, an *entity* is described by a non-empty set of attributes representing its permanent features, a set of goals that it wants to bring about, a set of capabilities that it is able to perform, and a set of motivations representing its preferences. Moreover, *agents* are entities whose set of goals is not empty, and *autonomous agents* are agents with non-empty sets of motivations. By omitting irrelevant details, we formalise them as follows.

$$
\begin{array}{|l}
\hline
\;Agent \underline{\hspace{8cm}} \\
\;\; capabilities : \mathbb{P} \, Action; \; goals : \mathbb{P} \, Goal \\
\;\; motivations : \mathbb{P} \, Motivation; \; beliefs : \mathbb{P}_1 \, Attribute \\
\hline
\;\; goals \neq \varnothing \\
\hline
\end{array}
$$

$$AutonomousAgent \mathrel{\widehat{=}} [Agent \mid motivations \neq \varnothing]$$

An agent may have access to certain norms, which are represented as data structures relating to social rules. *Norms* are mechanisms within a society that influence the behaviour of agents within it; they can be characterised by observing several different aspects. First, norms must be complied with by a set of *addressee* agents in order to *benefit* another set of agents (possibly empty). They specify what ought to be done and, consequently, they include *normative goals* that must be satisfied by addressees. Sometimes, these normative goals must be directly intended, whereas other times their role is to inhibit specific goals (as in the case of prohibitions). Second, norms are not always applicable, and their activation depends on the *context*; there may be *exceptions* when agents are not obliged to comply with the norm. Finally, in some cases, norms suggest the existence of a set of *sanctions* or *punishments* to be imposed when addressees do not satisfy the normative goal, and a set of *rewards* to be received when they do. Thus, the general structure of a norm can be formalised as follows.

$$
\begin{array}{|l}
\hline
\;\_\_\, Norm \,_____ \\
\; addressees, beneficiaries : \mathbb{P}\ Agent \\
\; context, exceptions : EnvState \\
\; normativegoals, rewards, punishments : \mathbb{P}\ Goal \\
\hline
\; addressees \neq \varnothing \wedge context \neq \varnothing \\
\hline
\end{array}
$$

Now, in order to know if a norm has been fulfilled, the satisfaction of its associated normative goals must be verified. This is true if the normative goals are a *logical consequence* of the current environmental state. This is formalised as follows.

$$
\begin{array}{|l}
\; logicalconsequence\_ : \mathbb{P}(EnvState \times EnvState) \\
\; fulfilled\_ : \mathbb{P}(Norm \times EnvState) \\
\hline
\; \forall n : Norm;\ st : EnvState \bullet \\
\; fulfilled\ (n, st) \Leftrightarrow (\forall g \in n.normativegoals \bullet logicalconsequence\ (st, g)) \\
\end{array}
$$

Moreover, a *normative agent* is an autonomous agent whose behaviour is shaped by the obligations it must comply with, prohibitions that limit the kind of goals that it can pursue, social commitments that have been created during its social life and social codes which may not carry punishments, but whose fulfillment could represent social satisfaction for the agent. All these responsibilities are represented by norms.

$$
\begin{array}{|l}
\;\_\_\, NormativeAgent \,_____ \\
\; AutonomousAgent \\
\; norms : \mathbb{P}\ Norm \\
\hline
\end{array}
$$

Sometimes, it is useful to observe norms not through the normative goals that ought to be achieved, but through the actions that can lead to the satisfaction of such goals. Then we can talk about actions that are either *permitted* or *forbidden* by a norm as follows. If there is a state that activates a norm, and the results of a particular action benefit the achievement of the associated normative goals, then such an action is *permitted* by the respective norm. Similarly, *forbidden* actions are those leading to a situation that contradicts or hinders normative goals. In general, it is not trivial to observe how the results of an action might benefit or hinder the achievement of normative goals, but to avoid drilling down into the intricate details of this, the associations between situation states that might either *benefit* or *hinder* goals are taken for granted. Moreover, we define two relations that hold among an action and a norm, which either permit or forbid it, as follows.

$$benefits\_, hinders\_ : \mathbb{P}(EnvState \times Goal)$$
$$permitted\_, forbidden\_ : \mathbb{P}(Action \times Norm)$$

$$\forall a : Action;\ n : Norm;\ \bullet$$
$$permitted\,(a, n) \Leftrightarrow (\exists g : n.normativegoals \bullet benefits\,(a\ n.context, g)) \land$$
$$forbidden\,(a, n) \Leftrightarrow (\exists g : n.normativegoals \bullet hinders\,(a\ n.context, g))$$

In other words, if an action is applied in the context of a norm, and the results of this action benefit the normative goals, then the action is permitted, otherwise the action is forbidden.

3   Institutional Powers

It is generally accepted that social structures define power relationships derived from the roles agents play in a norm-based system. In such systems there exist norms that entitle some agents to direct the behaviour of others. Therefore, as long as an agent wants to belong to such a system, it must recognise the power, and therefore the authority, of certain agents. We call these kinds of powers *institutional powers*, a term that we borrow from [11], and before analysing them we define a *normative multi agent system* as a set of normative agents controlled by a common set of norms (a better description can be found in [12]). In such systems four types of norms can be identified, namely, norms directed at controlling all agents(*normsNMAS*), norms directed at enforcing compliance with norms by applying punishments(*enforcenorms*), norms directed at encouraging compliance with norms by giving rewards (*rewardnorms*), and norms issued to allow the creation of new norms (*legislationnorms*). To effectively represent their function, the structure of the three last sets of norms is constrained as follows. First, enforcement norms are activated when a norm is not fulfilled in order to punish its offenders. By contrast, reward norms are activated when a norm is fulfilled, and their normative goals are aimed at rewarding compliant agents. Finally, legislation norms allow some agents to issue new norms. These constraints are represented in the relationships below.

$$enforce\_, reward\_ : \mathbb{P}(Norm \times Norm)$$
$$legislate\_ : \mathbb{P}\ Norm$$

$$\forall n_1, n_2 : Norm \bullet$$
$$enforce\,(n_1, n_2) \Leftrightarrow (\neg\ fulfilled(n_2, n_1.context) \land$$
$$n_2.punishments \subseteq n_1.normativegoals) \land$$
$$reward\,(n_1, n_2) \Leftrightarrow (fulfilled(n_2, n_1.context) \land$$
$$n_2.rewards \subseteq n_1.normativegoals) \land$$
$$legislate\,(n_1) \Leftrightarrow (\exists\ issuingnorms : Action \bullet permitted\,(issuingnorms, n_1))$$

Now, a normative multi-agent system is formally defined in the schema below. The first predicate states that all members must have adopted some of the norms of the system, the second makes explicit that addressees of norms must be members of the system, and the last predicates represent the constraints on each different set of norms.

```
┌─ NormativeMAS ──────────────────────────────────────────────
│ members : ℙ NormativeAgent
│ normsNMAS, enforcenorms : ℙ Norm
│ rewardnorms, legislationnorms : ℙ Norm
├──────────────────────────────────────────────────────────────
│ ∀ ag : members • ag.norms ∩ normsNMAS ≠ ∅
│ ∀ rg : normsNMAS • rg.addressees ⊆ members
│ ∀ en : enforcenorms • (∃ n : normsNMAS • enforce (en, n))
│ ∀ rn : rewardnorms • (∃ n : normsNMAS • reward (rn, n))
│ ∀ ln : legislationnorms • legislate (ln)
└──────────────────────────────────────────────────────────────
```

As we can observe, norms are in fact the way to *empower* agents by entitling them to punish, reward or legislate in a normative multi-agent system. In summary, it can be said that *institutional* powers are predetermined by norms that entitle agents to demand other agents to behave in a certain way. However we admit that those norms can change, and therefore these powers might disappear. At least four types of institutional powers in a norm-based system can be found: power to issue new norms, power to punish offenders of norms, powers to claim a reward, and powers to claim benefits from a norm.

Legal Power. This is the kind of power that legislators, as addressees of a legislation norm, have because they are entitled to issue new orders for the members of a normative multi-agent system. For instance, when the manager of a factory gives orders to workers under his control, we can observe that he is exerting the power acquired by the role he plays in the factory. Here, workers accept the manager's orders because they recognise his authority and therefore his power in the social structure. This kind of power is formally defined in the schema below, which states that an agent has *legal* power over another if the first is a legislator in the same normative system. Due to type compatibility, first a function to cast a normative agent as an agent is introduced.

```
│ theagent : NormativeAgent → Agent
│ legalpower_ : ℙ(NormativeAgent × NormativeAgent × NormativeMAS)
├──────────────────────────────────────────────────────────────
│ ∀ ag₁, ag₂ : NormativeAgent; nmas : NormativeMAS •
│   legalpower (ag₁, ag₂, nmas) ⇔ ((ag₂ ∈ nmas.members) ∧
│     (∃ ln : nmas.legislationnorms • theagent ag₁ ∈ ln.addressees))
```

Legal Coercive Power. It can be said that in a normative multi agent system, an agent has *legal coercive* power over another, if the first is legally allowed, through an *enforcement* norm, to punish the second when it fails to comply with a norm. Enforcement norms avoid the situation in which other agents coerce their peers. For instance, in a factory, only managers are entitled (by norms) to fire their workers, no worker can do so.

$$
\begin{array}{|l}
\hline
legalcoercivepower\_ : \mathbb{P}(NormativeAgent \times NormativeAgent \times Norm \\
\quad \times NormativeMAS) \\
\hline
\forall\, ag_1, ag_2 : NormativeAgent;\ n : Norm;\ nmas : NormativeMAS \bullet \\
legalcoercivepower\,(ag_1, ag_2, n, nmas) \Leftrightarrow ((n \in nmas.normsNMAS) \wedge \\
\quad (ag_2 \in nmas.members) \wedge (theagent\ ag_2 \in n.addressees) \wedge \\
\quad (\exists\, en : nmas.enforcenorms \bullet \\
\qquad ((theagent\ ag_1 \in en.addressees) \wedge enforce(en, n)))) \\
\end{array}
$$

Legal Reward Power. Once an agent complies with its responsibilities, it acquire the power to claim the reward offered. In fact, this is considered a right of the agent who satisfied a norm, and it becomes an obligation of the responsible agent for providing rewards.

$$
\begin{array}{|l}
\hline
legalrewardpower\_ : \mathbb{P}(NormativeAgent \times NormativeAgent \times Norm \\
\quad \times NormativeMAS \times EnvState) \\
\hline
\forall\, ag_1, ag_2 : NormativeAgent;\ n : Norm; \\
\quad nmas : NormativeMAS;\ st : EnvState \bullet \\
legalrewardpower\,(ag_1, ag_2, n, nmas, st) \Leftrightarrow (n \in nmas.normsNMAS \wedge \\
\quad (ag_1 \in nmas.members) \wedge (theagent\ ag_1 \in n.addressees) \wedge \\
\quad fulfilled\,(n, st) \wedge (n.rewards \neq \varnothing) \wedge \\
\quad (\exists\, rn : nmas.rewardnorms \bullet \\
\qquad (theagent\ ag_2 \in rn.addressees \wedge reward\,(rn, n)))) \\
\end{array}
$$

Consequently, an agent has *reward* power over another, if the first has already fulfilled a norm for which the second agent is responsible (through a rewarded norm) for providing a reward.

Legal Benefit Power. Agents who are expecting to receive the benefits of a norm for which non-compliance might be penalised are also empowered agents, because they can achieve something by using other agents' abilities. The benefits are guaranteed through legal enforcement of fulfillment. In other words, an agent has *benefit* power over another, if there is a satisfied norm for which the first is a beneficiary, the second an addressee, and there exists someone entitled to punish non-compliance with the norm.

$$
\begin{array}{|l}
\hline
legalbenefitpower\_ : \mathbb{P}(NormativeAgent \times NormativeAgent \times Norm \\
\quad \times NormativeMAS) \\
\hline
\forall\, ag_1, ag_2 : NormativeAgent;\ n : Norm;\ nmas : NormativeMAS \bullet \\
legalbenefitpower\,(ag_1, ag_2, n, nmas) \Leftrightarrow ((n \in nmas.normsNMAS) \wedge \\
\quad (ag_1 \in nmas.members) \wedge (theagent\ ag_1 \in n.beneficiaries) \wedge \\
\quad (ag_2 \in nmas.members) \wedge (theagent\ ag_2 \in n.addressees) \wedge \\
\quad (\exists\, rn : nmas.rewardnorms \bullet reward\,(rn, n))) \\
\end{array}
$$

4   Personal Powers

There are also powers derived from an agent's capabilities on the one hand, and from the goals of target agents on the other. These powers have been studied extensively as part of *Social Power Theory*, and are known as *personal powers* [4,3]. However, such powers have been limited to powers due to dependence among agents. Our work extends such theory by identifying other kinds of powers that are also a result of an agent's abilities. That is, some agents can either facilitate or impede the satisfaction of other agent goals. On the one hand we know that agents are entities with abilities to act. However, these capabilities are limited and, consequently, they may need other agents to succeed in the achievement of their goals. On the other hand, there are also situations in which, although possessing the needed abilities, agents cannot satisfy their goals because other agents hinder them. Both cases can lead to the creation of power. However, contrary to the cases presented in Section 3 where powers are given by the norms of the society, personal powers are given for their capabilities to satisfy goals.

Knowing if an agent can either facilitate or impede the achievement of some goals requires the evaluation of many aspects. For example, we can evaluate an agent's capabilities, its experience, its availability in the current state (which in turn depends on its goals), and even the relationships that such an agent has with other agents. However, this is a complex topic that we prefer to discuss in future work. At this moment, we define, and specify it without developing it further, a relationship that holds between an agent, a goal, and a specific state of the system when the agent is able to satisfy that goal in such an state. After that, two basic forms of power are defined by using it.

$$satisfy_- : \mathbb{P}(Agent \times Goal \times EnvState)$$

Facilitation Power. It can be said that an agent has the power to *facilitate* the achievement of another agent's goal, if the first has the means to satisfy a goal which, in turn, benefits the goal of the second.

$$facilitationpower_- : \mathbb{P}(Agent \times Agent \times Goal \times EnvState)$$

$$\forall\, ag_1, ag_2 : Agent;\ g_2 : Goal;\ st : EnvState \bullet$$
$$facilitationpower\,(ag_1, ag_2, g_2, st) \Leftrightarrow ((g_2 \in ag_2.goals)\ \wedge$$
$$(\exists\, g_1 : Goal \bullet (satisfy\,(ag_1, g_1, st) \wedge benefits(g_1, g_2))))$$

Being able to facilitate the satisfaction of goals creates dependence relations between agents with the relevant abilities and those without them. Therefore, a dependence relationship can also be defined in terms of powers and their absence, as follows.

$$depend_- : \mathbb{P}(Agent \times Agent \times Goal \times EnvState)$$

$$\forall\, ag_1, ag_2 : Agent;\ g : Goal;\ st : EnvState \bullet$$
$$depend\,(ag_1, ag_2, g, st) \Leftrightarrow (g \in ag_1.goals \wedge$$
$$\neg\, satisfy\,(ag_1, g, st) \wedge satisfy\,(ag_2, g, st))$$

These relations are, in general terms, equivalent to those given by Castelfranchi and colleagues [2,4,17], and a better and detailed definition of powers and dependence in terms of an agent's plans and capabilities can be found elsewhere [7,13,20]. However, for the purpose of this paper our definitions seem to be sufficient.

Illegal Coercive Power: There are also agents whose abilities are not used to benefit the goals of some agents, but to impede or hinder them. In these cases, power is expressed by an agent's capabilities to directly threaten the goals of others agents in order to obtain what they want. We call this *illegal coercive* because there is no norm that entitled these agents to coerce the others. On the contrary, this kind of power is generally forbidden, which is why although some agents have this kind of power, they scarcely use it. Formally, we say that an agent has illegal coercive power over another if it can satisfy a goal that can hinder one of the goals of the second agent.

$$illegalcoercivepower\_ : \mathbb{P}(Agent \times Agent \times Goal \times EnvState)$$

$$\forall ag_1, ag_2 : Agent;\ g_2 : Goal;\ st : EnvState \bullet$$
$$illegalcoercivepower\ (ag_1, ag_2, g_2, st) \Leftrightarrow ((g_2 \in ag_2.goals) \wedge$$
$$(\exists\ g_1 : Goal \bullet (satisfy\ (ag_1, g_1, st) \wedge hinders(g_1, g_2))))$$

Now, we describe situations in which these basic forms of powers are either overcome or related to other kinds of powers.

Comrade Power. One of the things that makes small groups work is the friendship relations that are created among its members. In this case, agents have the power to require help from any of the *comrades* of the group. In general, members of this group, know that they can ask for help from the rest without objection. This represents benevolence towards a *specific group* of agents. For example, a group of friends helping each other as a way of being identified as members of what they consider a special group of agents. Note that the conditions to have this kind of power are that both agents belong to the same group of agents, and that the agent over whom the power is exerted is able to facilitate the required goal.

$$comradepower\_ : \mathbb{P}(Agent \times Agent \times Goal \times \mathbb{P}\ Agent \times EnvState)$$

$$\forall ag_1, ag_2 : Agent;\ g : Goal;\ ags : \mathbb{P}\ Agent;\ st : EnvState \bullet$$
$$comradepower\ (ag_1, ag_2, g, ags, st) \Leftrightarrow ((ag_1 \in ags) \wedge (ag_2 \in ags) \wedge$$
$$(facilitationpower\ (ag_2, ag_1, g, st)))$$

Reciprocation Power. Reciprocation with previous actions has been considered as one of the key aspects underlying society cohesion [10]. Agents who have worked in support of another's goals generally expect to receive some reciprocal benefits, even if not explicitly mentioned. This represents an ethical matter in which agents show their gratitude to others. Formally, we say that an agent has the power of being *reciprocated* by other agent, if it has already fulfilled a norm whose benefits were enjoyed by the second, and the second has the power to facilitate one of the goals of the first.

$$reciprocationpower\_ : \mathbb{P}(NormativeAgent \times NormativeAgent \\ \times Norm \times EnvState)$$

$$\forall\, ag_1, ag_2 : NormativeAgent;\ n : Norm;\ st : EnvState \bullet \\ reciprocationpower\ (ag_1, ag_2, n, st) \Leftrightarrow (fulfilled\ (n, st) \wedge \\ (theagent\ ag_1 \in n.addressees) \wedge (theagent\ ag_2 \in n.beneficiaries) \wedge \\ (\exists\, g : ag_1.goals \bullet facilitationpower\ (ag_2, ag_1, g, st)))$$

Note that in contrast with *legal reward* power (described in Section 3), here the considered norms are not necessarily *system* norms, and the goal of the reciprocation is neither part of an offered reward nor the other agent's responsibility.

Exchange Power. Castelfranchi et al. state that dependence makes a network of relationships that might be used by agents to influence each other [4,5]. Among all possible forms of dependence relationships, one is of particular interest: *reciprocal dependence* occurs when an agent depends on another to satisfy a goal and vice versa. In this particular situation, both agents acquire what is called *exchange power* [6], because both of them have the power to offer something to benefit the goals of the other. In this way, any of the agents can start a negotiation process that finishes with the creation of a social commitment in which each part of the deal receives what it wants.

$$exchangepower\_ : \mathbb{P}(Agent \times Goal \times Agent \times Goal \times EnvState)$$

$$\forall\, ag_1, ag_2 : Agent;\ g_1, g_2 : Goal;\ st : EnvState \bullet \\ exchangepower\ (ag_1, g_1, ag_2, g_2, st) \Leftrightarrow ((g_1 \in ag_1.goals) \wedge (g_2 \in ag_2.goals) \\ \wedge depend\ (ag_1, ag_2, g_1, st) \wedge depend\ (ag_2, ag_1, g_2, st))$$

Before finishing, we emphasise that *no powers are eternal*. In the case of institutional powers, the authorities of a system are recognised as long as agents consider themselves members which, much of the time, is due to some of their goals being satisfied simply by being there. However, sometimes agents evaluate their society, or compare it with other societies, in order to know what might be more convenient for the satisfaction of their goals. As a result of this evaluation, agents might emigrate to other societies and, consequently, the norms that until now have influenced them can be abandoned, and authorities could lose their legal power. Personal powers are relativised to a particular situation in which some agent goals are either helped or hindered. Therefore, what is true in one situation may not remain true if an agent's interests, and therefore its goals, change. For example, *exchange power* disappears if one of an agent's goals is no longer considered important. In addition, it can also be said that *there are no absolute powers*, and therefore every kind of power has its own limitations.

5   Conclusion

The main contribution of this paper is a classification of dynamic power relationships that some agents can use to make other agents satisfy their goals. In our work, both powers acquired through the roles agents play in a society and powers that emerge from their own

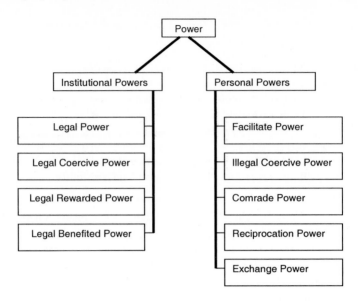

Fig. 1. Powers Taxonomy

capabilities are analysed (see Figure 1). We argue that agents must be able to recognise either their power, or their susceptibility to be influenced because power is, in some sense, only "in the mind". Agents that do not recognise these situations may not be influenced, but will suffer in the long term through less optimal interactions. In addition, if agents know where a situation of power comes from, the limits of such power can be established and therefore abusive situations can be avoided. For example, when a secretary gets a job, he is informed who is the boss, who has the power to control him and, consequently, the boss's orders are fulfilled. However, if he is unable to understand both where the boss's powers come from and where the boss's authority finishes, his submissiveness could be exploited by making him to do things beyond his own responsibilities. Clearly, there remain many questions to be answered. For example, issues relating to how this model impacts on the development or implementation of multi-agent systems have not been our main focus, but are important nonetheless.

Although our analysis builds on important work on power, dependence and norms [1,2,11,19], it goes beyond power due to dependence [4], or powers to legislate [11] in a society. In addition, in contrast to much work in which powers of agents are taken as absolute, our power situations have been relativised to both the society and the goals of agents. In the same way that power situations were identified in this paper, future work will be directed to analysing the conditions that enable agents to become influenced, and therefore willing to adopt both new norms and the goals of other agents.

Acknowledgments. The first author is supported by the Faculty Enhancement Program (PROMEP) of the Mexican Ministry of Public Education(SEP) and the Benemérita Universidad Autónoma de Puebla (México).

References

1. W. Balzer and R. Tuomela. Social institutions, norms and practices. In C. Dellarocas and R. Conte, editors, *Proceedings of the Workshop on Norms and Institutions in MAS at AGENTS'2000*, Barcelona, Spain, 2000.

2. C. Castelfranchi. Social power. A point missed in Multi-Agent, DAI and HCI. In Y. Demazeau and J. Müller, editors, *Decentralized A.I.*, pages 49–62. Elsevier Science Publishers, 1990.

3. C. Castelfranchi. All I understand about power (and something more). Technical report, ALFEBIITE Project, London, 2000.

4. C. Castelfranchi, M. Miceli, and A. Cesta. Dependence relations among autonomous agents. In E. Werner and Y. Demazeau, editors, *Decentralized A.I. 3*, pages 215–231. Elsevier Science Publishers, 1992.

5. R. Conte and C. Castelfranchi. Simulating multi-agent interdependencies. a two-way approach to the micro-macro link. In K. Troitzsch, U. Mueller, N. Gilbert, and J. E. Doran, editors, *Social Science Microsimulation*. Springer-Verlag, 1998.

6. K. Cook and M. Emerson. Power, equity and commitment in exchange network. *American Sociological Review*, 43(5):721–739, 1978.

7. M. d'Inverno and M. Luck. A formal view of social dependence networks. In C. Zhang and D. Lukose, editors, *Proceedings of the First Australian Workshop on DAI*, LNAI 1087, pages 115–129. Springer-Verlag, 1996.

8. M. d'Inverno and M. Luck. *Understanding Agent Systems*. Springer-Verlag, 2001.

9. J. French and B. Raven. The bases of social power. In D. P. Cartwright, editor, *Studies in Social Power*, pages 150–167. The University of Michigan, 1959.

10. A. Gouldner. The norm of reciprocity: A preliminar statement. *American Sociological Review*, 25(2):161–178, 1960.

11. A. Jones and M. Sergot. A formal characterisation of institutionalised power. *Journal of the IGPL*, 4(3):429–445, 1996.

12. F. López y López and M. Luck. Towards a model of the dynamics of normative multi-agent systems. In *Proceedings of the International Workshop on Regulated Agent-Based Social Systems: Theories and Applications (RASTA'02) at AAMAS'02*, pages 175–193, 2002.

13. F. López y López, M. Luck, and M. d'Inverno. A framework for norm-based inter-agent dependence. In *Proceedings of The Third Mexican International Conference on Computer Science*, pages 31–40. SMCC-INEGI, 2001.

14. F. López y López, M. Luck, and M. d'Inverno. Constraining autonomy through norms. In *Proceedings of The First International Joint Conference on Autonomous Agents and Multi Agent Systems AAMAS'02*, pages 674–681, 2002.

15. M. Luck and M. d'Inverno. Motivated behaviour for goal adoption. In C. Zhang and D. Lukose, editors, *Multi-Agents Systems. Theories Languages and Applications*, LNAI 1544, pages 58–73. Springer-Verlag, 1998.

16. M. Luck and M. d'Inverno. A conceptual framework for agent definition and development. *The Computer Journal*, 44(1):1–20, 2001.

17. M. Miceli, A. Cesta, and P. Rizzo. Distributed artifical intelligence from a socio-cognitive standpoint: Looking at reasons for interaction. *Artificial Intelligence and Society*, 9:287–320, 1996.

18. S. J. Ott. Power and influence. In S. J. Ott, editor, *Classic Readings in Organizational Behavior*, chapter V, pages 420–428. Brooks/Cole Publishing Company, USA, 1989.

19. A. Ross. *Directives and Norms*. Routledge and Kegan Paul Ltd., England, 1968.

20. J. Sichman, R. Conte, Y. Demazeau, and C. Castelfranchi. A social reasoning mechanism based on dependence networks. In A. Cohen, editor, *Proceedings of the 11th European Conference on Artificial Intelligence (ECAI94)*, pages 188–192. John Wiley & Sons, 1994.

21. J. M. Spivey. *The Z Notation: A Reference Manual*. Prentice Hall, 1992.

Distributed Agenda Management through Decentralised Vowels Co-ordination Approach

João L.T. da Silva* and Yves Demazeau**

Laboratoire LEIBNIZ-IMAG,
46, Avenue Felix Viallet
38031 Grenoble, France
{Joao-Luis.Tavares, Yves.Demazeau}@imag.fr

Abstract. This paper presents an application to a Distributed Agenda Management problem through a decentralised multi-agent co-ordination model. Each agent represents a user's personal agenda, which must to co-ordinate with other agendas in order to reach a joint commitment, such as a meeting scheduling, respecting user's privacy and local constraints. Constraints represent personal preferences and committed engagements that must be take into account during a search for a globally consistent schedule. The aim of this paper is to illustrate the application of the decentralised co-ordination model addressing distributed satisfaction constraints through negotiation, plan relations and social dependence.

1   Introduction

Advances in the Distributed Artificial Intelligence domain has provided the user with more flexible, dynamic and autonomous systems that are able to complex co-operation with each other. As a matter of fact, since distributed systems are spreading rapidly on the Internet the user needs more and more functionalities in order to manage heterogeneous and distributed knowledge. The Multi-Agent Systems (MAS) field has proposed techniques for co-ordination among artificial automated agents which provide those functionalities to real problems, as it has been reported in [1].

One of the applications that we are concerned with is of the Distributed Agenda Management domain. This application consists of multiple independent agents that represent an user's Agenda and that must co-ordinate themselves in order to solve a scheduling problem. This domain is open and highly dynamic since information such as meeting hours, user preferences or user priorities can change over time and even during the negotiation phase. Many works have addressed the problem of the distributed meeting scheduling [6,5,7,14,8] through Distributed Constraint Satisfaction Problem [18,17] or Distributed Resource Allocation [12] approaches.

---

* Suported by the CAPES/COFECUB, Brazil-France.
** CNRS Research Fellow, Grenoble, France.

F.J. Garijo, J.C. Riquelme, and M. Toro (Eds.): IBERAMIA 2002, LNAI 2527, pp. 596–605, 2002.

The purpose of our work is to specify a Distributed Agenda Manager where agents can manage calendar appointments and schedule meetings on behalf of user according its individual preferences and social dependencies, ruled by an organisational structure. The interest in take agenda management application through a decentralised multi-agent co-ordination approach lays on its natural distribution and the need for privacy of personal user information. For this matter, we provide a co-ordination model which is decentralised on the Vowels Paradigm and we illustrate a multi-agent specification for the agenda application under this approach.

2   The Vowels Co-ordination Model

Our decentralised co-ordination model is based on the Vowels paradigm, focusing particularly on plan relations and social dependence. The Vowels paradigm [4] describe a methodology to build multi-agent systems based on a componential principle to reason in terms of Agents, Environments, Interactions, Organisations and their dynamics as a core of a Multi-agent Oriented Programming approach.

This model is oriented to every component of a MAS, addressing some co-ordination approaches into an integrated way. At the Organisation level, we take Sichman's social reasoning mechanism [16] and we extend it to deal with planning techniques also at the Interaction level. The plan relations are borrowed from Martial's work [11] about co-ordination actions among planning agents. In this case, we have used potential plan relations at the Agent and Organisation levels through the extension of the DEPendence NETwork (DEPNET) from [16]. At the Environment level, we have associated a description of the activities, resources and world representation through a TÆMS-like approach [3]. In the next section, a short overview is presented about our research on the decentralised co-ordination model under Vowels methodology[1].

2.1   Co-ordination Requirement Dependencies

Our central claim is about relationships between plans, actions, goals, and specification of co-ordination dependencies. Dependence is defined through classes that describe co-ordination requirements concerning resource, goal, plan and action relationships. For instance, an action requirement could be related to *simultaneity constraints* (Mutex) or *producer/consumer conflicts*; with regards to co-ordination mechanisms, the former can be managed through scheduling techniques, while the latter is related to synchronisation.

In MAS, these dependencies account for multi-level constraints among multi-agent components: *personal constraints* at the Agent level; *situational constraints* at the Environment level; *relational constraints* at the Interaction level and *organisational constraints* at the Organisation level. We have proposed a co-ordination approach [2] that aims to decentralise the dynamic of MAS by splitting the control among MA components according their specifications and skills.

---

[1] A broader coverage of the model specification and description can be found in [2].

In our work, goal and plan requirements are deal with at the Agent level, while action and resource requirements are considered in the Environment component.

2.2   Co-ordination Model Description

(A)gent Level Co-ordination: at this level, a co-ordination problem is mainly concerned with plan synchronisation, action/resource dependencies, goal evaluation, and scheduling optimisation. We have taken into account *personal constraints* generated by the agent's internal reasoning, which is concerned with plan relationships and task dependencies. For our Agent level co-ordination, we have defined a hierarchical planning representation with additional description relationships, which extends to an internal representation approach in order to deal with social dependence [16].

   (E)nvironment Level Co-ordination: resource management and *situational constraints* at the level of tasks concerning multiple agents acting together are dealt with by the (E) component. To solve certain task and resource dependencies, we assume a relationship description at the task structure based on co-ordination mechanisms from Decker's GPGP approach [3]. Thus, methods to execute on the planning level take into account some relationships like *Enables, Facilitates, Cancel* and so on, which are represented into the task structure (local or global dependence network at the Organisation level). Resource relationships are taken as dependencies between plans as part of the action description that require these resources. Thus, co-ordination actions such as synchronisation can be triggered.

   (I)nteraction Level Co-ordination: this level is concerned with *relational constraints*, meaning multi-agent communication through message passing specification, protocol management, and negotiation requirements. In order to reach the negotiation requirements, we describe a set of plan relations based on co-ordination action taxonomy [11]. This leads us to the description of potential communication needs through an intersection procedure between the task structure (E) and the dependence network (O). Additionally, some constraints detected from these intersection operations may guide one in the choice of adequate protocols.

   (O)rganisation Level Co-ordination: the Organisation notion takes into account roles, relations between them and social dependence among agents [16]. A role is an abstraction of an agent behaviour which interacts with other roles. This behaviour is described through global goals and plans that play those roles in a MAS by using the same external description structure used into the agent model. At the social level, the roles interact with each other through relations and dependencies between them. These relations determine the existence of a link between two roles and the need for interaction between agents. Throughout this external description of other's skills and goals, we are able to cope with plan/action/resource relationships that embark on an implicit co-ordination by coalition formation through complementary needs between agents. Additionally, these coalitions will influence the local control at each multi-agent component in order to evaluate plan priorities and reschedule tasks.

3   Distributed Agenda Management

The Distributed Agenda Management approach, which we present in this paper, concerns temporal co-ordination and social dependence. We assume each Agenda as an autonomous agent acting for the service of a particular user. Hence, the main problem is to find out a local schedule as a result of a global consensus on distributed constraints among the agents. Constraints are defined through user preferences, internal task dependencies and external co-ordination requirements, such as time/resource availability and plan relationships.

Agenda agents can manage calendar appointments and schedule meetings on behalf of the user, according to its individual preferences and social dependencies ruled by an organisational structure. The Agenda agent must respect some privacy requirements of users and thus, reason with possibly incomplete information, which can be required only to meet some joint constraint. In the following section, we will specify the Distributed Agenda Management according to our multi-agent co-ordination model.

3.1   Vowels Specification

The problem lays on the classical domain of distributed constraint satisfaction and distributed resource allocation. Typically, the problem is the satisfaction of a common goal in a physical and/or temporal context, taking into account local constraints to meet a globally consistent solution. In this context, an agenda represents an user and takes into account his/her personal preferences in order to manage dependencies between local tasks and to satisfy distributed constraints during a meeting scheduling. We want to avoid exchanging all of his/her agenda information during the negotiation of an acceptable meeting for all the agents, so that a certain degree or privacy for the users can be guaranteed. For this matter, a decentralised approach is suitable because it allows a flexible local control, even though with more interactions, which lead us to take into account dependencies at the interaction level (negotiation and plan modification).

The agents (*hosts*) depend on one another (*attendees*) to accomplish their plan (*MeetingSchedule*), specifically with regard to a consistent schedule. There is a dependence between **A-O**, since the roles define some action/resource priorities. Between **A-I**, message deadlines and type of protocol define schedule optimisation. Dependencies between **O-E** are related to actions of certain roles, since some roles can have a distinct relationship with the environment (different action and perception patterns). For instance, a *host* can cancel meetings while *attendees* cannot. **A-E** dependence is represented through what actions to do and what about the resource status (calendar). An **(O-I)** dependence may respect the privacy information concerning some roles and constrain certain slot information in the message packet. A dependence between **I-E** assumes that in case of fault, **I** can inform **E** for cancel a calendar blocking action when a threshold to message confirmation has been reached.

3.2   Agenda-Agent Component Design

Into the (A) component we embark on meeting schedule heuristics and constraint management (personal user preferences and engagements already committed). Co-ordination among agents for meeting scheduling is defined in terms of dependencies computed through plan and resources modifications (time shifting and unavailable resources changing).

When the Agenda receives a goal from its user, a plan is chosen to satisfy this goal that relates plan dependencies and agent constraints to be satisfied. For instance, in a task/sub-task dependency, the task *ConfirmMeeting* depends on the environment relationship for the task *VerifyCalendar* in order to carry out the plan *ScheduleMeeting*. The agent infers that a situational constraint implements a co-ordination requirement and activates a distributed component that carries out such task at the Environment level.

As we claim in [2], agent goals are reached by associated plans which are composed by an ordered set of completed instantiated actions. Goals, such as *ScheduleMeeting* are represented by an AND hierarchy. Figure 1(a) shows that to achieve the *ScheduleMeeting* plan, the *VerifyCalendar* task must obtain a suitable time slot; the *ConfirmMeeting* task has to find out an agreement, and the *AppendMeeting* task may complete the schedule meeting requirements.

Desired appointments on user Agenda are described through a hierarchical planning approach in such way that agents start by exchange more abstract plans at a first negotiation level. If constraints are not solved, agents can proceed with the negotiation by refining only those abstract plans that have to be detailed. For instance, when an agent starts a negotiation cycle, it first blocks a time slot on the calendar. In the following, an *AppendMeeting* plan is engaged by the agent containing a *VerifyCalendar* task as showed at figure 1(a). The Calendar checks for available time slots and, if a temporal conflict exists, the plan is refined and the *blockInterval* action is expanded creating a dependency between the agent and the environment (Calendar).

Constraints through user preferences. Constraints are defined in terms of user preferences and committed engagements. For this matter, a meeting is defined as a future joint appointment which must be agreed by all participants concerning these constraints. Each user creates its own appointments according to its agenda status for the chosen time slots. These appointments can be individual tasks or meetings, which describe a goal achievable by their agendas. User preferences are categorised by temporal preferences which define priorities over time slots and contextual preferences which refer to personal and professional activities. Priorities are defined in terms of urgency and importance over activities. For instance, an "exam preparation" can be both highly urgent and important while "exercising" is important (for user healthy) but not so much urgent.

The user defines his/her own level of priority over appointments by assigning a combination of urgency and importance level to each activity to be scheduled. Temporal preferences can be setup by choosing work times for each day in the week, optional extended hours, weekends and holidays. Those last ones define how temporal constraints will be considered to negotiate over additional working times. Contextual preferences are defined through task responsibility and organisational structure.

3.3   Agenda-Environment Component Design

The environment is defined according to the group of agents and the calendar definition. At this level, the calendar represents action/resource constraints between agents. These constraints are described through temporal availability from calendar time slots as *unavailable, occupied* or *free*. An *unavailable* time slot is an interval that possesses a private appointment allocated by the user and it can not be considered to negotiation or relaxation. An *occupied* time slot is allocated to a public appointment, which can be negotiable or can be relaxed according to user preferences. Finally, a *free* slot time can accept a new appointment.

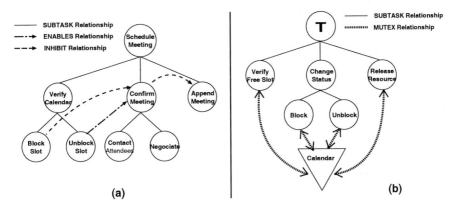

Fig. 1. (a) ScheduleMeeting plan representation, (b) Resource partial task structure.

In our approach we assume a description over resources and its relationship with the actions permitted by the environment through a task structure hierarchy. The figure 1(b) illustrates a partial task structure to check for resource availability (here, time slots, but also rooms and equipment). In this work, we use a finite state automaton model to describe the resource status (pre- and post-conditions of time slots) and a *mutex* relationship between tasks and resources.

3.4   Agenda-Interaction Component Design

The (I) component is in charge of managing protocols and priority interactions in terms of message passing. Agents need to exchange relevant information to achieve a globally consistent schedule. The (I) component deals with communication and protocol management. At the co-ordination level, we are concerned with how to choose adequate protocols according to dynamic situation and role allocation. Additionally, this level of co-ordination must guarantee some consistency during message passing. For instance, in a meeting scheduling task, if an attendee can not receive the message, all the related messages have to be cancelled. The protocol manager properly provides the atomicity of transactions.

According to dependence constraints, the interaction control may properly manage with distinct protocols for different kinds of information exchange. In the agent connection phase, for instance, the Interaction controller triggers an initial co-ordination mechanism of information gathering, which updates the external description (at agent level) of each one.

For our experiment, we have chosen to adapt Sian's co-operative learning protocol [15], because we only need to provide the agents with a simple consensus protocol. The protocol that we need is a simple one, since that a part of constraint management is taken in each component control. In this protocol, an agent elaborates a hypothesis about a believed information, which is shared with a group of associated agents. Each agent evaluates this hypothesis against its own beliefs and then confirms, modifies or rejects it. When the group reaches a consensus, they update their knowledge base with this new information. In our case, the hypothesis stands for a meeting request, which has to be agreed by all attendees or dropped in case of non-consensual result. Several meeting requests can be involved with different agent groups, so the Interaction model has to deal with concurrent scheduling.

At the Interaction level, we assume that relevant information must be exchanged to build local schedules. Here, we take a traditional meeting scheduling specification to provide the (I) component with the content of the message. We use the protocol management approach [10] which provides the (I) component with a methodology to assemble protocols based on micro-protocol components. In our approach, the Sian's negotiation protocol is described as following:

$$negotiate\,(h_i, A_i, m_i) \rightarrow propose\,(h_i, A_i, m_i)$$

Formally, we represent a meeting specification by the tuple: $m_i = (S_i, l_i, w_i, T_i)$.

The goal of a set of agents ($\mathcal{A}$) is to schedule a globally consistent meeting i (m_i). The meeting is proposed by a host ($h_i \in A_i$) who will interact with a set of attendees ($A_i \subseteq \mathcal{A}$) in order to find out a consensual schedule. The meeting is required to be schedule at the time interval (S_i) and with a required length in time unites (l_i). Time interval is defined by a couple $\langle date, time \rangle$ for *start* and *end* intervals, so ($S_i = \{\langle d_{start}, t_{start} \rangle, \langle d_{end}, t_{end} \rangle\}$). A priority is assigned to the meeting (w_i) that is directly related to local constraints to be evaluated and solved during co-ordination. Optionally, a free time set (T_i) by which the meeting can be scheduled is proposed by the host.

3.5   Agenda-Organisation Component Design

Co-ordination requirements, related to organisational constraints (cf. section 2.1), are concerned with role external description and the organisational structure.

The (O) component takes into account social relations between the participants in order to represent the organisational hierarchy and responsibilities between activities according to the roles that agents play. The agent belongs to a group, a set of roles, which defines the organisational structure of an institution or agent society. We assume that the organisational hierarchy and the responsibility influence the preferences during a negotiation to find a consensus. Hence, the role that an agent plays in the society (organisational hierarchy) can bias the search for a consistent schedule. For example, a meeting with the director has a higher priority than that with a colleague, whereas responsibility on a task such as *PrepareLecture* can be more important than an *OrganizeDesktop* task.

Each agent is accessible to the other participants by an external description, social dependencies [16] can be detected with regard to their goals and plans. In this way, the (O) component could manage a thematic group formation according to the meeting joint action (*ScheduleMeeting*) given a range of priorities related to the global importance for this scheduled meeting.

3.6   An Appointment Taking Example

A user decides to schedule a meeting for an important project and adds an appointment on his/her agenda, providing a time interval, a deadline to the meeting and a set of attendees. His/her Agenda starts by selecting a new *ScheduleMeeting* goal and calculating the constraints for this goal. The *VerifyCalendar* task is trigger to search for free time slots in the given interval. After that, *AppendMeeting* can be started by selecting *ContactAttendees* and *Negotiate* tasks. The *Negotiate* task will detect a dependency with the (I) component through a distributed component to trigger the negotiation protocol. The list of the each participant's *id* is selected by the *ContactAttendees* task while the protocol manager starts to send a $propose(h_i, A_i, m_i)$ to each $a \in A_i$. At this moment, a constraint is added to the agent's constraint set since the host (h_i) depends on the attendees (A_i) to achieve the $AppendMeeting(m_i)$ goal. The (I) component manages the protocol termination taking into consideration the dependency (A-I) which provides the host with the answers from the attendees.

When all attendees send $agree(a, h_i, m_i)$ to the host without any other constraint, the *AppendMeeting* goal can be reached and the *ScheduleMeeting* task is confirmed. If the host receives a $modify(a, h_i, m_i')$ message, a new cycle of *ScheduleMeeting* is started in order to take into account the constraints under the proposed meeting modification (m_i'). A confirmation is reached if everyone agree with the new meeting. If a $disagree(a, h_i, m_i)$ or $noopinion(a, h_i, m_i)$ is received, the meeting is dropped and a $cancel(h_i, A_i, m_i)$ is sent, concluding with the negotiation phase. The user is notify that his/her meeting was not possible.

To deal with constraints, the agent checks for free time slots into the meeting interval systematically. If no free slots are found, the agent checks for temporal constraints that could be relaxed, such as time preferences and weak commitments. This last one stands for occupied time slots that are checked for temporal and contextual constraints. That means, whether exists an individual event or a meeting with low priority that can be moved. For instance, a meeting with a person who owns a lower importance than the actual hosting is a good candidate to renegotiation.

4   Summary and Related Work

Distributed Agenda Management falls on classical Distributed Constraints Satisfaction Problem and it is mainly related to scheduling problems and distributed resource allocation. Some of these algorithms have claimed for an exchange of partial knowledge from each agent in order to take all constrained variables into account. In algorithms based on backtracking (synchronous/asynchronous backtracking, weak-commitment) agents have to communicate some tentative values assignment to their neighbours in order to detect whether they have reached a local-minimum. The Flexible Contracting Model approach [14] proposes several search biases which allow to properly evaluate alternative choices. Persistent conflicts are dealt through a hierarchical representation of calendars that enable a structured cancellation mechanism. However, these approaches neither assumes the privacy of the user's calendar information nor resource interdependencies and social dependence through organisation structure.

In this paper, we have illustrated a decentralised multi-agent model applied to a dynamic and over-constrained problem that addresses some of those points. The general model is based on dependencies between multi-agent components according to Vowels paradigm. This approach takes resource interdependencies and social dependence into account in order to detect and apply co-ordination mechanisms to achieve a globally consistent solution.

We have implemented this solution through Volcano platform [13], a JAVA Vowels-oriented multi-agent platform designed to assist the multi-agent system creation process. Up to now, we have implemented the (A) component and a graphical user interface to provide all agenda functionalities to the user. Interaction features are provide through an Interaction Protocol Management tool [10], which is placed on a basic inter-agent communication Router layer, from JATLite [9], in order to deal with negotiation and information gathering. The first version will be soon operational and we intend to validate it intensively into the MAGMA research group to manage the complex meeting interactions among the members. By the future, we intend to offer it as a free open source to the research community in order to validate in a large-scale real-life environment.

Acknowledgments. The authors would like to thank J-F. Rolland for providing the graphical user interface and a part of agent component implementation.

References

1. J.L. Tavares da Silva and Y. Demazeau. Multiagent centered real-time planning. In *III Iberoamerican Workshop on Distributed Artificial Intelligence and Multi-Agents Systems (SBIA/IBERAMIA'00)*, 131–142, Sao Paulo, Brazil, November 2000.

2. J.L. Tavares da Silva and Y. Demazeau. Vowels co-ordination model. In Cristiano Castelfranchi and W. Lewis Johnson, editors, *Proceedings of the 1st International Joint Conference on Autonomous Agents and Multiagent Systems (AAMAS'02)*, 1129–1136, Bologna, Italy, 2002. ACM Press.

3. K. Decker and V. Lesser. Generalized partial global planning. *International Journal on Intelligent Cooperative Information Systems*, 1(2):319–346, June 1992.

4. Y. Demazeau. Steps towards multi-agent oriented programming. In *1st International Workshop on Multi-Agent Systems (IWMAS'97)*, Boston, 1997.

5. P. Ferreira and J. Wainer. Scheduling meetings through multi-agent negotiating. In Maria Carolina Monard and Jaime Sichman, editors, *Proceedings of 15th Brazilian Symposium on Artificial Intelligence*, 126–135. Springer, 2000.

6. L. Garrido and K. Sycara. Multi-agent meeting scheduling: Preliminary experimental results. In Victor Lesser, editor, *Proceedings of the First International Conference on Multi–Agent Systems*. MIT Press, 1995.

7. T. Haynes and S. Sen. Satisfying user preferences while negotiating meetings. In *Second International Conference on Multi-Agent Systems*, page 440, 1996.

8. J. R. Jennings and A. J. Jackson. Agent-based meeting scheduling: A design and implementation. *Electronic Letters*, 31(5):350–352, March 1995.

9. H. Jeon, C. Petrie, and M.R. Cutkosky. JATLite: A java agent infrastructure with message routing. *IEEE Internet Computing*, 4(2):87–96, 2000.

10. J-L. Koning and M-P. Huget. A component-based approach for modeling interaction protocols. In H. Kangassalo, H. Jaakkola, and E. Kawaguchi, editors, *Proceedings of 10th European-Japanese Conference on Information Modelling and Knowledge Bases*, Saariselkä, Finland, May 8–11 2000. IOS Press.

11. F. Martial. *Coordinating plans of autonomous agents* Lecture Notes in Computer Science, Vol. 610. Springer-Verlag, New York, USA (1992).

12. P.J. Modi, H. Jung, M. Tambe, W-M. Shen, and S. Kulkarni. Dynamic distributed resource allocation: A distributed constraint satisfaction approach. In John-Jules Meyer and Milind Tambe, editors, *Pre-proceedings of the Eighth International Workshop on Agent Theories, Architectures, and Languages (ATAL-2001)*, 181–193, August 2001.

13. P-M. Ricordel and Y. Demazeau. Volcano, a vowels-oriented multi-agent platform. In *Proceedings of the International Conference of Central Eastern Europe on Multi-Agent Systems (CEEMAS 2001)*, Krakow, Poland, 2001.

14. S. Sen and E.H. Durfee. A formal study of distributed meeting scheduling: Preliminary results. In *Conference on Organizational Computing Systems*, Groups within Organizations, 55–68, 1991.

15. S.S. Sian. Adaptation based on cooperative learning in multi-agent systems. In Y. Demazeau and J.-P. Müller, editors, *Decentralized AI 2*, 257–272, Amsterdam, The Netherlands, 1991. Elsevier Science Publishers B.V.

16. J.S., R. Conte, C. Castelfranchi and Y. Demazeau. A social reasoning mechanism based on dependence networks. In A. G. Cohn, editor, *Proceedings of the Eleventh European Conference on Artificial Intelligence*, 188–192, Chichester, August 8–12 1994. John Wiley and Sons.

17. T. Tsuruta and T. Shintani. Scheduling meetings using distributed valued constraint satisfaction algorithm. In Werner Horn, editor, *Proceedings of the 14th European Conference on Artificial Intelligence (ECAI-2000)*, 383–387, Berlin, Germany, August 20–25 2000. IOS Press.

18. M. Yokoo and K. Hirayama. Algorithms for distributed constraint satisfaction: A review. *Autonomous Agents and Multi-Agent Systems*, 3(2):185–207, June 2000.

Meta-modelling in Agent Oriented Software Engineering

Jorge J. Gómez-Sanz and Juan Pavón

Dep. Sistemas Informáticos y Programación,
Univ. Complutense, 28040 Madrid, Spain
{jjgomez,jpavon}@sip.ucm.es
http://grasia.fdi.ucm.es

Abstract. The MESSAGE methodology has shown that the application of meta-models in the development of Multi-Agent Systems (MAS) facilitates the integration of current software engineering processes and the use of agent technology concepts in analysis and design activities. This paper presents an extension to the MESSAGE meta-models and how to conduct the modelling (i.e., instantiation of the meta-models into a specific MAS) following the Unified Software Development Process, especially considering the importance of an incremental development and the role of the different meta-model entities in this process. This process is illustrated by an example.

1   Introduction

Most of the existing agent development methodologies consider a development process of a short number of steps for analysis and design of the MAS, which may seem rather simplistic, especially when compared with standard development processes, such as the Unified Software Development Process [9]. Developing a Multi-Agent System (MAS) is more complex than a conventional object oriented application, as it has to cope with distributed intelligent entities. It is true that in some cases, like MaSE [4], the presence of a tool, such as an agentTool, simplifies the development process. However, this means risking a loss of flexibility because of the constraints of the underlying agent model. For instance, the idea of an agent in agentTool is that of a conventional process, whose behavior is specified as state machines (which is not convenient for deliberative agents). ZEUS [13] facilitates the development process by providing implemented solutions for planning, ontologies management, and communication between agents. When the MAS is a small one and when the problem is restricted to the academic domain, and for rapid prototyping, such tools are useful and a methodology of just a short number of steps sounds reasonable. However, an industrial development, involving a team of several engineers requires management of activities, a more detailed software development process, and the control of the cost involved in making a MAS work under real world workload.

A trend in current software methodologies is the provision of methods for incremental development. Though the idea is present in the development processes of existing agent methodologies, it is not clear how to achieve an incremental development using existing formalisms. For instance, GAIA [16] propose iterations of some development steps in order to comply with the specification of *roles*; however,

F.J. Garijo, J.C. Riquelme, and M. Toro (Eds.): IBERAMIA 2002, LNAI 2527, pp. 606–615, 2002.
© Springer-Verlag Berlin Heidelberg 2002

the formalism that gathers the information from iteration to iteration is not well suited for that task. GAIA uses card-like specifications that are textual descriptions of what is being modelled. Changes to such specifications are not trivial and may involve high costs. This lesson is well known in software engineering and that is why today developers use other formalisms, such as UML.

From this perspective of industrial software engineering, and trying to avoid the constraints of a specific agent model, the MESSAGE project [2] addresses the definition of an agent development methodology by identifying the generic elements required to build a MAS, organizing them in five views, and expressing them using a meta-modelling language. The resulting meta-models (one for each view) can be applied by integration into a well-proven software development process model, which in the case of MESSAGE is the Unified Software Development Process [9], although others could be considered.

The work presented in this paper is an extension to MESSAGE in several aspects. First, by providing a more detailed definition of the agent, organization, interaction, tasks and goal views of a MAS, and by adding the *Environment* view, which substitutes the *Domain* view from MESSAGE. Meta-models have been described using a meta-tool (METAEDIT+ [10]) to create specific editors for building MAS models (illustrations in this paper are taken from the application of such a tool), which allows the developer to work directly with agent concepts instead of specific implementation entities such as classes or rules. Another improvement to MESSAGE methodology is a more detailed definition of the activities required in the MAS analysis and design phases in the context of the Unified Software Development Process, and the provision of a path and supporting tools to obtain an implementation.

The next section discusses how meta-modeling supports the definition of a language for the development of a MAS using agent technology concepts, and which elements have to be considered in each view of the MAS. The third Section explains how meta-models are integrated into the development process, and which kind of activities are required for building a MAS. This is illustrated with a working example, in order to provide a practical insight into the proposed methodology. Finally, we present some conclusions. For further information and a detailed description of all the meta-models and the activities of the methodology visit our web site at http://grasia.fdi.ucm.es.

2   MAS Meta-models

The meta-models describe the entities that should be part of a MAS and their relationships. As such, the task of the MAS developer is to define models with specific instances of the entities from the meta-models. In the case of an object-oriented application a model is defined by a set of classes (instances of meta-classes) and their relationships. In the case of a MAS we are interested in the identification of types of organization, groups, workflows, agents, perceptions, interactions, mental state, goals, tasks, resources, etc., which are instances of the entities in the MAS meta-models. In this sense, the MAS meta-models provide a high level language for development MAS in terms of agent technology concepts (although in the end they have to be translated into computational terms such as classes, rules, neural networks, depending on the implementation technology).

In order to structure the specification of the MAS, we can consider several views (this separation of concerns is also applied in most of the existing MAS methodologies, for instance, Vowel engineering [14] and MASCommonKADS [7]), and therefore one meta-model for each one:

- **Agent meta-model.** Describes agent's responsibilities with tasks and roles. It also takes into account the control of the agent defining its goals and mental states required during execution. With instances of this model, we can define constraints in the freedom of action of the agent without it being restricted to a specific control paradigm.

- **Organization meta-model.** Organization is the equivalent of a system architecture. Following Ferber [5] and MESSAGE [6], there are structural relationships that are not restricted to hierarchies between roles. These structures are delegated to specialized entities, *groups*. In the organization model there are also power relationships among *groups, organizations,* and *agents*. Functionality of the organization is expressed using workflows which show consumer/producer associations between tasks as well as assignment of responsibilities for their execution, and resources associated to each.

- **Environment meta-model.** The environment defines the sensors and effectors of the agents. It also identifies available resources as well as already existing agents and applications.

- **Tasks and Goals meta-model.** As we base this on a BDI model and Newell's *principle of rationality* [12], it is important to justify the execution of tasks in terms of the goals that are achieved. We provide decomposition of tasks and goals. To relate both, there are specialised relationships that detail which information is needed to consider a goal to be solved or failed. Finally, this meta-model also provides low level detail of tasks in the system, describing which resources are needed in the execution, which software modules are used throughout the process, and which are the inputs and outputs in terms of entities of these meta-models.

- **Interaction meta-model.** Describes how coordination among agents takes place. It goes a step further than sequence diagrams (UML) in the sense that it reflects the motivation of the interaction and its participants. It also includes information about the mental state required in each agent throughout the interaction as well as tasks executed in the process. In this way, we can justify at design level why an agent engages in a interaction and why it should continue.

The generation of models from these meta-models is not trivial, since there are dependencies between different views. For instance, tasks appearing in workflows in an organization model should also appear in a Tasks and Goals model. That is why meta-models need to be integrated into a consistent software development process, as described in the next section.

The example in section 4 shows some of the concepts defined in the above meta-models in some detail. Note that for each entity in the meta-model there is a graphical representation that allows the developer to work at a higher level, i.e., with agent concepts instead of implementing specific artefacts. This is supported by a visual tool generated by a meta-tool from the meta-models specifications.

3   Integration in the Unified Software Development Process

For each meta-model, we have defined a set of activities (around seventy) in the software development process that lead to the final MAS specification. Initially, activities are organised in UML activity diagrams showing dependencies between them. Instead of showing these activities here, Fig. 1 summarises the results required in each phase of the Unified Software Development Process. Meta-models are used as specification language of the MAS the same way as UML does for object oriented applications. We have used a meta-tool, METAEDIT+, that takes as input the meta-models specifications and generates graphical tools that are used by the developer to produce models using the concepts described in the meta-models (for which we have also associated a graphical representation). Models developed using these graphical tools consist of the agent concepts described in the meta-models. The example in the next section shows some diagrams for a particular case study, and the iterative and incremental nature of the development process.

<table>
<tr><td colspan="2"></td><td colspan="3" align="center">PHASES</td></tr>
<tr><td colspan="2"></td><td>Inception</td><td>Elaboration</td><td>Construction</td></tr>
<tr>
<td rowspan="4">WORKFLOWS</td>
<td>Analysis</td>
<td>o   Generate use cases and identify actions of these use cases with interaction models.
o   Sketch a system architecture with an organization model.
o   Generate enviroment models to represent results from requirement gathering stage</td>
<td>o   Refined use cases
o   Agent models that detail elements of the system architecture.
o   Workflows and tasks in organization models
o   Models of tasks and goals to highlight control constraints (main goals, goal decomposition)
o   Refinements of environment model to include new environment elements</td>
<td>o   Refinements on existing models to cover use cases</td>
</tr>
<tr>
<td>Design</td>
<td>o   Generate prototypes perhaps with rapid application development tool such as ZEUS o Agent Tool.</td>
<td>o   Refinements in workflows
o   Interaction models that show how tasks are executed.
o   Models of tasks and goals that reflect dependencies and needs identified in workflows and how system goals are achieved
o   Agent models to show required mental state patterns</td>
<td>o   Generate new models

o   Social relationships that perfect organization behaviour.</td>
</tr>
</table>

Fig. 1. Results to be obtained in each phase of the development process

In the analysis-inception phase, organization models are produced to sketch how the MAS looks like. This result, equivalent to a MAS architecture, is refined late in the analysis-elaboration phase to identify common goals of the agents and relevant tasks to be performed by each agent. Task execution has to be justified in terms of organizational or agent's goals (with task-goal models). This leads to identify the results that are needed to consider a goal as satisfied (or failed). In the design-elaboration phase, more detail is added, by defining workflows among the different agents (with organization models), completing workflow definition with agent interactions (with interaction models), and refining agent's mental state as a consequence (with agent models). According to the Unified Software Development Process, the goal of elaboration phase is to generate a stable architecture, so only of the most significant use cases should be considered (the key functionality of the system). Remaining use cases, which are supposed to deal with special situations but that do not provide changes in the system architecture, are left to the construction phase.

According to Unified Software Development Process, the different iterations would point to a certain level of detail. We perform activities with an increasing level of detail in the products obtained so far. Testing and implementation phases have not been included in this paper. Testing should not be different from conventional software testing. We assume that use cases determine core functionality to be developed. From these use cases, test suites can be generated. Regarding implementation, we envision two choices: (1) consider generated models as a specification of the system like those generated by UML and perform the implementation manually; and (2) try to generate the code automatically from the specification. The first approach was carried out in the MESSAGE project [3]. The second option is oriented towards the encapsulation of the implementation so designers of MAS are not that interested in the code. Work in this line has already been done by ZEUS [13], AgentBuilder [8] and, recently, agentTool [15]. However, in most cases the target platform cannot be changed. The only one that supports this feature is agentTool.

To facilitate automated code generation, we use a complete MAS architecture made of components implemented in different languages. Current target languages include JAVA, Java Expert Ssystem Shell (JESS), April or PROLOG. We have also tried to generate a code for agent platforms, specifically JADE [1]. Our approach does not embed the final code into the application. Instead, it assumes that the source code of the architecture is marked up with tags. These tags are later substituted by data from the models according to a process defined by the developer. With meta-models and the supporting tool (METAEDIT+), it is easy to generate a representation of the models in other languages. In our case, we use PROLOG as intermediate representation of the meta-models. Later, and with another PROLOG program, we run the parameterisation procedure to generate the final system.

4   A Structured Development Example

The example shows a model of an organisation of personal agents to hep the user in managing the personal computer. The diagrams shown in this section have been generated directly from meta-models. The tool that supports meta-modeling allows work to be carried out in the same way as in a conventional software engineering tools. Also, the tool checks that during the development, models are defined exactly as conceived at the meta-model level.

4.1   Problem Statement

Managing a personal computer is a tiring task, as we know. Though operative systems facilitate the management of the computer, there is not too much management support for the tons of programs that today can be installed in a PC. Conventional support only includes tools to install/uninstall the program and detect collisions in the access to system resources (e.g. printers, files).

However, it is well known that there is also information overload in the PC. There are many programs producing information (e-mail, chat-programs, internet monitors, bookmarks, word-processors) without any more control than the user's orders. This leads to an information overload which causes user's desidia. For instance, users tend to spread their documents throughout the folders in one or many virtual (e.g. NFS) or physical (e.g. current hard disk) storage media. E-mail messages are stored forever in a forever growing in-box. Notifications of changes in some monitored URL are ignored again and again. Agents have been applied to solve some of these problems, especially those concerning email (Maxims [11]). However, what should be designed is one or several organizations of agents able to collaborate among themselves to deal with this information overload in the PC.

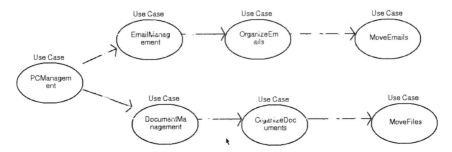

Fig. 2. Use case diagram that identifies relevant use cases in this case study

4.2 Analysis-Inception

We start identifying initial use cases oriented towards PC management (see Fig. 2). With these use cases we want to cover email and document management, and more specifically, organize information in the PC when the information is emails and files on the hard disk.

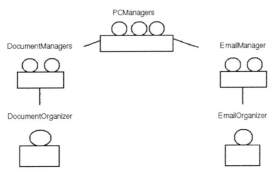

Fig. 3. Organization model of agents in the PC. Rectangles with one circle denote agents, rectangles with two circles, groups, and rectangles with three circles, organizations.

Organization is seen, in this case, as the allocation of files in different folders (email folders or hard disk folders). As readers may imagine, there is a strong chance that the system will grow, by adding new agents to deal with other PC management tasks or improving agent functionality by adding some collaboration between agents allocated in different PCs.

According to the initial specification, initially, there should be two kinds of agents: agents that organize user's email (*EmailOrganizer*) and agents that organize user's documents on the hard disk (*DocumentOrganizer*). As the system is expected to grow with different assistants for other PC management issues, it seems reasonable to start grouping these agents into two organizational structures: *Document Manager* and *Email Manager*. This tentative system architecture is sketched in Fig. 3.

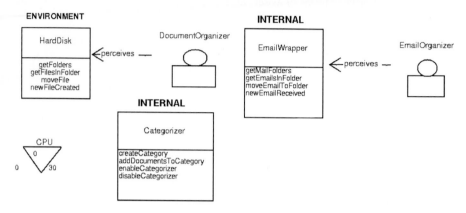

Fig. 4. Tentative environment model. Inverted triangles denote resource. Left number is the lower usage threshold, center number denotes expected initial value, right number is higher threshold. System applications are represented with the same symbol as UML objects.

The environment, the user's PC in this case, is modelled focussing on the aspects that are going to be modelled. These are files on the hard disk and an email application. To handle these aspects (see Fig. 4), we define application entities (*HardDisk* and *EmailWrapper*) and some expected methods. Among these, we highlight *newFileCreated* and *newEmailReceived* operations since with them we are able to define agent's perception (*perceives* associations). To be able to organize information, emails and files, we decided to apply a text mining tool that provides clustering and classification capabilities. As a requisite, we established that the use of CPU should not exceed 30 %, so that user's work is not disturbed.

After this study, we should return to the organization model and include this new information. Though it will not be shown here, changes include integrating *EmailWrapper* in the *EmailManager* group, *HardDisk* in *DocumentsManager*, and the *Categorizer* to both groups.

4.3 Design and Implementation–Inception

In this stage we make some prototypes to test the viability of the proposal using text-mining tools to classify emails and other text documents. To facilitate experiments, we assume that the user uses the Eudora email client, which stores emails and attachments separately (this facilitates the work of the text mining tool since binary files distort clustering results). To test user interaction, we develop an HTML prototype. Since agent interaction is not considered at this point in the development, we do not see any need to use any rapid application development agent tool (like ZEUS [13] or agentTool [15]).

4.4 Analysis-Elaboration

In this stage we continue adding details to each agent's specification. As a refinement of the *email organization* use case, we add a new scenario that considers relationships between emails and other user's documents. These related documents may improve email organization by providing more documents whose allocation can serve as a quality test.

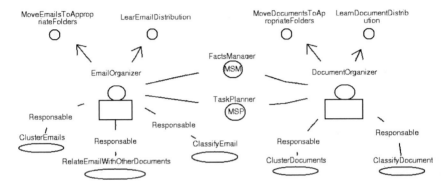

Fig. 5. *EmailOrganizer* and *DocumentOrganizer* description. MSM means *Mental State Manager* and MSP *Mental State Processor*. Ovals denote tasks. Circles denote goals.

Each agent is represented in Fig. 5. As one can seen, the functionality of both agents is quite similar. However, the domain of application of each task is completely different. Email structure includes mail headers and MIME types. Hard disk files, however, can be word documents, HTML pages, or GIF files, among others. As the categorizer tool performs final classification on ASCII documents, we need to process the different sources of information accordingly, and this is the purpose of these tasks.

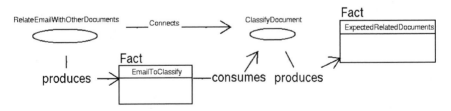

Fig. 6. Description of consumer-producer relationships between two tasks. Facts produced and consumed belong to the mental state of the agent.

To begin considering agent control, we assume that it will be composed of a mental state manager (to manage the knowledge of the agents) and a mental state processor (in charge of taking decisions upon current knowledge). In this case, we established that we would use facts as a unit of knowledge and that a task planner would decide what to do next. In order to justify this planner, a proper definition of tasks should be provided.

What Fig. 6 shows is that there is a workflow that relates *EmailOrganizer* tasks with *DocumentOrganizer* tasks. It also defines each task by the required inputs and the outputs that are produced. Information is lacking here about how new facts contribute to goal satisfaction, but this is part of the incremental specification. For the moment, it may be enough to know that these two tasks are related and what the nature of the relationship is. Note that during the specification of these tasks we discover mental entities that should exist in the mental state of the agent, so in fact we are defining control restrictions (*ClassifyDocument* cannot work until an *EmailToClassify* fact is present in the mental state of its responsible agent).

The process would continue identifying new goals and tasks, and modifying organization accordingly (indicating the existence of workflows and new resources, for instance). During the process, key interactions, like the one added between the two agents are associated with use cases and existing goals. These interactions are expected to be fully detailed during their design. Of course, the environment model may also change, since new applications may be required, for instance, to perform the transformation from word processing documents to ASCII documents.

4.5 Other Stages

In the design stage, the detail of the interactions increases, specifying which tasks are executed throughout the interaction and which mental states are required from each agent in each stage. Again new tasks or mental entities can be discovered during the design and so existing models should be modified to maintain consistence.

For reasons of brevity, other stages have been omitted. However, we would like to point out that the specification continues incrementally and that, in parallel, implementation starts from the construction stage.

5   Conclusions

The paper shows the generation of the specification of a MAS using meta-models. Though the development of the example specification has been summarised, it shows that it is possible to build MAS following an incremental and iterative software development process. Though the example cannot be compared with more serious problems, like coordination of robots in a factory, there has been experiments with problems of a similar degree of complexity, such as the coordination of hundreds of agents distributed throughout several computers in order to perform information personalization. Current application domains range from interface agents and planning agents to collaborative filtering systems.

Our experiments show that there are key differences with existing approaches. The most important is how the analysis and design are carried out in a similar way to conventional software engineering without simply falling into an object oriented trend.

From current specifications we have performed automated code generation of specific parts, like the interaction model. In future work we intend to complete code generation with different target MAS architectures, like ZEUS or JADE. Another goal is to include knowledge from experts in different agent fields in the methodology, such as real time or mobility.

References

[1]   Bellifemine, F., Poggi, A., and Rimassa, G. *JADE – A FIPA-compliant Agent Framework*. The Practical Application of Intelligent Agents and Multi-Agents. 1999.

[2]   Caire, G., Leal, F., Chainho, P., Evans, R., Garijo, F., Gomez-Sanz, J. J., Pavon, J., Kerney, P., Stark, J., and Massonet, P., *Agent Oriented Analysis using MESSAGE/UML*, in Wooldridge, M., Weiss, G., and Cianciarini, P. (eds.) *Agent-Oriented Software Engineering II* Springer Verlag, 2001.

[3]   Caire, G., Leal, F., Chainho, P., Evans, R., Garijo, F., Gomez-Sanz, J. J., Pavon, J., Kerney, P., Stark, J., and Massonet, P. *Eurescom P907: MESSAGE - Methodology for Engineering Systems of Software Agents*. http://www.eurescom.de/public/projects/P900-series/p907/default.asp. 2002.

[4]   DeLoach, S. *Analysis and Design using MaSE and agentTool*. Proceedings of the 12th Midwest Artificial Intelligence and Cognitive Science Conferece (MAICS). 2001.

[5]   Ferber, J. and Gutknecht, O. *A Meta-Model for the Analysis and Design of Organizations in Multi-Agent Systems*. Proceedings of the Third International Conference on Multi-Agent Systems (ICMAS98), IEEE CS Press. 1998.

[6]   Garijo, F., Gomez-Sanz, J. J., and Massonet, P. *Multi-Agent System Organization. An Engineering Perspective.*. MAAMAW 2001, Springer Verlag. 2001

[7]   Iglesias, C., Mercedes Garijo, M., Gonzalez, J. C., and Velasco, J. R., *Analysis and design of multiagent systems using MAS-CommonKADS*, in Singh, M. P., Rao, A., and Wooldridge, M. J. (eds.) *Intelligent Agents IV* LNAI Volume 1365 ed. Springer-Verlag: Berlin, 1998.

[8]   IntelliOne Technologies. *AgentBuilder*. http://www.agentbuilder.com . 2002.

[9]   Jacobson, I., Rumbaugh, J., and Booch, G., *The Unified Software Development Process* Addison-Wesley, 1999.

[10]   Lyytinen, K. S. and Rossi, M. *METAEDIT+ – A Fully Configurable Multi-User and Multi-Tool CASE and CAME Environment*. LGNS#1080. Springer-Verlag. 1999

[11]   Maes, P., *Agents that Reduces Work and Information Overload.*, *Readings in Intelligent User Interfaces* Morgan Kauffman Publishers, 1998.

[12]   Newell, A., *The knowledge level, Artificial Intelligence*, vol. 18 pp. 87–127, 1982.

[13]   Nwana, H. S., Ndumu, D. T., Lee, L. C., and Collis, J. C., *ZEUS: A Toolkit for Building Distributed Multi-Agent Systems, Applied Artificial Intelligence Journal*, vol. 1, no. 13, pp. 129–185, 1999.

[14]   Ricordel, P. M., *Programmation Orientée Multi-Agents , Développement et Déploiement de Systèmes Multi-Agents Voyelles*. Institut National Polytechnique de Grenoble, 2001.

[15]   Wood, M. and DeLoach, S. *Developing Multiagent Systems with agentTool*. 2000. ATAL 2000. LNAI 1986. Castelfranchi, C. and Lespérance, Y.

[16]   Wooldridge, M., Jennings, N. R., and Kinny, D., *The Gaia Methodology for Agent-Oriented Analysis and Design, Journal of Autonomous Agents and Multi-Agent Systems*, vol. 15. 2000.

Multi-agent Systems and Network Management – A Positive Experience on Unix Environments

Nelson dos Santos[1,2], Flávio Miguel Varejão[2], and
Orivaldo de Lira Tavares[2]

[1] Companhia Siderúrgica de Tubarão
Av. Brigadeiro Eduardo Gomes, s/n - Jardim Limoeiro
CEP 29164-280 – Serra - ES – Brasil
`nsantos@tubarao.com.br`
[2] Universidade Federal do Espírito Santo - UFES
Centro Tecnológico – Programa de Pós-Graduação em Informática
Av. Fernando Ferrari, s/n – Campus de Goiabeiras
CEP 29060-900 – Vitória – ES – Brasil
`{fvarejao, tavares}@inf.ufes.br`

Abstract. This paper presents an experiment of using a multi-agent system that improves the efficiency in network management on Unix environments. This system aims to decrease the financial damages occasioned by processing interruptions of the computational environment. The multi-agent system is based on a distributed and delegated management approach and it was developed using the GAIA methodology for analysis and design of agent-based systems. The agents architecture is based on activities and rule bases. The agents have lists of activities and apply their rule bases to accomplish them.

Keywords. Multi-agent system, network management, unix, intelligent agent, gaia methodology.

1 Introduction

Currently, the computational environment of many companies is composed by a great variety of hardware components, software, operating systems, etc. Depending directly on their computational environment, there are several applications (systems) that companies use to support their main businesses. The stability and readiness of this computational environment have become more important for increasing productivity and efficiency of companies. Slowness or even unavailability of some of the company most critical applications could be the result of any unstable or unavailable part of the computational environment, and can generate large financial damages [10] [12].

This article presents a work on how the multi-agent system-based technology [1] [3] can increase the readiness of computational environments. The multi-agent system has been gradually developed to deal with the different parts of computer network management. Initially, the experiments have only been performed on Unix environments. On these environments, a common problem that often causes damages to the stability of user applications is the *file system full* problem. We have chosen this

F.J. Garijo, J.C. Riquelme, and M. Toro (Eds.): IBERAMIA 2002, LNAI 2527, pp. 616–624, 2002.

problem to observe the multi-agent system performance. It happens when some disk space shared by many applications is 100% used. Then, some applications become unavailable and others have their response time significantly increased. The traditional way of handling this problem depends on human experts. Monitoring tools or complaining users notify the experts about the problem and they must identify the problem causes and take the corrective actions. The main pitfalls associated to this procedure are the possible unavailability of human experts (the problem may happen at any time, including during the night, weekends and holidays) and delays on the problem solving (the problem causes and their corrective actions may not be trivial). It is important to re-emphasize that delays on the file system unavailability increase the possibility of provoking a cascading effect over the overall network environment, suspending and aborting many other applications.

The multi-agent system was developed using the GAIA Methodology [18] for analysis and project of agent-based systems, and aiming the implementation of a multi-agent system in the Companhia Siderúrgica de Tubarão (CST)[1]. Due to the fact that it is a metallurgical company producing 24 hours a day, the main businesses in CST are supported by applications which must be maintained stable and available as long as possible. The multi-agent system is able to identify the causes of the file system full problem and take actions such as canceling processes and removing or reallocating files. As a result, new free disk spaces are generated and the environment availability is improved. The multi-agent system is composed by several specialized agents acting on different parts of the Unix environment. Each agent may react to a list of hierarchically ordered activities and have a knowledge base describing how to perform these activities.

Analysis of the log of our experiment has shown that the multi-agent system avoided that important financial and production control systems were interrupted and provided disk space for executing routine backup procedures (which, otherwise, would not be performed).

This article has the following structure: section 2 introduces a general view of the area of network management and services. Section 3 presents a description of the multi-agent system. Section 4 describes the experiment being performed. Finally, in section 5, the conclusions and some future work are presented.

2 Network Management Approaches

The main network management approach has been the IETF Management Structure (SNMP). The SNMP structure is based on a small group of concepts: agents or managed nodes (which represent elements of the network, as bridges, routers, switches, etc.), manager or network management system (which provides a set of operations to the network support team), managed information base – MIB (which represents the information that can be manipulated by each agent), the management

---

[1] http://www.cst.com.br

protocol - SNMP (the standard way of extracting management information from the systems) and the proxy (which allows the interaction of the SNMP structure with components that don't include this structure) [10] [12].

The SNMP structure is a centralized approach that uses distributed agents to collect manageable information. However, this approach has some problems when dealing with extensive and complex network models. The central manager may have some troubles for handling great amounts of manageable information and for managing a large number of geographically distributed sites [12] [16].

An alternative approach uses the "divide and conquer" strategy for promoting solutions based on distributed management and on delegation [12]. Several works use this approach, such as proposed by BRITES [2], GOLDSZMIDT [7] and OLIVEIRA [14]. In this approach, a main manager delegates the control to several distributed workstations and to more powerful agents. By promoting the collaboration among these agents, we have several management "islands". This procedure increases the reliability and failure tolerance of the network environment [12].

Another approach, considered by many researchers as the ideal solution for the complex network management, is the paradigm of mobile agents [4] [10]. The term Mobile Agent refers to autonomous programs that can move through the network, from node to node, and assume the knowledge of an agent, i.e., acting as users or other entities [15]. Many research investigations have been made in distributed network management and delegation [7], network services delivery [9], optimization of network traffic and network failure tolerance [11].

Whichever approach is adopted, it should aim to promote the pro-active concept in the network management. Several approaches have used this concept, such as, CHIU [5], DE FRANCESCHI [6] and HOOD [8].

3 The Multi-agent System

The multi-agent approach is based on distributed management and on delegation. The agents are permanently acting in specific parts of the computational environment, being able to solve from simple routine problems (of their strict domain) to even more complex problems that involve communications and activities among several agents. Our approach was based on the characteristics of the problem to be solved (the need of immediate actions instead of waiting for human intervention), as well as on the intelligent agents characteristics (autonomy to take actions, being always active and ready to take actions, capacity to act together with other agents, speed equivalent to the computational processors in which they are installed, etc.) [17].

The multi-agent system was developed using the GAIA[2] methodology [18] for analysis and design of systems based on agents. The multi-agent system includes the

---

[2] http://www.inf.ufes.br/~tavares/dsba

following roles: *ADMINISTRATOR, MONITOR, COORDINATOR* and *CONTROLL-ERS.*

The computational environment represented in figure 1 is composed of several hardware components that host multi-agent systems. Inside these hardware components, there are software components and other components that the system may control. The monitor role is also part of the computational environment and is represented by the monitoring tools, as shown by the "black box" in figure 1.

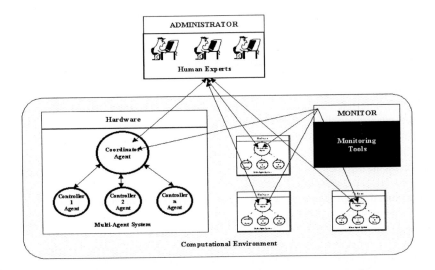

Fig. 1. Global Architecture

Each multi-agent system has an agent that coordinates the other controlling agents. These agents are responsible for the communications among the controlling agents and also allow the interaction between the multi-agent system and the human experts. In addition, they receive the information about the problems detected by the monitoring tools and distribute them to the appropriate controlling agents.

The controlling agents are responsible for the specific control of services and parts of the computational environment. For instance, we may have safety, database, response time, disk space, cleaning and printing service controllers. Researches approaches with similar architectures are found in the works of ABECK [1] and MARZO [13].

All agents have the same architecture. This feature allows the construction of a unique agent programming structure. The agent architecture is based on activities and rule bases. The agents should perform activities and apply their rule bases to accomplish them. The distinction between agents is expressed in their rule bases. Figure 2 shows that, if there is no longer any activity to be accomplished, the agents change their state to "sleeping". This state is disabled as soon as a new activity to be accomplished is sent to the agent or the sleeping time ceases.

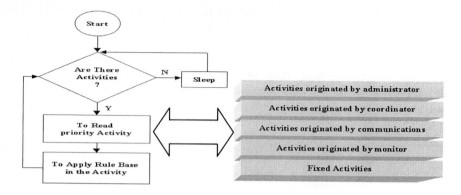

Fig. 2. Agent Behavior

Every agent selects the highest priority activity to perform at first, as may be observed in Figure 2. The fixed activities are executed after the "sleeping" state. The priorities sequence guarantees the compliance with the proposed hierarchical structure because an agent will always accomplish an activity generated by a human expert first, no matter how many fixed or communications activities it must have to accomplish in a given moment.

We developed a *coordinator*, a *disk space controller, a process controller*, and a *cleaning controller agent* for solving this problem. The disk space controller controls the allocation of the computer disk space in order to maintain the environment stability. The process controller agent is responsible for controlling all the processes executed in the computer, analyzing CPU consumption, looping states, process ownership and the interdependencies among the processes. The cleaning controller agent is responsible for controlling and optimizing the use of files inside the computer. It controls where the main files are and who is responsible for them. It also cleans the temporary files.

4 The Experiment

The experiment was divided into four steps: choosing an appropriate environment for the multi-agent system operation, choosing a problem with appropriate complexity, running the multi-agent system in the real environment during a period of three months and finally analyzing the results.

4.1 The Environment's Choice

We chose a part of the computational environment that was critical in terms of availability, involving a high level of complexity and demanding non trivial solutions and the participation of several controlling agents acting together to solve them. The Unix environment was the one chosen. The main applications assisting the metallurgical processes of CST use databases installed in Unix servers. The prototype was initially installed on eight Unix servers: two of development, one of endorsement and five of production (financial, supply, histories, control and supervision). The language chosen for the development of the agents was the language Korn Shell because it is native of the Unix environment (thus, computationally efficient) and easily allows the complete environment control.

4.2 The Problem's Choice

The *file system* problem usually happens when a Unix environment process saves (or is still saving) large files or a large number of small files in the disk area. This problem solution consists of canceling the process creating the files, whenever it is still active, and then removing or moving those files to some free disk area in the same computer or in another one. That problem allows a good observation of the multi-agent system operation since it demands the constant communication among the agents. Another important factor to the experiment is that the file system full problem often happens many times and at any time during a week, making possible real verification of the multi-agent system operation. Finally, the causes and solutions of the problem are very well defined, as well as the flow of communications and activities that the agents must execute.

4.3 Running the Multi-agent System

After being notified by the monitoring tools of some problem in some area of the environment, the multi-agent system reproduces actions that specialists would take to solve the problem. Basically, it identifies the files responsible for increasing the occupation rate and the processes using those files. Identified the processes and files, it cancels the processes and the area is cleaned by removing or moving the files.

Initially, the monitoring tool sends an activity for the coordinator agent informing the problem area and the current rate of occupation. In the experiment, the monitoring tool was configured to verify all the computer areas every 3 minutes and to send a message to the multi-agent system whenever, if some rate is above 95% of occupation.

The coordinator agent verifies the type of the activity to be executed and sends a message to the appropriate agent. In this particular case, the space disk controller agent is the responsible for coping with that activity. In the experiment, the coordinator agent knowledge base was fulfilled with solutions of several types of problems.

The space disk controller agent, after receiving the message, initially verifies if the problem continues to happen. If so, it tries to identify the problem causes. Identifying the causes, it sends messages to the coordinator agent for canceling processes and cleaning of files. It is the role of the coordinator agent to distribute the new activities to the appropriate agents. In the experiment, the problems reasons were precisely identified. They differed from problem to problem. The system is able to solve problems originated by one or more files. These files may also be generated by one or more processes. Difficulties found in the identification were due to the current lack of rights for investigation in certain directories or because the problem had already finished when the agent began the identification. In that case, the agent concluded that there was nothing to do.

The coordinator agent receives activities again, this time originated by the space disk controller agent and identifies which agents should be responsible for these activities.

The processes controller agent and the cleaning controller agent had in you're their own knowledge bases, countermands for the cancellation of certain processes as well as removal of certain files. In the experiment, when those countermands were identified, the specific agent cannot solve the activity and returns this information for the coordinator agent. The coordinator informs the space disk controller agent of the impediment for solving the problem. In this case, the space disk controller agent registers the impediment and informs the specialists about the found countermands. If there is no countermands, the process controller agent would usually cancel the requested processes and the cleaning controller agent would remove the appropriate files. We adopt the strategy of making the agents inform the specialists what they would have done to solve the problem, as well as informing the responsible for the affected systems of those actions. This strategy will be maintained until we consolidate the system acceptance. Up to now, the analysis of the actions taken by the multi-agent system were very positive. There was no indication of harmful actions taken over the environment.

At last, the controller agents send messages to the coordinator agent indicating the end of their activities execution. The coordinator agent sends this information to the space disk controller agent.

4.4 Analysis of Results

Table 1 shows a summary of the experiment current results.

Table 1. Current Results Obtained of the Experiment

Time of Operation of the Experiment	90 days – Feb until May of the 2002
Amount of Problems	78
Amount of Resolved Problems	68
Percentile of Resolved Problems	88%
Benefits reached by the system	Avoided that important financial and production control systems were interrupted; Provided disk space for executing routine backup procedures; Avoided problems of response time for maintaining critical file systems below 100% of occupation.

The results obtained by the experiment are very positive. Most of the problems and their causes were correctly identified. The multi-agent system was not only able to solve the problem where it does not have full rights for investigating directories and where the problem had already been finished at the moment of analysis.

5   Conclusions and Future Work

We have shown how an Artificial Intelligence based technology, not frequently used in the routine working environment of companies, can be of great value for keeping available the company computational environment.

The multi-agent system may avoid the interruption of parts of the industrial production, failures in financial operations that may provoke fines, spending human expert time for solving complex problems that began simple, time losses of users, failures on customers purchases, accidents with our without human losses, etc. The good results obtained by the multi-agent system have motivated claims from the human experts to include new and more complex problems to be solved by the system. New knowledge is being included to the agent rule bases and new agents are being constructed to attend these demands.

In the short term, we intend to add more controller agents to the Unix environment to evaluate the growing difficulties of an increasingly complex agent structure acting together. The next controllers will be the database ones (a type of omnipresent DBA), the safety ones (to control the access to the computers, invasions attempts, password control, etc.), the response time (to maintain the environment with suitable performance rates) and other specific services controllers. It is also our intention to develop in the medium term agents using a language compatible with other environments that can be controlled (NT, Netware, WEB, etc.). In the long term, we intend to endow the agents with a type of learning capacity, through the development of "curious" or "questioning" agents that register situations in which the multi-agent systems have failed. These agents will keep questioning the human experts about how these problems were solved. Another type of learning happens when the agents themselves inform the agents of the same type located in other hardware about alterations in their knowledge base. With the growing complexity of the knowledge bases, it would be ideal to have a way to make the agents themselves optimize these bases in order to get better solutions than the ones previously used. In this context, the agents will be able to teach the human experts.

References

1.   Abeck, S.; Koppel, A.; Seitz, J.; A Management Architecture for Multi-Agent Systems. Proceedings of the IEEE Third International Workshop on System Management. Newport, Rhode Island. Apr., 1998.
2.   Brites, A.; A Protocol-Independent Notation for the Specification of Operations and Management Applications. Proceedings DSOM'94, Fifth IFIP/IEEE International Workshop on Distributed Systems: Operations & Management. Oct. 1994.

624   N. dos Santos, F.M. Varejão, and O. de Lira Tavares

3. Brito, S.R.; Tavares, O. L.; Agentes Inteligentes: Definições, Aplicações e Comunicação. Revista Engenharia – Ciência & Tecnologia. ISSN 1414-8692. Vitória-ES, Ano 2, No. 9, p. 13-20; mar.-abr. 1999.
4. Buchanan, W.J.; Naylor, M.; Scott, A.V.; Enhancing Network Management using Mobile Agents. Proceedings of the 7th IEEE International Conference and Workshop on the Engineering of Computer Based Systems. Edinburgh, Scotland. Apr. 2000.
5. Chiu, T.; Getting Proactive Network Management from Reactive Network Management Tools. International Journal of Networks Management. Vol. 8, Issue 1, p. 12–17, 1998.
6. De Franceschi, A.S.M.; Rocha, M.A.; Weber, H.L.; Westphall, C.B.; Proactive Network Management Using Remote Monitoring and Artificial Intelligence Techniques. Proceedings of the 2nd IEEE Symposium on Computers and Communications (ISCC'97). Jul. 1997.
7. Goldszmidt, G.; Yemini, Y.; Delegated Agents for Network Management. IEEE Communications Magazine. Vol. 36 Num. 3, p. 66–71, Mar. 1998.
8. Hood, C.S.; JI, C.; Intelligent Agents for Proactive Fault Detection. IEEE Internet Computing. Vol. 2, No. 2, Mar./Apr. 1998.
9. Krause, S.; Magedanz, T.; Mobile Service Agents enabling Intelligence on Demand in Telecommunications. Proceedings of IEEE GLOBCOM'96, 1996.
10. Lipperts, S.; Enabling Alarm Correlation for a Mobile Agent Based System and Network Management - A Wrapper Concept. Proceedings of the IEEE International Conference on Networks. Brisbane, Australia. Oct., 1999.
11. Lopes, R.P.; Oliveira, J.L.; Software Agents in Network Management. Proceedings of the 1st International Conference on Enterprise Information Systems – ICEIS'99. Setúbal, Portugal. Mar. 1999.
12. Lopes, R.P.; Oliveira, J.L.; On the Use of Mobility in Distributed Network Management. Proceedings of the 33rd Hawaii International Conference on System Sciences. Maui, Hawaii, Jan., 2000.
13. Marzo, J-L.; Vilá, P.; Fabregat, R.; ATM Network Management based on a Distributed Artificial Intelligence Architecture. Proceedings of the fourth International Conference on Autonomous Agents. p. 171–172. Barcelona, Spain. Jun. 2000.
14. Oliveira, J.; Arquitectura para Desenvolvimento e Integração de Aplicações de Gestão. Tese de Doutorado. Universidade de Aveiro. Sep. 1995.
15. Pham, V; Karmouch, A., Mobile Software Agents: An Overview. IEEE Communications, Vol. 36, Num. 7, p. 26–37, Jul. 1998.
16. Sprenkels, R.; Martin-Flatin, J-P.; Bulk Transfer of MIB Data, The Simple Times, Vol. 7, Num. 1, Mar., 1999.
17. Wooldridge, M.; Jennings, N.R. Applications of the Intelligent Agents. In: N. R. Jennings, N. R.; Wooldridge, M. (Org.). Agent Technology: Foundations, Applications and Markets. New York: [s.n.], 1998.
18. Wooldridge, M.; Jennings, N.R.; Kinny, O. A Methodology for Agent-Oriented Analysis and Design. In: O. Etzioni, J.P. Muller, and J.Bradshaw, Editors: Agents'99: Proceedings of the Third Annual Conference on Autonomous Agents, p. 69–76, Seattle, WA, 1999.

Formal Specification of Opinions Applied to the Consensus Problem

Guillaume Vauvert and Amal El Fallah-Seghrouchni

LIPN-Univ. Paris, 13 av. Clement, 93430 Villetaneuse-France
{guillaume.vauvert,amal.elfallah}@lipn.univ-paris13.fr

Abstract. Agents are often lead to make collective decision (reaching a consensus about task or resource allocation, election, etc). This paper proposes a distributed protocol based on iterative exchange of opinions among strongly autonomous, weakly rational and heterogeneous agents. We prove that the protocol converges to a consensus while respecting agents' autonomy and fairness. First, a formalism to model agents' preferences, positions and opinions is developed. Then several operators required by the protocol are characterized (e.g. opinion cycle detector, aggregation operator, and consensus detector). Finally, the main experimental results we obtained when the protocol has been applied to the coalition formation problem in the e-commerce context.

Keywords: intelligent agents, preference, consensus, coalition formation
Topics: Multi-Agent Systems, Knowledge Representation, Decision Support Systems

1 Introduction

In Multi-Agent Systems (MAS), agents often have to reach a consensus. In e-commerce context, agents are strongly autonomous and weakly rational. Using this class of agents has several consequences on the design of protocols (as discussed in [1]). It is not possible to design a protocol that permits agents to act in any possible way. One way to restrict their behavior is to make assumptions about their internal state (*e.g.* a kind of rationality, a utility function), but that is incompatible with autonomy. An other way is to give a protocol to agents that agreed on it, and to control that they abide by it: agents are autonomous because no hypothesis about their internal state is made.

In a consensus problem, agents' autonomy is conflicting with a solution computed using an external operator basically because: 1) known operators cannot generally lead to a solution that satisfies every agent (a good solution on average as in [2] is not agreed by all agents, since some of them could prefer to try to earn more, even if they risk to lose more); 2) generally (*e.g.* [3]) operators are based on internal informations about agents (utility function, inmost preferences), which violates their autonomy and privacy.

To reach a consensus among agents who are motivated to satisfy their own preferences first, we propose a protocol which may be summarized as follows: 1) agents may start with different preferences; 2) agents exchange data to influence others' opinions; 3) an iterative process that incites agents to evolve their opinion at run-time and guarantees the consensus will be reached; 4) stops when a consensus is reached.

F.J. Garijo, J.C. Riquelme, and M. Toro (Eds.): IBERAMIA 2002, LNAI 2527, pp. 625–634, 2002.

This protocol rises three questions. First: what is to be exchanged ? Using resources suppose that all services are convertible into them. Argumentation is often used to convince the other agents by giving new information as a rational way to reach a consensus; but such a process assumes that agents have symbolic computation capabilities [4], time and inference abilities [5,6]. Such capabilities are not available for heterogeneous agents, and their normalization -as FIPA- is not practicable [1]. We choose to exchange agents' opinions represented as application, because: 1)it can be understood and processed by heterogeneous agents; 2)agents don't need to reveal their internal informations (which respects their autonomy). Over time, opinions should represent: 1)private preferences of an agent; 2)his current position (voluntarily influenced by other opinions) even if different from his private preferences; 3)a mean to influence other agents.

The second question is how to incite agents to modify their positions. Time cost could be used (by decreasing the incomes), but that implies that agents estimate a possibility using only money. Here, agents are allowed to change their preferences until all give the same opinion twice (a cycle is detected, see section 4). To avoid infinite processing, agents have then the possibility to form alliances. An alliance is a group of agents that decide to behave as a super-agent; its opinion is computed using an aggregation operator on opinions of its members (see section 5). If nobody decides to form an alliance, the MAS chooses the two nearest agents w.r.t. their preferences (using an operator not presented in this paper due to the lack of place and force them to ally. Autonomy is not violated, because: i) this sanction is known and agreed by agents at the beginning of the protocol; ii) constraints on agents' behaviors are weak and can be checked.

The third question concerns the consensus legitimity. We could use a vote to decide about a consensus, but that could make the process tedious and slow down the convergence (since unsatisfied agents may vote against the reached consensus). So, we suggest to use a criteria that is known and agreed initially by agents.

In this paper, we propose an approach based on the exchange of opinions and their evolution among strongly autonomous and weakly rational agents (section 2). The protocol we propose requires: i) a formalism to represent and handle agents' opinions (section 3); ii) a *cycle detector* to recognize a cycle (section 4); iii) an *aggregation operator* that computes the opinion of an alliance or more generally a group of agents (section 5); iv) a *chooser operator* that computes the preferred possibility once a consensus is reached (section 6); v) a *consensus detector* able to decide that a consensus has been reached (section 7). Section 8 presents experiments and results. Related work are presented in section 9. Section 10 concludes our paper and outlines our future work.

2   Our Approach

Conceptually speaking, in our protocol, two roles are distinguished (even if the same agent may play the two roles): the member who competes to perform tasks, and the representative of an alliance who plays the role of interface between his alliance and the other alliances, *i.e.* he receives opinions from his alliance's members, computes the aggregated opinion and send it to the others. Used symbols will be explained later.

The role of an Alliance's Member (AM). (Hypothesis: to begin with, each agent creates an alliance (cardinality 1) and supports two roles: member and representative.)

Main:
- $\diamond$ position $\omega = private\_preference(AM)$
- $\diamond$ AM sends his position ω and in the same time receives the positions of other agents
- $\diamond$ while a consensus is not reached do /*¬ ⋈*/
  - $\diamond$ if a cycle is detected then /*$\Theta = True$*/ then AM calls alliance formation
  - $\diamond$ AM computes his new position ω
  - $\diamond$ AM sends his position ω to his representative

Alliance formation:
- $\diamond$ process of proposition/acceptation of alliance formation
- $\diamond$ if no alliance is formed
  - $\diamond$ then the two nearest alliances ally /*chosen using nearest alliances chooser. This operator chooses the two alliances having the minimal distance between aggregated opinions of alliances (not presented in this paper because of the lack of space).*/

The role of an Alliance's Representative (AR).
- $\diamond$ AR receives the positions from the members of his alliance
- $\diamond$ AR computes the alliance's position /*using aggregation operator II*/
- $\diamond$ AR broadcasts the position of the alliance

3 Opinions

Notation: let A be a set of agents. Lower-case letters denote agents. S is a set of possibilities, Δ a set of preference's degrees, ς a set of conflict's level, Ω a set of opinions. The preference for a possibility c_1 over a possibility c_2 is the expression of the intensity of its author's will to have c_1 chosen instead of c_2. Then an on opinion is a set of preferences comparing every possibilities to every other one. To represent preferences, we propose to use *degrees* that range from -1 to 1: the closer to 1 a degree is, the more the first possibility is preferred to the second (and reciprocally). We don't use an order even partial as in the case of the most other approaches (see section 9), basically because the transitivity is not an inherent property of preferences in rational context. For example, an agent has the choice between three cars with two criteria, the price and the consumption $(c_1 = (\$10K, 8L)$, $c_2 = (\$14K, 6L)$ and $c_3 = (\$18K, 4L))$ and has the following rational rule: "If consumptions are close (less than $3L$), I choose the most expensive car (because it is more luxuous); else I choose the one that consumme the less."; the results are: $c_1 \preceq c_2$, $c_2 \preceq c_3$, and $c_3 \preceq c_1$, what is not transitive.

What happens at the group level ? The first idea is to compute the mean of the degrees $(\omega_{i,j}^{\{a,b\}} = (\omega_{i,j}^a + \omega_{i,j}^b)/2)$, but this formula leads to strange results: a preference of two agents with opposite degrees equals zero (*i.e.* indifference), while incompatible preference could be find. In fact, computing the average for a group leads to the the loss of too much information. To solve this problem, we propose to use the standard deviation that summarizes the dispersion of values.

In order to modelize finely these concepts about possibilities, we propose to distinguish different levels. Our formalism of opinions should be used to represent a private opinion, a computed position and an exchanged position (of agents and alliances).

Our formalism. A preference between two possibilities i and j is defined by a degree of preference $\delta_{i,j}$ and a level of conflict $\sigma_{i,j}$ (standard deviation).

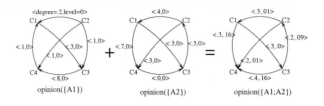

Fig. 1. Opinions and aggregation

Definition 1 (Opinion sets).
The set of possibilities is S, the set of degrees is $\Delta = [-1, 1]$ and the set of levels of conflict is $\varsigma = [0, 1]$.

Property 1 (Degree set). The set of degrees is: i) stable when computing the opposite; ii) continuous; iii) contains a unique element 0 that represents the indifference.

Interpretation:
 - A degree $\delta_{i,j}$ between i and j is interpreted as follows:
   - $0 < \delta_{i,j} \leq 1 \iff$ "I prefer i to j with a degree $\delta_{i,j}$"
   - $-1 \leq \delta_{i,j} < 0 \iff$ "I prefer j to i with a degree $-\delta_{i,j}$"
   - $\delta_{i,j} = 0 \iff$ "I have no preference between i and j"
 - A level of conflict $\sigma_{i,j}$ between i and j is interpreted as follows:
   - $\sigma_{i,j} = 0 \iff$ "everybody agrees the degree of preference" (low level of conflict)
   - $\sigma_{i,j} = 1 \iff$ "the maximum level of conflict is reached"
   - $\sigma_{i,j} < \sigma'_{i,j} \iff$ "opinion with level of conflict $\sigma_{i,j}$ is less conflicting than opinion with level $\sigma'_{i,j}$"

Definition 2 (Opinion). *An **opinion** $\omega \in \Omega$ is an application $\omega : S \times S \to \Delta \times \varsigma$ with the following properties:*
 - *$\forall i \in S, \omega_{i,i}^a = \langle 0, 0 \rangle$: a is indifferent to i and i;*
 - *$\forall (i, j) \in S^2, \omega_{i,j}^a = \langle \delta, \sigma \rangle \Rightarrow \omega_{j,i}^a = \langle -\delta, \sigma \rangle$: the degree is antisymmetric.*

4   Cycle Detector

In order to be sure that the process finishes, we have to detect when a situation happens twice (*i.e.* a cycle).

Characterization. The idea is to save the history (process) of the exchanged opinions and to detect similar situations called "views" (notation: $u \approx_v v$) thanks to the operator called "cycle detector" as follows.

Definitions 3 *View: A **view** v is an application $A \to \Omega$.*
History*: An **history** $h \in H$ is a sequence $(v_t)_{1 \leq t \leq T}$ of views, where T is the length of the history.*
Partial order on opinions*: A **partial order on opinions** $\succ_o$ is defined by: $\forall (\omega^a, \omega^b) \in \Omega^2, \omega^a \succ_o \omega^b \iff \forall (i, j) \in S^2, \delta_{i,j}^a \geq \delta_{i,j}^b \wedge \sigma_{i,j}^a \leq \sigma_{i,j}^b$.*
Partial order on views*: Let $(\omega^a)_{a \in A}$ the agents' opinions. A **partial order on views** $\succ_v$ is defined by: $\forall (v, v') \in V^2, v \succ_v v' \iff \forall (a, b) \in A^2, \omega^a \succ_o \omega^b$.*

Definition 4 (Cycle detector). *A* **cycle detector** Θ *is an application* $H \times \mathbb{R}^* \times \mathbb{R}^* \to$ *{False, True} characterized as:*

i) $\forall h \in H, h = (v_t)_{1 \leq t \leq T}, \exists t \in [1, T[, \forall a \in A, v_t(a) = v_T(a) \Rightarrow \Theta(h) = True$: *detects true cycles (i.e. when a situation happens twice);*

ii) $\forall (u, v) \in V^2, u \approx_v v \Rightarrow \forall (u', v') \in V^2, u \succ_v u' \succ_v v' \succ_v v, u' \approx_v v'$: *if u and v correspond to a cycle, then all the couples of views* (u', v') *situated between u and v must be detected as cycles too.*

Example of Our Distance Cycle Detector.

Definitions 5 **Opinion preference distance**: *An* **opinion preference distance** $|., .|_o^p$ *is an application* $\Omega \times \Omega \to \mathbb{R}$ *defined by:* $\forall (\omega, \omega') \in \Omega^2, |\omega, \omega'|_o^p = \max_{i,j} |\delta_{i,j} - \delta'_{i,j}|$.
Opinion conflict distance: *An* **opinion conflict distance** $|., .|_o^c$ *is an application* $\Omega \times \Omega \to \mathbb{R}$ *defined by:* $\forall (\omega, \omega') \in \Omega^2, |\omega, \omega'|_o^c = \max_{i,j} |\sigma_{i,j} - \sigma'_{i,j}|$.
View preference distance: *A* **view preference distance** $|., .|_v^p$ *is an application* $V \times V \to \mathbb{R}$ *defined by:* $\forall (v, v') \in V^2, |v, v'|_v^p = \max_{a \in A} |\omega_v^a, \omega_{v'}^a|_o^p$.
View conflict distance: *A* **view conflict distance** $|., .|_v^c$ *is an application* $V \times V \to \mathbb{R}$ *defined by:* $\forall (v, v') \in V^2, |v, v'|_v^c = \max_{a \in A} |\omega_v^a, \omega_{v'}^a|_o^c$.

Definition 6 (Distance cycle detector). *Let* $(\epsilon_p, \epsilon_c) \in \mathbb{R}^{*2}$ *be two thresholds.*
$\breve{\Theta}$ *is an application* $H \times \mathbb{R}^* \times \mathbb{R}^* \to$ *{False, True} defined by:*
$\forall h \in H, h = (v_t)_{1 \leq t \leq T}, \breve{\Theta}(h) = True \Longleftrightarrow \exists t \in [1, T-1],$
$|v_t, v_T|_v^p \leq \epsilon_p \wedge |v_t, v_T|_v^c \leq \epsilon_c.$

$\breve{\Theta}$ returns true if the two views are close enough considering both view preference distance (ϵ_p) and view conflict distance (ϵ_c).

Proposition 1. $\breve{\Theta}$ *is a cycle detector.*

5 Aggregation Operator

The main interest of our opinion model is its ability to compute naturally the opinions of a group contrary to other approaches. In fact, using a total order to modelize individual preferences prevents from computing groups' preferences with the same formalism. For example, if a_1 prefers 1 over 2, and a_2 prefers 2 over 1, what is the preference of a_1, a_2 ? In our framework and in MAS in general, opinions' aggregation is usefull to: i) estimate the opinion of a group, what may be used to choose which actions to be performed; ii) compute the new position of an agent (others' opinions are informations that an agent should take into account in order to evolve his private opinion). A way to do that is to aggregate the opinions of others with small weights (using a weighted aggregation, as defined in section 9).

Characterization. According to the rationality of the aggregation, we propose axioms necessarily respected by the aggregation operator.

Definition 7 (Aggregation operator). *Let $n \in \mathbb{N}^*$.*
*An **aggregation operator** $\amalg_n$ is an application $\Omega^p \to \Omega$ with the following properties:*
i) [Independence] $\amalg_n(\omega_{i,j}^1, \ldots, \omega_{i,j}^n) = f(\omega_{i,j}^1, \ldots, \omega_{i,j}^n)$: the aggregation of two opinions on two possibilities doesn't depend on opinions on other possibilities;
ii) [Everywhere defined] $\forall(\omega^1, \ldots, \omega^n) \in \Omega^n, \forall(i,j) \in S, \amalg_n(\omega_{i,j}^1, \ldots, \omega_{i,j}^n)$ is defined: all opinions could be aggregated;
iii) [Keep equality] $\amalg_2(\langle \delta, \sigma \rangle, \langle \delta, \sigma' \rangle) = \langle \delta, \sigma'' \rangle$;
iv) [Equity] $\forall \tau$ a permutation on $[1, n]$, $\amalg_n(\langle \delta_1, \sigma_1 \rangle, \ldots, \langle \delta_n, \sigma_n \rangle) = \amalg(\langle \delta_{\tau(1)}, \sigma_{\tau(1)} \rangle, \ldots, \langle \delta_{\tau(n)}, \sigma_{\tau(n)} \rangle)$: the result of the aggregation doesn't depend on the order of opinions;
v) [Opposition] $\amalg_2(\langle \delta, \sigma \rangle, \langle -\delta, \sigma' \rangle) = \langle 0, \sigma'' \rangle$: if two agents have opposite degrees, the result of aggregation is a null degree (but not the level of conflict);
vi) [Associativity] $\amalg_2(\amalg_2(\omega, \omega'), \omega'') = \amalg_2(\omega, \amalg_2(\omega', \omega''))$: an aggregated opinion must not depend on how the group has been formed (e.g. when agents join the group)

Example of Our Aggregation Operator.
Definition 8 (Aggregation of groups' opinions). *Let $(\omega_i)_{1 \leq i \leq n}$ be a sequence of opinions: $\forall i, \omega_i = \langle \delta_i, \sigma_i \rangle$.*
The quadratic mean is defined by: $\forall i, \overline{m}_i = \sigma_i^2 - \delta_i^2$.
We define $\breve{\amalg}((\omega_i)_{1 \leq i \leq n}) = \langle \delta, \sigma \rangle$ where: $\delta = \frac{1}{n}\sum_{i=1}^n \delta_i$, $\overline{m} = \frac{1}{n}\sum_{i=1}^n \overline{m}_i$ and $\sigma = \sqrt{\overline{m} - \delta^2}$

Remark 1. In statistic, given a standard deviation σ, m a mean and $\overline{m}$ a quadratic mean, from the Huygens/König formula, we deduce: $\sigma = \sqrt{\overline{m} - m^2}$. In this paper, $m = \delta$, so $\sigma = \sqrt{\overline{m} - \delta^2}$. The same formula are used to compute $\overline{m}_i = \sigma_i^2 - \delta_i^2$.

Proposition 2. $\breve{\amalg}$ *is an aggregation operator.*

An example of aggregation is given in figure 1. The opinions of the two agents at the left are aggregated into one opinion (the right one). Let us remark that the levels of conflict that vary from 0 to 0.16, depend on the closeness of degrees of preferences.

Definition 9 (Weighted aggregation). *Let $p \in \mathbb{N}^*$. A **weighted aggregation operator** $\tilde{\amalg}$ is an application $(\Omega \times \mathbb{R}^+)^p \to \Omega$ defined by: $\tilde{\amalg}((\omega_1, w_1), \ldots, (\omega_p, w_p))$ aggregates all opinions, replacing the degrees δ_i by $w_i \times \delta_i$ and the level of conflict σ_i by $w_i \times \sigma_i$.*

6 Chooser Operator

When a consensus is reached (the agents have close opinions), we have to find the preferred solution. This is why opinions will be aggregated using the chooser operator defined below. When preferences are formalized by a total order, there is a unique possibility preferred to all others. In partial orders, several maximal possibilities may exist. As we allow cycles (in the preference relation), generally there is no maximal preferred possibility. The difficulty is that we have to find a compromise between maximizing the degrees of preference and minimizing the level of conflict (w.r.t. other possibilities).
Characterization. The necessary axiom of a chooser operator is that if a best possibility exists, then this possibility will be chosen.

Definition 10 (Chooser operator). *Let* $E_{max} = \{i \in S/[\forall j \in S, \delta_{i,j} \geq 0] \wedge [\forall(k,l) \in S^2, (\delta_{i,j} \geq \delta_{k,l}) \wedge (\sigma_{i,j} \leq \sigma_{k,l})]\}$.
A **chooser operator** $\bigcirc$ *is an application* $\omega \rightarrow S$ *with the property: if* $E_{max} \neq \emptyset$, *then* $\bigcirc(\omega) \in E_{max}$

Example of Our Chooser. Generally, E_{max} is empty; so we defined several heuristics to make this choice. In the following, we present one of them called "degrees first, conflicts next".It's difficult to take into account the degree of preference and the conflict level in the same time, because we don't know which criteria must be used before the other; in this heuristics, we favor degrees.

Definitions 11 Weight of a possibility*: We call* **weight of a possibility** $i \in S$ *for the opinion* ω *the value* $w_\omega(i) = \frac{1}{|S|-1}\sum_{j \in S \setminus \{i\}} \delta_{i,j}$.
Efficient opinion*: An opinion* $\langle \delta, \sigma \rangle$ *is efficient if* $\nexists \langle \delta', \sigma' \rangle, \delta \geq \delta' \wedge \sigma \leq \sigma' \wedge (\delta > \delta' \vee \sigma < \sigma')$.
Degrees first, conflicts next*:*
  − *Step 1: Build the set of the best possibilities (I) as follows:*
Let $(w_i)_{i \in S}$ *be the sequence of weights of possibilities of S computed using def.11.*
Let $w_{max} = \max_i w_i$ *and let* $\epsilon \in \mathbb{R}^*$ *be a threshold.*
Let $I = \{i \in [1,n]/w_i \geq w_{max} - \epsilon\}$ *be the set of possibilities that are close to the maximum.*
  − *Step 2: K is a restriction of I such that K is a total order*
Let $\succeq_P$ *be the preference relation defined by* $\delta_{i,j} \geq 0 \Longleftrightarrow i \succeq_P j$.
Let Q be the set of relations between possibilities of I ordered by σ_i.
Let apply the process:
1- Let K be an empty partial order.
2- while $Q \neq \emptyset$ do
3- let $(i \succeq_P j) = min(Q)$; $Q \leftarrow Q \setminus \{i \succeq_P j\}$. /* less conflict*/
4- If $K \cup (i \succeq_P j)$ doesn't contain a cycle, then add the relation to K.
5- endwhile
We call "degrees first, conflicts next" the application $\omega_S \mapsto max(K)$.

Proposition 3. *The application "degrees first, conflicts next" is an opinion chooser.*

Example: let us apply this operator to the aggregated opinion of the figure 1. Step 1: let us compute the sequence of weights: $w_1 = (-.3+.3+.3)/3 = .1, w_2 = (.3-.2+.2)/3 = .1, w_3 = (-.3+.2+.4)/3 = .1$ and $w_4 = (-.3-.2-.4)/3 = -.3$; so $I = \{C_1, C_2, C_3\}$. Step 2 : $Q = \{C_1 \succeq_P C_3; C_2 \succeq_P C_1; C_3 \succeq_P C_2\}$ (remark: the most important relations form a cycle); $K_0 = \emptyset$, $K_1 = \{C_1 \succeq_P C_3\}$, $K_2 = \{C_1 \succeq_P C_3; C_2 \succeq_P C_1\}$ and $K_3 = \{C_1 \succeq_P C_3; C_2 \succeq_P C_1\}$. Finally, C_2 is the preferred car.

7 Consensus Detector

A consensus operator has to answer the question: do all agents agree ? The vote is often used: firstly, each agent chooses one possibility and the one that has the maximum of votes is elected. In some vote systems, agents may choose more than one possibility (often two), but all possibilities have the same weight. We propose to extend this system by aggregating all opinions into a lone one using an aggregation operator, and then by choosing a possibility by applying a chooser operator on the aggregated opinion.

Two parameters are taken into account: the degree of preference and the conflict level.

Characterization.

Definition 12 (Consensus detector). *A consensus detector $\bowtie$ is an application $\Omega \rightarrow$ {False, True} defined by:* $\bowtie (\omega) = True \Longleftrightarrow \forall (i,j) \in S^2, \sigma_{i,j} = 0$

It seems rational to impose that if one possibility is preferred by all agents, then this possibility will be elected.

Example of consensus detector.

Definition 13 (Epsilon consensus detector). *Let $\epsilon \in \mathbb{R}^*$.*
An epsilon consensus detector $\breve{\bowtie}_\epsilon$ is an application $\Omega \rightarrow$ {False, True} defined by:
$\forall (i,j) \in S^2, \sigma_{i,j} \leq \epsilon \Rightarrow \bowtie (\omega) = True$

Proposition 4. *For all $\epsilon \in \mathbb{R}^*$, $\breve{\bowtie}_\epsilon$ is a consensus detector.*

8   Experiments

We distinguish the coalition from alliance: some agents may ally because they are interested in the same solution, even if they don't collaborate in a coalition to fulfill a task.

Protocol of Experiment.   We have made several experiments, but we present here only the most significant result. In a reaching consensus problem, it is difficult to find an efficient strategy. In order to test our formalism and operators, we have built a family of strategies and organized a tournament between these strategies.

The problem chosen to test our strategies is an allocation of tasks in an e-commerce context (see [1,7]). Some sub-tasks have to be allocated to several agents who are not able to fulfill all tasks because they have limited skills (no agent meets all the requirements of a task). In our study, 7 agents have to share 8 sub-tasks among themselves, and 32 possibilities are assumed available.

Each agent chooses to take the others' opinions into account with a more or less great weight. At the beginning, it is in their interest to be rigid (*i.e.* do not take others' opinions into account) in order to influence the opinions of the others. At the end, they should better be flexible in order to have chance to be assigned a task. The question is: at what speed do I decrease my rigidity ? We define a strategy as a speed of decreasing. Formally, the rigidity r is defined by: $\forall a \in A, \forall \alpha \in [0,1], \forall t \in [1,T], r(t) = \exp^{-\alpha t}$. The agent computes his new opinion as follows:

- first, he aggregates the opinions of other agents: $\omega_m = \amalg(\{\omega'_b / b \in A \backslash \{a\}\})$;
- then he applies the weighted aggregation operator to aggregate his preferences weigthed by r and other agents' preferences weigthed by $1 - r$; as result, the strategy is defined by: $s_\alpha^a(t/10) = \tilde{\amalg}(< \omega_a, r >, < \omega_m, 1 - r >)$.

Each strategy α (used by one agent) is opposed to a strategy β (used by all other agents, *i.e.* uniform population). For each fight α against β, we compute the ratio of income (in comparison with the agent's maximal income) for the agent using the strategy α.

The results are presented as follows (see figure 2): the strategy α takes place on the X-axis, and the mean of percentages of income (for all agents that used the strategy α) on Y-axis. Each curve represents the set of results for a fixed value of β ($\beta \in [0.0, 0.2, \ldots, 1.0]$ represents strategies of other agents).

Results. Figure 2 gives the results of our experiments. It shows that, whatever the value

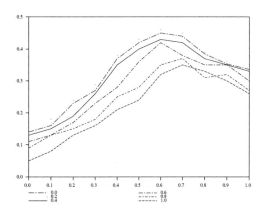

Fig. 2. Results of experiment

of β, the best strategy α remains around $\alpha = 0.7$. This result is interesting as it emphasizes that our protocol doesn't favor extremely rigid strategies. Such strategies don't lead to rational solutions, as when every agent is extremely rigid, the final solution is given by the chooser applied to the aggregated opinions at the first step, what amounts to use an external chooser operator. Symetrically, too flexible strategies, as one can expect, are not interested.

9   Related Work

In [8], Kenneth Arrow formalized the concept of preference by a binary relation $<$ (antisymmetric, transitive and not reflexive) in order to find a function of aggregation of preferences that respects the intuition. He proves that the only solution is a totalitarian system (one agent decides). This very strict modelization is not rich enough to represent some aspects of preferences: i) the indifference (no preference) is not modelized; ii) there is no level of preference (no intermediate degree); iii) a rational preference relation may be non-transitive (see section 3).

Many representations of preferences have been proposed in order to solve this impossibility problem [9]: i)as a preference ordering of the possibilities what results to a total order; ii)as a utility function: the result is a total order, but with a measure of the difference of preference between two possibilities that is richer than preferred/not preferred; iii)as a preferred relation with some degree of preference of any alternative over another: the degree is interpreted as a degree of credibility. The modelization of users' preferences [10] is based on several kinds of transitivities (more or less strict: min- or weak-transitivity, *etc.*) and two symbols (indifference and incomparability). We consider that the transitivity is not necessary for preference's modelization: in fact, K. Arrow's modelization refers to an absolute judgment, while a preference is relative.

Our formalism may be viewed as a generalization of several others. If we limit values of degrees to $\{-1, 0, 1\}$ and don't take the level of conflict into account, our formalism is equivalent to a total order (strict if we remove the 0). Incomparability when added leads to a partial order; in our approach, the semantics of the incomparability is a high level of conflict. To represent a valuation, we have to impose the constraint: $\delta_{i,j} \geq 0 \wedge \delta_{j,k} \geq 0 \Rightarrow \delta_{i,k} = \delta_{i,j} + \delta_{j,k}$.

10   Conclusion and Future Works

This paper introduces a new formalism of opinions and shows how use it in a consensus protocol for tasks' allocation among strongly autonomous, weakly rational and heterogeneous agents. This formalism permits fine representations of an agent's opinions (several degrees of preference and uncertainty) and of a group's one (several degrees of preference and levels of conflict) thanks to the aggregation operator. In the future, we will test other operators and more complex strategies in order to show the richness of our formalism.

References

1. Vauvert, G., El Fallah-Seghrouchni, A.: Coalition formation among strongly autonomous and weakly rational agents. In: Proc. of MAAMAW'2001, France (2001)
2. Shapley, L.S.: A Value for N-Person Game. In: Contributions to the Theory of Games. Princeton University Press (1953)
3. Zlotkin, G., Rosenschein, J.S.: Coalition, cryptography, and stability: Mechanisms for coalition formation in task oriented domains. In: Proc. of AAAI94, Washington (1994) 432–437
4. Kraus, S., Sycara, K., Evenchik, A.: Reaching agreements through argumentation: A logical model and implementation. Artificial Intelligence 104 (1998) 1–69
5. Konolige, K.: A Deduction Model of Belief. Pitman, London (1986)
6. Nirkhe, M., Kraus, S., Perlis, D.: Situated reasoning within tight deadlines and realistic space and computation bounds. In: Proc. of the 2nd Symposium On Logical Formalizations Of Commonsense Reasoning. (1993)
7. Vauvert, G., El Fallah-Seghrouchni, A.: A distributed algorithm for coalition formation among strongly autonomous and weakly rational agents. In: Proc. of IAT'2001, Japan (2001)
8. Arrow, K.: 1. In: The Origins of the Impossibility Theorem. Elsevier Science Publishers B. V., Amsterdam (1991) 1–4
9. Sen, A.: Collective Choice and Social Wellfare. Holden-Day (1970)
10. Dastani, M., Jacobs, N., Jonker, C., Treur, J.: Modeling user preferences and mediating agents in electronic commerce. In F. Dignum, C.S., ed.: Agent-Mediated Electronic Commerce. Volume 1991 of LNAI. Springer Verlag edn. (2001) 164–196

Practical NLP-Based Text Indexing

Jésus Vilares, F. Mario Barcala, Miguel A. Alonso, Jorge Graña, and
Manuel Vilares

Departamento de Computación, Universidade da Coruña
Campus de Elviña s/n, 15071 La Coruña, Spain
{jvilares,barcala}@mail2.udc.es   {alonso,grana,vilares}@udc.es
http://coleweb.dc.fi.udc.es/

Abstract. We consider a set of natural language processing techniques
based on finite-state technology that can be used to analyze huge
amounts of texts. These techniques include an advanced tokenizer, a
part-of-speech tagger that can manage ambiguous streams of words, a
system for conflating words by means of derivational mechanisms, and
a shallow parser to extract syntactic-dependency pairs. We propose to
use these techniques in order to improve the performance of standard
indexing engines.

1   Introduction

In recent years, there has been a considerable amount of interest in using Natural Language Processing (NLP) in Information Retrieval (IR) research, with
specific implementations varying from the word-level morphological analysis to
syntactic parsing to conceptual-level semantic analysis. In this paper we consider the employment of a set of practical NLP techniques built on finite-state
technology that make them adequate for dealing with large amounts of texts.
Finite-state technology is sometimes characterized as ad-hoc. However, we propose a sequence of finite-state based processes, where each stage corresponds to
intuitive linguistic elements, reflecting important universals about language:

- The existence of individual words and idioms forming each sentence.
- The existence of different categories of word carrying the semantics of the
  sentence: nouns, adjectives and verbs.
- The existence of semantic relations between words belonging to different
  categories (e.g. the noun corresponding to the action of a verb).
- The existence of basic syntactic structures relating words within a sentence,
  such as the noun-modifier, subject-verb or verb-object relations.

The scheme of the paper follows the processing stages shown in Fig. 1. Firstly,
in Sect. 2, we describe the preprocessor, an advanced tokenizer which accounts
for a number of complex linguistic phenomena, as well as for pre-tagging tasks.
Section 3 shows the tagger, which is based on Hidden Markov Models with
disambiguation and lemmatization capabilities. Next, in Sect. 4, we describe the
main morphological mechanisms of word formation, and their application to the
automatic generation of morphological families. Section 5 describes a shallow

F.J. Garijo, J.C. Riquelme, and M. Toro (Eds.): IBERAMIA 2002, LNAI 2527, pp. 635–644, 2002.

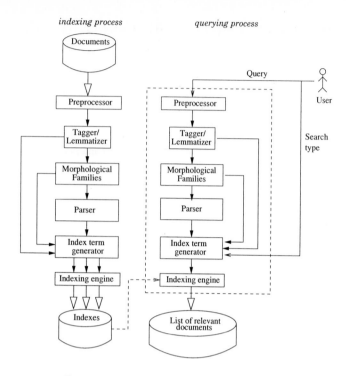

Fig. 1. General architecture of the system

parser working on syntactic and morpho-syntactic variants of noun phrases for the extraction of syntactic dependency pairs. The evaluation of the proposed techniques is performed in Sect. 6. Section 7 presents final conclusions.

2   The Preprocessor

Current taggers assume that input texts are correctly segmented in *tokens* or high level information units that identify every individual component of the texts. This working hypothesis is not realistic due to the heterogeneous nature of the application texts and their sources. For this reason, we have developed a preprocessor module [4,1], an advanced tokenizer which performs the following tasks:

Filtering. Texts are converted from source format (e.g. HTML or XML) to plain text, and delimiters are compacted (e.g. it removes multiple blanks or blanks at beginning of sentences).

Tokenization. Every individual word as well as every punctuation mark will be a different token, taking into account abbreviations, acronyms, numbers with decimals and dates in numerical format. For this purpose, we use two dictionaries, one of abbreviations and another one of acronyms, and a small set of rules to detect numbers and dates.

Sentence Segmentation. The general rule consists of separating a sentence when there is a dot followed by a capital letter. However, it must be taken into account certain abbreviations to avoid marking the end of a sentence at their dots.

Morphological Pretagging. The preprocessor tags elements whose tag can be deduced from the morphology of the word, and there is no more reliable way to do it. In this step, for instance, numbers and dates are identified.

Contraction Splitting. Contractions are split into their different tokens, assigning a tag to every one of them, by using external information on how contractions are decomposed. For instance, the Spanish contraction `del` (*of the*) is decomposed into the preposition `de` (*of*) and the article `el` (*the*).

Enclitic Pronouns. Verb stems are separated from their enclitic pronouns, tagging every one of them correctly. To perform this function, we need to consult a dictionary with as many verbal forms as possible, a dictionary containing the greatest possible number of verbal stems capable of presenting enclitic pronouns, a list with all the valid combinations of enclitic pronouns, and a list with the whole set of enclitic pronouns, together with their tags and lemmas. As an example, the Spanish word `comerlo` (*to eat it*) is decomposed in `comer` (which is the infinitive *to eat*) and `lo` (which is the pronoun *it*).

Expression Identification. The different tokens that make up an expression are joined together [2], using a dictionary with the expressions that are uniquely expressions, e.g. `a pesar de` (*in spite of*), and a dictionary of phrases that may be expressions or not, e.g. `sin embargo` (*however* or *without seizure*). The preprocessor simply generates the possible segmentations, and then the tagger selects one of those alternatives later.

Numeral Identification. Consecutive numerals are joined together in order to build a compound numeral and so obtain only one token. For instance, every component of `mil ciento veinticinco` (*one thousand one hundred and twenty-five*) is joined with the rest in the same way as the components of an expression. Unlike the case of expressions, the tag assigned by the preprocessor here is definitive.

Proper Noun Training. Given a sample of the texts that are going to be indexed, the preprocessor identifies the words that begin with a capital letter and appear in non-ambiguous positions, i.e. in positions where if a word begins with a capital letter then it is a proper noun. For instance, words appearing after a dot are not considered, and words in the middle of the text are considered. It also identifies sequences of capitalized words connected by some valid connectives like the preposition *of* and definite articles. The proper nouns detected are added to a trained dictionary.

Proper Noun Identification. Using a specific dictionary of proper nouns and the trained dictionary, we are able to detect proper nouns whether simple or compound, and either appearing in positions ambiguous or not. This task is explained in detail in [1].

The general structure of this first module is shown in Fig. 2. As we can see, there are two processing modes. Firstly, there is an off-line process, during

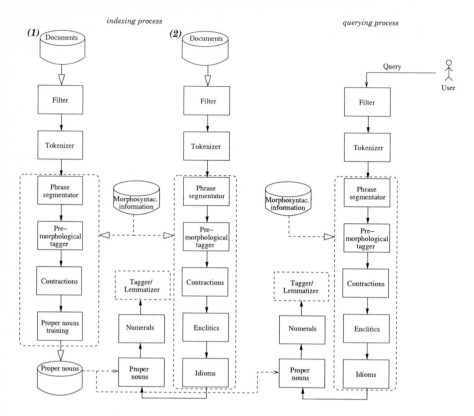

Fig. 2. General architecture of the preprocessor

indexing time, where the documents to be indexed are tagged. This off-line process consists of two steps. In the first step, a subset of the documents is used for proper noun training, and in a second step, the data obtained are employed to tag the entire document database. The other main processing mode is an on-line process during querying time where the query is tagged. The data obtained in the proper noun training phase during indexing process is also employed here for tagging the query.

3   The Tagger

A second order Hidden Markov Model (HMM) is used to perform part-of-speech tagging. The states of the model represent pairs of tags, and outputs represent the words. Transition probabilities depend on the states, thus pairs of tags. Output probabilities only depend on the most recent category. To be explicit, we use the Viterbi algorithm to calculate:

$$\arg\max_{t_1\ldots t_n} \prod_{i=1}^{n} [P(w_i|t_i) \times P(t_i|t_{i-2}, t_{i-1})]$$

for a given sentence of words $w_1 \ldots w_n$ of length n, where $t_1 \ldots t_n$ are elements of the tagset. Transition and output probabilities are estimated from a tagged corpus. As a first step, we use the maximum likelihood probabilities derived from relative frequencies. As a second step, contextual frequencies are smoothed and lexical frequencies are completed by handling words that do not appear in the training corpus but are present in external dictionaries.

Trigram probabilities generated from a corpus cannot be used directly because of the sparse-data problem, which means that there are insufficient instances for each trigram to reliably estimate the probability. The smoothing paradigm that delivers the best results is linear interpolation of unigrams, bigrams and trigrams. Therefore, we estimate a trigram probability as follows:

$$P(t_3|t_1,t_2) = \lambda_3\,\hat{P}(t_3|t_1,t_2) + \lambda_2\,\hat{P}(t_3|t_2) + \lambda_1\,\hat{P}(t_3)$$

where $\lambda_1 + \lambda_2 + \lambda_3 = 1$, so P again represents probability distributions. The values of λ_1, λ_2 and λ_3 are estimated by deleted interpolation.

Given an unknown word, its candidate tags and their probabilities are set according to the ending of the word in question. The probability distribution of a particular suffix is generated from all words in the training set that share the same suffix of some predefined maximum length. Probabilities are then smoothed by successive abstraction [9]. This method obtains a proper probability distribution for each tag and for each suffix length, as needed by the HMM.

Sometimes we have to deal with languages with very few available linguistic resources. Currently, the typical situation in Spanish processing is very short training texts, but very large dictionaries, since the morphology of the language is well-known and the effort made to formalize it has been much greater. The most intuitive way to integrate a dictionary is the Adding One method, which consists of using the dictionary as an additional tagged corpus where a frequency of 1 is assigned to each word-tag pair. However, this integration does not produce a coherent representation of the model we are estimating, and it can produce important alterations in the working parameters. This leads us to consider another method based on the Good-Turing formulas [7]. Every word-tag pair present only in the external dictionary can be seen as an event with null frequency in the training corpus, and the Good-Turing formulas are themselves a method able to assign probabilities greater than 0 to these rare but existing events. In addition, this technique produces less distortion of the model and increases the performance of the tagging process when the training corpus is small [5].

Due to the ambiguous segmentations obtained during preprocessing, as it was described in Sect. 2, this tagger must be able to deal with streams of tokens of different lengths: it not only has to decide the tag to be assigned to every token, but also to decide whether some of them form or not the same term, and assign the appropriate number of tags on the basis of the alternatives provided by the preprocessor. To perform this process, we consider the evaluation of every stream of tokens and their subsequent comparison, in order to select the most probable one, as indicated in [3]. It is also necessary to define some objective criterion for that comparison. When the tagging paradigm used is the framework of the hidden Markov models, as is our case, that criterion is the comparison of the normalization of the cumulative probabilities. One reason to support the use of hidden Markov models is that, in other tagging paradigms, the criteria for comparison may not be so easy to identify.

Once a text has been tagged, content words (nouns, verbs, adjectives) are extracted to be indexed. In this way we solve the problems derived from inflection in Spanish. Therefore, recall is remarkably increased. With regard to computational cost, the running cost of a lemmatizer-disambiguator is linear in relation to the length of the word and cubic in relation to the size of the tagset, which is a constant. As we only need to know the grammatical category of the word, the tagset is small and therefore the increase in cost with respect to classical approaches (stemmers) becomes negligible.

4   Morphological Families

Once inflectional variation has been solved, the next logical step is to solve the problems derived from derivational morphology. Spanish has a great productivity and flexibility in its word formation mechanisms by using a rich and complex productive morphology, preferring derivation to other mechanisms of word formation. We define a *morphological family* as the set of words obtained from the same morphological root through derivation mechanisms. It is expected that a basic semantic relationship will remain between the words of a given family, relations of the type process-result, e.g. *producción* (production) / *producto* (product), process-agent, e.g. *manipulación* (manipulation) / *manipulador* (manipulator), etc. In Spanish, the basic derivational mechanisms are: *prefixation*, preposing morphemes to the base; *emotive suffixation*, postposing morphemes that alter the base in some sort of subjective emotional way; *non-emotive suffixation*, postposing morphemes that change the meaning of the base fundamentally rather than marginally, often effecting a change of syntactic category; *back formation*, a morphological procedure to derive nouns from verbs by truncation; and *parasynthesis*, the simultaneous prefixation and suffixation of the base lexeme.

Many derivational morphemes have variable forms (*allomorphs*), sometimes phonologically determined, and others lexically imposed by convention or etymology. It must also be taken into account that morphological operations can also involve phonological alterations of the base [8].

Regular word formation patterns in Spanish can be obtained through the 'rules of word formation' [8] defined by generative phonology and transformational-generative grammars. Though this paradigm is not complete, it has been used to implement an automatic system for generation of morphological families with an acceptable degree of completeness and correction [11].

Given two words w and w' in the lexicon, we denote by $w \triangleright w'$ the fact that w' is obtained from w by means of some of the derivational mechanisms shown above. Given this, we compute the morphological family of w as its reflexive and transitive closure through derivation, denoted closure(w) and defined recursively as:

- $w \in$ closure(w).
- If $w \rhd w'$ then $w' \in$ closure(w).
- If $w' \rhd w$ then $w' \in$ closure(w).

The set of morphological families associated with a given lexicon is obtained by means of applying closure(w) to each word w in the lexicon.

In order to use morphological families for document conflation, once we have obtained the part of speech and the lemmas of the text to be indexed, we replace each of the lemmas obtained by a fixed representative of its morphological family, which is indexed [11]. In this way we are using the same index term to represent all words belonging to the same morphological family; therefore, semantic relations that exist between these words remain in the index because related terms are conflated to the same index term. With regard to computational cost, morphological families and their representatives are computed *a priori*, so they do not affect the final indexing and querying cost.

5   The Shallow Parser

Given a stream of tagged words, the parser module tries to obtain the *head-modifier* pairs corresponding to the most relevant syntactic dependencies:*noun-modifier*, relating the head of a noun phrase with the head of a modifier; *subject-verb*, relating the head of the subject with the main verb of the clause; and *verb-complement*, relating the main verb of the clause with the head of a complement.

It has to be noted that while the head-modifier relation may suggest semantic dependence, what we obtain here is strictly syntactic, even though the semantic relation is what we are really after.

The kernel of the grammar used by the parser is inferred from the basic trees corresponding to noun phrases and their syntactic and morpho-syntactic variants [6,10]:

Syntactic variants result from the inflection of individual words and from modifying the syntactic structure of the original noun phrase. Given a noun phrase, their syntactic variants are obtained by means of:
- *synapsy*, changing a preposition or adding or removing a determiner;
- *substitution*, employing modifiers to make a term more specific;
- *permutation* of words around a pivot element;
- employing *coordinating constructions* (copulative or disjunctive) with the modifier or with the modified term.

Morpho-syntactic variants differ from syntactic variants in that at least one of the content words of the original noun phrase is transformed into another word derived from the same morphological stem. They can be classified according to the nature of the morphological transformations applied to their words:
- *Iso-categorial:* morphological derivation process does not change the category of words, but only transforms one noun syntagma into another. There are two possibilities: noun-to-noun and adjective-to-adjective.

	stm	lem	fam	sdp
Average precision	0.2179	0.2214	0.2268	0.2931
Average recall	0.6335	0.6211	0.6397	0.5179

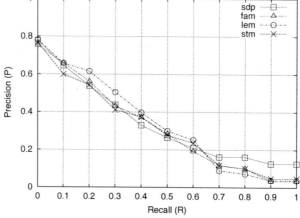

Fig. 3. Experimental results on a corpus of newspaper articles

- *Hetero-categorial:* morphological derivation does result in a change of the category of a word. There are also two possibilities: noun-to-verb and noun-to-adjective.

We must remark that syntactic variants involve inflectional morphology but not derivational morphology, whereas morpho-syntactic variants involve both inflectional and derivational morphology. In addition, syntactic variants have a very restricted scope (the noun phrase) whereas morpho-syntactic variants can span a whole sentence, including a verb and its complements.

Once the basic trees of noun phrases and their variants have been established, they are compiled into a set of regular expressions, which are matched against the tagged texts in order to extract the dependency pairs, which are used as index terms, as is described in [10]. In this way, we can identify dependency pairs through simple pattern matching over the output of the tagger/lemmatizer, dealing with the problem by means of finite-state techniques, leading to a considerable reduction of the running cost.

6   Evaluation

The lack of a standard evaluation corpus has been a great handicap for the development of IR research in Spanish.[1] This situation is changing due to the

---

[1] The test collection used in the Spanish track of TREC-4 (1995) and TREC-5 (1996), formed by news articles written in Mexican-Spanish, is no longer freely available.

incorporation in CLEF-2001[2] of a Spanish corpus (composed of news provided by a Spanish news agency) which is expected to become a standard. The techniques proposed in this paper have been integrated recently, therefore, we could not participate in CLEF-2001 edition, but we are prepared to join competition in 2002. Due to the unavailability of the CLEF corpus, we have chosen to test our techniques over the corpus used in [12], formed by 21,899 newspaper articles (national, international, economy, culture,...) with an average length of 447 words. We have considered a set of 14 natural language queries with an average length of 7.85 words per query, 4.36 of which were content words.

The techniques proposed in this article are independent of the indexing engine we choose to use. This is because we first conflate the document to obtain its index terms; then, the engine receives the conflated version of the document as input. So, any standard text indexing engine may be employed, which is a great advantage. Nevertheless, each engine will behave according to its own characteristics (indexing model, ranking algorithm, etc.). We have compared the results obtained, using SMART with the ltc-lnc weighting scheme as indexing engine, by four different indexing methods: stemmed text after eliminating stopwords (*stm*), lemmatized text (*lem*), text conflated by means of morphological families (*fam*) and syntactic dependency pairs (*sdp*). Results are shown in Fig. 3. We can observe that *lem* and *fam* slightly improve the precision of *stm*, with *fam* also improving recall. With respect to *sdp*, we must remark it shows an improvement in precision of 34.5% with respect to *stm*.

7   Conclusion

In this article we have proposed a set of practical natural language techniques to improve the performance of text indexing when applied to Spanish texts. These techniques include an advanced tokenizer for the right segmentation of texts which accounts for a number of complex linguistic phenomena, a part-of-speech tagger based on a stochastic model that can manage ambiguous streams of words and integrate external dictionaries, a system for identifying words related by derivational morphology, and a parser to extract head-modifier pairs. All of them are built on finite-state technology, so they are very efficient and can be applied to tasks in which huge amounts of text need to be analyzed, as is the case of information retrieval. Albeit our scheme is oriented towards the indexing of Spanish texts, it is also a proposal of a general architecture that can be applied to other languages with very slight modifications.

Acknowledgements. Supported in part by Plan Nacional de Investigación Científica, Desarrollo e Innovación Tecnológica (TIC2000-0370-C02-01), Ministerio de Ciencia y Tecnología (HP2001-0044) and Xunta de Galicia (PGIDT01PXI10506PN).

---

[2] http://www.clef-campaign.org

References

1. Fco. Mario Barcala, Jesús Vilares, Miguel A. Alonso, Jorge Graña, and Manuel Vilares. Tokenization and proper noun recognition for information retrieval. In *3rd International Workshop on Natural Language and Information Systems (NLIS 2002), September 2-3, 2002. Aix-en-Provence, France*, Los Alamitos, California, USA, 2002. IEEE Computer Society Press.
2. Jean-Pierre Chanod and Pasi Tapanainen. A non-deterministic tokeniser for finite-state parsing. In *Proceedings of the Workshop on Extended finite state models of language (ECAI'96)*, Budapest, Hungary, 1996.
3. Jorge Graña, Miguel A. Alonso, and Manuel Vilares. A common solution for tokenization and part-of-speech tagging: One-pass Viterbi algorithm vs. iterative approaches. In *Text, Speech and Dialogue*, Lecture Notes in Computer Science. Springer-Verlag, Berlin-Heidelberg-New York, 2002.
4. Jorge Graña, Fco. Mario Barcala, and Jesús Vilares. Formal methods of tokenization for part-of-speech tagging. In Alexander Gelbukh, editor, *Computational Linguistics and Intelligent Text Processing*, volume 2276 of *Lecture Notes in Computer Science*, pages 240–249. Springer-Verlag, Berlin-Heidelberg-New York, 2002.
5. Jorge Graña, Jean-Cédric Chappelier, and Manuel Vilares. Integrating external dictionaries into stochastic part-of-speech taggers. In Galia Angelova, Kalina Bontcheva, Ruslan Mitkov, Nicolas Nocolov and Nokolai Nikolov, editors, *Euro-Conference Recent Advances in Natural Language Processing. Proceedings*, pages 122–128, Tzigov Chark, Bulgaria, 2001.
6. Christian Jacquemin and Evelyne Tzoukermann. NLP for term variant extraction: synergy between morphology, lexicon and syntax. In Tomek Strzalkowski, editor, *Natural Language Information Retrieval*, volume 7 of *Text, Speech and Language Technology*, pages 25–74. Kluwer Academic Publishers, Dordrecht/Boston/London, 1999.
7. Frederick Jelinek. *Statistical Methods for Speech Recognition*. MIT Press, Cambridge, MA, 1998.
8. Mervyn F. Lang. *Spanish Word Formation: Productive Derivational Morphology in the Modern Lexis*. Croom Helm. Routledge, London and New York, 1990.
9. Christer Samuelsson. Morphological tagging based entirely on bayesian inference. In Robert Eklund, editor, *Proceedings of the 9th Nordic Conference on Computational Linguistics*, Stockholm, Sweden, 1993.
10. Jesús Vilares, Fco. Mario Barcala, and Miguel A. Alonso. Using syntactic dependency-pairs conflation to improve retrieval performance in Spanish. In Alexander Gelbukh, editor, *Computational Linguistics and Intelligent Text Processing*, volume 2276 of *Lecture Notes in Computer Science,*, pages 381–390. Springer-Verlag, Berlin-Heidelberg-New York, 2002.
11. Jesús Vilares, David Cabrero, and Miguel A. Alonso. Applying productive derivational morphology to term indexing of Spanish texts. In Alexander Gelbukh, editor, *Computational Linguistics and Intelligent Text Processing*, volume 2004 of *Lecture Notes in Computer Science*, pages 336–348. Springer-Verlag, Berlin-Heidelberg-New York, 2001.
12. Jesús Vilares, Manuel Vilares, and Miguel A. Alonso. Towards the development of heuristics for automatic query expansion. In Heinrich C. Mayr, Jiri Lazansky, Gerald Quirchmayr, and Pavel Vogel, editors, *Database and Expert Systems Applications*, volume 2113 of *Lecture Notes in Computer Science*, pages 887–896. Springer-Verlag, Berlin-Heidelberg-New York, 2001.

Definite Description Resolution Enrichment with WordNet Domain Labels*

Rafael Muñoz and Andrés Montoyo

Grupo de investigación del Procesamiento del Lenguaje y Sistemas de Información.
Departamento de Lenguajes y Sistemas Informáticos. Universidad de Alicante. Spain
{rafael,montoyo}@dsli.ua.es

Abstract. This paper presents a new method, based on semantic information, to resolve Definite Descriptions in unrestricted Spanish text. The method is performed in two consecutive steps. First, a lexical knowledge word domain sense disambiguation (WDSD) process is made. The text is tagged with a domain label instead of a sense label. Second, an algorithm to identify and to resolve the Spanish definite description is applied taking advantage of domain labels. In addition, this paper presents an experimental work that shows the advantage of using a WSD method in the Definite Description (DD) resolution process. Moreover, this experimental work proves that using WordNet Domain in unsupervised WSD method improves DD resolution.

1 Introduction

Coreference resolution consists of establishing a relation between an anaphoric expression and an antecedent. Different kinds of anaphoric expressions can be located in the text, such as pronouns, definite descriptions, adverbs, etc. In this paper, we focus on the treatment and resolution of definite descriptions[1].

Previos work such as [1,11,12] showed that most definite descriptions in the text are non-anaphoric. The treatment of DD has been made up of two different tasks. The first one, is focused on identifying the type of DD (anaphoric or non-anaphoric). And, the second task is focused on providing the antecedent of the anaphoric DD. Definite descriptions whose antecedents are full sentences or full paragraphs are treated like non-anaphoric DDs. In this work, we only establish the coreference of DDs whose antecedents are any kind of noun phrases (indefinite, definite, entity). Previous identification of non-anaphoric DD is useful only to apply the coreference resolution algorithm to anaphoric DDs. According to Frege [4], the identification of DD type cannot be carried out using structural information alone without comparison with previous candidates. Frege states that the reference property of a DD depends on semantic characteristics. A DD can only refer to a semantically compatible NP.

---

* This paper has been supported by the Spanish Government through the project TIC2000-0664-C02-01/02

[1] We only considered as DD the noun phrases headed by a definite article (el, la, los, las → *the*) or a demonstrative (este, esta, estos, estas → *this*, *these*).

F.J. Garijo, J.C. Riquelme, and M. Toro (Eds.): IBERAMIA 2002, LNAI 2527, pp. 645–654, 2002.
© Springer-Verlag Berlin Heidelberg 2002

The use of semantic information is associated to Word Sense Disambiguation (WSD). In relation to the WSD task several authors [14,7] have stated that for many applications the fine-grained sense distinctions provided by WordNet are not necessary. Therefore, we propose a way to deal with this problem starting with the hypothesis that many sense distinctions are not relevant for a DD resolution. Moreover, we want to investigate how the polysemy reduction caused by domain clustering can help to improve the DDs resolution. Because, a single domain label may group together more than one word sense, resulting in a reduction of the polysemy. Therefore, in this paper we propose to use a variant of the Specification Marks Method (SMM) [8] where for each word in a text a domain label is selected instead of a sense label.

2   Preprocessing and Resources

The Spanish text that is to be treated came from different files and is passed through a preprocessing stage. The first step in preprocessing consists of using a POS-tagger to automatically assign morphological information (POS tags). Next, it also performs a surface syntactic parsing of the text using dependency links that show the head-modifier relations between words. This kind of information is used for extracting NP's constituent parts, and these NP's are the input for a WSD module. This module returns all the head nouns with a domain sense assigned from all the head nouns that appear in the context of a sentence. This process is illustrate in Figure 1.

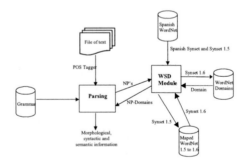

Fig. 1. Process and resources used by WSD module

The Figure 1 shows that the WSD module used the following resources:

- Spanish WN is a generic database with 30,000 senses. The Spanish WN will be linked through the English WN 1.5, so each English synonym will be associated with its equivalent in Spanish.
- WN 1.5 mapped to WN 1.6 is a complete mapping of the nominal, verbal, adjetival and adverbial parts of WN 1.5 onto WN 1.6 [3].

– WordNet Domain [6] is an extension of WN 1.6 where synsets are clustered by means of domain labels.

3   Domain Specification Marks Method

The WSD method used in this paper consists of a variant of the SMM, which we named Domain Specification Marks Method (DSMM), where for each head noun in a text a domain label is selected instead of a sense label. The SMM is applied for the automatic resolution of lexical ambiguity of groups of words, whose different possible senses are related. The disambiguation is resolved with the use of the Spanish WordNet lexical knowledge base. This method requires the we know how many of the words are grouped around a Specification Mark, which is similar to a semantic class in the WordNet taxonomy. The word sense in the subhierarchy that contains the greatest number of words for the corresponding Specification Mark will be chosen for the sense disambiguation of a noun in a given group of words. In this work [10] it has been shown that the SMM works successfully with groups of words that are semantically related. Therefore, a relevant consequence of the application of this method with domain labels is the reduction of the word polysemy (i.e. the number of domains for a word is generally lower than the number of senses for the word). That is, domain labels (i.e. Health, Sport, etc) provide a way to establish semantic relations among word senses, grouping then into clusters. Detailed explanation of the SMM can be found in [9].

Next, we describe the way to obtain the domain label of WordNet Domain from the word sense obtained by SMM. That is, SMM initially obtains the Spanish word sense and from this information has to apply the three following steps.

1. Starting from the Spanish word sense disambiguated by the SMM, we should obtain the corresponding synset in WN 1.5. For this task, we use the Spanish WN to disambiguate the Spanish word sense. It allows us to calculate the intersections in the Spanish synsets and the English synsets version 1.5. For example, the output of the SMM applied to the word "planta → *plant*" is the Spanish Synset "08517914" (planta#2). As the two WordNets are linked (i.e. they share synset offsets), therefore the intersection determines the synset of WordNet 1.5, which is "00008894" (Plant#2).

2. WN 1.5 is mapped with the WN 1.6, therefore the synsets obtained in step 1 are searched in this resource. Then, the synset 1.6 corresponding to the previous synset 1.5 is obtained. For example, the synset 1.5 "00008894" belonging to the sense "plant#2" is mapped to the synset 1.6 "00008864".

3. Finally, the synset 1.6 obtained in step 2 is searched for in the WordNet Domain, where the synsets have been annotated with one or more domain labels. For example, the synset 1.6 "00008864" belonging to the sense "plant#2" is searched for in the WN Domain giving the label "botany".

4   Coreference Resolution of Definite Description

Coreference resolution for DD presents different characteristics as pronouns. Three main differences can be pointed out: accessibility space, previous identification of non-anaphoric and different kinds of coreference (identity, part-of, set-member, set-subset). The accessibility space for pronouns is only a limited number of sentences. However, the accessibility space for DD represents a much greater number when encompassing the full text. For this reason, the number of potential candidates can be high for larger texts. If the coreference algorithm compares the DD to all candidates and the number is high then the algorithm becomes slow. Unlike other authors that reduce the number of previous sentences to be considered as the anaphoric accessibility space, our algorithm proposes the use of domain labels to group the NPs. This grouping is used to identify some non-anaphoric DD (remaining non-anaphoric will be classified by coreference algorithm) and to built the lists of candidates for each DD. A DD looks for its antecedent among the previous NPs with the same domain label. This fact makes possible the use of a full anaphoric space made up of all previous sentences and the reduction of comparisons. The coreference algorithm provides an antecedent of DD or it classifies the DD as non-anaphoric, if no candidate is found. The coreference algorithm is a system based on weighted heuristics. These heuristics study the relationship between heads and modifiers of both NP (candidate and DD). Moreover, DD can establish different kinds of relationships to their antecedents. DD can refer to the full antecedent (identity coreference) or a part of the antecedent (part-of, set-member, set-subset). Our algorithm resolves the identity and part-of coreference. The following section shows the algorithm in detail.

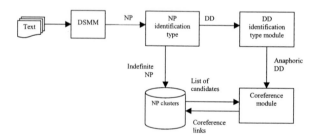

Fig. 2. Full system

4.1   Algorithm

The algorithm is focused on solving two tasks: non-anaphoric identification and coreference resolution. The algorithm takes advantage of DSMM (domain specification mark method) to solve both tasks. Two different modules are distinguished in the algorithm. The first module, Identification module, establishes the type of DD (anaphoric or non-anaphoric DD). A process of clustering is developed using the domain label proposed by DSMM. This module uses the Frege's idea of 'a word can only refer to a semantically compatible word'. Because of, a cluster is used in order to classify a DD between anaphoric and non-anaphoric. The second module, (Coreference resolution module), is only applied to anaphoric DD. This module is based on a weight-heuristic system to choose the antecedent or to re-classify the DD as non-anaphoric if no antecedent is found.

Identification module. The main goal of this module is to classify DDs between an anaphoric and non-anaphoric DD. For this reason, a prior task of identification of the NP type is done. The NP identification type is made by studying the first premodifier of NP. If the first modifier is a definite article or a demonstrative then the NP is classified as a DD. Otherwise, the NP is classified as an indefinite NP.

Every NP (DD and indefinite NP) is stored next to previous NPs with the same domain label. In addition, a virtual cluster is linked (label as v_link) to the NP (indefinite and non-anaphoric) made up of synonym, hyperonym, hyponym, meronym and holonym. All the words belonging to the virtual cluster do not necessarily appear previously in the text.

Moreover, the following process is only applied for DDs. If the DD is the first NP related to a domain label then the DD is classified as non-anaphoric. Otherwise, the coreference resolution mechanism is applied.

Coreference resolution module. The goal of this module is to identify the antecedent of a DD or re-classify the DD as non-anaphoric if no antecedent is found. The algorithm needs as input the DD and a list of candidates. The list of candidates used for this coreference resolution module is made up all NPs with the same domain labels excluding words from the virtual clusters. This virtual cluster is only used as a repository of words that are semantically related to the head noun of NP. The following steps are carried out: 1) The algorithm selects from the list of candidates those that have the same head noun as the anaphoric expression (DD). 2) If no candidate is selected then it goes through the virtual clusters that are related to the NP with the same domain label. The algorithm looks for the head noun of the anaphoric expression (DD). If it is found then the NP with the same domain label is selected as a candidate. 3) A weighting-heuristic algorithm is applied to choose the antecedent from the list of candidates or, if the candidate list is empty, then the DD is classified as non-anaphoric. The following heuristics are used:

- Identity coreference. The algorithm looks for previous noun phrases with the same head noun or a previous NP whose head noun is related using a synonym, hyperonym or hyponym relation and no incompatible modifiers. If one is found then both are linked using a identity coreference link (ic_link). Otherwise, the resolution process treats the anaphoric expression as a part-of coreference.

Hi1.- Same head. If a candidate has the same head noun as the DD then a value of 50 is added to the salience value (the red car, the car).

Hi2.- Synonym head. If the head noun of a candidate is a synonym of the head noun of the DD then a value of 45 is added to the salience value (the red car, the auto).

Hi3.- Hyper/hyponym head. If the head noun of a candidate is a hyperonym or hyponym of the head noun of the DD then a value of 35 is added to the salience value (the red car, the taxi).

Hi4.- Same modifier. A value of 10 is added to the salience value for each modifier that appears in both NP (candidate and DD) (the red car, the red auto).

Hi5.- Synonym modifier. A value of 9 is added to the salience value for each synonym modifier (the slow car, the lazy car)

Hi6.- Hyper/hyponym modifier. A value of 8 is added to the salience value for each hyper/hyponym modifier (the wood furniture, the mahogany furniture)

Hi7.- Antonym modifier. A value of -1000 is added to the salience value for each antonym modifier (the left ear, the right ear)

- Part-of coreference. Looking for a previous NP whose head noun is related using a meronym or holonym. If one is founded both are linked using a part-of coreference link (pc_link). The algorithm looks for the head noun at the virtual clusters linked by the same label.

Hp1.- Holo/meronym head. If the head noun of a candidate is a holo/meronym of the DD head noun then a value of 25 is added to the salience value (car, engine).

Hp2.- Head as modifier. If the head noun of DD is a modifier of candidate then a value of 10 is added to the salience value (the car, the car engine).

Hp3.- Synonym as modifier. If the head noun of DD is a synonym of a modifier of a candidate then a value of 9 is added to the salience value (the car, the auto engine).

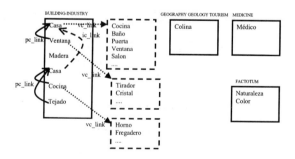

Fig. 3. NP clustering using WN Domain tag

If no candidate is selected as antecedent in identity coreference and part-of coreference then the DD is re-classified as non-anaphoric. And, if more than one candidate is proposed then the closest criteria is applied. Figure 3 shows the NP grouping after processing the following sentences: La casa de la colina era de un médico. Las ventanas eran de madera maciza. La casa estaba en plena naturaleza. La cocina era muy amplia y el tejado era de color rojizo.

Table 1. DD distribution

Corpus	Total	n-anaph DD	anaph DD	
			IC	PC
Training	560	340	164	56
Test	742	451	217	74
Total	1302	791	381	130

5   Experimental Work and Results

The experimentation data was taken from different HTML pages. In table 1 a distribution of DD in the corpora is shown. We distinguish anaphoric from non-anaphoric DD (n-anaph DD). Moreover, anaphoric DDs (anaph DD) are also divided into identity coreference (IC) and part-of coreference (PC). The test corpus was used to evaluate the identification of non-anaphoric DD (previous and full) and the coreference resolution (identity and part-of). Moreover, two experiments have been carried out. Obviously, the goal of the experimentation process is to evaluate the DD treatment. But, experiments were carried out to establish the influence of WSD module. The first experiment evaluates the full algorithm carrying on errors produced by WSD module. And, the second experiment evaluates the algorithm supervising the errors from WSD module.

Table 2. Identification of non-anaphoric values using test corpus

Exp.	Previous			Full		
	C	E	S%	C	E	S%
exp. 1	130	0	100	405	46	89.8
exp. 2	141	0	100	421	30	93.3

5.1   Experiments for Non-anaphoric Identification

Table 2 shows the values obtained in each experiment for the identification of non-anaphoric DD. In the first experiment, 130 non-anaphoric DD were correctly classified (C) obtaining a success rate (S) of 100%. This is due to the fact that the algorithm can only classify as non-anaphoric those DDs that cannot be compared with any other because they have the first word as their domain label. The 321 remaining non-anaphoric DD were treated by the coreference algorithm. If this coreference algorithm did not find an antecedent then the DD was re-classified as non-anaphoric. The full task of non-anaphoric identification (adding previous identification and coreference identification) obtained a success rate around 90%. In the second experiment, the algorithm obtained a small improvement in both stages (previous and full). For previous identification, 141 non-anaphoric DD were identified. And, the 310 remaining were treated by coreference algorithm. The full process achieved a success rate around 93%.

5.2   Experiments for Coreference Resolution

The evaluation of coreference algorithm involves the evaluation of two different kinds of coreference: identity and part-of. Other kinds of coreference such as set-member or set-subset are not solved by treating them as non-anaphoric DD. Moreover, identity coreference can be divided into two types: direct anaphora and bridging references[2]. According to this definition, part-of coreference is also a type of bridging reference. Table 3 shows the values obtained in each experiment for the coreference resolution. In the first experiment, the algorithm achieved a success rate of 76% for identity coreference and a success rate of 58.1% for part-of coreference. In the second experiment, both coreferences (identity and part-of) increased their values. Identity coreference achieved a success rate of 80.1% and part-of coreference achieved a success rate of 62.1%. The values achieved for identity coreference can be divided into two different types: direct anaphora and bridging reference. The algorithm achieved a 83% success rate for direct anaphora and a 64% success rate for identity bridging reference[3]

5.3   Comparative Results

The comparison of different approaches should be carried out using the same features. The main problem we found in this work was carrying out the comparison between two different languages (Spanish and English), the use of specific tools (partial or full parser, ontologies, lexical resources, etc). For this reason, we decided to carry out an indirect comparison with approaches extensively cited in the literature and a direct comparison with a baseline algorithm.

A baseline algorithm was developed for this experiment. A simple algorithm for DD resolution is taken as a baseline algorithm. This algorithm looks for each DD as the candidate, with the same head noun as the anaphoric expression (DD) choosing the closest. If no candidate is selected then the DD is classified as non-anaphoric. The values achieved for baseline algorithm are the same in

---

[2] DD with different head noun as their antecedent were called bridging references by Clark [2]

[3] We use this term to refer to DD with different head noun as their antecedent and establishing an identity coreference.

Table 3. Coreference values using test corpus

Exp.	Identity coref.			Part-of coref.		
	C	E	S%	C	E	S%
exp. 1	165	52	76	43	31	58.1
exp. 2	174	43	80.1	46	28	62.2

experiments 1 and 2 because this algorithm does not use semantic information. The success rate calculated for non-anaphoric identification was around 63% for baseline algorithm and around 90% for our algorithm without supervising the errors produced by DSMM (exp. 1) and 93% when supervising the DSMM' errors (exp. 2). The comparison made for coreference resolution shows the values achieved in two type of coreference: identity (IC) and part-of (PC) for both algorithms. The success rate calculated for identity coreference was around 56% for baseline algorithm and around 76% for our algorithm without supervising the errors produced by DSMM (exp. 1) and 80% supervising the DSMM's errors (exp. 2). Moreover, identity coreference can be divided into two types: direct anaphora and identity bridging reference. The identity bridging reference resolution needs to use semantic information, for this reason the value achieved by baseline algorithm is zero. The direct anaphora resolution is solved by both algorithm (baseline and our algorithm) achieving a success rate of 70% for baseline and 83% for our algorithm. The success rate calculated for part-of coreference was 0% for baseline algorithm because it does not use semantic information and around 58% for our algorithm without supervising the errors produced by DSMM (exp. 1) and 62% when supervising the DSMM's errors (exp. 2).

We selected for indirect comparative evaluation two approaches extensively cited in the literature. For non-anaphoric identification, we used Vieira & Poesio 'algorithm [13] and Bean & Rillof [1]. And, for coreference resolution, we used Vieira & Poesio 'algorithm [13] and Kameyama [5]. For non-anaphoric identification, our algorithm achieved a better score (93%) than Bean & Rillof algorithm (86%) and Vieira & Poesio (72%). For coreference resolution, our algorithm achieved similar values for direct anaphora as Vieira & Poesio, around 83% and for bridging reference our algorithm (65%) is better than Poesio & Vieira (28%). The bridging reference values of our algorithm included identity bridging reference and part-of coreference due to Vieira & Poesio work does not separately show these values. Moreover, Kameyama's work shows an overall value for coreference resolution task at 59%.

6   Conclusions

We have introduced a DD algorithm based on semantic information to identify non-anaphoric DD and to solve anaphoric DD. In addition to typical semantic information (synonym, hyperonym, etc.), domain labels are used to cluster NPs. This clustering helps us to establish a mechanism for previous non-anaphoric identification and to reduce the number of candidates. Experimental work shows that the use of WSD improves the values of DD resolution tasks. Our algorithm resolves two different types of coreference, identity and part-of, achieving better values than others work developed for English.

References

1. D. L. Bean and E. Riloff. Corpus-based Identification of Non-Anaphoric Noun Phrases. In *Proceedings of the 37th ACL*, pages 373–380, 1999.
2. H. H. Clark. Bridging. In P. Johnson-Laird and P Wason, editors, *Thinking: readings in cognitive science*, pages 411–420. Cambridge UP, 1977.
3. J. Daudé, L. Padró, and G. Rigau. A Complete WN1.5 to WN1.6 Mapping. In *Proceedings of the NAACL Workshop WordNet and Other Lexical Resources: Applications, Extensions and Customisations.*, pages 83–88, 2001.
4. G. Frege. Sobre sentido y referencia. In Luis Ml. Valdés Villanueva, editor, *La búsqueda del significado: Lecturas de filosofía del lenguaje.* 1892.
5. M. Kameyama. Recognizing Referential Links: An Information Extraction Perspective. In Mitkov, R. and Boguraev, B., editor, *Proceedings of ACL/EACL Workshop on Operational Factors in Practical, Robust Anaphora Resolution for Unrestricted Texts*, pages 46–53, 1997.
6. B. Magnini and G. Cavaglia. Integrating subject field codes into WordNet. In *Proceedings of the LREC-2000*, 2000.
7. B. Magnini and C. Strapparava. Experiments in Word Domain Disambiguation for Parallel Texts. In *Proceedings of the ACL Workshop on Word Senses and Multilinguality*, 2000.
8. A. Montoyo and M. Palomar. Word Sense Disambiguation with Specification Marks in Unrestricted Texts. In *Proceedings of the DEXA-2000, 11th International Workshop on Database and Expert Systems Applications*, pages 103–107. IEEE Computer Society, September 2000.
9. A. Montoyo and M. Palomar. Specification Marks for Word Sense Disambiguation: New Development. In Gelbukh, editor, *Proceedings of the CICLing-2001*, LNCS, pages 182–191, 2001.
10. A. Montoyo, M. Palomar, and G. Rigau. WordNet Enrichment with Classification Systems. In *Proceedings of the NAACL Workshop WordNet and Other Lexical Resources: Applications, Extensions and Customisations.*, pages 101–106, 2001.
11. R. Muñoz, M. Palomar, and A. Ferrández. Processing of Spanish Definite Descriptions. In O. Cairo et al., editor, *Proceeding of MICAI*, volume 1793 of *LNAI*, pages 526–537, 2000.
12. M. Poesio and R. Vieira. A Corpus-Based Investigation of Definite Description Use. *Computational Linguistics*, 24:183–216, 1998.
13. R. Vieira and M. Poesio. An Empiricall Based System for Processing Definite Descriptions. *Computational Linguistics*, 26(4):539–593, 2000.
14. Y. Wilks and M. Stevenson. Word sense disambiguation using optimised combination of knowledge sources. In *Proceedings of COLING-ACL'98*, 1998.

A Hidden Markov Model Approach to Word Sense Disambiguation

Antonio Molina, Ferran Pla, and Encarna Segarra

Departament de Sistemes Informàtics i Computació
Universitat Politècnica de València (Spain)
{amolina,fpla,esegarra}@dsic.upv.es

Abstract. In this work, we propose a supervised approach to Word Sense Disambiguation which is based on Specialized Hidden Markov Models and the use of *WordNet*. Our approach formulates the disambiguation process as a tagging problem. The specialization process allows for the incorporation of additional knowledge into the models. We evaluated our system on the *English all-words* task of the *Senseval-2* competition. The performance of our system is in line with the best approaches for this task.

1 Introduction

Word Sense Disambiguation (WSD) consists of selecting the semantic sense of a word from all the possible senses given by a dictionary. It is well known that semantic information can be useful to solve different tasks such as parsing, machine translation, language understanding, information retrieval, etc. For example, a term-based information retrieval system answers the query *plants that live in the sea* with all the documents that contain the terms *plant, live* or *sea* regardless of their meaning. Some of these documents contain the term *plant* with the meaning "life form" and others contain the term *plant* with the meaning "factory". It would be interesting for the information retrieval system to give only the documents in which the term *plant* appears with the meaning "life form". To do this, the system should use a WSD module in order to obtain the correct sense of the ambiguous terms in the query.

WSD is a difficult task for various reasons. First, there is no consensus on the concept of sense, and consequently, different semantic tag sets can be defined. Second, the modeling of contextual dependencies is complicated because a large context is generally needed and sometimes the dependencies among different sentences must be known in order to determine the correct sense of a word (or a set of words). Also, the lack of common evaluation criteria makes it very hard to compare different approaches. In this respect, the knowledge base *WordNet* [1] and the *SemCor*[1] corpus [2] are the most frequently used resources.

---

[1] The *SemCor* corpus and the knowledge base *WordNet* are freely available at
http://www.cogsci.princeton.edu/~wn/

F.J. Garijo, J.C. Riquelme, and M. Toro (Eds.): IBERAMIA 2002, LNAI 2527, pp. 655–663, 2002.

WordNet is a large-scale hand-crafted lexical knowledge base. English nouns, verbs, adjectives and adverbs are organized into synonym sets, each representing one underlying lexical concept. *WordNet* provides all the possible senses for a certain word. These senses are sorted according to their frequency in the *SemCor* corpus. This corpus, which consists of 676,546 words, has been semantically annotated using the senses of *WordNet* and manually supervised.

There has been a wide range of approaches to the WSD problem (a detailed study can be found in [3] and [4]). In general, you can categorize them into knowledge-based and corpus-based approaches. Under the knowledge-based approach the disambiguation process is carried out using information from an explicit lexicon or knowledge base. The lexicon may be a machine-readable dictionary, such as the *Longman Dictionary of Contemporary English*, a thesaurus, such as *Rodget's Thesaurus*, or large-scale hand-crafted knowledge bases, such as *WordNet* [5,6,7,8,9,10].

Under the corpus-based approach, the disambiguation process is carried out using information which is estimated from data, rather than taking it directly from an explicit knowledge base. In general, disambiguated corpora are needed to perform the training process, although there are a few approaches which work with raw corpora. Machine learning algorithms have been applied to learn classifiers from corpora in order to perform WSD. These algorithms extract certain features from the annotated corpus and use them to form a representation of each of the senses. This representation can then be applied to new instances in order to disambiguate them [11,12,13].

In the framework of corpus-based approaches, successful corpus-based approaches to POS tagging which used Hidden Markov Models (HMM) have been extended in order to be applied to WSD. In [14], they estimated a bigram model of ambiguity classes from the *SemCor* corpus for the task of disambiguating a small set of semantic tags. Bigram models were also used in [15]. The task of sense disambiguating was carried out using the set of synsets of *WordNet* and using the *SemCor* corpus to train and to evaluate the system.

Senseval[2] competition can be viewed as the most important reference point for WSD. The last edition of this competition has shown that corpus-based approaches achieve better results than knowledge-based ones. Around 20 different systems participated in the *English all-words* task. The three best systems used supervised methods and they achieved a precision which ranked between 61.8% and 69.0%. The system *SMUaw* by Rada Mihalcea achieved the best precision (69.0%). It used a hybrid method which combined different knowledge sources: the *WordNet*, the *SemCor* corpus and a set of heuristics in order to obtain a set of sense-tagged word-word pairs. The second system in the competition (*CNTS-Antwerp*) by Veronique Hoste used a voting strategy in order to combine different learning algorithms, such as memory-based learning and rule induction. It used *SemCor* to train the different classifiers and obtained a precision of 63.6%. The *Sinequa-LIA-HMM* system by E. Crestan, M. El-Beze and C. Loupy achieved a

[2] Information about the latest edition of *Senseval* competition can be found at http://www.sle.sharp.co.uk/senseval2/

precision of 61.8%. It used a second-order HMM in a two-step strategy. First, it determined the semantic category associated to a word. Then, it assigned the most probable sense acording to the word and the semantic category. In addition, it used an alternative approach based on classification trees for certain words. The next two systems in the ranking by D. Fernández-Amorós (*UNED-AW-U*) used an unsupervised approach obtaining a precision of 55.0% and 56.9%. They constructed a relevance matrix from a large colecction of English books, which was used to filter the context of the words to be disambiguated. The rest of the systems, which are mainly based on unsupervised methods, gave a significantly lower performance than the methods mentioned above. Only a few of them gave a precision which was higher than 50%; however, they had a very low recall.

Some conclusions can be established from all these works. WSD is still an open problem in Natural Language Processing because the performance of the different systems is not satisfactory enough. In addition, the semantic resources available are not sufficient, because the number of senses is very large and anno-tated corpora do not have enough data to estimate appropriate models. Although this aspect specially affects corpus-based approaches, these achieve better results than knowledge-based ones.

In this paper we present a corpus-based approach to WSD based on Special-ized HMM [16]. We chose this approach because it has been successfully applied to solve other Natural Language Processing problems such as Part-of-speech (POS) tagging [17] and chunking [18]. A preliminary evaluation of our WSD system was conducted on the *SemCor* corpus [19]. In that case, the precision results (70.39%) were not very satisfactory because our system performed much like the Baseline (we considered a system that assigned the most frequent sense in the *SemCor* corpus given a lemma and its POS as Baseline). In order to get a more objective analysis of the performance of our system, we selected the *English all-words* task of the *Senseval-2* competition.

The paper is organized as follows: in Sections 2 and 3, we describe the WSD system proposed and the learning process of the system. In Section 4, we present the experimental work conducted on the *Senseval-2 English all-words* task. Fi-nally, we present some concluding remarks.

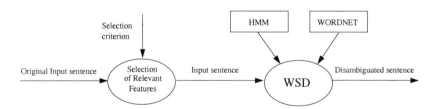

Fig. 1. System Description

2   Description of the WSD System

We consider WSD to be a tagging problem which we propose to solve by using a HMM formalism. Figure 1 shows a scheme of the WSD system developed. The system has two components: *WordNet* and the HMM.

WordNet is used to know all the possible semantic tags associated to an input word. If the input word is unknown for the model (the word has not been seen in the training data set) the system takes the first sense provided by *WordNet*.

We can formulate the tagging process as a maximization problem. Let $\mathcal{S}$ be the set of sense tags considered, and $\mathcal{W}$, the vocabulary of the application. Given an input sentence, $W = w_1, \ldots, w_T$, where $w_i \in \mathcal{W}$, the tagging process consists of finding the sequence of senses $(S = s_1, \ldots, s_T$, where $s_i \in \mathcal{S})$ of maximum probability on the model, that is:

$$\widehat{S} = \arg\max_S P(S|W)$$

$$= \arg\max_S \left(\frac{P(S) \cdot P(W|S)}{P(W)} \right); \; S \in \mathcal{S}^T \tag{1}$$

Due to the fact that this maximization process is independent of the input sequence, and taking into account the Markov assumptions for a first-order HMM, the problem is reduced to solving the following equation:

$$\arg\max_S \left(\prod_{i:1\ldots T} P(s_i|s_{i-1}) \cdot P(w_i|s_i) \right) \tag{2}$$

The parameters of equation 2 can be represented as a first-order HMM where each state corresponds to a sense s_i, $P(s_i|s_{i-1})$ represent the transition probabilities between states and $P(w_i|s_i)$ represent the probability of emission of symbols, w_i, in every state, s_i. The parameters of this model are estimated by maximum likelihood from semantic annotated corpora using an appropriate smoothing method.

Different kinds of available linguistic information can be useful to solve WSD. In particular, the available annotated corpora provide the following input features: words, lemmas and the corresponding part-of-speech tags. The first system step (see Figure 1) consists of applying a *selection criterion* to the original input sentence in order to choose the features which are relevant to the task. In our system, the vocabulary of the input sentence to the WSD module consists of the concatenation of its relevant features. The *selection criterion* is decided in the learning phase as we will show in Section 3.

Therefore, the disambiguation process is as follows: first, the original input sentence is processed in order to select its relevant features providing the input sentence; then, the semantic tagging is carried out through the Viterbi algorithm using the estimated HMM and *WordNet*.

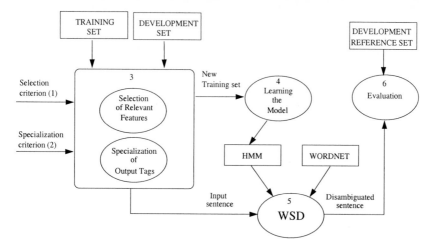

Fig. 2. Learning Phase Description

3   Description of the Learning Phase

The learning process of a Specialized HMM [16,18] is similar to the learning of a basic HMM. The only difference is that Specialized HMM are based on an appropriate definition of the input information to the learning process. This information consists of the input features (words, lemmas and POS tags) and the output tag set (senses) provided by the training corpus. A specialized HMM is built according to the following steps (see Figure 2):

1. To define which available input information is relevant to the task (*selection criterion*).
2. To define which input features are relevant to redefine or *specialize* the output tag set (*specialization criterion*). This specialization allows the model to better capture some restrictions relevant to the task.
3. To apply the chosen criteria to the original training data set to produce a new one.
4. To learn a model from the new training data set.
5. To disambiguate a development data set using that model.
6. To evaluate the output of the WSD system in order to compare the behavior of the selected criteria on the development set.

These steps are done using different combinations of the input information in order to determine the best selection and specialization criteria. From our experimental work, the best *selection criterion* consists of a concatenation of the lemma (l_i) and the POS[3] (p_i) associated to the word (w_i) as input vocabulary, if w_i has a sense in *WordNet*. For the words which do not have a sense in *WordNet*,

---

[3] We mapped the POS tags to the following tags: 1 for nouns, 2 for verbs, 3 for adjectives and 4 for adverbs.

we only consider their lemma (l_i) as input. Therefore, in our HMM, $l_i \cdot p_i$ or l_i are the symbols emitted in the states. For example, for the input word *interest* which has an entry in *WordNet* and whose lemma is *interest* and whose POS is *NN*, the input considered in our system is *interest·1*. If the word does not have a sense in *WordNet*, such as the article *a*, we consider its lemma *a* as input.

With respect to the *specialization criterion* we made the following decisions. We defined the output semantic tag set by considering certain statistical information which was extracted from the annotated training set. In the *SemCor* corpus, each annotated word is tagged with a *sense_key* which has the form *lemma%lex_sense*. In general, we considered the *lex_sense* field of the *sense_key* associated to each lemma as the semantic tag in order to reduce the size of the output tag set. This does not lead to any loss of information because we can obtain the *sense_key* by concatenating the lemma to the output tag. For certain frequent lemmas, we considered a more fine-grained semantic tag: the *sense_key* or *synset*. These choices were made experimentally by taking into account a set of frequent lemmas, $\mathcal{L}_s$, which were extracted from the training set.

For instance, the input *interest·1* is tagged with the semantic tag *1:09:00::* in the training data set. If we estimate that the lemma *interest* belongs to $\mathcal{L}_s$, then the semantic tag is redefined as *interest·1:09:00::*.

For the words without semantic information (tagged with the symbol *notag*), we tested several transformations: to consider their POS in the states, to consider their lemma or to consider only one state for all these words. The approach that achieved the best results consisted of specializing the states with the lemma. For example, for the word *a* the output tag associated is *a·notag*.

4   Experimental Results

We conducted some experiments on the *English all-words* task of the *Senseval-2* competition. This competition did not provide any training corpora for this task, so we used as training data the part of the *SemCor* corpus which is semantically annotated and supervised for nouns, verbs, adjectives and adverbs (that is, the files contained in the Brown1 and the Brown2 folders of *SemCor* corpus). The semantic tag set consists of 2,193 different senses which are included in *WordNet*. The corpus contains 414,228 tokens (359,732 word forms); 192,639 of these tokens have a semantic tag associated to them in the corpus and 162,662 are polysemic. We used 10% of the training corpus as a development data set. The test data set provided by *Senseval-2* consisted of three Penn TreeBank documents which contained 2,473 sense-tagged words. POS information was extracted directly from the corresponding Penn TreeBank documents.

In the experiments, we used *WordNet* 1.6 as a dictionary which supplies all the possible semantic senses for a given word. Our system disambiguated all the polysemic lemmas, that is, the coverage of our system was 100% (therefore, precision[4] and recall[5] were the same). For unknown words (words that did not appear in the training data set), we assigned the first sense in *WordNet*.

We compared the following models. The unigram (UNI) and bigram (BIG) models are basic HMMs which take into account an input vocabulary that only consists of lemmas. UNIpos and BIGpos are models which were learnt using only the best *selection criterion*. UNIesp and BIGesp are also learnt using this *selection criterion* and have been specialized using the best *specialization criterion*.

To build the specialized models, we selected the set of lemmas $\mathcal{L}_s$ beforehand. The *specialization criterion* consisted of selecting the lemmas whose frequency in the training data set was higher than a certain threshold (other specialization criteria could have been chosen, but frequency criterion usually worked well in other tasks as we reported in [18]). In order to determine which threshold maximized the performance of the model, we conducted a tuning experiment on the development set. For the BIGesp model, the best performance was obtained using a threshold of 20 ($|\mathcal{L}_s|$ was about 1,600 lemmas).

Table 1. Precision results for the *English all-words* task in *Senseval-2*. 100% of the words were tagged.

Model	Precision
UNI	40.00%
UNIpos	52.30%
UNIesp	58.80%
BIG	50.10%
BIGpos	58.20%
BIGesp	60.20%

The results for the *English all-words* task are shown in Table 1. The UNIpos and BIGpos models improved the performance of the basic models (UNI and BIG), showing that the POS information is important in differentiating among the different senses of a word. In addition, both Specialized models (UNIesp and BIGesp) outperformed the non-specialized ones. The best performance was achieved by the Specialized Bigram model (BIGesp) with a precision of 60.20%, which was slightly higher than the Baseline precision (58.0%). This result is in line with the results provided for the best systems in *Senseval-2*. This comfirms that Specialized HMMs can be applied to WSD, as successfully as they have been applied to other disambiguation tasks. The most similar approach to our system (Sinequa-LIA-HMM) achieved a result which was slightly better (61.8%), but it combined the HMM model with a classification tree method to disambiguate some selected words.

---

[4] precision = # of correctly disambiguated words / # of disambiguated words
[5] recall = # of correctly disambiguated words / # of words to be disambiguated

5 Conclusions

In this paper, we have proposed a Word Sense Disambiguation system which is based on HMM and the use of *WordNet*. We made several versions of our WSD system. Firstly, we applied classic unigram and bigram models and, as we had expected, the bigram model outperformed the unigram model. This is because the bigram model better captures the context of the word to be disambiguated. Secondly, we incorporated POS information to the input vocabulary which improved the performance and showed the relevance of this information in WSD. Finally, we specialized both the unigram and the bigram models in order to incorporate some relevant knowledge to the system. Again, as we expected, specialized models improved the results of the non-specialized ones.

From the above experimentation, we conclude that the BIGesp model is the best model. This model gave a precision of 60.20% in the *English all-words* task of the *Senseval-2* competition, which was only outperformed by the three best systems for the same task. This is a good result taking into account that our WSD system is mainly an adaptation of our POS tagging and chunking systems. This adaptation consists of an appropriate definition of the relevant input information and the output tag set.

Finally, we think that we could improve our WSD system through a more adequate definition of the selection and specialization criteria. To do this, a larger training data set, which is close to the task, would be necessary. Moreover, this definition could be done using linguistic knowledge as well.

Acknowledgments. This work has been supported by the Spanish research projects CICYT TIC2000–0664–C02–01 and TIC2000–1599–C01–01.

References

1. Miller, G.A., Beckwith, R., Fellbaum, C.D., Gross, D., Miller, K.J.: WordNet: An on-line lexical database. International Journal of Lexicography **3** (1990) 235–244
2. Miller, G.A., Chodorow, M., Landes, S., Leacock, C., Thomas, R.G.: Using a Semantic Concordance for Sense Identificaction. In: Proceedings of the ARPA Workshop on Human Language Technology. (1994) 240–243
3. Ide, N., Véronis, J.: Word Sense Disambiguation: The State of the Art. Computational Linguistics **24** (1998) 1–40
4. Resnik, P., Yarowsky, D.: Distinguishing systems and distinguishing senses: new evaluation methods for Word Sense Disambiguation. Natural Language Engineering **6** (2000) 113–133
5. Lesk, M.: Automated Sense Disambiguation using Machine-readable Dictionaries: How to tell a pine cone from an ice cream cone. In: Proceedings of the 1986 SIGDOC Conference, Toronto, Canada (1986) 24–26
6. Yarowsky, D.: Word-sense Disambiguations Using Statistical Models of Roget's Categories Trained on Large Corpora. In: Proceedings of the 14th International Conference on Computational Linguistics, COLING, Nantes, France (1992) 454–460

7. Voorhees, E.: Using WordNet to Disambiguate Word Senses for Text Retrieval. In: Proceedings of the 16th Annual International ACM SIGIR Conference on Research and Development in Information Retrieval, Pittsburgh (1993) 171–180

8. Resnik, P.S.: Using Information Content to Evaluate Semantic Similarity in a Taxonomy. In: Proceedings of the 14th International Joint Conference on Artificial Intelligence, IJCAI, Montreal, Canada (1995) 448–453

9. Agirre, E., Rigau, G.: Word Sense Disambiguation Using Conceptual Density. In: Proceedings of the 16th International Conference on Computational Linguistics, COLING, Copenhagen, Denmark (1996)

10. Stevenson, M., Wilks, Y.: The Interaction of Knowledge Sources in Word Sense Disambiguation. Computational Linguistics **27** (2001) 321–349

11. Yarowsky, D.: Decision Lists for Lexical Ambiguity Resolution: Application to Accent Restoration in Spanish and French. In: Proceedings of the 32nd Annual Meeting of the Association for Computational Linguistics, Las Cruces, NM, ACL (1994) 88–95

12. Ng, H.T.: Exemplar-Base Word Sense Disambiguation: Some Recent Improvements. In: Proceedings of the 2nd Conference on Empirical Methods in Natural Language Processing, EMNLP. (1997)

13. Escudero, G., Márquez, L., Rigau, G.: A comparison between supervised learning algorithms for Word Sense Disambiguation. In: Proceedings of CoNLL-2000 and LLL-2000, Lisbon, Portugal (2000)

14. Segond, F., Schiller, A., Grefenstette, G., Chanod, J.P.: An Experiment in Semantic Tagging using Hidden Markov Model Tagging. In: Proceedings of the Joint ACL/EACL Workshop on Automatic Information Extraction and Building of Lexical Semantic Resources, Madrid, Spain (1997) 78–81

15. Loupy, C., El-Beze, M., Marteau, P.F.: Word Sense Disambiguation using HMM Tagger. In: Proceedings of the 1st International Conference on Language Resources and Evaluation, LREC, Granada, Spain (1998) 1255–1258

16. Molina, A., Pla, F., Segarra, E.: Una formulación unificada para resolver distinto problemas de ambigüedad en PLN. Revista para el Procesamiento del Lenguaje Natural (to be published) (2002)

17. Pla, F., Molina, A.: Part-of-Speech Tagging with Lexicalized HMM. In: proceedings of International Conference on Recent Advances in Natural Language Processing (RANLP2001), Tzigov Chark, Bulgaria (2001)

18. Molina, A., Pla, F.: Shallow Parsing using Specialized HMMs. Journal of Machine Learning Research **2** (2002) 595–613

19. Molina, A., Pla, F., Segarra, E., Moreno, L.: Word Sense Disambiguation using Statistical Models and WordNet. In: Proceedings of 3rd International Conference on Language Resources and Evaluation, LREC2002, Las Palmas de Gran Canaria, Spain (2002)

A Simple Connectionist Approach to Language Understanding in a Dialogue System*

María José Castro and Emilio Sanchis

Departament de Sistemes Informàtics i Computació
Universitat Politècnica de València
Camí de Vera s/n, 46022 València, Spain
{mcastro,esanchis}@dsic.upv.es

Abstract. A contribution to the understanding module of a domain-specific dialogue system is presented in this work. The task consists of answering telephone queries about train timetables, prices and services for long distance trains in Spanish. In this system, the representation of the meaning of the user utterances is made by means of *frames*, which determine the type of communication of the user turn, and by their associated *cases*, which supply the data of the utterance.
We focus on the classification of a user turn given in natural language in a specific class of frame. We used multilayer perceptrons to classify a user turn as belonging to a frame class. This classification can help in the posterior processes of understanding and dialogue management.

1   Introduction

The construction of dialogue systems applied to limited domain information systems is an important objective in the area of human language technologies. The advance in the design and analysis of the different knowledge sources involved in a spoken dialogue system, such as speech processing, language modeling, language understanding, or speech synthesis, has led to the development of dialogue system prototypes. Some characteristics of these systems are telephone access, limited semantic domains and mixed initiative [1,2,3].

A contribution to the understanding module of the BASURDE dialogue system [4] is presented. The task consists of answering telephone queries about timetables, prices and services for long distance trains in Spanish. In this system, the representation of the meaning of the user utterances is made through *frames*, which determine the type of communication of the user turn, and with *cases*, which supply the data of the utterance. The understanding module gets the output of the speech recognizer (sequences of words) as input and supplies its output to the dialogue manager. In this work, we are restricted to dealing with text data, that is, the correct transcription of each utterance. The semantic representation is strongly related to the dialogue management. In our approach,

---

* This work has been partially supported by the Spanish CICYT under contracts TIC2000-0664-C02-01 and TIC2000-1153.

F.J. Garijo, J.C. Riquelme, and M. Toro (Eds.): IBERAMIA 2002, LNAI 2527, pp. 664–673, 2002.

the dialogue behavior is represented by means of a stochastic network of *dialogue acts*. Each dialogue act has three levels of information: the first level represents the general purpose of the turn, the second level represents the type of semantic message (the frame or frames), and the third level takes into account the data supplied in the turn.

In this work, we focus on the process of classification the user turn in terms of the second level of the dialogue act, that is, the identification of the frame or frames given in the turn. This classification will help us to determine the specific data supplied in the sentence in a later process.

2   Artificial Neural Networks for Language Understanding

Language understanding tasks have usually been based on symbolic architectures, which use explicit rules that operate on symbols [5]. In contrast, machine learning techniques for inferring structural models have also been applied to this field. Specifically, hidden Markov models and stochastic regular grammars have been successfully used in the understanding module of dialogue systems [6,7].

Recently, artificial neural networks have been used in language understanding, but most of the connectionist language models implemented until now have had severe limitations. Understanding models have been limited to simple sentences with small lexica (see [8] for a revision of understanding and production neural network models).

We used multilayer perceptrons (MLPs) for simple language understanding. The number of input units was fixed by the size of the input lexicon (natural language of a restricted-semantic task). There was one output unit corresponding to each class to classify the sentences by their meaning.

3   The Dialogue Task

The final objective of this dialogue system is to build a prototype for information retrieval by telephone for Spanish nation-wide trains [9,4]. Queries are restricted to timetables, prices and services for long distance trains. Several other European dialogue projects [10,11,1] selected the same task.

A corpus of 200 person-to-person dialogues corresponding to a real information system was recorded and analyzed. Then, four types of scenarios were defined (departure/arrival time for a one-way trip, departure/arrival time for a two-way trip, prices and services, and one free scenario). A total of 215 dialogues were acquired using the Wizard of Oz technique. From these dialogues, a total of 1,460 user turns (14,902 words) were obtained. An example of two user turns is given in Figure 1 (see the *Original sentence*).

3.1   Labeling the Turns

The definition of dialogue acts is an important issue because they represent the successive states of the dialogue. The labels must be specific enough to show the different intentions of the turns in order to cover all the situations, and they must be general enough to be easily adapted to different tasks. If the number of labels is too high the models will be underestimated because of the sparseness of the training samples. On the other hand, if we define a set of just a few labels only general purposes of the turn can be modeled.

The main feature of the proposed labeling is the division into three levels [12]. The first level, called *speech act*, is general for all the possible tasks. The second and third level, called *frames* and *cases*, respectively, are specific to the working task and give the semantic representation. With this structure, the labeling is general enough to be applied to other tasks and specific enough to cover all the possible situations in the dialogue.

First level: *speech act*
The first level takes into account the intention of the segment (i.e., the dialogue behavior) and has a unique value. For this level, we define the following values, which are common to every task:

> *Opening, Closing, Undefined, Not understood, Waiting, Consult, Acceptance, Rejection, Question, Confirmation, Answer.*

Second level: *frames*
The second level is specific to each task and represents the type of message supplied by the user. This information is organized in *frames*. A total of 16 different classes of frames were defined for this task:

> *Departure_time, Return_departure_time, Arrival_time, Return_arrival_time, Price, Return_price, Length_of_trip, Train_type, Return_train_type, Services, Confirmation, Not_understood, Affirmation, Rejection, Closing, New_data.*

Third level: *cases*
The third level is also specific to the task and takes into account the data given in the sentence. Each frame has a set of slots which have to be filled to make a query or which are filled by the retrieved data after the query. The specific data which fills the slots is known as *cases*. This level takes into account the slots which are filled by the specific data present in the segment, or the slots being used to generate the segment corresponding to an answer. To complete this level, it is necessary to analyze the words in the turn and to identify the case corresponding to each word. Examples of cases for this task are: *Origen, Destination, Departure_time, Train_type, Price* ...

An example of the three-level labeling for some user turns is given in Figure 1. We will center our interest on the second level of the labeling, which is used to guide the understanding process. Note that each user turn can be labeled with more than one frame label (see the second example of Figure 1).

Original sentence:	Quería saber los horarios del Euromed Barcelona–Valencia. [I would like to know the timetables of the Euromed train from Barcelona to Valencia.]
1st level (speech act):	*Question*
2nd level (frames):	*Departure_time*
3rd level (cases):	*Departure_time* (*Origen:* barcelona, *Destination:* valencia, *Train_type:* euromed)

Original sentence:	Hola, buenos días. Me gustaría saber el precio y los horarios que hay para un billete de tren de Barcelona a La Coruña el 22 de diciembre, por favor. [Hello, good morning. I would like to know the price and timetables of a train from Barcelona to La Coruña for the 22nd of December, please.]
1st level (speech act):	*Question*
2nd level (frames):	*Price, Departure_time*
3rd level (cases):	*Price* (*Origen:* barcelona, *Destination:* la_coruña, *Departure_time:* 12-22-2002) *Departure_time* (*Origen:* barcelona, *Destination:* la_coruña, *Departure_time:* 12-22-2002)

Fig. 1. Example of the three-level labeling for two user turns. The Spanish original sentence and its English translation are given.

3.2   Lexicon and Codification of the Sentences

For classification purposes, we are concerned with the semantics of the words present in the user turn of a dialogue, but not with the morphological forms of the words themselves. Thus, in order to reduce the size of the input lexicon, we decided to use categories and lemmas:

1. General categories: city names, cardinal and ordinal numbers, days of the week, months.
2. Task-specific categories: departure and arrival city names, train types.
3. Lemmas: verbs in infinitive, nouns in singular and without articles, adjectives in singular and without gender.

In this way, we reduced the size of the lexicon from 637 to 311 words. Finally, we discarded those words with a frequency lower than five, obtaining a lexicon of 138 words. Note that sentences which contained those words are not eliminated from the corpus, only those words from the sentence are deleted. An example of the preprocessing of the original sentences is illustrated in Figure 2 (see *Original sentence* and *Preprocessed sentence*).

We think that for this task the sequential structure of the sentence is not fundamental to classifying the type of frame.[1] For that reason, the words of a sentence were all encoded with a local coding: the input of the MLP is formed by 138 units, one for each word of the lexicon. When the word appears in the sentence, its corresponding unit is set to 1, otherwise, its unit is set to 0. An example is given in Figure 2 (see from *Original sentence* to *Input local codification*).

3.3   Extended Frames and Multiple Frames

A total of 16 different frames were defined for the task (see Section 3.1). Each user turn can be labeled with more than one frame label (as in the second example of Figures 1 and 2). We wanted to perform two types of classification experiments: a maximum a posteriori approach and a multiple a posteriori approach.

For the strict maximum a posteriori approach to classification, only one class was desired for each turn. To do so, we extended the frames classes, defining a new class for each different combination of classes: if a given turn is labeled with the classes *"Price"* and *"Departure_time"*, a new class is defined as *"Price&Departure_time"*. Finally, we discarded those turns labeled with a class with a frequency lower than five (a total of 1,338 user turns were selected), obtaining 28 frame classes (11 original frame classes and 17 extended frame classes). For each training sample, the corresponding output unit to the frame class is set to 1.

For the multiple a posteriori approach to classification, the desired outputs for each training sample are set to 1 for those (one or more) frame classes that are correct and 0 for the remainder. As we wanted to compare both approaches to classification (extended and multiple frames), the same data (1,338 user turns) which comprised only 11 original frame classes was used.

An example of codification of the frames as *extended frames* or *multiple frames* is illustrated in Figure 2.

4   The Classification Problem

In this work, we focus on the classification of a user turn given in natural language (categorized and leximized) in a specific class of frame. Multilayer perceptrons are the most common artificial neural networks used for classification. For this purpose, the number of output units is defined as the number of classes, C, and the input layer must hold the input patterns. Each unit in the (first) hidden layer forms a hyperplane in the pattern space; boundaries between classes can be approximated by hyperplanes. If a sigmoid activation function is used, MLPs can form smooth decision boundaries which are suitable to perform classification tasks [13]. The activation level of an output unit can be interpreted as an approximation of the a posteriori probability that the input pattern belongs to

---

[1] Nevertheless, the sequential structure of the sentence is essential in order to *segment* the sentence into slots to have a real understanding of the sentence.

Original sentence:	Quería saber los horarios del Euromed Barcelona–Valencia. [I would like to know the timetables of the Euromed train from Barcelona to Valencia.]
Preprocessed sentence:	querer saber horario del tipo tren nom ciudad origen nom ciudad destino [want know timetable of train type from city name to city name]
▷ *Input local codification:*	00000000000000000000000001000000000000000000000010000 00000000000000000000000001100000000000000000000001000 0001000000000000000100000000000000 (7 active input units)

2nd level (frames):	Departure time	
Extended frame:	Departure time	
▷ *Output codification:*	000000000000000010000000000000	(one of 28 classes)
Multiple frames:	Departure time	
▷ *Output codification:*	00000100000	(one of 11 classes)

Original sentence:	Hola, buenos días. Me gustaría saber el precio y los horarios que hay para un billete de tren de Barcelona a La Coruña el 22 de diciembre, por favor. [Hello, good morning. I would like to know the price and timetables of a train from Barcelona to La Coruña for the 22nd of December, please.]
Preprocessed sentence:	hola bueno d'ia me gustar saber precio y horario que haber para billete de tren nom ciudad origen nom ciudad destino numero de nom mes por favor [hello good morning like know price and timetable of train from city name to city name for date of month name please]
▷ *Input local codification:*	00000000001100000000000101000000000000000000011001010000 00000000000100000000000000001111000100000001001000010000 0001000000000000000001000000010 0 (20 active inputs units)

2nd level (frames):	Price, Departure time	
Extended frame:	Price&Departure time	
▷ *Output codification:*	000000000000000000000001000	(one of 28 classes)
Multiple frames:	Price, Departure time	
▷ *Output codification:*	00000100010	(two of 11 classes)

Fig. 2. Example of the codification of two user turns (codification of the preprocessed sentence and codification of the type of frames) for both extended frames and multiple frames. The Spanish original sentence and its English translation are given.

the corresponding class. Therefore, an input pattern can be classified in the class $i^\star$ with maximum a posteriori probability:

$$i^\star = \operatorname*{argmax}_{i \in C} \Pr(i|x) \approx \operatorname*{argmax}_{i \in C} g_i(x, \omega), \qquad (1)$$

where $g_i(x, \omega)$ is the i-th output of the MLP given the input pattern, x, and the set of parameters of the MLP, ω. The set of classes C are the 28 extended frames.

On the other hand, we desired to test multiple outputs (if only the original frames are used, a user turn can be labeled with more than one frame). To perform this type of experiment, after training the MLP with multiple desired classes, an input pattern can be classified in the classes $I^\star$ with a posteriori probability above a threshold $\mathcal{T}$:

$$I^\star = \{i \in C' \mid \Pr(i|x) \geq \mathcal{T}\} \approx \{i \in C' \mid g_i(x, \omega) \geq \mathcal{T}\}, \qquad (2)$$

where, as before, $g_i(x, \omega)$ is the i-th output of the MLP given the input pattern, x, and the set of parameters of the MLP, ω. The set of classes C' are the 11 simple frame classes.

5   Experiments

We used multilayer perceptrons to classify a user turn (codified as explained in 3.2) as belonging to a unique frame class (*extended frames*) or as belonging to a set of classes (*multiple frames*). The number of input units was fixed by the size of the lexicon of the sentences (138 words). There was one output unit corresponding to each frame class (28 classes for the extended frame experiments and 11 classes for the multiple frame experiments).

The dataset (1,338 user turns) was randomly splitted into training (80%) and test (20%) sets.

5.1   Training the Artificial Neural Networks

The training of the MLPs was carried out using the neural net software package "SNNS: Stuttgart Neural Network Simulator" [14]. In order to successfully use neural networks, a number of considerations had to be taken into account, such as the network topology, the training algorithm, and the selection of the parameters of the algorithm [13,14,15]. Tests were conducted using different network topologies of increasing number of weights: a hidden layer with 2 units, two hidden layers of 2 units each, two hidden layers of 4 and 2 units, a hidden layer with 4 units, etc. Several learning algorithms were also tested: the incremental version of the backpropagation algorithm (with and without momentum term) and the quickprop algorithm. The influence of their parameters was also studied. Different combinations of learning rate (LR) and momentum term (MT), as well as different values of the maximum growth parameter (MG) for the quickprop algorithm, were proved. In every case, a validation criterion (20% of the training data was randomly selected for validation) was used to stop the learning process and to select the best configuration.

5.2   Selecting the Best Configuration of MLP

Extended Frame Experiments

We trained different MLPs of increasing number of weights using the standard backpropagation algorithm (with a sigmoid activation function and a learning

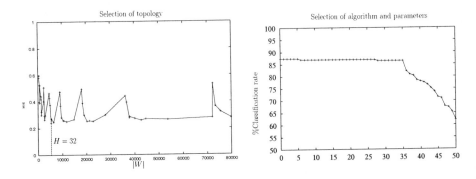

Fig. 3. Extended frame experiment. **a)** Mean square error (MSE) of the validation data with different MLPs of increasing number of weights. $|W|$ is the number of weights of each MLP. **b)** Percentage of validation user turns correctly classified with MLPs of one hidden layer of 32 units trained with different algorithms and parameters. Results are ordered from the best to the worst performance.

rate equal to 0.2), selecting the best topology according to the mean square error (MSE) of the validation data (see Figure 3a). The minimum MSE of the validation data was achieved with an MLP of one hidden layer of 32 units.

We followed our experimentation with MLPs of this topology, training MLPs with several algorithms: the incremental version of the backpropagation algorithm (with and without momentum term) and the quickprop algorithm. Different combinations of learning rate (LR = 0.05, 0.1, 0.2, 0.3, 0.4, 0.5) and momentum term (MT = 0.1, 0.2, 0.3, 0.4, 0.5) as well as different values of the maximum growth parameter (MG = 1.75, 2) for the quickprop algorithm were proved. The performance on the validation data of each trained net is shown in Figure 3b. The best result on the validation data was obtained with the MLP trained with the standard backpropagation algorithm (LR = 0.3).[2]

Multiple Frame Experiments

The same scheme was followed to train MLPs with multiple outputs: different MLPs of increasing number of weights using the standard backpropagation algorithm (with a sigmoid activation function and a learning rate equal to 0.2) were trained and the best topology according to the MSE of the validation data was selected (see Figure 4a). As in the previous experiment, the minimum MSE of the validation data was achieved with an MLP of one hidden layer of 32 units.

We followed our experimentation with MLPs of this topology, training MLPs with several algorithms (same proofs as before). The performance on the validation data of each trained MLP is shown in Figure 4b. The highest classi-

---

[2] The same performance was achieved with six different configurations; we decided to select the configuration with the lowest MSE.

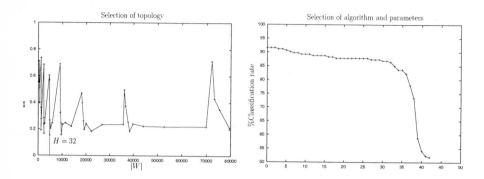

Fig. 4. Multiple frame experiment. **a)** Mean square error (MSE) of the validation data with different MLPs of increasing number of weights. $|W|$ is the number of weights of each MLP. **b)** Percentage of validation user turns correctly classified with MLPs of one hidden layer of 32 units trained with different algorithms and parameters. Results are ordered from the best to the worst performance.

fication rate of the validation data was obtained with the MLP trained with the backpropagation with momentum (LR=0.4 and MT=0.3).[3] In this type of experiment, the threshold $\mathcal{T}$ was also fixed using the validation data.

5.3   Final Experiment: Testing the Best MLPs

Once we had selected the best combination of topology, learning algorithm and parameters for the MLPs of both types of experiments, according to the classification rate of the validation data, we proved the trained MLP with the test data, obtaining a percentage of classification equal to 83.96% for the extended frame approach and a percentage equal to 92.54% for the multiple frame approach. We think that the multiple frame experiment achieves better performance due to the fact that the number of training samples is very low and the data is better employed with this approach.

6   Conclusions

The results obtained show that, with the correct transcription of each utterance (text data is used for the experiments), using a connectionist approach to language understanding is effective for classifying the user turn according the type of frames. This automatic process will be helpful to the understanding module of the dialogue system: firstly, the user turn, in terms of natural language, is classified into a frame class or several frame classes; secondly, a specific understanding model for each type of frame is used to segment and fill the cases of

---

[3] The same performance was achieved with three different configurations; we decided to select the configuration with the lowest MSE.

each frame. This could be specially useful when we deal with speech data (with errors from the speech recognition module) instead of written data.

References

1. L. Lamel, S. Rosset, J. L. Gauvain, S. Bennacef, M. Garnier-Rizet, and B. Prouts. The LIMSI Arise system. *Speech Communication*, 31(4):339–354, 2000.
2. J. Glass and E. Weinstein. Speech builder: facilitating spoken dialogue system development. In *Proceedings of Eurospeech'01*, volume 1, pages 1335–1338, 2001.
3. CMU Communicator Spoken Dialog Toolkit (CSDTK). http://www.speech.cs.cmu.edu/communicator/.
4. A. Bonafonte et al. Desarrollo de un sistema de diálogo oral en dominios restringidos. In *Primeras Jornadas de Tecnología del Habla*, Sevilla (Spain), 2000.
5. S. K. Bennacef, H. Bonneau-Maynard, J. L. Gauvain, L. Lamel, and W. Minker. A Spoken Language System for Information Retrieval. In *Proceeedings of the 3th International Conference in Spoken Language Processing (ICSLP'94)*, pages 1271–1274, Yokohama (Japan), 1994.
6. H. Bonneau-Maynard and F. Lefèvre. Investigating stochastic speech understanding. In *Proceedings of IEEE Automatic Speech Recognition and Understanding Workshop (ASRU'01)*, 2001.
7. Emilio Sanchis, Fernando García, Isabel Galiano, and Encarna Segarra. Applying dialogue constraints to the understanding process in a Dialogue System. In *Proceedings of fifth International Conference on Text, Speech and Dialogue (TSD'02)*, Brno (Czech Republic), 2002.
8. Douglas L. T. Rohde. *A Connectionist Model of Sentence Comprehension and Production*. PhD thesis, Computer Science Department, School of Computer Science, Carnegie Mellon University, Pittsburgh, PA, 2002.
9. A. Bonafonte et al. Desarrollo de un sistema de diálogo para habla espontánea en un dominio semántico restringido. Technical report, Spanish project from the Comisión Interministerial de Ciencia y Tecnología (TIC98-0423-CO6), 1998–2001. URL: `gps-tsc.upc.es/veu/basurde/`.
10. H. Aust, M. Oerder, F. Seide, and V. Steinbiss. The Philips automatic train timetable information system. *Speech Communication*, 17:249–262, 1995.
11. L. F. Lamel et al. The LIMSI RailTail System: Field trail of a telephone service for rail travel information. *Speech Communication*, 23:67–82, 1997.
12. C. Martínez, E. Sanchis, F. García, and P. Aibar. A labeling proposal to annotate dialogues. In *Proceedings of third International Conference on Language Resources and Evaluation (LREC'02)*, 2002.
13. D. E. Rumelhart, G. E. Hinton, and R. J. Williams. Learning internal representations by error propagation. In D. E. Rumelhart and J. L. McClelland, editors, *PDP: Computational models of cognition and perception, I*, pages 319–362. MIT Press, 1986.
14. A. Zell et al. *SNNS: Stuttgart Neural Network Simulator. User Manual, Version 4.2*. Institute for Parallel and Distributed High Performance Systems, University of Stuttgart, Germany, 1998.
15. C. M. Bishop. *Neural networks for pattern recognition*. Oxford University Press, 1995.

Wide–Coverage Spanish Named Entity Extraction*

Xavier Carreras, Lluís Màrquez, and Lluís Padró

TALP Research Center, LSI Department
Universitat Politècnica de Catalunya
Jordi Girona, 1–3, E-08034, Barcelona
{carreras,lluism,padro}@lsi.upc.es

Abstract. This paper presents a proposal for wide-coverage Named Entity Extraction for Spanish. The extraction of named entities is treated using robust Machine Learning techniques (AdaBoost) and simple attributes requiring non-linguistically processed corpora, complemented with external information sources (a list of trigger words and a gazetteer). A thorough evaluation of the task on real corpora is presented in order to validate the appropriateness of the approach. The non linguistic nature of used features makes the approach easily portable to other languages.

1 Introduction

There is a wide consensus about that Named Entity Extraction is a Natural Language Processing (NLP) task which provides important knowledge not only for anaphora and correference resolution, but also to improve the performance of many applications, such as Information Extraction, Information Retrieval, Machine Translation, Query Answering, Topic detection and tracking, etc.

From 1987 to 1999, the *Message Understanding Conferences* (MUC), devoted to Information Extraction, included a *Named Entity Recognition* task, which *de facto* determined what we usually refer to with the term *Named Entity*, and established standard measures for the accuracy of a system performing this task.

In MUC, the Named Entity Recognition task is divided into three subtasks: the Name Extraction (ENAMEX), the Time Extraction (TIMEX), and the Number Extraction (NUMEX) tasks. The first consists of recognizing and classifying the names for persons, locations and organizations. The second refers to the extraction of temporal expressions (dates, times), and the last one deals with monetary and percentage quantities.

The techniques used in systems addressing this task cover a wide spectrum of approaches and algorithms traditionally used in NLP and AI. Some systems rely on heavily data-driven approaches [3,1], while others use only hand–coded

---

* This research has been partially funded by the Spanish Research Department (HERMES TIC2000-0335-C03-02, PETRA TIC2000-1735-C02-02), by the European Comission (NAMIC IST-1999-12392), and by the Catalan Research Department (CIRIT's consolidated research group 1999SGR-150 and CIRIT's grant 1999FI 00773).

F.J. Garijo, J.C. Riquelme, and M. Toro (Eds.): IBERAMIA 2002, LNAI 2527, pp. 674–683, 2002.

knowledge, [4,2,15,9]. Finally, there are also hybrid systems combining corpus evidence and hand-coded knowledge, or external information sources [16,5,10].

We approach the task excluding the equivalent to the NUMEX and TIMEX tasks in MUC (i.e., we do not consider time or numerical expressions, which being frequent and easy to detect and classify, have the effect of raising the final accuracy figures). In addition, the task we approach is somewhat more difficult than MUC ENAMEX since we consider not only PERSON, LOCATION, and ORGANIZATION classes, but also a fourth category OTHER which includes named entities such as documents, measures and taxes, titles of art works —cinema, music, literature, painting, etc.— and others.

The system uses Machine Learning (ML) components for the recognition and classification of simple entities. The ML modules use a large set of extremely simple contextual and orthographic information, which do not require any previous linguistic processing. A thorough experimental evaluation is presented confirming the validity of the approach proposed. We also test whether the NE classification performance significantly improves when using external knowledge sources (such as gazetteers or lists of trigger words).

The system performance has been compared to other approaches and ported to languages other than Spanish in the framework of the *CoNLL'02 Shared Task* (see [12,8] for details). Results show that our approach ranks among the top performing systems in the competition.

The overall organization of the paper is the following: Section 2 presents the addressed task. Sections 3 and 4 are devoted to describe the algorithms and sources of information used to recognize and classify NEs. Section 5 describes the experimental evaluation of the model in a general Spanish corpus from a news agency. Finally, section 6 presents the main conclusions of the work and outlines some directions for future research.

2 Named Entity Extraction

In what respects to NE extraction, two sub-tasks must be approached: Named Entity Recognition (NER) —consisting of detecting the boundaries for each entity— and Named Entity Classification (NEC) —consisting of deciding whether the NE refers to a person, a location, an organization, etc. See figure 1 for a real example from the corpus described in section 5.1.

Según informó el (Departamento)$_{ORG}$ *que dirige el consejero* (Inaxio Oliveri)$_{PER}$ *, los representantes de la* (Consejería)$_{ORG}$ *y de las universidades del* (País Vasco)$_{LOC}$*,* (Deusto)$_{ORG}$ *y* (Mondragón)$_{ORG}$ *estudiaron los nuevos retos de estos centros educativos.*

Fig. 1. Example of Spanish text including several Named Entities

We follow the approach of performing each task as soon as the necessary information is available. In this way, NER is performed during morphological analysis, since it requires only context information on word forms, capitalization patterns, etc. NEC is performed after the morphological analysis and before the tagging since no significant improvement were obtained when adding lemma and PoS information. Thus, NER and NEC tasks are performed sequentially.

Formally, NER can be seen as the task of segmenting a sequence of words into non–overlapping and non–recursive chunks (i.e., the NEs). From this point of view, a NE is defined by its starting and ending points. There are several possible classification models for this task:

- OpenClose: Two classifiers are used: one classifier to decide if a certain word in the sentence opens a new NE and another one to decide if it closes an already opened NE.
- IOB: A single classifier decides whether each word is the beginning of a NE (B tag), if it is a component of a NE, but not the first word (I tag), or if it is outside a NE (O tag).

There are several ways of using these classifiers to perform the NER task. The simplest and most efficient way consists in exploring the sequence of words in a certain direction and applying the *open* and *close* classifiers (or, alternatively, the IOB classifier) coherently. This greedy approach is linear in the number of words of the sentence. Given that the classifiers are able to provide predictions, which may be translated into probabilities, another possibility is to use dynamic programming for assigning the sequence of tags that maximize a global score over the sequence of words, taking into account the coherence of the solution [11,7]. In this work, for simplicity and efficiency reasons, the greedy approach has been followed. Initial experiments on applying global inference have provided no significant improvements.

Finally, it is worth noting that NEC is simply a classification task, consisting of assigning the NE type to each potential, and already recognized, NE. In this case, all the decisions are taken independently, and the classification of a certain NE cannot influence the classification of the following ones.

3 Learning the Decisions

The AdaBoost algorithm has been used to learn all the binary decisions involved in the extraction of NEs. The general purpose of the AdaBoost algorithm is to find a highly accurate classification rule by combining many *base* classifiers. In this work we use the generalized AdaBoost algorithm presented in [14], which has been applied, with significant success, to a number of problems in different research areas, including NLP tasks [13]. In the following, the AdaBoost algorithm will be briefly sketched —see [14] for details.

Let $(x_1, y_1), \ldots, (x_m, y_m)$ be the set of m training examples, where each x_i belongs to an input space $\mathcal{X}$ and $y_i \in \mathcal{Y} = \{+1, -1\}$ is the class of x_i to be learned. AdaBoost learns a number T of base classifiers, each time presenting the base learning algorithm a different weighting over the examples. A base classifier is seen as a function $h : \mathcal{X} \to \mathbb{R}$. The output of each h_t is a real number whose sign is interpreted as the predicted class, and whose magnitude is a confidence rate for the prediction. The AdaBoost classifier is a weighted vote of the base classifiers, given by the expression $f(x) = \sum_{t=1}^{T} \alpha_t h_t(x)$, where α_t represents the weight of h_t inside the combined classifier. Again, the sign of $f(x)$ is the class of the prediction and the magnitude is the confidence rate.

The base classifiers we use are decision trees of fixed depth. The internal nodes of a decision tree test the value of a boolean predicate (e.g. "the word *street* appears to the right of the named entity to be classified"). The leaves of a tree define a partition over the input space $\mathcal{X}$, and each leave contains the prediction of the tree for the corresponding part of $\mathcal{X}$.

In [14] a criterion for greedily growing decision trees and computing the predictions in the leaves is given. Our base learning algorithm learns trees following this criterion, having a *maximum_depth* parameter as the stopping criterion. These base classifiers allow the algorithm to work in a high dimensional feature space that contains conjunctions of simple features.

4   Information Sources and Features

The features used to take the decisions in NER and NEC tasks can be obtained from untagged text and may be divided into context features and external knowledge features. For the latter, we used a 7,427 trigger-word list typically accompanying persons, organizations, locations, etc., and a 10,560 entry gazetteer containing geographical and person names. These lists have been semi–automatically extracted from lexical resources and corpora.

Due to the nature of AdaBoost, all features are binarized, that is, there is a feature for each possible word form appearing at each position in the context window. It is well-known that the AdaBoost algorithm is able to appropriately deal (i.e., efficiently and preventing overfitting to the training examples) with the large feature spaces created by this representation of examples.

4.1   NER Features

All features used for training the classifiers in the NER task, refer to context. Contrary to the NEC task, it has been empirically observed that the addition of knowledge from gazetteers and trigger words provides only very weak evidence for deciding the correct segmentation of a NE.

Since the basic AdaBoost algorithm is designed for binary classification problems, we have binarized the 3–class IOB problem by creating one binary problem for each tag. Therefore, each word in the training set —labelled as I, O, or B— defines an example, which is taken as positive for its class and negative for the rest. The following features are used to represent these examples:

- The form and the position of all the words in a window of ±3 words, and including the focus word (e.g., *word*(-1)="estadio").

- An orthographic feature and the position of all the words in the same ± 3 window. These orthographic features are binary and not mutually exclusive and consider whether the $\pm i$_th word is: *initial-caps, all-caps contains-digits, all-digits alphanumeric, roman-number, contains-dots, contains-hyphen acronym, lonely-initial, punctuation-mark, single-char, function-word,* and *URL*.
- I, O, B tags of the three preceding words.

In the OpenClose scheme, the *open* classifier is trained with the words at the beginning of the NEs as positive examples, and the words outside the NEs as negative examples. The feature codification is the same as in the IOB case.

The *close* classifier is trained only with examples coming from words internal to the NEs, taking the last word of each NE as a positive example, and the rest as negative examples. In this case, the decision of whether a certain word should close a NE strongly depends on the sequence of words between the word in which the NE starts and the current word (i.e., the structure of the partial NE). For the words in a [-2,+3] window outside this sequence, exactly the same features as in the IOB case have been considered. The specific features for the inner sequence are the following:

- Word form and orthographic features of the focus word and the word starting the NE.
- Word form and orthographic features of the words inside the sequence taking its position with respect to the current word.
- Length in words of the sequence.
- Pattern of the partial entity, with regard to capitalized or non-capitalized words, functional words, punctuation marks, numbers, and quotations.

4.2   NEC Features

A binary classifier is trained for each NE class. Each training occurrence is used as a positive example for its class and as a negative example for the others. All classifiers use the following set of features:

- Context features: Form and position of each word in a ± 3–word window (e.g. *word*(-2)="presidente").
- Bag-of-words features: form of each word in a ± 5–word window of five words left and right of the entity being classified. (e.g., "banco" $\in$ *context*).
- NE inner features: Length (in words) of the entity being classified, pattern of the entity with regard to acronyms, numbers, capitalized words, prepositions, determiners, and punctuation marks.
- Trigger word features: Class and position of trigger words in a ± 3–word window. Pattern of the entity immediate left context, with regard to punctuation marks, prepositions, determiners, trigger words denoting person, location, or organization, or other entities, and trigger words denoting geographical origin,
- Gazetteer features: Class (geographical, first name, or surname) and position of gazetteer words in a ± 3 window. Class in gazetteer of the NE being classified and class in the gazetteer of its components.

5   Evaluation

5.1   The EFE Spanish Corpus

The EFE[1] corpus used for the evaluation of the whole named entity processing system is a large unrestricted collection of over 3,000 news agency articles issued during year 2000. It contains 802,729 words, which contain over 86,000 hand tagged named entities. A corpus subset containing 65,000 words (4,820 named entities) is reserved for evaluation tests and the remaining is used as training material.

For the NER task only a subset of 100,000 words of the training set has been used[2]. Both in NER and NEC, features occurring less than 3 times in the training corpus have been filtered out. The exact number of examples and features derived from the training corpus for each binary decision is described in table 1.

Table 1. Sizes and proportions of positive examples and feature sets in the NER and NEC binary decisions

NER	#Exs.	#Feat.	#Pos.examples
open	91,625	19,215	8,126 (8.87%)
close	8,802	10,795	4,820 (54.76%)
I	97,333	20,526	5,708 (5.86%)
O	97,333	20,526	83,499 (85.79%)
B	97,333	20,526	8,126 (8.35%)

NEC	#Exs.	#Feat.	#Pos.examples
PERSON	61,266	22,465	12,976 (21.18%)
LOCATION	61,266	22,465	14,729 (24.04%)
ORGANIZ.	61,266	22,465	22,947 (34.46%)
OTHER	61,266	22,465	10,614 (17.32%)

5.2   Experimental Methodology

We trained the system using different feature sets and number of learning rounds, using base classifiers of different complexities, ranging from stumps (simple decision trees of depth 1) to decision trees of depth 4.

The evaluation measures for NER are: number of NE beginnings correctly identified (B), number of NE endings correctly identified (E), and number of complete NEs correctly identified. In the last case, recall (R, number of entities correctly identified over the number of expected entities), precision (P, number of entities correctly identified over the number of identified entities), and F-measure ($F_1 = 2 \cdot P \cdot R/(P + R)$) are computed.

The evaluation for NEC task includes the accuracy of the binary classifiers for each category, and the evaluation of the combined classifier, which proposes the final decision based on the outcomes of all binary classifiers. The combination performance is measured in terms of recall, precision, and F_1. The accuracy (Acc) of the system when forced to choose one class per entity is also evaluated.

---

[1] *Agencia EFE* is the official Spanish news agency.
[2] It has been empirically observed that using a bigger corpus does not result in a better performance, while the number of examples and features greatly increase.

5.3 NER Results

Figure 2 contains the performance plots (F_1 measure) with respect to the number of rounds of the AdaBoost algorithm in the I, O, B binary decisions of the NER task. Note that decision trees perform significantly better than stumps and that a further increasing of the depth of the trees provides a small gain. Also, it can be noticed that all NER binary classifiers are quite accurate, with F_1 measure over 96%. The learning curves present a satisfactory behaviour, with no significant overfitting with larger number of rounds, and achieving maximum performance after a quite reduced number of rounds. Exactly the same properties hold for the curves (not included) corresponding to the open and close classifiers.

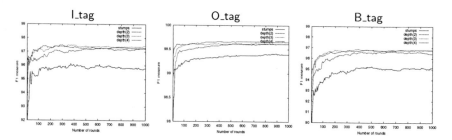

Fig. 2. F_1 measure w.r.t. the number of rounds of the I, O, B classifiers of NER task

Table 2 contains the results of the OpenClose and IOB approaches on the whole NER task, using depth–3 base classifiers. It can be observed that both variants perform significantly better than the baseline MACO+ [6]. The MACO+ NE module is a heuristic rule based NE recognizer, which takes into account capitalization patterns, functional words and dictionary lookup.

The performance of the OpenClose scheme is slightly worse than the IOB. This can be explained by the fact that when the *close* classifier wrongly decides not to end a NE then its output for the following words becomes unpredictable, since it enters into a situation not seen in the training phase.

This is confirmed by an additional experiment with a modified scheme consisting of applying the OpenClose scheme but after each negative prediction of the *close*, the I classifier is asked to confirm whether the following word is still inside the NE. If the I classifier gives a positive answer then the process continues normally, otherwise it is assumed that the *close* classifier was wrong. The positive answers of the *close* classifier are never questioned, since it is very accurate in its predictions. As it can be seen in table 2, this scheme (OpenClose&I) achieves the best results on the task.

Finally, table 3 presents the NER results depending on the length of the NE to recognize, as well as depending on whether the entity begins with uppercase or lowercase letter. As it could be expected, the performance degrades with the length of the sequence to be detected (specially on recall). However, a reasonable high accuracy can be expected for NEs of length up to six words. The set of

Table 2. Results of all methods in the NER task

Method	B	E	P	R	F_1
Maco+	90.83%	87.51%	89.94%	87.51%	88.71%
OpenClose	94.61%	91.54%	92.42%	91.54%	91.97%
IOB	95.20%	91.99%	**92.66%**	91.99%	92.33%
OpenClose&I	**95.31%**	**92.14%**	92.60%	**92.14%**	**92.37%**

NEs that begin with a lowercase word poses a very challenging problem for the NER module, specially due to the very shallow semantic treatment of the training examples (captured only through the word forms, without any kind of generalization). We find very remarkable the precision achieved by the system on this subset of words (85.40%). The recall is significantly lower (63.93%), basically because in many occasions the *open* classifier does not have enough evidence to start a NE in a lowercase word.

Table 3. Results of OpenClose&I on different subsets of the NER task

Subset	#NE	B	E	P	R	F_1
length=1	2,807	97.04%	95.80%	94.64%	95.65%	95.15%
length=2	1,005	99.30%	93.73%	94.01%	93.73%	93.87%
length=3	495	93.74%	88.69%	91.65%	88.69%	90.14%
length=4	237	89.45%	84.81%	84.81%	84.81%	84.81%
length=5	89	87.64%	76.40%	77.27%	76.40%	76.84%
length=6	74	93.24%	79.73%	81.94%	79.73%	80.82%
length=7	22	59.09%	54.55%	60.00%	54.55%	57.14%
length=8	22	77.27%	68.18%	88.24%	68.18%	76.92%
length=9	11	90.91%	72.73%	80.00%	72.73%	76.19%
length=10	3	66.67%	33.33%	50.00%	33.33%	40.00%
uppercase	4,637	96.42%	93.25%	92.81%	93.25%	93.03%
lowercase	183	67.21%	63.93%	85.40%	63.93%	73.13%
TOTAL	4,820	95.31%	92.14%	92.60%	92.14%	92.37%

5.4   NEC Results

The binarization of the NEC problem used in this work consists of a binary classifier for each class (*one-vs-all* scheme). All NEC binary classifiers achieve an accuracy between 91% and 97% and show very similar learning curves (not included) in terms of number of rounds. As in the NER task, decision trees significantly outperform stumps.

With respect to the complete NEC system, the combination of binary decisions is performed selecting the classes to which binary predictors assigned a positive confidence degree. The system can be forced to give exactly one prediction per NE by selecting the class with higher confidence degree.

The results of all NEC systems are presented in table 4 (left part). The *basic* row refers to the model using context word, bag-of-words, and NE features as described in section 4.1. Results when the models include features obtained from lists of trigger words (*tw*) and gazetteers (*gaz*) are also presented. As a baseline we include the results that a dumb *most-frequent-class* classifier would achieve.

In all cases, the use of extra information improves the performance of the system, both in the binary decisions and in the final combination. The best result is achieved when both external resources are used, pointing out that each of them provides information not included in the other. Although the individual performance of the binary classifiers is over 91%, the combined classifier achieves an accuracy of about 88%.

Table 4. Results of all feature sets in the NEC task assuming perfect NE segmentation (left part), and using the real output of the NER module (right part)

Method	P	R	$F1$	Acc	P	R	$F1$	Acc
Most frequent	39.78%	39.78%	39.78%	39.78%	37.47%	37.47%	37.47%	37.47%
basic	90.19%	84.44%	87.22%	87.51%	83.84%	79.39%	81.55%	81.85%
basic+tw	90.11%	84.77%	87.36%	88.17%	85.08%	79.30%	82.09%	82.15%
basic+gaz	90.25%	**85.31%**	87.71%	88.60%	85.05%	79.57%	82.22%	82.15%
basic+tw+gaz	**90.61%**	85.23%	**87.84%**	**88.73%**	**85.32%**	**79.80%**	**82.47%**	**82.31%**

Finally, the complete system is evaluated by testing the performance of the NEC classifier on the output of the NER module. Again, table 4 (right part) presents the results obtained. Performance is rather lower due to the error propagation of the NER module and to the worst-case evaluation, which counts as misclassifications the entities incorrectly recognized.

6   Conclusions and Further Work

We have presented a Named Entity Extraction system for Spanish based on robust Machine Learning techniques. The system relies on the usage of a large set of simple features requiring no complex linguistic processing. The performance of the learning algorithms is fairly good, providing accurate and robust NE recognizers and classifiers, which have been tested on a large corpus of running text. By adding extra–features from a gazetteer and a list of trigger words the performance has been further improved. The validity of the presented approach and its portability to other languages have been tested in the *CoNLL* competition framework [12,8] with very good results.

Some lines of improvement currently under research include:

- Classification algorithms other than AdaBoost must be tested at NE extraction. Although this task fits well AdaBoost capabilities, other algorithm such as Support Vector Machines may offer similar or better performances.
- Although the initial experiments have not reported good results, we think that the use of global inference schemes (instead of the one-pass greedy approach used in this paper) for assigning the sequence of tags deserves further investigation.

 – NEC: The combination of the four binary classifiers obtains lower performance than any of them. Further combination schemes must be explored, as well as the use of multi-label AdaBoost algorithms.

References

1. J. Aberdeen, J. Burger, D. Day, L. Hirschman, P. Robinson, and M. Vilain. MITRE: Description of the *ALEMBIC* System Used for MUC-6. In *Proceedings of the 6th Messsage Understanding Conference*, 1995.
2. D. E. Appelt, J. R. Hobbs, J. Bear, D. Israel, M. Kameyama, A. Kehler, D. Martin, K. Myers, and M. Tyson. SRI International FASTUS System MUC-6 Test Results and Analysis. In *Proceedings of the 6th Messsage Understanding Conference*, 1995.
3. D. M. Bikel, S. Miller, R. Schwartz, and R. Weischedel. Nymble: A High Performance Learning Name-Finder. In *Proceedings of the 5th Conference on ANLP*, Washington DC, 1997.
4. W. J. Black, F. Rinaldi, and D. Mowatt. FACILE: Description of the NE System Used for MUC-7. In *Proceedings of the 7th MUC Conference*, 1998.
5. A. Borthwick, J. Sterling, E. Agichtein, and R. Grishman. NYU: Description of the MENE Named Entity System as Used in MUC-7. In *Proceedings of the 7th Message Understanding Conference*, 1998.
6. J. Carmona, S. Cervell, L. Màrquez, M. Martí, L. Padró, R. Placer, H. Rodríguez, M. Taulé, and J. Turmo. An Environment for Morphosyntactic Processing of Unrestricted Spanish Text. In *Proceedings of the 1st LREC*, Granada, Spain, 1998.
7. X. Carreras and L. Màrquez. Boosting Trees for Clause Splitting. In *Proceedings of the 5th CoNLL Conference*, Tolouse, France, 2001.
8. X. Carreras, L. Màrquez, and L. Padró. Named entity extraction using AdaBoost. In *Proceedings of the Sixth CoNLL*, Taiwan, Taipei, 2002.
9. G. R. Krupka and K. Hausman. IsoQuest, Inc.: Description of the NetOwl^{TM} Extractor System as Used for MUC-7. In *Proceedings of the 7th Message Understanding Conference*, 1998.
10. A. Mikheev, C. Grover, and M. Moens. Description of the LTG System Used for MUC-7. In *Proceedings of the 7th Message Understanding Conference*, 1998.
11. V. Punyakanok and D. Roth. The Use of Classifiers in Sequential Inference. In *Proceedings of the 13th NIPS Conference*, 2000.
12. E. T. K. Sang. Introduction to the CoNLL-2002 shared task: Language-independent named entity recognition. In *Proceedings of the Sixth Conference on Natural Language Learning*, Taiwan, Taipei, 2002.
13. R. E. Schapire. The boosting approach to machine learning. an overview. In *Proceedings of the MSRI Workshop on Nonlinear Estimation and Classification*, Berkeley, CA, 2001.
14. R. E. Schapire and Y. Singer. Improved Boosting Algorithms Using Confidence-rated Predictions. *Machine Learning*, 37(3), 1999.
15. R. Weischedel. BBN: Description of the PLUM System as Used for MUC-6. In *Proceedings of the 6th Messsage Understanding Conference*, 1995.
16. S. Yu, S. Bai, and P. Wu. Description of the Kent Ridge Digital Labs System Used for MUC-7. In *Proceedings of the 7th Message Understanding Conference*, 1998.

Terminology Retrieval: Towards a Synergy between Thesaurus and Free Text Searching*

Anselmo Peñas, Felisa Verdejo, and Julio Gonzalo

Dpto. Lenguajes y Sistemas Informáticos, UNED
{anselmo,felisa,julio}@lsi.uned.es

Abstract. Multilingual Information Retrieval usually forces a choice between free text indexing or indexing by means of multilingual thesaurus. However, since they share the same objectives, synergy between both approaches is possible. This paper shows a retrieval framework that make use of terminological information in free-text indexing. The Automatic Terminology Extraction task, which is used for thesauri construction, shifts to a searching of terminology and becomes an information retrieval task: *Terminology Retrieval*. Terminology Retrieval, then, allows cross-language information retrieval through the browsing of morpho-syntactic, semantic and translingual variations of the query. Although terminology retrieval doesn't make use of them, controlled vocabularies become an appropriate framework for terminology retrieval evaluation.

1 Introduction

The organization of information for later retrieval is a fundamental area of research in Library/Information Sciences. It concerns to understand the nature of information, how humans process it and how best to organize it to facilitate use. A number of tools to organize information have been developed, one of them is the information retrieval thesaurus. A thesaurus is a tool for vocabulary control. Usually it is designed for indexing and searching in a specific subject area. By guiding indexers and searchers about which terms to use, it can help to improve the quality of retrieval. Thus, the primary purposes of a thesaurus are identified as promotion of consistency in the indexing of documents and facilitating searching. Most thesauri have been designed to facilitate access to the information contained within one database or group of specific databases. An example is the ERIC[1] thesaurus, a gateway to the ERIC documents database containing more than 1.000.000 abstracts of documents and journal articles on education research and practice. Via the ERIC interface, one can navigate the thesaurus and use the controlled vocabulary for more accurate and fruitful search results. Thesaurus were a resource used primarily by trained librarians obtaining good performance. However nowadays on-line database searching is carried out by a wider and less specialized audience of Internet users and recent studies [4]

---

[1] http://www.ericfacility.net/extra/pub/thessearch.cfm

* This work has been partially supported by European Schools Treasury Browser project (ETB, http://www.eun.org/etb) and HERMES project (TIC2000-0335-C03-01).

F.J. Garijo, J.C. Riquelme, and M. Toro (Eds.): IBERAMIA 2002, LNAI 2527, pp. 684–693, 2002.

claim that most end-users obtained poor results, missing highly relevant documents. Nevertheless there is a strong feeling in the documentalist field that the use of a thesaurus is a central issue for raising the quality of end-users results [7] specially in a multilingual context where natural language ambiguity increases, producing additional problems for translingual retrieval. A multilingual thesaurus guarantees the control of the indexing vocabulary, covering each selected concept with a preferred term, a descriptor, in each language, and ensuring a very high degree of equivalence among those terms in different languages. However, multilingual thesauri construction and maintenance is a task with a very high cost, which motivates the exploration of alternative approaches based on free text indexing and retrieval.

In this paper, on one hand, we show how NLP techniques have a part to play both in thesaurus construction and in free text searching in specialized collections; on the other hand, we describe an evaluation framework for an NLP-based full-text multilingual search system where a thesaurus resource is used as a baseline. The structure of the paper is the following: Section 2 reports the developed methodology implying NLP techniques to support the construction of the European Schools Treasury Browser (ETB) multilingual thesaurus in the field of education. This methodology easily shifts to a new strategy with IR shared objectives: *terminology retrieval*. Section 3 introduces Website Term Browser (WTB) [5], a browsing system that implements this strategy for searching information in a multilingual collection of documents. The system helps users to cross language barriers including terminology variations in different languages. In order to assess the performance of WTB we have designed an evaluation framework for the *terminology retrieval* task, that takes profit of the ETB multilingual thesaurus. Section 4 presents this evaluation framework and shows the results obtained. The conclusion points out a direction in which NLP techniques can be a complement or an alternative to thesaurus based retrieval.

2 From Terminology Extraction to Terminology Retrieval

Thesaurus construction requires collecting a set of salient terms. For this purpose, relevant sources including texts or existing term lists have to be identified or extracted. This is a task combining deductive and inductive approaches. Deductive procedures are those analyzing already existing vocabularies, thesauri and indexes in order to design the new thesaurus according to the desired scope, structure and level of specificity; inductive approaches analyze the real-world vocabularies in the document repositories in order to identify terms and update the terminologies. Both approaches can be supported by automatic linguistic techniques. Our work followed the inductive approach to provide new terminology for the ETB thesaurus, starting with an automatic Terminology Extraction (TE) procedure [6]. Typically, TE (or ATR, Automatic Terminology Recognition) is divided in three steps [2], [3]:

1. Term extraction via morphological analysis, part of speech tagging and shallow parsing. We distinguish between one word terms (mono-lexical terms) and multi-word terms (poly-lexical terms), extracted with different techniques detailed in [6].
2. Term weighting with statistical information, measuring the term relevance in the domain.
3. Term selection. Term ranking and truncation of lists by thresholds of weight.

These steps require a previous one in which relevant corpora is identified, automatically collected and prepared for the TE task. After collecting terms, documentalists need to decide which ones are equivalent, which are finally selected and which other terms should be introduced to represent broad concepts or to clarify the structure of semantic relations between terms. The main semantic relations are hierarchical (represented as BT and NT) and RT to express an associative relationship. To support documentalists decisions, a web-based interface making use of hyperlinks was provided. Through this interface, access to candidate terms contexts as well as their frequency statistics were provided.

This was the methodology employed to term extraction task and thesaurus construction. However, while the goal in the Terminology Extraction is to decide which terms are relevant in a particular domain, in a full text search users decide which are the relevant terms according to their information needs, i.e. the user query gives the relevant terms. In this case, the automatic terminology extraction task oriented to text indexing should favor recall rather than precision of the extracted terms. This implies:

1. Terminology list truncation is not convenient.
2. Relaxing of poly-lexical term patterns is possible.

And also suggests a change of strategy. From a thesaurus construction point of view, TE procedure shifts to *term searching* becoming a new task: *terminology retrieval*. From a text retrieval perspective, *retrieved terminology* becomes an intermediate information level which provides document access bridging the gap between query and collection vocabularies even in different languages. This framework, shared for both tasks, needs:

1. A previous indexing to permit phrase retrieval from query words.
2. Expansion and translation of query words in order to retrieve terminology variations (morpho-syntactic, semantic and translingual).

This strategy has been implemented in the WTB described in the next section.

3   Website Term Browser

The system, *Website Term Browser* (*WTB*) [5], applies NLP techniques to perform automatically the following tasks:

1. Terminology Extraction and indexing of a multilingual text collection.
2. Interactive NL-query processing and retrieval.
3. Browsing by phrases considering morpho-syntactic, semantic and translingual variations of the query.

Terminology Extraction and Indexing. The collection of documents is automatically processed to obtain a large list of terminological phrases. Detection of phrases in the collection is based on syntactic patterns. Selection of phrases is based on document frequency and phrase subsumption. Such processing is performed separately for each language (currently Spanish, English, French, Italian and Catalan). We reused, in a relaxed way, the terminology extraction procedure originally meant to produce a terminological list to feed a thesaurus construction process[6].

Query processing and retrieval. Cross-language retrieval is performed by translating the query to the other languages in the collection. Word translation ambiguity can be drastically mitigated by restricting the translation of the components of a phrase into words that are highly associated as phrases in the target language [1]. This process is generalized in the Website Term Browser as follows:

1. Lemmatized query words are expanded with semantically related words in the query language and all target languages using the EuroWordNet lexical database [8] and some bilingual dictionaries.

2. Phrases containing some of the expanded words are retrieved. The number of expansion words is usually high, and the use of semantically related words (such as synonyms) produce a lot of noise. However, the retrieval and ranking of terms via phrasal information discards most inappropriate word combinations, both in the source and in the target languages.

3. Unlike batch cross-language retrieval, where phrasal information is used only to select the best translation for words according to their context, in this process all salient phrases are retained for the interactive selection process.

4. Documents are also ranked according to the frequency and salience of the relevant phrases they contain.

Browsing by phrases. *Figure 1* shows the WTB interface. Results of the querying and retrieval process are shown in two separate areas: a ranking of phrases that are salient in the collection and relevant to the user's query (on the left part) and a ranking of documents (on the right part). Both kinds of information are presented to the user, who may browse the ranking of phrases or directly click on a document.

Phrases in different languages are shown to users ranked and organized in a hierarchy according to:

1. Number of expanded terms contained in the phrase. The higher the number of terms within the phrase, the higher the ranking. In the monolingual case, original query terms are ranked higher than expanded terms.

2. Salience of the phrase according to their weight as terminological expressions. This weight is reduced to within-collection document frequency if there is no cross-domain corpus to compare with.

3. Subsumption of phrases. For presentation purposes, a group of phrases containing a sub-phrase are presented as subsumed by the most frequent sub-phrase in the collection. That helps browsing the space of phrases similarly to a topic hierarchy.

Figure 1 shows an example of searching. The user has written the English query *"adult education"* in the text box. Then, the system has retrieved and ranked related terminology in several languages (Spanish, English, French, Italian and Catalan). This terminology was extracted automatically during indexing, and now has been retrieved from the query words and their translations. In the example, the user has selected the *Spanish* tab as target language where there are three different top terms (folders): *"formación de adultos"*, *"adultos implicados en el proceso de enseñanza"* and *"educación de adultos"*. The second one (*"adultos implicados en el proceso de enseñanza"*) is not related to the concept in the query, but the *term browsing facility* permits to discard it without effort. Top term folders contain morpho-syntactic and semantic variations of terms. For example, the preferred Spanish term in the ETB thesaurus is *"educación de adultos"*. However, in this case, besides the preferred term, *WTB* has been able to offer some variations:

- *Morpho-syntactic variation*: *"educación permanente de adultos"*, *"educación de personas adultas"*.
- *Semantic variation*: *"formación de adultos"*, *"formación de personas adultas"*

In the example, the user has expanded the folder *"educación de adultos"* and has selected the term *"educación de las personas adultas"*, obtaining (on the right handside) the list of documents containing that term.

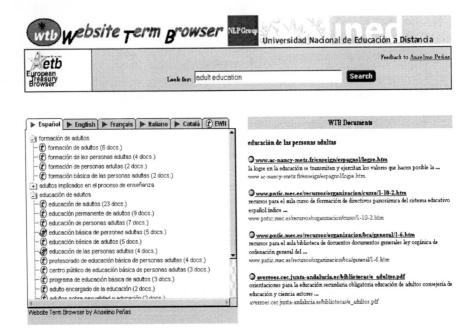

Fig. 1. Website Term Browser interface

4   Evaluation

The usefulness of *term browsing* versus document ranking was already evaluated in [5] from the users perspective. Now the evaluation is aimed to establish the system coverage for translingual terminology retrieval compared with the use of a multilingual handcrafted thesaurus for searching purposes. The second main point of this evaluation aims to study the dependence between the quality of our results, the quality of used linguistic resources and the quality of WTB processing. While NLP techniques feed Terminology Extraction and thesaurus construction, now a thesaurus becomes a very useful resource to give feedback and evaluate the linguistic processes in a retrieval task.

The evaluation has been performed comparing the WTB terminology retrieval over a multilingual web pages collection, with the European Schools Treasury Browser (ETB) thesaurus. The multilingual collection comprises 42,406 pages of several European repositories in the educational domain (200 Mb) with the following distribution: Spanish 6,271 docs.; English 12,631 docs.; French 12,534 docs.; Italian 10,970 docs.

	ESP	ENG	FRA	ITA
	terapia	therapy	thérapie	terapia
therapy	-terapeutico -terapia -terapéutica	-therapy -treatment	-thérapie -traitement	-cura -curar -terapia -trattamento
terapia	-terapeutico -terapia -terapéutica	-therapeutics -therapy -treatment	-thérapie -traitement	-cura -curar -terapia -trattamento
thérapie	-terapeutico -terapia -terapéutica	-therapy -treatment	-thérapie -traitement	-cura -curar -terapia -trattamento
terapia	-terapeutico -terapia -terapéutica	-therapeutics -therapy -treatment	-thérapie -traitement	-cura -curar -terapia -trattamento

Fig. 2. Interface for qualitative evaluation of terminology retrieval (mono-lexical terms)

The ETB thesaurus alpha version used in the evaluation has 1051 descriptors with its translations to each of the five considered languages (English, Spanish, French, Italian and German). German hasn't been considered in the evaluation because no linguistic tools were available to us for that language. Each ETB thesaurus descriptor has been used as a WTB query. The thesaurus preferred translations have been compared with the WTB retrieved terms in each language. In such a way, precision and recall measures can be provided. Approximately half of the thesaurus descriptors are phrases (poly-lexical terms) which can be used to evaluate the WTB terminology retrieval. Thesaurus mono-lexical terms permit the coverage evaluation of linguistic resources used in the expansion and translation of query words.

Qualitative evaluation. *Figure 2* shows the interface for the qualitative evaluation. This interface is aimed to facilitate inspection on the system behavior, in order to detect errors and suggest improvements on WTB system. The first column contains the thesaurus terms in each language (in the example, *therapy, terapia, thérapie and terapia)*. Each of them are the preferred terms, or descriptors, in the thesaurus and have been used as WTB queries. The retrieved terms in each target language are shown in the same row. For example, when searching WTB with *therapy* (English term), in the first column, the system retrieves *terapeutico, terapia y terapéutica*, in Spanish (same row, second column); it also retrieves *therapy* and *treatment* in English (same row, third column).

Quantitative evaluation. If the preferred term in the thesaurus has been retrieved by WTB, then it is counted as a correctly retrieved term. Then, precision and recall measures can be defined in the following way:

- *Recall*: number of retrieved descriptors divided by the number of descriptors in the thesaurus.
- *Precision*: number of retrieved descriptors divided by the number of retrieved terms.

Figure 2 shows that there are correct terms retrieved by WTB different from the preferred terms (descriptors) in the thesaurus. Hence, the proposed recall and precision measures are lower bounds to the real performance. For example, among the retrieved terms by the English query *"adult education"*, only the Spanish term *"educación de adultos"* adjusts to the preferred term in the thesaurus. However, there are some morpho-syntactic variations *("educación de adultas", "educación de los adultos")*, semantic variations *("formación de adultos")*, and related terms *("formación básica de las personas adultas")* which are correctly retrieved terms but not counted as such.

WTB retrieved terms have been directly extracted from texts and, for that reason, recall will depend on the coverage of thesaurus descriptors in the test collection. Although the test collection is very close to the thesaurus domain, it's not possible to guarantee the presence of all thesaurus terms in all languages in the collection. Indeed, thesaurus descriptors are indexes to abstract concepts, which are not necessarily contained in the texts being indexed. *Table 1* shows the coverage of thesaurus descriptors in the test collection where exact matches have been considered (including accents).

Table 1. Thesaurus descriptors in the test collection

Coverage	Spanish	English	French	Italian
Mono-lexical descriptors found in the collection	84.3%	81.9%	82.3%	81.1%
Poly-lexical descriptors found in the collection	56.5%	57.5%	54.2%	42.6%

Mono-lexical term retrieval. Since mono-lexical term expansion and translation only depend of lexical resources, potential retrieval capabilities can be evaluated independently of the collection, just counting the mono-lexical thesaurus descriptors present in the lexical resources used (EuroWordNet lexical database and bilingual dictionaries). This comparison gives and idea of the domain coverage by the lexical resources. *Table 2* shows presence of thesaurus descriptors in the lexical resources (monolingual case, in diagonal) and their capability to go cross-language. The first column corresponds to the source languages and the first row corresponds to the target languages. The cell values correspond to the percentage of mono-lexical thesaurus descriptors recovered in the target language from the source language descriptor. *Table 2* shows that recall for the Spanish/ English pairs is significantly higher than the rest. The reason is that Spanish and English languages have been complemented with bilingual dictionaries while French and Italian only use EuroWordNet relations. Since monolingual cases show a good coverage, numbers point out that there is a lack of connections between different language hierarchies in EuroWordNet. In conclusion, with the currently used resources, we can expect a poorer behavior of WTB translingual retrieval implying French and Italian.

Table 2. Potential recall of mono-lexical descriptors with WTB lexical resources

Recall	Spanish	English	French	Italian
Spanish	91.6%	83.7%	60.9%	64.3%
English	80.4%	97.2%	63.9%	63.9%
French	66.3%	61.8%	85.5%	55.9%
Italian	67.9%	62.2%	53.9%	96.7%

Poly-lexical term retrieval. WTB poly-lexical term retrieval depends of the previously extracted phrases from the document collection and therefore, depends on the coverage of thesaurus descriptors in the test collection. Coverage of thesaurus descriptors in the test collection in the monolingual case (*Table 1, last row*), gives an upper bound for recall in the translingual cases. *Table 3* show WTB recall for each pair of languages in percentage over this upper bound for the target language.

Table 3. WTB recall in % respect collection coverage (poly-lexical terms)

Recall	Spanish	English	French	Italian
Spanish	63.1%	45.8%	19.9%	16.3%
English	40.2%	66.5%	14.7%	7.4%
French	12.5%	15.6%	40.3%	7.8%
Italian	17.1%	17.2%	8.9%	39.3%

As shown in *Table 3* English/ Spanish pairs show better behavior than other pairs of languages. The reason for this relies in that poly-lexical term retrieval is based in the combination of mono-lexical terms, and this depends on the lexical resources used. Again, just in the case of English/ Spanish pairs, EuroWordNet has been complemented with bilingual dictionaries and, for that reason, these pairs of languages present the best behavior in both mono and poly-lexical term retrieval. However, differences between mono and poly-lexical terms recall need further consideration. While mono-lexical terms correspond to nouns, which are well covered by EuroWordNet hierarchies, most poly-lexical terms include adjective components which aren't covered so well by EuroWordNet. This lack has been also corrected only for English/ Spanish pairs using bilingual dictionaries and this is an additional factor for a better recall.

The best recall is obtained for Spanish as source language. The reason relies in that, for this language, WTB uses a morphological analyzer which gives all possible lemmas for the query words. All these lemmas are considered in expansion, translation and retrieval. In this way, possible lemmatization errors are avoided both in query and texts, and increases the number of possible combinations for poly-lexical term retrieval. However, the recall values are quite low even in monolingual cases and thus, a broader study explaining loss of recall is needed. As said, WTB poly-lexical term retrieval depends on the previous extracted phrases and thus, not only depends on the test collection, but also on phrase extraction, indexing and retrieval procedures. *Table 4* shows the loss of recall due to phrase extraction and indexing procedures. There are several factors which lead to a loss of recall:

1. *Phrase extraction procedure.* Loss of recall due to not exhaustive syntactic patterns and wrong part-of-speech tagging. The loss of recall due to a wrong phrase extraction procedure is represented by the differences between first and second rows and oscillates between 2.8% for Spanish and 17.3% for French.
2. *Phrase indexing.* Loss of recall due to wrong phrase components lemmatization. The loss of recall due to wrong indexing (mainly wrong lemmatization of phrases components in texts) oscillates between 2% for English and 34% for French.
3. *Phrase retrieval.* Loss of recall due to wrong lemmatization, expansion and translation of query words, and wrong discarding in phrase selection and ranking of terms. WTB discards retrieved terms with document frequency equal to 1 in order to improve precision in the terms shown to users. This fact produces a loss of recall between 12.9% for Spanish and 36.7% for Italian.
4. *Mismatching caused by accents and case folding.* WTB doesn't need to separate documents in different languages. For this reason the loss of recall due to accents mismatching is difficult to quantify here because it produces a big confusion

between languages. For example, there are lots of terms in English equal to the French ones without accents. Similar occurs between Italian and Spanish.

All this factors show that not only lexical resources must be improved, but also linguistic processing tools as lemmatizers and part-of-speech taggers.

Table 4. Loss of recall in WTB poly-lexical term retrieval by steps in the processing

Poly-lexical descriptors	Spanish	English	French	Italian
found in the collection	56.5%	57.5%	54.2%	42.6%
found among extracted phrases	54.9%	50.1%	44.8%	40.0%
(loss of recall due to phrase extraction)	(-2.8%)	(-12.9%)	(-17.3%)	(-6.1%)
retrieved with WTB	40.9%	49.1%	29.2%	26.4%
(loss of recall)	(-27.6%)	(-14.6%)	(-46.1%)	(-38%)
(loss of recall due to phrase indexing)	(-25.5%)	(-2%)	(-34.8%)	(-34%)
retrieved with WTB discarding df=1	35.6%	38.2%	21.8%	16.7%
(loss of recall)	(-36.9%)	(-33.5%)	(-59.7%)	(-60.7%)
(loss of recall due to phrase selection)	(-12.9%)	(-22.1%)	(-25.3%)	(-36.7%)

Regarding precision, in the worst case, there is one preferred descriptor in average among ten retrieved terms, and three in the best case. Term discrimination is an easy and very fast task which is helped in the WTB interface through the term organization into hierarchies. In fact, about 70% of the retrieved relevant descriptors are retrieved in the top level of the hierarchies. This is a good percentage to ensure fast discrimination of retrieved terms.

5   Conclusions

Terminology Retrieval gives a shared perspective between terminology extraction and cross-language information retrieval. From thesaurus construction point of view, the Automatic Terminology Extraction procedures shift to term searching. From text retrieval perspective, *retrieved terminology* becomes an intermediate information level which provides document access crossing the gap between query and collection vocabularies even in different languages. This strategy has been implemented in the Website Term Browser. The evaluation framework for *terminology retrieval* has been established in this paper, being able to detect where processing and resources can be improved. While NLP techniques feed Automatic Terminology Extraction for thesaurus construction, now, in a retrieval framework, a thesaurus provides a baseline for *terminology retrieval* evaluation and gives feedback on the quality, coverage and use of the linguistic tools and resources.

The qualitative evaluation shows that WTB is able to retrieve a considerable amount of appropriate term variations not considered in the thesaurus. Thus, terminology retrieval becomes a very good complement to thesauri in the multilingual retrieval task. The quantitative evaluation results are a lower bound of the real recall and precision values because correct term variations, different from the preferred thesaurus descriptors, are not taken into account. Results show a high dependence of WTB terminology retrieval with respect to the used linguistic resources showing that EuroWordNet relations between different languages must be improved. Results also show the loss of recall due to phrase extraction, indexing and retrieval processes.

Future work must study the loss of recall due to accent mismatching. We conclude that, when appropriate resources and linguistic tools are available, WTB show a reasonable good behavior, although there is place for improvement.

Future work will refine the evaluation framework and include the study of infrequent thesaurus descriptors (especially those not found in the collection). For these purposes, the construction of a new test collection is planned querying Internet search engines with the thesaurus descriptors. The crawling of the listed documents will ensure a collection with a thesaurus coverage of 100% and will permit separate processing and results for each language including accent mismatching evaluation.

References

1. Ballesteros, L. and Croft W. B. Resolving Ambiguity for Cross-Language Information Retrieval. Proceedings of the 21st ACM SIGIR Conference. 1998
2. Bourigault, D. Surface grammatical analysis for the extraction of terminological noun phrases. Proceedings of 14th International Conference on Computational Linguistics, COLING'92. 1992; 977–981.
3. Frantzi, K. T. and S. Ananiadou. The C-value/NC-value domain independent method for multiword term extraction. Natural Language Processing. 1999; 6(3)
4. Hertzberg, S. and Rudner L. The quality of researchers' searches of the ERIC Database. Education Policy Analysis Archives. 1999.
5. Peñas, A. Gonzalo J. and Verdejo F. Cross-Language Information Access through Phrase Browsing. Proceedings of NLDB 2001, Madrid, Lecture Notes in Informatics (LNI), (GI-Edition). 2001; P-3:121–130.
6. Peñas, A. Verdejo F. and Gonzalo J. Corpus-based Terminology Extraction applied to Information Access. Corpus Linguistics 2001; Lancaster, UK. 2001.
7. Trigari, M. Multilingual Thesaurus, why? E. Schools Treasury Browser. 2001.
8. Vossen, P. Introduction to EuroWordNet. Computers and the Humanities, Special Issue on EuroWordNet. 1998.

Mixed Parsing of Tree Insertion and Tree Adjoining Grammars

Miguel A. Alonso[1], Vicente Carrillo[2], and Víctor J. Díaz[2]

[1] Departamento de Computación, Universidade da Coruña
Campus de Elviña s/n, 15071 La Coruña (Spain)
`alonso@udc.es`
[2] Departamento de Lenguajes y Sistemas Informáticos, Universidad de Sevilla
Avda. Reina Mercedes s/n, 41012 Sevilla (Spain)
`{carrillo, vjdiaz}@lsi.us.es`

Abstract. Adjunction is a powerful operation that makes Tree Adjoining Grammar (TAG) useful for describing the syntactic structure of natural languages. In practice, a large part of wide coverage grammars written following the TAG formalism is formed by trees that can be combined by means of the simpler kind of adjunction defined for Tree Insertion Grammar. In this paper, we describe a parsing algorithm that makes use of this characteristic to reduce the practical complexity of TAG parsing: the expensive standard adjunction operation is only considered in those cases in which the simpler cubic-time adjunction cannot be applied.

1 Introduction

Tree Adjoining Grammar (TAG) [4] and Tree Insertion Grammar (TIG) [6] are grammatical formalisms that make use of a tree-based operation called adjunction. However, adjunctions are more restricted in the case of TIG than in the case of TAG, which has important consequences with respect to the set of languages generated and the worst-case complexity of parsing algorithms:

- TAG generates tree adjoining languages, a strict superset of context-free languages, and the complexity of parsing algorithms is in $\mathcal{O}(n^6)$ for time and in $\mathcal{O}(n^4)$ for space with respect to the length n of the input string.
- TIG generates context-free languages and can be parsed in $\mathcal{O}(n^3)$ for time and in $\mathcal{O}(n^2)$ for space.

Albeit the powerful adjunction provided by TAG makes it useful for describing the syntax of natural languages, most of the trees involved in wide coverage grammars like XTAG [3] do not make use of such operation, and so a large portion of XTAG is in fact a TIG [6]. As the full power of a TAG parser is only put into practice in adjunctions involving a given set of trees, to apply a parser working in $\mathcal{O}(n^6)$ time complexity when most of the work can be done by a $\mathcal{O}(n^3)$ parser seems to be a waste of computing resources. In this paper, we propose a mixed parser that takes the best of both worlds: those parts of the grammar that

F.J. Garijo, J.C. Riquelme, and M. Toro (Eds.): IBERAMIA 2002, LNAI 2527, pp. 694–703, 2002.
© Springer-Verlag Berlin Heidelberg 2002

correspond to a TIG are managed in $\mathcal{O}(n^3)$ time and $\mathcal{O}(n^2)$ space complexity, and only those parts of the grammar involving the full kind of adjunction present in TAG are managed in $\mathcal{O}(n^6)$ time and $\mathcal{O}(n^4)$ space complexity.

1.1   Tree Adjoining Grammars

Formally, a TAG is a 5-tuple $\mathcal{G} = (V_N, V_T, S, \boldsymbol{I}, \boldsymbol{A})$, where V_N is a finite set of non-terminal symbols, V_T a finite set of terminal symbols, S the axiom of the grammar, $\boldsymbol{I}$ a finite set of *initial trees* and $\boldsymbol{A}$ a finite set of *auxiliary trees*. $\boldsymbol{I} \cup \boldsymbol{A}$ is the set of *elementary trees*. Internal nodes are labeled by non-terminals and leaf nodes by terminals or the empty string ε, except for just one leaf per auxiliary tree (the *foot*) which is labeled by the same non-terminal used as the label of its root node. The path in an elementary tree from the root node to the foot node is called the *spine* of the tree.

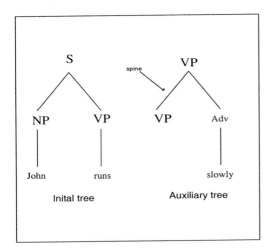 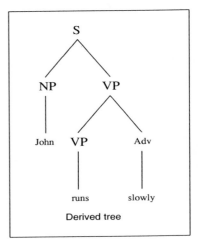

Fig. 1. Adjunction operation

New trees are derived by *adjunction*: let γ be a tree containing a node N^γ labeled by A and let β be an auxiliary tree whose root and foot nodes are also labeled by A. Then, the adjunction of β at the *adjunction node* N^γ is obtained by excising the subtree of γ with root N^γ, attaching β to N^γ and attaching the excised subtree to the foot of β. We illustrate the adjunction operation in Fig. 1, where we show a simple TAG with two elementary trees: an initial tree rooted S and an auxiliary tree rooted VP. The derived tree obtained after adjoining the VP auxiliary tree on the node labeled by VP located in the initial tree is also shown.

We use $\beta \in \mathrm{adj}(N^\gamma)$ to denote that a tree β may be adjoined at node N^γ of the elementary tree γ. If adjunction is not mandatory at N^γ then $\mathbf{nil} \in \mathrm{adj}(N^\gamma)$

where **nil** $\notin \boldsymbol{I} \cup \boldsymbol{A}$ is a dummy symbol. If adjunction is not allowed at N^γ then $\{\mathbf{nil}\} = \mathrm{adj}(N^\gamma)$.

1.2   Tree Insertion Grammars

We can consider the set $\boldsymbol{A}$ as formed by the union of the sets $\boldsymbol{A}_L$, containing *left auxiliary trees* in which every nonempty frontier node is to the left of the foot node, $\boldsymbol{A}_R$, containing *right auxiliary trees* in which every nonempty frontier node is to the right of the foot node, and $\boldsymbol{A}_W$, containing *wrapping auxiliary trees* in which nonempty frontier nodes are placed both to the left and to the right of the foot node. Given an auxiliary tree, we call *spine nodes* to those nodes placed on the spine and *left nodes* (resp. *right nodes*) to those nodes placed to the left (resp. right) of the spine. The set $\boldsymbol{A}_{SL} \subseteq \boldsymbol{A}_L$ (resp. $\boldsymbol{A}_{SR} \subseteq \boldsymbol{A}_R$) of *strongly left* (resp. *strongly right*) auxiliary trees is formed by trees in which no adjunction is permitted on right (resp. left) nodes and only strongly left (resp. right) auxiliary trees are allowed to adjoin on spine nodes. Figure 2 shows three derived trees resulting from the adjunction of a wrapping, left and right auxiliary tree, respectively.

In essence, a TIG is a restricted TAG where auxiliary trees must be either strongly left or strongly right and adjunctions are not allowed in root and foot nodes of auxiliary trees.

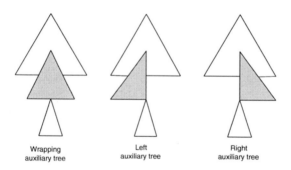

Fig. 2. TAG vs. TIG adjunction operation

1.3   Notation for Parsing Algorithms

We will describe parsing algorithms using *Parsing Schemata*, a framework for high-level descriptions of parsing algorithms [8]. A *parsing system* for a grammar G and string $a_1 \ldots a_n$ is a triple $\langle \mathcal{I}, \mathcal{H}, \mathcal{D} \rangle$, with $\mathcal{I}$ a set of *items* which represent intermediate parse results, $\mathcal{H}$ an initial set of items called *hypothesis* that encodes the sentence to be parsed, and $\mathcal{D}$ a set of *deduction steps* that allow new items to be derived from already known items. Deduction steps are of the form $\frac{\eta_1,\ldots,\eta_k}{\xi}$ *cond*, meaning that if all antecedents η_i of a deduction step are present and the conditions *cond* are satisfied, then the consequent ξ should be generated by the parser. A set $\mathcal{F} \subseteq \mathcal{I}$ of *final items* represent the recognition of a sentence. A *parsing schema* is a parsing system parameterized by a grammar and a sentence.

In order to describe the parsing algorithms for tree-based formalisms, we must be able to represent the partial recognition of elementary trees. Parsing algorithms for context-free grammars usually denote partial recognition of productions by dotted productions. We can extend this approach to the case of tree-based grammars by considering each elementary tree γ as formed by a set of context-free productions $\mathcal{P}(\gamma)$: a node N^γ and its children $N_1^\gamma \ldots N_g^\gamma$ are represented by a production $N^\gamma \to N_1^\gamma \ldots N_g^\gamma$. Thus, the position of the dot in the tree is indicated by the position of the dot in a production in $\mathcal{P}(\gamma)$. The elements of the productions are the nodes of the tree.

To simplify the description of parsing algorithms we consider an additional production $\top \to \mathbf{R}^\alpha$ for each $\alpha \in \mathbf{I}$ and the two additional productions $\top \to \mathbf{R}^\beta$ and $\mathbf{F}^\beta \to \perp$ for each $\beta \in \mathbf{A}$, where $\mathbf{R}^\beta$ and $\mathbf{F}^\beta$ correspond to the root node and the foot node of β, respectively. After disabling $\top$ and $\perp$ as adjunction nodes the generative capability of the grammars remains intact. We introduce also the following notation: given two pairs (p,q) and (i,j) of integers, $(p,q) \leq (i,j)$ is satisfied if $i \leq p$ and $q \leq j$ and given two integers p and q we define $p \cup q$ as p if q is undefined and as q if p is undefined, being undefined in other case.

2   A Mixed Parser for TIG and TAG

In this section we define a parsing system $\mathrm{P_{Mix}} = \langle \mathcal{I}_{\mathrm{Mix}}, \mathcal{H}_{\mathrm{Mix}}, \mathcal{D}_{\mathrm{Mix}} \rangle$ corresponding to a mixed parsing algorithm for TAG and TIG in which the adjunction of strongly left and strongly right auxiliary trees[1] will be managed by specialized deduction steps, the rest of adjunctions will be managed with the classical deduction steps included in most of TAG parsers [1].

For $\mathrm{P_{Mix}}$, we consider a set of items $\mathcal{I}_{\mathrm{Mix}} = \mathcal{I}_{\mathrm{Mix}}^{(a)} \cup \mathcal{I}_{\mathrm{Mix}}^{(b)} \cup \mathcal{I}_{\mathrm{Mix}}^{(c)}$ formed by the union of the following subsets:

- A subset $\mathcal{I}_{\mathrm{Mix}}^{(a)}$ with items of the form $[N^\gamma \to \delta \bullet \nu, i, j \mid p, q \mid adj]$ such that $N^\gamma \to \delta\nu \in \mathcal{P}(\gamma)$, $\gamma \in \mathbf{I} \cup \mathbf{A}$, $0 \leq i \leq j$, $(p,q) = (-,-)$ or $(p,q) \leq (i,j)$, and $adj \in \{\mathrm{true}, \mathrm{false}\}$. The two indices with respect to the input string i and j indicate the portion of the input string that has been spanned from δ (see figure 3). If $\gamma \in \mathbf{A}$, p and q are two indices with respect to the input string that indicate that part of the input string recognized by the foot

---

[1] Given the set $\mathbf{A}$ of a TAG, we can determine the set $\mathbf{A}_{SL}$ as follows: firstly, we determine the set $\mathbf{A}_L$ examining the frontier of the trees in $\mathbf{A}$ and we set $\mathbf{A}_{SL} := \mathbf{A}_L$; secondly, we eliminate from $\mathbf{A}_{SL}$ those trees that permit adjunctions on nodes to the right of their spine; and thirdly, we iteratively eliminate from $\mathbf{A}_{SL}$ those trees that allow adjoining trees in $\mathbf{A} - \mathbf{A}_{SL}$ on nodes of their spine. $\mathbf{A}_{SR}$ is determined in an analogous way.

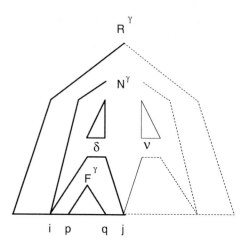

Fig. 3. Graphical representation of items

node of γ if it is a descendant of δ. In other case $p = q = -$ representing they are undefined. Therefore, this kind of items satisfy one of the following conditions:

1. $\gamma \in \boldsymbol{A} - (\boldsymbol{A}_{SL} \cup \boldsymbol{A}_{SR})$, $\delta \neq \epsilon$, $(p, q) \neq (-, -)$ and δ spans the string
$a_{i+1} \ldots a_p \ \mathbf{F}^\gamma \ a_{q+1} \ldots a_j$

2. $\delta \neq \epsilon$, $(p, q) = (-, -)$ and δ spans the string $a_{i+1} \ldots a_j$.

The last boolean component of items is used to avoid several adjunctions on a node. A value of true indicates that an adjunction has taken place on the node N^γ and therefore further adjunctions on the same node are forbidden. If $adj = $ true and $\nu \neq \epsilon$, it means that a strongly left auxiliary tree $\beta \in \boldsymbol{A}_L$ has been adjoined at N^γ. If $adj = $ true and $\nu = \epsilon$, it means that an auxiliary tree has been adjoined at N^γ. A value of false indicates that no adjunction was performed on that node. In this case, during future processing this item can play the role of the item recognizing the excised part of an elementary tree to be attached to the foot node of a right auxiliary tree. As a consequence, only one adjunction can take place on a node, as is prescribed by the tree adjoining grammar formalism.

– A subset $\mathcal{I}_{\text{Mix}}^{(b)}$ with items of the form $[N^\gamma \to \bullet v, j, j \mid -, - \mid \text{false}]$ such that $M^\gamma \to \delta \nu \in \mathcal{P}(\gamma)$, $\gamma \in \boldsymbol{I} \cup \boldsymbol{A}$ and $0 \leq i \leq j$. The last boolean component indicates any tree has been adjoined at N^γ.

– A subset $\mathcal{I}_{\text{Mix}}^{(b)}$ with items of the form $[N^\gamma \to \bullet v, i, j \mid -, - \mid \text{true}]$ such that $M^\gamma \to \delta \nu \in \mathcal{P}(\gamma)$, $\gamma \in \boldsymbol{I} \cup \boldsymbol{A}$, $0 \leq i \leq j$ and there exists a $\beta \in \boldsymbol{A}_{SL}$ such that $\beta \in \text{adj}(N^\gamma)$ and $\mathbf{R}^\beta$ spans $a_{i+1} \ldots a_j$ (i.e. β has been adjoined at N^γ). In this case, i and j indicate the portion of the input string spanned by the left auxiliary tree adjoined at N^γ.

The hypotheses defined for this parsing system encode the input string in the standard way: $\mathcal{H}_{\text{Mix}} = \{ [a, i-1, i] \mid a = a_i, 1 \leq i \leq n \}$.

The set of deduction steps is formed by the following subsets:

$$\mathcal{D}_{\text{Mix}} = \mathcal{D}_{\text{Mix}}^{\text{Init}} \cup \mathcal{D}_{\text{Mix}}^{\text{Scan}} \cup \mathcal{D}_{\text{Mix}}^{\epsilon} \cup \mathcal{D}_{\text{Mix}}^{\text{Pred}} \cup \mathcal{D}_{\text{Mix}}^{\text{Comp}} \cup$$

$$\mathcal{D}_{\text{Mix}}^{\text{AdjPred}} \cup \mathcal{D}_{\text{Mix}}^{\text{FootPred}} \cup \mathcal{D}_{\text{Mix}}^{\text{FootComp}} \cup \mathcal{D}_{\text{Mix}}^{\text{AdjComp}} \cup$$

$$\mathcal{D}_{\text{Mix}}^{\text{LAdjPred}} \cup \mathcal{D}_{\text{Mix}}^{\text{LAdjComp}} \cup \mathcal{D}_{\text{Mix}}^{\text{RAdjPred}} \cup \mathcal{D}_{\text{Mix}}^{\text{RAdjComp}} \cup \mathcal{D}_{\text{Mix}}^{\text{LRFoot}}$$

The parsing process starts by creating the items corresponding to productions having the root of an initial tree as left-hand side and the dot in the leftmost position of the right-hand side:

$$\mathcal{D}_{\text{Mix}}^{\text{Init}} = \frac{}{[\top \to \bullet R^{\alpha}, 0, 0 \mid -, - \mid \text{false}]} \quad \alpha \in I \wedge S = \text{label}(R^{\alpha})$$

Then, a set of deductive steps in $\mathcal{D}_{\text{Mix}}^{\text{Pred}}$ and $\mathcal{D}_{\text{Mix}}^{\text{Comp}}$ traverse each elementary tree while steps in $\mathcal{D}_{\text{Mix}}^{\text{Scan}}$ and $\mathcal{D}_{\text{Mix}}^{\epsilon}$ scan input symbols and the empty symbol, respectively:

$$\mathcal{D}_{\text{Mix}}^{\text{Pred}} = \frac{[N^{\gamma} \to \delta \bullet M^{\gamma} \nu, i, j \mid p, q \mid adj]}{[M^{\gamma} \to \bullet \upsilon, j, j \mid -, - \mid \text{false}]} \quad \begin{array}{l} \textbf{nil} \in \text{adj}(M^{\gamma}) \vee \\ (\exists \beta \in A_{SL} \cup A_{SR}, \; \beta \in \text{adj}(M^{\gamma})) \end{array}$$

$$\mathcal{D}_{\text{Mix}}^{\text{Comp}} = \frac{\begin{array}{c} [N^{\gamma} \to \delta \bullet M^{\gamma} \nu, i, j \mid p, q \mid adj], \\ {[M^{\gamma} \to \upsilon \bullet, j, k \mid p', q' \mid adj']} \end{array}}{[N^{\gamma} \to \delta M^{\gamma} \bullet \nu, i, k \mid p \cup p', q \cup q' \mid adj]}$$

$$\text{with } (\textbf{nil} \in \text{adj}(M^{\gamma}) \wedge adj' = \text{false}) \vee$$
$$(\exists \beta \in A, \; \beta \in \text{adj}(M^{\gamma}) \wedge adj' = \text{true})$$

$$\mathcal{D}_{\text{Mix}}^{\text{Scan}} = \frac{\begin{array}{c} [N^{\gamma} \to \delta \bullet M^{\gamma} \nu, i, j \mid p, q \mid adj], \\ {[a, j, j+1]} \end{array}}{[N^{\gamma} \to \delta M^{\gamma} \bullet \nu, i, j+1 \mid p, q \mid adj]} \quad a = \text{label}(M^{\gamma})$$

$$\mathcal{D}_{\text{Mix}}^{\epsilon} = \frac{[N^{\gamma} \to \delta \bullet M^{\gamma} \nu, i, j \mid p, q \mid adj]}{[N^{\gamma} \to \delta M^{\gamma} \bullet \nu, i, j \mid p, q \mid adj]} \quad \epsilon = \text{label}(M^{\gamma})$$

The rest of steps are in charge of managing adjunction operations. If a strongly left auxiliary tree $\beta \in A_{SL}$ can be adjoined at a given node M^{γ}, a step in $\mathcal{D}_{\text{Mix}}^{\text{LAdjPred}}$ starts the traversal of β. When β has been completely traversed, a step in $\mathcal{D}_{\text{Mix}}^{\text{LAdjComp}}$ starts the traversal of the subtree corresponding to M^{γ} and sets the last element of the item to true in order to forbid further adjunctions on this node.

$$\mathcal{D}_{\text{Mix}}^{\text{LAdjPred}} = \frac{[M^{\gamma} \to \bullet \upsilon, i, i \mid -, - \mid \text{false}]}{[\top \to \bullet R^{\beta}, i, i \mid -, - \mid \text{false}]} \quad \beta \in \text{adj}(M^{\gamma}) \wedge \beta \in A_{SL}$$

$$\mathcal{D}_{\text{Mix}}^{\text{LAdjComp}} = \frac{\begin{array}{c} [M^{\gamma} \to \bullet \upsilon, i, i \mid -, - \mid \text{false}], \\ {[\top \to R^{\beta} \bullet, i, j \mid -, - \mid \text{false}]} \end{array}}{[M^{\gamma} \to \bullet \upsilon, i, j \mid -, - \mid \text{true}]} \quad \beta \in A_{SL} \wedge \beta \in \text{adj}(M^{\gamma})$$

If a strongly right auxiliary tree $\beta \in \mathbf{A}_{SR}$ can be adjoined at a given node M^γ, when the subtree corresponding to this node has been completely traversed, a step in $\mathcal{D}_{\text{Mix}}^{\text{RAdjPred}}$ starts the traversal of the tree β. When β has been completely traversed, a step in $\mathcal{D}_{\text{Mix}}^{\text{RAdjComp}}$ updates the input positions spanned by M^γ taking into account the part of the input string spanned by β, and sets the last element of the item to true in order to forbid further adjunctions on this node.

$$\mathcal{D}_{\text{Mix}}^{\text{RAdjPred}} = \frac{[M^\gamma \to v\bullet, i, j \mid p, q \mid \text{false}]}{[\top \to \bullet R^\beta, j, j \mid -, - \mid \text{false}]} \quad \beta \in \mathbf{A}_{SR} \wedge \beta \in \text{adj}(M^\gamma)$$

$$\mathcal{D}_{\text{Mix}}^{\text{RAdjComp}} = \frac{\begin{array}{c}[M^\gamma \to v\bullet, i, j \mid p, q \mid \text{false}], \\ [\top \to R^\beta\bullet, j, k \mid -, - \mid \text{false}]\end{array}}{[M^\gamma \to v\bullet, i, k \mid p, q \mid \text{true}]} \quad \beta \in \mathbf{A}_{SR} \wedge \beta \in \text{adj}(M^\gamma)$$

No special treatment is given to the foot node of strongly left and right auxiliary trees and so, it is simply skipped by a step in the set $\mathcal{D}_{\text{Mix}}^{\text{LRFoot}}$.

$$\mathcal{D}_{\text{Mix}}^{\text{LRFoot}} = \frac{[\mathbf{F}^\beta \to \bullet \bot, j, j, \text{false}]}{[\mathbf{F}^\beta \to \bot\bullet, j, j, \text{false}]} \quad \beta \in \mathbf{A}_{SL} \cup \mathbf{A}_{SR}$$

A step in $\mathcal{D}_{\text{Mix}}^{\text{AdjPred}}$ predicts the adjunction of an auxiliary tree $\beta \in \mathbf{A} - (\mathbf{A}_{SL} \cup \mathbf{A}_{SR})$ in a node of an elementary tree γ and starts the traversal of β. Once the foot of β has been reached, the traversal of β is momentary suspended by a step in $\mathcal{D}_{\text{Mix}}^{\text{FootPred}}$, which re-takes the subtree of γ which must be attached to the foot of β. At this moment, there is no information available about the node in which the adjunction of β has been performed, so all possible nodes are predicted. When the traversal of a predicted subtree has finished, a step in $\mathcal{D}_{\text{Mix}}^{\text{FootComp}}$ re-takes the traversal of β continuing at the foot node. When the traversal of β is completely finished, a deduction step in $\mathcal{D}_{\text{Mix}}^{\text{AdjComp}}$ checks if the subtree attached to the foot of β corresponds with the adjunction node. The adjunction if finished by a step in $\mathcal{D}_{\text{Mix}}^{\text{Comp}}$, taking into account that p' and q' are instantiated if and only if the adjunction node is on the spine of γ. It is interesting to remark that we follow the approach of [5], splitting the completion of adjunction between $\mathcal{D}_{\text{Mix}}^{\text{AdjComp}}$ and $\mathcal{D}_{\text{Mix}}^{\text{Comp}}$.

$$\mathcal{D}_{\text{Mix}}^{\text{AdjPred}} = \frac{[N^\gamma \to \delta \bullet M^\gamma v, i, j \mid p, q \mid \text{adj}]}{[\top \to \bullet R^\beta, j, j \mid -, - \mid \text{false}]} \quad \beta \in \mathbf{A} - (\mathbf{A}_{SL} \cup \mathbf{A}_{SR}) \wedge \beta \in \text{adj}(M^\gamma)$$

$$\mathcal{D}_{\text{Mix}}^{\text{FootPred}} = \frac{[\mathbf{F}^\beta \to \bullet \bot, k, k \mid -, - \mid \text{false}]}{[M^\gamma \to \bullet v, k, k \mid -, - \mid \text{false}]} \quad \beta \in \mathbf{A} - (\mathbf{A}_{SL} \cup \mathbf{A}_{SR}) \wedge \beta \in \text{adj}(M^\gamma)$$

$$\mathcal{D}_{\text{Mix}}^{\text{FootComp}} = \frac{\begin{array}{c}[\mathbf{F}^\beta \to \bullet \bot, k, k \mid -, - \mid \text{false}], \\ [M^\gamma \to v\bullet, k, l \mid p', q' \mid \text{false}]\end{array}}{[\mathbf{F}^\beta \to \bot\bullet, k, l \mid k, l \mid \text{false}]} \quad \beta \in \mathbf{A} - (\mathbf{A}_{SL} \cup \mathbf{A}_{SR}) \wedge \beta \in \text{adj}(M^\gamma)$$

$$\mathcal{D}_{\text{Mix}}^{\text{AdjComp}} = \frac{\begin{array}{c}[\top \to R^\beta\bullet, j, m \mid k, l \mid \text{false}], \\ [M^\gamma \to v\bullet, k, l \mid p', q' \mid \text{false}]\end{array}}{[M^\gamma \to v\bullet, j, m \mid p', q' \mid \text{true}]} \quad \beta \in \mathbf{A} - (\mathbf{A}_{SL} \cup \mathbf{A}_{SR}) \wedge \beta \in \text{adj}(M^\gamma)$$

The input string belongs to the language defined by the grammar if a final item in the set $\mathcal{F} = \left\{\, [\mathsf{T} \rightarrow \mathbf{R}^{\alpha} \bullet, 0, n \mid -, - \mid \text{false}] \mid \alpha \in \boldsymbol{I} \,\wedge\, S = \text{label}(\mathbf{R}^{\alpha}) \,\right\}$ is generated.

3 Complexity

The worst-case space complexity of the algorithm is $\mathcal{O}(n^4)$, as at most four input positions are stored into items corresponding to auxiliary trees belonging to $\boldsymbol{A} - (\boldsymbol{A}_{SL} \cup \boldsymbol{A}_{SR})$. Initial trees and strongly left and right auxiliary trees contribute $\mathcal{O}(n^2)$ to the final result. With respect to the worst-case time complexity:

- TIG adjunction, the adjunction of a strongly left or right auxiliary tree on a node of a tree belonging to $\boldsymbol{I} \cup \boldsymbol{A}_{SL} \cup \boldsymbol{A}_{SR}$, is managed in $\mathcal{O}(n^3)$ by steps in $\mathcal{D}_{\text{Mix}}^{\text{RAdjComp}}$ and $\mathcal{D}_{\text{Mix}}^{\text{Comp}}$.
- Full TAG adjunction is managed in $\mathcal{O}(n^6)$ by deduction steps in $\mathcal{D}_{\text{Mix}}^{\text{AdjComp}}$, which are in charge of dealing with auxiliary trees belonging to $\boldsymbol{A} - (\boldsymbol{A}_{SL} \cup \boldsymbol{A}_{SR})$. In fact, $\mathcal{O}(n^6)$ is only attained when a wrapping auxiliary tree is adjoined on a spine node of a wrapping auxiliary tree. The adjunction of a wrapping auxiliary tree on a right node of a wrapping auxiliary tree is managed in $\mathcal{O}(n^5)$ due to deduction steps in $\mathcal{D}_{\text{Mix}}^{\text{Comp}}$. The same complexity is attained by the adjunction of a strongly right auxiliary tree on a spine or right node of a wrapping auxiliary tree, due to deduction steps in $\mathcal{D}_{\text{Mix}}^{\text{RAdjComp}}$.
- Other cases of adjunction, e.g. the adjunction of a strongly left or right auxiliary tree on a spine node of a tree belonging to $(\boldsymbol{A}_L - \boldsymbol{A}_{SL}) \cup (\boldsymbol{A}_R - \boldsymbol{A}_{SR})$, are managed in $\mathcal{O}(n^4)$.

4 Experimental Results

We have incorporated the parsing algorithms described in this paper into a naive implementation in Prolog of the deductive parsing machine presented in [7].

As a first experiment, we have compared the performance of the Earley-like parsing algorithms for TIG [6] and TAG [1] with respect to TIGs. For this purpose, we have designed two artificial TIGs G_l (with $\boldsymbol{A}_{SR} = \emptyset$) and G_r (with $\boldsymbol{A}_{SL} = \emptyset$). For a TIG, the time complexity of the adjunction completion step of a TAG parser is $\mathcal{O}(n^4)$, in contrast with the $\mathcal{O}(n^2)$ and $\mathcal{O}(n^3)$ complexities of left and right adjunction completion for a TIG parser, respectively. Therefore, we expected the TIG parser to be considerably faster than the TAG parser. In effect, for G_l we have observed that the TIG parser is up to 18 times faster than the TAG parser, but in the case of G_r the difference becomes irrelevant.

These results have been corroborated by a second experiment performed on artificial TAGs with the Mixed (P_{Mix}) and the TAG parser: the performance of the Mixed parser improves when strongly left auxiliary trees are involved in the analysis of the input string.

In a third experiment, we have taken a subset of the XTAG grammar [3], consisting of 27 elementary trees that cover a variety of English constructions:

Table 1. XTAG results, in seconds, for the TAG and Mixed parsers

Sentence	TAG	Mixed	Reduction
Srini bought a book	0.61	0.49	19.67%
Srini bought Beth a book	0.77	0.71	7.79%
Srini bought a book at the bookstore	0.94	0.93	1.06%
he put the book on the table	0.83	0.71	14.46%
the sun melted the ice	0.71	0.66	7.04%
the ice melted	0.44	0.38	13.64%
Elmo borrowed a book	0.55	0.49	10.91%
a book borrowed	0.39	0.33	15.38%
he hopes Muriel wins	0.93	0.77	17.20%
he hopes that Muriel wins	1.26	1.16	7.94%
the man who Muriel likes bought a book	2.14	1.48	30.84%
the man that Muriel likes bought a book	1.21	1.04	14.05%
the music should have been being played for the president	1.27	1.26	0.79%
Clove caught a frisbee	0.55	0.49	10.91%
who caught a frisbee	0.55	0.44	20.00%
what did Clove catch	0.60	0.55	8.33%
the aardvark smells terrible	0.44	0.38	13.64%
the emu thinks that the aardvark smells terrible	1.48	1.32	10.81%
who does the emu think smells terrible	0.99	0.77	22.22%
who did the elephant think the panda heard the emu said smells terrible			
	3.13	2.36	24.60%
Herbert is more livid than angry	0.50	0.44	12.00%
Herbert is more livid and furious than angry	0.50	0.50	0.00%

relative clauses, auxiliary verbs, unbounded dependencies, extraction, etc. In order to eliminate the time spent by unification, we have not considered the feature structures of elementary trees. Instead, we have simulated the features using local constraints. Every sentence has been parsed without previous filtering of elementary trees. Table 1 shows the results of this experiment. The application of the Mixed parser results in a reduction in time that varies in percentage from 31% to 0%, depending on the kind of trees involved in the analysis of each sentence.

5   Conclusion

We have defined a parsing algorithm which reduces the practical complexity of TAG parsing by taking into account that a large part of actual TAG grammars can be managed as a TIG.

This parsing algorithm does not preserve the correct prefix property [5]. It is possible to obtain a variant satisfying this property by means of the introduction of an additional element h into items, which is used to indicate the position of the input string in which the traversal of the elementary tree involved in each item was started. The worst-case space complexity increases to $\mathcal{O}(n^5)$ but the worst-case time complexity remains $\mathcal{O}(n^6)$ if we modify steps $AdjComp_0$ and Comp as indicated in [5].

The performance of the algorithm could be improved by means of the application of practical optimizations, such as the replacement of the components p and q of items $[N^\gamma \to \delta \bullet \nu, i, j \mid p, q \mid adj] \in \mathcal{I}_{\text{Mix}}^{(a)}$ by the list of all adjunctions that are still under completion on N^γ [2], albeit this modification can increase the worst-case complexity of the algorithm.

Acknowledgements. Supported in part by Plan Nacional de Investigación Científica, Desarrollo e Innovación Tecnológica (TIC2000-0370-C02-01), Ministerio de Ciencia y Tecnología (HP2001-0044) and Xunta de Galicia (PGIDT01PXI10506PN).

References

1. Miguel A. Alonso, David Cabrero, Eric de la Clergerie, and Manuel Vilares. Tabular algorithms for TAG parsing. In *Proc. of EACL'99, Ninth Conference of the European Chapter of the Association for Computational Linguistics*, pages 150–157, Bergen, Norway, June 1999. ACL.
2. Eric de la Clergerie. Refining tabular parsers for TAGs. In *Proceedings of Language Technologies 2001: The Second Meeting of the North American Chapter of the Association for Computational Linguistics (NAACL'01)*, pages 167–174, CMU, Pittsburgh, PA, USA, June 2001.
3. Christy Doran, Dania Egedi, Beth Ann Hockey, B. Srinivas, and Martin Zaidel. XTAG system — a wide coverage grammar for English. In *Proc. of the 15th International Conference on Computational Linguistics (COLING'94)*, pages 922–928, Kyoto, Japan, August 1994.
4. Aravind K. Joshi and Yves Schabes. Tree-adjoining grammars. In Grzegorz Rozenberg and Arto Salomaa, editors, *Handbook of Formal Languages. Vol 3: Beyond Words*, chapter 2, pages 69–123. Springer-Verlag, Berlin/Heidelberg/New York, 1997.
5. Mark-Jan Nederhof. The computational complexity of the correct-prefix property for TAGs. *Computational Linguistics*, 25(3):345–360, 1999.
6. Yves Schabes and Richard C. Waters. Tree insertion grammar: A cubic-time parsable formalism that lexicalizes context-free grammar without changing the trees produced. *Computational Linguistics*, 21(4):479–513, December 1995. Also as Technical Report TR-94-13, June 1994, Mitsubishi Electric Research Laboratories, Cambridge, MA, USA.
7. Stuart M. Shieber, Yves Schabes, and Fernando C. N. Pereira. Principles and implementation of deductive parsing. *Journal of Logic Programming*, 24(1–2):3–36, July-August 1995.
8. Klaas Sikkel. *Parsing Schemata — A Framework for Specification and Analysis of Parsing Algorithms*. Texts in Theoretical Computer Science — An EATCS Series. Springer-Verlag, Berlin/Heidelberg/New York, 1997.

Task Oriented Dialogue Processing Using Multiagents Theory⋆

Norton Trevisan Roman and Ariadne Maria Brito Rizzoni Carvalho

Instituto de Computação, Unicamp, Caixa Postal 6176,
13083–970 Campinas, SP, Brazil
{norton, ariadne}@ic.unicamp.br

Abstract. This paper describes a multiagent system for natural language processing that deals with task oriented dialogue processing in Portuguese. The system is based on Discourse Structure Theory, on Centering Theory and on Lochbaum's work on modeling the Intentional Structure of the discourse. The dialogue takes place between the user and the system in such a way that the user plays the role of one participant and the system plays the other. Together, both the system and the user collaborate to achieve the goal the user had in mind when he/she initiated the dialogue.

1 Introduction

This paper describes a multiagent system for natural language processing based on Discourse Structure Theory [2], on Centering Theory ([1], [4], [6], [7], [9]) and on Lochbaum's work on modeling the Intentional Structure of the discourse ([10], [11]).

The system deals with task oriented dialogue processing in Portuguese in which the user plays the role of one participant in the dialogue and the system plays the other. Together, both the system and the user collaborate to achieve the goal the user had in mind when he/she initiated the dialogue. The goal is something the system must identify by itself while the dialogue develops, and, possibly, which cannot be completely determined until the dialogue is finished.

The scenario is a simple home security system that records the status of the house's windows and doors, that is, if they have been opened and, if so, when that happened. The user can ask the system either about what happened when he/she was absent, or simply for monitoring the house's possible entrances.

The interaction between the system and the user happens through utterances in natural language typed by the user. The system tries to evaluate the user's utterance in order to determine its logical content and, after doing so, it responds to the user with either an action or another utterance.

Also, the system is responsible for generating subdialogues, in case it needs extra information to more accurately determine the logical content of the user's

---

⋆ This work has been sponsored by FAPESP (Fundação de Amparo à Pesquisa do Estado de São Paulo)

F.J. Garijo, J.C. Riquelme, and M. Toro (Eds.): IBERAMIA 2002, LNAI 2527, pp. 704–713, 2002.

utterance, or when it is necessary for the system and the user to solve some problem that may arise in the communication.

The system is composed of four independent but interactive main structures, as shown in Fig. 1: the Linguistic Structure, which is responsible for the linguistic analysis of the utterance, and that generates the corresponding logical form of the utterance [12]; the Attentional Structure, responsible for keeping track of the system's and user's focus of attention [2]; the Intentional Structure, responsible for determining the intentions that lie behind each utterance and how these intentions fit into the context formed by the previous utterances; and the Task Structure, which is a repository for the syntactic and semantic information needed to build the corresponding logical form of the utterance [12]. In Sect. 3 it will be presented an example showing how these four structures act and interact to analyse an user's utterance.

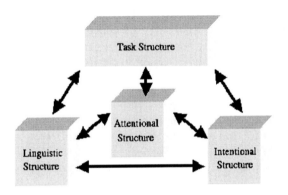

Fig. 1. System's general architecture

Although Grosz and Sidner have already defined the structures that would be necessary for dialogue processing [2], they have only modeled part of the Attentional and Intentional Structures. The Attentional Structure modeling deals only with the global focus of the dialogue, which is the set of the entities relevant to the overall discourse [7]. The Intentional Structure was completely modeled by Lochbaum in her PhD Thesis [11], using Shared Plans Theory, proposed by Grosz [5],

The work presented here added to the original Attentional Structure proposed by Grosz and Sidner [2] a new element - the Centering Theory [9] - which deals with the immediate focus, that is the entities with which an individual utterance is most centrally concerned [7]. Therefore, the Attentional Structure is not only responsible for the global focus of the dialogue, but also for the immediate one.

As well as completely modeling the Linguistic Structure for Portuguese, this work added a fourth structure to the three original ones – the Task Structure –

which is responsible for keeping all the information necessary for the system to work at first place, for example the dictionary.

The addition of this structure brought to the system the interesting feature that, in order to change the scenario completely, it would be only necessary to change or update this structure, since the interaction between the user and the system happens through a task oriented dialogue [12].

Finally, the main contribution of this work was to integrate the four structures – the Linguistic Structure, modeled in this work; the Attentional Structure, modeled by Grosz and Sidner [2] and augmented in this work; the Task Structure, created in this work, and the Intentional Structure, modeled by Lochbaum [11] – into a multiagent system, so that the structures could be seen and evaluated while working together.

The remaining of this paper is organized as follows. Section 2 describes at a higher level the behavior of the system's structures and shows the interaction among them; Section 3 presents an example showing how the four structures carry an utterance's processing; Section 4 shows two dialogues between the user and the system; and, finally, in Section 5 a conclusion is presented.

2   System's Description

As already mentioned, the system is composed of four independent but interactive main structures: the Linguistic Structure, the Attentional Structure, the Intentional Structure and the Task Structure. In this section these structures will be better explained, emphasizing their roles in the dialogue's processing so that the system can achieve the desirable results.

2.1   Task Structure

The Task Structure is a repository for the syntactic and semantic information carried out by the words in the utterance and needed to build the corresponding logical form of that utterance. So, this structure acts as a system's database, providing information to the other three structures [12].

The information is kept in two basic inner structures: the dictionary, which contains the words the system recognizes, together with syntactic and semantic information about them; and the recipe book, which contains the recipes – sets of sub-actions and constraints for an action such that the doing of those sub-actions under those constraints constitute the doing of the action itself ([8],[11])). All this information is managed by an agent responsible for answering the requests made by other structures. These requests, as well as any other communication among the agents, are made through speech acts.

2.2   Attentional Structure

The main function of the Attentional Structure is to keep track of the focus of attention of the discourse participants, recording the entities and intentions that are more salient in the discourse, as it develops. These factors make this structure a very important one in a search for a pronoun referent and ellipsis reconstruction [12].

The Attentional Structure represents two distinct foci in the discourse: the global focus, which carries the information and intentions relevant to the overall discourse, and the immediate focus, which deals with the identification of the entity that an individual utterance is most centrally concerned [4].

The modeling and representation of the global focus in this structure is made by means of a Focus Space Stack, whose behavior and modeling can be found in ([2], [12]). The immediate focus is modeled using a stack, which keeps track of the three last utterances in the dialogue. The information kept in the stack is concerned with the entities these three utterances brought to the focus of attention of the discourse participants. More information about the kind of information the stack records and how it deals which such information can be found in [12].

The Attentional Structure is passive in the sense that it only reacts to orders and requests coming from other structures. When it receives a request for the entities currently in focus, it searches in the immediate focus stack and, if a match is not found, it searches in the Focus Space Stack, returning the entity found to the requesting structure (in this case, the Linguistic Structure). In fact, that is the way this structure provides referents for pronouns and for ellipsis reconstruction. This request may also come from the Intentional Structure, wanting to know the intention which is currently in focus. So, the Attentional Structure searches for a match in the Focus Space Stack, returning the intention found to the requesting structure.

But the Attentional Structure does not deal with requests only; it also receives information from the Linguistic Structure about new entities that should be part of the current focus, as well as information from the Intentional Structure about new intentions carried on by the dialogue's utterances. In this case, the Attentional Structure is responsible for updating the information kept in both stacks to reflect the new information brought to the dialogue.

2.3 Intentional Structure

The Intentional Structure is responsible for the effective "comprehension" and manipulation of the intentions that lie behind each utterance in the dialogue. As each utterance is analyzed, the Intentional Structure has to determine the way it contributes to the overall dialogue purpose ([12], [2], [11]).

The modeling of the Intentional Structure was made by Lochbaum [11], using Shared Plans Theory developed by Grosz and Sidner [3]. So, the system presented here uses Lochbaum's system to implement this structure, with some adaptations in order to fit the other structures.

Lochbaum's modeling deals with recipes represented as a graph and, for each utterance in the dialogue, it determines how this utterance contributes to the previous ones, according to the model presented by Grosz and Sidner in [2]. For more details on Lochbaum's work see ([10], [11]).

When the Intentional Structure receives the currently focused intention, it asks the Task Structure to send a recipe for this intention and, then, tries to fit the user's utterance into this recipe, determining how this utterance contributes to the intention currently in focus.

After determining the role the user's utterance has in the previous discourse, the Intentional Structure sends this new scenario back to the Attentional Structure, so that it can make the proper arrangements to reflect it, and, then, the Intentional Structure gives the user an appropriate feedback, either executing some action, or sending to the user a natural language message, according to the actions not yet executed in the recipe it has for the currently focused intention.

So, when the system executes an action, it is actually executing the sub-actions that compose that action, in a pre-established order. If the executed action is a sub-action of some other action's recipe, when the system executes this sub-action, it verifies, also, whether the action which the sub-action is part of was completely executed, or if there are still sub-actions to be executed.

This verification is crucial for determining the next utterance's role in the dialogue context, because if there are still sub-actions to be executed, the next utterances in the dialogue must be concerned with this subject; otherwise, the dialogue would not have satisfied all intentions that it conveys.

2.4   Linguistic Structure

The Linguistic Structure is responsible for generating the corresponding logical form of the utterance.

When the user types an utterance, the Linguistic Structure consults the Task Structure to obtain the syntactic category and the semantic meaning of every word in the utterance. It may obtain various possible meanings for the utterance, depending on the ambiguity of the words.

After that, the Linguistic Structure chooses one of the different meanings which were generated and searches for possible occurrences of pronouns and ellipsis (the way it chooses among the possible meanings and the searching algorithm are beyond the scope of this paper, and are fully described in [12]).

When the Linguistic Structure finds a pronoun or an ellipsis, it asks the Attentional Structure for entities that could serve as referents and, after receiving these referents, it completes the generation of the logical form of the utterance.

Therefore, the Linguistic Structure is responsible for doing the parsing, which happens through the interaction among the agents that compose this structure.

Before sending the utterance's logical form to the Intentional Structure, the Linguistic Structure sends to the Attentional Structure the entities that were more salient in the utterance, either because they were explicitly mentioned, or because they were implicitly referred to (as, for example, when an ellipsis is found), so that the Attentional Structure can update its internal representation of the discourse's focus of attention.

3   A Simple Example

The system's general architecture is shown in Fig. 2. In order to "understand" an user's utterance, the system does as follows. Suppose the utterance is "Was it opened at anytime at all?".

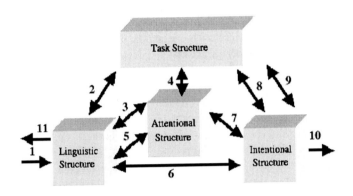

Fig. 2. System's general architecture

The utterance is read by the Linguistic Structure (1) which, then, tries to build the logical form of that utterance, solving the pronoun references and detecting and reconstructing the elliptical phrases. In the example, the Linguistic Structure identifies that the type of request made by the user is a question and, then, in (2) it asks the Task Structure for the syntactic category and the semantic representation of every word in "Was it opened at anytime at all?"

When the Task Structure finds an answer, it sends it back to the Linguistic Structure. If it cannot find a representation of some word in the database, it sends an error message to the Linguistic Structure, which in turn transmits it to the user (11). It is worth noticing that the words that compose the utterance are ambiguous. For instance, "opened" could be either a verb or an adjective. Both meanings and the syntactic classification for "opened" are sent to the Linguistic Structure.

Having the syntactic classification for every word in the utterance, the Linguistic Structure detects a pronoun, "it", and contacts the Attentional Structure (3) to solve the reference. The Attentional Structure, with the help of the Task Structure (4), finds a referent ("back door") and sends it back to the Linguistic Structure. If such a referent was not found, the Attentional Structure would send an error message to the Linguistic Structure, which, in turn, would send an error message to the user (11). At the moment the system is only capable of dealing with simple elliptical nouns and with a subset of the pronouns found in Portuguese.

Now, since the Linguistic Structure has all the elements needed to build the utterance's logical form, it does it. If a logical form could not be built, possibly because the syntactic structure of the utterance was not accepted by the system, the Linguistic Structure would send the user an error message. In the example, the Linguistic Structure understands the utterance as meaning "the user wants to know whether or not the entity 'back door' was opened at the time 'anytime' ".

After the logical form of the user's utterance has been built, the Linguistic Structure sends the entities that were more salient in the utterance to the Attentional Structure (5) (in this case, "back door"), which updates its internal structures to reflect the addition of this entity to the current focus of the dialogue. Then, the Linguistic Structure sends the logical form of the user's utterance to the Intentional Structure (6).

The Intentional Structure, in turn, tries to situate the logical form in the overall discourse context. To do so, it consults the Attentional Structure to find out which intention is currently in focus (7). When it receives this intention, it asks the Task Structure for a recipe for that intention (8), so that the Intentional Structure can determine how the user's utterance contributes to the intention that is currently in focus. Having the recipe for the intention currently in focus (9), the Intentional Structure tries to fit the user's intention, that is "the user wants to know whether or not the entity 'back door' was opened at the time 'anytime' ", in that recipe and, then, tries to execute it.

Depending on the action currently in focus, the execution of this recipe can either lead to the execution of some action or to send the user a reply. The answers produced by the system are actually actions or utterances to communicate some information, and are part of the intention's recipe.

So, for instance, if the system's intention is to communicate the user some fact, in the intention's recipe there will be an act for the system to perform such as "write X on the screen", where X is the information the system needs to present to the user in the form of a predefined natural language sentence.

Therefore, the system is incapable of generating sentences containing pronouns and ellipsis and, when it does use them, it is because the recipe for the information the system wants to convey has a pre-built natural language sentence that contains a pronoun or an ellipsis.

In the given example, the recipe tells the Intentional Structure to search a database for all the entries matching the entity "back door" and to show the user the entities found, or to reply "no" if none were found.

Since there is such an entity in the database, the system executes the action, giving the user an appropriated answer (10).

4   Sample Dialogues

In order to test the system described here, two dialogues were generated (Figs. 3 and 4). These dialogues show some interesting features about the system. It is worth mentioning that the dialogues were generated in Portuguese. Figs. 3 and 4 actually show English translations of those dialogues; so, there can be some differences in the dialogue's processing.

```
(1)  User     – What happened after 14:00?
(2)  System – The back door was opened at 14:30.
(3)  User     – Show it.
(4)  System – <action>
(5)  User     – Show me the front door now.
(6)  System – <action>
(7)  User     – Was it opened at anytime at all?
(8)  System – No.
(9)  User     – OK. Go on.
(10) System – At 15:00 the back window was opened
```

Fig. 3. First dialogue between the user and the system.

```
(1) User     – Show me the door.
(2) System – Which one?
(3) User     – The frontal one.
(4) System – I can't. The camera is off. You'll have to turn it on.
(5) User     – How?
(6) System – Go to the main room, the camera is on the table. Push
                  the "on" button.
(7) User     – Done.
(8) System – <action>
```

Fig. 4. Second dialogue between the user and the system.

The first dialogue (Fig. 3) is very simple and shows a single basic intention (the user asking about the facts that happened after 2 o'clock) and interruptions made by the user to obtain extra information about the focus of attention (utterance 3) or to change the focus (utterance 5). After the user has satisfied his/her curiosity, he/she asks the system to go on in the interrupted segment (utterance 9), which the system does immediately (utterance 10).

The second dialogue (Fig. 4) shows what happens when something goes wrong. In the first utterance, the user asks the system to show him/her a door. The system, then, tries to identify the object "door". As it finds more than one object that could fit that entity, the system asks the user to identify the object among the ones it already knows (utterance 2).

After the object has been identified, the system detects a hardware problem that it cannot solve. So, the system transmits this information to the user (utterance 4).

The user, then, asks the system for a recipe on how to solve the problem (utterance 5), which the system gives in utterance 6. After solving the problem, the user communicates that fact to the system (utterance 7), so that the system can execute the user's order.

5   Conclusion and Future Work

This work showed a multiagent natural language processing system whose objective was to verify the practical use of Grosz and Sidner's Discourse Theory [2], and the Shared Plans modeling for the Intentional Structure made by Lochbaum [11], verifying the integration and interaction among these structures.

It is argued that the Attentional Structure, as described in [2], proved to be insufficient for carrying discourse processing since it only deals with global focus. Therefore, Centering Theory [9] was added to the Attentional Structure so that it could supply the system's need for some mechanism to deal with the immediate focus.

Besides, as an extension to Grosz and Sidner work, it was introduced a fourth structure – the Task Structure – which is claimed to bring to the system some flexibility since, in order to change the system's scenario, it would only be necessary to change or update this structure. Also, a Linguistic Structure for Portuguese language was developed and implemented.

The dialogues in Sect. 4 give an example of the system's behavior. Particularly, the results obtained with pronoun reference resolution and ellipsis reconstruction were very promising.

Another interesting feature of the system is that it was devised and implemented under a multiagents point of view. Following Lochbaum's [11] and Grosz and Sidner's [3] ideas, the system as a whole is considered an agent, being the user the other one. The system, in turn, is composed of smaller agents, responsible for the system's correct functioning. So, each structure is composed of other agents that are responsible for performing a subset of the actions that the structure as a whole needs to perform, allowing each structure's tasks to be distributed among its composing agents. Such a view has simplified the planning task as well as the system's design enormously. For example, parsing is done as a consequence of the interaction among some agents in the Linguistic Structure. The parser itself does not physically exist in the system, although its functionalities still remain.

As future research, the Linguistic Structure must be improved, so that it can deal with other difficult linguistic phenomena. At the moment, ellipsis reconstruction is very simple; the system can only deal with simple elliptical nouns. Also, pronoun resolution must be improved so that the system can deal with cataphora resolution.

An automatic generator must be designed and implemented in order for the system to communicate with the user in a more natural way. Also, the system must be augmented so that it can recognize cue phrases in the dialogue.

Finally, the system must be tested in different scenarios, in order to better evaluate the claimed flexibility of the Task Structure.

Acknowledgments. We would like to thank Heloisa Vieira da Rocha and Vera Lúcia Strube de Lima for their valuable comments on a previous version of this work.

References

1. Gordon, P., Grosz, B., Gillion, L.: Pronouns, Names, and the Centering of Attention in discourse. Cognitive Science 3(17) (1993) 311–347
2. Grosz, B., Sidner, C.: Attention, Intentions, and the Structure of Discourse. Computational Linguistics 12(3) (1986) 175–204
3. Grosz, B., Sidner, C.: Plans for Discourse. Intentions in Communication. P. R. Cohen, J. L. Morgan e M. E. Pollack (eds.). MIT Press, Cambridge MA (1990) 417–444
4. Grosz, B., Joshi, A., Weinstein, S.: Centering: A framework for Modeling the Local Coherence of Discourse Computational Linguistics 2(21) (1995) 203–225
5. Grosz, B., Kraus, S.: Collaborative Plans for Complex Group Action. Artificial Intelligence 86(2) (1996) 269–357
6. Grosz, B., Ziv, Y.: Centering, Global Focus, and Right Dislocation. Centering in Discourse. M. Walker, A. Joshi e E. Prince (eds.). Oxford University Press (1998) 293–307
7. Grosz, B., Hunsberge, L., Sidner, C.: Lost Intuitions and Forgotten Intentions. Centering in Discourse. M. Walker, A. Joshi e E. Prince (eds.). Oxford University Press (1999) 39–51
8. Grosz, B., Kraus, S.: Planning and Acting Together. AI Magazine 4(20) (1999)
9. Joshi, A., Kuhn, S.: Centering Logic: The Role of Entity Centered Sentence Representation in Natural Language Inferencing. Proceedings of the International Joint Conference on Artificial Intelligence (1979) 435–439
10. Lochbaum, K.: A Collaborative Planning Approach to Discourse Understanding. Technical Report TR-20-93. Harvard University, Cambridge MA (1993)
11. Lochbaum, K.: Using Collaborative Plans to Model the Intentional Structure of Discourse. PhD Thesis. Technical Report TR-25-94. Harvard University, Cambridge MA (1994)
12. Roman, N.: Estudo de Diálogos Orientados à Tarefa Usando a Teoria de Multiagentes. Master Science Dissertation. University of Campinas, Campinas SP Brazil (2001)

Automatic Adaptation of a Natural Language Interface to a Robotic System

Ramón P. Ñeco, Óscar Reinoso, José M. Azorín
José M. Sabater, M. Asunción Vicente, and Nicolás García

Dpto. Ingeniería, Miguel Hernández University, Avda. Ferrocarril s/n, 03202 Elche
(Alicante), Spain `ramon.neco@umh.es`
`http://lorca.umh.es`

Abstract. This paper shows an application of four neural networks architectures for the automatic adaptation of the voice interface to a robotic system. These architectures are flexible enough to allow a non-specialist user to train the interface to recognize the syntax of new commands to the teleoperated environment. The system has been tested in a real experimental robotic system applied to perform simple assembly tasks, and the experiments have shown that the networks are robust and efficient for the trained tasks.

1   Introduction

Learning of natural language can be divided in two different tasks: (1) learning of the syntax and (2) learning of the semantics. In the case of learning the syntax, the objective is to extract a set of grammatical rules, starting from a sequence of examples of sentences grammatically correct (and possibly of sentences grammatically incorrect). In the case of the semantics, the objective is to obtain an association between the emitted commands and the corresponding internal representation of those commands (intermediate language to a robot in the experiments presented in this paper).

The automatic learning of the syntax, also known as *grammatical inference*, has been studied from the theoretical point of view in numerous works [1], [2]. There exists two sets of learning techniques: symbolic and connectionist. The symbolic techniques try to obtain the grammatical rules directly from each learning example, while the connectionist technique obtains the grammar's model as a neural network. Most works that learn the semantics try to learn the meanings of new words from examples, in the symbolic paradigm [3], but some authors have also developed neural networks solutions [4]. In this paper, we show how neural networks architectures can be used to adapt the grammar of a natural language interface to a robotic system.

2   The System

As in all teleoperated robotic applications, the experimental system considered here consist of a remote environment, as well as a local environment that control

F.J. Garijo, J.C. Riquelme, and M. Toro (Eds.): IBERAMIA 2002, LNAI 2527, pp. 714–723, 2002.
© Springer-Verlag Berlin Heidelberg 2002

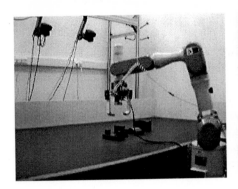

Fig. 1. Teleoperated system used for the experiments on natural language.

and supervise the remote environment. The devices that interact with the task have been located in the remote area (figure 1). The elements of the remote environment are the following: A robotic arm (Mitsubishi PA-10) of 7 degrees of freedom, that executes the commands emitted by the operator; a computer that acts as the robot controller; a computer for image processing; wide range area cameras; and a camera located at the end of the robotic arm, to obtain more precise visual information in the manipulation of the objects on the part of the robot.

In the local environment all the elements such that the operator can interact to send and to receive the commands to the remote environment can be found. These elements are the following: graphic computation system, by means of which the operator knows in real time the state of the task and can control in a complete way the remote system; a master device; and a computer for speech recognition that make the speech recognition together with the natural language processing so that the operator can command the teleoperated system using voice commands [5].

2.1   Formal Grammars and Grammatical Inference

We give in this section a short introduction to formal grammars, grammatical inference and natural language. For a more detailed description we recommend, for example, [6]. A grammar G is a four-tuple (N, T, P, S) where N and P are sets of terminals and nonterminals symbols comprising the alphabet of the grammar, P is a set of production rules, and S is the start symbol of the grammar. The language $L(G)$ associated to this grammar is the set of strings of the terminal symbols that the grammar recognizes. We define *grammatical inference* as the procedures that can be used to obtain the production rules of an unknown grammar G (the *syntax*) based on a finite set of strings of $L(G)$ (and possibly also a finite subset of the complement of $L(G)$). In this paper we apply grammatical inference using neural networks in order to learn the syntax of new commands in a natural language interface to a teleoperated robot.

Natural language processing has traditionally been handled using symbolic methods and recursive processes. The most used of these symbolic methods are based on finite-state descriptions such as n-grams or hidden Markov models. However, finite-state models cannot represent hierarchical structures as found in natural language commands to a robot. Recurrent and feedforward neural networks have been used for several small natural language problems [7], [8]. Also, in speech recognition some neural network models have been used to account for a variety of phenomena in phonology, morphology and role assignment [8], [9]. The main motivation for the work presented in this paper was the fact that a natural interface to a robot needs to be flexible enough to allow the users to adapt the underlying system grammar.

Some authors have addressed the problem of induction of simple grammars - e.g. [10] - and there has been some interest in learning more than regular grammars with recurrent neural networks, such as recursive auto-associative memories (RAAMs) [11] or recurrent neural networks tied to external trainable stacks [12]. In all these works the grammars learned were not large, while other authors such as [13] tried to learn considerably more complex grammars. However, in the last case the obtained grammars where not intuitively interpretable from a logical point of view. In the practical applications presented in this paper, the phrases to be analyzed are not too large so we expected that a connectionist architecture can learn the syntax of new commands not included initially in the designed interface.

In the next sections the results obtained in the training of two categories of recurrent neural architectures for grammatical inference in the robotic application will be described. Section 3 describes the first category of experiments, performed using simple recurrent networks. In the second category of experiments, described in section 4, a combination of recurrent nets will be used in order to obtain a "neural" interpretation of the presented command.

3   Simple Recurrent Networks

This section describes the application of three recurrent neural network architectures : (1) totally connected recurrent network [14]; (2) Elman recurrent network [15]; and (3) Back-Tsoi network [16].

3.1   Network Architectures

Totally Connected Network. The architecture of this network consists of three layers, shown in Figure 2 (left): One input layer in which the code of the input sentence is introduced; one hidden layer that represents the internal state of the network; and one output layer where the network stores the result, which is the feedback toward the nodes in the hidden layer. The output of node k in the output layer is given by the following expression:

$$y_k = f\left(\sum_{y=0}^{N_l-1} w_{ki}h_i\right) \tag{1}$$

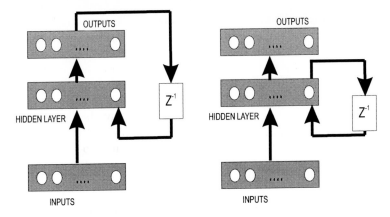

Fig. 2. Totally connected and Elman networks.

where f is a sigmoid function, N_l is the number of nodes of the hidden layer, w_{ki} is the weight of the connection between the node i of the hidden layer and the node k in the output layer, and h_i is the activation of the node i of the hidden layer which in turn is computed according to the following expression:

$$h_k = f \left(\sum_{i=0}^{N_e-1} w_{ki}e_i + \sum_{i=0}^{N_s-1} v_{ki}s_i \right) \tag{2}$$

where e_i is the input corresponding to node i in the input layer, s_i is the activation of node i in the output layer, w_{ki} is the value of the connection between the node i in the input layer to the node k in the hidden layer, and v_{ki} is the value of the connection between node i in the output layer to node k in the hidden layer.

Elman Recurrent Network. The second network architecture considered for the learning of the syntax is an Elman recurrent network, also known as simple recurrent net (SRN) [15]. This network has feedback from each node in the hidden layer toward all the nodes of the same layer. In Figure 2 an scheme of this architecture is shown.

The dynamics of this net is given by the following expression:

$$s_k = f \left(\sum_{l=1}^{D} w_{kl}e_l + \sum_{l=0}^{H} v_{kl}s_l(t-1) \right) \tag{3}$$

where s_k is the activation of the node k in the hidden layer, v_{kl} is the value of the connection between the node l of the input layer and the node k in the hidden layer, v_{kl} is the value of the recursive connection between the node 4 of the hidden layer and the node k of the hidden layer, and $s_l(t-1)$ is the value of the node l of the hidden layer at the previous discrete time step. Starting from s_k at time t, the output of the net is obtained according to the following expression:

$$y_p = f\left(\sum_{l=0}^{H} v_{lp}^{(2)} s_l(t)\right) \tag{4}$$

where v_{lp} is the value of the connection between the node l of the hidden layer and the node p of the output layer, and $s_p(t)$ is the value of the node p of the hidden layer at the current time step t. The error measure used is the quadratic error, given by the expression

$$E(t_1, t_2) = \sum_{t=t_1}^{t=t_2} E(t) = \sum_{t=t_1}^{t=t_2} \frac{1}{2}\sum_{p=1}^{M}(d_p(t) - y_p(t))^2 \tag{5}$$

Back-Tsoi Network. The third architecture used in the experiments is the FIR net of Back-Tsoi [16] (FIR, Finite-duration Impulse Response). The basic idea of this architecture is the inclusion of a FIR and a gain term in each synapsis. The net has L processing layers, excluding the input layer, without feedback. In the layer l there exists N_l nodes. The output of the node k in layer l at the time step t, $k = 1, 2, \cdots, N_l, l = 0, 1, \cdots, L$, is given by the following expression:

$$y_k^l(t) = f\left(x_k^l(t)\right) \tag{6}$$

where f is a sigmoid function, computed according to the expression:

$$x_k^l(t) = \sum_{i=0}^{N_l-1} c_{ki}^l(t) \sum_{j=0}^{N_b} w_{kij}^l(t) y_i^{l-1}(t-j) \tag{7}$$

3.2   Training and Experiments

The experiments with these three architectures used sets of 124 training commands, positives and negatives. All these commands have been or imperative sentences or declarative sentences describing situations of the robot's environment. The training commands are shown to each one of the nets one to one, applying the two learning algorithms that are described next for each time of training. The learning is considered successful when one of the following conditions is completed:

1. The quadratic error is less than an established value.
2. A maximum number of steps is reached, considering in this case that the net has failed in the learning of the grammar corresponding to the training samples.

The number of units in the output layer of each net was set to 2. One of these two units is called the *acceptance unit*, while the other one is called the *rejection unit.* The network is trained in such a way that the desired value of the output units for a grammatically correct sentence (a positive example) is a value close to 1 in the case of the acceptance unit and a value close to 0 in the case of the rejection unit.

For the input to each net pattern, the data are encoded in a window of fixed size constituted by segments included in c possible clusters, where c is the number of different grammatical categories (noun, verb, adverb, etc.). The training samples are labelled using thesse categories. For the training of the nets two types of algorithms have been used: Backpropagation through time (BPTT) [18] for the recurrent nets and the classic backpropagation for the non-recurrent network.

The results obtained for these three networkss are described next. In Table 1 the rates of correct recognition cases are shown on the group of commands used for training the networks, and in Table 2 the same rates are shown for commands not presented in the training samples. The experiments corresponding to Table 2 have been carried out generating 500 commands syntactically correct or incorrect. The maximum number of iterations in the learning algorithms has been set to 3500 in all the cases.

Table 1. Successful rates for training commands

	Large input window	Small input window
Totally connected network	90	95
Elman network	100	100
BT FIR network	100	70

Table 2. Sucessful rates for generalization commands

	Large input window	Small input window
Totally connected network	50	60
Elman network	70	85
BT FIR network	65	55

The results have been obtained for a window size of 2 words in the case of the small window, and a size of 8 words for the case of the large window. In all the cases 10 nodes have been used in the hidden layer. What is interesting in these experiments is that for the natural language processing task in the robot's teleoperation is feasible the use of one of these three nets to extract new grammatical rules which are added to the rules initially considered in the teleoperation interface. This property is very useful to make the interface easily adaptive for the operator.

4   Compound Recurrent Network

Another possibility of using recurrent neural nets for grammatical learning consists on applying the capacity that these systems have to learn distributed codes
of input sequences. Some authors called this approach of obtaining an internal
"neural" code of a data structure *holistic computation* [1].

4.1   Network Architecture

The general idea of the use of autoassociative nets for syntactic analysis is summarized in Figure 3. Connectionist or neural representations are obtained for the
input sentence and for its syntactic tree. The analysis is then made by a correspondence between the representation of the sentence with the representation of
its syntactic structure (holistic transformation). The input sentence is encoded

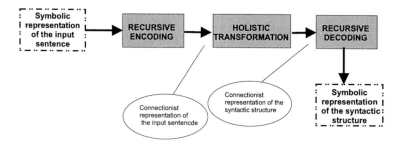

Fig. 3. Autoassociative nets for syntactic analysis.

using RAAM networks (Recusive Autoassociative Memories) [17]. The encoder
is, therefore, a recursive function that takes as input a vector of $[0,1]^N \times [0,1]^K$.
The implementation of the encoder is carried out as a simple perceptron:

$$r_i(t) = g\left(\sum_{j=1}^{N} W_{ij}^{rr} r_j(t-1) + \sum_{j=1}^{N} W_{ik}^{ru} u_k(t) + W_i^r \right) \qquad (8)$$

where W_{ij}^{rr} are the recursive weights, W_{ik}^{ru} are the weights connecting the input
and hidden units, W_i^r is the bias corresponding to the i-th hidden unit, and g is
a sigmoid function.

   The net has, therefore, $N + K$ input units, and N output units. With this
formulation of the encoder, an input sentence i with length L_i can be encoded
placing a binary representation of the first terminal symbol in the K first input
units, and a representation of the empty string in the N remaining units. Then,
the encoder produces an internal representation for the first symbol in its N
hidden units. The activations of the hidden units are copied recursively in the

last N input units, placing the representation of the second terminal symbol of the sentence in the K first input units. This process is repeated until the encoder has processed all the terminal symbols of the input sentence, obtaining a representation for the sentence in the N hidden units of the net. The encoder of the syntactic tree operates in a similar way.

4.2   Training and Experiments

This architecture has been trained with sentences used in the natural language interface to the robot. A total number of 80 sentences have been used together with their corresponding syntactic analysis trees. A random subset of 60 sentences has been chosen for training, while the 20 remaining sentences have been used to check the generalization capacity. The length of the longest sentence has been of 15 words, and the more complex tree analysis had 5 levels. The network has been trained using the BPTT algorithm [18] for the encoders, and the standard backpropagation algorithm the net that performs the transformation between the representation of the input sentence and the representation of the syntactic analysis tree. The generalization obtained in the experiments has been of 100 % in all the cases.

Experiments to show the error recovery capability of the network have also been made. The types of errors that have been introduced in the sentences for the recovery capacity experiments are the following:

1. *Substitution* of a input terminal for another terminal that does not make sense in the sentence. This substitution simulates the situation in which the voice recognizer fails to recognize a word in the sentence.
2. *Insertion* of a new terminal symbol in the sentence. This simulates the inclusion of some incorrect sound, emitted by the user, and that the voice recognizer has recognized as the nearest word to the signal received by the microphone.
3. *Deletion* of a terminal symbol of the sentence. The recovery of this error depends on the importance of the terminal eliminated in the semantics of the sentence.

With these modifications types on the 60 original training sentences, a test set of 40 sentences has been obtained for each type of errors. These input sentences are entered to the network that has been trained. In the experiments a sentence is considered correctly recovered if the two following conditions are completed: [1]:

1. The generated tree corresponds to a correct sentence from the syntactic point of view.
2. The sentence corresponding to the tree doesn't differ much from the erroneous sentence.

The second condition is justified since if a small recognition error had taken place in the sentence, the analysis tree should not differ much from the analysis tree corresponding to the original sentence without errors. In the experiments, the condition 2 is considered satisfied if two (sub)conditions are completed:

1. The length of the sentence corresponding to the generated tree is correct or differs in one symbol from the correct sentence.
2. The maximum number of terminal symbols with errors is 2.

The percentages of recovery errors following the previous conditions is shown in the Table 3. The best generalization results have been obtained for a total of $N = 9$ input neurons.

Table 3. Error recovery rates

Substitution	Insertion	Deletion
91%	71%	76 %

5   Conclusions

The experiments presented in this paper have shown that the use of autoassociative networks is useful to obtain additional grammatical rules to those that exist originally in the grammar, with the objective that the voice interface can adapt its syntactic structure to new environments or new users. This method is not considered appropriate to obtaining the initial grammar (and, therefore an initial grammar design is needed). The experiments also have shown that sentence encoding using RAAM networks is a quite robust technique for the experienced task.

In general, the connectionist analyzers can learn the grammatical regularity that exists in the training sentences in a inductive way. As a consequence, the application of any explicit analysis algorithm is not assumed. This characteristic is relevant in natural language phenomena which are difficult to capture with formal grammars or with transition nets and difficult to analyze with symbolic algorithms.

The main problem in the applicability of these nets is its lack of scalability to adapt to complex problems. In spite of this important disadvantage, these techniques are still very useful in the adaptation of the grammars initially designed in the system. Also, in the teleoperation application, the problem of scalability lack is more limited because the natural language expressions (commands to the robot) are not too long.

Acknowledgements. This work has been supported by the Spanish Government inside the Plan Nacional de Investigacion Cientifica, Desarrollo e Innovacion Tecnologica 2000-2003 through project DPI2001-3827-C02-02.

References

1. Shin Ho, E.K., Wan, L.C.: How to Design a Connectionist Holistic Parser. Neural Computation 11, p. 1995-2016 (1999).
2. Lawrence, S., Giles, C.L., Fong, S.: Natural Language Grammatical Inference with Recurrent Neural Networks. IEEE Transactions on Knowledge and Data Engineering (2000).
3. Regier, T.: A Model of the Human Capacity for Categorizing Spatial Relations. Cognitive Linguistics 6-1 (1995), pp. 63–88.
4. Stolcke, A., Ries, K., Coccaro, N., Shriberg, E., Bates, R., Jurafsky, D., Taylor, P., Martin, R., Van Ess-Dykema, C., Meteer M.: Dialogue Act Modeling for Automatic Tagging and Recognition of Conversational Speech. Computational Linguistics 26(3), pp. 339–373 (2000).
5. Ñeco, R.P., Reinoso, O., Garcia, N., Aracil, R.: A Structure for Natural Language Programming in Teleoperation. In: Proc. of the 6th International Conference on Control, Automation, Robotics and Vision, Singapur, December 2000.
6. Jurafsky, D., Martin, J.H.: Speech and Language Processing. Prentice Hall. (2000).
7. Stolcke, A.:Learning feature-based semantics with simple recurrent networks, TR-90-015, ICSI, Berkeley, California (1990).
8. St. John, M.F., McClelland, J.: Learning and applying contextual constraints in sentence comprehension, Arificial Intelligence 46 (1990) 5–46.
9. MacWhinney, B., Leinbach, J., Taraban, R., McDonald, J.: Language learning: cues or rules?, Journal of Memory and Language 28 (1989) 255–277.
10. Watrous, R., Kuhn, G.: Induction of finite-state languages using second-order recurrent networks, Neural Computation 4(3) (1992).
11. Sperduti, A., Starita, A., Goller, C.: Learning distributed representations for the classification of terms. Proceedings of the International Joint Conference on Artificial Intelligence (1995) pp. 509–515.
12. Zeng, Z., Goodman, R., Smyth, P.: Discrete recurrent neural networks for grammatical infence. IEEE Transactions on Neural Networks 5(2) (1994) 320–330.
13. Giles, C.L, Horne, B., Lin, T.: Learning a class of large finite state machines with a recurrent neural network. Neural Networks 8(9) (1995) 1359–1365.
14. Narendra, K.S., Parthasarathy, K.: Identification and control of dynamical systems using neural networks. IEEE Trans. on Neural Networks, 1(1):4–27 (1990).
15. Elman, J.L.: Distributed representations, simple recurrent networks and grammatical structure, Machine Learning, 7(2/3):195–226 (1991).
16. Back, A.D., Tsoi, A.C.: FIR and IIR synapses, a new neural network architecture for time series modelling Neural Computation, 3(3):337–350 (1991).
17. Pollack, J.B.: Recursive distributed representations, Artificial Intelligence, 46, 77-105.
18. Williams, R.J., Zipser, D.:Gradient-based learning algorithms for recurrent connectionist networks, in Chauvin, Y., Rumelhart, D.E. (eds.), Backpropagation: Theory, Architecture, and Applications. Erlbaum, Hillsdale, NJ, (1990).

Semantic Comparison of Texts for Learning Environments

Patricia Gounon[1] and Benoît Lemaire[2]

[1] L.I.U.M., University of Maine, France
Patricia.Gounon@univ-lemans.fr
[2] L.S.E., University of Grenoble 2, France
Benoit.Lemaire@upmf-grenoble.fr

Abstract. This paper presents a method for comparing a student essay and the text of a course. We first show that the comparison of complex semantic representations is better done with sub-symbolic formalisms than symbolic ones. Then we present a method which rely on Latent Semantic Analysis for representing the meaning of texts. We describe the implementation of an algorithm for partitionning the student essay into coherent segments before comparing it with the text of a course. We show that this pre-processing enhances the semantic comparison. An experiment was performed on 30 student essays. An interesting correlation between the teacher grades and our data was found. This method aims at being included in distance learning environments.

1 Introduction

There is a huge demand nowadays for intelligent systems being able to assess student texts produced in distance learning environments. Students at a distance want assessments on the course they just work on. Multiple-choice questions can be found in most of the existing learning environments but their design is very time-consuming and they are quite rigid. Free text assessment is much more precise but require sophisticated AI techniques.

The specificity of the problem is that the student texts need to be assessed with respect to a domain, corresponding to a course. For instance, a student text about "the financial crash of 1929" need to be assessed with respect to a correct representation of that domain in order to detect missing information or, inversely, parts with too much details. One could imagine to assess student texts with respect to an ontology or any symbolic description of the domain but very few domains are represented in such formalisms. Most of the courses being taught are represented as... texts. Therefore, the challenge is to compare a text to another text. Since the phrasing will not be the same in both texts, the comparison need to be performed at the semantic level.

One way to achieve that goal is to automatically transform each text, the student text and the reference text, into a semantic representation and to compare both representations. The question is: which knowledge representation formalisms to rely on? And which comparison method to use?

F.J. Garijo, J.C. Riquelme, and M. Toro (Eds.): IBERAMIA 2002, LNAI 2527, pp. 724–733, 2002.

After describing various approaches of that problem, we briefly present a statistical model of semantic knowledge representation, called Latent Semantic Analysis (LSA). We relied on this model to partition a text into paragraphs. We then used this segmentation to design a method for assessing a student text. For each method, we performed an experiment with real student texts.

2   Knowledge Representation

2.1   Symbolic Approaches

Artificial intelligence has produced many expressive languages for representing the meaning of words. Some of them are symbolic approaches, other can be called sub-symbolic. All the symbolic formalisms have basically the same structure: each concept is associated with a node which is linked to other nodes, thus describing the relations between nodes. Semantic networks [14] are a well-known example of such formalism. Description logics [2] rely also on this formalism while being more formal and rigourous. The main advantage of these approaches is that the representation is explicit: it is possible, even for a non-computer scientist, to understand the meaning of a node as well as its relations with other nodes. The drawback, however, is that the main part of the knowledge needs to be coded (or at least verified) by a human, even if a system can assist that task.

2.2   Latent Semantic Analysis

LSA is more a sub-symbolic approach since the knowledge representation is not so explicit. LSA represents the knowledge by assigning high-dimensional vectors to words and pieces of texts. To do so, LSA analyses huge corpus of texts divided into paragraphs. The underlying idea is that:

- two words are semantically similar if they appear in similar paragraphs;
- two paragraphs are semantically similar if they contain similar words.

This kind of mutual recursion is implemented by a singular value decomposition algorithm applied to a word-paragraph matrix. This huge matrix is then reduced to 300 dimensions. The aim of this paper is not to describe this algorithm which is presented in details elsewhere [3].

Once the whole corpus has been analyzed and all vectors created, it is straightforward to compare two words or two pieces of texts or a word and a piece of text at the semantic level. The measure of similarity is just the cosine of the angle between the corresponding vectors. Therefore, the similarity between two words or two set of words is a number between -1 (lowest similarity) and 1 (highest similarity). In spite of a lack of syntactical analysis, this measure of semantic similarity has been proven successful in various experiments [4,5,10]. Basically, if the corpus is big enough, LSA has performances on semantic judgement between pairs of words that compare with human ones. It is worth noting that the number of dimensions plays an important role. Experiments show that performances are maximal for dimensions around 300 [4].

We believe that such a representation of the meaning of words can be used for representing knowledge, provided that a knowledge source can be represented by a piece of text, that is a set of words. Therefore, a knowledge source can be represented by a vector in the high-dimensional space defined by LSA.

2.3   Comparison of Both Approaches

As we mentioned above, symbolic approaches of knowledge representation have the great advantage of being explicit. Therefore, various reasoning methods can rely on these representations. However, knowing whether one representation is semantically similar to another one is not obvious because this formalism is not intended for comparison but rather for description. Therefore, most of the methods used for comparing representations are based on surface features : number of common nodes, subsumption relations, etc. This is often the case in the field of machine learning or case-based reasoning. The representation is rich but the comparison is poor. In the other way, LSA representations are not suited for drawing inferences since they are not explicit. However, they are better at making semantic comparisons between entities. In other words, the symbolic approach make absolute representations while LSA provides relative representations. Our goal being to compare representations and not drawing inferences, LSA seemed to us an interesting model of knowledge representation.

Another advantage of LSA is that any new text can be given quickly a new representation, provided that the words are part of the initial corpus with a sufficient frequency. This is not exactly the case with symbolic representations: building a representation from a novel text might be difficult.

LSA is a fully automatic method: there is no need to code knowledge by hand. As we will show, our system can therefore be used in any domain, provided that there exists texts describing that domain.

3   Assessing a Student Essay with LSA

Assessing a student essay with LSA implies that a high-dimensional space is computed from a text describing the domain. Usually, this text is a course. Additionnal texts in the same domain might be required to ensure the accurracy. Each word of the domain will then be represented by a vector.

Several environments rely on LSA to assess a student essay. The essay is usually represented as a 300-dimensions vector. It is compared with other vectors representing several reference texts or parts of reference texts. The feedback to the student is usually composed of (1) a global assessment score; (2) an indication of the topic that are (or not) well covered by the essay;

Intelligent Essay Assessor (IEA) [7,8] is a system which is based on reference texts that are pre-graded essays. Two kinds of assessments are proposed:

- an holistic score corresponding to the score of the closest pre-graded essay;
- a gold standard score which relies on an expert essay.

An experiment with 188 student essays led to a correlation of 0.80 between IEA grades and human grades. However, this system provides no advice on the student essay, which is important for the student to improve the text.

Apex [11] performs a semantic comparison between the essay and the parts of the course previously marked as relevant by the teacher. The whole student essay is successively compared with each of these parts. For instance, if the student has to write a text from the question "What were the consequences of the financial crash of 1929?", the essay will be compared with the following sections of the course: *The political consequences, Unemployment and poverty, The economical effects,* etc. An experiment with 31 student essays in the domain of Sociology of Education led to a correlation of 0.51 between Apex grades and teacher grades.

Select-a-Kibitzer [15] automatically assesses a student essay and provides feedback on the text. The system is not intended to assess whether the student knows a domain, like in the previous approach. Its goal is rather to assess the task of text composition. Therefore, students are required to write a text on a topic like: "if you could change something about school, what would you change?". Select-A-Kibitzer is based on reference texts that are prototypical sentences of what students usually say about school (food, teachers, school hours, etc.).

Despite interesting correlations with human scoring, these approaches suffer from not taking into account the semantic structure of the essay. Two essays that would have the same sentences but organized differently would get the exact same score. This is not acceptable since it is known that the way the essay is structured is an important predictor of the student comprehension of the domain. Moreover, relying on the essay structure would enhance the feedback to the student by providing a more precise assessment. In particular, the student would be advised if one part of the essay seems to cover several topics.

The goal is therefore to go from a n-to-1 comparison to a n-to-m comparison (cf. Fig 1). We need to segment the essay into coherent parts. One way would be to identify each carriage return indicating the end of a paragraph. However, this approach is not fully reliable since students do not usually segment properly their essays, especially if they have trouble to organize what they know about the domain. Therefore, we need to segment student paragraphs from the content.

4   Partitioning a Text

4.1   Related Work

Several methods were designed for partitioning texts into coherent units. A first set of approaches is based on the identification of term repetitions. The idea is that there is a lexical cohesion within a unit. A new unit implies the use of new words. Therefore, term repetition should be an indicator of the lexical cohesion. Hearst [9] implemented such an algorithm and found interesting correlations with human judgements. Reynar [12] relied on a dotplotting algorithm for detecting lexical cohesion. Beefmann [1] also worked at the lexical level but implemented a feature selection algorithm, a method often used in machine learning, to detect

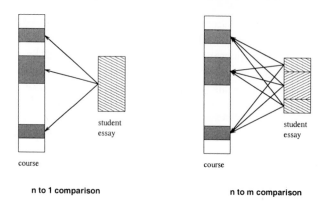

Fig. 1. Two ways of comparing a course and a student essay.

topic boundaries. Salton and Allan [13] relied on a statistical method for representing the similarities and the relations between paragraphs on a map. This technique allows the visualization of groups of similar paragraphs.

All of these approaches suffer from not being explicit. In particular, it is hard to explain to the student why topic breaks have been defined at positions X or Y. Moreover, these methods do not really work at the semantic level, which is what is required for student texts.

Another method was proposed by Foltz et al. [6]. It is based on the semantic comparison of adjacent sentences. The idea is that segment boundaries can be defined each time a low similarity is found between adjacent sentences since it should be an indication of a topic shift. Foltz et al. realized an experiment from a psychology textbook to determine whether LSA can detect automatically the ends of chapters. They found that LSA identified half of the ends of chapters.

4.2   Our Method

This last method was applied to textbooks but we did not know whether it would work for student essays. So, we decided to implement and test this method. A high-dimensional space was then computed by LSA from the text of the course.

The first step to partition a text is therefore to make a comparison between all pairs of adjacent sentences. Each sentence needs to be represented by a vector. It is worth noting that this vector does not exist beforehand since the sentence did not usually appear in the corpus. LSA computes a new vector for each sentence by just adding the vectors of each word of the sentence. Given the vectors of two sentences, it is therefore possible to compute a semantic similarity between them. This measure returns a coefficient of similarity between -1 and 1. At the end, we have a sequence of coefficients that we use in a second step to identify local minima. Instead of just looking for a low coefficient, we compare each sequence of 3 consecutive coefficients to determine whether the second is lower than the previous and the next ones. A local minimum is an indication of a topic shift in the text. To test this method, we realized an experiment.

4.3   Experiment 1

The goal of this experiment is to compare the topic breaks found by our method with those defined by the students by means of the paragraph structure.

Procedure. This first experiment is not concerned with comparing student essays with the course. Inputs are just student essays. However, we need to process the text of the course for computing the high-dimensional semantic space. We submitted LSA with 30 student essays in the same domain in which all paragraph ends were deleted.

Results. The goal of this test was to determine how LSA would partition a text. Although we know that the way students segment essays into paragraphs is far from being optimal, we decided to compare both information sources. We wanted to know whether LSA would find the same breaks as the student. The results concern in particular the number of correct and supplementary cuts. The percentage of error made by LSA was 60%. This means that LSA made several breaks that were not in the initial text. The score of correct breaks was thus 40%. We decided to analyse more precisely these results. Information retrieval researchers make use of several measures to determine the precision of a query: precision and recall. They are based on the following values, for each essay:

1. REL is the number of breaks determined by the student;
2. RET is the number of breaks determined by LSA;
3. RETREL is the number of correct breaks, which is defined here by the number of breaks found by both LSA and the student.

Precision corresponds to the number of common breaks in relation to the number of breaks determined by LSA:

$$precision = \frac{RETREL}{RET}$$

Recall corresponds to the number of common breaks in comparison with the number of breaks determined by the student:

$$recall = \frac{RETREL}{REL}$$

We found a recall of 41% as well as a precision of 34%. These results bring us to put several questions that we develop in the following section.

Comments. The goal of this experiment was to determine whether LSA can retrieve the initial structure of a text. Results indicated that, although they are far better than random, they do not correspond well with the student breaks. The main reason is that the student texts were not expert texts: they were written by people who were in the process of learning a domain. We could not expect them to provide ideal text. Since all student texts were real exam essays, it is also possible that some factors like stress or time pressure might have interfered.

It should be possible to enhance the method by using a local minimum threshold to increase the accurracy of the partitioning. When we compare three consecutive coefficients, the difference between two coefficients can be quite small. In that case, it is probably not a real topic shift. Therefore, another solution would be to indicate a coefficient of certitude for each paragraph after partitioning a text. It can be a coefficient indicating the degree of certitude of each paragraph. More work will be done in that direction in the near future.

5 Comparing Texts

The previous section presented a method for partitioning a text based on the LSA model. Now, the question is: how to take into account the structure of the essay that the previous method identified? In other words, how to assess an essay composed of several paragraphs?

5.1 How to Assess a Student Essay Composed of Several Paragraphs?

To assess a student essay, we relied on the text of the course. This text contained seven chapters and 56 units in the domain of Sociology of Education. We also used an exam question concerning 14 units of this course marked as relevant by the teacher. Contrary to other approaches that we presented above, the assessment is not realized with pre-graded essays.

The first question is: how to evaluate each unit of course? To do that, we compared each paragraph of the essay with each unit of the course. So, we obtained, for each paragraph, several coefficients of semantic similarities between -1 and 1. In the example described in Figure 2, the first paragraph of the essay was compared with each one of the 6 relevant units of the course. This first paragraph was given the following values: 0.02, 0.09, 0.45, 0.08, 0.01, 0.09.

The second question is: how to grade the essays based on these different coefficients? For each unit, we look for the paragraph which covered it the best. In the figure, each best similarity coefficient is marked with a circle. For instance, the unit 1 is best described by the third paragraph. For each paragraph, we have several possibilities:

- only one unit is covered (paragraph 1 in the example). It means that the paragraph is probably coherent. Its grade is the semantic similarity provided by LSA between the paragraph and the course unit (0.45 in the example). In addition, the student is informed that this paragraph is OK.
- several units were developed in the paragraph (paragraphs 3 et 4 in the example). This indicate a paragraph which is not very coherent since it covers several topics. In that case, the grade for that paragraph is the average of the semantic similarity between the essay and the relevant units (0.31 and 0.19 for paragraphs 3 and 4 of the example). The student is warned that these paragraphs need to be revised since they cover several topics.

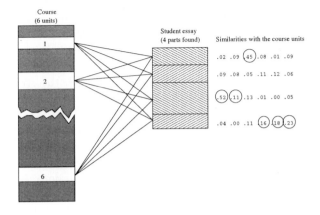

Fig. 2. Example of comparison between student essay and course

- no units were found (paragraph 2 of the example). It means that the paragraph does no seem to cover any relevant topic. A message is then provided to the student for requiring a modification of the paragraph.

The grade of the essay is the average of the grades of its paragraphs. This measure between -1 and 1 is converted into a letter from A to E.

Concerning the feedback, more information is given to the student concerning the assessment of the essay :

- the way LSA structured the essay by highlighting the breaks in the text;
- for each of these paragraphs, the course units that seem to have been covered;
- for each of these paragraphs, a grade between A and E;
- a global grade between A and E;
- an indication of the rank of this global grade with respect to the grade of other students. For instance: "You are in the first 25%". This measure is probably more reliable than the absolute global grade. In fact, it is possible that the absolute global grade does not correspond well with the grades given by teachers.

These methods were implemented in an interface written in PHP. The LSA procedures, written in C, were kindly provided by Telcordia Technologies. To test this method, we realized an experiment only concerned with the global grade.

5.2 Experiment 2

The goal of this experiment was to compare the grades given by our system with those given earlier by the teacher.

Procedure. We used the text of the course mentioned before, composed of seven chapters and 56 units and the same exam question, corresponding to 14 units of the course. The same 30 student essays were involved.

732   P. Gounon and B. Lemaire

Results and comments. A correlation of 0.62 ($p < .001$) between the system grades and the teacher grades was found. This result is coherent with other researches comparing human and computer grades or even grades produced by two human judges on literary domains.

We compared this result with a test performed with the Apex system described earlier. This test concerned the same exam question and the same student essays. A correlation of 0.51 ($p < .001$) between Apex grades and teacher grades was found [11]. It means that it was useful to structure the student essay before computing the similarity with the text of the course.

It is worth noting that we are not interested in the grade per se. It is an objective value that can be easily compared with human data, but the student could be much more interested in the overall feedback which indicates the parts of the essay where the student should work on to enhance the text. In the previous systems, the student was informed about the topics that were not well covered but the student did not know where to make the modification in the text. Our system provides this indication.

6   Conclusion

We presented in this paper a method for partitioning a text into coherent segments which allows the comparison of a student essay and the text of a course. This segmentation gives better results than usual approaches in which the student essay is considered as a whole. This method has been implemented in a Web-based environment. Students at a distance can connect to the system and learn a domain by writing and revising their essay. This method can be used in any literary domain, provided that there exists texts describing that domain. Figures, tables or even mathematical formulas are obviously not taken into account.

We relied on the LSA model to represent the knowledge contained in both the text of a course and a student essay. Results are in the same vein as those found in the literature: LSA seems to be an interesting model of semantic representation of textual knowledge.

Improvements can be done at various levels. First, the method for partitioning the essay and comparing it with the course could be improved by using thresholds for rejecting low similarities. It would also be interesting to test the system with different domains and different teachers. An experiment with real students working on-line would also be very informative, especially for the design of the interface. One more improvement would consist in asking the student to validate the segmentation of the essay. The student would agree or not on the breaks defined by the system. The assessment part would then be based on this segmentation. The result of this step would possibly be more accurate.

It is worth noting that our goal is not just to provide grades but rather to help students at a distance to learn a domain by writing and revising free texts. A grade is a general information which can be useful but it cannot help the student to revise the essay. For this reason, the other kinds of feedback are highly valuable. These feedbacks were possible because of the segmentation of the essay. This way of learning a domain by writing and revising a text is intended to be included in Web-based learning environments, which are currently mainly based on multiple-choice questions, a method which is domain-dependent and, moreover, quite time-consuming.

Acknowledgments. We would like to thank V. Barré, C. Choquet, A. Corbière, P. Dessus and P. Tchounikine for their comments on an earlier version of this paper.

References

1. Beefermann D., Berger A., and Lafferty J.D.: Statistical models for text segmentation. *Machine Learning*, **34**(1-3) (1999) 177–210.
2. Borgida A.: On the relative expressive power of description logics and predicate calculus. *Artificial Intelligence*, **82**, (1996) 353–367.
3. Deerwester S., Dumais S.T., Furnas G.W., Landauer T.K., and Harshman R.: Indexing by Latent Semantic Analysis. *Journal of the American Society for Information Science*, **41**(6) (1990) 391–407.
4. Dumais S.T.: Improving the retrieval of information from external sources. *Behavior Research Methods, Instruments and Computers*, **23**(2) (1991) 229–236.
5. Foltz P.: Latent Semantic Analysis for text-based research. *Behavior Research Method, Instruments and Computer*, **23**(2) (1996) 229–236.
6. Foltz P., Kintsch W., and Landauer T.K.: The measurement of textual coherence with Latent Semantic Analysis. *Discourse Processes*, **25** (1998) 285–307.
7. Foltz P.W., Laham D., and Landauer T.K.: Automated essay scoring: Applications to educational technology. In: *Proceedings of the ED-MEDIA Conference*, Seattle, (1999).
8. Foltz P.W., Laham D., and Landauer T.K.: The intelligent essay assessor: Applications to educational technology. *Interactive Multimedia Electronic Journal of Computer-Enhanced Learning*, **1**(2) (1999).
9. Hearst M.: Multi-paragraph segmentation of expository text. In: *32nd. Annual Meeting of the Association for Computational Linguistics*, Las Cruces, (1994) 9–14.
10. Landauer T.K. and Dumais S.T.: A solution to Plato's problem: The Latent Semantic Analysis theory of acquisition, induction and representation of knowledge. *Psychological Review*, **104** (1997) 211–240.
11. Lemaire B. and Dessus P.: A system to assess the semantic content of student essays. *Journal of Educational Computing Research*, **24**(3) (2001) 305–320.
12. Reynar J.C.: An automatic method of finding topic boundaries. In: *Meeting of the Association for Computational Linguistics*, (1994).
13. Salton G. and Allan J.: Automatic text decomposition and structuring. *Information Processing and Management*, **32**(2) (1996) 127–138.
14. Sowa J.F.: *Principles of Semantic Networks: Exploration in the Representation of Knowledge*. Morgan Kaufman, 1991.
15. Wiemer-Hastings P. and Graesser A.: Select-a-kibitzer: A computer tool that gives meaningful feedback on student compositions. *Interactive Learning Environments*, **8**(2) (2000) 149–169.

I-PETER: Modelling Personalised Diagnosis and Material Selection for an Online English Course

Timothy Read[1], Elena Bárcena[2], Beatriz Barros[1], and Felisa Verdejo[1]

Depts.: [1]Lenguajes y Sistemas Informáticos, [2]Filologías Extranjeras y sus Lingüísticas
UNED, Madrid, Spain
[1]{tread, felisa, bbarros}@lsi.uned.es, [2]mbarcena@flog.uned.es

Abstract. In this paper the underlying knowledge model and architecture of I-PETER (Intelligent Personalised English Tutoring EnviRonment) are presented. This system has been designed for the on-line distance learning of English where too many students restrict the teacher's possibilities to provide individualised guidance. I-PETER is made up of four domain models that represent linguistic and didactic knowledge: the conceptual framework related to linguistic levels and knowledge stages, and the educational content and study strategies. The student model represents the knowledge that the student has learnt, the study strategies, and his/her profile. A student's command of English is evaluated by interpreting his/her performance on specific linguistic units in terms of three related criteria, rather than by a general linguistic competence ranking. Evaluation consists of a diagnostic task model which assesses student performance, taking the form of a Bayesian network, and a selection mechanism that proposes appropriate materials and study strategies.

1 Introduction

As in other educational areas, interactive on-line environments for learning English enable students to work without having the teacher present. In a distance learning context they represent an advance over their book-based counterpart, since as well as their inherently interactive nature, they enable both the teacher to add new content as the course progresses according to the students' general needs (e.g., summaries, extra exercises, and mock exams to help them prepare for the final exam), and the students to make use of the communication facilities (e.g., e-mail, net-news) to contact the teacher or peers for help. For reasons like these, courses based upon interactive on-line environments are being adopted in a wide range of distance learning institutions.

A problem present with all taught courses is that, as the number of students grows, it becomes progressively harder for the teacher to maintain control of the overall learning process of the group: follow the progress of individual students, identify their difficulties, provide help and guidance accordingly, and introduce modifications in the way in which the material is being studied to adapt to individual needs. Due to the typically large number of students in on-line distance learning courses (in the case of the UNED, the various English courses can have between 350 and 15,000 students),

F.J. Garijo, J.C. Riquelme, and M. Toro (Eds.): IBERAMIA 2002, LNAI 2527, pp. 734–744, 2002.

and the additional communication difficulties (e.g., there is no face-to-face contact or non-verbal feedback), the teacher becomes more of an administrator, being able to deal with only a small number of problems that certain students present via e-mail or telephone calls (not always the ones that really require the help!). A related problem present in all courses is that they do not take into account the profile, learning goals, and other features and needs of individual students.

The research presented in this paper has three objectives. Firstly, the structural decomposition of both the linguistic domain knowledge and student linguistic competence in such a way as to capture and represent the underlying conceptual content and student model. This is necessary in order to design an intelligent personalised English tutoring environment for use in a distance learning context where, as mentioned above, a very high number of students limits teacher interaction drastically. Secondly, the analysis of the results of student interactions with the system, in order to encounter study strategies (considered in terms of conceptual units and materials) which are particularly effective or ineffective, and that can be used appropriately by the system to improve student progress and learning. Thirdly, based partly on the previous objective, the automatic detection (or prediction) of students who are having (or may have) difficulties with the material in order to help the teacher know who needs help. This last objective is still work in progress and, as such, is not discussed here.

Throughout the three decades of CALL[1] research, different approaches have been developed, from the earliest vocabulary and grammar trainers to multimedia and Web-based workbenches that reflect the current interest in communicative intent and functions within Linguistics and eclectic pedagogic frameworks. Combined with these are research strategies taken from different areas, including Computational Linguistics (e.g., parsing student input and/or generating natural language), Artificial Intelligence (e.g., knowledge-based systems, student modeling), Cognitive Psychology, Psycholinguistics, Human-Computer Interaction, etc. [2], [9]. While progress has been made in the area of interactive on-line learning, the authors' experience is that it is currently unfeasible to design the perfect tutoring system. It is possible however, to solve a subset of problems present in a particular educational domain. In this paper a system called I-PETER[2], based to some extent upon the previously mentioned disciplines, is presented as a proposal for representing and organizing the domain knowledge and student model necessary for personalized English distance learning.

This paper starts with a description of the different pedagogic parameters that have been taken into account for the design of I-PETER. Secondly, the linguistic and didactic domain modelling undertaken for this system is presented together with details of the student model and the tasks of diagnosis and selection. Thirdly, the functionality of the system and its underlying architecture are briefly presented. Fourthly and finally, some conclusions are offered together with plans for future work.

---

[1] CALL: Computer Assisted Language Learning
[2] I-PETER: *Intelligent Personalised English Tutoring EnviRonment*

2   The Pedagogic Foundations of I-PETER

The design of I-PETER takes into consideration such pedagogic issues as: the influence of mother tongue in second language acquisition, the need to treat the tuition of sublanguages separately, the existence of personal preferences for language learning vs. acquisition, and the relevance of error analysis. However, there is one particular pedagogic issue that is crucial for the overall design of this system: student knowledge modelling.

On-line language courses are typically organised according to an idealised degree of quasi-native 'linguistic competence' that a student must reach at the end of his/her studies. To achieve this, the 'mass of knowledge' that the student needs to command is typically categorized into stages such as: stage 1… stage n, beginners', intermediate, advanced, etc. These classifications reflect attempts to group together students with roughly the same level of English knowledge, and they are deeply engrained into the educational system, as well as being a motivational factor for students. However, while it is relatively easy to organize students into, for example, three, four, or even ten stages of linguistic knowledge, the reality is that the subset of English known by students that have been assigned a given stage can vary greatly within the different linguistic levels (some may have a considerable vocabulary due to extensive reading in English; others may be fluent in their production for having been immersed in the speaking community although with a poor knowledge of grammar, etc.). Inevitably, the potential progress of some students within a given group can be slowed (e.g., there are some topics that they will not need to practice), while others will fail to fully acquire certain language items due to insufficient underlying knowledge. Furthermore, the decision to move students up to a higher stage is typically based upon some sort of average mark made up from the results of test questions which measure a few linguistic skills. This practice inevitably leads to 'holes' in the students' knowledge. In the authors' experience, a more useful approach for the classification of student knowledge and progress relates three dimensions, rather than the general notion of 'degree of linguistic competence'. These interacting dimensions are defined to be: 'linguistic level', 'knowledge stage', and 'learning phase', as shown in figure 1.

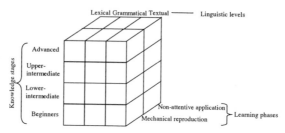

Fig. 1. Relationship between the three dimensions that make up the problem domain

Firstly, knowledge stage is the term used to classify the students' linguistic knowledge (as above). The difference lies in the scope of application, because it is applied to the narrower fields of discrete linguistic conceptual units, and only from there can it be generalised to a linguistic level and the student's general competence. In this system the stages are: beginners', lower intermediate, upper intermediate, and advanced. The number of stages chosen could have been larger to reflect more subtle divisions, but such fine granularity is unnecessary in this multidimensional knowledge classification.

Secondly, the linguistic level corresponds approximately to the generally accepted distinction (with some variance) amongst linguists regarding the structural composition of language. These levels are: lexicon (the level of words, their orthography and meaning, either in isolation, in locutions, and in the context of other elements), grammar (the level of morphology and syntax at phrasal, clausal and sentential level) and discourse (the level of text and composition; a supra-sentential level). I-PETER does not currently consider the oral aspect of the language (phonetics and phonology).

Thirdly, the learning phase corresponds to the extent to which the knowledge has been internalised by the student. This knowledge is made up of a set of concepts (e.g., verbs, simple sentences; see figure 3), and sub-concepts (e.g., for verbs: conjugation, internal composition, collocations, complementation), where each sub-concept is in itself a set of items (e.g., for verbal conjugation: simple present, simple past; see figure 4), and sub-items (e.g., for simple past: regular and irregular verbs). Conventional single topic-based exercises are typically used to help the student learn a particular linguistic item, and its subsequent evaluation, to check that it has been understood (learnt). However, they can be misleading because mechanical attentive practice of a particular item does not ensure that it has been really interiorised (acquired), so that the student is ready to use it correctly (and creatively) in other (non-attentive) contexts [8]. Furthermore, even though an item appears to have been acquired, it may be the case that this is a temporal phenomenon, and that it is subsequently forgotten due to lack of sufficient usage immediately after its acquisition. I-PETER attempts to avoid the dangers of monitorised practice and short-term memory learning by distinguishing two learning phases: mechanical reproduction and non-attentive application, and using multiple topic-based exercises that provide extra practice and 'secretly' test previously learnt items as well as the current item under study.

3   Knowledge Models Used in the System

I-PETER is made up of a set of knowledge models that include domain and student knowledge, the interactions between which can be seen in figure 2. The **domain model** of the problem is made up of two linguistic models (M1 and M2) together with two didactic models (M3 and M4):

M1: The **concepts** that make up the knowledge domain for learning English and their relation to the linguistic levels. In this model, as can be seen in figure 3, the 'mass of knowledge' to be learnt has been organized into a set of concepts. These have

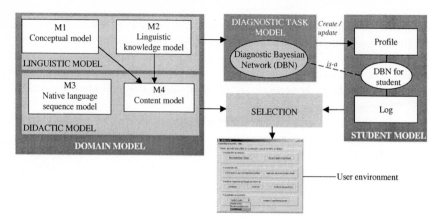

Fig. 2. Interaction of the knowledge models within I-PETER

been established together with their percentage correspondences at each linguistic level, to reflect the type of knowledge that the student is progressively gaining within the field of Linguistics as s/he works on a given topic (for example: learning a list of the irregular verbs is both a vocabulary and grammar task; certain conjunctions are used both to join clauses [grammar level in this system] and sentences [text level]). Furthermore, by having concepts linked to the linguistic levels, more precise information will be available regarding the knowledge and progress of each student.

M2: The **linguistic knowledge** that relates each sub-concept to a set of items and sub-items for each stage at which they are typically taught[3]. In this system, a concept represents a general category of linguistic knowledge which, in turn, is made up of sub-categories of actual study elements or units (items). In figure 4 part of this knowledge model is shown for the concept verb and its sub-concept verb conjugation (including mood, tense, aspect, person, and number). The items and sub-items of this sub-concept are mapped to the four knowledge stages represented in this system. It is recommended, for example, that a typical advanced student studies such verb tenses as future perfect continuous and conditional continuous.

M3: The **native language sequence model**. This model represents instructional strategies in the form of the set of sequences of conceptual units, materials, and exercises most appropriate depending upon the speaker's own native language which, in the authors' experience, should be a determining factor in syllabus design.

M4: The **educational content**: theoretical explanations, examples, and exercises for this domain. Different types of content are stored to offer students a wide range of learning options and practice depending, among other things, upon previous interactions and results. The content of this model is classified in terms of these criteria to

---

[3] This is the general structure of linguistic content found in the majority of language courses and text books prepared without taking into account native language effects and interferences or learning preferences and restrictions.

Concepts	Linguistic levels %		
	Grammatical	Lexical	Textual
Nouns	50	50	-
Determinants	80	20	-
Pronouns	80	20	-
Adjectives	50	50	-
Adverbs	65	35	-
Verbs	50	50	-
Prepositions	80	20	-
Conjunctions	80	10	10
Simple sentences	100	-	-
Complex sentences	80	-	20
Reading	20	60	20
Contexts	25	25	50

Sub-concept	Knowledge stage	Item	Sub-item
Verb conjugation	Beginners'	Simple present	Lexical verbs
		Simple present	Primary verbs
		Present continuous	
	Lower-intermediate	Future shall/will	
		Future be going to-	
		Simple past	Regular verbs
		Simple past	Irregular verbs I
		Present perfect	Regular verbs
		Present perfect	Irregular verbs I
		Past perfect	Regular verbs
		Past perfect	Irregular verbs I
		Modal verbs I	
		Conditional	
	Upper-intermediate	Simple past	Irregular verbs II
		Past continuous	
		Present perfect continuous	
		Present perfect	Irregular verbs II
		Past perfect	Irregular verbs II
		Future perfect	
		Conditional perfect	
		Modal verbs II	
		Past perfect continuous	
	Advanced	Future continuous	
		Future perfect continuous	
		Future be going to- continuous	
		Conditional continuous	
		Conditional perfect continuous	

Fig. 3. Principal concepts for learning English and their relation to the linguistic levels (**M1**)

Fig. 4. The linguistic knowledge of this domain for the sub-concept verb conjugation, relating items and sub-items to the student's knowledge stage (**part of M2**)

enable correct selection and ensure efficient retrieval. The templates used to declare the structure and content of the didactic material in this system are shown in figure 5. The material in the knowledge model M4 is made up of two types of elements: firstly, a set of conceptual units (concepts, sub-concepts, items, and sub-items), together with

CONCEPTUAL UNITS: Concept / Sub-concept / Item / Sub-item			
KNOWLEDGE STAGE			
THEORETICAL EXPLANATION			
ILLUSTRATIVE EXAMPLES			

TYPE OF EXERCISE			
CONCEPTUAL UNITS TESTED: Mechanical / Non-attentive [list of conceptual material that can be tested with this exercise and the type of test]			
DETAILS OF THE EXERCISE			
CORRECT ANSWER	EFFECT: (item/sub-item, % mod.)	EFFECT: (item/sub-item, % mod.)	
INCORRECT ANSWERS:			
a EXPLANATION a	EFFECT: (item/sub-item, % err.)	EFFECT: (item/sub-item, % err.)	ERROR TYPE: f, s or u
b EXPLANATION b	EFFECT: (item/sub-item, % err.)	EFFECT: (item/sub-item, % err.)	ERROR TYPE: f, s or u
c EXPLANATION c	EFFECT: (item/sub-item, % err.)	EFFECT: (item/sub-item, % err.)	ERROR TYPE: f, s or u

Fig. 5. The frame for the content model (**M4**)

their theoretical explanations and illustrative examples; and secondly, a set of related exercises. As can be seen in figure 5, these include information about the types of units they test, either mechanically or non-attentively. Since open production exercises (where the student is free to write) are currently beyond the scope of tutoring systems (due to the inherent intractability of natural language) [5], this system uses three generally acknowledged types of closed exercises: 'multiple-choice', 'filling in the gaps', and 'modifying the form and/or order of a word or sequence of words' [7]. The system is not only capable of interpreting the correct answers but also the erroneous ones. It distinguishes between three types of error: formal (surface mistakes in the construction of a word or a larger linguistic unit, including spelling mistakes), semantic (mistakes with the meaning of a word or a larger linguistic unit), and usage (mistakes of adequacy related to communicative context), and establishes a relation between each of these and the most likely knowledge stage at which they occur.

The **student model**, the structure of which can be seen in figure 6, stores the information that pertains to each student, such as his/her preferences and restrictions (e.g., native language, learning goals) and the knowledge that the student has learnt. This profile is another determining factor for the selection of the materials within the didactic model that are most appropriate for him/her. It can be accessed and partially modified by the student at any time. There is also a log (or record) of the student activities and interactions with the system that represents the way in which the different materials within the system have been studied (e.g., sequence, time, results).

PERSONAL INFORMATION			
LOGIN	PASSWORD	NATIVE LANGUAGE: Romance / Germanic / Slavic	
TYPE OF ENGLISH: General / Scientific / Technical / Business / Legal / Formal		INITIATIVE: Student / System / Mixed	
OBJECTIVE: Fill knowledge gap / Improve knowledge stage / Improve linguistic level / Practise conceptual unit			
DEGREE OF THEORETICAL EXPLANATION: Standard / Minimum		OTHER PREFERENCES / RESTRICTIONS	
KNOWLEDGE STAGE:	LINGUISTIC LEVELS:	CONCEPTUAL UNITS:	LEARNING PHASE:
Beginners' Lower-intermediate Upper-intermediate Advanced	Lexical Grammatical Textual	Concept Sub-concept Item Sub-item	Mechanical reproduction Non-attentive application

Fig. 6. The frame for the student profile

The **diagnostic task model** represents how the teacher evaluates the student, and it is implemented as a Bayesian network [11]. This approach has been selected since it appears that this probabilistic mechanism, that combines evidence to form an overall probability, is closest to the way a real teacher heuristically assesses a student [1], [3], [10] both through correct performance and error identification and analysis.

This network is used to **diagnose** the presence of holes in the linguistic knowledge of the student in terms of the degree of membership of a particular knowledge stage and linguistic level. The domain models M1 and M2 (see figure 2) are implicitly represented in the structure of the network. As figure 7 shows, for the sub-concept verb

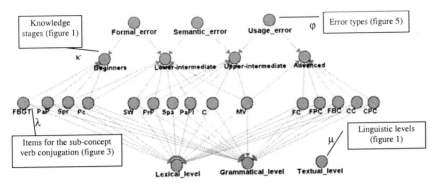

Fig. 7. Bayesian network for the diagnosis of student errors

conjugation[4], this network is made up of four distinct types of nodes. The items that make up the sub-concept are represented as the row of nodes marked as ③ in the figure and, as can be seen, influence the nodes marked as ② (knowledge stages) and ④ (linguistic levels). Furthermore, there is another row of nodes (marked as ① in the figure), which represent the types of errors committed and influence the nodes marked as ②. In this part of the overall network, the node that corresponds to the textual level is not connected to any of the sub-concept nodes since the concept verb has no direct relation to it, as reflected in figure 3.

The student profile is created at the beginning of the course by preference selection together with an optional stage test, based upon the results generated by the diagnostic task model. Each time the student works in the environment, his/her actions and results are added to the log, and the diagnostic task model updates the student profile accordingly. Subsequently, the **selection** of appropriate material is undertaken in terms of the information contained in the profile. Firstly, a selection criterion is established by combining this information with the M3 sequence model. Secondly, a subset of the most appropriate material is proposed for the student by the application of this criterion to the M4 content model. This selection criterion also takes into account heuristic information such as the time that has gone past since the student last worked with this type of material and any other didactic criteria specified by the teacher.

4   System Functionality and Architecture

The main client interface to I-PETER can be seen on the right hand side of figure 8 (marked as ①). The student uses this interface to express and review his/her preferences and restrictions, choose the type of material that s/he wants to study, or simply inspect the information that the system has about his/her progress (presented visually

---

[4] Only the nodes that correspond to the sub-concept verb conjugation are included in this figure for the sake of legibility. It should be noted that all the concepts represented in figure 3 would be included in the complete network.

as a set of points within the cube of figure 1 for each concept, sub-concept, etc., as selected), a feature aimed at involving and motivating the student [4].

As can be seen in figure 8 (marked as ②), the learning process can be undertaken in three ways: trying to improve or fill holes in existing knowledge stages, improve a particular knowledge stage or linguistic level, or practice specific items and sub-items, although it is also possible to let the system take the initiative. In the example in this figure, once the student selects that s/he wants to practice conditional verbs, the window shown on the left side of the figure opens, presenting the student with the theoretical explanation of the linguistic item together with a set of selected exercises (marked as ③ in the figure) that the student can use to test his/her understanding. Once the student answers a question, by selecting the answer thought to be correct, feedback can be requested, where the system presents information about the correct answer together with an explanation for each erroneous case. It should be noted, as an example of what has been discussed previously in this paper regarding the learning phases, that exercise 1 shown in the figure is interpreted by the system as a mechanical reproduction test for conditional verbs and also a non-attentive test for simple past verbs, thereby assessing also how well the student has acquired the latter.

The architecture of the system is presented below[5] in figure 9. As can be seen, it has been developed using a JNLP-based (Java Network Loading Protocol) client-server model for three reasons. Firstly, to limit potential server load problems given the large number of students, and to make use of the processing power that is typically wasted on a standard client PC used as a Web browser platform. Secondly, to permit a more sophisticated user environment than that which is possible in a standard HTML-based Web interface (without the use of a Java applet interface, which in itself has problems – see the third reason). Thirdly and finally, JNLP enables Java applications to be downloaded (the first time they are used) and run locally from a client computer. The advantage of JNLP over applets is that, once downloaded to the client, the next time that the user wants to run the application it is not necessary to download it again, and if there are any differences between the version on the client machine and the server, only those parts of the application that have been changed are downloaded, thereby maintaining the user version up to date.

5   Conclusions and Future Work

In this paper I-PETER has been presented, a proposal for organizing and representing the knowledge necessary for English distance learning in a personalized tutoring system. The traditional division of linguistic knowledge into simple levels has been extended to distinguish between three learning dimensions: the knowledge stage, the linguistic level, and the learning phase of the student. The domain knowledge has been

---

[5] The sequence Bayesian network is included in the architecture diagram for the sake of completeness, even though, as noted in the following section, it is still under development and, as such, not detailed in this paper.

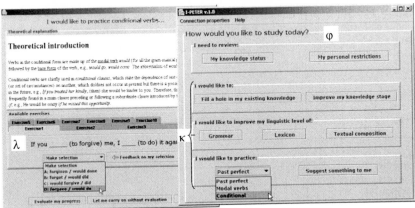

Fig. 8. Two parts of the user interface of I-PETER

structured into two parts: a linguistic model which relates units of knowledge to linguistic levels and knowledge stages, and a didactic model that contains course materials and a set of appropriate study sequences according to the student's native language. The diagnostic task model used here is a Bayesian network, which was selected because it enables the real-world heuristic evaluation of student ability to be modelled in an explicit and plausible manner. This work represents an original contribution with respect to other previous systems [7], since the three dimensional classification model provides a fine-grained representation of the knowledge levels and needs of a student beyond the general and vague concept of linguistic competence typically used. The system uses this diagnostic model to interpret student performance and subsequently selects and organises the material for him/her.

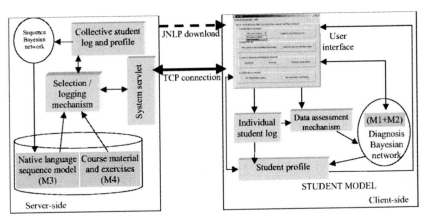

Fig. 9. The architecture of I-PETER

In the ongoing development of this system, work is being undertaken to explore the way in which a second Bayesian network could be used to detect particular domain features, such as effective learning sequences (to be incorporated in M3) and potential problems that students might encounter with the system. This work looks promising, but no conclusions can be drawn yet because more student data is required.

References

1. Bunt, A. & Conati, C. "Assesing Effective Exploration in Open Learning Environments using Bayesian Networks". *ITS'2002* (2002)
2. Chapelle, C. "CALL in the year 2000: Still in search of research paradigms?". *Language Learning and Technology*, vol. 1, no. 1 (1997)
3. Conati C., VanLehn K. "POLA: a Student Modeling Framework for Probabilistic On-Line Assessment of Problem Solving Performance". In *Proc. of UM-96*, Univ. Hawaii (1996)
4. Dimitrova, V. & Dicheva, D. "'Who is who': the roles in an intelligent system for foreign language terminology learning". *British Journal of Edu. Technology*, vol. 29, no. 1 (1998)
5. Harrell, W. "Language learning at a distance via computer". *International Journal of Instructional Media*, vol. 23, no. 3 (1999)
6. Heift, T. & Nicholson, D. "Web Delivery of Adaptive and Interactive Language Tutoring". *International Journal of Artificial Intelligence in Education*, vol. 12 (to appear in 2002)
7. Kohn, K. "Distributive language learning in a computer-based multilingual communication environment". In H. Jung & R. Vanderplank (eds.) *Barriers and Bridges: Media Technology in Language Learning*. Frankfurt: Peter Lang (1994)
8. Krashen, S.D. *Second Language Acquisition and Second Language Learning*. London: Prentice-Hall (1988)
9. Levy, M. *Computer-Assisted Language Learning*. Oxford: Clarendon Press (1997)
10. Millán, E. *Sistema bayesiano para modelado del alumno*. Ph.D. Thesis, U. Málaga (2000)
11. Pearl, J. *Probabilistic Reasoning in Intelligent Systems: Networks of Plausible Inference*. San Mateo, CA: Morgan-Kaufmann (1988)

An Agent-Based System for Supporting Learning from Case Studies

Marta C. Rosatelli[1], John A. Self[2], and Tulio V.D. Christofoletti[3]

[1]Graduate Program in Informatics, Catholic University of Santos
R. Dr. Carvalho de Mendonça, 144/5º andar, Santos-SP, 11070-906, Brazil
rosatelli@unisantos.br
[2]Computer Based Learning Unit, University of Leeds, Leeds, LS2 9JT, UK
jas@cbl.leeds.ac.uk
[3]Department of Informatics and Statistics, Federal University of Santa Catarina
Cx.P. 476, Florianópolis-SC, 88040-900, Brazil
tulio@inf.ufsc.br

Abstract. A main issue in collaborative learning is providing support and monitoring both the individual learners and the group activities. In this sense, there is a variety of functions that might be accomplished by a collaborative learning support system. Some examples are: knowledge diagnosis and evaluation, group and individual feedback, student and group modelling, and so on. LeCS (Learning from Case Studies) is a collaborative case study system that provides a set of tools and accomplishes some functions that together support learners during the development of a case study solution. This paper gives an overview of LeCS, focusing on the system design and architecture. The LeCS design is based on our model of supporting the learning from case studies method in a computer-based environment and in a distance learning context. The LeCS architecture is agent-based and includes three kinds of agents.

1 Introduction

A main issue in collaborative learning is providing support and monitoring both the individual learners and the group activities. In this sense, there is a variety of functions that might be accomplished by a collaborative learning support system. Some examples are: knowledge diagnosis and evaluation, group and individual feedback, student and group modelling, and so on. The usual problem in most Intelligent Tutoring Systems (ITS) of generating appropriate feedback and determining the contents of this feedback is also present in this kind of systems. This is specially critical in a distance learning context.

LeCS (Learning from Case Studies) [1] is a collaborative case study system for distance learning that provides a set of tools and accomplishes some functions that together support learners during the development of a case study solution. This paper gives an overview of LeCS, focusing on the system design and architecture. The design of LeCS is based on our model [1] of supporting the learning from case studies method in a computer-based environment and in a distance learning context. The LeCS architecture is agent-based and includes three kinds of agents.

F.J. Garijo, J.C. Riquelme, and M. Toro (Eds.): IBERAMIA 2002, LNAI 2527, pp. 745–754, 2002.

The paper is organised as follows. In the next section we outline some related work. In the section thereafter, we present LeCS: first, we give an overview about the learning from case studies method and a methodology to develop the case study solution; then, we describe LeCS and its graphical user interface with the student; next, the LeCS architecture and functions accomplished by each kind of agent are detailed. Finally, we present the conclusions and directions for future work.

2   Related Work

The work presented in this paper introduces the case study element, which is particularly novel in ITS research. Learning from case studies is well established as an educational method in the traditional classroom [2]. However, the characteristics of case studies activities have led to their relative neglect in the ITS and Artificial Intelligence in Education areas. On the other hand, this work shares characteristics with other approaches used in these areas: agent-based ITS (e.g., [3]), work on collaboration (e.g., [4]), and work on supporting the problem solving process at a distance (e.g., [5]).

Particularly concerning collaborative and intelligent distance learning, LeCS has features that are quite similar to COLER's [6, 7]. COLER is a web-based collaborative learning environment in the domain of database design that uses the Entity-Relationship modelling formalism. Like LeCS, it focuses on both individual and collaborative learning, and on an agreement by the group on a joint solution for a collaborative task, it monitors the students' participation and encourages them to discuss their differences, and it generates advice to the students concerning issues such as group participation, group discussion, feedback, and reflection.

Furthermore, LeCS also shares similarities with systems that use pedagogical agents. In particular we may cite TEATRIX [8], which is a learning environment designed to help children, and their teachers, in the process of collaborative story creation. In TEATRIX the characters represented does not play the role of a tutor or a learning companion but rather they are actors in a play. Likewise, in LeCS the character represented plays the role of the case instructor.

3   LeCS: Learning from Case Studies

3.1   The Learning from Case Studies Method

Learning from case studies [2] is typically used in the business schools to train the students in disciplines that contain open-ended problems. Such kind of problems usually present complex, realistic situations, and demand cognitive flexibility to cope with them. The case method is used when the situated nature of cognition in the learning process and/or learning in ill-structured domains is required [9].

The case method has been widely used for years in a variety of disciplines, e.g., law, engineering, business, and management. The common characteristic between such disciplines is that they introduce the kinds of problem that no analytical technique or approach is suitable to solve, with no „correct" or clear-cut solution.

A central issue in the case method is the case discussion. It is so important that the case method is often referred to as the process of teaching by holding discussions, as opposed to lectures or labs. The case discussion process is described as fluid and collaborative and is intrinsically related to the instructor's role in the case method. The case study text will basically furnish raw material for the case discussion.

The case instructor role - different from the teacher in the traditional classroom - is to lead the process by which the individual students and the group explore the complexity of a case study and develop the case solution. He or she maximises the opportunities for learning by asking the appropriate questions during the discussion, rather than having a substantive knowledge of the field or case problem.

The case method application in the traditional classroom consists roughly of presenting a case study that introduces a problem situation to a group of learners who are supposed to discuss the case and find a solution to it.

The Seven Steps approach [10] is a methodology used to carry out the case solution development. It proposes that the case study solution be developed step-by-step. Thus, it guides the case solution development splitting it into parts. Each step of the approach has its own goal and suggests an activity to be carried out by the learners in order to achieve such goal. The steps, goals, and related activities are listed below:

- Step 1. Understanding the situation: to relate important information.
- Step 2. Diagnosing problem areas: to list problems.
- Step 3. Generating alternative solutions: to list solutions.
- Step 4. Predicting outcomes: to list outcomes.
- Step 5. Evaluating alternatives: to list pros and cons.
- Step 6. Rounding out the analysis: to choose.
- Step 7. Communicating the results: to present the case solution.

3.2 LeCS Description

LeCS provides a set of tools and accomplishes some functions that together support the learners during the development of the case solution. The tools are a browser, a chat, a text editor, and a representational tool. The support LeCS provides consists of representing the solution path taken by the learners and making interventions concerning the following aspects of the case solution development:

- *the time that the learners spend on each step of the Seven Steps approach* [10];
- *the learners' degree of participation in the case discussion*;
- *the misunderstandings that the learners might have about the case study*, and
- *the coordination of the group work*.

LeCS was implemented in the Delphi language and has a client-server architecture. The server hosts sessions and the client interacts with sessions. A session is associated with a group of students working collaboratively on the solution of a case study. The clients run on the students' machines. The server can run on one of the student's machine or alternatively on a different machine.

Graphical User Interface: Student. The LeCS graphical user interface with the student displays the following components shown in Fig. 1: a pull down menu, a participants list, a browser, a solution graphical representation, a text editor, a chat, and a system intervention area.

The pull-down menu includes among others: (1) a case studies library containing the set of case studies available; and (2) the forms, where the learners fill out the agreed group answer to each step question. There is a form to each step. The forms are numbered and each entry corresponds to a component sentence of the step answer.

The participants list shows all the group participants that are working on a case study. The participants who are on-line at a particular moment - logged on a certain session - have their names annotated with the green colour whereas the ones that are logged off are annotated in red. The participants can carry out tasks directly with another participant (send a message or see the information available about him or her) just by clicking on the button corresponding to his or her name (cf. Fig. 1). Also, a timer is included in this area.

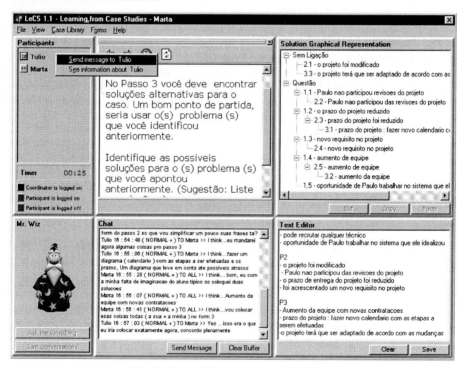

Fig. 1. The LeCS graphical user interface.

The browser is used to access the web pages that display the teaching and learning materials and that guide the learners through the system use. The browser window is the only one that can be drag and dropped and customised by the user.

The solution graphical representation area shows the tree that is generated by the system during the case solution development. The representation is displayed graphically as a directory tree. The nodes of the tree are numbered with the forms correspondent numbers, which are followed by the correspondent textual answer.

The text editor is an individual space where the learners can edit their individual answers. It is used to answer individually the questions posed by the system, i.e., during the part of the solution process when individual learning takes place. The individual answers edited with this tool are supposed to be used when the learners participate in the case discussion (when collaborative learning takes place).

The chat tool is quite similar to the traditional programs of this kind and is where the case study discussion takes place. The participant can, besides writing free text, (1) express his or her emotional state; (2) direct his or her message to the whole group or to a particular participant (although this message is visible by all the group); and (3) make use of sentence openers [11, 12] to scaffold conversation and facilitate the process of reaching an agreement in the case discussion.

The intervention area includes an interface agent (a Microsoft-based agent) that can be characterised as an animated pedagogical agent [13]. All the interventions that LeCS makes are presented through this agent.

3.3 Architecture

The LeCS agent-based [14] architecture (Fig. 2) is organised in a federated system. Its agents can be classified either as interface, reactive, and/or hybrid [15]. The agents communication is based on an Agent Communication Language [16]. The messages exchanged between the agents use the KQML (Knowledge Query and Manipulation Language) format [17]. The communications structure establishes that the communication does not happen directly between agents, but rather through a facilitator. The facilitator is a special program – implemented as an agent – that keeps the information about each agent in the system, and is responsible for routing the messages, working as a broker. In addition, two databases were implemented: in the first one, the facilitator stores all the necessary information in order to route the messages; in the second one, it logs all the exchanged messages. The LeCS architecture includes three classes of agents: interface agent, information agent, and advising agent. There is one information agent and one advising agent running during a session, but as many interface agents as there are participants logged on.

Interface Agent. The interface agent (cf. Fig. 1) can be characterised as an animated pedagogical agent [13]. It resides on the participant machine and all the system interventions are presented through it. A resources database contains the agent address, the name by which it is known, and its network mapping. A history database is implemented to log everything the interface agent does, including the communications with the user and the other agents. The information agent and the advising agent also have these same kinds of databases.

In addition, the interface agent stores information about the individual users: what is typed in the text editor, the number of contributions in the chat, the current step he or she is working on, the answer to each step question, and the time spent on each step (these last two functions are accomplished just by the interface agent of the group coordinator). Based on this information, the interface agent generates the interventions about timing and participation.

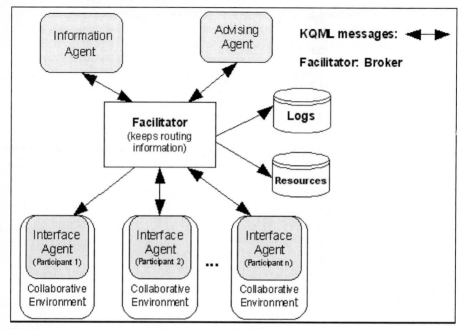

Fig. 2. The LeCS agent-based architecture.

Timing Intervention. The timing intervention consists of warning the learners when they exceed the time limit established for on-line collaborative work, which is a function of both the total time estimated for the solution of the case study and the time to respond to the particular step they are working on. The interface agent stores this information and monitors the time spent by the learners in each step. An example of a timing intervention is „You are taking too long to complete this step".

Participation Intervention. The interface agent is responsible for identifying and intervening regarding a low degree of participation of the individual learners in the case solution development. This is denoted by a small percentage of contributions during the case discussion. To accomplish this, the interface agent monitors the learners' contributions in the chat per step. If a learner remains silent for more than 50% of the estimated time for working on a particular step, the interface agent generates an intervention inviting the learner to participate. An example of a participation intervention is „Would you like to contribute to the discussion?".

Information agent. This agent stores information that is divided into two different categories: didactic material and knowledge bases. Didactic material consists of HTML pages, images, and text. The knowledge bases refer to the domain and the pedagogical knowledge: the interventions about case-specific utterances and the representation of the case solution developed by the group of students. The information agent also stores the chat interactions. Both the interface and the advising agents access the information agent.

Case-Specific Intervention. The interventions that LeCS makes about the learners' case-specific utterances are based on what is modelled in the domain knowledge base concerning the case study. In order to represent this knowledge we have adapted the idea of constraint-based modelling (CBM) [18]. CBM proposes that a domain be represented as constraints on correct solutions. As such, it is appropriate to the identification of case-specific utterance patterns that characterise a learner misunderstanding the case study contents.

In CBM [18] the unit of knowledge is called a state constraint and is defined as an ordered pair $<Cr, Cs>$, where (1) Cr is the relevance condition that identifies the class of problem states for which the constraint is relevant, and (2) Cs is the satisfaction condition that identifies the class of relevant states in which the constraint is satisfied. For our purposes, Cr is a pattern that indicates that a particular sentence is a case-specific utterance and Cs is the correct case-specific utterance. The semantics of a constraint is: if the properties Cr hold, then the properties Cs have to hold also (or else something is wrong). In LeCS, when „something is wrong" it means that there is a learners' misunderstanding of this sentence and hence the system should initiate an intervention.

In order to initiate the intervention LeCS checks for any violations of what is modelled. If the satisfaction pattern of a relevant constraint is not satisfied, then that state violates the constraint. The problem states are the input sentences, i.e., the sentences that compose the group answers to each step question entered by the group coordinator in the forms. The intervention consists of stating the correct sentence.

Graphical User Interface: Case Instructor. The LeCS graphical user interface for the case instructor allows modelling a case study to be worked on with the system. The case editor is used to edit the case study text. The constraints editor is used to edit the set of constraints for the case study. Thus, prior to run time, besides editing the case study text, the case instructor edits the constraints regarding each particular case study using the forms provided by the constraints editor (see Fig. 3). The system interventions concerning case-specific utterance patterns are generated based on these constraints. It is important to note that in the current implementation the order in which the words are used by the learners does not make any difference to the system response. Also, the constraints editor allows the case instructor to edit as many constraints as he or she deems necessary or appropriate for a given case study. In addition, it allows the modelling of more than one word to each constraint, through the use of the logic operators *and* and *or*, when the case instructor intends to contemplate different words that the students might use.

Advising Agent. The advising agent has engines to reason about the user actions, and to recognise situations in which some support is needed. With the information provided by the interface agent it executes an algorithm to generate the solution tree representation, and identifies the case-specific utterance patterns that denotes a learners' misunderstanding of the case study. When applicable, it generates an intervention about the misunderstanding, and sends the request of an intervention to the interface agent. It also generates and requests interventions to the interface agent concerning the coordination of the group work and the jumping of a step.

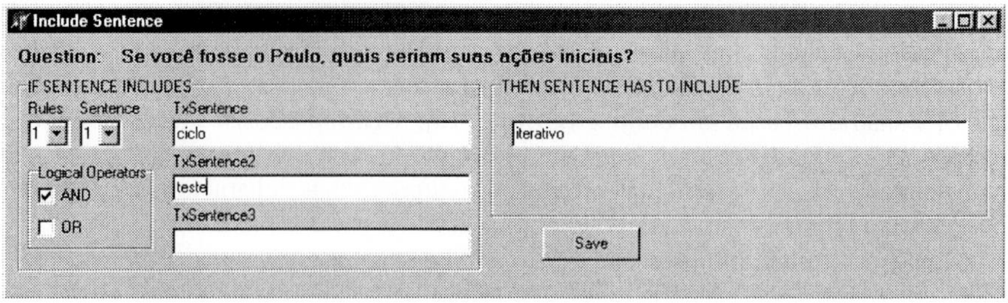

Fig. 3. The LeCS graphical user interface for the case instructor.

Solution Development Representation. LeCS dynamically generates a knowledge representation, a tree data structure [19] that represents the case solution development according to the Seven Steps approach [10]. The solution tree represents the solution path taken by the group to solve the case study and is presented to the learners on the user interface. Thus, at each step, what is displayed represents the case solution developed so far by the group (cf. Fig. 1). The objective is to help the learners choose the best envisaged solution. All the group participants see the same representation.

In order to generate this representation the connections between the tree nodes (the arcs) have to be obtained, i.e., the system has to link a node in a given level to its parent node in the previous level through some kind of reasoning. A set of if-then rules define our heuristics to make these connections [20]. Such rules, which were derived from an empirical study [21], are implemented by an algorithm.

In this algorithm the tree nodes are labelled by the sentences and the arcs are labelled by the rules. Inputs are the outcomes of each step, namely the sentences that compose the group's joint answers to each step question, which are entered in the forms. The root of the tree corresponds to the question posed by the case study and the levels represent the Seven Steps [10]. Each node refers to a component sentence of the group's answer to that step question. The algorithm has a procedure to compare the answers of two subsequent levels (steps), which aims to find out which sentence in the previous level is related to the sentence that is being analysed in the current level.

The procedure to compare the sentences verifies if a set of keywords in a sentence of a given level is also included in a sentence of the previous level. This set of keywords is defined in every step when the group coordinator fills out the form with the group's joint answer to the step question. Thus, the set of keywords of a level n sentence is compared with the words of a level $n-1$ sentence, word by word, until either one of the keywords is found, or the set of keywords is finished. In the former case (i.e., if a keyword is found) the nodes are linked. The expansion of a node is then represented precisely when it is linked with its parent node in the previous level.

Next, provided that the interface agent informs the advising agent about which step the learners are currently working on, one level is added to the tree, and the procedure to compare the sentences is executed again. The final state of the tree represents all (ideally) alternative solutions that can be generated through the Seven Steps approach.

Group Coordination Intervention. LeCS coordinates the group through the Seven Steps [10]. To accomplish this, when starting a session the group should define a coordinator: a group member who is responsible for filling out the forms with the group's joint answers to the step questions. In this way, the contributions gleaned from the various participants regarding the step answers are integrated into the joint answers. This means that the forms are disabled to all the other group members except the coordinator, and LeCS coordination function is accomplished based on the group coordinator actions. He or she, in a certain sense, defines to the system the pace in which the group proceeds in the solution development. Thus, once the coordinator fills out the forms of a particular step question and moves on to the next step, the system „knows" which step the group should be working on. For instance, if any of the learners access a web page different from the one referring to that step, the system will prompt him or her a notification, warning that the group is working on a different step. An example of this kind of intervention is „The group is working on step x". At any time during the solution process the group can decide to change its coordinator.

Missing Step Intervention. LeCS does not constrain the learners by requiring them to complete all the Seven Steps [10]. We believe this behaviour is avoided by the solution tree representation and the answers that the group is supposed to enter in every step. However, if the learners still jump a step, LeCS intervenes notifying the group. An example of this kind of intervention is „You have just jumped step x".

4   Conclusion and Future Work

In this paper we have presented LeCS, an agent-based system for supporting learning from case studies. We provided a theoretical background about the learning from case studies method and gave an overview of the system, describing its graphical user interface, agent-based architecture, and agents' functions.

As future work we plan to test LeCS with pairs of subjects in an experiment along the same lines as the empirical study described in [21]. In LeCS next version we intend to make the adjustments indicated by these experimental results and to tackle issues such as the recognition of many solution paths and student modelling.

Acknowledgements. This research is funded by grant no. 68.0057/01-3, Kit Enxoval, ProTem-CC, CNPq, Brazil.

References

1. Rosatelli, M.C., Self, J.A., Thiry, M.: LeCS: A Collaborative Case Study System. In: Frasson, C., Gauthier, G., VanLenh, K. (eds.): Intelligent Tutoring Systems. Springer-Verlag, Berlin (2000) 242–251
2. Christensen, C.R., Hansen, A.J.: Teaching with Cases at the Harvard Business School. In: Christensen, C.R., Hansen, A.J. (eds.): Teaching and the Case Method: Text, Cases, and Readings. Harvard Business School, Boston, MA (1987) 16–49

3. Shaw, E., Ganeshan, R., Johnson, W.L., Millar, D.: Building a Case for Agent-Assisted Learning as a Catalyst for Curriculum Reform in Medical Education. In: Lajoie, S.P, Vivet, M. (eds.): Artificial Intelligence in Education. IOS Press, Amsterdam (1999) 509–516

4. Mühlenbrock, M., Hoppe, H.U.: A Collaboration Monitor for Shared Workspaces. In: Moore, J.D., Redfield, C.L. Johnson, W.L. (eds.): Artificial Intelligence for Education. IOS Press, Amsterdam (2001) 154–165

5. Greer, J., McCalla, G., Cooke, J., Collins, J., Kumar, V., Bishop, A., Vassileva, J.: The Intelligent Helpdesk: Supporting Peer-Help in a University Course. In: Goettl, B.P., Halff, H.M., Redfield, C.L., Shute, V.J. (eds.): Intelligent Tutoring Systems. Springer-Verlag, Berlin (1998) 494–503

6. Constantino-González, M.A., Suthers, D.D.: A Coached Collaborative Learning Environment For Entity-Relationship Modeling. In: Frasson, C., Gauthier, G., VanLenh, K. (eds.): Intelligent Tutoring Systems. Springer-Verlag, Berlin (2000) 324–333

7. Constantino-González, M.A., Suthers, D.D., Icaza, J.I.: Designing and Evaluating a Collaboration Coach: Knowledge and Reasoning. In: Moore, J.D., Redfield, C.L. Johnson, W.L. (eds.): Artificial Intelligence for Education. IOS Press, Amsterdam (2001) 176-187

8. Prada, R. Machado, I.,Paiva, A.: TEATRIX: Virtual Environment for Story Creation. In: Frasson, C., Gauthier, G., VanLenh, K. (eds.): Intelligent Tutoring Systems. Springer-Verlag, Berlin (2000) 464–473

9. Shulman, L.S.: Toward a Pedagogy of Cases. In: Shulman, J.H. (ed.): Case Methods in Teacher Education. Teachers College Press, Columbia University, New York, NY (1992) 1–30

10. Easton, G.: Learning from Case Studies. Prentice Hall, London (1982)

11. McManus, M.M., Aiken, R.M.: Monitoring Computer-Based Collaborative Problem Solving. Journal of Artificial Intelligence in Education 6 (4) (1995) 307–336

12. Robertson, J., Good, J., Pain, H.: BetterBlether: The Design and Evaluation of a Discussion Tool for Education. International Journal of Artificial Intelligence in Education 9 (1998) 219–236

13. Lester, J.C., Converse, S.A., Stone, B.A., Kahler, S.E., Barlow, S.T: Animated Pedagogical Agents and Problem-Solving Effectiveness: A Large-Scale Empirical Evaluation. In: du Boulay, B., Mizoguchi, R. (eds.): Artificial Intelligence in Education. IOS Press, Amsterdam (1997) 23–30

14. Franklin, S., Graesser, A.: Is It an Agent or Just a Program? A Taxonomy for Autonomous Agents. In: Müller, J., Wooldridge, M.J., Jennings, N.R. (eds.): Intelligent Agents III. Springer-Verlag, Berlin (1997) 21–35

15. Nwana, H.S.: Software Agents: An Overview. The Knowledge Engineering Review 11 (3) (1996) 205–244

16. Genesereth, M.R., Ketchpel, S.P: Software Agents. Communications of the ACM 147 (1994) 48–53

17. Labrou, Y., Finin, T.: A Proposal for a New KQML Specification. Tech. Rep. CS-97-03, Computer Science and Electrical Engineering Department, University of Maryland Baltimore County (1997)

18. Mitrovic, A., Ohlsson, S.: Evaluation of a Constraint-Based Tutor for a Database Language. International Journal of Artificial Intelligence in Education 10 (1999) 238–256

19. Russell, S.J., Norvig, P.: Artificial Intelligence: A Modern Approach. Prentice Hall, Englewood Cliffs, NJ (1995)

20. Rosatelli, M.C., Self, J.A.: A Collaborative Case Study System for Distance Learning. International Journal of Artificial Intelligence in Education 13 (2002) to appear

21. Rosatelli, M.C., Self, J.A.: Supporting Distance Learning from Case Studies. In: Lajoie, S.P., Vivet, M. (eds.): Artificial Intelligence in Education. IOS Press, Amsterdam (1999) 457–564

Emergent Diagnosis via Coalition Formation

Carine Webber[*] and Sylvie Pesty

Laboratoire Leibniz – IMAG
46, avenue Felix Viallet
38031 Grenoble Cedex France
{Carine.Webber, Sylvie.Pesty}@imag.fr
http://www-leibniz.imag.fr/

Abstract. This paper presents a mechanism of coalition formation where agents solve a problem of diagnosis. Our approach considers that a diagnosis may be seen as the result of an emergent process where findings (at a microscopic level) are interpreted by entities (at a macroscopic level). At the micro-level agents interact and form coalitions. At the macro-level specialized agents are able to interpret coalition formation and infer a diagnosis. Our domain of application is student modelling and in this framework we conceive it as a diagnosis task where a 'state of conceptions' is ascribed to a student based on his/her problem-solving activities.

1 Introduction

According to Maxion, diagnosis is a form of high-level pattern recognition of symptoms or symbols and it may be one emergent property of certain complex systems [6]. Usually diagnosis is defined as a process of identifying a situation or a system condition from its intrinsic characteristics. Additionally, a diagnosis may allow a system to adapt itself to the immediate constraints of the environment, to resources reallocation, and to the different categories of users.

Essentially, we assume that a diagnosis is a process where microscopic observable findings are recognised by macroscopic entities and they may determine global system's behaviour. For instance, in the case of user-adapted applications, a limited set of elements observed from user interactions may permit a system to diagnose the user's level of expertise and adjust its behaviour according to it. In this case, the level of expertise ascribed to a user could be the result of a diagnosis process.

Systems having multiple interacting components and a behaviour that cannot be simply inferred from the behaviour of the components are qualified as complex [9]. Diagnosis, as a product, may be an emergent property of some complex systems. Multi-agent approach brings some advantages for modelling complex systems since: (1) its application is not dependent on the number of agents (contrarily to certain approaches where a large number of elements is necessary); (2) agents can have heterogeneous behaviours; (3) interactions of different levels of complexity are allowed; (4)

---

[*] Scholar of Capes/Cofecub, Brazil.

F.J. Garijo, J.C. Riquelme, and M. Toro (Eds.): IBERAMIA 2002, LNAI 2527, pp. 755–764, 2002.

it is applicable to several domains (social sciences simulations, computational economy, ecology, physics, and so on).

The idea that systems constituted of several agents having simple behaviour (a behaviour described by a few rules, for instance) can show a dynamic global behaviour having properties not easily predictable (even if the external condition are known) is exploited in this paper. A few examples have demonstrated such emergent and unpredictable behaviour. For instance, simulations in the domain of voting theory have shown how parties emerge from voters' choices [8,11]. Also, experiments in computational economics have illustrated the emergence of markets based on the behaviour of agents representing costumers and vendors [12] as well as the emergence of social classes and social norms [1]. In a similar fashion, the two domains apply coalition formation mechanisms to simulate and study social behaviours. But beyond simulation purposes, coalitions are as well applied to problem solving. Task allocation has been one of the most applicable examples of coalition formation [10]. Most recently, electronic marketplace has shown to enclose enough dynamic aspects to constitute an excellent testbed for mechanisms of coalition formation.

The work we describe here considers diagnosis as a problem-solving task and we propose to solve it by coalition formation. In addition, we assume that user modelling, more specifically student modelling, is a process of diagnosing the 'state of conceptions' hold by an student in interaction with a learning environment [13]. The diagnosed conceptions are ascribed to the student and kept in his/her student model to guide pedagogical decisions (the choice of problems, advices, etc.) of Baghera, a distance learning environment [13]. The framework we propose for student modelling is based on the model of conceptions [2], developed in mathematics education.

This paper is organised as follows. Next section briefly describes the theoretical framework of our approach. Third section introduces the multi-agent systems for diagnosing conceptions. Fourth section describes the elements composing the system and mechanisms for coalition formation. Finally, some experiments realised are described.

2 Theoretical Framework

2.1 Emergence

An emergent system is characterised by having a behaviour that cannot be predicted from a centralised and complete description of the component units of the system [5]. In emergent systems, the overall behaviour is the result of a great number of interactions of agents obeying very simple laws. The overall behaviour cannot be anticipated by simple reduction to individual behaviours, following a logico-deductive model, but it is rather conditioned by the immediate surroundings, like other agents and objects in the environment.

Very often the definition of emergence is attached to the notion of levels and detection [3]. For this reason diagnosis can be effectively seen as an emergent property of certain complex systems, since in a diagnosis process lower-level symptoms or symbols are recognised by higher-level entities [6]. Note that emergent objects have a representation distributed over many different elements. Each of these elements may take part of many different objects simultaneously. This may be observed in the classifier systems proposed by Forrest [5], in the system for diagnosis of communication networks [6], and in the emergence of conceptions discussed in this paper.

2.2 Conception Theory

Conception theory was developed in mathematics education with a cognitive and didactical foundation [2]. In this model a conception is characterised by a quadruplet C (P, R, L, Σ) where:

-P represents a set of problems;
-R represents a set of operators involved in the solutions of problems from P;
-L is a representation system allowing the representation of P and R;
-Σ is a control structure (details are given at section 3.1).

An element from any set can contribute to the characterisation of several different conceptions; for example two conceptions may share problems in their domain of validity or may have common operators. For the sake of brevity it is not possible to give in this paper more details about this theory. However, we propose the examples presented in figures 1 and 2.

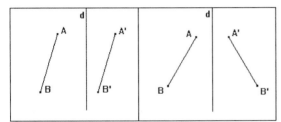

Fig. 1. Parallelism   **Fig. 2.** Reflection

Figure 1 presents a construction made by a student holding a misconception stating that "if two line segments are symmetrical then they are parallel". Figure 2 was constructed by a student holding the correct conception of reflection.

In order to illustrate how diagnoses occur, we examine the problem described on figure 3.

Problem statement: Let ABC be an equilateral triangle. A' is symmetrical to A with respect to line d. L is the middle point of [AB], M is the middle point of [BC], and N is the middle point of [AC]. P is the intersection point of lines (LM) and (CA'). O is the intersection point of lines (NM) and (BA'). What is the symmetrical line segment of [NM] with respect to line d? Construct your proof.

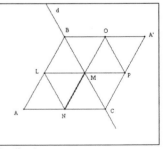

Fig. 3. A problem in the domain of reflection

In this problem students are asked to prove, using geometrical properties of reflection, that the line segment [NM] has a symmetrical object with respect to the axis d. Let's consider one strategy to solve it, which consists on proving each step from table 1. In the case of step 6, we consider four alternatives (6.a, 6.b, 6.c and 6.d) in order to exemplify how students holding different conceptions would express the solution. First, consider the proof composed by steps 1-2-3-4-5-6.a where the student has proven that [OM] is the symmetrical line segment of [NM]. This solution, by the operators used to construct it (6.a1-6.a7), characterizes the so-called misconception of 'central symmetry'.

Table 1. Possible strategies to solve the problem

1		A'BC is an equilateral triangle
2		ABA'C is a lozenge ([AB]//[CA'] and [BA']//[AC])
3		[AB]//[CA']; [AB]//[NO]; [NO]//[CA']
4		O is the middle point of [A'B]
5		P is the middle point of [A'C]
6.a	1	M is its own symmetrical point with respect to d
	2	As [AC]//[BA'] and
	3	N is the middle point of [AC] and
	4	O is the middle point of [A'B] and
	5	Line segments [NM] and [OM] have the same size
	6	O is the symmetrical point of N
	7	So, [OM] is the symmetrical line segment of [NM] with respect to point M
6.b	1	M is its own symmetrical point with respect to d
	2	Line segments [NM] and [PM] have the same size
	3	[NP] is perpendicular to axis d
	4	P is the symmetrical point of N
	5	So, [PM] is the symmetrical line segment of [NM] with respect to d
6.c	1	As [NO] // [CA'] and [NM]//[PA']
	2	As [NM] and [PA'] are parallels and have the same size, they are symmetrical.
	3	P is the symmetrical point of N
	4	A' is the symmetrical point of M
	5	So, [PA'] is the symmetrical line segment of [NM] with respect to d
6.d	1	As [NO] // [CA'] and [NM]//[CP]
	2	As [NM] and [CP] are parallels and have the same size, they are symmetrical.
	3	P is the symmetrical point of N
	4	A' is the symmetrical point of M
	5	So, [CP] is the symmetrical line segment of [NM] with respect to d

The second alternative (1-2-3-4-5-6.b) gives the correct answer ([PM] is the symmetrical segment of [NM]) and its attached to the conception of reflection. Third (1-2-3-4-5-6.c) and forth (1-2-3-4-5-6.d) alternatives, even though they give different answers, they characterize the same misconception of 'parallelism'. In these cases (6.c and 6.d), students state that *two line segments are symmetrical if they are parallel and have the same size* and it is possibly an inversion of the correct operator, which states that *two parallel line segments having the same size are symmetrical with respect to a parallel axis.*

It is important to note that a diagnosis is based on a sequence of problems solved by the student. Different problems in a well-oriented sequence permit the construction of a student model having enough information to characterize student's conceptions in a specific domain of knowledge [13].

2.3 Voting Theory

Voting models are widely used in social sciences and have their roots in Game Theory. Social sciences research about voting has been investigating new approaches to studying voting schemes, voter behaviour, and the influences of manipulation of votes and insincere voting. Studies based on simulation of elections have led to models providing explanations to voter behaviour, so as explanations to group decisions and coalition formation.

In the domain of multi-agent systems, voting theory has been used as a technique for reaching consensus in a negotiation process and group-decision making [7]. In the simulation of coalitions formation, agents have been used to demonstrate how it occurs from individual voter preferences [8].

Furthermore, it has been shown that emergent structures can be resultant of a voting process. Schreiber [8] has demonstrated through multi-agent simulations that elites and parties are emergent consequences of the behaviour and preferences of voters.

In essence our interest in voting theory relies on the possibility of capturing group decision as well as modelling the influence of an agent preference over the preferences of the rest of agents.

Our approach is based on spatial models of simulation of voting behaviour. Spatial voting theory has its origins in the field of Political Science [11]. This model assumes that political issues can be quantified and therefore voters and candidates can be represented by points in a so-called *issue space*. Similarly, each candidate is described by a platform position in the issue space.

Usually this space is viewed as the Euclidian vector space R^I having I dimensions. Each voter is represented by a vector in the issue space, called ideal point that represents its opinion on each issue. In these models, voters form coalitions with other voters close to them in the issue space. Coalitions start with a small number of voters and possibly form coalitions with other coalitions to increase their potential. A hierarchy of coalitions is built until a coalition is created with the majority of voters. The coalition with the majority rules and the competing coalitions adapt platforms to gain greater support. Each voter may represent a single voter or a team of voting people. Agents may be voters or coalitions and, in the last case, they may represent an aggregation of voters but having no votes by themselves. The action in this model takes place only in the issue space.

3 Multi-agent Architecture

We have employed the AEIO methodology [4] for the multi-agent-oriented analysis and design of our diagnosis system. This methodology considers the problem to be modelled as composed by four elements: Agents, Environment, Interactions and Organization. The first step of the methodology consists in defining the four elements and then they can be formalised.

We propose a multi-agent system where, at a microscopic level, agents behave and interact and, at a macroscopic level, coalitions emerge. The emergence of coalitions is interpreted as the emergence of a diagnosis of student's conceptions.

The conception theory allows to model student's conceptions. However, conceptions are not elements possible to be directly observed. Observable elements are operators used by student, the problem solved, the language used to express them, and theoretical control structures. For this reason, the micro-level is composed by elements (from the quadruplet) defining a conception. At the macro-level, conceptions can be seen as sets of agents of four categories: problems, operators, language and control. Each element from the quadruplet is the core of one particular agent.

3.1 Agents

An agent, in a given time slot, can be either active or inactive. This state can vary according to changes it perceives in its environment. The first action of any agent is to check whether the element it represents is present in the environment. In the presence of the element, the agent becomes satisfied. Once satisfied, the agent takes part in the issue space and it is able to form coalitions. Notice that an agent knows previously to which conceptions the element it represents belongs. A description of the role of each category of agents is given below.

Problem Agents. A problem agent becomes satisfied when the category of problems it represents is present in the environment. In the domain of reflection, a category of problems is described by four didactical variables named: line of symmetry orientation, segment orientation, angle formed between line of symmetry and line segment and intersection formed between the line of symmetry and line segment. The combination of the different values that these didactical variables could take, leads to problems of different complexity, allowing to focus on different aspects of the learning of reflection and most important, allowing the expression of different conceptions.

Operator Agents. An operator agent becomes satisfied when the element r of R it represents, is present in the solution constructed by the student. An operator transforms a problem in a new problem. A sequence of operators leads to the problem solution. An example of an operator is as follows: *if two symmetrical objects have one point in common, then this point belongs to the axis of symmetry.*

Language Agents. A language agent becomes satisfied when the element l of L it represents, is present in the solution constructed by the student. It can be a grammar, a graphical representation, or an alternative way of expression allowing the description of the problem and the solution. Given that our problems ask for the construction of a proof, the language is based on a grammar (for reasons of brevity it is not presented here).

Control Agents. A control agent becomes satisfied when the element s of Σ it represents, is present in the solution constructed by the student. During problem solving, learners choose operators, validate actions and validate the final result. Each of these three decisions is guided by control structures. Control elements are perceptive when attached to the fact that the learner makes assertions based on something "seen" on the screen and uses this information to take and validate decisions. On the other hand, control structures are theoretical when a learner bases decisions and validations on knowledge previously acquired. Reflection involves many visual elements of control; for instance, a learner holding the conception of parallelism may accept that a problem is correctly solved when the image line segment "looks" parallel to the original line segment. In the case of our system, we consider only theoretical controls and some perceptive controls that can be expressed by means of a proof.

3.2 Environment

The environment represents the external world that agents have to deal with and it co-evolves with the agents. In the environment there is a representation of the problem solved by the student, the proof corresponding to the student's solution and the issue space where coalition formation takes place.

3.3 Interactions

Agents interact with the environment and through these interactions they transform the environment (issue space). Such transformation generates changes in agents' behaviours. The cycle of interactions continues indefinitely until no more coalitions can be formed or merged.

3.4 Organisations

We apply a dynamic approach to conceive organisations. We consider that agents form dynamically coalitions when they are needed to solve a problem. Our approach of coalitions formation is based on emergent approach. Moreover, it is considered that once the problem is solved, coalitions are not applicable anymore for a later processing.

In the next section we proceed with the formalisation of the most relevant components of the model.

4 Formal Description

4.1 Environment

The environment is described by a set $\mathsf{Env} = \{PR, SP, IS\}$ where PR represents the problem that the student has solved, SP represents the proof constructed by the student as a solution to the problem PR and IS is the issue space. The space of votes $\mathbb{R}^I$ is the Euclidian space having I dimensions. The number of conceptions to be diagnosed determines the number of space dimensions. Voters are represented by a position in the space corresponding to their 'opinions' about candidate conceptions. A position is represented by a vector $v \in \mathbb{R}^I$.

4.2 Diagnosis Problem

Given a set of conceptions $C = \{c_1,...,c_i\}$, a set of n agents $A = \{a_1,...,a_n\}$ and a set representing the state of the environment $Env = \{PR, SP, IS\}$, the problem we propose to solve consists in assigning one or more (possibly concurrent) groups G of agents (G $\subset$ A) representing the state of student's conceptions reflected in the environment.

4.3 Agent

Let C be a set of conceptions $\{c_1,c_2...,c_n\}$. Consider that any conception c_i in C is defined by a quadruplet (P_i,R_i,L_i,Σ_i) where :
- P_i is a set of problems $\{p_1,p_2,...,p_n\}$ of c_i ;
- R_i is a set of operators $\{r_1,r_2,...,r_n\}$ of c_i ;
- L_i is a grammar for the expression of P_i and R_i of c_i ;
- Σ_i is a set of control structures $\{\sigma_1,\sigma_2,..., \sigma_n\}$ of c_i.

Let A be a set of agents $\{a_1,...,a_n\}$. Let K_i be a set of n candidate conceptions $\{k_{11}, k_{12}...,k_{in}\}$ for an agent a_i where $K_i \subset C$. Let E be a set of elements $\{e_1,..., e_n\}$ from the conceptions formalisation and assume that e_i is the element in the core of an agent a_i. About any element e_i it is known that $e_i \in P_i | e_i \in R_i | e_i \in L_i | e_i \in \Sigma$. Let Q_i be the set of acquaintances of an agent a_i (acquaintances are detailed later in this paper). Finally, V is the set of votes $\{v_{1k},...,v_{ik}\}$ given by the agent to preferred candidate conception from K_i. An agent a_i is defined by : an identifier N_i , an internal state $S_i \in$ {satisfied, unsatisfied}, a set of acquaintances Q_i a set of candidates conceptions K_i , an element e_i , a satisfaction function $f_i(e_i, Env)$ and a vector V_i representing its starting position in the Euclidian space $\mathbb{R}^l$.

4.3.1 Agent Behaviour

Agents are created in an unsatisfied state and the satisfaction function may change its state to a satisfied one. When an agent becomes satisfied, it creates its vector to be added to the issue space. Since it is situated in the issue space, its acquaintances are set (section 4.3.2). Agents start forming coalitions with each member of its acquaintances list. Any agent may take part in any number of coalitions. Once an agent takes part in proposed coalitions, it can accept or refuse it. Besides, an agent tries to merge coalitions in which it takes part into. And finally, agents are free to enter and leave coalitions at any time. When it is not possible anymore for an agent to execute any of these actions, the agent stops. The major steps of the algorithm defining the behaviour of an agent are as follows: (1) initialise the data structure; (2) calculate agent's power of voting; (3) set agent's acquaintances; (4) while (list of proposed coalitions is not empty): (4.1) propose coalitions; (4.2) accept coalitions; (4.3) refuse coalitions; (4.4) calculate coalition's utility; (4.5) merge coalitions; and (4.6) abandon a coalition.

4.3.2 Finding Acquaintances

The most important feature of an agent is its voting vector, representing its choice of candidate conceptions. Its acquaintances represent a list of agents that are spatially located close to it in the issue space.

Let a_α and a_β be two different agents. Let V_α and V_β be vectors representing respectively the positions of a_α and a_β in the space $\mathbb{R}^l$. Let Q_α and Q_β be the set of acquaintances (initially empty) of respectively a_α and a_β. We assume that a_α and a_β are acquaintances if they satisfy the neighbourhood condition.

Neighbourhood condition is calculated by the formula of Euclidian distance between the two vectors V_α and V_β. The two agents satisfy the condition if the distance is a value under a specific threshold and in this case, $a_\beta \in Q_\alpha$ and $a_\alpha \in Q_\beta$. Otherwise, a_α and a_β are not acquaintances to each other.

4.4 Coalition Formation

A coalition is a nonempty subset Co of A and it has as utility value the sum of utilities of all agents belonging to it. We follow the traditional approach of coalition formation in the domain of multi-agent systems [7].

The initial number of coalitions is reduced since the initial coalitions are formed between any two agents situated spatially close in the issue space. When agents form a coalition it has a status of proposed coalition and when it is accepted by all of its members it becomes an accepted coalition.

5 Experiment and Final Considerations

We have run a diagnosis considering the proof presented at section 2.2 (steps 1-2-3-4-5-6c). The multi-agent system is composed of 101 agents, distributed as follows: 60 operator agents, 30 problem agents and 11 control agents. As explained before, agents become active if the element represented is found in the proof. For this experiment, 13 agents (1 problem agent, 10 operator agents and 2 control agents) have become active. The issue space has 4 dimensions, representing 4 conceptions on reflection (central symmetry, oblique symmetry, parallelism and reflection). Vectors of agents' opinions have 1 in each dimension representing a good candidate and 0 otherwise. The threshold for calculating acquaintances was 1.

In the end of this experiment two coalitions have emerged. The greatest number of coalitions, reached at interaction number 150, was of 134 coalitions. Coalition formation was stopped when this number was reduced to 2 coalitions and no relevant changes in the system were observed. The coalition having the greatest utility is considered the winner. Among the 13 agents involved in the diagnosis process, 10 of them took part of the winner coalition. In this experiment, the winner represents the misconception of parallelism; the second coalition represents the conception of reflection (the correct one). The result is satisfactory and it indicates that the student possibly holds the misconception of parallelism. We interpret the fact that a weak coalition (representing reflection) has appeared as a result of correct operators and properties present in the student's proof; they certainly must have a weight in the diagnosis process. However, incorrect operators have appeared as well and they have induced the diagnosis of parallelism by forming the strongest coalition.

As long as the diagnosis process is over, macro-agents (belonging to Baghera main multi-agent system) take pedagogical decisions based on it. For instance, tutor agents may propose new problems to confirm a diagnosis or propose a problem where incorrect procedures of resolution fail, according to pedagogical strategies.

The main challenge of this work has been to define and implement a computational framework to model student's conception supported by a theory developed in the domain of mathematics education. We start assuming that a diagnosis is a kind of problem-solving task. We have proposed in this paper to solve it by coalition formation. However, other approaches, such as those based on probabilistic models (Bayesian networks, for instance) have been studied and will be the object of new implementations.

References

1. Axtell, R., Epstein, J., Young, H.P. The emergence of classes in a multi-agent bargaining model. Center on Social and Economics Dynamics, Working paper no.9, February 2000.
2. Balacheff N., Gaudin N. Modelling students conceptions – the case of functions. Mathematical Thinking and Learning – an International Journal, 2002. (to appear).
3. Bonabeau, E.; Dessalles, J.; Grumbach, A. Characterizing Emergent Phenomena (1): A critical review. In: Revue Internationale de Systémique, vol.9, n°3, 1995, pp. 327–346.
4. Demazeau, Y. From Interactions to Collective Behaviour in Agent-Based Systems. In: Proceedings of the 1st. European Conference on Cognitive Science. Saint-Malo, France, 1995.
5. Forrest, S. Emergent Computation. Physica D 42, 1990. Elsevier Science Publishers, North-Holland.
6. Maxion, R.A. Toward diagnosis as an emergent behavior in a network ecosystem. In: Physica D 42, 1990, pp. 66–84. Elsevier Science Publishers, North-Holland.
7. Sandholm, T.W. Distributed Rational Decision Making. In: Multiagent Systems: A Modern Introduction to Distributed Artificial Intelligence, Weiβ, G., MIT Press, 1999. pp.201–258.
8. Schreiber, D. The emergence of parties: an agent-based simulation. In: The Annual Meeting of the Midwestern Political Science Association, Chicago, Illinois, 2000.
9. Schweitzer, F.; Zimmermann, J. Communication and Self-Organisation in Complex Systems: A Basic Approach. In: Knowledge, Complexity and Innovation Systems (Eds. M.M. Fischer, J. Frohlich) Advances in Spatial Sciences. Springer, Berlin 2001, pp.275–296.
10. Shehory, O.; Kraus, S. Task allocation via coalition formation among autonomous agents. In: Proceedings of IJCAI'95, Montreal. pp.655–661.
11. Stadler, B.M.R. Adaptative Platform Dynamics in Multi-Party Spatial Voting. Adv.Complex Systems (1999) vol.2, 101–116.
12. Vriend, N.J. Self-Organization of Markets: An Example of a Computational Approach. Computational Economics, 1995, Vol. 8, No. 3, pp. 205–231.
13. Webber, C.; Pesty, S.; Balacheff, N. A multi-agent and emergent approach to learner modelling. In: ECAI 2002 - Proceedings of the 15th European Conference on Artificial Intelligence. F. van Harmelen (ed.), IOS Press, Amsterdam, 2002. pp.98–102.

Adaptive Bayes

João Gama and Gladys Castillo

[1] LIACC, FEP – University of Porto
Rua Campo Alegre, 823
4150 Porto, Portugal
jgama@liacc.up.pt
[2] Department of Mathematics
University of Aveiro
Aveiro, Portugal
gladys@mat.ua.pt

Abstract. Several researchers have studied the application of Machine Learning techniques to the task of user modeling. As most of them pointed out, this task requires learning algorithms that should work on-line, incorporate new information incrementality, and should exhibit the capacity to deal with concept-drift. In this paper we present Adaptive Bayes, an extension to the well-known naive-Bayes, one of the most common used learning algorithms for the task of user modeling. Adaptive Bayes is an incremental learning algorithm that could work on-line. We have evaluated Adaptive Bayes on both frameworks. Using a set of benchmark problems from the UCI repository [2], and using several evaluation statistics, all the adaptive systems show significant advantages in comparison against their non-adaptive versions.

Keywords: User Modeling, Machine Learning, Adaptive Bayes, Incremental Systems

1 Introduction

The task of user modeling is a challenging one for machine learning. Observing the user behavior is a source of information that machine learning systems can use to build a predictive model of user future actions. This is a challenging task because it requires incremental techniques that should work on-line. Moreover, as pointed out in [14]:

> User modeling is known to be a very dynamic modeling task - attributes that characterize a user are likely to change over time. Therefore, it is important that learning algorithms be capable of adjusting to these changes quickly.

Nowadays, with the explosion of the World Wide Web, has increased the need of tools for automatic acquisition of user profiles, retrieval of relevant information, personalized recommendation, etc. All these tasks could use learning techniques. One of the machine learning algorithms most used in these tasks is naive Bayes

F.J. Garijo, J.C. Riquelme, and M. Toro (Eds.): IBERAMIA 2002, LNAI 2527, pp. 765–774, 2002.
© Springer-Verlag Berlin Heidelberg 2002

[13,11,10]. Naive Bayes has been studied both on pattern recognition literature [5] and in machine learning [9]. Suppose that $P(Cl_i|\boldsymbol{x})$ denotes the probability that example $\boldsymbol{x}$ belongs to class i. The zero-one loss is minimized if, and only if, x is assigned to the class Cl_k for which $P(Cl_k|\boldsymbol{x})$ is maximum [5]. Formally, the class attached to example x is given by the expression:

$$argmax_i P(Cl_i|\boldsymbol{x}) \tag{1}$$

Any function that computes the conditional probabilities $P(Cli|x)$ is referred to as discriminant function. Given an example $\boldsymbol{x}$, the Bayes theorem provides a method to compute $P(Cl_i|\boldsymbol{x})$: $P(Cl_i|\boldsymbol{x}) = P(Cl_i)P(\boldsymbol{x}|Cl_i)/P(\boldsymbol{x})$

$P(\boldsymbol{x})$ can be ignored, since it is the same for all the classes, and does not affect the relative values of their probabilities. Although this rule is optimal, its applicability is reduced due to the large number of examples required to compute $P(\boldsymbol{x}|Cli)$. To overcome this problem several assumptions are usually made. Depending on the assumptions made we get different discriminant functions leading to different classifiers. In this work we study one type of discriminant function that leads to the naive Bayes classifier.

1.1   The Naive Bayes Classifier

Assuming that the attributes are independent given the class, $P(\boldsymbol{x}|Cl_i)$ can be decomposed into the product $P(x_1|Cl_i) * ... * P(x_a|Cl_i)$. Then, the probability that an example belongs to class i is given by:

$$P(C_i|\boldsymbol{x}) \propto P(Cl_i) \prod_j P(x_j|Cl_i) \tag{2}$$

which can be written as:

$$P(Cl_i|\boldsymbol{x}) \propto log(P(Cl_i)) + \sum_j log(P(x_j|Cl_i)) \tag{3}$$

The classifier obtained by using the discriminant function 2 and the decision rule 1 is known as the naive Bayes Classifier. The term naive comes from the assumption that the attributes are independent given the class.

1.2   Implementation Details

All the required probabilities are computed from the training data. To compute the prior probability of observing class i, $P(Cl_i)$, a counter, for each class is required. To compute the conditional probability of observing a particular attribute-value given that the example belongs to class i, $P(x_j|Cl_i)$, we need to distinguish between nominal attributes, and continuous ones. In the case of nominal attributes, the set of possible values is a enumerable set. To compute the conditional probability we only need to maintain a counter for each attribute-value and for each class. In the case of continuous attributes, the number of possible values is infinite. There are two possibilities. We can assume a particular distribution for the values of the attribute and usually the normal distribution is assumed. As alternative we can discretize the attribute in a pre-processing phase. The former has been proved to yield worse results than the latter [3]. Several methods for discretization appear in the literature. A good discussion about discretization is presented in [4]. In [3] the number of intervals is fixed to $k = min(10; nr.\ of\ different\ values)$ equal width intervals. Once the attribute has been discretized, a counter for each class and for each interval is used to compute the conditional probability.

All the probabilities required by equation 3 can be computed from the training set in one step. The process of building the probabilistic description of the dataset is very fast. Another interesting aspect of the algorithm is that it is easy to implement in an incremental fashion because only counters are used.

Domingos and Pazzani [3] show that this procedure has a surprisingly good performance in a wide variety of domains, including many where there are clear dependencies between attributes. They argue that the naive Bayes classifier can approximate optimality when the independence assumption is violated as long as the ranks of the conditional probabilities of classes given an example are correct. Some authors[7,8] suggest that this classifier is robust to noise and irrelevant attributes. They also note that the learned theories are easy to understand by domain experts, most due to the fact that the naive Bayes summarizes the variability of the dataset in a single probabilistic description, and assumes that these are sufficient to distinguish between classes.

2   Iterative Bayes

In a previous article [6] we have presented an extension to naïve Bayes. The main idea behind Iterative Bayes is to improve the probability associated with predictions. The naive Bayes classifier builds for each attribute a two-contingency table that reflects the distribution on the training set of the attribute-values over the classes. Iterative Bayes iterates over the training set trying to improve the probability associated with predictions on the training examples.

2.1   An Illustrative Example

Consider the Balance-scale dataset. This is an artificial problem available at the UCI repository [2]. This data set was generated to model psychological experimental results. This is a three-class problem, with four continuous attributes. The attributes are the left weight, the left distance, the right weight, and the right distance. Each example is classified as having the balance scale tip to the right, tip to the left, or to be balanced. The correct way to find the class is the greater of $left\_distance \times left\_weight$ and $right\_distance \times right\_weight$. If they are equal, it is balanced. There is no noise in the dataset.

Because the attributes are continuous the discretization procedure of naive Bayes applies. In this case each attribute is mapped to 5 intervals. In an experiment using 565 examples in the training set, we obtain the contingency table for the attribute $left\_W$ that is shown in Table 1.

Table 1. A naive Bayes contingency table

Attribute: left_W (Discretized)					
Class	I1	I2	I3	I4	I5
Left	14.0	42.0	61.0	71.0	72.0
Balanced	10.0	8.0	8.0	10.0	9.0
Right	86.0	66.0	49.0	34.0	25.0

After building the contingency tables from the training examples, suppose that we want to classify the following example:

```
left_W:1, left_D: 5, right_W: 4, right_D: 2, Class: Right
```

The output of the *naive Bayes* classifier will be something like:

```
Observed Right Classified Right   [ 0.277796 0.135227 0.586978 ]
```

It says that a test example that it is observed to belong to class *Right* is classified correctly. The following numbers are the probabilities that the example belongs to each one of the classes. Because the probability $p(Right|x)$ is greater, the example is classified as class *Right*. Although the classification is correct, the *confidence* on this prediction is low (59%). Moreover, taking into account that the example belongs to the training set, the answer, although correct, does not seems to fully exploit the information in the training set.

The method that we propose begins with the contingency tables built by the standard naive Bayes scheme. This is followed by an iterative procedure that updates the contingency tables. The algorithm iteratively cycle through all the training examples. For each example, the corresponding entries in the contingency tables are updated in order to increase the confidence on the correct class. Consider again the previous training example. The value of the attribute left_W is 1. This means that the values in column $I1$ in table 1 are used to compute the probabilities of equation 2. The desirable update will increase the probability $P(Right|x)$ and consequently decreasing both $P(Left|x)$ and $P(Balanced|x)$. This could be done by increasing the contents of the cell (I1;Right) and decreasing the other entries in the column I1. The same occurs for all the attribute-values of an example. This is the intuition behind the update schema that we follow. Also the amount of correction should be proportional to the difference $1 - P(C_{predict}|x)$. The contingency table for the attribute *left_W* after the iterative procedure is given in figure 2[1]. Now, the same previous example, classified using the contingency tables after the iteration procedure gives:

```
Observed Right Classified Right   [ 0.210816 0.000175 0.789009 ]
```

---

[1] The update rules tries to maintain constant the number of examples, that is the total sum of entries in each contingency table. Nevertheless we avoid zero or negative entries. In this case the total sum of entries could exceed the number of examples.

Table 2. A naive Bayes contingency table after the iteration procedure

Attribute: left_W (Discretized)				
Class	I1	I2	I3	I4	I5
Left	7.06	42.51	75.98	92.26	96.70
Balanced	1.06	1.0	1.0	1.0	1.08
Right	105.64	92.29	62.63	37.01	20.89

The classification is the same, but the confidence level of the predict class increases while the confidence level on the other classes decreases. This is the desirable behavior.

The iterative procedure uses a hill-climbing algorithm. At each iteration, all the examples in the training set are classified using the current contingency tables. The evaluation of the actual set of contingency tables is done using equation 4:

$$\frac{1}{n}\sum_{i=1}^{n}(1.0 - max_j p(C_j|x_i)) \tag{4}$$

where n represents the number of examples and j the number of classes. The iterative procedure proceeds while the evaluation function decreases. To escape from local minimum we allow some more iterations till the maximum of a user-defined look-ahead parameter.

The pseudo-code for the adaptation process is shown in Figure 1. To update the contingency tables, we use the following heuristics:

1. If an example is correctly classified then the increment is positive, otherwise it is negative. To compute the value of the increment we use the following heuristic: $(1.0 - p(Predict|x))$ if the example is correctly classified and $-P(Predict|x)$ if the example is misclassified.
2. For all attribute-values observed in the given example, the increment is added to all the entries for the predict class and $increment/\#Classes$ is subtracted to the entries of all the other classes. That is, the increment is a function of the confidence on predicting class $Predict$ and of the number of classes.

The contingency tables are updated each time a training example is seen. This implies that the order of the training examples could influence the final results. This update schema guarantees that after one example is seen, the probability of the prediction in the correct class will increase. Nevertheless, there is no guaranty of improvement for a set of examples.

The starting point for Iterative Bayes is the set of contingency tables built by naïve Bayes. In these work we study Adaptive Bayes, an algorithm that use the update schema of Iterative Bayes in an incremental mode.

```
Function AdaptModel (Model, Example, Observed, Predicted)
//Compute the increment
If(Predicted<>Observed) Then   delta = (1-P(Predicted|Example))
Else                           delta = - (P(Predicted|Example))

// the increment is used to update the contingency tables
For each Attribute
  For each Class
    If (Class == Predicted) Then
          Model(Attribute,Class,AttributeValue) += delta
      Else
          Model(Attribute,Class,AttributeValue) -= delta/#Classes
    Endif

  Next Class
Next Attribute
return: Model
End
```

Fig. 1. Pseudo-code for the Adaptation Model function.

3   Adaptive Bayes

Given a decision model and new classified data not used to built the model what should we do? Most of the time a new decision model is built from the scratch. Few systems are able to adapt the decision model given new data. The naïve Bayes classifier is naturally incremental. Nevertheless most interesting problems are not stationary, that is the concepts to learn could change over time. In these scenarios forget old data to incorporate concept drift is a desirable property. An important characteristic of Iterative Bayes is the ability to adapt a given decision model to new data. This property can be explored in the context of concept-drift. The update schema of Iterative Bayes could be used to an incremental adaptive Bayes able to deal with concept drift.

We consider two adaptive versions of naïve Bayes: incremental adaptive Bayes and on-line adaptive Bayes. The former built a model from the training set updating the model (the set of contingency tables) once after seeing each example (there is no iterative cycling over the training set). The latter works on an on-line framework: for each example the actual model makes a prediction. Only after the prediction the true decision (the class of the example) is known.

The base algorithm for the incremental adaptive Bayes is presented in figure 2. The base algorithm for the on-line adaptive Bayes is presented on figure 3[2].

---

[2] In the initialization step the contingency tables are initialized randomly with the constrain that for all attributes the sum of the entries for each class is constant.

```
Function IncrementalBayes(Training Set, Adaptive)
inputs: The training set, Adaptive Mode

Initialization: Model = initialise all counters to zero
For each Example in the Training Set
    IncrementCounters(Model, Example, Observed)
    If Adaptive=TRUE Then AdaptModel(Model, Example, Observed, Predicted)
  Next Example
Return Model
End
```

Fig. 2. Pseudo-code for the Incremental Adaptive Bayes.

3.1 Discussion

The adaptive step of our algorithm has clear similarities with the gradient descent method used to train a perceptron. For example, both use an additive update schema. The perceptron learning procedure uses the gradient vector of partial derivatives of the parameters. Adaptive Bayes don't use derivatives, but uses a *likelihood* function that increases at each step. Under this perspective, the method could be related with the generalized Expectation-Maximization approach[12] that only requires an improvement of the likelihood function. As pointed out in [1] *"the gradient-based approach is closely related to a GEM algorithm, but this relation remains unclear."*.

4 Experimental Evaluation

We have evaluated all variants of Adaptive Bayes in a set of benchmark problems from the UCI repository [2]. The design of experiments for the incremental

```
Initialisation: Model = Randomly  initialise all counters

Function OnLineBayes(Example, Model, Adaptive)
   Predicted <- PredictClass(Model, Example)
   Observed <- Class of Example
   IncrementCounters(Model, Example, Observed)
   If Adaptive = TRUE Then AdaptModel(Model, Example, Observed, Predicted)
   Return Model
End
```

Fig. 3. Pseudo-code for the On-Line Adaptive Bayes.

versions of the algorithms is the standard 10-fold cross validation. All the algo-rithms incrementally built a model from the training set and the model is used to classify the test set. The evaluation statistics is the average of the 10 error rates. While the incremental naive Bayes should generate exactly the same model as its batch version, the adaptive Bayes could generate a different model. For the on-line versions, the experimental set-up was designed as follows. All the avail-able data is presented to the algorithm in sequence. Each example is classified with the actual model. After the prediction the algorithm modifies its decision model. The evaluation statistic is the percentage of misclassified examples. This process is repeated ten times using different permutations of the dataset.

For each dataset the algorithm has access to some information about the problem domain. This information is similar to the information existing in the file *.names* used in C4.5. For each attribute it is known the name, the type, and the set of possible values for each nominal variable. Moreover, for each continuous variable the algorithm also knows the *range* of possible values.

The results are presented on table 3. The best accuracy achieved on each dataset is shown in bold. A summary of evaluation statistics is presented on table 4. The first and second lines present the average and geometric mean of the error across all datasets. The third line shows the average rank of incremental and on-line models, computed for each dataset by assigning rank 1 to the best algorithm and 2 to the second best. The fourth line shows the average ratio of the error rate. This is computed for each dataset as the ratio between the error of the adaptive model and the non-adaptive model. The sixth line shows the number of significant differences using the *Wilcoxon Matched-Pairs signed-rank test* with p-value less than 0.99. The Wilcoxon Test is also used to compare the error rate of pairs of algorithms across datasets[3]. The last line shows the *p values* associated with this test for the results on all datasets.

All evaluation statistics shows the advantage of using the proposed adapta-tion process. The adaptive process seems to be more advantageous in the on-line framework. The reader should take into account that we cannot compare the results between the incremental and on-line versions: the performance statistics are very different.

We should note that the computational complexity of all the algorithms is the same: $O(n)$ where n represents the number of examples[4].

5   Conclusions and Future Work

Several researchers have studied the application of Machine Learning techniques to the task of user modeling. Learning algorithms for user modeling should work on-line, incorporate new information in an incremental way, and with the capac-ity to deal with concept-drift.

---

[3] Each pair of data points consists of the estimate error on one dataset and for the two learning algorithms being compared.

[4] Assuming that the number of examples is much greater than the number of at-tributes.

Adaptive Bayes 773

Table 3. Comparison between adaptive versus non-adaptive naive Bayes on incremental and on-line frameworks.

Dataset	Incremental		On-Line	
	Naive Bayes	Adaptive	Naive Bayes	Adaptive
Adult	17.671 ±0.6 +	**14.748 ±0.5**	17.818 ±0.1 +	**14.870 ±0.1**
Australian	**13.750 ±0.4**	13.839 ±0.5	14.899 ±0.5	**14.841 ±0.6**
Balance	**8.539 ±0.3**	8.747 ±0.4	14.560 ±0.8	**14.160 ±0.7**
Banding	22.822 ±1.1	**21.542 ±1.1**	23.740 ±1.6	**23.529 ±1.1**
Breast	**2.659 ±0.1**	2.774 ±0.1	**3.119 ±0.3**	3.176 ±0.2
Cleveland	**18.035 ±0.6**	18.134 ±1.0	**18.581 ±1.1**	18.977 ±1.1
Credit	14.060 ±0.3	**13.869 ±0.3**	15.652 ±0.8	**15.449 ±0.4**
Diabetes	23.763 ±0.6	**23.203 ±0.7**	25.547 ±0.7	**24.674 ±0.8**
German	**24.400 ±0.5 −**	25.510 ±0.6	**26.710 ±0.5**	27.620 ±0.4
Glass	36.900 ±1.5	**35.710 ±1.8**	42.570 ±2.1	**41.916 ±1.4**
Heart	17.407 ±0.7 +	**16.370 ±0.8**	18.556 ±1.7	**18.370 ±2.2**
Hepatitis	19.308 ±1.1 +	**16.348 ±0.9**	21.097 ±1.9 +	**19.226 ±1.7**
Ionosphere	11.158 ±0.6	**10.437 ±0.5**	13.903 ±1.2 +	**12.108 ±0.9**
Iris	**6.133 ±0.5**	6.133 ±0.5	10.133 ±1.6	**9.867 ±1.3**
Letter	29.989 ±1.2 +	**28.262 ±1.3**	33.075 ±0.2 +	**31.907 ±0.3**
Mushroom	4.766 ±0.0 +	**1.307 ±0.0**	5.695 ±0.1 +	**2.008 ±0.1**
Satimage	18.943 ±0.1 +	**15.942 ±0.2**	19.133 ±0.2 +	**16.306 ±0.2**
Segment	10.948 ±0.2 +	**8.965 ±0.3**	13.312 ±0.7 +	**11.416 ±0.5**
Shuttle	3.052 ±0.6	**2.704 ±0.3**	3.173 ±0.2 +	**2.897 ±0.1**
Sonar	24.505 ±1.8 +	**22.759 ±2.3**	27.500 ±2.9	**26.635 ±2.3**
Vehicle	40.191 ±0.8 +	**37.866 ±1.2**	42.411 ±1.1 +	**39.870 ±0.7**
Votes	9.820 ±0.2 +	**8.760 ±0.4**	10.207 ±0.5 +	**9.149 ±0.7**
Waveform	19.076 ±0.2 +	**15.615 ±0.3**	19.961 ±0.6 +	**16.904 ±0.4**
Wine	4.258 ±0.6 +	**3.176 ±1.0**	8.258 ±1.9	**7.303 ±2.0**

Table 4. Summary of Results.

Dataset	Incremental		On-Line	
	Naive Bayes	Adaptive	Naive Bayes	Adaptive
Arithmetic Mean	16.76	15.53	18.73	17.63
Geometric Mean	13.40	11.79	15.55	14.03
Average Rank	1.75	1.25	1.88	1.12
Error Ratio	1	0.91	1	0.92
Nr. Wins	6	18	3	21
Nr. Significant Wins	1	12	0	11
Wilcoxon Test	−	0.0002	−	0.0006

In this paper we have studied the behavior of adaptive Bayes, a new incremental algorithm based on naive Bayes that could work on-line. Adaptive Bayes uses the same adaptation strategy used in Iterative Bayes - a batch classifier. The main idea behind Iterative Bayes is to improve the probability associated with predictions. This strategy is used on Adaptive Bayes to guide the adaptation process. In a set of benchmark datasets, the adaptation process shows clear advantages over the non-adaptive naive-Bayes both on incremental and on-line frameworks.

The next step of this work is to incorporate the on-line adaptive Bayes in a WEB based teaching system.

Acknowledgments. Gratitude is expressed to the financial support given by the FEDER, the Plurianual support attributed to LIACC, and ALES project (POSI/39770/SRI/2001).

References

1. John Binder, Daphne Koller, Stuart Russel, and Keiji Kanazawa. Adaptive probabilistic networks with hidden variables. *Machine Learning*, 29:213–243, 1997.
2. C. Blake, E. Keogh, and C.J. Merz. UCI repository of Machine Learning databases, 1999.
3. Pedro Domingos and Michael Pazzani. On the optimality of the simple Bayesian classifier under zero-one loss. *Machine Learning*, 29:103–129, 1997.
4. J. Dougherty, R. Kohavi, and M. Sahami. Supervised and unsupervised discretization of continuous features. In A. Prieditis and S. Russel, editors, *Machine Learning Proc. of 12th International Conference*. Morgan Kaufmann, 1995.
5. R.O. Duda and P.E. Hart. *Pattern Classification and Scene Analysis*. New York, Willey and Sons, 1973.
6. J. Gama. Iterative Bayes. In S. Arikawa and K. Furukawa, editors, *Discovery Science - Second International Conference*. LNAI 1721, Springer Verlag, 1999.
7. I. Kononenko. Semi-naive Bayesian classifier. In Y. Kodratoff, editor, *European Working Session on Learning -EWSL91*. LNAI 482 Springer Verlag, 1991.
8. P. Langley. Induction of recursive Bayesian classifiers. In P.Brazdil, editor, *Proc. of European Conf. on Machine Learning*. LNAI 667, Springer Verlag, 1993.
9. Tom Mitchell. *Machine Learning*. MacGraw-Hill Companies, Inc., 1997.
10. Kamal Nigam, Andrew Kachites Mccallum, Sebastian Thrun, and Tom Mitchell. Text Classification from Labeled and Unlabeled Documents using EM. *Machine Learning*, 39:1–32, 2000.
11. Michael Pazzani and Daniel Billsus. Learning and revising user profiles: the identification of interesting web sites. *Machine Learning*, 27:313, 1997.
12. Brian D. Ripley. *Pattern Recognition and Neural Networks*. Cambridge University Press, 1996.
13. Mia Stern, Joseph Beck, and Beverly Woolf. Naive bayes classifiers for user modelling. In *Proceedings of the User Modelling Conference*. Morgan Kaufmann, 1999.
14. G. Webb, M. Pazzani, and D. Billsus. Machine learning for user modelling. *User Modelling and User-adapted Interaction*, 11:19–29, 2001.

A Dynamic Scheduling Algorithm for Real-Time Expert Systems

Antonio M. Campos and Daniel F. García

Department of Informatics
University of Oviedo
Campus de Viesques, Asturias 33271, SPAIN
{campos, daniel}@atc.uniovi.es

Abstract. Computational characteristics of real-time expert systems have been the subject of research for more than a decade. The computation time required to complete inferences carried out by expert systems present high variability, which usually leads to severe under-utilization of resources when the design of the schedule of inferences is based on their worst computation times. Moreover, the event-based aperiodic activation of inferences increases the risk of transient overloads, as during critical conditions of the controlled or monitored environment the arrival rate of events increases. The dynamic scheduling algorithm presented in this article obtains statistical bounds of the time required to complete inferences on-line, and uses these bounds to schedule inferences achieving highly effective utilization of resources. In addition, this algorithm handles transient overloads using a robust approach. During overloads our algorithm completes nearly as many inferences as other dynamic scheduling algorithms, but shows significantly better effective utilization of resources.

1   Introduction

The potential benefits of using expert systems in real-time environments has sparked research on algorithms and techniques to fulfill the temporal requirements and overcome the limitations of using expert systems in these environments. Various research projects have addressed the high variability of time required to complete inference processes, and the inexistence of tight bounds for inference time [1], [2], [3]. In addition to this formal research, the demand by industry for adequate software development tools has motivated the appearance of fast inference engines and complete development environments, such as G2 (by Gensym Corp.), Cogsys KBS (by Cogsys Ltd.) or Rtie (by Talarian Corp.). Some of these tools are suitable for building expert systems for on-line continuous operation or soft real-time expert systems.

The applicability of some of these tools for building real-time expert systems for automating or monitoring complex industrial processes has been evaluated. Although some of the tools claim to be the definitive solution for developing real-time expert systems, most of them do not recognize the concept of a real-time task as a computation that must satisfy a time restriction. So, management of temporal requirements in design decisions is complicated. Furthermore, the scheduling policy

F.J. Garijo, J.C. Riquelme, and M. Toro (Eds.): IBERAMIA 2002, LNAI 2527, pp. 775–784, 2002.

is a key element of the design to fulfill the temporal requirements in real-time systems. Few of the commercial tools provide the system designer with any scheduling mechanisms. Some of them only allow the application of static priorities to the rules, which does not provide sufficient predictability of the system. In addition, when a real-time expert application developed with commercial tools must co-exist with other applications in the same computer, there is no a clear way of knowing how the expert application is using computer resources. This makes it impossible to control CPU assignment among all running applications. Clearly, there is a need for a specific real-time expert system based on a compact (embeddable) and easily connectable architecture, which is perfectly integrated in the operating system, and allows scheduling inferences following a well-defined policy.

The solution presented in this work involves serializing the use of a single inference engine by all the tasks in the system. This approach allows the use of a fast, general-purpose inference engine without truth maintenance support, because the working memory content will not be corrupted by the preemption of one running inference by another. In real-time expert systems, data input/output duration can usually be considered negligible when compared to inference duration. Thus, the behavior of our real-time expert system can be analyzed as the problem of scheduling a set of inference tasks, whose main characteristic is a highly variable computation time, in a non-preemptive way. The arrival of tasks, associated to changes in the environment, is aperiodic. This characteristic, added to the highly variable computation time of tasks, makes dynamic scheduling necessary. In addition, event-based aperiodic arrival of tasks can easily lead to transient overload conditions, related to critical conditions of the environment to be monitored or controlled. During these transient overloads the performance of a real-time expert system must be predictable. In summary, a dynamic, non-preemptive scheduling algorithm for tasks with aperiodic arrival and highly variable computation times, with graceful degradation during transient overloads, has been developed and evaluated.

The rest of the paper is structured as follows. In the next section the system model is presented. Section 3 presents the scheduling algorithm. The final sections describe the load and performance metrics used and include the results obtained.

2   System Model

The real-time expert system is composed of a set of n tasks, called intelligent tasks, $\{\tau_1, \tau_2, \ldots, \tau_n\}$. Intelligent tasks are invoked aperiodically by events (stimulus) received from the environment, and produce a corrective reaction to this environment through the adequate interface. Arrival times, a_i, of events are not known in advance (the system is *non-clairvoyant*), and there is no lower bound on the duration between occurrences of the same event. Worst-case computation times, c_i, of the intelligent tasks are not known in advance (the high variability of execution time makes bounds obtained by static analysis very pessimistic), but an on-line estimation of the worst-case computation time, $\hat{c}_i$, will be calculated, as is described later. Each intelligent task must meet a time restriction defined by its relative deadline, d_i. If a task does not meet this requirement, the task is said to have failed. Missing a deadline would not jeopardize the behavior of the system, although the benefit of executing a task that misses its deadline is zero (*firm* tasks). In this first approach, the benefit (the utility) of executing a task before its deadline has been considered constant for each task. Thus, an intelligent task, τ_i, is defined by the 4-tuple $(a_i, \hat{c}_i, d_i, u_i)$, where a_i is the arrival time of the event that invokes the task, $\hat{c}_i$ is a estimation of the worst-case computation time, d_i is the relative deadline of the task and u_i is the benefit obtained if the task execution finishes prior to its deadline.

Intelligent tasks are broken down into three activities: *data acquisition, inference* and *actuation*. During *data acquisition*, data from the environment are obtained and pre-processed. During *inference*, conclusions about the environment are obtained sharing a single unit resource in exclusive mode, the *inference kernel*. Only the inference activity of one task can be executed by the system at a time. *Actuation* applies corrective actions over the environment if necessary. In general, the resources used by acquisition and actuation activities of tasks do not require exclusive access. So two or more of these activities of different tasks can use resources concurrently. The usage of resources by both data acquisition activities and actuation activities are negligible compared with the consumption of resources of the inference activity (in particular, the highest consumption of resources, up to 90%, takes place during the pattern-matching phase [4] of the inference activity).

In summary, at a given moment, t, the expert control system can be modeled as a set of n firm aperiodic tasks $\{\tau_1, \tau_1, ..., \tau_n\}$, defined by 4-tuples $(a_i, \hat{c}_i, d_i, u_i)$, which compete for the use of an exclusively usable single unit resource, the *inference kernel*.

The sum of the utilities of all the tasks in the set is the total value of the task set. The task set is said to be feasible when all the tasks of the set can be completed before their deadlines. If one or more tasks fail, the system is said to be overloaded.

3   Scheduling Algorithm

The goal of an algorithm that schedules the execution of intelligent tasks is to find a schedule for a given task set which obtains as high a value as possible, while fulfilling the restrictions imposed by the environment and the internal architecture of the expert system itself. In this paper we assume that the expert system runs in a uniprocessor machine.

Exclusive access imposed by the inference kernel makes the problem of finding a feasible schedule NP-Hard [5]. It is well known that optimal pre-emptive scheduling algorithms for uniprocessor systems are not optimal when preemption is not allowed, as with Lowest Laxity First algorithm [6], or remain optimal but under more restrictive conditions, as with Earliest Deadline First (EDF) algorithm. EDF was proven to be optimal in a non-preemptive task model if the processor does not remain idle while there are tasks waiting to be executed [7][8]. As the expert system is non-clairvoyant, there is no reason to remain idle while there are tasks waiting in the system, so the EDF algorithm is optimal in the sense of feasibility. In addition, deadline scheduling means that it is not necessary to know computation times of tasks in advance, ratifying the EDF selection. Unfortunately, the performance of EDF is dramatically reduced in overload conditions, so the effect of a transient overload can be catastrophic [9]. This risk is unacceptable for most real-time applications, and in particular for real-time expert systems, as overload conditions are normally related to critical conditions in the environment

Overloads can be handled using two basic techniques [10]. The first technique, *guarantee*, handles overloads by using acceptance tests, and rejecting tasks that makes the task set unfeasible. The second technique, *robust*, is an extension of the first technique, in which rejected tasks enter a reject queue from where they can be rescued for execution or finally discarded.

The best effort technique is not adequate for real time expert systems with non-preemptive restrictions, as it does not predict overloads. If EDF is used running without overload prediction, catastrophic situations will result. Nor are guarantee techniques adequate because of the high variability of the execution time of intelligent tasks. Consequently, using guarantee techniques there is a risk of under-utilization of resources. So, only robust-like approaches are able to achieve adequate scheduling for this kind of system.

Our algorithm uses statistical information, obtained on-line, about the intelligent tasks in order to detect a system overload. If the system is not overloaded, the intelligent task to run is selected following EDF policy. If, on the contrary, an overload is detected, the task to execute is selected as a function of the probability of success and the expected utility. Tasks remain in the system until they have missed their deadlines.

3.1   Overload Detection

The high variability of the computation time of intelligent tasks reduces the validity of the feasibility analysis of the complete set of tasks in the expert system. It is quite normal to have time after executing one intelligent task or to miss a deadline due to an unexpectedly long computation, so feasibility analysis loses validity as the number of executed tasks of the analyzed set increases. Also, as intelligent tasks can share data stored in the working memory of the real-time expert system, the computation time of intelligent tasks can be influenced by the computation of previous tasks. The aperiodic arrival of new intelligent tasks can also make long feasibility analysis invalid. Thus, this work predicts overloads after the execution of every task using all the tasks in the system, but considering only one-task-ahead execution, as is explained below.

Let $\alpha \in \Re$, $0 \le \alpha < 1$ be the maximum admissible probability of missing a deadline, chosen at design time. If $\hat{c}_i$ is an estimator of the worst-case computation time of task τ_i with a *confidence* *level* of $1-\alpha$ (that is $P(c_i \le \hat{c}_i) \ge 1-\alpha$ $0 \le \alpha < 1$), the laxity, L_i, of the task τ_i, defined in (1), can be obtained at any instant, t.

$$L_i = a_i + d_i - \hat{c}_i - t \tag{1}$$

If the laxity of the task is negative, the probability that task τ_i will fail is given by (2).

$$L_i < 0 \Rightarrow P(\tau_i \ fails) > \alpha \tag{2}$$

Before executing a task, the laxities of all the tasks in the system are calculated. If the laxity of even one task, i.e. τ_i, is negative, the expert system is considered overloaded because the probability of failing when executing τ_i is inadmissible.

Tchebychef's inequality [11] allows us to estimate the worst-case execution time of intelligent tasks using the sample mean and the sample variance of the past execution times of the tasks.

Let $\hat{\mu}_i$ and $\hat{\sigma}_i^2$ be the sample mean and the sample variance of task τ_i after $n+1$ samples of c_i, obtained recursively using (3) and (4).

$$\hat{\mu}_i = \hat{\mu}_{i,n+1} = \hat{\mu}_{i,n} + \frac{c_{i,n+1} - \hat{\mu}_{i,n}}{n+1} \tag{3}$$

$$\hat{\sigma}_i^2 = \hat{\sigma}_{i,n+1}^2 = \left(1 - \frac{1}{n}\right)\hat{\sigma}_{i,n}^2 + (n+1)(\hat{\mu}_{i,n+1} - \hat{\mu}_{i,n})^2 \tag{4}$$

If both $\hat{\mu}_i$ and $\hat{\sigma}_i^2$ are finites, given $k \in \Re, k \geq 1$ Tchebychef's inequality gives a lower bound of the probability that c_i belongs to an interval centered in $\hat{\mu}_i$ and with radius $k\hat{\sigma}_i$, as holds (5).

$$P(\hat{\mu}_i - k\hat{\sigma}_i \leq c_i \leq \hat{\mu}_i + k\hat{\sigma}_i) \geq 1 - \frac{1}{k^2} \tag{5}$$

From (5), (6) and (7) immediately follow.

$$P(c_i \leq \hat{\mu}_i + k\hat{\sigma}_i) - P(\hat{\mu}_i - k\hat{\sigma}_i \leq c_i) \geq 1 - \frac{1}{k^2} \tag{6}$$

$$P(c_i \leq \hat{\mu}_i + k\hat{\sigma}_i) \geq 1 - \frac{1}{k^2} + P(\hat{\mu}_i - k\hat{\sigma}_i \leq c_i) \tag{7}$$

As $P(\hat{\mu}_i - k\hat{\sigma}_i \leq c_i) \geq 0$, (8) can be obtained from (7).

$$P(c_i \leq \hat{\mu}_i + k\hat{\sigma}_i) \geq 1 - \frac{1}{k^2} \tag{8}$$

That is, for each value of $k \in \Re, k \geq 1$, computation time c_i of task τ_i is known to be lower than $\hat{\mu}_i + k\hat{\sigma}_i$ with a probability of $1 - 1/k^2$. From (8) we also get (9), where the value $1 - \alpha$ is the confidence level of the bound.

$$P(c_i \leq \hat{\mu}_i + k\hat{\sigma}_i) \geq 1 - \frac{1}{k^2} = 1 - \alpha \quad k \geq 1, \ 0 \leq \alpha < 1 \tag{9}$$

So, the worst-case computation time, $\hat{c}_i$, of task τ_i can be estimated using (10) with a confidence level of $1 - \alpha$.

$$\hat{c}_i = \hat{\mu}_i + k\hat{\sigma}_i = \hat{\mu}_i + \alpha^{-1/2}\hat{\sigma}_i \qquad (10)$$

Tchebychef's inequality makes no suppositions about probability distribution of computation time, so bounds obtained are usually pessimistic. As (8) also neglects the value of $P(\hat{\mu}_i - k\hat{\sigma}_i \leq c_i)$, bounds are even more pessimistic. Thus, it is not necessary to choose high values of k to obtain bounds of adequate confidence. We have determined empirically that a value of $k = 2$ or, what is the same, a confidence level of $1 - \alpha = 0.75$ are adequate for most cases.

3.2 Scheduling Policy during Overloads

If the system is overloaded, EDF must be replaced by a more adequate scheduling policy. We have observed that during overloads the result of executing a task with low probability of success is even worse for non-preemptive than for preemptive systems. If a task cannot be preempted once scheduled, all the tasks of the system may miss their deadlines if their laxity is small. For this reason, during overloads tasks are run taking their probability of success into account.

The benefit of executing tasks must also be taken into account, as it can not be the same for all tasks. Thus, in some situations it is preferable to execute a task with a lower probability of success but which will provide greater benefit if it succeeds. Locke [12] observed experimentally that running the tasks with the greatest values of the ratio u_i / c_i allows the system to achieve a utility at least as high as with any other policy.

The dynamic priority of the tasks, p_i, obtained using (11) summarizes both factors, and so was chosen as the policy to select tasks to be run during overloads.

$$p_i = \frac{L_i + \hat{c}_i}{\hat{c}_i} \cdot \frac{u_i}{\hat{c}_i} \qquad (11)$$

Tasks with high utility and high (positive) laxity have high values of p_i. Tasks with low utility and low (negative) laxity have values of p_i near zero: a task remains in the system until its deadline is missed, and at that moment $L_i = a_i + d_i - \hat{c}_i - t = -\hat{c}_i \Rightarrow L_i + \hat{c}_i = 0$.

4   Results

The results achieved using the scheduling policy presented in this work are measured using two performance metrics, the *completed task ratio* CTR (the count of tasks completed before their deadlines divided by the total number of task arrivals) and the *effective processor utilization* EPU (the time consumed executing tasks completed before their deadlines, divided by the total time consumed). Only these two measurements have been included as in most cases the number of tasks completed and the value of the effective processor utilization is enough to analyze the behavior of a system during overloads [16]. The results presented are obtained by assigning the same constant utility of 1 to all the tasks in the system. So another broadly used metric, the *hit value ratio* [10], is not included as it coincides with the completed task ratio.

Results are obtained for various sets of tasks, composed of a number of tasks, n, of 10, 25 or 50 intelligent tasks. Only results for the case of $n = 10$ are presented (see Fig. 2), as they can be safely extrapolated to the cases of 25 and 50 tasks. Computation time of tasks are random variables distributed following an Erlang distribution [17], whose probability density function is shown in (12), with $k = 2$ and variable mean value $\bar{c}_i = k / \lambda_i$.

$$f(c_i) = \frac{\lambda_i^k c_i^{k-1} e^{-\lambda x}}{(k-1)!} \quad c_i \geq 0 \tag{12}$$

Mean computation time of tasks, $\bar{c}_i$, varies uniformly from a value of 1 to a value of $\bar{c}_{max}$, where $\bar{c}_{max}$ takes the values 1, 10, 25 or 50. Relative deadlines of tasks, d_i, are defined by (13).

$$d_i = \bar{c}_i + 4 \cdot \bar{c}_i \tag{13}$$

The mean load of the system, $\bar{L}$, (see (14)), ranges from a value of 0.5 to a value of 1.5, where f_i is the arrival rate of each intelligent task.

$$\bar{L} = \sum_i \bar{c}_i f_i \tag{14}$$

For each value of n, $\bar{c}_i$ and $\bar{L}$ arrival rates of tasks, f_i, are obtained using (15).

$$f_i = \frac{\bar{L}}{\bar{c}_i \cdot n} \tag{15}$$

Each intelligent tasks contributes equally to the load of the system with a demand value of $\bar{L}/n$.

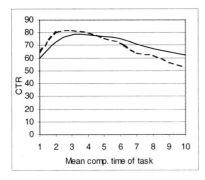 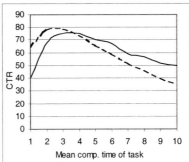

Fig. 1. CTR for each task of the set with $\bar{L} = 1.25$ (left) and $\bar{L} = 1.5$ (right).

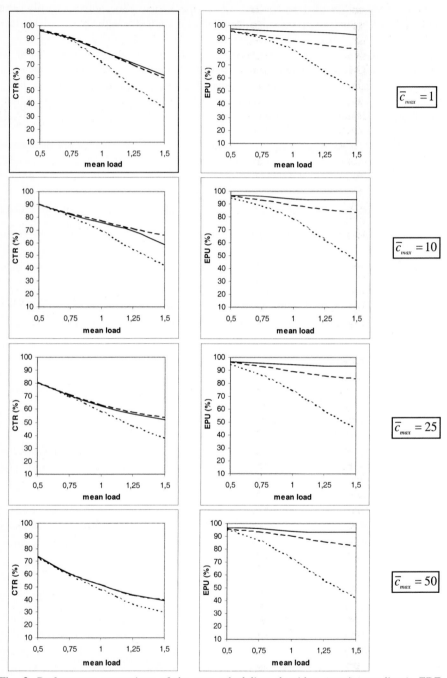

Fig. 2. Performance comparison of the new scheduling algorithm (continuous lines), EDF (dotted lines) and MVD (dashed lines) for $n = 10$ tasks.

The results are obtained from simulations of 180000 time units in length, divided in 30 batches of 6000 time units each, which assures a significance level of the measurements presented greater than 90%. Figures include results obtained by scheduling tasks following our scheduling policy, EDF policy and maximum expected $u_i / \hat{c}_i$ policy (or maximum value density, MVD). EDF has been included for reference, and it is very important to take into account the fact that tasks are removed from the system when they miss their deadline, which dramatically improves EDF performance during overloads.

Comparing the behavior of the new algorithm with the behavior of the EDF algorithm, the validity of overload detection can be affirmed, as the new algorithm behaves as well as EDF when the mean load is low, and degrades gracefully when the mean load increases. It can also be observed that the new algorithm achieves nearly the same value of CTR as the MVD algorithm, while the EPU is always better.

The better behavior of the MVD can be explained by analyzing the CTR of tasks individually for high values of the mean load, shown in Fig. 1. With $n = 10$, $\overline{c}_{max} = 10$, and values of mean load $\overline{L} = 1.25$ and $\overline{L} = 1.5$, MVD shows preference for tasks with short computation time (dashed lines), which improves the count on completed tasks with respect to the new algorithm (continuous lines), which improves the balance between the number of tasks with long and short computation time scheduled.

5   Conclusions

This work presents a new scheduling algorithm designed to be coupled with a specific real-time expert system architecture, whose main characteristic is the serialization of inferences. The algorithm exploits the observation that in non-preemptive systems deadline misses cause high performance degradation and the well-known properties of the MVD scheduling. As its performance analysis shows, the algorithm achieves highly effective utilization of resources, and nearly as high a task completion ratio as the MVD algorithm.

References

1. Barachini, F., "Frontiers in Run-Time Prediction for the Production-System Paradigm", *AI Magazine*, Vol. 15, No. 3, pp. 47-61, Fall 1994.
2. Wang, R., H. and Mok, A. K., "Response-Time Bounds of Rule-Based Programs under Rule Priority Structure", *Proc. IEEE Real-Time Systems Symposium*, pp. 142-151, 1994.
3. Cheng, A. M. K and Chen, J., "Response Time Analysis of OPS5 Production Systems", *IEEE Transactions on Knowledge and Data Engineering*, Vol. 12, No. 3, pp. 391–498, May-Jun 2000.
4. Forgy, C. L., "On the Efficient Implementacion of Production Systems", *PhD Thesis, Carnegie-Mellon University*, 1979.
5. Lenstra, J. K. and Rinnooy Kan, A. H. G., "Optimization and Approximation in Deterministic Sequencing and Scheduling: A Survey", *Annals of Discrete Mathematics*, Vol. 5, pp. 343-362, 1977.

6. George, L., Rivierre, N. and Spuri, M., "Preemptive and Non-Preemptive Real-Time Uni-Processor Scheduling", *Rapport de Reserche RR-2966, INRIA*, Le Chesnay Cedex, France, 1996.
7. Jeffay, K., Stanat, D. F. and Martel, C. U., "On Non-Preemptive Scheduling of Periodic and Sporadic Tasks with Varying Execution Priority", *Proc. IEEE Real-Time Systems Symposium*, pp. 129-139, 1991.
8. George, L., Muhlethaler, P. and Rivierre, N., "Optimality and Non-Preemptive Scheduling Revisited", *Rapport de Reserche RR-2516, INRIA*, Le Chesnay Cedex, France, 1995.
9. Locke, C. D., "Best Effort Decision Making for Real-Time Scheduling", *PhD Thesis, Carnegie-Mellon University, Computer Science Department*, Pittsburgh, PA, 1986.
10. Butazzo, G., *Hard Real-Time Computer Systems, Predictable Scheduling Algorithms and Applications*, Chapter 8, Kluwer Academic Publishers, 1997. ISBN: 0-7923-9994-3.
11. Hardy, G., Littlewood, J. E. and Pólya, G., "Tchebychef's Inequality", *Inequalities, Second Edition, Cambridge Mathematical Library*, pp. 43-45 and 123, Feb. 1998. ISBN 0-521-35880-9.
12. Jensen, E., D., Locke, C. D. And Tokuda, H., "A Time-Driven Scheduling Model for Real-Time Operating Systems", *Proc. IEEE Real-Time Systems Symposium*, pp. 112-122, 1985.
13. Gordon, A., *The COM and COM+ Programming Primer*, Prentice Hall, 2000. ISBN: 0130850322.
14. Shepherd, G., "COM Apartments", *Visual C++ Developers Journal*, Vol. 2, N. 1, February/March 1999.
15. Gärdenfors, P., and Rott, H., "Belief Revision", in Gabbay, D., Hogger, C. J. and Robinson, J. A., editors, *Handbook of Logic in Artificial Intelligence and Logic Programming*, Vol. 4, pp. 35-132. Clarendon Press, Oxford.
16. Baruah, S. K., Haritsa, J. and Sharma, N., "On-Line Scheduling to Maximize Task Completions", *Proc. IEEE Real-Time Systems Symposium*, pp. 228-236, 1994.
17. Erlang, A. K., "The Theory of Probabilities and Telephone Conversations", *Nyt Tidsskrift for Matematik B*, Vol. 20, 1909.

A Process Knowledge-Based Controller for Maneuverability Improvement of a Nonlinear Industrial Process

Salvador Carlos De Lara Jayme[1], Raul Garduño Ramírez[1],
Marino Sánchez Parra[1], Luis Castelo Cuevas[1], and Marco Antonio Carretero R.[2]

[1] Instituto de Investigaciones Eléctricas, Gerencia de Control e Instrumentación.
Av. Reforma No. 113, Col. Palmira, Temixco. 62490 Morelos, México
{sdelara, rgarduno, msanchez, lcastelo}@iie.org.mx
http://www.iie.org.mx/uci/
[2] Instituto Politécnico Nacional (IPN) SEPI-ESIME-IPN.
Unidad "Adolfo López Mateos"
Av. IPN s/n, Col. Lindavista, 07738, Méx, D.F. Edif. 5 3er. Piso
{macarretero}@hotmail.com

Abstract. This paper is concerned with the formulation of a process knowledge based controller (PKBC) for maneuverability improvement of non-linear processes operation. The capacity for empirical knowledge acquisition from artificial intelligence systems was utilized in the development of the strategy. The PKBC is a neuro-fuzzy system obtained from process data. The GT 5001 type is the selected nonlinear process, for speed control during startup operation, where the GT has to follow a specific speed path that imposes tight regulation requirements for the control system, including fast response and precision. The proposed control strategy is a feedforward-feedback one. In the feedback path a PID controller is used. In the feedforward path a PKBC provides most of the control signal for wide-range operation, diminishing the control effort on the PID controller. Simulation tests were carried on a dynamic mathematical model of the GT, and demonstrate the maneuverability improvement concerning the startup speed response.

1 Introduction

Industrial processes are dominated by nonlinear and time-varying behavior presented during changes in operating conditions and operation modes. Throughout the process behavior, startup, normal operation and shutdown, the conventional controllers have to lead the process to the desired target. These controllers belong to the PID class and have been widely used in various industrial control applications. Their almost universal use is mainly attributed to their simple structure and robust performance in a wide range of operating conditions. However, real industrial processes may have character-

F.J. Garijo, J.C. Riquelme, and M. Toro (Eds.): IBERAMIA 2002, LNAI 2527, pp. 785–794, 2002.

istics such as high-order, dead-time, nonlinearity, etc. which make the PID controller inaccurate because they are designed only to regulate the process for an operating point. Additionally, these processes may also be affected by parameter variations, noise and load disturbances.

Although operators are able to control complicated nonlinear and time varying systems after a long acquired experience, PID controllers are not good at coping with non-linearity, operational constraints and interaction between process variables [1]. In these cases the operator, based on his experience on the process, has to tune-up the controller parameters to reject the disturbances. This can lead to a good controller for disturbances rejection, but a malfunctioning controller for regulation purposes. To overcome the regulation problem, a reference feedforward control is proposed to free the PID controller of set-point tracking chores to almost exclusively deal with these events, in a more effective way.

Successful implementation of the fuzzy logic technology has become an even greater interest in the field and currently new applications, as reported in this paper, are emerging every day [8, 9]. Benefits in using fuzzy logic for control in place or besides of conventional methods in that they are easy to design, easy to implement, and generally more robust than conventional controllers [10].

The feedforward fuzzy controller is a wide range nonlinear static mapping of the reference signal and the control signal, which approximates a process steady state inverse model. The mathematical formulation of the process model is a complex and difficult task, so we take advantage of the fuzzy systems universal approximation property, to obtain a good process representation. The feedforward fuzzy controller is designed off-line from input-output data measurements using a neural network learning method, resulting in a neurofuzzy feedforward controller

Previous approaches on real applications for power control [2], considered a constant feedforward action, which is only valuable for an operating point. In this paper a wide-range feedforward controller implemented as a fuzzy system. Thus, main difference with previous approaches is the variable reference feedforward action, providing a variable gain based on the operating point throughout the unit operating range.

This paper is organized in four sections; Section 2 describes the PKBC formulation, which is based on input-output process data along the whole operating range of the process, Section 3 presents the knowledge acquisition process for the PKBC design, Section 4 shows a case study based on the gas turbine operation. Simulation tests were carried out with a dynamic mathematical model of a GE-5001 Turbogas unit. Speed control over the whole operating range shows a better performance overcoming the change on the operating point during startup. Finally, Section 5 summarizes and concludes this work.

2 PKBC Formulation

The PKBC is a fuzzy controller with a TSK (Takagi-Sugeno-Kan) inference fuzzy system where the consequents of the inference rules are a linear combination of the system inputs. The design problem is based on the constant consequent values determination and the membership functions parameters in the antecedent part of each rule. This problem is resolved by using a neural supervised learning procedure from a collection of process input-output data. The convenience of this design procedure resides on the obtained fuzzy inference systems that can be directly implanted, without additional adjustment and may be utilized as a base design to improve the process performance.

Several methods may be used to design the PKBC from input-output data. The combination of neural networks and fuzzy systems in a homogenous structure, synthesizes both techniques advantages in a complementary way. Neural network learning characteristics make easy the fuzzy system tuning. We can find several methods to synthesize fuzzy systems, including GARIC, NEFCON, FuNe, ANFIS, etc [3]. The method known as adaptive neuro-fuzzy inference system (ANFIS) was used here [4]. This technique allows the implementation of multi-input single output first order TSK-type model with weighted average defuzzification.

The PKBC is based on the TSK [5] model that is the best suited for implementation purposes, since it significantly reduces complexity at the output defuzzyfication layer, using input-related output hyper planes instead of output membership functions. The ANFIS method allows first order TSK controller design with the following IF-THEN rules:

$$IF\ u_1\ is\ A_1^j\ and \cdots and\ u_n\ is\ A_n^j\ THEN\ b_i = g_i(.)$$
$$b_i = g_i(.) = a_{i,0} + a_{i,1}(u_1)^2 + \cdots + a_{i,n}(u_n)^2 \tag{1}$$

where An represent the input fuzzy sets, $a_{i,n}$ are the constants and $j=1,2,...n$ is the rule number in the fuzzy processor. For the functional fuzzy system the crisp output is obtained by the discrete center-of-mass defuzzyfier:

$$y = \frac{\sum_{i=1}^{R} b_i \mu_i}{\sum_{i=1}^{R} \mu_i} \tag{2}$$

where μ_i represent the membership values of the inputs.

Given an arbitrary set of inference rules, the ANFIS method adjust the membership functions An, and the $a_{i,n}$ constants of the consequent part by a neural learning standard process until the desired input-output pattern set is reproduced. To accomplish this, the TSK fuzzy system is represented as a feedforward neural network with n inputs, N rules, with five layers with N neural processing units in layers L_1 to L_4, and a single neural unit in layer five, L_5. Layer 0 with n distribution units is not considered as a neural processing layer (Figure 1).

The implementation of the controller is based on the structure depicted in figure 2, which consists of a feedforward and feedback control processors. The feedback control processor is a PID based controller that provides the control signal u_{fb}, and it is designed for disturbances rejection. The feedforward control processor provides the control signal u_{ff}, and it is designed to provide the maneuverability needed during the startup operation.

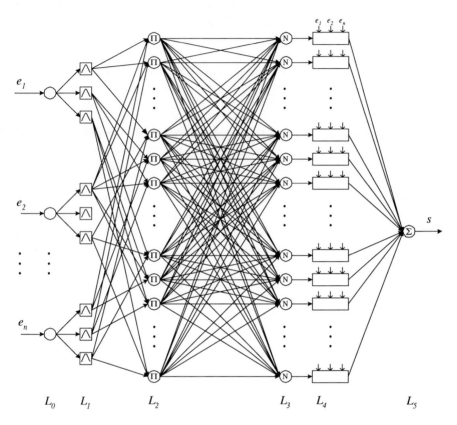

Fig. 1. TSK fuzzy-system structure as a feedforward neural-network

The initial idea of the control structure comes from the two degrees of freedom linear control system [6]. For the feedforward path the PKBC proposed is based on the inverse steady state behavior is approximated, as a fuzzy system, using input-output process data along the whole operating range of the nonlinear industrial process. This configuration permits to maneuver the process to follow the reference, while the feedback controller reduces disturbances.

3 Knowledge Acquisition

Fuzzy systems theory proposes a systematic method for mapping human knowledge into an input-output nonlinear relation. The operator's process knowledge can be represented by a PKBC integrated to the existing control strategy. The implementation of the PKBC is based on the steady-state data along the operation range of the nonlinear process.

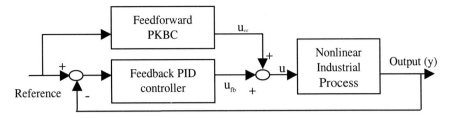

Fig. 2. Feedforward/feedback control configuration.

The inverse model is obtained by measuring the steady state process behavior. The input to the PKBC is given by the current output of the nonlinear process, and the output of the PKBC is given by the current demand to the process (control valve). Once the PKBC is designed, and included in the control system, its input is supplied by the reference (setpoint) to obtain the feedforward contribution to the final control element demand (control valve).

A classical feedback control loop, one input one output, is shown in figure 3, where r, u, and y are the reference, the control and the output signals respectively. w is the disturbance effect on the control loop, $G(s)$ and $G_c(s)$ are the process and controller transfer functions, and s is the Laplace operator. The closed loop transfer function is:

$$Y(s) = [1 + G(s)G_c(s)]^{-1}[G(s)G_c(s)R(s) + W(s)] \qquad (3)$$

where $R(s)$, $W(s)$, and $Y(s)$ are the Laplace transfer functions of r, w, and y, respectively.

Clearly, only by $G_c(s)$ design is difficult to achieve a precise reference pursuit (speed regulation), $Y(s)=R(s)$. In order to accomplish this, a feed forward control path may extend the control loop from the reference, as shown in figure 4. The closed loop function would be:

$$Y = [1 + GG_c]^{-1} [(GG_r + GG_c)R + (GG_c)W] \qquad (4)$$

where, G_r is the feed forward control transfer function, omitting for brevity the Laplace operator dependency.

In theory, G_r can be designed as:

$$G_r = G^{-1} \qquad (5)$$

to accomplish a perfect following for reference changes, and G_c can be designed to compensate for disturbances effects.

Feedforward and feedback controllers can be complementary. Feedforward control actions allows fast following on reference signal changes. Feedback control actions give a corrective action over a lower time scale to compensate for model inaccuracies presented by the feedforward control, measurements errors and non-measured disturbances.

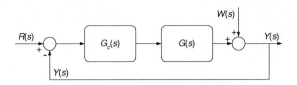

Fig. 3. Typical closed control loop.

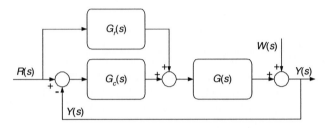

Fig. 4. Loop with feedforward control trajectory.

4 Case Study: Gas Turbine Operation

4.1 Combustion Turbine System Description

Figure 5 shows the main components of the GT system: a starting device, the air compressor, the gas turbine and the generator. All are on a common shaft. The starting device is an induction motor which accelerates the turbine from initial start, through fuel ignition and light off, and continue to aid acceleration to about 25% of rated speed; at this point the fuel combustion process maintains acceleration and the starting motor is turned off. The compressor accepts filtered inlet air from the environment and passes it through 17 stages to produce a compression ratio, which yields a discharge pressure of combustion airflow. Three bleed valves bypass portion of the compressor air during startup to produce stabilizing turbine acceleration and avoid the *surge* phenomenon. An Inlet Guide Vane (IGV) at the front of the compressor is modulated to improve GT performance.

The combustion chamber burns natural gas in the proper air mixture to provide hot gases for the two-stage power turbine. The fuel throttle valve is controlled to develop speed turbine following the speed profile first, and megawatt generation later, within appropriate turbine exhaust gasses temperature limits.

As driving force of the electric generator, safety, availability, and efficiency are important factors to be searched with an effective control system to:
- Restore stability of turbine operation after a disturbance and to obtain precision response in normal operation
- Follow the acceleration startup curve to minimize fuel consumption before synchronization and minimize the high vibration periods

- Keep the main variables of the unit, temperature and pressure, close to the operating limits without exceeding them to preserve the unit

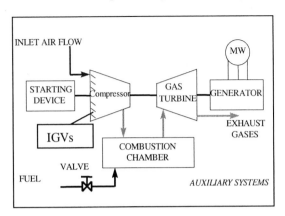

Fig. 5. Combustion Turbine System

The operation procedures of the GT generate important process disturbances, fig. 6:

Starting motor outage: when the speed path follows the desired acceleration pattern and reaches the 25% of rated speed, the starting motor goes out. Then the GT experiences a speed disturbance that the control system has to overcome. This is shown by an exhaust temperature variation that may cause thermal shock in the gas turbine mechanical parts

Bleed valves closing and IGVs opening: When the GT reaches the 95% of rated speed the bleed valves close and the IGVs open. The combined effect increases the combustion chamber's pressure, decreases the exhaust gases temperature and consequently the GT experiences another speed disturbance, over-speed transient, which needs to be corrected by the control system.

4.2 Simulation Results

The simulation platform was the Matlab/Simulink programming environment, where the GT dynamic mathematical model was developed [7]. The design data was obtained by GT simulation under feedback control. This PID feedback controller was tuned to get the best process response. Once the tuning process was finished, the simulation established the training data.

The inverse model of the GT was obtained by measuring the steady state process behavior. The input to the PKBC is given by the output speed of the GT, and the desired output of the PKBC is given by the current demand to the control valve.

After several essays with different membership partitions and forms, the resulting system is a one-input one-output fuzzy system, composed of seven rules, seven triangular membership functions and seven crisp values. Performance of the FF path to reproduce the inverse static behavior of the process was verified by reproducing the

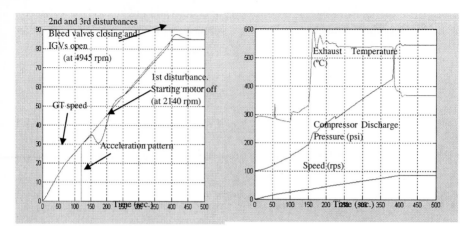

Fig. 6. Process disturbances.

steady state data of figure 7. The universal approximation property of fuzzy systems is confirmed.

Once the PKBC is designed, and included in the control system, its input is supplied by the acceleration startup reference curve to obtain the feedforward contribution to the control valve. A typical startup operation is shown in figure 8, where the turning speed and the speed reference are shown.

The speed response with the PKBC follows the speed reference without disturbances effects over the operation. Almost all the control effort over the process is given by the PKBC, and the FB control signal (PID controller) realizes disturbance compensation, as shown in figure 9. The main component of the final control signal is the feedforward contribution, while the feedback controller contributes the regulation of the controlled variable about the commanded trajectory.

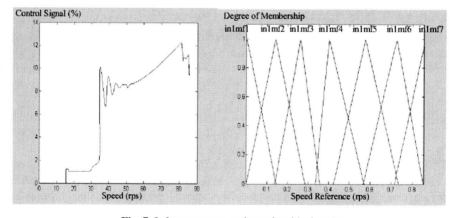

Fig. 7. Inference curve and membership functions.

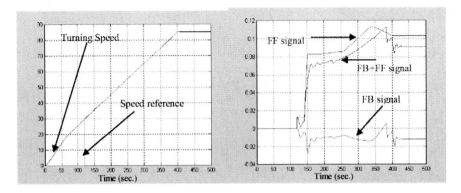

Fig. 8. GT startup operation.   **Fig. 9.** Control signals behavior.

5   Summary and Conclusions

In this paper, a PKBC for maneuverability improvement of a non-linear industrial process, such as a gas turbine for power generation, was presented.

Training data for feedforward fuzzy controller design was obtained from the process controlled by a conventional PID, with no process model requirement at all. A neural network learning technique, available in Matlab, was used for controller's parameters tuning, resulting in a neurofuzzy feedforward controller.

The results show that the PKBC (feedforward control) signal successfully drives the process close to the desired state through wide-range operating maneuvers. On the other side, the feedback controller (FB) signal compensates for disturbances about the reference speed. This is due to the PKBC nature, which maps the steady-state behavior over the operating range.

After simulation tests have been realized the following phase of this work are: the extension of this strategy for load control, an analysis of performance robustness and, the real-time platform tests. The real-time platform test will be composed of an industrial controller, an operator interface and a dynamical simulator, which will emulate the real process.

Acknowledgement. The authors thank Dr. Salvador Gonzalez C. and Ing. Rafael Chavez T. at IIE for their support to develop neurofuzzy controls; research in this paper was conducted under project 11983.

References

1. R. Babuska, H.B. Verbruggen and H. Hellendoorn. "Promising Fuzzy Modeling and Control Methodologies for Industrial Applications". Proceedings European Symposium on Intelligent Techniques ESIT'99, AB-02, Crete, Greece, June 1999.
2. Garduno-Ramirez, Raul, and Sanchez-Parra, Marino. "Control System Modernization: Turbogas Unit Case Study", Proceedings of IFAC Symposium on Control of Power Plants and Power Systems, Vol.2, December, 1995, Cancun, Mexico, pp. 245–250.
3. Nauck, D., F. Klawonn, and R. Kruse (1997). Foundations of Neuro-Fuzzy Systems. John Wiley & Sons.
4. Jyh-Shing Roger Jang. "ANFIS: Adaptive-Network-Based Fuzzy Inference System". IEEE Trans. On Systems, Man and Cybernetics. Vol. 23, no. 3, pp. 665–685, May 1993.
5. Passino, K. Fuzzy Control. Addison-Wesley Longman, Inc. 1998.
6. Raul Garduno-Ramirez, Kwang Y. Lee. "Wide Range Operation of a Power Unit via Feedforward Fuzzy Control". IEEE Trans. On Energy Conversion. Vol. 15, No.4, pp. 421–426. December 2000.
7. Marco Antonio Carretero Reyes, Salvador De Lara Jayme, Raúl Garduño Ramírez and Domitilo Libreros. "Sistema para Desarrollo y Validación de Algoritmos de Control para Turbinas de Gas". Reunión de Verano de Potencia. RVP'2001. Acapulco, Gro., Mexico. The Institute of Electrical and Electronics Engineers. IEEE Seccion Mexico.
8. Bonissone, P.P., Badami, V., Chiang, K.H., Khedkar, P.S., Marcelle, K.W., Schutten, M.J., "Industrial Applications of Fuzzy Logic at General Electric". Proc. IEEE, Vol. 83, No.3, March 1995, pp. 450–456.
9. Momoh, J.A. and Tomsovic, K., "Overview and Literature Survey of Fuzzy Set Theory in Power Systems", IEEE Transactions on Power Systems, Vol. 10, No.3, August 1995, pp. 1676–1690.
10. Mandani, E.H., "Twenty Years of Fuzzy Control: Experiences Gained and Lessons Learned", Fuzzy Logic Technology and Applications, Robert Marks, Ed. IEEE Technical Activities Board, pp. 19–24, 1994.

An Architecture for Online Diagnosis of Gas Turbines

Luis de Jesús González–Noriega and Pablo H. Ibargüengoytia

Instituto de Investigaciones Eléctricas
Av. Reforma 113, Palmira
Temixco, Mor., 62490, México
ljgon@hotmail.com / pibar@iie.org.mx

Abstract. Diagnosis systems are becoming an important requirement in these days given the complexity of industrial systems. This article presents an architecture for online diagnosis based on probabilistic reasoning. Probabilistic reasoning utilizes a model of the system that expresses the probabilistic relationship between the main variables. Thus, the values of some variables are utilized as evidence and the propagation provides an inferred value of other variables. Comparing the inferred value with the real one, an abnormal condition can be detected. Next, an isolation phase is executed in order to find the root cause of the abnormal behavior.

This article presents the design of an architecture that performs online diagnosis of gas turbines of combined cycle power plants. The architecture was designed utilizing some of the classes of the Spanish *elvira* project as a double experiment: (i) to test a general purpose, probabilistic reasoning package elvira in a real application in a real time environment and (ii) to test a previously developed theory for diagnosis in a gas turbine.

1   Introduction

Given the high costs and the difficulties for building new electric generation plants, the current trend consists in increasing the performance, availability and reliability of the actual installations. The performance refers to the amount of mega watts that can be generated with a unit of fuel. The availability refers to the hours that the central stops generating, and the reliability refers to the probability of counting with the different equipment in the plant.

Diagnosis is the technique utilized in several fields devoted to find faults, to explain abnormal behavior or to detect a faulty component in a system. Sometimes, engineers acquire data from a working process in order to analyze it off line, and detect the faulty component or the cause of the abnormal behavior. Other diagnosis systems run in line, i.e., they collect data and reason about the responses of the system. Some diagnosis systems predict the occurrence of a failure while others only explain the causes once that the fault has been propagated.

The diagnosis architecture presented in this paper is part of a larger system formed by a monitor, an optimizer, a diagnoser and an intelligent planning

F.J. Garijo, J.C. Riquelme, and M. Toro (Eds.): IBERAMIA 2002, LNAI 2527, pp. 795–804, 2002.
© Springer-Verlag Berlin Heidelberg 2002

module. When the monitor detects that the process works normally, it runs the optimizer in order to increase the performance of the process, e.g., the generation of more mega watts with less fuel. On the opposite, when the diagnoser detects an abnormal behavior, it identifies the faulty component and starts the intelligent planning that generates advices to the operator in order to return the plant to its normal state. This optimizer and diagnosis system are devoted to enhance the performance and availability indices.

The diagnosis system utilizes probabilistic reasoning for the detection and isolation of faults. It is based on the reasoning that an experimented operator carries out when some sensors of the plant present abnormal readings given the rest of signals. The operator may infer a fault in a sensor given the readings of the related variables. The first step is to acquire a probabilistic model of the process that relates the variables, i.e., a Bayesian network. Then one by one, the variables are predicted through probabilistic propagation and compared with the real value. If significant deviation is presented, then an apparent fault is detected. The isolation of the fault is carried out using a special property of the Bayesian networks called the Markov blanket.

The diagnosis architecture is based on the *elvira project*[1]. The input for the system is a sample with data of one execution of the process without any failure. With the data, the learning module of elvira generates a Bayesian network representing the probabilistic relationship between all the variables considered. Once a model is established, the system runs in real time, i.e., it reads data from the process and detects faulty components. The output of the diagnosis is a vector with the probability of failure of all the variables considered.

The next section explains a previously developed theory for probabilistic validation of important variables.

2   Probabilistic Diagnosis Model

The probabilistic diagnosis model requires the construction of a Bayesian network relating all the variables in the system being diagnosed. For example, Fig. 1 shows a probabilistic model of a process where variables g and a *cause* variable t, and this variable together with p affect the behavior of variable m.

The diagnosis consists of two operations: (i) *basic validation* and (ii) *isolation*. The former operation detects the presence of a fault while the later isolates the faulty element. This corresponds to the FDI (Fault Detection and Isolation) technique utilized in industry. These operations are made cyclically with all the variables in a model. Both, the detection and isolation modules utilize a Bayesian network. The detection is made using the Bayesian network representing the probabilistic relations between the variables as in the example of Fig. 1. This is called the detection network. The isolation network is explained below.

The *basic validation* consists in the estimation of the value of a variable according to the values of other related variables. A particular variable is taken as

---

[1] information about this project can be consulted in http://www.ia.uned.es/ēlvira.

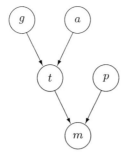

Fig. 1. A Bayesian network of certain process.

the hypothesis while the related variables act as the evidence. Thus, the propagation in the Bayesian network provides the posterior probability distribution of the variable's estimated value, given other variables. This distribution can then be used to infer if the variable has a proper value or if it shows an abnormal behavior.

For example, for the validation of variable m in Fig. 1, a posterior probability distribution $P(m \mid t, p)$ is calculated[2]. The real value of m is compared with the probability distribution and a conclusion is obtained. However, if the validation of a variable is accomplished utilizing a faulty variable then a false conclusion is expected. A basic validation algorithm then, can only tell if a variable has a potential fault, but (without considering other validations) it can not tell if the fault is real or apparent. The *fault isolation* module distinguishes between apparent and real faults, isolating the faulty variable.

The isolation module functions as follows. When a faulty variable exists, the fault will be manifested in all the related variables. The most closely related variables for each variable in a Bayesian network are those in its *Markov blanket*. A Markov blanket (MB) is defined as the set of variables that makes a variable independent from the others. In a Bayesian network, the following three sets of neighbors are sufficient for forming a MB of a node: the set of direct predecessors, direct successors, and the direct predecessors of the successors (i.e. parents, children, and spouses) [4]. For example, consider the Bayesian model of Fig. 1. The MB of t consists of the set $\{g, a, p, m\}$, while MB of p consists only of $\{m, t\}$.

The set of variables that constitutes the MB of a variable can be seen as a protection of this variable against changes of variables outside the blanket. Additionally, the *extended Markov blanket* of a variable v_i written $EMB(v_i)$, is formed by its MB plus the variable itself. Utilizing these concepts, if a fault exists in one of the variables, it will be revealed in all the variables in its EMB. On the contrary, if a fault exists outside a variable's EMB, it will not affect the estimation of that variable. It can be said then, that the EMB of a variable acts as its protection against other faults, and also protects others from its own

---

[2] Notice that the value of a and g are not required since they are conditionally independent of m given t.

failure. This assumes that all the variables in the MB are instantiated. The *fault isolation* module utilizes this property to update a probability of failure vector (one for each variable) and hence, to distinguish the real faulty variable [2].

The isolation utilizes a probabilistic causal model relating the real and apparent faults [4]. Fig. 2 shows the causal network corresponding to the example of Fig. 1. This is called the isolation network.

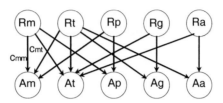

Fig. 2. Probabilistic causal model for fault isolation. R_i represents the real fault in sensor i while A_j represents the apparent fault in sensor j.

The node R_m represents the real fault in variable m while A_p represents the apparent fault in variable p. The arcs denote causality, i.e., an apparent failure in variable m (node Am) is *caused* by the existence of a real fault in one of the nodes m, t or p^3. This set happens to be the $EMB(m)$. Thus, given more evidence about the state of apparent faults in the variables, the posterior probability value of real fault nodes will tend either to zero or one.

The probabilistic diagnosis theory developed in [2,3] can be summarized as follows. After a cycle of basic validation of all variables is completed, a set S of apparent faulty variables is obtained. Thus, based on the comparison between S and the EMB of all variables, the following situations arise:

1. If $S = \phi$ there are no faults.
2. If S is equal to the EMB of a variable X, and there is no other EMB which is a subset of S, then there is a *single real fault* in X.
3. If S is equal to the EMB of a variable X, and there are one or more EMBs which are subsets of S, then there is a real fault in X, and possibly, real faults in the variables whose EMBs are subsets of S. In this case, there are possibly *multiple undistinguishable* real faults.
4. If S is equal to the union of several EMBs and the combination is unique, then there are *multiple distinguishable* real faults in all the variables whose EMB are in S.
5. If none of the above cases is satisfied, then there are multiple faults but they can not be distinguished. All the variables whose EMBs are subsets of S could have a real fault.

For example, consider the network shown in Fig. 1 and its corresponding probabilistic causal model shown in Fig. 2. Suppose a failure in the value of

---

³ The parameter c_{ij} correspond to the *noisy–or* condition [4,3].

variable p. The basic validation of m will produce an apparent fault given that its estimation was made using an erroneous value. This imply the instantiation of node Am in Fig. 2 as true. At this point, the probability of failure will show an estimation of the most suspicious real faulty nodes. Following the procedure for all nodes, will result in the detection of apparent faults in nodes m, p, and t. Thus, instantiating those apparent fault nodes in Fig. 2 will provide the posterior probability of all real fault nodes $R_{variable}$. In this example, a high probability value in node Rp will be obtained.

This theory assumes that all the variables in the MB are insaniated when a variable is validated. This is not always feasible in model–based diagnosis. However, the influence of an instantiation of a variable outside its MB is not too strong. So it is considered that a faulty variable only affects the variables in its MB and the previous theory can be applied.

3   The Diagnosis Architecture

At the highest level, the architecture is a typical intelligent system, i.e., it contains a knowledge base, an inference mechanism and the output. The knowledge base is a Bayesian network representing the probabilistic model that relates all the variables. The network is constructed from a data set and using an automatic learning program. The inference mechanism is the propagation methods of elvira, and the output is a vector with the probability of failure of all the variables. From a functional point of view, the diagnosis has two tasks: fault detection and fault isolation.

Figure 3 shows the most general architecture. The learning module receives a data set and produces a Bayesian network to be utilized by the detection module. This module is the inference mechanism mentioned above. The detection module reads data from the plant through the real time data acquisition module. Real time data is utilized as evidence in the propagation, so apparent faults are detected as explained in section 2. The list of apparent faults is the input to the isolation module. The isolation module utilizes a causal model and produces the final output of the diagnosis system, namely, a vector with the probability of failure of all the variables in the system. This vector is transmitted to the graphical user interface (GUI) for indication to the operator of the plant. Notice that the diagnosis is carried out in a cycle between the detection and isolation modules until all the variables have been diagnosed. The proposed architecture described in this paper includes only the modules inside the dashed square. They are described in the following sections.

3.1   Learning Module

The learning process starts with the acquisition of historical data from the process without faults. Normally, the variables monitored in industrial processes are continuous, i.e., discretization is required. When the sampled information has been discretized, the **K2Learning** class from elvira is utilized. The elvira's

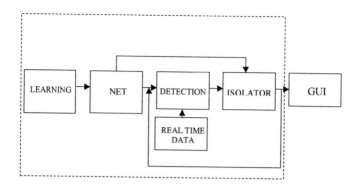

Fig. 3. High level architecture of the diagnosis system.

learning module produces a file with the resulting Bayesian network in elvira's format (*detection.elv*). Figure 4 shows the steps needed in the learning process.

Fig. 4. Learning the probabilistic model for diagnosis.

Creating a Bayesian network object in elvira requires a network description in elvira's format. This format is an ascii description of the nodes and arcs, their characteristics and the parametric information. For the detection module, the network is obtained with the learning module mentioned above. The isolation network is formed with the detection network and the Markov blanket property of Bayesian networks as explained in section 2. Figure 5 shows that, once the elvira format has been defined, a syntactic and semantic validation is required. The syntactic analysis is made with the **parser** class, indicating if an error is found. Next, the **network** class reads the network description in memory and generates a Bnet object. The Bnet object is the basis for the probabilistic inference described next.

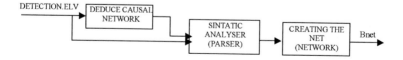

Fig. 5. Acquisition of the Bayesian networks for diagnosis.

3.2   Detection Module

The detection module compiles a Bnet object it with the **bnet** class and loads the network in memory. The validation consists in the prediction of a variable's value given all the related variables. Thus, the value of the related variables are read and compared with the ranks of values generated in the discretization step of the variable. This discrete value forms the evidence for the **evidence** class. Next, the **propagation** class is called to obtain the posterior probability of the validated variable given all the evidence. The real value of the variable is compared with the probability distribution and if the deviation is higher than a specific threshold, then an apparent failure is detected. This process is repeated with all the evidence for each variable and for all variables. Figure 6 shows this process.

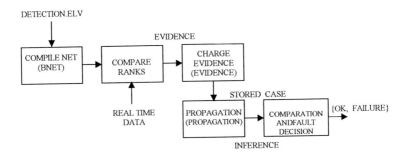

Fig. 6. Fault detection module.

3.3   Isolation Module

The isolation module also utilizes a Bnet object, an evidence information and generates a posterior probability distribution. The Bnet object is obtained from the isolation causal network deduced as indicated in Fig. 5. The evidence is the occurrence of an apparent fault obtained in the detection module. The propagation of probabilities in the isolation module provides the final output of the diagnosis system, namely, the probability of being faulty of all the variables in the system. The next section presents an experiment of a diagnosis of gas turbines utilizing the proposed architecture.

4   Diagnosis of Gas Turbines

A gas turbine consists fundamentally of four main parts: the compressor, the combustion chamber, the turbine itself and the generator. Combustion is produced in the combustion chamber producing high pressure gases at high temperature. The expansion of these gases produces the turbine rotation with a torque that is transmitted to the generator in order to produce electric power output. The control valve regulates the gas fuel in the combustion chamber and is commanded by the control system, and its aperture can be read by a position sensor. The temperature at the blade path, is taken along the circumference of the turbine. Other important variables, measured directly through sensors are the mega watts generated and the turbine speed in revolutions per minute.

The architecture has been utilized in diagnosis experiments in a gas turbine simulator at the laboratory. The simulation executed for this experiment consists in a load increasing from 2 MW to 23 MW. Six analog signals were sampled every half second so a number of 2111 records were obtained during the 20 minutes that this procedure took.

The learning module of *elvira* with the K2 algorithm [1] were executed utilizing the data table with the seven variables. Figure7 shows the resulting Bayesian network involving the six variables.

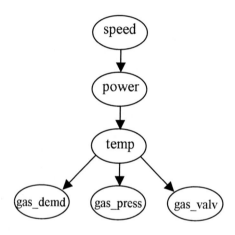

Fig. 7. Bayesian network learned from the experiment.

The *speed* variable represents the measure of the velocity of the turbine in revolutions per second (RPS). The *power* variable is the measure of the mega watts generated, *temp* is the exhaust gas temperature in the turbine, variable *gas_press* is the gas fuel pressure, *gas_valv* is the position of gas control valve, and variable *gas_demd* is the gas valve demand.

According to the experts, the model can be interpreted as follows. The velocity or mechanical work produces mega watts and this generation is related with heat. The temperature is related with the demand of gas, the aperture of the valve and the pressure of the fuel. Notice that the direction of the arcs represents probabilistic relationship between any pair of nodes and not necessarily a *causal* relation. Several tests were made with different discretization values in order to see the best result in the learning process.

Figure 8 shows the isolation network that corresponds to the probabilistic network of Fig. 7.

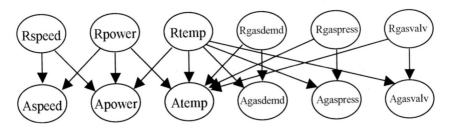

Fig. 8. Isolation network for the example of the gas turbine.

Consider the following scenario. The plant is generating and incrementing the demanded load. The demand of gas (*gas_demd*) is at 57.11 units, corresponding to state s3, the gas pressure (*gas_press*) is at 152.26, and the gas fuel position (*gas_valv*) is at 56.85 units or s3 state. The exhaust gas temperature (*temp*) is at its 337.46 degrees and the gas turbine speed (*speed*) is at its 5085 rpm or the s5 state. Thus, instantiating those nodes in the network of Fig. 7, and propagating probabilities, the following results are obtained in the power variable: $P(power = s2) = 100$ %, and 0 in the rest of the power value intervals. In this case, the propagation enforces the value of *power* variable to the interval corresponding to the state s2.

Now, consider a failure in the electric generator or a failure in the power generation sensor, in the above scenario. Table 1 shows the diagnosis process. The second column indicates the result of the basic validation step, i.e., it provides the probability of finding an apparent fault. The third column indicates the result of the detection module according to the value of second column. This result is the value of *ok* or *failure* indicated in Fig. 6. The following 6 columns indicate the posterior probability of the *Real* fault nodes in the isolation network (Fig. 8). They are in fact, the ultimate output of the diagnosis system: the probability of failure of each variable. First, variables *gas_demd*, *gas_press* and *gas_valv* are validated. The propagation of probabilities indicates a flat distribution in these variables, and the real value coincide in an interval with a real probability to be correct, i.e., $P(gas\_demd = correct) = 88$ %, $P(gas\_press = correct) = 54$ %, and $P(gas\_valv = correct) = 75$ %,. This implies the instantiation of nodes *Agasdemd*, *Agaspress* and *Agasvalv* with no apparent faults in the isolation network of Fig. 8.

Notice the first row in the table. With the propagation after *Agasdemd* was instantiated as *ok*, the probability of failure vector shows that the variables *temp* and *gas_demd* have a 9 % probability of failure, i.e., they are free of faults while the rest of the variables are completely uncertain (50 %). After the three first variables have been validated, the results indicate that the temperature reading is securely correct, the gas variables are very low suspicious, the speed is still uncertain and the power starts to be the faulty variable. As expected from the theory, the last step in the validation cycle confirms that the faulty variable is indeed the *power*.

Table 1. Diagnosis experiment simulating a failure in the power generation.

variable validated	$P(app.failure)$ (%)	state assigned	R_{speed}	R_{power}	R_{temp}	$R_{gasdemd}$	$R_{gaspress}$	$R_{gasvalve}$
gas_demd	88	ok	50	50	9	9	50	50
gas_press	54	ok	50	50	1	9	9	50
gas_valv	75	ok	50	50	0	9	9	9
$temp$	86	nok	50	80	0	15	15	15
$power$	20	nok	57	90	0	13	13	13
$speed$	1	ok	26	81	1	15	15	15

5 Conclusions and Future Work

This paper has presented a proposed architecture for the diagnosis of industrial processes. The architecture is formed by a detection module and a isolation
module. Both modules utilize probabilistic reasoning. The first, requires a probabilistic model that represents the conditional dependence and independence of
all the variables in the process. The isolation module utilizes a special property of
the Bayesian networks, namely the Markov blanket. A causal network is formed
utilizing the first model and the Markov blanket of every variable.

The architecture was implemented utilizing the elvira software. It is a software package devoted to the probabilistic reasoning and decision support. The
main classes of elvira were integrated to the diagnosis architecture and were initially tested with the diagnosis of six variables model in a gas turbine of a power
plant.

The next step in this project is the fully utilization of this architecture in
the diagnosis and optimization of a complete power plant. First, the selection
of the most common failures reported in power plants is required. Next, the
specification of all the variables involved and the probabilistic model is obtained
with the learning tools Finally, with the installation of the architecture and the
acquisition of the process data, faults can be detected and isolated *inline*.

References

1. G.F. Cooper and E. Herskovits. A bayesian method for the induction of probabilistic
   networks from data. *Machine Learning*, 9(4):309–348, 1992.
2. P.H. Ibargüengoytia, L.E. Sucar, and S. Vadera. A probabilistic model for sensor
   validation. In E. Horvitz and F. Jensen, editors, *Proc. Twelfth Conference on Uncertainty in Artificial Intelligence UAI-96*, pages 332–339, Portland, Oregon, U.S.A.,
   1996.
3. P.H. Ibargüengoytia, L.E. Sucar, and S. Vadera. Any time probabilistic reasoning
   for sensor validation. In G.F. Cooper and S. Moral, editors, *Proc. Fourteenth Conference on Uncertainty in Artificial Intelligence UAI-98*, pages 266–273, Madison,
   Wisconsin, U.S.A., 1998.
4. J. Pearl. *Probabilistic reasoning in intelligent systems: networks of plausible inference*. Morgan Kaufmann, Palo Alto, Calif., U.S.A., 1988.

STeLLa v2.0: Planning with Intermediate Goals

Laura Sebastia, Eva Onaindia, and Eliseo Marzal

Dpto. Sistemas Informaticos y Computacion
Universidad Politecnica de Valencia
{lstarin, onaindia, emarzal}@dsic.upv.es

Abstract. In the last few years, AI planning techniques have experimented a great advance. One of the reasons for this big expansion is the International Planning Competition (IPC), which enforces the definition of language standards as PDDL+ and new benchmarks. In this paper, we present the new features of STeLLa, a planner that participated in the last IPC, held in Toulouse last April. STeLLa is a forward search planner that builds intermediate goals to ease the resolution of the planning problem.

1 Introduction

The field of planning in AI has experimented great advances over the last few years. Problems that seemed unsolvable, can be solved now in a few seconds. Obviously, this motivates the researchers to increase the complexity of the problems to be solved by their planners. This way, some of the domains tested in the last International Planning Competition 2002 (IPC2002) came out as a combination of the domains used in the previous planning competition (AIPS'00), like blocksworld, logistics, etc. thus increasing the difficulty of the problems[1]. Moreover, other domains exhibiting new features such as the use of numerical values or durative actions were also defined.

In this paper, we present STeLLa v2.0, a planner which participated in the STRIPS track at the IPC2002. This version uses a new problem-solving approach that consists of computing the set of subgoals to be achieved at each time step. Solving a planning problem can be stated as successively decomposing the problem into a set of intermediate goals. STeLLa's goal is then to find the (parallel) actions to reach those intermediate goals. That is, STeLLa obtains parallel plans and tries to minimize the overall number of actions in the plan.

Under this new approach, efforts are simply concentrated in obtaining the literals in the next intermediate goal set and then finding the set of actions to reach those literals from the previous state. The issue of how to build these intermediate goals is fully detailed in Section 3, but we can anticipate that STeLLa uses *landmarks* graphs (LG) to create those intermediate goals. The idea of using LGs was firstly introduced in [5] and was extended in [6]. In both

---

[1] The definition of these new domains and the results obtained by the participating planners in the IPC2002 can be found in www.dur.ac.uk/d.p.long/competition.html.

F.J. Garijo, J.C. Riquelme, and M. Toro (Eds.): IBERAMIA 2002, LNAI 2527, pp. 805–814, 2002.
© Springer-Verlag Berlin Heidelberg 2002

papers, a landmark is defined as a literal that must be true in every solution plan. The process extracts a set of landmarks which are later ordered under the concept of "reasonable order", obtaining a LG.

This paper is organized as follows. Section 2 summarizes some basic concepts about landmarks and LGs. Our technique to build intermediate goals is explained in Section 3 and how STeLLa uses the obtained intermediate goals in order to find the solution is shown in Section 4. Section 5 gives the results obtained in the IPC2002 and Section 6 concludes by summarizing the strong and weak points of this framework and the future work.

2 Concepts about Landmarks and Orders

Definition 1. *A* **STRIPS action** *o is a triple $o = \langle \mathsf{Pre}(o), \mathsf{Add}(o), \mathsf{Del}(o) \rangle$ where $\mathsf{Pre}(o)$ are the preconditions of o, $\mathsf{Add}(o)$ is the Add list of o and $\mathsf{Del}(o)$ is the Delete list of the action, each being a set of atoms. The result of applying a single STRIPS action to a state S when $\mathsf{Pre}(o) \subseteq S$ is defined as follows:*

$$Result(S, \langle o \rangle) = (S \cup \mathsf{Add}(o)) \setminus \mathsf{Del}(o)$$

The result of applying a sequence of actions to a state is recursively defined as:

$$Result(S, \langle o_1, \ldots, o_n \rangle) = Result(Result(S, \langle o_1, \ldots, o_{n-1} \rangle), \langle o_n \rangle).$$

Definition 2. *A* **planning task** *$\mathcal{P} = (\mathcal{O}, \mathcal{I}, \mathcal{G})$ is a triple where $\mathcal{O}$ is the set of actions, and $\mathcal{I}$ (the initial state) and $\mathcal{G}$ (the goals) are sets of atoms.*

The process to build a LG consists of two steps [6]: (1) extracting the set of landmarks and (2) ordering the obtained set of landmarks.

Definition 3. *Given a planning task $\mathcal{P} = (\mathcal{O}, \mathcal{I}, \mathcal{G})$, a fact l_i is a* **landmark** *in $\mathcal{P}$ iff l_i is true at some point in all solution plans, i.e., iff for all $P = \langle o_1, \ldots, o_n \rangle, \mathcal{G} \subseteq Result(\mathcal{I}, P) : l_i \in Result(\mathcal{I}, \langle o_1, \ldots, o_i \rangle)$ for some $0 \le i \le n$.*

Definition 4. *The* **side-effects** *of a landmark l_i are defined as:*
$side\_effects(l_i) = \{\mathsf{Add}(o) - \{l_i\} \mid o \in \mathcal{O}, l_i \in \mathsf{Add}(o)\}$

The extraction process is straightforward. First, a Relaxed Planning Graph[2] (RPG) is built. Then, all top level goals are added to the LG and posted as goals in the first level at which they were added in the RPG. Each goal is solved in the RPG starting from the last level. For each goal g in a level, all actions achieving g are grouped into a set and the intersection I of their preconditions is computed. We also compute a set U formed by the union of these preconditions

---

[2] A RPG is a Graphplan Planning Graph [1] where the Delete list of the actions is ignored.

which do not belong to I. This set is called **disjunctive set**. For all facts p in I we post p as a goal in the first RPG level where p is achieved. When all goals in a level are achieved, we move on to the next lower level. The process stops when the first (initial) level is reached.

Definition 5. *Let l_i, l_j be two landmarks. l_i and l_j are* **consistent** *if there exists a possible state $S/l_i \in S \land l_j \in S$.*

We use the TIMinconsistent function [3], which returns whether two literals are consistent or not. Once the set of landmarks has been extracted, they are ordered according to the following orders, which in turn define an LG:

Definition 6. *A* **natural order** *is established between two landmarks l_i, l_j ($l_i <_n l_j$) when in every solution plan it is necessary to solve l_i to achieve l_j, that is, l_i is a precondition of all the actions that satisfy l_j.*

Definition 7. *A* **weakly reasonable order** *is established between two landmarks l_i, l_j ($l_i <_{wr} l_j$) in the following cases:*

- *if l_i and l_j are naturally ordered before the same node l_k and $\exists$ landmark x: $x <_n l_i \land$ TIMinconsistent$(x, l_j) =$ TRUE*
- *if there exists some other landmark x, and x and l_j are ordered before the same node; and there is an ordered sequence of $<_n$ orders that post l_i before x; and $\exists$ landmark y: $y <_n l_i \land$ TIMinconsistent$(y, l_j) =$ TRUE*
- *if $\exists$ landmark x: $l_i <_n x \land l_j <_{wr} x \land$ TIMinconsistent$(side\_effects(l_j), l_i) =$ TRUE*

A weakly reasonable order between two landmarks $l_i <_{wr} l_j$ states that it is better to satisfy l_i before l_j because if l_j is achieved first it might be eventually deleted by l_i.

Definition 8. *A* **LG** *is a graph (N, E) with three types of nodes:*

- simple node: $l_i \in N$ *as a simple node if l_i is a landmark.*
- disjunctive node: $l_i \in N$ *as a disjunctive node if l_i is a disjunctive set.*
- conjunctive node: $[l_i, l_j] \in N$ *as a conjunctive node if l_i is a side-effect of l_j and viceversa*

The set of edges E for a **LG** *is built as follows. Let l_i, l_j be simple or disjunctive nodes and $[l_n, l_m]$ be a conjunctive node:*

- *If $l_i <_n l_j \lor l_i <_{wr} l_j \to E = E \cup (l_i, l_j)$*
- *$\forall l_k/(l_k, l_n) \in E \lor (l_k, l_m) \in E \to E = E \cup (l_k, [l_n, l_m])$*

We consider that a *landmark* is any of the elements in N and we will use the notation $l_i < l_j$ throughout the rest of the paper to refer an edge (l_i, l_j) in the LG.

It is important to remark the fact that, both the process for extracting landmarks and calculating the orders are approximate computations, that is, not every landmark in a problem or all the orders between the obtained landmarks are extracted. For this reason the information in the LG may not be complete.

3   Building Intermediate Goals

This section explains how to build the intermediate goals.

Definition 9. *An* **intermediate goal** $\mathcal{IG}$ *is the set of literals that should be achieved next from the current state.*

Definition 10. *A* **fringe** $\mathcal{F}$ *is an* $\mathcal{IG}$ *whose literals can be reached by applying only one action for each literal.*

Currently, STeLLa v2.0 focuses on building fringes instead of intermediate goals. The reason is that it is easier to build subplans to reach the corresponding fringe than the IG, although some more reasoning is required for building a fringe than for building an IG, as we will explain later on.

The first step for obtaining a fringe is creating the LG between the current state and the top level goals. Then, all the landmarks whose predecessors nodes in the LG belong to the current state are included in $\mathcal{F}$. More formally, let $LG(N, E)$ be the current LG and $l_i \in N$, $l_i \in \mathcal{F}$ if $\forall l_j \in N/l_j < l_i, l_j \in$ current state. Due to the incompleteness of the LG it might be the case that it is not possible to achieve all the landmarks in $\mathcal{F}$. This happens in any of the two following cases:

1. **One or more literals have to be postponed due to inconsistency or optimality criteria.** A literal $l_i \in \mathcal{F}$ can be delayed in the following cases:
   a) $\exists l_j \in \mathcal{F}$ / TIMinconsistent(l_i, l_j) = TRUE
   b) $\exists l_j \in \mathcal{F}$ / TIMinconsistent(l_i, l_j) = FALSE but the producer actions for each literal are mutually exclusive, that is, they cannot be executed at the same time from the current state
   c) Even though l_i is consistent with all the other literals and its producer actions would not cause any conflict, it may be the case that the achievement of this literal at this moment would lead to a non-optimal plan.
2. **One or more literals need more than one action to be reached.** In this case, a regression process is performed to compute the new fringe.

3.1   Postponing Literals

In this section, we focus on case 1. In order to avoid inconsistency or to reduce the addition of redundant actions in the plan, the solution is to add new orders between the literals in $\mathcal{F}$:

Inconsistency Orders (Cases 1a and 1b)

By **inconsistency orders** we refer to those orders that must be established between two landmarks to solve cases 1a and 1b.

Definition 11. *A literal l_i* **can be delayed** *if for every landmark following l_i there is at least a precedessor landmark l_k which is neither in the fringe nor in the current state:* $\forall l_j/l_i < l_j, \exists l_k/l_k < l_j \land l_k \notin \mathcal{F} \land l_k \notin$ currentstate.

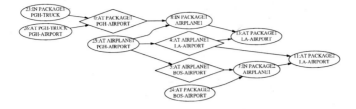

Fig. 1. Example of the order type 1 in the `logistics` problem

Fig. 2. Example of the order type 2 in the `logistics` problem

We now define three types of inconsistency orders. The first two types are aimed at solving case 1a and type 3 covers case 1b.

Type 1: If TIMinconsistent(l_i, l_j) = TRUE $\wedge$ can-be-delayed(l_j)$\wedge$
$\neg$can-be-delayed(l_i) then $l_i < l_j$.

Figure 1 shows an example where this order can be applied[3]. In this example,
$\mathcal{F}$={(at package1 pgh-airport), (at airplane1 la-airport), (at airplane1 bos-airport)}.
Let's take l_i=(at airplane1 la-airport) and l_j=(at airplane1 bos-airport), as a pair
of inconsistent literals. l_i can be delayed because (at package1 la-airport) has a
predecessor landmark, (in package1 airplane1), which is neither in $\mathcal{F}$ nor in the
current state. However, l_j cannot be delayed since the only previous landmark
for (in package2 airplane1) belongs to the current state. Therefore, (at airplane1
bos-airport) should be achieved before (at airplane1 la-airport).

Type 2: If TIMinconsistent(l_i, l_j) = TRUE $\wedge$ $\exists l_k / l_i <_{wr} l_k \wedge l_j <_n l_k$ then
$l_i < l_j$.

The intuition behind this type of order is as follows. A natural order $l_j <_n l_k$
states that l_j is a precondition for l_k, that is, l_j must be true immediately before
l_k. Therefore, if l_i is inconsistent with l_j, it seems reasonable to achieve l_i before
so that l_j does not have to be reachieved after l_i.

Figure 2 shows an example of the order type 2. In this case, l_i={at airplane1
la-airport}, l_j={at airplane1 bos-airport} and l_k={at package1 bos-airport}, then
l_i should be achieved in first place so that l_j is true just before satisfying l_k.

Type 3: If TIMinconsistent(l_i, l_j) = FALSE $\wedge$ $\exists l_k / l_k < l_i \wedge l_k < l_j \wedge$
TIMinconsistent(l_j, l_k) = TRUE $\wedge$ TIMinconsistent(l_i, l_k) = FALSE then $l_i < l_j$.

---

[3] The nodes in diamond indicate the landmarks that belong to $\mathcal{F}$.

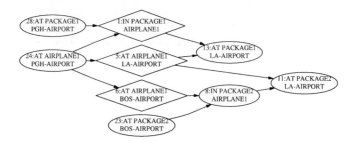

Fig. 3. Example of the order type 3 in the `logistics` problem

Figure 3 shows an example where this order is applied. In this example, $\mathcal{F}$={(in package1 airplane1), (at airplane1 la-airport), (at airplane1 bos-airport)}. If we take l_i=(in package1 airplane1), l_j=(at airplane1 la-airport) and l_k=(at airplane1 pgh-airport), since l_j and l_k are inconsistent and l_i and l_k are not, then l_j should be delayed. Otherwise, we could not achieve (in package1 airplane1) without reachieving (at airplane1 pgh-airport).

Optimality Orders (Case 1c)

The reasonable orders discovered when building the LG are aimed to reduce the number of actions in the final plan. Since not all these reasonable orders are found, we define some additional orders so as to improve the quality of the final plan. It is remarkable the fact that, while the inconsistency orders are defined between pairs of literals in $\mathcal{F}$, the optimality orders refer to a single literal.

Type 4: If the producer action of a landmark removes a literal which is required later on in the planning process, this landmark should be delayed. More formally, let l_i be a landmark in $\mathcal{F}$ and $P = \{l_j/l_j < l_i \wedge \mathsf{TIMinconsistent}(l_i, l_j) = \mathsf{TRUE}\}$. If $\exists p \in P/out-degree(p) > 1 \wedge \exists l_k \notin \mathcal{F}/p < l_k \wedge \mathsf{TIMinconsistent}(p, l_k) = \mathsf{FALSE}$ then l_i is delayed.

Figure 4 shows an example where this optimality order should be applied. Let's consider the node (at airplane1 la-airport) as l_i. Then, P ={(at airplane1 pgh-airport)}, and so is p. The out-degree of p is 2, setting l_k to (in package1 airplane1). l_k and p are consistent, so l_i has to be delayed. If we analyse this problem, we realise that if the literal (at airplane1 la-airport) is satisfied before (in package1 airplane1), we would have to achieve (at airplane1 pgh-airport) again for (in package1 airplane1), thus adding one more action.

Type 5: Let l_i be a landmark in $\mathcal{F}$. If $\exists l_j/l_i <_n l_j \wedge \exists l_k < l_j \wedge$ $\mathsf{TIMinconsistent}(l_i, l_k) = \mathsf{TRUE} \wedge l_k \notin$ current state then l_i is delayed.

In the example shown in Figure 5, if we consider (at airplane1 la-airport) as l_i, (at package2 la-airport) as l_j and (at airplane1 bos-airport) as l_k, the conditions above hold and, therefore, (at airplane1 la-airport) should be delayed. In this case, it is better going first to Boston to collect `package2` and then transport both packages to la-airport, their final destination. Otherwise, if airplane1 headed la-

Fig. 4. Example of the order type 4 in the `logistics` problem

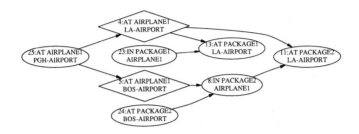

Fig. 5. Example of the order type 5 in the `logistics` problem

airport before bos-airport, then the plan would have one more action as it would be necessary to go to Boston from LA and then back again.

3.2   More-Than-One-Action Literals

As we said above, it might be the case that a literal in $\mathcal{F}$ cannot be reached by applying only one action from the current state. In this case, we perform a regression process that approaches the current fringe $\mathcal{F}$ to the current state. If we were working with $\mathcal{IG}$, we would not need to perform this regression process. This is done by finding the set of literals $\mathcal{F}'$ that should be reached before $\mathcal{F}$. This intermediate fringe is computed as follows:

```
G' = ∅
Forall the literals lᵢ ∈ F
    1. Select an action A that achieves lᵢ
    2. G' = G' ∪ Pre(A)
Build a new fringe F' from I to G'
If F' is a correct fringe, then return F'
Else Regression (I, F')
```

The selection of the action $\mathcal{A}$ is very important because a wrong selection may not lead to the best fringe. This can have a high impact in the final solution since it can cause the planner to add redundant actions, as the results in Section 5 will show.

4   Using the Intermediate Goals

In this section, we present the complete algorithm implemented in STeLLa .

Algorithm STeLLa $(\mathcal{I}, \mathcal{G}) \rightarrow$ plan $\mathcal{P}$ organized in time steps

---

$\mathcal{C} = \mathcal{I}$; *time* = 0
While $\mathcal{G} \not\subset \mathcal{C}$
    1. Compute fringe $\mathcal{F}$
    2. Compute the set of actions $\mathcal{A}$ that solve $\mathcal{F}$
    3. If $\mathcal{A} = \emptyset$ return $\mathcal{P} = \emptyset$
    4. Execute $\mathcal{A}$, obtaining the new $\mathcal{C}$
    5. $\mathcal{P}_{time} = \mathcal{A}$
    6. *time* = *time* + 1
return $\mathcal{P}$

While the planner has not reached the goals, it computes the next fringe $\mathcal{F}$. Then, the set of actions $\mathcal{A}$, necessary to solve the fringe, is computed. If $\mathcal{A}$ is empty the planner returns an empty plan. Otherwise, this set of actions is executed over $\mathcal{C}$, obtaining the new current state.

The most important difference between the current version and STeLLa v1.0 [7] is that in the latter the fringe after step 1 in the algorithm above, could contain inconsistent literals whereas in STeLLa v2.0 $\mathcal{F}$ is totally consistent. So, in the previous version it was necessary to create consistent subsets of goals from $\mathcal{F}$. Moreover, as no regression process was used the planner could reach a dead-end when the literals in the fringe could not be achieved in only one action.

5   Experiments

In this section, we summarize the experiments performed with STeLLa v2.0 for the IPC2002. We compare these results with the planners that were awarded a prize in this competition:

- The quality version of LPG planner [4] which exhibited a *distinguished performance of the first order* in the fully-automated track.
- MIPS [2] which exhibited a *distinguished performance* in the fully-automated track.
- VHPOP [8] which was awarded the *best newcomer* prize.

Table 1 shows only the results for the problems STeLLa was able to solve in the Depots and Driverlog domains out of 20 problems. For the Zeno and Satellite domains (Table 2), STeLLa was able to solve almost all of the problems.

We can see that in all domains the results obtained by STeLLa are comparable in terms of time steps and number of actions with the other planners. In terms of time[4], the performance of STeLLa varies along the domains. Although our main

---

[4] In the Driverlog we have considered only those problems solved by STeLLa, whereas in the Zeno and Satellite domains the time in average is computed over the problems solved by each planner.

Table 1. Depots and Driverlog problems (time steps / number of actions).

Depots					Driverlog			
	LPG	VHPOP	MIPS	STeLLa		LPG	VHPOP	MIPS	STeLLa
pfile1	8/10	8/10	12/13	6/11	pfile1	7/7	7/7	7/7	7/7
pfile2	12/15	12/15	9/16	9/16	pfile2	14/20	11/21	18/22	20/28
pfile3	21/27	/	21/34	17/33	pfile3	7/12	8/13	12/18	8/13
pfile8	21/35	/	27/48	30/56	pfile4	11/16	11/16	9/19	17/30
pfile10	13/24	/	22/34	25/30	pfile5	11/18	8/18	17/25	10/22
pfile13	19/25	/	18/25	11/30	pfile6	10/17	5/11	7/13	9/16
					pfile7	7/13	8/15	9/15	10/21
					pfile8	11/22	13/25	15/27	18/38
					pfile9	13/23	14/22	14/24	13/26
					pfile10	11/17	9/21	11/21	27/35
					Time in avg.	6986	1966	135	3426

Table 2. Zeno and Satellite problems (time steps / number of actions).

Problem	Zeno				Satellite			
	LPG	VHPOP	MIPS	STeLLa	LPG	VHPOP	MIPS	STeLLa
pfile1	1/1	1/1	1/1	1/1	8/9	8/9	8/9	8/9
pfile2	5/6	6/6	5/6	7/9	12/13	12/13	12/13	12/13
pfile3	5/6	5/6	7/9	5/6	10/11	10/11	10/11	10/11
pfile4	7/8	7/8	9/10	11/13	17/18	20/22	17/18	17/18
pfile5	7/11	9/12	11/16	11/15	14/16	15/16	14/16	15/19
pfile6	6/12	7/12	11/15	10/15	10/20	18/21	12/21	10/26
pfile7	8/15	7/16	6/16	6/16	12/21	13/25	14/23	19/26
pfile8	7/12	9/13	8/12	8/15	14/26	12/29	14/27	21/26
pfile9	7/23	10/21	10/25	16/32	10/30	/	10/35	13/31
pfile10	9/30	9/25	16/32	10/31	27/30	21/37	18/35	23/48
pfile11	6/15	6/16	8/18	9/18	27/32	13/33	13/35	23/40
pfile12	16/33	10/25	12/26	13/28	22/43	29/47	/	49/71
pfile13	16/38	10/27	9/33	11/35	22/61	24/64	22/60	43/84
pfile14	18/45	/	15/41	10/41	18/42	22/41	19/44	25/51
pfile15	11/54	/	14/54	23/61	16/48	19/50	17/50	19/56
pfile16	16/63	/	/	21/65	26/51	35/52	/	28/74
pfile17	45/96	/	/	46/131	28/43	22/43	/	27/70
pfile18	25/91	/	38/79	/	18/32	18/32	/	16/35
pfile19	59/113	/	/	27/117	25/75	/	/	/
pfile20	37/126	/	/	56/148	25/110	/	/	/
Time in avg.	164612	11380	43515	268315	13370	11528	34125	33981

concern is the plan quality, the performance in average is quite competitive for most of the domains.

One remarkable aspect is that STeLLa obtains sometimes better results for more complex instances than LPG. This is because the LG provides a more global view of the planning problem than local search planning.

It is also important to remark that STeLLa v2.0 obtains similar results to the previous version for those domains where regression is not needed. That is, both planners exhibit the same performance but the new version can solve a broader range of problems.

6   Conclusions and Further Work

In this paper we have presented the new version of STeLLa that participated in the IPC2002. STeLLa v2.0 offers a new planning approach consisting in building intermediate goals. However, the process to compute the intermediate goals is not reliable enough because of the regression step which may not lead to the best fringe.

Our ongoing work consists of building successive intermediate goals without being subject to be fringes. This way, if we can assure that these intermediate goals drive to an optimal plan, then solving a planning problem can be viewed as solving several subproblems each consisting in achieving the next intermediate goal.

Acknowledgement. This work has been partially funded by the Spanish Government CICYT project DPI2001-2094-C03-03 and by the Universidad Politecnica de Valencia projects UPV-2001-0017 and UPV-2001-0980.

References

1. A. Blum and M. Furst. Fast planning through planning graph analysis. *Artificial Intelligence*, 90(1-2):281–300, 1997.
2. S. Edelkamp. Symbolic pattern databases in heuristic search planning. In *Proceedings of the Sixth Int. Conference on AI Planning and Scheduling (AIPS'02)*. AAAI Press, 2002.
3. M. Fox and D. Long. The automatic inference of state invariants in TIM. *Journal of Artificial Intelligence Research*, 9:367–421, 1998.
4. A. Gerevini and I. Serina. Lpg: a planner based on local search for planning graphs. In *Proceedings of the Sixth Int. Conference on AI Planning and Scheduling (AIPS'02)*. AAAI Press, 2002.
5. J. Porteous and L. Sebastia. Extracting and ordering landmarks for planning. In *19th Workshop of the UK Planning and Scheduling Special Interest Group*, 2000.
6. J. Porteous, L. Sebastia, and J. Hoffmann. On the extraction, ordering, and usage of landmarks in planning. In *Recent Advances in AI Planning. 6th European Conference on Planning (ECP'01)*. Springer Verlag, 2001.
7. L. Sebastia, E. Onaindia, and E. Marzal. STeLLa: An optimal sequential and parallel planner. In *Proceedings of the 10th Portuguese Conference on Artificial Intelligence (EPIA'01)*. Springer Verlag, 2001.
8. H. Younes and R. Simmons. On the role of ground actions in refinement planning. In *Proceedings of the Sixth Int. Conference on AI Planning and Scheduling (AIPS'02)*. AAAI Press, 2002.

Scheduling as Heuristic Search with State Space Reduction

Ramiro Varela and Elena Soto

Centro de Inteligencia Artificial.
Universidad de Oviedo. Campus deViesques. E-33271 Gijón. Spain.
Tel. +34-8-5182032. FAX +34-8-5182125.
http:\\www.aic.uniovi.es

Abstract. In this paper we confront the Job Shop Scheduling problem by means of an A* algorithm for heuristic state space searching. This algorithm can guarantee optimal solutions, i.e. it is admissible, under certain conditions, but in this case it requires an amount of memory that grows linearly as the search progresses. We hence start by focusing on techniques that enable us to reduce the size of the search space while maintaining the ability of reaching optimal schedules. We then relax some of the conditions that guarantee optimality in order to achieve a further reduction in the number of states visited. We report results from an experimental study showing the extent to which this reduction is worth carrying out in practice.

1 Introduction

State space searching is a classic artificial intelligence technique suited to problems involving deterministic actions and complete information. It has a number of interesting properties, such as the ability to guarantee optimal solutions and the possibility of exploiting domain knowledge to guide the search. Unfortunately, even when a great amount of knowledge is available at a reasonable computational cost, the total cost of a search process is prohibitive, since the number of explored nodes grows linearly with the size of the search space, even for small problem instances. For this reason, a number of techniques are usually employed to reduce the effective search space with the subsequent loss of optimality.

In this paper we confront the Job Shop Scheduling (JSS) problem by means of an A* heuristic search algorithm [6,7]. Firstly, we use a technique that enables us to restrict the search space to the set of active schedules. This is a subset of feasible schedules to a given problem that contains at least one optimal solution. In order to do so, we exploit the strategy of the well-known G&T algorithm [4]. As we will see in the reported experiments, this technique combined with a classic heuristic can solve small problem instances to optimality. We then exploit two more methods aimed at further reducing the number of states expanded during the search. The first one consists in a reduction of the search space that limits the search to a subset of the active schedules. The second is a weighted heuristic

F.J. Garijo, J.C. Riquelme, and M. Toro (Eds.): IBERAMIA 2002, LNAI 2527, pp. 815–824, 2002.

method that assigns more reliance to the heuristic estimation during the first stage of the search. It becomes clear that neither of the aforementioned methods maintains admissibility, i.e. the guarantee of reaching optimal solutions. However, the effect can be controlled in both cases by means of parameters. We report results from an experimental study in which we calculate the value of the parameters that produce the optimal solution at the lowest cost of the search.

The rest of the paper is organized as follows. In Section 2, we formally describe the JSS problem. In Section 3, we present a version the G&T algorithm, the so-called hybrid G&T, and show how this algorithm can be adapted by means of a parameter to define a search space representing either the whole set or a subset of active schedules. In Section 4, we summarize the main characteristics of the A* algorithm, as well as the heuristic strategies that we used in the experiments. In Section 5, we report the results from our experimental study. Finally, the main conclusions are summarized in Section 6, where we also propose a number of ideas for further work.

2 The Job Shop Scheduling Problem

JSS requires scheduling a set of jobs $\{J_1,...,J_n\}$ on a set of physical resources or machines $\{R_1,...,R_q\}$. Each job Ji consists of a set of tasks or operations $\{t_{i1},...,t_{imi}\}$ to be sequentially scheduled. Each task has a single resource requirement and a fixed duration or processing time du_{il} and a start time st_{il} whose value must be determined. We assume that there is a release date and a due date between which all the tasks have to be performed.

Furthermore, the problem presents two non-unary constraints: *precedence constraints* and *capacity constraints*. Precedence constraints, defined by the sequential routings of the tasks within a job, translate into linear inequalities of the type: $st_{il} + du_{il} \leq st_{il+1}$ (i.e. st_{il} before st_{il+1}). Capacity constraints, which restrict the use of each resource to only one task at a time, translate into disjunctive constraints of the form: $st_{il} + du_{il} \leq st_{jk} \vee st_{jk} + du_{jk} \leq st_{il}$ (two tasks that use the same resource cannot overlap). The most widely used goal is to come up with a feasible schedule

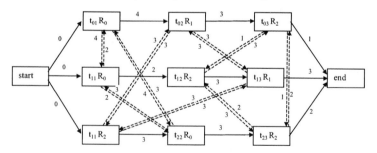

Fig. 1. A directed graph representation of a JSS problem instance with three jobs. The release date is 0 and the due date is 15. The resource requirement of each task is indicated within the boxes. Arcs are weighted with the processing time of the task at the outcoming node.

such that the completion time of the whole set of tasks, i.e. the makespan, is minimized.

In the following, a problem instance will be represented by a directed graph $G = (V, A \cup E)$. Each node of the set V represents a task of the problem, with the exception of the dummy nodes *start* and *end*, which represent tasks with processing time 0. The set of arcs A represents the precedence constraints and the set of arcs E represents the capacity constraints. The set E is decomposed into subsets E_i with $E=\cup_{i=1..m}E_i$, such that there is one E_i for each resource R_i. The subset E_i includes an arc (v,w) for each pair of tasks requiring the resource R_i. Figure 1 depicts an example with three jobs $\{J_0,J_1,J_2\}$ and three physical resources $\{R_0,R_1,R_2\}$. Solid arcs represent the elements of the set A, whereas dotted arcs represent the elements of the set E. The arcs are weighted with the processing time of the task at the source node. The dummy task *start* is connected to the first task of each job; and the last operation of each job is connected to the node *end*.

A feasible schedule is represented by an acyclic subgraph Gs of G, $Gs=(V,A \cup H)$, where $H=\cup_{i=1..m}H_i$, H_i being a Hamiltonian selection of E_i. The makespan of the schedule is the cost of a critical path. A critical path is a longest path from node *start* to node *end*. When this value is less than or equal to the due date, the schedule is a solution to the problem. Therefore, finding a solution can be reduced to discovering compatible Hamiltonian selections, i.e. orderings for the tasks requiring the same resource or partial schedules, that translate into a solution graph Gs without cycles whose critical path does not exceed the due date. Figure 2 shows a graph representing a feasible solution to the problem of Figure 1.

3 The G&T Algorithm and the State Space for the JSS Problem

This is the well-known algorithm proposed by Giffler and Thomson in [4]. Here we present a variant called *hybrid G&T* that is based on a chromosome-decoding schema proposed by Bierwirth and Mattfeld in [2] within the framework of a Genetic Algorithm. This schema is in turn inspired by a proposal made by Storer, Wu and Vaccari in [11] for state space searching. In principle, the G&T is a greedy algorithm that builds up a schedule for a given problem by scheduling one task at a time. In each iteration, a subset of tasks B is determined such that no matter how a

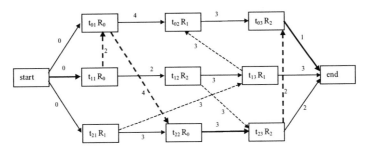

Fig. 2. A feasible schedule for the problem of Figure 1. The boldface arcs show the critical path whose length, i.e. the makespan, is 12.

task is selected from B to be scheduled next, the resulting schedule is *active*. Active schedules are a subset of feasible schedules in which no operation could be started earlier without delaying some other operation. It is easy to prove that the set of active schedules contains at least one optimal schedule. Thus, a search constrained to the whole set of active schedules is exhaustive, while keeping the size of the search space much smaller than a search over the whole set of feasible schedules.

Figure 3 shows the hybrid G&T algorithm. This is a variant of the genuine G&T in which a narrowing mechanism is introduced that enables a reduction of set B in each iteration. This is controlled by a reduction parameter $\delta \in [0,1]$; when $\delta=1$, sentence 6 has a null narrowing effect and hence we have the original G&T algorithm. In this case, it is possible to envisage a non-deterministic sequence of operation selections that gives rise to an optimal schedule. Otherwise, i.e. if $\delta<1$, the search is restricted to a subset of the active schedules; thus guaranteeing the existence of such a sequence is no longer possible. As pointed out in [2], the algorithm produces a *non-delay* schedule at the extreme $\delta=0$. Non-delay scheduling means that no resource is kept idle when it could start processing some operation.

Given its non-deterministic nature, the G&T algorithm can be particularized in many ways by fixing a selection criterion at step 7. For example, it has been widely used in the context of Genetic Algorithms as a decoding schema and is usually combined with some dispatching rule to design a greedy, non-optimal algorithm.

In this paper, we use the G&T algorithm to define a search space that can be

Algortithm G&T hybrid

   1. A = *set containing the first task of each job;*
   while $A \neq \emptyset$ **do**
   2. *Determine the task $\theta' \in A$ with the shortest completion time if scheduled in the current state, that is $t\theta' + du\theta' \leq t\theta + du\theta$, $\forall \theta \in A$;*
   3. *Let M' be the resource required by θ', and B the subset of A whose tasks require M';*
   4. *Delete from B every task that cannot start at a time lower than $t\theta' + du\theta'$;*
   5. *Determine task $\theta'' \in B$ with the lowest possible start time $t\theta''$;*
   /* *the least start time of every operation in B, if it is selected next, is a value of the interval $[t\theta'', t\theta'+du\theta']$ */
   6. *Reduce the set B such that*
      $$B = \{ \theta \in B \mid t\theta < t\theta'' + \delta((t\theta'+du\theta') - t\theta'') \}, \delta \in [0,1]\};$$
   /* *now the interval is reduced to $[t\theta'', t\theta'' + \delta((t\theta'+du\theta') - t\theta'']$ */
   7. *Select $\theta^* \in B$ and schedule it at its lowest possible start time to build a partial schedule corresponding to the next state;*
   8. *Delete θ^* from A and insert the next task of θ^* in that set if θ^* is not the last task of its job;*
   endwhile;

Fig. 3. The hybrid G&T algorithm; $t\theta$ stands for the start time of operation θ and $du\theta$ for its processing time.

explored by a state space search algorithm such as backtracking or best first (BF). This idea was used for instance in [5] and consists in the following two steps, bearing in mind that the initial state s represents a null partial schedule $PS_\varnothing$:

1. At a state n representing a partial schedule PS_T for a set of tasks T, calculate a set B as done by the G&T algorithm in an analogous situation.
2. For each task $t \in B$, generate a successor n' of n with a partial schedule $PS_{T'}$, T' being $T \cup \{t\}$, by scheduling t at its lowest start time from the partial schedule PS_T.

Hence the branching factor of the state space is given by the average value of the cardinality of set B over the whole set of states. This branching factor is expected to be much lower than the one obtained with other approaches like, for example, those proposed in [9] and [1], which might be found to be impractical for an admissible search, even for a small problem instance. On the other hand, the cost $c(n,n')$ is given by the difference $C_{max}(PS_{T'}) - C_{max}(PS_T)$, where $C_{max}(PS_T)$ is the maximum completion time of a task in the partial schedule PS_T. It is easy to prove [10] that the state space generated in this way is a tree.

The state space proposed in [9] consists in selecting an unscheduled operation at a given state and then considering all the possible starting times compatible with the current partial schedule. For each one of these start times, a new partial schedule is built by scheduling the current task at this time. This strategy requires the establishment of a due date for each job so that the current set of possible start times could be restricted to a finite set. This set is initially determined from the release and due dates and the precedence constraints and is further reduced as long as the search continues.

On the other hand, the state space proposed in [1] consists in reductions of the constraint graph of the problem by means of various types of commitments that can be asserted and retracted; for example, fixing a start time of an operation or posting a precedence constraint between activities. In this case, the approach generalizes the JSS problem to other situations where, for example, one goal might be to minimize the number of resources used. In both cases, good experimental results are achieved using a backtracking search guided by means of smart, powerful heuristics. However, it becomes clear that both of the cited schemas are not suitable for an admissible search like A*, due to the fact that the branching factor is so high that it is impractical to store all the states required.

4   The A* Algorithm

The A* algorithm is a general BF heuristic search for graphs [6,7], though the algorithm is much simpler if the state space is a tree. It starts from an initial state s, a set of goal nodes and a transition operator SCS such that for each node n of the search space, $SCS(n)$ provides the set of successor states of n. Each transition from a node n to a successor n' has a positive cost $c(n,n')$. The algorithm searches for a solution path from the node s to one of the goal states. At any one time, there is a set of candidate nodes to be expanded which are maintained in an ordered list

OPEN; this list is initialized with the node *s*. Then in each iteration, the node to be expanded is always the one in *OPEN* with the lowest value of the evaluation function *f*, defined as *f(n)=g(n)+h(n)*; where *g(n)* is the minimal cost known to date from the node *s* to the node *n*, (of course if the search space is a tree, the value of *g(n)* does not change, otherwise this value has to be updated as long as the search progresses) and *h(n)* is a heuristic positive estimation of the minimal distance from *n* to the nearest goal.

The A* algorithm has a number of interesting properties, most of which depend on the heuristic function *h*. First of all, the algorithm is complete. Moreover, if the heuristic function underestimates the actual minimal cost, *h*(n)*, from *n* to the goals, i.e. *h(n)≤h*(n)*, for all nodes, the algorithm is admissible, i.e. the return of an optimal solution is guaranteed. The heuristic function *h(n)* represents knowledge about a specific problem domain, therefore if complete knowledge were available at an assumable computational cost (at most polynomial on the problem size), i.e. *h(n)=h*(n)*, the best solution could be found by expanding the lowest number of nodes possible. Unfortunately, this is rarely the case, and in practical cases we have to look for the best underestimation whose computational cost is assumable. This is because another interesting property of the algorithm is that if we have two admissible heuristics *h1* and *h2*, such that *h1(n)<h2(n)*, *h2* is said to be more informed than *h1* and it can be proved that in this case every node expanded by *h2* is also expanded by *h1*. It is then said that the algorithm using *h2* dominates the one using *h1*.

The most common technique for discovering admissible heuristics is problem relaxation [7]. This consists in relaxing some of the problem constraints so as to obtain a relaxed problem that can be solved to optimality, or at least a good underestimation can be made, in polynomial time. Then the solution cost of the relaxed problem is taken as the real problem cost estimation. In the case of the JSS problem, the constraints that can be relaxed are precedence and capacity constraints. Two problem relaxations are common: in the first, every capacity constraint is relaxed; whereas in the second, every precedence constraint is relaxed. It is easy to see that the cost of the optimal solution in the first case can be calculated in linear time. In the second case, however, the relaxed problem has a similar complexity to that of the original problem, although a reasonably good underestimation of its optimal cost can also be calculated in linear time. It is clear that the two aforementioned relaxations are quite strong, hence the relaxed problem is actually much simpler than the original one and the resulting heuristic is thus not too informed. Unfortunately, as far as we know, lower relaxed versions of the problem cannot be solved in an acceptable amount of time. Even though the heuristics obtained from the two relaxations mentioned above cannot be strictly compared, they are both expected to perform similarly in square problems, i.e. problems with an equal number of jobs and resources. However, the second heuristic will probably perform better for problem instances with much more jobs than resources, whereas in the opposite case, the first heuristic will probably do so.

In the experimental study described in the next section we consider the first of the aforementioned heuristics, which is calculated for a state *n* corresponding to a partial schedule PS_T of a subset of tasks *T*, as follows:

$$h_p(n) = MAX_{J \in JOBS} \left\{ C^J_{max}(PS_T) + \sum_{\theta \in US(J)} du_\theta \right\} - C_{max}(PS_T),\tag{1}$$

where *JOBS* is the set of jobs of the problem instance, $C^J_{max}(PS_T)$ is the completion time of the last scheduled task of job J at node n, $US(J,n)$ is the set of unscheduled tasks of job J at node n and du_θ is the processing time of task θ.

Although the heuristic h_p is clearly an underestimation of the optimal cost, the difference $h^*(n)-h_p(n)$ is not expected to be uniform for all nodes along the search process. Nevertheless, this difference is expected to be quite large at the beginning of the search, subsequently decreasing as the search progress and tends to be null at the end. This leads us to use the following dynamic weighted heuristic technique: a weighting factor $P(n)$ is introduced into the h component of the evaluation function f, so that this function is $f(n)=g(n)+P(n)h(n)$. The value of $P(n)$ depends on the depth of the node n. In this paper, we propose the following value:

$$P(n) = K - \left(K * \frac{depth(n)}{N * M} \right) + 1,\tag{2}$$

where $K \geq 0$ is the weighting parameter, *depth(n)* is the number of tasks scheduled at state n, N is the number of jobs and M is the number of resources. It is clear that for values of $K>0$, the aforementioned function f is not guaranteed to be admissible, since the component $P(n)h(n)$ might overstimate the value of $h^*(n)$. However, for some value of K, this component is expected to be a good aproximation of $h^*(n)$. Weighted heuristic search is widely used; for instance, a dynamic weighted method is proposed in [8] that guarantees that the cost of the solution does not worsen more that a factor ε with respect to the optimal. In [3], a static method is proposed that uses a constant weighting factor W for planning problems; this method guarantees a worsening factor not higher than W. And a dynamic method similar to ours is used in [5] for the JSS problem in conjunction with a limited memory schema and a non-admissible heuristic obtained from a classic dispatching rule that overestimates the optimal cost.

5   Experimental Results

In this section we report results from an experimental study on a set of JSS problems instances. We used the prototype implementation proposed in [10], which is coded in C++ language and developed in Builder C++ 5.0 for Windows. The hardware platform was a Pentium III at 900 Mhz. and 125 Mbytes of RAM. The first problem of the test bed was problem FT06; this is a small problem obtained from the OR library (http://www.ms.ic.ac.uk/info.html). The remaining problem instances were generated by us, as the problem instances from the OR library and other conventional repositories are too large to be solved to optimality by our implementation in an acceptable amount of time.

Table 1. Experimental results from the problem instance FT06 with heuristics h_0 and h_p

Heuristic	Reduction parameter δ	Number of generated nodes	Number of expanded nodes	Branching Factor	Cost of the reached solution	Run time (hh:mm:ss)
h_0	0.0	89,129	66,141	1.26	57	09:03:34
	0.1	89,129	66,141	1.26	57	09:03:34
	0.2	160,575	127,765	1.26	57	57:23:32
	0.3	-	-	-	-	>125:00:00
h_p	0.0	4,662	3,651	1.27	57	4
	0.1	4,662	3,651	1.27	57	4
	0.2	9,170	6,797	1.35	57	10
	0.3	**5,395**	**4,007**	**1.35**	**55**	**5**
	0.4	8,061	5,702	1.41	55	8
	0.5	11,340	7,589	1.49	55	10
	0.6	14,163	9,225	1.54	55	13
	0.7	21,841	13,571	1.61	55	19
	0.8	26,056	15,399	1.69	55	23
	0.9	28,127	16,134	1.74	55	25
	1.0	**28,127**	**16,134**	**1.74**	**55**	**25**

Table 1 shows the results obtained with problem FT06, running the algorithm with the heuristics h_0 and h_p and considering values of the parameter δ ranging in the interval [0.0,1.0]. As expected, heuristic h_0 is unable to solve the problem. On the other hand, heuristic h_p can solve the problem to optimality, even with a space reduction given by $\delta=0.3$. In this case, we can observe a significant reduction in the number of expanded and generated nodes, the branching factor and the running time, as long as the parameter δ decreases from 1.0 to 0.3. For values of δ under 0.3, the number of expanded nodes is higher in some cases, as the search space does not contain an optimal solution.

Figure 4 shows the evolution of the branching factor over the depth of the search space for 2 values of the parameter δ. As we can see, a value of $\delta=0.3$ produces a slightly lower branching factor over the first levels than $\delta=1.0$, which translates into a lower overall number of both generated and expanded nodes. Here,

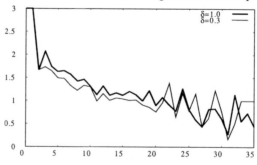

Fig. 4. Evolution of the branching factor over the depth of the search tree for two values of the parameter δ.

Table 2. Experimental results from the problem instance FT06 with heuristic h_p and different values of δ and K. In every case is the optimal solution reached, except with $K=0.3$. In this case, a solution with cost 58 is reached with either value 1.0 or 0.3 of δ.

K	$\delta = 0.3$		$\delta = 1.0$	
	Number of Generated Nodes	Number of Expanded Nodes	Number of Generated Nodes	Number of Expanded Nodes
0.00	5,395	4,007	28,127	16,134
0.05	1,715	1,279	9,397	5,472
0.10	1,092	806	5,257	3,013
0.15	812	598	2,545	1,466
0.20	313	237	599	333
0.25	156	109	563	313
0.30	210	165	574	339

the branching factor at depth N is calculated as the quotient of the number of states generated at depth $N+1$ and N respectively.

Table 2 shows the reduction in the number of nodes generated and expanded for increasing values of K. Here we consider the limit values of δ that generate an exhaustive search space (one containing an optimal solution). As we can see, the number of generated and expanded nodes clearly decreases while the optimal solution is still reached, with the exception of value $K=0.3$, for which a suboptimal solution is reached.

Table 3 shows the results of an experimental study on a set of 10 problem instances of size 6×6 with random job sequences and processing times generated at random in the interval [5,95] from a uniform probability distribution. For each one of the problems, we report the number of nodes expanded for the limit values of δ and K. First for values $\delta=1$ and $K=0$, which are the only values that guarantee optimality. Then for every instance, we kept $K=0$ and decreased the parameter δ down to the lowest value (δmin) that produces an optimal solution. After that, maintaining the value of δmin, the value of K is augmented to the largest value,

Table 3. Experimental results from the set of 10 problem instances

Prob. Inst.	Best solution	Number of Expanded Nodes				δmin	Kmax	
		$\delta=1$, $K=0$	δmin, $K=0$	$\delta=1$, Kmax	δmin, Kmax		$\delta=1$	δmin
0	468	14,018	3,373	14,018	3,373	0.4	0.0	0.0
1	514	1,843	717	1,843	717	0.4	0.0	0.0
2	458	60,276	32,621	56,953	31,674	0.7	0.1	0.1
3	561	3,235	280	457	102	0.0	0.2	0.2
4	545	2,535	543	139	64	0.2	0.3	0.5
5	450	1,337	219	175	48	0.2	0.2	0.2
6	600??	-	-	-	-	-	-	-
7	471	11,627	118	11,627	118	0.8	0.0	0.0
8	481	11,120	481	1776	44	0.0	0.1	0.6
9	477	55,939	27,268	7,141	5,172	0.7	0.5	0.5

Kmax(δmin), that produced an optimal solution. And finally, keeping *δ=1*, the value of *K* is also augmented to the largest value, *Kmax(δ=1)*, that produced an optimal solution. As we can see, the variations of *δ* and *K* allowed without loss of optimality are not the same for all problems and the actual computational cost of obtaining the optimal schedule varies significantly from one problem to another. In fact, problem instance number 6 could not be solved to optimality. The best solution we were able to obtain was by running the algorithm with *δ=0.9* and *K=0.5*, after expanding 62328 states.

6   Conclusions

The main conclusion of the experiments reported above is that in real problems it is possible to reduce the size of the search space as well as to weight the heuristic evaluation function to some extent up to a certain point given by the values *(δmin, Kmax(δmin))* in such a way that the optimal solution is obtained by expanding a number of states much lower than the number of states expanded with values *(1,0)*. Unfortunately, determining the limit values *(δmin, Kmax(δmin))* for a given problem instance is not trivial; it is a new search problem in the two-dimensional space *(δ,K)*. As future work, we plan to study a systematic way to envisage these values and experiment with other techniques to further reduce the search space and accurately weighting the heuristic function in order to improve efficiency so that bigger problem instances can be solved.

References

1. Beck, J. Ch., and Fox, M. S. Dynamic problem structure analysis as a basis for constraint-directed scheduling heuristics. Artificial Intelligence 117, 31-81 (2000).
2. Bierwirth, Ch., and Mattfeld D. C., Production Scheduling and Rescheduling with Genetic Algoritms. Evolutionary Computation 7 (1), 1-17 (1999).
3. Bonet, B., Geffner, H., Planning as Heuristic Search, Art. Intelligence 129, 5-33, (2001).
4. Giffler, B. Thomson, G. L. Algorithms for Solving Production Scheduling Problems. Operations Reseach 8, 487-503 (1960).
5. Hatzikonstantis, L. and Besant, C. B., Job-Shop Scheduling Using Certain Heuristic Search Algorithms. Int. J. Adv. Manuf. Tecnol. 7, 251-261 (1992).
6. Nilsson, N., Principles of Artificial Intelligence, Tioga, Palo Alto, CA, 1980.
7. Pearl, J., Heuristics, Morgan Kauffman, San Francisco, CA, 1983.
8. Pohl, I., Practical and theoretical considerations in heuristic search algorithms, Machine Intelligence 8, Ed. E. W. Elcock and D. Michie, Ellis H. Ltd., Chich., G.B., 1977.
9. Sadeh, N., Fox, M.S., Variable and Value Ordering Heuristics for the Job Shop Scheduling Constraint Satisfaction Problem. Artificial Intelligence 86, 1-41 (1996).
10. Soto, Elena, Resolución de problemas de Satisfacción de Restriciones con el Algoritmo A*. Proyecto fin de carrera nro. 1012076. ETSII e II de Gijón. Univ. de Oviedo. (2002).
11. Storer, R., and Talbot, F. New search spaces for sequencing problems with application to job shop scheduling. Management Science 38, 1494-1509 (1992).

This work has been partially supported by FICYT under project PB-TBI01-04

Domain-Independent Online Planning for STRIPS Domains

Oscar Sapena and Eva Onaindía

Departamento de Sistemas Informáticos y Computación,
Universidad Politécnica de Valencia, Spain
{osapena,onaindia}@dsic.upv.es

Abstract. SimPlanner is an integrated tool for planning and execution-monitoring which allows to interleave planning and execution. In this paper we present the on-line planner incorporated in SimPlanner. This is a domain-independent planner for STRIPS domains. SimPlanner participated in the IPC 2002, obtaining very competitive results.

1 Introduction

Off-line planning generates a complete plan before any action starts its execution [15]. This forces to make some assumptions that are not possible in real environments like, for example, that actions are uninterruptable, that their effects are deterministic, that the planner has complete knowledge of the world or that the world only changes through the execution of actions.

On the other hand, on-line planning allows to start execution while the planner continues working in order to improve the overall planning and execution time [15]. Nowadays there are only some few approaches for planning in dynamic environments and/or with incomplete information [8]:

- *Conditional planning*: there exists two approaches in conditional planning. The first one is based on those problems where the next action to be executed in a plan can depend on the result of previous sensing actions, that is, on information obtained by means of actions during execution time [11]. The second approach tries to consider all the possible contingencies which can happen in the world [2]. Although this solution is untractable in complex environments, it is interesting for particularly dangerous domains. *Probabilistic planning* is a more moderate variant, since it generates conditional plans only for the most likely problems [4].
- *Parallel planning and execution*: this approach separates the planning process from the execution [6]. The execution module is able to react to the environment without the necessity of a plan. The planner is in charge of modifying the behavior of this module in order to increase the satisfaction probability of the objectives.
- *Interleaving planning and execution*: this approach allows quick and effective responses to changes in the environment, and it has been adopted by many researchers [1] [13].

F.J. Garijo, J.C. Riquelme, and M. Toro (Eds.): IBERAMIA 2002, LNAI 2527, pp. 825–834, 2002.

SimPlanner is an integrated tool for planning and execution, and it is based on this latter approach. The on-line planner generates a sequence of actions to reach the goals, while the execution module carries out these actions and provides the planner with sensing information. With this new incorporated information, the planner updates its beliefs about the world.

2   Objectives

SimPlanner is aimed to be an integrated tool for planning and execution monitoring. SimPlanner has been developed to work under several domains and not only for particular robot environments. Because SimPlanner is thought to be a domain-independent tool, we have chosen PDDL 2.1 [7] as the planning language for domain and problem specification. SimPlanner only uses level one of PDDL[1] (without disjunctive preconditions neither conditional effects), although extending it to support levels 2 and 3[2] is quite simple.

Our second objective is to design a fast planner so that SimPlanner is able to react rapidly to exogenous events. Moreover, planning should consume less time than the execution, otherwise the behavior of the system could demean and even lose the chance to reach the goals [12]. If this objective is accomplished, the planner will have additional time to optimize the part of the plan that has not been executed yet. Plan quality is not so relevant in dynamic environments as it is not worth spending lots of time in computing a good plan when it may get invalid shortly after execution starts [10].

The objective of this work is to illustrate the working of the on-line planner integrated in SimPlanner. For this reason, the rest of the SimPlanner modules will only be briefly commented in the following section.

3   SimPlanner Overview

The SimPlanner tool is thought to be used in real environments such as the intelligent control of robots. However, it has initially been implemented as a simulator in order to check its behavior without the necessity of integrating it in different several domains.

The on-line planner is responsible for generating, in an incremental way, a plan to achieve the goals. As soon as the planner calculates the first action, the plan can begin to be executed. Starting from this moment, the planning and execution processes continue working in parallel.

Monitoring is the process of observing the world and trying to find discrepancies between the physical reality and the beliefs of the planner [5]. Contrary to the classic planning, monitoring is needed for different reasons [11]:

 – The planner can have an incomplete knowledge of the world in the initial state.

---

[1] Corresponding to the ADL level of the McDermott's PDDL.
[2] Levels 2 and 3 extend level 1 through numeric variables and durative actions.

- The effects of the actions can be, sometimes, uncertain.
- Exogenous actions produced by external agents can take place.

There exists mainly two types of plan execution monitoring [8]: *action monitoring* checks that preconditions are valid before the action execution and that its effects have taken place as expected. The *environment monitoring* tries to acquire information of the world that can condition the rest of the planning process. Monitoring is, therefore, domain-dependent. Since SimPlanner is being used at the moment as a simulator, this information is input in the system by the user. The user is who decides what information the robot receives and which unexpected events that happen in the world are communicated.

When an unexpected event is detected, the calculated plan is checked in order to assure that it is still valid [5]. If this is the case, the execution simply continues. Otherwise the replanning module is invoked. The replanner tries to reuse as much of the calculated plan as possible without losing the quality of the final plan. A fully detailed description of the replanning module can be found in [14]. After this step, the on-line planner starts again.

4   The Online Planner

This work is focus to illustrate the sequential on-line planner integrated in Sim-Planner. The planner is based on a depth-first search, with no provision for backup. The reason for not using a complete search algorithm is, once again, the necessity of finding very rapidly the first set of actions to be executed. However, the use of a complete search as iterative deepening could be used at some particular times when there is enough slack time for planning. The planning decisions (inferred actions) are consequently irrevocable in SimPlanner. This approach speeds up the planning process, but presents two shortcomings:

- *Dead-ends*: it is possible to reach a state which it is impossible to achieve the goals from [5].
- *Loops*: in spite of the mechanism SimPlanner uses to detect a previous reached state, the planner can get stuck in a loop which prevents the planner from finding a solution.

Therefore, the planner is not complete, but these shortcomings are acceptable in most of cases due to the advantages it offers against classical off-line planners. Moreover, it is possible to improve the planning performance by taking advantage of the time gained by the planner during the execution.

The overall working scheme is shown in Figure 1. A planning problem $P = (O, I, G)$ is a triple where O is the set of actions, I the initial state and G the top-level goals. This algorithm starts from the current state S_0, which initially corresponds to I. The planner calculates the next action to be executed. The current state S_0 is updated by applying this action. This algorithm will be executed repeatedly until all the goals are achieved ($G \subset S_0$).

The SimPlanner planning algorithm can be divided into four main steps:

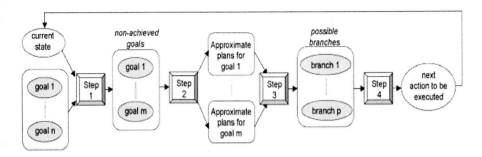

Fig. 1. SimPlanner planner working scheme

1. *Non-achieved goals selection*: the non-achieved goals are those which are not true in the current state ($\{g_i : g_i \in G \wedge g_i \notin S_0\}$).
2. *Calculation of the approximate plans*: an approximate plan is computed for each non-achieved goal g_i separately, i.e., P is decomposed in m planning subproblems $P_1 = (O, S_0, g_1)$, $P_2 = (O, S_0, g_2)$, ..., $P_m = (O, S_0, g_m)$.
3. *Grouping of the approximate plans*: approximate plans are grouped according to their initial actions. Each of these groups is called a *branch* and, all the approximate plans in a *branch* share, at least, the same first action.
4. *Selection of the action to be executed*: the branches are ordered according to a conflict checking criteria. The next action to be executed will be the first action of the branch ordered in the first place.

Steps two and four are the most complex tasks, so they are fully detailed in the next sections.

4.1   Calculation of the Approximate Plans

The computation of an approximate plan is incrementally performed in three stages. The starting point is to build a *Relaxed Planning Graph* (RPG). The second stage generates a special type of graph named *Backward Graph* (BG) and the final stage is aimed at extracting the approximate plans from the BG.

First stage: RPG

The RPG is a graph based on a GraphPlan-like expansion [3] where delete effects are ignored. The first level of the RPG is a literal level which contains all the literals that are true in the current state S_0. The expansion of the RPG finishes when a literal level containing all top-level goals is reached, or when it is not possible to apply any new action. This type of relaxed graph is commonly used in heuristic search based planners [9] as it allows to easily extract admissible heuristics to guide the search.

Second Stage: BG

The BG is a graph whose nodes represent sets of subgoals and whose edges denote *clusters* of actions. SimPlanner uses a regression process to create a BG for each non-achieved top-level goal g_i.

Definition 1 *A cluster for a literal l_i $(C(l_i))$ is the set of actions of the RPG which produce l_i: $C(l_i) = \{a_i : a_i \in RPG \land l_i \in Add(a_i)\}$*

In this regression process, clusters of actions are applied over subgoals, i.e., the *application* of a cluster $C(l_i)$ in a subgoal set yields a situation in which l_i is achieved [16].

Definition 2 *The application of a cluster $C(l_i)$ to a subgoal set S returns a new subgoal set S' defined as:*
$$S' = Result(C(l_i), S) = S - Add(C(l_i)) + Prec(C(l_i)), \text{ where}$$
$$Add(C(l_i)) = \cap Add(a_i), \forall a_i \in C(l_i), \text{ and}$$
$$Prec(C(l_i)) = \cap Prec(a_i) \notin S_0, \forall a_i \in C(l_i)$$

Definition 3 *A BG is defined as a tuple (N, E) where nodes are sets of subgoals and edges represent clusters of actions between two subgoal sets S and S'. An edge is represented as $S' \xrightarrow{C(l_i)} S$.*

The first level of a BG is formed by a single node, corresponding to the top-level goal g_i. Each node in the BG is expanded by applying clusters of actions to each literal in the node. The BG expansion continues until an empty node is reached. The following algorithm shows, in a more formal way, the BG creation process for a particular goal g_i:

$N = \emptyset, E = \emptyset$
$n_0 = \{g_i\}$
$N = N \cup n_0$
$End = false$
while $\neg End$ **do**:
    $N' = N$
    for every non-expanded node $n \in N'$ **do**:
        for every subgoal $l \in n$ **do**:
            $n_{new} = Result(C(l), n)$
            if $n_{new} = \emptyset$ **then** $End = true$ **endif**
            $N = N \cup n_{new}$
            $E = E \cup n_{new} \xrightarrow{C(l)} n$
        endfor
    endfor
endwhile
return (N, E)

Third stage: extracting approximate plans

Once the BG is created, our next goal is to select a single action from each cluster. The BG can be viewed as a set of independent sequences of clusters which reversely applied to a top-level goal g_i lead to an empty set of subgoals.

Definition 4 *A path in a BG = (N,E) (BGpath) is defined as a possible sequence of clusters in the BG. The reverse application of this sequence to a top-level goal leads to an empty set of subgoals:*

$$BGpath = \{C(l_1), C(l_2), ..., C(g_i)\}:$$
$$S_1 \xrightarrow{C(l_1)} \emptyset, S_2 \xrightarrow{C(l_2)} S_1, ..., \{g_i\} \xrightarrow{C(g_i)} S_n \in E$$

For each BGpath in a BG, SimPlanner creates as many sequences of actions as possible combinations can be formed with the actions in the clusters of the BGpath. Each sequence of actions is called an approximate plan.

Definition 5 *An approximate plan (AP) is a possible sequence of actions extracted from a BGpath. Any action in the AP belongs to the cluster located in the same position within the sequence:*
$$AP = \{a_1, a_2, ..., a_n\} : a_j \in C(l_j) \wedge C(l_j) \in BGpath$$

Because the number of APs obtained from a BGpath can be very large, SimPlanner applies a heuristic function to select the best-valued approximate plans. This heuristic function uses a conflict-checking procedure to set a value to each possible AP. A conflict $(Conflict(a_j, a_i))$ occurs when an action a_j ordered before a_i deletes a precondition of a_i and there is no intermediate action which restores that literal. The heuristic function (h) is incrementally applied while the approximate plans are being computed. Initially, the function is applied over the first action of each AP, following over the first two actions of each AP and so on. The application of h over a partial AP, which is made up of the first i actions, is defined as follows:

$$h(AP_{1..i}) = \begin{cases} i - j, & \text{if } \exists a_j : (a_j < a_i \wedge Conflict(a_j, a_i)) \wedge \\ & \quad (\nexists a_k : a_j < a_k < a_i \wedge Conflict(a_k, a_i)) \\ \infty, & \text{if } \forall a_j < a_i, \nexists Conflict(a_j, a_i) \end{cases}$$

The algorithm used to return the best-valued APs is detailed below. Notice that all the APs have the same length $(length(BGpath))$, i.e. the same number of actions. This is due to all the APs are obtained from paths in the same BG, which also have the same length.

```
L = set of all first partial APs = {AP_{1..1}}
for i = 2 to length(BGpath) do:
    for all AP_{1..i-1} ∈ L do:      // Expansion of each partial AP in L
        L = L - AP_{1..i-1}
        AP_{1..i} = AP_{1..i-1} ∪ ComputeNextAction(AP_{1..i-1})
        L = L ∪ AP_{1..i}
    endfor
    max_value = max(h(AP_{1..i})), ∀AP_{1..i} ∈ L
    L = L - {AP_{1..i} : AP_{1..i} ∈ L ∧ h(AP_{1..i}) < max_value}
endfor
return L
```

The resulting set L only contains a small set of all approximate plans obtained from a BG. Additionally, some further criteria are used to reduce even more the number of APs generated for each goal:

- Actions in the plans are reordered, as some plans are sometimes permutations of the same sequence of actions.
- The executability of each AP is checked, inserting additional actions if necessary. Those plans with a lower number of executable actions are rejected.

4.2   Selection of the Action to Be Executed

Approximate plans are grouped into branches forming a tree topology. All the APs in a branch begin with the same action, which is the root node of the tree. Gradually, APs in a branch diverge to reach their own objectives.

Then, these branches are ordered in order to find out which branch must be executed in the first place. A branch B_1 is ordered before a branch B_2 in the following situations:

- *Flexible orders*: let's suppose that the first action of branch B_1 produces literal p, and this literal is not deleted throughout the rest of the branch. If the first action of branch B_2 needs and also deletes literal p, then branch B_1 is ordered before branch B_2. This type of situations often occurs in domains like *Logistics*[3], *Zeno-Travel*[4], *DriverLog*[4], etc. Flexible orders are very useful, for example, to order the *load* and *unload* actions in transportation domains before moving the involved vehicle.
- *Non-flexible orders*: let's suppose that both branches have an action that needs and deletes literal p. This is a non-flexible order since it is not possible to order these actions unless an additional action which restores p is inserted between them. If this additional action is found in only one of the branches, then this branch is ordered before the other one. This type of situations often occurs in domains where there exists very strong interactions between the goals, such as *BlocksWorld*[3], *Depots*[4], *FreeCell*[3], etc.

After applying this process, SimPlanner rejects those branches which are not ordered at first place. If there is more than one branch left, some additional criteria are applied in order to select a single branch. For example, if the goals achieved by a branch B_1 is a subset of the goals achieved by another branch B_2, B_1 is discarded. Another rule is to remove those branches with a lower number of executable actions, etc.

The first action of the selected branch is inserted at the end of the final plan. The plan generation finishes when all the goals are achieved.

5   Results

SimPlanner has been tested on a wide range of domains: *Blocksworld*, *Logistics*, *Monkey*, etc. Moreover, SimPlanner planner participated in the 2002 International Planning Competition (IPC2002). All the data shown in this section are

---

[3] Domains used in the IPC 2000 (http://www.cs.toronto.edu/aips2000)
[4] Domains used in the IPC 2002 (http://www.dur.ac.uk/d.p.long/competition.html)

extracted from the results of this competition [5]. The most similar planner to SimPlanner in the competition was FF-Speed [9] as it is designed to return sequential plans very quickly. In fact, FF-Speed is probably the fastest planner in its category, at the expense of a loss in the quality of the generated plans.

The graphics (Figures 2 and 3) show a comparative between SimPlanner planner and FF-Speed for the *Depots* and *Satellite* domains. *Depots* domain is a combination of the *Logistics* and the *Blocksworld* domains, and the *Satellite* domain consists in planning and scheduling a set of observation tasks between multiple satellites. An additional serie showing the time that SimPlanner takes to compute the first action to execute (*SP 1st action*) is also included in these graphics. The times obtained by SimPlanner and FF-Speed are quite similar. FF-Speed is, in general, a bit faster than SimPlanner, although its behaviour is more unpredictable (SimPlanner scales up very well as the size and complexity of the problems increase). But the main contribution of SimPlanner is that it is able to compute the first action of a plan very quickly (only a few tenths of seconds in relatively big problems). As the problem resolution is close to the goals, computation time for deducing an action is shorter and shorter. This feature allows the planner to quickly interact in dynamic environments and get the plan adapted to the new situations which can arise (unexpected events, changes in the goals, etc.)

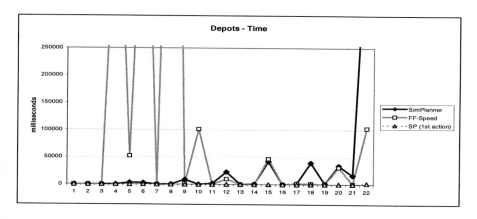

Fig. 2. Time for the *Depots* domain

With regard to the quality of plans, in general SimPlanner produces longer plans than FF-Speed (Figure 4). The planning approach used by SimPlanner makes difficult to compute high quality plans.

However, since execution usually takes longer than planning, SimPlanner can take advantage of this extra time to optimize the remaining plan. Also it is

[5] Full results of IPC2002 available at
http://www.dur.ac.uk/d.p.long/competition.html

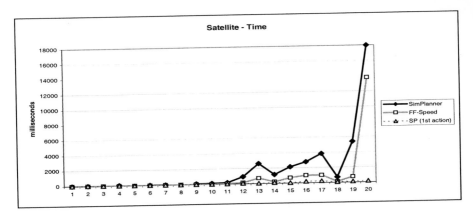

Fig. 3. Time for the *Satellite* domain

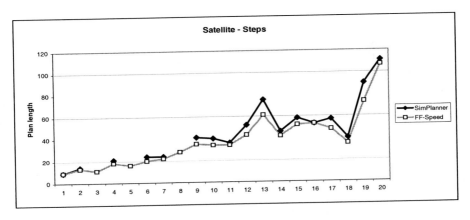

Fig. 4. Quality of the plans for the *Satellite* domain

possible to adjust the heuristics used by the planner to minimize the error rate in the action selection process. What we have presented here is still a preliminary version of the on-line planner so it can be improved in many different ways.

6   Conclusions and Future Work

SimPlanner is a planning tool for working in dynamic environments or with incomplete information. It allows to monitor a plan execution, to recover from changes in the environment and to adapt the plan to the new needs in fractions of a second. The results of the first version of the integrated on-line planner show that it is able to work very efficiently in a wide range of domains.

We are currently extending SimPlanner to handle numeric variables and functions. This is a very important feature in those domains in which distances and consumable resources (batteries, fuel, etc.) are necessary. In these domains, such as intelligent control of robots, it is also important to be able to handle actions with different durations.

On the other hand, we are working on the integration of SimPlanner in a real environment of mobile robots. Aspects that arise in real environments (like what variables to monitor, how to react when the execution is interrupted, etc.) should be handled, producing a more complex and versatile tool.

Acknowledgements. This work has been partially funded by the Spanish Government CICYT project DPI-2001-2094-C03-03 and by the Technical University of Valencia projects UPV-2001-0017 and UPV-2001-0980.

References

1. J.A. Ambros-Ingerson and S. Steel. 'Integrating planning, execution and monitoring.' *In Proceedings of AAAI-88*, 83–88, (1988).
2. E.M. Atkins, E.H. Durfee, and K.G. Shin. 'Detecting and reacting to unplanned-for world states.' *Papers from the 1996 AAAI Fall Symposium*, 1–7, (1996).
3. A. Blum and M. Furst. 'Fast planning through planning graph analysis.' *Artificial Intelligence*, **90**, 281–300, (1997).
4. J. Blythe. 'Planning with external events.' *Proceedings of the 10th Conference on Uncertainty in Artificial Intelligence*, 94–101, (1994).
5. G. De Giacomo and R. Reiter. 'Execution monitoring of high-level robot programs.' *Principles of Knowledge Representation and Reasoning*, 453–465, (1998).
6. M. Drummond, K. Swanson, J. Bresina, and R. Levinson. 'Reaction-first search.' *In Proceedings of the IJCAI-93*, 1408–1414, (1993).
7. M. Fox and L. Derek. 'PDDL2.1': An extension to PDDL for expressing temporal planning domains. *In http://www.dur.ac.uk/d.p.long/IPC/pddl.html*, (2002).
8. K.Z. Haigh and M. Veloso. Interleaving planning and robot execution for asynchronous user requests. *Papers from the AAAI Spring Symposium*, pages 35–44, 1996.
9. J. Hoffman and B. Nebel. 'The FF planning system: Fast planning generation through heuristic search.' *In JAIR*, **14**, 253–302, (2001).
10. Y. Lespérance and H.K. Ng. 'Integrating planning into reactive high-level robot programs.' *In Proc. of International Cognitive Robotics Workshop*, 49–54, (2000).
11. H. Levesque. 'What is planning in the presence of sensing?' *Proceedings AAAI*, 1139–1146, (1996).
12. T.S. Li and J.C. Latombe. 'On-line manipulation planning for two robot arms in a dynamic environment.' *In Proceedings of the 12th Annual IEEE International Conference on Robotics and Automation*, 1048–1055 (1995).
13. I.R. Nourbakhsh. *'Interleaving Planning and Execution for Autonomous Robots.'* Kluwer Academy Publishers, 1997.
14. E. Onaindia, O. Sapena, L. Sebastia, and E. Marzal. 'SimPlanner: an execution-monitoring system for replanning in dynamic worlds.' *Proceedings of EPIA-01, Lecture Notes in Computer Science*, 393–400, (2001).
15. F. Terpstra, A. Visser, and B. Hertzberger. 'An on-line planner for MARIE', *In Proc. of Irish Conference on A.I. and Cognitive Science*, 199–209, (2001).
16. D.S. Weld. 'An introduction to least commitment planning,' *AI Magazine*, **15**(4), (1994).

A Pomset-Based Model for Estimating Workcells' Setups in Assembly Sequence Planning

Carmelo Del Valle, Miguel Toro, Rafael Ceballos, and Jesús S. Aguilar-Ruiz

Dept. Lenguajes y Sistemas Informáticos, Universidad de Sevilla,
Avda. Reina Mercedes s/n, 41012 Sevilla, Spain
{carmelo, mtoro, ceballos, aguilar}@lsi.us.es

Abstract. This paper presents a model based on pomsets (partially ordered multisets) for estimating the minimum number of setups in the workcells in Assembly Sequence Planning. This problem is focused through the minimization of the makespan (total assembly time) in a multirobot system. The planning model considers, apart from the durations and resources needed for the assembly tasks, the delays due to the setups in the workcells. An A* algorithm is used to meet the optimal solution. It uses the *And/Or* graph for the product to assemble, that corresponds to a compressed representation of all feasible assembly plans. Two basic admissible heuristic functions can be defined from relaxed models of the problem, considering the precedence constraints and the use of resources separately. The pomset-based model presented in this paper takes into account the precedence constraints in order to obtain a better estimation for the second heuristic function, so that the performance of the algorithm could be improved.

1 Introduction

Assembly planning is a very important problem in the manufacturing of products. It involves the identification, selection and sequencing of assembly operations, stated as their effects on the parts. The identification of assembly operations usually leads to the set of all feasible assembly plans. The number of them grows exponentially with the number of parts, and depends on other factors, such as how the single parts are interconnected in the whole assembly, i.e. the structure of the graph of connections. In fact, this problem has been proved to be NP-complete [1]. The identification of assembly tasks is carried out analyzing the graph of connections and taking into account the geometry of parts and the properties of contacts between parts [2] [3].

Two kinds of approaches have been used for searching the optimal assembly plan. One, the more qualitative, uses rules in order to eliminate assembly plans that includes difficult tasks or awkward intermediate subassemblies. Another approach, the more quantitative, uses an evaluation function that computes the merit of assembly plans. There are various of these proposals in [4].

The criterion followed in this work is the minimization of the total assembly time (*makespan*) in the execution of the plan in a multirobot system, supposed the estimations of the durations of each possible task as well as of the necessary resources to carry out them [5]. This approach allows using the results in different stages of the

F.J. Garijo, J.C. Riquelme, and M. Toro (Eds.): IBERAMIA 2002, LNAI 2527, pp. 835–844, 2002.
© Springer-Verlag Berlin Heidelberg 2002

whole planning process, from the design of the product and of the manufacturing system, to the final execution of the assembly plan.

The rest of the paper is organized as follows: Section 2 describes the problem of assembly sequence planning and the model used. Section 3 shows the proposed A* algorithm, as well as the two basic heuristics taken from relaxed models of the problem. The pomset-based model for estimating more accurately the minimum number of setups in the assembly machines is exposed in Section 4. Section 5 presents some of the results obtained, and some final remarks are made in the concluding section.

2   Assembly Sequence Planning

The process of joining parts together to form a unit is known as assembly. An assembly plan is a set of partially ordered assembly tasks, which allows the whole assembly of a product. Each task consists of joining a set of sub-assemblies to give rise to an ever larger sub-assembly. A sub-assembly is a group of parts having the property of being able to be assembled independently of other parts of the product. An assembly sequence is an ordered sequence of the assembly tasks satisfying all the precedence constraints. Each assembly plan corresponds to one or more assembly sequences.

And/Or graphs have been used for a representation of the set of all feasible assembly plans for a product [6]. The *Or* nodes correspond to sub-assemblies, the top node coinciding with the whole assembly, and the leaf nodes with the individual parts. Each *And* node corresponds to the assembly task joining the sub-assemblies of its two final nodes producing the sub-assembly of its initial node. In the *And/Or* graph representation of assembly plans, an *And/Or* path whose top node is the *And/Or* graph top node and whose leaf nodes are the *And/Or* graph leaf nodes is associated to an assembly plan, and is referred to as an assembly tree. An important advantage of this representation, used in this work, is that the *And/Or* graph shows the independence of assembly tasks that can be executed in parallel. Figure 1 shows an example of this representation. *And* nodes are represented as hyperarcs.

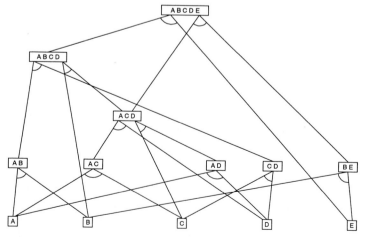

Fig. 1. *And/Or* graph of product ABCDE.

The problem is focused on searching an optimal assembly sequence, i.e. an ordering of an assembly plan (one of the *And/Or* trees of the *And/Or* graph). The evaluation of solutions implies a previous estimation of the durations and resources (robots, tools, fixtures…) needed for each assembly task in the *And/Or* graph. Another factor taken into account here, is the time necessary for changing tools in the robots, which is of the same order as the execution time of the assembly tasks and therefore cannot be disregarded as in Parts Manufacturing. $\Delta_{cht}(R,T,T')$ will denote the time needed for installing the tool T in the robot R if the tool T' was previously installed. Notice that any change of configuration in the robots can be modeled in this way.

3   Algorithm Description

An algorithm based on the A* search [7] has been developed, which has two well-differentiated parts: one of them studies the sequential execution of assembly tasks, and the other solves the parallel execution of assembly tasks (the representation through the *And/Or* graph allows a natural study of this stage). This is actually the most complex section, because the execution of tasks involved in the assembly of a sub-assembly is not independent of the rest, and can influence the execution of tasks in the other part of the assembly.

Because of the *And/Or* graph's structure, the assembly problem can be studied, starting from the final situation (the whole assembly) and going towards the initial one (the individual parts). This way, we will solve the opposite problem, that of disassembly, but supposing assembly tasks, so that the solution of the original problem can be made reversing the solution obtained by the algorithm.

Heuristic functions based on the execution of tasks taken only from the part of the tree below the node, and the time remaining for the use of tools and robots (supposing the minimum number of tool changes, in order to maintain the algorithm as A*) have been used in order to expand the minimum number of nodes and avoid redundant nodes.

3.1   Sequential Execution of Tasks

An A* algorithm to search for the global assembly plan can be implemented in the following way. Beginning with an initial node whose state represents the complete assembly realization, and therefore corresponds to the root node of the *And/Or* graph (complete assembly), all its possible successors are generated, whose states will represent the execution at the end of the assembly process of the tasks corresponding to the *And* nodes coming from the root node of the *And/Or* graph.

Two types of nodes may be generated, depending on the destination *Or* nodes of each chosen *And* node. If at least one of these *Or* nodes corresponds to an individual part, the assembly process will continue to be sequential, and the node resulting from the expansion may be treated as the initial node, where the node corresponding to the non-trivial sub-assembly will take the place of the root node.

If, on the other hand, the application of the task involves two non-trivial sub-assemblies, in the resulting plan (or plans in general) the task arrangement is not totally specified (various possible sequences exist for each assembly plan), or tasks may be carried out in parallel. There is also an interdependence amongst the sub-assemblies, because they potentially use the same set of resources. The treatment of this type of nodes has therefore to be undertaken in a different way from those corresponding to sequential task execution, and this will connect with the second part of this algorithm.

The evaluation function used for the nodes generated in the sequential stage is

$$f(n) = g(n) + h(n) \tag{1}$$

$g(n)$ being the time accumulated in the execution of tasks corresponding to the state of node n, including the delays in the necessary tool changes and in the transportation of intermediate subassemblies, and $h(n)$ being an optimistic estimation of the remaining time in which to complete the global process. ($h(n)$ should be a lower bound of the remaining time for the algorithm to be A*.) Due to the fact that various different plans (and therefore different task sets which would complete the assembly process) may be reached from node n, a detailed study would be computationally costly, and therefore

$$h(n) = durMin \cdot \log_2\left(a(n)+1\right) \tag{2}$$

has been chosen, $a(n)$ being the number of tasks necessary to complete the assembly plan, and $durMin$ the minimum duration of tasks. As can be seen, it is also impossible to determine the minimum number of tool changes without a detailed study, and therefore when estimating $h(n)$ it is assumed to be zero.

All the assembly trees (task precedence trees) are obtained for the "parallel" nodes, and are studied separately. The function $h(n)$ corresponding to each tree is defined in the following subsection.

3.2   Parallel Execution of Tasks

The objective of this part of the algorithm is to determine the total minimum time for the execution of the precedence trees obtained in the previous section. In order to do this, an A* algorithm is used again. Now, the nodes of the expansion tree present partial information about the execution of the assembly process. Concretely, at each expansion step only one assembly task is introduced, and its processing time will affect only one of the workstations, the same state being retained by the other workstations.

The state corresponding to a node of the expansion tree is represented by using the tasks available for introduction in the state of the next step, termed "candidates", and their earliest starting times, denoted $est(J_i)$. At the same time, the last tool used is included for each robot, denoted $lastTool(R_j)$, as well as the final time of use, denoted $lastTime(R_j)$.

The evaluation function for the nodes obtained by this algorithm is similar to (1), being now $g(n)$ the largest of the earliest starting times of $cand(n)$, the set of candidates, and the final times of the already finished in n without successors. The function $h(n)$ must be an optimistic estimation of the time remaining, taking into account the slacks between $g(n)$ and the different times describing the state of n. Two different heuristic functions have been defined in this work, taken from relaxed models of the problem in which some constraints have been disregarded.

The heuristic function h_1: precedence of tasks. It corresponds to an estimation of the time remaining if the interdependencies between different branches in the tree are not taken into account. It is looked at only in depth. It can be defined as follows:

$$h_1(n) = \max\left(0, \max_{J_i \in cand(n)} \left(h_1(J_i) - e(n, J_i)\right)\right) \tag{3}$$

where

$$e(n, J_i) = g(n) - est(n, J_i) \tag{4}$$

$$h_1(J) = dur(J) + \max_{J_i \in suc(J)} \left(h_1(J_i) + \tau\left(J_i, R(J), T(J)\right)\right) \tag{5}$$

$$\tau(J, R, T) = \max\left(0, \max_{J_i \in suc(J)} \left(h_1(J_i) + \tau\left(J_i, R(J), T(J)\right) - h_1(J)\right)\right) \tag{6}$$

In the above expressions, n is an expansion node, J is an assembly task, and $e(n, J)$ is the existing time slack. $R(J)$ and $T(J)$ are the robot and tool necessary for the execution of task J, and $dur(J)$ is its duration. $\tau(J, R, T)$ is the added delay, due to the fact that the tool T is being used by robot R in task J and successors, because of the necessary tool changes. The equation (6) defines $\tau(J, R, T)$ when $R \neq R(J)$. In the case $R = R(J)$, $\tau(J, R, T)$ is defined as $\Delta_{cht}(R, T(J), T)$ (that could be zero if $T = T(J)$).

Notice that $h_1(J)$ does not depend on the expansion nodes, and thus allows one to calculate a lower bound prior to using the A* algorithm.

The heuristic function h_2: use of resources. It corresponds to an estimation of the time needed if only the remaining usage times of the tools in each robot are taken into account, further supposing the number of tool changes to be at a minimum. It can be defined as follows:

$$h_2(n) = \max_{robots}\left(h_2(n, R_i) - e(n, R_i)\right) \tag{7}$$

where

$$e(n, R) = g(n) - lastTime(n, R) \tag{8}$$

and $h_2(n, R_i)$ is the minimum time of use of robot R_i without considering the task precedence constraints. If each tool is associated with only one robot, the calculation of $h_2(n, R)$ is equivalent to the traveling salesman problem, when considering the tools not yet used and an initial node corresponding to the last used tool in the robot R:

$$h_2(n, R) = \sum_{H_j \in R} \sum_{J_i \in cand(n)} h_2(J_i, T_j) + \left(n\Delta_{cht}(R)\right) \tag{9}$$

with $h_2(J, T)$ the remaining time of usage of tool T by task J and its successors. The term $\left(n, \Delta_{cht}(R)\right)$ refers to the time needed for the tool changes. In the usual case that tool changing times do not depend on the type of tool, it can be calculated easily:

$$\left(n, \Delta_{cht}(R)\right) = N_{cht}(n, R) \cdot \Delta_{cht}(R) \tag{10}$$

where $N_{cht}(n, R)$ is the number of tool changes needed in R for the remaining tasks for completing the assembly from n, and $\Delta_{cht}(R)$ is the duration of a simple tool change in R. Without considering any precedence information, an in order to maintain the admissibility of the heuristic, it must be supposed that the remaining tools will be installed only once in the estimation of $N_{cht}(n, R)$.

4   The Pomset-Based Model

The heuristic h_2 does not consider any information about precedence of tasks, and, in order to meet an admissible heuristic, it must be supposed that every tool will be installed once, so that the number of tool changes is minimized. The heuristic h_3 is based on h_2, but it estimates more accurately the number of tool changes. For that, a pomset-based model is used that reflects some of the precedence constraints of the problem.

Given a precedence tree of tasks, the tasks using the same robot must be done sequentially. For each sequence of tasks using the same robot, it can be defined a sequence of tools, in the same order as that of the tasks which use them. Because we are only interested in the tool changes, we must transform that sequence of tools in another one substituting consecutive repetitions of the same element for an instance of it. These sequences will be denoted as *sequences of tools*.

The objective is to find, for each robot, the minimum number of times that each tool must be installed, but estimated in the more realistic way possible. Figure 2 shows a simple example: for the precedence tree of tasks (a), the precedence tree of usages of tools in the robot R1 is shown (b); in order to minimize the number of tool changes, T1 must be installed once, so that (c) represents the constraint precedence graph of tools, each node corresponding to possibly more than one consecutive usage of the tool. Finally, (d) represents the *pomset*[1] corresponding to a simplified model of (c), maintaining only the precedence constraints referring to the tool in the top node.

The data structure pomset was introduced by Pratt [8] in the specification of concurrent programs. An alignment is a sequence of the elements of the pomset satisfying the ordering constraints. In our pomset-based model, not all the possible alignments from the pomset will correspond to valid sequences of tools, because of the constraints that have been disregarded. For example, the pomset in Figure 2 (d) has an alignment {T2,T3,T2,T1}, which does not correspond to any possible sequences of tool formed from (c). However, this in not the main purpose, but the number of tool changes, which is related to the cardinality of the pomset.

According to the previous comments, the pomset can be defined as a tuple $< \mathcal{B}, \mathcal{F} >$, $\mathcal{B}$ being a multiset containing the same elements (and multiplicity) as the optimal sequence of tools taken from the precedence tree. On the other hand, $\mathcal{F}$ denotes the set of tools which can appear the first in any optimal sequence.

Two basic operations are needed in the recursive definition of the pomsets (one for each robot) for a precedence tree. The first operation, denoted *push*, allows adding one element to the pomset, proceeding from the root node. The other operation, denoted *merge*, is about merging the pomsets from the subtrees.

The pomset $< \mathcal{B}, \mathcal{F} >$ corresponding to a precedence tree whose root node is the task J and robot R, denoted $\mathcal{P}(J, R)$, is given by

---

[1] *pomset* = partially ordered multiset. A multiset is a set in which the elements can be repeated.

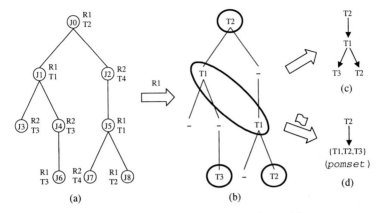

Fig. 2. An example of a pomset from the model.

$$\begin{aligned}
P(J,R) &\equiv \begin{cases} <\{T(J)\},\{T(J)\}> & \text{if } suc(J)=\varnothing \\ push\big(T(J),P(J_1,R)\big) & \text{if } suc(J)=\{J_1\} \\ push\big(T(J),merge\big(P(J_1,R),P(J_2,R)\big)\big) & \text{if } suc(J)=\{J_1,J_2\} \end{cases} \\
(R=R(J)) &
\end{aligned} \tag{11}$$

if R is the robot used by J. If robot R is not the used by J, then the pomset is defined by

$$\begin{aligned}
P(J,R) &\equiv \begin{cases} \varnothing & \text{if } suc(J)=\varnothing \\ P(J_1,R) & \text{if } suc(J)=\{J_1\} \\ merge\big(P(J_1,R),P(J_2,R)\big) & \text{if } suc(J)=\{J_1,J_2\} \end{cases} \\
(R \neq R(J)) &
\end{aligned} \tag{12}$$

The operation *push* is defined by

$$push\big(x,<B,\mathcal{F}>\big) \equiv \begin{cases} <B,\{x\}> & \text{if } x\in\mathcal{F} \\ <B\uplus\{x\},\{x\}> & \text{if } x\notin\mathcal{F} \end{cases} \tag{13}$$

that shows that the set of first elements must contain the element pushed only, and that and instance of this element must be added (operator $\uplus$, multiset additive union) when the element does no belong to the set of first elements of the original pomset, reflecting the corresponding additional change tool.

The operation *merge* is defined by

$$merge(P_1,P_2) \equiv \begin{cases} <B_1\cup B_2,\mathcal{D}_\mathcal{F}(P_1,P_2)> & \text{if } \mathcal{D}_\mathcal{F}(P_1,P_2)\neq\varnothing \\ <B_1\cup B_2,\mathcal{F}_1\cup\mathcal{F}_2> & \text{if } \mathcal{D}_\mathcal{F}(P_1,P_2)=\varnothing \end{cases} \tag{14}$$

where

$$\mathcal{D}_\mathcal{F}(P_1,P_2) \equiv (\mathcal{F}_1\cap\mathcal{F}_2)\cup\mathcal{D}'_\mathcal{F}(P_1,P_2)\cup\mathcal{D}'_\mathcal{F}(P_2,P_1) \tag{15}$$

and

$$\mathcal{D}'_\mathcal{F}(P_i,P_j) \equiv \{x\in\mathcal{F}_i \mid \#(x,B_i) > \#(x,B_j)\} \tag{16}$$

The multiset union operator $\cup$ is defined taking the maximum multiplicity of each element, so that is the adequate operator for the resultant multiset from the merge of the pomsets. The resultant set of first elements is formed according to the concept of *dominance*. Figure 3 shows two cases. The symbol $\otimes$ represents the merge operator,

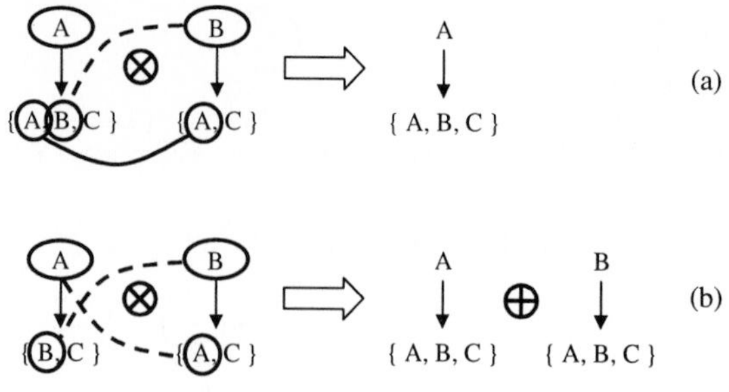

Fig. 3. An example of dominance.

and $\oplus$ is used for expressing the different possibilities we can obtain. In (a), we can obtain a pomset without increasing the number of instances of each element, because the element A in $\mathcal{F}_1$ has more instances in $\mathcal{B}_1$ than in $\mathcal{B}_2$, so we say that A is *dominant*. Moreover, B is not dominant because it cannot appear as first element in any optimal sequence of tools, i.e. without increasing the number of instances. In this situation, $\mathcal{D}_{\mathcal{F}}(\mathcal{P}_1, \mathcal{P}_2)$ is not empty, so we can determine the set of first elements without any problems. In case (b), A and B are not dominants, but the set of first elements cannot be empty. Notice that the optimal sequences can be taken from two different pomsets, in which the number of instances for A and B are different, expressing that the first element in an optimal sequence can be A or B, and depending of which is choosed, it has an additional instance. We say that there is an indetermination in the number of instance of A and B. The model proposed in this work makes a simplification about this aspect (see eq. (14)), so that the number of instances of A and B are not increased, and both appear as possible first element in an optimal sequence. This way, the resultant heuristic is admissible, but losing accuracy. On the other hand, if an element is present in the set of first elements in both pomsets, it must be present in the set of first elements in the resultant pomset.

A last operation must be defined for the pomset structure, for obtaining the number of tool changes. This operation is denoted as *ntrans*, and for the model proposed in this work is defined as the number of elements of the multiset less one:

$$ntrans(\mathcal{P}) = \sum_{x \in \mathcal{B}} \#(x, \mathcal{B}) - 1 \tag{17}$$

Finally, the new heuristic h_3 is defined in the same way as h_2 (eq. (9)), but in the calculation of $(n, \Delta_{cht}(R))$ (eq. (10)), the term $N_{cht}(n, R)$ is now estimated more accurately. If the candidate tasks in n are $J_1, ..., J_m$, and T is the last tool used in R,

$$N_{cht}(n, R) = ntrans\left(push\left(T, merge\left(\mathcal{P}(J_1, R), ..., \mathcal{P}(J_m, R)\right)\right)\right) \tag{18}$$

5   Results

The algorithm has been tested in a variety of situations, considering different product structures (number of parts, number of connections between parts), different types of

And/Or graphs (number of sub-assemblies, number of assembly tasks for each sub-assembly), and different assembly resources (number of robots, number of tools).

The results in Tables 1-4 correspond to a hypothetical product of 30 parts, with 396 *Or* nodes and 764 *And* nodes in the *And/Or* graph. The number of linear sequences is about 10^{21}. The tables show the effect of having more or less resources for assembling the product in the performance of the algorithm. The results refer to 10 different combinations of durations and resources for assembly tasks.

The heuristic functions defined present two different effects in calculating $h(n)$. The estimation made from h_1 is due to the most unfavorable candidate task. In the other hand, h_2 and h_3 shows an additive effect, because of the uses of robots by all candidate tasks. Therefore, two new heuristic functions can be defined from the com-

Table 1. Results for 2 robots and 2 tools/robot

Heuristic	Nodes visited			Time (ms)			N-Pr	N-F	% Error
	Ave	Max	Min	Ave	Max	Min			
h_1	41492	89189	2520	19429	30590	180	4	6	0,990
h_2	9316	42775	32	1422	6420	0	5	0	0,000
h_3	617	3019	32	176	870	0	2	0	0,000
$max(h_1, h_2)$	16385	71585	32	4291	30050	0	4	1	0,248
$max(h_1, h_3)$	3422	30506	32	3257	31470	0	1	1	0,248

Table 2. Results for 2 robots and 4 tools/robot

Heuristic	Nodes visited			Time (ms)			N-Pr	N-F	% Error
	Ave	Max	Min	Ave	Max	Min			
h_1	40093	56108	3020	25025	30930	710	2	8	2,648
h_2	5311	19398	267	790	4230	50	1	0	0,000
h_3	1458	6120	32	198	930	0	1	0	0,000
$max(h_1, h_2)$	5078	19009	387	1143	4450	60	1	0	0,000
$max(h_1, h_3)$	1303	4805	32	418	1870	0	1	0	0,000

Table 3. Results for 4 robots and 2 tools/robot

Heuristic	Nodes visited			Time (ms)			N-Pr	N-F	% Error
	Ave	Max	Min	Ave	Max	Min			
h_1	16905	85540	32	2357	11700	0	1	0	0,000
h_2	2751	7195	32	263	710	0	2	0	0,000
h_3	1781	7011	32	533	2030	0	3	0	0,000
$max(h_1, h_2)$	804	2098	32	99	220	0	2	0	0,000
$max(h_1, h_3)$	794	2098	32	148	330	0	2	0	0,000

Table 4. Results for 4 robots and 4 tools/robot.

Heuristic	Nodes visited			Time (ms)			N-Pr	N-F	% Error
	Ave	Max	Min	Ave	Max	Min			
h_1	22697	93376	32	6084	30530	0	4	1	0,302
h_2	1808	5907	128	197	660	0	1	0	0,000
h_3	1072	5014	119	396	2260	0	1	0	0,000
$max(h_1, h_2)$	1765	5907	32	278	980	0	2	0	0,000
$max(h_1, h_3)$	1062	5014	119	396	2260	0	1	0	0,000

bination of both effects, taking the most realistic estimation, $\max\left(h_1(n),h_2(n)\right)$ and $\max\left(h_1(n),h_3(n)\right)$.

The use of A* algorithms presents some problems. The most important is the storage space that could be occupied. The algorithm was adapted so that it uses a depth-first search periodically for finding a new solution whose value could be used for pruning the search tree. Another improvement was done in order to detect symmetries, so that redundant nodes are avoided.

Apart from the number of nodes visited and execution times, the tables show how many times the optimal solution was found by a depth-first movement (N-Pr), how many times the algorithm did not find the optimal solution in 30 seconds, when the available memory was exhausted (N-F), and the error rate.

6   Conclusions

A model for the selection of optimal assembly sequences for a product in a generic multirobot system has been presented. The objective of the plan is the minimization of the total assembly time. To meet it, the model takes into account, in addition to the assembly times and resources for each task, the times needed to change tools in the robots.

A pomset-based model has been proposed for estimating the number of workcells' setups needed in Assembly Planning. The model is used in the definition of a heuristic function for an A* algorithm. The result is a more informed heuristic than the one which was based on, due to the combination of two kinds of constraints, the precedence constraints and the use of the resources.

References

1. R.H. Wilson, L. Kavraki, T. Lozano-Pérez and J.C. Latombe. Two-Handed Assembly Sequencing. *Int. Jour. of Robotic Research*. Vol. 14, pp. 335-350, 1995.
2. L.S. Homem de Mello and A.C. Sanderson. A Correct and Complete Algorithm for the Generation of Mechanical Assembly Sequences. *IEEE Trans. Robotic and Automation.*Vol 7(2), 1991, pp. 228-240.
3. T. L. Calton. Advancing design-for-assembly. The next generation in assembly planning. *Proc. 1999 IEEE International Symposium on Assembly and Task Planning*, pp. 57-62, Porto, Portugal, July 1999.
4. M. H. Goldwasser and R. Motwani. Complexity measures for assembly sequences. *Int. Journal of Computational Geometry and Applications*, 9:371-418, 1999.
5. C. Del Valle and E.F. Camacho. Automatic Assembly Task Assignment for a Multirobot Environment. *Control Eng. Practice*, Vol. 4, No. 7, 1996, pp. 915-921.
6. L.S. Homem de Mello and A.C. Sanderson. And/Or Graph Representation of Assembly Plans. *IEEE Trans. Rob. Automation*. Vol. 6, No. 2, pp. 188-199, 1990.
7. J. Pearl. Heuristics: Intelligent Search Strategies for Computer Problem Solving. Reading, MA, Addison-Wesley, 1984.
8. V.R. Pratt. Modeling Concurrency with Partial Orders. *Int. Journal of Parallel Programming*. Vol. 15, No. 1, pp. 33-71, Feb 1986.

New Methodology for Structure Identification of Fuzzy Controllers in Real Time

H. Pomares, I. Rojas, and J. González

Department of Computer Architecture and Computer Technology. University of Granada
(Spain)

Abstract. This paper presents an innovative approach to self-adaptation of the structure of a neuro-fuzzy controller in real time. Without any off-line pretraining, the algorithm achieves very high control performance through the iteration of a three-stage algorithm. In the first stage, coarse tuning of the neuro-fuzzy rules (both rule consequents and membership functions of the premises) is accomplished using the sign of the dependency of the plant output with respect to the control signal and an overall analysis of the main operating regions. In stage two, fine tuning of the rules is achieved based on the controller output error using a gradient-based method. Finally, the third stage is responsible of modifying the structure of the controller, proposing that input variable which should get a new membership function in order to improve the control policy in an optimum way.

1   Introduction

The problem of adjusting the parameters of a control system based on the control performance in real time without any off-line pretraining is one of the most important issues in intelligent systems research. The main difficulty encountered when dealing with this topic is that the plant behavior is a priori unknown, i.e., neither the plant model nor its differential equations are available.

As is well known, fuzzy logic controllers have proved successful in a number of applications where no analytical model of the plant to be controlled is available [2], [3]. Among the different ways of implementing a fuzzy controller, adaptive neuro-fuzzy controllers are, at least in principle, able to deal with unpredictable or unmodeled behaviors, which made them outperform non-adaptive control policies when the real implementation is accomplished [5].

Recent approaches in this field are presented in [1] and [8]. In the very interesting approach proposed by Andersen et al. [1], fine tuning of the controller rules (both consequents and premises) is accomplished through the controller output error. Since the plant output error reduction is not directly pursued, this method requires the existence of a previously-tuned controller. This problem is overcome in [6] where a SOC-based adaptation block works concurrently with the controller output error method to achieve global learning of the controller parameters. Nevertheless, none of the afore-mentioned works are capable of dealing with the problem of the automatic structure identification of the main neuro-fuzzy controller.

F.J. Garijo, J.C. Riquelme, and M. Toro (Eds.): IBERAMIA 2002, LNAI 2527, pp. 845–854, 2002.
© Springer-Verlag Berlin Heidelberg 2002

In this paper, the main drawbacks of the above presented approaches are overcome by the use of a three-stage approach to automatically identify the optimum neuro-fuzzy controller structure and tune the main fuzzy controller parameters in a systematic way. The main features of the proposed algorithm are:

- It needs neither a model of the plant to be controlled nor its differential equations.
- Both fuzzy rules consequents and membership functions in the premises are fine tuned to provide a high performance control policy.
- No initial guesses about the controller parameters are needed. The controller can run in a standalone manner from the start with no off-line pretraining.
- Since this is a direct control policy, no plant model is created during the control process. Furthermore, no great amount of data needs to be collected from the plant, enabling the algorithm to work with high speed control processes.

2   Statement of the Problem

The main goal of this paper is to achieve real time control of a system which, in general, may be non-linear and whose exact differential equations are unknown. Furthermore, we assume there is no model of the plant available so there cannot be any off-line pre-training of the main controller parameters. Starting from this "void" neuro-fuzzy controller, we attempt to achieve the identification of the main controller and optimize the controller's rules and the parameters defining it in order to translate the state of the plant to the desired value in the shortest possible time.

In mathematical terms, the system or plant to be controlled can be expressed in the form of its differential equations or, equivalently, by its difference equations, provided these are obtained from the former with the use of a short enough sampling period

$$y(k+d) = f(y(k),...,y(k-p),u(k),...,u(k-q)) \tag{1}$$

where d is the delay of the plant and f is an unknown continuous and derivable function. The restriction usually imposed on plants is that they must be controllable, i.e., that there always exists a control policy capable of translating the output to the desired value (within the operation range). This means that there must not be any state in which the output variable does not depend on the control input. Therefore, the partial derivative of the plant output with respect to the control signal must never be cancelled and as the plants are, in particular, derivable and continuous with respect to the control input, this derivative must have a constant sign, i.e., the plant must be monotonic with respect to the control signal. Thus, we can assume there exists a function F such that the control signal given by

$$u(k) = F(\bar{x}(k)) \tag{2}$$

with

$$\bar{x}(k) = (r(k),y(k),...,y(k-p),u(k-1),...,u(k-q)) \tag{3}$$

and $r(k)$ being the desired output at instant k, is capable of reaching the set point target after d instants of time, i.e., $y(k+d) = r(k)$.

3   Overview of the 3-Stage Algorithm

In the proposed algorithm, no information is needed about the equations that govern the plant, although it is necessary to know the monotonicity of its output with respect to the control signal, the delay of the plant (which can nearly always be taken as 1 if we use a sampling period that is not very small) and the inputs that can have a significant influence on the plant output.

For the main neuro-fuzzy controller, we will use a complete rule-based fuzzy system [4], with rules of the form:

$$IF\ x_1\ is\ X_1^{i_1}\ AND\ ...\ AND\ x_N\ is\ X_N^{i_N}\ THEN\ u=R_{i_1 i_2...i_N} \tag{4}$$

where X_v^j is the j-th membership function of variable x_v, N is the number of input variables and $R_{i_1 i_2...i_N}$ is a scalar value. The fuzzy inference method, as is commonly used in all neuro-fuzzy systems, uses the product as T-norm and the centroid method with sum-product operator as the defuzzification strategy, i.e., the weighted average deffuzzification method. Thus, the output of our neuro-fuzzy controller is given by:

$$u(k) = \hat{F}(\vec{x}(k)) = \frac{\sum_{i=1}^{n_{rules}} R_i \cdot \mu_i(\vec{x}(k))}{\sum_{i=1}^{n_{rules}} \mu_i(\vec{x}(k))} =$$

$$= \frac{\sum_{i_1=1}^{n_1}\sum_{i_2=1}^{n_2}\cdots\sum_{i_N=1}^{n_N}\left(R_{i_1 i_2...i_N} \cdot \prod_{m=1}^{N} \mu_{X_m^{i_m}}(x_m^k)\right)}{\sum_{i_1=1}^{n_1}\sum_{i_2=1}^{n_2}\cdots\sum_{i_N=1}^{n_N}\left(\prod_{m=1}^{N} \mu_{X_m^{i_m}}(x_m^k)\right)} \tag{5}$$

where n_v is the number of membership functions defined in variable x_v.

In this paper, the membership functions are triangular functions with pair-wise overlap, i.e. each variable has a non zero membership value in at most two fuzzy sets. To define such a configuration, commonly known as a Triangular Partition (TP), [4], [9], [11], only the centres of the membership functions need to be stored, since the slopes of the triangles are calculated according to the centres of the surrounding membership functions.

Figure 1 shows the general flowchart of the algorithm proposed to accomplish the control task. Since no initial control parameters are available, the control process is carried out in three stages:

In the first stage [8], a coarse tuning of the neuro-fuzzy controller parameters is accomplished based on the plant output error. With a SOC-like algorithm, fuzzy rule consequents are adapted after taking into account the sign of the dependence of the plant output with respect to the control signal and the plant delay in a reward/penalty manner. Meanwhile, the error distribution throughout the operating regions is measured periodically in order to provide enough information for coarse tuning of the membership functions (MFs) defined in the premises of the fuzzy rules.

Once coarse convergency is achieved in the first stage, the algorithm switches to the second stage [8]. All fuzzy rule parameters are then fine tuned using as information source the controller output error via a gradient-based algorithm. After convergency of the second stage, if the control policy is not under the pre-defined specifications, the algorithm switches to the stage responsible of modifying the main controller structure. This process is accomplished by examining the data taken from the plant during the previous steps.

4   Parameter Optimization (Stages i & ii)

This section summarizes the method presented in [8] for the adjustment in real time of the parameters of the main neuro-fuzzy controller for a fixed topology. As stated in

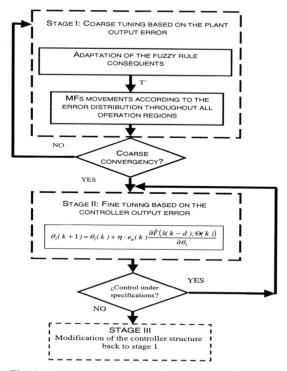

Fig. 1. Flowchart of the proposed control algorithm

that paper, this process comprises two main stages: the first one is responsible of a coarse tuning of both the rule consequents and rule antecedents (i.e., the membership functions). The second one is in charge of the fine tuning of all of them. These are described in the two next sub-sections.

4.1   Stage I: Coarse Tuning of the Main Controller Parameters

The main problem when real time control strategies must be faced lies in the fact that, as the internal functioning of the system to be controlled is unknown, we are unaware of how to modify the controller's parameters. As stated in [12], the monotonicity of the plant provides valuable information on how to adapt the consequents of the fuzzy rules. To modify these, we need only take into account the rules really used to obtain $u(k)$ as the neuro-fuzzy controller output. It is evident that with the kind of information available from the plant, only a relatively coarse control can be applied to the system. In this first stage of the algorithm, coarse adaptation of the fuzzy rule consequents is accomplished by evaluating the current state of the plant and proposing a correction of the rules responsible for the existence of such a state, either as a reward or as a penalty, in the following way (see Eq. (4)):

$$\Delta R_{i_1 i_2 \ldots i_N}(k) = C \cdot \mu_{i_1 i_2 \ldots i_N}(k-d) \cdot e_y(k) =$$
$$C \cdot \mu_{i_1 i_2 \ldots i_N}(k-d) \cdot (r(k-d) - y(k)) \quad (6)$$

where, as in [12], this modification is proportional to the degree with which the rule was activated in achieving the control output $u(k-d)$ now being evaluated at instant k. In the above expression, $r(k-d)$ is the set point required of the plant output at instant $k-d$ and $y(k)$ is the current plant output. Note that it would be incorrect to use $r(k)$, as the rules that are activated at instant $k-d$ serve to achieve the desired value $r(k-d)$ and not $r(k)$. C is used for normalization purposes, and its absolute value can be determined off-line by: $|C| = \Delta u / \Delta y$, where Δy is the range in which the plant output is going to operate and Δu is the range of the controller's actuator. Finally, the sign of C depends on the monotonicity of the plant, i.e., if the plant output increases (decreases) with increasing values of the control signal, C is positive (negative).

Using the above SOC-like algorithm, only the consequents of the fuzzy rules can be tuned. However, the distribution of the membership functions also has a strong influence on the performance of the control process, making it necessary to optimize them. When a generic controller is working in real time, it is very common for there to exist certain operating regions that are more important than others. On the other hand, it is not uncommon to find operating regions which the system never reaches. In all these cases, it is very convenient to re-structure the MF configuration in order to concentrate fuzzy rules in the most important regions and to avoid unnecessary effort on less important ones. The idea proposed in [8] to overcome this problem is based on trying to find a MF configuration which distributes a certain performance criterion homogeneously throughout the operating regions. In this case, the performance criterion is the integral of the square error (ISE). Thus, the more a certain operating region is activated the more frequently this region will contribute to the ISE. This contribution must be compensated with smaller plant output errors. Conversely, less activated regions can be allowed bigger plant output errors. In order to implement this idea, we have to define a period of time T' during which the ISE is computed. Thus, the centre of the j-th membership function of input variable v can be associated with a "slope" p_v^j of the form:

$$p_v^j = \frac{1}{r_y^2} \left(\begin{array}{l} \int_t^{t+T'} dt \cdot e^2(\bar{x}(t)) / x_v(t) \in \left[c_v^{j-1}, c_v^j \right[\quad - \\ \int_t^{t+T'} dt \cdot e^2(\bar{x}(t)) / x_v(t) \in \left[c_v^j, c_v^{j+1} \right[\end{array} \right) \quad (7)$$

which represents the difference between the contribution of the preceding operating region and the succeeding one to the integral of the square error during the period of time T'. A positive value for such a slope means that the contribution to the left hand sector is greater than that to the right and so the centre must be moved to the left to counteract this effect. The parameter r_y, (the plant output range) has been introduced as a normalization factor. As the order of the centres cannot be allowed to vary, we perform the following movement:

$$\Delta c_v^j = \begin{cases} \dfrac{c_v^{j-1}-c_v^j}{2}\dfrac{p_v^j}{p_v^j+\dfrac{1}{T_v^j}} & \text{if } p_v^j \geq 0 \\[4ex] \dfrac{c_v^{j+1}-c_v^j}{2}\dfrac{\left|p_v^j\right|}{\left|p_v^j\right|+\dfrac{1}{T_v^j}} & \text{if } p_v^j < 0 \end{cases} \qquad (8)$$

in which the temperature T_v^j of the centre c_v^j, indicates how far the centre is moved within the limits of possible movement. Thus, for very high temperatures the centres will move large distances, while at low temperatures these movements will be very small.

Finally, the whole stage finishes when centre locations are modified below a certain threshold value. Since stage I is used only to coarse tune the controller fuzzy rules, a typical value of 5% of the range of every input variable is selected in this paper.

4.2 Stage II: Fine Tuning of the Main Controller Parameters

In this second stage, we use a gradient-based methodology in order to achieve a fine tuning of the main controller parameters. For this purpose, we base our approach on the algorithm proposed by Andersen et al. [1]: when the controller provides a control signal at instant k, $u(k)$ and the output is evaluated d sampling periods later $y(k+d)$, the error committed at the plant output is not the only information that may be obtained. Regardless of whether or not this was the intended response, we now know that, if the same transition from the same initial conditions but now with $r(k) = y(k+d)$ is ever required again, the optimal control signal is precisely $u(k)$. Therefore, at every sampling time, we do get an exact value of the true inverse function of the plant [10]. In mathematical terms, the control signal exerted at the plant at instant k is given by (see Eq. (5)):

$$u(k) = \hat{F}\left(\bar{x}(k);\Theta(k)\right) \qquad (9)$$

where $\Theta(k)$ represents the set of parameters that define the controller at instant k (rules plus membership functions) and $\bar{x}(k)$ is given by Eq. (3). After d iterations, we obtain at the plant output the value $y(k+d)$. If we now replace the input vector $\bar{x}(k)$ by:

$$\bar{x}(k) \equiv (y(k+d),y(k),...,y(k-p),u(k-1),...,u(k-q)) \qquad (10)$$

an expression that only differs from $\bar{x}(k)$ in the first element, where $y(k+d)$ replaces $r(k)$, we obtain the following datum belonging to the actual inverse plant function:

$$u(k) = F\left(\hat{x}(k)\right) \qquad (11)$$

The neuro-fuzzy controller is now tested d iterations afterwards to see if it does indeed output a signal equal to $u(k)$ when required to drive the plant through this same transition. Instead of producing a control signal $u(k)$, however, the controller outputs the signal:

$$\hat{u}(k) = \hat{F}\left(\hat{x}(k); \Theta(k+d)\right) \tag{12}$$

Thus, the controller output is in error by

$$e_u(k) = u(k) - \hat{u}(k) \tag{13}$$

It is important to note that, although $\hat{u}(k)$ is produced by the controller, it is not applied to the plant. Its only purpose is to calculate $e_u(k)$. Another important remark is that, since this datum belongs to the current state of the plant, it is expected, by continuity, that reducing the control output error implies a reduction in plant output error. Thus, in each iteration k the error in the output of the controller is computed, where the magnitude to be minimized is given by:

$$J(k) \equiv \frac{1}{2}e_u^2(k-d) = \frac{1}{2}\left[u(k-d) - \hat{F}\left(\hat{x}(k-d); \Theta(k)\right)\right]^2 \tag{14}$$

Therefore, the parameters of the main neuro-fuzzy controller are optimized in each iteration in the following way:

$$\Delta\bar{\Theta}(k) = -\eta(k) \cdot \nabla_\Theta J(k) \tag{15}$$

5   Identification of the Main Controller Topology (Stage iii)

The modification of the main neuro-fuzzy controller in real time is a key topic that has never been tackled in depth in the literature. Thus far, the majority of the adaptive neuro-fuzzy systems proposed in the bibliography are based on neuro-fuzzy controllers with a fixed number of membership functions. The reason for this is straightforward since this is a very complex task.

In order to accomplish this issue, it is necessary to get as much information as possible from all the operating regions through which the plant has proceeded. For that reason, due to the fact that all operations must be made in real time from no initial information, this must be compiled during the very control process.

In this section, we take advantage of the real data belonging to the actual inverse function of the plant that we have used in the previous stage. For this purpose, we define a grid in the input space and store the most recent datum belonging to each of the hypercubes defined by that grid, substituting a pre-existing datum in this hypercube. By these means, real data from the plant are stored in a memory M which contains a uniform representation of the inverse function of the plant. Once this task is accomplished, we can use the methodology proposed in [7] in order to obtain the information about which input variable should increase the number of its membership functions. In mathematical terms, this procedure decomposes the domain of the input variables (except that of the variable we are analyzing, in this case x_v) into infinitesimal intervals of the form:

$$\left[x_1, x_1+dx_1\right] \times \cdots \times \left[x_{v-1}, x_{v-1}+dx_{v-1}\right] \times \left[D_v^-, D_v^+\right] \times$$

$$\left[x_{v+1}, x_{v+1}+dx_{v+1}\right] \times \cdots \times \left[x_N, x_N+dx_N\right] \tag{16}$$

where D_v^-, D_v^+ are the lower and upper limits of the domain of variable v, and we consider each one of them individually as one-dimensional subfunctions of variable x_v using the MFs already defined in that variable. As this is a fixed configuration, and the problem is linear, the approximation process can be done in a straightforward manner, and a one-dimensional function is obtained:

$$F^{v}_{x_1,\ldots,x_{v-1},x_{v+1}\ldots,x_N}\left(x_v\right) \tag{17}$$

which approximates the error surface in the region considered using the MFs of variable x_v and without the influence of the ones defined in the other variables. If function (17) is capable of accurately approximating the error surface in its definition domain, we conclude that, as far as this region is concerned, there is no need to insert a new membership function into variable x_v. Conversely, if this approximation is poor then there is a high degree of responsibility of variable x_v in the error existing in that region.

By adding all the approximation errors with respect to the error surface for each infinitesimal region, we can compute an index reflecting the degree of responsibility of variable x_v in the existing global error:

$$J_v = \int_{X_1} dx_1 \cdots \int_{X_{v-1}} dx_{v-1} \int_{X_{v+1}} dx_{v+1} \cdots$$
$$\int_{X_N} dx_N \left[\int_{X_v} dx_v \left(e(\vec{x}) - F^{v}_{x_1,\ldots,x_{v-1},x_{v+1}\ldots,x_N}\left(x_v\right) \right)^2 \right] \tag{18}$$

where $e(\vec{x})$ is the error surface, i.e., the error between the original function and the one approximated by the current neuro-fuzzy system. Finally, we compute these approximation indexes for each input variable and compare; the input variable with highest J_v is the one selected to increment the number of membership functions.

6   Simulations

This section presents a simple example showing the functioning of the above-described algorithm. Consider the system described by the following difference equation:

$$\Pi_5 \equiv y(k+1) = \frac{1.5\, y(k-1)\, y(k)}{1 + y^2(k-1) + y^2(k)} +$$
$$0.35\, \sin\left(y(k-1) + y(k) \right) + 1.2\, u(k) \tag{19}$$

and assume its output must follow random set-points in the range [-4,4]. For this input range, this plant happens to be very difficult to control in a optimum. As input variables, the desired plant output r(k), the actual plant output y(k) and the two previous outputs y(k-1) and y(k-2) are used. The period T' for this case has been selected as 500 epochs, which is estimated to be sufficient to compute the ISE values. In Table 1, the evolution of the control process is presented for the whole algorithm proposed, starting from a "void" neuro-fuzzy system, i.e., only one membership function defined for each input variable and thus, only one constant output which is initially set to zero.

As can be seen from the table, the first decision that the third stage of the algorithm makes is to use the set point r(k) as input variable. It must be taken into account that, although the main controller is not using initially r(k), the auxiliary systems do use it

Table 1. Evolution of the proposed algorithm.

	r(k)	y(k)	y(k-1)	y(k-2)	
Config.	J_1	J_2	J_3	J_4	MSE*1000 after stage II
1x1x1x1	0.485	0.144	0.126	0.0154	6493
2x1x1x1	0.0320	0.201	0.194	0.0324	307.4
2x2x2x1	0.0233	0.105	0.105	0.0216	108.8
2x3x3x1	0.0148	0.0681	0.0687	0.0140	88.11
2x4x4x1	0.00975	0.0228	0.0235	0.00968	12.3
2x5x5x1	0.00816	0.137	0.0138	0.00862	5.17
2x6x6x1	0.00754	0.0956	0.0964	0.00787	1.74

and that is the reason why the control process can be accomplished even with only one rule (the system will behave as a pure adaptative controller, with no learning).

Nevertheless, once two MFs are defined for the first variable, the algorithm starts adding new MFs in y(k) and y(k-1) and never in y(k-2). This is the optimum evolution since if we take a look at equation (19), we can check that the control output u(k) varies linearly with r(k), that it does not depend on y(k-2) and that its dependency with respect to y(k) and y(k-1) is exactly the same.

7   Conclusions

In this paper, a new algorithm to automatically identify the structure of a neuro-fuzzy controller and self-tune all its parameters without any off-line pretraining has been proposed. Using a three-stage approach, the methodology is capable of obtaining optimum configurations and optimum parameter values for the fuzzy rules (both rule consequents and membership functions defined in the premises) both in real time. Starting from a "void" main neuro-fuzzy controller, coarse tuning is achieved based on the plant output error. When the algorithm switches to the second stage, fine tuning of the fuzzy rules is accomplished by using controller output error as the information source. Finally, the third stage is responsible of finding a more suitable main controller topology.

Acknowledgements. This work has been partially supported by the Spanish CICYT Project DPI2001-3219.

References

[1]   H.C.Andersen, A.Lotfi, A.C.Tsoi, "A new approach to adaptive fuzzy control: The Controller Output Error Method", IEEE Trans. Syst. Man and Cyber.- Part B, vol.27, no.4, pp.686–691, August 1997.

[2]   J.A.Bernard, "Use of rule-based system for process control", IEEE Contr. Syst. Mag., vol. 8, no. 5, pp. 3–13, 1988.

[3]   Y.Kasai, Y.Morimoto, "Electronically controlled continuously variable transmission", in Proc. Int. Congr. Transport. Electron., Dearborn, MI, pp. 69–85, Oct. 1988.

[4]   C.C.Lee, "Fuzzy logic in control systems: fuzzy logic controller – Part I,II", IEEE Trans. Syst. Man and Cyber., vol.20, no.2, pp.404–435, 1990.

[5]   R.Ordoñez, J.Zumberge, J.T.Spooner, and K.M.Passino, "Adaptive Fuzzy Control: Experiments and Comparative Analyses", IEEE Trans. Fuzzy Systems, vol.5, no.2, pp.167–188, May 1997.

[6]   H.Pomares, I.Rojas, F.J. Fernández, M.Anguita, E.Ros, A.Prieto, "A New Approach for the Design of Fuzzy Controllers in Real Time", Proc. 8th Int. Conf. Fuzzy Systems, Seoul, Korea, pp.522–526, Aug. 1999.

[7]   H.Pomares, I.Rojas, J.González, A.Prieto, "Structure Identification in Complete Rule-Based Fuzzy Systems", to appear in IEEE Trans. Fuzzy Systems.

[8]   H.Pomares, I.Rojas, J.González, F.Rojas, M.Damas, F.J.Fernández, "A Two-Stage Approach to Self-Learning Direct Fuzzy Controllers", to appear in Int. J. Approximate Reasoning.

[9]   H.Pomares, I.Rojas, J.Ortega, J.Gonzalez, A.Prieto, "A Systematic Approach to a Self-generating Fuzzy Rule-table for Function Approximation", IEEE Trans Syst., Man and Cyber., vol.30, no.3, pp.431–447, June 2000.

[10]   D.S.Reay, "Comments on 'A new approach to adaptive fuzzy control: the controller output error method'", IEEE Trans. Syst., Man, Cyber.-Part B, vol. 29, no. 4, pp. 545–546, Aug. 1999.

[11]   E.H.Ruspini, "A new approach to Clustering", Info Control, no.15, pp. 22–32, 1969.

[12]   I.Rojas, H.Pomares, F.J.Pelayo, M.Anguita, E.Ros, A.Prieto, "New methodology for the development of adaptive and self-learning fuzzy controllers in real time", International Journal of Approximate Reasoning, vol.21, pp.109–136, 1999.

Comparing a Voting-Based Policy with Winner-Takes-All to Perform Action Selection in Motivational Agents

Orlando Avila-García and Lola Cañamero

Adaptive Systems Research Group
Department of Computer Science, University of Hertfordshire
College Lane, Hatfield, Herts AL10 9AB, UK
{O.Avila-Garcia,L.Canamero}@herts.ac.uk

Abstract. Embodied autonomous agents are systems that inhabit dynamic, unpredictable environments in which they try to satisfy a set of time-dependent goals or motivations in order to survive. One of the problems that this implies is action selection, the task of resolving conflicts between competing behavioral alternatives. We present an experimental comparison of two action selection mechanisms (ASM), implementing "winner-takes-all" (WTA) and "voting-based" (VB) policies respectively, modeled using a motivational behavior-based approach. This research shows the adequacy of these two ASM with respect to different sources of environmental complexity and the tendency of each of them to show different behavioral phenomena.

1 Introduction

In the mid 80's, a new approach emerged in artificial intelligence (AI) to study intelligence in the context of "complete", embodied autonomous agents [5]. This new paradigm is highly inspired in biology, animal behavior (ethology), neuroscience and evolutionary biology, and has been termed "behavior-based AI" or "animat[1] approach" [14,12]. The animat approach is appropriate for the class of problems that require a system to autonomously fulfill several time-dependent goals or motivations in a dynamic, unpredictable environment. The main problem in this area is to build architectures for an autonomous agent that will result in the agent demonstrating adaptive, robust and effective behavior. Specifically, two related subproblems have to be solved [9]: The problem of action (or behavior) selection and the problem of learning from experience. This research is focused on the first issue.

Action selection consists in making a decision as to what behavior to execute in order to satisfy internal goals and guarantee survival in a given environment and situation. This implies resolving conflicts between competing behavioral alternatives. We have modeled two action selection mechanism (ASM) using a motivational behavior-based approach that follows the architecture proposed in [6]. This means that the agent's behavior is driven by motivational states—impulses to action based on bodily needs. There are

---

[1] Animat is shorthand for "artificial animal"

F.J. Garijo, J.C. Riquelme, and M. Toro (Eds.): IBERAMIA 2002, LNAI 2527, pp. 855–864, 2002.

several ways in which the set of motivations can lead to the execution of a behavior, since the same behavior may be able to satisfy more than one motivation and the satisfaction of one motivation may lead the arousal of another. In this paper, we present an experimental comparison of two action selection architectures implementing approaches that are often regarded as opposite in the literature: "winner-takes-all" (WTA) and "voting-based" (VB). With a WTA policy the animat will execute the behavior that satisfies its highest motivation in the best way. This means that only the highest motivation drives behavior selection. With a VB policy, all the motivations have influence on the final selection since the animat will execute the behavior that best satisfies a subset of motivations at the same time. In previous work [4,3] we did a systematic study and comparison of four architectures that differed along a few relevant parameters; however, only the differences between the two architectures we present here (WTA and VB) were significant enough, giving rise to more stable results and differences in behavior. Drawing on the notion of viability [1], used within the animat approach for different purposes [12,13,2], we have defined several complementary viability indicators to assess behavior selection performance, and we have analyzed our results in terms of some interesting behavioral phenomena that [8] proposes as desirable features of architectures to achieve flexible behavior selection.

2   The Valimar Environment

In order to test our architectures, we have created a typical behavior selection environment, called Valimar, in which our robot must select among and perform different activities in order to survive. The platform we have used is Webots 3.0 (www.cyberbotics.com), a very realistic 3D mobile robot simulator allowing users to create different environments with continuous space and complex physics. For these experiments, we have used Kheperas fitted with a color camera on their top to create two species of robots—Nessas (green Kheperas) and Enemies (red Kheperas). *Nessas* are more complex creatures used to implement the two behavior selection architectures described in Section 3. *Enemies* have the same sensors and actuators as Nessas, but they have a much simpler architecture and behavior (their main goal is to attack Nessas), since their only role is to introduce dynamism in the environment. Neither Nessas nor Enemies can remember the location of objects, and they also lack any planning capabilities. Valimar is surrounded by a wall and contains cylindrically-shaped objects of different colors: food (yellow) and water (blue) sources, nests (purple), obstacles (gray), dull blocks (red), and our two species of robots. Since Enemies and dull blocks have the same color, Nessas can mistake one for another.

3   Architectures for Behavior Selection

The architectures we have studied are neither strictly flat (parallel) nor hierarchical (structured), but a combination of both that lies more on the flat side. They consist of two layers—motivational and behavioral—that lead to a two-step computation of intensity. This computation is parallel within each layer, but motivational intensity must be computed prior to the calculation of behavioral intensity. Both architectures have the same elements but differ in how these are linked together in their arbitration mechanism.

3.1   Elements

Sensing and acting. The robots are equipped with the following *external sensors*: eight infrared proximity sensors and eight binary collision sensors; a radio emitter/receiver used to transmit and detect the attack of another robot ($pain_e$); and a color camera returning a RGB pattern of 90×90 pixels used to detect direction and discriminate objects. Object learning and recognition is performed by a combination of three ART1 neural networks, each of them specialized to detect patterns in one of the RGB components. In addition to external sensors, we have programmed *internal sensors* to perceive the values of physiological variables. Navigation (including obstacle avoidance) is controlled by a neural network that improves over time through Hebbian learning.

Physiology. The robots have a synthetic physiology of survival-related essential variables that must be kept within a range of values for the robot to stay alive. They thus define a physiological space [11] or viability zone [12] within which survival (continued existence) is guaranteed, whereas transgression of these boundaries leads to death. Nessa's essential variables are: damage, energy, glucose, moisture, internal pain[2] ($pain_i$), and stress.

External stimuli. In addition to internal variables, behavior selection is also influenced by the presence of external stimuli that affect the motivational state of the robot. There are six types of external stimuli to which Nessas can react: the different (colors of the) objects in the environment plus external pain ($pain_e$).

Motivations. Motivations constitute urges to action based on bodily needs related to self-sufficiency and survival. They implement a homeostatic process to maintain an essential physiological variable within a certain range. A feedback detector generates an error signal—the drive—when the value of this variable departs from its ideal value (setpoint), and this triggers inhibitory and excitatory controlling elements (in this case, the execution of behaviors) to adjust the variable in the adequate direction. The error is a number normalized in the interval $[0, 1]$, where 0 indicates no error and 1 results when the actual value of the variable overflows/underflows the upper/lower limit, in which case the robot dies. Each motivation receiving an error signal from its feedback detector receives an intensity (activation level) proportional to the magnitude of the error. Several motivations can be active at the same time, with varying degrees of intensity. Nessa's motivations are characterized by: a controlled (essential) physiological variable, a drive to increase or decrease the level of the controlled variable, an (external) incentive stimulus that can increase the motivation's intensity, and a behavioral tendency of approach or avoidance towards the stimulus. Table 1 (left) shows Nessas' motivations with their drives and incentive stimuli.

Behaviors. Our behaviors are coarse-grained subsystems implementing different competencies, similarly to those proposed in [8,6]. Following the usual distinction in ethology [10], Nessas have consummatory (goal-achieving) and appetitive (goal-directed)

---

[2] Pain has a double characterization as internal and external stimulus. Internal pain receives its value from externally felt pain but has more inertia, decreasing more slowly and lasting longer.

behaviors. A consummatory behavior is executed only if it has been selected by the motivational state of the robot and its incentive stimulus is present. If the stimulus is not present, an appetitive behavior is activated to search for it. The execution of a behavior has an impact on (increases or decreases) the level of specific physiological variables. Behaviors can be activated and executed with different intensities that depend on the intensities of the motivations related to them. The intensity with which a behavior is executed affects motor strength (speed of the wheels) and the modification of physiological variables (and hence the duration of the behavior). Table 1 (right) shows Nessas' behaviors.

Table 1. Nessas' motivations (left) and behaviors (right; names in italics indicate appetitive behaviors, the rest are consummatory).

Motivation	Drive	Incentive stimulus
Confusion	$\downarrow stress$	nest
Excitement	$\downarrow energy$	enemy
Fatigue	$\uparrow energy$	nest
Hunger	$\uparrow glucose$	food
Overmoisture	$\downarrow moisture$	none
Overnutrition	$\downarrow glucose$	none
Repair	$\downarrow damage$	nest
Self-protection	$\downarrow pain_i$	enemy, $pain_e$
Thirst	$\uparrow moisture$	water

Behavior	Stimulus	Effects
Avoid	none	$\downarrow energy, \downarrow glucose, \downarrow moisture, \downarrow pain, \uparrow stress$
Attack	enemy	$\downarrow energy, \downarrow glucose, \downarrow moisture, \downarrow pain, \downarrow stress$
Drink	water	$\downarrow energy, \downarrow glucose, \uparrow moisture$
Eat	food	$\downarrow energy, \uparrow glucose, \downarrow moisture$
Rest	none	$\uparrow energy, \downarrow glucose, \downarrow moisture$
RunAway	enemy	$\downarrow energy, \downarrow glucose, \downarrow moisture, \downarrow pain, \uparrow stress$
Search	none	$\downarrow energy, \downarrow glucose, \uparrow stress, \downarrow moisture$
Sleep	nest	$\downarrow damage, \uparrow energy, \downarrow glucose, \downarrow stress, \downarrow moisture$
Wander	none	$\downarrow energy, \downarrow glucose, \downarrow moisture$

3.2   Arbitration Mechanisms

Motivations and behaviors are connected indirectly through physiological variables, i.e., motivations take into account the effects that the execution of a behavior will have on the physiology to make their selection. Our architectures differ in the way these elements interact to select the behavior that the robot must execute. In the WTA approach, the main selection is made at the level of motivations, and a single motivation is selected to be in charge of selecting the behavior that best satisfies it. In the VB approach the main decision is made at the level of behaviors, and each behavior receives activation from all the motivations that will result affected by its execution, and behavior selection is postponed until behavioral intensity has been computed. In this case, all the behaviors are considered for the final selection, and the robot can satisfy several goals simultaneously.

The behavior selection loops are as follows.
Behavior selection loop in WTA. At every cycle (simulation step):

1. The winner motivation j_{winner} is calculated.
   a) For each motivation j:
      i. Compute the intensity of the drive as proportional to the error of its controlled variable (e_{vj}).
      ii. Compute the effect of the presence of external stimuli on the intensity of the motivation: $a_j = \sum(s_k \times u_{jk})$, where s_k is the intensity of stimulus k, and u_{jk} is the weight between j and k.
      iii. $m_j = e_{vj} + a_j$ is the final intensity of j.
   b) The motivation with highest intensity is selected.
2. The intensity of each behavior linked (through the physiology) with the winner motivation is computed as $b_i = m_{j_{winner}} \times f_{iv}$, where $b_i, m_{j_{winner}}$ are the intensities of behavior i and the winner motivation, respectively, and f_{iv} is the effect that the execution of behavior i has on v, which is the physiological variable controlled by j_{winner}.
3. The behavior with highest intensity is selected to be executed.

Behavior selection loop in VB. At every cycle (simulation step):

1. Calculate the intensity of each motivation j:
   a) Compute the intensity of the motivation's drive as proportional to the error of its controlled variable (e_{vj}).
   b) Compute the effect of the presence of external stimuli on the intensity of the motivation j: $a_j = \sum(s_k \times u_{jk})$, where s_k is the intensity of stimulus k, and u_{jk} is the weight between j and k.
   c) $m_j = e_{vj} + a_j$ is the final intensity of j.
2. The intensity of each behavior is computed as $b_i = \sum(m_j \times f_{iv})$, where b_i, m_j are the intensities of behavior i and motivation j, respectively, and f_{iv} is the effect that the execution of behavior i has on v, the physiological variable controlled by j.
3. The behavior with highest intensity is selected to be executed.

4   Experiments

4.1   Viability Indicators

We have used the notion of viability [1] as general criterion to assess behavior selection performance. The values (upper and lower boundaries) of the robot's essential variables define a physiological space [11] or viability zone [12] within which survival (continued existence) is guaranteed, whereas transgression of these boundaries leads to death. The behavior of the robot is thus viable when it keeps the values of the essential variables within the boundaries of the physiological space.

In our opinion, however, this notion of viability is too vague to provide a direct criterion to measure the goodness or performance of a behavior selection architecture, as it leaves several possibilities open. For example, the performance of a behavior selection architecture can be simply assessed in terms of the time it allows the robot to remain viable (survive) in a given environment. Longer life spans usually indicate better behavior selection performance but this correlation is not necessarily straightforward, since the "life quality" or "well-being" of the robot can be very different during its life span depending on how viability is preserved during that period. A robot can live a long life with poor "life quality" if the values of its essential variables are kept close to the critical zone (near the boundaries) of the physiological space for a long period. On the contrary, it can live a shorter life that ended due to "accidental" factors (e.g., the attack of one or several predators or the absence of resources) during which it had good viability in terms of "well-being" if the values of its essential variables remained close to their ideal values. "Life quality" or "well-being" can also have different interpretations. It can for example be measured in terms of global internal stability or "comfort" that takes into account the average level of satisfaction of all the essential variables simultaneously. It can also be seen in terms of how "balanced" the satisfaction of the different physiological needs is, since the same level of comfort and life span can be achieved e.g., by satisfying one or few motivations to a high degree while keeping the rest close to the critical zone, or by satisfying all the motivations in a more homogeneous way.

We have therefore used three indicators of viability to measure and compare the performance of our architectures:

Life span: The time that the robot survived (remained viable) during each run normalized with the total simulation time, $S_{life} = t_{life}/t_{simul}$, where t_{life} is the number of simulation steps that the robot lived and t_{simul} is the total simulation time measured in number of simulation steps.

Overall comfort: The average level of satisfaction of all the essential variables, measured at each step as $c_{step} = 1 - (Err/n)$, where Err is the total sum of errors of the robot's physiological variables normalized between $[0, 1]$ with n (the worst error possible in each step), which corresponds to the sum of the intensities of the motivations' drives $(Err = \sum(e_{vj}))$, and n is the number of compatible motivations[3]. Average control for a run is given by $C = \sum_1^{t_{life}}(c_{step})/t_{life}$, where t_{life} is the number of simulation steps that the robot lived.

Physiological balance: The homogeneity with which the different physiological needs are satisfied, measured at each step as $b_{step} = 1 - (Unb/max_{unb})$, where Unb is the variance of the errors of the robot's physiological variables normalized between $[0, 1]$ with max_{unb} (the worst variance possible in each step), which corresponds to the variance of the intensities of the (compatible) motivations' drives $(Unb = \sigma^2(e_{vj}))$. Average balance for a run is given by the mean of steps. Average physiological balance for a run is given by $B = \sum_1^{t_{life}}(b_{step})/t_{life}$.

4.2   Method

We have explored the effects of three sources of environmental complexity on the behavior and performance of our architectures: *Number of objects* (the more populated a world is, the more complex navigation and perception are), *availability of resources* (the fewer resources a world contains, the more difficult and costly it is to obtein them), and *dynamism* (Enemies that can attack and kill Nessas, and also hamper foraging activities). To vary these sources of complexity, we created four Valimar settings (Table 2) with different elements sparsely distributed across the world.

---

[3] Two motivations are compatible if they do not control the same variable in opposite directions.

Table 2. Elements of the four Valimar worlds.

Worlds	Water sources	Food sources	Nests	Obstacles	Dull blocks	Enemies	Nessas
V1	4	4	2	2	2	0	1
V2	1	1	1	0	1	0	1
V3	2	2	1	2	0	1	1
V4	2	2	1	2	0	2	1

We tested the two architectures in 30 sets of runs for each Valimar world (V1, V2, V3, V4), each set being comprised of a run for each architecture. This made a total of 240 runs (about 45 hours), each run lasting 10,000 simulation steps.

4.3   Results

Figure 1 shows average performance of both architectures in the four Valimar worlds in terms of life span (left), overall comfort (center), and physiological balance (right).

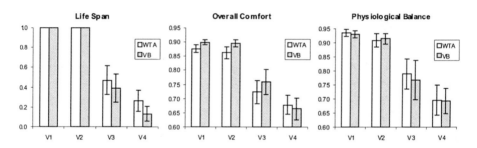

Fig. 1. Average performance of the two architectures in the four Valimar worlds in terms of life span (left), overall comfort (center), and physiological balance (right). Mean confidence intervals shown are calculated with a 95% confidence level.

Analysis of variance (using ANOVA Single Factor) showed that the difference of each architecture across worlds is statistically highly significant (99%) in terms of our three viability indicators. Considering both architectures, these three indicators show significant differences between static (V1, V2) and dynamic (V3, V4) worlds.

In static worlds, the life span obtained by the both architectures is very similar. In terms of overall comfort, there is a clear tendency that shows that VB obtains better results than WTA, although they obtain very similar results in terms of physiological balance. In the dynamic world with one Enemy, big confidence intervals indicate that similarities among architectures in terms of life span might be due to external factors (e.g., the ability of the Enemy to find and attack Nessa) to a big extent. A clear difference appears in the world with two Enemies, where WTA outperforms the VB architecture. Mean confidence intervals of the other indicators show that dynamism affects them too much to be significant when analyzed separately in dynamic worlds, and results have to be nuanced by taking into account life span. It would seem, then, that the trend observed in static worlds appears in dynamic worlds as well.

4.4   Discussion

Let us now discuss some phenomena commonly studied in animal decision making (see e.g., [10]) that we have observed in our simulations, and that allow us to better understand the differences between architectures and how they deal with different properties of the environment. Some of these phenomena have been proposed by [8] as desirable features of architectures to achieve flexible behavior selection.

Reactivity (openness). WTA is more reactive to changes in the environment than VB because only one motivation drives behavior selection. Since with a VB policy all the motivations influence the behavior selection, being thus the decision more "democratic", it usually takes longer for VB to satisfy the most urgent physiological need (motivation) and to react to external changes. Therefore, WTA deals better with quick and unpredictable (physiological and external) environmental changes.

Stability of a sequence of behaviors occurs when behavioral intensities are (nearly) similar for all the sequence. A non-stable sequence results in sudden changes[4] in the robot's velocity and modification of its variables. WTA, being more reactive as it uses a single motivation to drive behavior selection, was the less stable architecture.

Displacement behaviors appear in a competition between two motivations highly activated when a third motivation less activated and unrelated to the current context drives behavior selection. This phenomenon was only observed in VB, as its "voting-based" policy, together with the fact that links between motivations and behaviors can be positive (excitatory) or negative (inhibitory), can lead to *mutual inhibition* (cancellation) of two motivations with high intensity.

Opportunism management. WTA is less opportunistic than VB as a consequence of the way in which the influence of external stimuli are taken into account. In WTA each external stimulus is computed only once to calculate the intensity of the winner behavior because it only influences the highest activated motivation. However in VB the same external stimulus can be computed more than once—as many times as motivations contribute towards calculating the intensity of a particular behavior. This may explain the fact that the performance of VB in terms of overall comfort seems to be the same in static worlds in spite of the shortage of resources in V2, while with a WTA policy this indicator is affected.

Situations of self-protection are more difficult to deal with when Nessas are executing a consummatory behavior next to a resource, as they are more exposed to Enemies, which can attack them on the back, where they are not detected, and block them against resources, as shown in Figure 2. This roughly corresponds to what [8] denotes as *varying attention*—the fact that animals pay lower attention to danger when they are in an extreme motivational state, e.g. very hungry. WTA, being more reactive (like a simple emotional system), is the best in this case, while VB is more often trapped in these situations due to its lower reactivity.

---

[4] Recall that the intensity of the winner behavior has an impact on motor strength and on how physiological variables are modified (and therefore on the duration of the behavior).

Fig. 2. Nessas (lighter Kheperas) attacked and blocked by Enemies next to a nest.

Maximizing efficiency of behavioral choice, i.e., executing the behavior that best contributes towards approaching the ideal zone of the physiological space, is usually considered an important desideratum for behavior selection mechanisms. The extent to which maximization is achieved is directly related to the amount of "information" available to each architecture about the effect that the execution of the behavior will have on the physiology. WTA uses less information than VB, since it only takes into account the effects of behavior execution on one motivation to make the selection, while VB considers the (positive and negative) effects of behavior execution on all motivations. Executing a behavior that satisfies several motivations simultaneously (VB) is more efficient in static worlds in terms of overall comfort than executing a behavior that only satisfies one goal (WTA), as reflected by our results in Figure 1. However, maximizing efficiency does not necessarily lead to better results in terms of physiological balance and life span, again referred to static worlds, but leads to poorer reactivity and therefore presents drawbacks in dynamic worlds, as seen above.

5   Conclusion and Future Work

We have presented a study comparing the performance of two different motivated behavior selection architectures (WTA and VB) in environments with varying degrees and types of complexity. The indicators used have shown significant differences in the behavior of both architectures between static and dynamic worlds. Interestingly, WTA and VB obtained highly similar results in terms of physiological balance, and complementary ones in terms of life span and overall comfort. We have demonstrated that a "winner-takes-all" policy is more adequate for unpredictable and dynamic environments since it is the most reactive, while a "voting-based" policy is more adequate for static and predictable worlds since in each step it takes the most efficient decision.

   To continue this study we envisage several directions for future work. First, we plan to perform quantitative analyses of the different behavioral phenomena observed (opportunism, displacement behaviors, etc.) in order to better understand the differences between architectures. Second, we intend to study the optimization mechanisms underlying "winner-takes-all" versus "voting-based" architectures, to better understand our results in terms of overall comfort and physiological balance. Third, we would like to extend our model of motivational states to consider other aspects that contribute to homeostatic regulation in addition to behavior execution, in particular physiological regulation. Fourth, we want to increase the complexity of the world in terms of dynamism to take into account not only the presence of enemies but also extinction and mobility of resources. Finally, we plan to add basic emotions to our behavior selection architectures, following the design proposed by [6,7], and compare the performance of both architectures with and without emotions in both more static and highly dynamic worlds.

Acknowledgments. We are grateful to Elena Hafner for her contribution to earlier stages of this research. Orlando Avila-García is supported by a research scholarship of the University of Hertfordshire.

References

1. Ashby, W.R. (1952). *Design for a Brain: The Origin of Adaptive Behavior*. London: Chapman and Hall.
2. Aubin, J.P. (2000). Elements of Viability Theory for Animat Design. In J.A. Meyer, A. Berthoz, D. Floreano, H. Roitblat, and S.W. Wilson, eds., *Proc. Sixth Intl. Conf. on Simulation of Adaptive Behavior*, 13–22. Cambridge, MA: MIT Press.
3. Avila-García, O. and Cañamero, L.D. (2002). A comparison of Behavior Selection Architectures Using Viability Indicators. In *Proc. International Workshop on Biologically-Inspired Robotics: The Legacy of W. Grey Walter*. 14–16 August 2002, Bristol HP Labs, UK (in press).
4. Avila-García, O., Hafner, E., and Cañamero, L. (2002). Relating Behavior Selection Architectures to Environmental Complexity. In *Proc. Seventh Intl. Conf. on Simulation of Adaptive Behavior*. Cambridge, MA: MIT Press (in press).
5. Brooks, R.A. (1991). Intelligence without reason. In J. Mylopoulos, R. Reiter (eds.), *Proc. 12th Intl. Joint Conf. on Artificial Intelligence (IJCAI)*, 569–595. San Mateo, CA: Morgan Kaufmann.
6. Cañamero, L.D. (1997). Modeling Motivations and Emotions as a Basis for Intelligent Behavior. In W.L. Johnson, ed., *Proc. First Intl. Conf. on Autonomous Agents*, 148–155. New York: ACM Press.
7. Cañamero, L.D. (2002). Designing Emotions for Activity Selection in Autonomous Agents. In R. Trappl, P. Petta, S. Payr, eds., *Emotions in Humans and Artifacts*. Cambridge, MA: MIT Press (in press).
8. Maes, P. (1991). A Bottom-Up Mechanism for Behavior Selection in an Artificial Creature. In J.A. Meyer and S.W. Wilson, eds. *Proc. First Intl. Conf. on Simulation of Adaptive Behavior*, 238–246. Cambridge, MA: MIT Press.
9. Maes, P. (1995). Modeling Adaptive Autonomous Agents. In C.G. Langton, ed., *Artificial Life: An Overview*, 135–162. Cambridge, MA: MIT Press.
10. McFarland, D. (1995). *Animal Behaviour*, 3rd. edition. Harlow, England: Longman.
11. McFarland, D. and Houston, A. (1981). *Quantitative Ethology*. London: Pitman.
12. Meyer, J.A. (1995) Artificial Life and the Animat Approach to Artificial Intelligence. In M. Boden, ed., *Artificial Intelligence*. Academic Press.
13. Steels, L. (1997). A Selectionist Mechanism for Autonomous Behavior Acquisition. *Robotics and Autonomous Systems*, 20(2/4): 117–131.
14. Wilson, S.W. (1985). Knowledge Growth in an Artificial Animal. In J.J. Grefenstette (ed.), *Proc. of the First Intl. Conf. on Genetic Algorithms and their applications*, 16–23. Hillsdale, NJ. Lawrence Erlbaum.

Bayesian Approach Based on Geometrical Features for Validation and Tuning of Solution in Deformable Models

Francisco L. Valverde[1], Nicolás Guil[2], and Jose Muñoz[1]

[1]Department of Computer Science
[2]Department of Computer Architecture
University of Malaga
29071 Malaga, Spain
valverde@uma.es

Abstract. A local deformable-model-based segmentation can be very helpful to extract objects from an image, especially when no prototype about the object is available. However, this technique can drive to an erroneous segmentation in noisy images, in case of the active contour is captured by noise particles. If some geometrical information (a priori knowledge) of the object is available, then it can be used to validate the results and to obtain a better segmentation through a refining stage. A Bayesian approach is proposed to evaluate the solution of segmentation performed by a deformable model. The proposed framework is validated for vessel segmentation on mammograms. For that purpose a specific geometric restriction term for vessels on mammograms is formulated. Also a likelihood function of the contour and the image is developed. Our model avoids manual initialization of the contour using a local deformable model to obtain an initial contour approximation.

1 Introduction

A local deformable-model-based segmentation scheme can overcame some limitations of the traditional image processing techniques and no model template about the object is needed. The inherent continuity and smoothness of the models can compensate for gaps and other regularities in object boundaries. Unfortunately, this technique presents problems in noisy images. However, if some information of the model such us geometrical features is available, then some problems caused by the noise or edges from another objects in the image can be solved using a global deformable model.

Several segmentation-scheme based on snakes (local deformable model) have been developed for noisy images [1,2] but none of them are applicable for segmentation in images with granular noise (macro-particles) or when objects are superimposed. We present a model that is adequate for those cases where some geometrical information about the object is available.

Our model is applied to vessel segmentation in mammograms. Vessel detection is essential in many applications in radiology and, in mammograms is a fundamental step for elimination of vascular false positives.

F.J. Garijo, J.C. Riquelme, and M. Toro (Eds.): IBERAMIA 2002, LNAI 2527, pp. 865–874, 2002.
© Springer-Verlag Berlin Heidelberg 2002

This paper is organized as follows. In the next section a brief review of previous work on geometrical deformable models is given. The limitations of these proposed methods and some open problems are pointed out. Our new approximation to a geometrical (global) deformable model is presented in Section 3, where a Bayesian approach of the geometrical constraints is described. In section 4, two different algorithms, global minimization and fast global minimization are proposed. In Section 5 the results show that our new geometrical deformable model is helpful to segment objects with granular noise or another superimposed objects. Finally, in Section 6, conclusions are presented.

2   Geometrical Deformable Models

Deformable models are a useful tool for image segmentation. They can be classified, according to the information held by the model [3], in local deformable models and global deformable models. Local deformable models manage information to pixel level taking into account only a close pixel neighborhood. However, global deformable models can use information from any location in the image. Local deformable models are faster to converge and they do not need a template of the object to be segmented. The most popular approach to local deformable model is the "snake" by *Kass et al*[4]. Unfortunately, they are very sensitive to noise. On the other hand, global deformable models have slower convergence than local deformable models and usually they need a template of the object. However, global deformable models are more robust and less sensitive to noise than local models.

Geometrical deformable models are a particular case of global deformable models that use geometric information of the object. Geometrical models have been used for a number of applications in image segmentation. Continuous geometric models consider an object boundary as a whole and can use the a priori knowledge of object shape to constrain the segmentation problem. Wang and Gosh [5] proposed a geometrical deformable model based on the curve evolution theory in differential geometry. Burger et al [6] used a geometrical priori knowledge information for the segmentation of the aorta. Delibasis and Undrill [7] developed a geometric deformable model for anatomical object recognition. And Clarysse and Friboulet [8] proposed a 3-D deformable surface model with geometrical descriptors for the recognition of the left-ventricular surface of the heart. Shen and Davatzikos [9] used an attribute vector to characterize the geometric structure around each point of the snake and only affine-segment transformations of a standard shape are allowed during convergence process. This restriction permits a faster convergence but a close object initialization has to be carried out. In addition, some kind of objects can not be properly represented using this standard shape.

Our geometric model avoids guided initialization by using a previous local deformable model where no user interaction is required.

3   Description of Geometric Deformable Model

In the segmentation task, we assume the object to be detected is represented by a contour(x) in an image(z). A polygon (or vector) representation of an object is a representation where the contour is defined by a set of nodes giving coordinates of contour points in a circular (clockwise) manner. Between each node, the contour is defined by a straight line (or some spline-curves).

The Bayesian paradigm consist of four successive stages:

1. Construction of a prior probability distribution $\pi(x)$ where x is the contour of the object. Priori knowledge is included in $\pi(x)$.

2. Combining the observed image z with the underlying contour x through a conditional probability density $f(z\,|\,x)$.

3. Constructing the posterior density $p(x\,|\,z)$ from $\pi(x)$ and $f(z\,|\,x)$ by Bayes Theorem giving

$$p(x\,|\,z) \propto \pi(x)\ f(z\,|\,x) \tag{1}$$

4. Base any inference about the contour x on the posterior distribution $p(x\,|\,z)$

Prior knowledge is usually present on the contour to be recognized. This prior knowledge is associated to features as shape, size, orientation, etc.

In Bayesian analysis, all kinds of inference are calculated from the posteriori probability $p(x\,|\,z)$. Finding the maximum a posteriori (MAP) estimation is the most used choice of inference. Constraints on contours are, for this approach, designed through energy-functions. The energy-function consists of internal energy and external energy, where the internal energy is related to geometric features of the contour and external energy is related the contour and the image. Assume $U(x)$ is the total energy of the contour represented by x, and given by

$$U(x; z) = U_{int}(x) + U_{ext}(x; z) \tag{2}$$

where U_{int} is the internal energy while U_{ext} is the external energy (depending on the observed image z). Then, a prior model is defined by

$$\pi(x) = \frac{1}{Z_{int}} e^{-U_{int}(x)} \tag{3}$$

where Z_{int} is a normalization constant guaranteeing the prior model to be a proper probability distribution.

Assume further that the likelihood for the observed image z given x is defined by

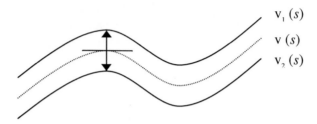

Fig. 1. Vessel geometric model

$$f(z \mid x) = \frac{1}{Z_{ext}} e^{-U_{ext}(x;z)} \tag{4}$$

where Z_{ext} is a normalization constant similar to Z_{int}. The posterior probability for the contour conditioned on the image is then

$$\pi(x \mid z) \propto \pi(x) f(z \mid x) \propto e^{-U_{int}(x)-U_{ext}(x;z)} = e^{-U(x;z)} \tag{5}$$

verifying that minimization of the energy function corresponds to maximization of the posterior distribution, that is, finding the Maximum a posteriori (MAP) solution.

This Bayesian framework is proposed in order to evaluate the contour solution through a posteriori probability (APP) according to the $p(x \mid z)$ function and a threshold of reliability θ_p. The prior model, where the geometrical information is incorporated, is discussed in section 3.1 and the probability densities for observed image are presented in section 3.2.

3.1 Prior Model and Geometrical Information

Let's consider that the contour x has a polygon representation $x = (p_0, p_1, ..., p_{n-1})$ (contour of n points) with $p_0 = p_n$ and where p_i gives the coordinates of a point on the contour. A priori knowledge is present in the prior model through the $\pi(x)$ distribution from Eq. 3. The *a priori* distribution should capture the knowledge available about x. A common assumption is that the energy-function is built up by potentials measuring local and global characteristics. To incorporate the *a priori*

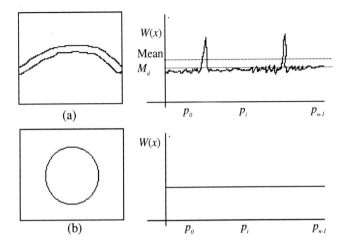

Fig. 2. Width function $W(x)$ for a vessel shape (a), and a circle shape(b)

geometrical information in the Bayesian approach, a new potential, U_{geom}, is considered to capture the geometrical information. Then,

$$U_{int}(x) = \alpha \cdot U_1(x) + \beta \cdot U_2(x) + \gamma \cdot U_{geom}(x) \qquad (6)$$

where $U_1(x)$ and $U_2(x)$ are the typical continuity and curvature term respectively [4]. In addition, $U_{geom}(x)$ is the geometrical restriction term, and α, β and γ parameters are regularization factors . In the following the term U_{geom} is developed.

3.1.1 Geometrical Constraints

Geometrically, a vessel can be defined as two parallel edges having a distance between them (width of the vessel) within a range. Let's consider that $v(s)$ with $s \in [a,b]$, is the axis curve of the vessel. Then, the edges of the vessel, $v_1(s)$ and $v_2(s)$ (Figure 1), can be defined as:

$$v_1(s) = v(s) + \frac{\lambda}{2} \frac{\nabla v(s)}{\|\nabla v(s)\|}, y \qquad (7)$$

$$v_2(s) = v(s) - \frac{\lambda}{2} \frac{\nabla v(s)}{\|\nabla v(s)\|},$$

with $s \in [a,b]$, where $\nabla v(s)$ is the gradient vector of s and λ is the width of the vessel. That is, the two edges and the axis have the same gradient vector in a point s.

Given a contour point p_i , we say that fp_i is the frontal point of the p_i, if fp_i is the contour point that intercept the line of gradient direction (perpendicular direction to the contour) of the point p_i. Then, we define the width of the contour at a point p_i , $W(p_i)$, as:

$$W(p_i) = distance(p_i, fp_i) \qquad (8)$$

that is, the distance between p_i and its frontal point. The width function of a vessel is represented in Figure 2a. Note that this function is dependent of the beginning point p_0. Also can be observed that this function is almost flat but two peaks. Because an image has limited dimensions, just a fragment of the vessel is present in it, and two additional edges are produced where the vessel crosses the borders of the image. These edges produce the two peaks in the width function of the vessel.

Most values of the width function are closer to the medium value (M_d) than to the mean value of the function because the median value is less sensitive to extreme values (two peaks in width function) than the mean value. Then we can think that a shape is more similar to a vessel shape in the way that its width function is more similar to a flat width function. However a circle shape has a flat width function (Figure 2b), then additional features such us compactness or elongation have to be taken into account. Finally, the U_{geom} potential function is defined as:

$$U_{geom}(x) = \mu \frac{\sum_{i=0}^{n-1} |W(p_i) - M_d|}{n \cdot \sigma_{Max}} + \lambda \frac{C(x)}{4\pi} \qquad (9)$$

where the first term is an estimation of the normalized deviation of the $W(p_i)$ function and σ_{Max} is the maximum deviation possible of $W(p_i)$. Similarly, $C(x) = area/(perimeter)^2$ is the fractal dimension of the object and is minimal for a disk-shaped region. The parameters μ and λ are regularization factors between both terms, and they must verify $\mu + \lambda = 1$ in order to be keep the term U_{geom} normalized.

3.2   Probability Densities for Image Data

The probability density $f(z|x)$ is related to the specification of the observed image data. In our approach it is defined through an external energy, which depends on the contour and the observed image. The external energy function connects the contour to the image features were defined through potentials along the contour. Thus, a generic external energy function can be defined as:

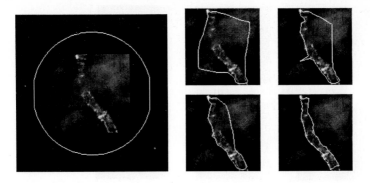

Fig. 3. Initial contour and results with the local deformable model

$$U_{ext}(x;z) = -\sum_{i=0}^{n-1} h(p_i;z) \qquad (10)$$

where $h(p_i, z)$ is some local measure from the observed image z at location p_i (contour pixel). Usually, measure is based on grey-levels itself or some gradient value. In many cases, the complexity of the segmentation process does necessary to take into account not only the observed measurements along the contour but also the gray level inside and outside the contour. For example, the average gray-level inside the object is very different from the average outside the object. Such information can be very useful but it will increase the time of computation with respect to the local measures. In this case, an alternative model is to assume one distribution function f_1 for the pixels inside the object, and another distribution f_2 for the pixels outside the object, then

$$U_{ext}(x:z) = -\left| \frac{\sum\limits_{p_j \in R_1} g(p_j)}{|R_1|} - \frac{\sum\limits_{p_k \in R_2} g(p_k)}{|R_2|} \right| \qquad (11)$$

where R_1 and R_2 are the sets of pixels inside and outside the contour, respectively, being R_1 and R_2 specified by x. Moreover, $g(p_i)$ is the gray value of the pixel p_i in the image.

4 Minimization

As pointed in previous section, maximizing the posterior distribution corresponds to minimizing the energy function. Optimal solutions are usually hard to find. Minimization algorithms can be based on dynamic programming [10], variational calculus [4] or iterative exploration [11], which is the most popular approach. We use

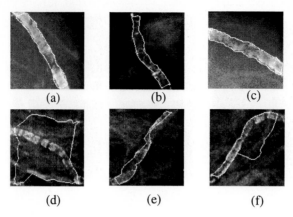

(a)   (b)   (c)

(d)   (e)   (f)

Fig. 4. Results obtained with regular snake for noisy images

this approach for our model. This method consists in dynamically move the contour towards the optimal solution. In the following the initial contour and iterative exploration of our methods are presented

4.1 Initial Contour

Usually, deformable global models have longer computation time than local deformable models. A critical factor in computation time is the initial contour. Some systems require a human operator to draw an initial contour close to the object. In our model, this requirement is avoided using a initial contour provided by a local deformable model, where no initial contour close to the solution is required (see example of fig 3).

Previous to geometrical deformable model application, the contour approximation (initial contour) provided by the local model is evaluated through the a posteriori probability (APP) of the contour. If the APP of the initial contour is high (above a reliable threshold, θ_p) $p(x \mid z) \geq \theta_p$, then no tuning is needed (Fig 4 a-c). However, a low APP (below the reliable threshold) indicates that a tuning of the solution need to be performed through the geometrical model (Fig 4 d-f) here presented.

4.2 Iterative Exploration

An easy way to minimize a global deformable model is an algorithm that moves the contour points looking for a position of lower energy value. A neighborhood of M x M of each contour point is explored and the point is moved to the location with lowest energy value. This operation is performed for every point of the contour at each iteration until the convergence criterion is done. The convergence criterion is based on the percentage of points moved in the current iteration. If this value is less than C, Where C is the convergence threshold, the algorithm finishes. This algorithm can be resumed as:

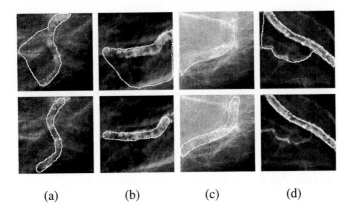

(a)   (b)   (c)   (d)

Fig. 5. Results. Initial contour approximation with local model (upper) and tuning by geometric deformable model (bottom)

```
Until Convergence criterion do
   For Pᵢ = 1 to N do
      Explore energy value U(x) in M x M neighborhood of Pᵢ
      Move Pᵢ to the location with minimum energy value
   End For
End Until
```

5   Results

The new approach to a geometrical deformable contour segmentation has been validated in a database of mammograms by detecting vessels on the images. These images (called Regions of interest ROI) have a size of $L \cdot L$, begin $L = 128$ pixels with 1024 gray levels. A local deformable for noisy image segmentation [2] was applied to a database of 200 ROIs. Some result images are shown in Figure 4. In 24 ROIS the local deformable model was not able to segment the vessel correctly because it was captured by noise particles, as shown in Figure 4(a-c).

The threshold probability θ_p for the evaluation was empirically set to 0.65 and $\sigma_{Max} = \sqrt{2} \cdot L$, which is the diagonal of the ROI Image. The α, β and γ parameters were also empirically adjusted to $\alpha = 0.1$, $\beta = 0.1$ and $\gamma = 1$.

Results of some images obtained with the geometric deformable model are presented in Figure 5. The upper row corresponds to the initial contour (from local deformable model), and the bottom row corresponds to the tuning by the geometric model. The algorithms were implemented in a Pentium II 450 Mhz, running Red Hat 6.0 linux operating system. The local deformable model spent 0.20 seconds per image in average. The global deformable model spent 2 seconds in average per image.

6 Conclusions and Future Works

In this paper we have proposed a global deformable model that uses the geometrical information as a priori knowledge of the object. This geometrical deformable model refines the solution of a local deformable model when the local information is not enough for segmenting the object. This situation can arise due to noise perturbation or other objects in the image. Also a Bayesian framework of the model is provided in order to evaluate the contour (initial estimation and solution) through a posterior probability. A specific geometrical restriction term and a likelihood function for contour vessels in mammograms are developed. An automatic initial contour for the geometric deformable model is provided for a local deformable model, avoiding manual initialization. Finally, a minimization algorithm based on iterative exploration is proposed.

As future works we propose the following points: A faster minimization algorithm because computation of the U_{geom} term makes the convergence algorithm very slow. Moreover, an algorithm for automatic parameter adjusting could be very useful.

References

1. Choi, Wai-Pak; Lam, Kin-Man, and Siu, Wan-Chi. An adaptive active contour model for highly irregular boundaries. Pattern Recognition. 2001; vol 34(2):323–331.
2. Valverde, F. L.; Guil, N., and Munoz, J. A deformable model for image segmentation in noisy medical images. IEEE International Conference on Image Processing, ICIP 2001. 2001:82–85.
3. Cheung, K.; Yeung, D., and Chin, R. On deformable models for visual pattern recognition. Pattern Recognition. 2002; vol 35:1507–1526.
4. Kass, M.; Witkin, A., and Terzopoulos, D. Snakes : Active Contour Models. International Journal of Computer Vision. 1987:321–331.
5. Wang H. and Gosh, B. Geometric active deformable models in shape modelling. IEEE Transactions on Image Processing. 2000; vol 9(2):302–307.
6. Rueckert, D.; Burger, P.; Forbat, S. M., and Mohiaddin, R. D. Automatic traking of the aorta in cardiovascular mr images using deformable models. IEEE Transactions on Med Imaging. 1997; vol 16(5):581–590.
7. Delibasis, H and Undrill, P. E. Anatomical object recognition using deformable geometric models. Image and Vision Computing. 1994; vol 12(7):423–433.
8. Clarysse, P; Friboulet, D, and Magnin, I. E. Tracking geometrical descriptors on 3-D deformable surfaces – aplication to the left ventricular surface of the heart. IEEE Transactions on Med Imaging. 1997; vol 16(4):392–404.
9. Shen, D. and Davatzikos, C. An adaptive-Focus deformable model using statisitical and geometric information. IEEE Transactions on Patterns Analysis and Machine Intelligence. 2000; vol 22(8):906–912.
10. Amini, A. A.; Weymouth, T. E., and Jain, R. C. Using dynamic programming for solving variational problems in vision. IEEE Transactions on Patterns Analysis and Machine Intelligence. 1990 Sep; vol 12(9):855–866.
11. Williams, Donna J. and Shah, Mubarak. A fast algorithm for active Contours and Curvature Estimation. Computer Vision, Graphics and Image Processing. 1992; vol 55(1):14–26.

Recognition of Continuous Activities

Rocío Díaz de León and L. Enrique Sucar

ITESM-Campus Cuernavaca

Av. Paseo de la Reforma #182-A, colonia Lomas de Cuernavaca, C. P. 62589

Temixco, Morelos, México

Office phone +52 777 3297169

Fax +52 777 3297168

{rtdiaz,esucar}@campus.mor.itesm.mx

Abstract. The recognition of continuous human activities performed with several limbs is still an open problem. We propose a novel approach for recognition of continuous activities, which considers the direction change between frames to track the motion of several limbs and uses a Bayesian network to recognize different activities. The approach presented can recognize activities performed at different velocities by different people. We tested the model with real image sequences for 3 different activities performed on a continuous way.

Keywords: Bayesian networks, human activity recognition, multiple motions, continuous activity recognition

1 Introduction

Performing an activity can imply that a human moves one or several limbs at the same time. In the case of sports, for example, when an athlete throws a ball he or she has to move his arms and legs at the same time. A good throw requires coordination between the limb movements. In order to recognize activities like this, we need to use a model able to work with information from different sources. Given a sequence of images we can extract information about the activity and then recognize it. Therefore, we require good models to represent and classify the activities. In this work we propose a human activity recognition model based on Bayesian networks. A Bayesian network realizes the classification of activities by associating the limb movements with different activities. The proposed model includes several outstanding aspects:

- Characterization of the activity based on its global trajectory in order to overcome occlusion and noise.
- Recognition of activities performed moving several limbs at the same time.

F.J. Garijo, J.C. Riquelme, and M. Toro (Eds.): IBERAMIA 2002, LNAI 2527, pp. 875–881, 2002.
© Springer-Verlag Berlin Heidelberg 2002

- Recognition of activities performed with different velocities.
- Representation and recognition of different activities using just one model.
- Recognition of activities performed on a continuous way.

The relevant previous work is commented in the next section. We describe our model to represent activities in section 3. The recognition network is presented in section 4. Experimental results are summarized in section 5. In section 6 we give some conclusions and directions for future work.

2   Related Work

When we want to recognize human activities we have to consider two aspects: representation and recognition. The former has been dealt in different ways. The human body and the activities have been modeled like silhouettes [1] and like temporal templates [2]. However, by trying to represent an activity with a silhouette pose, the silhouette extraction is a problem when shadows exist or there are many objects in the environment. In the representation with temporal templates, it is considered the global movement of the body, so that a change in the movement of some limb, no previously defined, will indicate a different activity.

The recognition process has been done using two main approaches: non-probabilistic and probabilistic. The work of Ayers and Mubarak [3] is an example of the non-probabilistic approach. They recognize human actions in an office environment. Their system works if it has a previous description of the environment. It can not work in unpredictable environments. In order to overcome the uncertainty or the changes in the environment the probabilistic approach has been developed. The most used probabilistic models in human activity recognition are hidden Markov models [4], [5]. Alternative probabilistic models are Bayesian networks [6]. Their application in computer vision has focused in the description of high level information. Probabilistic methods can deal with uncertainty and changes in the way the activity is performed.

In activity recognition, some situations make the recognition process more difficult. Sometimes one limb hides the other (auto-occlusion). This makes more difficult to follow the activity and the recognition process fails because of missing information. Another situation that we have to consider is that people perform the activities with different velocities and in different ways. All the previous works that recognize activities with hidden Markov models define one model for each activity. Previous works do not analyze the coordination between the movements of different limbs (multiple motions). So far the recognition of activities performed in a continuous way has not been achieved. In the next sections we describe a model that deals with the previous problems.

3   Activity Modeling

The first step in human activity recognition is to represent the activities that we want to recognize. Basically, we consider that when a person performs an activity we can have a global trajectory of each limb describing the movement. The global trajectory of a limb is its position sequence (X,Y,Z) obtained when the activity is performed just once. The beginning and the end position of the activity can change. We initially consider activities performed with the arms only. We use color landmarks in the wrists to tract the motion of each limb (simplifying the low level segmentation process) and apply a color detection process to get each landmark (figure 1). Then we extract its center of mass (we initially consider its position in just one plane, X-Y) to get the wrist position in each frame and track the activity trajectory. In this way the position of each limb is known every instant.

Working only with the X, Y positions of the landmarks' centroids is very susceptible to the distance between the person and the camera. Therefore, we calculate the direction of motion between two consecutive frames using the X, Y positions. The directions are discretized in 8 sections as shown in the figure 2. When there is no movement between frames we assign a value of zero. The problem here is how to determine how many frames are required to represent an activity since an activity is performed with different velocities by different persons or even by the same person. The activities that we are considering can be performed in at most one second. The frame rate employed is 15 frames per second. The movement of each limb has a direction sequence describing an activity. The most important aspect in sequence is the direction changes. Based on statistics from different activities by different people, we obtained that in a sequence of 15 frames at most there are 7 direction changes. So in a window of 15 frames we look for at most 7 direction changes (figure 3). These directions are used in the recognition network, presented in the next section.

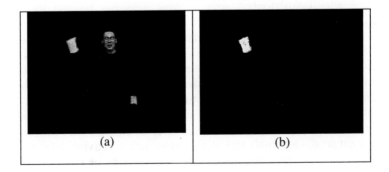

Fig. 1. (a) Original image with landmarks in the wrist. (b) Landmarks after using a color detection process

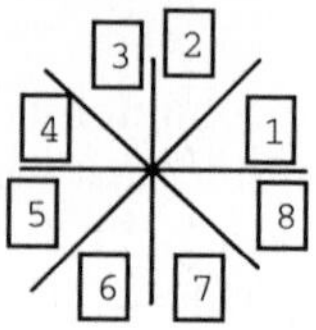

Fig. 2. Discretized directions of motion between frames

5	5	5	4	4	4	8	8	8	1	1	1	2	5	5
1	2	3	4	5	6	7	8	9	10	11	12	13	14	15

Fig. 3. Example of a window with direction changes. The first row shows direction changes. In this example there are 6 direction changes (5, 4, 8, 1, 2, 5). The second row indicates the frame number

4   Recognition Network

Activity recognition starts by capturing an image sequence in which one person is performing some activity. The model in figure 4 shows a Bayesian network [7] in which the root nodes represent the activities that are going to be recognized and the leaf nodes represent the direction changes (observations) obtained from a window of 15 frames. If in the window there are less than 7 direction changes we instantiate with a zero the nodes without direction change. Considering the direction changes we are representing activities performed with different velocities because the activity is characterized by its direction changes no by its velocity. We are considering that the activities to be recognized can be performed with one or both arms. The node values at the lower levels change according to the change of the activity direction reflecting the evolution of the limb motion. We use seven nodes leaf associated to each hand in order to describe the global trajectory of the hand movement (notice that those nodes are connected in a sequential way). If some observation is missing in one or several of such nodes, when we propagate this network obtains the probability of the unobserved leaf nodes, providing the most probable trajectory. The network is able to track the motion of each limb and at the same time recognize the most probable activity. The nodes in the middle give information about the type of movement of each arm.

The leaf nodes in the network are instantiated by the observations in each window, and then the probabilities are propagated [8] in the network in order to get the posterior probabilities of the root nodes. The root nodes have two possible values

(*Yes,No*) for each activity. In this way we can recognize several activities performed at the same time. After propagation, several nodes can have a high probability in its value "*Yes*". Also, the network is able to recognize when the movement of several limbs form an activity. This implies that there is coordination between the limb motions.

The Bayesian network model is applied in a window of 15 frames, and then displaced 3 frames to realize a continuous recognition. The activities to be recognized can take less than 15 frames. We do not need to mark the beginning and the end of the activity. The frames that generate a high probability in one or more of the root nodes indicate when an activity considered in the model is performed.

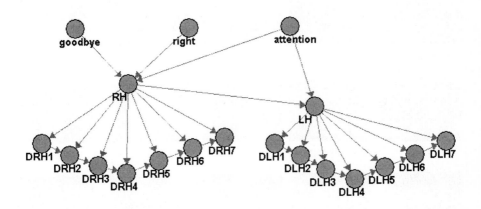

Fig. 4. Recognition network. The root nodes represent the activities to be recognized. The middle nodes contain information about the movement of each arm. The leaf nodes have the direction changes

5 Experimental Results

We trained the network with videos of 5 persons performing 3 types of activities: *goodbye, move right* and *attract the attention. Attract the attention* is a compound activity in which the movement of both arms is required. This involves the recognition of multiple motions. Every person performed the activities with different velocities so the number of direction changes needed to represent the global activity varied. We tested the activity recognition system using continuous activities. For example, figure 5 shows part of a sequence that had 378 frames where the person performed the three activities in a continuous way. The system was able to recognize correctly the activities *goodbye* and *attract the attention* in different sections of the test sequences. In some sections the system did not recognized the activity, but it did not give a wrong classification, neither.

880   R. Díaz de León and L.E. Sucar

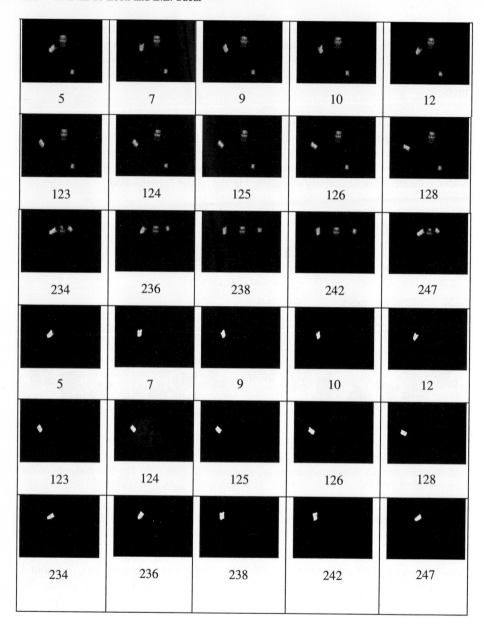

Fig. 5. In the 3 first rows, an image sequence is showed with a color landmark in both wrists. In the 3 bottom rows, the color landmark is depicted after applying a color detection process on the original images. The number below is the frame number in one continuous sequence of the activities "*goodbye* (5-12), *move right* (123-128) and *attract the attention* (234-247)"

6 Conclusions

We have developed a model that can recognize compound activities (performed with several limbs at the same time). It can recognize different activities performed continuously at different speeds and by different persons by using a window to get the direction changes of global activity trajectory. We made an analysis on how many direction changes are enough to have a general activity representation, and concluded that a reduced number of changes are sufficient for representing an activity and for its recognition. We developed a system that uses a Bayesian network for continuous recognition. With only one model we were able to model and to recognize different activities.

We consider that the system is robust with respect to the distance of the person to the camera and its position in the image as it was tested. Given that we are only considering know the X, Y coordinates, it will be affected by the view angle.

Future work will test the recognition network and the window displacement in order to improve the continuous recognition.

References

1. Ismail Haritaoglu, David Harwood, and Larry S. Davis, "Ghost: A Human Body Part Labeling System Using Silhouettes", Fourteenth International Conference on Pattern Recognition, Brisbane, August, 1998.
2. James W. Davis and Aarón F. Bobick, "The Representation and Recognition of Action Using Temporal Templates," IEEE Conference on Computer Vision and Pattern Recognition (CVPR'97), 1997.
3. Douglas Ayers and Shah Mubarak, "Monitoring Human Behavior in an Office Environment," Interpretation of Visual Motion Workshop, CVPR'98, june 1998.
4. Christoph Bregler, "Learning and Recognizing Human Dynamics in Video Sequences," Proceedings IEEE Conference on Computer Vision and Pattern Recognition, San Juan, Puerto Rico, june, 1997.
5. Junji Yamato, Jun Ohya and Kenichiro Ishii, "Recognizing Human Action in Time-Sequential Images Using Hidden Markov Model," IEEE, 1992.
6. Stephen Intille and Aaron Bobick, "A Framework for Recognizing Multi-Agent Action from Visual Evidence," M.I.T. Media Laboratory Perceptual Computing Section Technical Report No. 489, 1999.
7. Richard Neapolitan, "Probabilistic Reasoning in Intelligent Systems: Theory and Algorithms," New York: Wiley, 1989.
8. Steve B. Cousins, William Chen, Mark E. Frisse, "CABeN: A Collection of Algorithms for Belief Networks" Medical Informatics Laboratory, Washington University, 1990.

Kinematic Control System for Car-Like Vehicles

Luis Gracia and Josep Tornero

Department of Systems and Control Engineering, Polytechnic University of Valencia,
Camino de Vera s/n, 46022 Valencia, Spain
{luigraca, jtornero}@isa.upv.es

Abstract. In this paper, we have highlighted the importance of the WMR model for designing control strategies. In this sense, the differential model has been used as reference model in order to design the control algorithm. After the control has been design, new actions will be generated for each additional wheel of the real vehicle (non-differential model). This new approach simplifies the overall control systems design procedure. The examples included in the paper, illustrate the more outstanding issues of the designed control. Moreover, we have particularized this control for the line tracking based on a vision system. A velocity control in the longitudinal coordinate has been implemented instead of a position control because we have no longitudinal information. Also, we have simulated and validated this control, studying the effect of the sampling time on the WMR behavior.

1 Introduction

The automation of industrial processes is frequently based on the use of wheeled mobile robots (WMRs). In particular, WMR are mainly involved in the tracking of references. In this sense, the kinematic control of a WMR is very useful for getting this reference tracking. We have focused our research in a car-like vehicle and considered the differential model as reference model in order to design the control.

Section II describes several alternatives for controlling the WMRs. The Kinematic models, achieved in the previous work [3], are discussed in Section III. The kinematic control is obtained in Section IV and its restrictions are checked through a complete simulation included in Section V. Moreover, we particularize in Section VI the achieved control to a specific application: the line tracking based on a vision system. The simulation results of line tracking, obtained in Section VII, validate the kinematic control developed. Finally, Section VIII remarks the most important contributions and more outstanding issues of the present research.

2 Control of Wheeled Mobile Robots

2.1 Kinematic Control versus Dynamic Control

For WMR, kinematic control calculates the wheel velocities (in the rotation and orientation axles) for tracking the reference, while the dynamic control calculates the wheel accelerations (or torques). These control actions (velocities or accelerations / torques) are used as references for the low-level control loops of the motors.

F.J. Garijo, J.C. Riquelme, and M. Toro (Eds.): IBERAMIA 2002, LNAI 2527, pp. 882–892, 2002.

The WMR dynamic control has the following drawbacks: 1) the required analysis and computation become very complex; 2) it is very sensitive to uncertainties in model parameters; 3) inertial sensors are robustless, inaccurate and expensive and 4) estimators are also inaccurate and expensive.

On the contrary, the WMR kinematic control is simpler and valid as long as the WMR linear and angular velocities have low values (no slip) as usual in industrial environments.

2.2 WMR Control Based on Geometric Methods

This control consists on applying control actions in such a way that the WMR follows a curve that connects its present with an objective position along the reference. For instance, in [7] and [9] circulars arcs and 5th-order polynoms are used, respectively.

Note that this control forces a point-to-point trajectory tracking (pursuit), so it is difficult to guarantee the stability for a particular trajectory. In fact, the main drawback of this control is to find the optimum adjustment, depending on the trajectory, of some *pursuit* parameters for a good reference tracking.

2.3 WMR Control Based on Linear Approximations

Another possibility is to obtain a linear approximation model of the WMR around an equilibrium point and, then, design a classical linear control. Continuous-time as well as discrete-time model can be generated for this linear approximation.

The drawback of this approach is the robustless of the closed-loop control systems when we get away of the equilibrium point, even leading to instability. From the experience on WMR, we can see that the validity range is very small. As an example, [2] develops a WMR continuous direction control based on a linear approximation.

2.4 WMR Control Based on Non-linear Techniques

If we use the WMR non-linear model (either the continuous or the discrete model), we have to find the non-linear control action that guarantees the system stability. For instance, [5] applies a WMR kinematic adaptative discrete control where several parameters of the algorithm are experimental adjusted.

Moreover, stability may be guaranteed through the existence of a *Lyapunov* function, based on the designed control algorithm, that fulfils the *Lyapunov* theorem for stability. For instance, [6] applies a WMR dynamic continuous control where exists a *Lyapunov* function.

2.5 WMR Control Based on State Feedback Linearization

Also, a state feedback linearization of the WMR non-linear model (either the continuous or the discrete model) allows us to apply, in a second stage, a classical control for a reference tracking: point-to-point tracking, trajectory tracking, etc.

Nevertheless, this control has the drawback of singularities, which invalidate the linearization. However, if there are no singularities or they are never achieved, this control is very suitable. So, we will consider this option.

3   WMR Kinematic Model

We focus our research in a car-like vehicle, very common in many WMR applications. From a practical point of view, a unique steerable equivalent wheel (Fig. 1) is used instead the two steerable wheels which are related through the *Ackerman* mechanism. Therefore, we consider the car-like vehicle as a tricycle vehicle.

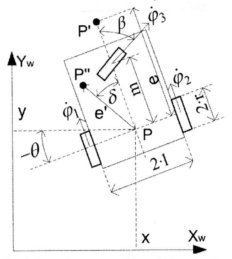

Fig. 1. Equivalent of a car-like vehicle (tricycle)

The meaning of the variables in Fig. 1 is: **P**: Midpoint of the fixed wheels axle; (X_w, Y_w): World coordinate system; (x, y): Position of the point **P** with respect to the world coordinate system; θ: Vehicle orientation with respect to the world coordinate system; (x, y, θ): Vehicle posture; **P'**: Point attached to the WMR that tracks the reference; e: Distance between **P** and **P'**; **P''**: Generic point of the vehicle, characterized by δ and e'; r: radius of the wheels; $2 \cdot l$: Fixed wheels separation; m: Distance between **P** and the center of the equivalent steerable wheel; $\dot\varphi_1, \dot\varphi_2$: Angular velocities of the fixed wheels; β: Angle of the equivalent steerable wheel; $\dot\varphi_3$: Angular velocity of the equivalent steerable wheel.

3.1   Differential Model (Fixed Wheels Driven)

In this case, we achieved in [3] the following kinematic model of the vehicle:

$$
\begin{pmatrix} \dot x \\ \dot y \\ \dot\theta \end{pmatrix} = \frac{r}{2 \cdot l} \begin{pmatrix} l \cdot \sin(\theta) & l \cdot \sin(\theta) \\ l \cdot \cos(\theta) & l \cdot \cos(\theta) \\ 1 & -1 \end{pmatrix} \cdot \begin{pmatrix} \dot\varphi_1 \\ \dot\varphi_2 \end{pmatrix}, \quad \beta = \arctan\left(\frac{(m/l) \cdot (\dot\varphi_1 - \dot\varphi_2)}{(\dot\varphi_1 + \dot\varphi_2)} \right), \dot\varphi_3 = \frac{m}{2 \cdot l} \cdot \frac{(\dot\varphi_1 - \dot\varphi_2)}{\sin(\beta)} \,.
$$

$$\text{(1a)}$$
$$\text{(1b)}$$
$$\text{(1c)}$$

The angular velocity $\dot{\varphi}_3$ can auto adjust, supposing that exists enough friction between the floor and the wheel, without slip. Nevertheless, the angle β cannot auto adjust without slip, since it is necessary to adjust it through the value of $\dot{\beta}$, which is obtained in (2) derivating (1b). Then, we control $\dot{\varphi}_1$ and $\dot{\varphi}_2$, and $\dot{\beta}$ for no slip.

$$\dot{\beta}=\frac{2\cdot m}{l}\cdot\cos^2(\beta)\cdot\frac{\ddot{\varphi}_1\cdot\dot{\varphi}_2-\ddot{\varphi}_2\cdot\dot{\varphi}_1}{(\dot{\varphi}_1+\dot{\varphi}_2)^2}\ . \tag{2}$$

3.2 Tricycle Model (Steerable Wheel Driven)

In this case, we achieved in [3] the following kinematic model of the vehicle:

$$\begin{pmatrix}\dot{x}\\\dot{y}\\\dot{\theta}\end{pmatrix}=\frac{r}{m}\cdot\begin{pmatrix}m\cdot\sin(\theta)\cdot\cos(\beta)\\m\cdot\cos(\theta)\cdot\cos(\beta)\\\sin(\beta)\end{pmatrix}\cdot(\dot{\varphi}_3),\ \begin{pmatrix}\dot{\varphi}_1\\\dot{\varphi}_2\end{pmatrix}=\begin{pmatrix}\cos(\beta)+\dfrac{l}{m}\cdot\sin(\beta)\\\cos(\beta)-\dfrac{l}{m}\cdot\sin(\beta)\end{pmatrix}\cdot\dot{\varphi}_3\ . \begin{matrix}(3a)\\[20pt](3b)\end{matrix}$$

The angular velocities $\dot{\varphi}_1$ and $\dot{\varphi}_2$ can auto adjust, supposing enough friction between the floor and the wheel, with no slip. Then, we control $\dot{\varphi}_3$ and $\dot{\beta}$.

3.3 Practical Kinematic Model

Both above models relate $\dot{\varphi}_1$ and $\dot{\varphi}_2$ with $\dot{\varphi}_3$ through (2b) and (3b). So we can use (1a) or (3a) without distinction, and finally obtain the angular/s velocity/es of the real driven wheel/s. If we name $\mathbf{X}$ to the posture (state) and $\mathbf{u}$ / $\mathbf{u'}$ to the inputs, we can rewrite (1a) and (3a) as:

$$\dot{\mathbf{X}}=B(\mathbf{X})\cdot\mathbf{u} \tag{4a}$$

$$\dot{\mathbf{X}}=B(\mathbf{X},\smallint\mathbf{u'})\cdot\mathbf{u'}\ . \tag{4b}$$

Note that (4a) depends linearly on the inputs, which makes easier a state feedback linearization. Therefore, we use as practical model (1a). In any case, when controlling the WMR, we must act over $\dot{\beta}$, as describes (2), for no slip. Nevertheless, if the velocities of the fixed wheels vary discontinuously there will be slip, since we cannot apply an infinite control action.

4   State Feedback Linearization and Control for a Car-Like Vehicle

4.1 State Feedback Linearization

According to [1], we can linearize as many states as inputs with a static state feedback. In particular, as we have two inputs in (1a) we can linearize two states. Therefore, we would be able to control two state variables. If we consider as reference a trajectory in a two-dimensional space, it is enough to control two state variables, which would correspond to the WMR point coordinates that track the reference. Note that the WMR orientation is not completely free, since if we specify a path we indirectly obligate a WMR orientation.

Now, we develop a static state feedback linearization for the generic system (4a).

First, we make the state transformation $\mathbf{h}(\mathbf{X})$, being $\mathbf{z_1}$ the new states to be linearized, and $\mathbf{k}(\mathbf{X})$ completes the difeomorphism transformation.

$$\mathbf{Z} = \begin{pmatrix} \mathbf{z_1} \\ \mathbf{z_2} \end{pmatrix} = \begin{pmatrix} \mathbf{h}(\mathbf{X}) \\ \mathbf{k}(\mathbf{X}) \end{pmatrix} . \tag{5}$$

Then, the new state equation is:

$$\dot{\mathbf{Z}} = \begin{pmatrix} \dot{\mathbf{z}}_1 \\ \dot{\mathbf{z}}_2 \end{pmatrix} = \begin{pmatrix} \dfrac{\partial(\mathbf{h}(\mathbf{X}))}{\partial \mathbf{X}} \cdot \mathbf{B}(\mathbf{X}) \\ \dfrac{\partial(\mathbf{k}(\mathbf{X}))}{\partial \mathbf{X}} \cdot \mathbf{B}(\mathbf{X}) \end{pmatrix} \cdot \mathbf{u} = \begin{pmatrix} \tilde{\mathbf{h}}(\mathbf{X}) \\ \tilde{\mathbf{k}}(\mathbf{X}) \end{pmatrix} \cdot \mathbf{u} = \begin{pmatrix} \tilde{\mathbf{h}}(\mathbf{Z}) \\ \tilde{\mathbf{k}}(\mathbf{Z}) \end{pmatrix} \cdot \mathbf{u} . \tag{6}$$

Therefore, the actions (7) linearize $\mathbf{z_1}$ so that $\mathbf{w}$ assigns its dynamic behavior.

$$\mathbf{u} = \tilde{\mathbf{h}}(\mathbf{X})^{-1} \cdot \mathbf{w} . \tag{7}$$

In order to get a stable control: a) we have to assign a stable dynamics; b) the non-linearized states must be bounded (what is fulfilled always for the model (1a)); and c) singularity conditions, which depend on the singularity of $\tilde{\mathbf{h}}(\mathbf{X})$, must not arise.

4.2 Linear Control for Trajectory Tracking

We can assign, with $\mathbf{w}$, different kind of controls (8a,b,c), where $\tilde{\mathbf{z}}_1 = \mathbf{z}_{1\text{ref}} - \mathbf{z}_1$ is the error and matrices $\mathbf{A}$ and $\mathbf{B}$ state the dynamics of the system.

$$\mathbf{w}_a = \mathbf{A} \cdot \tilde{\mathbf{z}}_1 , \; \mathbf{w}_b = \dot{\mathbf{z}}_{1\text{ref}} + \mathbf{A} \cdot \tilde{\mathbf{z}}_1 , \; \mathbf{w}_c = \dot{\mathbf{z}}_{1\text{ref}} + \mathbf{A} \cdot \tilde{\mathbf{z}}_1 + \mathbf{B} \cdot \int \tilde{\mathbf{z}}_1 . \tag{8a,b,c}$$

The option: (8a) is a point-to-point control where we close the loop with a proportional feedback; while (8b) is a trajectory control where we close the loop with a proportional feedback plus a derivative feedforward; and (8c) is an integral trajectory control where we close the loop with a proportional and integral feedback plus a derivative feedforward. So, considering (6) and (7) in (8a,b,c), we have:

$$\dot{\mathbf{z}}_1 + \mathbf{A} \cdot \tilde{\mathbf{z}}_1 = 0 , \; \dot{\tilde{\mathbf{z}}}_1 + \mathbf{A} \cdot \tilde{\mathbf{z}}_1 = 0 , \; \ddot{\tilde{\mathbf{z}}}_1 + \mathbf{A} \cdot \dot{\tilde{\mathbf{z}}}_1 + \mathbf{B} \cdot \tilde{\mathbf{z}}_1 = 0 . \tag{9a,b,c}$$

Then, the point-to-point control (8a) has, according to (9a), a non-null velocity error (permanent error for a ramp reference) and an infinite acceleration error (for a parabola reference), so it is not acceptable.

Nevertheless, the trajectory controls (8b,c) have, according to (9b,c), null permanent error for any continuous reference. It is interesting to remark that (8c) allows us to assign an oscillating dynamics, while with (8b) there is not any oscillation. The non-oscillating behavior is selected for WMRs.

4.3 Particularization for a Car-Like Vehicle

First, we apply a transformation $\mathbf{h}(\mathbf{X})$ to obtain a generic point $\mathbf{P}''$ of the WMR:

$$\mathbf{z_1} = \mathbf{h}(\mathbf{X}) = \mathbf{P}'' = \begin{pmatrix} P''_x \\ P''_y \end{pmatrix} = \begin{pmatrix} x + e\cdot\sin(\theta - \delta) \\ y + e\cdot\cos(\theta - \delta) \end{pmatrix}. \tag{10}$$

Then, operating the matrix $\tilde{\mathbf{h}}(\mathbf{X})$ and its singularity are:

$$\tilde{\mathbf{h}}(\mathbf{X}) = \frac{r}{2\cdot l} \cdot \begin{pmatrix} \begin{matrix} l\cdot\sin(\theta) \\ +e\cdot\cos(\theta-\delta) \end{matrix} & \begin{matrix} l\cdot\sin(\theta) \\ -e\cdot\cos(\theta-\delta) \end{matrix} \\ \begin{matrix} l\cdot\cos(\theta) \\ -e\cdot\sin(\theta-\delta) \end{matrix} & \begin{matrix} l\cdot\cos(\theta) \\ +e\cdot\sin(\theta-\delta) \end{matrix} \end{pmatrix}, \quad \left|\tilde{\mathbf{h}}(\mathbf{X})\right| = r\cdot e\cdot\cos(\delta) = 0 \rightarrow \begin{cases} e' = 0 \\ \delta = \pm\pi/2 \end{cases}. \tag{11a}$$
$$\tag{11b}$$

According to (11b), the dynamics of the WMR points on the axle of the fixed wheels cannot be linearized. Then, we can choose any WMR point as a tracking point as long as it does not belong to the axle of the fixed wheels. So, taking as a tracking point $\mathbf{P}'$, which has $\{e' = e, \delta = 0\}$ (it could be for instance the center of the vehicle), the kinematic control results as follows,

$$\mathbf{u} = \tilde{\mathbf{h}}(\mathbf{X})^{-1}\cdot\mathbf{w} = \begin{pmatrix} \dot{\varphi}_1 \\ \dot{\varphi}_2 \end{pmatrix} = \frac{1}{r\cdot e}\cdot\begin{pmatrix} \begin{matrix} l\cdot\cos(\theta) \\ +e\cdot\sin(\theta) \end{matrix} & \begin{matrix} e\cdot\cos(\theta) \\ -l\cdot\sin(\theta) \end{matrix} \\ \begin{matrix} -l\cdot\cos(\theta) \\ +e\cdot\sin(\theta) \end{matrix} & \begin{matrix} e\cdot\cos(\theta) \\ +l\cdot\sin(\theta) \end{matrix} \end{pmatrix}\cdot\left[\begin{pmatrix} \dot{P}'_{x\_ref} \\ \dot{P}'_{y\_ref} \end{pmatrix} - \begin{pmatrix} a_x & 0 \\ 0 & a_y \end{pmatrix}\cdot\begin{pmatrix} (x + e\cdot\sin(\theta)) \\ - P'_{x\_ref} \\ (y + e\cdot\cos(\theta)) \\ - P'_{y\_ref} \end{pmatrix}\right]. \tag{12}$$

where a_x and a_y state the dynamics (poles) of the tracking error in the X and Y axis.

In the designed control (12), the angular velocities of the fixed wheels are continuous (restriction for no slip in the steerable wheel) if the reference trajectory varies smoothly along the time, what means a smooth path.

Note that the kinematic control designed produces, provided that $\mathbf{P}'$ tracks a smooth paths, continuous curvature paths in $\mathbf{P}$ (since the angle of the steerable wheel varies continuously) without explicit them like in [8].

5 Simulation of the Kinematic Control Designed

We show two examples for the kinematic control designed in a simulation environment. Both of them have $r = 0.2$m, $e = 2$m, $l = 0.8$m, $a_x = a_y = 2$ s^{-1}. Moreover, the first example has $m = 4$m, $x_0 = 0$, $y_0 = 4$m, $\theta_0 = 180°$, and the second example $m = 2$m, $x_0 = y_0 = \theta_0 = 0$. {m $\equiv$ meters, s $\equiv$ seconds, ° $\equiv$ degrees }.

The reference of the first example is a semi-circumference followed by a straight line. We can see that the designed control works properly: $\mathbf{P}'$ tracks the reference

(Fig. 2a) and the constant rate of the tracking error is 2s (Fig. 2b). Note that the angle β required for no slip varies continuously, so exists a control action (although it varies instantaneously in the non-differentiable points of β, e.g. $t \cong 6.5$ s) that produces this evolution. Nevertheless, we must initialize the angle β as it corresponds.

The reference of the second example has a non-smooth point. Apparently the designed control works properly: $\mathbf{P'}$ tracks the reference (Fig. 3a) and the constant rate of the tracking error is 2s (Fig. 3b). But the angle β for no slip undergoes two discontinuities (Fig. 3b). The value of the first discontinuity is π, and it is avoided calculating the *arctan* of (1b) in four quadrants.

Nevertheless, the second discontinuity, produced when $\mathbf{P'}$ is on the non-smooth point of the reference, means an unrealizable control action. For preventing the slip in this situation, we should stop the WMR and reorient the steerable wheel.

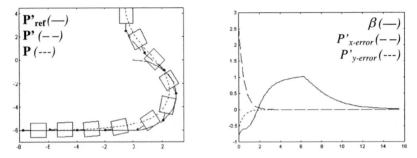

Fig. 2. First example: a) paths described b) signals evolution

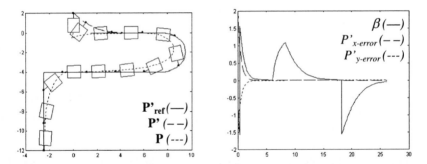

Fig. 3. Second example: a) paths described b) signals evolution

Note that $\mathbf{P}$ describes a smooth path, although it has a curvature discontinuity when $\mathbf{P'}$ is on the non-smooth point of the reference (Fig. 3a). So, a differential WMR (i.e. without steerable wheel) is able to track with $\mathbf{P'}$ non-smooth references.

Moreover, there is a maneuver (change in the direction of the movement) in the beginning of the tracking (Fig.3a). This denotes that the kinematic control designed does not distinguish between forward or backward tracking. So, we should orientate the WMR to the reference, to avoid a backward tracking, with a previous trajectory.

Also, simulation results show excessive tracking error if the center of the vehicle is considered. This is avoided just locating $\mathbf{P'}$ over the center of the vehicle.

6 Kinematic Control for the Line Tracking with a Vision System

The WMR positioning $\{\psi, h\}$ with respect to a line (Fig. 4), obtained with the vision system of [4], is related with the WMR posture as follows:

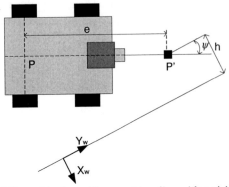

Fig. 4. WMR positioning with respect to a line with a vision system

$$\begin{pmatrix} x \\ y \\ \theta \end{pmatrix} = \begin{pmatrix} -(e \cdot \sin(\psi) + h) \\ \text{Indeterminated} \\ \psi \end{pmatrix} . \tag{13}$$

Then, x and θ are directly observables with $\{\psi, h\}$ and y is not. Also, from (1a):

$$\begin{pmatrix} \dot{x} \\ \dot{y} \\ \dot{\theta} \end{pmatrix} = \mathbf{B}(\theta) \cdot \mathbf{u} . \tag{14}$$

Therefore, we cannot either observe y indirectly, since it does not affect x or θ. On the other hand, we can rewrite the control action (17) as:

$$\mathbf{u} = \tilde{\mathbf{h}}^{-1}(\theta) \cdot \left(\dot{\mathbf{P}}'_{\mathbf{ref}} - \mathbf{A} \cdot \begin{pmatrix} P'_x(\theta, x) - P'_{x\_ref} \\ P'_x(\theta, y) - P'_{y\_ref} \end{pmatrix} \right) . \tag{15}$$

According to (15), the state feedback linearization depends on θ, while the dynamics assignment $\mathbf{w}$ uses (in general) x, y and θ. Then, as we have no y information (due to a vision limitation) we particularize the dynamics assignment so that we apply a velocity control (instead of a position control) in the y direction. Then, (15) results:

$$\mathbf{u} = \tilde{\mathbf{h}}^{-1}(\theta) \cdot \left(\dot{\mathbf{P}}'_{\mathbf{ref}} - \begin{pmatrix} a_x \cdot (P'_x(\theta, x) - P'_{x\_ref}) \\ 0 \end{pmatrix} \right) = \frac{1}{r \cdot e} \cdot \begin{pmatrix} l \cdot \cos(\theta) & e \cdot \cos(\theta) \\ +e \cdot \sin(\theta) & -l \cdot \sin(\theta) \\ -l \cdot \cos(\theta) & e \cdot \cos(\theta) \\ +e \cdot \sin(\theta) & +l \cdot \sin(\theta) \end{pmatrix} \cdot \begin{pmatrix} -a_x \cdot (x + e \cdot \sin(\theta)) \\ \dot{P}'_{y\_ref} \end{pmatrix} . \tag{16}$$

This control means to track the line with a velocity v_{ref}. Using (13) in (16) we get:

$$\mathbf{u} = \begin{pmatrix} \dot{\varphi}_1 \\ \dot{\varphi}_2 \end{pmatrix} = \frac{1}{r \cdot e} \cdot \begin{pmatrix} l \cdot \cos(\psi) + e \cdot \sin(\psi) & e \cdot \cos(\psi) - l \cdot \sin(\psi) \\ -l \cdot \cos(\psi) + e \cdot \sin(\psi) & e \cdot \cos(\psi) + l \cdot \sin(\psi) \end{pmatrix} \cdot \begin{pmatrix} a_x \cdot h \\ v_{ref} \end{pmatrix} . \tag{17}$$

Moreover, taking into account the processing time of the vision system, the kinematic control de control (17) is implemented in a discrete way. Then, we must guarantee the stability for discrete control actions. Then, using the rectangle approximation in (9) and considering constant the WMR orientation between samples (T):

$$\frac{d(\mathbf{z}_1(t))}{dt} \approx \frac{\mathbf{z}_1(k+1) - \mathbf{z}_1(k)}{T}, \tilde{\mathbf{h}}(\psi(t)) \approx \tilde{\mathbf{h}}(\psi(k)) . \tag{18a}$$

$$\tag{18b}$$

Then, it is straightforward that the dynamics of the discrete error is:

$$\tilde{\mathbf{z}}_{k+1} - (\mathbf{I} - T \cdot \mathbf{A}) \cdot \tilde{\mathbf{z}}_k = 0 . \tag{19}$$

Therefore, the discrete poles a_d related to the continuous poles a_c are:

$$a_d = 1 - T \cdot a_c . \tag{20}$$

The above expression is useful to assign an adequate dynamics. Moreover, in order to validate the approximations of (18), overcoat (18b), we have to assign a dynamics slower than the sampling time.

Other posing is to use the kinematic model (1a) for positioning the WMR when we have no positioning from the vision system so that we use a so fast sampling time as we need.

7 Simulation of the Kinematic Control Designed for Line Tracking

Next, we show several simulated examples for the control designed in the previous section. All of them have: $r = 0.05$m, $e = 0.39$m, $l = 0.17$m, $m = 0.3$m, $v_{ref} = 0.1$m/s, $x_0 = -0.3$m, $y_0 = \theta_0 = 0$. Also, we have estimated a sampling time of T = 0.5s for the image processing.

The first and second examples have $a_x = 0.3\text{s}^{-1}$, which means that we assign a dynamics around 7 times slower than sampling time of the control, what is acceptable. Their simulations ratify this, since the tracking is well performed (Fig. 5a,b).

Moreover, to prove robustness control, we have introduced in the second example a random noise (bounded to 2cm in WMR separation and 3° in WMR orientation), giving weak oscillations on the control action (Fig. 5e).

The third example has $a_x = 0.8\text{s}^{-1}$, which means that we assign a tracking dynamics around 2.5 times slower that the sampling time of the control, what is in the limit of an admissible value. In fact, the tracking error describes (Fig. 5c) a small oscillation and the control actions (Fig. 5f) are more drastic, so that we watch the beginning of a non-stable dynamics.

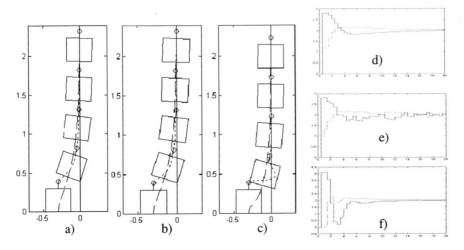

Fig. 5. Simulations of the control designed for line tracking

Moreover, another problem arises when we assign a fast dynamics: the reference line may disappear from the plane image of the vision system, especially if the tracking point does not match the cross between the axis of the camera and the floor.

8 Conclusions

In this paper, we have tried to highlight the importance of the WMR model for designing control strategies. In this sense, the differential model has been used as reference model in order to design the control algorithm. After the control has been design, new action will be generated for the additional wheels of the real vehicle (non-differential model). This new approach simplifies the overall control design procedure. The simulated examples, illustrate the more outstanding issues of the control.

Moreover, we have particularized this control for the line tracking based on a vision system. A velocity control in the longitudinal coordinate has been implemented instead of a position control, as we have no longitudinal information. Also, we have simulated and validated this control, studying the effect of the sampling time on the WMR behavior.

Acknowledgments. This research has been partially funded by the Spanish Government (Ministerio de Ciencia y Tecnología): Research Projects DPI2000-0362-P4-05 and DPI2001-2689-C03-02.

References

1. d'Andréa-Novel B., et al.: Control of Nonholonomic Wheeled Mobile Robots by State Feedback Linearization, The International Journal of Robotics Research Vol. 14 (1995).
2. O'Connor, M., Bell, T., Elkaim, G., Parkinson, B.: Automatic steering of farm vehicles using GPS, In Proceedings of 3rd Intl. Conference on Precision Agriculture 767–778 (1996).
3. Gracia, L., Tornero, J.: Application of Kinematic Modeling Methods to Wheeled Mobile Robots, WSES International Conference on Mathematics and Computers in Physics (2001).
4. Gracia, L., Tornero, J.: Vision-based system for Self-positioning and Calibration, WSEAS International Conference on Signal Processing, Robotics and Automation (2002).
5. Inoue, K., et al.: Estimation of place of Tractor and Adaptative Control Method of Autonomous Tractor using INS and GPS, In Proceedings of Biorobotics pp27–32 (1997).
6. Lyshevski, S. E., Nazarov, A.: Lateral Maneuvering of Ground Vehicles: Modeling and Control, In Proceedings of the American Control Conference (2000).
7. Ollero, A., García-Cerezo, A., Martínez, J: Fuzzy Supervisory Path Tracking of Mobile Robots, Control Engineering Practice Vol. 2 num. 2 pp 313–319, Pergamon Press (1994).
8. Scheuer, A., Laugier, Ch.: Planning Sub-Optimal and Continuous-Curvature Paths for Car-Like Robots, International Conference on Intelligent Robots and Systems (1998).
9. Shin, D.: High Performance Tracking of Explicit Paths by Roadworthy Mobile Robots, Ph. D. Dissertation, Carnegie Mellon University (1990).

Habituation Based on Spectrogram Analysis

Javier Lorenzo and Mario Hernández

IUSIANI*
Edificio del Parque Tecnológico
Univ. of Las Palmas de G.C. – Spain
jlorenzo@dis.ulpgc.es

Abstract. In this paper we present a habituation mechanism which includes a modification of the Stanley's habituation model with the addition of a stage based on spectrogram to detect temporal patterns in a signal and to obtain a measure of habituation to these patterns. This means that this measure shows a saturation process as the pattern is perceived by the system and when it disappears the measure drops. The use of the spectrogram simplifies the detection of the temporal patterns which can be detected with naive techniques. We have carried on some experiments both a synthetic signal and real signals like readings of a sonar in a mobile robot.

1   Introduction

Habituation and novelty detection can be thought as the two sides of the same problem because habituation begins when novelty finishes. Novelty detection is related with the discovery of stimuli not perceived before and habituation is related with the saturation process that living beings exhibit when the same stimulus is shown repeatedly, so habituation serves as a novelty filter [1]. Marsland [2] defines habituation as "a way of defocusing attention from features which are seen often". Both process are involved in social interaction where robots and multimodal interfaces have to deal with a large amount of stimuli from the environment so it needs to filter it and to focus on *interesting* ones and leave out the rest. Therefore, there are two problem to solve: what is interesting? and when and how long a stimuli is interesting?. The former is task-dependent so it is considered to be outside the scope of this work. The answers to the latter questions are given by novelty detection and habituation.

With regard to the habituation, it has received great attention in the physiological and psychological areas. In the physiological area, some researchers have investigated the mechanisms of habituation of animals. One of the most known works in this area is the study of the Aplysia's gill-withdrawal reflex [3] which led to the discovery physiological changes that are responsible for its habituation. Crook and Hayes [4] comment the study carried out on two monkeys (*macaca mulatta*) by Xiang and Brown who identified neurons that exhibit a habituation mechanism since their activity decreases as the stimulus was shown repeatedly.

---

* Institute of Intelligent Systems and Numerical Applications in Engineering

F.J. Garijo, J.C. Riquelme, and M. Toro (Eds.): IBERAMIA 2002, LNAI 2527, pp. 893–902, 2002.

There are some models of habituation, although the proposed by Stanley [5] to simulate the habituation data obtained from the cat spinal cord is widely used. This model describes the decrease in the synaptic efficacy y by the first-order differential equation

$$\tau \frac{dy(t)}{dt} = \alpha(y_0 - y(t)) - S(t) \tag{1}$$

where y_0 is the normal, initial value of y, $S(t)$ represents the external stimulation, τ is the time constant that governs the rate of habituation and α regulates the rate of recovery. Equation (1) ensures that the synaptic efficacy decreases when the input signal $S(t)$ increases and returns to its maximum y_0 in the absence of an input signal.

The model given by (1) can only explain short-term habituation, so Wang [6] introduced a model to incorporate both short and long-term habituation using an inverse S-shaped curve,

$$\tau \frac{dy(t)}{dt} = \alpha z(t)(y_0 - y(t)) - \beta y(t)S(t) \tag{2}$$

$$\frac{dz(t)}{dt} = \gamma z(t)(z(t) - l)S(t) \tag{3}$$

where α, y_0 and τ have the same meaning than in (1) and β regulates the habituation and $z(t)$ decreases monotonically with each activation of the external stimulation $S(t)$ and model the long term habituation. Due to this effect of $z(t)$ after a large number of activations, the recovery rate is slower.

The organization of the rest of this paper is as follows. In section 2 some works about the use of the habituation and novelty concepts in different areas are commented. Section 3 introduces the spectrograms like elements to detect temporal patterns in signal. The implementation of the proposed method is explained in section 4 and finally some experiments are presented in section 5.

2   Related Works

The concept of habituation (or novelty detection) has been used in different areas like fault diagnosis, learning of temporal signals or learning in mobile robotics. In the latter one, some works are based on mechanisms of storage that act as short-term memories, therefore all the patterns not included in this memory are considered novel. Marsland [7] proposes an approach using as memory mechanism a SOM neural network. To add the short-term memory to the original network architecture, each neuron of the SOM is connected to an output neuron with a habituable synapses based on the model (1). To solve the drawback of the limited number of patterns that can be stored in a fixed size SOM, Marsland [8] proposes a modification of the HSOM to add nodes as they are required giving as result the GWR network. Ypma and Duin [9] also uses a SOM neural network as a novelty detector in the area of fault diagnosis. They give the the SOM a memory function as Marsland, but they compare the stored patterns with the

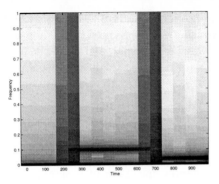

Fig. 1. Spectrogram of a signal

new using a new measure of map goodness. Crook and Hayes [4] also propose novelty detection based on a neural network, specifically a Hopfield network. The presence or absence of a pattern in the network is detected computing the energy of it, which has a fix computational cost, instead of recalling the pattern, which take several cycles.

Dasgupta and Forrest [10] propose a method for novelty detection using the negative selection algorithm that comes from the self-nonself discrimination that exhibits the immune system. The immune system has developed a mechanism to detect any foreign cell (novelty). This mechanism has detectors which are strings that do match with no own cell, so a match implies a shift in the normal behaviour pattern and it normally corresponds to a foreign cell. In the work of Dasgupta and Forrest a set of detectors is generated according to the normal behaviour of the system and then if a pattern matches with a detector, it means that there exists a deviation in the normal behaviour, that is, it is novel. Habituation has also been used to train neural networks which realizes dymanic classification. The neural network of Stiles and Gosh [1] make uses of habituation units as input to a feedforward network to encode temporal information as well for classifications problems. The output of these habituation units is governed by the model (1) with its own value of α and τ for each unit. Chang [11] also makes use of model (1) to add a habituation mechanism to a neural network that learns obstacle avoidance behaviours. The habituation mechanism improves the performance of the learned behaviour when the robot is placed in a narrow hallway, reducing the oscillations that it exhibits without the habituation mechanism.

3   Spectrogram as Temporal Patterns Detector

In some systems, it is necessary to have a habituation mechanism to temporal pattern. For example a waving hand can catch the eye of a multimodal user interface but after a while without any other stimuli the system will exhibit a lack of interest in the waving hand, or if a face appears in its visual field, the system reacts focusing its attention in the face, but if it keeps static for a long time it can be a picture not a person. In this situations, it is necessary to provide the system of a mechanism that habituates to this repetitive or static location.

Here, an approach based on the spectrogram of the location of the stimulus is proposed. The spectrogram is a time-frequency distribution of the signal which is based on the Fourier Transform with a sliding window [12]. The following equation

$$\Phi(t, f) = \left| \int_{-\infty}^{\infty} x(\tau) \exp^{(t-\tau)^2/T^2} \exp^{-j2\pi f\tau} d\tau \right|^2 \tag{4}$$

gives the definition of a spectrogram with a Gaussian window function of half-width T, and it is the power spectrum of a signal which corresponds to the squared magnitude of the Fourier transform of the windowed signal. The window can have others forms apart from the Gaussian one. In Figure 1 we have the spectrogram of the signal that appears in Figure 2, where darker areas correspond to higher power, so it can be observed that the frequency of the signal is changing twice over the time.

In the proposed approach, it is exploited the fact that temporal patterns of the stimulus have a specific pattern in the spectrogram. In the previous example, a fixed frequency signal corresponds to a straight line parallel to the time axe in the spectrogram, and the length of this line gives a clue about the time the stimulus is present.

4 Implementation

In this section the implementation of the proposed method is explained. The aim is to detect if the stimulus keeps a constant or repetitive location in the sensory space. To illustrate the method we utilise the test signal shown in Figure 2 which can be considered as the horizontal position of a stimulus in the visual field of a camera. This stimulus keeps a constant position at pixel 9 (12 sec.), then it oscillates around pixel 12 with a frequency of 2.5 Hz (18 sec.) and finally it moves to pixel 6 and oscillates with a frequency of 1 Hz (15 sec.)

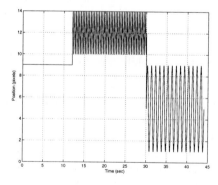

Fig. 2. Test signal

If we use the model of habituation (1) with the test signal, we get the response of Figure 3 which does not exhibit a habituation process in spite of the repetitive movement can produce habituation in some systems.

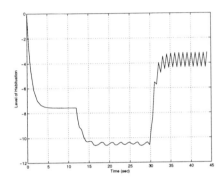

Fig. 3. Habituation model response to test signal

So it is necessary to add a previous stage to the model in order to capture the repetitive nature of the stimulus movement. This stage is based on a time-frequency distribution like the spectrogram, but in this case we do not have the complete signal to compute it, so the power spectral distribution (psd) is computed using the Fast Fourier Transform (FFT) in a window and then the power of the signal is obtained. The window to compute the spectrogram is slided as the positions of the stimulus are obtained, for example from a visual process. The psd gives the power of the signal at different frequencies so if we keep a trace of the frequency associated to the maximum power we can get the signature in the spectrogram and detect certain temporal patterns in the signal. Figure 4 shows the signature obtained with a rectangular window of width 256 as we have explained for the test signal. From analysis of the signature we can identified clearly three zones, each one corresponds to a different movement of the stimulus: one from 0 to 12 secs., the second from 13 to 31 secs. and the last from 33 to 44 secs. We have to note that there exists a delay between the change of the frequency in the spectrogram and the actual change in the signal. This delay obeys to the size of the window used to compute the FFT.

The identification of each of the previous zones in the spectrogram allows us to detect regularities in the position of the stimulus in the sensor space. Specifically, in Figure 4 each horizontal straight line corresponds to a periodical movement with constant frequency. To detect these horizontal lines we use a simple technique of fitting a straight line and then compute its slope; horizontal areas has zero slope. If we compute the slope of a fitted line using 10 points in the graph 4 and represent the absolute value of it, we get the graph 5, where it can be observed that the areas where the slope is null corresponds to the areas of interest in the spectrogram.

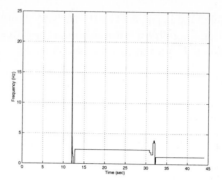

Fig. 4. Frequency of maximum power of the test signal using a window of size 256

Once, the areas of interest are identified in the spectrogram with a value of zero, the habituation model (1) can be fed and it will exhibit the desired behaviour of saturation after a while of being the stimulus in the same position or oscillating around a given one with a constant frequency (Fig. 6).

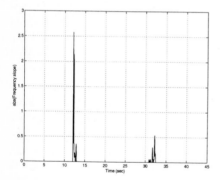

Fig. 5. Absolute value of the line fitted to the frequency graph

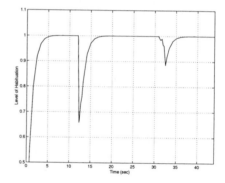

Fig. 6. Results of the habituation model after the detection of constant frequency movement ($\alpha = 1.0$, $\tau = 1.05$)

5   Experiments

In this section we show the results obtained with the habituation method we propose in this work. The first experiment corresponds to a problem of visual stimulus habituation. We present to a camera a yellow card (Fig. 7) and we move it after a while. Since the study of complex visual routines is out of scope of this work, we choose the yellow colour because it makes easy the detection

Fig. 7. Environment for the visual habituation experiment

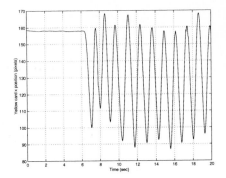

Fig. 8. Position in the x coordinate of
the yellow card

of the card in the office environment where the experiments where carried out.
For each frame of 384x288 pixels, we compute the position of the card and then
we apply the algorithm described in section 4. The values of the x-coordinate is
shown in figure 8 and the changes in frequency considered as changes in the slope
of the fitted straight line are shown in figure 9. When the yellow card starts to
move (6 secs.) there is a period where the frequency do not stabilises, but after
4 seconds the frequency is constant and it is detected correctly and the system
habituates to this movement as is shown in figure 10.

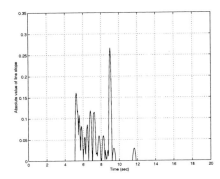

Fig. 9. Slope of the straight line fitted
to the frequency change in the visual
habituation experiment

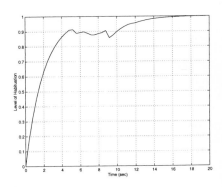

Fig. 10. Habituation level for the visual problem ($\alpha = 0.5, \tau = 1.0$)

This experiment was designed to study the habituation method proposed in
this work in an environment of mobile robots and it consists of a mobile robot
traversing in straight line the environment shown in Figure 11 and detecting the
distance to the wall where there are holes/doors. The readings of the right sonar
(Fig. 12) exhibits a repetitive pattern with noise due to the nature of the sensor

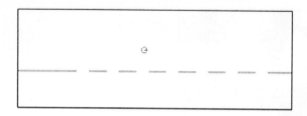

Fig. 11. Environment for the robot experiment

(sonar). The frequency of the pattern is very low because the update rate of the sonars is 2Hz in this robot (Pioneer2) so the difference in frequency between the flat wall and the wall with doors is small (Fig. 13) and it affects to the change in slope of the fitted line (Fig. 14). The fact of having a small change in slope forces to decrease the parameter α to a value of 0.1 in the model (1) to slow down the recovery rate and thus introducing a break in the habituation curve (Fig. 15) when the robot leaves the flat wall.

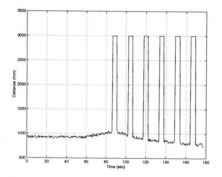

Fig. 12. Readings of the robot's right sonar along the corridor

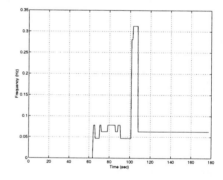

Fig. 13. Frequencies of maximum power for the corridor traverse problem

6   Conclusions and Future Work

In this work we have proposed a method to obtain a habituation measure to temporal patterns based on the use of a time-frequency distribution of the signal prior to a habituation model. The use of the spectrogram is due to the fact that temporal patterns in the signal domain correspond to signatures in the spectrogram which are easily detected by naive techniques like the study of the slope of a fitted straight line. Besides with the power spectrum distribution, the spectrogram can be computed incrementally so the habituation measure

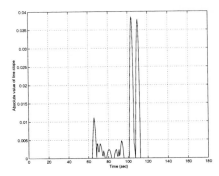

Fig. 14. Slope of the straight line fitted to the frequency change in the robot problem

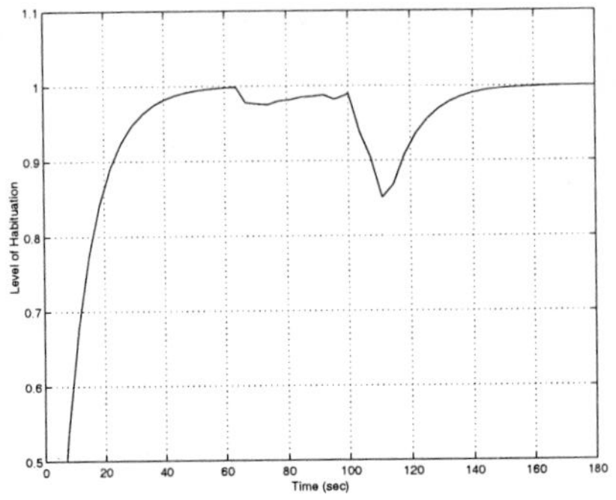

Fig. 15. Habituation level as the robot traverse the corridor ($\alpha = 0.1$, $\tau = 1.0$)

is obtained with a delay that depends of the window size used to compute the power spectrum distribution. We have tested the proposal in a problem of mobile robots using as signal the readings of the sonar which are noised and detecting correctly the two different zones in the corridor that the robot traverses.

The use of the model proposed by Stanley as habituation mechanism, implies the need of adjusting the parameters α and τ to control the recovery rate which depends in this proposal of the difference in frequency of the temporal patterns of interest. Therefore, a future work is to obtain a relation between the difference in frequency and the optimum α value to avoid to tune it by hand. Also, it is necessary to extend the study to other temporal patterns apart from those with constant frequency and the effect of those patterns in the spectrogram.

Acknowledgements. This work has been partially supported by Canary Islands Regional Government under Research Project PI2000/042.

References

1. Stiles, B., Ghosh, J.: A habituation based neural network for spatio-temporal classification. In: Proceedings of the 1995 IEEE Workshop In Neural Networks for Signal Processing, Cambridge, MA (1995) 135–144
2. Marsland, S., Nehmzow, U., Shapiro, J.: A model of habituation applied to mobile robots. In: Proceedings of TIMR 1999 – Towards Intelligent Mobile Robots, Bristol (1999)
3. Castellucci, V., Pinsker, H., Kupfermann, I., Kandel, E.R.: Neuronal mechanisms of habituation and dishabituation of the gill-withdrawal reflex in *Aplysia*. Science **167** (1970), 1745–1748,
4. Crook, P., Hayes, G.: A robot implementation of a biologically inspired method ofr novelty detection. In: Proceedings of TIMR 2001 – Towards Intelligent Mobile Robots, Manchester (2001)

5. Stanley, J.: Computer simulation of a model of habituation. Nature **261** (1976) 146–148
6. Wang, D.: Habituation. In Arbib, M.A., ed.: The Handbook of Brain Theory and Neural Networks. MIT Press (1995) 441–444
7. Marsland, S., Nehmzow, U., Shapiro, J.: Detecting novel features of an environment using habituation. In: From Animals to Animats, The Sixth International Conference on Simulation of Adaptive Behaviour, Paris (2000)
8. Marsland, S., Nehmzow, U., Shapiro, J.: Novelty detection in large enviroments. In: Proceedings of TIMR 2001 – Towards Intelligent Mobile Robots, Manchester (2001)
9. Ypma, A., Duin, R.P.W.: Novelty detection using self-organizing maps. In Kasabov, N., Kozma, R., Ko, K., O'Shea, R., Coghill, G., Gedeon, T., eds.: Progress in Connectionist-Based Information Systems. Volume 2. Springer, London (1997) 1322–1325
10. Dasgupta, D., Forrest, S.: Novelty detection in time series data using ideas from immunology. In: Proceedings of the 5th International Conference on Intelligent Systems, Reno (1996)
11. Chang, C.: Improving hallway navigation in mobile robots with sensory habituation. In: Proc. of the Int. Joint Conference on Neural Networks (IJCNN2000). Volume V., Como, Italy (2000) 143–147
12. Holland, S., Kosel, Tadej amd Waver, R., Sachse, W.: Determination of plate source, detector separation fron one signal. Ultrasonics **38** (2000) 620–623

Dynamic Schema Hierarchies for an Autonomous Robot

José M. Cañas and Vicente Matellán

Universidad Rey Juan Carlos, 28933 Móstoles (Spain)
{jmplaza,vmo}@gsyc.escet.urjc.es

Abstract. This paper proposes a behavior based architecture for robot control which uses dynamic hierarchies of small schemas to generate autonomous behavior. Each schema is a flow of execution with a target, can be turned on and off, and has several parameters which tune its behavior. Low level schemas are woken up and modulated by upper level schemas, forming a hierarchy for a given behavior. At any time there are several awake schemas per level, running concurrently, but only one of them is activated by environment perception. When none or more than one schema wants to be activated then upper level schema is called for arbitration. This paper also describes an implementation of the architecture and its use on a real robot.

1 Introduction

It is not science fiction to see a mobile robot guiding through a museum[1], navigating in an office environment, serving as a pet[2], or even playing soccer[3]. Today we've got best sensors and actuators ever. But how are they combined to generate behaviors? The hardware improvements have made clear the importance of a good control architecture, making it a critical factor to obtain the goal of autonomous behavior.

Robot control architecture can be defined as the organization of robot sensory, actuation and computing capabilities in order to generate a wide set of intelligent behaviors in certain environment. Architectures answer to a main question: what to do next? (action selection), as well as another questions like what is interesting in the environment? (attention), etc. Advances in architecture will lead to even more complex behaviors and increasing reliable autonomy.

In next section main proposals in robot control architectures will be reviewed. Section 3 presents our approach, Dynamic Schema Hierarchies, including its action selection mechanism, its reconfiguration abilities and how perception is organized in this proposal. The software architecture developed to implement DSH is commented on section 4. Some conclusions and future lines end the paper.

---

[1] Minerva: http://www.cs.cmu.edu/~minerva
[2] Aibo:http://www.aibo.com
[3] Robocup: http://www.robocup.org/

F.J. Garijo, J.C. Riquelme, and M. Toro (Eds.): IBERAMIA 2002, LNAI 2527, pp. 903–912, 2002.
© Springer-Verlag Berlin Heidelberg 2002

2   Robot Control Architectures

2.1   Deliberative Architectures

Symbolic AI has influenced on mobile robotics from its beginnings, resulting in the deliberative approach. This makes emphasis on world modeling and planning as deliberation for robot action. In mid eighties this was the main paradigm for behavior generation. The control architecture was seen as an infinite information loop: Sense-Model-Plan-Act (SMPA). In modeling step sensor data are fused into a central world representation, which stores all data about environment, maybe in a symbolic form. Most robot intelligence lie in the planning step, where a planner searched in the state space and found a sequence operators to reach some target state from the current one. Act were seen as a mere plan execution.

There was a single execution flow and a functional decomposition of the problem, where the modules called functions from other modules (vision module, path planning module).

2.2   Behavior Based Architectures

Rooted in connectionist theories in mid eighties new approaches which exhibited impressive demos on real robots were proposed. The common factor of such works was the distribution of control in several basic behavior units, called levels of competence, schemas, agents, etc.

Each behavior unit is a fast loop from sensor to action, with its own partial target. There is no central representation, each behavior processes its own sensory information. Additionally, there are no explicit symbols about the environment. The emphasis is put in real world robots (embodiment) and in interaction with the environment (situated).

Distribution of control poses the additional problem of behavior coordination. Each behavior has its own goal, but usually enters in contradiction with another one. How is the final actuation calculated (action selection)?. There are two major paradigms: arbitration and command fusion. Arbitration establishes a competition for control among all the behaviors and only the winning one determines the final actuation. Priorities, activation networks from Pattie Maes [13] and state based arbitration [3] fall in this category. Command fusion techniques merge all the relevant outputs in a global one that take into account all behavior preferences. Relevant approaches in command fusion include superposition[2], fuzzy blending [15] and voting [14]. Coordination is always a difficult issue.

We will present here in more detail two foundational works leaving apart extensions and refinements. They contain main relevant ideas of the approach.

Brook's subsumption. In 1986 Rodney Brooks proposed a layered decomposition of behavior in competence levels [6]. Since then many robots have been developed using this paradigm (Herbert, Toto), showing a great proficiency in low level tasks such as trash cans collecting, local navigation, etc. A competence level is an informal specification of a desired class of behaviors for a robot. Each level is implemented by a net of Finite State Machines (FSM), which have low bandwidth communication channels to exchange signals and small variables.

Low levels provide basic behaviors, i.e. avoid obstacles, wander, etc.. More refined behaviors are generated building additional levels over the existing ones. All levels run concurrently, and upper levels can suppress lower level outputs and replace their inputs. This is called subsumption and gives name to the architecture. This action selection mechanism uses fixed priorities hardwired in the FSM net.

Arkin' schemas. Following Arbib ideas [1], Ronald Arkin proposed a decomposition of behavior in schemas [2]. His architecture, named AuRA, contains two types of units: motor schemas and perceptive ones. "Each motor schema has an embedded perceptual schema to provide the necessary sensor information" [2].

For instance, the output of a navigation motor schema is a vector with the desired velocity and orientation to advance. The navigation behavior was obtained by the combination of avoid-moving-obstacles, avoid-static-obstacles, stay-on-path and move-to-goal schemas. Each schema can be implemented as a potential field, delivering a force vector for each location in the environment. The commanded movement is the superposition of all fields [2].

Extensions to Arkin's approach include the sequencing of several complex behaviors. A Finite State Acceptor is used for arbitration, where each state means the concurrent activation of certain schemas and triggering events are defined to jump among states [3].

2.3   Hybrid Approaches

The trend in last years is an evolution to hybrid architectures that combine the strengths of both paradigms. For instance, planning capabilities and fast reactivity, because they both are important for complex tasks on real reliable robots.

A successful approach is the layered 3T-architecture [5], based on Firby's RAP [9]. The control is distributed in a fixed hierarchy of three abstraction levels that run concurrently and asynchronously. Upper layer includes deliberation over symbolic representations and makes plans composed of tasks. The intermediate level, called sequencer, receives such tasks and has a library of task recipes describing how to achieve them. It activates and deactivates sets of skills to accomplish the tasks. Skills compose the reactive layer. Each one is a continuous routine that achieve or maintain certain goal in a given context (it is situated).

3   Dynamic Schema Hierarchies

We propose an approach named Dynamic Schema Hierarchies (DSH) that is strongly rooted in Arbib [1] and Arkin ideas [2]. The basic unit of behavior is called schema. Control is distributed among a hierarchy of schemas.

An *schema* is a flow of execution with a target. It can be turned on and off, and accepts several input parameters which tune its own behavior. There are perceptual schemas and motor schemas. Perceptual ones produce pieces of information that can be read by other schemas. These data usually are sensor observations or relevant stimuli in current environment, and they are the input for motor schemas. Motor schemas access to such data and generate their outputs, which are the activation signal for other low level schemas (perceptual or motor) and their modulation parameters.

All schemas are *iterative* processes, they perform their mission in iterations which are executed periodically. Actually, the period of such iterations is a main modulation parameter of the schema itself. Digital controllers are an example of such paradigm, they deliver a corrective action each control cycle. Schemas are also *suspendable*, they can be deactivated at the end on one iteration and they will not produce any output until they are resumed again.

A perceptual schema can be in only two states: SLEPT or ACTIVE. When ACTIVE the schema is updating the stimuli variables it is in charge of. When SLEPT the variables themselves exist, but they are outdated. The change from SLEPT to ACTIVE or vice versa is determined by upper level schemas.

For motor schemas things are a little bit more tricky, they can be in four states: SLEPT, CHECKING, READY and ACTIVE. A motor schema has preconditions, which must be satisfied in order to be ACTIVE. CHECKING means the schema is awake and actively checking its preconditions, but they don't match to current situation. When they do, the schema passes to READY and tries to win action selection competition against other READY motor schemas in the same level and so become ACTIVE. Only ACTIVE schemas deliver activation signals and modulation parameters to lower level schemas.

Schemas can be implemented with many different techniques: simple rules from sensor data, fuzzy controllers, planners, finite state machines, etc. The only requirement is to be iterative and suspendable. In the case of a planner, the plan is enforced to be considered a resource, an internalized plan [14] instead of a symbolic one. This is because the schema has to deliver an action proposal each iteration.

3.1   Hierarchy

Schemas are organized in hierarchies. These hierarchies are dynamically built. For instance, if an ACTIVE motor schema needs some information to accomplish its target then it activates relevant perceptual schemas (square boxes in figure 1) in order to collect, search, build and update such information. It may also awake a set of low level motor schemas (circles) that can be useful for its purpose because implement right reactions to stimuli in the environment. It modulates them to behave according to its own target and put them in CHECKING state. Not only the one convenient for current situation, but also all the lower motor schemas which deal with plausible situations. This way low level schemas are recursively woken up and modulated by upper level schemas, forming a unique hierarchy for a given global behavior.

At any time there are several CHECKING motor schemas running concurrently per level, displayed as solid circles in figure 1 (i.e. schemas 5, 6 and 7). Only one of them per level is activated by environment perception or by explicit parent arbitration, as we will see on 3.2. The ACTIVE schemas are shown as filled circles in figure 1 (1, 6 and 15). For instance motor schema 6 in figure 1 is the winner of control competition at the level. It awakes perceptual schemas 11, 16 and motor schemas 14, 15, and sets their modulation parameters.

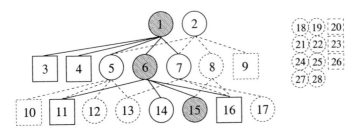

Fig. 1. Schema hierarchy and pool of SLEPT schemas

Schemas unused for current task rest in a pool of schemas, suspended in SLEPT state, but ready for activation at any time. They appear as dashed squares and circles in figure 1 (schemas 8, 9, 10, 12, 13, 17, 18, etc.). Actually, schemas 10, 12, and 13 are one step away from activation, they will be awaken if schema 5 passed to ACTIVE in its level.

Sequence of behaviors can be implemented with DSH using a motor schema coded as a finite state machine. Each state corresponds to one step in the sequence, and makes a different set of lower schemas to be awaken. It also activates the perceptual schemas needed to detect triggering events that change its internal state.

3.2   DSH Action Selection

At any time the ACTIVE perceptual schemas draw a perceptual subspace (attention subspace) that corresponds to all plausible values of relevant stimuli for each level (displayed as white areas in figure 2). It is a subset of all possible stimuli, because it doesn't include the stimuli produced by SLEPT perceptual schemas (shadowed area in figure 2). This subspace is partitioned into activation regions, which are defined as the areas where the preconditions of a motor schema are satisfied. Parent schema sets its child motor schemas activation regions to be more or less non overlapping.

A given situation corresponds to one point in such subspace, and may lie in the activation region of one motor schema or another. Only the corresponding motor schema will be activated, so situation activates only one schema per level among CHECKING ones. This is a coarse grained arbitration based on activation regions.

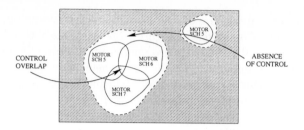

Fig. 2. Perceptual space, attention subspace and activation regions

Despite such coarse grained arbitration may appear situations where more than one motor schema for a level satisfy their preconditions (activation regions overlap in figure 2). Even situations where none of them are READY for activation, that is, not covered by any activation region (absence of control). Child schemas detect such control failures checking their brothers' state, and then parent is called for fine grained arbitration. Parent can change children parameters or just select one of them as the winner of control competition is its level. This is similar to context dependent blending [15], the parent schema knows the context for that arbitration, and so it can be very behavior specific.

The action selection mechanism in DSH has a distributed nature. There is no central arbiter as in DAMN [11], just parent and children. There is a competition per level, that occurs once every child iteration. This allows fast reconfiguration if situation changed.

It is a commitment between purposiveness top-down and reactive motivations. Only schemas awaken from upper level are allowed to gain control, but finally perceived situation chooses one and only one winner among them per level. The winner schema has double motivation, task-oriented and situation-oriented. Schemas without any of them don't add enough motivation for their activation and remain silent, CHECKING or SLEPT. Activation flows top-down in the hierarchy, similar to architecture proposed by Tinbergen and Lorenz [12] for instinctive behavior in animals. Addition of motivation and lateral inhibition among same level nodes also appear in such ethological architectures.

3.3   Perception

In DSH motor schemas make their decisions over information produced by perceptual schemas. Perception is distributed in perceptual schemas, each one may produce several pieces of such information. They exist because at least one motor schema eventually needs the information they produce. It can be sensor data that the schema collects, or more complex stimuli about environment or the robot itself built by the schema (for instance a map, a door, etc.). All the events or stimuli that we want to take into account in the behavior require a computational effort to detect and perceive them. DSH includes them in the architecture as perceptual schemas, each one searches for and describes its stimulus when present, updating internal variables.

Due to hierarchical activation in DSH, perception is situated, and context dependent. Perceptual schemas can be activated at will. The ACTIVE ones focus only on stimuli which are relevant to current situation or global behavior (attention). This filters out huge amounts of useless data from the sensors, i.e. shadowed area in figure 2. It makes the system more efficient because no computational resource is devoted to stimuli not interesting in current context.

There can be symbolic stimuli if they are convenient for the behavior at hand. These abstract stimuli must be grounded, with clear building and updating algorithms from sensor data or other lower level stimuli. Actually, different levels in perceptual schemas allow for abstraction and compounded stimuli: perceptual schemas can have as input the output of other perceptual schemas.

3.4   Reconfiguration

For a given task certain hierarchy generates the right robot behavior. The net of schemas builds relevant stimuli from sensor data and reacts accordingly to environment state. If the situation changes slightly, currently ACTIVE schemas can deal with it and maybe generate a slightly different motor commands. If the situation changes a little bit more maybe one ACTIVE schema is not appropriate anymore and the environment itself activates another CHECKING motor schema, that was ready to react to such change.

In the case of bigger changes they cause a control conflict at a certain level. In that case, the parent is called for arbitration and may decide to sleep useless schemas, wake up another relevant ones, change its children modulation, or propagate the conflict upwards forcing a hierarchy reconfiguration from upper level. The mechanism to solve conflicts may vary from one schema to another (fuzzy logic, simple rules, etc.). This reconfiguration may add new levels or reduce the number of them. This can be seen as a dynamic controller, composed of several controllers running in parallel and triggering events that change completely the controllers net. Each event requires a corresponding perceptual schema to detect it. This is similar to discrete state arbitration from [3], but accounts for hierarchy of schemas not only for a single level.

The levels are not static but task dependent as in TCA task trees [16]. These changes must be designed to work properly. Schemas don't belong to any level in particular. They can be located in a different level, probably with other parameters, for another global behavior. This way the schemas can be reused in different levels depending on the desired final behavior.

4   Implementation Issues

We have used a small indoor robot, composed of a pioneer platform, and a off-the-shelf laptop under Linux OS (figure 3). The robot is endowed with a 16 sonar belt, bumpers, and two wheel encoders for position estimation. We have added a cheap webcam connected through USB to the computer. Two DC motors allow robot movements.

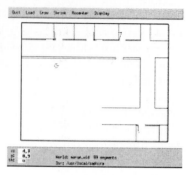

Fig. 3. Supercoco, our robot and Saphira© simulator

A software architecture has been developed to test the cognitive architecture proposed. All our code is written in ANSI-C. We have developed two socket servers which make available camera images, motor commands, raw sonar, bumper, and encoder data to client programs through message protocol. These servers can be connected both to robot simulator (Saphira environment [10]) or real platform, so the same control program can run seamlessly on real robot or on the simulator (without vision). The use of a simulator is very convenient for debugging. Additionally, the laptop is wireless connected, so the control program for real robot could run on-board, or in any other computer.

The DSH control program is a single client process, but with many kernel threads inside. Each schema is implemented as a thread (we use standard Posix threads on Linux) which periodically executes an iteration function. Communication between different threads is done through regular variables, because all the threads share virtual memory space. Motor schemas read variables updated by perceptual schemas, and low level schemas read their own parameters set by a higher level schema.

To implement SLEPT state we have used pthread `condition variables`. Each schema has an associated `condition variable`, so it can sleep on it when needed consuming no CPU cycles. Any schema may ask another one to be halted writing on a shared variable. The next time that recipient schema executes its iteration it will be suspended on its `condition variable`. The schema can be resumed when another thread signal on its condition variable. Typically the parent schema sets the child parameters and then wakes it up signalling on its condition variable.

Activation regions and arbitration are implemented as callback functions. Every iteration the motor schema calls its activation region function to check whether current situation matches its preconditions or not. Parent schema defines the activation region functions for each of its children. Additionally on each iteration the motor schema also checks the state of its brothers in the level to detect control overlaps or control absences. In such case, arbitration functions are invoked to solve the conflict.

4.1   Example

As an example we describe the `gotopoint` behavior developed using DSH: the robot reaches its destination point in the local environment and makes detours around obstacles if needed. It has been implemented as a parent motor schema that activates two perceptual schemas and three motor ones: `stop`, `followwall` and `advance`.

`Stop schema` stops the robot if obstacles are too close. This is the default schema in case of control absence. `Followwall schema` accepts sonar data and moves the robot parallel to closest obstacle. `Advance schema` moves it in certain orientation, faster if there are no obstacle in such angle, and turning to get it if needed. Activation regions are set in parent schema: if there is an obstacle closer than 100 cm in goal angle then `followwall schema` is activated, otherwise `advance schema` sends its motor commands. If a sudden obstacle gets closer than 20 cm then `stop schema` wins control competition.

First perceptual schema collects sonar and encoder data, and second one calculates distance to closest obstacle in goal angle. Actually it can calculate such distance in any orientation, but parent schema modulates it to do it in goal one. Parent schema read encoder data and computes relative distance and orientation to destination from current robot location. When detects the robot is over the target point it suspends all its child schemas.

`Followwall schema` alone makes the robot to follow walls. So this is an example of schema reusing. Used with a different activation region an together with other schemas can help to achieve another global behavior.

5   Conclusions

A new architecture named DSH has been presented, which is based on dynamic hierarchies of schemas. Perception and control are distributed in schemas, and grouped in abstraction levels. These levels are not general but task dependent which allow greater flexibility than fixed hierarchies. Perceptual schemas build relevant information pieces and motor schemas take actuation decisions over them in continuous loops.

It shares features with both deliberative and behavior based approaches, and avoids centralized monitor of 3T paradigm. It offers uniform layer interface and distributed context dependent monitor at every level. It may use symbolic stimuli when needed, directly grounded on sensor data or even on other stimuli, growing in abstraction. Also the absence of a central world model overcomes the SMPA bottleneck and avoids the need for such complete model before starting to act. The perception is task oriented, which avoid useless computation on non interesting data.

Timely reactions to environment changes are favored by low level loops and fast arbitration and reconfiguration capabilities. Deliberative schemas can be used too, but they are enforced to deliver an action recommendation each iteration. This prevents the use of plans as programs and enforces its use as resources for action.

A distributed arbitration is used for schema coordination. Each schema is the arbiter for its children, defining non overlapping activation regions. This combines top down (target oriented) and bottom up (environment oriented) motivations for action selection.

The architecture is extensible. Adding a new schema is quite easy, it requires to define the schema parameters and its iteration, arbitration functions. Also all previous schemas can be reused as building blocks for new behaviors.

We are working to perceive more abstract stimuli, specially vision based (in particular doors) and to extend the schema repertoire with more abstract ones, as narrow door traversal.

References

1. Arbib, M.A., Liaw, J.S.: Sensorimotor transformations in the worlds of frogs and robots. Artificial Intelligence, **72** (1995) 53–79
2. Arkin, R.C.: Motor Schema-Based Mobile Robot Navigation. The International Journal of Robotics Research, **8(4)** (1989) 92–112
3. Arkin, R.C., Balch, T.: AuRA: Principles and Practice in Review. Journal of Experimental and Theoretical Artificial Intelligence, **9(2-3)** (1997) 175–188
4. Ali, K.S., Arkin, R.C.: Implementing Schema-theoretic Models of Animal Behavior in Robotic Systems. Proceedings of the 5th International Workshop on Advanced Motion Control, AMC'98. IEEE, Coimbra (Portugal) (1998) 246–253
5. Bonasso, R.P., Firby, R.J., Gat, E., Kortenkamp, D., Miller, D.P., Slack, M.G.: Experiences with an Architecture for Intelligent, Reactive Agents. Journal of Experimental and Theoretical Artificial Intelligence, **9(2)** (1997) 237–256
6. Brooks, R.A.: A Robust Layered Control System for a Mobile Robot. IEEE Journal of Robotics and Automation, **2(1)** (1986) 14-23
7. Corbacho, F.J., Arbib, M.A.: Learning to Detour. Adaptive Behavior, **5(4)** (1995) 419–468
8. Firby, R.J.: Building Symbolic Primitives with Continuous Control Routines. Proceedings of the 1st International Conference on AI Planning Systems AIPS'92. (1992) 62–69
9. Firby, R.J.: Task Networks for Controlling Continuous Processes. Proceedings of the 2nd International Conference on AI Planning Systems AIPS'94. AAAI (1994) 49–54
10. Konolige, Kurt: Saphira Software Manual. SRI International, 2001
11. Langer, D., Rosenblatt, J.K., Hebert, M.: A Behavior-Based System for Off-Road Navigation. IEEE Journal of Robotics and Automation, **10(6)** (1994) 776-782
12. Lorenz, K.: Foundations of Ethology. Springer Verlag (1981)
13. Maes, P.: How to Do the Right Thing. Connection Science Journal (Special Issue on Hybrid Systems), **1(3)** (1989) 291–323
14. Payton, D.W., Rosenblatt, J.K., Keirsey, D.M.: Plan Guided Reaction. IEEE Transactions on Systems Man and Cybernetics, **20(6)** (1990) 1370–1382
15. Saffiotti, A.: The uses of fuzzy logic in autonomous robot navigation. Soft Computing, **1** (1997) 180–197
16. Simmons, R.G.: Structured Control for Autonomous Robots. IEEE Transactions on Robotics and Automation, **10(1)** (1994) 34–43
17. Tyrrell, T.: The Use of Hierarchies for Action Selection. Journal of Adaptive Behavior, **1(4)** (1993) 387–420

Monte Carlo Localization in 3D Maps Using Stereo Vision

Juan Manuel Sáez and Francisco Escolano

Robot Vision Group
Departamento de Ciencia de la Computación e Inteligencia Artificial
Universidad de Alicante
{jmsaez, sco}@dccia.ua.es
http://rvg.dccia.ua.es

Abstract. In this paper we present a Monte Carlo localization algorithm that exploits 3D information obtained by a trinocular stereo camera. First, we obtain a 3D map by estimating the optimal transformations between two consecutive views of the environment through the minimization of an energy function. Then, we use a particle-filter algorithm for addressing the localization in the map. For that purpose we define the likelihood of each sample as depending not only on the compatibility of its 3D perception with that of the observation, but also depending on its compatibility in terms of visual appearance. Our experimental results show the success of the algorithm both in easy and quite ambiguous settings, and they also show the speed-up in convergence when visual appearance is added to depth information.

1 Introduction

Current approaches to solve the problem of localizing a robot with respect to a map that approximately describes the environment are widely based on sonar sensors [1] [2].Such a map is usually build from an occupation grid [3], that is, a bidimensional grid in which each cell contains the probability that its associated space is occupied by an obstacle. In order to obtain such a grid one needs to know robot's motion (odometry), but this information becomes more and more uncertain as the robot moves. Current techniques, like [2], relying on the EM algorithm [4] attempt to deal with such uncertainty and in most cases these approaches, like Monte Carlo methods [6] or bootstrap filters [7] are particular cases of the so called particle filters.

How to translate the latter approaches to deal with 3D maps? Moravec defined in [8] a method to build a 3D occupation grid (3D evidence grid) from several stereoscopic views and outlined the benefits of such research in other robotic problems like path planning and navigation. Current efforts in this area follow different directions. On one hand it is attempted to obtain the geometric primitives that describe the map through the Hough transform [9]: aligning these primitives and conveniently mapping their texture it is possible to build a poligonal model. On the other hand, stereo is exploited to build 2D long-range

F.J. Garijo, J.C. Riquelme, and M. Toro (Eds.): IBERAMIA 2002, LNAI 2527, pp. 913–922, 2002.

sensors [10], that is only the Z component is considered. Other researchers use 3D information to build a topological map with landmarks like 3D corners [11]. In other works long-range laser scanners are used to obtain point clouds of the environment [14] [15].

In this contribution we exploit the mapping method presented in [12] to build a 3D occupation grid from a set of stereo views of the environment and we address the adaptation of particle filters to solve the task of localizing the robot with respect to that grid. As we also code appearance information in the grid, it is possible to evaluate the contribution of visual appearance to the localization tasks. The paper is organized as follows: Section 2 describes the approach followed to obtain the 3D map; in section 3 we outline the elements of the Bayesian approach (posterior, likelihood) and present our particle-filter algorithm; in section 4 we show four representative experiments; finally, section 5 contains our conclusions and future works.

Fig. 1. Digiclops camera and Pioneer mobile robot.

2   3D Maps of the Environment

2.1   Observations and Actions

Our observations are taken by a Digiclops trinocular stereo camera, with a resolution of 640x480 pixels and a frame rate of 14fps, mounted on a Pioneer mobile robot (see Figure 1). An observation v_t performed at instant t consists of k_t points of the 3D environment. For each one we register both their three spatial coordinates and their local appearance (grey level) in the left image (reference image):

$$v_t = \{p_1, p_2, ... p_{k_t}\}, p_i = (x_i, y_i, z_i, c_i). \tag{1}$$

Assuming a flat ground and also that the camera is always normal to the ground plane, its allowed motions are constrained to: translation along the X axis (horizontal), translation along the Z axis (depth) and rotation with respect to Y axis (vertical). Thus, robot's pose φ_t at instant t is defined by its coordinates

(x, z) in the XZ plane and the rotation α around Y, whereas a given robot action a_t is defined by the increments with respect to the previous pose:

$$\varphi_t = (x_t, z_t, \alpha_t), a_t = (\Delta x_t, \Delta z_t, \Delta \alpha_t). \tag{2}$$

Then, a robot trajectory (exploration) is defined by a sequence of $t - 1$ actions, that is $A^{t-1} = \{a_1, a_2, \ldots, a_{t-1}\}$ and t associated observations $V^t = \{v_1, v_2, \ldots, v_t\}$.

2.2 Composing the 3D Map

The 3D mapping process of a given environment consists of registering a set of observations V^t along a trajectory A^{t-1}. In order to integrate all the observations in the same 3D map we assume that the robot's initial pose, and thus the origin of the coordinate system of the map, is $\varphi_1 = (0, 0, 0)$. As this pose is associated to observation v_1, to map any observation v_k of the trajectory we need to know its pose, which may be obtained by accumulating all previous actions: $\varphi_k = \sum_{i=1}^{k-1} a_i$. Once the pose $\varphi_k = (x_k, z_k, \alpha_k)$ is estimated we multiply all points in v_k by the matrix 3:

$$T_{\varphi_k} = \begin{bmatrix} \cos(-\alpha_k) & 0 & \sin(-\alpha_k) & x_k \\ 0 & 1 & 0 & 0 \\ -\sin(-\alpha_k) & 0 & \cos(-\alpha_k) & z_k \\ 0 & 0 & 0 & 1 \end{bmatrix} \tag{3}$$

Integrating all observations over the same geometric space we obtain a first approximation to the map of the environment composed by a high-density 3D point cloud. This cloud is post-processed to remove replicated points (consider that each observation may produce 11,000 points) and also to discard outliers. Our map model is a geometric version of the Moravec's model [8].

We divide the bounding box of the point cloud $L = \{p_1, p_2, \ldots p_m\}$ in a 3D grid of voxels of constant size T_c (length of each edge of the cube). For each voxel enclosing a number of points greater than U_c we take a prototype (average) resulting a 3D matrix E in which we store the prototypes of each voxel in the grid.

In Figure 2 we show a map of our department. After integrating 187 observations we obtain a point cloud of 2,294,666 points. Setting $T_c = 8cm$ and $T_c = 15cm$ we obtain two maps of 25,637 and 19,809 prototypes respectively. In both cases $U_c = 3$. As stereo errors are not correlated in time, the integration process yields noise-free maps.

2.3 Action Estimation

Action estimation is key both for map building and localization. Thus, we apply the energy minimization method described in [12]. Such a method searches the action that minimizes a given distance between two clouds of 3D points. Here, we

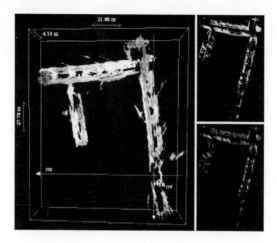

Fig. 2. Example of a map of our department. Left: point cloud after integrating all observations. Right: two maps with different thresholds.

highlight such a distance. Given the observations v_k and v_{k+1}, and the unknown action a_k, we define $\tilde{v}_k$ and $\tilde{v}_{k+1}$ as the observations mapped respectively to $\varphi_k = \sum_{i=1}^{k-1} a_i$ and $\varphi_{k+1} = \varphi_k + a_k$. Action a_k is the one that minimizes $D(\tilde{v}_k, \tilde{v}_{k+1})$, a distance $D(v_a, v_b)$ between two clouds of points v_a and v_b defined as follows:

$$D(v_a, v_b) = \frac{\sum_{i=1}^{K_a} D_{pp}(p_i, P(p_i, v_b))}{K_a}, \tag{4}$$

where $p_i \in v_a$ and $P(p_i, v_b)$ is the closest point to p_i in v_b, that is:

$$P(p_i, v_b) = \arg \min_{p_m \in v_b} \|(x_i, y_i, z_i) - (x_m, y_m, z_m)\|. \tag{5}$$

Finally, $D_{pp}(p_a, p_b)$ is the distance in terms of 3D coordinates and image appearance between points p_a and p_b:

$$D_{pp}(p_a, p_b) = \|(x_a, y_a, z_a) - (x_b, y_b, z_b)\| + \gamma|c_a - c_b|, \tag{6}$$

being γ a penalization constant defined so that both terms lie in the same range.

Given the latter distance, minimization is performed through Simulated Annealing [13] properly initialized: In order to reduce the number of iterations required to converge, we tend to start to search from the previous action. Moreover, as the cost of evaluating the distance is quadratic with the number of points we use a reduced version of the original clouds: We divide each depth image in cells of constant size and then we choose a prototype of each cell. The prototype is the disparity value d_C that minimizes the sum of differences between the disparities of the cell $C = \{d_1, d_2, \ldots d_n\}$:

$$d_C = \arg \min_{d \in C} \sum_{i=1}^{N} |d - d_i| \tag{7}$$

For instance, in Figure 3, we show the original 640x480 image, its associated depth image with 47,202 valid points, and the reduced 160x120 depth image with 1,520 valid points, assuming cells of 4x4 pixels.

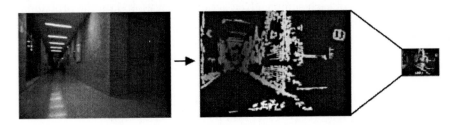

Fig. 3. Obtaining reduced views for action estimation.

In this work, the action estimation is a local process, that is prone to early erroneous estimations. We are currently investigating in globally consistent approaches.

3   Localization in the 3D Map

3.1   Posterior Term

Given a 3D map M obtained as explained in the latter section, we have adapted the CONDENSATION (CONDitional DENSity propagATION) filter proposed in [5] to the task of obtaining a sample-based estimation of the posterior probability density function $p(\varphi_t|V^t, A^{t-1})$ that measures the probability of the current pose φ_t given the sequence of observations $V^t = \{v_1, v_2 \dots v_t\}$ and actions $A^{t-1} = \{a_1, a_2 \dots a_{t-1}\}$ performed over M.

3.2   Likelihood Term

The CONDENSATION algorithm consists of estimating the latter posterior through a sampling process. Each sample represents a localization/pose hypothesis φ_i, and we denote its likelihood given an observation v_j by $p(\varphi_i|v_j)$.

Given the distance between the observation v_j, mapped in the pose hypothesis φ_i, and the map M, that is $D(\tilde{v}_j, M)$, the likelihood of such a pose is defined as the exponential expression:

$$p(\varphi_i|v_j) = e^{-\frac{D(\tilde{v}_j,M)}{\sigma^2}} \tag{8}$$

3.3   The CONDENSATION Algorithm

The CONDENSATION algorithm encodes the current posterior probabilityof a pose $p(\varphi_t|V^t, A^{t-1})$ given t observations $V^t = \{v_1, v_2 \dots v_t\}$ and $t-1$ actions

$A^{t-1} = \{a_1, a_2 \dots a_{t-1}\}$ as a set of N samples $(\varphi_1, \varphi_2 \dots \varphi_N)$ and their associated probabilities $(\omega_1, \omega_2, \dots \omega_N)$ attending to their likelihoods.

Initially the samples set is chosen attending to the prior distribution $p(\varphi_0)$. Then, the iteration associated to instant t consists of three steps: (1) compute the predicted pose of each sample given action a_{t-1}; (2) update the probabilities of each sample given the new pose and the current observation v_t; (3) build a new set considering the latter probabilities:

CONDENSATION Algorithm

Input: $M_{t-1} = \{(\varphi_{t-1}^1, \omega_{t-1}^1), (\varphi_{t-1}^2, \omega_{t-1}^2), \dots (\varphi_{t-1}^N, \omega_{t-1}^N)\}$
Output: $M_t = \{(\varphi_t^1, \omega_t^1), (\varphi_t^2, \omega_t^2), \dots (\varphi_t^N, \omega_t^N)\}$

1. **Prediction:** given action a_{t-1} the predicted pose for each sample $\varphi_{t-1}^i \in M_{t-1}$ is given by

$$\breve{\varphi}_t^i = \varphi_{t-1}^i + a_{t-1} + \epsilon, \quad i = 1, 2, \dots N$$

where $\epsilon = (N(0, \sigma_x), N(0, \sigma_z), N(0, \sigma_\alpha))$.

2. **Update:** Given the observation v_t the new probability $\breve{\omega}_t^i$ for each sample $\breve{\varphi}_t^i \in \breve{M}_t$ is given by

$$\breve{\omega}_t^i = p(\breve{\varphi}_t^i | v_t), \quad i = 1, 2, \dots N.$$

3. **Resampling:** build a new set of N samples resampling (with substitution) the set $\breve{M}_t$ in such a way that each sample $\breve{\varphi}_t^i$ is chosen with a probability proportional to $\breve{\omega}_t^i$:

$$(\varphi_t^i, \omega_t^i) \leftarrow \text{Sample from } \breve{M}_t, \quad i = 1, 2, \dots N.$$

Then normalize the probabilities ω_t^i of the samples in M_t to satisfy $\sum_{i-1}^N \omega_t^i = 1$, that is

$$\omega_t^i \leftarrow \frac{\omega_t^i}{\sum_{j=1}^N \omega_t^j}, i = 1, 2, \dots N$$

Robot localization is seen as an iterative process along step-by-step exploration. Assuming that N is high enough to capture the true location of the robot, the algorithm tends to concentrate all samples around that location as the robot moves around following, in this case, a first-order Markov chain over the action space. We consider that the algorithm has converged when the dispersion $\psi(M_t)$ is below a give threshold U_d and the highest probability $\max(\omega_t^i)$ is greater than another threshold U_v (to deal with situations in which the initial sample is too sparse). We define dispersion $\psi(M_t)$ in terms of the averaged distance between the 2D coordinates of all pairs of samples in the set M_t:

$$\psi(M_t) = \sum_{\varphi_i \in M_t} \sum_{\varphi_j \in M_t} \frac{\|(x_t^i, z_t^i) - (x_t^j, z_t^j)\|}{N^2} \tag{9}$$

3.4   Process Optimization

The bottleneck of the algorithm is the computation of the likelihood function for all the samples in the set. More precisely, the estimation of the closest prototype to each transformed point. In order to reduce the computation load, we build offline an extended map $\hat{E}$ in which each voxel stores the coordinates of the closer prototype (non-void cell) in the 3D matrix that registers M. Being $p_m = (x_m, y_m, z_m, 0)$ the minimal coordinates of all points in the map, the cell (i_a, j_a, k_a) in M associated to any point p_a is given by:

$$M(i_a, j_a, k_a) = (\lfloor \frac{x_a - x_m}{T_c} \rfloor, \lfloor \frac{y_a - y_m}{T_c} \rfloor, \lfloor \frac{z_a - z_m}{T_c} \rfloor) \tag{10}$$

M may be transformed into $\hat{E}$ though registering the closer prototype among its direct neighbors and then propagate such computation for each of them until all the space is covered. Then at each (i, j, k) we will have the closest prototype to the center $p_c(i, j, k) = (x_m + iT_c + \frac{T_c}{2}, y_m + jT_c + \frac{T_c}{2}, z_m + kT_c + \frac{T_c}{2})$ of that cell:

$$\hat{E}(i, j, k) = \arg \min_{p_r \in M} \|(x_r, y_r, z_r) - p_c(i, j, k)\|. \tag{11}$$

In Figure 4 we show a 2D sketch corresponding to 6 of the 79 iterations needed to extend the map in Figure 2 using $T_c = 15cm$ and $U_c = 3$.

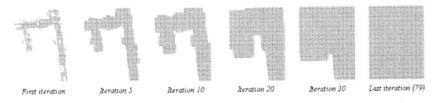

First iteration   Iteration 5   Iteration 10   Iteration 20   Iteration 30   Last iteration (79)

Fig. 4. Growing process for obtaining $\hat{E}$.

4   Experiments and Validation

In this section we will show our four most representative experiments addressed to validate the method. In all cases we use the map in Figure 2 with $T_c = 15cm$ and $U_c = 3$.

Experiment 1: First of all, the robot explores a unambiguous part of the environment (the top right corner). Using 2000 samples for pose estimation, at the 6th iteration, $\varphi_* = (2.01m, -17.94m, 276.70°)$ is the sample with highest probability, being the real pose of the robot $\varphi_r = (2.05m, -17.97m, 277.66°)$. Each iteration consumes an averaged time of 2.55 secs in a Pentiun III 900Mhz. In Figure 5 we show several iterations of this experiment.

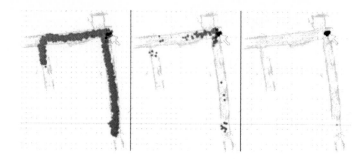

Fig. 5. Experiment 1: Iterations 1, 3 and 6 of CONDENSATION (from left to right) over a easy part. The arrow indicates the actual robot's position.

Experiment 2: Now, the robot explores an ambiguous part of the environment (the long corridor on the right). In Figure 6 we show several iterations of this experiment and in Figure 7 the evolution of the samples dispersion. We also are using 2000 samples for pose estimation. In the 10th iteration the sample with highest probability is $\varphi_* = (0.80m, -7.71m, 189.92°)$ being the real pose of the robot $\varphi_r = (0.74m, -7.70m, 190.73°)$.

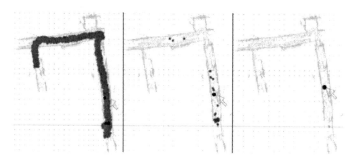

Fig. 6. Experiment 2: Iterations 1,4 and 10 of CONDENSATION (from left to right) over an ambiguous trajectory.

Experiment 3: In order to evaluate the contribution of visual appearance we have repeated the latter experiment without considering that component ($\gamma = 0$). This results are in a lower convergence rate. Such a rate is even lower when we also discard the Y component (Figure 7).

Experiment 4: In this case our purpose is to analyze the stability of the algorithm with respect to the number of samples considered. We repeat the second experiment but using only 500 samples, and the result is shown in Figure 8. The samples are finally clustered in an incorrect position, revealing the dependence of the approach on the number of samples.

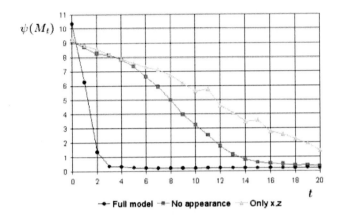

Fig. 7. Experiment 3: Evolution of the convergence rate for the complete algorithm, without appearance and without the Y component.

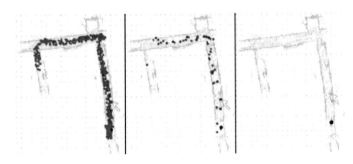

Fig. 8. Experiment 4: Iterations 1, 2 and 5 of the CONDENSATION algorithm with only 500 samples.

5   Conclusions and Future Work

In this paper we have adapted the CONDENSATION algorithm to the task of localizing a robot in a 3D map build by means of a stereo camera. We have designed a geometric map that encodes both 3D and appearance information and we have developed an auxiliar structure that contributes to reduce the temporal complexity of sampling. In our experiments we have evaluate the performance of the approach in real situations in which the map does not necessarily coincide with the environment and real perceptions may contain significant differences with respect to the data stored in the map.

As we can see in the experiments, to obtain a good localization it is necessary to mantain a minimum concentration of samples. Now, the number of samples and the time to compute them are directly proportional to the size of the map. We are currently working on different hierarchical representations for reducing the search in more complex maps.

On the other hand, we are investigating both the definition and consideration of 3D landmarks and the use of more elaborated information of appearance like PCA or ICA models.

References

1. S. Thrun et al: Probabilistic Algorithms and the interactive museum tour-guide robot Minerva. International Journal of Robotics Research Vol 19 N° 11. November 2000.
2. D. Gallardo: Aplicación del muestreo bayesiano en robots móviles: estrategias para localización y extracción de mapas de entorno. Tesis doctoral. Universidad de Alicante, Junio de 1999.
3. F.Dieter, W. Burgard, S. Thrun: The dynamic window approach to collision avoidance. IEEE Robotics and Automation Magazine, 1997.
4. A. Dempster, A. Laird, D. Rubin: Maximum likelihood from incomplete data via the EM algorithm. Journal of the Royal Statistical Society. Series B 39, 1 38, 1977.
5. M. Isard, A. Blake: Visual tracking by stochastic propagation of conditional density. European Conf. Computer Vision. Cambridge, England, Apr 1996.
6. D. Fox, W. Burgard, F.Dellaert, S. Thrun: Monte Carlo Localization: Efficient Position Estimation for Mobile Robots. Sixteenth National Conference on Artificial Intelligence (AAAI), Orlando, Florida, 1999.
7. D.Gallardo, F.Escolano, R.Rizo, O. Colomina, M. Cazorla: Estimación bayesiana de características en robots móviles mediante muestreo de la densidad a posteriori. I Congrés Català d'Intel.ligència Artificial. Tarragona, Octubre de 1998.
8. H.P. Moravec: Robot spatial perception by stereoscopic vision and 3D evidence grids. TR The Robotics Institute Carnegie Mellon University. Pittsburgh, Pennsylvania, 1996.
9. L. Iocchi, K. Konolige, M. Bajracharya: Visually realistic mapping of planar environment with stereo. Seventh International Symposium on Experimental Robotics (ISER'2000). Hawaii 2000.
10. D. Murray, J. Little: Using real-time stereo vision for mobile robot navigation. Computer Vision And Pattern Recognition (CVPR'98). Santa Barbara CA, June 1998.
11. S. Se, D. Lowe, J. Little: Vision-based mobile robot localization and mapping using scale-invariant features. IEEE International Conference on Robotics and Automation. Seoul, Korea May 2001.
12. J.M. Sáez, F. Escolano, E. Hernández: Reconstrucción de mapas 3D a partir de información estéreo utilizando un enfoque de minimización de energía. IX Conferencia de la Asociación Española para la Inteligencia Artificial (CAEPIA 2001). Gijón, Noviembre 2001.
13. S. Kirkpatrick, C.D. Gellatt, M.P. Vecchi: Optimization by simulated annealing. Science, 220:671-680, 1983.
14. Y. Liu, R. Emery, D. Chakrabarti, W. Burgard, S. Thurn: Using EM to learn 3D models of indoor enviroments with mobile robots. Eighteenth International Conference on Machine Learning. Williams College, June 2001.
15. V. Sequeira, K.C. Ng, E. Wolfart, J.G.M Gonçalves, D.C. Hogg: Automated 3D reconstruction of interiors with multiple scan-views. Electronic Imaging '99, IS&T/SPIE's 11th Annual Symposium. San Jose, California, USA, January 1999.

3D Complex Scenes Segmentation from a Single Range Image Using Virtual Exploration

P. Merchán[1], A. Adán[2], S. Salamanca[1], and C. Cerrada[3]

[1]Escuela de Ingenierías Industriales, Universidad de Extremadura, Avda. de Elvas s/n,
06071 Badajoz, Spain
{pmerchan,ssalaman}@unex.es
[2]Escuela Superior de Informática, Universidad de Castilla-La Mancha, Ronda de Calatrava
5, 13071 Ciudad Real, Spain
aadan@inf-cr.uclm.es
[3]ETSI Industriales, UNED, Ciudad Universitaria s/n, 28040 Madrid, Spain
ccerrada@ieec.uned.es

Abstract. In this paper we present a method for automatic segmentation of 3D complex scenes from a single range image. A complex scene includes several objects with: irregular shapes, occlusion, the same colour or intensity level and placed in any pose. Unlike most existing methods which proceed with a set of images obtained from different viewpoints, in this work a single view is used and a 3D segmentation process is developed to separate the constituent parts of a complex scene. The method is based on establishing suitable virtual-viewpoints in order to carry out a new range data segmentation technique. For a virtual-viewpoint a strategy [3D range data] – [2D projected range data] – [2D segmentation] – [3D segmented range data], is accomplished. The proposed method has been applied to a set of complex scenes and it can be said that the results guarantee the benefits of the method.

1 Introduction

Image segmentation is one of the most important subjects in image processing which finds wide applications in pattern recognition and 3D vision. It consists of partitioning the image into its constituent parts and extracting these parts of interest (objects). Until now a wide variety of different segmentation algorithms have been developed. Criteria used in the image-partitioning process are largely dependent on the nature of the input data, the desired high-level task and the nature of the scene.

In complex scenes, there are usually occluded surfaces in the image obtained from a view point, that is why most of the techniques developed until now use sets of data (intensity images or range images) taken from different viewpoints to obtain a complete model of the scene [1], [2], [3], [4], [5]. In these techniques, the problem of the camera positioning to reduce the number of views, known as the *Best-Next-View* problem, arises.

When we say "3D segmentation", two environments can be referred to single scenes or complex scenes. In the first case, 3D segmentation involves isolated objects, scenes with no occlusion, intensity image segmentation techniques of stereo pairs, etc.

F.J. Garijo, J.C. Riquelme, and M. Toro (Eds.): IBERAMIA 2002, LNAI 2527, pp. 923–932, 2002.

Segmentation means to extract features or primitives of the object. Different strategies are applied to perform these tasks. In general, approaches can be categorized into two types: edge-based approaches and region-based approaches. In edge-based approaches, the points located on the edges are first identified, followed by edge linking and contour processes. Edges or contours could segment the scene. In region-based approaches a number of seed regions are first chosen. These seed regions grow by adding neighbour points based on some compatibility threshold [6], [7], [8], [9]. In [10] a segmentation approach of range images is proposed. They use curved segments as segmentation primitives instead of individual pixels. So the amount of data is reduced and a fast segmentation process is obtained. A simulated electrical charge distribution is used in [11] in order to establish the surface curvature of the objects.

3D Segmentation of complex scenes is a bigger problem in computer vision. In the worst case, a complex scene includes: objects with irregular shapes; objects viewed from any direction, objects with self-occlusion or partially occluded by other objects and uniform intensity/colour appearance. In our case, we are concerned with complex scenes and range images to solve this problem. Range images have been used most frequently in 3D object recognition tasks and a lot of progress has been made in this field. Although several techniques based on modelling have been applied to segment parts of the scene using range data [12], [13], [14], [15], there are very few researchers working on segmentation/recognition based on range data processing. Therefore nowadays it is widely accepted that recognition of a real world scene based on a single range view is a difficult task.

In this paper, we present a region-based segmentation method for partitioning a complex scene image into meaningful regions (objects). To do this, we use a single range data image. In the next section, we will have a glance at the whole process. In section 3 and section 4, we describe two main stages: scene exploration and scene segmentation, respectively. Next, in section 5, experimental results achieved with the application of the proposed method to a set of real range images are shown. Finally, in section 6 we conclude and discuss limitations and future research.

2 Overview of the Process

As it has been said, we use a single view of the scene for separating all its constituent objects. The proposed segmentation scheme is an iterative process composed of three successive steps:

1. *Range data obtaining*: We use real range images obtained with a gray range finder. For the first iteration, range data are the scene surface points given by the sensor. For following iterations, the new range data will be the old range data without the range data segmented in the last iteration.
2. *Scene exploration*: A virtual camera is placed in the scene for exploring the range data and a procedure for searching for an appropriate virtual viewpoint is accomplished. The strategy developed to choose these viewpoints will be explained in section 3.

3. *Scene Segmentation*: Taking into account a virtual viewpoint, 2D data orthogonal projection is taken to perform a segmentation process. When the segmentation of the processed 2D image has been finished, an inverse transformation is accomplished to reassign each 2D segment to its corresponding 3D segment in the scene.

The process is iteratively executed until there are no objects in the scene. For each iteration several possibilities can be given:

- No segmentation. It means that for the current exploration viewpoint it is not possible to segment any part of the current scene data.
- Segmentation. The current scene is segmented into several parts. For each segmented part there are two possibilities :
    - The segmented part corresponds to an object.
    - The segmented part corresponds to more than one object. In this case each segment will be considered as a new range image for step 1.

3 Scene Exploration

In this section we will explain how the election of the virtual viewpoint is made. We use the mesh of nodes created by tessellating the unit sphere in order to limit the number of viewpoint candidates. Nowadays we have considered a tessellated sphere formed by 320 nodes with 3-connectivity (see Fig. 1.a) where each node N defines the viewpoint ON, O being the centre of the sphere. As it has been said before, we are interested in the projected image of the range data over the viewpoint chosen. Since a viewpoint and its opposite provide the same projected image of the scene we only consider the half-tessellated-sphere.

Probability between 0 and 1 is associated to each node N according to the topological organization proposed in [16], [17]: the *Modeling Wave Set*, MWS. Before explaining the probability mapping procedure, a short reference about MWS will be given.

MWS structure organizes the nodes of the tessellated sphere as disjointed subsets, each one containing a group of nodes spatially disposed over the sphere as a closed quasi-circle (see Fig. 1.b). Each of the disjointed subsets is called *wave front*, WF. To build a *modelling wave* MW, a node of the tessellated sphere must be chosen as the origin of the structure. This node, called *initial focus*, constitutes the first *wave front* WF_1 of the MW and will be used to identify it. Then, the remaining WF are sequentially obtained by building rings of nodes over the sphere until it is completely covered.

MW structure is used for updating the probabilities P associates to the nodes (viewpoints) for each iteration. For the t iteration, we select the node with the highest value of probability as the appropriate viewpoint. The viewpoint chosen defines an initial focus $WF_1(t)$ and its corresponding MW(t) (Fig. 1.b). After the process and taking into account the result of the segmentation, the map of probabilities is updated for iteration t+1 as follows:

- $P(WF_1(t+1))=0$. The old focus probability is assigned a value 0 because we will not use this node (or viewpoint) any more. It does not matter if we have segmented regions or not.

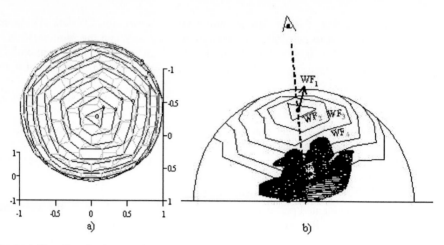

Fig. 1. a) Tessellated sphere and a MW drawn over it. b) Exploration viewpoint defined by a node of the sphere and the associate MW structure

- If the iteration is successful (segmented regions), we consider the nodes around the focus as *good* points to be selected for future segmentations and we increase the probability associated to the closest neighbours of WF_1. The nearest WF to WF_1 will have the highest increase. In this case the expression used for updating is the following:

$$P(WF_i(t+1)) = \frac{P(WF_i(t)) + (1 - 0.2i)}{v_{max}}, \quad i = 2,3,4,5. \tag{1}$$

where v_{max} is the maximum value among the obtained after summing the term *(1-0.2i)* to the old probabilities.

- If the iteration is not successful (no segmented regions), we consider the nodes around the focus as *bad* points to be selected for future segmentations. So we decrease the probability associated to the close neighbours of WF_1. The nearest WF to WF_1 will have the highest reduction. The expression used in this case is:

$$P(WF_i(t+1)) = \frac{P(WF_i(t)) - (1 - 0.2i)}{v_{max}}, \quad i = 2,3,4,5. \tag{2}$$

When the probability values have been changed, the t+1 iteration begins and the node with the highest value of probability is again selected as the appropriate viewpoint. Figure 2 illustrates the general procedure. Then the process continues with the next step, the scene segmentation.

For the first iteration, the map of probabilities must be imposed in an arbitrary manner because scarce information about *good* or *bad* viewpoints is known beforehand. It is just known that the viewpoint (or node) defined by the camera N_c is a *bad* viewpoint and consequently its neighbour nodes should be as well. Therefore, we can model this situation as the 0 iteration where: all nodes have probability 1, the viewpoint chosen is N_c and it is not successful. So in the first iteration $P(N_c)=0$ and N_c neighbour probabilities will be close to zero. Next an arbitrary node with probability 1 will be selected as the first viewpoint and the whole process will be run.

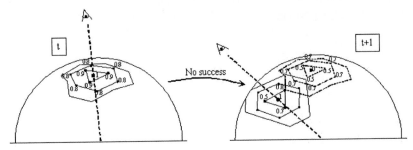

Fig. 2. Probability distribution and updating after a iteration step

4 Scene Segmentation

To obtain the constituent objects of the scene, we perform a transformation of the 3D data and the segmentation is made on a 2D image. The sequence developed to reach this objective is explained in Fig. 3.a).

The process begins with a 3D →2D transformation using the viewpoint chosen in the previous step. This conversion provides a multidimensional structure that stores the information of the relationship between every 3D point and its respective 2D pixel. We call this structure *multipixel matrix* (see Fig. 3.b). It is an array of two-dimensional matrixes. The first matrix stores the indexes of the projected points corresponding to the 2D black pixels. Since there may be points whose projection match up to the same 2D pixel, we must accumulate the information of each one in order not to lose any of them when the inverse transformation is made. To do this, we develop the multipixel matrix in such a way that each vector in the third dimension (*depth* in Fig. 3.b) stores all the 3D points with identical 2D projection.

With the projected points I_p we conform a 2D image with the purpose of carrying out a specific image processing. So 2D image size and a conversion to a binary image I_1 are given. Then we run a 2D region-based segmentation algorithm over the binary image. If the viewpoint is appropriate several binary disjointed segments of the image will be obtained and the algorithm will continue. On the contrary, if there are no disjointed segments, the result will be negative and a new viewpoint must be selected. We call I_2 the 2D segmented image.

After the segmentation phase, we define the regions on the original projected image from these segments I_{sp}. The binary conversion is undone and the regions on the recovered 2D image are found. Once we have segmented regions on the 2D projection, the information stored in the multipixel matrix is used to carry out the inverse transformation. This way, if the algorithm has segmented disjointed regions in the projected image, the corresponding 3D points will be extracted at the end of the iteration. Each disjointed region is considered as the viewed part of an object in the scene and consequently as a 3D segment.

The segmented parts are removed from the scene for the next iteration and a new scene is again explored. The process continues searching a new viewpoint with the remaining data. At the same time and in the same way, each segmented part could become a new range image for exploring if the number of data-points of the segment is high enough. So a segmentation distributed strategy could be achieved if necessary.

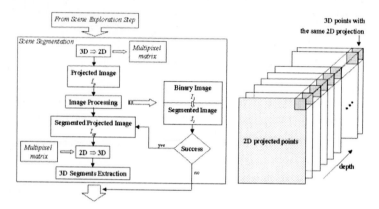

Fig. 3. a) Scene segmentation chart. b) Multipixel matrix structure

Fig. 4 shows an example illustrating the successive phases in the segmentation process. It begins at the first iteration. In a) intensity image and the corresponding range image of the scene are shown. An exploration viewpoint is chosen following section 3 and the corresponding projected range-data are plotted in b). After 2D image processing we deal with the image I_1 and perform the segmentation. As it can be seen in c) several segments are extracted. Then we recover the 3D points corresponding to each segment (d) and we identify them. Finally these points are removed to the original range image and the new range data for the next iteration is shown in e).

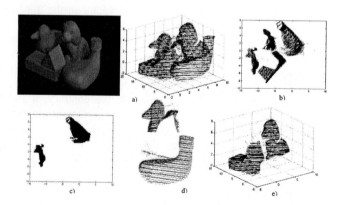

Fig. 4. Segmentation process. Example

5 Experimental Results

We have tested our algorithm on a set of real data images. The scenes are composed of several objects that can have irregular shapes. The objects are viewed from any direction and there are objects with self-occlusion or partially occluded by other objects. Moreover, the objects have been painted with the same colour.

The entire segmentation algorithm has been implemented in a Pentium III 1 GHz machine. The results achieved with some of the scenes have been summarized in Table 1. The intensity images of the scenes numbered in the first column as *Scene no.1* up to *Scene no. 5* can be seen in Fig. 5. Table 1 illustrates, in the second column, the total number of points that compose the input range images, which has been called N_T. In the third column the number of objects that constitute the scenes (Ob) are shown. The number of iterations of our algorithm needed to separate all the objects in the scenes, denoted I, appears in column four. Scene no. 5 takes a higher number of iterations than the others due to its higher occlusion complexity. In the next column, we have registered the number of points belonging to each segmented 3D object once the process has terminated, N_{Ob}. The last column reveals the quantity of points that has been lost during the process showing the percentage with respect to the initial data. As it can be seen, this number is low enough to confirm the goodness of our method. The average time taken by the algorithm to complete the process is 50 seconds.

Table 1. Results presentation

	N_T	Ob	I	N_{Ob}					$N_L(\%)$
				$Ob1$	$Ob2$	$Ob3$	$Ob4$	$Ob5$	
Scene no. 1	29932	4	4	10520	4234	8439	6527	-	0.71
Scene no. 2	24632	5	3	5014	6177	3349	5047	4905	0.57
Scene no. 3	19661	5	3	5453	3131	3638	5821	1424	0.98
Scene no. 4	16737	5	2	3327	3027	4008	3294	2786	1.5
Scene no. 5	22936	4	18	6539	3746	8778	2822	-	4.58

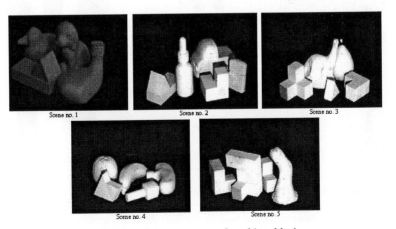

Scene no. 1   Scene no. 2   Scene no. 3

Scene no. 4   Scene no. 5

Fig. 5. The five scenes analyzed in table 1

Figs. 6 and 7 exemplify the results achieved after the segmentation algorithm has been run on two scenes. In Fig. 6.a) we show the intensity image of scene number 2. The range image obtained with the range finder of such a scene is shown in b). This range image constitutes the input data to the segmentation process. Fig. 6.c) displays the viewpoint selected among the possible candidates and in (d) the projected image obtained with this viewpoint can be seen. Fig. 6.e) shows three objects segmented at this iteration. In Fig. 6.f) we show the new scene to be analyzed after the elimination of the segmented objects and the viewpoint that gives the projected image shown in Fig. 6.g). Range data of each segment recovered at the end of the iteration is exposed in Fig. 6. h).

As it mentioned in section 4, sometimes the extracted segment corresponds to more than one object of the scene. This situation is contemplated by the method in the following manner: the algorithm automatically detects that such circumstances have taken place and performs a new segmentation over those segments starting from *Scene Exploration*. The probability values considered to select the viewpoint are those existing in the iteration in which the region was segmented. This occurred, i.e., in scene number 3. The four objects segmented after a number of iterations are shown in Fig. 7. b) to e). As it can be seen the segment in e) corresponds to two objects. Fig. 7.f) and g) illustrate the two objects obtained when the algorithm continues its execution recursively.

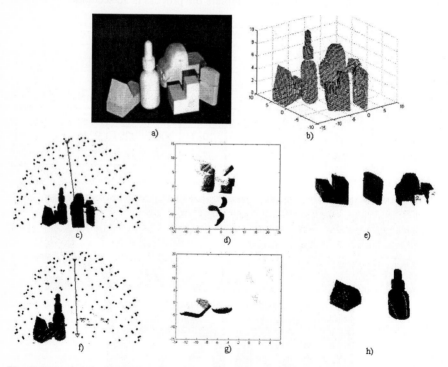

Fig. 6. Input data image and resultant segmentation. a) Intensity image of scene no.2. b) Range image of the same scene. c) Selected viewpoint among the possible candidates. d) Projected image obtained. e) Segmented object no.1, 2 and 3. f) Resultant scene after the segmentation and new viewpoint. g) Corresponding projected image. h) Segmented object no.4 and 5.

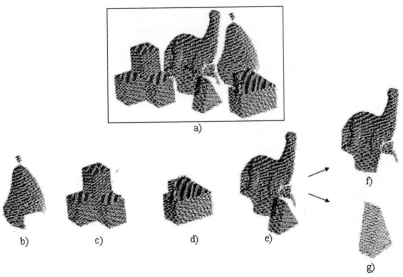

Fig. 7. Input data image and resultant segmentation. a) Range image of scene no. 3. b) to d) Segmented objects no. 1 to 3. e) Segmented region composed of two objects. f) and g) Segmented regions no. 4 and 5

6 Conclusions

In this paper, a method for automatic segmentation of 3D complex scenes has been presented. Contrasting most existing techniques, which proceed with a set of images obtained from different viewpoints, an important feature of our approach is that we use a single range image to separate the constituent parts of a 3D complex scene, which can include several objects with irregular shapes, occlusion, the same colour and place in any pose. This is achieved by applying a new strategy based on the selection of virtual-viewpoints that let us develop a range data segmentation algorithm over 2D projected images. Next, an inverse transformation is executed to relocate each 2D segment to its corresponding 3D object in the scene.

Experiments carried out on a set of real range images have proved the validity of our method. They have shown that it can successfully be used to perform the segmentation of a 3D scene. Nowadays we are improving this strategy for scenes with a higher number of objects and occlusion complexity.

References

1. Banta, J.E., Zhien, Y, Wang, X. Z., Zhang, G., Smith, M.T., and Abidi, M.A.: A "Best-Next-View" Algorithm for Three-Dimensional Scene Reconstruction Using Range Images. Proceedings SPIE, Vol. 2588, (1995), 418–429
2. Pito, R.: A Solution to the Next Best View Problem for Automated CAD Acquisition of Free-form Objects Using Range Cameras. Proceedings SPIE Symposium on Intelligent Systems and Advanced Manufacturing, Phila, PA, (1995).

3. Curless, B., and Levoy, M.: A Volumetric Method for Building Complex Models from Range Images. SIGGRAPH96, Computer Graphics Proceedings, (1996).
4. Massios, N. A., and Fisher, R. B.: A Best Next View Selection Algorithm Incorporating a Quality Criterion. Proceedings of the 6th British Machine Vision Conference, (1998), 780–789.
5. Reed, M. K. and Allen, P. K.: Constraint-Based Sensor Planning for Scene Modeling. IEEE Transactions on Pattern Analysis and Machine Intelligence, Vol. 22, no.12, (2000), 1460–1467.
6. Zhang, Y. J.: Evaluation and comparison of different segmentation algorithms. Pattern Recognition Letters, Vol. 18, Issue 10, (1997), 963–974.
7. Hoover, A., Baptiste, G. J., Jiang, X., Flynn, P. J., Bunke, H., Goldgof, D. B., Bowyer, K, Eggert, D. W., Fitzgibbon, A., and Fisher, R. B., An Experimental Comparison of Range Images Segmentation Algorithms. IEEE Transactions on Pattern Analysis and Machine Intelligence, Vol. 18, no.7, (1996), 673–689.
8. Stamos, I. and Allen, P. K.: 3-D Model Construction using Range and Image Data. Proceedings of IEEE International Conference on Computer Vision and Pattern Recognition, Vol. I, South Carolina, (2000), 531–536.
9. Huang, J. and Menq, C.H.: Automatic Data Segmentation for Geometric Feature Extraction From Unorganized 3-D Coordinate Points. IEEE Transactions on Robotics and Automation, Vol. 17, no. 3, (2001), 268–279.
10. Jiang, X., Bunke, H. and Meier, U.: High Level Feature Based Range Image Segmentation. Image and Vision Computing, 18 , (2000), 817–822.
11. Wu, K. and Levine, M. D.: 3D part Segmentation Using Simulated Electrical Charge Distributions. IEEE Transactions on Pattern Analysis and Machine Intelligence, Vol. 19, no.11, (1997), 1223–1235.
12. Benlamri, R.: Range Image segmentation of scenes with occluded curved objects. Pattern Recognition Letters 21, (2000), 1051–1060.
13. Lee, K.M., Mee, P. and Park, R.H.: Robust Adaptive Segmentation of Range Images. IEEE Transactions on Pattern Analysis and Machine Intelligence, Vol. 20, no.2, (1998) , 200–205.
14. Johnson A. and Hebert M.: Using Spin Images for Efficient Object Recognition in Cluttered 3D Scenes. IEEE Transactions on Pattern Analysis and Machine Intelligence, Vol. 21, no. 5, (1999), 433–449.
15. Marchand, E. and Chaumette, F.: Active Vision for Complete Scene Reconstruction and Exploration. IEEE Transactions on Pattern Analysis and Machine Intelligence, Vol. 21, no. 1, (1999), 433–449.
16. Adán, A., Cerrada, C. and Feliu, V.: Modeling Wave Set: Definition and Application of a new Topological Organization for 3D Object Modeling. Computer Vision and Image Understanding, Vol. 79, (2000), 281–307.
17. Adán, A., Cerrada, C. and Feliu, V.: Automatic pose determination of 3D shapes based on modeling wave sets: a new data structure for object modelling. Image and Vision Computing, Vol. 19, (2001), 867–890.

Recognizing Indoor Images with Unsupervised Segmentation and Graph Matching

Miguel Angel Lozano and Francisco Escolano

Robot Vision Group
Departamento de Ciencia de la Computación e Inteligencia Artificial
Universidad de Alicante, Spain
{malozano, sco}@dccia.ua.es
http://rvg.dccia.ua.es

Abstract. In this paper we address the problem of recognizing scenes by performing unsupervised segmentation followed by matching the resulting adjacency region graph. Our segmentation method is an adaptive extension of the Asymetric Clustering Model, a distributional clustering method based on the EM algorithm, whereas our matching proposal consists of embodying the Graduated Assignement cost function in a Comb Algorithm modified to perform constrained optimization in a discrete space. We present both segmentation and matching results that support our initial claim indicating that such an strategy provides both class discrimination and individual-within-a-class discrimination in indoor images which usually exhibit a high degree of perceptual ambiguity.

1 Introduction

Scene recognition is a key element in mobile robotics tasks like self-localization or exploration. Current approaches can be broadly classified as holistic [1] [2] [3] [4] and region-based[5] [6] [7]. Holistic methods exploit texture,color, and shape statistics without identifying objects previously. For instance, Torralba and Sinha propose a low dimensional representation that encodes statistics of Gabor filters' outputs and it is suitable for distinguishing views associated to specific parts of the environment [2]. On the other hand, region-based approaches allow the access to objects properties at the cost of incrementing the computational load due to the need of segmenting the images. One recent example is Carson et al's Blobworld framework [7], which relies on grouping pixels with similar features in regions and then use their characteristic statistics for identifying images with similar regions. We conjecture that inside indoor environments, which tend to be very ambiguous, the integration of segmentation and structural matching provides not only good recognition results at the class level, that is, distinguishing between views of corridor-A and of room-123, but at the individual level, allowing us to discriminate which part of corridor-A are we visiting. As this requires an extra cost and thus, the main contribution of this work is to provide effective and efficient segmentation and matching algorithms to that purpose.

F.J. Garijo, J.C. Riquelme, and M. Toro (Eds.): IBERAMIA 2002, LNAI 2527, pp. 933–942, 2002.
© Springer-Verlag Berlin Heidelberg 2002

Our segmentation module, described in Sect.2, relies on the Asymetric Clustering Model (ACM) proposed by Hoffman and Puzicha [8] [9], a distributional strategy that outperforms the classical K-means approach. We extend this model by making it adaptive, that is, able of identifying the optimal number of texture+color classes, and adaptivity is facilitated by the EM nature of the approach [10]. On the other hand, our proposal to region-matching is to embody the quadratic cost function proposed by Gold and Rangarajan in their Graduated Assignment approach [11], in the Comb Algorithm, a random search method proposed by Li [12], and adapt it to ensure matching constraints. In Sect.3 we present several recognition results that support our initial claim about class and individual performance. Our conclusions and future work issues are summarized in Sect.4.

2   Unsupervised Segmentation

2.1   EM Algorithm for Asymetric Clustering

Given N image blocks $x_1, \ldots, x_N$, each one having associated M possible features $y_1, \ldots, y_M$, the Asymetric Clustering Model (ACM) maximizes the log-likelihood

$$L(I, q) = -\sum_{i=1}^{N} \sum_{\alpha=1}^{K} I_{i\alpha} KL(p_{j|i}, q_{j|\alpha}) \,, \tag{1}$$

where: $p_{j|i}$ encodes the individual histogram, that is, the empirical probability of observing each feature y_j given x_i; $q_{j|\alpha}$ is the prototypical histogram associated to one of the K classes c_α; $KL(p_{j|i}, q_{j|\alpha})$ is the symmetric Kullback-Leibler divergence between the individual and the prototypical histograms; and $I_{i\alpha} \in \{0, 1\}$ are class-membership variables.

As $p_{j|i}$ are fixed, one must find both the most likely prototypical histograms $q_{j|\alpha}$ and membership variables $I_{i\alpha}$. Prototypical histograms are built on all individual histograms assigned to each class, but such an assignment depends on the membership variables. Following the EM-approach proposed by Hoffman and Puzicha, in which the class-memberships are hidden or unobserved variables, we start by providing good initial estimations of both the prototypes and the memberships, feeding with them an iterative process in which we alternate the estimation of expected memberships with the re-estimation of the prototypes.

Initialization. Initial prototypes are selected by a greedy procedure: First prototype is assumed to be a block selected randomly, and the following ones are the most distant blocks from any of the yet selected prototypes. Given these initial prototypes $\hat{q}_{j|\alpha}^0$, initial memberships $\hat{I}_{i\alpha}^0$ are selected as follows:

$$\hat{I}_{i\alpha}^0 = \begin{cases} 1 & \text{if } \alpha = arg\min_\beta KL(p_{j|i}, \hat{q}_{j|\beta}^0) \\ 0 & \text{otherwise} \end{cases}$$

E-step. Consists of estimating the expected membership variables $\hat{I}_{i\alpha} \in [0,1]$ given the current estimation of the prototypical histogram $q_{j|\alpha}$:

$$\hat{I}_{i\alpha}^{t+1} = \frac{\hat{\rho}_\alpha^t \exp\{-KL(p_{j|i}, \hat{q}_{i|\alpha})/T\}}{\sum_{\beta=1}^{K} \hat{\rho}_\beta^t \exp\{-KL(p_{j|i}, \hat{q}_{i|\beta})/T\}} \text{ , being } \hat{\rho}_\alpha^t = \frac{1}{N}\sum_{i=1}^{N}\hat{I}_{i\alpha}^t , \qquad (2)$$

that is, the probability of assigning any block x_i to class c_α at iteration t, and T the temperature, a control parameter which is reduced at each iteration (we are using the deterministic annealing version of the E-step, because it is less prone to local maxima than the un-annealed one).

M-step. Given the expected membership variables $\hat{I}_{i\alpha}^{t+1}$, the prototypical histograms are re-estimated as follows:

$$\hat{q}_{j|\alpha}^{t+1} = \sum_{i=1}^{N} \pi_{i\gamma} p_{j|i} \text{ , where } \pi_{i\alpha} = \frac{\hat{I}_{i\alpha}^t}{\sum_{k=1}^{N} \hat{I}_{k\alpha}^t} , \qquad (3)$$

that is, the prototype consists of the linear combination of all individuals $p_{j|i}$. The weights of such a combination are the ratios $\pi_{i\alpha}$ between the membership of each individual to c_α and the sum of all memberships to the same class. This is consistent with a distributional-clustering strategy.

Adaptation. Assuming that the iterative process is divided in epochs, our adaptation mechanism consists of starting by a high number of classes K_{max} and then reducing such a number, if proceeds, at the end of each epoch. At that moment we select the two closest prototypes $\hat{q}_{j|\alpha}$ and $\hat{q}_{j|\beta}$ as candidates to be fused, and we compute h_α the heterogeneity of c_α

$$h_\alpha = \sum_{i=1}^{N} KL(p_{j|i}, q_{j|\alpha})\pi_{i\alpha} , \qquad (4)$$

obtaining h_β in the same way. Then, we compute the fused prototype $\hat{q}_{j|\gamma}$ by applying Equation 3 and considering that $I_{i\gamma} = I_{i\alpha} + I_{i\beta}$, that is

$$\hat{q}_{j|\gamma} = \sum_{i=1}^{N} \pi_{i\gamma} p_{j|i} . \qquad (5)$$

Finally, we fuse c_α and c_β whenever $h_\gamma < (h_\alpha + h_\beta)\mu$, where $\mu \in [0,1]$ is a merge factor addressed to facilitate class fusion. After such a decision a new epoch begins. A minimal number of iterations per epoch are needed to reach a stable partial solution before trying two fuse two other classes.

2.2   Segmentation Results

Considering indoor images of 320×240 pixels, the feature extraction step consists on recovering texture and color statistics at blocks of size 32×32, that is, of radius 16 pixels. These blocks are taken each 8 pixels, that is, there is a partial overlap of 25%, providing $N = 37 \times 27 = 999$ blocks per image. Texture features rely on 8 Gabor filters with 4 orientations $(0, 45, 90,$ and 135 degrees) and 2 scales $(\sigma = 1.0$ and $\sigma = 2.0,$ corresponding to 7×7 and 13×13 windows respectively). Filter-output frequencies associated to each filter are registered in histograms of 16 equally spaced bins. Thus, there are $8 \times 16 = 128$ texture features per block, which are completed with 16 more features provided by the histogram associated to the first HSB color component (hue or chromaticity) inside the block. Consequently, the overall number of features is 144.

The unsupervised clustering algorithm proceeds through 10 epochs of 10 iterations each (100 iterations). Temperature range is fixed to $[1.0 \dots 0.05]$, that is, each iteration t, T value is $0.095 + e^{-t} + 0.05$. On the other hand, the merge factor μ is set to 0.8, and to $K_{max} = 10$. In Fig. 1 we compare the segmentation results obtained with and without adaptation. After clustering we proceed to group neighboring blocks belonging to the same class in homogeneous regions. Small regions (those with less than $\nu = 20$ blocks) are removed and absorbed by the more similar region in its neighborhood).

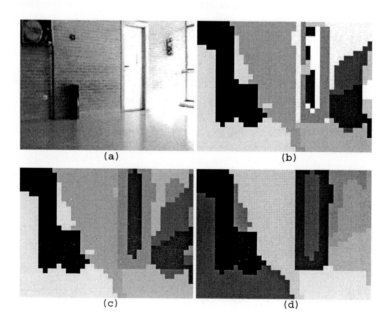

Fig. 1. *Segmentation results.* (a) Input indoor image.(b) Non-adaptive segmentation. (c) Adaptive segmentation. (d) After removing spurious blocks in (c).

3   Graph Matching

3.1   Stochastic Search for Assignment

Given an input segmented image we build an undirected data graph $G_D = (V_D, E_D)$ with one vertex $a \in V_D$ per region and one edge $(a, b) \in E_D$ per pair of adjacent regions. Similarly, we consider a stored graph $G_S = (V_S, E_S)$ with vertexes $i \in V_S$ and edges $(i, j) \in E_D$. Then, the adjacency matrices D and S of both graphs are defined by

$$D_{ab} = \begin{cases} 1 & \text{if } (a, b) \in E_D \\ 0 & \text{otherwise} \end{cases} \quad \text{and} \quad S_{ij} = \begin{cases} 1 & \text{if } (i, j) \in E_S \\ 0 & \text{otherwise .} \end{cases}$$

A feasible solution to the graph matching problem between G_D and G_S is encoded by a matrix M of size $|V_D| \times |V_S|$ with binary variables

$$M_{ai} = \begin{cases} 1 & \text{if } a \in V_D \text{ matches } i \in V_S \\ 0 & \text{otherwise} \end{cases}$$

satisfying the constraints defined respectively over the rows and columns of M

$$\sum_{i=1}^{|V_S|} M_{ai} \leq 1, \forall a \quad \text{and} \quad \sum_{a=1}^{|V_D|} M_{ai} \leq 1, \forall i . \tag{6}$$

Cost Function. Gold and Rangarajan formulated the problem in terms of finding the feasible solution M that maximizes the following cost function,

$$F(M) = \sum_{a=1}^{|V_D|} \sum_{i=1}^{|V_S|} \sum_{b=1}^{|V_D|} \sum_{j=1}^{|V_S|} M_{ai} M_{bj} C_{aibj} , \tag{7}$$

where $C_{aibj} = D_{ab} S_{ij}$, that is, when $a \in V_D$ matches $i \in V_S$, and also $b \in V_D$ matches $j \in V_S$, it is desirable that edges $(a, i) \in E_D$ and $(b, j) \in E_S$ exist, that is, that $M_{ai} = M_{bj} = 1$. However, this cost only encodes structural compatibility between both graphs. In order to enforce the preference of matching vertexes (regions) with compatible features (texture and color) we redefine C_{aibj} as

$$C_{aibj} = D_{ab} S_{ij} \exp\{-KL(q_a, q_i)\} , \tag{8}$$

where $q_a = q_{j|\alpha(a)}$ and $q_i = q_{j|\alpha(i)}$ are respectively the prototypical histograms of the classes of vertexes a and i.

Constrained Maximization. Gold and Rangarajan's deterministic annealing algorithm proceeds by estimating the averaged matching variables at each temperature T, while enforcing the satisfaction of matching constraints for the rows and columns of the candidate solution. Our preliminary matching experiments with this method showed that it assigns each vertex with another one with similar structure but this does not usually ensures that the mapping is globally consistent. This is why we replaced annealing phase by a global strategy, a modified Comb (Common structure of the best local maxima) algorithm, originally applied to labeling problems in MRF models, which explores the set of extended feasible solutions. An extended feasible solution is a matching matrix $\hat{M}$ with one more row and one more column, corresponding to slack variables (which are very useful to deal with noisy nodes), whose rows and columns add up to the unit, that is, a permutation matrix of binary variables.

The Comb algorithm maintains a population $P = \{\hat{M}^{(1)}, \ldots, \hat{M}^{(L)}\}$ with the L (experimentally set to 10 individuals) best local maxima found so far. Such a population is initialized according to an uniform distribution over the space of feasible solutions. Each iteration begins by selecting, also randomly, a pair of local maxima $\hat{M}^{(a)}$ and $\hat{M}^{(b)}$. As this method relies on the assumption that local maxima share some matching variables with the global maxima, it derives a new candidate to local maximum $\hat{M}^{(0)}$ by combining the latter pair. Such a combination consists of (i) retaining common variables, (ii) randomly generating new values for components with different variables and (iii) ensuring that the result is still a permutation matrix. This provides the starting point of a hill-climbing process which consists of randomly changing the value at a component while ensuring that the resulting matrix satisfies the matching constraints and then testing whether it provides a better solution. If so, a new hill-climbing step begins. Otherwise, if after $A = 10$ attempts it is not possible to improve the current matrix a new local maximum $\hat{M}^*$ is declared. Such a local maximum updates P as follows: If

$$F(\hat{M}^*) > \hat{M}^{worst} \text{ where } \hat{M}^{worst} = \arg\min_{\hat{M} \in P} F(\hat{M}), \qquad (9)$$

then the worst local maximum so far $\hat{M}^{worst}$ is replaced by $\hat{M}^*$. Otherwise the population does not change. Such an updating rule ensures that the quality of the individuals in P is improved, expecting that such an improvement eventually reaches the global maximum. Thus, if we detect that the quality of P can not be improved we assume that the algorithm has found the global maximum (the best local maximum so far). The algorithm also terminates when the latter termination condition is not satisfied after $I = 1000$ iterations.

3.2   Recognition Results

In order to test the adequacy of our approach in scene recognition, we have build two subjective classes of images, each one registering different viewpoints of two different places (natural landmarks) in our lab (see Fig. 2): class-A (images A1,A2,A3, and A4) and class-B (B1 and B2). Sample matching results between images of the same class (A1 and A2) and of different classes (A1 and B1) are showed in Fig. 3. The main question addressed here is whether these classes are not subjective but real classes. In Table 1 we show the best costs for each

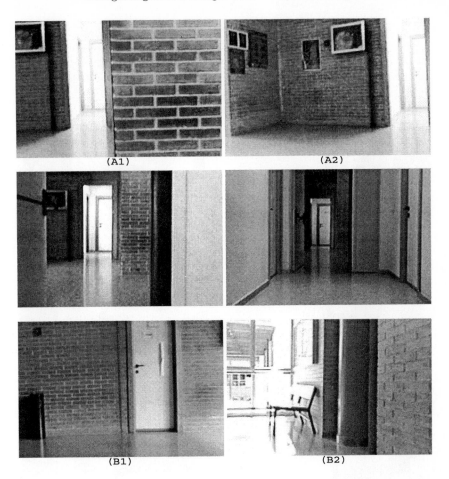

Fig. 2. Experimental set. Images A1 (first reference), A2 (15-degrees-rotation), A3 (2-meters-backwards), A4 (4-meters-backwards), B1 (second reference) and B2 (90-degrees-rotation

matching. Self matchings appear in boldface, matching between class-A images are emphasized, whereas matchings between class-B images, and between class-A and class-B images appear in normal text. We also show the a sort list of the three preferred matchings for each image (row in the matrix). Each image not only prefers itself, as expected, but its second and third choices are images in the same subjective class, when possible). In the case of B1 and B2, their third choice is A4, the more distant image from the first reference A1. Furthermore, we also show the degrees of ambiguity of the first and second matchings (ratios between the best costs of the second and the first matching, and between the best costs of the third and the second ones, respectively) and these degrees tend to be low at least for the winner matching.

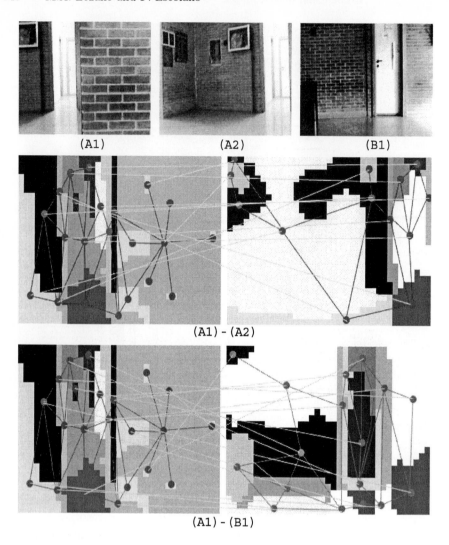

(A1)   (A2)   (B1)

(A1) - (A2)

(A1) - (B1)

Fig. 3. Matching results. Top: Images A1 , A2, and B1; Middle: Matching between A1 and A2; Bottom: Matching between A1 and B1. The co-occurrence of structure and appearance is key for discrimination.

Such a good performance is due to the co-occurrence of structural and appearance information between viewpoints of the same landmark. However, when we relax such a constraint and evaluate each matching only on behalf of structural compatibility, classes A and B are no longer distinct. In Table 2 we see that in many cases a given image does not prefer itself or even an image of the same subjective class. Furthermore, the analysis of the degrees of ambiguity reveals that the highest ambiguity in the latter case (0.62) is even lower that the current lowest ambiguity, reaching even 1.0 in the case of B2.

The averaged segmentation time was of 7.1 secs. in an ATHLON-XP-1700 processor, whereas the averaged processing time of the graph-matching step was of 4.8 secs, given an averaged size of 22 nodes per graph.

Table 1. Cost matrix when fusing structure and appearance.

	A1	A2	A3	A4	B1	B2	Sorted Preferences	Ambiguities
A1	**1.55**	*0.96*	*0.42*	*0.15*	0.03	0.01	A1, A2, A3	0.62, 0.44
A2	*1.07*	**2.92**	*0.49*	*0.20*	0.02	0.01	A2, A1, A3	0.37, 0.46
A3	*0.36*	*0.49*	**2.66**	*0.23*	0.02	0.03	A3, A2, A1	0.18, 0.73
A4	*0.20*	*0.23*	*0.29*	**1.47**	0.03	0.19	A4, A3, A2	0.20, 0.79
B1	0.03	0.03	0.03	0.04	**3.06**	0.68	B1, B2, A4	0.22, 0.06
B2	0.01	0.01	0.03	0.19	0.68	**2.00**	B2, B1, A4	0.34, 0.28

Table 2. Cost matrix when using only structural information.

	A1	A2	A3	A4	B1	B2	Sorted Preferences	Ambiguities
A1	**1.73**	*1.69*	*1.66*	*1.30*	1.76	2.00	B2, B1, A1	0.88, 0.98
A2	*1.85*	**2.92**	*1.33*	*1.69*	1.24	1.00	A2, A1, A3	0.63, 0.72
A3	*1.50*	*1.16*	**2.66**	*0.83*	1.66	2.00	A3, B2, B1	0.75, 0.83
A4	*1.30*	*1.24*	*1.83*	**1.80**	1.29	2.00	B2, A3, A4	0.92, 0.98
B1	1.65	1.54	1.66	1.65	**3.41**	2.00	B1, B2, A3	0.59, 0.83
B2	2.00	1.00	2.00	2.00	2.00	**2.00**	B1, B2, A3	1.00, 1.00

4 Conclusions

There are two main contribution in this paper: the adaptation and integration of state-of-the-art algorithms for unsupervised clustering and graph matching to the context of scene recognition, and the finding that this framework provides promising results for addressing the appearance-based localization problem in indoor environments. Future work includes the automatic inference of visual landmarks in the environment as well as the development of incremental localization algorithms which perform scene clustering adaptively.

References

1. Szummer, M., Picard, R.W.: Indoor-outdoor image classification. In Proc. IEEE Int. Workshop on Content-based Access of Image adn Video Databases (1998)
2. Torralba, A., Sinha, P.: Recognizing Indoor Scenes. AI Memo 2001-015, CBCL Memo 202, Cambridge, MA (2001)

3. Vailaya, A., Figueiredo, M.A.T., Jain, A.K., Zhang, H.-J.: Image Classification for Content-Based Indexing. IEEE Trans. on Image Processing, Vol. 10, No. 1 (2001) 117–130.
4. Kroese, B.J.A., Vlassis, N., Bunschoten, R., Motomura, Y.: A Probabilistic Model for Appearance-based Robot Localization. Image and Vision Computing, Vol. 19, No. 6 (2001) 381–391.
5. Lipson, P., Grimson, E., Sihna,P.: Configuration Based Scene Classification in Image Indexing. In Proc. IEEE CS Conference on Computer Vision and Pattern Recognition. Puerto Rico (1997) 1007–1013
6. Huet, B., Hancock, E.R.: Relational Object Recognition from Large Structural Libraries. Pattern Recognition (2002)
7. Carson, C., Belongie, S., Greenspan, H., Malik, J. : Blobworld: Image segmentation using Expectation-Maximization and its application to image querying. IEEE Trans. on Pattern Analysis and Machine Intelligence (2002)
8. Hofmann, T., Puzicha, J.: Statistical Models for Co-occurrence Data. MIT AI-Memo 1625 Cambridge, MA (1998)
9. Puzicha, J.: Histogram Clustering for Unsupervised Segmentation and Image Retrieval. Pattern Recognition Letters, 20, (1999) 899–909.
10. Figueiredo, M.A.T, Leitao, J.M.N, Jain, A.K.: On Fitting Mixture Models. In: Hancock, E.R., Pelillo, M. (eds.): Energy Minimization Methods in Computer Vision and Pattern Recognition. Lecture Notes in Computer Science, Vol. 1654. Springer-Verlag, Berlin Heidelberg New York (1999) 54–69.
11. Gold, S., Rangarajan, A.: A Graduated Assignement Algorithm for Graph Matching. IEEE Trans. on Pattern Analysis and Machine Intelligence, Vol. 18, No. 4 (1996) 377-388.
12. Li, S.Z.: Toward Global Solution to MAP Image Estimation: Using Common Structure of Local Solutions. In: Pelillo, M., Hancock, E.R.(eds.): Energy Minimization Methods in Computer Vision and Pattern Recognition. Lecture Notes in Computer Science, Vol. 1223. Springer-Verlag, Berlin Heidelberg New York (1997) 361–374.

Vision-Based System for the Safe Operation of a Solar Power Tower Plant

M. López-Martínez, M. Vargas, and F.R. Rubio

Dpto.Ingeniería de Sistemas y Automática.
Escuela Superior de Ingenieros.
Universidad de Sevilla, SPAIN.
{mlm,vargas,rubio}@cartuja.us.es

Abstract. In this paper several vision-based systems for the operation of a solar power tower plant are shown. These systems detect the presence of clouds next to the sun and compute a field coverture factor which features the area of the heliostat field that is shadowed by them. This cloud detection process is fundamental in order to preserve the integrity of the solar central receiver located at the top of the tower of these solar plants. These systems prevent the rupture of the receiver by thermal stress.

1   Introduction

Solar power provides an energy source which varies independently and cannot be adjusted to suit the desired demand. Although solar radiation does have predictable seasonal and daily cyclic variations, it is also affected by unpredictable disturbances caused by atmospheric conditions such as cloud coverture, humidity and air transparency. The ability to predict when a cloud will cover the field is one of the main problems in the operation of the solar power tower plants. In this kind of plants there is a heliostat field that reflects the solar radiation to a central receiver located at the top of a tower. At normal operating conditions the mean temperature of the receiver reaches up to 800ºC. When a cloud covers the sun, a sudden reduction of radiation occurs, and consequently the temperature of the receiver goes down. Besides this, at the moment the cloud lets the sun shine again, the receiver will suffer a thermal shock. If this phenomenon occurs several times the receiver will get damaged due to thermal stress. In this paper a system capable of detecting the presence of clouds next to the sun is presented. This system will send this information to the master control which, in turn, will order several heliostats to turn away, so that the receiver temperature can decrease before the cloud covers the sun, and hence will reduce the risk of the receiver rupture. In [4] and [3] advanced master controls of solar plants are shown.

In this paper three different aspects are presented: A method for the location and tracking of the sun based on artificial vision. Then, an algorithm for the segmentation of clouds based on artificial vision. Finally, a geometric method

F.J. Garijo, J.C. Riquelme, and M. Toro (Eds.): IBERAMIA 2002, LNAI 2527, pp. 943–952, 2002.
© Springer-Verlag Berlin Heidelberg 2002

to determine, using the captured images, which zones of the heliostat field are shadowed by clouds.

When vision-based methods are used, the following characteristics have to be considered: The brightness in the scene changes with the day hour and with the orientation of the camera. The brightness distribution of the sky is not uniform and there is a descending gradient towards the horizon. The clouds have a random form and a random luminosity.

These characteristics make more difficult the segmentation of the elements present in the scene. In order to help the segmentation process, the color information of each element has been used [5].

This paper is organized as follows: Section 2 describes the method used to locate the sun. In section 3 a method to segment the clouds surrounding the sun is given. Section 4 presents a method to estimate the area of the heliostat field that is covered by clouds. Conclusions are given in section 5.

2   Sun Location Procedure

High concentration solar systems require the sun to be tracked with high accuracy. Normally, heliostat positioning control used to follow the sun is made based on computation of the solar vector in open loop like done in [1]. In the system proposed in this paper, the solar vector is also employed in an upper level to position a pant-tilt platform, but a second control level is added, based on the detection of the sun through vision methods in a closed-loop (figure 1). The color information of the image has been used to make the detection process

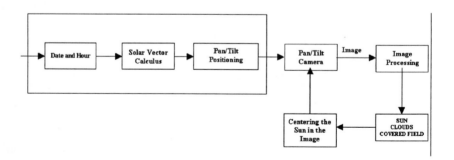

Fig. 1. Positioning System Diagram.

easier. The HSV color decomposition has been chosen because it enables to distinguish among the hue, saturation and value of each element of the scene [5]. The high variation of these color components in the different elements in the scene will help in the segment process.

After a thorough study of the HSV components in the image of the sun, clouds and sky, the following characteristics have been determined.

Value: When the sun is visible, its value is over 90% of the absolute maximum.

Saturation: The Clouds and the Sun have a similar saturation but the sky's one is clearly different.

Hue: The sky is blue and the sun is yellow, however the clouds used to be of many colors.

According to this, it is proposed to use the Value to do a preliminary segmentation, and in a second step to verify it through the Saturation and Hue components.

The detailed procedure for the sun location is as follows:

First of all, the image has to be captured (figure 2) and its color model has to be transformed into HSV, so that the three needed components are available (figure 2). Next, a Wiener filter will be applied at each color component. Notice that the saturation will be used in a complementary form 1-S, which represents a color with high content of white with a highly valued index. The algorithm applies a threshold of 93% to the Value Image. This image will be denoted Threshold Value Image (TVI) and will be used next(figure 3). The next step consists in applying edge detection using the Sobel Method. The algorithm calculates the minimum value of the image and applies a threshold slightly upper to it. This takes advantage of the fact that the statistical distribution of the Sun Value fits to a gaussian one. Therefore the sun appears with the lowest levels in the edge detection(figure 4). Next, a median filter is applied to the resultant binary image (figure 3). The algorithm identifies connected regions and removes those of less size (figure 5). It also calculates the mass center and the characteristic length of the resultant region. This length will be taken as the initial estimation of the sun radius (figure 5).

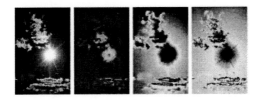

Fig. 2. From left to right Sun and Clouds Image. Decomposition H,S,V with Wiener Filter

The algorithm increases or decreases the sun radius using the information of the Value component, and varies the center position until the sun circle fits with the TVI mentioned before (figure 6). It also adjusts the position and radius of the sun inside the circle, that has been previously calculated with the Value information, using the information of the Saturation component. The algorithm calculates the mass centre of those zones which have a saturation higher than the average saturation, and calculates the characteristic length of the sun using

Fig. 3. From left to right, Threshold in Value Component, Threshold in edges over it, median filter

Fig. 4. From left to right, edge detection in columns, rows, and fusion of them

Fig. 5. From left to right, Connected regions, Bigger Region, Mass Center

this average saturation (figures 7 and 8). As a final step, the algorithm verifies the sun position using the Hue component (figure 7), transforms the image into RGB and represents over it the sun circle (figure 9). It also represents the sun as an artificial image, using a gaussian node (figure 9).

Fig. 6. From left to right, Initial Sun Circle, Final Circle, Mass Center

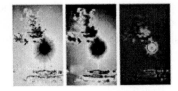

Fig. 7. From left to right, Sun Circle in Value, Sun circle in Saturation, Sun in Hue

Fig. 8. From left to right, Mass Center in Saturation, Internal Circle in Saturation, Sun Circle in Saturation

Fig. 9. From left to right, Sun Circle, Sun as a gaussian node in several color representations

3   A Method to Segment the Clouds

As mentioned before, in order to preserve the integrity of the receiver, it is necessary to detect and identify the clouds next to the sun. The proposed method makes that possible, and also determines the minimum distance between them at each instant.

The method is described in several steps: The algorithm computes the edge image starting from the original Value image. Figure 11 shows how the edges of the clouds appear very clear. This fact will be used to generate an automatic threshold using statistical information like the image histogram and its probabilistic distribution. The curve slope changes sharply when reaching a particular value. This value is chosen as the threshold (figure 10). After this, a median filtering is applied to the resultant image (figure 11). Next, the algorithm computes the growth of regions in the edges of the clouds using the saturation image and excluding the position of the sun (figure 12). In the following step, the algorithm detects connected regions and labels them (figure 12). It also calculates the minimum distance from each cloud to the sun, and saves these points (figure 13). Finally, the algorithm represents a grid around the sun and labels its elements (figure 13).Both procedures, the sun and cloud segmentation, have been achieved taking into account only the static information of the images. In order to improve these procedures it will be added the dynamic information in a similar way as the ones shown in [4] and [6].

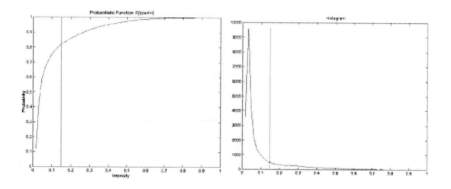

Fig. 10. Automatic Threshold for the edge detection of clouds based on the slope of the probabilistic function.

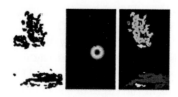

Fig. 11. From left to right, Edges Image, Thresholded Image, Median Filter

Fig. 12. From left to right, Growth of clouds using Saturation, Clouds with Gaussian Node, labeled clouds

Fig. 13. From left to right, Minimum distance Sun-Clouds, Labeled Regions, Clouds and Regions

The following step is to associate a region of the image next to the sun to a region of the heliostat field. In this way, when a particular region of the image is covered by a cloud, that means that a cloud is covering a specific region of the field. That will be shown in the next section.

4 A Method to Determine the Coverture of the Heliostat Field

A vision-based method to determine which regions of a heliostat field are covered by clouds, is presented in this section.

Several methods can be used in order to estimate the altitude of a cloud: They are mainly stereo vision and infrared vision. The method presented here is based on infrared vision. It is well known that the atmosphere temperature varies with the altitude. The higher altitudes, the lower temperatures. Obviously, this same principle applies to the temperature of the clouds. In figure 14a, the variation of temperature as a function of the altitude and the type of cloud, is shown. Ground and clouds temperatures will be measured with an infrared camera. Using this information the clouds altitude can be estimated.

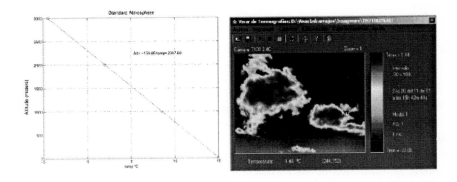

Fig. 14. Standard Atmosphere and Infrared Image

Figure 14b shows an infrared image in which the estimated temperature is under than 2°C. Therefore, using the hypothesis of standard atmosphere, the estimated altitude is 2km.

Using the information about the segmentation of the sun and the clouds, the covered field area will be estimated. In order to achieve this, a template, which represents the field as if it was seen from fixed axis, will be used. A triangle will be taken as the field template, which will change its form as a function of the solar time (figure 15a). The size of this triangle will depend on the estimation of the cloud altitude.

In this way, with an image of the sun, the surrounding clouds, and the altitude estimation, it will be possible to estimate the covered field area. In order to calculate the triangle, which represents three points of the field as seen from a camera located in the sun, the field has been projected taking into account the elevation and azimuth angles. These angles have been calculated using the algorithm in [1], which gives the solar vector.

As a first approximation, it has been considered that the solar vector is the same for the three points of the triangle due to the huge distance between the sun and the earth.

On the other hand, the field with the orientation of the solar vector, has been projected at a parallel plane to the ground at the altitude of the clouds H (figure 15b). Next, each point of this projection has been prolonged towards the position of the camera and over the image plane. As it is known, the image plane is perpendicular to the optical axis of the camera. The camera attitude is controlled so that the sun is in the center of the image. Therefore, in the image, the sun corresponds to the camera which is located in the mass center of the triangle that delimits the heliostat field.

Analyzing figure 15a, the following geometric relations can be established in order to obtain the attitude of the triangle as a function of θ_{Solar}, the azimuth angle of the sun taking the East as reference.

$$d_{1S} = d_{1C} \cdot cos(\theta)$$
$$d_{3S} = -d_{3C} \cdot cos(\frac{\pi}{2} - \theta - \alpha_3)$$
$$d_{4S} = d_{4C} \cdot sin(\theta - \alpha_4)$$
$$d_{CS1} = -d_{1C} \cdot sin(\theta)$$
$$d_{CS3} = -d_{3C} \cdot sin(\frac{\pi}{2} - \theta - \alpha_3)$$
$$d_{CS4} = d_{4C} \cdot cos(\theta - \alpha_4) \tag{1}$$

The signs have been defined in this way in order to make easier the correspondence of the triangle in the image and the triangle in the field. In the center of the image, where the sun will be located, an axis system has been situated. As mentioned before, this point corresponds to the situation of the camera. Similarly, the following equations (obtained from figure 15b) allow to locate the triangle as a function of the elevation angle of the sun, φ_{solar}.

$$d_{CC'} = \frac{H}{sin(\varphi)}$$

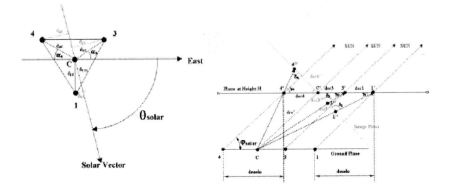

Fig. 15. From left to the right, Heliostat field plant sight and Azimuth angle of the sun. Heliostat field – Projection over the image plane

$$d_{suelo} = \frac{H}{tan(\varphi)}$$

$$\widehat{d_{SC4}} = d_{suelo} - d_{SC4}$$

$$\gamma_4 = arctan(\frac{H}{\widehat{d_{SC4}}})$$

$$\delta_4 = \frac{\pi}{2} + \varphi - \gamma_4$$

$$d_{SC4''} = \frac{sin(\gamma_4)}{sin(\delta_4)} \cdot d_{SC4} \qquad (2)$$

With these expressions, the triangle that represents the heliostat field, can be drawn over the image of the sun. If a cloud covers part of the triangle then the corresponding part of the field will be covered.

5   Conclusions

A method to segment the sun and the clouds and determine geometrically the covered area in a heliostat field has been shown.

This information is fundamental to achieve a correct operation of the solar power tower plant, and will let the master control system to take into account these factors, in order to reduce the number of heliostats aiming to the receiver and decrease the incident radiation when clouds are about to shade the heliostat field.

Acknowledgements. The authors would like to thank CICYT for supporting this work under grant DPI2001-2424-C02-01.

References

1. M.Blanco-Muriel, D.C.Alarcón-Padilla. "Computing the solar vector", *Solar Energy*, Vol. 70, No. 5, pp. 431–441, (2001).
2. F.J.García-Martín, M.Berenguel, E.F.Camacho. "Heuristic knowledge-based heliostat field control for the optimization of the temperature distribution in a volumetric receiver", *Solar Energy*, Vol. 66, No. 5, pp. 355–369, (1999).
3. E.F.Camacho, M.Berenguel, F.R.Rubio. "Advanced Control of Solar Plants", *Springer-Verlag*, London, (1997).
4. Ma, W.Y., Manjunath B.S. "Edge Flow: A Framework of Boundary Detection and Image Segmentation".(1997).
5. Deng Y., Manjunath B.S. "Color Image Segmentation". (1999).
6. Ridder, C., Munkelt Olaf. "Adaptive Background Estimation and Foreground Detection using Kalman-Filtering".(1995).
7. Ceballos Sierra, F.J. "Visual C++: Programación Avanzada en Win32".(1999)

Author Index

Lecture Notes in Artificial Intelligence (LNAI)

Lecture Notes in Computer Science

Vol. 2476: A.H.F. Laender, A.L. Oliveira (Eds.), String Processing and Information Retrieval. Proceedings, 2002. XI, 337 pages. 2002.

Vol. 2477: M.V. Hermenegildo, G. Puebla (Eds.), Static Analysis. Proceedings, 2002. XI, 527 pages. 2002.

Vol. 2478: M.J. Egenhofer, D.M. Mark (Eds.), Geographic Information Science. Proceedings, 2002. X, 363 pages. 2002.

Vol. 2479: M. Jarke, J. Koehler, G. Lakemeyer (Eds.), KI 2002: Advances in Artificial Intelligence. Proceedings, 2002. XIII, 327 pages. (Subseries LNAI).

Vol. 2480: Y. Han, S. Tai, D. Wikarski (Eds.), Engineering and Deployment of Cooperative Information Systems. Proceedings, 2002. XIII, 564 pages. 2002.

Vol. 2483: J.D.P. Rolim, S. Vadhan (Eds.), Randomization and Approximation Techniques in Computer Science. Proceedings, 2002. VIII, 275 pages. 2002.

Vol. 2484: P. Adriaans, H. Fernau, M. van Zaanen (Eds.), Grammatical Inference: Algorithms and Applications. Proceedings, 2002. IX, 315 pages. 2002. (Subseries LNAI).

Vol. 2485: A. Bondavalli, P. Thevenod-Fosse (Eds.), Dependable Computing EDCC-4. Proceedings, 2002. XIII, 283 pages. 2002.

Vol. 2486: M. Marinaro, R. Tagliaferri (Eds.), Neural Nets. Proceedings, 2002. IX, 253 pages. 2002.

Vol. 2487: D. Batory, C. Consel, W. Taha (Eds.), Generative Programming and Component Engineering. Proceedings, 2002. VIII, 335 pages. 2002.

Vol. 2488: T. Dohi, R. Kikinis (Eds), Medical Image Computing and Computer-Assisted Intervention – MICCAI 2002. Proceedings, Part I. XXIX, 807 pages. 2002.

Vol. 2489: T. Dohi, R. Kikinis (Eds), Medical Image Computing and Computer-Assisted Intervention – MICCAI 2002. Proceedings, Part II. XXIX, 693 pages. 2002.

Vol. 2491: A. Sangiovanni-Vincentelli, J. Sifakis (Eds.), Embedded Software. Proceedings, 2002. IX, 423 pages. 2002.

Vol. 2493: S. Bandini, B. Chopard, M. Tomassini (Eds.), Cellular Automata. Proceedings, 2002. XI, 369 pages. 2002.

Vol. 2495: C. George, H. Miao (Eds.), Formal Methods and Software Engineering. Proceedings, 2002. XI, 626 pages. 2002.

Vol. 2496: K.C. Almeroth, M. Hasan (Eds.), Management of Multimedia in the Internet. Proceedings, 2002. XI, 355 pages. 2002.

Vol. 2498: G. Borriello, L.E. Holmquist (Eds.), UbiComp 2002: Ubiquitous Computing. Proceedings, 2002. XV, 380 pages. 2002.

Vol. 2499: S.D. Richardson (Ed.), Machine Translation: From Research to Real Users. Proceedings, 2002. XXI, 254 pages. 2002. (Subseries LNAI).

Vol. 2502: D. Gollmann, G. Karjoth, M. Waidner (Eds.), Computer Security – ESORICS 2002. Proceedings, 2002. X, 281 pages. 2002.

Vol. 2503: S. Spaccapietra, S.T. March, Y. Kambayashi (Eds.), Conceptual Modeling – ER 2002. Proceedings, 2002. XX, 480 pages. 2002.

Vol. 2504: M.T. Escrig, F. Toledo, E. Golobardes (Eds.), Topics in Artificial Intelligence. Proceedings 2002. XI, 432 pages. 2002. (Subseries LNAI).

Vol. 2506: M. Feridun, P. Kropf, G. Babin (Eds.), Management Technologies for E-Commerce and E-Business Applications. Proceedings, 2002. IX, 209 pages. 2002.

Vol. 2507: G. Bittencourt, G.L. Ramalho (Eds.), Advances in Artificial Intelligence. Proceedings, 2002. XIII, 418 pages. 2002. (Subseries LNAI).

Vol. 2508: D. Malkhi (Ed.), Distributed Computing. Proceedings, 2002. X, 371 pages. 2002.

Vol. 2509: C.S. Calude, M.J. Dinneen, F. Peper (Eds.), Unconventional Models in Computation. Proceedings, 2002. VIII, 331 pages. 2002.

Vol. 2510: H. Shafazand, A Min Tjoa (Eds.), EurAsia-ICT 2002: Information and Communication Technology. Proceedings, 2002. XXIII, 1020 pages. 2002.

Vol. 2511: B. Stiller, M. Smirnow, M. Karsten, P. Reichl (Eds.), From QoS Provisioning to QoS Charging. Proceedings, 2002. XIV, 348 pages. 2002.

Vol. 2514: M. Baaz, A. Voronkov (Eds.), Logic for Programming, Artificial Intelligence, and Reasoning. Proceedings 2002. XIII, 465 pages. 2002. (Subseries LNAI).

Vol. 2516: A. Wespi, G. Vigna, L. Deri (Eds.), Recent Advances in Intrusion Detection. Proceedings, 2002. X, 327 pages. 2002.

Vol. 2517: M.D. Aagaard, J.W. O'Leary (Eds.), Formal Methods in Computer-Aided Design. Proceedings, 2002. XI, 399 pages. 2002.

Vol. 2519: R. Meersman, Z. Tari, et al. (Eds.), On the Move to Meaningful Internet Systems 2002: CoopIS, DOA, and ODBASE. Proceedings, 2002. XXIII, 1367 pages. 2002.

Vol. 2521: A. Karmouch, T. Magedanz, J. Delgado (Eds.), Mobile Agents for Telecommunication Applications. Proceedings. 2002. XII, 317 pages. 2002.

Vol. 2522: T. Andreasen, A. Motro, H. Christiansen, H. Legind Larsen (Eds.), Flexible Query Answering. Proceedings 2002. XI, 386 pages. 2002. (Subseries LNAI).

Vol. 2526: A. Colosimo, A. Giuliani, P. Sirabella (Eds.), Medical Data Analysis. Proceedings 2002. IX, 222 pages. 2002.

Vol. 2527: F.J. Garijo, J.C. Riquelme, M. Toro (Eds.), Advances in Artificial Intelligence – IBERAMIA 2002. Proceedings 2002. XVIII, 955 pages. 2002. (Subseries LNAI).

Vol. 2535: N. Suri (Ed.), Mobile Agents. Proceedings 2002. X, 203 pages. 2002.